ENTERTAINMENT LAW

MELVIN SIMENSKY
Member of New York Bar
Adjunct Professor of Law
New York University School of Law

and

THOMAS D. SELZ
Member of New York Bar
Adjunct Professor of Law
New York University School of Law

> Contemporary Casebook Series

 **Matthew Bender**
IRWIN

MATTHEW BENDER & CO.
EDITORIAL OFFICES
11 PENN PLAZA, NEW YORK, NY 10001   (212)967-7707
2101 WEBSTER ST., OAKLAND, CA 94612   (415)446-7100
1275 BROADWAY, ALBANY, NY 12202   (518)487-3000

Printed on recycled paper

LAW SCHOOL PUBLICATIONS

ADVISORY BOARD

To my son, Daniel, in the
hope that he will always know the
joys of learning

Thomas D. Selz

For my wonderful son Adam

Melvin Simensky

PERMISSIONS AND ACKNOWLEDGMENTS

PERMISSIONS

The following authors, publishers and organizations have granted permission to reprint copyrighted material:

American Film

Kirk Honeycutt "Whose Film is it Anyway?" (May, 1981), pp. 34–36, 38–39, 70–71. Copyright © 1981 by American Film.

Bantam Books

Louis L'Amour, "Letter to Booksellers from Louis L'Amour," Publisher's Weekly (July 29, 1983), p. 16. Copyright © 1983 by Bantam Books.

Entertainment Law Reporter

Analysis of *In the Matter of the Arbitration Between Directors Guild of America, Inc. and King-Hitzig Productions, No. 00892*, Entertainment Law Reporter (May 15, 1981), pp. 1–2. Copyright © 1979 by Entertainment Law Reporter.

"Arbitrators Find that the Directors of 'Jaws 2' and 'King of the Gypsies' Were Entitled to Credit in Certain Advertisements"; Entertainment Law Reporter (October 5, 1979), p. 2. Copyright © 1979 by Entertainment Law Reporter.

New York Law Journal

Martin Schoenfeld, "Art Law" (June 21, 1978), pp. 1, 3. Copyright © 1978 by the New York Law Journal.

New York Magazine

Ron Chernow, "The Perils of the Picture Show: Fade-out on an Era" (August 22, 1977), pp. 28–33. Copyright © 1977 by Ron Chernow.

Mario Puzo, "Hollywood's Raid on Israel, or Idi Amin's Revenge" (October 4, 1976), pp. 46–49. Copyright © 1976 by Mario Puzo.

William Wolf, "High Noon for Directors" (December 29, 1980–January 5, 1981), pp. 50–51. Copyright © 1981 by News Group Publications, Inc.

Steven Ginsberg, "Richard Pryor's $40-Mil Col Pact for Cash and Clout" (May 25, 1983), pp. 1, 86. Copyright © 1983 by Variety.

"Hollywood Backs Govt. in Court" (October 12, 1977), pp. 55, 74. Copyright © 1977 by Variety.

"Home Box Office's Suits Say Directors Guild Impedes Progress" (July 26, 1978), p. 41. Copyright © 1978 by Variety.

Richard Hummler, "Authors, Producers Break Off Confabs" (November 25, 1981), pp. 97, 105. Copyright © 1981 by Variety.

Dave Kaufman, "Feds Probe TV Block Booking by Syndicators" (August 2, 1978), pp. 1, 58. Copyright © 1978 by Variety.

Cynthia Kirk, "LP Deals Changing Drastically Sez Lawyer; Artists Bear Brunt of Industry's Economic Woes" (December 22, 1982), p. 50. Copyright © 1982 by Variety.

"Litigation Could Derail N.Y. Tracks" (August 31, 1977), p. 3. Copyright © 1977 by Variety.

"Orion to Track Exclusively in Westwood at Facelifted UACI 4" (September 7, 1983), p. 31. Copyright © 1983 by Variety.

"Par Signs Simpson, Bruckheimer to a 3-Year Exclusivity" (August 10, 1983), pp. 3, 34. Copyright © 1983 by Variety.

Dale Pollock, "Dustin Hoffman Persists in Suit on 'Creative Control'; Spurns FAP's Olive Branch" (July 19, 1978), pp. 4, 30. Copyright © 1978 by Variety.

"Rogers Sues Liberty for 44 Mil, Claiming Label Shortchanged Him" (October 28, 1981), p. 63. Copyright © 1981 by Variety.

Ken Terry, "Variable Record Pricing Comes of Age" (August 31, 1983), pp. 101, 104. Copyright © 1983 by Variety.

"They Pay Us Less and They Pay Us Last" (June 15, 1977), pp. 7, 30. Copyright © 1977 by Variety.

"$3.7-Billion Record for 1983" (January 11, 1984), pp. 7, 83. Copyright © 1984 by Variety.

Will Tusher, "Abuses of 'Star Power' Put Into Focus" (June 29, 1977), pp. 37, 50. Copyright © 1977 by Variety.

"Walter Hill Disowns 'Warriors,' Goldman Defends Necessary Cuts" (October 1, 1980), p. 39. Copyright © 1980 by Variety.

ACKNOWLEDGMENTS

The authors gratefully acknowledge the assistance of the following people and companies in making this work possible: Ronald Sandberg, Esq., and the Dramatists Guild, Inc.; Alexander Gigante, Esq., and Simon & Schuster; J. Marshall Wellborn, Esq., and the National Broadcasting Company; Richard Zimbert, Esq., and Joshua Wattles, Esq., and Paramount Pictures Corporation; Lyman Gronemeyer, Esq., and Twentieth Century-Fox Film Corporation; and David M. Berman, Esq., and Warner Bros. Records Inc.

The authors also wish to thank the following people for their assistance in the preparation of the manuscript: Sunita Sachdev and Diane Gholson.

Special Acknowledgment

The authors gratefully express their
appreciation to Steven Gordon, Esquire, of the
New York Bar, for his valuable assistance
in the research and case editing of this book.

PREFACE

Entertainment law, as practiced in the United States, is that body of principles governing activities within the entertainment industry in this country. This industry has five branches: movies, television, live theater, music, and print publishing. Among these branches there are common issues, such as the structure of power relationships within the branches; the importance of credit or billing; the methods of structuring compensation and related issues; creative control and the interests at stake in seeking to obtain or restrict such control; the different methods by which rights in creative product may be transferred; and representations, warranties and indemnities relating to risks particularly characteristic of the entertainment world.

To understand the principles which apply to these various issues throughout the entertainment industry, practitioners of entertainment law must first understand the business practices which exist in the different branches of the industry. The principles of entertainment law, after all, are merely aids for resolving disputes which arise among business people in the industry. To use these aids effectively, however, it is essential to understand the business issues at stake for the parties to the dispute.

An understanding of business practices, and of the principles which comprise entertainment law, can be obtained from a number of sources: case law, sample individual agreements, collective bargaining agreements, and newspaper and magazine articles that describe day-to-day activities within the industry.

This casebook is designed to use all of these sources which, when considered in light of selected questions, will illuminate the principles of entertainment law.

In using the source material, the reader should be looking not only at the holding of a case or major point of an article. In addition, the reader should be considering the materials from a business point of view: What were the business assumptions of the people described in the source material? What did each party expect to happen from a business standpoint? What went wrong? Was there a way in which the problem might have been anticipated in advance, and if so, what could have been done either to avoid the problem, or to assist the parties in expecting and reacting to the problem?

For pedagogical purposes, the business considerations reflected in the materials may, in fact, be more important than the actual holding of a case or point of an article. The holding in a case often relates only to the resolution of a particular dispute, rather than to an understanding of the business principles at work, and the reason business expectations were disappointed. What is newsworthy in an article may not be the general business practices or assumptions, but rather a particular way in which such practices are operating.

The source material is an invitation to thought, speculation and imagination. The authors of this casebook hope that its readers may find in their use of this work a sense of fascination with the study of entertainment law which we, as authors, have been fortunate enough to experience.

TABLE OF CONTENTS

Part I

ENTERTAINMENT INDUSTRY CONCEPTS

Chapter 1

STRUCTURE OF UNITED STATES
ENTERTAINMENT INDUSTRY

Chapter 4

COMPENSATION

Part III

APPLICATION OF
ENTERTAINMENT INDUSTRY CONCEPTS

Part I

ENTERTAINMENT INDUSTRY
CONCEPTS

CHAPTER 1

STRUCTURE OF UNITED STATES ENTERTAINMENT INDUSTRY

Introduction

The study of entertainment law should begin by considering the role of law, and of the lawyer, in the entertainment industry. The initial materials in this chapter, therefore, explore the functions which an entertainment lawyer performs, and the similarities and differences between those functions and the functions performed by agents.

This chapter will also consider practical realities which may limit the enforceability, and therefore the role, of contracts in the entertainment industry.

Mastery of such entertainment law subjects as credit, compensation, artistic control, grant of rights, and representations, warranties and indemnities also requires an understanding of the basic structure of the United States entertainment industry. This understanding is necessary in order to deal effectively with potentially conflicting business interests when entertainment law issues arise in a particular situation.

A starting point in considering the business forces within the entertainment industry is to analyze the industry in terms of its subject matter branches, and then to analyze the functional sectors within each branch. The landmark *Paramount* case, which suggests these functional sectors within the movie branch of the industry, is used as the vehicle for investigating these sectors as they appear in all branches of the industry, and for analyzing the relative power of each sector within its branch and the reasons for such power.

Anti-competitive practices are also discussed in *Paramount*. This chapter explores the reasons for such practices and their possible continuation even today. Legal and practical power considerations are also reviewed in the context of one of the ASCAP anti-trust cases, in which the court analyzes the role of ASCAP.

The relationships involved in creating and financing entertainment projects are crucial to the operation of the industry. These relationships, and their legal and practical ramifications, are also considered in this chapter.

Lastly, this chapter will consider limitations on power from a practical

3

point of view, in light of the creative processes needed to supply the industry
with the product essential to keep it operating.

Required Reading

H. A. Artists & Associates, Inc. v. Actors' Equity Assn. 451 U.S. 704 (1981).

" 'They Pay Us Less, & They Pay Us Last,' " *Variety* (June 15, 1977), pp. 7,
30.

Will Tusher, "Abuses of 'Star Power' Put Into Focus," *Variety* (June 29,
1977), pp. 37, 50.

Edwin McDowell, "Sagan Sells First Novel to Simon & Schuster," *The New
York Times* (January 13, 1981), p. C16.

United States v. Paramount Pictures, Inc., 334 U.S. 131 (1948).

"Hollywood Backs Govt. in Court," *Variety* (October 12, 1977), pp. 55, 74.

Martin Schoenfeld, Art Law, *New York Law Journal* (June 21, 1978), pp. 1, 3.

Herbert Mitgan, "2 Hoffa Books Pose Publishing Problem," *The New York
Times* (June 29, 1978), p. C15.

Lawrence Cohn, "Big Pix Now 25% of Majors' Sked," *Variety* (January 11,
1984), pp. 1, 87.

"$3.7–Billion Record For 1983," *Variety* (January 11, 1984), pp. 7, 83.

Cynthia Kirk, "LP Deals Changing Drastically, Sez Lawyer; Artists Bear
Brunt of Industry's Economic Woes," *Variety* (December 22, 1982), p.
50.

"Par Signs Simpson, Bruckheimer To A 3-Year Exclusivity," *Variety* (August
10, 1983), pp. 3, 34.

"Litigation Could Derail N.Y. Tracks," *Variety* (August 31, 1977), p. 3.

"Orion To Track Exclusively In Westwood At Facelifted UACI 4," *Variety*
(September 7, 1983), p. 31.

Dave Kaufman, "Feds Probe TV Block Booking By Syndicators," *Variety*
(August 2, 1978), pp. 1, 58.

Ron Chernow, "The Perils of the Picture Show: Fade-out on an Era," *New
York Magazine* (August 22, 1977), pp. 28–33.

Ring v. Spina, 148 F.2d 647 (2d Cir. 1945).

CBS v. ASCAP, 400 F. Supp. 737 (S.D.N.Y. 1975).

"Brooks' 'Endearment' Welcome At Par — But At Studio's Price," *Variety* (November 10, 1982), p. 48.

"Despite 'Officer's' Success, Hackford Finds His Next Pic Turned Around At Par To Col," *Variety* (May 11, 1983), pp. 32, 52.

All contracts and union agreements referred to in the chapter "Concepts."

CONCEPTS

1. What does an entertainment lawyer do?

2. What is the role of an agent in the entertainment industry, and how does that role differ from that of an entertainment lawyer? What does *H.A. Artists v. Actors' Equity* (p. 6) suggest about a response to this question?

3. What do the following articles suggest about the role of contracts in the entertainment industry:

    — *Variety*: 6/15/77 (p. 17); 6/29/77 (p. 21).

    — *The New York Times*: 1/13/81 (p. 24).

4. *U.S. v. Paramount* (p. 26).

    (A) What are the three sectors of the movie branch of the entertainment industry?

    (B) In light of the following articles, what are the analogues of these sectors in the other branches of the entertainment industry, *e.g.*, in the live theatrical, television, music and book publishing branches:

    — *Variety*: 10/12/77 (p. 49).

    — *New York Law Journal*: 6/21/78 (p. 51).

    — *The New York Times*: 6/29/78 (p. 55).

    (1) What is occurring in each article?

    (2) What are the three sectors in each entertainment industry branch?

    (C) What sector of these branches has the most leverage and why? Considering the articles in 4(B), what consequences follow from the situations discussed in such materials?

    (D) What anti-competitive practices did *Paramount* discuss?

    (E) What are some of the reasons distributors might be tempted to engage in anti-competitive practices? Consider the following articles:

— *Variety*: 1/11/84 (p. 58); 1/11/84 (p. 62); 12/22/82 (p. 63); 8/10/83 (p. 66).

(F) Which of the practices found violative of the anti-trust laws in *Paramount* are still with us, and why? Consider:

— *Variety*: 8/31/77 (p. 68); 9/7/83 (p. 70); 8/2/78 (p. 70).

— *New York Magazine*: 8/22/77 (p. 71).

5. *Ring v. Spina* (p. 78).

(A) What does the Minimum Basic Production Contract purport to be?

(B) What is the relationship between playwright and producer?

(C) Why is this relationship a problem for playwrights?

(D) What does this circumstance suggest about a possible problem for creative people throughout the entertainment industry?

(E) What makes the Minimum Basic Production Contract enforceable?

(F) As indicated in the opinion, what other branch of the entertainment industry is likely to have a structure similar to the live theatrical branch?

6. *CBS v. ASCAP* (p. 84).

(A) What gives ASCAP its power?

(B) Why are other associations or guilds not as powerful?

7. What is one major limit on the power of distributors due to the nature of the entertainment industry? Consider *Variety* article of 11/10/82 (p. 140). Under what circumstances is the effectiveness of this limitation reduced? See *Variety* article of 5/11/83 (p. 143).

H. A. ARTISTS & ASSOCIATES, INC. v. ACTORS' EQUITY ASSN.
451 U.S. 704 (1981)

JUSTICE STEWART delivered the opinion of the Court.

The respondent Actors' Equity Association (Equity) is a union representing the vast majority of stage actors and actresses in the United States. It enters into collective-bargaining agreements with theatrical producers that specify minimum wages and other terms and conditions of employment for those whom it represents. The petitioners are independent theatrical agents who place actors and actresses in jobs with producers. The Court of Appeals for the Second Circuit held that the respondents' system of regulation of theatrical agents is immune from antitrust liability by reason of the statutory labor exemption from the antitrust laws, 622 F. 2d 647.[2] We granted certiorari to consider the availability of that exemption in the circumstances presented by this case. 449 U. S. 991.

I

A

Equity is a national union that has represented stage actors and actresses since early in this century. Currently representing approximately 23,000 actors and actresses, it has collective-bargaining agreements with virtually all major theatrical producers in New York City, on and off Broadway, and with most other theatrical producers throughout the United States. The terms negotiated with producers are the minimum conditions of employment (called "scale"); an actor or actress is free to negotiate wages or terms more favorable than the collectively bargained minima.

Theatrical agents are independent contractors who negotiate contracts and solicit employment for their clients. The agents do not participate in the negotiation of collective-bargaining agreements between Equity and the theatrical producers. If an agent succeeds in obtaining employment for a client, he receives a commission based on a percentage of the client's earnings. Agents who operate in New York City must be licensed as employment agencies and are regulated by the New York City Department of Consumer Affairs pursuant to New York law, which provides that the maximum commission a theatrical agent may charge his client is 10% of the client's compensation.

In 1928, concerned with the high unemployment rates in the legitimate theater and the vulnerability of actors and actresses to abuses by theatrical agents,[3] including the extraction of high commissions that tended to undermine collectively bargained rates of compensation, Equity unilaterally established a licensing system for the regulation of agents. The regulations permitted Equity members to deal only with those agents who obtained Equity licenses and thereby agreed to meet the conditions of representation prescribed by Equity. Those members who dealt with nonlicensed agents were subject to union discipline.

The system established by the Equity regulations was immediately chal-

---

[2] The basic sources of organized labor's exemption from federal antitrust laws are §§ 6 and 20 of the Clayton Act, 38 Stat. 731 and 738, 15 U. S. C. § 17 and 29 U. S. C. § 52, and §§ 4, 5, and 13 of the Norris-LaGuardia Act, 47 Stat. 70, 71, and 73, 29 U. S. C. §§ 104, 105, and 113.

[3] Such vulnerability was, and still remains, particularly acute for actors and actresses without established professional reputations, who have always constituted the overwhelming majority of Equity's members.

lenged.[4] In *Edelstein v. Gillmore*, 35 F. 2d 723, the Court of Appeals for the Second Circuit concluded that the regulations were a lawful effort to improve the employment conditions of Equity members. In an opinion written by Judge Swan and joined by Judge Augustus N. Hand, the court said:

> "The evils of unregulated employment agencies (using this term broadly to include also the personal representative) are set forth in the defendants' affidavits and are corroborated by common knowledge. . . . Hence the requirement that, as a condition to writing new business with Equity's members, old contracts with its members must be made to conform to the new standards, does not seem to us to justify an inference that the primary purpose of the requirement is infliction of injury upon plaintiff, and other personal representatives in a similar situation, rather than the protection of the supposed interests of Equity's members. *The terms they insist upon are calculated to secure from personal representatives better and more impartial service, at uniform and cheaper rates, and to improve conditions of employment of actors by theater managers.* Undoubtedly the defendants intend to compel the plaintiff to give up rights under existing contracts which do not conform to the new standards set up by Equity, but, as already indicated, *their motive in so doing is to benefit themselves and their fellow actors in the economic struggle.* The financial loss to plaintiff is incidental to this purpose." *Id.*, at 726 (emphasis added).[6]

The essential elements of Equity's regulation of theatrical agents have remained unchanged since 1928.[7] A member of Equity is prohibited, on pain

---

[4] The challenge was grounded on allegations of common-law tortious interference with business relationships.

[6] For contemporary descriptions of agent abuses of actors and actresses, see generally A. Harding, The Revolt of the Actors (1929). See also New Rules for Actors, N. Y. Times, Sept. 24, 1928, p. 20, col. 3; The New Republic, Oct. 24, 1928, p. 263. Cf. *Ribnik v. McBride*, 277 U. S. 350, 359–375 (Stone, J., joined by Holmes and Brandeis, JJ., dissenting) (general abuses by employment agencies, particularly at times of widespread unemployment). The Court's decision in *Ribnik* v. *McBride* was overruled unanimously in *Olsen* v. *Nebraska*, 313 U. S. 236.

[7] The petitioners do not dispute this. The regulations have undergone revision in some details, largely as a result of negotiations between Equity and Theatrical Artists Representatives Associates (TARA), which until shortly before this litigation began was the only association voicing the concerns of agents with regard to their representation of Equity members. Until their voluntary resignation in late 1977, most of the petitioners were members of TARA. The petitioners are now members of the National Association of Talent Representatives (NATR). Unlike TARA, which functions only in the legitimate theater field, NATR also functions in the fields of motion pictures and television. In those fields, agents operate under closely analogous agent regulations maintained by the Screen Actors' Guild and the American Federation of Television and Radio Artists.

The history of the negotiations and disputes between Equity and TARA are described in the opinion of the District Court in the present case. 478 F. Supp. 496, 498 (SDNY).

of union discipline, from using an agent who has not, through the mechanism of obtaining an Equity license (called a "franchise"), agreed to comply with the regulations. The most important of the regulations requires that a licensed agent must renounce any right to take a commission on an employment contract under which an actor or actress receives scale wages.[8] To the extent a contract includes provisions under which an actor or actress will sometimes receive scale pay—for rehearsals or "chorus" employment, for example—and sometimes more, the regulations deny the agent any commission on the scale portions of the contract. Licensed agents are also precluded from taking commissions on out-of-town expense money paid to their clients. Moreover, commissions are limited on wages within 10% of scale pay,[9] and an agent must allow his client to terminate a representation contract if the agent is not successful in procuring employment within a specified period.[10] Finally, agents are required to pay franchise fees to Equity. The fee is $200 for the initial franchise, $60 a year thereafter for each agent, and $40 for any subagent working in the office of another. These fees are deposited by Equity in its general treasury and are not segregated from other union funds.

In 1977, after a dispute between Equity and Theatrical Artists Representatives Associates (TARA)—a trade association representing theatrical agents, see n. 7, *supra*—a group of agents, including the petitioners, resigned from TARA because of TARA's decision to abide by Equity's regulations. These agents also informed Equity that they would not accept Equity's regulations, or apply for franchises. The petitioners instituted this lawsuit in May 1978, contending that Equity's regulations of theatrical agents violated §§ 1 and 2 of the Sherman Act, 26 Stat. 209, as amended, 15 U. S. C. §§ 1 and 2.

---

[8] The minimum, or "scale," wage varies. In August 1977, for example, the minimum weekly salary was $335 for Broadway performances, and $175 for performances off Broadway. Scale wages are set by a collective-bargaining agreement between Equity and the producers, to which the agents are not parties. When an agent represents an actor or actress whose professional reputation is not sufficient to demand a salary higher than scale, the agent hopes to develop a relationship that will become continually more remunerative as the performer's professional reputation grows, and with it the power to demand an ever higher salary. No agent is required to represent an actor or actress whom he does not wish to represent.

[9] It is Equity's view that commissions in the industry are not necessarily related to efforts by the agents, and that an agent often functions as little more than an "order taker," who is able to collect a percentage of a client's wages for the duration of a show for doing little more than answering a producer's telephone call. Indeed, an agent may collect a commission on the salary of an actor or actress he represents even if the client obtains the job without the agent.

[10] Equity argues that this restriction is necessary because there is an incentive for agents to represent as many actors and actresses as possible—and not necessarily to serve them all well—because an agent receives a commission whenever his client is employed at a salary higher than scale, regardless of the extent of his involvement in obtaining employment for the client.

B

The District Court found, after a bench trial, that Equity's creation and maintenance of the agency franchise system were fully protected by the statutory labor exemptions from the antitrust laws, and accordingly dismissed the petitioners' complaint. 478 F. Supp. 496 (SDNY). Among its factual conclusions, the trial court found that in the theatrical industry, agents play a critical role in securing employment for actors and actresses:

> "As a matter of general industry practice, producers seek actors and actresses for their productions through agents. Testimony in this case convincingly established that an actor without an agent does not have the same access to producers or the same opportunity to be seriously considered for a part as does an actor who has an agent. Even principal interviews, in which producers are required to interview all actors who want to be considered for principal roles, do not eliminate the need for an agent, who may have a greater chance of gaining an audition for his client.

> . . . .

> "Testimony confirmed that agents play an integral role in the industry; without an agent, an actor would have significantly lesser chances of gaining employment." *Id.*, at 497, 502.

The court also found "no evidence to suggest the existence of any conspiracy or illegal combination between Actors' Equity and TARA or between Actors' Equity and producers," and concluded that "[t]he Actors Equity franchising system was employed by Actors' Equity for the purpose of protecting the wages and working conditions of its members." *Id.*, at 499.

The Court of Appeals unanimously affirmed the judgment of the District Court. It determined that the threshold issue was, under *United States* v. *Hutcheson*, 312 U. S. 219, 232, whether Equity's franchising system involved any combination between Equity and any "non-labor groups" or persons who are not "parties to a labor dispute." 622 F. 2d, at 648–649. If it did, the court reasoned, the protection of the statutory labor exemption would not apply.

First, the Court of Appeals held that the District Court had not been clearly erroneous in finding no agreement, explicit or tacit, between Equity and the producers to establish or police the franchising system. *Ibid.* Next, the court turned to the relationship between the union and those agents who had agreed to become franchised, in order to determine whether those agreements would divest Equity's system of agency regulation of the statutory exemption. Relying on *Musicians* v. *Carroll*, 391 U. S. 99, the court concluded that the agents were themselves a "labor group," because of their substantial "economic inter-relationship" with Equity, under which "the union [could] not eliminate wage

competition among its members without regulation of the fees of the agents."
622 F. 2d, at 650, 651. Accordingly, since the elimination of wage competition
is plainly within the area of a union's legitimate self-interest, the court
concluded that the exemption was applicable.[11]

After deciding that the central feature of Equity's franchising system—the
union's exaction of an agreement by agents not to charge commissions on
certain types of work—was immune from antitrust challenge, the Court of
Appeals turned to the petitioners' challenge of the franchise fees exacted from
agents. Equity had argued that the fees were necessary to meet its expenses in
administering the franchise system, but no evidence was presented at trial to
show that the costs justified the fees actually levied. The Court of Appeals
suggested that if the exactions exceeded the true-costs, they could not legally
be collected, as such exactions would be unconnected with any of the goals of
national labor policy that justify the labor antitrust exemption. Despite the
lack of any cost evidence at trial, however, the appellate court reasoned that
the fees were sufficiently low that a remand to the District Court on this point
"would not serve any useful purpose." *Id.*, at 651.

II

A

Labor unions are lawful combinations that serve the collective interests of
workers, but they also possess the power to control the character of competition in an industry. Accordingly, there is an inherent tension between national
antitrust policy, which seeks to maximize competition, and national labor
policy, which encourages cooperation among workers to improve the conditions of employment. In the years immediately following passage of the
Sherman Act, courts enjoined strikes as unlawful restraints of trade when a
union's conduct or objectives were deemed "socially or economically harmful." *Duplex Printing Press Co.* v. *Deering*, 254 U. S. 443, 485 (Brandeis, J.,
dissenting). In response to these practices, Congress acted, first in the Clayton
Act, 38 Stat. 731, and later in the Norris-LaGuardia Act, 47 Stat. 70, to
immunize labor unions and labor disputes from challenge under the Sherman
Act.

Section 6 of the Clayton Act, 15 U. S. C. § 17, declares that human labor "is
not a commodity or article of commerce," and immunizes from antitrust
liability labor organizations and their members "lawfully carrying out" their
"legitimate object[ives]." Section 20 of the Act prohibits injunctions against

---

[11] The Court of Appeals recognized that even if there had been an agreement between Equity
and a "non-labor group," the agreement might still have been protected from the antitrust laws
under the "non-statutory" exemption. 622 F. 2d, at 649, n. 1. See *Connell Construction Co.* v.
Plumbers & Steamfitters, 421 U.S. 616, 622. . .

specified employee activities, such as strikes and boycotts, that are undertaken in the employees' self-interest and that occur in the course of disputes "concerning terms or conditions of employment," and states that none of the specified acts can be "held to be [a] violatio[n] of any law of the United States." 29 U. S. C. § 52. This protection is re-emphasized and expanded in the Norris-LaGuardia Act, which prohibits federal-court injunctions against single or organized employees engaged in enumerated activities, and specifically forbids such injunctions notwithstanding the claim of an unlawful combination or conspiracy. While the Norris-LaGuardia Act's bar of federal-court labor injunctions is not explicitly phrased as an exemption from the antitrust laws, it has been interpreted broadly as a statement of congressional policy that the courts must not use the antitrust laws as a vehicle to interfere in labor disputes.

In *United States* v. *Hutcheson*, 312 U. S. 219, the Court held that labor unions acting in their self-interest and not in combination with nonlabor groups enjoy a statutory exemption from Sherman Act liability. After describing the congressional responses to judicial interference in union activity, *id.*, at 229–230, the Court declared that

> "[s]o long as a union acts in its self-interest and does not combine with non-labor groups, the licit and the illicit under § 20 [of the Clayton Act] are not to be distinguished by any judgment regarding the wisdom or unwisdom, the rightness or wrongness, the selfishness or unselfishness of the end of which the particular union activities are the means." *Id.*, at 232 (footnote omitted).

The Court explained that this exemption derives not only from the Clayton Act, but also from the Norris-LaGuardia Act, particularly its definition of a "labor dispute," *supra*, in which Congress "reasserted the original purpose of the Clayton Act by infusing into it the immunized trade union activities as redefined by the later Act." 312 U. S., at 236. Thus under *Hutcheson*, no federal injunction may issue over a "labor dispute," and "§ 20 [of the Clayton Act] removes all such allowable conduct from the taint of being a 'violation of any law of the United States,' including the Sherman [Act]." *Ibid.*[16]

The statutory exemption does not apply when a union combines with a "non-labor group." *Hutcheson*, *supra*, at 232. Accordingly, antitrust immunity is forfeited when a union combines with one or more employers in an effort to restrain trade. In *Allen Bradley Co.* v. *Electrical Workers*, 325 U. S. 797, for

---

[16] See also *Apex Hosiery Co.* v. *Leader*, 310 U. S. 469. There, in the Term preceding that in which the *Hutcheson* case was decided, the Court reasoned that the Sherman Act prohibits only restraints on "commercial competition," 310 U. S., at 497, 499, 510–511—or those market restraints designed to monopolize supply, control prices, or allocate product distribution—and that unions are not liable where they merely further their own goals in the labor market.

example, the Court held that a union had violated the Sherman Act when it combined with manufacturers and contractors to erect a sheltered local business market in order "to bar all other business men from [the market], and to charge the public prices above a competitive level." *Id.*, at 809. The Court indicated that the union efforts would, standing alone, be exempt from antitrust liability, *ibid.*, but because the union had not acted unilaterally, the exemption was denied. Congress "intended to outlaw business monopolies. A business monopoly is no less such because a union participates, and such participation is a violation of the Act." *Id.*, at 811.

B

The Court of Appeals properly recognized that the threshold issue was to determine whether or not Equity's franchising of agents involved any combination between Equity and any "non-labor groups," or persons who are not "parties to a labor dispute." 622 F. 2d, at 649 (quoting *Hutcheson*, 312 U. S., at 232).[20] And the court's conclusion that the trial court had not been clearly erroneous in its finding that there was no combination between Equity and the theatrical producers[21] to create or maintain the franchise system is amply supported by the record.

The more difficult problem is whether the combination between Equity and the agents who agreed to become franchised was a combination with a "nonlabor group." The answer to this question is best understood in light of *Musicians* v. *Carroll*, 391 U. S. 99. There, four orchestra leaders, members of the American Federation of Musicians, brought an action based on the Sherman Act challenging the union's unilateral system of regulating "club dates," or one-time musical engagements. These regulations, *inter alia*, enforced a closed shop; required orchestra leaders to engage a minimum number of "sidemen," or instrumentalists; prescribed minimum prices for local engagements;[22] prescribed higher minimum prices for traveling orchestras; and permitted leaders to deal only with booking agents licensed by the union.

---

[20] Of course, a party seeking refuge in the statutory exemption must be a bona fide labor organization, and not an independent contractor or entrepreneur. See *Meat Drivers* v. *United States*, 371 U. S. 94; *Columbia River Packers Assn.* v. *Hinton*, 315 U. S. 143. See generally 1 P. Areeda & D. Turner, Antitrust Law § 229c, pp. 195–198 (1978). There is no dispute about Equity's status as a bona fide labor organization.

[21] As the employers of Equity's members, producers are plainly a "nonlabor group." Employers almost always will be a "nonlabor group," although an exception has been recognized, for example, when the employer himself is in job competition with his employees. See *Musicians* v. *Carroll*, 391 U. S. 99 (orchestra leaders who both lead an orchestra and play an instrument).

[22] These consisted of a minimum scale for sidemen, a "leader's fee," which was twice the sidemen's scale in orchestras of at least four, and an additional 8% for social security, unemployment insurance, and other expenses. In addition, if a leader did not appear but

Without disturbing the finding of the Court of Appeals that the orchestra leaders were employers and independent contractors, the Court concluded that they were nonetheless a "labor group" and parties to a "labor dispute" within the meaning of the Norris-LaGuardia Act, and thus that their involvement in the union regulatory scheme was not an unlawful combination between "labor" and "nonlabor" groups. The Court agreed with the trial court that the applicable test was whether there was "job or wage competition or some other economic interrelationship affecting legitimate union interests between the union members and the independent contractors." *Id.*, at 106.

The Court also upheld the restrictions on booking agents, who were *not* involved in job or wage competition with union members. Accordingly, these restrictions had to meet the "other economic interrelationship" branch of the disjunctive test quoted above. And the test was met because those restrictions were " 'at least as intimately bound up with the subject of wages' . . . as the price floors." *Id.*, at 113 (quoting *Teamsters v. Oliver*, 362 U. S. 605, 606). The Court noted that the booking agent restrictions had been adopted, in part, because agents had "charged exorbitant fees, and booked engagements for musicians at wages . . . below union scale."[23]

C

The restrictions challenged by the petitioners in this case are very similar to the agent restrictions upheld in the *Carroll* case. The essential features of the regulatory scheme are identical: members are permitted to deal only with agents who have agreed (1) to honor their fiduciary obligations by avoiding conflicts of interest, (2) not to charge excessive commissions, and (3) not to book members for jobs paying less than the union minimum.[25] And as in

---

designated a subleader, and four or more musicians performed, the leader was required to pay from his leader's fee 1.5 times the sidemen's scale to the subleader.

[23] The Court did not explicitly determine whether the second prong of the *Hutcheson* test for the statutory exemption had been met, *i. e.*, whether the union had acted in its "self-interest." But given its various findings that the challenged restrictions were designed to cope with job competition and to protect wage scales and working conditions, 391 U.S., at 108, 109, 110, 113, it clearly did so *sub silentio*.

[25] Indeed, the District Court in *Carroll*, whose judgment was affirmed by this Court "in its entirety," 391 U.S., at 114, drew parallels with the restrictions at issue in the present case. The court noted that "[a]pparently, similar abuses by booking agents existed in other fields too. *Edelstein v. Gillmore*, 35 F. 2d 723, 726 (2d Cir. 1929) (actors)." *Carroll v. AFM*, 241 F. Supp. 865, 892 (SDNY).

The petitioners argue that theatrical agents are indistinguishable from "numerous [other] groups of persons who merely supply products and services to union members" such as landlords, grocers, accountants, and lawyers. But it is clear that agents differ from these groups in two critical respects: the agents control access to jobs and negotiation of the terms of employment. For the actor or actress, therefore, agent commissions are not merely a discretionary expenditure of disposable income, but a virtually inevitable concomitant of obtaining employment.

Carroll, Equity's regulation of agents developed in response to abuses by employment agents who occupy a critical role in the relevant labor market. The agent stands directly between union members and jobs, and is in a powerful position to evade the union's negotiated wage structure.

The peculiar structure of the legitimate theater industry, where work is intermittent, where it is customary if not essential for union members to secure employment through agents, and where agents' fees are calculated as a percentage of a member's wage, makes it impossible for the union to defend even the integrity of the minimum wages it has negotiated without regulation of agency fees. The regulations are "brought within the labor exemption [because they are] necessary to assure that scale wages will be paid. . . . " *Carroll*, 391 U. S., at 112. They "embody . . . a direct frontal attack upon a problem thought to threaten the maintenance of the basic wage structure." *Teamsters* v. *Oliver*, 358 U. S. 283, 294. Agents must, therefore, be considered a "labor group," and their controversy with Equity is plainly a "labor dispute" as defined in the Norris-LaGuardia Act: "representation of persons in negotiating, fixing, maintaining, changing, or seeking to arrange terms or conditions of employment, regardless of whether or not the disputants stand in the proximate relation of employer and employee." 29 U. S. C. § 113 (c).

Agents perform a function—the representation of union members in the sale of their labor—that in most nonentertainment industries is performed exclusively by unions. In effect, Equity's franchise system operates as a substitute for maintaining a hiring hall as the representative of its members seeking employment.

Finally, Equity's regulations are clearly designed to promote the union's legitimate self-interest. *Hutcheson*, 312 U. S., at 232. In a case such as this, where there is no direct wage or job competition between the union and the group it regulates, the *Carroll* formulation to determine the presence of a nonlabor group—whether there is " 'some . . . economic interrelationship affecting legitimate union interests . . . ,' " 391 U. S., at 106 (quoting District Court opinion)—necessarily resolves this issue.

D

The question remains whether the fees that Equity levies upon the agents who apply for franchises are a permissible component of the exempt regulatory system. We have concluded that Equity's justification for these fees is inadequate. Conceding that *Carroll* did not sanction union extraction of franchise fees from agents,[29] Equity suggests, only in the most general terms, that the fees are somehow related to the basic purposes of its regulations:

---

[29] See *Carroll*, 241 F. Supp., at 881. We have, in fact, found no case holding that a union may extract such fees from independent agents who represent union members.

elimination of wage competition, upholding of the union wage scale, and promotion of fair access to jobs. But even assuming that the fees no more than cover the costs of administering the regulatory system, this is simply another way of saying that without the fees, the union's regulatory efforts would not be subsidized—and that the dues of Equity's members would perhaps have to be increased to offset the loss of a general revenue source. If Equity did not impose these franchise fees upon the agents, there is no reason to believe that any of its legitimate interests would be affected.[31]

III

For the reasons stated, the judgment of the Court of Appeals is affirmed in part and reversed in part, and the case is remanded for proceedings consistent with this opinion.

It is so ordered.

JUSTICE BRENNAN, with whom THE CHIEF JUSTICE and JUSTICE MARSHALL join, concurring in part and dissenting in part.

I join all but Part II-D of the Court's opinion. That part holds that respondents' exaction of a franchise fee is not a "permissible component of the exempt regulatory system." *Ante*, at 722. Rather, I agree with the Court of Appeals that the approximately $12,000 collected annually in fees is not "incommensurate with Equity's expenses in maintaining a full-time employee to administer the system," 622 F. 2d 647, 651 (CA2 1980), and thus is not "unconnected with any of the goals of national labor policy which justify the antitrust exemption for labor," *ibid*.

The Court justifies its conclusion by suggesting that, since the union could increase its dues to offset the revenue lost from invalidation of the fee system, "there is no reason to believe that any of [the union's] legitimate interests would be affected," if the fee system were found to violate the antitrust laws. *Ante*, at 722. The union could of course raise its dues, but the issue here is whether the conceded antitrust immunity of the franchising system includes the franchise fee.

I find somewhat incongruous the Court's conclusion that an incident of the

---

[31] The respondents offer union hiring hall fees as an analogy in support of Equity's collection of franchise fees. In that context, the respondents argue, without citation, that a union may impose reasonable fees, upon employers to meet the costs of maintaining a union-run hiring hall. But even if the respondents' statement of labor law is correct, the analogy would not be persuasive. Assuming that hiring hall fees are so imposed, the fees are borne by parties who directly benefit from the employment services of the hiring halls and are collected by the entities that provide them. That is not true in the present case.

The view expressed in the separate opinion filed today as to who are the beneficiaries of the franchising system will undoubtedly surprise the agents who brought this lawsuit . . .

overall system constitutes impermissible regulation, but that agents in general may be significantly regulated because they are not a "nonlabor group." This incongruity is highlighted by the similarity between union hiring halls and the franchising system, a similarity which the Court itself acknowledges: "Equity's franchise system operates as a substitute for maintaining a hiring hall as the representative of its members seeking employment." *Ante*, at 721. The Court disregards this similarity in concluding that the franchising system does not "directly benefit" the agents who are required to pay the fees. *Ante*, at 722, n. 31. It reaches this conclusion by incorrectly assuming that the only parties who directly benefit from the hiring hall and the franchising system are employers and employees and producers and actors, as the case may be. But surely the agents also benefit from the franchising system, which provides an orderly and protective mechanism for pairing actors who seek jobs with producers who seek actors. The system is thus the means by which the agents ultimately receive their commissions; it is as much the source of their livelihood as it is that of the actors.

Because the fee is an incident of a legitimate scheme of regulation and because it is commensurate in amount with the purpose for which it is sought, I would also affirm this holding of the Court of Appeals.

" 'THEY PAY US LESS, & THEY PAY US LAST' "
Variety (June 15, 1977), p. 7

INDIE DISTRIBS RE U.S. THEATRES

"We're mad as hell," indie producers and distributors on the East Coast seem to be saying, "and we're not going to take it anymore."

In interview after *Variety* interview, the indies recite a litany of marketplace woes—from slow- (and even non-) paying exhibitors and lazy sub-distributors to lack of major circuit playoff and sharply rising "cooperative" advertising costs.

While the complaints are all too familiar, the indies' apparent passion for corrective action isn't. This time, they are saying, this time we're going to do something.

Just what isn't completely clear but recent actions initiated by East Coast indies offer some clues. In N.Y. City, for example, the largely dormant International Film Importers & Distributors Assn. of America is being reorganized and revived.

Excommunication

That started last fall when IFIDA was threatened with being kicked out of the film industry's film rating apparatus, supervised by the Motion Picture Assn. of America.

IFIDA traditionally had representatives on the rating appeals board and its policy review committee, the body which sets the film rating guidelines. The MPAA, representing major production-distribution companies, and the National Assn. of Theatre Owners, repping exhibs, also have representatives on the board and the committee.

But, it was suggested, since IFIDA was really only a paper organization and didn't reflect the interests of the active indies, it shouldn't have role in the rating process. That galvanized local IFIDA members into action. New officers were elected—Joseph Brenner, Jerry Pickman and Lew Mishkin on the board of governors; Carl Peppercorn, treasurer and Sam Sherman, membership chairman.

More importantly, IFIDA got pledges of active support from such companies as Sam Arkoff's American International Pictures and Roger Corman's New World Pictures. IFIDA is now mulling the possibility of opening a Los Angeles office to corral more West-Coast based indies into the ranks.

Says Mishkin

The significance of all this isn't just that IFIDA successfully maintained its representation in the rating system. Let Mishkin of William Mishkin Motion Pictures Inc. explain: "the threat of being booted out of the ratings system got us together but the most important thing now is the need for action on the economic issues."

And then there's the case of Earl Owensby. For years now, independent producers and distribs have been muttering privately about the supposedly shabby treatment they get from the MPAA-supervised rating system. In essence, they claim, PG (parental guidance advised) films from the major companies will be certified PG by the rating board, but PG films from indies often wind up with an R (restricted) or worse from the rating people.

There seems to be one rating standard for the majors and another—and less flexible—one for the indies, some of them complain sottovoce. (The MPAA, of course, has gone out of its way many times to disprove that impression. But the feeling among indies has lingered. -Ed.)

A Yodel From Dixie

With Owensby, a producer based in Shelby, North Carolina, the feeling lingered so pervasively, he complained loudly to his congressman. Public hearings were called—with some fanfare—by a subcommittee of the House

Small Business Committee to investigate the alleged discrepancy in the ratings system.

The committee hearings are winding down somewhat inconclusively (the MPAA again successfully defended its province) but the sight of Assn. heavyweights being dragooned into a Congressional hearing room to prove the Simon-purity of rating certifications must have pleased more that one disgruntled indie.

But it's the economic issues, of course, that most concern the indies quizzed by *Variety*. The nature (and size) of independent operations will always mean they'll be the tail wagged by the dog dominated by the major companies. No one has any illusions about the possibility of altering that reality.

Conditions Get Harsher

Even so, more indies seem to be saying that conditions of doing business are getting unduly harsh and some correction is needed. Joseph Green, the veteran indie who heads the Joseph Green Pictures distribbery, is the most blunt about things. Exhibitors are "SOB's" says he.

"They are taking from the poor to pay off the rich." What he is referring to is the fact that theatremen are too often telling indie distribs that by the time the hefty advances and guarantees are paid major companies for their bigger pictures (and increasingly, even for smaller films), there's nothing left over. Waits of six months for due rentals are not uncommon, says Mishkin.

Brenner says his company in the last year filed more suits against exhibs for alleged overdue rentals than in the preceding 30 years he's been in business.

As To Ad Costs

Mishkin and Ernest Gruenberg of Gamma III agree that advertising costs are escalating precipitously. "It's becoming harder and harder to compete (with major companies in terms of blurb outlays)," Gruenberg opines.

One reason for this, according to Mishkin, is that because the major companies are successfully extracting hefty advances, they're more likely to compensate a bit by throwing more coin into "cooperative" ad efforts with exhibs. Latter have come to expect the indies to be as generous, Mishkin observes.

Arthur Manson, the N.Y.-based consultant and former Warners exec, says: "There's a need for a lot of dough behind the release of a film." That's a hard, economic fact-of-life for indies these days.

Sam Sherman, President of Independent International Pictures, says that in the face of rising business costs, indies have to "do well just to stay alive. A good year, like we're having, means we survive, not that we can retire."

He is particularly vocal about late-paying exhibs, especially those not affiliated with the major chains. Rental payment delays range from 60 days to 18 months, Sherman opines. Some independent exhibs actually bank on indie distribs going out of business "so they won't have to pay at all," he adds.

That's the main reason why Sherman is now an officer of the newly reorganized IFIDA. "We hope to enforce fair payment, both in terms of payment times and rental scales, for our members," says Sherman. His company, 10 years old this year, has a long record of original production, and is currently distributing "Cinderella 2000" and "Uncle Tom's Cabin," the latter a restitching of an earlier European film. Sherman says "Uncle Tom" grossed more than $1,000,000 since March, making it the highest crossing indie pic in the country.

Although the much-vaunted product shortage is widely interpreted as a plus for the indies, things aren't just that simple, according to those quizzed. Ray Silver of Midwest Films says he found that holes in major company release schedule permitted playoff of his wife's (Joan Micklin) "Hester Street" on many circuits at "top terms."

But Mishkin claims exhibs consistently pay lower terms to pix from indies, one of the things, he adds, that he hopes the newly organized IFIDA will look into. Films from the independents require, asserts Mishkin in effect, larger ad costs to launch to play at lower rental terms for which the distrib won't see for a considerable period following the completion of the playdate. No wonder East Coast indies are mad.

One issue of primary concern to both distribs and producer is the tougher scramble for product. "Unless you have a breakthrough film, everything is confined to mediocre business," avers Jerry Frankel of New World Pictures. "The public no longer accepts what were known as 'B movies' that were formerly the foundation of the independent's existence."

Finding "suitable properties" is a big headache for Film Ventures International, the successful indie based in Atlanta, Ga.

Edward Montoro, the company president, [notes] that although films are available, there's a lack of "grossable product." By that he means a non-sexpo outing that doesn't sufficiently interest major distribs yet which has a "hook" to get the public out of the house, away from the tube and into the theatre.

(Film Ventures, for an indie, deals in a big way. For its latest release, the $1,750,000 "Day of the Animals," the company obtained some $2,000,000 in advance guarantees, spent $750,000 on network tv buys in addition to local buys, and opened the pic at some 450 situations across the country, says Montoro. Pic has been sold to CBS-TV for "seven figures," he adds.)

Production is becoming attractive to more and more indie distribs. New

Line Cinema's Robert Shaye reports that his company is currently selling its first feature, "Stunts," (he just returned from Cannes where foreign territories were captured), and is planning two more, "Killer" and "Natural Forces." ("Stunts," a murder-mystery about stuntmen, bowed in L.A. at 87 houses on June 2.)

Competing with the majors for film acquisitions is increasingly a losing battle, says Shaye. "They're like juggernauts; giant bureaucracies like whole governments."

Brenner reports his company is mulling at least one coproduction. Gruenberg says Gamma III "is arranging" for financing of new properties mainly via corporate U.S. and foreign tax deferral deals. He was the only one quizzed who mentioned so-called "shelters."

Film Ventures, Mishkin, Midwest Films, Independent-International and New Line finance their films internally, say toppers at the companies. The loss of the "tax shelter" wasn't a chief complaint among those indies quizzed, although its absence on a broad scale certainly is a limiting factor in the production finance picture.

Budgets for indie films are in at least the $1,500,000 to $2,000,000 range. "You can't get away with anything less anymore," avers Montoro. The trick, say the indies, is to get every penny up on the screen. That in turn gets trickier as ad and other film launch factors get more costly.

So between the "grossable" product shortage, higher production budgets, higher ad and launching costs, lower rentals from bookings that are months late in returning, the East Coast indies report tougher times. Indies have always gambled on winning at higher odds, but this year they seem to be telling the industry that the odds are getting too high— and they mean to do something about it.

Will Tusher, "ABUSES OF 'STAR POWER' PUT INTO FOCUS"
Variety (June 29 1977), p. 37

CONTRACT BUSTING A RED-HOT ISSUE

Hollywood, June 28.

A sleeper glamour issue—focusing on asserted abuses of star power—is about to come awake in the final stages of Screen Actors Guild negotiations with the Assn. of Motion Picture & Television Producers and the Universal-Paramount bargaining unit, The Alliance.

Up to now, it's been mostly management responding to SAG demands. But the employers, goaded by aggrieved television producers, are poised to insist on safeguards against alleged contract busting by the recalcitrant likes of Farrah Fawcett-Majors, Lee Majors and Paul Michael Glaser.

SAG's chief negotiator, national executive secretary Chester L. Migden, won't tip the guild's hand on the controversial question, but has indicated that he is steeled to come to grips with it.

Universal, where series stars have engaged in periodic uprisings, has perhaps a larger stake in the issue than any other major studio. Twentieth Century-Fox—not precisely a stranger to contract jumping—is not all that far behind.

MCA president Sid Sheinberg declines comment, deferring to v.p. Tom Wertheimer who is representing Universal at the bargaining table. Wertheimer also ducks comment, taking cover behind the no-talk pledge of both sides in the discussions which have days to go before the current pact expires coincident with the deadline for reaching an agreement.

Nolan Speaks Up

AMPTP executive v.p. Joseph Adelman similarly passes up the invitation to express himself on the issue, but SAG president Kathleen Nolan does not elect to sidestep the issue. During the recent ABC affiliates meeting in Los Angeles, she was sought out by Fred Pierce, president of ABC Television, who communicated his feeling that the SAG should tighten policing of overscale series stars who treat their contracts with disdain.

Three top ABC series—"Charlie's Angels" (FF Majors), "Six Million Dollar Man" (Lee Majors) and "Starsky & Hutch" (Glaser)—are or were locked into disputes with stars who have balked at returning for another season. Abe Vigoda, of "Barney Miller" and "Fish," has been in a running battle with executive producer Danny Arnold over extra-curricular assignments. (Glaser has since returned to work.)

In recent years, NBC (and Tandem Productions) has dealt with walkouts by Redd Foxx and unacceptable salary demands by Demond Wilson on "Sanford & Son." CBS (also via Tandem) had its share of headaches—now long since resolved—with Carroll O'Connor and Sally Struthers.

Nolan speaks out strongly for the integrity of contracts, but she is careful to assert SAG's intention of verifying alleged contract violations before applying pressure—or sanctions—to bring offending performers in line.

On Honoring The Contract

"Yes, indeed, the SAG takes a dim view of any party breaching a contract," Nolan says. "I was not talking specifics to any one case when I spoke to Mr.

Pierce. I do know that both sides, the actor and the producer, had better have an opportunity of time to know what contract provides for, and then honor it.

"Where applicable under the agreement, the guild has been called upon in the past to arbitrate contract disputes, and will continue to do so in the future. The actor has a responsibility, and in my opinion most often lives up to it. However, if there is a dispute we will use the good offices of the guild to hear the facts and make the determination."

SAG's performance, to date, has not left too favorable an impression on Bill Hayes, attorney for Spelling-Goldberg Productions.

Calls It A Sag Copout

"The guild has always kind of copped out in that regard," Hayes declares. "When you get above a certain amount, they leave it up to lawyers and representatives (agents) and try not to get involved if they can keep from it because the things that apply to a star in a series rarely apply to most guild members.

"We have not had much success in getting the guild to police their members . . . because the areas of policing fall into the category . . . where a star will indulge himself on the set and get temperamental and walk off, or delay production, or cause overtime and things like that. It's just difficult to deal with on a practical level unless a union representative is on the set."

Hayes concedes that there have been instances when SAG has done just that. Occasionally, he warrants, such monitoring has produced more professional behavior. But he insists the process has been hit or miss at best.

How Do You Prove It?

"It's a difficult problem," Hayes submits, "because the guild can't keep a representative on all the sets all the time. At the same time, it's very difficult to prove up things like that dealing with a star. If a star causes some expense and you deduct it from the check, the star will deny doing it . . . You get into a rhubarb with your star and the practicalities overrule the legalities."

His conclusion: SAG policing "has rarely worked." Nevertheless, Hayes, who is with Executive Business Management, sees it as the best of limited recourse short of going to the courts.

"My advice to producer clients," he says, "has been that if they have an actor or an actress that is giving them trouble, they ask the guild to have a representative on the set for observation."

Hayes doesn't suggest that a remedy for contract shirking by series stars lies with SAG alone. He says there's urgent need for an industrywide "integrity reappraisal" involving not only SAG but the agents, attorneys and managers of misbehaving stars. He suggests a need for wall-to-wall upgrading of professionalism. And in so doing, he does not even entertain the hard-line notice of slamming the door on renegotiation.

Would Reappraise Walkouts

"There's no question," Hayes grants, "that actors can have their financial benefits improved when they get into a successful show. Even going back 30 years, the studios, when they had stock players, would amend an agreement . . . if an actor hit and became a star. So that's nothing new. But this business of walking out on agreements, putting people over a barrel, and putting them through all the nonsense and expense they have to go through—that's something the industry generally should reappraise and try to get some professional integrity on."

But while Hayes—noting Pierce's conversations with Nolan—agrees on pressuring SAG to assume greater responsibility, he admits coming up short on specifics.

'Shake Them Up A Bit'

"Obviously," he says, "SAG should do anything and everything it possibly can, and there may indeed be some way they can do something. But we have not been able to find a way for SAG to police the star of a series unless the star is a continuing bad boy or bad girl. Then you can get SAG to put an observer on the set, and have a talk with them and shake them up a little bit."

But when the grievances go full blown and a star walks out on a contract, Hayes feels the guild should take a strong— certainly a stronger—enforcement position. However, he claims that even when SAG moves to enter such cases the representation founders on ritual insistence by attorneys that their seemingly recalcitrant stars have a sound case.

"That," proposes Hayes, "is not necessarily true. Usually, it's just a hook that some lawyer finds to hang it on."

———————

Edwin McDowell, "SAGAN SELLS FIRST NOVEL TO SIMON & SCHUSTER"

The New York Times (January 13, 1981), p. C16

Carl Sagan, the astronomer and bestselling author, has negotiated a $2 million contract with Simon & Schuster for a first novel, to the chagrin of his current publisher, Random House. Simon & Schuster won the book at auction after publishers were told by Mr. Sagan's agent that the four-book contract the author signed with Random House in 1976 applied only to works of nonfiction.

"Random House was quite resentful," according to Scott Meredith, Mr. Sagan's literary agent, who conducted the auction for rights to the novel. "But there is no question that Carl eventually will deliver two more books of nonfiction to them." His first two books for Random House under the present contract were "The Dragons of Eden," which won a Pulitzer Prize in 1978, and "Cosmos," a current best seller, which is tied in with the Public Broadcasting Service series of the same name.

That interpretation of the contract is seconded by Charles Rembar, the lawyer for Mr. Meredith and Mr. Sagan, but Random House has a different view. "It's Sagan's position that the contract applies only to books of nonfiction," Anthony M. Schulte, the company's executive vice president, said. "It is not our position, but we chose not to argue it."

Other Disagreements

There are other areas of disagreement as well. Mr. Meredith said Random House had bid on the novel, and, along with other publishers, "was in it to the end."

Mr. Schulte said, "We did not bid for the book." He declined to elaborate on the discrepancy between his and Mr. Meredith's recollection of events, nor would he elaborate on why Random House had chosen not to contest what it regards as a misinterpretation of the contract.

One well-placed publishing source said Random House probably felt that, even if it won in the courts, the fight could seriously erode relations with Mr. Sagan, a valuable literary resource. "It goes back to the old saying about half a loaf being better than none," the source said.

The 45-year-old Mr. Sagan is a television personality and publishing phenomenon. "The Dragons of Eden," his first title under the four-book, $250,000 contract, has sold 200,000 copies in hard-cover and more than one million in paperback.

115-Page Outline for Novel

His latest book, "Cosmos," has been on The New York Times best-seller list since Nov. 9. Even with 395,000 copies in print, demand is so brisk that Random House has ordered a fifth printing of 57,000, and it is trying to borrow copies from England and book clubs. Mr. Sagan's other books include "Other Worlds," published by Bantam Books.

Copies of the 115-page outline for the proposed novel, "Contact," about man's first encounter with extraterrestrial beings, were hand-delivered to officials of nine publishing houses Dec. 5, 1980, according to Mr. Meredith. The auction remained open two weeks.

A few days after the outlines were delivered, Mr. Meredith said he and his editorial director, Jack Scovil, were invited to Random House headquarters on East 52d Street to meet with Robert L. Bernstein, chairman and president; Jason Epstein, editorial director, and Anne Freedgood, Mr. Sagan's editor at Random House.

Not Especially Friendly

"We had a gentlemanly but not especially friendly get-together," Mr. Meredith said. "They seemed surprised when I pointed out that the contract called for four books of nonfiction. I think there was grave disappointment on Random House's part, and I understand it completely. But there was grave disappointment on my part that they didn't come up to snuff financially."

The movie rights to "Contact," scheduled for publication in the fall of next year, have been purchased by Polygram Pictures. Mr. Meredith said the movie was tentatively budgeted at $40 million and was scheduled for release at Christmas 1983.

Motion Picture

UNITED STATES v. PARAMOUNT PICTURES, INC.
334 U.S. 131 (1948)*

MR. JUSTICE DOUGLAS delivered the opinion of the Court.

These cases are here on appeal from a judgment of a three-judge District Court holding that the defendants had violated § 1 and § 2 of the Sherman Act, 26 Stat. 209, as amended. 50 Stat. 693, 15 U.S.C. §§ 1, 2, and granting an injunction and other relief. 66 F. Supp. 323; 70 F. Supp. 53.

The suit was instituted by the United States under § 4 of the Sherman Act to prevent and restrain violations of it. The defendants fall into three groups: (1) Paramount Pictures, Inc., Loew's, Incorporated, Radio-Keith-Orpheum Corporation, Warner Bros. Pictures, Inc., Twentieth Century-Fox Film Corporation, which produce motion pictures, and their respective subsidiaries or affiliates which distribute and exhibit films. These are known as the five major

---

* Together with No. 80, *Loew's, Incorporated* v. *United States*; No. 81, *Paramount Pictures, Inc.* v. *United States*; No. 82, *Columbia Pictures Corp.* v. *United States*; No. 83, *United Artists Corp.* v. *United States*; No. 84, *Universal Corp.* v. *United States*; No. 85, *American Theatres Assn., Inc.* v. *United States*; and No. 86, *Allred* v. *United States*, also on appeal from the same court.

defendants or exhibitor-defendants. (2) Columbia Pictures Corporation and Universal Corporation, which produce motion pictures, and their subsidiaries which distribute films. (3) United Artists Corporation, which is engaged only in the distribution of motion pictures. The five majors, through their subsidiaries or affiliates, own or control theatres; the other defendants do not.

The complaint charged that the producer defendants had attempted to monopolize and had monopolized the production of motion pictures. The District Court found to the contrary and that finding is not challenged here. The complaint charged that all the defendants, as distributors, had conspired to restrain and monopolize and had restrained and monopolized interstate trade in the distribution and exhibition of films by specific practices which we will shortly relate. It also charged that the five major defendants had engaged in a conspiracy to restrain and monopolize, and had restrained and monopolized, interstate trade in the exhibition of motion pictures in most of the larger cities of the country. It charged that the vertical combination of producing, distributing, and exhibiting motion pictures by each of the five major defendants violated § 1 and § 2 of the Act. It charged that each distributor-defendant had entered into various contracts with exhibitors which unreasonably restrained trade. Issue was joined; and a trial was had.

First. Restraint of Trade— (1) *Price Fixing.* Per Se

No film is sold to an exhibitor in the distribution of motion pictures. The right to exhibit under copyright is licensed. The District Court found that the defendants in the licenses they issued fixed minimum admission prices which the exhibitors agreed to charge, whether the rental of the film was a flat amount or a percentage of the receipts. It found that substantially uniform minimum prices had been established in the licenses of all defendants. Minimum prices were established in master agreements or franchises which were made between various defendants as distributors and various defendants as exhibitors and in joint operating agreements made by the five majors with each other and with independent theatre owners covering the operation of certain theatres.[4] By these later contracts minimum admission prices were often fixed for dozens of theatres owned by a particular defendant in a given area of the United States. Minimum prices were fixed in licenses of each of the

---

[4] A master agreement is a licensing agreement or "blanket deal" covering the exhibition of features in a number of theatres, usually comprising a circuit.

A franchise is a licensing agreement, or series of licensing agreements, entered into as part of the same transaction, in effect for more than one motion picture season and covering the exhibition of features released by one distributor during the entire period of the agreement.

An independent as used in these cases means a producer, distributor, or exhibitor, as the context requires, which is not a defendant in the action, or a subsidiary or affiliate of a defendant.

five major defendants. The other three defendants made the same requirement in licenses granted to the exhibitor-defendants. We do not stop to elaborate on these findings. They are adequately detailed by the District Court in its opinion. See 66 F. Supp. 334–339.

The District Court found that two price-fixing conspiracies existed—a horizontal one between all the defendants; a vertical one between each distributor-defendant and its licensees. The latter was based on express agreements and was plainly established. The former was inferred from the pattern of price-fixing disclosed in the record. We think there was adequate foundation for it too. It is not necessary to find an express agreement in order to find a conspiracy. It is enough that a concert of action is contemplated and that the defendants conformed to the arrangement. *Interstate Circuit* v. *United States*, 306 U.S. 208, 226–227; *United States* v. *Masonite Corp.*, 316 U.S. 265, 275. That was shown here.

On this phase of the case the main attack is on the decree which enjoins the defendants and their affiliates from granting any license, except to their own theatres, in which minimum prices for admission to a theatre are fixed in any manner or by any means. The argument runs as follows: *United States* v. *General Electric Co.*, 272 U.S. 476, held that an owner of a patent could, without violating the Sherman Act, grant a license to manufacture and vend, and could fix the price at which the licensee could sell the patented article. It is pointed out that defendants do not sell the films to exhibitors, but only license them and that the Copyright Act (35 Stat. 1075, 1088, 17 U.S.C. § 1), like the patent statutes, grants the owner exclusive rights.[5] And it is argued that if the patentee can fix the price at which his licensee may sell the patented article, the owner of the copyright should be allowed the same privilege. It is maintained that such a privilege is essential to protect the value of the copyrighted films.

We start, of course, from the premise that so far as the Sherman Act is concerned, a price-fixing combination is illegal *per se. United States* v. *Socony-Vacuum Oil Co.*, 310 U. S. 150; *United States* v. *Masonite Corporation, supra.* We recently held in *United States* v. *Gypsum Co.*, 333 U. S. 364, 400, that even patentees could not regiment an entire industry by licenses containing price-fixing agreements. What was said there is adequate to bar defendants, through their horizontal conspiracy, from fixing prices for the exhibition of films in the movie industry. Certainly the rights of the copyright owner are no greater than those of the patentee.

Nor can the result be different when we come to the vertical between each

---

[5] See note 12, *infra.*

distributor-defendant and his licensees. The District Court stated in its findings:

> "In agreeing to maintain a stipulated minimum admission price, each exhibitor thereby consents to the minimum price level at which it will compete against other licensees of the same distributor whether they exhibit on the same run or not. The total effect is that through the separate contracts between the distributor and its licensees a price structure is erected which regulates the licensees' ability to compete against one another in admission prices."

That consequence seems to us to be incontestable. We stated in *United States* v. *Gypsum Co., supra*, p. 401, that "The rewards which flow to the patentee and his licensees from the suppression of competition through the regulation of an industry are not reasonably and normally adapted to secure pecuniary reward for the patentee's monopoly." The same is true of the rewards of the copyright owners and their licensees in the present case. For here too the licenses are but a part of the general plan to suppress competition. The case where a distributor fixes admission prices to be charged by a single independent exhibitor, no other licensees or exhibitors being in contemplation, seems to be wholly academic, as the District Court pointed out. It is, therefore, plain that *United States* v. *General Electric Co., supra*, as applied in the patent cases, affords no haven to the defendants in this case. For a copyright may no more be used than a patent to deter competition between rivals in the exploitation of their licenses. See *Interstate Circuit* v. *United States, supra*, p. 230.

(2) *Clearances and Runs.*

Clearances are designed to protect a particular run of a film against a subsequent run.[6] The District Court found that all of the distributor-defendants used clearance provisions and that they were stated in several different ways or in combinations: in terms of a given period between designated runs; in terms of admission prices charged by competing theatres; in terms of a given period of clearance over specifically named theatres; in terms of so many days' clearance over specified areas or towns; or in terms of clearances as fixed by other distributors.

The Department of Justice maintained below that clearances are unlawful *per se* under the Sherman Act. But that is a question we need not consider, for

---

[6] A clearance is the period of time, usually stipulated in license contracts, which must elapse between runs of the same feature within a particular area or in specified theatres.

Runs are successive exhibitions of a feature in a given area, first-run being the first exhibition in that area, second-run being the next subsequent, and so on, and include successive exhibitions in different theatres, even though such theatres may be under a common ownership or management.

the District Court ruled otherwise and that conclusion is not challenged here. In its view their justification was found in the assurance they give the exhibitor that the distributor will not license a competitor to show the film either at the same time or so soon thereafter that the exhibitor's expected income from the run will be greatly diminished. A clearance when used to protect that interest of the exhibitor was reasonable, in the view of the court, when not unduly extended as to area or duration. Thus the court concluded that although clearances might indirectly affect admission prices, they do not fix them and that they may be reasonable restraints of trade under the Sherman Act.

The District Court held that in determining whether a clearance is unreasonable, the following factors are relevant:

(1) The admission prices of the theatres involved, as set by the exhibitors;

(2) The character and location of the theatres involved, including size, type of entertainment, appointments, transit facilities, etc.;

(3) The policy of operation of the theatres involved, such as the showing of double features, gift nights, give-aways, premiums cut-rate tickets, lotteries, etc.;

(4) The rental terms and license fees paid by the theatres involved and the revenues derived by the distributor-defendant from such theatres;

(5) The extent to which the theatres involved compete with each other for patronage;

(6) The fact that a theatre involved is affiliated with a defendant-distributor or with an independent circuit of theatres should be disregarded; and

(7) There should be no clearance between theatres not in substantial competition.

It reviewed the evidence in light of these standards and concluded that many of the clearances granted by the defendants were unreasonable. We do not stop to retrace those steps. The evidence is ample to show, as the District Court plainly demonstrated, see 66 F.Supp. pp. 343–346, that many clearances had no relation to the competitive factors which alone could justify them.[7] The

---

[7] Thus the District Court found:

"Some licenses granted clearance to sell to all theatres which the exhibitor party to the contract might thereafter own, lease, control, manage, or operate against all theatres in the immediate vicinity of the exhibitor's theatre thereafter erected or opened. The purpose of this type of clearance agreements was to fix the run and clearance status of any theatre

clearances which were in vogue had, indeed, acquired a fixed and uniform character and were made applicable to situations without regard to the special circumstances which are necessary to sustain them as reasonable restraints of trade. The evidence is ample to support the finding of the District Court that the defendants either participated in evolving this uniform system of clearances or acquiesced in it and so furthered its existence. That evidence, like the evidence on the price-fixing phase of the case, is therefore adequate to support the finding of a conspiracy to restrain trade by imposing unreasonable clearances.

The District Court enjoined defendants and their affiliates from agreeing with each other or with any exhibitors or distributors to maintain a system of clearances, or from granting any clearance between theatres not in substantial competition, or from granting or enforcing any clearance against theatres in substantial competition with the theatre receiving the license for exhibition in excess of what is reasonably necessary to protect the licensee in the run granted. In view of the findings this relief was plainly warranted.

Some of the defendants ask that this provision be construed (or, if necessary, modified) to allow licensors in granting clearances to take into consideration what is reasonably necessary for a fair return to the licensor. We reject that suggestion. If that were allowed, then the exhibitor-defendants would have an easy method of keeping alive at least some of the consequences of the effective conspiracy which they launched. For they could then justify clearances granted by other distributors in favor of their theatres in terms of the competitive requirements of those theatres, and at the same time justify the restrictions they impose upon independents in terms of the necessity of protecting their film rental as licensor. That is too potent a weapon to leave in the hands of those whose proclivity to unlawful conduct has been so marked. It plainly should not be allowed so long as the exhibitor-defendants own theatres. For in its baldest terms it is in the hands of the defendants no less than a power to restrict the competition of others in the way deemed most desirable by them. In the setting of this case the only measure of reasonableness of a clearance by Sherman Act standards is the special needs of the licensee for the competitive advantages it affords.

Whether the same restrictions would be applicable to a producer who had not been a party to such a conspiracy is a question we do not reach.

Objection is made to a further provision of this part of the decree stating that "Whenever any clearance provision is attacked as not legal under the provisions of this decree, the burden shall be upon the distributor to sustain

---

thereafter opened not on the basis of its appointments, size, location, and other competitive features normally entering into such determination, but rather upon the sole basis of whether it were operated by the exhibitor party to the agreement."

the legality thereof." We think that provision was justified. Clearances have been used along with price fixing to suppress competition with the theatres of the exhibitor-defendants and with other favored exhibitors. The District Court could therefore have eliminated clearances completely for a substantial period of time, even though, as it thought, they were not illegal *per se*. For equity has the power to uproot all parts of an illegal scheme—the valid as well as the invalid—in order to rid the trade or commerce of all taint of the conspiracy. *United States* v. *Bausch & Lomb Co.*, 321 U. S. 707, 724. The court certainly then could take the lesser step of making them *prima facie* invalid. But we do not rest on that alone. As we have said, the only justification for clearances in the setting of this case is in terms of the special needs of the licensee for the competitive advantages they afford. To place on the distributor the burden of showing their reasonableness is to place it on the one party in the best position to evaluate their competitive effects. Those who have shown such a marked proclivity for unlawful conduct are in no position to complain that they carry the burden of showing that their future clearances come within the law. Cf. *United States v. Crescent Amusement Co.*, 323 U.S. 173, 188.

(3) *Pooling Agreements; Joint Ownership.*

The District Court found the exhibitor-defendants had agreements with each other and their affiliates by which theatres of two or more of them, normally competitive, were operated as a unit, or managed by a joint committee or by one of the exhibitors, the profits being shared according to prearranged percentages. Some of these agreements provided that the parties might not acquire other competitive theatres without first offering them for inclusion in the pool. The court concluded that the result of these agreements was to eliminate competition *pro tanto* both in exhibition and in distribution of features,[8] since the parties would naturally direct the films to the theatres in whose earnings they were interested.

The District Court also found that the exhibitor-defendants had like agreements with certain independent exhibitors. Those alliances had, in its view, the effect of nullifying competition between the allied theatres and of making more effective the competition of the group against theatres not members of the pool. The court found that in some cases the operating agreements were achieved through leases of theatres, the rentals being measured by a percentage of profits earned by the theatres in the pool. The District Court required the dissolution of existing pooling agreements and enjoined any future arrangement of that character.

These provisions of the decree will stand. The practices were bald efforts to

---

[8] A feature is any motion picture, regardless of topic, the length of film of which is in excess of 4,000 feet.

substitute monopoly for competition and to strengthen the hold of the exhibitor-defendants on the industry by alignment of competitors on their side. Clearer restraints of trade are difficult to imagine.

There was another type of business arrangement that the District Court found to have the same effect as the pooling agreements just mentioned. Many theatres are owned jointly by two or more exhibitor-defendants or by an exhibitor-defendant and an independent.[9] The result is, according to the District Court, that the theatres are operated "collectively, rather than competitively." And where the joint owners are an exhibitor-defendant and an independent the effect is, according to the District Court, the elimination by the exhibitor-defendant of "putative competition between itself and the other joint owner, who otherwise would be in a position to operate theatres independently." The District Court found these joint ownerships of theatres to be unreasonable restraints of trade within the meaning of the Sherman Act.

The District Court ordered the exhibitor-defendants to disaffiliate by terminating their joint ownership of theatres; and it enjoined future acquisitions of such interests. One is authorized to buy out the other if it shows to the satisfaction of the District Court and that court first finds that such acquisition "will not unduly restrain competition in the exhibition of feature motion

---

[9] *Theatres jointly owned with independents:*

Paramount	993
Warner	20
Fox	66
RKO	187
Loew's	21
Total	1287

Theatres jointly owned by two defendants:

Paramount-Fox	6
Paramount-Loew's	14
Paramount-Warner	25
Paramount-RKO	150
Loew's-RKO	3
Loew's-Warner	5
Fox-RKO	1
Warner-RKO	10
Total	214

Of the 1287 jointly owned with independents, 209 would not be affected by the decree since one of the ownership interests is less than 5 per cent, an amount which the District Court treated as *de minimis.*

pictures." This dissolution and prohibition of joint ownership as between exhibitor-defendants was plainly warranted. To the extent that they have joint interests in the outlets for their films each in practical effect grants the other a priority for the exhibition of its films. For in this situation, as in the case where theatres are jointly managed, the natural gravitation of films is to the theatres in whose earnings the distributors have an interest. Joint ownership between exhibitor-defendants then becomes a device for strengthening their competitive position as exhibitors by forming an alliance as distributors. An express agreement to grant each other the preference would be a most effective weapon to stifle competition. A working arrangement or business device that has that necessary consequence gathers no immunity because of its subtlety. Each is a restraint of trade condemned by the Sherman Act.

The District Court also ordered disaffiliation in those instances where theatres were jointly owned by an exhibitor-defendant and an independent, and where the interest of the exhibitor-defendant was "greater than five per cent unless such interest shall be ninety-five per cent or more," an independent being defined for this part of the decree as "any former, present or putative motion picture theatre operator which is not owned or controlled by the defendant holding the interest in question." The exhibitor-defendants are authorized to acquire existing interests of the independents in these theatres if they establish, and if the District Court first finds, that the acquisition "will not unduly restrain competition in the exhibition of feature motion pictures." All other acquisitions of such joint interests were enjoined.

This phase of the decree is strenuously attacked. We are asked to eliminate it for lack of findings to support it. The argument is that the findings show no more than the existence of joint ownership of theatres by exhibitor-defendants and independents. The statement by the District Court that the joint ownership eliminates "putative competition" is said to be a mere conclusion without evidentiary support. For it is said that the facts of the record show that many of the instances of joint ownership with an independent interest are cases wholly devoid of any history of or relationship to restraints of trade or monopolistic practices. Some are said to be rather fortuitous results of bankruptcies; others are said to be the results of investments by outside interests who have no desire or capacity to operate theatres, and so on.

It is conceded that the District Court made no inquiry into the circumstances under which a particular interest had been acquired. It treated all relationships alike, insofar as the disaffiliation provision of the decree is concerned. In this we think it erred.

We have gone into the record far enough to be confident that at least some of these acquisitions by the exhibitor-defendants were the products of the unlawful practices which the defendants have inflicted on the industry. To the extent that these acquisitions were the fruits of monopolistic practices or restraints of trade, they should be divested. And no permission to buy out the other owner should be given a defendant. *United States* v. *Crescent Amusement Co.; Schine Chain Theatres, Inc.* v. *United States.* Moreover, even if lawfully acquired, they may have been utilized as part of the conspiracy to eliminate or suppress competition in furtherance of the ends of the conspiracy. In that event divestiture would likewise be justified. *United States* v. *Crescent Amusement Co.* In that situation permission to acquire the interest of the independent would have the unlawful effect of permitting the defendants to complete their plan to eliminate him.

Furthermore, if the joint ownership is an alliance with one who is or would be an operator but for the joint ownership, divorce should be decreed even though the affiliation was innocently acquired. For that joint ownership would afford opportunity to perpetuate the effects of the restraints of trade which the exhibitor-defendants have inflicted on the industry.

It seems, however, that some of the cases of joint ownership do not fall into any of the categories we have listed. Some apparently involve no more than innocent investments by those who are not actual or potential operators. If in such cases the acquisition was not improperly used in furtherance of the conspiracy, its retention by defendants would be justified absent a finding that no monopoly resulted. And in those instances permission might be given the defendants to acquire the interests of the independents on a showing by them and a finding by the court that neither monopoly nor unreasonable restraint of trade in the exhibition of films would result. In short, we see no reason to place a ban on this type of ownership, at least so long as theatre ownership by the five majors is not prohibited. The results of inquiry along the lines we have indicated must await further findings of the District Court remand of the cause.

(4) *Formula Deals, Master Agreements, and Franchises.* Rules of Reason

A formula deal is a licensing agreement with a circuit of theatres in which the license fee of a given feature is measured, for the theatres covered by the agreement, by a specified percentage of the feature's national gross. The District Court found that Paramount and RKO had made formula deals with independent and affiliated circuits. The circuit was allowed to allocate playing time and film rentals among the various theatres as it saw fit. The inclusion of theatres of a circuit into a single agreement gives no opportunity for other theatre owners to bid for the feature in their respective areas and, in the view of the District Court, is therefore an unreasonable restraint of trade. The District Court found some master agreements[10] open to the same objection.

---

[10] See note 4, *supra.*

Those are the master agreements that cover exhibition in two or more theatres in a particular circuit and allow the exhibitor to allocate the film rental paid among the theatres as it sees fit and to exhibit the features upon such playing time as it deems best, and leaves other terms to the discretion of the circuit. The District Court enjoined the making or further performance of any formula deal of the type described above. It also enjoined the making or further performance of any master agreement covering the exhibition of features in a number of theatres.

The findings of the District Court in these respects are supported by facts, its conclusion that the formula deals and master agreements constitute restraint of trade is valid, and the relief is proper. The formula deals and master agreements are unlawful restraints of trade in two respects. In the first place, they eliminate the possibility of bidding for films theatre by theatre. In that way they eliminate the opportunity for the small competitor to obtain the choice first runs, and put a premium on the size of the circuit. They are, therefore, devices for stifling competition and diverting the cream of the business to the large operators. In the second place, the pooling of the purchasing power of an entire circuit in bidding for films is a misuse of monopoly power insofar as it combines the theatres in closed towns with competitive situations. The reasons have been stated in *United States* v. *Griffith* and *Schine Chain Theatres, Inc.* v. *United States,* and need not be repeated here. It is hardly necessary to add that distributors who join in such arrangements by exhibitors are active participants in effectuating a restraint of trade and a monopolistic practice. See *United States* v. *Crescent Amusement Co., supra.*

The District Court also enjoined the making or further performance of any franchise. A franchise is a contract with an exhibitor which extends over a period of more than a motion picture season and covers the exhibition of features released by the distributor during the period of the agreement. The District Court held that a franchise constituted a restraint of trade because a period of more than one season was too long and the inclusion of all features was disadvantageous to competitors. At least that is the way we read its findings.

Universal and United Artists object to the outlawry of franchise agreements. Universal points out that the charge of illegality of franchises in these cases was restricted to franchises with theatres owned by the major defendants and to franchises with circuits or theatres in a circuit, a circuit being defined in the complaint as a group of more than five theatres controlled by the same person or a group of more than five theatres which combine through a common agent in licensing films. It seems, therefore, that the legality of franchises to other exhibitors (except as to block-booking, a practice to which we will later advert) was not in issue in the litigation. Moreover, the findings on franchises are clouded by the statement of the District Court in the opinion that franchises "necessarily contravene the plan of licensing each picture, theatre by theatre, to the highest bidder." As will be seen hereafter, we eliminate from the decree the provision for competitive bidding. But for its inclusion of competitive bidding the District Court might well have treated the problem of franchises differently.

We can see how if franchises were allowed to be used between the exhibitor-defendants each might be able to strengthen its strategic position in the exhibition field and continue the ill effects of the conspiracy which the decree is designed to dissipate. Franchise agreements may have been employed as devices to discriminate against some independents in favor of others. We know from the record that franchise agreements often contained discriminatory clauses operating in favor not only of theatres owned by the defendants but also of the large circuits. But we cannot say on this record that franchises are illegal *per se* when extended to any theatre or circuit no matter how small. The findings do not deal with the issue doubtlessly due to the fact that any system of franchises would necessarily conflict with the system of competitive bidding adopted by the District Court. Hence we set aside the findings on franchises so that the court may examine the problem in the light of the elimination from the decree of competitive bidding.

We do not take that course in the case of formula deals and master agreements, for the findings in these instances seem to stand on their own bottom and apparently have no necessary dependency on the provision for competitive bidding.

(5) *Block-Booking.*

Block-booking is the practice of licensing, or offering for license, one feature or group of features on condition that the exhibitor will also license another feature or group of features released by the distributors during a given period. The films are licensed in blocks before they are actually produced. All the defendants, except United Artists, have engaged in the practice. Block-booking prevents competitors from bidding for single features on their individual merits. The District Court held it illegal for that reason and for the reason that it "adds to the monopoly of a single copyrighted picture that of another copyrighted picture which must be taken and exhibited in order to secure the first." That enlargement of the monopoly of the copyright was condemned below in reliance on the principle which forbids the owner of a patent to condition its use on the purchase or use of patented or unpatented materials . . . The court enjoined defendants from performing or entering into any license in which the right to exhibit one feature is conditioned upon the licensee's taking one or more other features.[11]

---

[11] Blind-selling is a practice whereby a distributor licenses a feature before the exhibitor is

We approve that restriction. The copyright law, like the patent statutes, makes reward to the owner a secondary consideration. In *Fox Film Corp.* v. *Doyal*, 286 U. S. 123, 127, Chief Justice Hughes spoke as follows respecting the copyright monopoly granted by Congress, "The sole interest of the United States and the primary object in conferring the monopoly lie in the general benefits derived by the public from the labors of authors." It is said that reward to the author or artist serves to induce release to the public of the products of his creative genius. But the reward does not serve its public purpose if it is not related to the quality of the copyright. Where a high quality film greatly desired is licensed only if an inferior one is taken, the latter borrows quality from the former and strengthens its monopoly by drawing on the other. The practice tends to equalize rather than differentiate the reward for the individual copyrights. Even where all the films included in the package are of equal quality, the requirement that all be taken if one is desired increases the market for some. Each stands not on its own footing but in whole or in part on the appeal which another film may have. As the District Court said, the result is to add to the monopoly of the copyright in violation of the principle of the patent cases involving tying clauses.[12]

---

afforded an opportunity to view it. To remedy the problems created by that practice the District Court included the following provision in its decree:

> "To the extent that any of the features have not been trade shown prior to the granting of the license for more than a single feature, the licensee shall be given by the licensor the right to reject twenty per cent of such features not trade shown prior to the granting of the license, such right of rejection to be exercised in the order of release within ten days after there has been an opportunity afforded to the licensee to inspect the feature."

The court advanced the following as its reason for inclusion of this provision:

> "Blind-selling does not appear to be as inherently restrictive of competition as block-booking, although it is capable of some abuse. By this practice a distributor could promise a picture of good quality or of a certain type which when produced might prove to be of poor quality or of another type—a competing distributor meanwhile being unable to market its product and in the end losing its outlets for future pictures. The evidence indicates that trade-shows, which are designed to prevent such blind-selling, are poorly attended by exhibitors. Accordingly, exhibitors who choose to obtain their films for exhibition in quantities, need to be protected against burdensome agreements by being given an option to reject a certain percentage of their blind-licensed pictures within a reasonable time after they shall have become available for inspection."

We approve this provision of the decree.

[12] The exclusive right granted by the Copyright Act, 35 Stat. 1075, 17 U. S. C. § 1, includes no such privilege. It provides, so far as material here, as follows:

"That any person entitled thereto, upon complying with the provisions of this Act, shall have the exclusive right:

"(d) To perform or represent the copyrighted work publicly if it be a drama or, if it be a dramatic work and not reproduced in copies for sale, to vend any manuscript or any record

It is argued that *Transparent-Wrap Machine Corp.* v. *Stokes & Smith Co.,* 329 U.S. 637, points to a contrary result. That case held that the inclusion in a patent license of a condition requiring the licensee to assign improvement patents was not *per se* illegal. But that decision, confined to improvement patents, was greatly influenced by the federal statute governing assignments of patents. It therefore has no controlling significance here.

Columbia Pictures makes an earnest argument that enforcement of the restriction as to block-booking will be very disadvantageous to it and will greatly impair its ability to operate profitably. But the policy of the antitrust laws is not qualified or conditioned by the convenience of those whose conduct is regulated. Nor can a vested interest in a practice which contravenes the policy of the anti-trust laws receive judicial sanction.

We do not suggest that films may not be sold in blocks or groups, when there is no requirement, express or implied, for the purchase of more than one film. All we hold to be illegal is a refusal to license one or more copyrights unless another copyright is accepted.

(6) *Discrimination.*

The District Court found that defendants had discriminated against small independent exhibitors and in favor of large affiliated and unaffiliated circuits through various kinds of contract provisions. These included suspension of the terms of a contract if a circuit theatre remained closed for more than eight weeks with reinstatement without liability on reopening; allowing large privileges in the selection and elimination of films; allowing deductions in film rentals if double bills are played; granting moveovers[13] and extended runs; granting road show privileges;[14] allowing overage and underage;[15] granting unlimited playing time; excluding foreign pictures and those of independent producers; and granting rights to question the classification of features for rental purposes. The District Court found that the competitive advantages of these provisions were so great that their inclusion in contracts with the larger circuits and their exclusion from contracts with the small independents consti-

---

whatsoever thereof; to make or to procure the making of any transcription or record thereof by or from which, in whole or in part, it may in any manner or by any method be exhibited, performed, represented, produced, or reproduced; and to exhibit, perform, represent, produce, or reproduce it in any manner or by any method whatsoever;"

[13] A moveover is the privilege given a licensee to move a picture from one theatre to another as a continuation of the run at the licensee's first theatre.

[14] A road show is a public exhibition of a feature in a limited number of theatres, in advance of its general release, at admission prices higher than those customarily charged in first-run theatres in those areas.

[15] Underage and overage refer to the practice of using excess film rental earned in one circuit theatre to fulfill a rental commitment defaulted by another.

tuted an unreasonable discrimination against the latter. Each discriminatory contract constituted a conspiracy between licensor and licensee. Hence the District Court deemed it unnecessary to decide whether the defendants had conspired among themselves to make these discriminations. No provision of the decree specifically enjoins these discriminatory practices because they were thought to be impossible under the system of competitive bidding adopted by the District Court.

These findings are amply supported by the evidence. We concur in the conclusion that these discriminatory practices are included among the restraints of trade which the Sherman Act condemns. See *Interstate Circuit* v. *United States, supra,* p. 231; *United States* v. *Crescent Amusement Co., supra,* pp. 182-183. It will be for the District Court on remand of these cases to provide effective relief against their continuance, as our elimination of the provision for competitive bidding leaves this phase of the cases unguarded.

There is some suggestion on this as well as on other phases of the cases that large exhibitors with whom defendants dealt fathered the illegal practices and forced them onto the defendants. But as the District Court observed, that circumstance if true does not help the defendants. For acquiescence in an illegal scheme is as much a violation of the Sherman Act as the creation and promotion of one.

Second—Competitive Bidding.

The District Court concluded that the only way competition could be introduced into the existing system of fixed prices, clearances and runs was to require that films be licensed on a competitive bidding basis. Films are to be offered to all exhibitors in each competitive area.[16] The license for the desired run is to be granted to the highest responsible bidder, unless the distributor rejects all offers. The licenses are to be offered and taken theatre by theatre and picture by picture. Licenses to show films in theatres in which the licensor owns directly or indirectly an interest of ninety-five per cent or more are excluded from the requirement for competitive bidding.

Paramount is the only one of the five majors who opposes the competitive bidding system. Columbia Pictures, Universal, and United Artists oppose it. The intervenors representing certain independents oppose it. And the Department of Justice, which apparently proposed the system originally, speaks strongly against it here.

At first blush there is much to commend the system of competitive bidding.

---

[16] Competitive bidding is required only in a "competitive area" where it is "desired by the exhibitors." As the District Court said, "the decree provides an opportunity to bid for any exhibitor in a competitive area who may desire to do so."

The details of the competitive bidding system will be found in 70 F. Supp. pp. 73–74.

The trade victims of this conspiracy have in large measure been the small independent operators. They are the ones that have felt most keenly the discriminatory practices and predatory activities in which defendants have freely indulged. They have been the victims of the massed purchasing power of the larger units in the industry. It is largely out of the ruins of the small operators that the large empires of exhibitors have been built. Thus it would appear to be a great boon to them to substitute open bidding for the private deals and favors on which the large operators have thrived. But after reflection we have concluded that competitive bidding involves the judiciary so deeply in the daily operation of this nation-wide business and promises such dubious benefits that it should not be undertaken.

Each film is to be licensed on a particular run to "the highest responsible bidder, having a theatre of a size, location and equipment adequate to yield a reasonable return to the licensor." The bid "shall state what run such exhibitor desires and what he is willing to pay for such feature, which statement may specify a flat rental, or a percentage of gross receipts, or both, or any other form of rental, and shall also specify what clearance such exhibitor is willing to accept, the time and days when such exhibitor desires to exhibit it, and any other offers which such exhibitor may care to make." We do not doubt that if a competitive bidding system is adopted all these provisions are necessary. For the licensing of films at auction is quite obviously a more complicated matter than the like sales for cash of tobacco, wheat, or other produce. Columbia puts these pertinent queries: "No two exhibitors are likely to make the same bid as to dates, clearance, method of fixing rental, etc. May bids containing such diverse factors be readily compared? May a flat rental bid be compared with a percentage bid? May the value of any percentage bid be determined unless the admission price is fixed by the license?"

The question as to who is the highest bidder involves the use of standards incapable of precise definition because the bids being compared contain different ingredients. Determining who is the most responsible bidder likewise cannot be reduced to a formula. The distributor's judgment of the character and integrity of a particular exhibitor might result in acceptance of a lower bid than others offered. Yet to prove that favoritism was shown would be well-nigh impossible, unless perhaps all the exhibitors in the country were given classifications of responsibility. If, indeed, the choice between bidders is not to be entrusted to the uncontrolled discretion of the distributors, some effort to standardize the factors involved in determining "a reasonable return to the licensor" would seem necessary.

We mention these matters merely to indicate the character of the job of supervising such a competitive bidding system. It would involve the judiciary in the administration of intricate and detailed rules governing priority, period of clearance, length of run, competitive areas, reasonable return, and the like.

The system would be apt to require as close a supervision as a continuous receivership, unless the defendants were to be entrusted with vast discretion. The judiciary is unsuited to affairs of business management; and control through the power of contempt is crude and clumsy and lacking in the flexibility necessary to make continuous and detailed supervision effective. Yet delegation of the management of the system to the discretion of those who had the genius to conceive the present conspiracy and to execute it with the subtlety which this record reveals, could be done only with the greatest reluctance. At least such choices should not be faced unless the need for the system is great and its benefits plain.

The system uproots business arrangements and established relationships with no apparent overall benefit to the small independent exhibitor. If each feature must go to the highest responsible bidder, those with the greatest purchasing power would seem to be in a favored position. Those with the longest purse—the exhibitor-defendants and the large circuits—would seem to stand in a preferred position. If in fact they were enabled through the competitive bidding system to take the cream of the business, eliminate the small independents, and thus increase their own strategic hold on the industry, they would have the cloak of the court's decree around them for protection. Hence the natural advantage which the larger and financially stronger exhibitors would seem to have in the bidding gives us pause. If a premium is placed on purchasing power, the court-created system may be a powerful factor towards increasing the concentration of economic power in the industry rather than cleansing the competitive system of unwholesome practices. For where the system in operation promises the advantage to the exhibitor who is in the strongest financial position, the injunction against discrimination[17] is apt to hold an empty promise. In this connection it should be noted that, even though the independents in a given competitive area do not want competitive bidding, the exhibitor-defendants can invoke the system.

Our doubts concerning the competitive bidding system are increased by the fact that defendants who own theatres are allowed to pre-empt their own features. They thus start with an inventory which all other exhibitors lack. The latter have no prospect of assured runs except what they get by competitive bidding. The proposed system does not offset in any way the advantages which the exhibitor-defendants have by way of theatre ownership. It would seem in fact to increase them. For the independents are deprived of the stability which flows from established business relationships. Under the proposed system they can get features only if they are the highest responsible bidders. They can no longer depend on their private sources of supply which

---

[17] The competitive bidding part of the decree provides: "Each license shall be granted solely upon the merits and without discrimination in favor of affiliates, old customers or others."

their ingenuity has created. Those sources, built perhaps on private relationships and representing important items of good will, are banned, even though they are free of any taint of illegality.

The system was designed, as some of the defendants put it, to remedy the difficulty of any theatre to break into or change the existing system of runs and clearances. But we do not see how, in practical operation, the proposed system of competitive bidding is likely to open up to competition the markets which defendants' unlawful restraints have dominated. Rather real danger seems to us to lie in the opportunities the system affords the exhibitor-defendants and the other large operators to strengthen their hold in the industry. We are reluctant to alter decrees in these cases where there is agreement with the District Court on the nature of the violations. *United States* v. *Crescent Amusement Co., supra,* p. 185; *International Salt Co.* v. *United States,* 332 U.S. 392, 400. But the provisions for competitive bidding in these cases promise little in the way of relief against the real evils of the conspiracy. They implicate the judiciary heavily in the details of business management if supervision is to be effective. They vest powerful control in the exhibitor-defendants over their competitors if close supervision by the court is not undertaken. In light of these considerations we conclude that the competitive bidding provisions of the decree should be eliminated so that a more effective decree may be fashioned.

We have already indicated in preceding parts of this opinion that this alteration in the decree leaves a hiatus or two which will have to be filled on remand of he cases. We will indicate hereafter another phase of the problem which the District Court should also reconsider in view of this alteration in the decree. But out of an abundance of caution we add this additional word. The competitive bidding system was perhaps the central arch of the decree designed by the District Court. Its elimination may affect the cases in ways other than those which we expressly mention. Hence on remand of the cases the freedom of the District Court to reconsider the adequacy of decree is not limited to those parts we have specifically indicated.

Third. Monopoly, Expansion of Theatre Holdings, Divestiture.

There is a suggestion that the hold the defendants have on the industry is so great that a problem under the First Amendment is raised. Cf. *Associated Press* v. *United States,* 326 U. S. 1. We have no doubt that moving pictures, like newspapers and radio, are included in the press whose freedom is guaranteed by the First Amendment. That issue would be focused here if we had any question concerning monopoly in the production of moving pictures. But monopoly in production was eliminated as an issue in these cases, as we have noted. The chief argument at the bar is phrased in terms of monopoly of exhibition, restraints on exhibition, and the like. Actually, the issue is even narrower than that. The main contest is over the cream of the exhibition business—that of the first-run theatres. By defining the issue so narrowly we do not intend to belittle its importance. It shows, however, that the question here is not *what* the public will see or *if* the public will be permitted to see certain features. It is clear that under the existing system the public will be denied access to none. If the public cannot see the features on the first-run, it may do so on the second, third, fourth, or later run. The central problem presented by these cases is which exhibitors get the highly profitable first-run business. That problem has important aspects under the Sherman Act. But it bears only remotely, if at all, on any question of freedom of the press, save only as timeliness of release may be a factor of importance in specific situations.

The controversy over monopoly relates to monopoly in exhibition and more particularly monopoly in the first-run phase of the exhibition business.

The five majors in 1945 had interests in somewhat over 17 per cent of the theatres in the United States—3,137 out of 18,076.[18] Those theatres paid 45 per cent of the total domestic film rental received by all eight defendants.

In the 92 cities of the country with populations over 100,000 at least 70 per cent of all the first-run theatres are affiliated with one or more of the five majors. In 4 of those cities the five majors have no theatres. In 38 of those cities there are no independent first-run theatres. In none of the remaining 50 cities did less than three of the distributor-defendants license their product on first run to theatres of the five majors. In 19 of the 50 cities less than three of the distributor-defendants licensed their product on first run to independent theatres. In a majority of the 50 cities the greater share of all of the features of defendants were licensed for first-run exhibition in the theatres of the five majors.

In about 60 per cent of the 92 cities having populations of over 100,000, independent theatres compete with those of the five majors in first-run exhibition. In about 91 per cent of the 92 cities there is competition between independent theatres and the theatres of the five majors or between theatres of the five majors themselves for first-run exhibition. In all of the 92 cities there

---

[18] The theatres which each of the five majors owned independently of the others were: Paramount 1,395 or 7.72 per cent; Warner 501 or 2.77 per cent; Loew's 135 or .74 per cent; Fox 636 or 3.52 per cent; RKO 109 or .60 per cent. There were in addition 361 theatres or about 2 per cent in which two or more of the five majors had joint interests. These figures exclude connections through film-buying or management contracts or through corporations in which a defendant owns an indirect minority stock interest.

These theatres are located in 922 towns in 48 States and the District of Columbia. For further description of the distribution of theatres see Bertrand, Evans, and Blanchard, The Motion Picture Industry—A Pattern of Control 15–16 (TNEC Monograph 43, 1941).

is always competition in some run even where there is no competition in first runs.

In cities between 25,000 and 100,000 populations the five majors have interests in 577 of a total of 978 first-run theatres or about 60 per cent. In about 300 additional towns, mostly under 25,000, an operator affiliated with one of the five majors has all of the theatres in the town.

The District Court held that the five majors could not be treated collectively so as to establish claims of general monopolization in exhibition. It found that none of them was organized or had been maintained "for the purpose of achieving a national monopoly" in exhibition. It found that the five majors by their present theatre holdings "alone" (which aggregate a little more than one-sixth of all the theatres in the United States), "do not and cannot collectively or individually, have a monopoly of exhibition." The District Court also found that where a single defendant owns all of the first-run theatres in a town, there is no sufficient proof that the acquisition was for the purpose of creating a monopoly. It found rather that such consequence resulted from the inertness of competitors, their lack of financial ability to build theatres comparable to those of the five majors, or the preference of the public for the best-equipped theatres. And the percentage of features on the market which any of the five majors could play in its own theatres was found to be relatively small and in nowise to approximate a monopoly of film exhibition.[19]

---

[19] The number of feature films released during the 1943-44 season by the eleven largest distributors is as follows:

| | No. of Films | Percentages of Total | |
		With "Westerns" included	With "Westerns" excluded
Fox	33	8.31	9.85
Loew's	33	8.31	9.85
Paramount	31	7.81	9.25
RKO	38	9.57	11.34
Warner	19	4.79	5.67
Columbia	41	10.32	12.24
United Artists	16	4.04	4.78
Universal	49	12.34	14.63
Republic	–29 features –30 "Westerns"	14.86	8.66
Monogram	–26 features –16 "Westerns"	10.58	7.76
PRC	–20 features –16 "Westerns"	9.07	5.97
Totals	397 335 without "Westerns"	100.00	100.00

Even in respect of the theatres jointly owned or jointly operated by the defendants with each other or with independents, the District Court found no monopoly or attempt to monopolize. These joint agreements or ownership were found only to be unreasonable restraints of trade. The District Court, indeed, found no monopoly on any phase of the cases, although it did find an attempt to monopolize in the fixing of prices, the granting of unreasonable clearances, block-booking and the other unlawful restraints of trade we have already discussed. The "root of the difficulties," according to the District Court, lay not in theatre ownership but in those unlawful practices.

The District Court did, however, enjoin the five majors from expanding their present theatre holdings in any manner. It refused to grant the request of the Department of Justice for total divestiture by the five majors of their theatre holdings. It found that total divestiture would be injurious to the five majors and damaging to the public. Its thought on the latter score was that the new set of theatre owners who would take the place of the five majors would be unlikely for some years to give the public as good service as those they supplanted "in view of the latter's demonstrated experience and skill in operating what must be regarded as in general the largest and best equipped theatres." Divestiture was, it thought, too harsh a remedy where there was available the alternative of competitive bidding. It accordingly concluded that divestiture was unnecessary "at least until the efficiency of that system has been tried and found wanting."

It is clear, so far as the five majors are concerned, that the aim of the conspiracy was exclusionary, i. e. it was designed to strengthen their hold on the exhibition field. In other words, the conspiracy had monopoly in exhibition for one of its goals, as the District Court held. Price, clearance, and run are interdependent. The clearance and run provisions of the licenses fixed the relative playing positions of all theatres in a certain area; the minimum price provisions were based on playing position—the first-run theatres being required to charge the highest prices, the second-run theatres the next highest, and so on. As the District Court found, "In effect, the distributor, by the fixing of minimum admission prices, attempts to give the prior-run exhibitors as near a monopoly of the patronage as possible."

It is, therefore, not enough in determining the need for divestiture to conclude with the District Court that none of the defendants was organized or has been maintained for the purpose of achieving a "national monopoly," nor that the five majors through their present theatre holdings "alone" do not and cannot collectively or individually have a monopoly of exhibition. For when the starting point is a conspiracy to effect a monopoly through restraints of trade, it is relevant to determine what the results of the conspiracy were even if they fell short of monopoly.

An example will illustrate the problem. In the popular sense there is a monopoly if one person owns the only theatre in town. That usually does not, however, constitute a violation of the Sherman Act. But as we noted in *United States v. Griffith,* and see *Schine Chain Theatres, Inc. v. United States,* even such an ownership is vulnerable in a suit by the United States under the Sherman Act if the property was acquired, or its strategic position maintained, as a result of practices which constitute unreasonable restraints of trade. Otherwise, there would be reward from the conspiracy through retention of its fruits. Hence the problem of the District Court does not end with enjoining continuance of the unlawful restraints nor with dissolving the combination which launched the conspiracy. Its function includes undoing what the conspiracy achieved. As we have discussed in *Schine Chain Theatres, Inc. v. United States,* the requirement that the defendants restore what they unlawfully obtained is no more punishment than the familiar remedy of restitution. What findings would be warranted after such an inquiry in the present cases, we do not know. For the findings of the District Court do not cover this point beyond stating that monopoly was an objective of the several restraints of trade that stand condemned.

Moreover, the problem under the Sherman Act is not solved merely by measuring monopoly in terms of size or extent of holdings or by concluding that single ownerships were not obtained "for the purpose of achieving a national monopoly." It is the relationship of the unreasonable restraints of trade to the position of the defendants in the exhibition field (and more particularly in the first-run phase of that business) that is of first importance on the divestiture phase of these cases. That is the position we have taken in *Schine Chain Theatres, Inc. v. United States,* in dealing with a projection of the same conspiracy through certain large circuits. Parity of treatment of the unaffiliated and the affiliated circuits requires the same approach here. For the fruits of the conspiracy which are denied the independents must also be denied the five majors. In this connection there is a suggestion that one result of the conspiracy was a geographical division of territory among the five majors. We mention it not to intimate that it is true but only to indicate the appropriate extent of the inquiry concerning the effect of the conspiracy in theatre ownership by the five majors.

The findings of the District Court are deficient on that score and obscure on another. The District Court in its findings speaks of the absence of a "purpose" on the part of any of the five majors to achieve a "national monopoly" in the exhibition of motion pictures. First, there is no finding as to the presence or absence of monopoly on the part of the five majors in the *first-run* field for the entire country, in the *first-run* field in the 92 largest cities of the country, or in the *first-run* field in separate localities. Yet the *first-run* field, which constitutes the cream of the exhibition business, is the core of the present cases. Section 1 of the Sherman Act outlaws unreasonable restraints irrespective of the amount of trade or commerce involved (*United States* v. *Socony-Vacuum Oil Co.,* 310 U.S. 150, 224, 225, n.59), and § 2 condemns monopoly of "any part" of trade or commerce. "Any part" is construed to mean an appreciable part of interstate or foreign trade or commerce. *United States* v. *Yellow Cab Co.,* 332 U.S. 218, 225. Second, we pointed out in *United States* v. *Griffith, ante,* p. 100, that "specific intent" is not necessary to establish a "purpose or intent" to create a monopoly but that the requisite "purpose or intent" is present if monopoly results as a necessary consequence of what was done. The findings of the District Court on this phase of the cases are not clear, though we take them to mean by the absence of "purpose" the absence of a specific intent. So construed they are inconclusive. In any event they are ambiguous and must be recast on remand of the cases. Third, monopoly power, whether lawfully or unlawfully acquired, may violate § 2 of the Sherman Act though it remains unexercised (*United States* v. *Griffith, ante,* p. 100), for as we stated in *American Tobacco Co.* v. *United States,* 328 U. S. 781, 809, 811, the existence of power "to exclude competition when it is desired to do so" is itself a violation of § 2, provided it is coupled with the purpose or intent to exercise that power. The District Court, being primarily concerned with the number and extent of the theatre holdings of defendants, did not address itself to this phase of the monopoly problem. Here also, parity of treatment as between independents and the five majors as theatre owners, who were tied into the same general conspiracy, necessitates consideration of this question.

Exploration of these phases of the cases would not be necessary if, as the Department of Justice argues, vertical integration of producing, distributing, and exhibiting motion pictures is illegal *per se.* But the majority of the Court does not take that view. In the opinion of the majority the legality of vertical integration under the Sherman Act turns on (1) the purpose or intent with which it was conceived, or (2) the power it creates and the attendant purpose or intent. First, it runs afoul of the Sherman Act if it was a calculated scheme to gain control over an appreciable segment of the market and to restrain or suppress competition, rather than an expansion to meet legitimate business needs. *United States* v. *Reading Co.,* 253 U.S. 26, 57; *United States* v. *Lehigh Valley R. Co.,* 254 U.S. 255, 269–270. Second, a vertically integrated enterprise, like other aggregations of business units (*United States* v. *Aluminum Co. of America,* 148 F. 2d 416), will constitute monopoly which, though unexercised, violates the Sherman Act provided a power to exclude competition is coupled with a purpose or intent to do so. As we pointed out in *United States* v. *Griffith, ante,* p. 100, 107, n. 10, size is itself an earmark of monopoly power. For size carries with it an opportunity for abuse. And the fact that the power created by size was utilized in the past to crush or prevent competition is potent evidence that the requisite purpose or intent attends the presence of monopoly power. See *United States* v. *Swift & Co.*, 286 U.S. 106, 116; *United States* v. *Aluminum Co. of America, supra*, p. 430. Likewise bearing on the question whether monopoly power is created by the vertical integration, is the nature of the market to be served (*United States* v. *Aluminum Co. of America, supra*, p. 430), and the leverage on the market which the particular vertical integration creates or makes possible.

These matters were not considered by the District Court. For that reason, as well as the others we have mentioned, the findings on monopoly and divestiture which we have discussed in this part of the opinion will be set aside. There is an independent reason for doing that. As we have seen, the District Court considered competitive bidding as an alternative to divestiture in the sense that it concluded that further consideration of divestiture should not be had until competitive bidding had been tried and found wanting. Since we eliminate from the decree the provisions for competitive bidding, it is necessary to set aside the findings on divestiture so that a new start on this phase of the cases may be made on their remand.

It follows that the provision of the decree barring the five majors from further theatre expansion should likewise be eliminated. For it too is related to the monopoly question; and the District Court should be allowed to make an entirely fresh start on the whole of the problem. We in no way intimate, however, that the District Court erred in prohibiting further theatre expansion by the five majors.

The Department of Justice maintains that if total divestiture is denied, licensing of films among the five majors should be barred. As a permanent requirement it would seem to be only an indirect way of forcing divestiture. For the findings reveal that the five majors could not operate their theatres full time on their own films.[21] Whether that step would, in absence of competitive bidding, serve as a short-range remedy in certain situations to dissipate the effects of the conspiracy . . . is a question for the District Court. [District Court was reversed and case was remanded—Ed.]

"HOLLYWOOD BACKS GOVT. IN COURT"
Variety (October 12, 1977), p. 55

The Justice Dept. cheered on by Hollywood, is preparing its case against the

---

[21] The District Court found, "Except for a very limited number of theatres in the very largest cities, the 18,000 and more theatres in the United States exhibit the product of more than one distributor. Such theatres could not be operated on the product of only one distributor."

way the television networks currently do business with program producers, and even partial victories by the Government when U.S. District Court judge Robert Kelleher in Los Angeles issues his decisions will dramatically change the shape of the industry.

The latest prelude to battle was sounded by Justice last month when it submitted voluminous identifications of evidence in support of its antitrust contentions (*Variety*, Sept. 14), and the networks will respond later this month. A reading of the Government documents discloses a great deal of new information that Justice is eliciting in an attempt to encircle the networks (see separate compilation). There are many points of attack:

Litany of Woe

—The way tv series are tied up for many years, with license fees rising only predetermined levels, as low as 2% per year and usually no higher than 5% per year.

—The way the webs prohibit the sale of current shows for stripping on other networks, though they themselves will strip the shows with no apparent impact on primetime ratings.

—The way webs prohibit series spinoffs from going to other networks.

—The current latitude networks have for internal production.

—The way the networks have tied many performers to exclusive contracts.

—The control the networks exercise over the creative elements in productions.

—The way the webs have developed control over a great deal of the best production facilities.

Money's At Stake

Those arguments haven't been proven, of course: that's what the judge must consider. But there's no doubt whatever that most, if not all, Hollywood production executives believe they are unfairly and illegally bound by network control. The end concern, naturally, is money. As one exec of a major production house said last week. "If the network controls the property, the creative elements, the stars and the below-the-line facilities, then it controls the price."

The court must not only consider whether Justice has a strong enough case to warrant continued proceedings. Also in the balance is the proposed consent decree between Justice and NBC. The suit now concerns only ABC and CBS, since NBC has negotiated a separate peace. But a number of Hollywood firms have asked to intervene in the consent decree; they think that NBC is giving up very little and getting Federal protection in return, since virtually everything that NBC now does would be allowed. Currently unrestricted primetime production capability would be held to two and one-half hours, but "Little House On The Prairie" is its only current prime-time effort. What's more, news and sports are exempt, and a lot of marginal programming can be put under those twin umbrellas. The web's option term on series would also be trimmed to four years, but with the option of tagging on another year.

After sitting on the case for years, Justice filed its antitrust suit in 1972, only to have it dismissed without prejudice because of the Nixon Administration's proven bias against the television networks. The current case was resubmitted under the Ford Administration in 1974, and the recent Justice filings resulted from a court order on June 21 this year to identify the evidence in support of its allegations prior to the start of depositions. There's obviously a long road ahead. Justice said it "has not had the opportunity to elicit testimony from present or former employees of ABC or CBS. Further, there are over 7,000 documents which CBS has withheld on grounds of privilege, the claim of which plaintiff is now challenging. Finally, both CBS and ABC are still in the process of producing documents concerning talent and literary property exclusivity, and none of these documents have been evaluated . . . " The documents Justice has received are not even indexed yet, the JD indicated.

Meanwhile, though Hollywood is supporting the Justice efforts as best it can, many production execs are worried. They have to continue doing business with the networks while they testify against web abuses, and not even Hollywood is entirely free of paranoia — to say nothing of justifiable concern about tainting business and personal relationships. As long as the case remains alive, there are going to be nervous moments.

Martin Schoenfeld, "ART LAW"
New York Law Journal (June 21, 1978), p. 1

Recording Artists
And Exclusive Contracts

The advent of the Beatles marked the birth of the self-contained recording group. Many artists today not only sing and play instruments but are also successful composers. Since a substantial financial investment is required to create a successful record album, record company executives must look with favor upon the self-contained artist who adds more than one dimension to a work.

Of course, even the most talented artist generally requires guidance and assistance to advance his career in the entertainment market.[1] He, therefore, joins with a personal manager who is asked to promote the artist, to help find employment,[2] to assist in the selection of the artist's best material, to act as confidant, and to give financial advice. A number of budding entertainers who come to Volunteer Lawyers for the Arts with contractual questions are also dependent upon their managers for financial assistance to purchase instruments, to pay for demonstration records and sometimes even to meet their day to day living expenses.

At the outset, the manager will require that a contract be signed granting him the exclusive right to represent the artist in the entertainment field, and providing a commission for him, either on a straight or sliding scale percentage, based upon artist's gross earnings. In addition, it has become common for many managers to obtain from their clients exclusive recording contracts which may then be assigned to major recording companies. The recording agreement provides that in exchange for royalty payments, the client will render services as a recording artist to the manager, his affiliates or assigns, for the purpose of producing master recordings.

Managers are cognizant of the fact that most major record companies have publishing arms and that as a partial return for their investment in a new artist they may require that the artist's songs become part of their own publishing catalogue. Therefore, a manager will often tie in an exclusive songwriter's agreement with the recording contract. The songwriter's agreement provides for royalty payments to the artist while granting to the manager, his affiliates or assigns, the publishing rights to the artist's original musical compositions.

The Frey Case

The validity of such a tying arrangement was the subject of a recent lawsuit. *Frey v. Warner Bros. Music Co., Inc.*[3] This Federal action was commenced in California by members of the popular recording group professionally known as the "Eagles." The facts, simply stated, were that in September, 1971, at the direction and request of their manager, the group entered into an exclusive recording agreement with Asylum Records and an exclusive songwriter's

---

[1] The Beatles were no exception. Their manager, Brian Epstein, played a large role in their rise to success. See P. McCabe & R. D. Schonfeld, Apple to the Core (1972).

[2] Generally, agents, rather than managers, find work for the artist since they are licensed to do so. However, as an incidental function of his total management duties, the manager may seek employment for his client. See Pine v. Laine, 36 App. Div. 2d 924, 321 NYS 2d 303 (1st Dep't 1971), aff'd 31 NY 2d 988, 293 NE 2d 824, 341 NYS 2d 448 (1973), N.Y. Gen. Bus. Law Section 171 (8) (McKinney 1977).

[3] 77 Civ. 1724 (C.D. Cal.)

contract with Companion Music. Their manager, well known in the recording industry, was a principal in both companies.

There was a clause in the songwriter's contract stating in part: "This Agreement is being entered into contemporaneously with the execution of an Exclusive Artist's Recording Agreement . . . and . . . is made and entered into in consideration for the execution of said Exclusive Artist's Recording Agreement . . . " Subsequently, this songwriter's agreement was assigned to Warner Bros. Music Co., Inc., while its parent company, Warner Communications Inc., acquired Asylum Records which held the recording contract.

The plaintiffs, alleging that defendants were economically powerful and prominent in the music field, contended that the group would not have been allowed to enter into the recording agreement had they refused to enter into the songwriter's contract. They claimed that this constituted a tying arrangement (the recording contract being the tying product and the songwriter's agreement the tied product), intended to limit competition in the music publishing industry in violation of the Sherman Act.[4]

The principal evil of tying arrangements which are forbidden is the use of power in one market to acquire power in, or otherwise distort, a second market.[5] It is a violation per se of Section 1 of the Sherman Act when a defendant, who ties the availability of one product to the purchase of another, has sufficient market power over the tying product and forecloses a substantial quantity of commerce in the tied product.[6] Further, there is a non-per se infringement where it can be shown by a more thorough examination of the purposes and effects of the practices involved, that the general standards of the Sherman Act have been violated.[7]

Dismissal Denied

The defendants in *Frey* moved to dismiss the complaint for failure to state antitrust claims upon which relief could be granted. Their motion was denied.[8] The action was eventually settled before trial. Thus, the issue of whether or not the tying arrangement was illegal remains undecided.

It appears from the opinion of Judge Hill, denying defendants' motion, that

---

[4] 15 U.S.C. 1 (1975). Plaintiffs also alleged several causes of action for breach of contract and fiduciary duty. However, since total diversity of citizenship between the parties was lacking, the court, citing United Mine Workers v. Gibbe, 383 U.S. 715 (1966), dismissed the pendent claims without prejudice to their being filed in State court.

[5] Fortner Enterprises v. U. S. Steel, 394 U.S. 495, 519 (1968) (dissenting opinion).

[6] Id. at 498–499.

[7] Id. at 500.

[8] Frey v. Warner Bros. Music Co., Inc., 77 Civ. 1724 (C.D. Cal. memorandum opinion Aug. 16, 1977).

plaintiffs would, nevertheless, have been hard pressed to prove their claims at trial. The judge declared that in establishing the requisite economic power in the relevant market, plaintiffs had not and could not state a per se violation of the Sherman Act on the theory that their manager was unique in that relevant market. Plaintiffs could have proceeded on other theories such as defendants' size in the market or their ability to impose tying arrangements on a number of persons in the market. However, it was further declared that it was the economic power of the manager and his entities at the time of the signing of the 1971 contracts that was relevant in determining whether defendants had sufficient economic power in the tying market to impose the tie of the songwriter's agreement:

Regarding a non-per se violation, Judge Hill declared that plaintiffs would have to specifically delineate the relevant product and geographic markets, the share of the market controlled by the defendants in 1971, and the percentage of the market subject to the tying restraints.

Although proving their claims would not have been easy, it was not necessarily impossible. Attorneys and others in the music business should therefore be made aware of the "Eagles" action which may be the precursor of future cases where the facts are only slightly different.

In interpreting the antitrust laws, the courts are not bound by formal concepts of contract law.[9] Where, however, there is no illegality for violation of any statute or public policy, then unless the parties actually failed to come to an understanding regarding essential contract terms, it is established that the artist's exclusive agreements with his manager will generally be upheld.[10] Keeping this in mind, when an artist is intent upon signing a series of agreements with his manager, there are several clauses which his counsel may add for his protection.

First, the agreements should be conditioned upon the manager's obtaining for his artist within a specified period of time a record contract with an established company whose recordings are at least nationally distributed. It should be agreed that if such condition precedent is not met, the various contracts with the manager shall terminate.

Second, there should be a provision that the manager cannot enter into any binding contracts or make any assignments or other commitments on behalf of the artist without first informing him of the terms thereof and without obtaining the artist's prior approval.

---

[9] U.S. v. Phosphate Export Ass'n., 393 U.S. 199, 208 (1968).

[10] See Pawlowskl v. Woodruff. 122 Misc. 695, 203 NYS 819 (N.Y. Co. 1924), aff'd 212 App. Div. 871, 208 NYS 912 (1st Dep't 1925); Mandel v. Liebman, 303 N.Y. 88, 100 NE 2d 149 (1951); In Re Waterson, Berlin & Snyder Co., 48 F. 2d 704 (2d Civ. 1931).

Third, and possibly more significant to an artist than a pecuniary advance, there should be a requirement that once completed, the artist's recording will be released commercially within a certain period of time. A company required to release a record rather than being able to leave it on the shelf generally tries harder to sell that record.

Songwriter's Protection

Fourth, along the same line but regarding publishing rights, there should be a clause in the songwriter's agreement which gives the artist a right to recapture his compositions if within a specified period of time his music is not printed and distributed.

Fifth, and especially where an advance is not paid, an artist's recording agreement with his manager should provide that after the deduction and recoupment of recording costs, all royalties, moneys or other consideration derived from or in any way related to that agreement, including the sale, assignment or other use of masters recorded thereunder will be divided between artist and manager on an equal basis. While a manager may argue that he is making the initial capital investment, it must be remembered that only with the artist's labor and talent can a profit be made. Indeed, the risk which a manager sometimes takes is quite insignificant compared to the profit he stands to make.

Sixth, the artist should be assured that for his efforts the manager will not be compensated more than once. Where there are tying arrangements with the manager, he should be required to acknowledge that whenever he is compensated by virtue of the recording or songwriter's contract, in that regard, he will not additionally be entitled to a manager's commission.

Seventh, and finally, it should be clearly stated in the management contract that the artist reserves the right to hire the services of accountants, lawyers or other financial representatives.

While it goes without saying that even the most unrecognized talent is entitled to his attorney's best effort in contract negotiations, counsel should also keep in mind the old maxim that today's unknown artist may be tomorrow's new superstar.

Herbert Mitgang, "2 HOFFA BOOKS POSE PUBLISHING PROBLEM"
The New York Times (June 29, 1978), p. C15

Two forthcoming books on the same controversial subjects — James R.

Hoffa and the International Brotherhood of Teamsters' covert role in American political and criminal life—have pitted their authors and publishers in a behind-the-scenes contest, with possible broad implications for publishing independence or suppression.

Both publishing houses are now racing to reach bookstores early in October and, long before then, to try to sell magazine syndication, book-club and paperback rights. The decision about these rights could be decided in the next few weeks, with only one of the books expected to make it big.

Three publishing houses are actually involved: Simon & Schuster, New Republic Books, publishing affiliate of The New Republic magazine, and Paddington Press. When Simon & Schuster discovered that New Republic Books — which it distributes—had a book coming out on a similar theme to one of its own, it asked New Republic to postpone publication until next year. As a result, Paddington Press acquired the New Republic book and put it back into competition for the fall.

Troubles of Independents

At issue is not censorship, but a growing trend to contractual arrangements in which smaller publishers use larger ones to sell their books. The Hoffa books, according to the publishing community, point up the difficulties involved for independent houses in today's marketplace.

The first book is "The Hoffa Wars: Teamsters, Rebels, Politicians and the Mob" by Dan E. Moldea, to be published by Paddington, a small but vigorous independent house with offices in New York and London; its books are distributed by Grosset & Dunlap.

The second is "The Teamsters" by Steven Brill, to be published by Simon & Schuster, which is owned by the Gulf and Western Industries conglomerate.

Mr. Moldea is a 28-year-old investigative reporter. While going to the University of Akron and later doing graduate teaching at Kent State University, he worked part time as a truck driver and loader for teamsters' Local No. 24 in Akron.

He signed a contract for a book last September with New Republic Books of Washington, with publication scheduled for October. With the help of grants from the Fund for Investigative Journalism, he proceeded full time on his manuscript. He and his editor, Joan Tapper, worked closely and satisfactorily in shaping the book to meet the publishing date, according to both of them.

But there was an essential fact to be reckoned with: New Republic Books are distributed by Simon & Schuster, which had its own book, "The Teamsters," about to be listed in the same catalogue for this fall's list.

Offer Rebuffed

In the middle of last February, Mr. Brill called Mr. Moldea and offered to share some facts on two conditions — that "The Teamsters" be credited and that "The Hoffa Wars" be delayed until next year.

"Then the hardball started," Mr. Moldea said. "I told Brill that I didn't need his help and that I was willing to let the public be the judge."

The bad news came for Mr. Moldea in March, when New Republic informed him that Simon & Schuster would not distribute his book this fall in competition with "The Teamsters."

"We have a clause in our distribution contract with Simon & Schuster" Martin Peretz, New Republic publisher said, "saying that if a conflict arose between one of their books and ours, they could ask us to delay publication. There was no battle over it—it's there in black and white, a clear stipulation. I very much regret it because it's a powerful book."

Because New Republic could no longer publish on its contractual time, Mr. Moldea talked to his lawyers, Michael Allen and Stephen Martindale, who put him in touch with Paddington. New Republic released the author and received back its advance.

"Early in April," Mr. Moldea said, "I flew up to New York from Washington to meet John Marqusee, Paddington's publisher, who told me he would fight to keep the October publication date. He liked the book and doubled my advance to $10,000."

Different Focuses

Richard E. Snyder, president of Simon & Schuster, said: "I was surprised when I heard that New Republic was selling its book to Paddington. We requested them to postpone it, not to sell it."

Publishing sources familiar with the contents of "The Hoffa Wars" and "The Teamsters" say that Mr. Moldea's book is more about Mr. Hoffa and that Mr. Brill's is more of a historical work. Both follow Lester Velie's "Desperate Bargain," published last year by The Reader's Digest Press. It covered labor corruption and Mr. Hoffa's career.

"The Hoffa Wars" includes information derived from and three and a half hour taped interview that Mr. Moldea was allowed to make with suspects in the case of the missing teamsters' leader.

This interview was conducted Oct. 25, 1976, in the hall of teamsters' Local No. 560, dominated by the recently convicted Anthony (Tony) Provenzano, in Union City, N.J. Included on the author's tapes was an interview with Salvatore Briguglio, who was killed March 21 by six bullets on a street corner in Little Italy.

Mr. Moldea writes in the "The Hoffa Wars" that he has been beaten and that his [sic] was vandalized during his investigations. He played a tape recording for The New York Times of a conversation he had with a reform teamsters' official that included warnings to him to "cool it" because his life was in danger.

Brill Cites Different Threat

Mr. Brill also says he has been threatened—by an official of the Federal Bureau of Investigation—for supposedly not sharing a taped "confession" about the Hoffa murder. "Please stress that I have no such tape— it's just not true," Mr. Brill said.

The Simon & Schuster author graduated from the Yale University Law School in 1976 and now writes a law column for Esquire magazine. "My book is less than 10 percent about Hoffa," he said. "In some respects, it's a very positive story about the teamsters. In fact, I've had an offer to go to work for the teamsters as a public-relations consultant—which I turned down."

To arouse interest, Simon & Schuster is resorting to the familiar technique of not divulging its contents before publication. However, Mr. Snyder permitted himself to describe the book as "definitive."

Publishing lawyers said that a number of small houses availed themselves of the sales and marketing forces of the major publishers in an arrangement similar to that between New Republic and Simon & Schuster. The lawyers said that the attempted delay of the Moldea book was one of the first examples of possible loss of independence— with implicit censorship—where there is a conflict on a controversial nonfiction book.

Lawrence Cohn, **"BIG PIX NOW 25% OF MAJORS' SKED"**
Variety (January 11, 1984), p. 1

35 PROJECTS TO COST AT LEAST $14,000,000 EACH

In 1984 the major distributors will be releasing an unprecedented quantity of big-budget pictures, presently targeted at 25% of their total release schedule.

As displayed on the accompanying chart of upcoming films costing $14,000,000 or more (compared to the majors' current budget average of about $11,300,000 per picture), the 35 or so big-ticket films in the works for next year include many independent productions. This factor, combined with the majors' heavy reliance upon outside investor funding via schemes such as the SLM, Delphi and other offerings, has served to substantially reduce the risk involved in expensive films.

Collectively, they do represent increased financial exposure and inflated inventories for the majors, all of which (except for Disney, whose large-scale animation film "The Black Cauldron" as well as "Return To Oz" will not be finished before 1985) have at least two megabuck films apiece for 1984. WB leads the pack with 10 big-budget films next year, while Universal will release seven.

It is worth recalling that the majors will also be releasing at least 100 modestly budgeted pictures during 1984, including many highly commercial properties (e.g., comedies) which did not require large production expenditures. As in 1983, when pictures costing $10,000,000 and under, such as "Flashdance," "Mr. Mom," "Risky Business," "Terms Of Endearment" and "National Lampoon's Vacation" finished high on the annual rentals tally, low-budget films can be expected to bail out their higher-priced brethren at each studio this coming year.

The estimates of negative costs on the chart are based upon published reports, interviews with the films' producers and in some cases *Variety*'s conservative estimates based on known talent costs, shooting (and re-shooting) schedules and physical production factors. The major studios are quite reticent about releasing budget figures for individual pictures.

The return to big-budgets began in 1976 (sparked by such indie projects as "A Bridge Too Far," "King Kong" and "Apocalypse Now"). The majors had adhered to a self-imposed moratorium on megabuck films which lasted from 1971 through 1975, during which time a ceiling of $15,000,000 per film was adhered to. This period of belt-tightening had followed the spurt of $20,000,000-plus pictures made in the late 1960s as roadshow spectaculars, which had resulted in big losses and massive inventory writeoffs at the end of the decade.

Indicative Of Competition

The abundance of such special films for 1984 reflects the heated-up competition for the consumer dollar being waged currently by the film companies, with new "major" Tri-Star entering the fray and relative newcomer Orion Pictures weighing in with three independently made megabuck pictures on its release sked.

In retrospect, although 1983 was a record-setting year at the b.o., it represented a relatively conservative set of mainly modestly budgeted film releases.

The drastically increased level of production spending is reflected in the films which emerged during the current Christmas season. The majors' 15 wide releases at Yuletide in 1983 had an aggregate negative cost of about $180,000,000, which swells to a still-modest $233,000,000 when limited year-end releases "The Right Stuff," "Star 80," "Never Cry Wolf" and "The Dresser" are added in.

By contrast, the nine major distributors (including Tri-Star) have targeted an extraordinary $370,000,000 in production budgets for some 18 features currently planned to open wide at Christmas 1984, more than doubling 1983's investment level. Just six of these films, already in production or pre-production, will cost about $175,000,000 by themselves: "Dune," "The Cotton Club," "2010: Odyssey II," "Kansas City Jazz," "The River" and "Lady-hawke."

Missing from the already crowded Christmas 1984 schedule is the Salkinds' independent project "Santa Claus," budgeted at a whopping $50,000,000, bankrolled via overseas pre-sale arrangements. Due to have started shooting this month in London, the megabuck fantasy film instead rolls next August for release at Christmas 1985, with Tri-Star handling domestic release.

1984's Spectaculars

The 35 or so megabuck films for 1984 are generally designed as "spectaculars," aimed at special attraction releases, and costly due to their massive physical productions (often involving period recreations) and extended shooting schedules, as well as special effects. Also notable on the chart are a number of superstar vehicles, costly due to talent salaries and other above-the-line expenses.

To avoid the risk of never being released domestically (a fate that befell, for example, "Roar," "Virus" and "Red Bells" in recent years), almost all indie projects in this budget range hook up with a major distributor before commencing production.

Confounding any comparison of the absolute scale of these films is their having been made under differing studio arrangements. "Dune," for example, has been rumored to be costing in excess of $60,000,000, though its backers, Dino DeLaurentiis Corp. and Universal Pictures, will admit to only (!) $40,000,000-plus.

Direct Cost Only

Unlike the in-house studio projects (such as "Greystoke," "Ghostbusters" and "The River") which include a studio overhead charge ranging from 15-30% in their negative costs, "Dune" and other independently produced projects are carried at their direct cost only. Also, Paramount and Orion do not affix an overhead charge to the cost of individual pictures. Twentieth Century-Fox applies a variable rate based on actual yearly operating costs, while Columbia, Universal, Warner Bros., MGM-UA and Walt Disney use fixed rates in the 15-30% range. Thus, if "Dune" had been made routinely at most studios, the film would have an additional $10,000,000-plus built into its negative cost to cover studio overhead.

Upcoming Big-Buck Pictures

The following films, either completed or currently in production, have budgets in excess of $14,000,000 and are due for release during 1984, except where noted.

Title, Prod-Distrib	Estimated Negative Cost
"Dune" (DeLaurentiis/U)	$40,000,000+
"The Cotton Club" (Evans/Orion)	40,000,000+
"Greystoke, Legend Of Tarzan" (WB)	40,000,000
"Once Upon A Time In America" (Wishbone/Ladd/WB)	38,000,000
"Supergirl" (Salkinds/WB)	30,000,000
"A Woman For All Time" (Sovinfilm/Poseidon Par)	30,000,000+
"Ghostbusters" (Columbia)	29,000,000
"The Bounty" (DeLaurentiis/Orion)	28,000,000
"Rhinestone" (20th-Fox)	28,000,000
"Indiana Jones & The Temple Of Doom" (Lucasfilm/Par)	27,000,000
"The Never-Ending Story" (Neue Constantin/WB)	27,000,000
"The Black Cauldron" (Disney/Buena Vista, 1985 release)	25,000,000
"2010: Odyssey II" (MGM-UA)	25,000,000
"Stick" (U)	22,000,000
"Ladyhawke" (WB/20th)	21,000,000
"Return To Oz" (Disney/BV, 1985 release)	20,000,000
"The River" (U)	20,000,000
"Streets Of Fire" (RKO/U)	19,500,000
"The Natural" (Tri-Star)	19,000,000
"A Passage To India" (Thorn EMI/Col)	17,500,000
"Cannonball II" (Golden Harvest/WB)	17,000,000
"Buckaroo Banzai" (Sherwood/20th)	17,000,000
"Baby" (Disney/Buena Vista)	16,000,000
"Star Trek III: The Search For Spock" (Par)	16,000,000
"Sheena, Queen Of The Jungle" (Col/Thorn EMI)	16,000,000
"Swing Shift" (WB)	16,000,000
"Conan II, King Of Thieves" (DeLaurentiis/U)	16,000,000
"The Last Starfighter" (Lorimar/U)	15,000,000
"Amadeus" (Zaentz/Orion)	15,000,000
"The Little Drummer Girl" (WB)	15,000,000

"Sahara" (Cannon/MGM-UA)   15,000,000
"The Killing Fields" (Goldcrest/WB)   15,000,000
"The Muppets Take Manhattan" (Tri-Star)   14,000,000
"The Lonely Guy" (U)   14,000,000

"YEAR-END BIZ HOLDS TO CONSTANT: CORE OF HITS CROP OF LOSERS"

Variety (January 11, 1984), p. 7

Hollywood.

There's a lesson in the recent year-end domestic film boxoffice season, and it's got nothing to do with the weather or the national economy or the day-placement of certain holidays. Simply this: the year-end b.o. season is very static, year-in and year-out, and forcing too many films on the market dilutes the performance of all but the top three hits.

Over the past seven years, the number of U.S. film tickets sold in the last four weeks of the year has been steady within 5% of 92,000,000.

Last month there were 22 major releases competing for holiday season business. In the comparable period of 1982, the number was 18. (In both years there were a few autumn holdovers in the totals.)

The numbers show that there were three or four too many new wide-released pics last month. It's rather difficult for even the most avid filmgoer to digest more than six to eight films over the very limited (about 25 days) year-end period.

. . . .

Of course nobody knows for certain in advance what the hits will be, but a certain amount of common sense ought to restrain the release of too much product.

Talk all you want about the weather, but keep in mind that "Sudden Impact" grossed $41,900,000 over the holidays, virtually the same as did "Tootsie" a year earlier with $39,900,000 through New Year's.

And the holiday season portion of $29,700,000 for "Terms Of Endearment" (of its overall $39,800,000 cumulative at year-end) matches the $30,500,000 for "The Toy" a year earlier.

Further, the $22,100,000 for "Scarface" is near the $24,600,000 for "48 Hrs." a year back. In all cases these films ranked comparably over the year-end b.o. season. (Their later life in the new year is not the subject under discussion.)

The top eight pics in both year-end holiday seasons took 75-80% of the business, a pattern noted in prior years as well.

Sharp Drop

But following the eighth-ranking film, there usually is a sharp drop into mediocre performance. And last month there were three or four more such wimps than before. This tail end of the market enriches only film laboratories and tv time sales departments.

The year-end holidays—make no mistake—are very lucrative. But the *overall* level of business is remarkably constant from year to year, and the short time-base forces selective filmgoing decisions. The addition of just three or four too many major wide releases has a devastating effect on the ecology. (It's a far different story in summer, when the time base is more than 100 days in length and a high level of b.o. potential exists for nearly four months.)

As any child soon learns, the "weather" is the phoniest excuse in show business. And the most enduring—*Murf.*

Cynthia Kirk, "LP DEALS CHANGING DRASTICALLY, SEZ LAWYER; ARTISTS BEAR BRUNT OF INDUSTRY'S ECONOMIC WOES"
Variety (December 22, 1982), p. 50

Hollywood, Dec. 21.

The depressed economic climate in the record industry since 1979 has dramatically changed the parameters of artist-diskery negotiations, music biz attorney Lee Phillips told the UCLA Entertainment Symposium Dec. 10.

Contract points which were once dealt with in a matter of minutes are now critical bargaining areas, says Phillips, and many of the traditional "givens" of a record deal are no more, for both new and established artists alike.

Diskeries are caught in a squeeze, he said, between rising production-marketing costs and consumer resistance to price hikes. As a result, Phillips said, it's the artist, rather than the consumer, "who bears most of the consequences of the depressed" industry.

Given production costs which can approach or exceed $500,000, and Phillips' estimate that only 16-20% of all LPs released ever reach a break-even point on those costs, diskeries are slashing product commitments in artist pacts, in hopes of hedging their financial bets a bit.

Now "a thing of the past," for example, are two and three-LP deals for newcomers, he said. Instead, singles deals or EP pacts are becoming more common, while for established performers, who used to command five or 10-album deals, three or four LPs are now the rule, he said.

Royalty rates are being affected as well, he said. While in the peak sales year of 1978, newcomers might be able to secure as much as a 14-15% rate, today it's more like 7-10%, while for superstars, who in 1978 could demand and get 19-20% royalty rates, the level is more likely 13-16% today. Yet, said Phillips, "even those superstar expectations . . . are more and more being dashed in this difficult and competitive environment."

Increasingly, he said, pacts include escalation clauses for royalties, in recognition of the fact that marketing and promotion costs, for example, are higher early on in an LP's release. Lowest sales level at which escalators will kick in, he estimated, is 250,000 units, with 500,000 units sold being the more common kick-off point.

Lower Advances

Likewise, the days of firm, and hefty advances are past, Phillips said. Today, diskeries tend to make advances based upon a percentage of earnings from prior LPs, with floors and ceilings built into the contracts. This, he said, forces the artist to assume some of the risks inherent in today's disk market.

In general, the minimums guaranteed under this method are "far less" than the advances offered in contracts signed in 1978 or before, he said. On the other hand, the ceilings protect labels from "aberrationally large selling LPs which would up the next album's advance astronomically and unrealistically, given the general state of the market at present."

Also affected by today's disk biz climate, Phillips said, are mechanical copyright royalties. While the statutory rate has jumped from 2-¾ cents to 4 cents, diskery use of the so-called "controlled compositions clause," which covers performer-penned tunes, can reduce that take by 25%.

Diskeries can't absorb the increase in mechanicals from 12½¢ to 40¢ for a 10-song LP, says Phillips, and thus insist on a 30¢ per LP ceiling, via the clause. As a result, even if an LP contains 12 performer-controlled songs, the 30¢ ceiling remains in effect. Phillips estimates that the 10¢ per-album saving represents "tens of millions of dollars per year" to a record company overall.

But, since the mechanical rate is due to increase in the future, signing pacts now with controlled compositions clauses will mean performer-writers will get substantially less than three-quarters of the minimum statutory rate in years to come, he noted.

Artist Penalized

Another way in which performers are affected by the clause is when they record tunes by other writers, for which the diskery must pay the full statutory rate. If, as a result, mechanicals exceed the maximum level under the controlled compositions clause, those overages may be deducted from other royalties and sums due the artist under his contract.

Phillips made two suggestions in reference to mechanicals and the controlled compositions clause. He urged artists to seek mechanicals on all "free goods" given to retailers and to seek a modification of the clause in the area of songs co-written with outside writers, so that the other songwriter would get the full statutory rate.

One section of a recording contract long glossed over is now quite critical, said Phillips. In the past, contracts required delivery of "technically satisfactory" masters. That language is being changed to "commercially satisfactory," a phrase which makes it possible for diskeries to reject LPs.

Given this possibility, contract negotiations should settle the issue of who will bear the re-recording costs, and in what manner.

Another contract area which has undergone significant change in recent years is tour support. Once a frequently promised item, diskery deficit financing of tours is virtually extinct today.

Of growing importance to artists are such new technology areas as video and satellite-fed home delivery of LPs to consumers.

In the latter regard, although diskery costs may be significantly reduced by such systems, some labels are already including clauses in their pacts covering this area and promising the same royalty levels as paid under the "old" distribution system, which Phillips argues is not fair.

David Berman, business affairs veepee at Warner Bros. Records, which has such a clause, argued at the symposium that diskeries may net less than they do at retail via this delivery system. He added, however, that in some quarters of his company, consideration is being given to offering a straight percentage of receipts formula in this area.

"PAR SIGNS SIMPSON, BRUCKHEIMER TO A 3-YEAR EXCLUSIVITY"

Variety (August 10, 1983), p. 3

Hollywood, Aug. 9.

Former Paramount Pictures production president Don Simpson and veteran line producer Jerry Bruckheimer, who teamed to coproduce Par's current hit film "Flashdance," have signed an exclusive three-year deal to develop and produce film and television projects for Paramount. The duo will soon have as many as 20 properties in active development and are expected to make more than two features for the studio each year.

The new deal has Paramount totally bankrolling the pair's substantial production activity, which already includes a list of 11 original feature ideas now being scripted by various writers. It is also anticipated Simpson-Bruckheimer Prods. will have yet another picture rolling in the fall, the elements of which are just now falling into place.

The pair are moving more slowly in the television area though they say there are also a number of projects there now under consideration. Though neither has worked in television, Simpson is a self-proclaimed tv buff whom Par Pictures president Michael Eisner was eager to get working in the area.

"I believe they'll be productive in both films and television," Eisner said. "When I was at ABC our swing into first place was not with established people but with new people. Paramount's success has been with new people in many areas. I think Don knows exactly what kinds of program we're interested in. Already we have two of the three networks interested in them (Simpson and Bruckheimer) as a team."

Simpson and Bruckheimer will still have to get Par's ultimate approval for the films and tv programs they make, though Simpson claims they'll have "a lot of latitude in the choice of talent and in the nature of films." Because he once ran Paramount's feature development activities, Simpson said he felt "we're not going to become involved in things Paramount isn't going to make."

In terms of development, the pair predicted a three-to-one ratio in terms of projects they get started and then eventually wind up as films. With the cost of development estimated in the area of $75,000-$150,000 per property, Paramount will be giving the producers a healthy amount of funds to get their pictures off the ground.

Latest Longterm Lockup

The new deal follows a spate of longterm agreements Paramount has made in the last few months with such talent as Eddie Murphy, director Dan Curtis, actress Cynthia Rhodes and former Par Television prez turned producer Gary Nardino. Though Paramount has stayed away from making such pacts in previous years, Eisner said there is no particular conclusion to be drawn from the so recent occurrences.

"We might make 50 deals in 50 days and then maybe not another such deal for another five years," he said. "We're just looking for original, unique and different projects from people. It's a business of making movies—not deals."

Interestingly, all of the 11 films Simpson and Bruckheimer now have in development are original ideas, rather than scripts based on novels or film remakes. "One of the problems and reasons behind movies failing is that they're not based on new ideas," Simpson offered. "We have much more on the upside working this way and I think our personal aptitude is more in that area."

Development Roster

Among Simpson and Bruckheimer's projects are "The Receptionist," a dramatic comedy written by Katherine Reback, who did a final script polish on "Flashdance." It focuses on a female receptionist and has been compared in tone in Paul Mazursky's "An Unmarried Woman."

"City Kids" is a contemporary drama on urban high school kids written by Richard Price ("Wanderers," "Bloodbrothers") while "The Bully" is a courtroom drama penned by Mark Medoff. The duo are also developing "Top Gun" with writers Jim Cash and Jim Epps, who penned the upcoming "Dick Tracy." It is based on a California magazine article on a training school for naval aviators.

Simpson and Bruckheimer additionally have a deal with Monty Python troupe member Eric Idle to direct and write a comedy entitled "Rutland Islands" and another with producer Martin Elfand on "Harry," a contemporary comedy by David Andrus about a man who invents a robot.

Dan Petrie Jr. is now writing "Beverly Hills Cop," a character action piece about an inner city policeman who works in Beverly Hills while National Lampoon writers Tod Carroll and Ted Mann are scripting "Weekend Warriors," a contempo military comedy.

"Prism," a modern action adventure story centering on an American agent is being penned by Hampton Fancher while a writer is just being firmed on another project, "Teen Detective." Latter is also the case on "Christmas Story," a picture that will have an emphasis on music.

Simpson and Bruckheimer plan to stay involved with each of their pics through the marketing stage (they respectively began their careers in publicity and advertising) though they admit that Paramount will have the final say in those matters.

"LITIGATION COULD DERAIL N.Y. TRACKS"
Variety (August 31, 1977), p. 3

ON TOP OF UATC SUIT, COMES RKO-STANLEY

Strain following the United Artists Theatre Circuit $58,500,000 antitrust suit filed last month in New York Federal Court for the Southern District against 20th-Fox, RKO-Stanley Warner and Mann Theatres is starting to be felt throughout the entire New York metropolitan area.

RKO-Stanley Warner last week (23) slapped a $60,000,000 trebled antitrust counterclaim against United Artists circuit and related plaintiffs in the same court, and further proceeded to name Century Theatres, Loews (and related companies) Theatres, Metro, Warner Brothers, Universal and United Artists Pictures as third party defendants.

All are charged with having "rigged" the N.Y. metropolitan market with violation of sections of the Clayton and Sherman Antitrust acts, forcing RKO into an inferior stature in the market place and controlling the flow of firstrun features into the area.

Perhaps most significant of all, what began in September, 1975 as the clashing of wills between two iron-willed individuals—Peter Myers, 20th-Fox's sales veep, and Salah Hassanein, UTAC's exec veepee—over the playoff of Fox product in the New York market in 1976, not only resulted in ruptured business relations thereafter, but has now exploded into a courtroom fight that could very well drag the entire New York marketplace up to the witness stand. There, each others' secrets of how the backs are scratched may become interesting bedtime reading for everyone—the trade, the public, the Justice Department in Washington.

The RKO suit perhaps even more directly than the UATC suit takes on the whole subject of tracks—the relatively fixed constellation of theatres that play a given distributor's product—acknowledging in public papers that pictures are rarely, if ever, sold "theatre by theatre, without discrimination, solely on the merits," the guidelines set out by the 1948 Consent Decree achieved by the U.S. Justice Dept.

Forced Tandems

After nearly three pages of chronicling combinations and conspiracies to cut RKO out of serious competition in the N.Y. marketplace since 1970, RKO claimed in one almost virginal passage that from "time to time" it was forced to play on tracks set by UATC, Loews and Century in order to get any product at all. Loews, suit alleged, had approached RKO in 1973 with instructions to relinquish firstrun dealings with Warners and Universal, except as Loews called the shots.

RKO attorneys further named the tracks (which may be a first for papers filed in court by a participant), confusing a couple of generic terms, such as "showcase" and "selected" with actual tracks, such as "Red Carpet," "Flagship" and "Blue Ribbon."

"Premiere," which was the progenitor of all showcase tracks in the early Sixties but is now defunct, was included, but the Deluxe I&II used by Columbia and Paramount, and the Fox track, used by RKO along with Mann, General Cinema and independents, were omitted. The Gold Medal, American International track used by RKO, was listed as "Gold Circle."

The RKO suit arrived on the scene almost on the heels of a visit by Myers into the New York area met with Hassanein to try to settle the suit—on the advice of Fox attorneys who reportedly warned that a major public brouhaha could dash a hoped for rise in Fox stock calculated at $10, to over $30 per share.

The Myers-Hassanein face-off ended in a shouting match, observers report, over Hassanein's demand that Fox put another 30-plus runs of "Star Wars" (the picture that put the severely strained Myers-Hassanein relationship beyond the pale and into the courtroom when it was not awarded to UATC) into UATC immediately in exchange for UATC's dropping the original suit. No dice; both parties are said to be anxious to go to the mat, sources say.

A Trade Question?

By bringing in Warner's, UA, Metro, Universal—companies that service UATC—and going further afield to name Loews and Century circuits, has RKO added fuel to the fire begun by UATC that will somehow consume them all, including Columbia, Paramount, American International, General Cinema—you name it—which have thus far remained outside the legal inferno?

"If this thing goes to court—actually goes to court," one showman warned, "it will destroy everything as we know it in the distribution of pictures in New York. The walls of the temple will come tumbling down for sure," he sighed. "Nobody should have pointed any fingers. Everybody's as guilty as hell."

"ORION TO TRACK EXCLUSIVELY IN WESTWOOD AT FACELIFTED UACI 4"

Variety (September 7, 1983), p. 31

Hollywood, Sept. 6.

Beginning this Christmas, Orion Pictures will open its films in Los Angeles' Westwood Village exclusively at the United Artists Communications Inc.'s four-plex, which will be extensively renovated and redubbed the UA Coronet.

Per UACI prexy-chief executive officer Robert Naify, the outlet, currently known as the UA Cinema Center, will be completely remodeled inside and out at a cost of $800,000. The two larger auditoria, with 631 seats apiece, will be equipped with new 35m and 70m projectors as well as Dolby and THX (Lucasfilm) sound systems.

Orion domestic distribution exec v.p. Eugene Tunick described his company's relationship with UACI in Westwood as a "marriage" that will have advantages for both parties. Orion will now be assured of venues in which to showcase its films in the L.A. market's most intense filmgoing center, and UACI will now have a flow of product from a major company for theatres which, at least until now, have been on the low end of the Westwood totem poll.

First Orion pic set to open in the made-over houses will be "Gorky Park" on Dec. 16. Set to follow in 1984 are "Broadway Danny Rose" on Jan. 27, "Amadeus" (in 70m) on Feb. 15 and "The Hotel New Hampshire" in March.

Relationship will not, in practice, be entirely exclusive, at least on UACI's end, since there will inevitably be breaks in Orion's release sked when other company's pics can be booked. But Orion has first dibs, at least on the two big screens.

Dave Kaufman, "FEDS PROBE TV BLOCK BOOKING BY SYNDICATORS"

Variety (August 2, 1978), p. 1

Hollywood, Aug. 1.

U.S. Dept. of Justice's antitrust division has launched an investigation into tv block booking practices, and has begun contacts with some L.A. stations seeking documentation of allegations regarding such deals by syndicators.

Confirmation that a preliminary investigation is now underway was made by Barbara Reeves, in charge of the L.A. office of the antitrust division, which covers the entire southwest. While confirming reports of such a probe, Reeves said, "That's all we can say at this time."

JD probers set up appointments, beginning last week, with local indie channels, indies being the principal buyers of syndicated product. It's reported the investigation was inspired by reports that Paramount TV, about to release "Laverne and Shirley" for syndication, has indicated to potential buyers that "Mannix," also a Par TV series, would be expected to be part of any such deal.

Series of Meetings

JD sources have indicated they want to determine the facts on that situation, and to see "if the industry is moving in that direction," commented one source close to the situation.

Meanwhile probing on the packaging practices of syndicators is getting underway, with a meeting held last week between JD reps and KTLA, and one today (Tues.) between JD probers and KHJ-TV.

KCOP and KTTV, L.A.'s other indie stations, haven't been contacted as yet by the Justice Dept.

Par TV Service has been mulling syndication of "Mannix," the private eye series starring Mike Connors, for some time, and said some months ago the show would likely be put into distribution this summer. Studio sources have said the current anti-violence sentiment in tv has been a deterrent regarding release of the series, which ran for about eight years on CBS-TV.

"Laverne," on the other hand, is a torrid property eagerly being sought by stations around the country, including indies in L.A.

Ron Chernow, "THE PERILS OF THE PICTURE SHOW: FADE-OUT ON AN ERA"
New York Magazine (August 22, 1977), p. 28

Theater owners may feel a special kinship these days to the flaming skyscrapers, omnivorous sharks, and collapsing cities that dominate their screens. For cinemas are starting to fold around New York with the grim momentum of a disaster film.

The signs of doom are small but ubiquitous: The old, plush theater is suddenly converted into a complex of "screening rooms"; ushers no longer shepherd patrons to their seats; pictures stay on the marquee for months at a time; retreads like *The Godfather* reappear in local theatres after being aired on TV; dollar cinemas disappear; *The Sting* is resurrected at Radio City Music

Hall after a spate of rock and gospel shows; movie palaces like the Ziegfeld, the Criterion, and Loews Astor Plaza stand idle for weeks at a time; and porno pops up in once respectable theaters.

Such trends signal a crisis that threatens not only to bankrupt many theaters but to alter the nature of the American film business. In industry argot, that crisis is termed the "product shortage." It means that Hollywood studios are not cranking out enough films, especially first-rate ones, to satisfy all available movie screens. And in this seller's market, movie theaters across America are being slaughtered. In fact, the Saturday-night "picture show" may soon become a thing of the past, as small-town theaters are squeezed out of business by the giant, urban-oriented distributors.

In the metropolitan area alone, an estimated two dozen cinemas have closed in the past two years, and many others have had to shut temporarily for lack of product. The Walter Reade organization—operator of the Baronet-Coronet, the Waverly, the Little Carnegie, and other popular New York houses—filed for bankruptcy in January. In three years, the Reade colossus has shriveled from a national chain of 80 theaters to fewer than 30.

To anyone who remembers Hollywood in its palmy days, the shrinkage of the film business seems incredible. Before television, the major studios each produced about 50 films annually, feeding them to their theatre chains. But the seven companies that direct the industry today—Paramount, Universal, Columbia, MGM, Twentieth Century-Fox, United Artists, and Warner Bros.—each make only a dozen or so films per year. The term *studio* has become a misnomer, for the seven "majors" finance and distribute films created by independent producers at least half of the time.

There's no lack of cynical exhibitors who think that the product shortage has been deliberately created, since it is more profitable for the majors to market a dozen films a year apiece than their former 50. And in recent years, the studios have been swallowed up by conglomerates—Paramount by Gulf & Western, Universal by MCA, etc.—more concerned with profits than with imperishable art.

So while theaters starve for film, these companies are rolling up record profit margins. On the strength of *A Star Is Born* and *The Enforcer*—scarcely a pair of masterpieces—Warner Bros. raked in an unprecedented $50 million in domestic film rentals in the first quarter in 1977. And riding the crest of *Rocky, Carrie, The Pink Panther Strikes Again, and Network*, United Artists took in $46 million in rentals for the first quarter, nearly *double* what it made in the initial quarter last year.

Strange as it may seem to film addicts, pictures are marketed as coldly as any commodity. To some extent, the price paid for a film fluctuates with the size of each season's celluloid crop. In today's seller's market, the majors are extracting exorbitant rental terms from movie theaters hungry for product. Most moviegoers assume that the theater owner pockets the $3.50 or so charged for each ticket. For the most part, however, the theaters now take only a small fraction of that money, funneling most of it to the distributors. Meanwhile, they're going broke.

To fathom this paradox, one must return to the 1920's, when Paramount tycoon Adolph Zukor started the practice of distributors' skimming off a percentage of box-office receipts. The percentage "split" between film company and theater is a function of supply and demand. When there is a glut of films, theater owners have the upper hand and can negotiate a larger slice—which was the case in the 1960s. But the power balance has seesawed. Distributors now often siphon off up to *90 percent* of the box-office take, leaving the crumbs to the theaters. Once limited to a few Hollywood spectaculars, such lopsided splits are fast becoming the standard deal for even mediocre films. This past year, for instance, Columbia dictated such tough terms for undistinguished fare like *The Eagle Has Landed* and *Fun With Dick and Jane*.

The 90/10 split is a bit of an oversimplification. Before the booty is divided, the theater owner gets to deduct his house expenses—dubbed the "nut." But many of the 90/10 contracts also carry a tiny clause guaranteeing the distributor a minimum of 70 percent of the first week's gross *under any circumstances*—even if it nibbles at the nut.

On top of this, theater managers complain that the majors haven't allowed them to revise their nut for inflation. "My nut was established two or three years ago and everything has gone up," said one Queens theater owner. "When I complain to the distributors, they say, 'Go ahead, screw yourselves.' " A Nassau County exhibitor grumbled that his house expenses had been frozen at their 1972 level.

Some of the majors seem secretly gleeful about the rash of retail closings and are unsympathetic to exhibitors' woes, perhaps because they remember the buyer's markets of the fifties and sixties, when the theater owners skinned *them*. Asked about the exhibitor's contention that they hadn't been allowed to update their nuts for three or five years, Bruce Snyder, the modish young Atlantic Division branch manager for Twentieth Century-Fox, retorted coolly, "That's right. And in two more years it will be an honest figure." The distributors almost uniformly feel that the house nuts are padded; of course, exhibitors claim the opposite.

But the declining number of films can be explained without resorting to theories of venal studios. The fundamental fact of life in the film business is that it must fill the gaps left by TV—graphic sex, sadistic violence, and obscenity. These elements often work together best in the big-budget disaster pictures. Toss in some million-dollar stars who seldom appear on television, and the TV fiend has an incentive to visit the corner cinema.

"Television can't deliver you a Dustin Hoffman or an Al Pacino," says Ray Silver, independent producer of *Hester Street* and *Between the Lines.* "And it can't deliver you a war or certain themes not permitted on television. It can't give you the raucous comedy of a Mel Brooks or the sophisticated comedy of A Woody Allen"—at least not on first run. "So movies tend to go after those very special areas that television can't handle. And they tend to be large films with what the studios hope will be large, explosive national-audience potential."

So the bottom line is this: The more high-budget movies the studios churn out, the smaller their total film output will be. And that means a product shortage.

The majors don't cast their few pearls on the market arbitrarily. It's axiomatic in the film business that the biggest throngs turn out during the summer holidays and at Christmas and Easter. Therefore, the distributors conduct saturation ad campaigns and spill the best pictures at these times. But this tactic leaves exhibitors stranded as soon as the holiday tide ebbs. Everyone in the industry parrots the same sentiment: The studios are now in a sixteen-weeks-a-year business, the movie houses in a 52-weeks-a-year business. And the theaters find that they simply cannot recoup their yearlong losses during the holiday flurries.

Asked about the product shortage, studio executives hark back to 1948. In the famous Paramount case of that year, the federal government divested the studios of their theater chains. Executives argue that before that time, they had an incentive to supply a steady stream of product. Also, assured of playing time at their own theaters, they could afford to do art pictures of a more esoteric nature. But in the wake of the Paramount decision, and with the growing competition from "free" and cable TV, the studios have had to concentrate on mass-audience films released at peak holiday periods.

Most exhibitors spend less time analyzing the product shortage than figuring out how to cope with it. A favorite tactic has been to gut the interiors of those big Byzantine cinemas and create a warren of screening cubicles. This way, one cashier, one ticket taker, etc., can service two or three screens, spreading out the overhead.

"All of the old-fashioned single, large theaters are going to go under," says Bernard Goldberg, executive vice-president of Golden Theatre Management, operator of the Quad Cinema in the Village and six other New York City houses." "A traditional large theater cannot meet its overhead with the film rentals it has to pay. There aren't enough top-grossing pictures for them to show. Either they will divide the theater into two, three or four screens—which is what we've done at the Quad—or go under."

Who decides which theaters will screen the few prize pictures? The crux of transactions between distributors and exhibitors is the mysterious bidding rite, which rivals papal elections for secrecy and intrigue. Each exhibitor privately submits a bid stating, among other things, what percentage he will hand over to the studio. But many independent exhibitors suspect that powerful theater chains are given preferential treatment. Since the bids are never disclosed, paranoid fantasies are given full rein. A whole mythology has sprung up around the bidding process.

"When you bid for a film, you don't submit a sealed envelope, then sit around a table and open up the envelopes," says Ralph Donnelly, vice-president of RKO—Stanley Warner Theatres. "It's all done late at night in some dark room someplace." Exhibitors will tell you darkly about the "five o'clock look"—when distributors supposedly usher favored clients into their offices after the bidding closes at 5 P.M. These customers, so the story goes, are then given a chance to top the high bid. It's difficult to find a local independent who doesn't think that the bidding system is bent, if not plain crooked. "Most of the time the bidding is a farce," said one.

When confronted with such charges of discrimination, the majors are armed with a glib explanation. They claim that in addition to bids, they study the track record of the theater and simply calculate where they will net the most profit. Since the rich chains have shiny new theaters in profitable locations, they reportedly walk off with the trophies. In theory, the majors entertain bids on all pictures; in actuality, they book certain clusters of theaters—"tracks"—year-round. Ordinarily, theaters balk at being "locked up" by the majors, but with the product shortage, most are only too happy to be their kept mistresses.

In April, the Justice Department outlawed "split agreements"—an exhibitors' tactic of carving up territory and bidding only on pictures from certain distributors. Though the impact of this ruling is still far from clear, it seems possible that it will terminate the honeymoon between distributors and theaters on their tracks. Twentieth Century-Fox has already said that it will switch to a pure bidding system.

In the Paramount case, the government also prohibited an unscrupulous practice called "block-booking." For years the studios had been negotiating package deals, forcing theaters to screen a couple of flops in exchange for the latest Oscar winner. Some exhibitors say that this practice has again reared its head. Distributors profess shock and astonishment at the thought.

"Oh, no," said one horrified ex-sales executive for a major studio. "That's

30-year-old history. No distributor would care a damn about a picture that didn't gross."

But Marvin Goldman, president of the National Association of Theatre Owners, suggested in a recent speech that the studios have indeed returned to the predatory strategies of the forties: " . . . There is more than the customary amount of kowtowing to a distributor's demand on one picture in order to get a second. The practice has become much more frequent. If a theater owner does not agree to terms or extended playing time on a current feature, he can't get the next. Some of this has always been in practice, but the attitude today is completely adamant without any room for argument."

The controversy over block-booking erupted into legal warfare in July. United Artists Theaters spearheaded a lawsuit against Twentieth Century-Fox, distributor of the fantastically successful *Star Wars,* charging Fox with forcing certain cinemas owned by RKO-Stanley Warner and Mann Theatres into contracts for exhibiting only Fox first-run features.

This isn't to say that exhibitors are all little white lambs. Independent theaters charge that theater chains will sometimes bully distributors into giving them a hot picture despite higher bids by independents. In such cases, say independents, the chain will threaten to forgo future films released by the distributor. Or else it will promise to take a couple of duds. So the sword can cut both ways.

Theater owners must possess finely tuned instincts for the tastes of their local audience. Traditionally, they've been able to prescreen films and assess their appeal before bidding, and this has often been a crucial part of the business. But many theater owners are now flying blind and being forced to bid on unfinished pictures. In some cases, they are effectively financing these pictures by pledging tens of thousands of dollars in nonrefundable "guarantees" on the strength of cast and synopsis alone. In the case of a blockbuster like *Star Wars*, for example, Fox reportedly sought a $50,000 guarantee from every theater. To finance a pair of $25-million extravaganzas—*A Bridge Too Far* and the upcoming *Apocalypse Now*—United Artists got money commitments from movie theaters that virtually safeguard its investment in both films. Based on the sluggish showing of *A Bridge Too Far*, U.A. must feel lucky to have the security of the up-front money for its other war epic.

Theater owners can also consult *Variety* for a picture's box-office performance at comparable theaters around the country, although in the past this has proven something less than a surefire method. "Most of *Variety* is lies, absolute lies," says Charlie Carmello, a veteran film production manager now with Gemini Images ad agency. "There's a three- or four-week period of suckering everyone in. When they put a figure of $170,000 in one theater recently, my God, you wouldn't have enough seats. If you charged $50 a person, you couldn't make that much money from one theater." Of course, *Variety* can't hire spies to police the 20,000 screens across America but must rely on data supplied by distributors.

Through this sort of dice-rolling, many New York cinemas dropped thousands last year on box-office duds like *Lucky Lady* and *Nickelodeon*. In their beggarly posture brought about by the product squeeze, theaters have also had to agree to extended first runs of six, ten, or even twelve weeks for pictures they've never seen. (This overexposure on "first run" was what killed many dollar cinemas.) If theaters want to extricate themselves from a long, losing run, they must pay a pullout fee equivalent to what the film would have earned for the remainder of its stay.

Many editorial writers have focused upon the porno explosion as a symptom of moral degeneracy in America. But there is a simple economic explanation. The product shortage and extortionate rental terms have driven many theater owners into the arms of smut merchants. Porno distributors offer not only product but seductively soft terms: Theater owners can keep the bulk of the box-office gross, and they don't have to fork over guarantees or hold unpopular pictures for prolonged runs. If Hollywood doubled its output of films, many porno houses would gladly switch to family entertainment.

And what of the future? Some film pundits say not to worry, that the business has always suffered its boom-and-bust cycles. But there are reasons to believe that the theaters' present hardships are the first stage of a terminal decline. Again, the explanation has to do with television and the conglomerate control of the majors.

After spending many years dreading the inroads of television, some studios have, in effect, defected to the enemy. The same conglomerates that make films also produce television shows. Some observers note that the peak TV and movie seasons conveniently alternate. When theater attendance tapers off in September, TV ratings soar with the new fall schedule. And for the entertainment conglomerates, a dollar of TV profit is a lot easier to collect than a dollar from movie theaters.

In March, a federal court of appeals ruled that the Federal Communications Commission didn't have the right to regulate pay TV. One upshot of the decision will be that cable TV, along with the major networks, will be able to bid for first-run pictures. The handwriting on the wall is clear. Thousands of atomized theater owners bidding against the concerted strength of "free" or cable TV networks probably won't stand a chance. The distributors will cry all the way to the bank. They'll be able to sell one or a handful of prints instead of several hundred—and be able to make the same money. They'll be able to slash sales personnel, pare down their vast distribution mechanism, and still boost profits.

The thesis that the conglomerates are cannibalizing themselves has been given some credence by the court battle over the Sony Betamax color television tape recorder. Unlike other machines that simply allow a playback of television films, the Betamax permits permanent taping. Universal Pictures and Walt Disney Productions have been trying to get a court order to stop the sale of these machines, contending that consumers would pirate their copyrighted films and wipe out their resale value.

But apparently not all the studios feel equally threatened. Sony has allied itself with Paramount Pictures in a venture called the Sony-Paramount Home Entertainment Center, which would include the taping technology being combated by Universal and Disney. The strange partnership would suggest that Paramount is content to let the home supplant the theater as the primary distribution outlet. There are also movements afoot by other companies to sell relatively recent feature films in the form of "video discs."

Fortunately, theater owners aren't leaping into the graves being dug for them by the majors. A trade group called the National Independent Theater Exhibitors has declared war against the studios with a campaign to produce low-budget films by pooling funds from theater owners.

I must say I hope it succeeds. Moviegoing is one of the few tribal rituals left in America. The musty smell of the seats, the taste of the popcorn, the giant faces on the screen have all shaped our experience of film. The cinema is one of the few places where we can be close to a crowd and yet keep our urban anonymity intact. I think we'll all miss slouching in that impenetrable darkness. For what will be the chances for fantasy and escape when we sit in our rooms, fiddling with our Japanese machines?

Ron Chernow is a free-lance writer.

RING v. SPINA
148 F.2d 647 (2d Cir. 1945)

Before EVANS and CLARK, Circuit Judges.

CLARK, Circuit Judge.

This is an appeal from an order of the District Court vacating a temporary injunction and denying a motion for such injunction pending trial in an action for treble damages under the Sherman Act, as amended, 15 U.S.C.A. § 15, and for other relief. Defendants Spina, Heyman, and Hannan are authors of a theatrical production called "Stovepipe Hat." The other defendants are Pauker, agent of these authors, and The Dramatists' Guild of the Authors' League of America, Inc., an association said to include substantially all the playwrights in the country. Restraint of trade is alleged to be accomplished by means of the Guild's Minimum Basic Agreement, which a producer or "manager" must sign before any Guild members, such as the authors herein, may license or sell to him their works. The Basic Agreement, among other things, fixes the minimum terms under which the Guild permits any of its members to lease or license a play, including the minimum advance payments and the minimum royalties to be paid by a manager. It limits contracts by both managers and authors to those made under its own terms, and between managers and members, both of whom are "in good standing" with the Guild.[1] It also provides that any dispute shall be finally adjudicated by arbitration.

It appears from the moving papers that plaintiff signed this Minimum Basic Agreement after he had invested $50,000 in the play. He came into the venture first by association with, later by taking over the rights of, one Gaumont, who had entered into a "Production Contract" with the three authors on February 7, 1944, whereby Gaumont was to produce the play upon stated royalties and other payments—all subject to the provisions of the Basic Agreement. Then plaintiff on May 4, 1944, to safeguard his investment, and upon his agreement to advance the balance necessary for the show to open in New Haven, May 18, 1944, attempted to enter into an agreement with the authors on the basis of Gaumont's contract with them; but they signed only on condition that their lawyer would later approve. Their lawyer held, however, that this contract could not be made with plaintiff, a non-Guild member; and it was destroyed. Thereupon plaintiff, as he says, "against his will and under the coercive pressure of the monopolistic practice and rules and regulations" of the Guild, signed its Basic Agreement, in order that he might protect his part in the venture. The play did open in New Haven, and then went on to Boston, preparatory to going to Philadelphia and then to New York City; and plaintiff put up an additional $75,000, as he alleges. A dispute having arisen as to changes which plaintiff thought should be made in the play, the authors then took the position that plaintiff had breached the Basic Agreement by making changes without consent of the authors, contrary to its provisions, and hence that the production contract was terminated. The play was then forced to

---

[1] Thus Art. I, Sec. 2, "Member's Right to Contract," provides: "None of the members of the Guild shall, without its consent, make any contract granting rights to produce and present a play upon the speaking stage in the United States except under the terms of this Basic Agreement and only with a Manager who is in good standing with the Guild. The names of Managers in good standing shall be filed with the Secretary of the Guild, and any Manager or Member of the Guild shall be entitled, upon written demand, to be informed of the names of Managers in good standing. The Guild shall have the right to notify its Members and Managers as and when any Manager has ceased to be in good standing." Like restrictions govern the "Manager's Right to Contract" under Art. I, Sec. 1.

close and the authors requested arbitration of the dispute pursuant to the arbitration clauses of the Basic Agreement. Thereupon plaintiff commenced this action and asked for a temporary injunction, which was first granted pending a further hearing, but later denied after the hearing had been held.

The motion for a temporary injunction pending trial asked that defendants be enjoined from proceeding with arbitration or otherwise enforcing the Basic Agreement and from interfering with plaintiff's production of the show, and that royalties be withheld pending assessment of damages in this action. In denying the motion the District Court stated that not enough facts had been furnished to indicate that the Basic Agreement was void under the Sherman Act, that the transactions here involved were not in interstate commerce, and that relief should be denied, since the parties were in pari delicto and since plaintiff was seeking at the same time to be awarded rescission and enforcement of a contract.

The granting or denial of an interlocutory injunction is usually relegated to the discretion of the District Court, which an appellate tribunal is reluctant to disturb. But here the trial court's denial of the injunction was based in substantial measure upon conclusions of law which can and should be reviewed because of their basic nature in this litigation. The case then should be remanded for action by the District Court in the light of the legal principles thus enunciated.

Plaintiff attacks the Basic Agreement for its provisions for compulsory arbitration, for price fixing, and for dealing with only Guild members. It is now well settled that a contract covering a large part of an industry will be void and illegal under the Sherman Act for such restrictive agreements and that these constitute adequate proof of a combination in restraint of trade. The agreement also forbids outright sale of radio, television, and other subsidiary rights in the play prior to its stage presentation; and even thereafter such sales still require the Guild's written approval. These and similar provisions in the Basic Agreement indicate an attempt to control the industry; and the affidavit of Richard Rodgers, president of the Guild, tends to admit that such is the purpose of the organization. We think we must hold that there is a showing prima facie of an agreement in restraint of trade. We need not go further at this time before a trial has established the extent of the restraint, except perhaps to suggest that, in view of the repeated statement by the Supreme Court that a "price-fixing combination" is "illegal per se under the Sherman Act", it is difficult for us to see now how this Basic Agreement can be upheld, at least in its entirety.

The District Court, however, stressed the point that there can be no recovery under the Sherman Act where the restraint fails to involve transactions in interstate commerce. But we disagree with the conclusion below that the restraint in question was not of commerce among the several states. The District Court relied particularly upon the cases of Hart v. B. F. Keith Vaudeville Exchange, 2 Cir., 12 F.2d 341, certiorari denied 273 U.S. 703, 704, 47 S.Ct. 97, 71 L.Ed. 849, and Federal Base Ball Club of Baltimore v. National League, 259 U.S. 200, 42 S.Ct. 465, 66 L.Ed. 898, 26 A.L.R. 357. These cases held that contracts for the personal services for exhibition purposes of vaudeville and baseball artists were not in interstate trade or commerce, even though the actual exhibitions were to take place in different states.

Even if we thought that this present case concerned only a musical play being prepared in the provinces for Broadway, we should doubt the presently controlling force of these precedents. Employment contracts for separate exhibitions seem to us quite different from the substantial business of readying a musical comedy through tryouts on the road for New York production. There must be the securing of services of countless actors, actresses, members of choruses, and others, of scenery, music, and appropriate lighting, then the strenuous activities required to weld all these parts into a delectable whole, the judicious advertising, and all the other details to such a production, so extensive in fact that it seems not unusual for a single play to be separately incorporated as a business corporation. And the road tryouts—here, from New Haven to Boston to Philadelphia—are an essential part of the fashioning of a perfect product for the Broadway trade. Moreover, there is no doubt of the steadily expanding content of the phrase "interstate commerce" in recent years; and hence there is no longer occasion for applying these earlier cases beyond their exact facts. The Supreme Court has not hesitated to regard the distribution of motion picture films as interstate commerce, Interstate Circuit, Inc. v. United States, 306 U.S. 208, 59 S.Ct. 467, 83 L.Ed. 610; and it may seem invidious to draw a different conclusion as to a stage production.

But much more is here involved than merely an agreement for the production of a single play; under attack is a broad plan for controlling the dramatic productions of the country. It is clear that the plaintiff in an anti-trust suit need not himself be in interstate commerce. It is sufficient that the combination which is the cause of his injury seeks to restrain such commerce. Here the purpose of the Basic Agreement seems not at all in doubt; it is in effect admitted by the Guild's president in his affidavit, although he calls it a "minimum collective bargaining agreement" "to produce a fair return for the labor of its members who write plays for a living." But the cases cited earlier show that a price-fixing combination is not saved by the high purpose for which it is conceived. So far as the moving papers go, they thus show that this is in fact a system of control of theatrical productions wherever produced or transported throughout the country and even in foreign lands. That it also encompasses local incidents does not deprive it of its interstate character.

The Guild contends, however, that it is a labor union, and thus attempts to bring itself within the exception of § 17 of the Sherman Act, as amended, 15 U.S.C.A. § 17. It is true that this exception has recently received a broad interpretation in the light of its original purpose. United States v. Hutcheson, 312 U.S. 219, 61 S.Ct. 463, 85 L.Ed. 788 . . . ; Allen Bradley Co. v. Local Union No. 3, 2 Cir., 145 F.2d 215, now before the Supreme Court, 65 S.Ct. 433. But as we pointed out in the last case cited, 145 F.2d 215, 223, while the parties to the dispute may not always be employers and employees, yet the exception will not apply unless an employer-employee relationship is "the matrix of the controversy." Here not only are the disputing parties not in an employer-employee relationship, but, unlike the Allen Bradley case, the controversy cannot concern itself with conditions of employment, since none of the parties affected are in any true sense employees. An author writing a book or play is usually not then even in any contractual relation with his producer. If and when he does contract, he does not continue in the producer's service to any appreciable or continuous extent thereafter. Normally the author appears more nearly like the fishermen entrepreneurs of the Hinton [Columbia River Packers Ass'n. v. Hinton, 315 U.S. 143, 62 S.Ct. 520, 86 L.Ed. 750] case or the doctors in the American Medical Association (American Medical Ass'n. v. U.S., 317 U.S. 519, 63 S.Ct. 44, 87 L.Ed. 497) case than workmen banded together in a union. The minimum price and royalties provided by the Basic Agreement, unlike minimum wages in a collective bargaining agreement, are not remuneration for continued services, but are the terms at which a finished product or certain rights therein may be sold. And no wages or working conditions of any group of employees are directly dependent on these terms. We think the exception therefore inapplicable.

Plaintiff also calls attention to the fact that the parties herein are citizens of different states, and hence he claims also the right to recover under state laws prohibiting combinations in restraint of trade, such as N. Y. General Business Law, Consol. Laws N.Y., c. 29, § 340. In view of the conclusion we have reached as to the applicability of federal law, we find it unnecessary to consider this further claim at this time.

The District Court was also of the view that plaintiff's participation in any possible combination, as evidenced by his signing of the Basic Agreement, was sufficient to require denial of relief. As appears above, plaintiff, having invested $50,000 with Gaumont, took over the latter's production contract with the authors and, before he invested more, endeavored to enter into a direct contract with them. But he found this impossible until he in turn became a member of the Guild in good standing by signing the Basic Agreement. The rules of the Guild permitted no other course. Thus, he had to sign to save his $50,000 investment and to safeguard his further attempts to bring the venture to fruition. This seems to us a prima facie showing of economic coercion. We do not think it an answer to say that he knew of this Basic

Agreement at the time he dealt with Gaumont. It seems a fair conclusion that the real compulsion for his quite personal commitment came when he found himself actively engaged in plans to take over the venture personally.

It is well settled that where one party to an illegal contract acts under the duress of another the parties are not in pari delicto. And in actions for triple damages under the Sherman Act a showing of economic duress similar to that asserted here has been held sufficient proof that the plaintiff is not a party to the monopoly.

Where the parties stand actually and truly in pari delicto, the law should leave them where it finds them. But here even without a showing of economic coercion as the final step in forcing him to sign the Basic Agreement, plaintiff is precisely the type of individual whom the Sherman Act seeks to protect from combinations fashioned by others and offered to such individual as the only feasible method by which he may do business. Considerations of public policy demand court intervention in behalf of such a person, even if technically he could be considered in pari delicto. Indeed, this is a general principle applicable beyond the anti-trust field. Any other conclusion would mean that for many, perhaps most, victims of restraint of trade, private remedies under the Sherman Act would be illusory, if not quite non-existent.

Finally, we disagree with the District Court's comment that plaintiff's action fails because he seeks at the same time rescission and enforcement of a contract. This comment is in point only as to a very small part of plaintiff's extensive prayers for relief, which were based upon an extremely detailed, if not verbose, complaint. But plaintiff is entitled to state his claims in detail if he chooses, and rely upon the court to award him such judgment as his case deserves; and at trial he will not be bound by his prayers. Since these prayers are not binding at this time, no extensive discussion of the point is called for now. As a matter of fact, it is not improbable that any question as to immediate production of the play by any one, and particularly by plaintiff, a lawyer not a producer, is academic. But should the point ever become important, the trial court may find it possible to separate the rights and duties under the specific production contract assigned to plaintiff from the more far-reaching provisions of the Basic Agreement incorporated therein by a general reference. More broadly still, plaintiff's situation is that of one seeking recovery of a loss due to having been forced to buy goods at a price artificially raised by an illegal combination. It is a main purpose of the Sherman Act to prohibit such a consequence, and redress should not be limited to the activities of public officials. As we have seen, this is a statutory private right of action, and hence is not based upon rescission of the contract; even if a technical analysis should show a result substantially equivalent thereto, yet mere legal theory cannot defeat appropriate remedies granted by law. . . . Of course, plaintiff may not recover three times the amount of his loss up to the present time and then keep all profits if he ever should produce the play. But this limitation goes merely to the amount of his potential recovery and fails to indicate that he cannot recover at all.

So far, therefore, as the underlying principles of law are concerned, we think plaintiff showed prima facie grounds of potential recovery. The District Court did not, however, pass upon the facts in controversy. It is true that much of the story herein is shown by documentary evidence, though the amount actually invested by plaintiff and the proximate cause for the failure of the production seem in serious dispute. Nothing we have said should be considered to foreclose adjudication of these issues, although the parties and the court may be disposed in the interest of expeditious dispatch of this litigation to agree to try the case upon the merits at the same time further hearing is held upon the proceedings for a temporary injunction. Meanwhile we think the ends of justice will be served by continuing the present restraining order—granted by this court to the same effect as the original preliminary injunction below—until hearing and decision upon the facts are had by the District Court. The order as entered was much less broad than that moved for by plaintiff; its main effect is to suspend arbitration proceedings pending adjudication of the validity of the contracts. No good purpose will be served by forcing the parties to the time and expense of arbitration while this question remains unsettled; and serious legal problems may develop if an arbitration is had, and thereafter the contracts are held invalid.

Judgment reversed and cause remanded for proceedings consistent with this opinion.

COLUMBIA BROADCASTING SYSTEM, INC. v. AMERICAN SOCIETY OF COMPOSERS
400 F. Supp. 737 (S.D.N.Y. 1975)

LASKER, District Judge.

In this age of change the quality of life has been fundamentally altered and influenced by the development of the automobile, the computer and television.

Millions of viewers spend untold hours weekly viewing television. During the larger part of that time the viewer is a listener to programs which utilize music, whether as background, as theme or as a feature. This case relates to the method by which networks are licensed to use copyrighted music on television.

The Columbia Broadcasting System (CBS)[1] brings this antitrust action

_____

[1] CBS is engaged in a number of businesses, only one of which is the operation of the CBS

against the American Society of Composers, Authors and Publishers (ASCAP), Broadcast Music, Inc. (BMI) and their members and affiliates.[2] It complains that the present system by which ASCAP and BMI issue blanket licenses for the right to perform any or all of the compositions in their repertories over the CBS network in exchange for a flat annual fee violates the Sherman Act, 15 U.S.C. §§ 1 and 2. The complaint seeks an injunction under § 16 of the Clayton Act, 15 U.S.C. § 26, directing ASCAP and BMI to offer CBS performance right licenses on terms which reflect the nature and amount of CBS' actual use of music, or in the alternative, enjoining them from offering blanket licenses to any television network. CBS also seeks a declaration of copyright misuse under the Declaratory Judgment Act, 28 U.S.C. §§ 2201, 2202.

I.

Introduction

A. The Parties

Prior to ASCAP's formation in 1914 there was no effective method by which composers and publishers of music could secure payment for the performance for profit of their copyrighted works. The users of music, such as theaters, dance halls and bars, were so numerous and widespread, and each performance so fleeting an occurrence, that no individual copyright owner could negotiate licenses with users of his music, or detect unauthorized uses. On the other side of the coin, those who wished to perform compositions without infringing the copyright were, as a practical matter, unable to obtain licenses from the owners of the works they wished to perform. ASCAP was organized as a "clearinghouse" for copyright owners and users to solve these problems. The world of music has changed radically since 1914. Radio and television broadcasters are the largest users of music today; they "perform" copyrighted music before audiences of millions. In 1975 ASCAP and BMI licensed these large users, including CBS and the other networks as well as smaller ones such as concert halls and background music services.

Because of the multitude of performances of music they generate each year, virtually all radio stations and television networks secure the rights to perform the music they use by a "blanket" license. An ASCAP blanket license gives

---

television network (CTN). Although the parties distinguish between CBS and CTN in their post-trial submissions, for the sake of clarity we refer throughout this opinion to both the parent corporation and the network as "CBS."

[2] The other named defendants are certain members of ASCAP, as representative of the class of ASCAP's members; and certain BMI affiliates, as representative of the class of BMI affiliates. The case has heretofore been declared a class action against both classes.

the user the right to perform all of the compositions owned by its members as often as the user desires for a stated term, usually a year. Convenience is the prime virtue of the blanket license: it provides comprehensive protection against infringement, that is, access to a large pool of music without the need for the thousands of individual licenses which otherwise would be necessary to perform the copyrighted music used on radio stations and television networks in the course of a year. Moreover, it gives the user unlimited flexibility in planning programs, because any music it chooses is "automatically" covered by the blanket license.

ASCAP's current membership includes some 6,000 publishing companies and 16,000 composers. Its members have granted ASCAP, as their licensing agent, the nonexclusive right to license users to perform the compositions owned by them. ASCAP provides its members with a wide range of services. It maintains a surveillance system of radio and television broadcasts to detect unlicensed uses, institutes infringement actions, collects revenues from licensees and distributes royalties to copyright owners in accordance with a schedule which reflects the nature and amount of the use of their music and other factors.

BMI, a non-profit corporation, was organized in 1939 by members of the radio broadcasting industry, including CBS. It is affiliated with approximately 10,000 publishing companies and 20,000 writers and functions in essentially the same manner as ASCAP. Although CBS sold back its BMI stock to the corporation in 1959, BMI is still owned entirely by broadcasters.

As a practical matter virtually every domestic copyrighted composition is in the repertory of either ASCAP, which has over three million compositions in its pool, or BMI, which has over one million. Like ASCAP, BMI offers blanket licenses to broadcasters for unlimited use of the music owned by its "affiliates." Almost all broadcasters hold blanket licenses from both ASCAP and BMI.

As is generally known, CBS operates one of three national television networks, as well as AM and FM radio stations in seven major cities. It has held blanket licenses from ASCAP for its radio broadcast operations since 1928, and from BMI since soon after that organization was founded in 1939. It has held ASCAP and BMI blanket licenses for its television network on a continuous basis since the late 1940's.

CBS supplies television programs to approximately two hundred affiliated television stations throughout the country, and telecasts about 7,500 programs per year. Many of these programs make use of copyrighted music which is recorded on the soundtrack. However, CBS does not produce most of the programs seen on its network. Instead it purchases the right to broadcast programs produced by independent television production companies, known as "program packagers." Most of the popular prime-time serials fall into this category. In addition CBS itself produces a television serial ("Gunsmoke"), two day-time serials, a number of "specials," usually variety shows, as well as news, public affairs and sports programs.

Agreements between program packagers and CBS normally stipulate the price at which the packager will produce a program in a series and furnish it to CBS for broadcast. Pursuant to the agreements, packagers are responsible for obtaining and furnishing to CBS most rights necessary for the use of copyrighted music by the network, such as the right to record a copyrighted song in synchronization with the film or video tape ("synch" rights). However, program packagers do not, in the present scheme of things, furnish to CBS the right to *perform* the copyrighted music for profit as part of a television broadcast. Ever since television became commercially practicable in the late 1940's, CBS has obtained such "performance" rights for packaged programs, as well as for the programs it produces itself, from ASCAP and BMI by purchasing blanket licenses. From time to time it has renewed its licenses after negotiations with ASCAP and BMI. In the history of the parties the fee for the blanket license has been expressed in terms of a percentage of CBS' advertising revenues. For example, for many years prior to the institution of suit, the BMI blanket license fee remained at 1.09% of net receipts from sponsors after certain deductions. This resulted in payment to BMI of about $1.6 million in 1969. For access to ASCAP's considerably larger repertory, CBS paid about $5.7 million in 1969. Averaging the total of $7.3 million paid by CBS in that year over 7,500 programs, its cost for ASCAP or BMI music runs about $1,000. per program. Of course, as detailed later, many of CBS' programs, such as news and public affairs shows, use no music at all; while others, such as variety shows, use a great deal. $1,000. is a small fraction of the total cost of the program. CBS pays about $200,000. for each episode of a one hour variety show or dramatic serial, and as much as $750,000. for a made-for-TV movie. Since the commencement of this action, CBS has held interim blanket licenses from ASCAP and BMI at a total annual cost of some $6 million.

B. The Consent Decrees

Neither ASCAP nor BMI is a stranger to antitrust litigation. In 1941 the government sued ASCAP for antitrust violations. The action resulted in a consent decree which largely governs ASCAP's relationships with licensees such as CBS and other users. As amended in 1950, the decree requires ASCAP to offer a "per program" license to broadcasters in addition to the blanket license it has traditionally offered. Both forms of license grant the right to use any or all of the works in ASCAP's repertory. However, the blanket license allows use of the entire inventory for a designated period of time, usually a year, for which the user pays a flat fee, while the per program license permits use of the entire repertory but requires payment only with respect to programs which actually make use of copyrighted music. The 1950 decree mandatorily enjoins ASCAP to set its fees for these licenses in a manner which gives the user a genuine choice between them, and prohibits it from requiring or influencing the prospective licensee to negotiate for a blanket license before negotiating for a per program license.[3] If ASCAP and the licensee are unable to agree on a fee, the latter may apply to the United States District Court for

---

[3] The 1950 decree states in part that ASCAP is:

(B) Ordered and directed to issue to any unlicensed radio or television broadcaster, upon written request, per program licenses, the fee for which

(1) In the case of commercial programs, is, at the option of ASCAP, either (a) expressed in terms of dollars, requiring the payment of a specified amount for each program in which compositions in the ASCAP repertory shall be performed, or (b) based upon the payment of a percentage of the sum paid by the sponsor of such program for the use of the broadcasting or telecasting facilities of such radio or television broadcaster,

(2) in the case of sustaining programs, is at the option of ASCAP, either (a) expressed in terms of dollars, requiring the payment of a specified amount for each program in which compositions in the ASCAP repertory shall be performed, or (b) based upon the payment of a percentage of the card rate which would have been applicable for the use of its broadcasting facilities in connection with such program if it had been commercial, and

(3) subject to the other provisions of Section VIII, takes into consideration the economic requirements and situation of those stations having relatively few commercial announcements and a relatively greater percentage of sustaining programs, with the objective that such stations shall have a genuine economic choice between per program and blanket licenses;

(C) Enjoined and restrained from requiring or influencing the prospective licensee to negotiate for a blanket license prior to negotiating for a per program license.

VIII. Defendant ASCAP, in fixing its fees for the licensing of compositions in the ASCAP repertory, is hereby ordered and directed to use its best efforts to avoid any discrimination among the respective fees fixed for the various types of licenses which would deprive the licensees or prospective licensees of a genuine choice from among such various types of licenses.

IX. (A) Defendant ASCAP shall, upon receipt of a written application for a license for the right of public performance of any, some or all of the compositions in the ASCAP repertory, advise the applicant in writing of the fee which it deems reasonable for the license requested. If the parties are unable to agree upon a reasonable fee within sixty (60) days from the date when such application is received by ASCAP, the applicant therefore may forthwith apply to this Court for the determination of a reasonable fee and ASCAP shall, upon receipt of notice of the filing of such application, promptly give notice thereof to the Attorney General. In any such proceeding the burden of proof shall be on ASCAP to establish the reasonableness of the fee requested by it. Pending the completion of any such negotiations or proceedings, the applicant shall have the right to use any, some or all of the compositions in the ASCAP repertory to which its application pertains, without payment of any fee or other compensation, but subject to the provisions of Sub-section (B) hereof, and to the final order or judgment entered by this Court in such proceeding . . .

the Southern District of New York for determination of a "reasonable fee." In such proceedings, ASCAP bears the burden of establishing the reasonableness of the fee it requests.

Finally, ASCAP's licensing authority is not exclusive. The 1950 decree provides that music users may bypass ASCAP entirely, and negotiate for a license directly with the composer or publisher holding the copyright.[4]

Under the terms of a consent decree entered in 1966 in *United States v. BMI* (S.D.N.Y.), BMI is required to offer a per-program license in addition to a blanket license. The difference in the terms of these licenses must be justified by "applicable business factors."[5] Although the form of the BMI decree differs from that of the ASCAP decree, the parties have stipulated that CBS could secure direct licenses from BMI affiliates with the same ease or difficulty, as the case may be, as from ASCAP members. (CX 3)

C. CBS' Complaint

CBS does not allege that ASCAP and BMI have violated the terms of the consent decrees. It claims, rather, that the licensing alternatives which the decrees specify are not flexible enough to meet its needs, and are not realistically available to it. Thus, CBS' complaint charges that the blanket license "compels" it to pay performance royalties with respect to television programs which use no music and that the per-program license requires it to pay the

---

[4] The Decree provides:

IV. Defendant ASCAP is hereby enjoined and restrained from:

(A) Holding, acquiring, licensing, enforcing, or negotiating concerning any rights in copyrighted musical compositions other than rights of public performance on a non-exclusive basis;

(B) Limiting, restricting, or interfering with the right of any member to issue to a user nonexclusive licenses for rights of public performance;

[5] The BMI consent decree provides in part:

(B) Defendant shall, upon the request of any unlicensed broadcaster, license the rights publicly to perform its repertory by broadcasting on either a per program or per programming period basis, at defendant's option. The fee for this license shall relate only to programs (including announcements), or to programming periods, during which a licensed composition is performed. The fee shall be expressed, at defendant's option, either (1) in dollars, (2) as a percentage of the revenue which the broadcaster received for the use of its broadcasting facilities or (3) in the case of sustaining programs or programming periods, as a percentage of the applicable card rate had the program or programming period been commercially sponsored. In the event defendant offers to license broadcasters on bases in addition to a per program or per programming period basis, defendant shall act in good faith so that there shall be a relationship between such per program or such per programming period basis and such other bases, justifiable by applicable business factors including availability, so that there will be no frustration of the purpose of this section to afford broadcasters alternative bases of license compensation.

same royalty for a program which uses a single copyrighted composition as for one which uses many. (Complaint ¶¶ 14,19). In other words, CBS asserts that defendants are "using the leverage inherent in [their] copyright pool to insist that plaintiff pays royalties on a basis which does not bear any relationship to the amount of music performed." (Complaint ¶ 19) As to the third alternative specified in the consent decrees—the possibility of bypassing ASCAP and BMI entirely and seeking licenses for the specific compositions it wishes to perform directly from the copyright proprietors—CBS alleges that any attempt by it "to acquire such a large body of rights from the [individual copyright proprietors] . . . would be wholly impracticable . . . " (¶ 15)

CBS' disenchantment with the blanket licensing system takes form in several legal claims: first, that the writer and publisher members of ASCAP and BMI have combined through their common licensing organizations to eliminate price competition among themselves and, by pooling the grant of their respective licenses through ASCAP and BMI, to fix the price which a television network must pay to secure the rights; second, that ASCAP and BMI insist on granting only blanket licenses and have therefore imposed an unlawful tie-in, in that CBS is required to purchase the rights to music it does not want to buy in order to secure the rights to music it does want; third, that by forming pools of music and requiring CBS to deal with the common licensing agent of the pools, the writer and publisher members and affiliates of ASCAP and BMI are engaging in a concerted refusal to deal directly with CBS; fourth, that through ASCAP and BMI the writers and publishers are guilty of monopolization, both attempted and achieved; and fifth, that the activities described constitute copyright misuse.

Despite this rather imposing line-up of charges, the central issue in the case is not complex. The essence of CBS' claim is that ASCAP and BMI are illegal combinations whose purpose and effect is to exact royalties from CBS for music it does not wish to license. The validity of the claim turns on whether CBS is in fact compelled to take a blanket license from the licensing organizations in order to secure the performance rights it needs. ASCAP and BMI contend that CBS is not compelled to do so, but has, in common with the ABC and NBC television networks and virtually all radio broadcasters, found it most convenient to license music by the blanket method. Defendants argue that if CBS no longer wishes to secure performance rights through centralized agents such as ASCAP and BMI, it can obtain the necessary rights directly from the individual members and affiliates of ASCAP and BMI by negotiating with them for performance rights to the particular compositions it wants. As defendants view the case, if CBS is to prevail it must prove that direct licensing with members of the alleged combination is an unfeasible alternative to the blanket license. Proof that licenses could not be obtained directly from copyright proprietors, despite the fact that ASCAP and BMI are required by consent decrees to permit their members and affiliates to license their compositions to users directly, would support the inference that defendants have formed illegal combinations in order to foreclose competition in the market for performance rights to music for network use. Conversely, proof that direct licensing is a feasible alternative method by which CBS could satisfy its music needs would undercut its claims that copyright proprietors have combined to monopolize the market for performance rights and have used their leverage to fix prices and impose unlawful tie-ins.

CBS vigorously disagrees with this view of the case. It argues, as though it could have moved for summary judgment years ago, that ASCAP and BMI are guilty of per se violations of the antitrust laws because the blanket licensing system, which is the only method by which CBS and the other networks have ever licensed performance rights, has "thoroughly eliminated" price competition among copyright owners as a matter of historical fact. (CBS Post-Trial Brief at 15) CBS views the question of the feasibility of direct licensing as irrelevant to the issue whether defendants have restrained trade. It argues that the sole questions to be determined are (1) whether defendants' restraint is justified or reasonable in view of the unique economic setting of the music licensing market; and (2) whether licensing can be accomplished on a more competitive basis. We find CBS' analysis unpersuasive. Nevertheless, we set forth our views on the questions CBS raises because of their central importance to the case. To do this, we must retrace some of the steps taken to define the issues prior to the trial.

II.

The Issue Presented for Decision

A. ASCAP's Motion for Summary Judgment

At an earlier stage in the litigation ASCAP moved for summary judgment, relying principally on the decision in *K–91, Inc. v. Gershwin Publishing Corp.*, 372 F.2d 1 (9th Cir. 1967), *cert. denied*, 389 U.S. 1045, 88 S.Ct. 761, 19 L.Ed.2d 838 (1968). In *K–91* several members of ASCAP sued a radio broadcaster for infringement. The broadcaster admitted the infringement but defended on grounds similar to those asserted by CBS; that ASCAP is an unlawful combination engaged in price-fixing and block-booking of its members' compositions. In rejecting the claims, the Ninth Circuit observed that ASCAP does not fix prices because, under the 1950 consent decree, the United States District Court for the Southern District of New York is the ultimate price-fixing authority in the event of disagreement as to the reasonableness of ASCAP's fees. As to the other claims, the court observed:

"No contention is made here that ASCAP's actual activities do not comply with the decree. In short, we think that as a potential combination in restraint of trade, ASCAP has been 'disinfected' by the decree.

There is an additional reason why the activities disclosed by this record do not violate the antitrust laws. ASCAP's licensing authority is not exclusive. The right of the individual composer, author or publisher to make his own arrangements with prospective licensees are fully preserved [by the 1950 decree]." 372 F.2d at 4.

Although we agreed with the *K–91* court, and continue to agree, that the activities of ASCAP and BMI are not illegal per se, we denied ASCAP's motion for summary judgment because of a critical difference between the case presented in *K–91* and the one at hand. In *K–91* the parties stipulated that it would be virtually impossible for broadcasters and copyright proprietors to arrange separate licenses and payments for each radio performance of a copyrighted composition,[6] and no proposal was made to the court of a practicable alternative to blanket and per-program licenses. In contrast to *K–91*, CBS' claims are premised on the practicability of alternatives to the system now in effect. As noted earlier, CBS seeks an injunction either enjoining ASCAP and BMI even from offering blanket licenses or, in the alternative, and preferably, establishing what CBS calls a "per-use" system, by which ASCAP and BMI (rather than individual copyright owners) would be required to license individual compositions in accordance with a schedule of fees under court supervision.[7] Moreover, far from being a stipulated fact, the

---

[6] The United States adopted this position in its Memorandum of Amicus Curiae submitted in connection with the petition for writ of certiorari to the Supreme Court of the United States in *K–91*:

. . . There are over 4,100 AM and 1,744 FM broadcasting stations located in every part of the United States (FCC Ann.Rep., pp. 106, 110 (1966)). Most of these stations broadcast recorded music for a substantial part of their operating day. They may acquire ownership of any recording they wish, and in the present state of technology there appears to be no effective means by which the enormous number of separate performances broadcast each year by commercial stations across the nation can be accounted for by copyright holders. Nor is it feasible for these stations to deal on a "per piece" basis with the thousands of individual copyright holders across the country in order lawfully to exploit recorded music, for the value of the right to broadcast a single performance of one recorded composition is far less than the cost of negotiating a separate license. It would appear, therefore, that there must be some form of centralized licensing system which serves the mutual interests of copyright holders and of music users, and which enables the marketing of performing rights for recorded music to be effectively accomplished. (Memorandum at 9–10)

[7] Under the "per-use" system proposed by CBS, it would continue to license its music through ASCAP and BMI, but in a substantially different way than it does under the blanket license. CBS would pay ASCAP or BMI a specified fee for each performance of a composition in the pool (the "per-use reservoir"), plus an administrative fee. The fee for each use would be fixed in a schedule reflecting the nature of the use (theme, background or feature use) and other appropriate factors, such as duration of use, or the popularity of the composition. Thus, the fee

impracticability of CBS' "bypassing" ASCAP and BMI to secure licenses directly from copyright proprietors is the key factual issue in the case. Accordingly, we held that the feasibility of less restrictive alternatives to the blanket licensing system presented a genuine issue as to a material fact in the case and denied summary judgment to ASCAP.

Subsequent to determination of ASCAP's motion and in accordance with our holding, we ordered trial of the following specified issues:

"(i)   Whether defendants' conduct constitutes an actionable restraint of trade and compels the plaintiff as alleged in the complaint;

(ii)   Whether, if such restraint or compulsion exists, it is reasonable and justified or whether it may be achieved by less anticompetitive means."

B. CBS' "Per Se" Contention

Despite our earlier holding that the activities of ASCAP and BMI are to be judged by the rule of reason and the specification of the issues to be tried in light of that holding, CBS now takes the position that the primary question presented for determination is whether the present system can be amended to operate on a more competitive basis. As noted earlier, it argues as to the first issue, that it has established an illegal restraint of trade as a matter of law because the blanket licensing arrangement has "thoroughly eliminated" price competition among copyright owners as a matter of historical fact. (CBS Post-Trial Brief at 15) Coming after an eight week trial and the accumulation of a bulky factual record, the timing of this contention is unusual. For the reasons stated below, we find it to be unmeritorious as well.

In support of its contention that ASCAP and BMI are illegal combinations merely because they offer blanket licenses, CBS cites cases in which sellers agreed among themselves as to the prices to be charged buyers for their products. See, e.g., *United States v. Socony-Vacuum Oil Co., Inc.*, 310 U.S. 150, 60 S.Ct. 811, 84 L.Ed. 1129 (1940); *United States v. Trenton Potteries Co.*, 273 U.S. 392, 47 S.Ct. 377, 71 L.Ed. 700 (1927). The cases are inapposite.

---

schedule would likely provide different prices for otherwise comparable uses of particular compositions. If the fee schedule could not be fixed by agreement between CBS and defendants, it would be set by the court.

Each copyright proprietor would have the right to "withdraw" any of his works from the per-use reservoir on reasonable notice or at periodic intervals (e.g. quarterly). However, the right of withdrawal would not extend to spontaneous or other unplanned uses, nor to music which was filmed or taped prior to withdrawal even though the performance occurred after withdrawal. CBS and its producers would remain free to negotiate a license for a composition directly from the copyright proprietor regardless whether it is in the reservoir or has been withdrawn. The per-use rate schedule would be adjusted at periodic intervals to reflect prices negotiated in direct licensing transactions.

Unlike the plaintiffs in the cited cases, CBS does not claim that the individual members and affiliates ("sellers") of ASCAP and BMI have agreed among themselves as to the prices to be charged for the particular "products" (compositions) offered by each of them. It makes the very different claim that a combination of individual sellers offering the entire pool of their products through a common sales agent at a negotiated package price is per se illegal, regardless whether the sellers are willing to sell their products on an individual basis.

The claim fails as a matter of law. In *Automatic Radio Co., Inc. v. Hazeltine Research, Inc.*, 339 U.S. 827, 70 S.Ct. 894, 94 L.Ed. 1312 (1950), the parties entered into an agreement by which Automatic Radio acquired a license for a ten year term to incorporate into its products any or all of several hundred patents held by Hazeltine. Automatic Radio was not obligated to use any of the patents in the manufacture of its products, but agreed in any event to pay Hazeltine royalties based on a percentage of its total sales. Automatic argued that the terms of the license constituted per se patent misuse and an illegal tying arrangement because the agreement exacted payment of a royalty on all sales whether or not its products used the patents, and in effect required it to purchase licenses for products for which it needed no license as well as for those which did. In rejecting the argument, the Court stated:

> "We cannot say that payment of royalties according to an agreed percentage of the licensee's sales is unreasonable. Sound business judgment could indicate that such payment represents the most convenient method of fixing the business value of the privileges granted by the licensing agreement. We are not unmindful that convenience cannot justify an extension of the monopoly of the patent. But as we have already indicated, there is in this royalty provision no inherent extension of the monopoly of the patent. Petitioner cannot complain because it must pay royalties whether it uses Hazeltine patents or not. What it acquired by the agreement into which it entered was the privilege to use any or all of the patents and developments as it desired to use them. If it chooses to use none of them, it has nevertheless contracted to pay for the privilege of using existing patents plus any developments resulting from respondent's continuous research. We hold that in licensing the use of patents to one engaged in a related enterprise, it is not *per se* a misuse of patents to measure the consideration by a percentage of the licensee's sales." 339 U.S. at 834, 70 S.Ct. at 898 (citations omitted).

In *Zenith Radio Corp. v. Hazeltine Research, Inc.*, 395 U.S. 100, 89 S.Ct. 1562, 23 L.Ed.2d 129 (1969) the Court refined the standards by which the validity of package licenses are to be judged. At issue in that case was the propriety of an injunction entered by the district court enjoining Hazeltine from:

"A. Conditioning directly or indirectly the grant of a license to . . . [Zenith] . . . under any domestic patent upon the taking of a license under any other patent *or upon the paying of royalties on the manufacture, use or sale of apparatus not covered by such patent.*" 395 U.S. at 133–34, 89 S.Ct. at 1582 (emphasis in original).

The quoted provision was directed at Hazeltine's proven policy of *insisting* upon acceptance of its standard five-year package license agreement covering some 500 patents, and reserving royalties based on Zenith's total radio and television sales whether or not the licensed patents were actually used in the products manufactured. The Court of Appeals had stricken the last clause of the quoted paragraph, relying on *Automatic Radio* for the proposition that conditioning the license upon payment of royalties on unpatented products was not misuse of the patent. The Supreme Court disapproved this construction of its earlier decision. It distinguished between the situation presented in *Automatic Radio*, in which the parties *agreed* on a package license "as a convenient method designed by the parties to avoid determining whether each radio receiver embodied [a Hazeltine] patent," and the situation in *Zenith*, where the patent holder *compelled* the licensee to choose between a package license conditioned on the payment of royalties on unpatented products, or no license at all. 395 U.S. at 135–37, 89 S.Ct. 1562.[8] In other words, the critical difference between an illegal licensing arrangement and a legal one is the fact of coercion or compulsion by the licensor.

We disagree with CBS that such compulsion inheres in the present licensing system as regulated by the consent decrees and that defendants are therefore guilty of per se violations. As noted earlier, CBS makes no claim that either ASCAP or BMI has violated any provision of the consent decrees. The terms of the decrees do not by any construction suggest that CBS is in fact compelled to take a blanket license. To the contrary, ASCAP and BMI are required to offer per program licenses under which a fee is charged only with respect to programs in which a composition within the repertory has been performed; and to structure the fees for blanket and per program licenses so that the user

---

[8] The Court amplified the distinction as follows:

If the licensee negotiates for "the privilege to use any or all of the patents and developments as [he] desire[s] to use them" he cannot complain that he must pay royalties if he chooses to use none of them . . . But we do not read *Automatic Radio* to authorize the patentee to use the power of his patent to insist on a total-sales royalty and to override protestations of the licensee that some of his products are unsuited to the patent . . .

We also think patent misuse inheres in a patentee's insistence on a percentage-of-sales royalty, regardless of use, and his rejection of licensee proposals to pay only for actual use. Unquestionably, a licensee must pay if he uses the patent. Equally, however, he may insist upon paying only for use, and not on the basis of total sales . . . 395 U.S. at 139, 89 S.Ct at 1585.

has a genuine choice between them. Apart from the licenses available from ASCAP and BMI, the decrees leave a music user free to obtain licenses directly from copyright owners. This factor alone markedly distinguishes the present case from *Zenith*, in which Hazeltine, as the sole supplier of the patents in issue, had, for all practical purposes, unlimited leverage in bargaining the terms of any license to them.

C. CBS' Theory of the Burden of Proof

- Taking a different tack, CBS also argues that "it is clear that [ASCAP and BMI] insist on licensing exclusively on a blanket basis" and that because they insist on such an "inherently restrictive" method of sale, they have the burden of proving the availability in the market place of acceptable substitutes, i. e., that CBS could obtain direct licenses sufficient to meet its needs from copyright proprietors. (CBS Post-Trial Brief at 15, 26–27) Neither the facts nor the law support the argument. As outlined later in this opinion, the evidence does not establish that ASCAP and BMI insist or have ever insisted on licensing on a blanket basis; and, of course, if they did, they would flatly violate the terms of the consent decrees.

In any event, the argument fails as a matter of law. CBS cites a number of cases for the proposition that a defendant who argues that the plaintiff can avoid injury by obtaining a substitute product bears the burden of proving such an assertion. . . .

To secure injunctive relief in a private antitrust suit, the plaintiff must prove an actual violation of the antitrust laws or that such violation is impending and that as a result the plaintiff is threatened with loss or injury. *Zenith Radio Corp. v. Hazeltine Research, Inc., supra*, and *Credit Bureau Reports, Inc. v. Retail Credit Co.*, 476 F.2d 989 (5th Cir. 1973). In the cases on which CBS relies, the plaintiff had indisputably established the first element, i. e., that the defendant had illegally denied him something he wished to purchase, for example, space in a fruit market, access to telephone poles for a cable TV installation, or an aircraft dealership. The defendant in those cases argued that the plaintiff had failed to establish the second element of its claim—injury or the threat of injury—because he had not proven that he could not avoid injury simply by purchasing a substitute product elsewhere in the market. The court in each case held that a plaintiff does not have the burden of proving the nonexistence of suitable alternatives in order to prove injury or the threat of injury, particularly when it is clear that no substitute will have the unique attributes of the product which the defendant denied the plaintiff. However, in none of the cases did the court suggest that the plaintiff does not have the burden of proving the first element: the restraint of trade itself.

Accordingly, the validity of CBS' argument that it does not bear the burden of proving that direct licensing is not a feasible alternative to the blanket license turns on whether the issue of "alternatives" relates to the element of restraint, or the element of injury. We believe that it relates to the first factor: that is whether ASCAP and BMI have restrained trade. In the cases just discussed, plaintiff alleged that the defendant would not sell him something which he wanted to purchase, and the defendant argued that the plaintiff was not injured by the refusal because market substitutes were available. The present case poses an entirely different claim. The alleged restraint of trade is not that CBS is excluded from purchasing the services offered by ASCAP and BMI, and told to find substitutes elsewhere; but that (1) they allegedly offer only blanket licenses, which CBS says it does not want; (2) have combined to make any effort to obtain an alternative form of license (such as direct licensing) unfeasible; and (3) thereby compel CBS to continue to take a blanket license and to pay for music which it does not want to buy. Unlike the situations in the cases on which it relies, CBS *does not want the organizational defendant-seller's product at all.* Far from spurning "substitute" products, CBS claims that the lack of a substitute constitutes an alleged restraint of trade. So much is clear when one considers the nature of the direct licensing alternative. It is not at all a "substitute" in the sense used in the "injury-avoidance" cases; it is another means of licensing (on an individual basis) the use of precisely the same music which CBS would perform if it purchased a blanket license. If direct licensing is realistically available, it would enable CBS to pay only for the music it uses and for no other music, and would demonstrate that CBS' complaint in this action is unjustified.

In sum, we adhere to our earlier conclusion, as embodied in the pre-trial order, that to prevail here CBS must prove that defendants' conduct in combining into ASCAP and BMI *compels* CBS to take a blanket license as alleged in the complaint. Proof that direct licensing is not a feasible alternative to the blanket license is an essential element of CBS' claim, on which it accordingly bears the burden of proof. Conversely, proof that CBS could obtain the necessary performance licenses directly from copyright proprietors would be fatal to its claim that they have pooled the rights to perform their music in a manner which illegally restrains trade in those rights. If the restraint is proven, only then do defendants have the burden of proving that the restraint is justified by the economic context in which music licensing for network television use takes place, and cannot be achieved by less anti-competitive means.

III.

The Stipulation as to Competitive Disadvantage

Prior to trial, the parties executed a stipulation which states in part:

" . . . There is a portion of the performance rights to ASCAP music appearing on [CBS] programs as to which it would be impracticable for [CBS] or such producers to negotiate for licenses directly with the owners of the performance rights of said music. [Without limiting the parties' rights to adduce and offer additional proof with respect to any subject, both parties specifically reserve the right to adduce and offer proof regarding the reasons for such impracticability.]" (CX 2, ¶ 13; bracketed portion in original.)

"If [CBS] chose not to have an ASCAP license, the producers of [CBS] programs did not obtain such licenses, and [NBC] and [ABC] had such licenses, to the extent that [CBS] or the producers of [CBS] programs did not otherwise obtain the performance rights to the ASCAP music which they desired to use on [CBS] programming, [CBS] would be at a competitive disadvantage vis-a-vis [NBC] and [ABC]."[9] (Id. ¶ 15)

CBS argues that, putting aside its proof at trial as to the impracticality of the direct licensing alternative, ASCAP and BMI have ceded the primary issue in the case by stipulating that CBS could not obtain direct licenses for all its music needs and that consequently, if it dropped its blanket license, it would be at a competitive disadvantage vis-a-vis networks which continued to hold such licenses.

We disagree with the contention that defendants have stipulated the case away. Paragraph 13 does not specify the "portion" of the compositions in the ASCAP repertory as to which it would be "impracticable" for CBS to license directly; and the extent of "impracticability" is critical to the feasibility of direct licensing. As detailed later in this opinion, the evidence establishes that musical compositions are substantially interchangeable and that for any proposed use there are several, if not scores, of compositions which are equally suitable. Accordingly, even if CBS had access to far less than all of the compositions in the ASCAP and BMI repertories, that would not in itself render direct licensing unfeasible.

Because a fair reading of Paragraph 13 does not indicate that ASCAP and BMI have admitted the unfeasibility of direct licensing, Paragraph 15 loses the dispositive force which CBS attributes to it. It is obvious that CBS might be at a competitive disadvantage vis-a-vis other networks if it held no music license. But that fact only raises, but does not settle, the question of what licensing methods are available to CBS. We regard the stipulation merely as an aid to the definition of the issues of the case. The extent of CBS' use of music, the kinds of compositions it needs, and the persons with whom it must deal to

---

[9] BMI has stipulated with CBS that with respect to the practicability of CBS' obtaining direct licenses from BMI writers and publishers, BMI and CBS are bound by the determination in this case with respect to the practicability of CBS' obtaining direct licenses from ASCAP writers and publishers.

negotiate licenses for them are factors whose relevance to the feasibility of direct licensing is only suggested by the stipulation, on which the parties reserved the right to offer proof. The decision in this case rests on the evidence as to those factors, not the stipulation itself. Accordingly, we turn to the question whether CBS is in fact "compelled" as alleged in the complaint.

IV.

Compulsion: The Quality of the Evidence

Defendants argue that CBS' case, which alleges the refusal of the defendants to license on terms which require CBS to pay only for the music it uses, falters at the threshold because CBS has not shown that it ever made a clear demand on defendants which they have rebuffed. It is true that several courts have imposed such a requirement in treble damage cases based on a conspiracy to deprive the plaintiff of a particular product.

Although we agree with CBS that it is not required as a condition to suit to have been unequivocally refused the kind of license it now seeks, defendants' argument highlights the unusual nature of CBS' claim and the kind of evidence on which it relies. CBS does not claim that it is compelled to take a blanket license because ASCAP and BMI, or individual copyright proprietors, have actually refused or threatened to refuse to negotiate with it for alternative methods of licensing. Instead, its position is that ASCAP and BMI *would* refuse to negotiate new forms of licenses whose fees are based on actual music use; and that individual copyright proprietors *would* refuse to deal with it on a direct licensing basis, or at least make it such a difficult proposition that CBS would be forced to resume its blanket license. Although proof of what might or might not occur under hypothetical circumstances in the future is customary when the plaintiff in a private antitrust action seeks to establish a threat of injury, CBS relies heavily on hypothetical proof in order to establish the existence of the restraint itself—the nonavailability of direct licensing.

The other side of the coin just described is that CBS has made no effort to obtain the kinds of licenses it now complains defendants are unwilling to grant. Although the absence of such evidence does not establish that CBS is not compelled to take a blanket license, we nevertheless regard it as highly relevant to that issue.

V.

The Break-Up of an Amicable Marriage

Until the institution of the present suit CBS appears to have lived quite happily with the blanket arrangement which it now disavows. Since 1929 it has obtained ASCAP blanket licenses for its various broadcast operations, the earliest one purchased on behalf of a radio station; and when CBS and other broadcasters established BMI in 1939, they agreed to take blanket licenses. Since its establishment in 1946, the CBS television network (CTN) has continuously held blanket licenses from ASCAP and BMI. Since 1950, CBS' negotiations with ASCAP for licenses for its television network have of course been conducted within the framework of the amended consent decree. Although, as noted earlier the terms of the 1950 decree prohibit ASCAP from negotiating a blanket license prior to determining whether the user would prefer a per-program license,[10] CBS has never applied for relief under the decree complaining that ASCAP insisted on blanket licenses. Nor has the court ever been required to set a "reasonable fee" for the blanket licenses negotiated by the parties from time to time. CBS has never negotiated or held a per-program license from ASCAP or BMI for its television network and has never attempted to fulfill its music requirements by bypassing either organization and securing performance rights directly from copyright owners.

This suit did not follow a breakdown in negotiations for a new form of license, but for a renewal of CBS' *blanket* license from BMI. In April, 1969, CBS and ASCAP submitted for court approval agreements providing for final license fees as adjusted for 1969 and several prior years. Because the payments provided for in the agreements would have had the effect of sharply widening the historical ratio between BMI and ASCAP fees from CBS, BMI's President, Edward Cramer, protested to Donald Sipes, CBS' Vice President in charge of business affairs for the network, that BMI would insist on maintaining parity with ASCAP. After several meetings between Sipes and Cramer in 1969 during which the latter was unable to negotiate higher fees, BMI gave notice on October 29, 1969 that it was exercising its right under the consent decree to terminate CBS' license, effective January 1, 1970.

CBS did not apply for relief under the decree. Instead, on December 19, 1969, more than a month and a half after BMI's notice of termination, and less than two weeks before termination would become effective, the President of the CBS television network, Robert D. Wood, wrote to ASCAP and BMI requesting each of them to "promptly submit to us the terms upon which you would be willing to grant a new performance rights license which will provide, effective January 1, 1970, for payments measured by the actual use of your music." This was the first such demand CBS had made. By letter dated December 23, 1969, Herman Finkelstein, ASCAP's general counsel, replied that ASCAP would consider the proposal at its next Board of Directors meeting on January 29, 1970; that it regarded CBS' letter as an application for a license in accordance with the consent decree; that CBS would in the meantime have an interim license for 60 days "at rates and terms to be

---

[10] See note 3, *supra*.

negotiated, or determined ultimately by the court;" and that representatives of ASCAP would meet with CBS counsel on January 12, 1970 to discuss the application further. (PX 201)

By letter dated December 23, 1969 Cramer replied to CBS' request on behalf of BMI and stated that "The BMI Consent Decree provides for several alternative licenses and we are ready to explore any of these with you." (PX 202) CBS did not, however, pursue the matter further. Instead it commenced this lawsuit a week later, on December 31, 1969.

Neither the history of the relationship between the parties nor the events leading to this action remotely suggest that CBS has been compelled to take a blanket license it did not want. Indeed, CBS does not even appear to have seriously considered available alternatives to the blanket license prior to the commencement of suit. CBS' Vice President in charge of business affairs and planning for the network, Donald Sipes, was its principal witness as to the undesirability of blanket and per program licenses, and the need for a license under which the fee would be based strictly on actual use. Sipes testified that he first decided to explore alternatives to the blanket license sometime in 1968 or 1969. Although he was almost completely unacquainted with the intricacies of music licensing, he spoke to only three people in the course of his exploration. Two of these, Robert Evans and John Appel were house counsel for CBS. Sipes spoke to them only in their capacity as counsel, and did not seek their advice on the business aspects of licensing. The third person Sipes consulted was Emil Poklitar, the CBS employee in charge of the clerical personnel who process music logs and case sheets submitted by program producers to be sure the necessary rights have been cleared. Poklitar is not a business man and his duties involve a narrow portion of the music licensing spectrum.

Despite Sipes' lack of expertise, neither he nor his colleagues at CBS consulted any music writers, publishers, television producers or any other expert in the field about possible alternatives to the blanket license. (Tr. 151, 204, 358, 371) No one at CBS ever conducted a feasibility study about presently available or proposed methods of licensing the music to be performed on its television network. (Tr. 156–57) Indeed, Sipes testified that he did not even speak to other CBS executives about alternatives to the blanket license; he considered the alternatives entirely on his own initiative. (Tr. 180, 369) In sum, CBS thought very little indeed about revising its licensing practices prior to Robert Wood's "demand" letter to ASCAP and BMI just prior to the commencement of this suit. The evidence described hardly supports CBS' contention that it has been compelled to take a blanket license. To the contrary, it suggests that CBS did not even view music licensing as a business problem until immediately prior to suit.

VI.

The Claim That the Structure of the Market Bars Direct Licensing

In the absence of direct evidence that ASCAP and BMI and their members and affiliates have refused to negotiate licenses which reflect actual music use, CBS' claim that it is compelled to take a blanket license hinges on proof that the direct licensing alternative which exists in theory under the consent decrees is not a viable method for securing the necessary performance rights.

CBS claims that it established at trial that the defendants have structured the market in such a way as to lock it into a blanket licensing arrangement and to make any attempt to license its music needs directly so prohibitively risky as to preclude it even from trying. The basic elements of this claim are illustrated by the following syllogism: First, it would be uneconomic for CBS to attempt direct dealing while it still holds a blanket license, because it would then be paying twice for the same music: that is, since the blanket license fee covers unlimited use of the ASCAP or BMI repertory, direct licensing transactions would involve the purchase of additional licenses for music already covered under the blanket arrangement. Second, because copyright proprietors and television networks have never engaged in direct dealing, the transactional machinery necessary to negotiate and clear direct licenses between CBS program producers and the large number of individual copyright proprietors has not been developed; and the absence of such machinery creates a "barrier" to direct licensing. Third, because the blanket license system insulates copyright proprietors from price competition among themselves, they have no incentive to create the necessary machinery, and indeed would refuse to deal with CBS if it attempted to license its needs directly. Fourth, the risk of a refusal to deal is particularly acute in relation to CBS' present inventory of programs and films, which contains a large number of performances of copyrighted music whose initial runs on television were licensed under a blanket license. If CBS dropped its blanket license, it would need to seek direct licenses for the music contained in any programs which it plans to rerun because a rerun constitutes a performance for profit. Accordingly, the CBS inventory would be vulnerable to "hold-ups" by copyright proprietors who could either refuse to license their music at all, or exact a premium price for it.

In sum, CBS claims to have established that because there is at present (1) no market machinery for direct dealing; (2) no expectation that it will be created; and (3) reason to believe that proprietors would refuse to deal with CBS, particularly with regard to programs in its existing inventory which it wishes to rerun, direct licensing is not a feasible alternative and defendants illegally compel CBS to continue to take a blanket license. To understand the evidence relating to these claims, it is necessary first to describe the nature and extent of CBS' use of music.

VII.

CBS' Use of Music

Music is used on network television in three principal ways: as theme, background or feature music. Theme music is the music used to introduce and close a program. Background music is used to complement action on the screen. Feature music is music used as "the main focus of audience attention" (PX 469); for example, a performer singing a song on a variety show. Occasionally, however, well-known compositions suitable for feature use may be used as background music, for example, "Tea for Two" as background to a tea party scene. CBS concedes that it would be a simple matter for it to obtain direct licenses for most of the theme and background music it uses, and that the key to the feasibility of the direct licensing method is whether it can obtain licenses for the feature music and some of the background music it needs. To understand why this is so, some familiarity with the manner in which television programs are produced is necessary.

As noted earlier, CBS itself produces virtually none of its "entertainment" programming. Apart from the news, public affairs, sports and special events programs—which CBS does produce and which make little use of music—the bulk of the programs broadcast over the network are acquired from independent program production companies, or "packagers." Some of the packagers are well-known Hollywood "majors," such as MGM, Universal and Paramount. Variety shows and some of the filmed serials are produced by smaller production companies, which are sometimes owned by the star of the show. For example, the "Mary Tyler Moore Show" is produced by MTM Company, Ms. Moore's own; and "The Carol Burnett Show" is produced by her husband's company.

Ordinarily, the music used on entertainment serials is almost exclusively theme and background music composed especially for the program. For example, after the program has been filmed or taped, the producer typically hires a background composer to view the film, decide which action requires musical background, score the music and arrange and conduct the music scored. The producer pays the writer a fee for this work and acquires the copyright from him, as an "employee for hire." Theme music is created the same way, but the same music is of course used from week to week over the life of the series.

The producers of most of CBS' regular programs own publishing subsidiaries which acquire the copyrights for the music which has been specially composed for the program. For example, CBS itself owns April Music, which in turn owns the rights to the background music used in "Gunsmoke." The producer of "The Carol Burnett Show" owns Burngood Music and Jocar, which acquire the music specially created for that show such as background music for comedy sketches. Major studios, such as Universal, own major publishing houses, such as Leeds Music, which in turn own the rights to music created for Universal's television programs. The publishing subsidiaries receive royalty distributions from ASCAP or BMI for performance of music on the shows created by their parent company. The royalties are of course a small fraction of the amount the producer receives from CBS for the program package itself. CBS may pay upwards of $200,000. for a one hour episode of a dramatic serial; the publisher's performance royalties for that program may amount only to about $1,500.

This description of the process by which theme and background music is created makes clear that CBS can easily acquire performance rights for such music as part of the same transaction by which it acquires the program itself. Because the program production company, or its publishing subsidiary controls the rights to music specially created for the program, CBS could license the right to perform that music at the same time and place as the overall right to televise the program.

In contrast to theme and background music, feature music is not usually composed especially for the program. Rather, it is music which has been previously composed, and is controlled by a publisher who is not connected with the program production company. Feature music, and theme and background music whose copyrights are controlled by an "outside" publisher, cannot of course be licensed as a part of the overall transaction by which CBS acquires the program. Instead, in order to obtain rights to such music, it would be necessary for CBS or the program producer to approach the publisher who owns the rights to the music in question. As noted earlier, it is the feasibility of obtaining the licenses to this "outside" music on which the viability of the direct licensing alternate substantially depends.

In order to establish how much of CBS' music needs would require "outside" direct licensing transactions (as opposed to "inside" transactions with the program producer or his publishing affiliate whose feasibility CBS generally concedes) both sides have introduced into evidence computer runs which they claim establish the extent of CBS' music use in the three basic categories. In general the computer runs and the testimony relating to music use verify what the average television viewer would assume. CBS' news and public affairs programs use virtually no music; the staple situation comedy, crime and drama series use almost exclusively theme and background music specially composed for the program; and feature and background music controlled by outside publishers not connected with the program producer is used regularly on a small group of programs: variety shows and variety specials, sports shows

(e. g., football halftime shows), late night talk shows, and the "Captain Kangaroo Show."

Although the parties are in agreement as to the general pattern of CBS' music use, they differ in their claims as to precisely how much music CBS uses in each category and how evenly its use of music is distributed over the program schedule.

We believe it fruitless and unnecessary to determine the question whether CBS or defendants have more accurately interpreted the data as to CBS' use of music. It is fruitless because, as both sides concede, the data of record do not permit complete analysis. It is unnecessary because the validity of the conclusions which the parties seek to draw does not at all hinge on the few percentage points which separate the parties. Thus, defendants argue that the available data show that some 85–90% of CBS' programs use only "inside" music which could be conveniently licensed through the program packager, or no music at all; and that the music for another 5% of the programs could be licensed by seeking performance rights from only one "outside" publisher. According to defendants, only 3–4% of CBS' schedule is made up of programs (such as variety shows) which make heavy use of outside music, requiring licenses from several outside publishers. Accordingly, defendants argue, CBS could acquire the necessary performance rights for nearly all of its programming without the creation of the "machinery" which CBS claims (as discussed below) is required to facilitate transactions between producers and publishers. This assertion is not inconsistent with CBS' argument that, even adopting defendants' figures, direct licensing for the few programs which do make heavy use of "outside" music would be impracticable in the absence of "machinery" to service the large number of transactions which would be required. In short, no matter whose figures are closer to the truth, the question would remain whether the lack of "machinery" destroys the feasibility of direct licensing as an alternative to the blanket license and constitutes an illegal restraint of trade.

VIII.

Are There "Mechanical" Obstacles to Direct Licensing?

A. The Legal Significance of "Machinery"

Prior to trial the parties stipulated that ASCAP members and BMI affiliates "have not established facilities or procedures" for processing requests by music users for direct licenses for performance rights. (CX 2, CX 3) CBS argues that the fact that the individual defendants have not established such "machinery" constitutes a "barrier" to direct licensing which compels it to take a blanket license. (CBS Post-Trial Reply Brief at 29). Putting aside the question of the kind of machinery CBS claims to be necessary and whether its absence does in fact make direct licensing of outside music unfeasible, we disagree with CBS that defendants' mere failure to have created machinery amounts, without more, to an illegal refusal to deal. (CBS Post-Trial Reply Brief at 27)

As outlined above, CBS has not, in the many years it has held blanket licenses, indicated a wish to fill its music needs by means of direct licensing. There is no evidence of substance that before bringing this suit it ever considered such an alternative in its own business planning. The only expression of its dissatisfaction with the blanket system was the "demand" letter sent by the network President, Robert Wood, two weeks before the commencement of this suit. That letter did not even refer to direct licensing, nor of course to obstacles, such as the lack of "machinery," which arguably prevented CBS from engaging in direct dealing with copyright proprietors. Rather, the letter related only to CBS' request for alternative methods of licensing *through ASCAP* and *BMI*. In short, there is no evidence that CBS gave any thought to the need for machinery, or noticed its absence, prior to this litigation.

It is simplistic, in view of these facts, to argue that "by virtue of [defendants'] preemption of the field, there are absolutely no facilities in existence for . . . direct licensing . . . " (CBS Proposed Findings at 37). The "field" consists of buyers as well as sellers, and by taking a blanket license for twenty years, CBS (as well as other broadcasters) has "preempted" any need for the machinery whose absence is now claimed to constitute an antitrust violation. We are unable to accept the proposition that defendants have had the obligation to create the framework for a direct licensing system, particularly in the absence of any indication that CBS would ever wish to use it. There is no evidence, and indeed CBS does not claim, that defendants have refrained from creating the necessary machinery for the purpose of injuring CBS. In these circumstances, the fact that defendants have so far done nothing to facilitate direct licensing does not support the conclusion that they are illegally restraining it.

B. Problems Allegedly Created by the Lack of "Machinery"

Putting aside the question whether the mere absence of machinery illegally restrains trade in the market for performance rights, CBS has failed to prove that there are substantial mechanical obstacles to direct licensing. CBS postulates that under its new proposed licensing system it would pass on the job of licensing "outside" music to the production companies. In such a case, inside music would be conveniently licensed through the program packager and its publishing subsidiary. However, the producer would take on the additional job of obtaining rights to the outside music to be used on the program by contacting the publishers in question (or their agents, as described below) and dealing for the performance rights.

CBS' principal witnesses as to the need for machinery were Robert Wright, associate producer of "The Carol Burnett Show," and Edward Vincent, a former staff member of several network programs. Wright and Vincent are in the position of those who would use whatever machinery is required for direct licensing. In general the testimony of these witnesses was not persuasive, and their views on machinery were vague and abstract.[11] (e. g., Tr. 482–83, 500, 687) Three basic claims emerge from their testimony. First, CBS asserts that the producer in a direct licensing world would sometimes have difficulty in identifying the publisher of a given composition in order to approach him for a license. The argument is based on the fact of life in the industry that publishers' catalogs shift as they buy and sell copyrights, so that the publisher listed on the sheet music or record label may no longer own the composition when the producer wants to license it. CBS further claims that even assuming the producer can locate the publisher, the negotiations will be beset by confusion because, as defendants concede, music publishers have no established procedures for dealing with requests for performance licenses. Accordingly, the argument goes, direct licensing would be impracticable until settled ways of negotiating licenses are developed and publishers train their staffs to handle licensing. Finally, even assuming the producer can speak to the publisher in a language he can understand, CBS claims that difficulty would be caused by provision in certain contracts between writers and publishers requiring that the writer's consent be obtained prior to the grant of a direct license by the publisher. A provision requiring such consent appears in the form contract of the American Guild of Authors and Composers (AGAC). CBS claims that ASCAP's computer runs of CBS' music use show that some 40% of the outside music it uses is written by AGAC composers, a figure we adopt arguendo; and that the need to obtain writer consents for the use of that music would delay direct licensing transactions and disrupt the tight production schedules under which some programs are produced, particularly variety shows.

For the reasons stated below, we find that CBS' claims as to the effect of

---

[11] We note in passing that most of the testimony of Wright and Vincent as to the need for "machinery" related to the peculiar needs of producers of CBS' few variety shows, which make unusually heavy use of outside music and are produced on short production schedules. CBS did not offer proof as to how the needs of variety show producers for "machinery" differ from the needs of producers of programs which use outside music less regularly and in more modest amounts, and in which speed is not of the essence in the licensing transaction. Accordingly, even if we found the testimony of Wright and Vincent to be more persuasive than we do, it would be of limited value to establish the extent of the "machinery" necessary for shows other than variety shows.

lack of machinery are without merit. There are two basic flaws in CBS' general approach. First, CBS' premise that it would abruptly cancel its blanket license and seek to fulfill all its music needs by direct licensing on the next day (see, e. g., Tr. 463, 633, 1874, 1912–13) is utterly unrealistic. If CBS took such a course there might well be problems of the kind just described. But this would not be proof that defendants have created obstacles which render direct licensing unfeasible. As noted earlier, nothing in the antitrust laws requires defendants to maintain well-oiled machinery for direct licensing for the benefit of CBS. Indeed, there is no support in the record for the proposition that CBS could even as a matter of internal business planning, switch over to direct licensing without a long period of advance preparation. Accordingly, to presuppose, as CBS does, that the feasibility of the direct licensing alternative is to be judged literally as of "tomorrow" miscasts the issue. The proper question, we believe, is whether such mechanical obstacles as exist could be remedied with a reasonable period prior to cancellation of the blanket license.

The second flaw in CBS' approach is that it postulates that new direct licensing machinery would of necessity be an edifice entirely distinct from the machinery which now exists for the purpose of licensing other kinds of rights in music, in which ASCAP and BMI do not deal. As outlined earlier, the program packager is responsible for obtaining all rights necessary to televise the program except performance rights, which CBS obtains from ASCAP and BMI. These rights include "synch" rights, that is, the rights required for any program which is to be rerun. Program producers now obtain "direct" licenses for synch rights from publishers through "machinery" created for that purpose. Similarly, movie producers obtain from publishers the right to record and perform the music they use, (i. e., "mechanical rights" or "mechanicals") and there is "machinery" for this purpose as well.

Thus, although CBS is literally correct that "there are absolutely no facilities in existence for the direct licensing of [performance] rights by music publishers or other proprietors" (CBS Proposed Findings at 37), it overstates the issue to assume that such facilities would have to be created "from scratch" (CBS Post-Trial Brief at 40). The narrow question in the first instance is whether, as ASCAP and BMI contend, the machinery which publishers and producers now use to license other kinds of music could be adapted to facilitate the licensing of performance rights as well.

C. A Look at Other Kinds of Machinery

Apart from television performance rights, other rights in copyrighted music include motion picture synchronization and performance rights, and television synchronization rights. While ASCAP and BMI do not deal in these rights, facilities to license these rights directly from copyright owner to user do exist.

The television synchronization right is the right to record copyrighted music on the soundtrack of a filmed or taped program. Such rights are required for programs which are to be rerun, as distinguished from those (such as sports events or certain "one-run" taped programs) which are regarded as "live" performances. The grant of TV "synch" rights is almost exclusively brokered through the facilities of Harry Fox Agency, Inc., which represents virtually every major publisher, about 3,500 in all. As outlined by Fox's Managing Director, Albert Berman, and by Robert Wright and Edward Vincent, who are members of producers' staffs, the typical "synch" rights transaction starts with a telephone call to Fox from the producer or from Bernard Brody or Mary Williams, synch rights agents located in Los Angeles who represent producers in their dealings with Fox. Because Fox has instructions regarding each publisher's fee structure, (or, more often, is familiar with it on the basis of past experience) it is usually able to quote prices over the telephone for the compositions which interest the producer. The entire transaction, including actual issuance of the license, is completed within two to three days at most. Fox issues several thousand television synchronization licenses annually, using a basic staff of only two employees.

A "movie rights" transaction consists of the licensing of the performance right *and* synch right in one package for use in a theatrical (as distinguished from television) motion picture. The versatile Fox Agency also represents publishers in the licensing of these rights. The negotiation is similar in form to the TV "synch" rights. As described by Marion Mingle, the Fox employee who handles movie rights, producers call or write to Fox requesting price quotations on a number of compositions. Mingle or her assistant then telephones the publisher and outlines the nature of the film and the kind of use which is to be made of the composition in question, so that he can quote the price for the rights. Generally, the producer either accepts or rejects the various quotations on the spot; sometimes, however, he may make a counter-offer which Mingle passes on to the producer. In general, Mingle can quote prices to the producer within two days. She and her assistant license several hundred movies each year.

D. Could Other Kinds of Machinery Help CBS?

As note earlier, CBS claims that the non-existence of direct licensing machinery in the television performance rights field would practically bar direct dealing in several critical aspects: the producer would have difficulty in identifying the copyright owner of a song which had been sold to another publisher; the AGAC writer-consent requirement would delay the licensing transaction and disrupt production schedules; and publishers would be unable to handle requests for licenses because they have no staffs or procedures for direct dealing in performance rights and have not created a central facility such as the Fox Agency to facilitate contact between producers and publishers. These claims dissolve in view of the evidence as to the licensing of other rights in music.

1. Finding Copyright Proprietors

In most cases the producer of a CBS show would have no difficulty identifying the "outside" publisher of a song for which he wants a performance license because he or his agent already deals directly with that publisher to obtain a synch license for the same song. As former CBS Vice President in charge of programming, Michael Dann noted, any program on tape or film is likely to be rerun, and program packagers usually obtain synch rights at the time the program is produced. Wright, who is on the staff of "The Carol Burnett Show," testified that problems in clearing synch rights are "rare." Edward Vincent, a former staff member of "The Jim Nabors Variety Hour," testified that the Bernard Brody Agency would have no difficulty in giving him the name and address of any copyright owner.

Even if lines of communication to obtain synch rights were not already established, there are several other ways in which a producer could identify the publisher of music he plans to use. Emil Poklitar, who works in CBS' music clearance department stated that CBS maintains a file containing the relevant information on over 100,000 compositions. Indeed, as Wright testified, publishers regularly barrage television producers with catalogs and brochures to promote the use of their music. Where they have not done so, there appears to be no reason why CBS could not simply request the catalogs of the major publishers. Finally, it should be stressed that in the vast majority of cases, the copyright owner listed on the sheet music or phonograph record is still the owner of the composition in question.

2. The AGAC Writer-Consent Requirement

Nor has CBS proven that the writer consent requirement in the AGAC form contract would cause significant delay in direct negotiations for performance rights. At present, publishers are required to obtain an AGAC writer's consent for television synch licenses for songs over ten years old, and movie synch licenses for vocal use of a composition. (3M PX 31) Although Leon Brettler, Vice President of Shapiro, Bernstein & Co., a major publisher, testified that he has occasional difficulty contacting a writer who is on vacation or has just changed residence, the record establishes that meeting the consent requirement rarely causes delay in the issuance of a license. In addition to Brettler, several publisher witnesses were asked if they had trouble getting in touch with their writers. For example, Edwin H. Morris, who owns a company bearing his name, testified he has had no difficulties in doing so. Salvatore Chiantia, of MCA Music, testified that he is routinely able to locate his writers and obtain their consent. The reason why publishers have little difficulty in contacting an AGAC writer and obtaining his consent promptly is not hard to fathom: writers are intensely eager to have their work performed on television. Many AGAC writers have simply given advance blanket consent to their publishers to avoid the risk that the producer will, because of time pressures, substitute a different song. As Chiantia stated in a letter to AGAC concerning consents for background uses (PX 84):

> " . . . if we are not able to give licenses to TV film producers at $25. per film, or if we have to obtain the written consent of each writer for each individual use, we would for all practical purposes never get the compositions from our catalogs into current TV films other than in a few rare instances. The writers who have given us their approval are aware of the competitive situation which exists in connection with the use of music in the filmed TV programs produced in Hollywood. It is because of that very reason that they gave us their okay to go ahead." (PX 84)

In the same vein, Louis Bernstein of Shapiro, Bernstein & Co. wrote AGAC:

> " . . . Please bear in mind that the authors and composers who come into our office are desperately hungry for performances, which means money from ASCAP. A good number of writers have urged us to get them these performances and stop worrying about the AGAC technicalities. Even so, 19 out of 20 writers would gladly give us any authorization in writing, but since we are dealing with several thousand writers, it becomes a difficult job to be so technical." (PX 162)

There is every reason to believe that most writers would either give their publishers blanket consent for performance licenses, or give it promptly on a use-by-use basis, just as they presently do regarding synch rights. As Chiantia testified:

> "It is no different than the situation with respect to synchronization rights. Why do you have any greater difficulty in this matter than you have in synchronization rights? There are certain synchronization rights that you need that I have to get my writer's permission on and you get them. Why suddenly do you have such a great problem in respect of getting performance licenses where you don't have that same problem in getting synchronization licenses." (Tr. 2970)

3. The Need For Centralized "Machinery"

Although CBS has failed to prove that producers seeking performance licenses could not identify copyright owners, or that the writer consent requirements would significantly delay direct licensing of performance rights, we agree that direct licensing on any major scale would require some central clearing machinery through which transactions could be brokered. Without such machinery, direct licensing might be mechanically feasible, but would be a bulky and inefficient system: for a program producer (or an agent such as the Brody Agency) to contact each of the publishers whose compositions interest him, for every program, would of course be distinctly time-consuming and expensive.

In the past, the Fox Agency has responded to publishers' needs for central "direct-licensing" machinery for new kinds of music rights by expanding its long roster of services. Defendants argue, accordingly, that music publishers would turn over the job of clearing television performance rights licensing to Fox as well. CBS replies that defendants oversimplify the problem of creating machinery because there can be no assurance that the Fox Agency will agree to take on the job of brokering performance rights. Of course, it is possible that Fox would refuse the opportunity to expand its business. But the lack of hard evidence on the point is chargeable to CBS, not defendants. Never having explored the feasibility of direct licensing, CBS has not given Fox any occasion to consider the possibility of brokering such licenses. In any event, there is no substantial basis for concluding that the Fox Agency would not expand its services to include television performance rights, just as it has expanded in the past to meet the need of publishers for a central agency for movie performance rights and television "synch" rights. However, even if Fox were unwilling to take on the job of brokering performance rights, the creation of a new agency modeled along the same lines need not be the imposing project CBS makes it out to be. Albert Berman, Fox's Managing Director, testified as follows:

"Q Mr. Berman, you were asked by Mr. Hruska on direct something about suppose publishers ask you to take over licensing of public performances on network television. Do you remember that question?

A Yes.

Q And as I understood it, you said that you wanted to make a study before giving a detailed answer.

A Yes.

Q Let me ask this, sir: Would the task be significantly different from the task you now have when licensing TV sync rights?

A Only in numbers. It is certainly much more formidable merely because the uses would be so much greater. But the job could be done, I assume, with enough people and enough physical equipment." (Tr. 973–74)

Berman did not testify, and CBS did not offer proof, as to how many people and how much physical equipment would be required. According to CBS' projections, which we adopt arguendo, the number of direct licensing transactions required each year from outside publishers would range from approximately four thousand to eight thousand. (The low figure is projected from a period in 1971 when CBS had three night-time musical variety series; the high figure is based on a period in 1970 when it had seven such programs. CBS does not make a projection for the season which began in the Fall of 1974, during which it offered only one variety serial, "The Carol Burnett Show.") The question is whether CBS' projection of some 4,000 to 8,000 transactions would entail a large number of complex tasks requiring a massive staff, or a simple task repeated four thousand times by a relatively modest one. CBS' posttrial submissions strain to give the impression that each time a producer wished to use a certain type of composition, Fox or its newly created equivalent in the performance rights field would have to contact several different publishers, who in turn would have to check whether the AGAC writers (if any) whose music is involved would give their consent to the grant of a license, and then begin active price negotiations for the song or songs in question. (CBS Post-Trial Brief at 37–44, Reply Brief at 39–40)

It is unrealistic to assume that such cumbersome procedures would be involved in a direct licensing world; indeed CBS' own papers offer the key to streamlining the job. As noted early in this opinion, CBS seeks as one form of relief in this suit the establishment, under court supervision, of what it calls a "per-use" system. Under the per-use system, as outlined by CBS,[12] musical compositions would continue to be licensed through ASCAP and BMI, but instead of taking a blanket license, CBS would license individual compositions, for which it would pay a specified fee for each use of music from the per-use "reservoir." The fee for each license would be fixed in a schedule reflecting the nature of the use (e. g., theme, feature or background) and other appropriate factors, such as duration of use. CBS suggests that one convenient way to set a fee schedule is to adopt the present formula by which ASCAP and BMI give royalty "credits" to their members and affiliates. (CBS Post-Trial Reply Brief at 71) The question which naturally arises, and CBS does not answer, is why publishers would not readily adopt the same concept of a fee schedule[13] under

---

[12] The outline of CBS' "per-use" proposal are set forth at note 7, *supra*.

[13] Instead of addressing itself to the feasibility of a fee schedule in a direct licensing world, CBS postulates that a central licensing agency for performance rights would require a "massive" staff because the negotiation of such rights would be more time-consuming and complex than the "cut-and-dried" negotiations which are the rule in the television "synch" rights field: setting a price for the former would involve factors such as the nature and duration of the use and the unique attributes of a particular song (e. g., "Happy Birthday"). The argument is without merit. It is true, as CBS points out, that in most cases television "synch" rights negotiations are fairly clean cut. However, synch rights *and* performance rights for movies are negotiated in a single package; and accordingly the nature of the movie rights transaction provides a more relevant basis for determining CBS' argument that performance rights negotiations would be a complicated matter. As described by Marion Mingle, who handles movie rights

a direct licensing system, in which case a centralized computer would store information as to prices as well as other necessary information for each publisher's catalog.

Of course, it is not for the court to propose a system for direct licensing. Nevertheless, on studious review of the record, we are left with the belief that careful planning would go far to remove any significant "mechanical" obstacles to direct licensing for performance rights. It is true, as CBS points out, that new personnel would have to be trained to handle the task. But the only evidence on the point indicates that new central machinery could be staffed primarily by clerical personnel, as it is at Fox. The period required to train such personnel is presumably measured in weeks or months, rather than years.

Such a finding is supported by CBS' own scenario as to how things would go in the event it prevailed in this suit: either of its proposed forms of relief—the establishment of its "per-use" system under ongoing court supervision; or a mandatory injunction against the issuance of blanket licenses to any network by ASCAP and BMI—would require the development of "machinery" at least as extensive and very much of the same pattern as that involved in a direct licensing system under the consent decrees. For example, if CBS won an injunction against the issuance of blanket licenses, it would of course be faced with the very same mechanical "barriers" to direct dealing of which it now complains so strenuously. Nevertheless, Donald Sipes, CBS' Vice President in charge of business affairs and planning for the network, freely conjectured that in such an event the lack of "machinery" would pose no problem because ABC–TV and NBC–TV would be "in the same boat":

> "A Under that assumption, all three networks are in the same boat. In other words, neither one of the three—that's bad English—but none of them have a competitive advantage, you see, over the others.
>
> Q Assuming that, then what?
>
> A Assuming that with a lot of struggle and some chaos up front, I think again that the machinery necessary to broker deals between the sellers and the buyers in this situation will spring up to fill that gap. There is a need, there is money to be made, and people will spring into that breach to fill that need and make it happen. And deals, direct deals will be made for musical compositions between buyers and sellers.

---

at the Fox Agency, the increased complexity of the performance rights transaction amounts to asking the producer about the nature of the intended use and passing on the information to the publisher. (Tr. 870–71, 876–77) Mingle testified that she can generally supply quotations to producers within two days and, as noted earlier, she and a single assistant handle all of the several hundred movie rights licenses Fox issues each year.

Now, I do believe, of course, that it will take some time for that machinery to develop up front, but of course all three networks in that situation would have that same problem.

Q Suppose, Mr. Sipes, the injunctive order, in other words the order prohibiting ASCAP and BMI from licensing television networks, the effective date of that order was deferred for a period of, let's say, a year. Would that remove the struggle you mentioned earlier in your answer? Would that solve the problem, in your mind?

A I think that during that time the machinery would develop, yes, sir." (Tr. 79–80)

As we view the matter, CBS is not entitled to relief in this suit simply for the purpose of insulating it from the risk of competitive disadvantage vis-a-vis other networks if it makes the business decision to experiment with a new method of music licensing. If CBS' Vice President in charge of the very subject at hand concedes that within one year suitable machinery would "spring up," no reason appears on this record why it could not in any event plan to change over to direct licensing, effective one year hence, without a court order to spur the effort.

CBS' sole response is that copyright proprietors would not of their own accord leave the safe haven of ASCAP and BMI and expend their resources to set up the machinery for direct dealing because they are afraid to engage in price competition for their works; and that only a court order could provide the "signal" that they must do so. The argument is unpersuasive. Assuming that copyright proprietors would in fact be willing to deal with CBS produc-ers—a conclusion we reach in the next section—they would logically create an efficient mechanism to facilitate it (as they have in the case of other music rights), if only to hold down their own costs. In any event, the cost of creating new machinery would be passed on to music users, just as it is at present through ASCAP, BMI and the Fox Agency.

In sum, as stated earlier, CBS might well have "machinery" problems if it cancelled its blanket license "tomorrow." But this is not proof that defendants have created "barriers" to direct licensing in order to compel CBS to take a blanket license; it is just as consistent with the fact, which the evidence establishes, that no one, including CBS, imagined that the blanket license would lose its charms until shortly before this suit. Because CBS does not claim that it would commence direct licensing tomorrow (although its counsel often questioned witnesses on the assumption that it would), the relevant question is whether the relatively modest machinery required could be devel-oped during a reasonable planning period. The evidence establishes beyond doubt that it could.

IX.

Would Copyright Owners Attempt to Thwart Direct Licensing?

A. The Nature of CBS' Proof

In the absence of proof that direct licensing is unfeasible because of mechanical obstacles CBS' case rests primarily on its claim that copyright proprietors would refuse to deal directly if CBS asked, or at least make it such an arduous and expensive proposition that CBS would be forced to resume the blanket arrangement. (CBS Post-Trial Reply Brief at 29) Indeed, in a substantial sense, the "disinclination issue," as it has come to be called in the course of the lawsuit, is the major factual issue in the case. As CBS' post-trial papers recognize, even questions such as mechanical feasibility hinge almost exclusively on the willingness or unwillingness of the defendants to smooth CBS' course or obstruct it, as the case may be. (See, e. g., CBS Proposed Findings at 45–47)

Such a claim is difficult to prove even in the best of cases, and the present suit is no exception. CBS' Vice President Donald Sipes testified that CBS has never sought a direct license. The three CBS witnesses who predicted that writers and publishers would refuse to deal with producers were Sipes, and producers Robert Wright and Edward Vincent. Their testimony on the point was unimpressive, particularly inasmuch as none of them had ever spoken to a publisher or a writer in relation to performance rights licensing. Vincent's direct testimony is representative:

> "Q Let's go back to the delays you said you anticipated getting a secretary on the telephone, et cetera. Don't you think that copyright proprietors are going to see to it that all those delays are removed in this world in which the CBS Television Network has cancelled its ASCAP-BMI license?
>
> A No, I don't believe that because I am assuming on the basis of this particular lawsuit, that ASCAP and BMI like things the way they are.
>
> If you are asking me to assume that they are going to have a parade for me if I tell them in front I am going to run an end run around their entire organization and attempt to deal direct and circumvent the ASCAP and BMI—
>
> THE COURT: I don't think that is the question Mr. Hruska asked you. I think he asked you whether you wouldn't expect the copyright owners to make quick arrangements to deal with you if CBS didn't have a—

A No, sir, I don't, and that's the reason I don't. I don't believe that they would want to see that particular system succeed.

THE COURT: Do you have any basis for saying that?

THE WITNESS: Well, as I began to state before, your Honor, there is a system under which they are operating now, which I assume for them is a very good system and that they like—" (Tr. 636–37)

. . . .

"THE WITNESS: Your Honor, it is my opinion that we are talking about members of a group, of a group that has banded together for a very specific reason, and they have sought the shelter of this group for good and reasonable reasons, again, I assume.

You are also asking me if I think that I am going to expect them to want to deal with me?

THE COURT: Yes, I am.

THE WITNESS: To come toward me and say, 'Yes, let's make a deal,' after I have circumvented their group.

No, your Honor, I don't believe that prudent business sense dictates that I should believe that.

THE COURT: I mean that's just on your general experience, you are saying that?

THE WITNESS: Yes, sir." (Tr. 639–40)

Despite the testimony of Sipes, Wright and Vincent that many if not most ASCAP members and BMI affiliates would be "disinclined" to deal directly with producers for performance rights, none of them could give the name of even one actual publisher or writer whom they thought would fall into that category. Sipes has never spoken to a copyright owner. (Tr. 204, 358). Wright, who is associated with "The Carol Burnett Show," was "confident" that ASCAP members would be reluctant to deal with him, but was certain that Joe Hamilton, who wrote the theme music for the show would be inclined to deal (Tr. 489). Edward Vincent, of the Jim Nabors show, stated that the two writers with whom he had actually worked would deal with him (Tr. 726). CBS' economist Franklin Fisher, also expressed the view that ASCAP members would be reluctant to deal but, like Sipes, he has never spoken to a writer or publisher (Tr. 4853).

In the absence of evidence that any ASCAP member or BMI affiliate has ever refused or even threatened to refuse to grant CBS direct performance rights for any composition, CBS offered evidence as to (1) the strong economic incentives which would deter copyright proprietors from direct dealing (2) the experience of the Minnesota Mining and Manufacturing Company (the "3M" incident) in direct licensing its music needs for a background music tape and tape-player which it marketed in the mid-1960's and (3) the ease with which defendants could thwart a direct licensing attempt by CBS, by exacting premiums for the licensing of music already taped or filmed, (music "in the can") which has until now been covered by a blanket license.

B. The Alleged Incentives to Refuse to Deal

CBS' Post-Trial papers postulate the fact, which we adopt arguendo, that participants in the market for performance rights are rational businessmen motivated by the wish to maximize profits. It excuses its failure to pursue alternatives to the blanket license by arguing that "no reasonably prudent manager of a television network" would subject his company to the risks involved. (CBS Proposed Findings at 33, 36) By a similar line of reasoning CBS contends that no prudent copyright proprietor would voluntarily relinquish the bargaining leverage and shield against price competition which ASCAP and BMI provide. According to CBS' theory of the case, these essentially hypothetical facts establish both the restraint (i. e., the unavailability of the direct licensing alternative) and the threat of loss (i. e., the economic risk involved in the attempt). We are skeptical of the validity of this general approach, for the issue is not what CBS or copyright proprietors perceive their respective risks to be, but whether CBS has established that its fear that copyright proprietors would in fact attempt to thwart a direct licensing attempt is justified. With that caveat, we turn to the relevant evidence.

It is true, as CBS relentlessly emphasizes, that most of the writer and publisher witnesses who testified, by deposition or at trial, expressed a strong preference for the blanket licensing system. The preference is no surprise in view of the fact that the blanket license is the only way in which performance rights have been marketed to television networks for nearly thirty years. Moreover, the writer-publisher testimony establishes that, from their standpoint, the system is trouble-free and self-executing and the financial rewards are satisfactory. None of them expressed the wish to exchange their present, relatively uncomplicated way of doing business for what they viewed as a new mode involving unfamiliar procedures and possible financial uncertainty.

CBS stresses selected portions of the deposition testimony of several publisher witnesses who expressed themselves vigorously when asked to comment on such questions as the possible prohibition of the blanket licensing system. Several common themes pervade the portions of their testimony which CBS stresses: the recognition that there is a large number of publishers and writers who would be competing for exposure on the CBS network; that many of them might face financial difficulties as a result of possible intense competition in a very limited market; and the strong preference for licensing through ASCAP and BMI, which have a measure of bargaining clout in dealing with CBS, the world's largest "consumer" of music.

We may agree that the cited testimony proves that writers and publishers prefer the present system and are apprehensive of dealing directly with CBS. However, this by no means proves the obverse: that copyright owners would refuse to deal with CBS if it discontinued its blanket license and insisted upon dealing on a direct licensing basis. Indeed, the snippets of testimony on which CBS relies are replete with the Darwinian imagery of cutthroat competition among hungry publishers and writers seeking network exposure. The colorful deposition testimony of Leon Brettler, an officer of Shapiro, Bernstein, Inc., is an example:

> "Q Do you think that there would be a good deal of price cutting by publishers in the licensing of performance rights to television networks?
>
> " . . .
>
> A In this case I haven't got the slightest hesitation of saying not that I know, but I am virtually positive there would be a deluge of price cutting bordering on the cutthroat nature that would lead to mutual self-annihilation.
>
> " . . .
>
> "I mean among us competitors who would be so desperate and jockeying for position, none of us having any strength, dealing with one huge user or an industry that is a huge user, consisting of three main entities and we only have those three doors open to us and all 4000 of us converging through that door, I think there would be tremendous amounts of concessions and price cutting and deals." (Dep. 295–98)
>
> . . . .
>
> "I think that it would have substantial impact across the board, even to the big companies . . . the largest music publisher is still David compared to the Goliath of the television industry. The so-called top ten are still Davids compared to Goliath and the only time that I have ever heard of David whipping Goliath was in the Bible. Usually Goliath swamps David." (Dep. 302–03)

We do not view this testimony as aiding CBS' case. It tends rather to establish that copyright owners would line up at CBS' door if direct dealing were the only avenue to fame and fortune.

More significant, however, is the fact that, when read in their entirety, the depositions take on an entirely different hue. For example, Brettler testified that "there is no question of the fact that we would negotiate something" if a producer requested performance rights (Dep. 184–85), and that "hordes" of other publishers would do the same. (Dep. 304–05) Edwin H. Morris, who operates another publishing company, expressed anxiety similar to Brettler's. However, far from stating that he would not deal with CBS, he testified:

> "Q Let us assume that telephone does ring, that you are approached by producers and/or network people who are interested in obtaining direct licenses to the compositions or various of the compositions in the Morris catalog. Do you talk to these people?
>
> A Yes.
>
> Q Do you invite them to come into your office?
>
> A I will even go to theirs." (Dep. 211–12)

The conclusion that CBS has failed to prove that the "disinclination" of writers and publishers to leave the blanket system would ripen into a refusal to deal directly is fortified by the trial testimony. Although most of the writers and publishers who testified expressed concern similar to those of CBS' deposition witnesses, all but one of them testified that he or his company would negotiate directly with CBS for performance rights, and most of them believed that their attitudes were representative of others in their position. For example, Arnold Broido, President of the Theodore Presser Company, testified:

> "Q . . .
>
> "Let us suppose there came a time when CBS no longer held licenses from ASCAP and BMI and came to you to negotiate or seeking to negotiate direct licenses with you for public performance of compositions in your repertory.
>
> What would be your reaction?
>
> A We would deal with them, of course.
>
> Q Would you tell us why?
>
> A Well, there is really very little else that we could do. We would have no choice in the matter. We would regret it because, obviously, it would be an inconvenience to us and we would regret the breaking of the relationship but we would deal with them." (Tr. 3492–93).

Broido also stated that:

> "the publishers would by and large talk with CBS or anyone else who came to them." (Tr. 3498)

Salvatore Chiantia, President of the Music Division of MCA, Inc., testified:

"My primary responsibility is to get my music played. To get it exposed. And if I have to go to CBS in a direct licensing scheme, I am going to go. I am not going to sit back and say, I hope you fail. I want you to use my music and I am going to try to make it work." (Tr. 2957)

"There are only three games in town. I have to play one of three games. If we are talking about television, there are only three games in town. If I am effectively cut out from one, I only have two more to play with." (Tr. 2947)

The response of the composers who testified was similar to that of the publisher witnesses. For example, the dean of American composers, Aaron Copland, expressed reluctance to change the blanket arrangement, but testified that he would engage in direct dealing if necessary:

"Q Now, it has been suggested in this lawsuit that in the event that the Columbia Broadcasting System Television Network for some reason or another no longer held a license from ASCAP and BMI it might come to you, as an individual copyright proprietor, as an individual composer, and seek a license from you for the right to perform your copyrighted work or works.

I would like to ask you, sir, whether if someone from Columbia came to see you you would be inclined or disinclined to deal with them or what would your reaction be?

A Well, I think I would be rather regretful about the need to individually concern myself with the licensing of a particular work, since the present arrangement takes care of a great many of those chores, as I would think of them, and it seems a comfortable arrangement as it now exists, from our standpoint at any rate.

Q If, however, the question were squarely put to you, will you deal with CBS or will you refuse to deal with CBS, what would your answer be?

A Well, I think my answer would be that of most composers. If they want to get a performance, they will do what is necessary to get the performance and if they have to deal with CBS, they would, I suppose, agree to deal with them." (Tr. 3485–86)

Composer John Green testified to the same effect:

"Q Mr. Green, suppose the following hypothesis. That CBS canceled its ASCAP blanket license and NBC and ABC continued to hold blanket licenses from ASCAP and suppose that either CBS or a producer of a CBS film series show came to you and sought to engage you to write the background and theme music for the show.

Would you be included or disinclined to negotiate with him for the writing of that music?

A I would be inclined to negotiate with him.

Q Do you have an opinion as to whether other background writers and composers would be inclined or disinclined to negotiate with CBS or its producers in that situation?

. . . .

Q Do you have an opinion?

A I know how I would like to answer that question. I don't have an opinion but I would be surprised if they didn't feel exactly as I do.

. . . .

Q Mr. Green, can you tell us why you would be inclined to negotiate with CBS or the producer of the CBS show in that situation?

A For the following reasons. I like to think that part of my motivation is aesthetic and artistic, but I am also a fellow who earns his living by the making of music in various forms. I am also an artist who derives only secondary pleasure from thinking how great my music is when I hear it in my head.

I like to hear it performed and I like to get paid for hearing it performed and you referred to [CBS]—would I be inclined to negotiate with [CBS] for the performance? Well, they are one of the principal outlets in the world for the performance of music and I want my music to be performed, I want the public to hear it, I want to get paid for it and I would be totally inclined to negotiate with anybody who would like to use it.

Q Mr. Green, you have also told us that in addition to your work as a background composer you have written songs in your music career.

Suppose in that situation we posited just a moment ago, CBS canceling its ASCAP license, suppose one of your publishers called you up and told you that the producer of a CBS variety show is interested in using one of your compositions, one of your songs, on a show, and he asked you for your opinion or view, would you be inclined to recommend that he license or negotiate with CBS or the producer or would you recommend that he not negotiate with CBS or its producer?

A I would recommend that he negotiate.

Q And why?

A Because I would want my song to be exposed and I would also want to derive the revenue that would come from such a source as [CBS] for that exposure." (Tr. 3457–60)

Perhaps it is not surprising that Walter Dean, who was called by CBS, was the only witness to testify that the publishers for whom he worked would probably refuse to grant licenses to CBS. The publishers are April and Blackwood, companies which CBS owns, and whose catalogs consist mostly of copyrights owned by CBS as well.

Although the testimony of the writer and publisher witnesses persuasively suggested that they would deal directly with CBS, at least *ex necessitate*, our conclusion that CBS has not proven that they would refuse to do so does not rest solely on their testimony. The extensive evidence on the nature of the music industry amply confirms the proposition.

The two most salient features of the television music market are the enormous value to copyright proprietors of network exposure and the markedly limited opportunities for securing it. Copyright proprietors are eager to have their music performed on television not simply to earn performance royalties distributed through ASCAP and BMI, but because a television performance before millions of viewers is the most effective way to sell phonograph records and sheet music, and to generate performances by other music users. No less than eleven witnesses testified to the compelling desire of writers and publishers to gain television exposure for their music. To that end, publishers regularly direct extensive promotional efforts toward the networks, including the mailing of advance copies of sheet music or recordings to producers, performers and musical directors of television shows. Some publishers use promotional brochures or other written materials; others solicit by telephone. The record establishes beyond doubt that even in what CBS characterizes as a comfortable, blanket license world devoid of price competition, television network performances are highly sought by copyright owners.

The eagerness, and occasional desperation, of copyright proprietors is heightened by the fact that there are so few opportunities to win the prize. There are only three television networks and, as noted earlier, few programs which make appreciable use of previously published music; most programs either use no music at all or "inside" theme and background music published by the producer. The testimony of Alan Shulman, Vice President of the Belwin Mills Publishing Corp., aptly summarizes the situation:

"Q Are any of your promotional activities aimed at getting your music played on network television?

A Yes. But there are very, very limited number of opportunities to do this. For example, because of the number—well, they are limited pretty much to the variety shows that appear on the television networks and these are fewer in number of recent years than they were previously.

Q Why are your opportunities limited to the various shows?

A Well, because the other shows are basically prerecorded. Prefilmed, et cetera. The series, et cetera, are done and produced beforehand and the music that is performed and synchronized and used in those programs are pretty much controlled by the producers of the particular program.

And these producers, in fact, very often are publishers themselves who control the publishing rights and, naturally, are not too happy to use other people's music unless they absolutely have to because there is income from it." (Tr. 3083–84)

In fact, apart from variety programs, producers seldom "have to" use "other people's music." With rare exceptions, a considerable number of copyrighted songs are suitable for any use a producer might have in mind. Although every copyrighted composition is philosophically or aesthetically "unique" and its uniqueness is dignified by copyright, virtually none of the four million compositions in the ASCAP and BMI repertories is unique in the mind of a television producer. CBS' producer witnesses Wright and Vincent, testified that "any number" of songs would fit a producer's intended use and that "there would always be, obviously, alternates." (Tr. 419, 586) Copyright proprietors are keenly aware that their compositions are substantially interchangeable with the compositions of other writers and publishers, a factor which could well be expected to dissipate any "disinclination" to deal with CBS, which might otherwise exist.

Moreover, CBS' enormous power within the music industry supports the testimony of the writers and publishers who said they would engage in direct licensing. CBS is far more than a television network. It is, as Michael Dann, former Senior Vice President of CBS in charge of programming testified, "The No. 1 outlet in the history of entertainment" and "the giant of the world in the use of music rights." (Tr. 3374) CBS is the largest manufacturer and seller of records and tapes in the world (Tr. 4615); it owns radio and television stations in a number of major metropolitan areas. On CBS' own theory that composers and publishers belong to the race of economic men, it is doubtful that any copyright owner would refuse the opportunity to have his music performed on CBS, much less wish to incur CBS' displeasure. It would risk not only the loss of CBS performance royalties, but royalties from the sale of records sold by CBS subsidiaries and from radio plays of their records on fourteen radio stations operated by CBS in the seven largest cities in the nation.

Moreover, many of the largest publishers are, like April and Blackwood, subsidiaries of large entertainment companies. A number of the named defendants or their parent corporations are program packagers or movie distributors who compete to sell their products to CBS. For example, Famous Music is owned by Paramount and Leeds Music is owned by Universal. The royalties received by these publishing subsidiaries are a small fraction of the amount CBS pays for the program or film. It would be a rhetorical question to ask whether such producers would risk the sale of a program package to CBS because of the disinclination of its publishing subsidiary to engage in direct dealing for the music performance rights.

C. The "3M Incident"

In support of its disinclination theory, CBS also relies heavily on the experience of the Minnesota Mining and Manufacturing Company (3M) which sought direct licenses from publishers in connection with its marketing, in the mid 1960's of a tape and tape player (the M–700 project) designed to provide 24 hours of background music. The M–700 was designed for use in small commercial establishments, such as restaurants, stores, and doctors' and dentists' offices. To this extent, the M–700 was similar to the packages offered by other vendors of background music services such as the well-known Muzak. In one important respect, however, it was different: 3M planned to sell its tape outright, while other vendors leased theirs for a limited term.

3M retained Allen Arrow, an attorney, to negotiate performance licenses for the M–700. Initially, Arrow approached ASCAP for licenses but during the ensuing discussions several problems arose. For example, ASCAP wanted, and 3M did not want, different rates for different classes of users. According to Arrow, ASCAP took the position that the consent decree, which prohibits it from discriminating between similarly situated licensees, barred it from offering a "one class" license because it would discriminate against vendors of background tape systems for larger establishments, such as Muzak and Seeburg. In addition, ASCAP found serious difficulty in 3M's proposal to sell its tape outright because ASCAP would be required, after the expiration of an initial three year license term, either to try to relicense 3M's customers for a renewal term or, if they refused, to fight a losing battle trying to police possible infringement in a number of small establishments whose individual royalty payments would amount to some $10. per year. Although 3M, as a potential user, was entitled to invoke the licensing and rate-fixing procedures available to it under the consent decree, Arrow testified that 3M chose not to take that course because of time pressures in assembling the project and other such factors. In the circumstances, ASCAP suggested to 3M that it deal directly with copyright proprietors.

There is considerable evidence that the publishers 3M approached viewed the M–700 proposal with some reservations. Some of them were concerned about the novel form of license 3M sought; others about the policing problem;

others about the amount of money involved; and still others about the implications of such a proposal for the traditional ASCAP structure and their customary way of doing business. Nevertheless, 3M signed contracts with 27 of the 35 publishers it approached. It obtained all of the music it needed within its time schedule at a cost of about three quarters of the amount of its first offer to ASCAP. Shortly thereafter, 3M began another successful program to obtain licenses for a second series of M–700 tapes.

Although the statistics do not favor its case, CBS stresses the fact that 3M was able to reach agreement with "only" 27 of the 35 publishers it approached. It argues that a large music user like CBS could be expected to meet considerably greater resistance in a direct licensing effort than 3M, whose rather modest needs for direct licenses could not have threatened to topple the ASCAP structure. Defendants, argue, on the other hand, that the 3M incident demonstrates that direct licensing is feasible. It points to the fact that, in the last analysis, 80% of the publishers 3M approached put aside whatever "disinclination" they might otherwise have had to direct dealing, and engaged in business negotiations over a business proposition.

We hesitate to give important weight to the 3M incident as evidence of the likelihood that copyright proprietors would attempt to frustrate CBS' efforts to engage in direct licensing. In the first place, 3M is hardly as large a music user as CBS. Moreover, it sought licenses for a highly fragmented group of small users, rather than for a huge television network. Finally, the form of license which 3M solicited, involving a package of compositions from a publisher for a three year term is not comparable to a license for one performance of a single composition before an audience of millions. In short, CBS and copyright proprietors would be trading for a very different horse than did 3M and the publishers which it approached. Moreover, the evidence as to the 3M incident was developed in large part through documents and deposition testimony; and included considerable hearsay in the testimony of Allen Arrow. We cannot give significant weight to arguments as to the state of mind (e. g., disinclination) of the publishers approached by 3M based on such evidence. Nevertheless, CBS has made the 3M incident a central part of its disinclination claim. For the reasons set forth below we find that the incident, if it proves anything at all, establishes that copyright proprietors would deal with CBS for direct licenses.

In our view, the bare fact that 8 of 35 publishers were unwilling to sign a contract with 3M has no legal significance; the only relevant question is why they did not. To the extent that the motivations of the unwilling publishers can be gleaned from this record, it appears that general opposition to direct licensing and loyalty to ASCAP played a very small part; and that in general where 3M's proposals were rejected there were legitimate business objections to them. We detail some of these below.

1. *3M's Negotiations With Publishers*

Chappell & Co., Inc. was the first publisher 3M approached. Initially, it found 3M's offer very attractive, but ultimately refused it because of concern that the sale of the M–700 tape would, in effect, put a perpetual free performing right in the hands of 3M's purchasers unless ASCAP licensed and policed those rights. Chappell's concerns appear to have been justified because, as matters turned out, only about a third of 3M's purchasers agreed to pay for licenses to use their tapes after expiration of the initial three year term.

3M next approached MPHC, a publishing company owned by Warner Brothers. MPHC's initial response was favorable, but the MPHC official authorized to make a final agreement was ill, and died during the course of negotiations. By the time he had been replaced, 3M had met its licensing needs. In 1967, 3M negotiated and reached oral agreement with MPHC for licenses covering a subsequent series of tapes, but 3M then decided not to consummate the transaction.

Like Chappell & Co., Famous Music Corp. expressed serious reservations about the possibility of policing the renewal term performance rights, and after consulting ASCAP it rejected 3M's proposal. In 1967, Famous resumed negotiations with 3M for a second tape series and a tentative agreement was reached, but 3M dropped the proposition because at that point it expected to make a bulk licensing agreement with ASCAP covering the second series, which as matters turned out, did not materialize.

The Edwin H. Morris Company did not accept the 3M proposal because it thought, in Morris' words, that 3M was "trying to get something for virtually nothing." (Dep. 131) The evidence establishes that Morris had completely misunderstood the amount of money 3M was actually offering; and that he would have negotiated if there had not been a failure in communication. (Dep. 129–31, 137–41)

Irving Berlin Music, Inc., initially turned down the 3M offer for reasons which are not clear. It appears to have been reluctant to license except through ASCAP, largely because 3M proposed to use too small a number of Berlin songs to make a different decision worthwhile. Berlin changed its mind as to the second tape series but again 3M backed out in anticipation of licensing these later tapes through ASCAP.

By the time 3M approached The Richmond Organization it had made sizeable deals with other publishers. Accordingly, it was unwilling to guarantee the use of a sufficiently large number of Richmond songs to make the transaction attractive. Negotiations broke down on that issue. For Richmond, as for other publishers, policing was a problem directly related to the number of songs to be used: above a certain threshold, the cost of relicensing and policing might have become economically worthwhile. For Richmond, that threshold was not reached. Subsequently, Richmond contacted 3M's representative to express its interest in the 3M program, but because 3M wished to use only about 12 Richmond songs, negotiations again fell apart.

In addition to these publishers, 3M failed to conclude agreements with Robbins, Feist & Miller, Bregman, Vocco & Conn, and Frank Music. The first two publishers were the only ones whose reluctance to deal appears to have been motivated from a sense of devotion to ASCAP. Frank Music refused 3M's offer for the initial series of tapes because, like Richmond Brothers, it was concerned about the related problems of policing and the number of tapes to be used. However, it approached 3M to negotiate a license for the second series of tapes and agreement was reached.

We conclude, that, at best, the 3M incident does not favor CBS' case. The publishers which 3M contacted were offered varying proposals and responded as they thought appropriate to their respective legitimate business interests. Four fifths of them accepted the proposal, the remainder rejected it; and some rejected it the first time around but sought to be included in 3M's second series. The evidence contains no breath of parallel conduct. Those who had fears relating to the problem of relicensing and policing proved to be justified in their fears. Virtually all the publishers responded to 3M's unusual proposal as essentially a clean-cut business proposition; none of them refused entirely to negotiate with 3M. On such a record, no general inference of unwillingness to engage in direct dealing with 3M can be drawn. Even if it could be, it would be unwarranted to impute any such inference to the very different circumstances prevailing in the market for performance rights to music used on CBS.

2. The AGAC Ploy

CBS also stressed the role played by The American Guild of Authors & Composers (AGAC) in the 3M incident in voicing opposition to the issuance of direct licenses by their publishers. AGAC, which is not a party to this action, is a trade association of some 2,400 composers whose traditional concern has been the problems of composers in dealing with their publishers, such as the proper calculation of royalties. About 8% of the writer members of ASCAP and writer-affiliates of BMI are AGAC members. During its 45 year history AGAC has on occasion complained to publishers or to ASCAP and BMI that the interests of its members were not being protected. However, it has never brought suit against anyone; its principal technique appears to be the enthusiastic use of rhetoric.

AGAC's role in the 3M incident fits this general pattern. Although AGAC responded to the news that publishers had granted licenses to 3M in its typically vociferous way, the actions it took in opposition to the 3M program were untimely and ineffective. 3M started to negotiate with publishers in October, 1964, and by June of 1965 had already licensed the first series of tapes. It was not until November of 1965 that AGAC sent a form letter to publishers protesting that they had failed to secure writer consent for certain songs covered by AGAC contracts and suggesting that publishers refrain from licensing 3M. However, the AGAC letter clearly had no impact on 3M's efforts: it was circulated after licenses had been obtained for the first series, and after the eight publishers who declined the 3M proposal had told 3M of their decision. To this day 3M has continued to obtain licenses for its M—700 series directly from publishers. AGAC has not even attempted to lobby against the practice since 1966.

As CBS points out, a "radical" wing of AGAC which styled itself the West Coast Committee, criticized the AGAC Council for its mild-mannered response to the 3M project, and one of its strident letters appears to advocate a conspiracy by publishers to refuse to deal. However, the central AGAC Council in New York rejected the proposals on the advice of its lawyers.

In sum, CBS has seriously overreacted to the role of AGAC and the West Coast Committee in the 3M incident. Although there is testimony which supports CBS' view that the feelings of some writers run high when talk of direct licensing is in the air, the significant facts are that AGAC took no effective action against the 3M project and refused to adopt the suggestion of the West Coast Committee that radical action was appropriate. These facts, together with the evidence of AGAC's declining influence over the past ten years, and the strong desire of writers to gain exposure for their work do not support any inference that AGAC would or could take effective action against a direct licensing effort by CBS.

D. The "Music in the Can" Problem

1. The Significance of "Music in the Can"

Television programs or movies which have been filmed or taped are said to be "in the can." Music recorded on the soundtrack of such films or tapes is called "music in the can." At any given time, CBS has a large inventory of programs or feature films, much of which it will rerun over the network. CBS argues that if it cancelled its blanket license, the proprietors of compositions in the can, knowing that the music could not practicably be removed from the soundtrack, would exact premium prices for performance licenses: CBS would be forced to pay these premiums or risk infringement litigation.

CBS claims that by virtue of their leverage, copyright owners of music in the can could easily thwart any direct licensing attempt; and this fact accounts for the "business judgment of the [CBS] management that an attempted by-pass of ASCAP is not a realistic alternative . . . " (CBS Proposed Findings at 60–61). We disagree with CBS' analysis. Putting aside the fact, noted earlier, that CBS does not appear to have considered the feasibility of direct licensing prior to this suit, evidence of the ease or difficulty with which the antitrust laws may be violated cannot be equated to proof that the violation will occur.

Indeed, even if CBS had proven that some copyright owners would attempt to extract a premium price for their music in the can, that fact alone would not, absent proof of parallel conduct, tend to establish that defendants have violated the antitrust laws. At any point in the normal course of its business, CBS has a sizeable inventory whose make-up is continuously shifting from one season to the next as old programs and films are "retired" and new ones replace them. CBS obviously knew, when it accumulated its current inventory[19] that some form of performance license would ultimately be necessary for the second runs of the programs and films within it. These circumstances, however, do not result from the fact that CBS has continuously taken a blanket license, by "compulsion" or otherwise. To the contrary, they flow from the networks' practice of rerunning films and programs. Regardless what system of licensing CBS uses, its inventory would be vulnerable to "hold-ups" every time CBS puts music in the can without obtaining performance rights for future runs of the program in question. The fact that CBS has failed to secure such rights for reruns of the present inventory is hardly the defendants' fault. No defendant has ever refused CBS a license for any music in the can or out, if for no other reason than that CBS has never asked.

In sum, *any* changeover to direct licensing, even in a world of complaisant composers and publishers equipped with sturdy "machinery" may subject the CBS inventory to hold-ups by the greedy ones among them. However, simple greed, independently expressed, does not constitute a restraint of trade.

In any event, CBS has not proven that its fears of a "hold-up" by copyright proprietors are justified. CBS' principal witnesses in support of its "in the can" theory were its Vice President in charge of business affairs and planning, Donald Sipes, and its economist, Franklin Fisher. Neither of them has ever met a copyright proprietor, nor is either more than cursorily acquainted with the music licensing field. As was true of their testimony on "disinclination," the basis for their conclusion that copyright owners would "hold-up" CBS for rights to music in the can was that it would be economically rational for them to do so (see, e. g., Tr. 1686–87). Even taken alone this is not persuasive evidence, and it is clearly outweighed by the more concrete proof offered by defendants. For example, Albert Berman of the Harry Fox Agency testified that television producers often prepare programs without synchronization licenses and negotiate such licenses *after* the programs are in the can without being "held-up."

---

[19] We note in passing that CBS acquired most of its in the can inventory after the commencement of this action (AX 326).

"A . . . There is a certain confidence on the part of producers that they will not be held up by publishers when they want to use a song after the fact.

Q Do you have any opinion as to what the basis is for that confidence?

A The basis is that the users and providers of music have to live together. Nobody wants to lock himself up in a closet and not have them used. The producers are aware of that. It is a common interest that would prompt this type of action." (Tr. 981a–82)

Moreover, although we need not reiterate at length the basis of our earlier conclusion that no copyright proprietors would wish to fall into CBS' disfavor, the publishers who testified as to the "in the can" problem confirmed that view. Their statements on the point were highly persuasive. For example, Salvatore Chiantia of MCA Music, Inc. testified as follows:

"A . . . I believe the question here is whether a music publisher would take advantage—let us discard the term holding up—whether a music publisher would take advantage of a situation in which something has already been recorded and a license is subsequently sought.

There have been any number of occasions when that has arisen in the licensing of mechanical reproduction and in the licensing of motion pictures, theatrical motion pictures.

Very often, a theatrical motion picture will be made and the song recorded and the synchronization license is subsequently sought. In those cases, speaking for MCA, we have never held up anybody. We have never been unreasonable. We have licensed.

In the cases of mechanical reproductions, there are cases in which recording companies actually record a song before ever asking for a license. In those cases we would certainly hold them up if we wanted to, but we don't because it would be bad business practice.

There are some people in our business who make a habit of being unreasonable. There are a number of people. You mentioned Happy Birthday before. There is another very famous person with whom I have done a great deal of business, who lives in Paris, who makes my life miserable because she refuses to allow me to license under certain circumstances.

Well, those people are generally identified and people watch for them. Certainly in my business of being a music publisher I don't know of any company that has ever had to say, 'Watch out for Chiantia or MCA; they'll get you.'

We know that we are in this business and we intend to stay in this business and the way we stay in the business is by establishing some kind of a rapport and good will with our users and customers.

. . . .

We want the door to remain open for us and if you start holding up record companies or the people with whom you do business, you are in real trouble." (Tr. 2895–98)

Even assuming, contrary to the evidence, that some publishers would be drunk with power at having CBS on the spot, CBS has overstated the dimensions of the problem. Most of its inventory is comprised of theatrical motion pictures (i. e., movies), most of whose music is theme and background music controlled by the film producer's affiliated publishing company (PX 994, AX 287, BX 167). The "problem" of licensing this music is similar to the problem of licensing the "inside" theme and background music for CBS' regular television programming: it can be obtained from the producer itself. Of course, the producer *could* hold out for a large premium, but only on pain of losing large sales of his principal product, movies, to one of only three potential network buyers. It does not need to be repeated that the price of music performance rights is a tiny fraction of the price of a program or film.

Most of the remainder of CBS' in the can inventory is regular programming which is often rerun in the course of a season. As discussed earlier, most of CBS' serials use only theme and background music owned by an inside publisher. The factors just described as to movies in the can apply equally to other programs in the can.

Unfortunately, CBS has not offered evidence regarding the average life span of a given inventory of programs and films (or of categories of such programs and films), or the portion of the inventory which it actually intends to rerun. The absence of such evidence renders the "in the can" argument even less acceptable. For example, it may be that some television serials have a basic life of one year; if so, that portion of the inventory would be "consumed" during the inevitable interval between CBS' notice of termination of its blanket license and the date on which it actually commenced direct licensing for all its needs. For these programs, as well as the programs or films which CBS does not intend to rerun, there would be no "in the can" problem because there would be no need for performance licenses.

2. Commercials "in the Can"

CBS also claims that television commercials containing copyrighted music present a similar "in the can" problem. Advertising agencies do not ordinarily purchase performance licenses for the music they use. Instead they get a free ride on the networks' blanket licenses. Accordingly, CBS argues that if it cancelled its blanket license, a number of commercials "in the can" could not be used unless either the advertising agency or CBS paid the premium license fee which CBS feels sure would be exacted. The claim is without merit. Only a fraction of television commercials use music at all. (AX 263, AX 264) In those which do, the copyright proprietor is normally the advertiser on whose behalf the music was made. As Paul Marks, ASCAP's Director of Operations testified, "most of the commercials use music that is written directly for those commercials, [by an 'inside' composer] and in the overwhelming majority of cases, almost all the cases, the writer grants all rights to the sponsor or the advertising agency and makes no reservation of any rights to receive ASCAP distributions." (Tr. 2548) Of course, the sponsor or the advertising agency is the last person who might be expected to hold up CBS for licenses to use the music in its commercials.

A minimal number of commercials use previously published music for which CBS or the advertising agency would have to obtain a performance license from an "outside" publisher. For example, of the 1300 commercials created by the J. Walter Thompson Advertising Agency in 1972, only 21 used copyrighted music (AX 263, AX 264), or less than 2%. As to this miniscule percentage, it is worth repeating that few music publishers would hold up CBS or the world's largest advertising agency for a premium if they hoped to have their music used in preference to that of another publisher. Indeed, because commercials have a normal life span of six to eighteen months (Tr. 1873) CBS might well avoid any problem otherwise posed by "commercials" in the can simply by giving reasonable notice of the cancellation of its blanket license: most of the commercials in question would have run their short life before CBS commenced a direct licensing system.

X.

A Word About Per-Program Licenses

As outlined earlier, CBS concedes that it could license the music for most of its entertainment programs without difficulty by requiring the program packager to deliver performance rights together with the rest of the package. A substantial portion of CBS' other programming, such as news and public affairs programs, makes little or no use of previously published music. As to these two large categories, therefore, CBS could license the music used on an other-than-blanket basis. The programs which make by far the heaviest use of "outside" published music are weekly variety shows and variety specials, late-night talk shows, and the "Captain Kangaroo Show," which in the aggregate comprise a very small portion of CBS' program schedule. Assuming, contrary to the evidence, that the changeover to direct licensing would necessarily meet with mechanical problems until the "machinery" was properly oiled and adjusted, such problems would be acute only in relation to the few shows, such as variety shows, which regularly use music of outside publishers and are produced on short production schedules. For such shows, where speed and efficiency in clearing performance rights may be at a premium, a per-program license, which the consent decrees require ASCAP and BMI to offer, could be a logical alternative. Such a license gives the user unlimited access to the entire repertory, but requires him to pay only with respect to programs which actually use ASCAP (or BMI) music.

Although CBS has never sought to negotiate with ASCAP or BMI for a per-program license, it argues that such a license is not a feasible alternative. The argument is based on the assumption that the provisions of the per-program license negotiated between ASCAP and an All Industry Committee of owners of local television stations would be imported wholesale into any per-program license for network television use. (CBS Proposed Findings at 108–09) The local television license form provides that the station can avoid paying a per-program license fee for certain uses (e. g., motion pictures) only by obtaining direct licenses for all of the music contained in the program and by giving ASCAP seven days' notice of the direct license. CBS claims that such a license would not meet its needs because of the possibility that for a given variety program it might be successful in obtaining direct licenses for, say, only 90% of the music it needs, but would still need to purchase a per-program license at the full rate to cover the remaining 10%.

The argument overlooks several critical facts. CBS is of course not bound to agree to the terms of the local station per-program license, nor may ASCAP or BMI insist on any particular terms. To the contrary, they are required by the respective consent decrees to offer per-program licenses on terms which are justified by applicable business factors[20] and which give the user a genuine choice between it and other forms of license, such as the blanket license. Because CBS has never sought to negotiate a per-program license, there is no way to know what its terms might be. For example, there is no legal obstacle and no evidence of an unmanageable factual obstacle which would prevent it from bargaining for a license which gave it "credit" (i. e., a reduced rate) where it had obtained direct licenses for part of the music to be performed on the program in question. Indeed, because the decrees enjoin ASCAP and BMI from interfering with the direct licensing of compositions,[21] on the face of it, it would appear that CBS could argue in consent decree proceedings, if necessary, that ASCAP and BMI are required to offer a per-program license whose price is reduced to reflect the number of direct licenses obtained for the program. In view of these facts CBS' claim that the per-program license is not

---

[20] See notes 3 and 5, *supra*.

[21] See note 4, *supra*; CX 3.

suitable for its needs is, at best, premature. Indeed, because CBS makes heavy use of "outside" music on very few programs, there appears to be no reason why CBS could not feasibly turn to a combination of direct licenses, for shows using inside music or outside music of the one or two publishers; and per-program licenses, for those programs on which it makes heavy use of outside music.

XI.

Summary of Findings

On review of the record, we conclude that CBS has not met its burden of proving that defendants illegally restrain trade in the market for performance rights for network television use, and compel it to take a blanket license as alleged in the complaint. CBS has failed to prove that there are significant mechanical obstacles to direct licensing. Nor has it established by credible evidence that copyright owners would refuse to deal directly with CBS if it called upon them to do so. To the contrary, there is impressive proof that copyright proprietors would wait at CBS' door if it announced plans to drop its blanket license.

Even assuming, contrary to the evidence, that many publishers and writers would initially adopt a wait-and-see attitude under a direct licensing system, it is clear on this record that any resistance they might manifest would quickly dissolve, and that CBS could easily fill its music needs in the meantime. The music industry is highly fragmented. There are over 3,500 publishers and many thousands of composers who are eager for exposure of their music, and well aware that their compositions are, with rare exceptions, highly inter-changeable with others. In such circumstances, for direct licensing to fail CBS would have to be met with extraordinarily coherent resistance by publishers and composers. There is no basis in the record for the inference that such a coherent response is likely to occur.

We are left with the strong impression that CBS has exaggerated the risks involved in dropping its blanket license and sought a legal solution to what is essentially a business problem. The risks which CBS claims are posed by direct licensing realistically exist only if CBS ignores its own axioms about "reason-ably prudent" network managers (e.g., CBS Post-Trial Brief at 33, 36) and abruptly cancels its blanket license. There is little question that if CBS took such a course, its licensing efforts would produce temporary confusion and disarray. However, the taking of such a voluntary "risk" cannot itself act as a predicate for defendants' antitrust liability. Conversely, and more significant, CBS has considerable control over the degree of risk which a direct licensing attempt would involve. Assuming a reasonable period of preparation prior to the commencement of full-scale direct licensing, there are a number of steps

CBS could take to assure the success of its efforts, particularly given its leverage with program packagers and, by extensions, with their publishing subsidiaries. For example, prior to cancellation of its blanket license, CBS might negotiate with the producers of its programs and films using "inside" music to secure favorable prices for licenses for music "in the can," and for music contained in new programs to be shown in the upcoming season; it could build up a large reservoir of music by requiring program packagers affiliated with major publishers to make their catalogs available for direct licensing in accordance with a fee schedule; it could negotiate with independent publishers for either "mini-blanket" licenses covering their catalogs or direct licenses using a fee schedule; it could send notices to all publishers of its intention to seek direct licenses for compositions in their catalogs; it could negotiate a per-program license with ASCAP and BMI whose fee would reflect the amount of music actually performed and failing that, it could bring proceedings under the consent decree.

There is an astonishing lack of evidence that CBS considered such possibilities, or even the feasibility of direct licensing as a general proposition before commencing suit. The fact that it did not do so does not in itself defeat its claims, but it has rendered the nature of its proof at trial largely speculative. CBS' evidence was for the most part addressed to such abstract issues as "disinclination," and brought out through the generous use of hypothetical questions. However, it is proof of the threat of actual anticompetitive conduct, not possible "disinclination" which violates the antitrust laws. CBS might have obtained such proof by attempting to negotiate direct licenses. The proof which it chose to offer instead, as to the alleged fear or disinclination of copyright proprietors to engage in direct dealing, is not sufficient to establish an illegal restraint of trade. Such evidence does not prove that CBS needs, as it claims, the "signal" of a judgment in this suit to bring about a direct licensing system; it indicates rather that CBS has the power to give a clearly audible signal itself.

XII.

Conclusions of Law

As stated early in this opinion, the pre-trial order specified the following issues:

"(i) Whether defendants' conduct constitutes an actionable restraint of trade and compels the plaintiff as alleged in the complaint;

(ii) Whether, if such restraint or compulsion exists, it is reasonable and justified or whether it may be achieved by less anticompetitive means."

The conclusion which inescapably follows from the evidence outlined in the body of the opinion is that CBS has failed to establish that defendants' conduct constitutes an actionable restraint and compels CBS to take a blanket license. The complaint alleges that defendants' acts and practices in licensing performance rights for network use constitute several distinct violations of the antitrust laws. Because CBS has failed to prove the factual predicate of its claims—the non-availability of alternatives to the blanket license—the complaint must be dismissed. We detail our conclusions of law below.

1. The claim that members and affiliates of ASCAP and BMI have illegally combined to eliminate price competition among themselves must be dismissed because CBS has failed to prove that copyright proprietors would not compete with one another on a price basis if CBS sought direct licenses from them.

2. The claim that members and affiliates of ASCAP and BMI have combined to fix the price at which CBS must license performance rights by licensing those rights only in a package must be dismissed because CBS has failed to prove either that it purchased blanket licenses under compulsion or that the price it paid was fixed. To the contrary, the record establishes that CBS has always negotiated the price for its licenses with ASCAP and BMI.[22] Moreover, CBS has not established that the individual defendants are unwilling to sell performance rights on a direct licensing basis at a negotiated price for each license.

3. The claim that ASCAP and BMI have conditioned the licensing to CBS of music that it wishes to use upon the licensing of music it does not wish to use must be dismissed because CBS has failed to establish (a) that there were two separate and distinct "products" (i. e., groups of compositions, of which CBS wanted to purchase only one); (b) that CBS negotiated with ASCAP or BMI to license only the "wanted" compositions; and (c) that ASCAP and BMI refused to negotiate on that basis and had to coerce CBS to license the "unwanted" compositions as a condition of licensing the "wanted" compositions.[23]

---

[22] We note, moreover, that contrary to CBS' claim that the blanket license fee is unrelated to the extent of the networks' use of music, the only evidence on the point indicates that the extent of CBS' music usage has always been a significant factor in negotiations for the fee paid on renewals of CBS' blanket license. (Tr. 3611, 3870–72).

[23] In its post-trial reply brief CBS raises a new and somewhat puzzling variation of its claim that ASCAP and BMI are guilty of imposing unlawful tie-ins. CBS points out that ASCAP and BMI offer their members the services of monitoring and policing music uses and collection and distribution of royalties, and claims that neither organization offers such services to any user of music, such as CBS, "*unless* the user accepts a blanket license; and offers none to any member *unless* that members sells through the blanket license" (CBS Reply Brief at 14, emphasis in original). The claim is without merit. As to the first branch of the argument—that ASCAP and BMI condition the sale of their "auxiliary" services to CBS on its purchase of a blank license, CBS cannot have been the victim of a tie-in because it has never purchased such services; only

4. The claim that ASCAP members and BMI affiliates are guilty of a group boycott by forming the ASCAP and BMI music pools and authorizing their licensing agents to license only on terms that foreclose CBS from dealing directly with copyright owners must be dismissed because CBS has failed to prove that the licensing authority of ASCAP and BMI is limited to such terms, is exclusive in fact or that copyright owners have refused or would refuse to deal with CBS directly on an individual basis.

5. The claim that ASCAP members and BMI affiliates are guilty of copyright misuse must be dismissed because CBS has failed to establish that the members or affiliates of ASCAP or BMI have refused or would refuse to license their compositions on a direct licensing basis, or otherwise used their collective leverage to compel CBS to license rights to music which it did not wish to license.

6. The claim that defendants are guilty of monopolization, both attempted and achieved, must be dismissed. The offense of monopolization consists of two elements: possession of monopoly power in the relevant market and willful acquisition or maintenance of that power as distinct from growth as a consequence of a superior product or historical accident. *United States v. Grinnell Corp.*, 384 U.S. 563, 570–71, 86 S.Ct. 1698, 16 L.Ed.2d 778 (1966). Attempted monopolization is established by a showing of specific intent to monopolize with a "dangerous probability" of succeeding. *Lorain Journal Co.*

---

members and affiliates of ASCAP and BMI have done so. If CBS' claim is construed more charitably to be that ASCAP and BMI would refuse to sell such services to CBS (which CBS could use to induce copyright proprietors to engage in direct dealing) *unless* CBS also purchased a blanket license, the claim still fails as a matter of law: CBS has never sought to purchase "only" services, and there is no evidence that if it did so ASCAP and BMI would condition their sale on the purchase of a license CBS does not want.

The claim that ASCAP and BMI condition the sale to their members and affiliates of their services as licensing agents on their "purchase" (through administrative charges against royalty distributions) of auxiliary services such as monitoring is also without merit. CBS has no standing to assert such a claim because the member or affiliate, rather than CBS, is the alleged victim of the tie. Putting aside the conceptual difficulties presented by CBS' position, there is no evidence that ASCAP and BMI have refused or would refuse to monitor uses and collect royalties on behalf of members and affiliates who engaged in direct negotiations and wished to have the convenience which a central agency offers. To the contrary, there is every reason to believe that ASCAP and BMI would want to preserve this branch of their business even if they were forced to forego the issuance of blanket licenses. In addition, there is no evidence that if necessary copyright proprietors would not readily forego such services to have their compositions performed on CBS. Copyright proprietors certainly do not indispensably need ASCAP or BMI to perform the function of collecting their royalties; the producer using the music would simply remit payment to the proprietor, or to Harry Fox or a similar organization. Nor does it appear that however convenient the present arrangement may be, the producer is indispensably dependent on ASCAP and BMI to monitor possible infringements by a large television network which performs music before millions of viewers; certainly CBS cannot be expected to argue the contrary.

v. United States, 342 U.S. 143, 153, 72 S.Ct. 181, 96 L.Ed. 162 (1951); *Swift & Co. v. United States,* 196 U.S. 375, 396, 25 S.Ct. 276, 49 L.Ed. 518 (1905). CBS has failed to prove these elements.

To begin with, we disagree with CBS' argument that the relevant market is the market for BMI and ASCAP blanket licenses. The proposition is based on a factual premise which is rebutted by the evidence: that blanket licenses are the sole method for securing performance rights. Manifestly, ASCAP and BMI are not the sole source of the performance rights CBS needs; they are merely the sole source of the blanket licenses which CBS does not want. A market whose only product CBS does not want to purchase cannot by definition, be a relevant market, and the monopolization of a market in which CBS does not want to buy (and in which, of course, it need not buy) cannot injure it.

The relevant market is the market for performance rights to compositions suitable for television network use. The classic test for determining the relevant market in suits brought under § 2 of the Sherman Act is whether products are "reasonably interchangeable by consumers for the same purposes." *United States v. E. I. duPont de Nemours & Co.,* 351 U.S. 377, 395, 76 S.Ct. 994, 1007, 100 L.Ed. 1264 (1956). Products are said to be interchangeable when they can be used for the same purpose, and when a purchaser is willing to substitute one for the other. *United States v. Chas. Pfizer & Co.,* 246 F.Supp. 464, 468 (E.D.N.Y.1965, Mishler, J.). It is evident (indeed it is CBS' premise in this suit) that a bundle of direct licenses for network performances, acquired on an individual transaction basis, is interchangeable with a blanket license permitting the use of exactly the same music. Moreover, because the evidence establishes that musical compositions are fungible, a virtually unlimited number of *combinations* of compositions (i.e., bundles of licenses negotiated on a direct basis) sufficient for CBS' music needs would be readily interchangeable with a blanket license. Accordingly, the relevant market includes *all* sellers of performance licenses for network use, including ASCAP and BMI, as sellers of blanket licenses, and individual copyright proprietors, as sellers of "direct" licenses.

CBS has not proven that ASCAP or BMI possesses, or has attempted to achieve monopoly power in the market for performance rights for network use. In *United States v. Grinnell Corp., supra,* 384 U.S. at 571, 86 S.Ct. at 1704, and *United States v. E. I. duPont de Nemours & Co., supra,* 351 U.S. at 391, 76 S.Ct. at 1005, the court defined "monopoly power" as the "power to control prices or exclude competition." CBS has not established that ASCAP and BMI have power to control the prices in the market for performance licenses. We have found that copyright proprietors would deal readily on a price basis; certainly the record does not establish that ASCAP and BMI could effectively control the prices at which such transactions take place. Indeed, as noted earlier, the power of ASCAP and BMI to control the price even of their own blanket or per-program licenses is sharply curtailed under the decrees.

Nor does ASCAP or BMI have the power to exclude competition: there is a high degree of interchangeability among compositions, and performance rights to any given type of composition are available from a number of sources if CBS chooses to tap them. In addition to the choice of a blanket license or a per-program license from ASCAP or BMI for any given type of group of compositions, any composition (or combination of compositions) or its practical equivalent could be licensed from several individual copyright proprietors.

Finally, there is no substantial evidence that ASCAP and BMI have attempted to monopolize the market for performance rights for network use. Although at present they are the sole suppliers of CBS' music needs, such a state of affairs has resulted not from any violation of the antitrust laws but because CBS has, since the advent of television, found it convenient to secure a blanket license which, by definition, can be practicably obtained only through a collective licensing agent. The fact that CBS now wishes to change its long standing business practices does not, without more, convert defendants into monopolists.

CBS has failed to prove that any activities of ASCAP and BMI and their members and affiliates threaten it "with loss or damage by reason of any violation of the antitrust laws" within the meaning of § 16 of the Clayton Act. Even assuming, contrary to the evidence, that CBS has established the possibility of an impending violation on the part of some individual defendants, it has not established the threat of loss or damage sufficiently to warrant the grant of an injunction against the issuance of blanket licenses to any television network, or establishing its proposed "per-use" system.

The foregoing constitutes our findings of fact and conclusions of law. The complaint is dismissed.

It is so ordered.

"BROOKS' 'ENDEARMENT' WELCOME AT PAR—BUT AT STUDIO'S PRICE"
Variety (November 10, 1982), p. 48

Hollywood, Nov. 9.

Shirley MacLaine and Debra Winger have been cast as mother and daughter in Paramount's "Terms Of Endearment," a comedy-drama focusing on the evolution of feelings between the two characters over a 25-year period. Jim

Brooks, whose credits include the creation of such television programs as "The Mary Tyler Moore Show," "Lou Grant" and "Taxi" in addition to the screenplay for "Starting Over," wrote the script from Larry McMurtry's novel and will make his directing debut. Lensing begins in March on Texas locales with Brooks coproducing with Martin Jurow.

The development of this particular property under Brooks' hand for the last two and a half years is a good illustration of what it takes for even top talent nowadays to bring an "unusual" picture to the screen.

Interested in making a film on a mother-daughter relationship, Brooks was approached in 1980 by a woman who had the rights to a novel about a mother and daughter in Texas and the special understanding they maintain over the years as their lives take different directions. Brooks was particularly intrigued by the characters created by McMurtry (author of "The Last Picture Show," "Hud") since they were far different from the "urban N.Y.-L.A. types" he had drawn in his other television and film work.

Par's 'Faith'

Paramount, for whom Brooks was working on "Taxi," eventually picked up the option on the tear-jerker novel for him and put the picture into development. He then spent six months writing the first draft screenplay after three months of research. He claims to be especially grateful to the company for its faith in the project during that time since after the option was up it had to decide whether to buy the book before reading a word Brooks had written.

Paramount was, however, unswerving about how much it would spend to make a picture one studio exec complained was "the only film I can't compare to something else I've read" (Brooks jokingly expresses alarm that he might have been "original"). The company held firm to not giving him a penny more than a $7,500,000 budget despite the fact that MacLaine had already agreed to do it.

Shopping Around

That seemed fine to Brooks until his script was budgeted and it came to far more than $7,500,000. Rather than give up the additional locales and textures he felt were essential to make the story work, he starting shipping at other studios.

He finally settled at United Artists where it was agreed he would make the picture at the cost he felt necessary. However, when Freddie Fields took over MGM-UA production reins UA passed the picture and Brooks was back to square one.

Back To Par

That meant returning to Paramount, where president Michael Eisner had said the film was always welcome — for a $7,500,000 budget. Brooks eventually figured out a way to cut down some of the costs and managed to obtain an additional $500,000 in financing outside of Paramount. He claims to accept Par's reticence of refusing to spend the additional money as the way of life in the business in light of economics.

"I realize I have a responsibility to make money for them," he says. "I feel very lucky. I have an enormous amount of freedom to do the film I want — as long as I stay on budget."

Although he admits preferring the creative end to packaging a picture, Brooks claims to have been no less troubled in the writing of "Endearment" than he was figuring out a way to get it physically made.

Between his tv chores he would break away for weeks at a time to interview women in Texas in order to get a feeling for McMurtry's characters. He had introductions from an actress friend who came from a prominent family in Houston and a journalist friend who knew the area. It was from hours of interviews that he fashioned MacLaine's character of Aurora, the type of mother who on one hand would do anything to protect her child from danger, but would also think nothing of not attending her wedding because she felt the groom was the wrong choice. A flirtatious romantic, her daughter Emma, a salt of the earth young woman.

MacLaine's Diversity

After agonizing over the writing for six months ("there were times where I was convinced I'd never come up with a way to solve it") Brooks says he then spoke to almost every prominent actress over the age of 45 ("the survivors of the survivors") about playing the role of Aurora. He decided on MacLaine quite early, seeing the divergent nature of her film roles ("Children's Hour," "Some Came Running"), active nightclub career, success as an author and film producer (she and Claudia Weill made one of the first American documentaries shot on mainland China) as the right complexity of character from which to approach Aurora.

Although he says he spoke to and liked Winger from the beginning, she was not signed until recently. Though the women have not met, Brooks thinks each have displayed a similar fiery style in their careers that is almost like mother and daughter "across a generation of acting."

Because of the sensitive nature of the characters, Brooks was granted a month of rehearsal time starting in mid-February before he begins his 10-week shoot.

As a first-time director, he'll be working closely with coproducer Jurow (who produced "Breakfast At Tiffany's" and the first "Pink Panther" film in addition to at one time heading the N.Y. William Morris office and serving as assistant d.a. in Dallas) on ironing out any logistical problems.

Brooks, who never directed any of the tv shows he is famous for, notes he will try to stress the comedic elements in his script during filming despite the often serious nature of the subjects he deals with. While some might argue that has been known to result in the type of pictures studios can find difficult to sell, he dismisses it as being the only way to work.

"People are always trying to think of shortcuts on making the kind of films people want to see," he observed. "But that doesn't work. The answer is to do the film you really want to do and just try to be good at it."

"DESPITE 'OFFICER'S' $UCCESS, HACKFORD FINDS HIS NEXT PIC TURNED AROUND AT PAR TO COL"
Variety (May 11, 1983), p. 32

Hollywood, May 10.

Taylor Hackford's first picture since "An Officer and A Gentleman," an action-romance loosely based on the 1947 film noir "Out Of The Past," is now shooting for Columbia in Mexico on a $10,000,000 budget with "Gandhi" director-producer Richard Attenborough joining Jeff Bridges, Rachel Ward and James Woods in one of the lead roles.

Attenborough plays a powerful Century City attorney who becomes involved in the intrigue surrounding the three principles. Love triangle between Bridges, Ward and Woods is set against a power struggle in contemporary L.A.

Although Hackford's "Officer" has grossed $124,000,000 at the domestic boxoffice, getting his followup picture off the ground was not as easy as one might expect. While common trade belief is that such a huge success automatically makes a director bankable, at least on his next project, Hackford's new picture (still untitled) was last month actually put into turnaround by Paramount — the studio for which he made "Officer."

Hackford, however, claims to bear no ill will for Paramount. He sees his situation as symptomatic of the way the film business functions.

"It's a myth that after a success like 'Officer' that you can do anything you want to," Hackford said from an office at Columbia. "What it does do is that it gets people to more easily give me money to develop ideas. But if I have a difficult subject that doesn't fall into traditional packaging concepts, I'll have trouble."

Par Turned It Around

The director first brought the project to Paramount, which put it into development after Hackford had scored some attention from his first feature, United Artists' "The Idolmaker." But at the same time Paramount was even more anxious to find a director for "Officer" in order for it to commence lensing before the threatened Directors Guild of America strike. Hackford signed on for "Officer" and meanwhile handed the "Out Of The Past" project to screenwriter Eric Hughes to pen, utilizing some of Hackford's ideas.

During "Officer"'s editing and marketing a script was realized and Hackford went on to raise half of the projected budget from independent financiers. Having come up with the idea and part of the money. Hackford said he also wanted to produce and eventually came to an understanding with Paramount to acquire the film domestically as a negative pickup.

Those plans went awry, said Hackford, when his financing fell through and Paramount declined to fully bankroll the picture. However, the next day he had a meeting with Col Pix prez Guy McElwaine who was interested in taking on the project with Col fully financing and retaining all rights. Hackford agreed, though he is still producer. William S. Gillmore, experienced line producer and former production exec with Zanuck-Brown serves as coproducer. Jerry Bick, who owned the rights to the 1947 pic, is exec producer.

Unusual Backdrops

Project is currently in the midst of shooting in Mexico for three weeks followed by eight weeks in L.A. Plan is to film the more romantic portions in several sacred Mayan ruins in Mexico and use L.A. locales for the more gritty, action-oriented segments of the story. Hackford says he's spent a great deal of time scouting unusual L.A. areas to film on that have not been used before.

Original film, directed by Jacques Tourneur and written by Dan Mainwaring based on his novel "Build My Gallows High," focused on gangster Kirk Douglas and his lover Jane Greer involving Robert Mitchum (who used to work for Douglas) in a series of unsavory occurrences. The new script casts Jeff Bridges as an ex-pro football player attracted to beautiful, rich Ward with Woods as a nightclub owner. Greer is also scheduled to play a role in the new picture.

Unlike his other two efforts, Hackford has final cut this time out. However, he cautions that the privelege is not as "final" as it sounds, since "you don't do your editing off in a corner without considering the people you're doing it for. You want them to like the movie so they'll want to enthusiastically market it."

The director credits Par Pictures prez Frank Mancuso with the substantial success of "Officer," since it was his idea to move its release to the summer and heavily screen it before it was brought before the public. Hackford's previous film, "Idolmaker" had been released by UA during the time the studio was spending substantial coin on "Heaven's Gate" and never had a solid campaign. The UA experience caused him to take a more active interest in "Officer" 's launch which carried over to his enthusiasm in placing his new project with Columbia.

Col's Marketing Savvy

"As a filmmaker you can work one and a half years on a picture and then in a week, with a bad campaign, it's gone," opined Hackford. "One of the reasons I felt comfortable at Columbia, aside from the creative freedom they were giving me, was their ingenuity at marketing. You want to be with people who know what they're doing."

While shooting this film, Hackford is developing another script at Columbia with Dustin Hoffman, "The Glory Boys." Although he claims that since "Officer" he has been offered numerous projects to direct for large amounts of money he has refused those offers in favor of working on his own material.

"The business is at a tough time and one has to probe oneself over and over again, despite success, what to do next. I think, because no one knows what people will go to see, that as a filmmaker you just have to hold to your own vision."

Supplemental Reading

U.S. v. Columbia Pictures Industries, Inc., 507 F. Supp. 412 (S.D.N.Y. 1980) (joint venturers preliminarily enjoined under the antitrust laws from establishing a pay television network where four of the five venturers were major motion picture companies).

U.S. v. Shubert, 348 U.S. 222 (1955) (federal antitrust law found applicable to producing, booking, and presenting legitimate theatre attractions on a multistate basis).

Allied Artists Picture Corp. v. Rhodes, 679 F.2d 656 (6th Cir. 1982) (state statutory provisions establishing a trade screening requirement and competitive bidding guidelines did not abridge free speech, nor violate copyright and antitrust laws).

General Cinema Corp. v. Buena Vista Distribution Co., 532 F. Supp. 1244 (C. D. Cal. 1982) ("split" arrangements by which participating theatre owners divided films for subsequent exhibition constituted *per se* antitrust violation).

Home Box Office, Inc. v. Directors Guild of America, Inc., 83 F.R.D. 423 (S.D.N.Y. 1979) (summary disposition denied in declaratory judgment action seeking to restrain Directors Guild of America from preventing HBO from negotiating directly with free-lance directors).

Buffalo Broadcasting Corp. v. ASCAP, 546 F. Supp. 274 (S.D.N.Y. 1982) ("blanket licensing" of music performance rights held an unreasonable restraint of trade in connection with non-network television).

CBS v. ASCAP, 562 F.2d 130 (2d Cir. 1977) ("blanket licensing" of music performance rights to television networks held a *per se* antitrust violation); *rev'g*, 400 F. Supp. 737 (S.D.N.Y. 1975); *rev'd sub nom.*, *BMI v. CBS*, 441 U.S. 1 (1979) ("blanket licensing" of music performance rights to network television not a *per se* antitrust violation; case remanded for review under rule of reason test); *on remand*, 620 F.2d 930 (2d Cir. 1980) ("blanket licensing" of music performance rights to networks not an antitrust violation under rule of reason test); *cert. denied*, 450 U.S. 470 (1981).

1 T. Selz & M. Simensky, *Entertainment Law* §§ 1.01–5.08 (1983).

Conant, "The Paramount Decrees Reconsidered," 44 *Law & Contemp. Probs.* No. 4, 79 (1981).

Note, "Blind Bidding and the Motion Picture Industry," 92 *Harv. L. Rev.* 1128 (1979).

Comment, "*CBS v. ASCAP*: Blanket Licensing and the Unresolved Conflict between Copyright and Antitrust Law," 13 *Conn. L. Rev.* 465 (1981).

Sobel, "CBS Tests its Clout: Network Asks Producers to Get "Direct" Music Performance Licenses from Composers and Publishers," 5 *Ent. L. Rep.* 4 (1983).

Note, "Labor Pains, Movies and the Antitrust Blues," 20 *U.C.L.A. L. Rev.* 142 (1972).

CHAPTER 2

ARTISTIC CONTROL

Introduction

One of the fundamental differences between the entertainment industry and other business enterprises is the creative nature of the manufacturing process. The creative process necessarily raises the question of who has control over decisions relating to the appearance and content of the final product. This chapter analyzes the conflicting interests involved in disputes over creative control.

In addition, industry practices involving creative controls are introduced and discussed. These practices reflect certain assumptions about who has ultimate artistic control. An attorney must understand these assumptions in order to be able to suggest contractual provisions to alter them, if appropriate, or to confirm and reinforce them in order to avoid future disagreements. Limitations on artistic control, from both a contractual and a practical point of view, are also examined.

Lastly, this chapter surveys the types of remedies available to the creator of an entertainment project if there is injury resulting from an exercise of artistic control to the creator's detriment.

Required Reading

C. Gerald Fraser, "TV Film Stirs Fight," *The New York Times* (July 13, 1978), p. C20.

Dale Pollock, "Dustin Hoffman Persists In Suit On 'Creative Control'; Spurns FAP's Olive Branch," *Variety* (July 19, 1978), pp. 4, 30.

"First Film Editor Ever As Speaker Deplores All That 'Auteur' Palaver," *Variety* (March 5, 1980), p. 40.

"Walter Hill Disowns 'Warriors,' Goldman Defends Necessary Cuts," *Variety* (October 1, 1980), p. 39.

Steven Ginsberg, "Richard Pryor's $40–Mil Col Pact For Cash and Clout," *Variety* (May 25, 1983), pp. 1, 86.

147

William Wolf, "High Noon for Directors," *New York Magazine* (December 29, 1980), pp. 50–51.

Preminger v. Columbia Pictures Corporation, 49 Misc. 2d 363, 267 N.Y.S.2d 594 (Sup. Ct. N.Y. Co.), *aff'd* 25 A.D.2d 830, 269 N.Y.S.2d 913 (1st Dept. 1966).

John J. O'Connor, "When Films Go Under the Knife," *The New York Times* (July 16, 1978), pp. 2, 26.

Seroff v. Simon & Schuster, Inc., 162 N.Y.S.2d 770 (Sup. Ct. N.Y. Co. 1957).

Gilliam v. American Broadcasting Companies, Inc., 538 F.2d 14 (2d Cir. 1976).

Sinatra v. Goodyear Tire and Rubber Co., 435 F.2d 711 (9th Cir. 1970).

Kirk Honeycutt, "Whose Film Is It Anyway?" *American Film* (May, 1981), pp. 34–36, 38–39, 70–71.

Kirk Honeycutt, "Getting Credit: The Scenario," *American Film* (May, 1981), pp. 38–39.

In the Matter of the Arbitration Between Directors Guild of America, Inc. and King-Hitzig Productions, No. 00892, as reported in 2 *Entertainment Law Reporter* 24 (May 15, 1981), p. 1.

"California Art Preservation Act," California Civil Code § 987 (West Supp. 1984).

"Artists' Authorship Rights Act," New York General Business Law §§ 228 m–q (McKinney 1983).

All contracts and union agreements referred to in the chapter "Concepts."

CONCEPTS

1. What is "artistic control"?

2. What are the conflicting interests in disputes over artistic control? Consider the following articles:
    — *The New York Times*: 7/13/78 (p. 150)

    — *Variety:* 7/19/78 (p. 151); 3/5/80 (p.153); 10/1/80 (p. 154); 5/11/83 (p. 143); 5/25/83 (p. 155)

    — *New York Magazine*: week of 12/29/80 (p. 157)

3. *Preminger v. Columbia* (p. 160); *The New York Times* article of 7/16/78 (p. 172)

    (A) What do the case and article indicate about industry practice?

(B) What and how much of Preminger's film was cut for TV exhibition?

(C) What would have happened in *Preminger* if key scenes had been cut or interrupted to meet time requirements?

(D) In *Preminger*, what was the importance of plaintiff's prior contracts?

(E) What do the *Preminger* case and *Variety* articles: 7/19/78 and 10/1/80 (pp. 151, 154) suggest about limits of final cut without specific contractual language to the contrary? What problems does *The New York Times* article: 7/16/78 (p. 172) suggest even if Contractual language is favorable?

4. *Seroff v. Simon & Schuster* (p. 174)

(A) What does Parag. 83(a) of Book Publishing Agreement (p. 874) indicate about artistic control in book publishing industry?

(B) What does *Seroff* indicate about limits in practice of author's artistic control?

    (1) How does this practice compare with the situation in the movie branch of the industry?

    (2) What do these practical limits suggest about a negotiating concern when dealing with artistic control?

(C) What harm does Seroff claim he has suffered?

    (1) What does *Gilliam v. ABC* (p. 181) suggest about a cause of action for *Seroff*?

    (2) Are the claims in *Gilliam* and *Preminger* similar? How do you account for the different results?

    (3) Is the *Gilliam* claim similar to the claim by Sinatra in *Sinatra v. Goodyear* (p. 193)?

    (4) What accounts for the different outcomes of *Gilliam* and *Sinatra*? What are the issues at stake? Why are the parties in litigation?

(D) What do *Preminger* and *Seroff* indicate about the role of contracts when dealing with artistic control?

(E) What is the role of union agreements? Compare the *American Film* article of 5/81 (p. 201), and the *Wolfen* decision (p. 212).

5. What do Parags. 78(b), 83 and 84 of Book Publishing Agreement (pp. 872, 874–875) indicate about reasons for not publishing a book?

(A) Why are advances repayable under Parags. 78(b) and 83(a), but not under 83(b) or 84?

(B) Compare these provisions with Minimum Basic Production Contract, Parag. SIXTH (a) (p. 716); Screenplay Loanout Agreement, Parags. 1.3, 9 (pp. 670, 677); Record Agreement, Parags. 4(a) and (b) (p. 799); and Network Television Agreement, Parag. 3(a) (p. 687).

(1)   Who has artistic control in each branch?

(2)   Why is this different in different branches of the industry?

(3)   How useful is such control to a record producer, TV network, film producer?

(4)   What does this suggest about the nature of artistic control?

(5)   At what stage does artistic control become meaningful?

6. What does *Variety* article: 5/11/83 (p. 143) suggest about possible limits on the exercise of artistic control from creator's viewpoint?

7. Do the "California Art Preservation Act" (p. 214) and the New York "Artists' Authorship Rights Act" (p. 217) have any application to the entertainment industry?

(A)   What are the significant differences between the two Acts?

(B)   How might the injunctive dangers under the Acts be avoided?

C. Gerald Fraser, "TV FILM STIRS FIGHT"
The New York Times (July 13, 1978), p. C20

A documentary film about blacks in Britain is the subject of a dispute between WGBH, a public-television station in Boston, and David Koff, the film's producer and director.

The issue, both sides agree, is to whom the film belongs: the station, which paid $160,000 to the producer to make the film, or the film maker, whose creativity and expertise the finished product represents.

The film is called "Blacks Britannica." It is a 57-minute presentation of the problems faced by blacks—Afro-West Indians, Africans, Indians and Pakistanis—who live in Britain. Said to number about 1.7 million, 3 percent of the British population, most of them arrived in Britain after World War II.

"Blacks Britannica" is scheduled to be broadcast Aug. 10 in Boston unless Mr. Koff succeeds in legally blocking the broadcast.

A significant portion of the film is devoted to relations between the British police and British blacks and the impact of the economic situation on the black population.

Mr. Koff is an independent film maker from California. The film's associate producer was Musindo Mwinyipembe, a Tanzanian-born woman who has lived in Britain since she was 6 years old, except for a couple of years she spent in the United States when she worked for "Black Journal," a Public Broadcasting Service series.

WGBH "wanted to make some changes," Mr. Koff said, "to make the message of the film clearer to an American audience. We are disputing their right to do that."

The film is to be shown on WGBH-TV as part of a series called, "World: Pictures From a Small Planet."

At issue, Louis Wiley, a producer on the "World" series, said is the arrangement of the film. He said that the basic problem is that historical materials are placed "midway in the film." WGBH officials felt, Mr. Wiley said, that "in order for Americans to know whom the film is about, who were these people, where did they come from, what was the basic problem," the historical matter needed to be brought up to the front of the film.

Dale Pollock, "DUSTIN HOFFMAN PERSISTS IN SUIT ON 'CREATIVE CONTROL'; SPURNS FAP's OLIVE BRANCH"
Variety (July 19, 1978), p. 4

Hollywood, July 18.

Despite denial of his request for a preliminary injunction to halt the release of "Agatha," actor Dustin Hoffman will press ahead with his civil suit against First Artists Productions and Warner Bros., seeking both several million dollars in damages and the termination of both firms' distribution rights to both "Agatha" and "Straight Time" due to an alleged "material breach of contract."

Behind the legal maneuverings between Hoffman's own Sweetwall Productions, First Artists and WB stands the key question of creative control and final cut of a picture. On the one side is an actor who traded his upfront salary for "creative and artistic control" on two pix; arrayed against him are two studios who allege he consistently spent too much time and money on the films, violating his contract and necessitating their stepping in to finish the pictures.

In the meantime, First Artists reports that post-production on "Agatha" has resumed in England, although declining to say who is supervising the scoring, editing and looping that is reportedly being done on the pic. "Agatha" is being readied for a fall release, possibly in October or November, after grinding to a standstill following the filing of Hoffman's suit last February.

"Straight Time," of course, was released this year to generally weak boxoffice response by Warner Bros. The denied injunction applied only to "Agatha,": Hoffman's civil suit will bring "Straight Time" into the courts, too. In the way of background, Hoffman joined other First Artists principals Paul Newman, Sidney Poitier, Barbra Streisand and Steve McQueen in September, 1972. Contrary to popular assumption, however, Hoffman never became a principal himself, failing to exercise various stock options which have since expired, according to First Artists attorney Robert Mirisch. His association with the production company was only for a two-picture agreement, although he did have the right to designate a member of the board of directors of FAP.

That designee was Hoffman's former business associate, Jarvis Astaire, whom Hoffman subsequently sued, along with FAP and WB, in February. Jarvis then filed a $3,500,000 countersuit in May, alleging Hoffman failed to pay him commissions on several business deals.

The 'If'

In the complaint filed with his lawsuit, Hoffman noticed his FAP deal called for him to sacrifice his "usual cash compensation" in exchange for creative and artistic control, including final cut. Only means by which these rights could be forfeited would be if costs of production got out of control during lensing.

FAP attorney Ted Olson said that was what the company was trying to prove in court, alleging the final "Agatha" budget of $3,041,000 was exceeded by $500,000 or more, well above what Olson says the contract specified as a 15% cost overrun. He also alleges the 49-day production schedule had stretched to 72 days by the time FAP took over the production, again over the 15% leeway specified in the contract.

"Contractual provisions such as these are standard," said Olson. "We presented evidence that demonstrated these are not unreasonable provisions. When it's apparent that production is out of control, there has to be some remedy."

Company's Logic

"The company (FAP) felt strongly," Olson continued, "in view of the experiences with 'Straight Time' that something had to be done. The string can be stretched only so far, then it has to snap."

While noting his client will not appeal the denial of the preliminary injunction, Hoffman's attorney, Bertram Fields, said the recent decision doesn't resolve the basic issue in the case, that of creative control, and the economic damages result when that right is taken away. "It's hard to quantify what will happen if a picture isn't well cut," said Fields, "but we feel in the case of 'Straight Time,' it's several million dollars."

Noting that Hoffman has had no participation on either picture since February, Fields said, "Our contention is by taking over the pictures improperly, First Artists and WB committed a major breach of contract. One of the remedies is termination of their distribution rights."

Admitting that the case may not go to trial until early 1979, Fields admitted the distribution question may be moot by that time. First Artists sources said they don't expect the case to end up in court for at least three or four years.

"But this absolutely terminates Mr. Hoffman's relationship with First Artists, and we remain confident we'll get substantial damages out of the civil action. This is an important case in the sense that it will establish the ease with which studios can take away creative rights once they're given.

"Studios have an enormous amount of economic power," Fields opined. "If you don't stand up and fight, you lose your rights. Mr. Hoffman is standing up and fighting."

FAP, for its part, is still holding out the olive branch, and requesting Hoffman's "participation" in the final stages of post-production work on "Agatha." Said FAP counsel Olson, "We've got nothing but sarcastic letters back. We're continuing to make those offers."

But Fields said there were conditions attached, claiming FAP said in essence, "You can come in and express your opinions, but we don't guarantee we'll listen."

"FIRST FILM EDITOR EVER AS SPEAKER DEPLORES ALL THAT 'AUTEUR' PALAVER"
Variety (March 5, 1980), p. 40

Chicago, March 4.

Railing against the notion that the director is the sole creator of a feature film, Ralph Rosenblum told the Midwest Film Conference here that the contributions of film editors are often ignored or misunderstood although many films are salvaged in the cutting room—"while the director paces the corridor outside chewing fingernails."

As among the best-known editors in the film industry—and author of the recently published "When the Shooting Stops and the Cutting Begins"— Rosenblum's appearance here was singular since he's the first editor ever to address the 12-year-old Conference.

Echoing many of the points stated in his book, Rosenblum crisply set forth his thesis that filmmaking is a "real democratic art" and the editor is a key member of a film's creative team.

Rosenblum discussed, with the aide of clips nicely used, his work on "The Night They Raided Minsky's," a film he worked on (and salvaged) for 11 months: Woody Allen's "Annie Hall" (he's done six Allen films over 10 years); "A Thousand Clowns" and on "Goodbye, Columbus."

The job of the film editor, he said, is "to make everybody involved in a film look wonderful—and then cover your tracks."

Invitation To Suicide

Rosenblum was most informative about first cuts of pics, the first formal assemblage of completed footage after production. "The first cut reveals all the problems of a film, and most filmmakers get suicidal when they see their first cut on the screen."

Of the 35 pics he's worked on, said Rosenblum, all have gone through "massive" editing after the first cut. "No film is ever released after the first cut." And, he said, directors aren't often around when the editing is done.

So much for the auteur theory?

"WALTER HILL DISOWNS 'WARRIORS,' GOLDMAN DEFENDS NECESSARY CUTS"
Variety (October 1, 1980), p. 39

Paris, Sept. 30.

In an open letter to French filmgoers, director Walter Hill disowned as his work the version of "The Warriors" that is currently playing here in a cut print.

CIC sheared off a total of 10 minutes as part of its campaign to free pic of the "X" for violence rating that had been slapped on it last year by the French review board.

Hill's letter, dated Sept. 3, appeared in French last week in L'Express news weekly. The text reads:

"Filmgoers of France:

The cuts made by the censor on "The Warriors" force me to reject all authorship of the version currently being shown in Paris.

I don't wish to make a special plea for my motion picture. I simply wish to add my name to the long list that believes what can happen to one film can happen to all films; that believes when one freedom is abridged all freedoms are endangered; that believes censorship is an insult to the dignity of the individual and an insult to the idea of democracy.—*Walter Hill.*"

Responding to Hill's letter, CIC head Daniel Goldman told *Variety* that he felt he had done the right thing in trimming certain scenes of the film in order to get it re-appraised by the review board. "If I spent over a year fighting for the film," he said "it's because I love it and think it would be a shame if it were not seen here. I don't believe the light cuts we made harm the film."

The cutting of the pic was harshly derided by some local critics who had seen the complete version last year at the Deauville Film Festival.

Particularly abridged by CIC were the early scenes depicting the gathering of N.Y.C. street gangs in the Bronx, and the call to rise up and take over the city. Some later sequences involving the "Warriors" battle with their antagonists were also edited.

Pic opened here August 27 and has been doing good boxoffice. It has totalled 119,060 entries in its first three weeks in Paris alone, and there have been no incidents reported as result of pic's subject matter.

Steven Ginsberg, "RICHARD PRYOR'S $40-MIL COL PACT FOR CASH & CLOUT"
Variety (May 25, 1983), p. 1

Hollywood, May 24.

Richard Pryor has entered into a five-year arrangement with Columbia Pictures that will make him one of the highest-paid and creatively independent entertainers in the film industry.

Pryor's deal with the studio gives him in excess of $40,000,000 over five years to support a new film production entity, Pryor Company, that will make four $5–6,000,00 budgeted pictures in which Pryor would produce but not necessarily star. As long as Pryor stays within budget limitations of those pics, he is said to have absolute creative control over all aspects of the projects he brings in.

In addition, Pryor has committed to star in a minimum of three Columbia features over the next five years where insiders say his average upfront salary will be $5,000,000 per picture. He will also receive a hefty percentage of the distributor's gross on each picture which will increase in relation to the rentals take.

Pryor's attorneys have been negotiating the deal with Columbia Pictures chairman Frank Price and prez Guy McElwaine (Pryor's onetime agent) for the last six months.

The overall agreement gives Pryor the opportunity to variously function as actor, producer, writer and director on his own films. He has for instance, spent the last month writing his own original screenplay (rumored to be about a comedian) which he may possibly direct.

In terms of acting, Pryor has an Oct. 1 start date to star in the title role in Col's "The Charlie Parker Story." The script based on the late jazz saxophonist, which has been in development for the last year and a half, has been written by Joel Oliansky with Pryor in mind and contributing ideas. Pic will be exec produced by William Sackheim in association with the Pryor Company (but it will not be one of Pryor's own four pics). Pryor will also get producer's credit.

Spring Plans

In the spring of 1984, Pryor is scheduled to costar with Gene Wilder in "Double Whoopee," a comedy written by Wilder, based on an idea from Pryor. Pic will be the first reteaming of the duo since the 1979 Col boxoffice hit, "Stir Crazy."

Also on tap for the comedian is "The Man Who Would Work Miracles," which is being done in association with Mace Neufeld Prods. and producer Roger Lewis. Michael Leeson, who penned Col's upcoming "The Survivors," is in the final stages of the screenplay.

As for his own company, Pryor's longtime friend, former football star and actor, Jim Brown, is coming aboard as president. Topper Carew, who is now coproducing Universal's "D.C. Cab," will serve as production vice-president—a slot that will basically see him handling line producing chores on all of the films.

The Pryor Company will officially headquarter at The Burbank Studios June 1 in a large suite of offices. Firm's development fund is termed "substantial," and is part of the $40,000,000 five-year package (which also includes pic budgets, overhead, salaries, etc.).

Pryor's overall commitment to Columbia is expected to amount to a minimum of one picture a year he stars in and another he produces, according to Colpix prez McElwaine. But even with all of that activity the deal still leaves Pryor the option of doing a film for another studio as an actor ·if he desires (and has time).

Longterm Blueprint

"We wouldn't ask Richard to put himself in the position to have to say no to a film he wants to do," McElwaine claimed. "We think of this as a longterm marriage where he has the opportunity to truly express his creativity. It's everything he has always wanted to do."

Indeed, the only real restrictions of the production deal are on the budgets of Pryor Co. pics. McElwaine says that as long as Pryor approached him with a film that meets the budget requirements he is free to make "anything he wants." Contractually, Col cannot turn him down. If there is a project that would require more money, then he is in a position of getting Col's approval. The entity is also free to develop any properties it sees fit, McElwaine added.

Though the Pryor deal is certainly one of the most lucrative in recent years, it is not terribly surprising considering the success he has had recently in films. Even Pryor films that have proved not to live up to creative expectations, have generated some significant degree of boxoffice power based on the comedian's name. His films over the last five years have included Col-Rastar's "The Toy" and "Richard Pryor Live On The Sunset Strip," as well as Par's "Some Kind Of Hero," Universal's "Bustin' Loose" and Col's "Stir Crazy."

William Wolf, "HIGH NOON FOR DIRECTORS"
New York Magazine
(December 29, 1980), p. 50

". . . *A tug-of-war has always existed between the studio bankrolling a film and the director. What should the balance be? . . .* "

"*Heaven's Gate* is merely the culmination of a series of over-budget fiascos that have already wrought a dramatic change," insists a high-level studio executive who prefers anonymity. "Control by the director is over—it's the end of that game. A readjustment has been taking place for the last six months."

Alan Ladd, former Twentieth Century-Fox production head, who now has his own company, doubts that the current furor will result in lasting changes, although he says it is too early to tell. He recalls the uproar in the late 1960s over costly bombs like *Star* and *Paint Your Wagon*. Low budgets were in, but only for a while.

My own belief is that the backlash will be tempered and temporary. Contracts will be tightened, and producers will dig in to avoid more Cimino-style debacles. But the nature of filmmaking is such that the money men can't make good films without the creative talent (and often with it), and the recent excesses are as much the result of producer incompetence as of *auteur* hubris.

But what should be the balance of control between the studio or independent producer bankrolling a film and the director in pursuit of artistic freedom? A tug-of-war has always existed. Long before *Heaven's Gate*, producer Ray Stark boasted to me of his riposte to an agent who had demanded the right of final cut for his director client: "Tell him that he can have final cut—at his circumcision." Understandably, a director like Robert Altman fears that *Heaven's Gate* "will now provide the excuse for the studios to say that the artists have had their day."

But in posing the issue of producer-director balance to various people involved in the filmmaking process, I found that differences are not as extensive or polarized as one might have expected; the realities necessitate a spirit of cooperation, which makes more sense than a producer-director Donnybrook.

For example, Woody Allen acknowledges directorial obligations while upholding directorial prerogatives: "It seems to me that there has to be mutual responsibility. The director agrees to work for a certain budget, and as long as he sticks to the budget, allowing for a few reasonable misjudgments, then it's imperative that he have 100 percent absolute, total control of the creation of the film. Once the studio agrees to go ahead on a project, whether it's budgeted at $1 million or $50 million, control of every phase of creation must be the director's. It's wrong to think that outside input is any more valid on a more expensive picture than on a less expensive one. The point for the studio is not to agree to the deal unless it has complete confidence in the director."

Writer Neil Simon places the onus for keeping a film within bounds on the studios. "Any sum in excess of $30-million should be spent on building a hospital, not making a movie—unless you're Francis Coppola, who I would trust with a hospital *and* a movie. At least the man had the courage to back his convictions with his own money. The heads of the studios are completely responsible for the indulgences now being practiced by filmmakers. They are quite capable of budgeting a film based on a script they are given. If they initially budget a film at $11 million and it balloons to $35 million, they deserve what they get for not pulling the plug.

"The rules haven't changed since the Greeks invented theater—the play's the thing. Start with a good solid story and script and there's no reason any film should run over to the extent we've seen in recent years—and if it does, the money would have been better spent on the hospital, since that's where most of the indulgent studio executives will end up anyway."

Producer Dino De Laurentiis, who is prone to high budgets (*Ragtime*, $25-million; *Flash Gordon*, $30 million; *King Kong*, $25 million), sees the matter of control as twofold—the contractual and the practical. "By contract I never give anyone artistic control, not even Bergman or Fellini. [He did give final cut to Altman on *Buffalo Bill and the Indians*.] But in practice I give Bergman and Fellini 100 percent artistic control. What's the point of making a film with them, or any other great director, if you don't leave them alone? With *Ragtime*, why have a brilliant director like Milos Forman if I don't rely upon him? [Altman, originally set to do *Ragtime*, was fired for refusing to cut *Buffalo Bill*.]

"There's something else that's important. The time to decide on the budget is when you read the script. I know if the budget is correct or not, allowing for being off about 10 percent. Fellini came to me with *Casanova* and said it would cost $4 million. I said, 'Federico, it will cost $8 million to $10 million.' I refused the film and was right. A picture like *Casanova* shouldn't cost that much, because it's hard to sell." Unlike Neil Simon, De Laurentiis contends that many studio executives don't know how to read a script for budget. "In my opinion, that was the problem with Cimino's picture."

Producers and directors with whom I talked frequently used phrases like "mutual respect" and "give-and-take." Robert Altman's image is that of an individualist who makes films to suit himself. But he says that while he has had final cut on a few films, it isn't usual. "I didn't have final cut on *Popeye*. There was no reason to expect it, as there were too many elements involved." He speaks warmly of his collaboration with producer Robert Evans, who in turn lays claim to extensive input and says that working with Altman was "the best collaboration I've ever had with a director."

Producer Lester Persky (*Hair, Yanks*) says the element of control also depends on who initiated the picture—the director or producer. He adds, "Although producers shouldn't exercise day-to-day control of the shooting, when a film begins to go over budget, a producer owes it to himself, the director, and the people financing the film to do something. But the worst thing would be if we went back to close studio supervision." About to begin *Lone Star* with Altman as director, Persky notes, "It's budgeted under $6 million; no wonder United Artists loves it."

Given the costly nature of filmmaking ($10 million is now considered the norm), directors cannot be totally free. No matter how much creative control is allowed them, there will be strictures dictated by budget. And should a new Cimino, Spielberg, Friedkin, Landis, or even a Kubrick acquire unusual clout as a result of extraordinary success or critical acclaim, one or two flops could do him in. And, allowing for inflation, on the next go-around you'll gasp at how anyone in a position of responsibility could allow a film to cost $75 million or $100 million.

Short of using his own money, a director's best guarantee of maximum freedom is to make films for modest budgets and avoid getting caught up in the mad, talent-corrupting Hollywood escalation syndrome. Playing that kind of Russian roulette can end in loss of integrity as well as loss of control.

PREMINGER v. COLUMBIA PICTURES CORPORATION
49 Misc. 2d 363, 267 N.Y.S.2d 594 (Sup. Ct. N.Y. Co. 1966)

ARTHUR G. KLEIN, Justice.

The interesting question presented for decision is the right of a producer, in the absence of specific contractual provision, to prevent, by injunction, minor cuts in his motion picture when shown on television and the usual breaks for commercials.

The litigation involves the production of the motion picture "Anatomy of a Murder".

The complaint alleges that plaintiff Preminger is a producer and director of motion pictures, including the motion picture involved; and plaintiff Carlyle Productions, Inc., a California corporation, was the owner of all rights to the picture, and Carlyle Productions, a limited New York partnership, its assignee; that Carlyle Productions, Inc. entered into a series of agreements with Columbia Pictures Corporation between 1956 and 1959, which are collectively referred to as the contract, copies of which are annexed to the complaint.

Defendant Columbia and defendant Screen Gems, Inc., its subsidiary, the complaint continues, have licensed over 100 television stations to exhibit the motion picture on television, and those license agreements purport to give the licensees the right to cut, to eliminate portions of the picture, and to interrupt the remainder of the picture for commercials and other extraneous matter.

Unless enjoined, the complaint asserts, defendants will

a)   detract from the artistic merit of "Anatomy of a Murder";

b)   damage Preminger's reputation;

c)   cheapen and tend to destroy "Anatomy"'s commercial value;

d)   injure plaintiffs in the conduct of their business;

e)   falsely represent to the public that the film shown is Preminger's film.

It is then alleged, and not denied, that "Anatomy" is one of a very few motion pictures with a rating of AA–1; that it has been licensed in blocks of 60–300 pictures; and that the others are artistically and commercially inferior to "Anatomy".

. . . .

Thus, the only question before the Court in this proceeding is the plaintiffs' right to a permanent injunction.

I

The plaintiffs plant themselves upon Article VIII of the contract, which provides:

> "You [Carlyle] shall have the right to make the final cutting and editing of the Picture, but you shall in good faith consider recommendations and suggestions with respect thereto made by us [Columbia]; nevertheless, you shall have final approval thereof, provided however that notwithstanding the foregoing, in the event that cutting or re-editing is required in order to meet censorship requirements and you shall fail or refuse to comply therewith, then we shall have the right to cut and edit the Picture in order to meet censorship requirements without obligation on our part to challenge the validity of any rule, order, regulation or requirement of any national, state or local censorship authority."

The import of the paragraph is that plaintiffs have the right to make the final "cutting and editing" of the picture; giving the defendants the right to make suggestions, only.

This article must be read, however, in juxtaposition with Article X of the contract, which provides as follows:

> "The rights herein granted, without limiting the generality of the foregoing, shall include and embrace all so-called 'theatrical' as well as 'non-theatrical' rights in the Picture (as those terms are commonly understood in the motion picture industry); and shall include the right to use film of any and all gauges. You hereby give and grant to us throughout the entire world the exclusive and irrevocable right during the term herein specified to project, exhibit, reproduce, transmit and perform, and authorize and license others to project, exhibit, reproduce, transmit and perform, the picture and prints thereof by television, and in any other manner, and by any other means, method or device whatsoever,

whether mechanical, electrical or otherwise, and whether now known or hereafter conceived or created."

This Article, it will be noted, which contains the specific grant of television rights, makes no reference to "cutting and editing."

In these circumstances the Court is inclined to the view that the right to the "final" cutting and editing, reserved to the plaintiffs, is limited to the original or theatrical production of the picture and not to showings on television; and that as to such showings, in the absence of specific contractual provision, the parties will be deemed to have adopted the custom prevailing in the trade or industry.

This view is confirmed by the authorities and fortified by the evidence.

II

We begin with the proposition that the law is not so rigid, even in the absence of contract, as to leave a party without protection against publication of a garbled version of his work. This, as pointed out by Frank, J., concurring in Granz v. Harris, 198 F.2d 585, at 589 (2 Cir., 1952) is not novel doctrine.

The Court "appreciates that the failure of the community . . . to protect their gifted men of letters led to tragedies which comprise scars in the history of civilization." Geller, J., in Seroff v. Simon & Schuster, 6 Misc.2d 383, 386–387, 162 N.Y.S.2d 770, 774 (N.Y.Co. 1957), affd. 12 A.D.2d 475, 210 N.Y.S.2d 479 (1st Dept.1960).

And in Granz, supra, the United States Court of Appeals for the Second Circuit held that publication of a truncated version of plaintiffs' phonograph recording should be enjoined. 198 F.2d 585, at 587–588.

In the case at bar, however, the contract must serve as a guide to the intention of the parties.

A

Thus, where the parties have particularized the terms of a contract, an apparently inconsistent general statement to a different effect must yield. Therefore, the clause in this contract, general in its terms, giving plaintiffs the right to "finally" cut and edit as to the original production of the motion picture, must yield to the specific clause with respect to television showing, which contained no such right.

B

So it is, too, that in the construction of a contract, weight will be given to the custom prevailing in the trade to which it refers.

This brings us to a review of the evidence, on which, of course, the burden of proof rests on the plaintiffs.

C

At the trial, extensive testimony was presented by both sides with respect to the normal customs prevailing in the television and motion picture industries as to the significance of the right to "final cut".

A review of the testimony demonstrates that, at least for the past fifteen years, the right to interrupt the exhibition of a motion picture on television for commercial announcements and to make minor deletions to accommodate time segment requirements or to excise those portions which might be deemed, for various reasons, objectionable, has consistently been considered a normal and essential part of the exhibition of motion pictures on television.

Implicit in the grant of television rights is the privilege to cut and edit.

D

No proof has been adduced that this cutting and editing would be done in such a manner as to interfere with the picture's story line.

The licensing agreements provide:

> "Licensee shall telecast each print, as delivered by Distributor, in its entirety. However, Licensee may make such minor cuts or elimination as are necessary to conform to time segment requirements or to the orders of any duly authorized public censorship authority and may add commercial material at the places and of the lengths indicated by Distributor, but under no circumstances shall Licensee delete the copyright notice or the credits incorporated in the pictures as delivered by the Distributor, provided, however, in no event may the insertion of any commercial material adversely affect the artistic or pictorial quality of the picture or materially interfere with its continuity. . . . "

Defendants' witnesses, Lacey of WCBS, Howard of WNBC and Gilbert of WABC, testified with respect to the practices customarily prevailing throughout the television industry. Plaintiffs' witnesses did not controvert the testimony concerning the customary practices in the trade with regard to interruptions for commercials, and minor cuts. As a matter of fact, Sherwin, one of plaintiffs' witnesses, the program director of KHJ, Los Angeles, testified, as had defendants' witnesses, that his station had never purchased any motion picture without the right to make interruptions as well as minor cuts. Whether or not, in an isolated instance, a picture was exhibited with less than the customary number of commercials is not determinative of the issue. We are concerned not with what might have happened in some rare instance but instead with what was the common practice and custom at the time the parties herein signed their contract.

Thus, Villante, a vice president of the Batten, Barton, Durstine & Osborn advertising agency, described a program known as the "Schaefer Award Theatre" which is handled by his advertising agency. This is a late show program in which feature films are shown without cuts, and with only four interruptions for commercial announcements. Villante acknowledged repeatedly that the Schaefer program was unique. In one instance, he stated, a picture called "The Nun Story" was shown on this same program without any interruptions for commercials whatsoever. He further testified that the purpose of deviating from usual industry practice in the case of this one program was not out of any concern for the rights of the producer, but rather as a public relations device to contribute to the public image of the Schaefer Company, and pursuant to agreement with said sponsor.

With respect to the expression "final cut", sufficient testimony was adduced to indicate that this phrase, as used in Article VIII of the contract, relates only to a phase in the production of the picture for theatrical showing and has no relation to the interruptions and minor cuts here under discussion. Even plaintiffs' own witnesses identified the "final cutting and editing" of a picture as the last stage in its production *for theatrical exhibition.* (emphasis supplied)

III

Although plaintiffs consistently refer to the practice of interrupting and making minor cuts as "mutilation", their own witnesses have conceded that the minor cuts customarily made in a television exhibition of a picture have such a minimal impact upon its overall effect that these are rarely even noticed.

Undisputed is the fact that not a single television station has ever failed to insist upon the right to interrupt for commercials. Similarly unrefuted is defendants' proof to the effect that no station ever purchased a motion picture without reserving to itself the right to interrupt for commercials and to make minor cuts.

IV

Plaintiff Preminger admitted that when he signed the agreement for "Anatomy of a Murder", he was aware that the practice of the television industry was to interrupt motion pictures for commercials and to make minor cuts. Aware of this practice, plaintiffs at the time the instant contract was signed nevertheless did not specifically provide for conditions other than those known to them to be prevalent in the industry.

Two contracts between Preminger and United Artists Corporation were received in evidence. These were contracts pertaining to "Man With a Golden Arm" and "The Moon Is Blue", the last two pictures produced by Preminger prior to "Anatomy of a Murder", which he made for Columbia. In both the contract for "The Moon Is Blue" and the contract for "Man With a Golden Arm", clauses appeared which demonstrate that Preminger was aware of the prevailing practice in the television industry with respect to interrupting motion pictures for commercials and making minor cuts therein for normal television purposes. These contracts further show that when Preminger desired to prevent television distribution in the normal manner, he so provided.

In the contract between the Carlyle corporation and United Artists Corporation, dated December 20, 1954, for "Man With The Golden Arm", it was expressly provided that United Artists' right "to make such changes, additions, alterations, cuts, interpolations and eliminations as may be required for the distribution of the picture in television" should be subject to the approval of Producer.

In similar fashion, the contract with United Artists Corporation with respect to "The Moon Is Blue", dated April 28, 1952, provided that United Artists' right "to make such changes, additions, alterations, cuts, interpolations, and eliminations as may be required for the distribution of the picture in television" should be "subject to the approval of Producer or its sales representative".

Both Preminger and United Artists were aware that granting the producer this right of approval was tantamount to giving him a veto power over ultimate television distribution of the film, for in other provisions of both of the above contracts it was expressly recognized that television distribution was not to take place without the producer's prior approval.

Plaintiffs' entry into the instant contract which failed to contain such a clause may be considered by the Court as evidence of the parties' intention.

V

Should a viewer resent the fact that the film is interrupted too often for commercials, and assuredly many do, this resentment would be directed at the station or the sponsor of the program. It is difficult to conceive how such resentment would be directed at the film's producer or director.

So standardized has the practice of interrupting films for commercials become, that guidelines have been established in the television industry as to the maximum number of commercials regarded as acceptable in a given time period.

VI

The television industry serves a great public need and its services have ofttimes, and perhaps at some financial sacrifice, been offered in the public interest. Despite such apparent unselfish public service, it should not be overlooked that the industry, like every other business, has as its primary objective the accumulation of profits. Sponsorship of programs, by advertisers, provides a station with its only source of revenue and though it ofttimes interrupts its programs with what some viewers feel to be an inordinate amount of advertising, since its primary purpose is to advertise the products of its sponsors, such interruptions in the absence of governmental or industry regulation can only be controlled by contractual arrangement.

It is of no import that some viewers may not approve of the advertising practices prevalent in the industry—that is, the number and types of commercials. However, the parties to this distribution agreement signed it knowing of the existence of such practices. The plaintiffs, as well as any independent producer or director, could have obviated this problem by specifically prohibiting such cuts or interruptions by contract. This, of course, might have had an adverse effect on the extent of television distribution—an eventuality which most producers would not welcome. Accordingly, in the absence of any contractual provision to the contrary, they must be deemed to have contemplated that what was permissible, under the existing practice, would continue in effect.

VII

The criterion for the determination of what the defendants were likely to do with respect to interrupting and cutting the subject film, in the absence of a specific contractual arrangement, was not what plaintiffs might disapprove of or dislike but, rather, what was the normal custom and practice in the industry.

The issues in the case, in the Court's view, are therefore issues of law: i. e. (1) whether plaintiffs may thwart the making of minor cuts or interpolations in the absence of specific contractual provision; the Court finds the answer to this question to be in the negative; and (2) whether, under this contract, in the light of the custom in the trade, plaintiffs left to the stationmasters the right to use their judgment and exercise their discretion, instead of plaintiffs', as to which minor cuts, eliminations, and interpolations are appropriate. In view of the variety of stations, localities, audiences, and commercials, the Court answers this question in the affirmative.

The running time of the full motion picture is 161 minutes. The brochure for WABC–TV advertised the picture to potential sponsors as a 100-minute feature. The stationmaster, however, testified, and the Court credits his testimony, that this was a mistake; that it was never intended to permit any such extensive cutting. This applies as well to the asserted cutting of the picture to 53 minutes. Obviously such cuts would not be minor and indeed could well be described as mutilation. Should such "mutilation" occur in the future, plaintiffs may make application to this Court for injunctive or other relief against such violation as they may be advised. Autry v. Republic Productions, supra, 213 F.2d 667, at 669: ["[W]e can conceive that some such cutting and editing could result in emasculating the motion pictures so that they would no longer contain substantially the same motion and dynamic and dramatic qualities which it was the purpose of the [artist] . . . to produce"]; Granz v. Harris, supra, 198 F.2d 585.

CONCLUSION

On this record, the Court holds that plaintiffs have not sustained their burden of establishing their right to injunctive relief.

To the extent, therefore, that the complaint seeks an injunction, it is dismissed; but without prejudice, as heretofore indicated.

. . . .

PREMINGER v. COLUMBIA PICTURES CORPORATION
25 A.D.2d 830, 269 N.Y.S.2d 913 (1st Dept. 1966)

PER CURIAM.

Judgment affirmed with $50 costs and disbursements to the respondents.

All concur except BENJAMIN J. RABIN. J., who dissents and votes to reverse in an opinion.

BENJAMIN J. RABIN, Justice (dissenting):

The Trial Court, at the outset of its opinion, purporting to state the "question for decision" stated as follows:

"The interesting question presented for decision is the right of a producer, in the absence of specific contractual provision, to prevent, by injunction, minor cuts in his motion picture when shown on television and the usual breaks for commercials."

Unfortunately, that statement does not present the "question" to be decided. It in effect states the Court's conclusion. Whether there is an "absence of specific contractual provision" is the basic question to be decided and it may not be taken as a premise.

It is because I believe that there is a "contractual provision", reserving to the plaintiffs (producers) and to the plaintiffs alone, the right to make any cuts in the motion picture involved, that I dissent. Moreover, the question presented does not involve the right to make only "minor cuts" in the motion picture. It is the assertion by the defendants (distributors) of the right to authorize unrestricted cuts—not merely "minor cuts"—that is put in issue by this lawsuit. The refusal to grant the injunction sought by the plaintiffs permits any television stationmaster, at will, to cut this picture down to the nebulous point, which the Trial Court calls "mutilation". It is also because I believe that such cutting is exactly what the contract seeks to guard against, that I dissent.

So let us start at the beginning rather than at the end. Is there a contractual provision with respect to cuts when the picture is shown on television?

The defendants are not the owners of the picture to do with it as they will. Ownership still lies with the plaintiffs. The defendants have only those rights—broad as they may be—as are given to them by the contract, subject, however, to whatever limitations the contract contains. Generally, the rights granted to defendants are the rights of distribution and exhibition, and those rights are contained in the main in Article 10 of the contract. The limitation with which we are chiefly concerned is contained in Article 8. In that article "the right to make the final cutting and editing of the picture" is reserved to the producer. That the distributor does not have the right to cut, or authorize cuts, in this picture, is conclusively demonstrated by the single exception contained in the same article which allows the distributor to cut or re-edit the picture, but only when it "is required . . . to meet censorship requirements and you [producer] shall fail or refuse to comply therewith." That article is as plain as plain can be. It states in simple language that with the single exception referred to, the distributor has no right to cut the picture, but that such right is reserved exclusively to the owner. We note what the Trial Court said in its opinion:

> "The import of the paragraph is that plaintiffs have the right to make the final 'cutting and editing' of the picture; giving the defendants the right to make suggestions, only."

How can it then be said that there is an "absence of specific contractual provision" preventing cuts in the motion picture by anybody but the producer when the picture is shown on television? To arrive at that conclusion the Court directs us to Article 10 of the contract which it says must be read in juxtaposition with Article 8. Of course, these two paragraphs must be read together. But how does Article 10 lead us to the conclusion reached by the Court "that the right to the 'final' cutting and editing, reserved to the plaintiffs, is limited to the original or theatrical production of the picture and not to showings on television . . . "? The answer advanced by the Court is that "This Article [10], it will be noted, which contains the specific grant of television rights, makes no reference to 'cutting and editing.' " It should also be noted that the same Article 10 contains "the specific grant" of theatrical rights without making "reference to cutting or editing." And yet, that the defendants have no right to cut when the picture is exhibited as a theatrical production is not only conceded but found by the Court. There is no distinction appearing in Article 10—or for that matter elsewhere in the contract—between the rights granted to the distributor for television and those granted for theatrical production. To be sure, Article 10 must be read together with Article 8. Reading them together we must find that the reservation of cutting rights in the producer, found in Article 8, applies to television production, as well as theatrical—Article 10 making no distinction between the two.

How then can cutting rights be found in the distributor in television production when, concededly, there are no such rights in theatrical production? The Trial Court relies on "custom prevailing in the trade and industry." It recognizes, however, that only in the "absence of specific contractual provision" may we consider custom. But here we do have a contractual provision and, consequently, there is no room for proof of custom contrary to such provision. While perhaps proof of custom may be availed of to explain the meaning of the words "cutting and re-editing"—although I think those words are plain enough—there certainly can be no allowance of testimony with respect to who should do the cutting or re-editing. The contract speaks clearly on that point—and that is the chief point in controversy. Custom, therefore, may not be used as a foundation for a finding that the distributors have a right to cut this picture at will in the face of the specific provision in the contract to the contrary.

However, testimony by an expert witness—of dubious qualification—was admitted in an attempt to prove a prevailing custom with respect to cutting in television production. But that witness did not testify that there is any custom prevailing where the parties have a contractual provision, such as we have here. Whatever the custom of the trade may be in other circumstances, it is of no force here, where the parties made their own provision with respect to the cutting rights.

The defendants introduced two agreements signed by the plaintiff Preminger with the United Artists prior to the signing of the contract in suit as "cogent evidence of Preminger's awareness of trade usage at the time." Examination of those two contracts proves an awareness by Preminger but one quite different than the one the plaintiffs try to show.

At the outset, it should be noted that the contracts referred to are contracts on printed forms. The paragraph on which the defendants rely is paragraph 19. The printed form, before interlineations were made, expressly gave to the distributor the right to make cuts in television productions. The language is as follows:

"United shall also have the right to make such changes, additions, alterations, cuts, interpolations and eliminations as may be required . . . for the distribution of the Picture in television . . . ."

If by custom, a distributor had the right to make television cuts, why the necessity to set forth expressly such rights in these form contracts? Paragraph 19 clearly indicates that it was on contract and not on custom that the distributors relied to make television cuts. The contracts being on printed forms indicate that they were in general or frequent use, pointing to a general recognition for the necessity of a specific grant to permit television cutting.

However, the defendants point to the interlineation of the words "subject to the approval of producer or its sales representatives", saying that such interlineation really makes the clause one forbidding cutting in television and conclude that not having inserted a similar clause in the contract here involved, Preminger must be deemed to have agreed to cutting rights in the distributor. The defendants arrive at the wrong conclusion. Not wishing to give the distributors unqualified rights of television cutting the producer inserted the interlined words to make the printed form conform to his wishes. Leaving that clause out of the contract in suit does not justify a conclusion that by doing so the producer did give the distributor the right to make television cuts. There was no point in including the clause of grant and then nullifying it by interlining words of withdrawal.

Leaving paragraph 19 out of the contract in issue is a clear indication that the producer did not wish to give the distributor any cutting rights whatsoever—not even the limited one contained in paragraph 19. Besides, leaving paragraph 19 out of the present contract did not leave a void with respect to cutting rights. Article 8, reserving to the producer all cutting rights without limitation, is in place and stead of paragraph 19. The United Artists' contract and this contract indicate that the producer was of one purpose—to retain cutting rights exclusively in himself, even with respect to television production. That purpose was clearly indicated in the United Artists' contract, which expressly reserved the right of approval in proposed television cutting in the producer and in this contract, which reserves to the producer all rights of cutting. The United Artists' contract is "cogent evidence of Preminger's awareness"—an awareness of the necessity of protecting himself by withholding from the distributors the right to cut the film in theatrical and television production alike.

Now let us apply the defendants' reasoning conversely. It appears that in a great percentage of Columbia contracts, where the distribution grants are given Columbia in words almost identical with those of Article 10 of this contract, there appears a clause specifically reserving to Columbia the following:

"the right in our sole discretion to cut, recut, edit, re-edit, and reassemble the Picture or any part or parts thereof . . . ".

Shall we not say that the failure of Columbia to insert a similar clause in this contract points to no right in Columbia to make the cuts as it usually reserved for itself in other contracts? Perhaps we could and perhaps we should.

In support of the defendants' position they point to that portion of article ten giving them the right to

"distribute and otherwise . . . deal in or with the Picture and all rights therein of every kind and nature, and prints or any part thereof . . . ".

They seize upon the words "or any part thereof" and seem to tangentially argue that these words give to the distributor the right to make cuts in television productions. Of course, the clause quoted and the words indicated apply to theatrical as well as television productions, there being no distinction made between the two. If the defendants be correct in their conclusion with respect to television, then they must take the same view with respect to theatrical productions. That they do not do and cannot do because it would make the reservation of cutting rights in the producer, appearing in article 8, absolutely meaningless. Therefore, they expressly claim no right in the distributor to cut theatrical productions despite the words "or any part thereof."

Reading article 10, together with article 8, as we are told we must, the only meaning we can gather from those words is that the producer parts not only with the right to exhibit or distribute the whole picture, but also parts with the right to exhibit or distribute any part thereof in the event the picture should be cut in the manner permitted by Article 8, i. e., by the producer. In other words, no right to exhibit or distribute remains in the producer with respect to the picture—not even in part. Reading the clause in that manner puts it in harmony with the rest of the contract and not at odds with it, as would appear if we would construe it as the defendants would have us do.

We must conclude that there is no way of finding a right in the distributor to cut or authorize cuts in the picture when it is exhibited on television, unless we write such a provision into the contract. That, the parties failed to do and apparently the producer refused to do, and, that the court may not do— particularly when the contract speaks so clearly against such a right.

The distributors not having such right, they should be enjoined from exercising any such claimed right.

Giving the plaintiffs the right to subsequently apply for an injunction in the event that there should be "mutilation" of the picture in the future, gives the plaintiffs no rights they did not always have quite apart from those reserved to them by the contract. To allow any one of the 103 television stationmasters to whom these defendants purport to have given the right to cut and delete parts of this picture at will to a point short of "mutilation" in order to meet their station requirements is to deprive the producer not only of his contract rights but also of his common law right to have the picture shown as he produced it. Particularly so when the contract requires that Preminger be identified as the producer and distributor in every exhibition of the picture. The exhibition of a garbled version under Preminger's name should by all means be enjoined (Granz v. Harris, 198 F.2d 585 (2d Cir. 1952).

In addition, the plaintiffs seek to prohibit the uncontrolled interruption of the exhibition of the picture for commercials. The producer made no provision in the contract for protection in that respect, as he did in connection with cutting. Nevertheless, it is conceivable that unlimited interruptions for commercials might tend to permit of a mutilated presentation of the picture to the detriment of the common law rights of the producer. Perhaps then the plaintiffs are entitled to some relief in that respect. The Court concluded that commercials have become so "standardized . . . that guidelines have been established in the television industry as to the maximum number of commercials regarded as acceptable in a given time period." However, those guidelines are just guidelines and do not give the plaintiffs adequate protection because they may be followed or disregarded by exhibitors at will. I appreciate the difficulty in fashioning proper relief, but difficulty in doing so does not justify the failure to give any relief. Accordingly, I would remand this phase of the case for the Court to make such provision as may be deemed sufficient to assure against interruptions by commercials to the extent that they would destroy the picture.

. . . .

John J. O'Connor, "WHEN FILMS GO UNDER THE KNIFE"
The New York Times (July 16, 1978), p. 2, 26

Trapped in the arrogance of television tampering, when is enough enough? For Robert Radnitz the moment of detonation came a few weeks ago after watching a two-part presentation of his "Where the Lilies Bloom" on CBS. Phoning this writer from his California office, Mr. Radnitz said he found his movie "butchered" and the result was "horrendous." In fact, I have not seen Mr. Radnitz's film, either intact or chopped up, but his cry of outrage is shockingly familiar to anyone in contact with the broadcasting industry.

When it comes to films, of the theatrical-release or the made-for-TV variety, the public very rarely sees what it thinks it is seeing. The more blatant examples can be found at the level of the local stations that rely heavily on old movies to fill schedule holes. Over the years, the movies have been snipped into differing specifications for a variety of programming needs. Today, many are almost unrecognizable, with not only whole scenes but whole sections deleted. Often only the skeleton remains, and even that might be missing an arm or a leg. My sharp-eyed and indefatigable colleague Howard Thompson, who writes the thumbnail reviews that appear in The Times' television listings, regularly downgrades presentations on a particular station because generally the films have been cut to the point of being meaningless.

Such mutilation, of course, merely reflects a total contempt for content. And that attitude reaches up into network levels. Some productions receive special care for the sake of a dollop of prestige or an occasional award, but the norm, the mediocre norm, is considered primarily as filler between money-making commercials. Just about everything is reduced to a "property" to be tinkered with mindlessly by executives who are essentially salesmen. In the made-for-TV genre, the process usually begins in the formative stages. Good, serious books are acquired for dramatizing and are subsequently mangled by people who get paid for coming up with trite ideas. There are hundreds of examples, but I shall single out only two: productions based on Doris Lund's "Eric" and on Barbara Mahoney's "A Sensitive, Passionate Man."

The dramatization of "Eric" was heralded in the promotional advertisements as "a true story." It then offered John Savage in the role of a young man dying of leukemia. The story was set somewhere around Seattle, and Eric was taking special treatment at a rather small local hospital. He kept his good looks to the end, and, of course, Mr. Savage was afforded several opportunities for romantic shots on waterside locations. The book, however, the "true story," was somewhat different. Mrs. Lund and her son Eric lived in New England. He was being treated at New York's Sloan-Kettering Memorial. He went to the city's singles bars until his physical condition deteriorated dramatically. There was little of the television "Eric" that had anything to do with the true story of the book.

In "A Sensitive, Passionate Man," a wife's harrowing and touching story of her alcoholic husband was turned into a slick vehicle for Angie Dickinson and David Janssen. Once again, there was a startling change in the setting. Mrs. Mahoney's true story, which for some reason was described in press releases for the TV dramatization as a novel, took place in Manhattan and the Hamptons. The TV movie shifted the locale to some nondescript, vaguely elegant slab of suburbia. More importantly, Mrs. Mahoney's tale of intense love and hate, compassion and resentment, confusion and fierce clarity was transformed into a tidy melodrama in which the color of Miss Dickinson's party-dress seemed as important as the pathos of alcoholism. Why did television acquire these two books? Perhaps it's cheaper than creating a story from scratch. Perhaps such works bring a built-in reading audience with them. Or, more likely, the practice has more to do with avarice and cynicism, with the conviction that everything is buyable and, once brought, nothing is sacred.

With theatrical-release films, the situation becomes slightly more complicated, largely because equally avaricious and cynical film studios are now in comfortable league with televisionland. On the one hand, in order to compete with television, the movie people offer their public products that contain more explicit sex and language. On the other, a sale to television for future presentation can be extremely profitable. The solution is devilishly simple. On major productions, two separate sound tracks are now regularly produced, one sprinkled with four-letter words for the sophisticates who stand in line for a hit, the other cleaned-up for television. On top of this, particular scenes might be shot twice—sexy and more sexy (which are also used for European distribution). So, for instance, the theatrically released "Saturday Night Fever," which has enough street-language to keep George Carlin in comedy routines for a year, will doubtlessly show up on television, for an astronomical price, in a state of sanitized acceptability. The TV presentation will cash in on the film's immense success at the box office, but the TV audience will be getting a significantly different product.

That is the well-taken point of Mr. Radnitz's complaint. This was the second time "Where the Lilies Bloom" had been telecast on CBS. Suddenly, it was being split in half for showings on successive Tuesdays and, Mr. Radnitz charges, cuts were made throughout the film. He was never called by anyone at the network for consultation. Noting that his other films were "Sounder" for the theaters and "Mary White" for television, Mr. Radnitz explains that his style is slow-paced, that "if my films work at all, they work visually." Cuts, therefore, are nearly always disruptive. Meanwhile, he notes, this second showing of "Where the Lilies Bloom" had been recommended in advance by many critics who assumed that the film was being repeated in its original form. But CBS's tinkering, according to Mr. Radnitz, made the critics' recommendations ridiculous. Mr. Radnitz is succinct: "The creator is being misused. The public is hoodwinked. There is a public trust here, and television has got to be called to task about it." Yes, it does—and has been, frequently. But little is likely to change until the industry is forced to realize that content is at least as important as selling soap. Until then, arrogance and ignorance will be facts of television life.

SEROFF v. SIMON & SCHUSTER, INC.
162 N.Y.S.2d 770 (Sup. Ct. N.Y. Co. 1957)

GELLER, Acting Supreme Court Justice.

This is an action in tort in the nature of libel brought by Victor Seroff, author of the biography "Rachmaninoff", against Simon & Schuster, Inc., his publisher, for damage allegedly done to his reputation as an author resulting from a distorted French translation of his book.

While there are authorities, as indicated herein, regarding the rights of an author in connection with alleged distortion in a domestic publication, neither counsel has cited nor has the court's independent research disclosed any authority dealing with the subject of a publisher's obligation and liability as to distortions in a foreign translation of a work previously published in a satisfactory domestic form.

In 1948, several years after the death of Sergei Rachmaninoff, Simon & Schuster commissioned Seroff, an author specializing in biographies of famous musicians, to write a book about the celebrated pianist-composer. The parties entered into a standard publishing contract, which provides:

"The Author Agrees:

"(a) to grant and hereby does grant, bargain, sell, convey, transfer, and set over unto the said Simon & Schuster, Inc., the sole and exclusive right to publish, print and put on the market the said work . . . in book form in the United States of America and in Canada, during the full term of copyright and all renewals thereof, and also grants to the Publisher the further rights hereinafter set forth:"

The contract as to the further rights, also states the following:

"additional rights . . . consist of all abridgement, translation, . . . and other publication and editorial rights . . . . All revenue derived from the sale of these rights shall be shared equally between the Author and the Publisher, . . . "

The book was published in 1950 and was favorably reviewed in this country. In accordance with its usual practice, Simon & Schuster sent copies of the book to various sales agents in other countries, including a leading sales agent in France. In 1953 a sale was consummated by Simon & Schuster through that agent with Editions Robert Laffont, a French publisher, of the exclusive right to publish and sell the book "in the French language throughout the world." Laffont hired a French translator and published the French version of the book in 1954. The French reviews were also favorable. Simon & Schuster's name does not appear in, nor did it participate in the translation, publication or distribution of the French version.

When Seroff, who speaks French fluently, was provided with a copy of the printed French book, he protested bitterly to Simon & Schuster of what he considered "a complete distortion of my English version and what is most distressing a flagrant falsification of my original text in the American edition."

He prepared a list of 134 alleged errors, mistranslations, distortions and changes, and also complained of the omission of the preface written by Virgil Thomson, as well as the index listing Rachmaninoff's musical works and bibliographical writings pertaining to him, which had given a scholarly tone to his book. He insisted that Simon & Schuster demand of Laffont recall of the books already sold and correction of new copies.

Simon & Schuster forwarded his letter to Laffont and asked the latter to take steps accordingly to avoid "serious harm." At this stage Simon & Schuster was of the opinion that at least some of the errors "appear to be quite serious." It offered to pay a limited sum to defray, in part, the expenses of a person named by Seroff, who would negotiate personally with Laffont in France in an endeavor to settle the matter, but this offer was rejected by Seroff's representative as inadequate for the purpose. Finally, when Laffont advised that his "specialists" had concluded, after a complete study of Seroff's complaints, that there were no errors and that he was firmly opposed to making any changes, Simon & Schuster offered to assign to Seroff any claim it might have against Laffont for whatever action Seroff desired to take against the French publisher, advancing to him the aforementioned limited sum for that purpose. Instead, Seroff sued Simon & Schuster.

Before reviewing the law, let us dispose of the factual issue of the translation itself. Considerable proof on this subject was adduced by both parties, including the testimony of experts and the submission of various French-English dictionaries. It is quite obvious that there are differences in a number of respects between the two versions. However, it does not necessarily follow that a mistranslation has been committed. A too literal translation would be avoided by any competent translator. There are nuances in one language which must be captured by the craftsman and expressed in the characteristic style of the other language, even though it may entail some deviation from the original. The question then becomes one of discrimination in the choice of the right word or phrase, the goal being to express the idea or mood of the original work in a style appropriate to the subject. In a proper translation, the translator, however, must be content with his role and not attempt to rewrite, revise or alter the ideas, mood or style of the original.

While most of the claimed errors are of a trivial nature and others not too serious in themselves, there are a few errors which constitute such significant deviations from the original that one is led to believe that the translator may have consciously sought to sensationalize and inject pungent language in order to make the book more attractive to a certain segment of the French public; or the translator, having a tendency in that direction, may have allowed himself free rein to express his own conception of what he believed were the implications in the original work. Probably Seroff, seriously disturbed when he first came across what must have seemed to him a deliberate distortion, reacted by becoming suspicious of every error, however slight, even such innocent slips as phonetic misspellings of Russian names in French.

Still, despite the favorable French reviews, it appears to the court that sufficient has been shown to establish such substantial alteration as would warrant the granting of some relief to an author who was entitled to and interested in the preservation and integrity of his work, if the parties responsible for the alteration of his work were before the court.

Turning to the law, the court recognizes the need to protect authors and others who work with intellectual rather than with tangible property. The court appreciates that the failure of the community, years ago, to protect their gifted men of letters led to tragedies which comprise scars in the history of civilization.

The failure of the English Courts of the period of the American Revolution to protect authors resulted in numerous tragedies poignantly described in Ball's, The Law of Copyright And Literary Property, Ch. I.

The theory upon which Seroff relies in this action is that Simon & Schuster "caused" by its acts and omissions the publication of the distorted French version. The precise lines of the theory have not been clearly defined by counsel but the proposed theory would appear to be analogous to what has been called the "moral right" of an author or artist to object to any deformation, mutilation or other alteration of his work.

Parenthetically, the term "moral right", though widely recognized in civil law countries, is not mentioned in our Copyright Act, nor is it expressly mentioned in the Universal Copyright Convention which came into force in the United States on September 16, 1955.

In the report of the Rappoteur-General Sir John Blake on the Inter-Governmental Copyright Conference in Geneva, wherein on September 16, 1952 the Convention was adopted, there is a direct reference to the desire of delegations "to avoid reference to 'droit moral'."

Nevertheless, a right analogous to "moral right", though not referred to as such, has been recognized in this country and in the common law countries of the British Commonwealth so that in at least a number of situations the integrity and reputation of an artistic creator have been protected by judicial pronouncements. The express grounds on which common law protection has been given include libel, unfair competition, copyright, and the right of privacy, with some groping toward what Roeder has called "a tort theory of a personal *sui generis* nature." Martin A. Roeder: The Doctrine of Moral Right, 53 Harv. L.R. 554, 576; Archbold v. Sweet, 1 M. & Rob. 162, 174 Eng.Rep. 55.

However, recognizing the existence of rights in artistic creators to defend themselves against the free or slipshod use of their creations, nevertheless, such rights may be transferred or surrendered by contract. It is the function of the court to determine the respective rights of the parties primarily by the contract that they made.

This is apparent from Judge Seabury's decision in the leading case of Clemens v. Press Publishing Co., 67 Misc. 183, 122 N.Y.S. 206, 207 (App. Term, 1910) where, while recognizing (though not by the name of "moral right") a right in authors to have the integrity of their writings protected, he simultaneously recognized the paramount rule of the law of contracts:

> "Even the matter of fact attitude of the law does not require us to consider the sale of the rights to a literary production in the same way that we would consider the sale of a barrel of pork. . . . While an author may write to earn his living, and may sell his literary productions, yet the purchaser, *in the absence of a contract which permits him so to do,* cannot make as free a use of them as he could do of the pork which he purchased.

> *"The rights of the parties are to be determined primarily by the contract which they make, and the interpretation of the contract is for the court.* If the intent of the parties was that the defendant should purchase the rights to the literary property and publish it, the author is entitled not only to be paid for his work, but to have it published in the manner in which he wrote it. The purchaser cannot garble it, or put it out under another name than the author's; nor can he omit altogether the name of the author, *unless his contract with the latter permits him so to do".* (Emphasis added.)

A classic example of a case where the integrity of an author would be protected is Archbold v. Sweet, supra, where Lord Tenterden held that an author could maintain an action for injury to his reputation against the publisher of a revised edition under the author's name of a work on criminal law, notwithstanding the ownership of the copyright in the publisher, where an employee of the publisher was responsible for errors appearing in the revised edition.

The control of "moral right" by the law of contracts under the present state of the law was accurately, though somewhat colloquially stated, by the late Prof. Zechariah Chafee, Jr., in Reflections on the Law of Copyright: II, 45 Col.L.Rev. 719, 729:

> "For the time being, we had better concentrate our energies on the pecuniary aspects of copyright. We have enough trouble there. After we get the issues of dollars and cents settled satisfactorily, we can go on to moral rights. . . . Meanwhile any copyright owner who really cares about his moral rights can protect them by inserting appropriate clauses in his contracts with publishers and producers, for example, by expressly

forbidding any alterations or ommissions made without his consent. He can do this until the copyright expires."

Plaintiff's right to some relief under a right analagous to a "moral right" being established, we turn then to the question of this defendant's duty with relation to that right under the contract between the parties.

The limits of that duty are contained in the contract of the parties and the implicit obligation arising therefrom. Seroff granted to Simon & Schuster the "additional" rights of translation and foreign publication, with the added proviso that all revenue derived from the "sale" of these rights was to be shared equally between them.

This would appear on its face to be an agreement between Seroff and Simon & Schuster to embark on a joint venture in regard to such "additional" rights, with Simon & Schuster to be the agent for the parties and under the normal obligations of a party acting in such capacity. We will discuss these obligations below.

Even assuming *arguendo* that this result would not be conclusively reached from a review of the contract *per se*, the established principles for interpreting a contract would lead to this same conclusion in the case at bar. Such established principles are set forth in Horby Realty Corp. v. Yarmouth Land Corp., 270 App.Div. 696, 697, 62 N.Y.S.2d 173:

> "Parol evidence is admissible to explain the meaning which custom or usage has given to words or terms as used in any particular trade or business or in any particular locality."

The evidence showed the existence of a trade practice followed by American publishers of the sale of foreign rights directly or through sales agents to foreign publishers, and the non-existence of any trade practice in connection with such sales calling for supervision by the American publishers of the foreign translations prior to their publication.

It appears that Seroff was familiar with this trade practice. His previous book "Shostakovitch" had been translated into Spanish and Portuguese, and his "The Mighty Five" had been translated into French. On neither of these books was he consulted about the foreign editions, nor did he see copies before the books appeared. Thus, Seroff knew, or should have known, that Simon & Schuster would handle the book exactly as it did.

Accordingly, there is no merit to plaintiff's contention that Simon & Schuster were remiss in their duty to him in failing to make provision in the sales contract with Laffont for the submission of a copy of the proposed French edition prior to its publication. Seroff must be deemed to have contemplated a "sale" of the foreign rights by Simon & Schuster in accordance with the practice of the publishing trade, absent any qualifications or directions concerning the "sale" in his publishing contract. The situation would have been different had there been inserted specific provisions, such as that Simon & Schuster were to supervise the accuracy of translations or that Seroff was to have that right prior to foreign publication.

However, as indicated above, the relationship established by the publishing contract concerning these "additional rights" was that of joint venture between Simon & Schuster and Seroff, with the former the active representative. This imposed upon Simon & Schuster the obligation to make a proper selection of prospective purchasers of Seroff's brain-child. The evidence conclusively showed that this obligation was completely fulfilled in the sale to Laffont. His reputation as a fine publisher was unimpeached. Included among his French editions are books by writers of such standing as Winston Churchill, Dwight D. Eisenhower, John Steinbeck and J. P. Marquand. It is unnecessary to determine whether any further duty devolved upon Simon & Schuster to take any steps to correct the situation after the mistranslations had been accomplished. No such issue is here raised or involved, or for which relief has been requested. It has been noted that it did take some steps in that direction, although without conceding any obligation therefor.

Plaintiff's entire case rests on the assumption that Simon & Schuster "caused" the distorted French version, and was therefore responsible for the libel thereby produced upon his reputation as an author. It is true that "as a general rule, all persons who cause or participate in the publication of libelous or slanderous matter are responsible for such publication"; but it must be shown "that the publication or participation of the person sought to be held liable related to the defamatory matter published, and not simply to the general communication of which the defamatory matter was a part." 53 C.J.S. Libel and Slander § 148. Thus, it has been held that when one sends some unobjectionable written material or information to another who distorts it into a "libel", the original party cannot be held responsible therefor. The situation would, of course, be different if one's own agent or employee had committed the distortion, since a principal or employer is responsible for the negligent or unskillful acts of his agent or employee. But Laffont is clearly not an agent of Simon & Schuster; he is a wholly independent publisher who bought the French rights, and is in fact an independent contractor.

Whatever the rights plaintiff may have against Laffont or the French translator, it is clear that he may not succeed against Simon & Schuster in this action to recover damages for injury to his reputation produced by the French version.

In view of this disposition, it is unnecessary to discuss the problem of damages or to determine whether special damages must be established in this kind of case.

Defendant is accordingly entitled to judgment dismissing the complaint. All motions upon which decision was reserved, except defendant's motion for judgment at the close of the entire case, are denied.

. . . .

GILLIAM v. AMERICAN BROADCASTING COMPANIES, INC.

538 F.2d 14 (2d Cir. 1976)

Before LUMBARD, HAYS and GURFEIN, Circuit Judges.

LUMBARD, Circuit Judge:

Plaintiffs, a group of British writers and performers known as "Monty Python," appeal from a denial by Judge Lasker in the Southern District of a preliminary injunction to restrain the American Broadcasting Company (ABC) from broadcasting edited versions of three separate programs originally written and performed by Monty Python for broadcast by the British Broadcasting Corporation (BBC). We agree with Judge Lasker that the appellants have demonstrated that the excising done for ABC impairs the integrity of the original work. We further find that the countervailing injuries that Judge Lasker found might have accrued to ABC as a result of an injunction at a prior date no longer exist. We therefore direct the issuance of a preliminary injunction by the district court.

Since its formation in 1969, the Monty Python group has gained popularity primarily through its thirty-minute television programs created for BBC as part of a comedy series entitled "Monty Python's Flying Circus." In accordance with an agreement between Monty Python and BBC, the group writes and delivers to BBC scripts for use in the television series. This scriptwriters' agreement recites in great detail the procedure to be followed when any alterations are to be made in the script prior to recording of the program. The essence of this section of the agreement is that, while BBC retains final authority to make changes, appellants or their representatives exercise optimum control over the scripts consistent with BBC's authority and only minor changes may be made without prior consultation with the writers. Nothing in the scriptwriters' agreement entitles BBC to alter a program once it has been recorded. The agreement further provides that, subject to the terms therein, the group retains all rights in the script.

Under the agreement, BBC may license the transmission of recordings of the television programs in any overseas territory. The series has been broadcast in this country primarily on non-commercial public broadcasting television stations, although several of the programs have been broadcast on commercial stations in Texas and Nevada. In each instance, the thirty-minute programs have been broadcast as originally recorded and broadcast in England in their entirety and without commercial interruption.

In October 1973, Time-Life Films acquired the right to distribute in the United States certain BBC television programs, including the Monty Python series. Time-Life was permitted to edit the programs only "for insertion of commercials, applicable censorship or governmental . . . rules and regulations, and National Association of Broadcasters and time segment requirements." No similar clause was included in the scriptwriters' agreement between appellants and BBC. Prior to this time, ABC had sought to acquire the right to broadcast excerpts from various Monty Python programs in the spring of 1975, but the group rejected the proposal for such a disjoined format. Thereafter, in July 1975, ABC agreed with Time-Life to broadcast two ninety-minute specials each comprising three thirty-minute Monty Python programs that had not previously been shown in this country.

Correspondence between representatives of BBC and Monty Python reveals that these parties assumed that ABC would broadcast each of the Monty Python programs "in its entirety." On September 5, 1975, however, the group's British representative inquired of BBC how ABC planned to show the programs in their entirety if approximately 24 minutes of each 90 minute program were to be devoted to commercials. BBC replied on September 12, "we can only reassure you that ABC have decided to run the programmes 'back to back,' and that there is a firm undertaking not to segment them."

ABC broadcast the first of the specials on October 3, 1975. Appellants did not see a tape of the program until late November and were allegedly "appalled" at the discontinuity and "mutilation" that had resulted from the editing done by Time-Life for ABC. Twenty-four minutes of the original 90 minutes of recording had been omitted. Some of the editing had been done in order to make time for commercials; other material had been edited, according to ABC, because the original programs contained offensive or obscene matter.

In early December, Monty Python learned that ABC planned to broadcast the second special on December 26, 1975. The parties began negotiations concerning editing of that program and a delay of the broadcast until Monty Python could view it. These negotiations were futile, however, and on December 15 the group filed this action to enjoin the broadcast and for damages. Following an evidentiary hearing, Judge Lasker found that "the plaintiffs have established an impairment of the integrity of their work" which "caused the film or program . . . to lose its iconoclastic verve." According to Judge Lasker, "the damage that has been caused to the plaintiffs is irreparable by its nature." Nevertheless, the judge denied the motion for the preliminary injunction on the grounds that it was unclear who owned the copyright in the programs produced by BBC from the scripts written by Monty Python; that there was a question of whether Time-Life and BBC were indispensable parties to the litigation; that ABC would suffer significant financial loss if it were enjoined a week before the scheduled broadcast; and that Monty Python had displayed a "somewhat disturbing casualness" in their pursuance of the matter.

Judge Lasker granted Monty Python's request for more limited relief by requiring ABC to broadcast a disclaimer during the December 26 special to the effect that the group disassociated itself from the program because of the editing. A panel of this court, however, granted a stay of that order until this appeal could be heard and permitted ABC to broadcast, at the beginning of the special, only the legend that the program had been edited by ABC. We heard argument on April 13 and, at that time, enjoined ABC from any further broadcast of edited Monty Python programs pending the decision of the court.

I

In determining the availability of injunctive relief at this early stage of the proceedings, Judge Lasker properly considered the harm that would inure to the plaintiffs if the injunction were denied, the harm that defendant would suffer if the injunction were granted, and the likelihood that plaintiffs would ultimately succeed on the merits. We direct the issuance of a preliminary injunction because we find that all these factors weigh in favor of appellants.

There is nothing clearly erroneous in Judge Lasker's conclusion that any injury suffered by appellants as a result of the broadcast of edited versions of their programs was irreparable by its nature. ABC presented the appellants with their first opportunity for broadcast to a nationwide network audience in this country. If ABC adversely misrepresented the quality of Monty Python's work, it is likely that many members of the audience, many of whom, by defendant's admission, were previously unfamiliar with appellants, would not become loyal followers of Monty Python productions. The subsequent injury to appellants' theatrical reputation would imperil their ability to attract the large audience necessary to the success of their venture. Such an injury to professional reputation cannot be measured in monetary terms or recompensed by other relief.

In contrast to the harm that Monty Python would suffer by a denial of the preliminary injunction, Judge Lasker found that ABC's relationship with its affiliates would be impaired by a grant of an injunction within a week of the scheduled December 26 broadcast. The court also found that ABC and its affiliates had advertised the program and had included it in listings of forthcoming television programs that were distributed to the public. Thus a last minute cancellation of the December 26 program, Judge Lasker concluded, would injure defendant financially and in its reputation with the public and its advertisers.

However valid these considerations may have been when the issue before the court was whether a preliminary injunction should immediately precede the broadcast, any injury to ABC is presently more speculative. No rebroadcast of the edited specials has been scheduled and no advertising costs have been incurred for the immediate future. Thus there is no danger that defendant's relations with affiliates or the public will suffer irreparably if subsequent broadcasts of the programs are enjoined pending a disposition of the issues.

We then reach the question whether there is a likelihood that appellants will succeed on the merits. In concluding that there is a likelihood of infringement here, we rely especially on the fact that the editing was substantial, i.e., approximately 27 per cent of the original program was omitted, and the editing contravened contractual provisions that limited the right to edit Monty Python material. It should be emphasized that our discussion of these matters refers only to such facts as have been developed upon the hearing for a preliminary injunction. Modified or contrary findings may become appropriate after a plenary trial.

Judge Lasker denied the preliminary injunction in part because he was unsure of the ownership of the copyright in the recorded program. Appellants first contend that the question of ownership is irrelevant because the recorded program was merely a derivative work taken from the script in which they hold the uncontested copyright. Thus, even if BBC owned the copyright in the recorded program, its use of that work would be limited by the license granted to BBC by Monty Python for use of the underlying script. We agree.

Section 7 of the Copyright Law, 17 U.S.C. § 7, provides in part that "adaptations, arrangements, dramatizations . . . or other versions of . . . copyrighted works when produced with the consent of the proprietor of the copyright in such works . . . shall be regarded as new works subject to copyright . . . ." Manifestly, the recorded program falls into this category as a dramatization of the script,[3] and thus the program was itself entitled to

---

[3] ABC has not argued that the principles of section 7 do not apply because Monty Python's copyright in its unpublished script is a common law copyright rather than a statutory copyright, which can exist only after publication. In any event, we find that the same principles discussed below with respect to derivative works adapted from material in which there is a statutory copyright also apply to material in which there is common law copyright. See *RCA Mfg. Co. v. Whiteman*, 114 F.2d 86, 88 (2d Cir.), *cert. denied*, 311 U.S. 712, 61 S.Ct. 393, 85 L.Ed. 463 (1940); 17 U.S.C. § 2.

The law is apparently unsettled with respect to whether a broadcast of a recorded program constitutes publication of that program and the underlying script so as to divest the proprietor of the script of his common law copyright. See 1 M. Nimmer, Copyright §§ 56.3, 57. Arguably, once the scriptwriter obtains the economic benefit of the recording and the broadcast, he has

copyright protection. However, section 7 limits the copyright protection of the derivative work, as works adapted from previously existing scripts have become known, to the novel additions made to the underlying work and the derivative work does not affect the "force or validity" of the copyright in the matter from which it is derived. Thus, any ownership by BBC of the copyright in the recorded program would not affect the scope or ownership of the copyright in the underlying script.

Since the copyright in the underlying script survives intact despite the incorporation of that work into a derivative work, one who uses the script, even with the permission of the proprietor of the derivative work, may infringe the underlying copyright. See *Davis v. E. I. DuPont deNemours & Co.*, 240 F.Supp. 612 (S.D.N.Y. 1965) (defendants held to have infringed when they obtained permission to use a screenplay in preparing a television script but did not obtain permission of the author of the play upon which the screenplay was based).

If the proprietor of the derivative work is licensed by the proprietor of the copyright in the underlying work to vend or distribute the derivative work to third parties, those parties will, of course, suffer no liability for their use of the underlying work consistent with the license to the proprietor of the derivative work. Obviously, it was just this type of arrangement that was contemplated in this instance. The scriptwriters' agreement between Monty Python and BBC specifically permitted the latter to license the transmission of the recordings made by BBC to distributors such as Time-Life for broadcast in overseas territories.

One who obtains permission to use a copyrighted script in the production of a derivative work, however, may not exceed the specific purpose for which permission was granted. Most of the decisions that have reached this conclusion have dealt with the improper extension of the underlying work into media or time, i.e., duration of the license, not covered by the grant of permission to the derivative work proprietor. Appellants herein do not claim that the broadcast by ABC violated media or time restrictions contained in the license

---

obtained all that his common law copyright was intended to secure for him; thus it would not be fair to find that publication of the derivative work divested the script of its common law protection. On the other hand, several types of performances from scripts have been held not to constitute divestive publication, see, e.g., *Uproar Co. v. NBC*, 81 F.2d 373 (1st Cir. 1936), and it is unclear whether a broadcast of the recording in itself constitutes publication. See M. Nimmer, supra, § 56.3. Since ABC has not objected to Monty Python's assertion of common law copyright in an unpublished script, we need not entertain the question on this appeal from denial of a preliminary injunction. We leave initial determination of this perplexing question to the district court of its determination of all the issues on the merits. This disposition is especially proper in view of the fact that, apart from the copyright claims, there will be a trial of the unfair competition claim.

of the script to BBC. Rather, they claim that revisions in the script, and ultimately in the program, could be made only after consultation with Monty Python, and that ABC's broadcast of a program edited after recording and without consultation with Monty Python exceeded the scope of any license that BBC was entitled to grant.

The rationale for finding infringement when a licensee exceeds time or media restrictions on his license—the need to allow the proprietor of the underlying copyright to control the method in which his work is presented to the public—applies equally to the situation in which a licensee makes an unauthorized use of the underlying work by publishing it in a truncated version. Whether intended to allow greater economic exploitation of the work, as in the media and time cases, or to ensure that the copyright proprietor retains a veto power over revisions desired for the derivative work, the ability of the copyright holder to control his work remains paramount in our copyright law. We find, therefore, that unauthorized editing of the underlying work, if proven, would constitute an infringement of the copyright in that work similar to any other use of a work that exceeded the license granted by the proprietor of the copyright.

If the broadcast of an edited version of the Monty Python program infringed the group's copyright in the script, ABC may obtain no solace from the fact that editing was permitted in the agreements between BBC and Time-Life or Time Life and ABC. BBC was not entitled to make unilateral changes in the script and was not specifically empowered to alter the recordings once made; Monty Python, moreover, had reserved to itself any right not granted to BBC. Since a grantor may not convey greater rights than it owns, BBC's permission to allow Time-Life, and hence ABC, to edit appears to have been a nullity.

ABC answers appellants' infringement argument with a series of contentions, none of which seems meritorious at this stage of the litigation. The network asserts that Monty Python's British representative, Jill Foster, knew that ABC planned to exclude much of the original BBC program in the October 3 broadcast. ABC thus contends that by not previously objecting to this procedure, Monty Python ratified BBC's authority to license others to edit the underlying script.

Although the case of *Ilyin v. Avon Publications, Inc.*, 144 F.Supp. 368, 373 (S.D.N.Y.1956), may be broadly read for the proposition that a holder of a derivative copyright may obtain rights in the underlying work through ratification, the conduct necessary to that conclusion has yet to be demonstrated in this case.[5] It is undisputed that appellants did not have actual notice of the

---

[5] Furthermore, the court in *Ilyin* specifically limited the theory to the situation in which ratification was used against a third-party infringer who claimed the proprietor of the derivative

cuts in the October 3 broadcast until late November. Even if they are chargeable with the knowledge of their British representative, it is not clear that she had prior notice of the cuts or ratified the omissions, nor did Judge Lasker make any finding on the question. While Foster, on September 5, did question how ABC was to broadcast the entire program if it was going to interpose 24 minutes of commercials, she received assurances from BBC that the programs would not be "segmented." The fact that she knew precisely the length of material that would have to be omitted to allow for commercials does not prove that she ratified the deletions. This is especially true in light of previous assurances that the program would contain the original shows in their entirety. On the present record, it cannot be said that there was any ratification of BBC's grant of editing rights. ABC, of course, is entitled to attempt to prove otherwise during the trial on the merits.

ABC next argues that under the "joint work" theory adopted in *Shapiro, Bernstein & Co. v. Jerry Vogel Music, Inc.*, 221 F.2d 569 (2d Cir. 1955), the script produced by Monty Python and the program recorded by BBC are symbiotic elements of a single production. Therefore, according to ABC, each contributor possesses an undivided ownership of all copyrightable elements in the final work and BBC could thus have licensed use of the script, including editing, written by appellants.

The joint work theory as extended in *Shapiro* has been criticized as inequitable unless "at the time of creation by the first author, the second author's contribution [is envisaged] as an integrated part of a single work," and the first author intends that the final product be a joint work. See 1 M. Nimmer, Copyright §§ 67–73. Furthermore, this court appears to have receded from a broad application of the joint work doctrine where the contract which leads to collaboration between authors indicates that one will retain a superior interest. In the present case, the screenwriters' agreement between Monty Python and BBC provides that the group is to retain all rights in the script not granted in the agreement and that at some future point the group may license the scripts for use on television to parties other than BBC. These provisions suggest that the parties did not consider themselves joint authors of a single work. This matter is subject to further exploration at the trial, but in the present state of the record, it presents no bar to issuance of a preliminary injunction.

Aside from the question of who owns the relevant copyrights, ABC asserts that the contracts between appellants and BBC permit editing of the programs for commercial television in the United States. ABC argues that the scriptwriters' agreement allows appellants the right to participate in revisions of the script only *prior* to the recording of the programs, and thus infers that BBC

---

work had no copyright in the underlying work. In this case, however, the proprietor of the underlying work, rather than the alleged infringer, contests the ratification.

had unrestricted authority to revise after that point. This argument, however, proves too much. A reading of the contract seems to indicate that Monty Python obtained control over editing the script only to ensure control over the program recorded from that script. Since the scriptwriters' agreement explicitly retains for the group all rights not granted by the contract, omission of any terms concerning alterations in the program after recording must be read as reserving to appellants exclusive authority for such revisions.[7]

Finally, ABC contends that appellants must have expected that deletions would be made in the recordings to conform them for use on commercial television in the United States. ABC argues that licensing in the United States implicitly grants a license to insert commercials in a program and to remove offensive or obscene material prior to broadcast. According to the network, appellants should have anticipated that most of the excised material contained scatological references inappropriate for American television and that these scenes would be replaced with commercials, which presumably are more palatable to the American public.

The proof adduced up to this point, however, provides no basis for finding any implied consent to edit. Prior to the ABC broadcasts, Monty Python programs had been broadcast on a regular basis by both commercial and public television stations in this country without interruption or deletion. Indeed, there is no evidence of any prior broadcast of edited Monty Python material in the United States. These facts, combined with the persistent requests for assurances by the group and its representatives that the programs would be shown intact belie the argument that the group knew or should have known that deletions and commercial interruptions were inevitable.

---

[7] *McGuire v. United Artists Television Productions, Inc.*, 254 F.Supp. 270 (S.D.Cal.1966), cited by appellee for the proposition that failure of a writer explicitly to reserve control over a recording of his script automatically forfeits that control, is inapposite. That case involved the question of whether a writer who had been granted an undetermined measure of "creative control" over the script could prevent editing of the film for insertion of commercials. The court found only that the parties had reached no agreement on the scope of the writer's "creative control." Here, however, that scope is clearly delineated by the agreement that retains for appellants those rights not granted to BBC, and hence, to BBC's licensees.

In a performer's agreement between Monty Python and BBC, the group warranted that any manuscript that it provided to BBC for performance would be either "original material of (its) own which (it) is fully at liberty to use for all purposes of this Agreement . . . or original material which (it) is fully at liberty to use for all purposes of this Agreement by reason of (its) holding all necessary licenses or permissions." ABC contends that somehow this clause provides an implicit right to edit for commercial television because that act would be consistent with the warranty that the parties are "fully at liberty" to use the scripts for any purpose. Judge Lasker found that the performer's agreement was wholly irrelevant to the issue of a preliminary injunction. While we need not express any opinion on that ruling at this time, it is obvious from a reading of the contract that the sole purpose of the clause relied upon by ABC is to hold BBC harmless from a claim by any party that the Monty Python scripts infringe upon another work.

Several of the deletions made for ABC, such as elimination of the words "hell" and "damn," seem inexplicable given today's standard television fare. If, however, ABC honestly determined that the programs were obscene in substantial part, it could have decided not to broadcast the specials at all, or it could have attempted to reconcile its differences with appellants. The network could not, however, free from a claim of infringement, broadcast in a substantially altered form a program incorporating the script over which the group had retained control.

Our resolution of these technical arguments serves to reinforce our initial inclination that the copyright law should be used to reorganize the important role of the artist in our society and the need to encourage production and dissemination of artistic works by providing adequate legal protection for one who submits his work to the public. See *Mazer v. Stein*, 347 U.S. 201, 74 S.Ct. 460, 98 L.Ed. 630 (1954). We therefore conclude that there is a substantial likelihood that, after a full trial, appellants will succeed in proving infringement of their copyright by ABC's broadcast of edited versions of Monty Python programs. In reaching this conclusion, however, we need not accept appellants' assertion that any editing whatsoever would constitute infringement. Courts have recognized that licensees are entitled to some small degree of latitude in arranging the licensed work for presentation to the public in a manner consistent with the licensee's style or standards. That privilege, however, does not extend to the degree of editing that occurred here especially in light of contractual provisions that limited the right to edit Monty Python material.

II

It also seems likely that appellants will succeed on the theory that, regardless of the right ABC had to broadcast an edited program, the cuts made constituted an actionable mutilation of Monty Python's work. This cause of action, which seeks redress for deformation of an artist's work, finds its roots in the continental concept of droit moral, or moral right, which may generally be summarized as including the right of the artist to have his work attributed to him in the form in which he created it. See 1 M. Nimmer, supra, at § 110.1.

American copyright law, as presently written, does not recognize moral rights or provide a cause of action for their violation, since the law seeks to vindicate the economic, rather than the personal, rights of authors. Nevertheless, the economic incentive for artistic and intellectual creation that serves as the foundation for American copyright law, cannot be reconciled with the inability of artists to obtain relief for mutilation or misrepresentation of their work to the public on which the artists are financially dependent. Thus courts have long granted relief for misrepresentation of an artist's work by relying on theories outside the statutory law of copyright, such as contract law, *Granz v.*

Harris, 198 F.2d 585 (2d Cir. 1952) (substantial cutting of original work constitutes misrepresentation), or the tort of unfair competition. Although such decisions are clothed in terms of proprietary right in one's creation, they also properly vindicate the author's personal right to prevent the presentation of his work to the public in a distorted form.

Here, the appellants claim that the editing done for ABC mutilated the original work and that consequently the broadcast of those programs as the creation of Monty Python violated the Lanham Act § 43(a), 15 U.S.C. § 1125(a).[10] This statute, the federal counterpart to state unfair competition laws, has been invoked to prevent misrepresentations that may injure plaintiff's business or personal reputation, even where no registered trademark is concerned. It is sufficient to violate the Act that a representation of a product, although technically true, creates a false impression of the product's origin. See *Rich v. RCA Corp.*, 390 F.Supp. 530 (S.D.N.Y.1975) (recent picture of plaintiff on cover of album containing songs recorded in distant past held to be a false representation that the songs were new); *Geisel v. Poynter Products, Inc.*, 283 F.Supp. 261, 267 (S.D.N.Y.1968).

These cases cannot be distinguished from the situation in which a television network broadcasts a program properly designated as having been written and performed by a group, but which has been edited, without the writer's consent, into a form that departs substantially from the original work. "To deform his work is to present him to the public as the creator of a work not his own, and thus makes him subject to criticism for work he has not done." In such a case, it is the writer or performer, rather than the network, who suffers the consequences of the mutilation, for the public will have only the final product by which to evaluate the work. Thus, an allegation that a defendant has presented to the public a "garbled," *Granz v. Harris*, supra (Frank, *J.*, concurring), distorted version of plaintiff's work seeks to redress the very rights sought to be protected by the Lanham Act, 15 U.S.C. § 1125(a), and should be recognized as stating a cause of action under that statute. See *Autry v. Republic Productions, Inc.*, 213 F.2d 667 (9th Cir. 1954); *Jaeger v. American Intn'l Pictures, Inc.*, 330 F.Supp. 274 (S.D.N.Y.1971), which suggest the violation of such a right if mutilation could be proven.

During the hearing on the preliminary injunction, Judge Lasker viewed the edited version of the Monty Python program broadcast on December 26 and

---

[10] That statute provides in part:

Any person who shall affix, apply, or annex, or use in connection with any goods or services, . . . a false designation of origin, or any false description or representation . . . and shall cause such goods or services to enter into commerce . . . shall be liable to a civil action by any person . . . who believes that he is or is likely to be damaged by the use of any such false description or representation.

the original, unedited version. After hearing argument of this appeal, this panel also viewed and compared the two versions. We find that the truncated version at times omitted the climax of the skits to which appellants' rare brand of humor was leading and at other times deleted essential elements in the schematic development of a story line.[12] We therefore agree with Judge Lasker's conclusion that the edited version broadcast by ABC impaired the integrity of appellants' work and represented to the public as the product of appellants what was actually a mere caricature of their talents. We believe that a valid cause of action for such distortion exists and that therefore a preliminary injunction may issue to prevent repetition of the broadcast prior to final determination of the issues.[13]

III

. . . .

For these reasons we direct that the district court issue the preliminary injunction sought by the appellants.

GURFEIN, Circuit Judge (concurring):

I concur in my brother Lumbard's scholarly opinion, but I wish to comment on the application of Section 43(a) of the Lanham Act, 15 U.S.C. § 1125(a).

I believe that this is the first case in which a federal appellate court has held that there may be a violation of Section 43(a) of the Lanham Act with respect to a common-law copyright. The Lanham Act is a trademark statute, not a copyright statute. Nevertheless, we must recognize that the language of Section 43(a) is broad. It speaks of the affixation or use of false designations of

---

[12] A single example will illustrate the extent of distortion engendered by the editing. In one skit, an upper class English family is engaged in a discussion of the tonal quality of certain words as "woody" or "tinny." The father soon begins to suggest certain words with sexual connotations as either "woody" or "tinny," whereupon the mother fetches a bucket of water and pours it over his head. The skit continues from this point. The ABC edit eliminates this middle sequence so that the father is comfortably dressed at one moment and, in the next moment, is shown in a soaked condition without any explanation for the change in his appearance.

[13] Judge Gurfein's concurring opinion suggests that since the gravamen of a complaint under the Lanham Act is that the origin of goods has been falsely described, a legend disclaiming Monty Python's approval of the edited version would preclude violation of that Act. We are doubtful that a few words could erase the indelible impression that is made by a television broadcast, especially since the viewer has no means of comparing the truncated version with the complete work in order to determine for himself the talents of plaintiffs. Furthermore, a disclaimer such as the one originally suggested by Judge Lasker in the exigencies of an impending broadcast last December would go unnoticed by viewers who tuned into the broadcast a few minutes after it began.

We therefore conclude that Judge Gurfein's proposal that the district court could find some form of disclaimer would be sufficient might not provide appropriate relief.

origin or false descriptions or representations, but proscribes such use "in connection with any goods or services." It is easy enough to incorporate trade names as well as trademarks into Section 43(a) and the statute specifically applies to common law trademarks, as well as registered trademarks. Lanham Act § 45, 15 U.S.C. § 1127.

In the present case, we are holding that the deletion of portions of the recorded tape constitutes a breach of contract, as well as an infringement of a common-law copyright of the original work. There is literally no need to discuss whether plaintiffs also have a claim for relief under the Lanham Act or for unfair competition under New York law. I agree with Judge Lumbard, however, that it may be an exercise of judicial economy to express our view on the Lanham Act claim, and I do not dissent therefrom. I simply wish to leave it open for the District Court to fashion the remedy.

The Copyright Act provides no recognition of the so-called *droit moral,* or moral right of authors. Nor are such rights recognized in the field of copyright law in the United States. See 1 *Nimmer on Copyright,* § 110.2 (1975 ed.). If a distortion or truncation in connection with with a use constitutes an infringement of copyright, there is no need for an additional cause of action beyond copyright infringement. *Id.* at § 110.3. An obligation to mention the name of the author carries the implied duty, however, as a matter of contract, not to make such changes in the work as would render the credit line a false attribution of authorship, *Granz v. Harris,* 198 F.2d 585 (2 Cir. 1952).

So far as the Lanham Act is concerned, it is not a substitute for *droit moral* which authors in Europe enjoy. If the licensee may, by contract, distort the recorded work, the Lanham Act does not come into play. If the licensee has no such right by contract, there will be a violation in breach of contract. The Lanham Act can hardly apply literally when the credit line correctly states the work to be that of the plaintiffs which, indeed it is, so far as it goes. The vice complained of is that the truncated version is not what the plaintiffs wrote. But the Lanham Act does not deal with artistic integrity. It only goes to misdescription of origin and the like. See *Societe Comptoir De L'Industrie Cotonniere Etablissements Boussac v. Alexander's Dept. Stores, Inc.,* 299 F.2d 33, 36 (2 Cir. 1962).

The misdescription of origin can be dealt with, as Judge Lasker did below, by devising an appropriate legend to indicate that the plaintiffs had not approved the editing of the ABC version.[1] With such a legend, there is no conceivable violation of the Lanham Act. If plaintiffs complain that their artistic integrity is still compromised by the distorted version, their claim does

---

[1] I do not imply that the appropriate legend be shown only at the beginning of the broadcast. That is a matter for the District Court.

not lie under the Lanham Act, which does not protect the copyrighted work itself but protects only against the misdescription or mislabelling.

So long as it is made clear that the ABC version is not approved by the Monty Python group, there is no misdescription of origin. So far as the content of the broadcast itself is concerned, that is not within the proscription of the Lanham Act when there is no misdescription of the authorship.

I add this brief explanation because I do not believe that the Lanham Act claim necessarily requires the drastic remedy of permanent injunction. That form of ultimate relief must be found in some other fountainhead of equity jurisprudence.

SINATRA v.
GOODYEAR TIRE & RUBBER CO.

435 F.2d 711 (9th Cir. 1970)

Before DUNIWAY, KILKENNY and TRASK, Circuit Judges.

TRASK, Circuit Judge:

This is an appeal brought by Nancy Sinatra from a summary judgement entered against her in favor of appellees, on her complaint against Goodyear Tire and Rubber Company based upon unfair competition, on the ground that there was no genuine issue as to a material fact. The district court's jurisdiction was founded on diversity of citizenship. 28 U.S.C. § 1332. This court has jurisdiction under 28 U.S.C. § 1291.

Plaintiff-appellant is a professional entertainer. She had made a recording of a song entitled "These Boots Are Made For Walkin' " which had become popular. The music, lyrics, and arrangement of this composition had been copyrighted with Criterion Music as the copyright proprietor.

The defendants Goodyear Tire and Rubber Company, a corporation, and Young and Rubicam, Inc., an advertising agency, conceived the idea of coining the phrase "wide boots" as a descriptive term for tires manufactured by defendant Goodyear. As part of a widespread advertising campaign based upon this "wide boots" theme, the defendants produced and exhibited six radio and television commercials centered around a musical background using the music and revised lyrics from "These Boots Are Made For Walkin' " in combination with the voice of a female singer who was not shown on the screen or identified by name. In the four television commercials, two had a group of female voices singing the song and two had a single female voice. All four had a male voice narrating the commercial with four girls dressed in high boots and "mod" clothes appearing briefly with rolling tires. Each of the two radio commercials had a single female voice singing the song and a male narrator giving the commercial.

The person who files the law suit says - - -

The complaint alleges that the song has been so popularized by the plaintiff that her name is identified with it; that she is best known by her connection with the song; that said song and the arrangement used by defendants "has acquired a secondary meaning"; that the defendants selected a singer whose voice and style was deliberately intended to imitate the voice and style of the plaintiff; and that the physical appearance and dress of the girls who appeared in fleeting views on the television commercials utilized the mannerisms and dress of the plaintiff. All of this, the complaint alleges, was intentionally accomplished for the purpose of deceiving the public into believing that the plaintiff was a participant in the commercials.

Plaintiff Sinatra further alleged that the defendant Young and Rubicam had previously contacted her agent in an effort to employ her on behalf of Goodyear but no contract was concluded.

She thereupon prayed for general and punitive damages, an accounting of all sales of Goodyear tires during the period the commercials were used and a reasonable royalty therefrom, together with a permanent injunction restraining defendants from further use of all of the commercials.

The defendants filed a motion to dismiss and a motion for summary judgment supported by affidavit and exhibits consisting of the film and tapes in question. The plaintiff filed her counteraffidavit and that of her agent.

Upon these papers the district court found that:

> "The performances of 'These Boots Are Made For Walkin' on each of said two radio commercials and four television commercials are anonymous; that is, there is no audio or visual representation, holding out, or inference that any of the commercials embody the performance or voice of any particular individual or individuals."

The Court thus concluded in part:

> "Defendants did not pass-off; that is, they did not mislead the public into thinking their commercials were the product of plaintiff or anyone else.

> "Imitation alone does not give rise to a cause of action; there is, therefore, no genuine issue of fact and defendants are entitled to Summary Judgment."

On appeal, Sinatra asserts that her complaint alleged the essential elements of the tort of passing-off and raised genuine issues as to material facts so that the district court erred in granting summary judgment. We disagree and affirm.

At the outset it must be remembered that this is not a copyright infringement case.[2] The copyright proprietor was Criterion Music. Criterion owned the copyright on the music, the lyrics and the arrangements of "These Boots Are Made For Walkin'." On March 3, 1967, and before the production of the commercials complained about, Criterion entered into a written agreement with Young and Rubicam on behalf of the defendant Goodyear for a license to use the composition, "including any arrangements thereof owned or controlled by you, music and/or lyrics. . . . " Complete rights were given for television and radio and for commercial use for advertising purposes on behalf of Goodyear. The written agreement with all of its provisions, warranties and representations was accepted and approved by Lee Hazelwood, designated as the author.

Neither is it a case where an actual tape or other recording of the voice of the plaintiff has been replayed. It is not falsely stated to be a Nancy Sinatra rendition. The defendant candidly admitted for purposes of the motion for summary judgment and the district court assumed that the vocal rendition was an imitation of plaintiff's recorded performance of this particular song.

The power to provide copyright protection for a limited time to the "Writings and Discoveries" of authors and inventors is one of the enumerated powers of Congress. The items designated by Congress to be within the Constitutional protection of "writings" were broadened to include a musical composition in 1831, and the author was given the exclusive right "to arrange or adapt it . . . ." When the Copyright Act was amended in 1909 it provided that any person complying with the provisions of the Act (i.e., obtaining a copyright) should have the exclusive right:

> "[t]o perform the copyrighted work publicly for profit if it be a musical composition; and . . . to make any arrangement or setting of it or of the melody of it in any system of notation or any form of record in which the thought of an author may be recorded and from which it may be read or reproduced."

Thus the author or composer was accorded copy protection, but no provision has yet been made in the Act for a performer's right, per se.

The appellant recognizes all of this and submits to this court the question as to whether or not she is entitled to relief from the alleged unfair competition by appellees.

---

[2] The complaint did not allege copyright infringement. Defendants acquired a license to use the copyrighted music, lyrics and arrangement of "These Boots Are Made For Walkin' " from Criterion Music, the copyright proprietor, on March 3, 1967. Rather, plaintiff alleges the international "passing-off" of the voice and mannerisms of others as her own for commercial exploitation.

Since this is a diversity action and reliance may not be based on the Federal Copyright Act, the law to be applied is the law of the state. The complaint indicates that the plaintiff is a resident of the State of California, the forum state. The defendants are both doing business in the State of California although one is alleged to be incorporated in Ohio and the other in New York. The wrong, if it occurred, is alleged to have occurred in many states since the advertising campaign was nationwide. None of the parties has urged that the law of any state other than that of the forum be applied. In the absence of any other showing we apply the law of the State of California.

Under the laws of California unfair competition is defined by code. As thus defined, unfair competition shall mean and include "unlawful, unfair or fraudulent business practice and unfair, untrue or misleading advertising. . . ."

An examination of the cases decided under the statute immediately disclosed an obvious distinction on the facts between this case and the great mass of unfair competition cases. There is no competition between Nancy Sinatra and Goodyear Tire Company. Appellant is not in the tire business and Goodyear is not selling phonograph records. There is no passing-off by the defendant of the plaintiff's products as its own either by simulation of name, slogan, device or other unfair trade practice.

No real assistance is therefore obtained from the California statute or cases decided under it. Neither counsel has relied upon the statute or the ordinary cases construing it. We turn then to an examination of the general authorities cited by Sinatra to determine if a cause of action exists.

Dean Prosser defines the tort of "passing-off" as involving the basic idea of competing for custom in the trade. Thus it is:

> "The making of some false representation to the public or to third persons, likely to induce them to believe that the goods or services of another are those of the plaintiff. . . . The test laid down in such cases has been whether the resemblance is so great as to deceive the ordinary customer acting with the caution usually exercised in such transactions, so that he may mistake one for the other." Prosser, Law of Torts 982-83 (1964).

Here we have a claim of an incidental or secondary passing-off. Appellant seeks to bring her case within the orbit of the traditional pattern of unfair competition by asserting that because some people would read her voice into the commercial the defendant has increased its sale of tires "by many millions of dollars."

Counsel has called attention to, and we have discovered, four cases which directly bear on appellant's claim. They are: Davis v. Trans World Airlines,

297 F. Supp. 1145 (C.D.Cal.1969); Lahr v. Adell Chemical Co., 300 F.2d 256 (1st Cir.1962); Sim v. H. J. Heinz Co., Ltd., [1958] 1 W.L.R. 313 (C.A.1959); and Gardella v. Log Cabin Products, Inc., 89 F.2d 891 (2d Cir.1937).

Gardella was the Aunt Jemima case. In it the defendants used a singer and an actor in an advertising campaign for Aunt Jemima Pancake Flour and Log Cabin Syrup over a radio station. They were presented under the name of "Aunt Jemima", a name which, with a picture of the character, had been registered as a trademark since 1890. The plaintiff was a state and radio performer who had used the name in many performances and in recordings. Although plaintiff obtained a recovery in damages in the district court, it was reversed because it was improperly based in part upon a claim under the state's Civil Rights law. The claim based upon unfair competition was sent back to be established, if at all, upon standards set out in the court's opinion. The court pointed out that although the name "Aunt Jemima" was used by both performers, the use of the name for the fictitious character was protected by the trademark registration and the only duty of the defendants was one of identification to prevent confusion with the theatrical Aunt Jemima who was the plaintiff and who had an established reputation and earning power as a performer. Absent confusion or deception, the court stated, imitation alone was not sufficient to sustain the claim. The court further suggested that so long as the pancake Aunt Jemima advertised her own products, imitation would not be deception. 89 F.2d at 897.

In *Sim, supra,* the Heinz Company developed an advertising program using speech from a cartoon figure. Alastair Sim, a well known actor, alleged that the advertiser employed another actor, Ron Moody, to make the vocal comments. Moody had in the past simulated the voice of Sim and the complaint was that he did so on these television commercials. The application for an injunction was denied on appeal. Lord Justice Hodson expressing some doubt said:

> "I would only add this. This is, on any view of the matter, a novel form of action of passing off. The plaintiff contends that his voice as an actor is part of his stock-in-trade and therefore is something which he is entitled to protect as part of his goods. No doubt that is an arguable case, but there are various questions to be determined in this action, which has not yet been tried, including the question whether this voice can in truth be regarded as a property and whether, in the circumstances of this case there could be said to be anything in the nature of unfair trade competition in a common field, where in the one case you have an actor who uses his voice in the performance of his particular occupation and, on the other hand, another actor who, in some way or other, uses his

voice to imitate a voice on television for advertising purposes." 1 W.L.R. at 319.

Lahr v. Adell Chemical Co., *supra*, was also a television commercial in which a cartoon duck was used to speak with a voice alleged to be the simulated voice of Bert Lahr, a successful professional entertainer. The complaint alleged three causes of action, for unfair competition, for invasion of privacy, and for defamation. An order dismissing the complaint for failure to state a claim was reversed on the basis of the claim of unfair competition. The court on appeal pointed out that the plaintiff had achieved stardom:

> "[I]n substantial measure because his 'style of vocal comic delivery which, by reason of its distinctive and original combination of pitch, inflection, accent and comic sounds,' has caused him to become 'widely known and readily recognized . . . as a unique and extraordinary comic character.' " 300 F.2d at 257.

The court held that the imposter was "stealing his thunder" and that on the face of the allegations the plaintiff was entitled to have his complaint go to trial. It was clear however that a cause of action for damage to reputation was not stated.

> "If every time one can allege, 'Your (anonymous) commercial sounded like me, but no so good,' and contend the public believed, in spite of the variance, . . . that his abilities had declined, the consequences would be too great to contemplate." 300 F.2d at 259.

It appears that *Lahr* was decided on the basis of a singular uniqueness of quality of voice that made his situation not just a difference of degree but a difference in kind.

> "We may agree with defendant that plaintiff has not shown any 'property' interest entitled to copyright protection. And we might hesitate to say that *an ordinary singer whose voice, deliberately or otherwise*, sounded sufficiently like another to cause confusion was not free to do so. Plaintiff here alleges a peculiar style and type of performance, unique in a far broader sense." 300 F.2d at 259 (emphasis supplied).

Because appellant relied so heavily upon *Lahr*, we point to a factual distinction, shared with *Sim*, that will have greater significance when seen in the light of *Sears* and *Compco*, discussed *infra*. In *Lahr* and *Sim* the defendants were not dealing in materials in which the defendants had a copyright. Or, to elaborate, in *Lahr* and *Sim* the plaintiffs claimed a "secondary meaning" in pure sound, their individual vocal characteristics.[11] The protection

---

[11] Gardella v. Log Cabin Products Inc., *supra*, is more difficult to distinguish upon the facts. The court there held that a "duty of identification" rested upon the defendant, the employer of the fictitious Aunt Jemima, and that the plaintiff, theatrical Aunt Jemima, must show actual

sought was not for the combination of sound together with copyrighted lyrics, melody and arrangement, as here. In this case appellant's complaint is not that her sound is uniquely personal; it is that the sound in connection with the music, lyrics and arrangement, which made her the subject of popular identification, ought to be protected. But as to these latter copyrightable items she had no rights. Presumably, she was required to obtain permission of the copyright owner to sing "Boots", and to make an arrangement of the song to suit her own tastes and talents. Had she desired to exclude all others from use of the song so that her "secondary meaning" with the song could not be imitated she could have purchased those rights from the copyright proprietor. One wonders whether her voice, and theatrical style, would have been identifiable if another song had been presented, and not "her song", which unfortunately for her was owned by others and licensed to the defendants.[12] But that case is not before us now.

Davis v. Trans World Airlines, *supra*, involved a television commercial where the airline used the music, lyrics and arrangement of a popular song "Up, Up and Away" to which it had acquired the rights from the copyright proprietor. Plaintiffs, a nationally known singing group called "The Fifth Dimension," had made a well known recording of the same song. The singing in the commercial was anonymous, as here. The district court held on a motion for summary judgment that there had been no passing-off and that imitation alone did not give rise to a cause of action.[13] In any event, *Davis* does not aid Sinatra for the court there denied recovery upon similar facts and a similar, if not identical, legal theory to that urged by Sinatra.

Across all of these cases fall the shadows of Sears, Roebuck & Co. v. Stiffel Co., 376 U.S. 225, 84 S.Ct. 784, 11 L.Ed. 2d 661 (1964), and Compco Corp. v. Day-Brite Lighting, Inc., 376 U.S. 234, 84 S.Ct. 779, 11 L.Ed.2d 669 (1964). In those two cases the Court announced, or we should probably more properly say, reaffirmed the "strong federal policy favoring free competition in ideas which do not merit [or qualify] for patent protection." Although both cases

---

confusion to establish a cause of action. *Gardella* was a pre-*Compco* case (see *infra*) and perhaps that is its only distinction.

[12] The tapes and the movies introduced as exhibits were viewed and heard by this court. To the untrained ear the sound of the voice carried no recognition, and no confusion of source. It was of professional quality but there was no readily identifiable accent (Maurice Chevalier), range, quality, (Lahr or Andy Devine), or pitch which would distinguish it to the ordinary listener from many others or identify it with any particular person. Although the actresses who appeared fleetingly and did not sing, wore boots, such props for this particular song carried no more originality than a snow scene for a rendition of "White Christmas."

[13] There was no appeal from the district court's decision. The question therefore remains an open one in this court.

involved imitation of patented articles the language of the Court spoke in broader terms.

> "But because of the federal patent laws a State may not, when the article is unpatented and *uncopyrighted*, prohibit the copying of the article itself or award damages for such copying." 376 U.S. at 232–233, 84 S.Ct. at 789. (emphasis supplied).

In both *Sears* and *Compco*, the unpatented articles of the plaintiff's were copied exactly by the defendants and sold as the defendant's articles without further identification.

> "What Sears did was to copy Stiffel's design and to sell lamps almost identical to those sold by Stiffel. This it had every right to do under the federal patent laws." 376 U.S. at 231, 84 S.Ct. at 789.

Nor do the copiers' motives make any difference. 376 U.S. at 238, 84 S.Ct. at 782.[15]

The Court made it very clear that just as a state could not encroach upon the federal patent laws directly it could not do so indirectly under the guise of enforcing its laws against unfair competition where those laws would clash with the federal objectives. Here, the defendants had paid a very substantial sum to the copyright proprietor to obtain the license for the use of the song and all of its arrangements. The plaintiff had not sought or obtained the same rights which would have protected the secondary meaning which she asserts. The resulting clash with federal law seems inevitable if damages or injunctive remedies are available under state laws. Moreover, the inherent difficulty of protecting or policing a "performance" or the creation of a performer in handling copyrighted material licensed to another imposes problems of supervision that are almost impossible for a court of equity.

An added clash with the copyright laws is the potential restriction which recognition of performers' "secondary meanings" places upon the potential market of the copyright proprietor. If a proposed licensee must pay each artist who has played or sung the composition and who might therefore claim unfair competition-performer's protection, the licensee may well be discouraged to the point of complete loss of interest. Finally as Judge Hand pointed out in his dissent in Capitol Records, Inc. v. Mercury Records Corp., 221 F.2d 657, 666–667 (2d Cir. 1955), to allow unfair competition protection where Congress has not given federal protection is in effect granting state copyright

---

[15] We note the caveat of Mr. Justice Harlan, concurring in the result, 376 U.S. at 239, 84 S.Ct. 779, in the event predatory practices should exist. While there is an inference of predatory business practices in the early attempts to bargain with Miss Sinatra through her agent, the terms upon which the negotiations took place might raise a question as to who was the predator.

benefits without the federal limitations of time to permit definite public domain use.

The judgment of the district court is affirmed.

Kirk Honeycutt, "WHOSE FILM IS IT ANYWAY?"
American Film (May, 1981), p. 34

"No area in the film or television industry is as bitterly contested as that of writing credits—and it's up to the Writers Guild jto give credit where due."

"She was so like all us writers when we first hit Hollywood—itching with ambition, panting to get your names up there: Screenplay by. Original story by. Hmph! Audiences don't know somebody sits down and *writes* a picture. They think the actors make it up as they go along."

—Sunset Boulevard

At the 1976 Academy Awards ceremony, writers Lawrence Hauben and Bo Goldman received Oscars for their collaboration in adapting Ken Kesey's novel *One Flew Over the Cuckoo's Nest* for the screen. Few people watching the telecast would have guessed that before that night, the two men had never met. In 1978 director Ronald Neame was so infuriated at the writing credits imposed on his film *Meteor* by the Writers Guild of America that he took out a full-page ad in the *Hollywood Reporter*, which explained how he believed the credits should read.

Last year film critics confronted two new works, *Rough Cut* and *Altered States*, written by those famous writers Francis Burns and Sidney Aaron, respectively. These were, in fact, pseudonyms for Larry Gelbart and Paddy Chayefsky. One of the most dazzling credit fights between writers in recent years involved *The Choirboys*. Joseph Wambaugh, who adapted his novel, and Christopher Knopf, who rewrote Wambaugh's script, *both* wanted their names taken off the film.

Welcome to Hollywood's version of a family feud. No area in the film or television industry is so thorny or bitterly contested as that of writing credits. Nearly every working writer in Hollywood has a horror story to tell about broken promises, stolen credits, or loss of fortune if not fame. The mere mention of a particular producer or fellow scenarist to a wounded writer can cause a personality transformation worthy of Dr. Jekyll.

Ironically, writers' credits are governed by their own union. The Writers Guild of America (WGA), a labor union representing more than eight thousand writers who work in television, film, and radio, handles all credit disputes. The guild is asked more than 150 times a year to resolve controversies between screenwriters and at least 300 times to intervene between television writers. Many of these disputes are technical in nature and can be routinely settled; others wind up in the WGA's credit arbitration process. [See side story, p. 212.]

"It's probably the most valuable function we perform," declares Leonard Chassman, executive director of the WGA. Yet few critics, moviegoers, or television viewers are aware of the arbitration process. What's even more surprising is that many writers and filmmakers are themselves ignorant of how the system actually works. How much do the credits which flash on the screen—often in such an unsightly clutter of writers' names that you can scarcely read them all—truly reflect authorship? How frequently do individuals get credit for work they really haven't done? "About ninety percent of the time, the system works very, very well," says Oscar-winning screenwriter Frank Pierson, guild vice-president and a member of the screen credits committee. "But ten percent of the time, people feel like they have been flayed alive."

Writers came late to the movie business. The first of their breed were gagmen and title writers in the silent era. Even after Jolson spoke and playwrights, journalists, and novelists came west, writers never enjoyed the authority or cachet of stars or directors. And today a writer on a set is a rare sight. "It's only the writer who gets gang-banged in this business," says screenwriter Steve Shagan, a two-time Oscar nominee. "You never see two directors or two cameramen on the screen. The writer puts everybody to work, but he's the disposable commodity."

For many years, writers' credits were determined by the production companies, often on a punitive, discriminatory, or nepotistic basis, without any recourse for the writer whatsoever. A producer's brother-in-law might get credit for a film, but not the person who worked for months on it. When the WGA negotiated its first Minimum Basic Agreement (MBA) with producers in 1942, control of credits was a key item. Nothing to this day, however, protects the writer's work—only his credit.

In theater, on the other hand, thanks to the protection of contracts designed and administered by the Dramatists Guild, the author of a play retains the copyright to his work. No one can change a word without his permission. However, a screen or television writer does not retain the copyright to his work; his employers do. He is a laborer hired to turn out a product, and that product can be altered at the whim of his employers. If anything, there is more rewriting now than ever before. "Credit arbitrations are becoming more complex and more time-consuming," says Leonard Chassman, "because of this [rewriting] trend. We've had films with twelve, thirteen, and fourteen writers on them."

"I've read arbitrations where the original writer did a helluva job," notes Christopher Knopf. "The script needs work, but he is never given an opportunity to follow through to a second and third draft. When the director is hired, he fires the original writer and brings in somebody else. He simply doesn't want the emotion of the writer who created the material on his neck. When those go to arbitration, they are very bitter." Such bitterness may strike the outsider as petty, egotistic squabbling. But more is at stake than just ego.

Money, for instance. The first two lines of the guild's credits manual read: "A writer's position in the motion picture or television industry is determined largely by his credits. His salary status depends on the quality and number of the screenplays, teleplays, or stories which bear his name." Most writers, especially newcomers, want their name on anything, regardless of quality. Writer-director John Carpenter freely admits his idea for *Eyes of Laura Mars* got "destroyed in various rewrites" after he left the picture. Yet he gladly took story and co-screenwriting credit, he says, because "I now have a credit on an $8 million film with Faye Dunaway. Whether good or bad, that gives me a certain amount of credibility in this town."

Most contracts now include contingency payment arrangements which increase a writer's fee or eligibility to participate in the film's profits if he gets a screen credit. The writer with a credit on a film also receives residual revenues. For instance, when the film is sold to television, he receives 1.2 percent of the adjusted gross receipts. With network licensing fees reaching as high as $10 million, that can be quite a bundle, especially if a writer has sole screen credit. If there are both screenplay and story credits, those responsible for the script receive seventy-five percent of the residuals, while the story credit is worth twenty-five percent.

However, the writer who gets the "Story by" credit holds a trump card of his own—a complex provision in the MBA called "separation of rights." In film he possesses publication rights for any paperback novelization. In television he has limited television sequel rights and certain dramatic, merchandising, and publishing rights. Pride of authorship can't be overlooked. However, "the problem you always run into with writers," says Knopf, "is that if you are a second writer, the moment you retype the script, you're convinced you've written everything."

There are those rare creatures who take their names off a show. Veteran writer Howard Rodman had his name removed from the television film *The Neon Ceiling*, the original pilot for "The Six Million Dollar Man," and the theatrical film *Madigan*. "In principle you take your name off because the script which comes out does not represent your work," he declares, "and, therefore, they [the producers] have no right to use it, and you have no right to put your name on it."

"Look, I'm sixty years old," Rodman continues. "I've worked my ass off to be a good writer. I'm still trying to be a better writer. My economic security lies in whatever craftsmanship and talent I have. I don't want that taken away from me. But over and above that, there is a matter of just sheer ego. I want what I have written to represent me—and only that."

In order to protect his financial interests, as well as to protect his home and loved ones from justifiably irate audiences, a writer may use a pseudonym, which he has registered with the WGA. Rodman signs many of his films as Henri Simoun. Christopher Knopf has registered, but never used, two pseudonyms: Bart Wideer, an anagram for Bad Rewrite, and Ted Sabat, an anagram for Bad Taste. Pseudonyms can only be used when a screenwriter has been paid less than $75,000 or a television writer less than three times the applicable minimum. It is assumed that writers paid more than those amounts are being hired partly for the value of their names and reputations.

Consequently, Joseph Wambaugh had to sue Universal to have his name removed from the film version of *The Choirboys*. "The guild wasn't able to do anything but support him morally," explains Naomi Gurian, WGA assistant executive director. The suit was based on an oral contract that no changes would be made in his script. Universal settled by taking his name off the script and giving him $1 million for his residual interests in the movie.

But the second writer, Christopher Knopf, protested to the WGA: He didn't want his name on the film alone. Knopf had done a little rewriting on Wambaugh's adaptation as a favor to director Robert Aldrich. He recalls cutting four scenes and writing a new, upbeat ending: "I swear to God, I don't think I changed three pages up until the end." Nevertheless, Wambaugh won the arbitration. "Joe's argument," says Knopf, "was that what he had set out to do had been changed by the upbeat ending, and I guess it had." Thus Knopf's name alone ended up on a film in which, Knopf says, "my total contribution was about five or six pages."

Credit should reflect authorship, which in the admittedly odd case of *The Choirboys*, it does not. So a question arises: In an art as collaborative as filmmaking, how often does the WGA's credit process represent, as John Carpenter puts it, "rules for the guild, not necessarily the truth"? The guild makes no bones about the fact that it tries to winnow the names down to as few as possible. "The basic cornerstone of our philosophy," says Chassman, "is that a multiplicity of credits diminishes the value of the writing credit. We have evolved a system that really narrows the number of writers who can share the final credits on a film."

The purity of this philosophy is soothing. Unfortunately, like the critics' auteur theory, it tends to ignore the realities of filmmaking. Scripts come not so much from the Muses as from story conferences involving producers, directors, actors, and writers. Rewriting is frequently done by second and third writers who may not contribute the exact percentage necessary to earn credit, yet who can make an inchoate script shootable.

"As a writer, I don't want to see my credit diluted," says Carl Gottlieb, whose credits include *Jaws* and *The Jerk*, "but as a guy called in to doctor scripts more than once, I would like to see some acknowledgement of what I did, short of a screenplay credit. Additional dialogue [a credit which the WGA has winnowed out] would be wonderful. Some people just can't write dialogue."

Limiting the writing credits can take some heat off producers. A film on which ten writers labored and received credit would tip off critics and those knowledgeable in the business that some production executive failed miserably in communicating with his writers. For the most part, however, production executives chafe at the WGA credit rules. Inasmuch as the arbitration system is totally dependent on written material, it can't adequately judge contributions made by other filmmakers.

"Nobody has yet sat down and worked out what it is a director does and what it is a writer does," says Howard Rodman. "In live television I once wrote a scene between Eddie Andrews and Nina Foch where a guy comes to propose marriage and she refuses him. But when those actors got through with the scene, it was far more than I had written. Now they made a genuine contribution over and beyond what I had written, but there is no way to arbitrate that. Film is a collaborative medium, and in that collaboration the rules are not well defined."

Frank Pierson disagrees: "The writing performed on a movie is done on paper. It's as ridiculous for a director to claim a writing credit from a writer to whom he made suggestions as for a writer to demand a share of the directing credit for suggestions he made or put in the screenplay."

Nevertheless, the story conference is often a bone of contention. When actor Richard Pryor claimed a story credit on *Which Way Is Up*, Carl Gottlieb protested and the case went to arbitration. Pryor was denied credit. "It was difficult because Pryor, the director, and myself spent long story sessions together at his place for several weeks," Gottlieb explains. "The script that emerged derived in large part from those conversations. I don't deny that. But I was the one who went home and wrote it. What I brought back was not a transcript of our conversations, but a script with dialogue, structure, and characters. People feel that because they sat in on the story session, they had significant input and they put their names on the script."

Undoubtedly, one of the bitterest disputes in recent years involved *The*

Rose. Not only was it a classic *Rashomon* situation, where everyone's memory filters events differently, but the final arbitrated credits, no matter how "fair" they are, cannot possibly reflect all the involvement and significant writing contributions on a project which went through nineteen drafts and five different directors.

In 1972 producer Marvin Worth hired Bill Kerby to write an original script called "The Pearl," based loosely on the life of Janis Joplin. When Twentieth Century-Fox agreed to finance the project, Worth hired Michael Cimino to direct. Kerby recalls that the three men then engaged in a "five-day brain-busting session," after which he wrote a second draft. "At this point," Kerby alleges, "Cimino evidently had all his notes transcribed, and then he registered them with the Writers Guild. As far as I can remember, they were notes by Cimino and Worth. My contention was that those notes represented ideas that all of us had."

Worth remembers things differently. "Cimino was dissatisfied with what Kerby was doing," he says. "Mike and I went and wrote a new outline for a new story and registered that at the Writers Guild. Bill Kerby was dismissed and Bo Goldman brought in as a writer. When Goldman's draft came in, I was told to put on it 'By Bo Goldman and Michael Cimino,' with the approval of Bo Goldman."

Kerby vigorously protested the credits Worth proposed for *The Rose*, as the film was by now called: "Story by Marvin Worth and Michael Cimino, Screenplay by Bo Goldman, Michael Cimino, and Bill Kerby." Then when the written material was submitted to the guild, Goldman, who ultimately wrote nine drafts, saw red: "What comes in is an outline that no one ever showed me. I realized that the ideas Cimino supplied [to me] were Bill Kerby's. So then I said, 'I don't feel that Cimino should get credit. Kerby should get story credit.' " So a rare special committee of three guild members met with all concerned, plus their attorneys, in order to determine whose name belonged on what scripts. Only then were all the scripts submitted for arbitration.

Worth, who has been a member of the guild for years, is adamant that his claim to story credit was valid, even though the WGA disallowed it. "I wrote at least forty pages before anybody came on as a writer. But the guild does not recognize something written on a person who lived." At the time, the forty pages, Worth recalls, "was about Janis Joplin, so it doesn't count. The [the WGA] refused to use it in arbitration." Ann Migden, the guild screen credits administrator, clarifies this point: "Credit cannot be granted where there is source material of a story nature, such as a biography or newspaper articles. But there as some times when a story credit is suitable in that case [of a living person], depending on if there is source material or not, and if a new story comes out of what somebody writes apart from source material."

Kerby's statement to the arbiters is indicative of the lengths to which writers go in credit disputes. He says, "I hired a story analyst to go through seven or eight drafts and point up the similarities and dissimilarities and also do a page and paragraph count. My statement ran, I think, twenty-three single-spaced pages and laid out my position the way a lawyer lays out a case. That's probably one of the reasons why I won." The final credits read: "Story by Bill Kerby, Screenplay by Bill Kerby and Bo Goldman."

Was Kerby's fight worth it? The paperback novelization rights sold for about $246,000. Kerby's share, under separation of rights, came to forty percent. Kerby did have one advantage in his fight: He was the first writer on the project. "There is in the [credit] rules and in the sentiments of the members of the arbitration panels and often our older and more experienced writers," explains Frank Pierson, "a strong bias toward the first writer. He was the guy that had to face the empty page and originate the whole thing."

The credits manual puts a special burden on subsequent writers in terms of demonstrating contributions to the final screenplay. The primacy of the first writer, many feel, is a knee-jerk reflex left over from the old studio-system days. "You're going to get a bunch of old hands," says Goldman, "who come from the old studio system, guys really kind of past their prime—although I wonder what their prime was, because they put in from nine to five at Columbia studios doing Dorothy Lamour movies—and they sit on arbitration committees, and they have this great rage against studios and directors and always see themselves as that first writer."

Whatever the psychology, the arbiters' judgements are always quantitative rather than qualitative. The quality of the first writer's work is never at issue, even though the lack thereof may be what caused the producer to hire another writer.

"When you're dealing with a union," says Howard Rodman, "the problem is that you cannot assume what probably is the truth—that some writers in that union are better than other writers. We don't say what's better or worse; we only say what is used. That's the basic premise in the whole arbitration."

"The first writer can do the worst job in the world," complains Goldman, "yet he is always in primary position. I can understand on an original, but on an adaptation from a novel, they're not his characters. On *One Flew Over the Cuckoo's Nest*, I was in second position, succeeding another writer. We used maybe his structure to some degree, but the structure is the structure of the novel!"

Other writers argue that to crack a book or play and to construct a film script that is cinematic is no small chore and fully deserves credit—even when the adapter has made minimal changes. "The matter of restraint and judgment is as much a part of an adaptation as anything else," insists Pierson.

"You benefit enormously by having the sense to leave what's going to work and not arbitrarily 'open up' a play or do other things you're always urged to do. That's a form of creative thinking.

A controversial new amendment to the screen credits manual, passed overwhelmingly late last year despite objections raised by a number of veteran members, has further codified the primacy of the first writer. In the event of a credit arbitration involving an original screenplay, the new rule states that the original writer must get at least a shared story credit, no matter how little of his work is used. "It is too sweeping," says Carl Gottlieb. "I don't feel the first writer is entitled to *that* much protection. If he creates the entire work on his own on 'spec,' then he deserves some kind of credit. But a writer commissioned to write something is not the creator of the project."

"I personally feel that's a disaster," agrees Pierson. "Credits should reflect who wrote what. But the fact of the matter is, we have searched the records and everybody's memory, and we've not yet come up with a case in which a writer of an original screenplay did not get credit."

Guild officials like to point out that none of the rules or procedures in its credits manual are considered rigid or inflexible, and that the percentages of contribution to the final screenplay necessary to receive credit serve only as guidelines. "A second writer could be called in and make only three changes on two different lines," says Naomi Gurian, "and have made such a major contribution to the thrust of the script to merit credit. On the other hand, writers may change every line a little bit and not merit credit, because all they did was play with words." Yet even on this score, individual arbiters interpret it the way they see fit.

"So often writers get credit for something that they haven't in fact done," says Ronald Neame, "or, at any rate, did a part of and should only get a second credit for." Such an instance, the English director says, led him to place the *Hollywood Reporter* ad challenging the story and shared screenplay credit of Edmund H. North for *Meteor*. Neame did not himself demand credit, but felt the arbiters' decision was unfair to Stanley Mann. "Stanley and I worked on that script based on an idea by one of the producers, Theodore Parvin. True, there were several other scripts, but when I joined Stanley, we started from page one, and I never read any other scripts."

"My quarrel with the present arbitration system," Neame continues, "is that the arbitration committee, while reading all those scripts and source materials, doesn't listen to the director. I feel if the director has been involved in the script, as all good directors should, he, probably more than anybody else, is the best judge of what the contributions of the various writers are. We should be given an ear and not made the enemy."

The WGA rejects such an idea flat out. "We do not want to turn arbitration into a court of law where testimony is taken," says Pierson. "We can't make judgments about who is telling the truth. Writing is writing, and we take as evidence only written material." Leonard Chassman makes another point: "It is highly possible that a director-producer may have a vested interest. There are contracts where moneys are contingent on the outcome of credit arbitration. So we feel sometimes a producer would advocate a certain credit because he, frankly, might save money."

Neame's use of the word "enemy" is not idle. As Gottlieb puts it, "I'm afraid our guild does see directors as the enemy." This hits hardest at the so-called hyphenates, writers who also direct or produce. If a production executive claims credit, unless the writing is done entirely without the collaboration of another writer, arbitration is automatic. What irritates the hyphenates is that the burden of proof in arbitration rests entirely on them. They must demonstrate a greater contribution than a "pure" writer to gain any screenplay credit.

Marvin Worth, a writer turned producer, does not mince words: "I feel the guild is very discriminatory against producers and directors who are hyphenates. Their attitude is terrible toward the guy who is not the pure writer. It's a dictatorship." Many writers and even guild officials agree. "It's like they're penalized for wanting to do more," says Bill Kerby.

"It's one of the most difficult areas for the guild," admits Naomi Gurian. "We have many writers who become directors or producers out of a basic need to control their own work. Once they do, then for them to get a writing credit when producing or directing a film where there were also other writers becomes a problem."

But whatever the problem, getting the writing credit is regarded in Hollywood as worth the struggle. The stakes are high—ego, reputation, and money are all on the line. Sometimes, though, *not* getting a writing credit is worth an equal struggle. Howard Rodman recalls one scene in his script for *Winning* which featured an actress in a bathing suit on a raft. The star decided her thighs were too heavy; so her manager, who was also a producer on the film, attacked the scene. When it was defended, he attacked the scene before it. "Pretty soon that whole section was attacked," he says, "and when I wouldn't rewrite it, someone else did."

Rodman wanted his name removed, but the studio refused. However, when he read the novelization of his script—which he regarded as pulp trash and which also had his name on it—he bypassed all the guild machinery and took a more elemental approach. "I informed them that I was the father of children and my name was not going to be on that. They said they couldn't do anything—it was published. I said, 'You take my name off or not only will I sue you, I'll *kill* you first.' " The title page was quickly removed from about five thousand paperback books.

Kirk Honeycutt, "GETTING CREDIT: THE SCENARIO"
American Film (May 1981), p. 38

When you're starting your career, having a written credit on a film is better than not having a credit, no matter what the film is," says screenwriter-critic Joseph McBride. "Your credit really is your bread and butter." Each year the Writers Guild is asked to resolve bread-and-butter disputes by arbitrating writers' credits on some 50 feature films and 160 television shows.

Here's how the process works. When a film finishes principal photography, the producer sends a suggested credit listing to the guild and all participating writers. If all parties agree, that's that (though if a producer or director is one of the suggested writers, arbitration is automatic). If a writer disagrees, however, he has twenty-four hours to request to see a final script; after he gets it, he has five days to register a protest with both the studio and the guild.

Now things get interesting. The guild assembles an arbitration panel of three writers, two of whom have some arbitration experience. (A contesting writer is allowed to strike a "reasonable" number of names from the guild's arbiter list.) Working anonymously, independently, without pay, and with the help of a consultant to interpret esoteric guild rules, the arbiters read all written material and source material submitted by the producer and then reach a decision. The amount of material they must read is sometimes staggering. Howard Rodman recalls reading eighteen drafts in one arbitration.

The types of credits awarded are arrived at by precentages that reflect the contribution to the final script. A second writer on an original screenplay, for example, must contribute fifty percent to receive screenplay credit. Story credit (defined as being "distinct from screenplay and consisting of basic narrative, idea, theme, or outline indicating character development and action") may not be shared by more than two writers. Screenplay credit (for the final script with scenes and dialogue) may not be shared by more than two writers, except as the result of arbitration, which may permit three names or two writing teams. (A team consists of two writers and is represented on the screen by the use of an ampersand: John Doe & Mary Roe.)

Most arbitration decisions are unanimous; if not, majority decision prevails. Although it's rare, a writer may request a review by the policy review board of the arbiters' decision to determine whether any serious deviation from guild policy occurred. This board can't overturn a decision, but may direct the panel to reconsider its decision or may form a new panel.

Although Christopher Knopf, a screenwriter and an arbiter, insists that "the arbitration structure in the guild is probably the purest and best thing the whole industry has going for itself," the system is not without flaws. Steve Shagan, who is on the screen credits committee, points out, "We can't seem to get the most proficient screenwriters, that is to say those writers who are technically and artistically highly skilled, to give up their time and energy and do an arbitration. Therefore, the arbitrations are done by people who are more or less in semiretirement." While television writers serve as arbiters only in areas they are familiar with—sit-coms, television movies, and so forth—no such match of genre and writer is made for screen arbiters. The guild also has no means of monitoring the arbiters' diligence.

For all the system's safeguards, it is still possible to steal credits. Abuse is more frequent in television, where producers and story editors can impinge on credits by doing unnecessary rewriting, but it can certainly happen in film, too.

A particularly sticky area in film arbitration is whether ideas by a producer or director constitute writing. "Somewhere input does become writing, and that can't be judged on the basis of written material," notes Carl Gottlieb. "That's where it's possible to steal a credit. As a writer, though, you're aware of the tricks. The first thing a lot of writers who rewrite a script do is change all character names. It *looks* different. Very often they reorganize the material in minor ways, like changing the order of scenes, so that it seems different. Others rewrite every line of dialogue. Some arbiters are taken in by all new dialogue, even though it's the same characters, relationships, and attitudes."

Then there is the "Moviola cut." Bill Kerby explains: "A producer screens the final film and has his secretary take down in shorthand the exact lines in the film. Occasionally, it hurts a writer's case, because actors change lines slightly and the producer can say, 'That's my draft.' "

"Another ploy producers pull," adds Frank Pierson, "is to try to stampede the situation by withholding all material until the last minute and suddenly dumping five tons of scripts on [the arbiters] and saying, 'Hurry up, hurry up, you've got to decide in forty-eight hours.' "

Recently, the guild encountered a case in which the final film did not accurately reflect the script the producer turned in as the final draft. This raised the still-unresolved question of whether, and under what circumstances, arbiters should view a print of the picture.

Bo Goldman sums up the whole question of arbitration this way: "Each case is unique, and it's a quasi-legal proceeding, and it's always, ultimately, unfair. But isn't life? The real credits should always read, 'Three-eighths one person and five-eighths another,' but how can you put that on the screen? Anybody in the business always knows who's written what anyway. I've never known anybody to get it wrong. Your Aunt Molly will get it wrong, but Ned Tanen or Sherry Lansing knows who did the script, even if your name isn't there. It's a tight little community."—K.H.

Kirk Honeycutt is the film critic for the Daily News in Los Angeles.

IN THE MATTER OF THE ARBITRATION BETWEEN DIRECTORS GUILD OF AMERICA, INC. AND KING-HITZIG PRODUCTIONS, No. 00892

as reported in
Entertainment Law Reporter 24 (May 15, 1981), p. 1

Movie director whose services are terminated after completion of principal photography has the right to consult with film's producers during post-production

DGA Arbitrator Edward Mosk has ruled that King-Hitzig Productions and Orion Pictures were entitled to terminate the services of director Michael Wadleigh after principal photography was completed on the film "Wolfen," but that King-Hitzig nevertheless was required to consult with Wadleigh regarding creative elements during post-production on the film.

The Directors Guild contended that once 100% of principal photography was completed, King-Hitzig had no right to terminate Wadleigh's services except for cause. Wadleigh was not notified of the grounds for his termination. According to King-Hitzig, Wadleigh had ordered unauthorized props for the film, inserted dialogue which was not in the screenplay, incurred unauthorized costs and had failed to follow the producer's instructions. Mosk found that these events did not justify the discharge of Wadleigh for "cause."

King-Hitzig also alleged that Wadleigh was responsible for the increased cost of the film. But Mosk noted that Wadleigh may not have been shown the budget, and there was no evidence that Wadleigh represented that he could complete the film within any special budget.

Mosk then found that King-Hitzig would have been entitled to remove Wadleigh even in the absence of cause if the producer had followed the "hotline" procedure of the DGA Collective Bargaining Agreement. Section 7-

502 of the agreement, which is entitled "Editing and Post-Production (Including Hotline)," states:

> Any director who prepares and has completed 90% of the scheduled principal photography of a theatrical motion picture . . . cannot be replaced, except for cause, until the following procedure (herein referred to as 'hotline') has taken place . . .

The section applies to events occurring after the director has completed 90% of the scheduled principal photography. Mosk concluded that the section would apply as well when 100% of principal photography is completed. But King-Hitzig did not use the "hotline" procedure at the time of Wadleigh's termination. Wadleigh was not given an opportunity to discuss his dismissal with a representative of the producer before being terminated. And a new director was not assigned to the film until the end of January. The delay was "inconsistent with the philosophy and objective of the Bargaining Agreement," stated Mosk. King-Hitzig argued that it did not need to employ a new director until post-production activities required the services of a director. Mosk found, however, that this interpretation "could provide an opportunity for a producer to act in bad faith to defeat the post-production creative rights of the first director." King-Hitzig therefore erred in dismissing Wadleigh without going though the hotline procedure.

While upholding the producer's right to terminate pursuant to hotline, Mosk also acknowledged the Directors Guild's concern about the erosion of the one director concept, and he determined that it was necessary to accommodate the first director's creative rights. Thus, Mosk ruled that all post-production consultation rights granted to directors by the collective bargaining agreement become vested when the director has completed 100% of principal photography. If a new director is then employed, the producer must consult with both directors. The first director must have a good faith opportunity at each meaningful stage of post-production to comment on a procedure before any irreversible step is taken, that is, at a time when it is still possible to make changes in accordance with the suggestions and vision of the first director if the producer finds there is merit in the suggestions.

Among the significant post-production procedures included by Mosk were optical effects, looping, dubbing of sound and/or music, negative cutting, and preview rights. Any inconvenience resulting from according such rights to two directors must be accommodated by the producer, Mosk ruled.

Mosk refused to reinstate Wadleigh as the director of "Wolfen." But King-Hitzig was required to provide Wadleigh with consultation rights and was required to invite him to all film previews. King-Hitzig was also ordered to pay $20,000 to Wadleigh and $20,000 to the DGA as damages for its violation of the hotline procedures of the collective bargaining agreement.

In the Matter of the Arbitration Between Directors Guild of America, Inc. and King-Hitzig Productions, No. 00892 (Before the Arbitration Tribunal of the Directors Guild of America, March 17, 1981)

"CALIFORNIA ART PRESERVATION ACT"
California Civil Code § 987 (West Supp. 1984)

§ 987. Preservation of works of art.

(a) Legislative findings and declaration.

The Legislature hereby finds and declares that the physical alteration or destruction of fine art, which is an expression of the artist's personality, is detrimental to the artist's reputation, and artists therefore have an interest in protecting their works of fine art against such alteration or destruction; and that there is also a public interest in preserving the integrity of cultural and artistic creations.

(b) Definitions.

As used in this section:

(1) "Artist" means the individual or individuals who create a work of fine art.

(2) "Fine art" means an original painting, sculpture, or drawing, or an original work of art in glass, of recognized quality, but shall not include work prepared under contract for commercial use by its purchaser.

(3) "Person" means an individual, partnership, corporation, association or other group, however organized.

(4) "Frame" means to prepare, or cause to be prepared, a work of fine art for display in a manner customarily considered to be appropriate for a work of fine art in the particular medium.

(5) "Restore" means to return, or cause to be returned, a deteriorated or damaged work of fine art as nearly as is feasible to its original state or condition, in accordance with prevailing standards.

(6) "Conserve" means to preserve, or cause to be preserved, a work of fine art by retarding or preventing deterioration or damage through appropriate treatment in accordance with prevailing standards in order to maintain the structural integrity to the fullest extent possible in an unchanging state.

(7) "Commercial use" means fine art created under a work-for-hire arrangement for use in advertising, magazines, newspapers, or other print and electronic media.

(c) Mutilation, alteration or destruction of a work.

(1) No person, except an artist who owns and possesses a work of fine art which the artist has created, shall intentionally commit, or authorize the intentional commission of, any physical defacement, mutilation, alteration, or destruction of a work of fine art.

(2) In addition to the prohibitions contained in paragraph (1), no person who frames, conserves, or restores a work of fine art shall commit, or authorize the commission of, any physical defacement, mutilation, alteration, or destruction of a work of fine art by any act constituting gross negligence. For purposes of this section, the term "gross negligence" shall mean the exercise of so slight a degree of care as to justify the belief that there was an indifference to the particular work of fine art.

(d) Authorship.

The artist shall retain at all times the right to claim authorship, or, for just and valid reason, to disclaim authorship of his or her work of fine art.

(e) Remedies.

To effectuate the rights created by this section, the artist may commence an action to recover or obtain any of the following:

(1) Injunctive relief.

(2) Actual damages.

(3) Punitive damages. In the event that punitive damages are awarded, the court shall, in its discretion, select an organization or organizations engaged in charitable or educational activities involving the fine arts in California to receive such damages.

(4) Reasonable attorneys' and expert witness fees.

(5) Any other relief which the court deems proper.

(f) Determination of recognized quality.

In determining whether a work of fine art is of recognized quality, the trier of fact shall rely on the opinions of artists, art dealers, collectors of fine art, curators of art museums, and other persons involved with the creation or marketing of fine art.

(g) Rights and duties.

The rights and duties created under this section:

(1) Shall, with respect to the artist, or if any artist is deceased, his heir, legatee, or personal representative, exist until the 50th anniversary of the death of such artist.

(2) Shall exist in addition to any other rights and duties which may now or in the future be applicable.

(3) Except as provided in paragraph (1) of subdivision (h), may not be waived except by an instrument in writing expressly so providing which is signed by the artist.

(h) Removal from building; waiver.

(1) If a work of fine art cannot be removed from a building without substantial physical defacement, mutilation, alteration, or destruction of such work, the rights and duties created under this section, unless expressly reserved by an instrument in writing signed by the owner of such building and properly recorded, shall be deemed waived. Such instrument, if properly recorded, shall be binding on subsequent owners of such building.

(2) If the owner of a building wishes to remove a work of fine art which is a part of such building but which can be removed from the building without substantial harm to such fine art, and in the course of or after removal, the owner intends to cause or allow the fine art to suffer physical defacement, mutilation, alteration, or destruction, the rights and duties created under this section shall apply unless the owner has diligently attempted without success to notify the artist, or, if the artist is deceased, his heir, legatee, or personal representative, in writing of his intended action affecting the work of fine art, or unless he did provide notice and that person failed within 90 days either to remove the work or to pay for its removal. If such work is removed at the expense of the artist, his heir, legatee, or personal representative, title to such fine art shall pass to that person.

(3) Nothing in this subdivision shall affect the rights of authorship created in subdivision (d) of this section.

(i) Limitation of actions.

No action may be maintained to enforce any liability under this section unless brought within three years of the act complained of or one year after discovery of such act, whichever is longer.

(j) Operative date.

This section shall become operative on January 1, 1980, and shall apply to claims based on proscribed acts occurring on or after that date to works of fine arts whenever created.

(k) Severability.

If any provision of this section or the application thereof to any person or circumstance is held invalid for any reason, such invalidity shall not affect any other provisions or applications of this section which can be effected without the invalid provision or application, and to this end the provisions of this section are severable.

"ARTISTS' AUTHORSHIP RIGHTS ACT"
New York General Business Law §§ 288 m–q (McKinney 1983)

§ 288–m. Definitions

Whenever used in this article, except where the context clearly requires otherwise, the terms below shall have the following meanings:

1. "Artist" means the creator of a work of fine art;

2. "Conservation" means acts taken to correct deterioration and alteration and acts taken to prevent, stop or retard deterioration;

3. "Person" means an individual, partnership, corporation, association or other group, however organized;

4. "Reproduction" means a copy, in any medium, of a work of fine art, that is displayed or published under circumstances that, reasonably construed, evinces an intent that it be taken as a representation of a work of fine art as created by the artist;

5. "Work of fine art" means any original work of visual or graphic art of any medium which includes, but is not limited to, the following: painting; drawing; print; photographic point or sculpture of a limited edition of no more than three hundred copies; provided however, that "work of fine art" shall not include sequential imagery such as that in motion pictures.

Added L.1983, c. 994 § 3.

§ 228–n. Public display, publication and reproduction of works of fine art

Except as limited by section two hundred twenty-eight-p of this article, no person other than the artist or a person acting with the artist's consent shall knowingly display in a place accessible to the public or publish a work of fine art of that artist or a reproduction thereof in an altered, defaced, mutilated or modified form if the work is displayed, published or reproduced as being the work of the artist, or under circumstances under which it would reasonably be regarded as being the work of the artist, and damage to the artist's reputation is reasonably likely to result therefrom.

Added L.1983, c. 994, § 3.

§ 228–o. Artists' authorship rights

1. Except as limited by section two hundred twenty-eight-p of this article,

the artist shall retain at all times the right to claim authorship, or, for just and valid reason, to disclaim authorship of his or her work of fine art. The right to claim authorship shall include the right of the artist to have his or her name appear on or in connection with the work of fine art as the artist. The right to disclaim authorship shall include the right of the artist to prevent his or her name from appearing on or in connection with the work of fine art as the artist. Just and valid reason for disclaiming authorship shall include that the work of fine art has been altered, defaced, mutilated or modified other than by the artist, without the artist's consent, and damage to the artist's reputation is reasonably likely to result or has resulted therefrom.

2. The rights created by this section shall exist in addition to any other rights and duties which may now or in the future be applicable.

Added L.1983, c. 994, § 3.

§ 228–p. Limitations of applicability

1. Alteration, defacement, mutilation or modification of a work of fine art resulting from the passage of time or inherent nature of the materials will not by itself create a violation of section two hundred twenty-eight-n of this article or a right to disclaim authorship under subdivision one of section two hundred twenty-eight-o of this article; provided such alteration, defacement, mutilation or modification was not the result of gross negligence in maintaining or protecting the work of fine art.

2. In the case of a reproduction, a change that is an ordinary result of the medium of reproduction does not by itself create a violation of section two hundred twenty-eight-n of this article or a right to disclaim authorship under subdivision one of section two hundred twenty-eight-o of this article.

3. Conservation shall not constitute an alteration, defacement, mutilation or modification within the meaning of this article, unless the conservation work can be shown to be negligent.

4. This article shall not apply to work prepared under contract for advertising or trade use unless the contract so provides.

5. The provisions of this article shall apply only to works of fine art knowingly displayed in a place accessible to the public, published or reproduced in this state.

Added L.1983, c. 994, § 3.

§ 228–q. Relief

1. An artist aggrieved under section two hundred twenty-eight-n or section two hundred twenty-eight-o of this article shall have a cause of action for legal and injunctive relief.

2. No action may be maintained to enforce any liability under this article

unless brought within three years of the act complained of or one year after the constructive discovery of such act, whichever is longer.

Added L.1983, c. 994, § 3.

Supplemental Reading

Dahl v. Columbia Pictures Corp., 12 Misc. 2d 574, 166 N.Y.S.2d 708 (Sup. Ct. N.Y. Co. 1957) (plaintiff restrained from controlling promotional use of her own likeness in film character role); *aff'd*, 7 A.D.2d 969, 183 N.Y.S.2d 992 (1st Dep't 1959).

Booth v. Colgate-Palmolive Co., 362 F. Supp. 343 (S.D.N.Y. 1973) (unauthorized imitation of voice in commercial not actionable).

Lahr v. Adell Chemical Co., 300 F.2d 256 (1st Cir. 1962) (unauthorized imitation of voice in commercial actionable as unfair competition).

Amarnick, "American Recognition of Moral Right: Issues and Options," 29 *Copyright L. Symp.* (ASCAP) 31 (1983).

DaSilva, "Droit Moral and the Amoral Copyright: A Comparison of Artists' Rights in France and the United States," 28 *Bull. Copyright Soc'y* 1 (1981).

Note, "Artworks and American Law: The California Art Preservation Act," 61 *B.U. L. Rev.* 1201 (1981).

Diamond, "Legal Protection for the "Moral Rights" of Authors and Other Creators," 68 *Trademark Rep.* 244 (1978).

Comment, "Protection of Artistic Integrity: Gilliam v. American Broadcasting Companies," 90 *Harv. L. Rev.* 473 (1976).

CHAPTER 3

CREDIT

Introduction

Credit, also called billing, is one of the two primary business points—along with compensation—which is, or should be, considered in *every* entertainment agreement. Credit is also frequently a subject of litigation, particularly in situations where credit provisions have not been adequately considered by the parties, or where one party has disregarded the exact letter of the contractual obligations.

In addition, credit may also be the basis for litigation between parties who have no contractual relationship. For example, lawsuits involving claims of invasion or abuse of rights of privacy or publicity are, in effect, lawsuits involving the unauthorized billing of a person's name, image or likeness for a project with which the person wishes not to be associated, or for which the person wishes to receive compensation.

There is a frequent assumption, particularly among persons unfamiliar with the industry, that disputes over credits or billing merely involve matters of ego. This chapter raises questions, and suggests possible answers, about the economic and psychological values of credit. It also explores the question of who has an interest in the value of credit, since credit may be of value to persons other than the one whose name is involved. Considering who has such an interest should permit the identification, and hopefully avoidance, of potential problems before they arise, or permit easier resolution if problems do in fact arise.

This chapter will also consider specific situations in which there is particular potential for the existence of troublesome credit problems, such as when there are multiple and possibly confusing credits.

Lastly, this chapter will explore, from both legal and practical perspectives, the remedies available to a party injured as the result of a breach of a credit obligation.

Required Reading

Geisel v. Poynter Products, Inc., 295 F. Supp. 331 (S.D.N.Y. 1968).

Paramount Productions, Inc. v. Smith, 91 F.2d 863 (9th Cir, 1937).

Curwood v. Affiliated Distributors, Inc., 283 F. Supp. 219 (S.D.N.Y. 1922).

"Arbitrators Find That The Directors of 'Jaws 2' and 'King of The Gypsies' Were Entitled To Credit In Certain Advertisements," *Entertainment Law Reporter* (October 15, 1979), p. 2.

Landon v. Twentieth Century-Fox Film Corporation, 384 F. Supp. 450 (S.D.N.Y. 1974).

Rich v. RCA Corporation, 390 F. Supp. 530 (S.D.N.Y. 1975).

Vargas v. Esquire, Inc., 164 F.2d 522 (7th Cir. 1947).

Perin Film Enterprises, Ltd. v. TWG Productions, Inc., No. _____ (S.D.N.Y. August 28, 1978).

Plaintiffs' Memorandum In Support of Motion For A Preliminary Injunction And Temporary Restraining Order.

Smith v. Montoro, 648 F.2d 602 (9th Cir. 1981).

Gold Leaf Group, Ltd. v. Stigwood Group, Ltd. (unpublished opinion) No. 11768/78 (Sup. Ct. N.Y. Co. October 4, 1978).

Aljean Harmetz, "Falk Says 'No' To Press Junket," *The New York Times* (June 15, 1978), p. C17.

Louis L'Amour, Advertisement, *Publisher's Weekly* (July 29, 1983), p. 16.

All contracts and union agreements referred to in the chapter "Concepts."

CONCEPTS

1. What is the economic value of credit?

    (A) What does the *American Film* article of May, 1981 (p. 201) suggest as to the groups of people to whom writing credits are valuable?

    (B) What does *Geisel v. Poynter* (p. 225) suggest about a response to this question?

    (C) What do Directors Guild of America Basic Agreement (1981), Parags. 8—203(a), (e) (p. 505) and Writers Guild of America Basic Agreement (1977), Parags. 1B1(b), 1C1(b) and 2A(1)-(3) (pp.530,531) suggest about a response to this question?

(1) Where and in what size does Directors Guild of America Basic Agreement (1981), Parags. 8–203(a), (e) (p. 505) require credit to appear?

(2) How does a person become a professional writer for purposes of the Writers Guild of America Basic Agreement, and what is the significance of such status?

2. *Paramount v. Smith* (p. 253)

(A) If the producer had wanted to give Smith a credit, what were the forms of credit available pursuant to the parties' contract?

(B) What other forms of credit exist for the author of an underlying work?

(C) What happens if there is a claim for credit by the author of an underlying work and a conflicting claim for "original screenplay" credit by the screenplay writer?

(1) What does *Curwood v. Affiliated Distributors* (p. 266) suggest about a possible answer?

(2) What does dissent in *Paramount* suggest about a possible answer?

(3) What does Writers Guild of America Basic Agreement (1977) and (1981), Theatrical Schedule A, Parags. 9 to 19 (pp. 580—594) suggest about a possible way to resolve this conflict?

(4) What is a practical approach to determining appropriate writing credit?

(D) For what other creative function are multiple credits possible? Why? See *Variety* article of 5/11/83 (p. 143).

3. What is a "possessory" credit? Who is likely to claim a "possessory" credit? What do Directors Guild of America Basic Agreement (1981), Parags. 8—203(a), (g)(i)(3), (ii) (p. 505); Writers Guild of America Basic Agreement (1977), Theatrical Schedule A, Parag. 22 exceptions (a), (b), (d) (p. 586), (1981) Parags. 22, 22(e) (p. 595) say about who is entitled to a possessory credit?

4. Looking at Directors Guild of America Basic Agreement (1981), Parag. 8–203(g)(i) (p. 505) and Writers Guild of America Basic Agreement (1977), Theatrical Schedule A, Parag. 22 exception (a) (p. 586):

(A) What are "teaser" and "trailer" ads? How does the Directors Agreement (p. 505) define "teasers"? What do arbitration decisions (p. 270) suggest about the danger of this type of definition?

(B) Why are these kinds of ads excluded from paid ad requirements?

(C) What would be excluded ads in live theatrical branch of the industry?

(D) Certain excluded ads have exclusions where credit must nevertheless be given—why?

(E) Which Guild—Directors Guild of America or Writers Guild of America—has fewer exclusions and why?

5. In Acquisition of Rights Agreement, why is Parag. 1.6 (p. 637) necessary? Given credit obligations of Parag. 11 (p. 642), is Parag. 1.6 necessary?

6. What are desirable limits on credit provisions? Consider:

— *Landon v. 20th Century Fox* (p. 272)

— *Rich v. RCA* (p. 274)

— *Vargas v. Esquire* (p. 275)

— *Geisel v. Poynter* (p. 225)

7. In what ways can credit obligations be evaded or abused? Consider Screen Actors Guild Codified Basic Agreement (1977), Parag. 25A (p. 605) and Directors Guild of America Basic Agreement (1981), Parag. 8–201 (p. 504), and the types of problems these provisions are designed to avoid.

8. From a comparison of Directors Guild of America Basic Agreement (1973), Article 2, Parag. 2–201 (p. 488), (1981) Article 2 (pp. 494–502); Writers Guild of America Basic Agreement (1970), Article 12A2 (p. 520), (1973) Article 12A2 (pp. 526–527), (1977) Articles 11E, 12A (pp. 531–533), 1981 Article 11E (p. 590); Screen Actors Guild Codified Basic Agreement (1977) Parag. 25 (pp. 605–606), Screen Actors Guild Television Agreement (1977) Parag. 54 (pp. 617–619), (1980) Parag. IV–5 (p. 625), what role have unions had with respect to remedies for breach of credit requirements?

(A) Why did unions need to negotiate these provisions if an injured person could sue?

(B) Why did it take the Screen Actors Guild until 1977 to achieve remedies acquired by the Directors Guild of America and the Writers Guild of America in 1973?

(C) In the Screen Actors Guild Codified Basic Agreement (1977), and in the Screen Actors Guild Television Agreement (1977), respectively, why have Parags. 25(C)(1), (2) (p. 605) and Parags. 54(b)(1), (2) (p. 618) been included? What do they contribute?

(D) What remedies do these union agreements offer for breach of a credit obligation?

9. What other remedies are available for breach of credit rights, and what are the legal theories available to support the remedies sought?

    (A) Consider the Memorandum in *Perin Film Enterprises v. TWG Productions* (p. 281) and *Smith v. Montoro* (p. 292).

    (B) In *Gold Leaf v. Stigwood,* an unreported decision, (p. 298):

        (1) What writing existed requiring credit for Frampton? What difference does it make how it was characterized?

        (2) What does Parag. 16.4 in the Screenplay Loanout Agreement (p. 680) suggest about the availability of the remedy sought in this case? Under what legal theories might the answer be different? Why?

    (C) See *The New York Times* article: 6/15/78 (p. 301).

    (D) See *Publisher's Weekly* advertisement: July 29, 1983 (p. 302).

10. Why are there credit obligations in movie, TV and live theatrical agreements, but not in recording, music publishing or book publishing agreements?

11. What are the different credit vehicles in each branch of the entertainment industry? What difference does it make?

    — Theatrical motion pictures?

    — Television?

    — Live theatrical?

    — Recording?

    — Book publishing?

GEISEL v. POYNTER PRODUCTS, INC.
295 F. Supp. 331 (S.D.N.Y. 1968)

OPINION

HERLANDS, District Judge:

Can an artist who sells his signed cartoon to a magazine validly object to the magazine's making and selling a doll which is truthfully advertised as based upon the cartoon? This, capsulated, poses the critical issue herein.

The Complaint

Plaintiff, Theodor Seuss Geisel, is the world-famous artist and author, whose nom de plume is "Dr. Seuss." In a complaint against the four defendants, filed March 8, 1968, plaintiff charged that the defendants manufactured and were advertising and selling dolls "derived from" . . . certain material which plaintiff "prepared for publication" . . . for the now defunct Liberty Magazine in 1932 and which was published in that magazine from June to December 1932; that, although plaintiff had nothing to do with the design or manufacture of the dolls, they were being advertised and sold as "Dr. Seuss" creations; and that the dolls are "tasteless, unattractive and of an inferior quality". . . .

On the basis of these and other allegations, plaintiff requested compensatory and punitive damages as well as an injunction enjoining defendants from using the name "Dr. Seuss" in any manner without plaintiff's consent, or in connection with any product not designed or approved by plaintiff.

In support of this prayer for relief, plaintiff pleaded five causes of action: (1) violation of Section 43(a) of the Lanham Act, 15 U.S.C. § 1125(a) (1964); (2) unfair competition, including violation of Section 368–d of the New York General Business Law, McKinney's Consol.Laws, c. 20; (3) violation of plaintiff's right of privacy as provided by the New York Civil Rights Law, McKinney's Consol.Laws, c. §§ 50, 51; (4) defamation; and (5) conspiracy with intent to injure plaintiff (prima facie tort).

The Preliminary Injunction

An order to show cause for a preliminary injunction was signed on March 8, 1968. On March 12, this Court heard argument on that motion, issued a temporary restraining order (which, in substance, restrained defendants from using the name "Dr. Seuss" in any manner in connection with any doll, toy or other product), and granted the parties leave to conduct discovery and to submit further papers.

On April 9, 1968, this Court concluded that there was a reasonable probability of plaintiff's success upon the trial of the Lanham Act (first) cause of action and issued a preliminary injunction restraining defendants as follow:

> "The defendants, their officers, agents, servants, employees and all persons acting under their control and each of them are hereby enjoined and restrained pendente lite from committing any of the following acts in connection with the manufacturing, displaying, advertising, distributing, selling or offering for sale of any doll, toy or other similar product:
>
> A. Representing that defendants' doll, toy or other similar product has been created, designed, produced, approved or authorized by plaintiff;

B. Describing defendants' doll, toy or other similar product as having been created, designed, produced, approved or authorized by plaintiff; or

C. Representing, describing or designating plaintiff as the originator, creator, designer, or producer of defendants' doll, toy or other similar products."

At the same time, the Court advanced the date of the trial on merits, pursuant to Rule 65(a) (2), Fed.R.Civ.P., to April 22, 1968. (See 283 F.Supp. 261, 268.)

Defendants' Basic Contentions

It would be useful to summarize defendants' basic contentions, as formulated in the pre-trial order. Defendants claim that they have the right to manufacture and sell the dolls in question for the reason that either (1) defendant Liberty Library Corporation—as successor-assignee of Liberty Magazine—owns complete rights, including copyright, in the cartoons published in 1932, and "the owner of copyright in cartoons has the exclusive right to make three-dimensional figures therefrom," or (2) the cartoons are in the public domain and, therefore, "anyone may use such cartoons as the basis for the three-dimensional figures." Defendants contend that the dolls are specifically "based on" Plaintiff's Exhibits 14A, 14B and 14C.

In addition, defendants argue that they have the right to state truthfully the relationship between plaintiff-cartoonist and the dolls, including the circumstance that the dolls were "based on, adapted from or inspired by" the plaintiff's Liberty Magazine cartoons. Finally, defendants have urged a variety of other defenses to the causes of action set forth in the complaint. . . .

This opinion contains the findings of fact and conclusions of law required by Rule 52(a), Fed.R.Civ.P.

Certain Undisputed Facts

Certain facts relating to the parties to this suit have been stipulated as not in dispute or are undisputed:

1. Plaintiff, Theodor Seuss Geisel (hereafter Geisel or plaintiff), is a well-known author and illustrator and a resident of La Jolla, California.

2. Defendant, Poynter Products Inc. (hereafter Poynter), is an Ohio corporation having its principal place of business at 7 Arcadia Place, Cincinnati, Ohio; it is engaged in the business of producing and selling toys and novelties. Its president and sole stockholder is Donald B. Poynter.

3. Defendant, Alabe Crafts, Inc. (hereafter Alabe), is an Ohio corporation having its principal place of business at 1632 Gest Street in

Cincinnati, Ohio; it distributes, among other things, the products of Poynter Products Inc.

4. Defendant, Liberty Library Corporation (hereafter Liberty), is a New York corporation with its principal place of business at 353 West 57th Street, New York, New York. Its president is Miss Lorraine Lester (Mrs. George Lessner). Its vice-president and treasurer is George Lessner. Its executive administrator is Robert Whiteman. The stock of Liberty is completely owned by Mr. and Mrs. Lessner.

5. Defendant, Linder, Nathan & Heide, Inc. (hereafter Linder), is a New York corporation having its principal place of business at 200 Fifth Avenue, New York, New York. It is engaged in selling toys and novelties to retailers; it acts as manufacturers' representative in New York City for defendant Alabe and others.

There is diversity of citizenship between the parties. The matter in controversy, exclusive of interest and costs, exceeds the sum of $10,000. It is not, therefore, necessary to decide whether there is an independent basis of jurisdiction.

The 1932 Agreement

At the trial, a substantial amount of the evidence concerned the nature of the 1932 agreement between plaintiff and Liberty Publishing Corporation (hereafter Liberty Magazine). Plaintiff contends that the evidence proves that plaintiff assigned to Liberty Magazine the title to the cartoons with their accompanying text

. . . with the understanding that Liberty would copyright this work as part of the entire issue of the magazines in which they appeared. It was understood, however, that while Liberty had the complete rights to publish these works in one issue of Liberty Magazine, Liberty held all other rights to this work (including the right to renew the copyright and the right to make other uses of the work) in trust of plaintiff." [P.T.O.]

Plaintiff presents this contention as an additional reason why he is entitled to the relief prayed for in the complaint.

On the other hand, defendants contend that the 1932 agreement provided for the transfer to Liberty Magazine of all or complete rights in the cartoons and accompanying text without reservation of any rights in plaintiff.

Certain facts relating to the 1932 transaction have been stipulated as not in dispute. The parties agree that, in 1932, plaintiff " . . . prepared and sold to Liberty Magazine material which was published in weekly issues of Liberty Magazine during the months of June through December 1932" (P.T.O.Stip.); that the material consisted of a series of twenty-three "cartoon essays" and that "each work [consisted of a page which] contained at least three cartoons and each cartoon contained several animal creations" (P.T.O.Stip.); that the material appeared in Liberty Magazine under the following titles: "Goofy Olympics," "Some Recent Developments in Zoology," "A Few Notes on Birds," "A Few Notes on the Coming Elections," "A New Idea in Taxation," "The Summer Problem and How to Solve Them," "A Few Notes on Torture," "Some Recent Inventions in the Offspring Field," "Educational Projects," "A Few Bright Spots on the Business Horizon," "Three Glorious Movements in the Clothing Field," "A Few Notes on Games," "The Rough Road to International Harmony," "House Cleaning the English Language," "A Few Hints on Hypnotism," "Some New Aids to Better Living," "A Few Notes on Origins," "A Few Notes on Fires," "A Few Hints on Navigation," "Is the Bird in Hand Really Worth Two in the Bush, Part I," "Is the Bird in Hand Really Worth Two in the Bush, Part II," "A Few Notes on Facial Foliage," "A Few Notes on Sleep." (P.T.O.Stip); and that plaintiff received $300 for each work (P.T.O.Stip.). . . .

There is also no dispute that the issues of Liberty Magazine in which the cartoons appeared were copyrighted by Liberty Magazine as entire issues (P.T.O.Stip.). Each issue contained the required notice of copyright; and Certificates of Copyright Registration were secured by Liberty Magazine (P.T.O.Stip.; Deft.Ex.). It is also agreed that "[n]o separate copyright was obtained . . . " by the plaintiff upon the cartoons (P.T.O.Stip.).

The only evidence describing the negotiations and consummation of the agreement between plaintiff and Liberty Magazine in 1932 was the testimony of plaintiff himself and of Leland Hayward. Hayward, presently a theatrical producer, was a literary agent from about 1929 to 1943. . . . According to plaintiff's and Hayward's testimony, one Ben Wasson approached plaintiff and asked whether he could represent him in seeking to place his work in magazines. Plaintiff agreed. . . . Prior to this conversation, in the 1920's and early 1930's plaintiff had sold other drawings to a number of magazines, including Judge, Vanity Fair, and the Saturday Evening Post. . . . During this period, plaintiff also drew cartoons for the Standard Oil Company of New Jersey to advertise a product known as "Flit." The "Quick, Henry the Flit" series appeared in magazines . . . , including Liberty Magazine. . . .

Ben Wasson, who did not appear as a witness, represented plaintiff in the negotiations with Liberty Magazine. . . . In so doing, Wasson acted as an employee of the Leland Hayward Agency. . . . Although Hayward did not personally handle the transaction, he recalls that he had one conversation with Fulton Oursler, then editor-in-chief of Liberty Magazine. Oursler stated that plaintiff was "popular" and that his work was "very suitable" for Liberty Magazine. . . . Hayward could not remember anything else said at that or any other time relating to the negotiations. . . . To the best of his recollection, there was no formal written contract executed in connection with this transaction . . ..

Plaintiff's only contact in 1932 with Liberty Magazine was a meeting of about fifteen minutes' duration with Fulton Oursler. . . . However, all that plaintiff recalls of the occasion is that Oursler said " . . . 'Glad to have you aboard,' or something like that". . . . Prior to that meeting, Wasson had told plaintiff of a "firm commitment" for plaintiff " . . . to do a number of pages, a small number of pages, because everything was sort of on a try-out basis . . . to see if they worked. I don't know how many pages they said they would buy, but they were $300 a piece". . . . From this and other evidence . . . the Court infers that the works which plaintiff sold to Liberty Magazine were not in existence at the time the contract was entered into; instead, they were created at Liberty Magazine's request.

The $300 payments were made by check to the Leland Hayward Agency, which deducted its commission as agent and then remitted the balance to plaintiff. . . .

Nothing was expressly said by either side during the negotiations regarding the scope of rights that Liberty Magazine obtained by the purchase of the material. . . . Plaintiff denies that the words "all rights" or "complete rights" were used by either side during the negotiations. . . .

This evidence demonstrates that plaintiff agreed to prepare cartoons for publication in Liberty Magazine; that the cartoons were published; that plaintiff received $300 a page; that the only copyright upon this material was in the name of Liberty Publishing Company; and that plaintiff did not *expressly* reserve any rights in the cartoons.

There is evidence, and the Court so finds, that, with certain exceptions which do not apply in this case, the custom and usage in 1932 in the magazine trade were that an agreement for the sale of a work between authors or their agents and magazines was oral and not a formal written contract. . . . The agreement was usually reached after *only* monetary terms were discussed. . . . This contrasts with the custom in the book publishing field in which similar contracts were written. . . .

If, arguendo, all rights in the cartoons were not assigned to Liberty Magazine in 1932, Liberty's copyright upon the entire issues of the magazine does not cover the cartoons. It would then follow that the cartoons would be in the public domain because admittedly they were *published* in 1932 without a separate copyright. . . . This result would transpire for the reason that a work can be copyrighted only by its "author or proprietor" (17 U.S.C. § 9); the "proprietor" can be the assignee but not the licensee of the right to use the work; and to be the assignee of the work, one must have been assigned all rights in the work.

Consequently, if the cartoons are not to be deemed in the public domain, it must be shown that all rights in the cartoons were assigned to Liberty Magazine in 1932. To escape from this logical dilemma plaintiff argues that, although legal title to the copyright was in Liberty Magazine's name as assignee-"proprietor", the copyright was held in trust for the cartoon's true or equitable owner, plaintiff. . . . Plaintiff, therefore, asks for judgment declaring that the defendants hold the copyright in trust for plaintiff and ordering that the copyright be assigned to plaintiff.[4]

Whether this trust relationship exists is primarily a question of fact dependent upon the circumstances of the case.

In this case, there was no *express* agreement that Liberty Magazine would hold the copyright in trust for plaintiff or that plaintiff reserved any rights in the cartoons. However, much evidence was offered by both sides with respect to the issue whether there was any settled and established custom and usage in the magazine publishing trade in 1932 by which any terms or conditions were implied in fact or understood to be part of a contract between an author or his agent and a weekly magazine; and if so, what were those implied-in-fact terms.

Evidence was also offered with respect to the issue whether there was any settled and established custom and usage concerning what the magazine was impliedly agreeing to in fact with respect to the extent of the magazine's use of the purchased material; and concerning the alleged practice of a magazine to hold its copyright in trust for the author and to reassign its copyright upon the request of the author.

Section 209 of the Copyright Law, 17 U.S.C. § 209 (1964), provides in relevant part that the certificate of copyright registration " . . . shall be admitted in any court as prima facie evidence of the facts stated therein.".

Plaintiff offered the testimony of three witnesses with respect to the above mentioned customs and usages in 1932 in the magazine publishing trade: Bennett Cerf, Leland Hayward and plaintiff himself.

Mr. Cerf has been a *book* publisher since 1925 and has himself written books as well as articles for periodicals. . . . Plaintiff's books are published by the firm of which Cerf is chairman of the board . . . ; and, in fact, plaintiff is the president of a division of that firm. . . . Mr. Cerf is an eminent personality in the field of *book* publishing. However, his testimony with respect to customs and usages in the *magazine* trade is found by the Court to be tenuous and unpersuasive. He repeatedly admitted his unfamiliarity with magazine customs . . . and with contracts between magazines and authors or their agents.

---

[4] There can be no doubt that the "proprietor" of a copyright upon the entire contents of a magazine may validly assign the copyright upon a single picture or article in that magazine. . . .

. . . Furthermore, some of his testimony presents internal inconsistencies and self-contradictions. . . .

Three witnesses called by defendants testified about the relevant customs and usages: Meyer Dworkin, Alfred Wasserstrom and Alden Norton. Mr. Dworkin, a retired attorney and accountant, was an adviser or "righthand man" to the head of Macfadden Publications, a magazine publisher, which purchased Liberty Magazine in 1931. Dworkin was associated with Macfadden Publications from 1919 until 1961 . . .

Alfred Wasserstrom, an attorney specializing in copyright and trademark law, is connected with the Hearst Corporation Legal Department. He has been with the Hearst Corporation since December 1933, when he was admitted to the bar. He has guest-lectured at law schools; is a member of the board of trustees of the Copyright Society of the U. S. A.; and is a member and chairman of the Copyright Committee of the Magazine Publishers Association . . .

Alden Norton, advisory editor of Argosy Magazine, is in charge of its foreign sales and rights and subsidiary rights. In 1932, he began working as an editor for Frank A. Munsey Company, a magazine publisher, and remained there until 1935, when he left to join Popular Publications, publisher of Argosy . . . While an editor in the 1930's, Norton dealt with authors and their agents with respect to literary purchases . . . He has also sold numerous stories and novels of his own to magazines since 1929 . . .

On the basis of the great weight of the credible evidence, the Court finds that during the relevant period it was the custom and usage in the magazine trade for the magazine to obtain a copyright upon the entire contents of the magazine . . . However, the author or artist *could* also obtain a separate copyright upon his particular work, as plaintiff did with respect to a "Quick, Henry the Flit" cartoon-advertisement which appeared in Liberty Magazine in 1931 . . .

Virtually all the testimony was in agreement on the proposition, which the Court finds established, that there was a settled custom and usage in the magazine publishing trade in the early 1930's by which a term or condition defining the scope of rights was implied in fact or understood to be part of the agreement between the author or his agent and the magazine . . . What that term or condition provided is a subject, however, about which the testimony is sharply conflicting.

Mr. Cerf testified that, if nothing was said with respect to scope of rights purchased, the term "always" implied in the agreement provided for the sale of "one-shot publication"—publication in one issue of the magazine—and return of the copyright thereafter upon the request of the author . . . He stated that the term "all rights" meant this understanding . . .

Mr. Cerf indicated that the basis of his knowledge of this custom or understanding was the "minimal" amount paid to plaintiff for the cartoons . . . He also testified that, if an author-artist received anything less than $1,000 a page in 1932 for his work, it meant that only one-time magazine rights were sold . . .

Although the price paid may be a circumstance probative of the scope of rights purchased by Liberty Magazine in 1932 . . . the clear preponderance of the credible evidence demonstrates that the price of $300 per page in 1932 was a "reasonable price for that particular year" in view of the near "panic" caused by the depression . . .

Mr. Hayward testified that the "standard practice" or usage in the magazine trade in 1932"was [for the material] to appear in one issue of the magazine or, in the case of a serialization, in several issues . . . The magazine was limited in its use of the material to single or serial publication " . . . and those rights are called 'complete rights'—or were" . . . He, and other witnesses, stated that the expressions "all rights" and "complete rights" had the same meaning . . . But, Mr. Hayward repeatedly stated that "all rights" did not mean "all" and that "complete rights" did not mean "complete" . . . rather, that these terms had a limited meaning . . . According to Mr. Hayward, "complete rights" in the magazine trade meant " . . . the complete right to publish that particular piece of material in a single issue or, in the case of serial rights, to publish parts of the material in several or more issues . . . Mr. Hayward also testified that, although the term "all rights" was not expressly used in negotiations, it was *"implicit" in the agreement* . . .

Mr. Hayward further asserted that after publication, the custom provided that the magazine " . . . would *always* assign the copyright to anyone the author requested" (emphasis added). The Magazine was thus the "custodian of the copyright" . . . He added that he had *never* heard of a magazine sharing the revenues gained on the material after the assignment back . . .

Plaintiff also testified that, in 1932 custom or usage implied in fact in the agreement a condition that the magazine would use the purchased material only in a single insertion in the United States and Canada . . . [5]

---

[5] The Court finds unconvincing plaintiff's testimonial assertions that there was a custom or usage in 1932 which *implied in fact* in the agreement a condition that the magazine would not alter or change a drawing; and that it was unheard of for a magazine publisher to tamper with *a single word* of a story or *a single line* of a drawing without the author's consent . . . This rejection of plaintiff's testimony does not suggest that such rights cannot be provided for, either expressly or impliedly, in a contract. The Court holds only that no such contractual provision was implied in fact in the Geisel-Liberty Magazine agreement.

The doctrine of "moral right" recognized by the civil law of many European and Latin American countries encompasses the right of an author or artist " . . . to object to any distortion, mutilation or alteration . . . " of his work even after the transfer of the copyright in

If believed in its entirety, the evidence adduced in behalf of plaintiff would prove that in 1932 custom or usage in the magazine trade implied in fact in the Geisel-Liberty Magazine agreement that (a) each cartoon could be used only in a single insertion in the magazine; that (b) thereafter the copyright was held in trust for plaintiff and would be reassigned to him at his request; and that (c) the term "all rights" or "complete rights," which was understood to mean (a) and/or (b), was "implicit" in the agreement.

Meyer Dworkin, called as a witness for defendants, testified that he did not recall, and, in fact, there "categorically" never was, any custom or understanding in 1932 whereby an author " . . . would reserve impliedly all rights except the right to have the magazine publish in that issue the particular work of art" . . . On the contrary, the custom was that "where the author said nothing and sold the manuscript to the company, the company would receive all rights . . . " He stated that this custom was understood by Liberty Magazine, Mcfadden Publications *and by the authors* who dealt with them . . . Mr. Dworkin defined "complete rights" as "all rights, full rights" . . . with no residual rights in anyone else . . .

Although Mr. Dworkin admitted that Liberty Magazine (or Mcfadden Publications) occasionally would reassign its rights to an author without charge, he stated that at other times the reassignment would be for a fee or for a share of the author's profits after the assignment back. Whether reassignment would be made and whether it would be made without payment depended upon who the author was and the purpose for which the assignment back was sought . . . Mr. Dworkin explained that sometimes reassignment would be made to retain the author's friendship and goodwill . . .

Alden Norton convincingly testified that, although every story purchased by a magazine was individually bargained for, " . . . if you sold me a story and you didn't ask for anything, you sold me all rights and it would say so on the check" . . . He also testified that, if there were no written or oral agreement and no legend on the check and the author or artist simply delivered the work to a magazine and was paid $300 a page, the custom and usage in 1932 provided that "[u]nless otherwise specified, [the author granted] all rights" . . . Mr. Norton rejected the assertion that, if nothing was said, only first publication rights were acquired by the magazine . . . He testified that, if all rights were not acquired, there were specific negotiations—i. e.,

---

his work. Berne Convention, article 6 bis [printed in Howell's Copyright Law 307, 310 (rev. Latman ed. 1962)] . . . However, the doctrine of moral right is not part of the law in the United States, see Vargas v. Esquire, Inc., 164 F.2d 522, 526 (7th Cir. 1947) . . . except insofar as parts of that doctrine exist in our law as specific rights—such as copyright, libel, privacy and unfair competition.

something *was said* . . . —and a lower price would be paid for the material
. . .

Mr. Norton's testimony indicates that the words "all rights" were a recognized term in the magazine trade in 1932. But he rejected plaintiff's contention that custom or usage gave these words a specialized meaning . . . As he said, "all rights" meant literally all rights [1361]—i.e., " . . . dramatic, movie, television, skywriting on Mars, anything you want to say . . . everything" . . . He also said that where "all rights" were purchased, the author " . . . retained absolutely nothing" . . .

Alfred Wasserstrom also testified persuasively that he knew of no custom or usage which gave the words "all rights" a specialized meaning in the magazine trade in 1935 . . . He agreed that the words "all rights" had a plain, colloquial English meaning [1372–1374, 1375]. Likewise, he testified that he knew of no custom or usage giving the words "complete rights" " . . . any meaning different from their ordinary, accepted English meaning . . .

Mr. Wasserstrom stated that there was no implied in fact term or condition, according to the custom or usage in 1935 in the magazine trade, that a magazine could use material . . . only for one insertion in the magazine . . .

Finally, he testified as to the alleged custom which implied a term in agreements between authors and magazines relating to reassignment of the copyright at the request of the author. He stated that such a custom existed in 1935 "[i]*f only limited rights were acquired* . . ." (emphasis added) . . . Thus, it was customary that, where the magazine purchased limited or restricted rights, such as serial rights, the copyright taken out by the magazine would be reconveyed to the author at his request . . . When such a reassignment of the copyright was made, the custom recognized that the magazine retained the limited rights (i.e. serial rights) originally acquired by the magazine . . . However, Mr. Wasserstrom stressed the fact that *no such custom*, whereby the magazine impliedly agreed to reassign the copyright at the author's request, *existed where all or complete rights were purchased by the magazine; or where nothing was said as to rights* . . . He agreed, on cross examination, that where limited rights were acquired, the author impliedly gave authority to the magazine to secure a copyright on the material as part of the copyright on the entire issue which " . . . would then be held for the benefit of both parties to the extent of their respective interests" . . .

On the basis of the clear preponderance of the credible evidence, the Court finds that the custom and usage in 1932 in the magazine trade implied in fact in the Geisel-Liberty Magazine agreement a provision whereby all rights or complete rights were assigned to Liberty Magazine . . .

In ordinary acceptance, the expressions "all rights" or "complete rights" have a nontechnical and literal meaning. Plaintiff has failed to sustain the burden of proof which is upon him when he seeks to impart to these words a connotation that is diametrically opposite to their plain, colloquial sense. The Court finds the testimonial assertions of plaintiff's witnesses, in this respect, to be incredible and factitious. The terms "all rights" and "complete rights," when understood according to their plain meaning, signify a totality of rights, including the right of reproduction or common law copyright and the right to secure statutory copyright without qualification.

Stated otherwise, the Court finds, on the basis of the overwhelming preponderance of the credible evidence, that there was no custom or usage which implied in fact in the agreement in issue that Liberty Magazine was restricted, in any way, as to the uses to which the cartoons might be put. The Court rejects the simplistic and unconvincing testimony of plaintiff's witnesses concerning a custom whereby the copyright in this case was being held in trust for plaintiff. Instead, the Court adopts the testimony of defendants' two disinterested expert witnesses, Alden Norton and Alfred Wasserstrom, as to the custom and usage in the magazine trade during the period in question. The Court finds both Norton and Wasserstrom, and their testimony, to be credible, reliable and persuasive.

Although corroboration for defendants' position—that all or complete rights were purchased by Liberty Magazine in 1932—is not necessary, corroboration is provided by Liberty's "permanent purchase record cards." Some of these cards were introduced into evidence by defendants . . . Each card specifies, among other things, the author's name, the title, the price paid, the date of purchase and date of publication, the "character" of the material (e. g. article, cartoon, etc.) and the rights purchased. There is a separate card corresponding to each page of plaintiff's cartoons which appeared in Liberty Magazine. Each of these cards relating to the Geisel-Liberty transaction expressly states that "complete" rights were purchased.

. . . .

Dworkin also testified that the same recital of rights which appeared on Liberty Magazine's cards was rubber-stamped as a legend on the check sent to the author or his agent . . . Although no cancelled check relating to this transaction was introduced into evidence, other checks of Liberty Magazine were . . . ; and the legends on those checks correspond to the description on the cards of the rights purchased . . .

Although oral agreements between authors or their agents and magazines were customary, the Court finds that it was also a custom or usage in 1932 that the scope of rights purchased by the magazine would be set forth in a legend on the check sent to the author or his agent . . . As Mr. Wasserstrom testified:

" . . . in '34, and for that matter, continuing to the present. There has been a reluctance to write out, say out, spell out at length the legal relationship as far as the acquisition of literary or artistic material is concerned and to merely memorialize it in somewhat eliptical fashion by a legend on a check, on the face of the check or on the back of the check or on the detachable voucher that accompanies a check." . . .

Although plaintiff . . . and his agent in 1932, Leland Hayward . . . , stated they were unfamiliar with this practice, Norton testified that Frank A. Munsey and Popular Publications and, in fact, other magazine publishers to which he sold articles as an author, had such an established practice . . . Wasserstrom testified that Hearst Corporation, which published several magazines, as well as other magazine publishers with which he was familiar, had such a practice . . . ; and Dworkin testified extensively to the same practice at Macfadden Publications, publisher of Liberty Magazine . . .

The permanent purchase record cards also circumstantially support defendants' position that complete rights or all rights had their literal meaning. Some of the cards indicated "complete" rights . . . ; another "complete, except book"; others stated first and second North American serial rights . . . ; and some included broadcast rights . . . together with serial rights.

Defendants have also introduced other circumstantial evidence . . . which tends to negate the testimonial assertions of plaintiff's witnesses that magazines "never" asked for, received or used rights to material for other than one-shot or serial publication in the magazine.

The ineluctable conclusion is that, when Liberty Magazine bought the cartoons in question from plaintiff, it purchased all rights, including the common law copyright and the right to secure statutory copyright without reservation of any rights in plaintiff.

Absent a reservation of the common law copyright or other rights, the copyright and all other rights pass with an absolute and unconditional sale. See Pushman v. New York Graphic Society, 287 N.Y. 302, 307–308, 39 N.E.2d 249 (1942) (painting);[11]

The parties formulate differently the rule of law deducible from the foregoing decisions,—the difference revolving around the point whether an implied reservation of rights may be as effective as an express reservation in precluding the transfer of all of the artist's rights. Regardless of the formulation, the evidence in the present case convincingly establishes only one conclusion: all rights (including the common law copyright) in the cartoons were transferred

---

[11] By statute effective September 1, 1966, the common law copyright in New York does not pass with the sale of the object or material *unless expressly so provided in a written instrument.* See Article 12–E of the New York General Business Law §§ 223, 224. (Emphasis added.) For legislative history, see L.1966, ch. 668, § 1.

to Liberty without any equitable or other rights reserved to plaintiff. Liberty's statutory copyright likewise is not subject to any equitable or other rights in plaintiff.

Although there is evidence in the record that plaintiff prepared the cartoons for Liberty *after* an agreement had been reached between his agent and the magazine, the Court does not rely on the cases relating to commissioned works of art.

The Dolls

Having decided that Liberty Magazine acquired *all* rights to the cartoons published in 1932, the Court now considers and determines what rights defendants have to make the dolls . . . and to what extent, if any, defendants may use the name "Dr. Seuss" in connection therewith.

Plaintiff's basic contentions are that defendants " . . . may not use plaintiff's name in any way in connection with the toy dolls because the toy dolls do not bear a sufficient relationship to the original work and differ in material respects from it"; and that "the toy dolls destroy the artistic integrity of plaintiff's original work and are so inferior in quality that the use of plaintiff's name in connection with them is disparaging and damaging to him." . . .

Additional details of the factual background of this litigation must be mobilized in order to consider the respective rights of the parties in proper context.

On September 1, 1949, Lorraine Lester entered into an option agreement with Liberty Magazine, Inc. . . . which, as amended on March 13, 1950 . . . , permitted her, upon certain conditions to exploit short story material which had appeared in Liberty Magazine during the period 1924 to 1949 for use in connection with radio, television and motion pictures. . . . The exclusive license agreement provided in part:

> "2. We shall make available for your inspection all short stories which have been published by Liberty. With respect to any stories selected by you of which we own all rights, your use thereof may commence immediately. As to any other stories selected by you, we will endeavor at your request to obtain all rights which may be required, but in no event will you be licensed to sue them hereunder until we have authorized such use." . . .

On September 20, 1949, Miss Lester signed an agreement assigning the option agreement . . . to Lester-Fields Productions, Inc. . . . , a company in which she was a principal . . .

In 1950, Miss Lester learned from Osborne B. Bond, the publisher of Liberty Magazine, that Liberty planned to cease publication . . . She thereupon entered into negotiations on behalf of Lester-Fields Productions, Inc. to acquire the magazine's "copyright library" . . . On August 10, 1950, Miss Lester received a letter from Liberty . . . accepting her prior oral offer to purchase the "rights to all material contained in the Library of Liberty Magazine, Inc. from May 10, 1924 to July, 1950, inclusive . . . "

Thereafter, on September 8, 1950 Lester-Fields and Liberty Magazine, Inc. entered into an agreement . . . terminating the 1949 option agreement with Miss Lester and providing in part as follows:

> "3. Liberty hereby sells, assigns and transfers to Lester any and all right, title or interest it may have in or to any and all of the stories and articles which have been published in Liberty Magazine from May 1924 to July 1950 inclusive, provided, however, that Liberty makes no representation as to the extent of its right, title or interest in and to such stories and articles."

The material referred to in that agreement included short stories, articles, cartoons and crossword puzzles which had appeared weekly in Liberty Magazine over a period of 26 years. . . . Approximately 17,000 literary properties were included . . . Lester-Fields also bought Liberty Magazine's permanent purchase record cards and checks covering the period of 1943 to 1950 . . .

On October 5, 1950, Lester-Fields assigned this agreement . . . to George Lessner, Lorraine Lester, Robert Fields and Samuel H. Evans . . . Fields subsequently assigned his interest to the others . . . Thereafter, on November 10, 1964, this agreement . . . was assigned to Liberty Library Corporation . . . Thus, defendant Liberty Library Corporation is successor to all the literary assets of Liberty Publishing Corporation, publisher of Liberty Magazine in 1932 . . .

In August 1964 Mr. Robert Whiteman called on Miss Lester in connection with film production. In the course of their conversation, he saw the 90 bound volumes of Liberty Magazine on her shelves; and, after discussion, suggested that he could help her make money by exploiting the literary properties contained in this magazine. . . . Thereafter, Whiteman entered into an agreement with Liberty Library, whereby Whiteman represented Liberty "on an exclusive basis" in exploiting the material from defendant Liberty Magazine . . .

Commencing in 1964, defendant Liberty embarked on a program of actively exploiting the material which had appeared in Liberty Magazine from 1924 to 1950. In the course of selecting material for sale or licensing, Whiteman came upon plaintiff's cartoons in the 1932 issues of Liberty Magazine . . . Whiteman checked the Liberty record cards and secured a copyright search on that material . . . After receiving expressions of interest in the cartoons, "as a matter of courtesy," Whiteman contacted Random House which referred him to plaintiff's agent, Mrs. Phyllis Jackson of Ashley Famous Agency. Whiteman showed her copies of the cartoons and of the copyright search and offered plaintiff the opportunity either to join with Liberty in exploiting the material or to repurchase the rights in the works . . . Whiteman agreed to keep her informed regarding any offers which he received with respect to the material . . . Subsequently, Whiteman informed her by letter of December 15, 1964, that he had received an offer for reprint rights to the material . . .

Prior to the letter of December 15th, Mrs. Jackson contacted plaintiff who rejected defendant Liberty's offer . . . After the December 15th letter, Mrs. Jackson wrote to plaintiff advising him to have his attorney write to defendant Liberty in an effort to prevent exploitation of the cartoon material . . . Thereafter, plaintiff's California attorney, Frank Kockritz, Esq., sent a telegram to defendant Liberty . . . advising it that plaintiff did not recognize Liberty's rights in the cartoons and reserving the right to institute a lawsuit.

After receiving the telegram, Whiteman consulted his attorneys and, on May 14, 1965, completed a transaction with Universal Publishing and Distributing Corporation . . . The agreement provided for licensing Universal to publish a paperback book of the Liberty "Dr. Seuss" cartoons [Pltf.Ex.; P.T.O.Stip.]. Universal subsequently wrote to plaintiff on June 6, 1966 asking plaintiff to retitle and revise his cartoons . . . Plaintiff rejected the proposal . . . ; Mrs. Jackson informed Universal; and plaintiff's attorney, Mr. Kockritz, sent a protest letter to Universal . . . However, Universal went ahead and published a paperback entitled "Dr. Seuss' Lost World Revisited" . . .

After publication, defendant Liberty again offered to sell its rights in the cartoons back to plaintiff . . . This final offer of defendant Liberty to sell its rights in the cartoons back to plaintiff was suggested by Arthur F. Abelman, Esq., who had previously discussed the matter with plaintiff's agent, Mrs. Jackson . . .

Finally, in 1967, Whiteman undertook to sell merchandising rights to the cartoons . . . Whiteman, who was experienced in licensing and merchandising items, including toys . . . , decided to grant a license to manufacture dolls based on the cartoons . . . Whiteman licensed defendant Poynter Products, Inc. because he had had successful dealings with Donald B. Poynter in the past and he considered Poynter to be " . . . a man of tremendous capabilities in the field of molding, sculpture, art, taste . . . " . . . The licensing agreement . . . was executed (on September 8, 1967), after Poynter had been shown the cartoons and informed of plaintiff's objection to the publication of the paperback book . . .

Donald B. Poynter was and is an experienced designer and manufacturer of toys, novelties and gift items, including items made for children . . . He had previously designed a variety of items based upon works of well known artists

. . . He had also produced puppets . . . ; "premiums," such as T-shirts and tags, given away by sponsors of children's radio and television shows; theatrical sets . . . and advertising artistic layouts for a large toy manufacturer . . .

In view of the protest telegram from plaintiff's attorney in 1964, Whiteman decided to submit everything done with respect to the dolls to Mr. Abelman. In fact, all meetings between Whiteman and Poynter took place in Mr. Abelman's office . . . In November 1967, Whiteman and Poynter came to Mr. Abelman's office to discuss design of the dolls . . . Poynter brought with him a hand sculptured styrofoam and papier-mâché model . . . of one of the cartoon "characters" . . . which he had prepared from "rough" sketches . . . Mr. Abelman found the prototype doll to be "reasonably acceptable and a faithful reproduction" . . . and Whiteman agreed . . .

At the meeting in November, 1967, Mr. Abelman also advised Poynter " . . . that under no circumstances should he consult any book written by Dr. Seuss, watch any television program by Dr. Seuss or use any material of Dr. Seuss outside the Liberty drawings in preparing the drawings for his dolls, and I told him that when he watched those drawings he should look at them very carefully, reproduce them as close as he possibly could, taking into account the fact that you are moving from a two-dimensional medium of paper and publishing into the three-dimensional medium of dolls" . . . In fact, the Court finds that Poynter used the cartoons *only* as they appeared in Liberty Magazine or in the paperback book . . . in the preparation and design of the dolls.

After the meeting, Poynter prepared additional models and then went to Japan for six weeks to work on the dolls and choose a manufacturer . . . By letter dated January 12, 1968 . . . , Poynter authorized the manufacture in Japan of a set of twelve small vinyl toy dolls designed from some of the creatures which appeared in the 1932 cartoons.

While in Japan and later when back in the United States, Poynter sculpted wax models of the dolls . . . These wax models became the basis of the molds in which the dolls were manufactured . . . During the design and manufacture of the dolls, minor changes were made so that the dolls which eventually were manufactured and sold were not precise copies of the original cartoons or of Poynter's initial transformation of the cartoons . . . These modifications reflected manufacturing techniques, cost and sales requirements, the availability and choice of plastics, aesthetic considerations . . . , and deviations representing Poynter's three-dimensional interpretative transmutation of the two-dimensional cartoons . . .

The dolls which were ultimately manufactured and sold . . . consist of six different vinyl figures, each of which comes in two different colors. At an earlier stage, Poynter made and rejected a stuffed doll version of the figures . . .

At a meeting in February 1968, Abelman, Whiteman and Poynter carefully examined each doll and compared it with the cartoons. Abelman expressed the opinion that Poynter . . . had done a very fine job of faithfully reproducing the cartoons in the doll medium, the three-dimensional medium" . . . Previously, Poynter had submitted to Abelman, by letter of December 30, 1967, prototypes of the "hang tag" . . . which was originally used with the dolls . . . Abelman approved the tag and suggested that a copyright notice also be permanently imprinted in the base of each doll . . . By letter dated February 16, 1968, Whiteman approved the dolls and the advertising material which he had viewed at the meeting . . .

Prior to March 12, 1968 (when the Court entered a temporary restraining order in this matter), defendants offered and sold the dolls using the name "Dr. Seuss" in the following ways:

> 1. It was engraved in very small letters on the vinyl bottom of each doll . . . with the statement: "From Original Illustrations of Dr. Seuss © 1932 Liberty Library Corporation Copyright Renewed © 1966 Poynter Products Inc., Cincinnati, Ohio Made in Japan." This was done pursuant to the suggestion of defendants' counsel . . .

> 2. A round hang tag [Pltf.Ex. 26] tied around the neck of each doll stated, on one side: "From the Wonderful World of Dr. Seuss—an original Merry Menagerie"; and, on the other side: "This is my _____ (you name it) from Dr. Seuss' Merry Menagerie." Mr. Abelman approved this tag . . .

The following are reproductions of both sides of this hang tag:

It is to be noted that the format of the name "Dr. Seuss" copies exactly the characteristic style of plaintiff's nom de plume as it appears in all his works.

As will be pointed out shortly, defendants discontinued the above wording and format after March 12, 1968.

3. The dolls were sold in a display carton . . . On the base of this carton was the statement: "Dr. Seuss' Merry Menagerie" and the words "Lovable . . . Huggable"; on the backboard attached to the base of the carton was the statement: "From the Wonderful World of Dr. Seuss . . . Everybody Loves 'em . . . From Original Illustrations by Dr. Seuss." This carton, as well as the hang tag, also contained Liberty Library and Poynter Products copyright notices. The carton contained a statement that defendant Alabe is the exclusive U.S.A. distributor. Although Abelman did not recall whether he approved the display box, he did approve the title "From the Wonderful World of Dr. Seuss" and the remainder of the text used . . .

4. The dolls were advertised on a handbill . . . which stated: "Dr. Seuss' Merry Menagerie" and "From the Wonderful World of Dr. Seuss . . . Everybody Loves 'em."

5. This handbill also contained the following statement on its reverse side:

"The Newest, Hottest Character Toy Line of 1968 . . . Dr. Seuss" . . .

6. The dolls were advertised or referred to in the Official Directory of the 65th Annual American Toy Fair (March 1968) held in New York . . . as "Dr. Seuss" toys.

7. The dolls were referred to on invoices of defendants Alabe and Linder . . . as "Dr. Seuss' Merry Menagerie." Defendant Alabe's personnel and Poynter referred to the dolls as "Dr. Seuss dolls" . . .

From March 12, 1968, when a temporary restraining order was entered in this action, until April 9, 1968, when a preliminary injunction was entered, defendants did not ship any of the dolls for sale . . . After the preliminary injunction was entered, defendants again began to offer the dolls for sale accompanied by revised labels and sales materials using the name "Dr. Seuss" in the following manner:

a. The hang tag tied around the neck of each doll . . . stated, on one side: "Wacky Merry Menagerie Everybody loves 'em"; and, on the other side: "Toys Created, Designed & Produced Exclusively by Don Poynter MERRY MENAGERIE Based on Liberty Magazine Illustrations by Dr. Seuss";

The following are reproductions of both sides of this revised hang tag:

It is to be noted that, subsequent to April 9, 1968, defendants discontinued using plaintiff's characteristic style of printing "Dr. Seuss".

b. The backboard of the display cartoon . . . :

"MERRY MENAGERIE

Toys Created, Designed	Based On Liberty
& Produced Exclusively	Magazine Illustrations
By Don Poynter	By Dr. Suess

The name "Dr. Seuss" and the name "Don Poynter" were in the same size and style of type. The base section of the cartoon . . . contained no mention of Dr. Seuss.

c. The revised handbill . . . read:

> "MERRY MENAGERIE. Toys Designed, Created & Produced Exclusively by Don Poynter Based on Liberty Magazine Illustrations by Dr. Seuss."

The name "Don Poynter" and the name "Dr. Seuss" were in the same size and style of type. In regular-size type in the handbill appeared the following copy:

> "These lovable, huggable little creatures are from original illustrations by the celebrated author-illustrator Dr. Seuss. These early drawings were featured in the famous Liberty Magazine. Now, from these drawings Don Poynter, the inventor of 'The Thing', has created, designed and produced the newest, cutest, most charming 'merry menagerie' to 'hit' the market in many years."

Extent of Defendants' Rights to Make the Dolls and To Use the Name "Dr. Seuss"

As the owner of a copyright on the two-dimensional cartoons, defendant Liberty Library has the right to make three-dimensional figures or dolls therefrom or to license another (e. g., defendant Poynter Products) to do so. See King Features Syndicate v. Fleischer, 299 F. 533, 535 (2nd Cir. 1924) (owner of copyright upon cartoon sued manufacturer of toy horse " . . . fashioned after, labelled, and sold as . . . " "Sparky", the cartoon character; *held:* there is a claim for copyright infringement because a three-dimensional toy figure can be a copy of a two-dimensional cartoon). As the Court of Appeals for this Circuit stated in *King Features Syndicate:*

> "Copying is not confined to a literary repetition, but includes various modes in which the matter of any publication may be adopted, imitated, or transferred with more or less colorable alteration" (299 F. at 535).

A copyright upon a work in one medium may be asserted affirmatively by the copyright owner to obtain protection against infringement accomplished in a different medium. . . .

A corollary of the rule just stated is that a copyright upon a work in one medium empowers the copyright owner to transform or copy the work into a different medium. More specifically, in this case the owner of the copyrighted two-dimensional cartoons has the right to make three-dimensional figures from the cartoons.

The manifest logic of the foregoing conclusion is demonstrated by assuming *arguendo* that the cartoons are in the public domain. In that suppositious situation, clearly defendants could copy the cartoons at will. In the present case, defendants, as owners of the copyrighted cartoons, cannot be in a less advantageous position.

Based upon a variety of legal theories set forth in the complaint, plaintiff's primary argument is that defendants' use of plaintiff's trade and pen name "Dr. Seuss" is wrongful.

1. *The Lanham Act and Unfair Competition Claims*

Plaintiff charges that defendants have violated Section 43(a) of the Lanham Act, 15 U.S.C. § 1125(a), and are guilty of unfair competition and of violating Section 368–d of the New York General Business Law. The counterargument advanced by defendants is that a series of federal cases involving trademark infringement and unfair competition establishes the defendants' indisputable right to use the name "Dr. Seuss" to describe truthfully the nature and origin of their product, the dolls.

In this area of federal trademark law, the governing principle was expounded by the Court of Appeals for this Circuit when it declared in Societe Comptoir De L'Industrie Cotonniere Etablissements Boussac v. Alexander's Department Stores, Inc., 299 F.2d 33, 36 (2nd Cir. 1962), aff'g, 190 F.Supp. 594 (S.D.N.Y. 1961), that registration of a mark:

" . . . bestows upon the owner of the mark the limited right to protect his good will from possible harm by those uses of another as may engender a *belief in the mind of the public that the product identified by the infringing mark is made or sponsored by the owner of the mark.* Champion Spark Plug Co. v. Sanders, 331 U.S. 125, 67 S.Ct. 1136, 91 L.Ed. 1386 (1947) citing with approval, Prestonettes, Inc. v. Coty, 264 U.S. 359, 44 S.Ct. 350, 68 L.Ed. 731 (1924). The Lanham Act does not prohibit a commercial rival's truthfully denominating his goods a copy of a design in the public domain, though he uses the name of the designer to do so. Indeed it is difficult to see any other means that might be employed to inform the consuming public of the true origin of the design.

Those cases involving sponsorship, whether trade-mark infringement or unfair competition, protecting the owner of the mark, are based upon a finding that *the defendant's goods are likely to be thought to have originated with, or to have been sponsored by, the true owner of the mark."* (Emphasis added.)

In *Prestonettes*, Coty, the owner of a registered trade-mark, sought to enjoin another from selling Coty's genuine products in smaller bottles and packages with Coty's name on it. The District Court issued a limited injunction which allowed the defendant to affix a label truthfully describing the relationship between defendant's product and Coty's product. The Court of Appeals issued a broad, absolute injunction restraining defendant from using Coty's marks *in any way* (as plaintiff requests in the case at bar). The Supreme Court reversed, holding that defendant could state the nature of the component parts of its product and the source from which it was derived. In doing so, defendant could use Coty's mark because " . . . [w]hen the mark is used in a way that *does not deceive the public* we see no . . . sanctity in the words as to prevent its [the mark] being *used to tell the truth"* (264 U.S. at 368, 44 S.Ct. at 351) (Emphasis added).

In *Champion Spark Plug*, defendant repaired and reconditioned Champion's used sparkplugs and sold them using the name "Champion". The Supreme Court, noting that, in fact, the plugs *were* plaintiff's, stated:

"Inferiority is immaterial so long as the article is clearly and distinctly sold as repaired or reconditioned rather than as new. The result is, of course, that the second-hand dealer gets some advantage from the trade mark. But under the rule of Prestonettes, Inc. v. Coty, . . . that is wholly permissible so long as the manufacturer is not identified with the inferior qualities of the product . . . . Full disclosure gives the manufacturer all the protection to which he is entitled." (331 U.S. at 130, 67 S.Ct. at 1139).

The doctrine of *Prestonettes* and *Champion Spark Plug*—that a trade name may be used by another as long as there is full and meticulously truthful disclosure communicating the actual character of the product—has been followed in a long line of decisions . . .

Another case that illuminates the problem before the Court is Chamberlain v. Columbia Pictures Corp., 186 F.2d 923 (9th Cir. 1951). There the Court affirmed the dismissal of a complaint by the heirs of Samuel Clemens against the defendant which had released a motion picture advertised as "A Story Only Mark Twain Could Tell," "Mark Twain's Tale of a Gamble in Hearts," and "Mark Twain's Favorite Story" and, therefore, assertedly conveyed the impression that Clemens had authored the picture. In fact, alleged plaintiff, the picture was of inferior quality; had only slight resemblance to Clemens' story; and was merely a "corny love story." The Court held that, because Clemens' story and, therefore, his name, were in the public domain, plaintiff had no monopoly in it and there could be no violation of plaintiff's rights; and that nothing in the advertisements could lead anyone to believe that the movie was plaintiff's business or that plaintiff was in any way connected with it (186 F.2d at 925). In the case at bar, plaintiff likewise has, to the extent that defendant Liberty Library owns all rights in the cartoons which appeared with the name "Dr. Seuss," no absolute monopoly in the name "Dr. Seuss."

With these guidelines as to the scope of the permissible use of the trade name "Dr. Seuss" in mind, the Court reaffirms, on the merits, that defendants violated Section 43(a) of the Lanham Act.[14] by their "use" of the name "Dr. Seuss" "in connection with" the advertising and sale of the dolls *prior to March 12, 1968* (when this Court issued a temporary restraining order). See Geisel v. Poynter Products, Inc., 283 F.Supp. 261 (S.D.N.Y.1968) (opinion on preliminary injunction). In the exercise of the Court's discretion the Court will make permanent that preliminary injunction.

---

[14] Section 43(a) of the Lanham Act, 15 U.S.C. § 1125(a) (1964), provides:

"§ 1125. *False designations of origin and false descriptions forbidden*

(a) Any person who shall affix, apply, or annex, or use in connection with any goods or services, or any container or containers for goods, a false designation of origin, or any false description or representation, including words or other symbols tending falsely to describe or represent the same, and shall cause such goods or services to enter into commerce, and any person who shall with knowledge of the falsity of such designation of origin or description or representation cause or procure the same to be transported or used in commerce or deliver the same to any carrier to be transported or used, shall be liable to a civil action by any person doing business in the locality falsely indicated as that of origin or in the region in which said locality is situated, or by any person who believes that he is or is likely to be damaged by the use of any such false description or representation."

On the present record, there is no showing of measurable damages because there is no proof of injury to plaintiff or of actual deception of a portion of the buying public. However, if plaintiff has reason to believe that these deficiencies can be remedied without substantial delay, the Court will, upon appropriate motion and showing, appoint a master to ascertain the amount of any measurable damages.

The critical question for decision is whether defendants' "use" of the name "Dr. Seuss" *after April 9, 1968* (when this Court issued a preliminary injunction) violates Section 43(a) of the Lanham Act. The Court holds that defendants' activities *after April 9th* do *not* constitute "a false designation of origin, or any false description or representation" within the meaning of Section 43(a).

While defendants' prior activities created a false impression that the dolls were designed, manufactured or authorized by plaintiff, no such impression was intended to be, is, or can be, created by defendants' "use" of the name "Dr. Seuss" *after* April 9th.

No actual deception or confusion of, or tendency to deceive, the public is possible. Defendants have, in fact, satisfied the criteria of full and meticulously truthful disclosure. The phrase "based on" or the word "based," as used by defendants after April 9th, like the phrases "derived from," "suggested by," or "inspired by," accurately characterizes the genetic link between the cartoons and the dolls. Differences between the two are readily discerned. The dolls are not exact reproductions or replicas of the cartoons. But these morphological differences are within the accepted limits in the licensed toy trade.

A comparison of other cartoon characters with the dolls or toys based on or derived from them discloses that some deviations between them, as between the cartoons and the dolls herein, are the inevitable result of the transmutation from two-dimensional drawings or cartoons to three-dimensional figures, manufacturing difficulties (including choice of material or medium), cost considerations, and aesthetic objectives (such as making the toy doll figures more "doll-like" or "huggable").

Plaintiff's experts, Charles M. Jones (of Metro-Goldwyn-Mayer's art department), Louis Lispi (art director of Walt Disney Productions), and Neil Estern (a noted sculptor) stated or implied that it is not possible to "base" a three-dimensional doll on a single two-dimensional cartoon drawing. This testimony is rejected by the Court as unsound and, indeed, belied by the demonstrated facts of this very case: the defendants have "based" their dolls on the plaintiff's cartoon characters. Despite the fantastic and imaginary character of plaintiff's cartoon animals . . . some of their "component parts" exist in nature . . . or did in prehistoric times . . . Consequently, Poynter was not working in primordial darkness when he had but one cartoon drawing upon which to base each doll.

To paraphrase the testimony of one of plaintiff's witnesses, the dolls are based on the cartoons in the same sense that a musical comedy may be based on a book despite obvious differences in the art forms and deviations in detail . . .

The Court does not adopt plaintiff's view that "based on" is a misrepresentation because it allegedly implies that plaintiff approved the dolls . . . Section 43(a) of the Lanham Act cannot be read as permitting such an inference as to defendants' actions *after* April 9th without deleting the word "false" from that statute. No such application of Section 43(a) is justified.

As to the claims of unfair competition, plaintiff cannot recover for the "appropriation" of the cartoons themselves because defendant Liberty Library owns the copyright and plaintiff has no rights in them.

Plaintiff argues that he is entitled to recover under New York law for the unauthorized use and appropriation of the name "Dr. Seuss" because of the false impression created that plaintiff sponsored or authorized defendants' dolls. Indubitably, one cannot attribute to an artist or author a work which the artist or author did not create or which substantially departs from his original work. See Granz v. Harris, 198 F.2d 585, 588 (2nd Cir. 1952). Indeed, the New York courts have sometimes enjoined truthful references to another's trade or business name where there was a tendency to deceive the public.

A salient fact in this case is that defendants own all rights, including the copyright, in the cartoons. That ownership must include some right to use the name "Dr. Seuss' because that name appeared on each of the pages of cartoons in Liberty Magazine. Although plaintiff did not design, manufacture or authorize the dolls, defendants have not, after April 9th, stated or implied that he did. In fact, defendants have truthfully stated plaintiff's relationship to the dolls. The Court reiterates that there is no tendency to deceive, or actual deception of, the public by virtue of defendants' use of the name "Dr. Seuss" after April 9th.

Plaintiff also claims that he is entitled to an injunction under Section 368–d of the New York General Business law.[16] That statute requires a showing of

---

[16] Section 368–d of the New York General Business Law, which by its terms creates only an injunctive remedy, provides:

"§ 368–d. *Injury to business reputation; dilution*

Likelihood of injury to business reputation or of dilution of the distinctive quality of a mark or trade name shall be a ground for injunctive relief in cases of infringement of a mark registered or not registered or in cases of unfair competition, notwithstanding the absence of competition between the parties or the absence of confusion as to the source of goods or services."

some measure of customer confusion. That showing has not been made herein with respect to defendants' post-April 9th conduct. In the ordinary case of "dilution" of a trade name, the parties are not in any contractual relationship involving the subject matter of the claim of dilution.

In this case, however, the applicability of the concept of dilution is precluded by the contractual relationship between the parties. Plaintiff's rights in the trade name "Dr. Seuss" are monopolistic as to all the world *except* as to defendant Liberty Library, who acquired all rights in the cartoons from plaintiff in 1932. Consequently, defendants cannot be considered to be diluting plaintiff's trade name.

Finally, the Court finds that there has been no showing of a "[l]ikelihood of injury to [plaintiff's] business reputation." The Court, therefore, concludes that the claim under Section 368–d of the New York Business Law must be dismissed.

2. *The Right of Privacy Claim*

Plaintiff also seeks relief pursuant to article 5 of the New York Civil Rights Law, §§ 50, 51, which creates a "right of privacy."[17]

Plaintiff consented neither to the manufacture and sale of the dolls nor to the use of the name "Dr. Seuss" therewith . . . In addition, it cannot be doubted that the name "Dr. Seuss" was " . . . used . . . for advertising purposes or for the purposes of trade . . . " within the meaning of Section 51. Neyland v. Home Pattern Co., Inc., 65 F.2d 363, 364 (2nd Cir.), cert. denied sub nom. Curtis Publishing Co. v. Neyland, 290 U.S. 661, 54 S.Ct. 76, 78 L.Ed. 572 (1933).

However, plaintiff cannot succeed under the right of privacy statute because that statute does not protect an assumed or trade name. Jaggard v. R. H. Macy & Co., 176 Misc. 88, 26 N.Y.S. 2d 829, 830 (Sup.Ct. 1941), aff'd sub

---

[17] Section 51 of the New York Civil Rights Law relevantly provides:

"§ 51. *Action for injunction and for damages*

Any person whose name, portrait or picture is used within this state for advertising purposes or for the purposes of trade without the written consent first obtained as above provided may maintain an equitable action in the supreme court of this state against the person, firm or corporation so using his name, portrait or picture, to prevent and restrain the use thereof; and may also sue and recover damages for any injuries sustained by reason of such use and if the defendant shall have knowingly used such person's name, portrait or picture in such manner as is forbidden or declared to be unlawful by the last section, the jury, in its discretion, may award exemplary damages. But nothing contained in this act shall be so construed as to prevent any person, firm or corporation, . . . from using the name, portrait or picture of any author, composer or artist in connection with his literary, musical or artistic productions which he has sold or disposed of with such name, portrait or picture used in connection therewith."

nom. Jaccard v. R. H. Macy & Co., 265 App.Div. 15, 37 N.Y.S.2d 570, 571 (1942).

In *Jaccard*, the plaintiff's actual name was "Ginette Jaggard" but she designed dresses under the assumed name of "Ginette de Paris". The court held that " . . . a name assumed for business purposes only . . . " is not within the protection of the statute . . .

In the case at bar, plaintiff's actual name is "Theodor Seuss Geisel." He began using the name "Seuss" in 1925 and added the "Dr." to create the name "Dr. Seuss" in 1927 . . . In fact, plaintiff stipulated that " 'Dr. Seuss' has been plaintiff's pen name and trade name since 1927 or 1928" [P.T.O. Stip.]. The Court holds that the name "Dr. Seuss" is an assumed name or pseudonym rather than a surname and is, therefore, not a protectible "name" within the meaning of Section 51 of the New York Civil Rights Law.

Defendants also argue that plaintiff cannot recover under the privacy statute because of the express statutory exception to Section 51. That exception is operative when three conditions are met: first, the plaintiff's name must be used by defendants " . . . with his literary . . . or artistic productions . . . "; second, the production must have been " . . . sold or disposed of . . . "; and third, the sale must have been " . . . with such name . . . used in connection therewith."

Clearly, the second and third conditions are met. Plaintiff "sold" the cartoons and the name "Dr. Seuss" appeared on each of them.

Plaintiff, however, contends that defendants have not satisfied the first condition for the reason that plaintiff "sold or disposed of" cartoons—*not* dolls—and the dolls are not substantially related to the cartoons. There is some superficial merit to this argument. However, the Court finds that the dolls are substantially related to the cartoons. Thus, the evident statutory purpose of the exception encompasses the circumstances of this case.

Decisions interpreting the statute have long held that, if a work is in the public domain, a concomitant of the right to copy that work is the right to use the name of the creator of the work in connection therewith, or, in other words, to state truthfully the creator's association with the product.

The case at bar presents an *a fortiori* situation: the copyright and all rights in the cartoons are held by defendants.

The Court, therefore, holds that all the conditions of the exception to Section 51 of the New York Civil Rights Law are met. That exception, as well as the trade name exception, requires dismissal of the right of privacy claim.

3. The Defamation Claim

Plaintiff argues that the dolls are "tasteless, unattractive and of an inferior quality" . . . and, therefore, sale of them with his trade or pen name holds him up to ridicule and contempt in his profession as a distinguished artist and author.

That plaintiff is a distinguished artist and author is not disputed [P.T.O.Stip]. The Court, however, rejects as unpersuasive and contrary to the preponderance of the credible evidence the testimony adduced in behalf of plaintiff that the dolls are "repellant" and of "inferior quality" . . . The Court finds that the execution of defendants' dolls was done with great care, skill and judgment by a qualified designer and manufacturer. In addition, the Court, on the basis of the entire record . . . and of its own close examination of the dolls, finds that they are attractive and of good quality. There is, therefore, no defamation.

This claim must also fail because defendants' activities *after April 9th do* not imply that plaintiff created, designed or approved of the dolls.

4. *Conspiracy to Injure (Prima facie Tort)*

Plaintiff alleges for his fifth and final cause of action essentially that defendants have conspired to commit all the other acts alleged with an intent to injure plaintiff. This claim has not been established.

The Court finds, on the basis of the great preponderance of the credible evidence, that with respect to the exploitation of plaintiff's cartoons by Liberty Library, Liberty's dealings with plaintiff's agent, Mrs. Jackson, reflect the good faith of defendant Liberty; and that all of the actions of defendant Liberty and of its licensee Poynter Products were under bona fide advice of experienced and competent counsel who had been specifically requested to remain in the role of advising defendants by plaintiff's agent . . . The Court reiterates that the designs and manufacture of the dolls were executed with great care and skill by persons with extensive experience.

Far from there being an intention to injure, the Court finds that defendants, at all stages of exploiting the Liberty Magazine cartoons, conducted themselves carefully and conservatively. There was no malice or intention to inflict injury on plaintiff.

It is important to note that plaintiff has not pleaded and proved special damages. There has been no showing that plaintiff was injured by defendants' conduct.

The prima facie tort claim must, therefore, be dismissed on the merits.

The same showing of good faith and reliance upon counsel which requires dismissal of the prima facie tort claim also requires dismissal, as a matter of discretion, of all claims for punitive damages.

Finally, plaintiff has offered no evidence of such participation by Alabe Crafts, Inc. and Linder, Nathan & Heide, Inc. in the accused acts as to make either of those defendants liable.

The Court denies costs to either party.

If any of the parties desire additional or supplemental findings of fact and conclusions of law, such additional or supplemental findings and conclusions shall be submitted to the Court and opposing counsel within five days from the date of the filing of this opinion.

Settle a judgment in accordance with the views expressed in this opinion.

PARAMOUNT PRODUCTIONS, INC. v. SMITH
91 F.2d 863 (9th Cir. 1937)

Before WILBUR, GARRECHT, and HANEY, Circuit Judges.

WILBUR, Circuit Judge, dissenting.

HANEY, Circuit Judge.

Judgment was rendered for appellee in his action against appellant for breach of contract, and the latter appealed.

It is admitted by the pleadings that appellee is the sole author of a story entitled "Cruise to Nowhere"; that appellee sold the story to appellant on April 29, 1933, for $2,500, as evidenced by a written contract containing the terms and conditions of the sale. This contract contains the following provisions:

> "Second: The Author hereby grants to the Purchaser all the motion picture rights throughout the world, in and to and in connection with the said story, together with the sole and exclusive rights to use, adapt, translate, subtract from, add to and change the said story and the title thereof in the making of motion picture photoplays and/or as a part of and/or in conjunction with any motion picture photoplay and/or to combine the said story with any other work, to use the said title and/or any similar title in conjunction with motion picture photoplays based upon the said story and/or other literary, dramatic and/or dramatico-musical works [works]. . . . "

> "Eighth: The Purchaser agrees to announce on the film of the motion picture photoplays that may be produced pursuant hereto that such motion picture photoplays are based upon or adapted from story written by the Author, or words to that effect."

In paragraph "Second," supra, by the use of the recondite and occult typographical jumble "and/or," a near approach to totality of confusion and unintelligibility has been accomplished, but, inasmuch as the determination of this appeal is dependent upon the construction of the eighth paragraph of the contract rather than the second, we abandon without regret all effort to determine, by reference to its written word, the meaning, if any there be, of the provisions of the second paragraph aforesaid.

The complaint alleged that in 1934 appellant completed the production and thereafter exhibited generally throughout the United States a "talking motion picture" under the title of "We're Not Dressing," which "was based upon, and adapted from, said original story of plaintiff herein, entitled 'Cruise to Nowhere' . . . "; that appellant violated the eighth provision of the contract quoted, in that appellant "wholly failed to announce upon said films, or at any of the public exhibitions thereof, that the same was either written by plaintiff, or that it was based upon, or adapted from, a story written by" appellee. Appellant admitted production and exhibition of the picture "We're Not Dressing," but denied the remainder of these allegations.

At the trial appellee introduced into evidence over appellant's objections a sheet showing production cost prepared by appellant's accounting department. This sheet contained the following:

"Production No. 983.
"Title 'We're Not Dressing'.
"From Story 'Cruise to Nowhere'."

The objection was "upon the ground that no proper foundation is laid to show that anyone connected with the accounting or auditing department, or that department itself, had anything to do with selecting either the title for a given picture, or determining whether a given picture should be based upon or adapted from a given story or not."

Appellee also offered in evidence an item released by the publicity department of appellant dated September 7, 1933, which contained the following statement: " 'We're Not Dressing' is an original story by Walton Hall Smith." Appellee also offered in evidence a similar item dated December 13, 1933, which stated in part:

"Francis Martin . . . today was assigned to write the screen adaptation of 'We're Not Dressing' to be produced soon . . .

"Others working on the story, an original by Walton Hall Smith called 'A Cruise to Nowhere,' are . . . "

Objection was made to both items on grounds identical with those urged against the admission of the production cost sheet, and counsel also stated: " . . . There is no foundation whereby the corporation may be bound, because, in order for the evidentiary matter to be an admission properly received as such, it must be made by one within the scope of his authority, and it must pertain to authority which he has."

The objections were overruled.

The trial court gave the following instruction to the jury: "Now, gentlemen, upon the evidence that the court has discussed a moment or so ago, upon the testimony as to earnings and the testimony as to failure on the part of the plaintiff to minimize the damages, there is an experience table of mortality that is applicable, and that may be used because in cases of this kind it is necessary to utilize the instruments that are possible or capable of utilization. One of these is that the experience table of mortality may be used if the jury concludes that it is proper to use it in the particular case; and under the American Experience Table of Mortality the expectant age of the defendant, under the stipulation that he is now 37 years of age, is 30.35 years. So that if you reach this question of damages you have the right to consider that together with all of the other elements that have been included in all of the instructions that have been heretofore given or that will be hereafter given in this case."

Upon the issues, the jury found in favor of appellee in the sum of $7,500. Judgment was entered on the verdict, from which judgment this appeal was taken.

Appellant contends that it was incumbent on appellee to prove that the accounting department and the publicity department was authorized to determine whether or not the picture produced was based upon or adapted from appellee's story. Appellant urges that, "in order to be binding upon the principal, admissions must be made by an agent while acting within the scope of his authority and must relate to matters to which that authority extends." Ferguson v. Basin Consolidated Mines, 152 Cal. 712, 713, 93 P. 867. The same rule is applicable with respect to admissions of an officer of the corporation. None of these cases is strictly in point. In each of them the person who made the admission was identified before the evidence was offered, or, in other words, it was known who made the admission. Here it is not denied that the admission was in fact made by some one for the corporation, but it did not appear who made the statement.

At the time the cost sheet was offered, there was no evidence as to the origin of the sheet, nor its content. There was proof that it was taken from the files of appellant, and produced by it. There was no proof, at the time it was offered, that it was made by or on behalf of any department. So far as the record shows, it might have been made by or on behalf of the board of directors, or by or on behalf of the production department, which appellant admits had authority to make such an admission. In other words, at the time the cost sheet was offered, the proof showed it was made for the corporation. If one agent or officer made it, it would have been made within his authority; if another agent or officer made it, it would not have been made within his authority.

There seems to be good ground for an exception to the rule mentioned. For example, suppose a prospectus is issued by a large corporation, which contains simply the corporate name at the end thereof, and in which an admission is made. If the rule mentioned is extended, then the person offering the prospectus would have to first prove who made the prospectus, before he could prove such person's authority. It is difficult to see how the party could prove such identity, short of questioning each officer, agent, and employee. Many corporations employ thousands of people. Such a rule would be impractical. Logic would compel admission as evidence of the admission so made, and, if the identity of the person who made the admission is thereafter proven, then the authority of the person should be proven, or the admission, on motion, stricken.

However, assuming without deciding, that the rule relied upon by appellant is applicable here, then we believe the error did not affect the substantial rights of appellant.

Appellant also contends that the cost sheet had no evidentiary value because the later evidence showed "that it was the practice of the accounting department to charge a story to a production when it had been bought for it, or for a specified star, whether the story was actually used or not. . . . " In the first place, this contention relates to the weight of the evidence and not to the admissibility thereof. In the second place, when such fact was proven, there was no renewal of the objection or a motion to strike. Therefore, no ruling of the trial court exists for review.

With respect to the publicity items it should be noted that both of them were issued before filming, and before the screen adaptation was written. We believe the error, if any, was cured by the repeated instructions of the trial court that the finished picture must have been based upon or adapted from appellee's story, since it was apparent to the jury that appellant may have changed its program. If the error was not cured, then it did not affect appellant's substantial rights.

Appellant specified the admission of certain other evidence as error, in specifications numbered 7 to 13, both inclusive. With respect to these appellant says in its brief: "We have no desire unduly to prolong this brief and hence the matters dealing with asserted error in the admission of evidence . . . detailed in [the specifications mentioned] will be submitted without argument." Under such circumstances, error is now shown, and we treat these specifications as abandoned.

With reference to the instruction hereinabove set forth, appellant says that mortality tables are inadmissible as evidence in such a case as this, and relies on Johnson v. Richards, 50 Idaho, 150, 294 P. 507, Snyder v. Great Northern Ry. Co., 88 Wash. 49, 152 P. 703, and Swope v. City of Seattle, 36 Wash. 113, 78 P. 607. Appellee contends that the instruction was proper on the authority of Turner v. Jackson, 139 Or. 539, 4 P.(2d) 925, 11 P.(2d) 1048. The California courts seem not to have passed on the question.

We believe the error, if any, did not affect the substantial rights of the parties, but was a technical error. The mortality table was not introduced into evidence. The court, judicially noting the table, simply instructed the jury to consider it with all the other evidence "if the jury contends that it is proper to use it in the particular case."

Appellant says that the primary question is whether or not the picture was based upon or adapted from appellee's story. That statement is only partially true. Our function is to ascertain whether or not there is any substantial evidence to sustain the verdict. Specifically, the question presented is whether or not there is any substantial evidence to sustain the finding of the jury that the picture "We're Not Dressing" was based upon or adapted from appellee's story, "Cruise to Nowhere."

An examination of the record discloses that the evidence was conflicting. Three of appellant's witnesses defined and distinguished between "based upon" and "adapted from." There was evidence showing that the picture produced was not based upon or adapted from appellee's story. We are not interested in such evidence, however, but only in the evidence of the opposite fact.

The cost sheet hereinabove discussed is some evidence of the fact found by the jury. Correspondence between officers of appellant had some months before filming was started indicates that appellant may have used the story. Appellee introduced a manuscript of his story into evidence, and read it to the jury. During the trial, the court and its attendants, the jury, appellee, and counsel for the parties saw a showing of the picture. The jury was able to make a comparison. Afterward, appellee testified, "I saw in the picture much of the plot which I originally had in mind; much of the basic idea." We believe this is sufficient to warrant submission of the issue to the jury, and, since the jury believed it, the verdict is supported thereby.

Finally, appellant urges that there is a lack of evidence to support the award of damages, in that there was no standard by which damages could be gauged. Appellee contends that the true rule on uncertainty of damages is that the prohibition is directed against uncertainty as to cause, rather than uncertainty as to measure or extent.

We do not believe the evidence is subject to the charge of uncertainty.

Appellee testified that he and another writer collaborated in writing a story and sold it without screen credit for $10,000, which the two writers divided. Appellee's story was sold for $2,500, but under a contract that required that he be given screen credit. From these figures, the jury might easily compute the advertising value of the screen credit. He also testified that he received screen credit for a play; that prior thereto his salary was $250 per week; and that afterward he received $350 per week at one time, and $500 per week for a period of two weeks, due to the screen credit he had received. That evidence is, if believed, likewise sufficient as a gauge for the measure of the damages.

Finding no error affecting the substantial rights of appellant, the judgment is affirmed.

WILBUR, Circuit Judge (dissenting).

I dissent. With reference to the question as to whether or not there was substantial evidence that the film play produced by the defendant was based upon a story written by the plaintiff entitled "Cruise to Nowhere" and purchased by the defendant for the purpose of screen production, I am unable to agree with the conclusion of my associates. In the first place, statements contained in the books of the corporation showing that the cost of the story purchased from the plaintiff was charged against the film play produced by the defendant was clearly admissible as a declaration against interest. The same is true with reference to the press release indicating that the defendant produced a screen play based upon plaintiff's story. These admissions might be sufficiently substantial to sustain the verdict were it not for the fact that other evidence supplements and explains these admissions and deprives them of any weight. Beyond question, the defendant purchased the plaintiff's story for film reproduction and went to work to adapt it for screen reproduction. The admissions above referred to were made during the preliminary stages of screen adaptation. But the evidence shows that it was later decided that plaintiff's story was not suitable for the type of production desired at that time, and that several screen writers were employed to write the scenario for reproduction. Later, when the play was produced, they were given credit for this work, and the plaintiff was not given the credit to which he deemed himself entitled under his contract with the defendant. That the story produced was vastly different from that purchased is clear from a comparison of the two stories. It follows that the admissions of the defendant made at the time when it was the intention to use plaintiff's story became valueless in determining whether or not they did in fact use his story. I conclude, therefore, that the admissions of the defendant that the produced story "We're Not Dressing" was based upon plaintiff's story "Cruise to Nowhere" are without probative value in determining whether or not the plaintiff was entitled to screen credit.

The provision of the contract relating to screen credit is quoted in the main opinion, and it is unnecessary to repeat it. It is a method of advertising to the public the fact that the production they are about to witness is the result of the ingenuity, inventive genius, and literary skill to the person to whom screen credit is given. Thus it is believed other motion picture producers will seek to avail themselves of the services of the person given screen credit to produce other stories for such reproduction. It is clear that to give screen credit to a person not reasonably entitled thereto would be a fraud upon the public, while, on the other hand, to deny the author his contract rights if the play produced is based upon his story would be a violation of the contract.

In view of these conflicting considerations it is clear that in construing the terms of the contract for screen credit some attention must be given to the question as to whether or not the giving of such credit to a play which has been substantially changed would in effect be a falsehood tending to deceive the public. It should be stated that this factor of the problem has not been urged by the appellant. The appellant has confined its contention to the proposition that a film play is not based upon a story unless it so far resembles the story that to produce it without authority from the author of the story would, if copyrighted, violate the copyright, and therefore relies upon such copyright cases as Harold Lloyd Corp. v. Witwer (C.C.A.) 65 F.(2d) 1.

We have, however, a different question involved in the two types of cases. In the copyright case we have an intent to appropriate a story without comparison by making changes for the purpose of camouflaging theft, whereas in the case at bar we have the defendant owning a story and making changes, not for the purpose of appropriating the property of another, but for the purpose of making the story more interesting and more profitable. Granting then, what seems obvious, that the changes in the plaintiff's story were made, not for the purpose of defrauding the plaintiff of his property, but for the purpose of adding to the interest and profit of the story, the question is, has the story been so far departed from in the play that it cannot reasonably be said to be based upon the plaintiff's story, having due regard to the rights of the plaintiff to credit for his achievement in producing the story, and the right of the public not to be deceived by reason of credit falsely given to an author.

With these facts in mind we must turn to a comparison of the film and the plaintiff's story, and from this comparison it must be determined whether or not there is so strong a resemblance between the two that the plaintiff was entitled to have the public informed through the screen production of the story that he was the author of the play, or, to put it in the words of the contract, that the play was based upon his story.

It is no doubt proper in such a case to assist the jury with the opinion of expert literary men and authors to indicate the points of resemblance and dissimilarity between the story and the play. I do not believe, however, that the fact that these experts may differ with relation to the literary value and the literary similarity of the story and the play would be such a conflict in the evidence as would justify and sustain a verdict where the story and the play were both presented to the jury for comparison. The trial judge and the appellate court should not be bound by the mere ipsa dixit of expert witnesses where the subject is one of general knowledge and the real question involved is not the impression conveyed by the picture to experts but the impression which the ordinary observer would receive. Harold Lloyd Corporation v. Witwer, supra.

I cannot believe that an extended analysis of the story and the play would be appropriate in a dissenting opinion in view of the conclusion which the majority of the court has reached. It will be sufficient to indicate my view to compare the testimony of Mr. George Marion, who claims to have written the story as it was finally screened, and the testimony of the plaintiff Marion testified:

"Mr. Glazer [the producer] and I talked it over five or six times. He gave me nothing in writing. He never wrote anything in connection with it; just a verbal conference. I am absolutely certain that Mr. Glazer did not write my story. I am certain that he did not write a line in the script that I have identified.

"Mr. Glazer's conferences with me were purely of a working nature, and as we went along I brought in material to him, and he discussed it, but there were no contributions beyond the idea of his background which already existed in my own story. ['Let's Go Native'.] The only contribution which he made to the working background of the story involved a group of people on a sea island. The idea of a boat starting out on a cruise and being wrecked was in 'Let's Go Native.' Naturally, he said something to me about it. He did so independent of my story. He told me that they had bought a story. He did not tell me what story they had bought. He never mentioned the name particularly, but he said they had purchased a piece of material which involved a shipwreck and people on a desert island. As I repeated before, I said I thought it was all right. I did know that they had bought a story based on this desert island scene. He did not tell me the substance of the story. He did not tell me a thing about it. He told me not to read it. He told me to write a script without reading the story as the story was being completely scrapped. It was a script. A script is the complete shooting continuity, including the actual dialogue and directions for the camera work on the set. An outline is simply the plot. It contains no dialogue. This script I wrote was not an outline. I never make outlines. I usually go right into the script after conversing with the producer. To a certain extent this script written by me was taken from the previous story of my own. There was a great deal of material in there which was original. The original material is simply gags and scenes in connection with characters and which Mr. Glazer said he would like to use. For instance, W. C. Fields. I did not discuss the name Jimmy with Mr. Glazer. I believe that when this script of mine was turned in, it was turned in under my name. It was simply turned in to the studio, because Mr. Glazer was not in the country at that time. I believe my several conversations with Mr. Glazer were had during the latter part of July and the first part of August. I don't know when he returned from his trip abroad because I was not working with that studio at that time. I had gone over to another studio and another job. In the usual course of work at the studio, if they think there is enough to the story and they want an adaptation job, they actually give us the material purchased to read, and contribute to it what we think is of value. After that, the adapter contributes to the best of his ability."

Smith testified as follows: "With the view of the motion picture 'We're Not Dressing' freshly in my mind, as regards the similarity of that picture to my story 'Cruise to Nowhere', I would state the following: I saw in the picture much of the plot *which I originally had in mind*; much of the basic idea. I had forgotten how close it was to *the original conception* that I had in mind for this story, which was that these characters—obviously, among the characters, there were principal characters—would be unexpectedly thrown against a background. It didn't make any difference what the background would be at the time, which would enable—I say the two principal characters—to discover in each other characteristics which they otherwise would never have known. Obviously, they would never have met. *That was the original idea.* I thought to use a shipwreck, which would give me that quality with an unexpectedness which none of the characters would have anticipated. So it would have been a complete surprise—thrown into the ocean and thrown upon an uninhabited island. That would permit my principal character, whom I called Jimmy June, to display talents which perhaps even he did not know he had. Those talents, and whatever ability he had would be observed by the girl. I purposely made him poor and made her rich. I did not have any specific heiress, because that was not necessary to a straight dramatic story. She did observe the qualities of the principal male character. She admired them in him, and thus through this primitive background they were drawn together. The story ended as a romance in marriage. . . . I know from my own experience in studio work, for an original story of this type, it is much more true to the finished film than anything I had ever seen. I mean they adhere closely to my plot . . . In other words, I know, without this original story this picture would never have been made. *The lean-tos the man built, the skill with which he built them, the obvious leadership and quality of the leader, the plot—I say again, basically is paralleled in the story 'Cruise to Nowhere' and the picture 'We're Not Dressing.'*" (Italics ours.)

Assuming that Marion wrote the photoplay as he testified, it is easy to account for such similarities as exist between the story and the photoplay without discrediting the plaintiff's testimony above quoted. We have, of course, nothing to do with the original idea he had in mind, nor with the original conception as to which he testified if they were not incorporated in his story, nor indeed with an idea so incorporated, for it is the author's treatment—the language he uses in the development of the idea that constitutes his literary property, not the idea itself. Without a detailed comparison of the story and the photoplay it is enough to say that the characters, the dialogue, the scenery are all original in the photoplay and differ from the story in substantially every detail. The things in common are the shipwreck, an uninhabited or desert island, the difficulties of life there, and the love story between a poor boy and a rich girl. The plaintiff disclaimed any originality in these points which are similar, as well he might.[1] I quote from his testimony in that regard as follows:

"I can't remember any situation such as the shipwreck, love affair, building a house, any situation which I claim to be original with me. There is a series of incidents in the story; there is a series of incidents in the picture; sometimes dissimilar, sometimes similar. I would say that the shipwreck is not original with me, of course, nor the love affair as such. This is a specific love affair between two characters who have been characterized as a poor boy and an heiress, and so forth. As regards incidents on the island, that is a group of incidents, too, and originality as to such incidents would be the manner in which they were handled. Certainly, I don't claim building a lean-to, building a house, is an original incident. I don't think there is any incident in the picture of life on that island, as an individual incident, that was original with me."

In my opinion there was no substantial evidence to go to the jury to show that the photoplay was based upon the plaintiff's story so that he was entitled to screen credit therefor as its author under his contract. Conclusions or opinion evidence tending to sustain the plaintiff's contention must fail in the teeth of the specific evidence furnished by a comparison of the actual story with the photoplay produced.

Damages.

If we assume there has been a breach of contract, there is no evidence of loss or damage proximately resulting therefrom. The evidence leaves the damages

---

[1] In this view he is corroborated by the appellant's witness Garland Greever, a professor of English at the University of Southern California: " . . . the similarities are in matters of a general nature. They are not peculiar to the picture or to the script. . . . they had been used many times."

to be determined by the jury by guess and speculation. The burden is upon the plaintiff to establish, not only the breach of the contract, but the damages, if any, proximately resulting therefrom, and, unless he has shown such damage, he is not entitled to recover.[2] It is clear that the contract for screen credit is in effect a contract to advertise the fact that the plaintiff was the author of the story reproduced on the screen. It seems clear that the damages he seeks in this action and the damages awarded are speculative in the absence of some proof as to special damages resulting from the breach of the contract. While the point seems self-evident, we are not without authority on the proposition that damages resulting from failure to advertise are speculative and that in the absence of some specific proof of damage plaintiff cannot recover. I refer without discussion to two or three of these authorities cited by the appellant: Stevens v. Yale, 113 Mich. 680, 72 N.W. 5; Tribune Co. v. Bradshaw, 20 Ill.App. 17; Winston Cigarette Mach. Co. v. Wells, etc., Co., 141 N.C. 284, 53 S.E. 885, 8 L.R.A.(N.S.) 255.

The plaintiff's contention is that, if his reputation had been enhanced by the advertisement that he had produced the story upon which the screen play was based, it would have been an advantage to him in securing other contracts of a similar nature and upon that hypothesis introduced evidence as to a past contract in which he had sold a story for less with screen credit than he had received for another story without screen credit. In the main opinion it is suggested that this evidence is not only pertinent to the inquiry but is a proper basis for determining damage. While it is manifest that favorable publicity of any kind in connection with the production of a screen play would be valuable to one seeking to sell a story or play, it is clear it would be impossible to measure the value of one story by the amount paid for an entirely different story even though the author is the same. There is no basis for comparison, and to permit the jury to determine the value of one play with or without screen credit by evidence of the value of another and entirely dissimilar play would evidently require the jury to enter the domain of speculation. The same

---

[2] This is a California contract and governed by the law of California.

The California Civil Code with relation to damages for breach of contract is as follows:

"Sec. 3300. For the breach of an obligation arising from contract, the measure of damages, except where otherwise expressly provided by this code, is the amount which will compensate the party aggrieved for all the detriment proximately caused thereby, or which, in the ordinary course of things, would be likely to result therefrom.

"Sec. 3301. No damages can be recovered for a breach of contract which are not clearly ascertainable in both their nature and origin."

Section 3358 of the California Civil Code provides:

"Notwithstanding the provisions of this chapter, no person can recover a greater amount in damages for the breach of an obligation than he could have gained by the full performance thereof on both sides."

thing may be said concerning the evidence referred to in the main opinion concerning the salary received by the plaintiff before and after he had obtained screen credit. There is no evidence that the increase in salary was due to the fact that screen credit had been given on a previous play. I think this evidence was too remote and speculative and should not have been received and that the conclusion of the jury from such evidence was based upon speculation and guess and not upon evidence.

There are other authorities which support the conclusion that in an action for damages for breach of contract the plaintiff cannot recover for loss of profits which he expected to acquire by reason of entering into other contracts which he claims to have been unable to do because of the breach of the contract. The appellant cites a number of cases in support of this general proposition, among them, Seymour v. McCormick, 16 How. (57 U.S.) 480, 14 L.Ed. 1024; Cincinnati Siemens-Lungren Gas Co. v. Western Siemens-Lungren Co., 152 U.S. 200, 14 S.Ct. 523, 38 L.Ed 411; Broadway Photoplay Co. v. World Film Corp., 225 N.Y. 104, 121 N.E. 756, 757; and Parke v. Frank, 75 Cal. 364, 17 P. 427. The decision in Broadway Photoplay Co. v. World Film Corporation was written by Judge Cardozo for the New York Court of Appeals. As it emphasizes the impossibility of comparing two dissimilar things as a basis for recovery of damages, I quote from the opinion as follows:

The comparison must be between feature pictures of the first run and feature pictures of later runs. The jury were so charged. They were charged that the plaintiff was 'limited to the difference in value between first run feature pictures and second or third run feature pictures, and not to the difference between feature pictures and other pictures.' But there is nothing in the evidence to supply a basis for the comparison. No law of averages, no constant or approximate uniformity of returns, can be gathered by induction from the sporadic and varying instances scattered through this record. The pictures of the first run are few in number. They disclose no semblance of equality in their returns when compared with one another. They disclose a like diversity when compared with pictures of later runs. . . .

"There can be no stable foundation for a verdict that is built on such assumptions. Nothing but guesswork can place the damages at $4,500, or any other fixed amount."

In the case of Bernstein v. Meech, 130 N.Y. 354, 29 N.E. 255, 257, defendant, the owner of a theater, contracted with plaintiff to bring a theatrical company to Buffalo to present four performances in defendant's theater. The parties were to share equally in the gross receipts. Plaintiff sued the defendant for breach of this contract. Plaintiff sought to recover his lost profits. This was denied him in the lower court, and he appealed. It was held that such profits were too speculative to be recovered in an action for breach of contract, the court stating, in part, as follows: "The value of the contract to the plaintiff was in the profits and in the amount of them which may have been realized over his expenses attending its performance. Those profits, not being susceptible of proof, were not the subject of recovery."

In a somewhat similar case, Todd v. Keene, 167 Mass. 157, 45 N.E. 81, the court said: "There are too many elements of uncertainty and conjecture to make it safe to rely upon opinions such as the plaintiff offered to give."

It follows that the jury should have been instructed to return a verdict in favor of the defendant because no breach of contract was proved and because no damages were proved.

The defendant also complains of an instruction by which the court informed the jury of the life expectancy of the plaintiff and instructed the jury that if in their judgment this life expectancy was relevant they should consider it in arriving at their verdict. Such an instruction might be considered harmless in some cases because a jury is presumed to know, that is, to take judicial notice of, the life expectancy of an individual, and it may be assumed, will apply this knowledge to any problem submitted to it where it is deemed by the jury to be germane to the solution. But the life expectancy of the plaintiff had no relation to the problem presented to this jury. They were to award such damages as the plaintiff had suffered up to the time of trial, or reasonably certain to result in the future. The court seemed to be of the impression that the failure to advertise the plaintiff in accordance with the terms of the contract may have permanently decreased his earning power and that such decreased earning power might be considered in arriving at a verdict. This was a direct invitation to the jury to speculate on the future possibilities of the defendant's earning capacity and upon the question of whether or not it would be affected by the defendant's breach of the contract. There was and could be no proof that he was permanently injured. As a matter of fact the evidence shows that the plaintiff abandoned his efforts in the moving picture line and withdrew from the field and devoted his time to writing a novel. Although he testified that he intended at some time to return to Hollywood for the purpose of engaging as an author in the moving picture industry, the testimony as to his change of occupation increases the speculative character of the jury's verdict based upon hypothetical losses due to a failure to secure contracts in the moving picture industry.

CURWOOD v. AFFILIATED DISTRIBUTORS, INC.

283 F. Supp. 219 (S.D.N.Y. 1922)

KNOX, District Judge. Plaintiff is the author of some 25 novels and numerous shorter stories. Some of the former, notably "The River's End" and "The Valley of Silent Men," have had a wide distribution, and have brought Mr. Curwood's name into favorable position before the novel-reading public.

In the main, the plots of complainant's fiction are laid in the Canadian Northwest, and frequently have as prominent characters thereof members of the Northwest Mounted Police. Most of the novels have been reproduced in motion pictures. These, too, have met with success, some of them having yielded rentals of more than $500,000. In connection with the exploitation of such pictures, Curwood's name has been prominently advertised and displayed. Unquestionably it is now associated by many moving picture distributors and patrons with stories having to do with forests, streams, snow, ice, and romance as they are, or are imagined to be, in the subarctic regions of this continent. That this association is of value to plaintiff may be indicated by testimony offered herein to the effect that the moving picture rights of one of plaintiff's stories sold for more than $50,000.

Defendants, Affiliated Distributors, Inc., William Nigh, Edwin Carewe Pictures Corporation, Charles C. Burr, and Edwin Carewe were interested in the making and exploitation of a Northwest Mounted Police Story which has been given the title "I Am the Law." Appreciating the value of complainant's name; when it was advertised that "I Am the Law" was based on James Oliver Curwood's latest story, "The Poetic Justice of Uko San," defendants set about to acquire the right to so advertise their picture. The means adopted therefor were as follows:

A number of years before he attained his present prominence as an author of fiction, Curwood wrote some stories for the Outing magazine. One of these was entitled "The Poetic Justice of Uko San." The tale had to do with three bears encountered by two men who were hunting in the north woods. Inasmuch as the only resemblance which the scenario and picture of "I Am the Law" bears to "The Poetic Justice of Uko San" is that the action of each takes place in northwestern Canada, there is no need to dwell upon the theme of the latter. When Curwood sold the story to Outing, moving picture rights were not valued as at present, and there is some question as to whether Curwood had retained such rights. At all events, outing had placed its rights to the story upon the market, and they were in the hands of a literary broker for sale. It appears that such rights, whatever might be their value as moving picture material, were not particularly desirable without the acquiescence of complainant.

Thereupon the defendant Burr entered into negotiation with Curwood's agent, Milligan, for the purchase of such rights. The price demanded by Milligan was $5,000. This figure was too large for Burr, and he declined the same, and then took steps to purchase the rights through the medium of the defendant Nigh. The latter got in touch with a literary broker named Maxine Alton. She in turn took up the matter with Milligan, with the result that upon March, 21, 1922, complainant made a contract with Nigh, the important part of which, for present purposes, reads as follows:

> "This is to ratify our understanding whereby James Oliver Curwood agrees, upon payment to him . . . of $1,000 and other valuable considerations, to relinquish all claim or claims he may have or have had in the screen rights to his story Poetic Justice of Uko San, and grants to you his permission, as far as he is concerned, to produce a feature motion picture of five reels or more from said story; it being understood that you are to select a capable man to elaborate on said story, with addition of characters, etc., however needed, and said production to be cast with a selected cast and to be produced in a first-class manner in every respect. . . . It is also understood that should you, either by act or omission, break the terms of the understanding as outlined in this letter, said understanding shall thereupon become null and void, and all moneys which shall have been paid to Mr. Curwood, and whatever benefit may have been derived by him under the terms of this letter, shall be retained by him without let or hindrance as liquidated damages, and from thenceforth shall become his sole and undisputed property. . . . "

The gist of Curwood's complaint is that, while Nigh was accorded the right to "elaborate" upon the story and reproduce it in moving pictures, he was not given the privilege to utterly disregard the same and yet use its name, and Curwood's authorship thereof, in connection with a wholly different story and picturization. It is claimed that what defendants have done, in advertising and producing their picture "I Am the Law" as being based upon Curwood's story "The Poetic Justice of Uko San," injures his standing, reputation, and prestige, and is in derogation of his civil rights, and, further, that the picture "I Am the Law" is a piratical adaptation of complainant's stories, "The River's End" and "The Valley of Silent Men."

Defendants admit the production of their picture, and also that the same is advertised in the manner complained of. It is, however, denied that plaintiff's stories, last mentioned, are pirated and plagiarized, and it is asserted, by way of defense, that Nigh's only purpose in buying the rights to "The Poetic Justice of Uko San" was to acquire authority to use Curwood's name in such picture as he, or his assignees, might choose to produce; that such purpose was thoroughly understood by Curwood, and that as a matter of fact, the picture

"I Am the Law" has been artistically produced by a selected cast; and, this having been done, complainant is in no position to object.

Much testimony has been offered by defendants in an effort to show, not only that Curwood was willing to sell his name, reputation, and prestige for hardly more than a normal sum, but also that such practice is a common one among authors of repute. It is said that Milligan, Curwood's agent, was flatly told by Miss Alton and by Burr that only the right to use Curwood's name was desired. Indeed, from defendants' evidence, it is charged that Curwood himself had previously negotiated for the sale of his name, in connection with stories not his own. Upon being asked why, if this were true, the real purpose of Nigh was not set forth in the contract, the witnesses giving the testimony just referred to replied that to pursue such course "wouldn't look nice."

Milligan and Curwood deny that any such statement of Nigh's purpose was communicated to them or that they suspected the same. As to the denial of Curwood, covering prior negotiations with Burr, I may say that it impressed me as being earnest and sincere, and had about it a tone of indignation that I believe not to have been feigned. He said:

> "Mr. Burr and I did have a conversation in his office regarding the sale of stories, in which he made the proposition to me of selling the use of my name, and that he would have another individual write a story to be exploited under my name. . . . The date I cannot remember, but I was in New York, and at the time Mr. Milligan was with me. . . . It was at a time when Mr. Burr was considering 'Little Miss "Tired-of-it-all"' 'A Nice Quiet Time,' 'The Governor's Daughter,' and 'The Yellow Back.' . . . Mr. Burr objected to the prices of these stories, and, while I cannot remember all the conversation had, I do remember one part of it very definitely, in which he said to me, 'Mr. Curwood, can you not give us something that we can use, so that we can put your name on a story, and we will have a story written up?' And I said 'No.' I said that no reputable author would prostitute his work in that way, because he could not be paid enough money to repay for prostituting his work in that way, because sooner or later it would get out, and, even if it did not get out, no reputable writer that I know of would defraud the public in that way. Then he brought up—and that was the only time that he brought it before me—the question of these stories, which for three years, your honor, I had been trying hard to keep from being produced. Those stories—there were four of them—were 'The Coyote,' 'Uko San,' 'A Poor Man's Chance,' and 'Test of a Code.' . . . We were hounded into the sale of these stories by the Alton Play Bureau and other interests. . . . I told Mr. Burr at that time positively that he could not use any of those stories. And Miss Alton, I do not see how she can forget the fact, because I was

very angry at the time; . . . once I talked with her and with a gentleman who was there. . . . I told them the situation, . . . that it would be a fraud to put those stories out before the public, that I would not allow them to be put on, and that I would sue."

Much more to the same effect might be quoted, but it is unnecessary, inasmuch as I believe that complainant did not contract for the mere sale of his name.

It is argued that "The Poetic Justice of Uko San" does not contain the elements upon which a five-reel "feature" picture might be founded, and that this tends to establish defendants' contention. As to this, there is conflicting testimony. Carewe, a successful moving picture director, says that the story is devoid of elements which would permit its elaboration into a feature picture. His testimony possesses no little weight. He is corroborated by Burr and others. Curwood, on the contrary, says that "Uko San" offers all the elements for a good animal picture of the emotional nature. He cites what was done with his story "Nomads of the North," the chief characters of which were a bear and a dog. I have concluded that an elaboration of "The Poetic Justice of Uko San" into a five-reel feature was not impossible. It is to be admitted that the task to a layman would seem difficult, but I do not consider it beyond the range of possibility in the hands of a person of skill and imagination.

And now as to what is acquired when one procures the right to elaborate upon an original story. Upon this much need not be said. I take it that, while scenery, action, and characters may be added to an original story, and even supplant subordinate portions thereof, there is an obligation upon the elaborator to retain and give appropriate expression to the theme, thought, and main action of that which was originally written. The unqualified grant of this right is, I should say, fraught with danger to a writer of standing, particularly when he inserts no provision for approval of such elaboration as may be made. Nevertheless, elaboration of a story means something other than that the same should be discarded, and its title and authorship applied to a wholly dissimilar tale.

Aside from all this, however, it does not seem probable that Curwood would risk his standing, prestige, and reputation as an author by the sale of his name for attachment to any picture that a purchaser might see fit to produce, and all this for $1,000. He is yet a young man; he has achieved success; he has reason to hope for much more, and upon the evidence before me I am wholly unable to believe that he would jeopardize it all, and sell his birthright for a proverbial mess of pottage. I will protest him by injunction against the present use of the name of "The Poetic Justice of Uko San," and his authorship thereof, in connection with the picture entitled "I Am the Law."

The question of damages sought by plaintiff against the defendants, together with his allegation that the picture "I Am the Law" infringes upon the copyright of "River's End," is reserved for further consideration.

"ARBITRATORS FIND THAT THE DIRECTORS OF 'JAWS 2' AND 'KING OF THE GYPSIES' WERE ENTITLED TO CREDIT IN CERTAIN ADVERTISEMENTS"
Entertainment Law Reporter (October 15, 1979), p. 2

The names of the directors of the films "Jaws 2" and "King of the Gypsies" were required to appear in certain advertisements for those films, according to two arbitration decisions recently made available. (The arbitrations were held in June and November of 1978.) Universal Pictures and Paramount Pictures Corporation claimed that the ads were "teasers" and that such identification was not required. The arbitrators concluded, however, that the ads in question lacked the necessary elements of "mystery" and "uncertainty" associated with teaser ads and upheld the Directors Guild position that the directors of the films were entitled to receive appropriate credit.

Both disputes arose under the DGA Memorandum-Basic Agreement of 1978. Article 8 of the Agreement covers directors' credits for theatrical motion pictures. Section 8-103 contains a list of exceptions to provisions requiring directors' credits in paid advertising, one of which is an exception for "so-called teaser advertising, as that term is used in the motion picture industry."

Universal pictures has prepared two ads for "Jaws 2." The "fin-moon" ad depicted a shark's fin with the moon in the background. The copy read, "Just when you thought it was safe to go back in the water" and included the title of the film and, in small type, "Coming to theatres everywhere June 16th." The other ad showed a large shark behind a woman waterskier, the "just when . . . " copy and the title "Jaws 2" in large lettering. The ads were not submitted to the DGA prior to public release as required under the 1978 Agreement.

Arbitrator Roger H. Davis, after reviewing several definitions of teaser advertising, noted that in general teaser are a series of ads which show various attributes of the product advertised. . . . The sketches . . . create an element of *mystery* in the public mind which becomes a challenge to solve, thereby heightening inquisitiveness about the product. . . .

Davis pointed out that a teaser ad could include the title of the film if the title would not be widely recognized by the public. He concluded, however, that the use of the title "Jaws 2" eliminated all mystery—a moviegoer's possible curiosity about the story differences between "Jaws" and "Jaws 2" would not supply this necessary element.

Therefore, Davis ordered Universal to replace the ads in question with ads containing "Directed by credit to Jeannot Szwarc. However, Universal was not required to pay any damages "because of the prior history of both parties . . . treating ads comparable to those prepared by Universal as 'teaser' ads . . . over the past 20 or 30 years."

In the matter involving "King of the Gypsies," Paramount had submitted a proposed advertisement for the film to the DGA. The ad depicted the head of a young man posed against a wall with the title of the film appearing in large capital letters above the head and "From Paramount for Christmas" and a small Paramount logo appearing below the head. The DGA rejected the ad. Paramount contending that the ad constituted a teaser ad, sought an arbitration ruling.

Paramount's position was that an effective teaser ad required the inclusion of the title of the film. According to Paramount, teaser ads include all prerelease advertising. Arbitrator Murray L. Schwartz disagreed, pointing out that the parties to the 1978 Agreement could have, but did not, adopt this definition of teaser advertising.

Schwartz noted that in previous hearings regarding credits in teaser ads, arbitrators stressed "the themes of stimulating curiosity by withholding identification of the product, keeping the observer guessing, nonidentification of the product being advertised, and the creation of mystery." He determined that a teaser ad "must create in the viewer a desire to know more about the subject . . . [and] look forward to the next advertisement for more information." A title will usually, although not always, "end the mystery."

Schwartz concluded that the Paramount ad was not a teaser because it did not "create a quantum of challenge to the viewer . . . ," and he ruled that if the ad were used by Paramount, the director would have to be given credit.

In the Matter of the Arbitration Between Directors Guild of America, Inc. and Universal City Studios, Inc., Before the Arbitration Tribunal of the Directors Guild of America, Inc. (undated)

In the Matter of the Arbitration Between Paramount Pictures Corporation and Directors Guild of America, Inc., Before the Arbitration Tribunal of the Directors Guild of America, Inc. (November 16, 1978)

LANDON v.
TWENTIETH CENTURY-FOX FILM CORPORATION
384 F. Supp. 450 (S.D.N.Y. 1974)

MEMORANDUM AND ORDER

LASKER, District Judge.

In 1944 Margaret Landon entered into an agreement with Twentieth Century-Fox Film Corporation (Fox) to sell, among other things, "motion picture rights" to her book entitled "Anna and the King of Siam". In 1972 Fox produced 13 films which were broadcast on the CBS Television network as a weekly serial entitled "Anna and the King."

This suit presents the question whether the 1944 agreement between Landon and Fox authorized Fox to produce and exhibit the 1972 series through defendant CBS. In addition to her assertion that the series infringed her copyright in the literary property "Anna and the King of Siam," Landon raises the novel claim that the 1944 agreement constituted a tying arrangement in violation of Section 1 of the Sherman Act, 15 U.S.C. § 1, on the grounds that Fox allegedly acquired the original copyright "on condition that" it also acquire the copyright renewal rights. She also argues that the assignment of the renewal copyright is unenforceable for lack of consideration. Landon's final claim is that production and exhibition of the television series constituted tortious misconduct on the part of defendants, that is, defamation, invasion of her right of privacy, misappropriation of literary property and wrongful attribution to Landon of credit for the series, which she claims to have "mutilated" her literary property.

Landon moves for summary judgment as to all claims against them, and to amend their answer to assert, as an affirmative defense to the antitrust count, the expiration of the applicable four year statute of limitations.

IV.

Landon's final claim charges that certain episodes in the 1972 television series "fail to retain and give appropriate expression to the theme, thought and main action of plaintiff's work," resulting in damage to her privacy and reputation and the literary property itself. . . . As fleshed out by the material in support of her motion, the basis of this allegation is that her book was a serious literary work concerned with the struggle for human rights, whereas the television series was light in tone, and punctuated with bursts of dubbed laughter from the audience.

It is undisputed that the television credits stated that the scripts were "based on" plaintiff's literary property, with screenwriting credit given to the actual authors of the series in the same titles as Landon's name appears.

For several reasons, the claim is insufficient as a matter of law. Even without permission from an author of the existence of a written agreement with him, any person may truthfully state that a work is "based on" or "suggested by" the work of that author. I Nimmer, Copyright, § 110.41 at p. 447; Geisel v. Poynter Products, Inc., 295 F. Supp. 331, 353 (S.D.N.Y.1968). Although plaintiff would have a valid claim against defendants if they had falsely attributed the authorship of the series to her, see Granz v. Harris, 198 F.2d 585, 589 (2d Cir. 1952), her claim must fail where, as here, she contract- ed to (1) *require* Fox to give her appropriate credit "for her contribution to the literary material upon which such motion pictures shall have been based" (1944 Agreement, Article X); and (2) grant Fox the right to:

> "reproduce . . . spoken words taken from and/or *based on* the text or theme, of said literary property . . . in . . . motion pictures, using for that purpose all *or a part of the theme*, text and/or dialogue contained in said literary property."

. . . .

> [and] "adapt one or more versions of said literary property, to add to and subtract from the literary property, change the sequence thereof, change the title . . . in connection with works or motion pictures *wholly or partially independent of said* literary property . . . *change the characters* . . . change the *description of the said characters*, and use all thereof in new versions, adaptations and sequels. . . . (Agreement, Article I, para- graphs (b), (c)). (emphasis added)

These provisions clearly grant Fox the right to alter the literary property substantially and to attribute to plaintiff credit appropriate to her contribu- tion. Accordingly, we find that Fox did not violate the agreement or engage in tortious conduct when it truthfully stated that the series was "based on" the property. See Shostakovitch. v. Twentieth Century-Fox Film Corp., 196 Misc. 67, 80 N.Y.2d. 575 (Sup.Ct.N.Y.Co.1948), aff'd, 275 App.Div. 692, 87 N.Y.S.2d 430 (1st Dept. 1949). Seroff v. Simon & Schuster, 6 Misc.2d 383, 388, 162 N.Y.S.2d 770 (Sup.Ct.N.Y.Co.1957), aff'd, 12 App.Div.2d 475, 210 N.Y.S.2d 49 (1st Dept. 1960).[2]

Plaintiff's motion for summary judgment is denied; defendants' motion to amend their answer is granted; defendants' motion for summary judgment dismissing the complaint is granted.

---

[2] We note in passing that Landon's complaint, a judicial admission, alleges at Paragraph 19 that "Defendant Fox did produce and make available to defendant CBS a series of television programs *based upon* the book" (emphasis supplied). The fact that plaintiff's own choice of language to describe her contribution to the series is almost identical to the wording of Fox's titles, supports our conclusion Fox fairly and accurately credited her.

It is so ordered.

———————

RICH AND CBS INC. v.
RCA CORPORATION
390 F. Supp. 530 (S.D.N.Y. 1975)

OPINION

MacMAHON, District Judge.

Plaintiffs, Charlie Rich and CBS Inc., seek a preliminary injunction enjoining RCA Corporation from using the current photograph or likeness of Rich on the jacket of a recently released phonograph record entitled "Charlie Rich—She Called Me Baby," containing authentic songs recorded by Rich some ten to fourteen years ago. Plaintiffs claim that defendant's use of Rich's current likeness on this album of old recordings violates Section 43(a) of the Lanham Act, 15 U.S.C. § 1125(a), since it misleads the public to believe that the record album contains recently recorded songs.

It is undisputed that the songs in the RCA album were recorded some ten to fourteen years ago, when Rich was under exclusive contract to RCA and prior to his current fame and success. It appears from the affidavits and exhibits that Rich's singing style and appearance has undergone considerable change over the last ten years. In contrast to his appearance at the time he was under contract to RCA, he now sports long hair and "mod" style clothing typical of his new image.

A likeness of the "current" Charlie Rich while performing appears on both the front and the back of the record jacket in question. The titles of the songs on the album are listed on the front and back of the record jacket, and four of the ten titles are followed by asterisks. In small type on the back of the jacket is an explanation that the asterisks indicate that the songs so marked are "previously released selections." The size and location of this explanation, however, make it visible only upon the closest inspection. It is far from obvious to a potential consumer who might be browsing through racks of record albums in search of a desirable recording. Moreover, it is not indicated anywhere on the album that these recordings were made over a decade ago. In fact, the only date appearing on the jacket is the copyright date, 1974.

The jacket is sealed with a transparent shrink wrap which prevents the consumer from examining the enclosed record prior to purchase. However, even if the consumer were able to inspect the record prior to purchase, he would glean no additional information since the affixed label neither mentions the dates of the recordings nor the fact that they were previously released. Again, the only date appearing on the label is the copyright date, 1974.

Section 43(a) of the Lanham Act provides in part:

> "Any person who shall affix . . . or use in connection with any goods . . . any false description or representation, including words or other symbols tending falsely to describe or represent the same, and shall cause such goods . . . to enter into commerce . . . shall be liable to a civil action . . . by any person who believes that he is or is likely to be damaged by the use of any such false description or representation."

In order to win a preliminary injunction, plaintiffs need not show that the public has been deceived or confused; the likelihood of deception and confusion is sufficient. We find that such a likelihood exists.

In light of all the indisputable facts, it is clear that the current picture of Rich on the record jacket, without a prominent notation that the songs in the album were recorded over a decade ago, is likely to deceive and confuse consumers as to the true contents of the package by misleading them to believe that the album contains songs recently recorded by Rich.

Furthermore, plaintiffs have shown a likelihood that continuance of defendant's deceptive packaging of its Charlie Rich album will cause irreparable injury in terms of loss of customers to CBS and damages to Rich's reputation. This injury is likely to be magnified unless defendant is enjoined from continuing its deceptive practice. The equities favor plaintiffs, and it is quite probable that plaintiffs will succeed on the merits if this action eventually proceeds to trial.

Accordingly, plaintiffs are entitled to a preliminary injunction enjoining defendant from further sales of the record album and tape recording "Charlie Rich—She Called Me Baby" in its present jacket bearing the current likeness of Rich. Settle order within fifteen (15) days.

VARGAS v. ESQUIRE, INC.
164 F.2d 522 (7th Cir. 1947)

MAJOR, Circuit Judge.

This appeal is from an order, entered December 17, 1946, dismissing plaintiff's complaint and supplemental complaint for failure to state a cause of action.

Plaintiff, an artist, sued to enjoin the reproduction of certain pictures made by him and delivered to defendant, a publisher, upon the ground that the same were wrongfully used in that they were published without the signature of plaintiff and without being accredited to him. Plaintiff also sued for damages on account of such publication alleged to violate his contract and his property right in the pictures and unfairly to represent them as the work of others. Defendant moved to dismiss on the ground that the plaintiff at the time of publication had no property right in the pictures and no right to control or to direct their disposition.

The facts alleged by the complaint center about and relate largely to two contracts of which the plaintiff and defendant were parties. The complaint sets forth that in June, 1940, the parties entered into a contract, . . . , wherein and whereby plaintiff was employed as an artist for three years, to produce art work for use by defendant in its publication and also for use in publications of a commercial nature, for a certain monthly compensation and in addition thereto a certain percent of the proceeds realized by defendant for work of a commercial nature. Under this contract plaintiff made and delivered certain pictures, one of which was reproduced each month, beginning October 1, 1940, in the magazine Esquire, published by defendant. Plaintiff also made and delivered twelve pictures each year, beginning in the fall of 1940, for a calendar published and sold the following year by defendant.

At first the pictures furnished bore plaintiff's name or signature, "Vargas," and they were reproduced and published with his name thereon. Later, by agreement of the parties, the name "Vargas" was changed to "Varga." Thereafter, the pictures made by plaintiff and published by defendant were called "Varga Girls," and the name of the plaintiff appearing thereon was "A. Varga." The name was used only in connection with pictures made by plaintiff and was thus used by the defendant until March 1, 1946. No name was on the pictures when they were furnished by plaintiff to the defendant.

The contract "Exhibit A," expired on June 30, 1943, but plaintiff continued to furnish pictures to defendant without a contract, which were published in the same manner was when the contract was in force, until May 25, 1945, when the parties entered into a second contract, "Exhibit B," attached to and made a part of the complaint.

On or about January 14, 1946, plaintiff notified the defendant that he was no longer bound by the contract, "Exhibit B," and refused to any longer furnish it with pictures. Defendant at that time had twenty pictures made by plaintiff which had not as yet been published. On February 11, 1946, plaintiff caused to be instituted in the United States District Court an action by which he sought a cancellation of such contract. On May 20, 1946, the court entered its decree, allowing the relief sought by the plaintiff, finding among other things that the contract had been fraudulently obtained by defendant and ordering the same cancelled and set aside as of January 10, 1946.

It was alleged that by reason of such publication by the defendant persons seeing said magazine came to know the work of the plaintiff and that as a result plaintiff became known to millions of persons, acquired a world-wide reputation and his name, "A. Varga," likewise became known throughout the world.

The complaint alleged that on March 1, 1946, the defendant published its magazine, Esquire, which contained a two-page reproduction of a picture made by the plaintiff. At the top thereof instead of the words, "The Varga Girl," appeared the words, "The Esquire Girl." The reproduction did not bear plaintiff's signature, "A. Varga," or any other signature. The supplemental complaint made a similar allegation as to a picture produced by plaintiff appearing in Esquire for the month of May, 1946. It was also alleged in the supplemental complaint that on October 1, 1946, defendant published a certain calendar enclosed in an outside envelope on which appeared the words and figures, "The 1947 Esquire Calendar 35¢ Copyright Esquire Inc. 1946 Printed in U. S. A." On the envelope was a reproduction of a picture painted for defendant by plaintiff. The calendar contained in said envelope was composed of the reproduction of twelve pictures of plaintiff made and intended to be used for the Varga Esquire 1947 calendar. Each of the said pictures bore the words, "The Esquire Girl Calendar." None of such pictures carried plaintiff's name or any name, word or legend indicating them to be the work of plaintiff or any other person.

All the pictures used by the defendant both in its magazine and in connection with its 1947 calendar were furnished by plaintiff to the defendant in accordance with the terms of "Exhibit B," prior to the time that plaintiff gave notice of its cancellation. All of such pictures had been paid for by the defendant in accordance with the terms of the contract, and as to those used in defendant's magazine, plaintiff had no further monetary interest. As to those used in connection with defendant's calendar, plaintiff was entitled to a share of proceeds derived from the sale thereof. There is no allegation, however, and no claim that defendant had refused to pay or is likely to refuse to pay to plaintiff his share of such proceeds.

It was further alleged that there was a duty upon the defendant to refrain from publishing reproductions of plaintiff pictures without their bearing his signature and giving him due credit; that defendant, in violation of its duty in this respect, published plaintiff's work without using his name and without giving him credit therefor, and that the same constituted a misrepresentation in that it represented the pictures to be the work of another and not that of plaintiff.

"Exhibit A" (the first contract) expired long prior to the inception of the instant controversy and we think it is of little consequence insofar as it affects the issues for decision. The rights of the parties must be determined from "Exhibit B" (the second contract), which was in effect at the time that plaintiff furnished the pictures to defendant which were reproduced by it subsequent to the time that plaintiff gave notice of cancellation of such contract.

In a preamble to "Exhibit B," it is stated that Vargas for approximately three years had been preparing and furnishing to Esquire drawings for use by Esquire in connection with its publications and other printed merchandise:

"In connection with certain of these drawings, the name 'Varga,' 'Varga Girl,' and similar names have been given national publicity by Esquire and have become well known to the public. Varga acknowledges that the success of the drawings has been due primarily to the guidance which Esquire has given him and to the publicity given to them by Esquire's publications . . . ."

The contract, after expressing the desire of the parties to enter into an agreement defining their mutual rights and obligations, contains a paragraph around which this controversy revolves and which we think is determinative of the issues involved. It provides:

"Vargas agrees for a period of ten years and six months, beginning January 1, 1944, as an independent contractor, to supply Esquire with not less than twenty-six (26) drawings during each six-months' period. . . . *The drawings so furnished, and also the name 'Varga', 'Varga Girl,' 'Varga, Esq.,' and any and all other names, designs or material used in connection therewith, shall forever belong exclusively to Esquire, and Esquire shall have all rights with respect thereto, including (without limiting the generality of the foregoing) the right to use, lease, sell or otherwise dispose of the same as it shall see fit,* and all radio, motion picture and reprint rights. Esquire shall also have the right to copyright any of said drawings, names, designs or material or take any other action it shall deem advisable for the purpose of protecting its rights therein." (Emphasis ours.)

Plaintiff's principal contention is that the publication of the reproductions of paintings produced by him, without his name appearing thereon, without credit to him and without any name appearing thereon, violated an implied agreement that the defendant would not do so. Plaintiff concedes that the contract defines defendant's rights in the pictures, but in his brief argues "that despite its broad generality, despite the fact that the defendant took all rights in the pictures, it is bound by the implied agreement not to publish them in the manner complained of."

Plaintiff cites and relies upon a number of cases in support of this alleged implied agreement. Uproar Co. v. National Broadcasting Co., 1 Cir., 81 F.2d 373; Kirke La Shelle Co. v. Armstrong Co., 263 N.Y. 79, 188 N.E. 163; Manners v. Morosco, 252 U.S. 317, 40 S.Ct. 335, 64 L.Ed 590. We have read these cases, and without attempting to discuss them in detail, we think they are inapplicable to the instant situation. In each of them an author signed a contract or license which conferred on the other party certain limited rights in a literary reproduction and reserved for the author the balance of the rights therein. The holding in each of these cases is to the effect that where certain of the rights to a literary composition were conferred and other rights retained, it would be implied that the author could not use the rights retained in such a way as to destroy or materially insure the rights conferred. Such a contractual situation is in marked contrast to that of the instant case where the plaintiff by plain and unambiguous language completely divested himself of every vestige of title and ownership of the pictures, as well as the right to their possession, control and use. The language by which the extent of the grant is to be measured, "shall forever belong exclusively to Esquire, and Esquire shall have all rights with respect thereto, including (without limiting the generality of the foregoing) the right to use, lease, sell or otherwise dispose of the same as it shall see fit," would appear to leave no room for a contention that any right, claim or interest in the pictures remained in the plaintiff after he had sold and delivered them to the defendant. Not only did plaintiff by the contract divest himself of all title, claim and interest in such drawings and designs, but also in the names "Varga," "Varga Girl," "Varga Esquire," when used in connection therewith.

Of the many cases where it has been sought to engraft an implied condition upon the terms of a written instrument, we like the rule announced in Domeyer v. O'Connell, 364 Ill. 467, at page 470, 4 N.E.2d 830, 832, 108 A.L.R. 476, where the language used is pertinent to the instant situation. The court stated:

"The rules concerning the construction of contracts are so well established as to require but brief attention. The object of construction is to ascertain the intention of the parties. . . . That intention is to be determined from the language used in the instrument and not from any surmises that the parties intended certain conditions which they failed to express. Where there is no ambiguity in the language used, from that, and that alone, may the intention of the parties be gathered. . . . An implied intention is one necessarily arising from language used or a situation created by such language. If such intention does not necessarily arise, it cannot be implied. On the other hand, absence of a provision from a contract is evidence of an intention to exclude such provision."

As already shown, we think there is no ambiguity in the granting language of the contract, nor can there be an implied intention from the language thus employed of an intention of the parties of any reservation of rights in the grantor. The parties had been dealing with each other for a number of years, and the fact that no reservation was contained in the contract strongly indicates that it was intentionally omitted. Such a reservation will not be presumed.

Plaintiff advances another theory which needs little discussion. It is predicated upon the contention that there is a distinction between the economic rights of an author capable of assignment and what are called "moral rights" of the author, said to be those necessary for the protection of his honor and integrity. These so-called "moral rights," so we are informed, are recognized by the civil law of certain foreign countries. In support of this phase of his argument, plaintiff relies upon a work by Stephen P. Ladas entitled "The International Protection of Literary and Artistic Property" (page 575, et seq.). It appears, however, that the author's discussion relied upon by plaintiff relates to the law of foreign countries. As to the United States, Ladas in the same work states (page 802):

"The conception of 'moral rights' of authors so fully recognized and developed in the civil law countries has not yet received acceptance in the law of the United States. No such right is referred to by legislation, court decision or writers."

What plaintiff in reality seeks is a change in the law in this country to conform to that of certain other countries. We need not stop to inquire whether such a change, if desirable, is a matter for the legislative or judicial branch of the government; in any event, we are not disposed to make any new law in this respect.

Plaintiff's third and last contention is that the manner of reproduction by defendant of plaintiff's work was such as to constitute a misrepresentation and was unfair competition. The concurring opinion of Mr. Justice Holmes in International News Service v. Associated Press, 248 U.S. 215, 246, 247, 39 S.Ct. 68, 63 L.Ed. 211, 2 A.L.R. 293; and Fisher v. Star Co., 231 N.Y. 414, 433, 132 N.E. 133, 136, 19 A.L.R. 937, are the only cases cited and relied upon as supporting this contention. We think that neither case affords any support for such theory. In both, the holding as to unfair competition rested on the premise that the defendants, without the consent or approval of the plaintiffs, had taken and used to their own advantage something in which the plaintiffs had a property right—more specifically, that the defendants had pirated or stolen plaintiff's property and used it in their business in competition with that of the plaintiffs. It is difficult to discern how there could be any pirating or unlawful taking of property in the instant case in view of the rights (heretofore discussed) which the plaintiff by contract conferred upon the defendant.

Plaintiff argues that the use of "Esquire Girl" as a title for the pictures was a representation that the author was someone other than the plaintiff. We do not agree with this contention. The title used was the name of the well-known and widely circulated magazine in which they were published, and we think the public would readily recognize the word "Esquire" referred to such magazine and not to the name of an artist.

More than that, as already shown, it was provided in the contract that both the pictures and the name "shall forever belong exclusively to Esquire, and Esquire shall have all rights with respect thereto including . . . the right to use . . . or otherwise dispose of the same as it shall see fit." This was the basis both upon which plaintiff was paid for his pictures and upon which Esquire acquired their possession and ownership. Under these circumstances, we are of the view that there was no unfair competition by the defendant in the manner of their use.

The order appealed from is affirmed.

Plaintiffs' Memorandum In Support Of Motion For A Preliminary Injunction And Temporary Restraining Order

UNITED STATES DISTRICT COURT
SOUTHERN DISTRICT OF NEW YORK

PERIN FILM ENTERPRISES, LTD. and RICHARD E. PERIN, Plaintiffs, v. TWG PRODUCTIONS, INC., GERBER/CARTER COMMUNICATIONS, INC., CHARLES S. GERBER and NICHOLAS LABORATORIES, INC., Defendants.	Civil Action No. . . . .

This is an action for injunctive and monetary relief based on defendants' malicious failure to compensate plaintiffs for their services as executive producer of the national syndicated television series called "For You . . . Black Woman", and for defendants' continuing failure to accord plaintiffs the screen credit as executive producer of the series which they have earned and deserve, as well as for defendants' unwarranted act of giving away to a third party an analagous and confusingly similar credit to the one which plaintiffs are entitled.

This memorandum is submitted in support of plaintiffs' motion for a preliminary injunction and temporary restraining order enjoining defendants from televising the series or causing it to be televised without giving plaintiffs a credit as "Executive Producer" in the list of credits televised at the end of each program in the series, and without removing therefrom the credit which is confusingly similar to the credit which plaintiffs deserve. Plaintiffs also seek to enjoin defendants from issuing, causing and/or participating in the issuance of advertising or promotional materials respecting the series without giving due credit to plaintiffs and without removing therefrom the unwarranted credit given to another.

THE FACTS

Plaintiffs, Perin Film Enterprises, Ltd. ("Perin Film") and Richard E. Perin ("Perin"), have been engaged in the independent production of television programs for the last three years. During that period, they have produced, among others, the critically acclaimed television specials called "The Apollo Presents" and the series of twelve television specials called "The Coral Jungle."

In September 1976, Perin agreed, at the request of defendant Charles S. Gerber ("Gerber"), to supervise and coordinate the entire production of the television series "For You . . . Black Woman" ("the series"), and generally to perform those functions respecting the series commonly associated with being its executive producer. Perin also agreed, at Gerber's request, to assist the series' producer in the performance of his own production functions, as well as to collaborate with the producer in developing the series. The series is a half-hour long weekly talk show presenting topics of special interest to black women, and is seen in New York and environs on WABC-TV on Sunday's from 2:30 to 3:00 P.M.

As executive producer charged by Gerber with the responsibility for the series' entire production, Perin figured prominently in getting the series broadcast, and in the success which the series then achieved. To that end, among other accomplishments, Perin was instrumental in selecting the series' hostess; in securing the services of a set designer; in hiring a technical facilities company; in establishing budgets and schedules; in determining the show's guests and contents; and in assisting Gerber to locate potential sponsors of the series.

The success of the series was and is in great measure attributable to Perin. This is especially true respecting "For You . . . Black Woman" because in addition to serving competently as its executive producer, Perin was also instrumental in developing the series, in helping to produce it, and in assisting to find stations to accept the series for broadcast. When many television programs fail to last more than one year, "For You . . . Black Woman" has already completed its first year's run and has recently commenced a second year's run beginning in or about July, 1978. Other indicia of the series' success are more fully set forth in the accompanying supporting affidavit of Perin sworn to on August 28, 1978.

The Credit Agreement and TWG's Representations and Inducements

In return for Perin's services as executive producer of the series, defendant TWG Productions, Inc. ("TWG"), Gerber's purported production arm, entered into an oral agreement with Perin and Perin Film ("the Credit Agreement") providing that TWG would accord Perin, or cause him to be accorded, a credit as "Executive Producer" in the list of credits televised at the end of each program in the series. In addition, TWG also represented and led Perin to believe that he would receive such credit.

In reliance upon the Credit Agreement and upon TWG's said representations and inducements, Perin thereafter performed services as executive producer of the series. In confirmation of the Credit Agreement and of TWG's representations and inducements, Perin subsequently received the credit as "Executive Producer" to which he was entitled at the end of each program in the series' first year run. Consistent with and reflecting both the Credit Agreement and TWG's said representations and inducements, Perin also received the same credit in newspaper articles promoting the series and in the press and promotional kit supplied to each television station broadcasting the series.

In continuing reliance upon both the Credit Agreement and upon TWG's representations and inducements to the same effect, Perin continued to perform services as executive producer of the series with respect to the first 22 of 36 programs scheduled for the series' second year run. When Perin undertook and performed the same executive producer services for the first 22 programs in the series' second year run that he had performed for the series' first year run, TWG, Gerber and/or Gerber's company, defendant Gerber/Carter Communications, Inc. ("Gerber/Carter"), knew, or should have known, that Perin would continue to rely on both the Credit Agreement and on TWG's representations and inducements and, more specifically, on TWG's past conduct in according him, or causing him to be accorded, the credit as "Executive Producer".

Notwithstanding the fact that Perin rendered the exact same services as executive producer of the first 22 programs in the series' second year run that he had rendered with respect to the series' first year run, and despite the satisfactory performance of these services, evidenced by the fact that the programs on which Perin worked have been and are continuing to be televised, TWG, pursuant to the direction, domination, and control of Gerber and/or Gerber/Carter, unlawfully breached the Credit Agreement and violated TWG's aforesaid representations and inducements to Perin (a) by failing to accord Perin, or causing him to be accorded, a credit as "Executive Producer" of the series for services he rendered in such capacity on programs that have been and are continuing to be televised during the series' second year run; and (b) by wrongfully substituting for Perin's credit a credit to Ms. Saint Charles Lockett, a consultant and/or employee of defendant Nicholas Laboratories, Inc. ("Nicholas"), called "Executive in Charge of Production", which is a credit comparable in stature and confusingly similar to Perin's credit as "Executive Producer", despite the fact that Ms. Lockett has failed to render services comparable to Perin's entitling her to receive the credit being accorded her.

Irreparable Injury to Plaintiffs

The correct attribution of credit is the only way that members of the entertainment industry, both performers and producers alike, can inform the public and others in their profession who serve as prospective employers, about their abilities and their association with a successful venture. Credit is the vehicle in the entertainment business by which one's name and reputation are established.

"For You . . . Black Woman" is a successful television series. Nevertheless, by not receiving a credit as the series' executive producer, both in advertising and promotional materials and in the credit list run at the end of each program, there is little Perin can do to identify his name with the success of the series, so as to enhance his professional standing and, therefore, his earning power. The failure to receive such a credit is especially damaging in Perin's situation, where he is just starting out as an independent producer. In this circumstance, it is self-evident that every credit, especially a good one, is an important credit.

In addition, the public has a right to know who performed services with respect to the production which it viewed. By TWG's according to Ms. Lockett a confusingly similar credit to the credit which Perin deserves, the public is being deceived into believing that Ms. Lockett performed executive producer functions respecting the series when this is not true because Perin performed those functions.

ARGUMENT

POINT I

Plaintiffs Are Entitled To A Preliminary Injunction And Temporary Restraining Order

The Court of Appeals for the Second Circuit has set forth the standards for obtaining a preliminary injunction as requiring that a plaintiff either establish a "clear likelihood of success on the law and facts" and "possible irreparable injury", *Columbia Pictures Industries, Inc.* v. *American Broadcasting Companies, Inc.*, 501 F. 2d. 894, 897, (2d Cir. 1974) or raise

> " ' . . . questions going to the merits so serious, substantial, difficult and doubtful, as to make them a fair ground for litigation and thus for more deliberate investigation' and 'the balance of hardships tips decidedly toward plaintiff' even though the plaintiff has not demonstrated a strong likelihood of success". *Omega Importing Corp.* v. *Petri-Kine Camera Company*, 451 F. 2d 1190, 1193, 1194 (2d Cir. 1971) citing Judge Frank in *Hamilton Watch Co.* v. *Benrus Watch Co.*, 206 F. 2d 738, 740 (2d Cir. 1953).

The instant case meets either of the relevant standards. Plaintiffs are entitled to an injunction enjoining the continued failure to accord them the television credit which they have earned and which in their business is fundamental to the development of their reputations, and that, in addition, is being subverted by a confusingly similar credit being accorded to Ms. Saint Charles Lockett. Plaintiffs seek the Court's exercise of its equitable powers to return the parties to the status quo when they had received such credit before defendants' false attribution of credit advances to such a point as to make final relief of little or no value.

POINT II

False Attribution Of Credit Is An Act Of Unfair Competition Supporting Injunctive Relief

Courts have long held that the failure to attribute credit to the person to whom it is entitled, so as to trade upon that person's skills and abilities, is an act of misrepresentation and constitutes unfair competition. *Prouty* v.*National Broadcasting Co.*, 26 F. Supp. 265 (D. Mass. 1939) holding:

> "[U]nfair competition is only 'a convenient name for the doctrine that no one should be allowed to sell his goods as those of another . . . ' It is the injury to the author and a fraud upon the reading public that constitutes the real offense alleged." 26 F. Supp. at 266.

In *Paramount Productions, Inc.* v. *Smith*, 91 F. 2d 863 (9th Cir. 1937), *cert.*

den., 302 U.S. 749 1937) a thoughtful dissent noted the fraudulent nature of giving a credit to a party to whom it is not entitled, and also set forth the reasons why the correct allocation of credit is so important to the person who deserves it:

> "[Screen credit] is a method of advertising to the public the fact that the production they are about to witness is the result of the ingenuity, inventive genius, and literary skill of the person to whom the screen credit is given. Thus it is believed other motion picture producers will seek to avail themselves of the services of the person given screen credit to produce other stories for such reproduction. It is clear that to give screen credit to a person not reasonably entitled thereto would be a fraud upon the public . . . " 91 F. 2d at 867.

Granz v. Harris, 198 F. 2d 585 (2d Cir. 1952) is directly in point. There, the parties had entered into a contract providing that defendant would use the credit-line "Presented by Norman Granz" in selling certain phonograph records which plaintiff produced. Following plaintiff's production of the records, defendant re-recorded the records, but in doing so, deleted some of the music contained on plaintiff's original recordings.

Plaintiff sued seeking, among other relief, an injunction against having defendant's abbreviated re-recordings attributed to him. The court held that the use of plaintiff's credit-line in connection with work that did not accurately represent his services and contributions constituted "false representation":

> "Disregarding for the moment the terms of the contract, we think that the purchaser of the master discs could lawfully use them to produce the abbreviated record and could lawfully sell the same provided he did not describe it as a recording of music presented by the plaintiff. If he did so describe it, he would commit the tort of unfair competition. But the contract required defendant to use the legend 'Presented by Norman Granz,' that is, to attribute to him the musical content of the records offered for sale. This contractual duty carries by implication, without the necessity of an express prohibition, the duty not to sell records which make the required legend a false representation . . . No specific damages were shown to have resulted. As such damages are difficult to prove and the harm to the plaintiff's reputation as an expert in the presentation of jazz concerts is irreparable, injunctive relief is appropriate." 198 F. 2d at 588.

Perin's situation in the instant case is the exact converse of the situation in *Granz*. While the defendant in *Granz* falsely attributed to plaintiff work that was no longer his, the defendants in the instant action have falsely attributed to Ms. Lockett work which is definitely not hers but Perin's.

Granz clearly makes actionable the injury to Perin and to the public in the instant action. In both cases, defendants' acts of falsely attributing credit caused injury to plaintiffs. Whether, as in *Granz*, false attribution occurs because a credit is given to a work which no longer represents the author, or, as with Perin, the author's work accurately supports a credit in his own name, but, instead, is falsely attributed to an undeserving party, in both situations the false attribution of credit results in plaintiffs being damaged and the public being defrauded. As Judge Frank pointed out in his concurring opinion in *Granz*:

> "The irreparable harm, justifying an injunction, becomes apparent when one thinks what would be the result if the collected speeches of Stalin were published under the name of Senator Robert Taft, or the poems of Ella Wheeler Wilcox [i.e. the collected work and services of Perin] as those of T. S. Elliot [i.e. were falsely accorded to Ms. Lockett] 198 F. 2d at 589.

As long ago as a hundred years, courts well understood the underlying rationale supporting the grant of injunctive relief in false attribution cases. Thus, in *Clemens* v. *Belford, Clark & Co.*, 14 Fed. 728, 731 (C.C.N.D. Ill. 1883), the court stated:

> "So, too, an author of acquired reputation, and, perhaps, a person who has not obtained any standing before the public as a writer may restrain another from the publication of literary matter purporting to have been written by him, but which, in fact, was never so written . . . no one has the right, either expressly or by implication, falsely or untruly to charge another with the composition or authorship of a literary production which he did not write. Any other rule would permit writers of inferior merit to put their compositions before the public under the names of writers of high standing and authority, thereby perpetuating a fraud not only on the writer whose name is used, but also on the public."

POINT III

False Attribution Of Credit Constitutes Unfair Competition In Violation Of The Lanham Act And Supports Injunctive Relief

The Lanham Act, in Section 43(a), 15 U.S.C. §1125(a), provides in pertinent part:

> "(a) Any person who shall affix, apply or annex, or use in connection with any goods or services, or any container or containers for goods, a false designation of origin, or any false description or representation, including words or other symbols tending falsely to describe or represent the same, and shall cause such goods or services to enter into commerce . . . shall be liable to a civil action . . . by any person who believes that

he is or is likely to be damaged by the use of any such false description or representation."

The Congressional intent in drafting Section 43(a) of the Lanham Act was not limited to the expansion of the Act's protection against infringement of trademarks, but also included the expansion of federal protection against acts of unfair competition. The intent of this chapter is to regulate commerce within the control of Congress by making actionable the deceptive and misleading use of marks in such commerce; [and] . . . to protect persons engaged in commerce against unfair competition . . . " 15 U.S.C. §1127.

Similarly, *Alfred Dunhill, Ltd.* v. *Interstate Cigar Company, Inc.*, 499 F. 2d 232, 236 (2d Cir. 1974) states:

"Section 43(a) of the Lanham Act was intended to expand the rights of those who were harmed by unfair competition. It was meant both to enlarge the category by activities which are proscribed by federal law and to expand the class of plaintiffs who could assert standing to sue under federal law . . . "

Section 43(a) is a "remedial provision" and is to "be broadly construed." *Geisel* v. *Poynter Products, Inc.*, 382 F. Supp. 261, 267 (S.D.N.Y. 1968).

False attribution of credit deceives the public and is an act of unfair competition constituting a violation of the Lanham Act. As stated by the Second Circuit in *Gilliam* v. *American Broadcasting Companies, Inc.*, 538 F. 2d. 14, 24, 25 (2d Cir. 1976), which observed that the complaint in *Granz* v. *Harris, supra* stated a cause of action under the Lanham Act:

"This statute [the Lanham Act], the federal counterpart to state unfair competition laws, has been invoked to prevent misrepresentations that may injure plaintiff's business or personal reputation, even where no registered trademark is concerned."

In *Rich* v. *RCA Corporation*, 390 F. Supp. 530 (S.D.N.Y. 1975), plaintiff Charlie Rich sought a preliminary injunction prohibiting defendant from using a then current photograph of Rich on the jacket of a then recently released album containing songs Rich recorded several years before then. Rich claimed that defendant's use of a current likeness on an album of old recordings violated the Lanham Act because it had a tendency to mislead the public into believing that the album contained recently recorded songs.

This Court preliminary enjoined further sales of the offending albums holding that it was unnecessary under the Lanham Act to show actual deception of the public, but merely that the offending item created a false impression and a likelihood of confusion and deception. See also *Gilliam, supra* at 24.

In the instant case, there is simply no question that giving Ms. Lockett a credit as "Executive in Charge of Production" of the series when she did nothing to warrant that credit caused confusion in the minds of the viewing public and prospective employers and creates a false impression (a) that she rendered substantial services to the series in the nature of an executive producer which was impossible because Perin performed those services at least with respect to the first 22 programs in the series' second year run; (b) that the credit accurately reflects her contributions; and (c) that she is in substantial measure a reason for the series' success.

Section 43(a) of the Lanham Act specifically created a new federal cause of action for "false designation of origin" of "any goods or services" entering interstate commerce. Thus, *Apollo Distributing Co.* v. *Apollo Imports, Inc.*, 341 F. Supp. 455, 458 (S.D.N.Y. 1972) makes actionable

> "a false designation . . . likely to cause confusion or to deceive purchasers that plaintiff is the source of origin of such merchandise . . . "

The failure to accord Perin a credit as executive producer of the series in conjunction with the erroneous substitution of a credit to Ms. Lockett as "Executive in Charge of Production" creates the false impression that she, and not Perin, is the "source of origin" for the services as executive producer performed with respect to the series.

Under the Lanham Act, defendants' conduct qualifies under either application of a "false designation of origin", i.e. of goods or of services. Failing to accord Perin his rightful credit and improperly according to Ms. Lockett an undeserved credit on a product, i.e. the film or tape of a television program seen in interstate commerce, constitutes the "false designation of origin" of goods. Similarly, such activity also constitutes the "false designation of origin" of services, i.e. the services as executive producer performed by Perin.

POINT IV

False Attribution Of Credit In Breach Of Contract
Supports Injunctive Relief

The breach of an agreement to give screen credit causes irreparable injury for which the remedy of damages at law is inadequate, the appropriate remedy being an injunction restraining exhibition of the particular motion picture without the required credit. *Poe* v. *Michael Todd Company*, 151 F. Supp. 801 (S.D.N.Y. 1957); *Granz* v. *Harris, supra* at 588. Although this Court, Weinfeld, J., denied plaintiff's preliminary injunction motion to restrain the exhibition of the motion picture *Around The World in Eighty Days* which plaintiff had brought because he had not been given screen credit for authorship of the screenplay, the Court noted that:

> "The plaintiff, however, has made a sufficient showing to warrant a

prompt trial since if he should sustain his burden of proof, the failure to give him credit would constitute irreparable injury. Not only would money damages be difficult to establish, but at best they would hardly compensate for the real injury done. A writer's reputation, which would be greatly enhanced by public credit for authorship of an outstanding picture, is his stock in trade; it is clear that irreparable injury would follow the failure to give him screen credit if in fact he is entitled to it." *Poe, supra* at 803.

The Court denied plaintiff's motion because of its finding that there were certain factual disputes, not present in the instant case, which made the grant of injunctive relief unwise. Included in these factual disputes was whether or not plaintiff's contribution to the film merited an award of screen credit. The Court also noted that the parties' oral contract did not include a promise to give plaintiff credit.

Unlike *Poe,* there is no question in the instant case, as more fully discussed below, that TWG was and is contractually obligated to accord Perin screen credit as executive producer of the series. There can also be no question that Perin's contributions to the series merited the award of such credit.

Perin performed the exact same services with respect to the first 22 programs in the series' second year run, when TWG failed to give him a screen credit as executive producer, as he had performed during the series' first year run, when he was given such credit. Although nothing had changed, Perin was given a credit in one situation but not in the other. Indeed, that Perin's level of competency remained unchanged is clearly evidenced by the fact that the programs in the series' second year run on which Perin worked are currently being televised. Under these circumstances, defendants cannot challenge the adequacy of Perin's performance in an effort to excuse their failure to accord him the credit he deserves.

De Bekker v. *Stokes,* 168 App. Div. 452, 153 N.Y.S. 1066 (2nd Dep't. 1915), *aff'd. mem.,* 219 N.Y. 573, 114 N.E. 1064 (1916) is directly in point. There, the parties had entered into a contract for the publication of a work to be prepared by the plaintiff under the name "Stokes' Encyclopedia of Music". Subsequently, defendant entered into an arrangement with a second party to have the work published as part of eight other volumes under the name "Encyclopedia of Music". Plaintiff sued for an injunction enjoining the publication of his work under any other name than the one originally agreed upon, alleging that to do otherwise constituted a breach of contract.

The court held that plaintiff's contract with the defendant supported the grant of injunctive relief, in that under the contract plaintiff had "the strict right to preserve the identity of his creation and to insist that it should be issued, if at all, by the Stokes Company [under the latter's name]." 168 App. Div. at 455.

POINT V

TWG's Contractual Obligation To Accord Perin A Credit

An Agent May Bind His Principal in Entering Into a Contract

The accompanying supporting affidavit of Perin clearly indicates the existence of a binding contract between Perin and TWG for the allocation of credit to Perin based on the agreement to that effect made between Perin and Mr. Frederick Dukes, the series' producer/director and TWG's agent. A principal is bound on a contract entered into by his agent on his behalf with his authorization, express or implied.

Agreement by Conduct

Perin's contract with TWG for the allocation of credit was thereafter confirmed by TWG's conduct of according Perin a credit as "Executive Producer" at the end of each program in the series' first year run. That Perin was accorded such credit cannot be disputed. To prove the existence of a binding contract arising from a course of conduct, it is necessary to look to the parties' objective manifestations of intent reflected in their express words and deeds viewed in the context of their surroundings circumstances, the situation of the parties, and the objectives the parties were striving to achieve.

Perin performed his duties as executive producer of the series in reliance upon his understanding that he would later be given a credit as the series' executive producer, which in fact occurred. Where a party relies upon an acceptance by conduct or act, performance becomes the test of acceptance.

TWG is Estopped From Denying Existence of a Contractual Obligation to Accord Perin Credit

In continuing reliance both upon his understanding that he would be accorded a credit as the series' executive producer and upon TWG's past conduct of actually according him such credit, Perin, prior to his unlawful termination, rendered the same services as executive producer for the first 22 programs in the series' second year run that he had performed during the series' first year run.

Accordingly, when Perin undertook and performed the same executive producer services during the series' second year run that he had performed for the series' first year run, TWG, Gerber and/or Gerber/Carter knew, or should have known, that Perin would continue to rely on defendants' past conduct in according him, or causing him to be accorded, an executive producer credit.

TWG, therefore, is estopped from denying existence of a contractual obligation on its part to accord Perin such credit. When a party is under a duty to speak, or when his failure to speak is inconsistent with honest dealings, and misleads another, then his silence must be deemed to be acquiesence or assent supporting the existence of a binding contract.

The doctrine of promissory estoppel clearly applies to the instant case. As set forth in the Restatement of Contracts, Section 90 (1932):

> "A promise which the promisor should reasonably expect to induce action or forebearance of a definite and substantial character on the part of the promisee, and which does induce such action or forebearance, is binding if injustice can be avoided only by enforcement of the promise." See also *Lloyd* v. *R.K.O. Pictures*, 280 P. 2d 295, 299 (2nd Dist., Div. 1, Calif. 1955); *Allegheny College* v. *National Chautauqua County Bank*, 246 N.Y. 369, 159 N.E. 173 (1927).

CONCLUSION

For the reasons set forth in plaintiffs' motion papers, it is respectfully submitted that plaintiffs' motion for a preliminary injunction and temporary restraining order should be granted in all respects.

Dated: New York, New York
      August 28, 1978

SMITH v. MONTORO
648 F.2d 602 (9th Cir. 1981)

PREGERSON, Circuit Judge:

This is an appeal from a judgement granting defendant's motion to dismiss under Fed.R.Civ.P. 12(b)(6) for failure to state a federal claim. The district court held that the complaint did not allege facts sufficient to constitute a violation of section 43(a) of the Lanham Act, 15 U.S.C. § 1125(a). Appellant argues that the district court erred since the acts alleged in the complaint are the economic equivalent of "palming off," or misuse of a trade name, thus meeting the district court's standard for stating a claim under section 43(a). For the reasons stated below, we reverse.

BACKGROUND

Paul Smith contracted to star in a film to be produced by Producioni Atlas Cinematografica ("PAC"), an Italian film company. The contract allegedly provided that Smith would receive star billing in the screen credits and advertising for the film and that PAC would so provide in any subsequent contracts with distributors of the film. PAC then licensed defendants Edward Montoro and Film Venture International, Inc. ("FVI") to distribute the film in this country under the name "Convoy Buddies." Plaintiff complains, however, that Montoro and FVI removed Smith's name and substituted the name of another actor, "Bob Spencer," in place of Smith's name in both the film credits and advertising material. Plaintiff alleges that, as a result of defendants' substitution, plaintiff has been damaged in his reputation as an actor, and has lost specific employment opportunities.

The complaint sought damages under several theories, including breach of contract, "false light publicity," violation of section 43(a) of the Lanham Act, and violation of Cal.Civ.Code § 3344 regarding commercial appropriation of a person's likeness. There being no diversity of citizenship, federal subject matter jurisdiction was based solely on plaintiff's Lanham Act claim. Plaintiff asserted that the district court had jurisdiction of the state law claims as a matter of pendent jurisdiction.

In proceedings held on May 1, 1978, the district judge explained his "tentative view" that defendants' motion should be granted and the complaint dismissed as "not stating a valid cause of action under the Lanham Act." While noting "there are many diverging interpretations of the Lanham Act" and that "some courts give a broad construction to it regarding it as a remedial kind of statute," the judge stated that "[i]t is my view . . . that the Lanham Act is limited in its scope and intent to merchandising practices in the nature of, or *economically equivalent* to, palming off one's goods as those of a competitor, and/or misuse of trademarks and trade names." (Emphasis added.) According to the district court, the acts alleged in the complaint

> are not the economic equivalent of palming off or misuse of a trademark or trade names. The acts are more in the nature of breaches of contract or tort which are properly the subject of state law. There is certainly in this case no intent to divert a competitor's business by misleading consumers. Plaintiff's claim is not that his name was misused, but that it wasn't used at all. Therefore, the nature of the misrepresentation alleged in this case, in my view, is not within the intended scope of the statute.

As an "alternative ground" for dismissal of the Lanham Act claim, the district court indicated that "there is an issue additionally of the plaintiff's standing to bring this suit under the Lanham Act since the plaintiff is not in any sort of competition with the defendants." Shortly after the hearing, the court issued a minute order stating that defendants' motion to dismiss was granted. Judgment was entered on May 5, 1978. The remaining state law claims were dismissed for lack of jurisdiction.

DISCUSSION

I. *Federal Claim*

A. *Elements of a Claim under Section 43(a)*

Section 43(a) of the Lanham Act, 15 U.S.C. § 1125(a), forbids the use of false designations of origin and false descriptions or representations in the advertising and sale of goods and services. The statute provides in pertinent part as follows:

> Any person who shall affix, apply, or annex, or use in connection with any goods or services . . . a false designation of origin, or any false designation or representation . . . and shall cause such goods or services to enter into commerce . . . shall be liable to a civil action . . . by any person who believes that he is or is likely to be damaged by the use of any such false designation or representation.

Appellant argues that defendants violated section 43(a) by affixing or using "a false designation or representation," i. e., another actor's name in place of appellant's, in connection with the movie's advertising and credits. Appellant claims standing under section 43(a) as a person "who believes that he is or is likely to be damaged" by the use of another actor's name in place of his. Thus, appellant's claim, although one of first impression, appears to fall within the express language of section 43(a).

The district court appears to have rejected appellant's argument on the ground that, to state a claim under section 43(a), a complaint must allege merchandising practices "in the nature of, or economically equivalent to, palming off . . . and/or misuse of trademarks and trade names."

"Palming off" or "passing off" is the selling of a good or service of one's own creation under the name or mark of another. Passing off may be either "express" or "implied." Express passing off occurs when an enterprise labels goods or services with a mark identical to that of another enterprise, or otherwise expressly misrepresents that the goods originated with another enterprise. Implied passing off occurs when an enterprise uses a competitor's advertising material, or a sample or photograph of the competitor's product, to impliedly represent that the product it is selling was produced by the competitor. Such practices have consistently been held to violate both the common law of unfair competition 43(a) of the Lanham Act.

To the extent that the district court's standard for section 43(a) claims could be read as limiting such claims to cases of palming off, such a narrow rule would be contrary to established case law. As one commentator has explained, the law of unfair competition and trademarks "has progressed far beyond the old concept of fraudulent passing off, to encompass any form of competition or selling which contravenes society's current concepts of 'fairness' . . . " 2 J. McCarthy, *supra*, § 25:1. *See also, e.g., L & L White Metal Casting Corp. v. Joseph*, 387 F.Supp. 1349, 1356 (E.D.N.Y.1975) ("The purpose of [section 43(a)] was to create a new federal cause of action for false representation of goods in commerce in order to protect persons engaged in commerce from, among other things, unfair competition, fraud and deception which had theretofore only been protected by the common law. While this section is broad enough to cover situations involving the common law 'palming off' of the defendants' products by the use of the plaintiff's photographs, it is also comprehensive enough to include other forms of misrepresentation and unfair competition not involving 'palming off.' ") (citations omitted).

The district court's ruling was entirely consistent with the vast majority of section 43(a) cases, however, to the extent that it indicated that a section 43(a) claim may be based on economic practices or conduct "economically equivalent" to palming off. Such practices would include "reverse passing off," which occurs when a person removes or obliterates the original trademark, without authorization, before reselling goods produced by someone else. *See* Borchard, *Reverse Passing Off—Commercial Robbery or Permissible Competition?*, 67 Trademark Rep. 1 (1977). Reverse passing off is accomplished "expressly" when the wrongdoer removes the name or trademark on another party's product and sells that product under a name chosen by the wrongdoer. See 1 R. Callman, *supra*, § 18.2(b)(1). "Implied" reverse passing off occurs when the wrongdoer simply removes or otherwise obliterates the name of the manufacturer or source and sells the product in an unbranded state. *Id.*

In the instant case, appellant argues that the defendants' alleged conduct constitutes *reverse* passing off and that appellant's complaint therefore stated a section 43(a) claim even under the district court's own standard. Appellees argue, however, that the protection afforded by the Lanham Act is limited to "sales of goods" and does not extend to claims that a motion picture shown to the public might contain false information as to origin.

The short answer to appellees' argument is that the Lanham Act explicitly condemns false designations or representations in connection with "*any goods or services.*" The prohibitions of this section have been applied to motion picture representations. *See, e.g., Dallas Cowboys Cheerleaders, Inc. v. Pussycat Cinema Ltd.*, 467 F.Supp. 366 (S.D.N.Y.), *aff'd*, 604 F.2d 200 (2d Cir. 1979). Moreover, the names of movie actors and other performers may, under certain circumstances, be registered under the Lanham Act as service marks[2] for

---

[2] The term "service mark" is defined in section 45 of the Lanham Act:

"[S]ervice mark" means a mark used in the sale or advertising of services to identify the services of one person and distinguish them from the services of others.

As to registration of a person's name as a service mark, *see also* sections 2(e)(3) and (f) of the Lanham Act, 15 U.S.C. §§ 1052(e) (3) and (f).

entertainment services. *See, e.g., Re Carson*, 197 U.S.P.Q.(BNA) 554 (Trademark Trial & App.Bd.1977); . . . Although appellant has not alleged that his name is registered as a service mark, registration of a trademark or service mark is not a prerequisite for recovery under section 43(a).

Appellant's allegations of "reverse passing off" are analogous to those of other complaints which have been held to state a cause of action under section 43(a). For example, in *Truck Equipment Service Co. v. Fruehauf Corp.*, 536 F.2d 1210 (8th Cir.), *cert. denied*, 429 U.S. 861, 97 S.Ct. 164, 50 L.Ed.2d 139 (1976), a farm equipment manufacturer used photographs of a competitor's grain trailer in its sales literature. In the photos, the competitor's labels were removed and the trailer was labeled as a product of the defendant. The court rejected the defendant-appellant's contention that the use of the photos was not a false representation prohibited by section 43(a), holding that the practice was "of the same *economic nature* as trademark infringement." 536 F.2d at 1216 (emphasis added). The court also noted that "The use of another's product, misbranded to appear as that of a competitor [i. e., reverse passing off], has been repeatedly found to be 'a false designation of origin' actionable under section 43(a)." *Id.*

In *John Wright, Inc. v. Casper Corp.*, 419 F.Supp. 292 (E.D.Penn.1976), *aff'd in relevant part sub nom. Donsco, Inc. v. Casper Corp.*, 587 F.2d 602 (3d Cir. 1978), the court stated that section 43(a) "prohibits 'reverse palming off.' i. e., conduct whereby the defendant purchases or otherwise obtains the plaintiff's goods, removes plaintiff's name and replaces it with his own." 419 F.Supp. at 325.[4] Similarly, in *FRA S.p.A. v. SURG–O–FLEX of America, Inc.*, 415 F.Supp. 421 (S.D.N.Y.1976), the court denied a motion to dismiss, and reaffirmed its previous grant of a preliminary injunction, based on allegations that a bandage manufacturer's former distributor violated section 43(a) by continuing to sell boxes of the manufacturer's bandages, after termination of the distributorship, by pasting the distributor's trademark over the manufacturer's name. Finally, in *Matsushita Electric Corp. v. Solar Sound Systems, Inc.*, 381 F.Supp. 64 (S.D.N.Y.1974), the court found a "clear violation" of section 43(a) based on the defendant's conduct in slightly modifying the control panel on plaintiff's radio, removing plaintiff's nameplate to substitute defendant's, and scraping off the embossed labeling on the back.

---

[4] In that case, involving competing manufacturers of reproductions of antique mechanical banks, the court found a violation of section 43(a) based on defendant's misleading advertisements for its banks. The advertisements contained pictures of the original antique banks from which defendant's reproductions were assertedly copied, and stated that the banks pictured were from the defendant's collection rather than the plaintiff's. Thus, although the court was quick to label, and condemn, the defendant's conduct as "reverse palming off," that conduct is more accurately described as "implied passing off." See 1 Callman, *supra,* §18.2(b)(1), at 294–95 (1980 Supp. to 3d ed.)

According to appellant's complaint, defendants not only removed appellant's name from all credits and advertising, they also substituted a name of their own choosing. Appellees' alleged conduct therefore amounts to *express reverse passing off*. As a matter of policy, such conduct, like traditional palming off, is wrongful because it involves an attempt to misappropriate or profit from another's talents and workmanship. Moreover, in reverse palming off cases, the originator of the misidentified product is involuntarily deprived of the advertising value of its name and of the goodwill that otherwise would stem from public knowledge of the true source of the satisfactory product. The ultimate purchaser (or viewer) is also deprived of knowing the true source of the product and may even be deceived into believing that it comes from a different source. . . .

In the film industry, a particular actor's performance, which may have received an award or other critical acclaim, may be the primary attraction for movie-goers. Some actors are said to have such drawing power at the box office that the appearance of their names on the theater marquee can almost guarantee financial success. Such big box office names are built, in part, through being prominently featured in popular films and by receiving appropriate recognition in film credits and advertising. Since actors' fees for pictures, and indeed, their ability to get any work at all, is often based on the drawing power their name may be expected to have at the box office, being accurately credited for films in which they have played would seem to be of critical importance in enabling actors to sell their "services," i. e., their performances. We therefore find that appellant has stated a valid claim for relief under section 43(a) of the Lanham Act.[6]

B. *Standing under the Lanham Act*

As an alternative ground for dismissal, the district court raised the issue of the plaintiff's standing to sue, . . . We reject this argument and hold that appellant is entitled to press his claim for "false representation" in federal court under section 43(a)

The Second Circuit has ruled that section 43(a) does not give standing to consumers . . . This reading of section 43(a) has been sharply criticized . . .

---

[6] In a case involving very similar facts, the district court denied a motion to dismiss and ruled orally that a cause of action for unfair competition under section 43(a) had been stated. *See Perin Film Enterprises v. TWG Productions*, 400 P.T.C. Journ. (10–19–78) A–13 (S.D.N.Y.1978). The plaintiff had served as executive producer of the television series "For You . . . Black Woman." During the second year of production, after having served as executive producer of the first 22 shows, plaintiff was dismissed and received no credit for his services. Instead, the name of employee of the show's underwriter was substituted as the "executive in charge of production." The parties entered into settlement negotiations shortly after the court's ruling, and the ruling was never subsequently embodied in published opinion.

At any rate, however, it is clear that appellant, as one in the business of providing his talents for use in the creation of an entertainment product, is uniquely situated to complain of injury resulting from a film distributor's misidentification of appellant's contribution to the product. According to one commentator, the "dispositive question" as to a party's standing to maintain an action under section 43(a) is whether the party "has a reasonable interest to be protected against false advertising." The vital interest of actors in receiving accurate credit for their work has already been described. Accordingly, we hold that appellant has standing to sue in federal court based on defendants' alleged violation of section 43(a).

II. *State Law Claims*

In addition to the claim under section 43(a), appellant's complaint alleged claims under state law for breach of contract, "false light publicity," and commercial appropriation of a person's likeness under Cal. Civ. Code § 3344. Since we are reversing the dismissal of appellant's Lanham Act claim, the dismissal for lack of jurisdiction of appellant's state law claims is also reversed. "One important benefit of section 43(a) is that it grants federal question jurisdiction totally apart from federal diversity jurisdiction." 2 J. McCarthy, *supra*, § 27:6.A. Thus, once in federal court under section 43(a), a plaintiff can allege related claims of unfair competition under common law and any available state statutory provisions.

CONCLUSION

As the district court stated, a section 43(a) claim may be based on practices or conduct "economically equivalent" to palming off. We find that appellant did state such a claim by alleging that defendants engaged in conduct amounting to "express reverse palming off." Since appellant also has standing to sue under section 43(a), the district court's dismissal of the complaint for failure to state a federal claim is reversed. The dismissal of the pendent state law claims is also reversed. *Reversed and remanded.*

GOLD LEAF GROUP, LTD. v. STIGWOOD GROUP, LTD.

Supreme Court, New York County
Index No. 11768/78

Opinion of the Court

RUBIN, J.:

Plaintiff, moves this court for an injunction, pendente lite, restraining defendant Stigwood Group Ltd. (Stigwood) from violating the written contractual "billing" rights of Peter Frampton (Frampton), one of the stars of a motion picture entitled "Sergeant Pepper's Lonely Hearts Club Band." Plaintiff corporation, of which Frampton is an officer, is the owner of Peter Frampton's motion picture services and recording services for motion picture soundtracks. The defendant corporation is the producer of the film.

The film took approximately two years to make at a cost of over $12,000,000.00. A significant part of the production package is an "original motion picture soundtrack" record album. The total cost of the project, which encompasses the film and record and includes promotion, now exceeds $20,000,000.00.

Plaintiff seeks a temporary injunction to prevent defendants from advertising the movie and the record in a manner according another starring group in the picture known as "the Bee Gees" the same billing credit line as Frampton. While the film itself credits Frampton "top billing", the advertising as to the film and the record accords "the Bee Gees" billing alongside and to the right of Frampton. Frampton claims that he has the right to have his name appear above "the Bee Gees" in connection with 1) the billing of the film, 2) the advertising of the film, 3) the art work on the cover of the record, 4) the advertising for the record and, 5) merchandising and subsidiary rights in connection with the film.

It appears that the billing provision of a contract is material in that it is not just a matter of status or prestige, but serves to protect and enhance the future marketability and commercial value of a star performer. While a dispute exists as to whether the writing, between the parties, on October 29, 1976, be termed a film/record contract as contended by plaintiff or a "deal memorandum" as contended by defendant, an agreement was signed wherein in Paragraph 4 the credit status of Frampton is set forth as follows:

> "Artist shall receive the sole star billing above the title of the photoplay in a size of type one hundred percent that of the credits of any other person."

In a subsequent modification it was agreed that the

Bee Gees name could be billed above the title, but below that of Frampton.

An injunction, pendente lite, is warranted when there is a showing of a likelihood of ultimate success on the merits, irreparable harm to movant absent granting of the preliminary injunction and a balancing of the equities . . . It is enough if the moving party makes a prima facie showing of his right to relief . . .

The language of the agreement, even as modified by the parties, gives Frampton sole star billing in the photoplay. It is further apparent that plaintiff considered Frampton's star billing to be of prime importance and would have withheld its consent to the agreement had its artist not been so recognized.

Defendant attempts to convince the court that billing alongside but to the left of the Bee Gees is recognized as "first star billing". However, the agreement gives to Frampton "sole star billing" and plaintiff is entitled to a fulfillment of its contractual obligations. The court is aware of defendants' desire to accord its clients a greater star status as the result of their sudden surge of popularity originating from the motion picture "Saturday Night Fever". However, in view of the contractual obligations, there is sufficient showing to enjoin defendant from billing or advertising the Bee Gees, other than on a line below Frampton, and in a size, type and prominence no greater than his in any billing or advertising concerning the motion picture "Sergeant Pepper's Lonely Hearts Club Band" . . .

The motion addressed to the record represents a different problem. While it may have been the intention of the plaintiff to have paragraph 4 of the agreement apply to the soundtrack recording, the agreement is not clear and convincing in this respect. Another agreement dated January 21, 1977, between defendants' recording subsidiary, RSO Records, Inc. and Frampton's recording agent, A & M Records, Inc. provides that Frampton's name be billed "in the same manner as the names of other artists are utilized in connection with said album". Furthermore, an agreement signed March 13, 1978, concerning worldwide merchandising and subsidiary rights is silent as to billing and advertising. There is, also, a question of whether plaintiff acquiesced in the design of the record album jacket. The proof required of defendants, for the purpose of this motion, is merely that they need only raise doubts of that liklihood that plaintiff will ultimately succeed in the action. It is incumbent upon the plaintiff to come forth with clear and convincing evidence dispelling such doubts. As to the soundtrack recording, this the plaintiff has failed to do.

Since the movie and soundtrack recording have already been released, it is evident that an early trial is warranted and necessary.

Accordingly, the motion for an injunction pedente lite is granted as to the motion picture and denied as to the soundtrack recording.

Settle order providing for an immediate trial.

Dated: October 4, 1978

Aljean Harmetz, "FALK SAYS 'NO' TO PRESS JUNKET"

The New York Times (June 15, 1978), p. C17

LOS ANGELES, June 14—Angered over the advertising campaign for his new film, "The Cheap Detective," Peter Falk has backed out of a New York press junket this week, leaving Columbia holding a $35,000 bag. Nearly 75 reporters and columnists will arrive in New York tomorrow to meet Peter Falk, but Peter Falk will be in Boston.

The advertisement that displeased Mr. Falk appeared in last Sunday's New York Times and Los Angeles Times. It showed a caricature of "cheap detective" Peter Falk cocking his thumb and forefinger as if they were a gun aimed at the picture's 15 other stars, who range alphabetically from Ann-Margret to Nicol Williamson.

"Peter's contract calls for him to be 'alone, separate and prominent,'" a Columbia spokesman said, "His name, doesn't have to be larger than the names of the other stars, but it must come first. For an earlier advertisement he had us draw a picture of him in a trenchcoat six times before he decided it looked enough like him. He didn't think this current ad made him prominent enough. And he wanted his name separated from all the other names."

"The Cheap Detective," which opens June 23 at the Coronet and Little Carnegie, was produced by Ray Stark from an original Neil Simon script. The film is in the same comedy detective genre as the earlier Stark-Simon "Murder by Death," with Mr. Falk playing the same kind of trenchcoated detective he played in the earlier film. That film's advertising featured caricatures drawn by Charles Addams.

"We chose a caricature for this teaser ad because we didn't want to cheat or confuse the audience," Mr. Stark said. "We didn't want them to think they were going to see a romantic Neil Simon comedy like "The Goodbye Girl." We spend hundreds of hours making such decisions. For actors to come in at the last minute and dot i's is capricious."

Mr. Stark, who has "great respect for Peter as an actor," was "surprised and shocked" at his star's refusal to go to New York for the press junket "because this picture is a marvelous vehicle for Peter, and any success the picture has also gives luster to him."

A Columbia executive who did not wish to be identified is rankled by the fact that "even though Peter Falk has been a big television star as Columbo, except for 'Murder by Death' he's hardly ever had a successful movie. Two-thirds of our money is going into television, and he is the focal point of those ads. But he still told us, 'Unless you change the billing, I won't come down.'"

Mr. Falk is in Boston, shooting his new movie, "Brinks," and could not be reached for comment.

Despite his absence, the press junket will go on as planned, with Eileen Brennan, James Coco and Dom DeLuise meeting the press without him.

Louis L'Amour, ADVERTISEMENT
Publisher's Weekly (July 29, 1983), p. 16

Los Angeles, California

Dear Booksellers:

As men and women who have sold and supported my books so faithfully over the last 30 years, I feel it's important to make you all aware of the most disturbing development in my career as a writer: the imminent publication of two completely unauthorized books of short stories bearing my name as author.

Imagine, as if it were not outrageous enough that this publisher I never even heard of would announce publication of my stories without even contacting me, they even refused my lawyers' request to tell me which of my stories they were using! I found this attempt to seize control of my work to be so appalling that for the first time in my career I went to court to protect my right to publish my writing as I see fit.

Unfortunately, although the court's decision has put restrictions on this publisher's presentation of my stories to the public, they still will be allowed to publish two short story collections over which I had no control and of which I do not approve.

I'm very proud of my short stories. In the 1940's and '50's I wrote a great many stories for a wide variety of magazines. I was writing as fast as I could in those days trying to sell as many stories as possible in order to feed my young family, and I didn't pay as much attention as I should have to some of the copyright paperwork. As a result, although the great majority of my stories are properly protected, there are some which are technically in the public domain.

I could have just compiled the public domain stories in their original form—as this other publisher will be doing—but I strongly believe that to do so would be a disservice to my many fans. I've grown as a writer since I created those early stories and I strive to give everyone who buys my books the best writing I can. Therefore, in 1975, I began a carefully planned ongoing publishing program to select and revise my stories, adding new introductions, notes of interest and connecting essays to enhance the volumes and to put the stories in historical perspective and to connect them to the themes I develop in my novels.

Now I'm forced to ask my real publisher, Bantam Books, to rush into print two authorized short story collections I have begun working on around the clock, so my readers won't be short-changed. One will be a collection of frontier stories and the other will contain detective stories.

So my fans won't be confused, I will make sure my authorized editions will bear the same titles and contain all of the stories in the unauthorized books, but I will also include additional stories plus the same kind of new material I've written especially for my five previous collections.

As far as I'm concerned and, I hope, as far as my fans are concerned, the two completely unauthorized editions of my stories do not exist. My authorized editions will be books on which I will be proud to put my name and pleased for my fans to read.

Thank you for all your support.

Sincerely,

Louis

Supplemental Reading

Clemens v. Press Publishing Co., 67 Misc. 183, 122 N.Y.S. 206 (N.Y. App. Term 1910) (sustaining publisher's refusal to credit author of purchased story).

Granz v. Harris, 198 F.2d 585 (2d Cir. 1952) (finding actionable the advertising of an edited recording as having been created by the same artist as the non-edited version).

Esquire, Inc. v. Varga Enterprises, 185 F.2d 14 (7th Cir. 1950) (publisher entitled to injunction prohibiting artist from using his name on drawings where the artist had sold the right to use such name to publisher).

Harris v. Twentieth Century-Fox Film Corp., 43 F. Supp. 119 (S.D.N.Y. 1942) (where writer had sold all rights in her story to defendant, and where writer's contract had not provided for attribution of a specific credit, defendant's attribution of "story research" credit to writer was not defamatory); *rev'd on other grounds*, 139 F.2d 571 (2d Cir. 1943).

Bonner v. Westbound Records, Inc., 49 Ill. App. 3d 543, 364 N.E.2d 570 (Ill. App. Ct. 1977) (restraining release of album under band's name where band's performance on album was distorted and, therefore, unrepresentative).

Hathaway, "American Law Analogues to the Paternity Element of the Doctrine of Moral Right: Is the Creative Artist in America Really Protected?" 30 *Copyright L. Symp. (ASCAP)* 121 (1983).

Berman & Rosenthal, "Screen Credit and the Law," 9 *U.C.L.A. L. Rev.* 156 (1962).

CHAPTER 4

COMPENSATION

Introduction

Compensation in the entertainment industry involves many more questions than how much money is to be paid over what period of time. These questions include, among others: Is money the only, or even best, form of compensation? What happens to promised money if a project is abandoned or if creative differences arise? What does it mean, legally and practically, if someone has a royalty, or a "piece of the profits"? This chapter explores non-monetary forms of compensation, as well as the variety of ways to structure monetary payments. The role of union agreements in setting minimums for a variety of forms of compensation is also considered.

In addition, this chapter presents an analysis of the "pay or play" concept, one of the fundamental business points in any entertainment contract negotiation. The meaning of "pay or play" and the justification for the arrangement are examined. Also discussed are exceptions to a "pay or play" obligation, as well as limitations on the "pay or play" requirement.

Contingent forms of compensation are characteristic of the industry. Therefore, this chapter explores not only the benefits, but also the possible dangers, to an obligor who seeks to lower fixed costs in exchange for making payments based on the success of an entertainment project.

Lastly, there is a detailed analysis of a sample net profits definition. Most forms of contingent compensation in the entertainment industry are governed by such contractual definitions. This analysis will indicate the care which must be taken in negotiating an agreement containing such definition; even a change in a few words may have dramatic financial repercussions.

Required Reading

Sigmon v. Goldstone, 116 A.D. 490, 101 N.Y.S. 984 (1906). *Parker v. Twentieth Century-Fox Film Corp.*, 3 Cal. 3d 176, 474 P.2d 689, 89 Cal. Rptr. 737 (1970).

"Arbitrator Gives Peter Hunt 134G In Merrick Case," *Variety* (April 16, 1980), pp. 3, 191.

Wood v. Lucy, Lady Duff-Gordon, 222 N.Y. 88 (1917).

Dodd, Mead & Co., Inc. v. Lilienthal, 514 F. Supp. 105 (S.D.N.Y. 1981).

Van Valkenburgh, Nooger & Neville Inc. v. Hayden Publishing Co., Inc., 30 N.Y.2d 34, 281 N.E.2d 142, 330 N.Y.S.2d 329 (1972).

Zilg v. Prentice-Hall, Inc., 717 F.2d 671 (2d Cir. 1983).

Arnold Productions, Inc. v. Favorite Films Corp., 176 F. Supp. 862 (S.D.N.Y. 1959).

Pinnacle Books, Inc. v. Harlequin Enterprises Limited, 519 F. Supp. 118 (S.D.N.Y. 1981).

Contemporary Mission, Inc. v. Famous Music Corporation, 557 F.2d 918 (2d Cir. 1977).

"Home Box Office's Suits Say Directors Guild Impedes Progress," *Variety* (July 26, 1978), p. 41.

Aljean Harmetz, "Film Figures Decry Profit-Sharing Evils," *The New York Times* (February 3, 1978), p. C35.

Mario Puzo, "Hollywood's Raid on Israel, or Idi Amin's Revenge," *New York Magazine* (October 4, 1976), pp. 46–49.

"Rogers Sues Liberty for $44 Mil, Claiming Label Shortchanged Him," *Variety* (October 28, 1981), p. 63.

Richard Hummler, "Authors, Producers Break off Confabs," *Variety* (November 25, 1981), pp. 97, 105.

Ken Terry, "Variable Record Pricing Comes of Age," *Variety* (August 31, 1983), pp. 101, 104.

All contracts and union agreements referred to in the chapter "Concepts."

CONCEPTS

1. What different benefits do people negotiate for in the entertainment industry? Consider *Sigmon v. Goldstone* (p. 311).

2. Why are clauses such as Parag. 6–101 (p. 502) of the Directors Guild of America Basic Agreement (1981) and Parag. 12 of the Screenplay Loan-out Agreement (p. 679) included in contracts?

   (A) What is the justification for such clauses from the artist's viewpoint?

   (B) What circumstances justify relieving a producer of his obligations under such clauses?

(C) Should these clauses guarantee payment of contingent compensation, e.g., deferrals and a share of net profits if they are part of a deal?

(D) If an artist is terminated after partial performance, should the answer to question 2.(C) change?

(E) What does *Parker v. Twentieth-Century Fox* (p. 313) indicate about the value of these clauses to an artist?

    (1) What issue might Fox have raised, but did not?

    (2) What contract provisions does case suggest are desirable from an artist's viewpoint? From a producer's viewpoint?

(F) What do *Variety* article of 4/16/80 (p. 322) and Directors Guild of America Basic Agreement (1981), Parag. 6–105 (p. 503) suggest about limitations on the clauses referred to in 2.?

3. In *Wood v. Lucy, Lady Duff-Gordon* (p. 323), what role did the exclusive agency nature of the relationship play in the decision?

(A) What is a comparable relationship in the motion picture, television, book publishing and live theatrical branches of the entertainment industry?

(B) Compare Book Publishing Agreement, Parags. SECOND C 63, 70 (pp. 855, 869, 870), Record Agreement, Parag. 3(a) (p. 795) and Merchandising Agreement, Parag. 4 (p. 843). What danger for the distributor is inherent in these paragraphs?

(C) What does *Dodd, Mead v. Lilienthal* (p. 324) suggest about the limits of the *Duff-Gordon* theory?

4. How do *Van Valkenburgh v. Hayden Publishing* (p. 329), *Zilg v. Prentice-Hall, Inc.* (p. 334) and *Arnold v. Favorite Films Corp.* (p. 343) relate to the danger considered in paragraph 3.(B) above?

(A) *Van Valkenburgh*

    (1) Was there an obligation by defendant to use reasonable efforts? What is the difference between "reasonable efforts" and "best efforts"?

    (2) Is a producer/distributor who pays a royalty based on sales precluded from dealing in competitive works?

    (3) Why did Hayden engage in competitive conduct?

(B) *Zilg*

    (1) What is a publisher's obligation under Judge Winter's ruling?

(2)   Under what circumstances would a breach of that obligation exist?

(C)   *Arnold*

(1)   What disturbed plaintiff?

(2)   How were films in this case distributed to television?

(3)   What were Favorite's gross receipts from television?

(4)   What potential problem is suggested by Nationwide's structure?

5.   What do Parag. 12 of the Screenplay Loanout Agreement (p. 679); Parag 50 of the Book Publishing Agreement (p. 867); Parag. 6(a) (but compare Parag. 7(a)) of the Record Agreement (pp. 805, 807) and Parag. SECOND of the Minimum Basic Production Contract (p. 709) have in common? What are the key words in each paragraph?

(A)   In Screenplay Loanout Agreement, is Parag. 12 necessary given Parag. 9 (p. 677)?

(B)   If artist is compensated based on sales, should a producer/ financier be obligated to exploit property?

(1)   Is answer different if only part of compensation is based on sales, e.g., contingent compensation?

(2)   Is answer different if there is an advance against royalties?

(3)   If product bombs, should producer be obligated to spend more money to exploit it?

6.   How can best efforts be measured? Compare *Pinnacle v. Harlequin* (p. 349) and *Contemporary Mission v. Famous Music Corporation* (p. 355).

(A)   Considering *Contemporary Mission*, what would comparable standards be in the movie and print publishing branches of the entertainment industry?

(B)   What is the danger to a producer/distributor from clear standards?

7. How does Parag. 16A8 of the Writers Guild of America Basic Agreement (1981) (p. 591) relate to Parag. 12 of the Screenplay Loanout Agreement (p. 679)? What changes were made in Parag. 16A8 in Writers Guild of America Basic Agreement (1981), as compared to the same paragraph in Writers Guild of America Basic Agreements (1977) (p. 557), (1973) (p. 527) and (1970) (p. 521)?

8. Directors Guild of America Basic Agreement (1981), Parags. 11–102, 11–201, 18–101 through 105 and 19–101 through 104 (pp. 506–518); Screen Actors Guild Codified Basic Agreement (1977), Parags. 4A, 5A, B, D (pp. 597–606); Screen Actors Guild Television Agreement (1977), Parags. 18(c), 19(a) through (c), 20(a) through (c) (pp. 608–617), (1980) Part I–5, 6, 7, 8, 9, Part V–3 and Part VI (pp. 622–628), (1983) Parags. 14, 36, 41 (pp. 628–9); Writers Guild of America Basic Agreement (1977), Parags. 15A3 (p. 533), 15B2 (p. 551), 15B13 (p. 553, Article 51 (p. 561) and Writers Guild of America Basic Agreement (1981), Article 51 (p. 593) all require additional payments ("residuals") based on release to markets other than market for which product was originally created. In light of these aforesaid guild provisions, consider the following:

(A) What are arguments favoring these residuals? Consider *Variety* article of 7/26/78 (p. 368).

(B) What are arguments against residuals? When does a distributor account to a producer? What is the danger to an independent producer from this arrangement?

(C) Why are Directors Guild of America Basic Agreement (1981), Parag. 19–109 (p. 518); Writers Guild of America Basic Agreement (1977), Parags. 15A3(g), 15B7 (pp. 539, 553); and Screen Actors Guild Television Agreement (1977), Parags. 18(f), 19(g) and 20(e) (pp. 610, 612, 617) included in such agreements?

(D) What would happen if Directors Guild of America Basic Agreement (1981), Parag. 4–110 (p. 502); and Writers Guild of America Basic Agreement (1977), Parags. 15B and 15B13c (pp. 551, 555) were not in in these agreements? Compare Screen Actors Guild Codified Basic Agreement (1977), Parag. 20 (p. 605); Screen Actors Guild Television Agreement (1977), Parags. 18(d) and 19(d) (pp. 610, 611; Screen Actors Guild Television Agreement (1980), Part I-8 (p. 624); and Screen Actors Guild Television Agreement (1983), Parag. 16 (p. 629).

9. What happens to the dollars you pay for a movie ticket?

10. What are the dangers in the standard definition of net profits? Examine, as set forth below, definition of net profits attached to Motion Picture Pre-Sale/Live Theatrical Financing Agreement (pp. 767–792). Consider *The New York Times* article of 2/3/78 (p. 369); *New York Magazine* article of 10/4/76 (p. 373). Compare these articles to *Variety* article of 10/28/81 (p. 381).

    (A) Why does a financier/distributor try to keep extra dollars?

    (B) How can a financier/distributor lower risk?

    (C) If an artist is entitled to 5% of 100% of net profits, consider the following questions in light of the above net profits definition:

        (1) What danger lies in Parag. I C (p. 776)?

        (2) What danger lies in Parag. II A2 (p. 777)?

        (3) Should distributor be entitled to write off four walling license losses? Consider Parag. II A5 (p. 777).

        (4) Why permit charitable contributions resulting in a tax benefit to distributor? Consider Parag. II B3 (p. 778).

        (5) What is the purpose of a distribution fee? Compare Parag. III (p. 778) and last clause of first paragraph of Parag. IV A (p. 779)?

        (6) What are the dangers in costs such as Parag. IV B, C and E (p. 779)?

        (7) Why permit trade dues? Consider Parag. IV J (p. 780)?

        (8) What is the purpose of overhead charges? Consider Parag. V B. (p. 781). Compare Parag. III and Parag. IV A (p. 779).

        (9) Should interest be permissible on overhead? Consider Parag. V C(1) (p. 782).

        (10) What is effect of Parag. V D (p. 782)?

        (11) What is danger in first sentence of Parag. VI B (p. 782)?

        (12) What is danger in second sentence of Parag. VI B (p.782)?

        (13) Consider Parag. VI (D) (p. 783)? What would happen if second paragraph were not in Agreement?

        (14) Dangers in Parag. VI E (p. 784)?

        (15) What would happen if second sentence in Parag. VI G (p. 784) were not in the Agreement?

        (16) What do Parag. VI I (p. 784) and Parag. VII B2 (p. 785)

indicate about remedies available to profit participant for a violation of his rights?

(17) What is the effect of Parag. VII C (p. 785)?

(18) Should a distributor have a right of buyout in Parag. VII D (p. 786)?

(19) What would happen if last clause in Parag. VIII K(1) (p. 789) were not in the Agreement?

(D) To what extent are complaints about creative accounting justified? Consider *Variety* article of 10/28/81 (p. 381).

(E) Consider *Variety* article of 11/25/81 (p. 382) about fears of creative accounting in live theatrical branch of the industry. In the context of the negotiation described in the article, what proposal could possibly have resolved the dispute by meeting both the producers' needs and the authors' fears?

(F) What is the danger to a recording artist from a change in business practices such as that described in *Variety* article of 8/31/83 (p. 385)?

SIGMON v. GOLDSTONE
116 A.D. 490, 101 N.Y.S. 984 (1906)

HOUGHTON, J. The plaintiff entered into an agreement in writing with the defendants, who are copartners, to serve them in the capacity of designer, pattern cutter, and foreman for the term of 21 months at a stipulated weekly salary. The plaintiff continued in the employ of the defendants for a little over 12 months, when, as he claims, the defendants wrongfully discharged him. He brings this action for damages for such breach of hiring. The defense is breach of the contract on the part of plaintiff, and that he voluntarily quit defendants' service. The record discloses that for some weeks prior to the alleged discharge considerable friction existed between the plaintiff and the defendants, and, instead of permitting him to do the work for which he was hired, they compelled him to sit during working hours in a dark room unemployed. This the plaintiff protested against, and consulted a lawyer, who waited upon the defendants at their place of business, and he and the plaintiff had an interview with one of the partners with respect to such alleged improper treatment. The plaintiff testifies that at the close of this interview such partner told both himself and the lawyer to get out of defendants' place of business. Thereupon the lawyer told plaintiff to come with him and both departed. On the same day plaintiff, through his attorney, by letter, notified the defendants that he tendered his services according to the contract. No offer to take the plaintiff back was made. The attorney who represented the plaintiff at the interview with defendants was sworn as a witness, and the learned trial court seems to have been led into the granting of a motion for nonsuit because the attorney would not swear positively that the command to get out of defendants' place of business was addressed specifically to the plaintiff. The attorney did testify that the command "to get out of here" was addressed to both himself and the plaintiff. The plaintiff, however, testified that the language was "both of you get out." In view of the testimony of the plaintiff that the defendants had endeavored to induce him to abandon his contract for a small money consideration, and the friction that existed, and the apparent anger on the part of defendants that the plaintiff had consulted an attorney, we think it was clearly a question for the jury to say whether the command to get out of defendants' place of business was addressed to the plaintiff as well as to his attorney.

No precise words are necessary to constitute a discharge. Any language by which an employé is notified that his services are no longer required is sufficient to operate as such. Whether the defendants did, or meant to, discharge plaintiff, or whether their language and conduct was such as to reasonably lead plaintiff to believe that he was discharged, was for the jury to determine from all the facts and circumstances. By the contract in question the defendants retained in their hands $5 per week of plaintiff's wages as a guaranty of faithful performance on his part. There had been an adjustment of this deposit, but at the time of the alleged discharge there remained in the hands of the defendants the sum of $70. Even if the plaintiff was not in fact discharged, as the record now appears, he would be entitled to recover this sum which he seeks by the second cause of action alleged in his complaint. A servant may abandon his service because of a breach of any of the express or implied provisions of his contract without liability for damages, as where the master assaults him or refuses to pay his wages as agreed, or requires him to perform services not contemplated by his contract of hiring, or does any act, or is guilty of any negligence prejudicial to the morals, reasonable comfort, safety, health, or reputation of the servant, which is in violation of the provisions of the contract of hiring, express or implied . . . The contract between plaintiff and defendants was that he should serve in the capacity of designer and cutter and foreman of defendants' manufacturing establishment at a salary comparatively large. In order thereafter to command this salary or a higher one, plaintiff must continue to be skillful and to enjoy a reputation for skill. It was one of the implied covenants of plaintiff's contract that he should be permitted to labor in the manner specified. It was a breach of this covenant for the defendants, without cause, to prohibit the plaintiff from doing any work and to shut him up in a dark room doing nothing, notwithstanding they continued to pay his weekly salary. This breach on the part of defendants entitled the plaintiff, prima facie, to recover the $70 in their hands, irrespective of whether or not he had any further action for breach of contract because of a wrongful discharge.

A nonsuit was therefore improper, not only on the ground that it was a question for the jury as to whether or not plaintiff had been discharged, but because plaintiff showed that there had been a breach on the part of defendants sufficient to relieve him from damages under his contract of hiring, whether he was discharged or not.

Upon both issues the plaintiff showed sufficient facts to put the defendants to their proofs, and the judgment must therefore be reversed, and new trial ordered, with costs to the appellant to abide the event. All concur.

PARKER v. TWENTIETH CENTURY-FOX FILM CORPORATION
3 Cal. 3d 176, 474 P.2d 689, 89 Cal. Rptr. 737 (1970)

BURKE, Justice.

Defendant Twentieth Century-Fox Film Corporation appeals from a summary judgment granting to plaintiff the recovery of agreed compensation under a written contract for her services as an actress in a motion picture. As will appear, we have concluded that the trial court correctly ruled in plaintiff's favor and that the judgment should be affirmed.

Plaintiff is well known as an actress, and in the contract between plaintiff and defendant is sometimes referred to as the "Artist." Under the contract, dated August 6, 1965, plaintiff was to play the female lead in defendant's contemplated production of a motion picture entitled "Bloomer Girl." The contract provided that defendant would pay plaintiff a minimum "guaranteed compensation" of $53,571.42 per week for 14 weeks commencing May 23, 1966, for a total of $750,000. Prior to May 1966 defendant decided not to produce the picture and by a letter dated April 4, 1966, it notified plaintiff of that decision and that it would not "comply with our obligations to you under" the written contract.

By the same letter and with the professed purpose "to avoid any damage to you," defendant instead offered to employ plaintiff as the leading actress in another film tentatively entitled "Big Country, Big Man" (hereinafter, "Big Country"). The compensation offered was identical, as were 31 of the 34 numbered provisions or articles of the original contract.[1] Unlike "Bloomer

---

[1] Among the identical provisions was the following found in the last paragraph of Article 2

Girl," however, which was to have been a musical production, "Big Country" was a dramatic "western type" movie. "Bloomer Girl" was to have been filmed in California; "Big Country" was to be produced in Australia. Also, certain terms in the proffered contract varied from those of the original.[2] Plaintiff was given one week within which to accept; she did not and the offer lapsed. Plaintiff then commenced this action seeking recovery of the agreed guaranteed compensation.

The complaint sets forth two causes of action. The first is for money due under the contract; the second, based upon the same allegations as the first, is for damages resulting from defendant's breach of contract. Defendant in its answer admits the existence and validity of the contract, that plaintiff complied with all the conditions, covenants and promises and stood ready to complete the performance, and that defendant breached and "anticipatorily repudiated" the contract. It denies, however, that any money is due to plaintiff either under the contract or as a result of its breach, and pleads as an affirmative defense to both causes of action plaintiff's allegedly deliberate

---

of the original contract: "We [defendant] shall not be obligated to utilize your [plaintiff's] services in or in connection with the Photoplay hereunder, our sole obligation, subject to the terms and conditions of this Agreement, being to pay you the guaranteed compensation herein provided for."

[2] Article 29 of the original contract specified that plaintiff approved the director already chosen for "Bloomer Girl" and that in case he failed to act as director plaintiff was to have approval rights of any substitute director. Article 31 provided that plaintiff was to have the right of approval of the "Bloomer Girl" dance director, and Article 32 gave her the right of approval of the screenplay.

Defendant's letter of April 4 to plaintiff, which contained both defendant's notice of breach of the "Bloomer Girl" contract and offer of the lead in "Big Country," eliminated or impaired each of those rights. It read in part as follows: "The terms and conditions of our offer of employment are identical to those set forth in the 'BLOOMER GIRL' Agreement, Articles 1 through 34 and Exhibit A to the Agreement, except as follows:

"1. Article 31 of said Agreement will not be included in any contract of employment regarding 'BIG COUNTRY, BIG MAN' as it is not a musical and it thus will not need a dance director.

"2. In the 'BLOOMER GIRL' agreement, in Articles 29 and 32, you were given certain director and screenplay approvals and you had preapproved certain matters. Since there simply is insufficient time to negotiate with you regarding your choice of director and regarding the screenplay and since you already expressed an interest in performing the role in 'BIG COUNTRY, BIG MAN,' we must exclude from our offer of employment in 'BIG COUNTRY, BIG MAN' any approval rights as are contained in said Articles 29 and 32; however, we shall consult with you respecting the director to be selected to direct the photoplay and will further consult with you with respect to the screenplay and any revisions or changes therein, provided, however, that if we fail to agree . . . the decision of . . . [defendant] with respect to the selection of a director and to revisions and changes in the said screenplay shall be binding upon the parties to said agreement."

failure to mitigate damages, asserting that she unreasonably refused to accept its offer of the leading role in "Big Country."

Plaintiff moved for summary judgment under Code of Civil Procedure section 437c, the motion was granted, and summary judgment for $750,000 plus interest was entered in plaintiff's favor. This appeal by defendant followed.

The familiar rules are that the matter to be determined by the trial court on a motion for summary judgment is whether facts have been presented which give rise to a triable factual issue. The court may not pass upon the issue itself. Summary judgment is proper only if the affidavits or declarations in support of the moving party would be sufficient to sustain a judgment in his favor and his opponent does not by affidavit show facts sufficient to present a triable issue of fact. The affidavits of the moving party are strictly construed, and doubts as to the propriety of summary judgment should be resolved against granting the motion. Such summary procedure is drastic and should be used with caution so that it does not become a substitute for the open trial method of determining facts. The moving party cannot depend upon allegations in his own pleadings to cure deficient affidavits, nor can his adversary rely upon his own pleadings in lieu or in support of affidavits in opposition to a motion; however, a party can rely on his adversary's pleadings to establish facts not contained in his own affidavits. Also, the court may consider facts stipulated to by the parties and facts which are properly the subject of judicial notice.

As stated, defendant's sole defense to this action which resulted from its deliberate breach of contract is that in rejecting defendant's substitute offer of employment plaintiff unreasonably refused to mitigate damages.

The general rule is that the measure of recovery by a wrongfully discharged employee is the amount of salary agreed upon for the period of service, less the amount which the employer affirmatively proves the employee has earned or with reasonable effort might have earned from other employment.[4] However, before projected earnings from other employment opportunities not sought or accepted by the discharged employee can be applied in mitigation, the employer must show that the other employment was comparable, or substantially similar, to that of which the employee has been deprived; the employee's rejection of or failure to seek other available employment of a different or inferior kind may not be resorted to in order to mitigate damages.

In the present case defendant has raised no issue of *reasonableness of efforts* by plaintiff to obtain other employment; the sole issue is whether plaintiff's

---

[4] Although it would appear that plaintiff was not *discharged* by defendant in the customary sense of the term, as she was not permitted by defendant to enter upon performance of the "Bloomer Girl" contract, nevertheless the motion for summary judgment was submitted for decision upon a stipulation by the parties that "plaintiff Parker was discharged."

refusal of defendant's substitute offer of "Big Country" may be used in mitigation. Nor, if the "Big Country" offer was of employment different or inferior when compared with the original "Bloomer Girl" employment, is there an issue as to whether or not plaintiff acted reasonably in refusing the substitute offer. Despite defendant's arguments to the contrary, no case cited or which our research has discovered holds or suggests that reasonableness is an element of a wrongfully discharged employee's option to reject, or fail to seek, different or inferior employment lest the possible earnings therefrom be charged against him in mitigation of damages.[5]

Applying the foregoing rules to the record in the present case, with all intendments in favor of the party opposing the summary judgment motion— here, defendant—it is clear that the trial court correctly ruled that plaintiff's failure to accept defendant's tendered substitute employment could not be applied in mitigation of damages because the offer of the "Big Country" lead was of employment both different and inferior, and that no factual dispute was presented on that issue. The mere circumstance that "Bloomer Girl" was to be a musical review calling upon plaintiff's talents as a dancer as well as an actress, and was to be produced in the City of Los Angeles, whereas "Big Country" was a straight dramatic role in a "Western Type" story taking place in an opal mine in Australia, demonstrates the difference in kind between the two employments; the female lead as a dramatic actress in a western style motion picture can by no stretch of imagination be considered the equivalent of or substantially similar to the lead in a song-and-dance production.

Additionally, the substitute "Big Country" offer proposed to eliminate or impair the director and screenplay approvals accorded to plaintiff under the

---

[5] Instead, in each case the reasonableness referred to was that of the *efforts* of the employee to obtain other employment that was not different or inferior; his right to reject the latter was declared as an unqualified rule of law. Thus, Gonzales v. Internat. Assn. of Machinists, *supra*, 213 Cal.App.2d 817, 823–824, 29 Cal.Rptr. 190, 194, holds that the trial court correctly instructed the jury that plaintiff union member, a machinist, was required to make "such *efforts* as the average [member of his union] desiring employment would make at that particular time and place" (italics added); but, further, that the court *properly rejected* defendant's *offer of proof* of the *availability of other kinds of employment* at the same or higher pay than plaintiff usually received and all outside the jurisdiction of his union, as plaintiff could not be required to accept different employment or a nonunion job.

In Harris v. Nat. Union, etc., Cooks and Stewards, *supra*, 116 Cal.App.2d 739, 761, 254 P.2d 673, 676, the issues were stated to be, inter alia, whether comparable employment was open to each plaintiff employee, and if so whether each plaintiff made a *reasonable effort* to secure such employment. It was held that the trial court *properly sustained an objection to an offer to prove a custom of accepting a job in a lower rank* when work in the higher rank was not available, as "The duty of mitigation of damages . . . does not require the plaintiff 'to seek or to accept other employment of a different or inferior kind.' " (p. 764 [5]. 254 P.2d p. 676.)

. . . .

original "Bloomer Girl" contract (see fn. 2, *ante*), and thus constituted an offer of inferior employment. No expertise or judicial notice is required in order to hold that the deprivation or infringement of an employee's rights held under an original employment contract converts the available "other employment" relied upon by the employer to mitigate damages, into inferior employment which the employee need not seek or accept.

Statements found in affidavits submitted by defendant in opposition to plaintiff's summary judgment motion, to the effect that the "Big Country" offer was not of employment different from or inferior to that under the "Bloomer Girl" contract, merely repeat the allegations of defendant's answer to the complaint in this action, constitute only conclusionary assertions with respect to undisputed facts, and do not give rise to a triable factual issue so as to defeat the motion for summary judgment.

In view of the determination that defendant failed to present any facts showing the existence of a factual issue with respect to its sole defense— plaintiff's rejection of its substitute employment offer in mitigation of damages—we need not consider plaintiff's further contention that for various reasons, including the provisions of the original contract set forth in footnote 1, *ante*, plaintiff was excused from attempting to mitigate damages.

The judgment is affirmed.

SULLIVAN, Acting Chief Justice (dissenting).

The basic question in this case is whether or not plaintiff acted reasonably in rejecting defendant's offer of alternate employment. The answer depends upon whether that offer (starring in "Big Country, Big Man") was an offer of work that was substantially similar to her former employment (starring in "Bloomer Girl") or of work that was of a different or inferior kind. To my mind this is a factual issue which the trial court should not have determined on a motion for summary judgment. The majority have not only repeated this error but have compounded it by applying the rules governing mitigation of damages in the employer-employee context in a misleading fashion. Accordingly, I respectfully dissent.

The familiar rule requiring a plaintiff in a tort or contract action to mitigate damages embodies notions of fairness and socially responsible behavior which are fundamental to our jurisprudence. Most broadly stated, it precludes the recovery of damages which, through the exercise of due diligence, could have been avoided. Thus, in essence, it is a rule requiring reasonable conduct in commercial affairs. This general principle governs the obligations of an employee after his employer has wrongfully repudiated or terminated the employment contract. Rather than permitting the employee simply to remain idle during the balance of the contract period, the law requires him to make a reasonable effort to secure other employment.[1] He is not obliged, however, to seek or accept any and all types of work which may be available. Only work which is in the same field and which is of the same quality need be accepted.[2]

Over the years the courts have employed various phrases to define the type of employment which the employee, upon his wrongful discharge, is under an obligation to accept. Thus in California alone it has been held that he must accept employment which is "substantially similar"; "comparable employment"; (Erler v. Five Points Motors, Inc. (1967); employment "in the same general line of the first employment"; "equivalent to his prior position"; "employment in a similar capacity"; employment which is "not . . . of a different or inferior kind . . ."

For reasons which are unexplained, the majority cite several of these cases yet select from among the various judicial formulations which contain one particular phrase, "Not of a different or inferior kind," with which to analyze this case. I have discovered no historical or theoretical reason to adopt this phrase, which is simply a negative restatement of the affirmative standards set out in the above cases, as the exclusive standard. Indeed, its emergence is an example of the dubious phenomenon of the law responding not to rational judicial choice or changing social conditions, but to unrecognized changes in the language of opinions or legal treatises. However, the phrase is a serviceable one and my concern is not with its use as the standard but rather with what I consider its distortion.

The relevant language excuses acceptance only of employment which is of a *different kind*. It has never been the law that the mere existence of *differences between two jobs in the same field* is sufficient, as a matter of law, to excuse an employee wrongfully discharged from one from accepting the other in order to mitigate damages. Such an approach would effectively eliminate any obligation of an employee to attempt to minimize damage arising from a wrongful

---

[1] The issue is generally discussed in terms of a duty on the part of the employee to minimize loss. The practice is long-established and there is little reason to change despite Judge Cardozo's observation of its subtle inaccuracy. "The servant is free to accept employment or reject it according to his uncensored pleasure. What is meant by the supposed duty is merely this: That if he unreasonably reject, he will not be heard to say that the loss of wages from then on shall be deemed the jural consequence of the earlier discharge. He has broken the chain of causation, and loss resulting to him thereafter is suffered through his own act." (McClelland v. Climax Hosiery Mills (1930) 252 N.Y. 347, 359, 169 N.E. 605, 609, concurring opinion.)

[2] This qualification of the rule seems to reflect the simple and humane attitude that it is too severe to demand of a person that he attempt to find and perform work for which he has no training or experience. Many of the older cases hold that one need not accept work in an inferior rank or position nor work which is more menial or arduous. This suggests that the rule may have had its origin in the bourgeois fear of resubmergence in lower economic classes.

discharge. The only alternative job offer an employee would be required to accept would be an offer of his former job by his former employer.

Although the majority appear to hold that there was a difference "in kind" between the employment offered plaintiff in "Bloomer Girl" and that offered in "Big Country", an examination of the opinion makes crystal clear that the majority merely point out differences between the two *films* (an obvious circumstance) and then apodically assert that these constitute a difference in the *kind* of *employment*. The entire rationale of the majority boils down to this: that the *"mere circumstances"* that "Bloomer Girl" was to be a musical review while "Big Country" was a straight drama "demonstrates the difference in kind" since a female lead in a western is not "the equivalent of or substantially similar to" a lead in a musical. This is merely attempting to prove the proposition by repeating it. It shows that the vehicles for the display of the star's talents are different but it does not prove that her employment as a star in such vehicles is of necessity different *in kind* and either inferior or superior.

I believe that the approach taken by the majority (a superficial listing of differences with no attempt to assess their significance) may subvert a valuable legal doctrine. The inquiry in cases such as this should not be whether differences between the two jobs exist (there will always be differences) but whether the differences which are present are substantial enough to constitute differences in the *kind* of employment or, alternatively, whether they render the substitute work employment of an *inferior kind*.

It seems to me that *this* inquiry involves, in the instant case at least, factual determinations which are improper on a motion for summary judgment. Resolving whether or not one job is substantially similar to another or whether, on the other hand, it is of a different or inferior kind, will often (as here) require a critical appraisal of the similarities and differences between them in light of the importance of these differences to the employee. This necessitates a weighing of the evidence, and it is precisely this undertaking which is forbidden on summary judgment.

This is not to say that summary judgment would never be available in an action by an employee in which the employer raises the defense of failure to mitigate damages. No case has come to my attention, however, in which summary judgment has been granted on the issue of whether an employee was obliged to accept available alternate employment. Nevertheless, there may well be cases in which the substitute employment is so manifestly of a dissimilar or inferior sort, the declarations of the plaintiff so complete and those of the defendant so conclusionary and inadequate that no factual issues exist for which a trial is required. This, however, is not such a case.

It is not intuitively obvious, to me at least, that the leading female role in a dramatic motion picture is a radically different endeavor from the leading female role in a musical comedy film. Nor is it plain to me that the rather qualified rights of director and screenplay approval contained in the first contract are highly significant matters either in the entertainment industry in general or to this plaintiff in particular. Certainly, none of the declarations introduced by plaintiff in support of her motion shed any light on these issues. Nor do they attempt to explain why she declined the offer of starring in "Big Country, Big Man." Nevertheless, the trial court granted the motion, declaring that these approval rights were "critical" and that their elimination altered "the essential nature of the employment."

The plaintiff's declarations were of no assistance to the trial court in its effort to justify reaching this conclusion on summary judgment. Instead, it was forced to rely on judicial notice of the definitions of "motion picture," "screenplay" and "director" (Evid.Code, § 451, subd. (e)) and then on judicial notice of practices in the film industry which were purportedly of "common knowledge." (Evid.Code, § 451, subd. (f) or § 452, subd. (g).) This use of judicial notice was error. Evidence Code section 451, subdivision (e) was never intended to authorize resort to the dictionary to solve essentially factual questions which do not turn upon conventional linguistic usage. More important, however, the trial court's notice of "facts commonly known" violated Evidence Code section 455, subdivision (a).[7] Before this section was enacted there were no procedural safeguards affording litigants an opportunity to be heard as to the propriety of taking judicial notice of a matter or as to the tenor of the matter to be noticed. Section 455 makes such an opportunity . . . mandatory and its provisions should be scrupulously adhered to. "Judicial notice can be a valuable tool in the adversary system for the lawyer as well as the court" (Kongsgaard, Judicial Notice (1966) 18 Hastings L.J. 117, 140) and its use is appropriate on motions for summary judgment. Its use in this case, however, to determine on summary judgment issues fundamental to the litigation without complying with statutory requirements of notice and hearing is a highly improper effort to "cut the Gordion knot of involved litigation." (Silver Land & Dev. Co. v. California Land Title Co. (1967) 248 Cal.App.2d 241, 242, 56 Cal.Rptr. 178, 179.)

The majority do not confront the trial court's misuse of judicial notice. They avoid this issue through the expedient of declaring that neither judicial

---

[7] Evidence Code section 455 provides in relevant part: "With respect to any matter specified in Section 452 or in subdivision (f) of Section 451 that is of substantial consequence to the determination of the action: (a) If the trial court has been requested to take or has taken or proposes to take judicial notice of such matter, the court shall afford each party reasonable opportunity, before the jury is instructed or before the cause is submitted for decision by the court, to present to the court information relevant to (1) the propriety of taking judicial notice of the matter and (2) the tenor of the matter to be noticed."

notice nor expert opinion (such as that contained in the declarations in opposition to the motion) is necessary to reach the trial court's conclusion. *Something*, however, clearly *is* needed to support this conclusion. Nevertheless, the majority make no effort to justify the judgment through an examination of the plaintiff's declarations. Ignoring the obvious insufficiency of these declarations, the majority announce that "the deprivation or infringement of an employee's rights held under an original employment contract" changes the alternate employment offered or available into employment of an inferior kind.

I cannot accept the proposition that an offer which eliminates *any* contract right, regardless of its significance, is, as a matter of law, an offer of employment of an inferior kind. Such an absolute rule seems no more sensible than the majority's earlier suggestion that the mere existence of differences between two jobs is sufficient to render them employment of different kinds. Application of such per se rules will severely undermine the principle of mitigation of damages in the employer-employee context.

I remain convinced that the relevant question in such cases is whether or not a particular contract provision is so significant that its omission create employment of an inferior kind. This question is, of course, intimately bound up in what I consider the ultimate issue: whether or not the employee acted reasonably. This will generally involve a factual inquiry to ascertain the importance of the particular contract term and a process of weighing the absence of that term against the countervailing advantages of the alternate employment. In the typical case, this will mean that summary judgment must be withheld.

In the instant case, there was nothing properly before the trial court by which the importance of the approval rights could be ascertained, much less evaluated. Thus, in order to grant the motion for summary judgment, the trial court misused judicial notice. In upholding the summary judgment, the majority here rely upon per se rules which distort the process of determining whether or not an employee is obliged to accept particular employment in mitigation of damages.

I believe that the judgment should be reversed so that the issue of whether or not the offer of the lead role in "Big Country, Big Man" was of employment comparable to that of the lead role in "Bloomer Girl" may be determined at trial.

"ARBITRATOR GIVES PETER HUNT 134G IN MERRICK CASE"
Variety (April 16, 1980), p. 3

Hollywood, April 15.

Peter Hunt has been awarded $134,000 in an arbitration with producer David Merrick, who hired and fired him in a week during last year's director shuffle on "Rough Cut."

Ruling on a quarrel brought by the Directors Guild of America against Merrick and Paramount, arbitrator Dixon Q. Dern assigned Hunt the full $150,000 he was promised for taking over the reins from director Don Siegel, less $10,000 already paid Hunt and $6,000 earned on other projects he couldn't have handled were he not fired from "Cut."

Case stems from Merrick's initial displeasure with Siegel, whom he wanted to fire but feared the reaction thereto of Burt Reynolds. Before firing Siegel, Merrick had some initial meetings with Hunt in London and had a long-distance telephone conversation with Hunt's agent, Martin Shapiro, about money and credits.

Dern noted, "Merrick made it clear in that conversation that he could not make a firm commitment for Hunt's services at that time because of his concern as to how Reynolds, the star of the picture, would react were the director of his choice, namely Don Siegel, to be removed from the motion picture."

But at some point right about that time, Dern held, it was agreed that, if hired, Hunt would receive $150,000 to be paid in 10 weekly installments of $10,000 each and the final $50,000 with the director's cut, plus points. Shapiro subsequently sent Merrick two telegrams pinning down the terms and in each referred to the deal as "pay or play."

Merrick's Rationale

On Aug. 11, Siegel was fired and Hunt was hired, reporting to work in London two days later. The following Friday, Hunt was fired and told that Siegel was being rehired. Merrick subsequently paid Hunt $10,000 for the week's work, contending he was only hired on a week-to-week basis.

"I find," Dern held, "that Shapiro's proposal to Merrick for Hunt's services contemplated that Hunt would direct the picture for the period required to complete it, that week-to-week employment was not discussed or negotiated between the parties, that when Merrick 'firmed up' Hunt's engagement he did not condition engagement upon any interpretation of the DGA Agreement relative to week-to-week employment and that, in fact, this issue was not raised until after Hunt had commenced services."

In addition to the $134,000 Merrick was ordered to pay $13,680 to DGA pension and welfare funds and held Par responsible if Merrick failed to pay the amounts.

WOOD v. LUCY, LADY DUFF-GORDON
222 N.Y. 88 (1917)

CARDOZO, J. The defendant styles herself "a creator of fashions." Her favor helps a sale. Manufacturers of dresses, millinery and like articles are glad to pay for a certificate of her approval. The things which she designs, fabrics, parasols and what not, have a new value in the public mind when issued in her name. She employed the plaintiff to help her to turn this vogue into money. He was to have the exclusive right, subject always to her approval, to place her indorsements on the designs of others. He was also to have the exclusive right to place her own designs on sale, or to license others to market them. In return, she was to have one-half of "all profits and revenues" derived from any contracts he might make. The exclusive right was to last at least one year from April 1, 1915, and thereafter from year to year unless terminated by notice of ninety days. The plaintiff says that he kept the contract on his part, and that the defendant broke it. She placed her indorsement on fabrics, dresses and millinery without his knowledge, and withheld the profits. He sues her for the damages, and the case comes here on demurrer.

The agreement of employment is signed by both parties. It has a wealth of recitals. The defendant insists, however, that it lacks the elements of a contract. She says that the plaintiff does not bind himself to anything. It is true that he does not promise in so many words that he will use reasonable efforts to place the defendant's indorsements and market her designs. We think, however, that such a promise is fairly to be implied. The law has outgrown its primitive stage of formalism when the precise word was the sovereign talisman, and every slip was fatal. It takes a broader view to-day. A promise may be lacking, and yet the whole writing may be "instinct with an obligation," imperfectly expressed (SCOTT, J., in *McCall Co.* v. *Wright*, 133 App. Div. 62; *Moran* v. *Standard Oil Co.*, 211 N. Y. 187, 198). If that is so, there is a contract.

The implication of a promise here finds support in many circumstances. The defendant gave an *exclusive* privilege. She was to have no right for at least a year to place her own indorsements or market her own designs except through the agency of the plaintiff. The acceptance of the exclusive agency was an assumption of its duties. We are not to suppose that one party was to be placed at the mercy of the other. Many other terms of the agreement point the same way. We are told at the outset by way of recital that "the said Otis F. Wood possesses a business organization adapted to the placing of such indorsements as the said Lucy, Lady Duff-Gordon has approved." The implication is that the plaintiff's business organization will be used for the purpose for which it is adapted. But the terms of the defendant's compensation are even more significant. Her sole compensation for the grant of an exclusive agency is to be one-half of all the profits resulting from the plaintiff's efforts. Unless he gave his efforts, she could never get anything. Without an implied promise, the transaction cannot have such business "efficacy as both parties must have intended that at all events it should have." But the contract does not stop there. The plaintiff goes on to promise that he will account monthly for all moneys received by him, and that he will take out all such patents and copyrights and trademarks as may in his judgment be necessary to protect the rights and articles affected by the agreement. It is true, of course, as the Appellate Division has said, that if he was under no duty to try to market designs or to place certificates of indorsement, his promise to account for profits or take out copyrights would be valueless. But in determining the intention of the parties, the promise *has* a value. It helps to enforce the conclusion that the plaintiff *had* some duties. His promise to pay the defendant one-half of the profits and revenues resulting from the exclusive agency and to render accounts monthly, was a promise to use reasonable efforts to bring profits and revenues into existence. For this conclusion, the authorities are ample.

The judgment of the Appellate Division should be reversed, and the order of the Special Term affirmed, with costs in the Appellate Division and in this court.

CUDDEBACK, McLAUGHLIN and ANDREWS, JJ., concur; HISCOCK, Ch. J., CHASE and CRANE, JJ., dissent.

Judgment reversed, etc.

DODD, MEAD & COMPANY, INC. v. LILIENTHAL
514 F. Supp. 105 (S.D.N.Y. 1981)

KEVIN THOMAS DUFFY, District Judge:

This is a motion and cross-motion for summary judgment brought by the parties pursuant to Rule 56 of Fed.R.Civ.P. The pertinent facts are undisputed.

Defendant Alfred M. Lilienthal ["Lilienthal"] is the author of a literary work entitled *The Zionist Connection*. On October 10, 1977, Lilienthal contracted with a publisher, Dodd Mead Co., Inc. ["Dodd Mead"], for the publication of his book. By means of this agreement, Lilienthal granted to Dodd Mead "the exclusive right of printing, publishing and selling in book form [*The Zionist Connection*] in the United States of America and its dependencies, also Canada and the Philippine Islands during the full term of copyright and all renewals thereof. . . . " Lilienthal also agreed that he would not, "without the consent of [Dodd Mead,] publish any abridged or other editions of the work or any book of similar or competing character."

Thereafter, Dodd Mead obtained a copyright registration in the name of Alfred M. Lilienthal, c/o Middle East Perspective, Inc. The certificate of copyright registration listed Dodd Mead as the registered agent of the author.

Dodd Mead printed and distributed 14,500 copies of the book between December 11, 1978 and October 10, 1979, and in addition Dodd Mead spent more than $66,000 in manufacturing and promoting the book. The work is currently listed in Dodd Mead's catalogues as well as in *Books In Print*.

In 1979, Lilienthal became dissatisfied with Dodd Mead's publication and marketing efforts. He learned that the book could not be found in many bookstores and that Dodd Mead had stated they would not print any additional books. As a result, he instituted an action upon the contract in New York State Supreme Court in September, 1979, claiming that Dodd Mead had failed to perform adequately under the contract. That action is still pending.

In December, 1979, defendants Lilienthal and Middle East Perspective, Inc. ["MEP"] published an edition of *The Zionist Connection* ["MEP edition"]. The only substantial difference in this edition from the Dodd Mead edition are the deletion of the name of Dodd Mead as publisher and the insertion of Middle East Perspective, Inc. in its place. There is no doubt that the two publications are otherwise identical.

Dodd Mead brought this federal action for damages and injunctive relief based on defendants' alleged piracy of their copyrighted work. In a decision dated July 14, 1980, I granted plaintiff's motion for a preliminary injunction restraining defendants from selling or printing copies of the MEP edition. *See* 495 F.Supp. 135 (S.D.N.Y. 1980). Plaintiff now moves for summary judgment to obtain a permanent injunction and to receive damages.

The issue of whether this court has subject matter jurisdiction to decide plaintiff's claim for copyright infringement has already been decided in the affirmative. *See* 495 F.Supp. at 137. An enforceable copyright in a literary work vests initially in the author or authors of the work. 17 U.S.C. § 201(a). "Any of the exclusive rights comprised in a copyright," however, "may be transferred in whole or in part by any means of conveyance." 17 U.S.C. § 201(d). The owner of such a right may "institute an action for any infringement of that particular right while he or she is the owner of it." 17

U.S.C. § 501(b). In this case, by contract between the parties, Dodd Mead is the owner of the exclusive right to print, publish and sell the work. Therefore, Dodd Mead, the owner of the exclusive right, is entitled to the protections and remedies of the Copyright Act.

The possible breach of contract by Dodd Mead does not necessarily affect its rights of exclusive publication. The defendants' state court action seeking damages for breach of contract acts to affirm the assignment of publication rights rather than avoid it. *See Sylvania Industrial Corp. v. Lilienfeld's Estate*, 132 F.2d 887, 893 (4th Cir. 1943). Thus, this court has jurisdiction to determine whether Lilienthal infringed the exclusive publication rights which had been assigned to Dodd Mead.

Defendants make three principal arguments in opposition to plaintiff's summary judgment motion and in support of their cross-motion for summary judgment. First, defendants argue that according to the terms of the contract between the parties, plaintiff retained the right to buy books at a substantial discount from the publisher and to re-sell them without restriction. When the plaintiff allegedly breached this term of the contract by refusing to print further copies of the book, they were entitled, defendants assert, to "cover" by printing up their own copies. Second, defendants argue that Dodd Mead abandoned the copyright and therefore cannot enforce it. Finally, defendants assert that Lilienthal's first amendment right to disseminate his work to the public precludes Dodd Mead's claim for copyright infringement. For the reasons that follow, these arguments are unavailing.

Defendants contend that a letter signed by S. Phelps Platt, Jr., president of Dodd Mead, six days before the parties entered into the publishing agreement, sets forth the essential terms of the parties' agreement which Dodd Mead supposedly breached. This letter states that Lilienthal agreed to purchase an initial order of not less than 3,000 copies of the first printing at 47 percent off the published retail price. In addition, Dodd Mead agreed that Lilienthal would have the continuing right to purchase books at the same discount on orders of 1,000 or more, and to purchase smaller quantities at a lower discount. Lilienthal asserts that the letter contained no restrictions on resale of the books and that, in fact, Dodd Mead encouraged Lilienthal to go out and sell the book. Finally, Lilienthal claims that Dodd Mead's letter expressed the publisher's continuing obligation to promote the book to "the maximum extent." [Lilienthal Affidavit ¶ 16, p.9].

An important issue raised by this argument is whether the October 4 letter is in any way incorporated into the October 10, 1977 agreement between the parties. This issue, which must be resolved under New York law, need not be disposed of here because even if the letter did constitute the agreement between the parties, Dodd Mead's actions in alleged breach of the agreement did not justify Lilienthal's publication of the book.

Lilienthal argues that Dodd Mead failed to adequately promote the book and to adequately distribute copies to bookstores around the country. Starting in the spring of 1979, Lilienthal began receiving letters from the public indicating that his book was not available in bookstores. Then, Lilienthal learned from his previous publisher that Dodd Mead did not intend to re-print the book. When Lilienthal requested an explanation by Dodd Mead, Dodd Mead stated in a letter dated September 18, 1979 that they did not intend to print more than the 12,500 copies of the book already printed until Lilienthal paid a $42,359.77 debt owed to Dodd Mead. Lilienthal then replied by letter to Dodd Mead stating that he had paid approximately this amount into an escrow account pending his accountant's analysis of the debt.

In October, 1979, Dodd Mead printed an additional 2,000 copies of the book. Lilienthal claims to have had no knowledge of this printing, at least until after October 23, 1979 when Lilienthal signed a contract with another printer to print approximately 2,000 copies of the book.

It is Lilienthal's contention that when Dodd Mead failed to publish the book at his request, he had the right to "cover" by substituting books printed at his own expense under the New York Uniform Commercial Code § 2–712. Lilienthal, however, has failed to demonstrate any breach of the contract by Dodd Mead which triggered a right to cover. There is no indication that Dodd Mead failed to meet specific orders for books made by Lilienthal in accordance with the October 4 letter. Lilienthal's major grievance is that Dodd Mead was not printing enough books to keep up with the public's demand. If proven, this may or may not have constituted a breach of contract. Such a determination, however, will have to be made in the state court action. In any case, Dodd Mead's alleged failure to meet the public demand did not permit Lilienthal to publish his own copies in contravention of the contract between the parties. Lilienthal's obvious remedy under these circumstances was to follow the terms of the contract which at paragraph 17 provided:

> If at any time during the continuance of this Agreement the work shall be out of print for six months in all editions, including reprints, whether under the imprint of the Publishers or another imprint, and if, after written notification from the Author, the Publishers shall fail to place the work in print within six months from the date of receipt of such notification, then this Agreement will terminate and all of the rights granted to the Publishers here under shall revert to the Author. The Author shall have the right for thirty days after such termination to purchase from the Publishers all copies or sheets (if any) remaining at the cost of manufacture and the plates and engravings of illustrations (if in

existence) at one-half their cost to the Publishers, including composition, all f.o.b. point of shipment.

Unfortunately, the record before me does not show that Lilienthal pursued this avenue. He cannot be permitted now to sue for damages on the contract and, at the same time, to breach the contract egregiously by printing his own copies.

Defendants' argument that Dodd Mead abandoned its exclusive right under the copyright is also without merit. In order for the holder of a copyright to abandon his rights thereunder, he must perform some overt act which manifests an intent to surrender rights in the copyrighted material. *Lottie Joplin Thomas Trust v. Crown Publishers, Inc.*, 456 F.Supp. 531, 535 (S.D.N.Y.1977), *aff'd*, 592 F.2d 651 (2d Cir. 1978); *National Comics Publications, Inc. v. Fawcett Publications, Inc.*, 191 F.2d 594, 598 (2d Cir. 1951); *see 3 Nimmer on Copyrights* § 13.06 (1978). Mere inaction or negative behavior will not suffice. *See Rohauer v. Killiam Shows, Inc.*, 379 F.Supp. 723, 730 (S.D.N.Y.1974), *rev'd on other grounds*, 551 F.2d 484 (2d Cir.), *cert. denied*, 431 U.S. 949, 97 S.Ct. 2666, 53 L.Ed.2d 266 (1977); *Marvin Worth Productions v. Superior Films Corp.*, 319 F.Supp. 1269, 1273 (S.D.N.Y.1970).

Here, Dodd Mead never abandoned the copyright in Lilienthal's work. Between December, 1978 and October, 1979, Dodd Mead printed 14,500 copies and spent more than $66,500 on its manufacturing and marketing. There is absolutely no evidence to suggest Dodd Mead intended to give up its exclusive rights in the book.

Finally, Lilienthal submits that his freedom of expression is being abridged, in violation of the first amendment, by Dodd Mead's enforcement of the copyright. The evidence proffered by Lilienthal, however, does not support this claim. There is no indication that he has been prevented from expressing his opinions. Ideas and opinions are not subject to copyright even though the specific form of expression may be. *Sid & Marty Krofft Television Productions, Inc. v. McDonald's Corp.*, 562 F.2d 1157, 1170 (9th Cir. 1977). Here, it is not Lilienthal's expression of a particular viewpoint to which Dodd Mead objects. Rather, the act complained of is the unauthorized reproduction and sale of a written work which Dodd Mead has acquired exclusive rights to distribute. There is no first amendment right on the part of Lilienthal to so egregiously breach an exclusive publication contract which he freely entered into.

Plaintiff's motion for summary judgment is therefore granted, and defendants' cross-motion for summary judgment is denied. The defendants are hereby permanently enjoined from publishing, selling, marketing or otherwise disposing of any copies of the book entitled *The Zionist Connection*. The case is referred to Magistrate Bernikow for an inquest to determine damages.

SO ORDERED.

VAN VALKENBURGH, NOOGER & NEVILLE INC. v. HAYDEN PUBLISHING CO., INC.

30 N.Y.2d 34, 330 N.Y.S.2d 329 , 281 N.E.2d 142 (1972)

BERGAN, Judge.

Plaintiff corporation is the copyright owner of a series of books on basic electricity, the publication of which is the subject of this litigation. Defendant Hayden Book Company, Inc. has merged with, and is the successor of, John F. Rider Publisher, Inc., which, under agreement with plaintiff, published the series. Defendant Hayden Publishing Company, Inc. is the owner of all the stock of the merged companies.

Although defendants are separate corporate entities, the court at Special Term found the parent company's officers and employees so controlled the actions of their subsidiaries in the present controversy that unitary liability to the plaintiff arising from the publication of the books could be imposed on both corporations. In this respect the Appellate Division affirmed the facts as found. It cannot be said as a matter of law on this record that if Hayden Book is liable the separate corporate entity of Hayden Publishing shields it from liability. For convenience, therefore, both defendants will here be called the "publisher" and the corporate plaintiff the "author".

Assuming facts most favorable to the author, consistently with the findings which have been affirmed by the Appellate Division, an agreement between the parties was entered into in November, 1954 for the publication of the electronics books. The publisher agreed to pay the author a royalty of 15% of the list price of books sold. The contract contained an undertaking by the publisher to use its "best efforts" in promotion of the books. Following upon execution of this agreement, a five-volume set entitled *Basic Electricity*, and a five-volume set entitled *Basic Electronics*, were published in 1954 and 1955; and in 1959 a sixth volume on transistors was added to *Basic Electronics*.

These publications were the publisher's best sellers and accounted for a substantial part of its income. In 1962 the author and publisher discussed a new and later edition of the author's works. The publisher asked a reduction in royalties if this were to be done. Financial discussions lasted about a year. It apparently became clear in the fall of 1963 that the author would not agree to a lower rate.

The publisher then hired Harry Mileaf and three other writers to prepare a new group of electronic books entitled *Electricity 1–7* and *Electronics 1–7*, the

"Mileaf" books. This effort was not disclosed to the author, but was "concealed", as plaintiff argues in this court. The Mileaf books utilized a very similar method of organizing, presenting and picturing the material. The agreements between the publisher and Mileaf and the other writers of the new group of books as to what they were to produce could well be regarded as an exact description of the author's existing books.

The publisher did not disclose to the author what it was doing, but when inquiry was made, on the basis of reports in the trade, the Mileaf enterprise was denied orally and in writing. The Mileaf books were published in 1966 and 1967. The publisher made efforts to sell them to customers who had been placing large orders for the author's books. The advertising for these books was very similar to that for the author's.

In 1967, when the publisher began to advertise Mileaf, the magazine advertisement of the author's works was suspended. There is a memorandum from the publisher's sales manager to its salesmen which notes that "a large portion of our time the past 8 weeks has been devoted to *ELECTRICITY 1–7* and *ELECTRONICS 1–7*". The Authors League of America, filing here a brief as *amicus*, makes this interesting commentary on the record: "The astounding pattern of Publisher's conduct, as disclosed and documented by the record, is probably without parallel in publishing history. Clearly it violates the 'best efforts' clause of the contract executed by the parties." The record on the whole seems to justify the factual finding that the publisher did not use its "best efforts" on the author's books after 1967.

On this record the court at Special Term, after a long trial, found the publisher occupied a fiduciary relationship to the author and that there had been a failure by the publisher to act in good faith in that relationship. Accordingly it found the author was entitled to a permanent injunction restraining the publisher from proceeding with the distribution and sale of the Mileaf books, and, indeed, ordered physical destruction of these books. The court directed an accounting to the author by the publisher of the profits of the Mileaf venture and a Referee's hearing for this purpose.

The Appellate Division, by a divided court, modified this decision in very material respects. It determined there was no fiduciary relationship between the parties but one of ordinary contract. It found there had been no breach by the publisher of the condition implicit in the contract to act in good faith; but that the publisher had breached its contractual undertaking to use its "best efforts" in promoting the author's books and hence was answerable in the money damages appropriate to a breach of contract.

Consistently with this, it reversed that part of the Special Term's order and judgment calling for a destruction of the Mileaf books and imposing a permanent injunction, and directed a hearing at the reference on the question of money damages allowing merely a temporary injunction until that question be determined. As to the "purely commercial" nature of the relationship and as to the absence of any fiduciary obligation of the publisher, the Appellate Division expressly reversed the factual findings made at Special Term and made new findings.

To decide this author-publisher controversy it is necessary to see just what the legal effect of the contract between them and the resulting relationships are, and especially what are the rights of a publisher as to the production of other works competing with the specific work of an author's.

There is implicit in all contracts—for book publishing or house building—an implied covenant of fair dealing and good faith. See, also, Kirke La Shelle Co. v. Armstrong Co., 263 N.Y. 79, p. 87, 188 N.E. 163, p. 167 where Judge Hubbs noted "in every contract there exists an implied covenant of good faith and fair dealing" . . .

It has already been observed that in this contract there was an undertaking by the publisher to use its "best efforts" to promote the author's works. Such a contract does not close off the right of a publisher to issue books on the same subject, to negotiate with and pay authors to write such books and to promote them fully according to the publisher's economic interests, even though those later publications adversely affect the contracting author's sales. This general freedom of publishing competition within the same house is demonstrated by the appellant publisher here and it is strongly argued by the Association of American Publishers, Inc. in its brief as *amicus*.

By analogizing the Federal cases growing out of patent and copyright licensing agreements which are governed by parallel principles, it will be observed that licensees are not deemed to limit themselves in their usual business enterprise to the promotion of the licensor's product, absent specific agreement to this effect; and an agreement to use due diligence or best efforts does not alone limit their activity to the licensor's interests.

This was noted by Justice Holmes in Eclipse Bicycle Co. v. Farrow, 199 U.S. 581, 26 S.Ct. 150, 50 L.Ed. 317, involving a coaster brake patent license owned by one Farrow. It was observed that the licensee's covenant "to use due business diligence in pushing their sale, did not preclude it from using any later invention, if one were made which superseded Farrow's and did not embody it" (p. 589, 26 S.Ct. p. 153).

Thus, too, in Thorn Wire Co. v. Washburn & Moen Co., 159 U.S. 423, 16 S.Ct. 94, 40 L.Ed. 205, it was held that an agreement of a licensee to "use reasonable and diligent efforts" to promote the barbed wire product did not impose an obligation not to sell barbed wire products under competitive patents (p. 449, 16 S.Ct. 94). Such a covenant cannot be "implied from the language used" (p. 450, 16 S.Ct. 94) . . .

But this general freedom of action of the publisher to produce competing works is not necessarily the answer to this litigation. Although a publisher has a general right to act on its own interests in a way that may incidentally lessen an author's royalties, there may be a point where that activity is so manifestly harmful to the author, and must have been seen by the publisher so to be harmful, as to justify the court in saying there was a breach of the covenant to promote the author's work.

This, of course, is essentially a fact value question and here the Appellate Division has found that there was a narrow breach in the failure of the publisher to use its best efforts. It did not find a breach of the implied condition of fair dealing. The Appellate Division specifically found that money damages resulting from the breach of this specific undertaking by the publisher in promotion of the author's work would afford "adequate relief".

There are cross appeals on certified questions . . . It seems clear that such an appeal brings up only questions of law and this is what the orders of the Appellate Division allowing the appeals expressly state. Thus the only issue that may be considered in this form of appeal is whether it could be found, as a matter of law, on the record that there was no fiduciary relationship; that there was a breach of a specific undertaking of the contract; and that money damages were a sufficient measure for the breach . . . Not any of those questions requires reversal here as a matter of law.

The argument of the publisher in this court that there was no damage cannot be determined from this record as a question of law. The publisher has compiled financial results from the record seeking to show the author's royalties and the sales of its books were about the same after, as before, the Mileaf publication began.

The publisher also contends that in the 18 months before the Mileaf publication began the total sales of the author's books were $435,000 and in a similar period after such publication for which there is evidence, the total sales were $433,600, and the total sales of both the author's and Mileaf books $615,200. Whether there was, in fact, damage to the author from the Mileaf publication will be decided at the reference.

If the action has been properly held to be one merely for breach of contract for which money damages afford a sufficient remedy, an injunction, even temporarily for the limited time fixed by the Appellate Division until the damages, if any, are determined, would normally be inappropriate absent some showing of imminent risk of frustration of a resulting judgment, such as insolvency or siphoning off of assets. But if the hearing on damages is conducted expeditiously, the court declines to interfere as a matter of law in this respect with the discretion of the Appellate Division.

The order of the Appellate Division should be affirmed, with costs to abide the event.

FULD, Chief Judge (dissenting in part).

I agree with Justice McNally, dissenting below, that the plaintiff is entitled not only to recover damages but also to a permanent injunction against continuance of the defendant publisher's wrong.

There was a continuing obligation on the publisher's part to use its "best efforts" to promote the object of the agreement between the parties, that is, to create a market for the plaintiff's books and to supply that market with its books. The defendant not only failed to use its best efforts but purposefully channeled those efforts into another and competing source that was more profitable for it. It created a market for its own books to the plaintiff's great detriment and to its own advantage. Whereas it paid the plaintiff a royalty of 15%, its obligations to the supplier of the new work entailed a payment of less than 3%. It also assumed the more favorable status of copyright owner of the new works, whereas the plaintiff was copyright owner of the original works. Both were intended for the same limited market; to the extent that one supplied that market, it necessarily replaced the other.

As a result of the defendant's deliberate undermining of the objectives of its agreement with the plaintiff, the only way to insure the plaintiff's unimpeded access to the market for its books and to prevent the defendant from taking advantage of its wrong—by replacing the plaintiff's books with its own—is by enjoining the further distribution of the defendant's books. Any resulting hardship to the defendant, directly or in its contractual relationship with third parties, has stemmed from the defendant's own wrongful conduct.

It is not necessary to decide whether or not the defendant's obligation to the plaintiff was a "fiduciary" one. It is sufficient that it was one which required a high degree of fair dealing which the defendant wholly and willfully disregarded for its own benefit. In my view, therefore, the trial court was entirely justified in concluding that damages, under the circumstances of this case, would be inadequate and that, as a consequence, injunctive relief was appropriate. Accordingly, I would modify the order appealed from to the extent of reversing so much thereof as denied injunctive relief.

. . . .

ZILG v. PRENTICE-HALL, INC.
717 F.2d 671 (2d Cir. 1983)*

WINTER, *Circuit Judge*:

Prentice-Hall, Inc. ("P-H") appeals from a judgment entered after a bench trial before Judge Brieant ordering it to pay damages of $24,250 plus prejudgment interest to the plaintiff, Gerard Colby Zilg, for breach of contract. Zilg cross-appeals the judgment in favor of E. I. DuPont de Nemours & Co., Inc. ("DuPont Company") on his claim of tortious interference with contract. We reverse as to Zilg's breach of contract claim against P-H and affirm the judgment in favor of the DuPont Company.

BACKGROUND

Gerard Colby Zilg is the author of *Dupont: Behind the Nylon Curtain*, an historical account of the role of the DuPont family in American social, political and economic affairs. Early in 1972, after one partially successful and several unsuccessful efforts to find a publisher for his proposed book, Zilg's agent introduced him to Bram Cavin, a senior editor in P-H's Trade Book Division. Cavin expressed interest in the book, and he and Zilg submitted a formal proposal to John Kirk, P-H's Editor-in-Chief at that time. Kirk approved the proposal, which described the future book as

> a thoroughly documented study of the major role the DuPont family has played in the development of modern America and its corporate and social institutions. After skimming lightly over the family's origins in France and its development of its gunpowder business up to and through the Civil War, the book will concentrate on the period after that conflict right down to the present day. The story—essentially one of money and power—is going to be told in human terms and in the lives of the members of the family and their actions. The family will be looked upon as a unit in its relations to the outside world. But it will also be shown to be, as many families frequently are, one torn by feuds and struggles over the money and the power.

As it passed through the editorial and corporate hierarchy, the proposal received a notation from P-H's publicity director that the book's potential for radio and television coverage was "slight to non-existent unless matter in [the] book is highly controversial and print [media] says so first."

P-H and Zilg executed a form contract which provided in relevant part:

> 3. The manuscript . . . will be delivered . . . by the AUTHOR to the

---

* The United States Supreme Court has subsequently rejected plaintiff's position, thereby affirming the decision below.

PUBLISHER in final form and content acceptable to the PUBLISHER.
. . .

4. When the manuscript has been accepted and approved for publication by the PUBLISHER . . . it will be published at the PUBLISHER'S own expense. . . .

12. The PUBLISHER shall have the right: (1) to publish the work in such style as it deems best suited to the sale of the work; (2) to fix or alter the prices at which the work shall be sold; (3) to determine the method and means of advertising, publicizing, and selling the work, the number and destination of free copies, and all other publishing details, including the number of copies to be printed, if from plates or type or by other process, date of publishing, form, style, size, type, paper to be used, and like details.

Zilg submitted the first half of his completed manuscript to Cavin in November, 1972, and the remainder a year later. Cavin authorized acceptance of the work on behalf of P-H, apparently without the participation of Peter Grenquist, who had become president of P-H's Trade Book Division sometime after execution of the contract but before submission of the manuscript. P-H's legal division scrutinized the manuscript for libelous content and concluded that, if a libel action were brought, P-H "would ultimately prevail" because the subject matter of the work was constitutionally privileged and the plaintiffs would have to prove actual malice. The division's opinion noted, however, that litigation against the DuPonts would be very costly.

A decision was made to accept the manuscript which was distributed to selected wholesalers, reviewers, and booksellers. Copies were also sent to the editorial director of the Book of the Month Club ("BOMC"). Although BOMC decided not to offer the book as a selection of its main club, a subsidiary, the Fortune Book Club, which appealed to a readership composed largely of business executives, did choose it as a selection.

A committee of various P-H department representatives, including the book's editor, met on March 28, 1974 to discuss production plans. The sales estimates of committee members varied from 12 to 15 thousand copies for the first year although by May two members were predicting sales of only 10 thousand. Estimates of from 15 to 20 thousand sales over a five year period were also made. Cavin, an ardent supporter of the book, made estimates of 20 to 25 thousand in the first year and 25 to 35 thousand over five years. The committee decided on a first printing of 15,000 copies at a retail price of $12.95 per copy. At a later meeting, the committee decided to devote roughly $15,000 to advertising.

Although the literary or scholarly merits of the book are not our concern, its nature, tone and marketability among various audiences are key facts in this litigation, for they bear upon the book's prospects for commercial success and illuminate the negative reactions which later set in at P-H. The book is a harshly critical portrait of the DuPont family and their role in American social, political and economic history. Indeed, it is a harshly critical portrait of that history itself. The reactions of readers and reviewers in the record indicate that the book is polarizing, the difference in viewpoint depending in no small measure upon the politics of the beholder. A significant number of readers regard the book as a strident caricature, drawing every conceivable inference against the DuPont family and firms with which members of the family were or are associated. One judge at BOMC, for example, described it as "300,000 words of pure spite." On the other hand, the book has a loyal band of admirers. It received a favorable review in many newspapers, including the *New York Times* Book Review section. Its comprehensiveness and the extensive research on which it was based were frequently noted. The book also has some appeal to another audience, namely readers with a taste for gossip about the rich and powerful, particularly readers in Delaware. Indeed, it was once first in non-fiction sales in that state.

In the American market, the book's appeal is somewhat limited by the fact that it is not a work critical of business on grounds that reform of capitalism is necessary in order to save it, a viewpoint with mainstream appeal. Rather, it presents a Marxist view of history. Also weighing against its overall marketability were its size (586 pages of text, 2 inches thick, three and one-half pounds), complexity (almost 200 family members with the surname DuPont and 170 years of American history) and price ($12.95 in 1974 dollars).

Prior to June, 1974, Grenquist appears not to have been aware of the nature and tone of the book, of the intensity of negative feeling it might arouse in some readers or of evidence of serious inaccuracies. He may have been reassured partly by Cavin's enthusiasm and partly by the book's selection by the Fortune Book Club. That selection itself remains something of a mystery since the Club's inside reader concluded it was "a bad book, politically crude and cheaply journalistic." However, instead of accepting his recommendation that it "be fed back to the author page by page," BOMC contracted with P-H to have it adopted by the Fortune Book Club.

In June, 1974, a chain of events was set in motion which apprised Grenquist of the negative aspects of Zilg's work. A member of the DuPont family obtained an advance copy of the manuscript from a bookseller and, predictably outraged, turned it over to the Public Affairs Department of the DuPont Company. Members of that department sought to locate individuals in P-H's management whom they knew personally in order to speak privately about the book, but to no avail. They advised the family member to do nothing before the book was published.

In July, the DuPont Company learned that the book had been accepted as a Fortune Book Club selection and decided to act before publication anyway. Harold Brown of DuPont ("DuPont-Brown") telephoned Vilma Bergane, a manager of Fortune Book Club, having received her name from the managing editor of *Fortune Magazine*. He told her that the book had been read by several persons, some of whom were attorneys, and that the book was "scurrilous" and "actionable." Bergane passed on a version of DuPont-Brown's remarks to F. Harry Brown, Editor-in-Chief of BOMC ("BOMC-Brown"). DuPont-Brown then told BOMC-Brown that DuPont family attorneys found the book abusive and that he was to try to locate someone at P-H with whom to discuss the book. He also told BOMC-Brown that the DuPont Company did not intend to throw its weight around. BOMC-Brown referred DuPont-Brown to Peter Grenquist at P-H.

Some days later, apparently in an effort to quash rumors or inaccurate messages to the contrary, DuPont-Brown phoned Grenquist to assure him that DuPont was not attempting to block publication of the book, initiate litigation, or even approach P-H in any kind of adversarial posture. One such rumor, allegedly passed on to Cavin by an editor at BOMC who does not remember the conversation, was that DuPont had gone to *Fortune Magazine* and threatened to pull all its advertising. *Fortune*, owned by Time, Inc., had no connection with the Fortune Book Club at this time.

Meanwhile, BOMC-Brown decided to look into the matter personally. Over the July 27-28 weekend, he "spent a horrible two days reading" the book and decided it was an unsuitable selection for the Fortune Book Club. He later stated he felt no pressure from the DuPont Company in reaching this decision. In view of the nature of the book and the Club's audience of business executives, his decision seems an inevitable result of his reading the book. BOMC immediately notified P-H of its decision not to distribute the book. The reason given was BOMC's belief that the book was malicious and had an objectionable tone.

P-H's own detailed examination of the manuscript may also have introduced or heightened skepticism on Grenquist's part. A toning down was found to be necessary even after the book was in page proof. Mistakes of fact, such as a statement that Irving S. Shapiro (DuPont's Chief Executive Officer) had served as an Assistant District Attorney in Queens County, New York, were discovered. More serious matters also came to light. The original manuscript attacked Judge Harold R. Medina for matters irrelevant to the DuPonts and in a fashion which the district court characterized as libelous. Zilg admitted at trial that there was no factual foundation for this attack. Some eyebrows at P-H may well have been raised when this passage was discovered and deleted, since it was not only unfounded but also irrelevant.

P-H continued to correct and tone down the book, hoping to reverse BOMC's decision not to offer it through the Fortune Book Club. A certain defensiveness also began to creep into P-H's attitude toward the book. On August 2, Grenquist circulated a memorandum which noted that questions had arisen regarding both the tone of the book and Zilg's approach and recommended that the adjective "polemical" henceforth be used because "[t]he book is a polemical argument and no pretense is made that it is anything else." More importantly, he also cut the first printing from 15,000 copies to 10,000, stating that 5,000 copies were no longer needed for BOMC. The proposed advertising budget was also slashed from $15,000 to $5,500.

Judge Brieant held that the DuPont Company had a constitutionally protected interest in bringing the "scurrilous" nature of the book and its unsuitability as a Fortune Book Club selection to the attention of senior officials at BOMC and P-H. He expressly found that the Company did not engage in coercive tactics but limited its actions to the expression of its good faith opinion.

As to P-H, Judge Brieant found that the publishing contract required the publisher to "exercise its discretion in good faith in planning its promotion of the Book, and in revising its plans." This obligation required that Prentice-Hall use "its best efforts . . . to promote the Book fully and fairly." He held that P-H breached this obligation because it had no "sound" or "valid" business reason for reducing the first printing by 5,000 volumes and the advertising budget by $9,500, which allowed the book to go briefly out of stock (although wholesalers had ample copies) just as it gained sales momentum. He expressly found that since BOMC did its own printing of club selections, the first printing cut could not be attributed to the cancellation of the BOMC order. He also found that the book would have sold 25,000 copies had P-H not taken these actions.

Having concluded that P-H had no sound or valid business reason for reducing the first printing and advertising budget, Judge Brieant held that P-H "privished" Zilg's book on the basis of the testimony of plaintiff's expert, William Decker. Decker testified that publishers often mount a wholly inadequate merchandising effort after concluding that a book does not meet prior expectations in either quality or marketability. Such "privishing" is intended to fulfill the technical requirements of the contract to publish but to avoid adding to one's losses by throwing "good money after bad."

DISCUSSION

We agree with Judge Brieant that DuPont did not tortiously interfere with Zilg's beneficial commercial relationships. We disagree, however, with his conclusion that P-H breached its contract with Zilg and reverse that judgment.

. . . .

2. *P-H's Breach of Contract*

We believe Judge Brieant's discussion of P-H's obligations under its contract with Zilg, and his finding of a breach of those obligations, is more troubling than his dismissal of the case against the DuPont Company. Judge Brieant read the contract in question to oblige P-H "to use its best efforts . . . to promote the Book fully. . . . " and found that the decision to cut the first printing and original advertising budget resulted in a loss of sales momentum when the book was briefly out of stock. These actions by P-H, he held, breached its agreement with Zilg because they lacked a sound or valid business reason.

Putting aside for the moment P-H's motive in slashing the first printing and advertising budget, we note that Zilg neither bargained for nor acquired an explicit "best efforts" or "promote fully" promise, much less an agreement to make certain specific promotional efforts. The contract here thus contrasts with that in issue in *Contemporary Mission, Inc. v. Famous Music Corp.*, 557 F.2d 918 (2d Cir. 1977), which contained specific promotional obligations with regard to a musical group. While P-H obligated itself to "publish" the book once it had accepted it, the contract expressly leaves to P-H's discretion printing and advertising decisions. Working as we must in the context of a surprising absence of caselaw on the meaning of this not uncommon agreement, we believe that the contract in question establishes a relationship between the publisher and author which implies an obligation upon the former to make certain efforts in publishing a book it has accepted notwithstanding the clause which leaves the number of volumes to be printed and the advertising budget to the publisher's discretion. This obligation is derived both from the common expectations of parties to such agreements and from the relationship of those parties as structured by the contract . . .

Zilg, like most authors, sought to take advantage of a division of labor in which firms specialize in publishing works written by authors who are not employees of the firm. Under contracts such as the one before us, publishing firms print, advertise and distribute books at their own expense. In return for performing these tasks and for bearing the risk of a book's failure to sell, the author gives a publisher exclusive rights to the book with certain reservations not important here. Such contracts provide for royalties on sales to the author, often on an escalating basis, *i.e.*, higher royalties at higher levels of sales.

While publishers and authors have generally similar goals, differences in perspective and resulting perceptions are inevitable. An author usually has a bigger stake in the success or failure of a book than a publisher who may regard it as one among many publications, some of which may lose money. The author, whose eggs are in one basket, thus has a calculus of risk quite different from the publisher so far as costly promotional expenditures are concerned. The publisher, of course, views the author's willingness to take large risks as a function of the fact that it is the publisher's money at peril. Moreover, the publisher will inevitably regard his or her judgment as to marketing conditions as greatly superior to that of a particular author.

One means of reconciling these differing viewpoints is "up-front" money—$6,500 in Zilg's case—which provides a token of the publisher's seriousness about the book. Were such sums not bargained for, acquisition of publishing rights would be virtually costless and firms would acquire those rights without regard to whether or not they had truly decided to publish the work.

However, up-front money alone cannot fully reconcile the conflicting interests of the parties. Uncertainty surrounds the publication of most books and publishers must be cautious about the size of up-front payments since they increase the already considerable economic risks they take by printing and promoting books at their own expense. Negotiating such matters as the number of volumes to be printed and the level of advertising efforts might be possible but such bargaining in the case of each author and each book would be enormously costly. There is never a guarantee of ultimate agreement, and if a set of negotiations fails over these issues, the bargaining must begin again with another publisher. Moreover, publishers must also be wary of undertaking obligations to print a certain number of volumes or to spend fixed sums on promotion. They will strongly prefer to have flexibility in reacting to actual marketing conditions according to their own experience.

The contract between Zilg and P-H was a printed form with formal and negotiated matters—*e.g.*, the parties' names and the amount of the advance to the author—typed in. Under the terms of the printed form, once P-H accepted the manuscript it was obliged to publish the book but had discretion to determine the number of volumes to be printed and the level of advertising expenditures. These clauses are, of course, interrelated and the extent to which the language regarding promotional efforts and the promise to publish modify each other is the central issue before us. In resolving it, we must attempt to preserve the major interests of both parties . . .

Once P-H had accepted the book, it obtained the exclusive right to publish it. Were the clause empowering the publisher to determine promotional expenses read literally, the contract would allow a publisher to refuse to print or distribute any copies of a book while having exclusive rights to it. In effect, authors would be guaranteed nothing but whatever up-front money had been negotiated, and the promise to publish would be meaningless. We think the promise to publish must be given some content and that it implies a good faith effort to promote the book including a first printing and advertising budget adequate to give the book a reasonable chance of achieving market success in light of the subject matter and likely audience. *See Contemporary Mission, Inc. v. Famous Music Corp.; cf. Van Valkenburgh Nooger & Neville, Inc. v. Hayden Publishing Co.,* 30 N.Y.2d 34, 281 N.E.2d 142, 330 N.Y.S.2d 329 (1972) (publication of competing works may be so foreseeably harmful to author's royalties as to breach covenant to promote the book).

However, the clause empowering the publisher to decide in its discretion upon the number of volumes printed and the level of promotional expenditures must also be given some content. If a trier of fact is free to determine whether such decisions are sound or valid, the publisher's ability to rely upon its own experience and judgment in marketing books will be seriously hampered. We believe that once the obligation to undertake reasonable initial promotional activities has been fulfilled, the contractual language dictates that a business decision by the publisher to limit the size of a printing or advertising budget is not subject to second guessing by a trier of fact as to whether it is sound or valid.

The line we draw reconciles the legitimate conflicting interests of publisher and author as reflected in the contractual language, for it compels the publisher to make a good faith effort to promote the book initially whether or not it has had second thoughts while relying upon the profit motive thereafter to create the incentive for more elaborate promotional efforts. Once the initial obligation is fulfilled, all that is required is a good faith business judgment. This is not an interpretation harmful to authors. Were courts to impose rigorous requirements as to promotional efforts, publishers would of necessity undertake to publish fewer books with unpredictable futures.

Given the line we draw, a breach of contract might be proven by Zilg in two ways. First, he might demonstrate that the initial printing and promotional efforts were so inadequate as not to give the book a reasonable chance to catch on with the reading public. Second, he might show that even greater printing and promotional efforts were not undertaken for reasons other than a good faith business judgment. Because he has shown neither, we reverse the judgment in his favor.

As to P-H's initial obligation, Zilg has not shown that P-H's efforts on behalf of his book did not give it a reasonable chance to catch on with the reading public. It printed or reprinted 13,000 volumes (3,000 over the volume of sales at which the highest royalty was triggered), authorized an advertising budget of $5,500 (1974 purchasing power), distributed over 600 copies to reviewers, purchased ads in papers such as the *New York Times* and *Wall Street Journal,* and made reasonable efforts to sell the paperback rights. The documentary record shows that Grenquist took a continued interest in marketing the book, made suggestions as to promoting it effectively and ordered that "rave reviews" be sent to BOMC as late as January, 1975.

The fact that initial decisions as to promotional efforts were trimmed is of no relevance absent evidence that the actual efforts made were so inadequate that the book did not have a reasonable chance to catch on with the reading public. The record is barren of such evidence. P-H's estimates of first year sales made at the peak of the book's standing within the firm were only 12,000-15,000. By May, before the BOMC reversal, the low estimate was 10,000. It can hardly be contended that an initial printing of 10,000 and reprinting of 3,000 is so low that it breaches the obligation to give the book a reasonable chance to sell. Plaintiff's expert, Decker, himself testified that these efforts were "perfectly adequate," although they were "routine" and P-H "did not follow through as they might have."

Judge Brieant found only that an "unexplained" reduction in the first printing and advertising budget caused the book to go out of stock for a brief period of time and prevented the exploitation of growing sales momentum. He thus did not find that P-H's promotional efforts gave the book no reasonable chance to sell. Rather, he found that sales momentum was generated but not adequately exploited because the book was briefly out of stock. That situation, however, was not an inevitable outcome of the size of the first printing since a timely reprinting would have prevented it. Indeed, Grenquist ordered a reprinting when over 10% of the original volumes were still in stock and a delivery delay in that reprinting led to the three week out of stock situation. Moreover, the book was always available from wholesalers although, as Judge Brieant found, book sellers prefer to buy from publishers who provide a discount.

The district court read the contract as imposing on P-H a continuing obligation to use "its best efforts . . . to promote the Book fully and fairly" and as empowering a trier of fact to second guess a publisher's judgments as to the soundness of the decisions made. We disagree. So long as the initial promotional efforts are adequate under the test we outline above, a publisher's printing and advertising decisions do not breach a contract such as that before us unless the plaintiff proves that the motivation underlying those decisions was not a good faith business judgment. Zilg failed to produce such evidence. His case was based on the theory that economic coercion by the DuPont Company caused P-H to reduce its promotional efforts. Judge Brieant found against him on this issue and, for the reasons stated above, we affirm this determination.

This district court's finding that the reduction of promotional efforts was not based on a sound or valid business reason thus does not support the conclusion that the contract was breached. The district court took a different view of the legal obligations imposed by the contract and its conclusion was based on its highly optimistic opinion of the marketability of Zilg's book. Even at the peak of the book's standing within P-H, at a time when the Fortune

Book Club was going to offer it as a selection and before the problems of tone and accuracy had come into focus, no one at P-H save Cavin thought the book would be as successful as the district court later found. P-H's March, 1974, estimate for five year sales, for example, was 15,000 to 20,000, the low estimate being closer to actual sales than the high estimate is to Judge Brieant's finding. Indeed, Judge Brieant's view of the book's potential is entirely inconsistent with Decker's definition of privishing—not throwing "good money after bad"—for he in essence found that P-H had managed to avoid a small bonanza by breaching its contract.

As explained above, we think the contract between P-H and Zilg left the decisions in question to the business judgment of the publisher, the author's protection being in the publisher's experience, judgment and quest for profits. P-H's promotional efforts were, in Decker's words, "adequate," notwithstanding the reduction of the first printing and the initial advertising budget. Indeed, those reductions, coming on the heels of BOMC's decision not to distribute the book, appear to be a rational reaction to that news. Decker himself testified that the Fortune Book Club selection was an important barometer of marketability since it was an independent judgment that the book had an audience. Zilg's contract with P-H did not compel the publisher to ignore the implications of BOMC's change of heart.

Affirmed in part, reversed in part.

. . . .

———————

ARNOLD PRODUCTIONS, INC. v. FAVORITE FILMS CORP.
176 F. Supp. 862 (S.D.N.Y. 1959)

THOMAS F. MURPHY, District Judge.

This is a diversity action by the owner of two motion pictures against two distributors, Favorite Films Corporation (hereinafter called Favorite), to whom it had granted the exclusive right to exploit the pictures in theaters and on television throughout the United States and Canada, and against Nationwide Television Corporation (hereinafter called Nationwide), whom Favorite sublicensed as its exclusive agent for the television exploitation of the films. The pictures in suit are reissues entitled, It Happened Tomorrow and Hangmen Also Die.

The complaint alleges that Favorite breached its contract in that (1) it failed to use its best efforts in the television exploitation of the films; (2) it failed to keep and maintain books relating thereto for plaintiff's inspection; (3) it breached the covenant against assignment. There is further alleged a conspiracy between Favorite and Nationwide to cheat and defraud plaintiff of its share of the proceeds from the television distribution of the pictures. No complaint is made with respect to the theater distribution of the films by Favorite.

Defendants deny the allegations and in addition, Favorite claims that plaintiff has waived any and all such breaches by its acceptance and retention of remittances sent to it by Favorite together with each monthly statement, both before and subsequent to the institution of this suit, and after it had been fully apprised of the facts complained of herein.

The contract between plaintiff and Favorite became effective on June 1, 1947 and provided that Favorite as licensee was to have the sole and exclusive right to reproduce, lease, license, sub-license, exhibit, rent, distribute and exploit the two photo-plays, for a period of seven years throughout the United States and Canada in theatrical and television markets. Favorite agreed "to use its best efforts diligently and in good faith to exploit the said photoplays and to obtain as wide a distribution thereof and as many exhibitions and bookings thereof as possible." Favorite also agreed to "keep at its place of business in New York City, full and correct books of account with respect to the gross receipts derived from said photoplays, and . . . to permit the licensor . . . the right of access to and inspection of such . . . books".

The license was personal and non-assignable without the consent in writing of the licensor, and was to be interpreted and governed by the law of the state of New York. Plaintiff retained the right to elect to terminate the license in the event of a breach of any of the conditions on the part of Favorite, and in such event to retake with or without legal process any and all property concerning the pictures, and to collect any and all monies due or to become due to the licensee from their exploitation. Plaintiff's share was to be 37½% of the gross proceeds and Favorite's 62 ½%.

On March 14, 1949, Favorite and Nationwide entered into an agreement whereunder Nationwide became the former's "sole and exclusive agent for the marketing and booking" of the two pictures on television, upon terms and conditions similar to those contained in the plaintiff-Favorite contract including a similar "best efforts" clause, except that the Nationwide license was limited to television distribution. Also, there were substantially identical provisions relating to the keeping and inspection of books; the personal nature and non-assignability of the license; the application of New York law, and the retention of the right to terminate the agreement with the same rights of repossession and collection of proceeds.

At the time of the negotiations between plaintiff's representative and Favorite, plaintiff was informed that Favorite was engaged in commercially exploiting and distributing re-issue motion pictures through the media of sub-licensees and sub-distributors, known as franchise holders, and that Favorite had some 30 such franchise holders throughout the United States and Canada. In fact it was through this network of agents that Favorite was expected to accomplish a wide distribution of the pictures, and moreover, accounted for its substantial share of the proceeds.

As we noted earlier, there is no complaint made here with respect to the theater distribution phase of Favorite's performance, and presumably, Favorite did utilize its network of franchise holders for that exploitation. The claim here relates to the television distribution, and more particularly with regard to the method of such distribution employed by Nationwide and, as alleged by plaintiff, Favorite's abandonment of that phase of exploitation to Nationwide which amounted in legal effect, it says to an assignment in disregard of the contractual prohibition against assignment.

The legal responsibility for the television exploitation would appear to be complicated somewhat further by the fact that Nationwide in turn, orally subleased the television distribution of these pictures to a subsidiary corporation, now dissolved, called Film Equities Corp. which apparently came into existence in early 1949. Film Equities was dissolved in March 1951 just prior to the institution of this suit, and was succeeded in the handling of plaintiff's films by another subsidiary of Nationwide, to wit, Unity, Inc., which was born almost simultaneously with the demise of Film Equities. These latter two entities each accounted directly to Favorite for its exploitation of the pictures retaining 25% of the proceeds, Nationwide receiving no part of the proceeds according to it. However, the evidence is clear that all three, Nationwide, Film Equities and Unity were owned by the same stockholders, had the same officers and occupied the same offices with the same personnel. We will treat them as one and the same legal entity for the purposes of this case.

We should dispose at the outset of the claim of conspiracy to defraud alleged to have existed between Nationwide and Favorite. Plaintiff has failed completely to support that claim. It has offered no evidence whatever to substantiate it and, accordingly, will be dismissed from further consideration.

Plaintiff's case rests upon the theory that the method of television distribution employed by Nationwide did not amount to the exercise of best efforts diligently to exploit the pictures on T.V., but on the contrary, was a breach of that obligation. In other words, Nationwide's failure in that respect would be Favorite's failure of its same obligation to plaintiff. We consider Nationwide, in the terminology under which it entered into the agreement with Favorite, as mere agent for the latter for the purpose of fulfilling part of Favorite's contract obligations to plaintiff. Similarly, the performance of Nationwide's subsidiaries would be Nationwide's performance, if not in fact, then on general equitable and agency principles. We will consider, as a practical matter, all of them as one when weighing the issue of "best efforts", and merely refer to defendant's performance in that regard.

Defendant marketed the pictures along with a group of other films in a "package" or "library" deal whereunder the T.V. station-buyer was given its choice to select from the group it leased, any picture it cared to exhibit; to play a picture as often as it cared to, during a stated contract term; and pay for the package, one lump sum, payable over the course of the contract, apparently averaging 12 to 18 months. If any picture in a group was not shown by the station owner, it was credited with no part of the lump sum. Those that were played were credited as follows: The total number of hours of television exhibition from that group was divided into the lump sum, and the quotient equalled the amount per hour to be apportioned to each picture for each hour that it was shown. Each "feature" was counted as one hour in length.

It did not appear that plaintiff's pictures failed to be exhibited under any contract, but we gather that they were usually shown one to three times during the course of any contract term. That is readily and practically understandable. Whatever the rental price there is a limit to the number of times the average film can be televised in a given area within a stated period.

Plaintiff does not say its pictures would have been played more often if marketed by defendant separately or other than in package deals, nor does plaintiff say defendant failed to widely distribute the pictures on T.V. Its principal complaint is that more money should have been obtained by a different method of selling. To prove this and its damages plaintiff relied upon the testimony of its expert witness who testified that he entered the T.V. field of motion picture distribution in the latter part of 1949 when it was becoming commercially profitable, and that he is familiar with the prices in all markets and with the customers who buy for T.V. exhibition. He classified the pictures in suit as "A" pictures or top film fare, solely on the basis of their cast, though he had not seen either of them except for a short time many years ago. Referring to an exhibit in evidence which is a typical example of the type of library or package deal negotiated by defendant, this witness was of the opinion that it was unfair to sell a "very decent group of 14 feature films" contained therein, including the plaintiff's two pictures, with "short subjects" also in the group. He said that "to have sold the 14 features by themselves as I had to do, would have brought more money". In his opinion library deals were not for the best interests of the pictures, and, that more money could be obtained if they were sold individually. Favorite's expert was of the opinion that package sales was the most profitable way to sell motion pictures for television exhibition. Besides cast, which to plaintiff's expert was the sole criterion, this witness stressed the ratings given to pictures, and specially published, to determine their salability. Other important factors he considered were whether or not the picture has been exhibited before in the particular

T.V. market, its age and its theatrical success (the uncontradicted testimony was that plaintiff's pictures were both financially unsuccessful). Without analogizing in these respects, but merely alluding to the similarity of equally popular casts, plaintiff's expert testified that he has sold individually, pictures comparable to plaintiff's in 1953, and procured such widely divergent prices as $3,000, $1,000, $700 and $300 per picture on terms allowing the station owner to play each picture four times in a period of 18 months.

Assuming that exploiting plaintiff's pictures in the manner defendant did constituted a breach of its agreement to exercise its best efforts, and accepting plaintiff's expert witness' testimony with respect to the amounts he received as stated above, we find that plaintiff nonetheless has failed to prove its damages with any possible degree of certainty, nor did the proof provide any reasonable basis of computation. There was presented to us just no way of ascertaining whether or not plaintiff's pictures would have brought more if sold individually and if so, how much. On the figures given us by plaintiff's expert we are left to speculate in a range anywhere from $300 to $3,000.

This case is not comparable to two recent decisions in this circuit wherein the defendants' tortious conduct, by its very nature, prevented the accurate ascertainment of the respective plaintiff's damages, which were undoubtedly sustained.

Here defendant performed under its contract and the complaint relates to the quality of that performance. Defendant has not prevented plaintiff from proving that it suffered damages, viz., the profits it could have grossed if defendant exploited the pictures as plaintiff says it should have. Plaintiff has simply not carried its burden.

Favorite had the contractual right to sub-license others for the exploitation of these pictures. It is fair to infer that Favorite sub-licensed some of its franchise holders for the theatrical distribution. It might have sub-licensed one or all of them for television distribution as well. It chose Nationwide as its exclusive agent for that purpose. The language employed in the Favorite-Nationwide agreement and the obligation of Nationwide to account to Favorite are not consistent with assignment. We hold that an assignment was not here proved. Nor did plaintiff satisfy its allegation of abandonment. In other words, we find that Favorite did not breach its agreement with plaintiff by its arrangement with Nationwide and that it was no more than a sub-agency, albeit an exclusive one, and within its contractual authority. It should be noted that Favorite exploited the pictures on T.V. through at least one other company (Telecast Corp.) for some 21 months before engaging Nationwide. The total T.V. income therefrom was $2,825. There does not appear to be any complaint with respect to Favorite's handling of these pictures during that period of time. From March 1949 when Nationwide took over, until July 1951 when this suit was filed, about 27 months, the total T.V. income was about $15,000. Merely from the figures quoted it would seem that Favorite had exercised good business judgment in engaging Nationwide. However, there has been some testimony to the effect that the television exhibition of motion pictures as a commercially profitable business, was only in its infancy between 1947–1949; that in the latter part of 1949 it just began to be lucrative.

There was no express provision in the agreement that Favorite was to license the pictures for T.V. exhibition separate and distinct from other motion pictures, nor has it been claimed that such a provision is implicit in the agreement. The exploitation of plaintiff's pictures in conjunction with others therefore was not of itself a breach of contract.

According to the testimony of Nationwide's secretary, all of the major distributors were selling pictures in the same package manner as Nationwide during the times in issue, and such was the most profitable way to market them. It appeared that plaintiff's expert handled between 30 and 40 films; Favorite's expert had a catalogue of about 140 pictures, and Nationwide's catalogue was still larger.

Concededly, plaintiff's expert did not handle large groups of pictures, nor did he know how to handle them. It may be that an industrious individual salesman, as he represented himself to be, could efficiently distribute single or small groups of pictures and secure higher prices for his wares than a firm like Nationwide, but we must analogize only with comparable companies or individuals. In ascertaining best efforts we would have to compare defendant's performance with the average, prudent comparable distributor in the T.V. market. A comparison of defendant's performance with that of the comparatively small scale operations of plaintiff's expert would not be valid. Defendant's expert testimony supports the manner and method utilized by it in marketing its catalogue of films in the television field, and, in effect, constitutes an endorsement of the package method as consistent with best efforts. We must either accept the testimony of defendant or consider that of plaintiff's expert as inapposite. In either case we are unable to find a failure to exercise best efforts under the circumstances.

The evidence allows a finding that Favorite in respect to T.V. distribution (and Nationwide, through Film Equities destruction of its books upon dissolution) breached the agreement with regard to the obligation to keep and maintain books for plaintiff's inspection. The books that were available were audited by plaintiff's accountant and no evidence relating thereto was introduced. While such a breach would perhaps entitle plaintiff to terminate the contract, that has long since become a moot remedy, and since plaintiff has made no attempt whatever to show damage flowing from this breach, none may be awarded.

Actually, plaintiff in its brief after trial points out that the contract has now expired and the films have been recaptured. It nevertheless is entitled to an accounting for all monies earned from the licensing of the films from the date of the last accounting.

Holding as we must that plaintiff has failed to sustain its burden, and that the complaint must be dismissed, except as to an accounting as above ordered, it is unnecessary to consider the question of waiver.

Judgment for defendants but without costs on all issues, except that relating to an accounting, and judgment for plaintiff directing defendants to account.

The above opinion is in lieu of findings of fact and conclusions of law pursuant to Rule 52(a) of the Federal Rules of Civil Procedure, 28 U.S.C.A.

PINNACLE BOOKS, INC. v. HARLEQUIN ENTERPRISES LIMITED
519 F. Supp. 118 (S.D.N.Y. 1981)

KEVIN THOMAS DUFFY, District Judge:

This is an action for a permanent injunction and damages resulting from the allegedly unlawful interference of defendant Harlequin Enterprises Limited ["Harlequin"] with the contractual relationship between plaintiff Pinnacle Books, Inc. ["Pinnacle"] and its most successful author, Don Pendleton ["Pendleton"]. Pinnacle claims that Harlequin induced Pendleton to breach his contract with Pinnacle and to enter into an agreement with Harlequin pursuant to which it will publish new books in or relating to a series of paperback men's action adventure books entitled "The Executioner" [sometimes referred to herein as the "Series"]. Pinnacle now moves for summary judgment.

I.

Pinnacle is a publisher of mass-market and trade paperback books. The company has offices in New York City and Los Angeles. It has been publishing "The Executioner" series since the inception of the series in 1969. Pinnacle has published thirty-eight different titles in "The Executioner" series and sold approximately twenty million copies. Pendleton, the author of the Series, is the copyright owner of the Series.

In 1976, Pinnacle and Pendleton entered into an agreement whereby Pinnacle agreed to publish books 29 through 38 in "The Executioner" series. The 1976 Agreement provided, *inter alia*, that Pendleton would not offer rights in "The Executioner" series to any other publisher until, after extending their best efforts, Pinnacle and Pendleton, were unable to agree on the terms of a new contract for the Series. In the event that the parties were unable to consummate a new contract, Pendleton was free to offer the Series to other publishers so long as any new publication did not occur for three months following the first publication of book 38 by Pinnacle. The pertinent provision provides:

> VII. The Author grants the Publisher the option to renew this contract for the books in THE EXECUTIONER series following the ten books covered hereby on terms to be agreed, and, if, after extending their best efforts, the parties are unable to reach an agreement thereon, then Author shall be free to offer rights in such other books in THE EXECUTIONER series to any other publisher, provided the publication thereof does not occur until the expiration of 3 months following the first publication of the tenth book hereunder.

The manuscript for the last book under the 1976 Agreement was delivered to Pinnacle on December 14, 1979. By that time, Andrew Ettinger, the Editorial Director of Pinnacle, had begun negotiations with Pendleton for an extension of the 1976 Agreement. These discussions between Ettinger and Pendleton occurred as early as September 8, 1978 and continued until November, 1979, at which time Ettinger left Pinnacle and joined Harlequin. According to Ettinger, he was unable to consummate a renewal of the 1976 Agreement before he left Pinnacle because an outstanding dispute between Pendleton and Pinnacle regarding foreign royalty rights had not been resolved. By late 1979, however, an acceptable resolution of the dispute had been reached and Pendleton was ready and willing to discuss an extension of the 1976 Agreement.

Negotiations between Pinnacle and Pendleton continued until about February 10, 1980. According to Pinnacle, the discussions had been congenial and the conditions established by Pendleton had either been satisfied in full or could have been met if the parties had proceeded with the negotiations in good faith and using their best efforts.

Meanwhile, Harlequin, a Canadian publisher and distributor of paperback books throughout the world, also had developed an interest in Pendleton. Having achieved spectacular success in the romance novel market, Harlequin was exploring the feasibility of entering the action/adventure line of book publishing. Ettinger, who was now affiliated with Harlequin, began meeting with Pendleton in early January, 1980, to discuss the possibility of Harlequin becoming Pendleton's publisher. On about February 10, 1980, Pendleton advised Pinnacle that, at Harlequin's invitation, he was planning to visit its Toronto headquarters where he expected Harlequin to discuss the possibility of licensing to it rights in "The Executioner" series. Pendleton also indicated that he wished to halt discussions on the Pinnacle offer until he heard from Harlequin. At the conclusion of his discussion with Harlequin, Pendleton signed a preliminary agreement to license the Series and its characters to Harlequin. On May 15, 1980, Pendleton signed the formal agreement with Harlequin pursuant to which twelve books in "The Executioner" series and four to six spin-offs from that Series would be published annually by Harlequin.

Pinnacle instituted this action in September, 1980, against Harlequin seeking injunctive and compensatory relief. Pinnacle alleges that Harlequin, although fully aware of Pendleton's contractual obligations to Pinnacle and that Pinnacle was still negotiating with Pendleton, induced Pendleton to break off negotiations with Pinnacle just as final agreement on new contract terms was near. Pinnacle now moves for summary judgment. Harlequin argues against the motion for summary judgment on the grounds that the option clause on which Pinnacle bases its case is unenforceable. Alternatively, Harlequin asserts that before the "best efforts" obligation can be enforced, an evidentiary hearing must be held to determine (i) the intention of the parties regarding the "best efforts" clause; (ii) the compliance of both parties with their obligations under the clause; and (iii) Harlequin's interference with Pendleton's performance under the clause.

DISCUSSION

To succeed in an action for interference with contractual relations, the plaintiff must establish first and foremost the existence of a valid contract.[1] *Nifty Foods Corp. v. Great Atlantic & Pac. Tea Co.*, 614 F.2d 832, 839 (2d Cir. 1980).

In the instant case, Pinnacle accuses Harlequin of interfering with the option clause in the 1976 Agreement. As noted above, that clause provides that, after Pendleton has fulfilled his obligation to deliver books 29 through 38 of "The Executioner" Series, the parties would use their "best efforts" to negotiate a new contract "on terms to be agreed" for delivery of an unspecified number of new Executioner books. Clause VII of the 1976 Agreement. Harlequin contends that this clause is unenforceable because either (i) it is nothing more than an unenforceable "agreement to agree"; or (ii) the material terms of the "best efforts" clause are too vague.

Harlequin's first contention that the "best efforts" clause is an unenforce-

---

[1] Plaintiff must also establish (i) the defendant's knowledge of that contract; (ii) the defendant's intentional procuring of a breach of that contract; (iii) but for the defendant's alleged inducement, the breach would not have occurred; and (iv) damages. *Special Event Entertainment v. Rockefeller Center*, 458 F.Supp. 72, 78 (S.D.N.Y.1978); *Israel v. Wood Dolsan Co.*, 1 N.Y.2d 116, 151 N.Y.S.2d 1, 134 N.E.2d 97 (1956).

able "agreement to agree" is inappropriate in this case. Clause VII of the 1976 Agreement does not require that any agreement actually be achieved but only that the parties work to reach an agreement actively and in good faith. *See Thompson v. Liquichimica of America, Inc.*, 481 F.Supp. 365, 366 (S.D.N.Y.1979).

Harlequin is correct, however, in arguing that the "best efforts" clause is unenforceable because its terms are too vague, "Best efforts" or similar clauses, like any other contractual agreement, must set forth in definite and certain terms every material element of the contemplated bargain. It is hornbook law that courts cannot and will not supply the material terms of a contract.

Essential to the enforcement of a "best efforts" clause is a clear set of guidelines against which the parties "best efforts" may be measured. *See Cross Properties v. Brook Realty Co.*, 76 A.D.2d 445, 454, 430 N.Y.S.2d 820, 825 (2d Dep't 1980). The performance required of the parties by a "best efforts" clause may be expressly provided by the contract itself or implied from the circumstances of the case. *See Bloor v. Falstaff Brewing Corp.*, 454 F.Supp. 258 (S.D.N.Y.1978), *aff'd*, 601 F.2d 609 (2d Cir. 1979) ("best efforts" under a distribution contract based on distributor's capabilities and prior merchandising of other similar products); *Perma Research & Development v. Singer Co.*, 402 F.Supp. 881 (S.D.N.Y.1975), *aff'd*, 542 F.2d 111 (2d Cir. 1976), *cert. denied*, 429 U.S. 987, 97 S.Ct. 507, 50 L.Ed.2d 598, ("best efforts" under a patent assignment based on company's financial and other capabilities). In the case at bar, there simply are no objective criteria against which either Pinnacle or Pendleton's efforts can be measured.

Pinnacle's argument that the parties' obligations under the "best efforts" clause are clear from the circumstances of the case is without merit. While it is possible to infer from the circumstances the standard of performance required by a "best efforts" clause where the parties have agreed to work toward a specific goal, *see, e.g., Bloor, supra; Perma Research & Development, supra*, it is not so here where the parties have agreed only to negotiate. The performance required by a contract to negotiate with best efforts, unlike the performance required by a distribution contract or a patent assignment, simply cannot be ascertained from the circumstances. Unless the parties delineate in the contract objective standards by which their efforts are to be measured,[4] the very nature of contract negotiations renders it impossible to determine whether the parties have used their "best" efforts to reach a new agreement. Certainly, no party to a negotiation, no matter what the circum-

---

[4] For instance, the parties could agree in the contract that "best efforts" means that they would not negotiate with others for a specific period of time or that one party has the right to match any offer received from another.

stances, is required to make a particular offer nor to accept particular terms. What each party offers or demands in the course of any negotiation is a matter left strictly to the business judgment of that party. Thus, absent express standards, a court cannot decide that one party's offer does not constitute its best efforts; nor can it say that the other party's refusal to accept certain terms does not constitute its best efforts.

In the instant case, therefore, where the parties agreed only to negotiate and failed to state the standards by which their negotiation efforts were to be measured, it is impossible to determine whether Pinnacle or Pendleton used their "best efforts" to negotiate a new agreement. For instance, there simply is no objective standard by which the court can determine whether Pinnacle's officer constituted its best efforts; nor can it decide whether Pendleton's participation in negotiations with Pinnacle for over a year were his best efforts. In short, the option clause is unenforceable due to the indefiniteness of its terms. Accordingly, Pinnacle's motion for summary judgment is denied.

In view of this decision which resolves the one basic issue underlying this case, I deem Harlequin's responsive papers as a cross-motion for summary judgment which motion is granted and the complaint dismissed. No costs are awarded.

SO ORDERED.

ON MOTION FOR REARGUMENT

By my opinion and order of May 13, 1981, the complaint herein was dismissed. The plaintiff now moves in effect for reargument and/or temporary injunctive relief pending the appeal of the May 13, 1981 order of this court.

The complaint is divided into five causes of action:

(1) unlawful interference by Harlequin with the plaintiff's contractual rights with Don Pendleton, author, under a 1976 Agreement and a 1979 Agreement executed between the author and the plaintiff;

(2) an intentional tort on the part of the defendant in that defendant maliciously deprived the plaintiff of rights to publish and distribute additional books by Pendleton, its most successful author;

(3) that, due to the contractual interference by the defendant and the intentional tort committed by the defendant, the plaintiff will suffer irreparable harm giving rise to equitable injunctive relief;

(4) that the defendant through the activities of Andrew Ettinger, a former editorial director of the plaintiff, in his position as an employee of the defendant breached fiduciary duties to the plaintiff and misappropriated plaintiff's ideas, thus, constituting unfair competition; and

(5) that because of the foregoing there is a continuing need for injunctive relief to prevent irreparable injury to the plaintiff.

The central question raised by this case involves the enforceability of the renewal clause of the 1976 contract between Pinnacle and Don Pendleton. Pendleton's obligations under the 1976 contract (if no reference is made to the renewal clause) were satisfied upon the delivery of the manuscript for the 38th book in the series to Pinnacle which occurred on December 14, 1979. In my opinion of May 13th, I held that the renewal clause is unenforceable.

The injunctive relief sought by the plaintiff is based solely upon the 1976 Agreement between plaintiff and Pendleton. As it appeared that the 1979 Agreement had never been executed or accepted by Pendleton, I was under the impression that the plaintiff had abandoned its claim under that alleged contract. Accordingly, upon determining that the renewal clause in 1976 contract is unenforceable, I dismissed the entire complaint.

It now appears, however, that the plaintiff believes that even if the renewal clause of the 1976 Agreement is unenforceable, they still have certain rights under the claimed 1979 Agreement. Plaintiff requests that my order of May 13 be modified so as to dismiss only those portions of the amended complaint which seek relief under the 1976 Agreement between the parties. While it appears, at this juncture, that plaintiff may have great difficulty in proving the claimed 1979 Agreement, I had no intention of depriving them of the right to litigate this matter. Accordingly, the opinion and order of May 13 is amended to restrict the relief therein to a dismissal of those portions of plaintiff's amended complaint which seek relief under the 1976 Agreement.

Plaintiff also seeks an order of this court affirmatively enjoining the defendant from publishing any of the books bearing the generic title "The Executioner" or from publicizing any such books pending the appeal of this case. It is the plaintiff's position that the appeal from my order will be in good faith and, indeed, I have no doubt that it will be so prosecuted. *See Thompson v. Liquichimica of America, Inc.*, 481 F.Supp. 365 (S.D.N.Y.1979). The plaintiff also argues that, should the defendant be permitted to proceed with publication prior to appeal, any damages incurred thereby will be most difficult of proof. It is suggested that should an order not be entered, the egg will be scrambled to such a point that should an appellant court disagree with my interpretation of the contract the parties could never be restored to the position they were in prior to the May 13, 1981 order of this court.

On the other hand, the contract whereby Harlequin obtained rights to books in "The Executioner" series from Don Pendleton was entered into many, many months ago and that the plaintiff had knowledge of that fact at or about the time that the contract was executed. Since then, Harlequin has expended large sums in order to prepare for this new venture in its business. The damage to Harlequin, should a stay be entered at this point, cannot be said to be insubstantial. It seems clear to me that the equities do not tip decidedly in favor of the plaintiff. *See Caulfield v. Board of Education of the City of New York,* 583 F.2d 605 (2d Cir. 1978). Accordingly, the requested affirmative injunction pending appeal is denied.

SO ORDERED.

CONTEMPORARY MISSION, INC. v. FAMOUS MUSIC CORPORATION
557 F.2d 918 (2d Cir. 1977)

MESKILL, Circuit Judge:

This is an appeal by Famous Music Corporation ("Famous") from a verdict rendered against it in favor of Contemporary Mission, Inc. ("Contemporary"), in the United States District Court for the Southern District of New York, after a jury trial before Judge Richard Owen. Contemporary cross-appeals from a ruling which excluded testimony concerning its prospective damages. The dispute between the parties relates to Famous' alleged breach of two contracts.

I. *The Facts.*

Contemporary is a nonprofit charitable corporation organized under the laws of the State of Missouri with its principal place of business in Connecticut. It is composed of a small group of Roman Catholic priests who write, produce and publish musical compositions and recordings.[1] In 1972 the group owned all of the rights to a rock opera entitled VIRGIN, which was composed by Father John T. O'Reilly, a vice-president and member of the group. Contemporary first became involved with Famous in 1972 as a result of O'Reilly's efforts to market VIRGIN.

Famous is a Delaware corporation with its headquarters in the Gulf + Western Building in New York City. It is a wholly-owned subsidiary of the Gulf + Western Corporation, and, until July 31, 1974, it was engaged in the business of producing musical recordings for distribution throughout the United States. Famous' president, Tony Martell, is generally regarded in the recording industry as the individual primarily responsible for the successful

---

[1] For a further description of the group see *Robert Stigwood Group, Ltd. v. O'Reilly,* 346 F.Supp. 376, 379 (D.Conn.1972), *rev'd,* 530 F.2d 1096 (2d Cir. 1976).

distribution of the well-known rock operas TOMMY and JESUS CHRIST SUPERSTAR.

The relationship between Famous and Contemporary was considerably more harmonious in 1972 than it is today. At that time, Martell thought he had found, in VIRGIN, another TOMMY or JESUS CHRIST SUPERSTAR, and he was anxious to acquire rights to it. O'Reilly, who was encouraged by Martell's expertise and enthusiasm, had high hopes for the success of his composition. On August 16, 1972, they executed the so-called "VIRGIN Recording Agreement" ("VIRGIN agreement") on behalf of their respective organizations.

The terms of the VIRGIN agreement were relatively simple. Famous agreed to pay a royalty to Contemporary in return for the master tape recording of VIRGIN and the exclusive right to manufacture and sell records made from the master. The agreement also created certain "Additional Obligations of Famous" which included, *inter alia*: the obligation to select and appoint, within the first year of the agreement, at least one person to personally oversee the nationwide promotion of the sale of records, to maintain contact with Contemporary and to submit weekly reports to Contemporary; the obligation to spend, within the first year of the agreement, no less than $50,000 on the promotion of records; and the obligation to release, within the first two years of the agreement, at least four separate single records from VIRGIN. The agreement also contained a non-assignability clause which is set out in the margin.[3]

On May 8, 1973, the parties entered into a distribution contract which dealt with musical compositions other than VIRGIN. This, the so-called "Crunch agreement," granted to Famous the exclusive right to distribute Contemporary's records in the United States. Famous agreed to institute a new record label named "Crunch," and a number of records were to be released under it annually. Contemporary agreed to deliver ten long-playing records and fifteen single records during the first year of the contract. Famous undertook to use its "reasonable efforts" to promote and distribute the records. Paragraph 15 of the Crunch agreement stated that a breach by either party would not be deemed material unless the non-breaching party first gave written notice to the defaulting party and the defaulting party failed to cure the breach within

---

[3] Paragraph 29 of the VIRGIN agreement provides, in full, as follows:

> This agreement shall not be assignable by FAMOUS, except in the voluntary sale of FAMOUS' entire business in which the present work is used, or in connection with a merger between FAMOUS and another business organization, or to a majority-owned subsidiary or division of FAMOUS engaged in the same business as FAMOUS, *all conditioned upon the execution and delivery to [Contemporary] of an agreement whereby the assignee agrees to be bound by the obligations of this Agreement.* (emphasis added).

thirty days. The notice was to specify the nature of the alleged material breach. The contract prohibited assignment by Contemporary, but it contained no provision relating to Famous' right to assign.

Although neither VIRGIN nor its progeny was ever as successful as the parties had originally hoped, the business relationship continued on an amicable basis until July 31, 1974. On that date, Famous' record division was sold to ABC Records, Inc. (ABC). When O'Reilly complained to Martell that Famous was breaking its promises, he was told that he would have to look to ABC for performance. O'Reilly met with one of ABC's lawyers and was told that ABC was not going to have any relationship with Contemporary. On August 21, 1974, Contemporary sent a letter to Famous pursuant to paragraph 15 of the Crunch agreement notifying Famous that it had "materially breached Paragraph 12,[4] among others, of [the Crunch] Agreement in that [it had] attempted to make a contract or other agreement with ABC-Dunhill Record Corporation (ABC Records) creating an obligation or responsibility in behalf of or in the name of the Contemporary Mission." This lawsuit followed.

II. *The Jury Verdict.*

Contemporary brought this action against several defendants and asserted several causes of action. By the time the case was submitted to the jury the only remaining defendant was Famous and the only remaining claims were that (1) Famous had failed to adequately promote the VIRGIN and Crunch recordings prior to the sale to ABC, (2) Famous breached both the VIRGIN and Crunch agreements when it sold the record division to ABC, and (3) Famous breached an oral agreement to reimburse Contemporary for its promotional expenses. The latter claim has no relevance to this appeal.

The district judge submitted the case to the jury in two parts: the first portion as to liability and the second concerning damages. The court's questions and the jury's answers as to liability and damages are set forth below:

Liability Questions

1. Has plaintiff established by a fair preponderance of the credible evidence that Famous breached the Virgin agreement by failing to adequately promote Virgin in its various aspects as it had agreed?

Yes.

---

[4] Paragraph 12 of the Crunch agreement provides, in full, as follows:

This agreement shall not be construed as one of partnership or joint venture, nor shall it constitute either party as the agent or legal representative of the other. Neither party shall have the right, power or authority to make any contract or other agreement, or to assume or create any obligation or responsibility, express or implied, in behalf of or in the name of the other party or to bind the other party in any manner for anything whatsoever.

2. If you find a failure to adequately promote, did that cause plaintiff any damage?

Yes.

3. Did the assignment of the Virgin contract by Famous to ABC cause any damage to the plaintiff?

Yes.

4. Did plaintiff establish by a fair preponderance of the credible evidence that Famous failed to use "its reasonable efforts consistent with the exercise of sound business judgment" to promote the records marketed under the Crunch label?

No.

5. Did plaintiff establish by a fair preponderance of the credible evidence that there was a refusal by ABC to perform the Crunch contract and promote plaintiff's music after the assignment?

Yes.

6. If your answer is "yes" to either 4 or 5 above, did such breach or breaches of the Crunch agreement cause plaintiff any damage?

Yes.

7. Did Tony Martell, on behalf of Famous, in talking to any member of plaintiff, make any agreement to reimburse plaintiff for the expense of its members promoting their music around the country?

Yes.

Damage Questions

1. To what damages is plaintiff entitled under the Virgin agreement?

$68,773.

2. To what damages is plaintiff entitled under the Crunch agreement?

$104,751.

3. To what unallocated damages as between the Virgin and Crunch and oral agreements is plaintiff entitled—if any?

$21,000.

4. To what damages, if any, is plaintiff entitled under the oral agreement?

$16,500.

III. *Discussion.*

On this appeal, Famous attacks the verdict on several grounds. Their first contention is that the evidence was insufficient to support the jury's response to liability question number 1. Their second contention is that the jury's response to liability question number 4 precludes a recovery for non-performance of the Crunch agreement. Their third contention is that Contemporary failed to comply with the notice provision of the Crunch agreement. Their final contention is that Contemporary is estopped from suing for a breach of the Crunch agreement. We find none of these arguments persuasive.

A. *The VIRGIN Agreement.*

Judge Owen charged the jury as a matter of law that Famous breached the VIRGIN agreement by assigning it to ABC without getting from ABC a written agreement to be bound by the terms of the VIRGIN agreement. A reading of paragraph 29 of the agreement[7] reveals that that charge was entirely correct, and Famous does not challenge it on this appeal. Famous vigorously contends, however, that the jury's conclusion, that it had failed to adequately promote VIRGIN prior to the sale to ABC, is at war with the undisputed facts and cannot be permitted to stand. In particular they argue that they spent the required $50,000[8] and appointed the required overseer for

---

[7] *See* note 3, *supra.*

[8] Martell testified that he was certain that over $50,000 had been spent. Melvin Schlissel, Famous' Vice-President of Finance, testified that in early 1973 he prepared a report that indicated that approximately $50,000 had been spent on the promotion of VIRGIN as of the date of the report. The report itself would have been admissible under the business records exception to the hearsay rule, Fed.R.Evid. 803(6), but the report had been lost, so the trial judge admitted oral proof of its contends, Fed.R.Evid. 1004. None of the parties recognized that the result was an oral business record—an apparent contradiction in terms. We express no view on the admissibility of an oral business record, for its admission is not claimed as error on this appeal.

Although Famous' proof that it spent over $50,000 was uncontradicted, the proof itself was not particularly strong; indeed, it was rather imprecise and self-serving. The jury could quite properly have concluded that the proof was insufficient.

Famous contends that Contemporary waived the $50,000 spending requirement. In return for an advance of $7,500, Contemporary agreed that

> Famous Music Corporation shall be relieved of its obligation to expend a minimum of $50,000.00 in the promotion of "Virgin" record sales if, as and when, in the sole option of Famous Music Corporation, such promotion shall cease to be effective and profitable.

This agreement did not operate as a present waiver of the spending requirement, as Famous contends. It granted Famous an option not to spend "if, as and when, in the sole option of Famous," the promotion became ineffective and unprofitable. Famous' argument is premised upon the notion that it had "absolute discretion concerning how much, if any, of the $50,000 to spend, and its opinion could not be challenged." This is not true. Under New York law there is implied in every contract a covenant of fair dealing and good faith . . . *see, e.g., Van Valkenburgh, Nooger & Neville, Inc. v. Hayden Pub. Co., Inc.*, 30 N.Y.2d 34, 45, 330 N.Y.S.2d 329, 333, 281 N.E.2d 142, 144, *cert. denied*, 409 U.S. 875, 93 S.Ct. 125, 34 L.Ed.2d 128 (1972). Thus, Famous' determination of effectiveness or profitability of promotion would have to be

the project.[9] The flaw in this argument is that its focus is too narrow. The obligations to which it refers are but two of many created by the VIRGIN agreement. Under the doctrine of *Wood v. Lucy, Lady Duff-Gordon*, 222 N.Y. 88, 118 N.E. 214 (1917), Famous had an obligation to use its reasonable efforts to *promote* VIRGIN on a nationwide basis. That obligation could not be satisfied merely by technical compliance with the spending and appointment requirements of paragraph 14 of the agreement. Even assuming that Famous complied fully with those requirements, there was evidence from which the jury could find that Famous failed to adequately promote VIRGIN. The question is a close one, particularly in light of Martell's obvious commitment to the success of VIRGIN and in light of the efforts that were in fact exerted and the lack of any serious dispute between the parties prior to the sale to ABC. However, there was evidence that Famous prematurely terminated the promotion of the first single record, "Got To Know," shortly after its release, and that Famous limited its promotion of the second record "Kyrie," to a single city, rather than promoting it nationwide.[10] Moreover, there was evidence that, prior to the sale to ABC, Famous underwent a budget reduction and cut back its promotional staff. From this, the jury could infer that the promotional effort was reduced to a level that was less than adequate. On the whole, therefore, we are not persuaded that the jury's verdict should be disturbed.

B. *The Crunch Agreement.*

There is no dispute that the sale of Famous' record division to ABC constituted an assignment of the Crunch agreement to ABC. The assignment of a bilateral contract includes both an assignment of rights and a delegation of duties. The distinctions between the two are important.

> Perhaps more frequently than is the case with other terms of art, lawyers seem prone to use the word "assignment" inartfully, frequently intending to encompass within the term the distinct [concept] of delegation . . . . An assignment involves the transfer of rights. A delegation involves the appointment of another to perform one's duties.

---

made in good faith. There is no indication that such a good faith determination was in fact made.

[9] It is clear that the personal overseer requirement was met. Martell himself was actively and extensively engaged in the promotional effort. In addition, Herb Gordon was clearly put in charge of the day-to-day supervision of the promotion. This adequately complied with the provisions of paragraph 14.

[10] We recognize that the limited promotion of "Kyrie" was a result of "test marketing," *i.e.*, the concentration of promotional efforts in one area before expanding the efforts to the rest of the country. However, because the promotion of "Kyrie" was thus limited, Famous only marketed three single records on a *nationwide* basis, and the contract required the nationwide promotion of four.

J. Calamari & J. Perillo, Contracts § 254 (1970) (footnote omitted). Famous' arguments with respect to the Crunch agreement ignore this basic distinction, and the result is a distortion of several fundamental principles of contract law.

It is true, of course, as a general rule, that when rights are assigned, the assignor's interest in the rights assigned comes to an end. When duties are delegated, however, the delegant's obligation does not end.

> [O]ne who owes money or is bound to any performance whatever, cannot by any act of his own, or by any act in agreement with any other person, except his creditor, divest himself of the duty and substitute the duty of another. "No one can assign his liabilities under a contract without the consent of the party to whom he is liable."
>
> This is sufficiently obvious when attention is called to it, for otherwise obligors would find an easy practical way of escaping their obligations
> . . . .

3 Williston on Contracts § 411 (3d ed. 1960) (footnote omitted). This is not to say that one may not delegate his obligations. In fact, most obligations can be delegated—as long as performance by the delegate will not vary materially from performance by the delegant.[11] The act of delegation, however, does not relieve the delegant of the ultimate responsibility to see that the obligation is performed. If the delegate fails to perform, the delegant remains liable.

Judge Owen correctly charged the jury that "after the assignment of the contract by Famous to ABC, Famous remained liable for any obligation that was not fulfilled by ABC." This was a correct statement of the law, and Famous' assault upon it, while valiant, is without merit.

Our conclusion also disposes of Famous' evidentiary argument. The argument is that since Famous is being held liable for a breach by ABC, and since the only proof of a breach by ABC was proof of ABC's repudiation, and since the evidence of repudiation was hearsay, there was no admissible proof of a breach by ABC, and, therefore, Famous cannot be held liable. This argument fails because it was unnecessary for Contemporary to prove that ABC breached, or repudiated, any obligation. All Contemporary was required to do was to prove that no one performed Famous' obligation to promote after the sale to ABC. This it clearly did. Performance by ABC would have been an affirmative defense for Famous, but in order to prevail it was not necessary for Contemporary to disprove an affirmative defense that was neither pled nor

---

[11] . . . .

Although the matter is not without considerable doubt, we shall assume, *arguendo*, that the duty to promote Contemporary's records was not sufficiently personal to bar its delegation. The fact that Martell worked for Famous rather than ABC, however, would appear to militate in favor of the opposite conclusion.

proved by Famous. Because Contemporary's proof of ABC's refusal to perform was unnecessary to make out its cause of action, we need decide whether that proof was admissible.

Famous also maintains that, even if there were a breach, Contemporary is barred from asserting it, because it failed to adequately comply with the notice requirement contained in the Crunch agreement. We find this argument unpersuasive. The letter sent by Contemporary to Famous shortly after the sale to ABC gave Famous adequate notice that Contemporary considered the contract to have been materially breached as a result of the sale, which had led to the "illegal seizure of our property from the marketplace," an obvious reference to evidence that the Crunch (and VIRGIN) record inventory had been removed from retail stores and shipped to ABC without notice to Contemporary, with probable harm to promotion and sales. Indeed, Famous' president, Martell, had advised O'Reilly of this fact before the latter's visit to ABC in early August 1974. While it is true that the letter directs Famous' attention to "Paragraph 12,[14] among others," and that a breach of paragraph 12 was not the basis for Contemporary's ultimate recovery, under the circumstances, it would be hypertechnical to upset the verdict on the ground that the notice was insufficient. We decline to construe the notice provision as if it were a common law pleading requirement under which every slip would be fatal. The purpose of the written notice requirement was to permit Famous within 30 days to cure any material breach. Contemporary's August 19, 1974, telegram, construed in the light of the earlier Martell-O'Reilly conversation with respect to the removal of the record inventory from retail stores was sufficient to place Famous under a duty to communicate immediately with ABC and to insure that the contract was being performed according to its terms. Had it done so, it would have found (as had O'Reilly a few days earlier) that ABC was not fulfilling Famous' obligations under the contract but was taking the position that it would not have anything to do with Contemporary. The problem for Famous, of course, was that, having sold its entire record division to ABC, it had stripped itself of its ability to cure the breach.

Famous' final contention is that Contemporary is estopped from suing for a breach of the Crunch agreement. According to Famous, because Contemporary has always claimed that the assignment was void *ab initio*, it is estopped to claim that Famous is vicariously liable for a breach by ABC, because if the assignment was void, ABC had no obligation which could have been breached. This argument is without merit because it is premised upon the mistaken notion that Famous is being held liable for a breach of ABC. Such is not the case. The basis for the recovery is not a breach by ABC, it is a breach by Famous after the sale to ABC.

---

[14] *See* note 4, *supra*.

IV. *The Cross-Appeal.*

During the trial, Contemporary sought to introduce a statistical analysis, together with expert testimony, in order to prove how successful the most successful of its single recordings, "Fear No Evil," would have become if the VIRGIN agreement had not been breached as a result of the sale to ABC. Based upon its projection of the success of that recording, Contemporary hoped to prove what revenues that success would have produced. Judge Owen excluded this evidence on the ground that it was speculative. *Freund v. Washington Square Press, Inc.*, 34 N.Y.2d 379, 357 N.Y.S.2d 857, 314 N.E.2d 419 (1974).

There can no dispute that Contemporary "is entitled to the reasonable damage flowing from the breach of" the VIRGIN agreement by Famous, and that "the measure of the damage is the amount necessary to put [Contemporary] in [the] exact position as [it] would have been if the contract had not been breached." *Perma Research & Dev. v. Singer Co.*, 542 F.2d 111, 116 (2d Cir.), *cert. denied*, 429 U.S. 987, 97 S.Ct. 507, 50 L.Ed.2d 598 (1976). Nor can there be any dispute as to the New York rules concerning the measure of proof required to prove the existence of damage and the measure of proof necessary to enable the jury to fix its amount. It is clear that the existence of damage must be certain—a requirement that operates with particular severity in cases involving artistic creations such as books, *Freund v. Washington Square Press, Inc., supra*, movies, *Broadway Photoplay Co. v. World Film Corp.*, 225 N.Y. 104, 121 N.E. 756 (1919), plays, *Bernstein v. Meech*, 130 N.Y. 354, 29 N.E. 255 (1891), and, by analogy, records. What all of these have in common is their dependence upon taste or fancy for success. When the existence of damage is uncertain or speculative, the plaintiff is limited to the recovery of nominal damages. On the other hand,

> if the plaintiff has given valuable consideration for the promise of performance which would have given him a chance to make a profit, the defendant should not be allowed to deprive him of that performance without compensation unless the difficulty of determining its value is extreme. Especially is this true where there is no chance of loss.

11 Williston on Contracts § 1346, at 242 (3d ed. 1968). Thus, under the long-standing New York rule, when the existence of damage is certain, and the only uncertainty is as to its amount, the plaintiff will not be denied a recovery of substantial damages. Moreover, the burden of uncertainty as to the amount of damage is upon the wrongdoer and the test for admissibility of evidence concerning prospective damages is whether the evidence has any tendency to show their probable amount. The plaintiff need only show a "stable foundation for a reasonable estimate of royalties he would have earned had defendant not breached." *Freund v. Washington Square Press, Inc., supra*, 34 N.Y.2d at

383, 357 N.Y.S.2d at 861, 314 N.E.2d at 421. "Such an estimate necessarily requires some improvisation, and the party who has caused the loss may not insist on theoretical perfection." *Entis v. Atlantic Wire & Cable Corp.*, 335 F.2d 759, 763 (2d Cir. 1964). "[T]he law will make the best appraisal that it can, summoning to its service whatever aids it can command." *Sinclair Rfg. Co. v. Jenkins Co.*, 289 U.S. 689, 697, 53 S.Ct. 736, 739, 77 L.Ed. 1449 (1933).

We are confident that under the principles enunciated above the exclusion of the evidence proffered by Contemporary was error. This is not a case in which the plaintiff sought to prove hypothetical profits from the sale of a hypothetical record at a hypothetical price in a hypothetical market. At the time of the sale to ABC, the record was real, the price was fixed, the market was buying and the record's success, while modest, was increasing. Even after the promotional efforts ended, the the record was withdrawn from the market-place, it was carried, as a result of its own momentum, to an additional 10,000 sales and to a rise from approximately number 80 on the "Hot Soul Singles" chart of Billboard magazine to number 61. It cannot be gainsaid that if someone had continued to promote it, and if it had not been withdrawn from the market, it would have sold more records than it actually did. Thus, it is certain that Contemporary suffered some damage in the form of lost royalties. The same is not true, however, of the existence of damage in the form of lost opportunities for concert tours, theatrical tours or similar benefits. While it is certain that some sales were lost as a result of the failure to promote, we cannot believe that under *Freund* the New York Courts would accept what Famous' counsel aptly described at trial as Contemporary's "domino theory" of prospective damages. The theory is that if "Fear No Evil" had become a "hit," its success would have stimulated additional sales of the full two-record VIRGIN album and would have generated sufficient popular acceptance to enable Contemporary to obtain bookings for a nationwide concert tour. We hold that these additional benefits are too dependent upon taste or fancy to be considered anything other than speculative and uncertain, and, therefore, proof of damage in the form of such lost benefits was properly excluded by Judge Owen. *Freund v. Washington Square Press, Inc., supra.*

We next turn to the question of whether the evidence as to the amount of lost royalties was relevant under the standards set out above. Because "Fear No Evil" ultimately reached number 61 on the record charts, Contemporary offered a statistical analysis of every song that had reached number 61 during 1974. This analysis showed that 76 percent of the 324 songs that had reached number 61 ultimately reached the top 40; 65 percent reached the top 30; 51 percent reached the top 20; 34 percent reached the top 10; 21 percent reached the top 5; and 10 percent reached number 1. If the trial judge had admitted this evidence, Contemporary was prepared to offer the testimony of an expert witness who could have converted these measures of success into projected sales figures. The sales figures could be converted into lost royalties in accordance with the terms of the VIRGIN agreement.

Famous vigorously maintains, and Judge Owen agreed, that the data was incomplete because it failed to account for such factors as the speed with which the various records rose upward (the most successful records generally rise quickly—passing number 61 in their third or fourth week—"Fear No Evil" had risen relatively slowly—number 61 in ten weeks); the reputations of the various artists performing the recordings (Contemporary had no prior hit records and was relatively unknown); and the size and ability of the company promoting the recordings. We agree that a more accurate prediction of the success of "Fear No Evil" would be likely to result if the statistical analysis accounted for these and other factors. The omission of these factors from Contemporary's study affects only the weight of the evidence, however, and not its admissibility. Evidence need not be conclusive in order to be relevant. Standing alone, the study tended to prove that it was more likely than not that "Fear No Evil" would be among the 51 percent of recordings that reached the top 20. If Famous wished to offer proof that would tend to cast doubt on the accuracy of that prediction, it would be free to do so. In this way, all of the evidence tending to show the probable amount of Contemporary's damages would be placed before the jury. While it is true that the jury would be required to speculate to some degree with respect to whether "Fear No Evil" would be within any particular percentage, such is the nature of estimation. If the amount of damage were certain, no estimation would be required. But the uncertainty exists, and since it is a product of the defendant's wrongful conduct, he will not be heard to complain of the lack of precision. *Entis v. Atlantic Wire & Cable Corp., supra,* 335 F.2d at 763.

Because *Freund* does not bar proof of lost royalties and because the proffered evidence was relevant on that issue, Fed.R.Evid. 401, Judge Owen was required to admit it, Fed.R.Evid. 402, unless he found that "its probative value [was] substantially outweighed by the danger of unfair prejudice, confusion of the issues, or misleading the jury." Fed.R.Evid. 403. It may be, for example, that "[i]n the frame within which [they were sought to be] used . . . the [statistics], though relevant, became an item of prejudicial overweight." *Marx & Co. v. Diners' Club, Inc.,* 550 F.2d 505, 511 & n.19 (2d Cir. 1977). Similarly, it may be that if Contemporary was unprepared to offer an analysis of factors other than the bare statistics, those statistics, standing alone, would be misleading and would therefore not provide a "stable foundation for a reasonable estimate of royalties" that would have been earned if Famous had not breached. *Freund v. Washington Square Press, Inc., supra,* 34 N.Y.2d at 383, 357 N.Y.S.2d at 861, 314 N.E.2d at 421. Because Judge Owen did not reach these issues, and because we believe it would be inappropriate for this Court to engage in Rule 403 balancing in the first instance, the case must be remanded to the district court for the purpose of making a Rule 403 determination. The resolution of that issue will, in turn, determine whether Contemporary should be given the new trial on the issue of damages which it seeks on its cross-appeal.

The judgment of the district court is affirmed in all respects except as to its ruling with regard to lost royalties, and the case is remanded to the district court for further proceedings in accordance with this opinion.

VAN GRAAFEILAND, Circuit Judge, concurring in part and dissenting in part:

Although I concur with much that has been said in Judge Meskill's carefully researched opinion, there are several points on which I find myself in disagreement with my colleagues. The first of these concerns the contractual requirement for notice of breach, and the second involves the majority's remand for further consideration of an evidentiary ruling. I will address each of these briefly.

Notice of Breach

When a businessman retains a lawyer to prepare a contract, he expects, and is entitled to expect, that the lawyer will incorporate such provisions therein as are necessary to protect his client's interests. Nothing is more frustrating to the conscientious lawyer than to painstakingly draft such provisions and then have a court brush them aside as "hypertechnical".

The attorneys for appellant very carefully provided that no failure to perform should be termed a material breach unless appellee should first deliver to appellant "a written notice specifying the . . . alleged failure to act constituting such claimed material breach and [appellant] shall have failed to cure the material breach within thirty (30) days after receipt by [appellant] of such written notice." Where such a clause exists, it is settled law that there can be no recovery unless the notice provided for has been given. This rule of law assumes particular importance where, as here, a contract has been assigned and the assignor's obligations assumed, because the notice which it requires guarantees the assignor an opportunity to remedy a defect in performance about which the assignor might not otherwise know.

The notice relied on in this case consisted of a telegram followed closely by a letter. The telegram stated in substance that the sale to ABC constituted a breach of contract and that suit would be filed against ABC immediately. The District Court has held that the sale did not constitute a breach of contract, and my colleagues do not quarrel with this holding. The inventory of records was, of course, included in the sale, and plaintiff's statement that this transfer constituted an illegal seizure did not make it so. The letter stated that defendant had breached the contract in that it attempted to make a contract with ABC "creating an obligation or responsibility in behalf of or in the name of the Contemporary Mission." Defendant had done no such thing. It is clear, therefore, that neither the letter nor the telegram pointed to any breach of contract which the defendant was given a thirty-day opportunity to cure.

The majority opinion states that the letter and telegram placed defendant under a duty to communicate with ABC to "insure that the contract was being performed"; and, that "[h]ad it done so, it would have found" that it was not. This, however, was the very procedure that the thirty-day notice of default was designed to eliminate.[1] Without going into unpleasant details, the record shows that plaintiff's members were not naive recluses venturing timidly into the commercial world, but were aggressive entrepreneurs who were strangers to neither contract negotiations nor litigation. I see no reason why they should not be bound by the specific provisions of their contract in the same manner as would any other businessmen.

Evidentiary Remand

Under the Federal Rules of Evidence, the trial judge continues to have wide discretion in his rulings, which will not be disturbed unless this discretion has been clearly abused. "Hardly anywhere does the inherent nature of an adversary trial commit so much to the careful, but wide and flexible, discretion of the trial judge as it does on questions of admissibility of evidence." 11 Wright & Miller, Federal Practice and Procedure § 2885, at 282 (1973).

Judge Owen gave thorough consideration to the plaintiff's exhibit which purported to show the sales history of some 324 records that were number 61 or better on the record chart during 1974. Indeed, he permitted plaintiff to put its vice president on the stand in the absence of the jury to attempt to lay a proper foundation for the exhibit's admission and exercised remarkable restraint during this procedure, in the face of conduct by the witness which bordered on the contemptuous. The testimony of the witness showed that the sales history of each record was dependent upon the reputation of the performing artist, the size and resources of the recording company, the quality of the music and recording and the speed with which the record rose on the record chart. The exhibit which plaintiff offered in evidence did not contain information as to any of these items. I see not abuse of discretion in the trial court's rejection of it.

---

[1] It should also be noted that no written notice of any sort was given to the assignee. An assignee of a contract stands in the shoes of his assignor and acquires the assignor's rights thereunder. *Tambro Fabrics Corp. v. Deering Milliken, Inc.*, 35 A.D. 469, 471, 318 N.Y.S.2d 764 (1st Dep't 1971); *see In re S & L Vending Corp. v. 52 Thompkins Avenue Restaurant, Inc.*, 26 A.D.2d 935, 274 N.Y.S.2d 697 (2d Dept. 1966). The right to a thirty-day notice of default was such a contractual right.

Evidence which may be arguably relevant should not be admitted if it tends, as here, to mislead rather than enlighten the jury. This is particularly true where figures are summarized in documents which "have a way of acquiring an existence of their own, independent of the evidence which gave rise to them." *Holland v. United States*, 348 U.S. 121, 128, 75 S.Ct. 127, 131, 99 L.Ed. 150 (1954). Evidence should also be excluded which leads to possible confusion, or tends to prolong the trial or distract the jury into side issues, such as excursions into the detailed history of 324 unrelated recordings. I am not sure that I understand what my colleagues are directing the District Court to do upon remand. My position simply is that there was no error in the trial court's ruling and there is therefore no necessity for any type of remand.

I agree with the majority that the question of liability as to the Virgin contract is a "close one", and, as a juror, I might well have reached a different conclusion than was reached below. However, I would affirm the judgment on the Virgin contract, both as to liability and amount. I would reverse so much of the judgment as awards damages under the Crunch agreement and such damages as are unallocated.

"HOME BOX OFFICE'S SUITS SAY DIRECTORS GUILD IMPEDES PROGRESS"
Variety (July 26, 1978), p. 41

Hollywood, July 25.

Time Inc.'s Home Box Office last week (10) filed two legal actions against the Directors Guild of America, one with the National Labor Relations Board and an antitrust suit in the Federal Court of New York.

The one before the NLRB charges violations of the NLRB Act in that the DGA has made inappropriate and excessive demands for its members that are totally blind to the realities of the media dynamics of the feevee biz, and further claims that the DGA has been nonresponsive at the negotiating table. The antitrust suit asks the federal court to look into the manner in which the DGA establishes prices to be paid to its members.

The DGA currently does not have a contract covering the production of programs directly for feevee. Over the last two years, Home Box Office has produced more than 50 original shows for feevee, most of them using DGA member directors. For the last six months, the DGA and Home Box Office have been negotiating in New York, trying to reach an agreement to cover the employment of DGA people in the production of feevee programs. These negotiations reportedly completely broke down late last week, which led to HBO filing for legal remedies.

HBO's actions stem directly from DGA's reminders to members—of the rule—part and parcel of the Guild's constitutional bylaws—that they may not work for a non-signatory company. Also alarming HBO and causing it to seek legal action, were DGA reminders to production companies with whom the feevee firm wants to work out a deal that if they intend to employ DGA people for programs to be produced directly for feevee, they must notify the Guild and negotiate a collective bargaining agreement covering the new medium.

HBO regards these written reminders as "boycott letters." DGA views it as an obligation—that no matter if a production is licensed to HBO itself or licensed to an outside firm for presentation on the HBO system—there's an obligation to bargain with the Guild.

Aljean Harmetz, "FILM FIGURES DECRY PROFIT–SHARING EVILS"

The New York Times (February 3, 1978), p. C13

HOLLYWOOD, Feb. 2—Movie-studio managements frequently drain off profits from the sale of films to television and to theaters abroad, leaving little remuneration for producers, actors, writers and other artists, according to industry craftsmen who have begun to complain publicly of being slighted.

Double billing and inventing expenses are common practices used help make profits "disappear," the creative workers charge.

Executives of the film companies deny that there are any irregularities in their financial practices. They say the expenses they charge to picture budgets are based on their overhead and distribution costs and, among other things, must reflect their losses on films that don't go over at the box office.

"The old adage about foreign sales is, 'Anything west of Catalina and anything east of Staten Island, the studio will bury," said Robert Aldrich, the independent producer and director known for such films as "The Choirboys," "The Longest Yard" and "The Dirty Dozen."

Audits Won't Pay for Accountants

"If you had enough money," Mr. Aldrich said, "you can go audit them in Bangkok. But there are so many ways of concealing money abroad that the audit usually won't pay for the accountants."

Until recently, when attention focused on the alleged embezzlement of 461,008 from Columbia Pictures by its president, David Begelman, the creative people in the industry have generally kept quiet on what they are now publicly saying have been decades of cheating by the studios. Increasingly, their criticism is becoming pointed and detailed.

Norman Lear, producer of the television series, "All in the Family," described double billing on expenses overseas as routine.

"If a major distributor has four pictures being produced in Europe and sends a representative to check them out," he said, "The chances are that the cost of the trip will be charged to each production."

Tony Curtis, the actor, said in an interview Wednesday on "The Stanley Siegel Show" on WABC-TV that studio executives sometimes include expenses for their own entertainment in production costs.

For example, Mr. Curtis said, "A producer goes to Acapulco to talk to another producer about a movie, but in reality he takes 14 little 'chicklets' along with him."

Changes In Overseas Taxation

Gerald Lipsky, a show-business lawyer, said that for years certain European countries used to withhold money from the studios for taxes.

These days, he said, "the monies are no longer withheld from the companies. But the studios continue to exclude them from the gross.

"If my client has a percentage of the gross receipts of his picture," Mr. Lipsky continued, "I made sure the studio has actually paid the taxes it deducts."

Sometimes, the creative people charge package sales of several films to television are devised in such a way that the films that made the most money in movie houses and made the package most desirable are allocated a disproportionate share of the profit.

"If a studio sells five movies to television," Peter Bart, the independent producer who made "Fun with Dick and Jane," said, "it decides how much revenue to allocate to each of the films. It usually dumps most of the television money on the films that have lost money rather than on the big money-making film that sold the whole television package."

Settlements and Anger

Mr. Bart's complaint was echoed by, among others, Warren Beatty, the actor, and Ross Hunter and Larry Turman, producers. Mr. Turman sued Avco-Embassy over his share of the profits from the sale to television of "The

Graduate." His case, like most other suits against the studios, was settled out of court.

This appears to have become an accepted way of doing business in the Hollywood of the 70's. And it is a situation that has fueled an undercurrent of anger among many in the industry.

"You have to fight to get back what's legally yours," said Sean Connery, who has starred in a number of James Bond films. "And all the time you're chasing to get the money to which you're entitled, the studio has the use of it."

"The new attitude seems to be," Brooks, director of "Looking for Mr. Goodbar," said, " 'Go ahead, sue. Take us to court.' The studios know it's going to take two or three years to get on a docket, and they can lend your money out at 18 percent."

Mr. Lipsky, the lawyer, pointed out that a new accounting practice permits the studios to hold on to the money for longer than previously.

"The motion picture companies used to account to you monthly," he said. "Now they account quarterly, and Universal is moving toward accounting semiannually."

Old Tie-In With Exhibitors

Daniel Sklar, an entertainment lawyer whose clients include the actress Lily Tomlin, attributes much of the problem to what he calls the old-fashioned, creaking, historically unsound insanity of motion-picture financing. "Hollywood was never designed to make money," he said. "The studios were set up originally simply as factories for the exhibition companies. M-G-M, for example, was set up to provide products for the Loews Theaters."

When the Justice Department forced separation of the exhibition chains from their studios, starting in 1948, the studios had to stand on their own feet as independent profit-making entities.

Robert Evans, former head of production at Paramount Pictures, is one independent producer who does not begrudge the studios the means they have chosen to use to turn a profit. "The companies are not in any way stealing from the picture makers," he said. Referring to a gambler's betting advantage, he added: "They have to have built-in vigorishes or they'd go broke. Who pays for the $21 million loss on 'Sorcerer?' The studio!"

A Weak Second Feature

Mr. Evans, who has 36 percent of the gross of his "Black Sunday," said his percentage was "not quite worth a ticket to the movies," despite the film's moderate success. Nor will he see any profit from his "Marathon Man," which, he says, cost $8 million and brought Paramount $35 million. "But that doesn't make the system wrong," he added.

Mr. Evans said: "To be successful as a profit participant, it's not enough to have made a film that makes money. You have to have a blockbuster."

Most creators who are supposed to share in the profits of their films are less generous toward the studios than Mr. Evans. Mr. Connery speaks bitterly about how "Columbia put out 'The Anderson Tapes' with a Mickey Mouse second feature, a disaster that didn't make a penny." "But Columbia allocated it 50 percent of the money every time they played together," Mr. Connery contended.

Mr. Sklar said certain distribution expenses defied "rational analysis." "I sold a picture to television once myself," he recalled. "The studio demanded a 10 percent fee and they didn't even make a phone call. I was told, 'That's the way we do it.' "

Mr. Connery, who along with his colleague, Michael Caine, has filed suit against Allied Artists Pictures charging that they were cheated of earnings due them from "The Man Who Would Be King," said that the accounting practice was accepted by everyone in the industry was "intolerable."

"I'm talking about millions of dollars," he added, "And every actor, producer and director in this town knows what I am talking about."

Allied Artists denies Mr. Connery's allegations, but concedes accounting procedures involving the film have been in dispute for more than a year.

"Studio overhead" is another tender subject to independent film makers. Mr. Sklar points out that the lights and cameras charged to each picture made at a studio "have already been paid for a hundred times over."

Mr. Brooks also told of trying to get Columbia to use the sound and editing equipment he owned:

"I wanted to lend it to the studio free of charge so that I could make my pictures for less money. They said, 'We don't want your equipment. We're going to rent you our equipment.' I said, 'Give me two extra days of shooting time instead.' They said, 'No, no, no.' It was Catch-22. They said, 'Renting equipment is our business.'

"Mr. Brooks added that when he made the same offer to Paramount on "Looking for Mr. Goodbar," the studio was delighted to accept it.

"The joke," Mr. Curtis said bitterly, "is that a movie costs $1 million, grosses $7 million, and then they say, 'Well, we just broke even.' "

"I have been cheated for years," he said in his televised interview. He cited "The Great Race," in which he appeared. He said it grossed $21 million. "It was supposed to cost $6 million," he said, "then I was told $8 million, then $11 million."

He said he had never been able to find out what the extra $5 million was for.

Mario Puzo, "HOLLYWOOD'S RAID ON ISRAEL, OR IDI AMIN'S REVENGE"
New York Magazine (October 4, 1976), p. 46

For the first time in the history of Israel, I fear for its survival. It is getting mixed up with Hollywood.

A few months ago the whole world, minus a few Arabs, was stunned with admiration when Israeli commandos flew 2,000 miles to Entebbe and rescued 100 hostages from a band of determined terrorists plus the whole Ugandan Army. Especially impressed were eight Hollywood moguls who immediately announced plans to immortalize the famous raid on film.

These eight moguls exerted all the charm for which they are famous in persuading Israel to cooperate in making the picture, each with his own particular company. Now, an Israel besieged by eight Hollywood moguls determined to be charming is in the position of a virgin washed ashore on a Devil's Island of convicted rapists.

What really worried me was the announcement by Israel that it may cooperate simply because income from a blockbusting movie would surely provide desperately needed foreign dollars. Those foreign dollars would buy bandages for the Israeli wounded, build more orange groves, buy tanks and modern fighter planes for an Israeli Army surrounded by 100 million Arabs. I hate to be a Jonah, but from some extensive research and a little bit of personal experience, I think Israel will be lucky to come out of the deal with enough dollars for two jeeps and a B-17.

What Israel does not yet understand is that movie studios have a religious veneration for the profits made by their films. Sure, Hollywood has donated millions of dollars to the Israeli cause, but now we are talking *business.* We are talking *deals.* In short, we are dealing in blood. A hundred studio lawyers will man the barricades to prevent any outside participants from getting their percentages. Specially trained kamikaze accountants with no fear of federal grand juries will dazzle Israeli eyes with Sten-gun balance sheets to cut them out of the profit pie. Top studio executives who have gone through special bypass operations that drain pity and mercy out of their blood will give Israel no quarter, literally as well as figuratively.

For example, to be personal, just this once, I have a 10 percent "net" of *Godfather II*, which grossed nearly 50 million dollars ($50,000,000). I will never see a penny. And I am not alone. Hundreds of actors, writers, and even some directors never see a cent of their percentages from successful movies.

Now it's hard to shed a tear for people like us who make a handsome living from our work. But what about the hero depicted in *Dog Day Afternoon*, the saga of an unsuccessful bank robber in love with a transvestite?

This was a story taken from real life. The hero signed away his rights for $7,500 and 1 percent of the net profits. The film ended up making 20 million bucks ($20,000,000). Then it was suddenly discovered that the hero, who had screwed up robbing a bank, had also screwed up by signing the "wrong" papers. He didn't even get his 1 percent ($200,000). Now you can really feel a little sorry for him. He was a Vietnam veteran. He married a pretty little girl who immediately ballooned up to 250 pounds. Then he fell in love with a transvestite, who demanded, instead of a box of chocolates or a diamond ring, money for a sex-change operation. So our hero tried to rob a bank, screwed that up, got his gun-toting buddy killed, and went to jail for a long stretch. When he got his $7,500 movie front money he gave it to his transvestite sweetheart, who got his sex-change operation; "she" then fell in love with another guy and broke off all communications with our hero. So there he is in prison, his wife and his children destitute, his true love, now really a girl, jilting him. A little pity? Never. Not Hollywood. The son of a bitch was a bank robber. Why should he get rich from his misdeeds?

Okay, let's try another case that I really can't vouch for; it sounds, even to me, a little too much. A famous producer made his studio hundreds of millions of dollars with a string of successful films. Finally he made one of the most successful movies of all time. His percentage would make him rich for the rest of his life. But the picture went $100,000 over budget.

Immediately 100 studio lawyers were put on 24-hours-a-day active duty. They went over every contract and they found a clause which implied that if the picture went over budget the producer could lose his percentage points. That was enough. The studio refused to pay and gleefully invited the producer to sue or accept a modest settlement. Rather than go to court for five years and fight that army of 100 lawyers, the producer took his settlement and moved to another studio.

Well, again, you can't feel too sorry for him as he stretches out by his swimming pool, surrounded by five blondes. Let's try again.

Years ago there was a very young, sweet, religious girl suddenly stricken by polio. She decided to go to the famous shrine at Lourdes and pray for a miracle cure so that she could become a singing nun. Sure enough, the miracle happened. She was cured. In addition, her body acquired the holy stigmata, the wounds of Christ on the Cross. With those stigmata she had a good chance of being declared a saint. She became the most famous person in the western world.

Hollywood immediately got on the scent. Millions of people would pay cash to see a girl bearing the holy stigmata on the silver screen. Hollywood envoys "romanced" her, as they say, and unluckily for her she agreed to accept a big hunk of the "net."

The movie studio wanted this film to have a truly authentic holy atmosphere. So it shot the picture in Lourdes. It turned out to be a gold-mine decision. Thousands of cripples visit Lourdes, and the producer used them all as extras. Naturally, since they were not really *able-bodied extras*, the movie studio paid them only $5 a day. The studio then charged the production of the picture $20 a day for each extra and put the difference in its pockets. This worked out very well. Because the use of thousands of extras at $20 a day (on the accounting balance sheet) so hiked the cost of the production that the candidate saint-star never saw a penny of her percentage deal.

And thinking that over, I guess you can't feel too sorry for her. She did get her one miracle.

One studio executive did express a little guilt. But the producer of the film set him right. Where did the girl rate a percentage of the movie? All she contributed was the faded stigmata, and a studio makeup artist could have done a much more convincing job. And remember all those cripples the studio gave jobs to.

I guess what Hollywood commits is what is called a "victimless crime." But Israel is a special case. Sure, the movie should be made. The story is a natural. A great story. The good guys win, a hundred innocent people are rescued from death, the excuse for violence is morally unassailable. You don't even have to be a Zionist to root for this picture. It's such a great story that even the Arabs will love it.

But Israel has to be very careful in making this deal. It must resist tempting offers like 100 percent of the net profits. It must not think of itself as a country but as a "creative, above-the-line item" in the world of moviemakers. Therefore, a *deal* must be made. Israel should then remember that this is a world which awarded a humanitarian award to a studio head who quite frankly admits that he is ruthless in protecting the interest of his studio, that he first makes the toughest deals possible and then asks what is wrong or unfair about that. True, he voices the essence of business-world morality. But his position reminds me of an argument my friend Marvin Winkler had with a boxer who was training for the Golden Gloves:

The boxer was 160 pounds of solid muscle, 22 years old, and moved so fast he *danced* the mile in under four minutes. Winkler was 160 pounds of solid fat because he religiously ate three pounds of chocolate a day. When the argument got really heavy, the boxer asked Winkler how much he weighed. Winkler said 160. The boxer said he also weighed 160, so they could step outside and settle the argument. The boxer said apologetically, "I never pick on a guy under my weight class." Marvin Winkler blinked and said, "Of course, neither would I. I was lying to you. I weigh 190."

But let us get down to realities. Israel will not be able to resist the offer of 100 percent of the "net" profits. Especially when the studio guarantees it that the picture will cost 10 million dollars ($10,000,000) and assures it that the picture will gross 50 million dollars ($50,000,000). Only eight movies in history have topped that high a gross. Israel will then ask for script approval and Hollywood will say, "Sure, of course" and the deal will be clinched. How can Israel say no? A potential $40-million profit and control of its movie image. Well, Israel will never see a dime.

Here's how it works. Any top-notch Hollywood executive knows a blockbuster movie must have two major stars. So let's say *The Entebbe Raid* is cast with Steve McQueen and Robert Redford. (Only the truly ignorant or possibly anti-Semitic will raise the problem that they do not look Jewish.) Steve McQueen costs $3 million up front and 10 percent of the gross. Robert Redford costs $2 million up front and 10 percent of the gross. That's five million bucks right there, just front money. Then we have the small fry.

Out of proper respect (public-relations-wise), you will have a get major actors to play the parts of Yitzhak Rabin and Moshe Dayan, or maybe even get them to play themselves. You'll need a top actor to play the terrorist leader and then maybe Helen Hayes to play one of the hostages. You need somebody really great to play President Amin. And how about the French airliner crew that elected to stay with the hostages when offered their release? You need a top French star to play the pilot. This all costs money.

Let's be very conservative and say that's another million dollars. But then there is a top director. He costs a million plus 10 percent of the gross. Well, maybe we can get him for 5 percent of the gross. (Notice how none of these people takes "net.")

That takes care of the "above-the-line costs" except for the hundred grand for the writers, which we won't even count. You won't need good writers. The story is there. All you need is a stitching job, a good "body and fenders" man, as they say in the movie business.

Now there is a "below-the-line" cost. The technicians, the camera crew, the soundmen, wardrobes, travel, sets, etc. Now remember this is a big, big production. Lots of explosions, lots of equipment, a lot of shooting days. I'll be very conservative and estimate "below the line" at $4 million. This brings the total cost of production to 10 million dollars ($10,000,000). As the movie studio guaranteed. And I think it really will be able to keep the cost down to this figure because the movie studio will con Israel into contributing its army as free extras, its military equipment, and even the huge crowd that welcomes the returning hostages and Entebbe heroes at the Tel Aviv air terminal.

Okay, so far it looks good. The picture comes in at $10 million. The gross rentals are $50 million. That leaves a net of 40 million dollars for Israel ($40,000,000). But now watch how this huge sum melts away. The studio charges 25 percent of the production cost on every movie for studio overhead. Twenty-five percent of $10 million is $2.5 million. Now remember, Redford and McQueen have 10 percent of the gross. That's $5 million for each of them. Another $10 million gone. Total: $12.5 million.

But in a picture like this, the first thing the studio has to do is knock out the competition. Remember those seven other production companies planning movies about Entebbe? You think they will give up their places at the trough without a fight? Yet it stands to reason that even a great story like Entebbe can't support eight different movies. So everybody will start suing each other. Legal fees will run at least a million dollars for the studio that wins. But you can't win in court. Eventually you have to buy everybody out. The deal will be gross percentages varying according to the strength of various opponents. Forget about trying to give these guys "net." That's like trying to sell a jeweler a zircon.

Altogether, the opposing companies will wind up with about 10 percent of the gross. That's $5 million gone again.

And of course there is the director. One hopes he has been chiseled down to 5 percent of the gross, but that's still $2.5 million. I almost forgot: That $1 million for legal expenses is added to the cost of the film. So 25 percent of that is charged for studio overhead. But that's only another 250 grand. We won't even count it. Hell, we don't even need it. Now let's see where we are at:

Gross receipts:	$50,000,000
Disbursements:	
Cost of film	$10,000,000
Percentage for Redford and McQueen	10,000,000
Percentage for buying off competition	5,000,000
Studio overhead charge	
(25 percent of cost)	2,500,000
Director (5 percent)	2,500,000
Legal costs	1,000,000
Producer (I forgot all about him)	500,000

Total (so far)	$31,500,000
Net (what's left for Israel):	$13,500,00

Not so fast. Do you really think this Hollywood movie studio is going to let a bunch of foreigners run off with that kind of money? *Its* money?

Now the time has come to tell you the real reason why movie studios make movies. They don't really want to make movies. To make movies you have to deal with creative people like directors, actors, and writers who are all a pain in the ass. Movie companies make movies so that they can be the *distributors.*

What is a distributor? He takes the completed movie and sells it to exhibitors who own movie houses. For this the distributor gets 35 percent of the gross domestic and up to 45 percent of the gross foreign. On our $50-million picture of the Entebbe raid the distributor will get between $17 million and $20 million. Let's be fair and say just $17 million. So:

Receipts:	$50,000,000
Disbursements:	
Previously listed	$31,500,000
Distributor	17,000,000
	——————
Total (so far)	$48,500,000
Net (what's left for Israel):	$ 1,500,000

Well, $1.5 million is not great, but it's something. But who the hell is Israel to get that kind of money?

Now what comes next may strike the ordinary layman as expenses that should be borne by the distributor, who, after all, has collected 17 million bucks. Remember, the distributor is the same guy who made the movie. (I really don't understand this part. Maybe the movies have the Big Fix going in Washington.) Remember, the movie business has special tax favors so that it gets back four tax-dollar exemptions for every dollar it loses in making a movie. That is why it has a distribution arm, a very heavy arm, that ensures the picture will show a loss. Anyway, here is the list of expenses that will wipe Israel out of its 100 percent net for ever and ever:

Domestic Distribution

(deducted from gross receipts)

Advertising	$5,000,000
Prints	1,000,000
Freight and insurance	
(Doesn't the distributor ever stop freeloading?)	100,000
Dues (For what?)	100,000

Taxes	100,000
Checking cost	50,000
Dubbing	20,000
Copyright (Really!)	60
Total	$6,370,060

So what we have now is the gross receipts of $50 million and disbursements of $48,500,000 plus this last disbursement of over 6 million dollars.

I won't even bother listing the foreign expenses in these categories which come to about half of domestic. So total domestic and foreign distribution costs easily come to $9 million.

Receipts:	$50,000,000
Disbursed:	57,500,000
Left for Israel:	Zip ($0)

In fact, this leaves the picture $7.5 million in the red, which serves a good many purposes. If the film is made under a tax-shelter deal, the movie company might get back a four-time exemption of that $7.5 million. Also, the picture could get a big TV sale, and that money is buried by the red ink. Incidentally, the *distributor* gets 30 percent of the gross of a TV sale even if the deal only takes one phone call from the studio to the TV network.

But, Hollywood would argue, look at the great public-relations benefit that Israel will receive from the film. Israelis will be heroes the world over. They will become a legend. But, again, this is not necessarily true. Hollywood has a brilliant record of turning great material into horribly distressing and offending movies. Even with script approval, Israel may not like this picture.

Script approval doesn't mean much. The casting, the directing, and most of all the final cut of the film will determine its point of view, the overall effect. What if the studio hires the wrong director? Some of the candidates mentioned are George Roy Hill, Sidney Lumet, Mark Robson. Heavyweights. My vote would go to George Roy Hill. He made *The Sting* and *Butch Cassidy and the Sundance Kid.* Huge moneymakers, fun to see. And George Roy Hill has no delusions of grandeur despite his use of three names. He knows his limitations. He never, never fools around with ideas or character development. He just gets Newman and Redford up there on the screen and lets them do their foolproof stuff. He banishes tragedy. Even when his heroes die in the final minute, by some amazing directorial art he turns it into a happy ending and you go out of the theater happy as a lark. Nevertheless, directors like George Roy Hill are fiercely proud about having final cut on their work. You never can tell what might happen. Remember that *Sting* and *Butch Cassidy* had outlaws as their heroes. What if Hill decides to cast Paul Newman as one of the terrorists? Or Godfrey Cambridge as Idi Amin? Cambridge is visually lovable on film. Will the state of Israel be ready for a lovable Amin in *its* movie story? But Hill gets my vote.

Sidney Lumet did a wonderful job on *Dog Day Afternoon*, but that was in New York City. Lumet is a camera poet shooting America's decaying urban landscape—not the best preparation for the lush greens and reds of Africa. And Lumet is socially aware. He may give us ten minutes of film that argues Israel's moral right to break international law when it invaded Uganda. He may give us another ten minutes of film showing the social and philosophical motivations of the terrorists. Not so terrible, except that it is not this movie. That's another movie.

As for Mark Robson, without SenSurround he's just another pretty Hollywood face.

What about cutting the film? The studios have to worry about America's huge black audience. You can't have the Israeli heroes slaughtering black Ugandan troops and expect American blacks to rush to the theater. The studio may finesse this by casting Sidney Poitier as the leader of an Israeli commando team. Or maybe even show how President Amin is not such a bad guy after all. Can Israel live with these accommodations?

Without a doubt Israel would forbid such proposals. But what if Moshe Dayan makes a big hit in his cameo role and Hollywood lures him away to become a movie star? What if a top Israeli commando officer proves so photogenic that he decides to make his future in films? Beverly Hills is a far cry from a kibbutz. Can Israel afford to lose such valuable manpower?

Of course, a miracle could happen. Let's say the picture grosses a hundred million bucks. Then the studio-accountant magicians will run out of places to hide the money. The studio will find a clause that will enable it to withhold payment and compel Israel to take it to court, the studio's hundred kamikaze lawyers waiting. In that case, my final bit of advice to Israel is this:

Get 200 of your toughest commandos. Load them into your armored transport planes with tanks and artillery. Land them on the lawn of the Beverly Hills Hotel and raise your standard. Thousands of writers, stars, directors, and actors will spring from their Malibu beach homes and Beverly Hills mansions to join your cause. You will march on the studio bank vaults together. Then, maybe, Israel will get its percentage.

Will Hollywood get mad? Never. When the smoke has cleared, eight moguls will fly to Tel Aviv with a great idea for another movie.

The title?

Entebbe II:
*The Raid on Beverly Hills**

"ROGERS SUES LIBERTY FOR $44 MIL, CLAIMING LABEL SHORTCHANGED HIM"

Variety (October 28, 1981), p. 63

Hollywood, Oct. 27.

Kenny Rogers, who is indisputably Liberty Records' biggest record seller, has filed a $44,000,000 breach of contract suit against that label, accusing it of failing to pay him the full amount of royalties due.

It is also Rogers' contention in the Los Angeles Superior Court suit that "general policies and practices" at the label with regard to royalties have affected "all or most" Liberty pactees in much the same manner.

Suit, which seeks $4,000,000 in general damages and $40,000,000 in punitive damages, cites 17 different "tactics" allegedly used by Liberty to pay out "substantially less" royalties than were due him.

In the area of free goods, Rogers says that the diskery mislabelled as "free goods" disks which should have been subject to royalties. Upon the return of these disks, Rogers alleges that royalties were deducted from his account, even though his account had not been credited for royalties upon the sale of these records.

In the area of promotional records, Rogers also accuses Liberty of mislabelling as promotional copies records which were actually sold and upon which royalties should have been paid.

Rogers' suit also alleges that Liberty bilked him in the following ways:

—Reducing his royalty payments by deducting a "packaging charge" from the retail price of each unit sold.

—Applying lower than agreed-upon rates when computing foreign royalties.

—Failing to account and pay royalties due for sales through the Columbia Record Club.

Note: Just after writing this piece, I learned that Warner Bros. will receive Israel's cooperation in making its version of the film. Israel might do well to have William Peter Blatty as its agent. Blatty is the only known writer (The Exorcist) who walked off with a good piece of the profits of his film. He is also suing Warner Bros., presumably for receipts that disappeared from his view in accounting.

—Deducting from royalties foreign taxes paid by Liberty.

—Refusing to supply Rogers' accountants with data necessary to verify record sales.

—Refusing to increase royalties with increases in retail list prices, as provided for in his pacts with the label.

—Refusing to pay escalated royalties as called for in his pacts.

—Failing to provide a timely accounting of foreign royalties due.

Suit contends that Liberty was apprised of these and other complaints on May 20 of this year. Rogers' Liberty pact is supposed to expire at year's end.

Richard Hummler, "AUTHORS, PRODUCERS BREAK OFF CONFABS"
Variety (November 25, 1981), p. 97

SPLIT ON REVISION OF ROYALTY TERMS

Talks between the Dramatists Guild and the League of N.Y. Theatres & Producers aimed at revising Broadway authors' financial compensation have broken off in disagreement. Prospects for a quick resumption of the discussions, which have been going on for almost four years, appear slight. There is no immediate threat of a production tieup, however.

The League's production committee, comprised of Richard Barr, League president, and Norman Kean, today (Tues.) submitted a report to the organization's executive committee. It's understood that they noted that an impasse has developed between the two groups and that League members shouldn't expect any imminent modification of the minimum basic agreement with the Guild. The League and the Guild last met June 10.

It had been believed that the League and the Guild were progressing toward a modification, which producers have been seeking for decades, in the basic agreement between the two groups. The most important provision of the pact is the minimum royalty structure of 10%, less $300, for authors of plays, and 6% for authors of musicals. Although the two groups had reached tentative agreement on several points, they weren't able to agree on a revised basic royalty structure.

A formula initially acceptable to both sides was discussed. It would have provided for authors to accept royalty waivers when their shows grossed less than 75% of capacity. The authors were willing to take a percentage of their full contractual royalty corresponding directly to the percentage of capacity grossed by the show.

For example, if a play with a weekly potential of $200,000 had grossed $126,000, or 63% of capacity, the authors would have received 63% of their full contractual royalty, or about $12,400 instead of $19,700. In weeks when the gross fell below 45% of capacity, authors' royalties would have automatically been reduced to $500 for straight plays and $1,500 for musicals. Full royalties would be paid on all shows grossing 75% of capacity or more.

The discussions foundered, however, on differing interpretations of weekly grossing potential at capacity. The producers' committee defined "gross capacity" as the equivalent of the weekly ticket manifest, i.e. the grossing potential represented by the full face value of every ticket for the weekly eight performances. The playwrights' delegation at first accepted that definition, but subsequently balked when they realized that weekly "gross capacity" is never actually achieved because of inevitable discounts for sales commissions to credit card companies and discount services. They insisted that the "net gross", rather than the "gross gross" be the basis of the royalty waiver agreement, and the producers held to the "gross gross" concept.

In addition to the revised royalty proposal, the Guild and the League had also reached tentative accord on substantially higher pre-production advances against royalties for authors. The new formula would have guaranteed authors of musicals 2½% of the total capitalization, and play authors 3% of the capitalization, payable upon full capitalization. Theoretically, that would mean about $50,000 as an advance for the authors of a $2,000,000 musical and $22,500 to the author of a $750,000 play. Prevailing advances are much smaller, often as low as $500 to a play author and $1,500 to musical authors.

In addition, the two committees had provisionally agreed to new terms on the sharing of subsidiary income between authors and productions. In return for increased advances and/or profit participation, authors would have reduced their share of subsidiary income. The current requirement of 21 performances for a show to share in subsidiary revenue was also to have been modified.

But those tentatively revised terms and the modified royalty structure are now moot in view of the breakoff of talks. Producers have been insistent for many years that the Guild's royalty minimums are unreasonably high and the primary reason for the steadily increasing length of time required for shows to recoup their investments. Authors tend to feel that they're being singled out unfairly and that their royalties aren't excessive in view of the length of time required to write plays and musicals and the relatively small amount of upfront payment.

"The idea of authors getting a fixed royalty, no matter what the show takes in, will eventually destroy this business" says Bernard Jacobs, president of the Shubert Organization and a fervent advocate of modified authors' royalties. "Because the underlying costs have risen so much it now costs about $200,000 a week for a musical to break, even *without* royalties. They've got to make some accommodation or we'll never be able to return anything to investors."

Jacobs and other producers also object to the uniform application of the Guild's minimum basic agreement for all playwrights. They argue that all playwrights aren't equally deserving of compensation.

"There is no problem about Peter Shaffer getting full royalties and a percentage of the profits, because 'Amadeus' deserves it," says Jacobs. "But the Dramatists Guild isn't full of Peter Shaffers."

Peter Stone, president of the Dramatists Guild and a member of the committee that held the talks with the League, defends the Guild's protectiveness of its royalty structure on the ground that the authors' organization has never asked for increased terms since it was established in the 1920s. He also charges that producers are attempting to penalize authors because they've been unwisely generous with other guilds and unions in recent years.

"Producers now take 2, 3 or 4% of the gross when they used to take nothing," says Stone. "Directors used to get 1% and now they get 3 to 5%. Choreographers used to get one-half percent and now they get 1%. Many scenic and costume designers now get a weekly royalty. The playwrights didn't make those deals, the producers did."

Stone says the authors are wary of accepting compensation on the basis of "net" figures. "I am not accusing any of the major producers of dishonesty, but can they assure me that none of the League members wouldn't use 'creative' bookkeeping? Accepting 'net' and 'profit' terms would bring Hollywood practices into the theatre, and there's not a picture going that doesn't involve some sort of legal action on the part of the profit participants against the producer. Why start it?"

If authors agreed to "net" compensation, Stone suggests, "we'd be arguing over every item in the budget. Why did you spend so much for the tv commercial? Does anybody want that to happen?"

Stone asserts that he regrets the Guild-League standoff "profoundly." He declares, "we're willing and anxious to discuss methods by which playwrights cooperate in the repayment of investments to backers in a speedier and more efficient manner. But it has to be reasonable.

In practice some producers have been successful in acquiring production rights to plays outside the aegis of the Guild, and others have tried to do so without success. It's not uncommon for authors to enter into "side agreements" outside the Guild agreement in which a schedule for royalty waivers and deferrals is accepted in advance of production. Authors also usually agree to waive or defer royalties in losing weeks.

The League-Guild talks were an attempt to formalize and codify such ad hoc economic modifications. The producers are convinced that the existing Guild royalty structure deters potential investors and invariably prolongs the period of recoupment. The collapse of the talks is a further important indication of the worsening economic climate in the commercial theatre, and possibly a sign that fewer shows will be produced in the future.

Ken Terry, "VARIABLE RECORD PRICING COMES OF AGE"
Variety (August 31, 1983), p. 101

LABELS GRAPPLE WITH NEW IDEAS

As a byproduct of the recent recession, the record labels have been forced, to varying extents, to adopt "variable pricing" strategies that would have been unthinkable during the boom years of the industry. A new pattern is starting to emerge in which new artist releases are priced at $5.98 or $6.98 list, albums by established acts come out at $8.98 list, and slower-moving catalog items are pegged at $5.98 or $6.98.

Of course, this is a very simplified view of the actual situation. First of all, many of the sub-$8.98 new artist releases are mini-LPs (also known as EPs), which contain fewer cuts than full-length albums. Secondly, the percentage of debut records that are not full-priced varies significantly from one diskery to another.

At CBS Records, according to Paul Smith, senior v.p./g.m. of marketing, about half of the new artist releases are priced at a wholesale level below the equivalent of $8.98 list (CBS has no list prices). Warner Bros. sales veepee Lou Dennis, on the other hand, says "not that many" tyro releases are $5.98 list mini-LPs or $6.98 list full-length disks. And at Polygram, senior v.p. of marketing Harry Losk estimates that no more than 5% of his company's new act releases come out at less than $8.98 list.

Looking at the overall release skeds of all the majors, however, it is increasingly evident that putting out debut LPs and mini-LPs at sub-$8.98 prices has become a very common, if not a standard practice.

Similarly, while Losk notes that "most of the companies have pretty scrupulously maintained a lot of catalog items at $8.98," they all have midlines consisting of catalog titles that are no longer selling up to earlier levels. WEA, which, alone among the majors, has raised its midline price from

$5.98 to $6.98, placed all $8.98 list LPs released before 1982 in its midline as of last Jan. 1. CBS, too, has a very substantial midline, to which it adds new selections on a regular bimonthly basis.

Recession Impact

The lower new artist and midline prices are a direct result of the precipitous plunge in record sales that began around 1979 and has only started to reverse itself this year. As Elliot Hoffman, a prominent disk biz attorney, puts it, "The fact is that records did get too expensive for a recession pocketbook."

Now that the economy seems to be recovering, label execs are loathe to rule out future price increases that would end the variable pricing situation. "Variable pricing is with us," Lou Dennis of Warners comments. "How long it will be with us I don't know. People are always testing new pricing concepts."

Similarly, Losk has mixed feelings about variable pricing. Lower-priced new artist releases, he says, have "met with varying degrees of success," depending largely on the music. ("If it's lousy, it won't sell at 99¢.") Although releasing debut disks at a lower price does encourage retailers to put them on the shelves, he avers, they'll still give most of their display space to the records that are happening on the charts. "We're not convinced that (low-priced new artist records) are the wave of the future," he states.

Smith of CBS, which largely pioneered variable pricing, is still bullish about the concept: "I think it's exactly the right way to go, and I hope it's a permanent rather than a temporary thing."

Smith points out that nearly every other industry patterns itself in such a way that its product is worth more at retail when it's hot. "The record industry is just now catching onto this idea," he says.

Deep Discounting

It is undoubtedly true that, before midlines came along, catalog was normally priced higher than hit records at retail, due to the deep discounting of hits which had become common across the country. Now, with so much catalog list-priced a few dollars lower than full-line hit product, the situation has become more equalized at retail. Hits are rarely selling for less than midlines, even on special sales, and are often selling for substantially more. According to Smith, in fact, at least three major chains have shelf-priced $8.98 list albums at $9.49, and many other dealers price full-line LPs at or near list.

Both Smith and Losk assert that deep discounting has become less widespread since the industry's go-go days. Smith notes there are fewer all-label and multi-label sales and that price slashing on hits has become "more selective." Dennis of Warner Bros. agrees that shelf prices have been "inching up," but he maintains that "sale prices are still very low" on a broad range of product.

Retailers confirm this view. Mike Weiner, a buyer for the Long Island-based Record World chain, says that 40–50 hit $8.98 LPs are usually on sale in his company's stores for prices ranging from $5.99–$6.99. In comparison, shelf price on $6.98 records is $6.49, and $5.98 items go for list price, unless they're on sale. Consequently, Weiner points out, the hits are often priced at around the same levels as the midline catalog and new artist releases.

Bob Varcho, catalog buyer for the Ohio-based Stark/Camelot chain, notes that, in his chain's stores, there's still a difference between midline and hit prices, even with discounting of the latter. Sale price on $8.98's varies from $6.99 to $7.99, compared with shelf price of $6.99 for $6.98 list and $5.99 for $5.98 list. Midlines rarely go on sale, he says, because they're already low-priced, but the hits are frequently put on sale to meet stiff competition in most of Camelot's markets.

A couple of years ago, recalls Varcho, catalog sold for a buck more than hits. Now Stark/Camelot can make more money out of lower-priced catalog than it can from discounted hits. The hot product is still being "given away," he says, and "you're still basically making money on catalog."

Lower Royalty Rate

Meanwhile, record companies are presumably making more money on slow-moving catalog pegged at $5.98 or $6.98 than at $8.98 list. Not only are sales often higher at the lower price, but royalties paid to artists are much lower. According to one experienced lawyer, the standard royalty rate for midlines is now only half of that on full-priced records; when midlines first appeared, in contrast, the rates were two-thirds to three-quarters of the full-priced percentage, he says. Of course, manufacturing costs are fixed, regardless of what the album is wholesaled for; but by the time a record goes into a midline, a diskery's investment in producing the LP has usually been recouped.

The attorney points out that the standard deal on placement of his album in a midline is "doubly disadvantageous" to an artist, because not only will he get paid on a lower list price, but at a reduced rate on that price. He believes that half-rate royalties are common even for top artists, who are generally more interested in negotiating a good deal on their upcoming releases.

David Werchen, another disk biz attorney, says that midline rates are negotiable, with a spread of up to 5% between full-price and mid-price royalty percentages. Thus, whereas an artist might get 12–14% on an $8.98 release, he could get as little as 7% on a $5.98 release.

Whether or not a new artist release will be priced at $8.98 list or at the $5.98/$6.98 level (with its cut-rate royalty) usually depends on the label's evaluation of the act's marketability. For instance, attorney Elliot Hoffman points out that, when Geffen Records was negotiating with Asia—"predictably a smash band"—he pushed hard for an initial $8.98 release, and Geffen went along with it.

With the average new band, though, states Hoffman, it doesn't make sense to "squeeze the record company" by insisting on an $8.98 release right away. "There is a life cycle for a rock band, and you have to nurture that, rather than strangling it for the sake of an artist's ego. A billboard on Sunset Strip might be a stupid thing."

Werchen, similarly, says that going with a $6.98 debut release might be "a wise decision" for a new act, since a mini-LP or lower-priced album might sell better and thus make a bigger impression than the same item priced at $8.98. "I don't think the total royalties generated by the first album are all that important," he says.

It appears that prices are not going to change radically in the record business until the economy starts booming again or until consumers chose to spend more of their entertainment dollars on records. As Paul Smith puts it, "There has been apprehension on the part of everybody to go to a $9.98 (full-line) price, and that hasn't changed."

Meanwhile, the labels seem to have every intention of maintaining their midlines and continuing their experiments with innovative pricing concepts for new artists. As long as these factors remain constant, variable pricing will be a fact of life in the record industry.

Supplemental Reading

Freund v. Washington Square Press, Inc., 34 N.Y.2d 379, 314 N.E.2d 419, 357 N.Y.S.2d 857 (1974) (author providing no foundation for reasonable estimate of future royalties could recover only nominal damages against publisher for refusal to publish).

Demaris v. G.P. Putnam's Sons, 379 F. Supp. 294 (C.D. Cal. 1973) (publisher entitled to withhold additional payment to author on basis of legal opinion that author's manuscript would subject publisher to liability).

Reback v. Story Productions, 15 Misc. 2d 681, 181 N.Y.S.2d 980 (Sup. Ct. N.Y. Co. 1958) (seller's contract with buyer, wherein seller conveyed exclusive rights in exchange for buyer's promise to pay a percentage of receipts from distribution, imposed an implied obligation to use buyer's best efforts to exploit the rights transferred), *aff'd*, 9 A.D.2d 880, 193 N.Y.S.2d 520 (1st Dep't 1959).

Payne v. Pathe Studios, Inc., 6 Cal. App. 2d 136, 44 P.2d 598 (Cal. Dist. Ct. App. 1935) (where film company agreed to engage actress for four weeks' work, but did not prevent her from taking other jobs, and actress was at all times ready, willing and able to perform the work but was not called on to do so, actress entitled to minimum contractual amount specified).

Hal Roach Studios, Inc. v. Film Classics, Inc., 68 F. Supp. 563 (S.D.N.Y.) (in determining whether disputed items should be included in contract phrase "gross receipts," court would be governed by contract, but as to matters not there specified, by evidence of custom and trade usage), *aff'd* 156 F.2d 596 (2d Cir. 1946).

Shanzer, "The Loss of Publicity as an Element of Damages for Breach of Contract to Employ an Entertainer," 27 *U. of Miami L. Rev.* 465 (1973).

Glucksman, "Art Resale Royalties: Symbolic or Economic Relief for Fine Artist," 1 *Cardozo Arts & Entertainment L.J.* 115 (1982).

Zechowy, "Cheaper by the Dozen: Unauthorized Rental of Motion Pictures, Video Cassettes and Videodisks," 34 *Fed. Com. L.J.* 259 (1982).

Luce, "Scuttling the Air Pirates: Theories of Pay Television Signal Theft Liability," 4 *Com. & the Law* 17 (1982).

CHAPTER 5

GRANT OF RIGHTS

Introduction

Since the entertainment industry depends substantially on the ability to reproduce artistic works in multiple copies, and to undertake widespread dissemination of artistic creations, copyright is a fundamental consideration of entertainment law. Equally important is the manner in which rights under copyright are transferred from one party to another. This chapter explores the ways in which such rights transfers may occur, and the implications of choosing one form of transfer over another.

The types of concerns which must be addressed when considering a grant of rights in an entertainment project are identified through examination of both contractual language and case law. The language of the agreements at issue in the cases will be explored to determine whether more careful thought and draftsmanship might have avoided the problems which arose.

Required Reading

Bartsch v. Metro–Goldwyn–Mayer, Inc., 270 F. Supp. 896 (S.D.N.Y. 1967), *aff'd* 391 F.2d 150 (2d Cir. 1968).

Bartsch v. Metro-Goldwyn-Mayer, Inc., 391 F.2d 150 (2d Cir. 1968).

Manners v. Morosco, 258 F. 557 (2d Cir. 1919), *rev'd* 252 U.S. 317 (1920).

Manners v. Morosco, 252 U.S. 317 (1920).

Warner Bros. Pictures, Inc. v. Columbia Broadcasting System, Inc., 216 F.2d 945 (9th Cir. 1954).

"A.C. Demands For Talent Exclusives Due for Legal Test," *Variety* (June 28, 1978), pp. 1, 99.

Lee A. Daniels, "Hardy Boys Named in Literary Suit," *The New York Times* (June 10, 1980), pp. A1, C9.

Namath v. Sports Illustrated, 80 Misc. 2d 531, 363 N.Y.S.2d 276 (Sup. Ct. N.Y. Co.), *aff'd* 48 A.D.2d 487, 371 N.Y.S.2d 10 (1st Dept 1975).

Namath v. Sports Illustrated, 48 A.D.2d 487, 371 N.Y.S.2d 10 (1st Dept 1975).

Cepeda v. Swift & Company, 291 F. Supp. 242 (E.D. Mo. 1968), *aff'd*, 415 F.2d 1205 (8th Cir. 1969).

Cepeda v. Swift and Company, 415 F.2d 1205 (8th Cir. 1969).

Factors Etc., Inc. v. Pro Arts, Inc., 579 F.2d 215 (2d Cir. 1978).

All contracts and union agreements referred to in the chapter "Concepts."

CONCEPTS

1. What are the differences among a work-for-hire, an assignment of rights and a license?

2. Which of the following agreements contain work-for-hire provisions, assignments of rights or licenses?

   — Book Publishing Agreement, Parags. FIRST C, THIRD A, 58, 84 (pp. 854, 855, 868, 875)

   — Minimum Basic Production Contract, Parags. FIRST (b), SECOND, SEVENTH (pp. 708, 709, 717)

   — Acquisition of Rights Agreement, Parags. 1, 13 (pp. 634–637, 643–644)

   — Screenplay Loanout Agreement, Parag. 2.3 (p. 673)

   — Record Agreement, Parag. 6(a) (p. 805)

   (A) What is the difference in the nature of rights granted in the various industries?

   (B) What would account for such differences?

3. In *Bartsch v. MGM* (p. 393), did plaintiff assign or license motion picture rights to MGM? Would it have made a difference?

4. In the following cases, what is the contractual grant of rights language? Did the contractual language accurately or inaccurately reflect the intention of the parties regarding the rights being conveyed? In each case, review the other provisions of the contract as reflected in the decisions, and consider what the parties could have done to make clearer their intentions about the rights conveyed:

   (A) *Manners v. Morosco* (p. 405)

   (B) *Warner Bros. v. CBS* (p. 416)

   Why do you think the parties failed to clarify their intentions?

5. In conveying rights, certain issues should be raised so that the intention of
    the parties can be accurately reflected. What are these issues as suggested
    by the following cases and articles:

    —   *Manners v. Morosco* (p. 405)

    —   *Warner Bros. v. CBS* (p. 416)

    —   *Rich v. RCA* (p. 274)

    —   *Variety*: 6/28/78 (p. 424)

    —   *The New York Times*: 6/10/80 (p. 425)

    —   *The New York Times*: 1/13/81 (p. 24)

6. *Namath v. Sports Illustrated* (p. 427), *Cepeda v. Swift* (p. 433) and
    Factors v. Pro Arts (p. 442) all seem to be dealing with a person's name,
    image, likeness, etc. What is the difference in these cases in the con-
    templated uses?

BARTSCH v.
METRO-GOLDWYN-MAYER, INC.
270 F. Supp. 896 (S.D.N.Y. 1967)
aff'd 391 F.2d 150 (2d Cir. 1968)

OPINION

FREDERICK van PELT BRYAN, District Judge:

This action for copyright infringement, brought under 17 U.S.C. § 101 et
seq., was tried before me without a jury. The dispute arises out of television
exhibitions by defendant of the motion picture "Maytime."

I.

Most of the factual background is not in dispute and is as follows: On June
1, 1914, certificate of copyright D–37173 was issued to Rudolf Bernauer and
Rudolph Schanzer as authors of a dramatic composition "Wie Einst Im Mai"
written in German with music by Walter Kollo and Willy Bredschneider.
Some time during the 1920's "Wie Einst Im Mai" was drawn upon as the basis
for the musical play or operetta "Maytime" which was copyrighted and
produced for the theatre. The operetta, with libretto and lyrics by Rita
Johnson Young and musical score by Sigmund Romberg, had a highly
successful Broadway run.

On January 23, 1930, Hans Bartsch, the late husband of the present
plaintiff, obtained exclusive motion picture rights for "Wie Einst Im Mai"

from the authors, Schanzer and Bernauer, and from several others owning interests in the composition. This grant in specific terms transferred to Bartsch "the sole and exclusive rights to use, adapt, translate, add to and change the said operetta or musical play and the title thereof in the making of motion picture photoplays, and to project, transmit and otherwise reproduce the said work or any adaptation or version thereof, visually and audibly by the art of cinematography or any other process analogous thereto, and to copyright, vend, license and exhibit such motion picture photoplays throughout the world . . . ." On May 12, 1930, Warner Bros. Pictures (Warner) obtained from Bartsch the exclusive right to make a motion picture based on "Wie Einst Im Mai" and "to project, transmit and otherwise reproduce the said musical play or any adaptation or version thereof visually and audibly by the art of cinematography or any process analogous thereto, and to copyright, vend, license and exhibit such motion picture photoplays throughout the world . . . "[4] Defendant Metro-Goldwyn-Mayer, Inc. (M.G.M.) succeeded to all of Warner's rights in "Maytime" and "Wie Einst Im Mai" by agreement dated February 27, 1935. *Young Romberg*

On October 31, 1935, Rudolph Schanzer assigned to Hans Bartsch all his right, title and interest in the "Wie Einst Im Mai" copyright and all renewals thereof. On January 10, 1938, Rudolph Bernauer made a similar grant transferring all his copyright interest and renewal rights in the work to Bartsch. On October 14, 1941, the Copyright Office issued a certificate of renewal of the "Wie Einst Im Mai" copyright to the authors Bernauer and Schanzer. On October 10, 1942, Bernauer in writing assigned his interest in the renewal copyright to Hans Bartsch. Schanzer made no additional transfer after the renewal copyright was registered; it appears, however, that the prior assignment of October 31, 1935, was sufficient in itself to transfer whatever interest he had in the renewal.

Bartsch died as a New York resident on July 10, 1953. His will was duly admitted to probate on September 3, 1952, and letters testamentary were on that day granted to plaintiff Irene Bartsch. Pursuant to the terms of the will Mrs. Bartsch, as executrix, transferred all of her husband's interest in the

---

[4] Def. Ex. B. provides in pertinent part: "Owner hereby grants and assigns unto Purchaser, its successors and assigns, the motion picture rights throughout the world, in and to a certain musical play entitled "WIE EINST IN MAI", . . . for the full period of all copyrights and any renewed and extended terms thereof, together with the sole and exclusive right to use, adapt, translate, add to, subtract from, interpolate in and change said musical play, and the title thereof, (subject so far as the right to use said title is concerned to Paragraph 7 hereof) in the making of motion picture photoplays and to project, transmit and otherwise reproduce the said musical play or any adaptation or version thereof visually and audibly by the art of cinematography or any process analogous thereto, and to copyright, vend, license and exhibit such motion picture photoplays throughout the world . . . "

"Wie Einst Im Mai" renewal copyright to herself. In this suit for infringement she seeks to enforce rights obtained under this assignment.

The following course of events led to this suit against M.G.M. for an alleged infringement of the renewal copyright: Some time during 1936 and 1937 defendant produced and commenced distribution and exhibition of the motion picture film entitled "Maytime". There is no question that the story of this motion picture is based in whole or in substantial part on the musical dramatic play of the same name written by Rita Johnson Young. The motion picture was first copyrighted on March 18, 1937; a renewal subsequently was issued on March 19, 1964.

On July 6, 1950, M.G.M. obtained a confirmation from G. Schirmer, Inc. of all rights under the "Maytime" renewal copyright—including the right to televise the motion picture. M.G.M. received a similar confirmation from Sigmund Romberg on July 26, 1950, assuring the transfer of all rights under the renewal copyright. This confirmation also specified the right to exhibit "Maytime" over television. On September 11, 1952, however, as the dispute between these parties crystallized, plaintiff confirmed to defendant only whatever rights under the "Wie Einst Im Mai" renewal copyright Hans Bartsch had originally granted to Warner in the original assignment of May 12, 1930. During 1958 defendant M.G.M. commenced licensing the motion picture "Maytime" for exhibition on television. Plaintiff charges that the licensing and exhibition of the "Maytime" film over television constitutes an infringement by the defendant, and she therefore seeks damages and injunctive relief under the copyright law.

II.

The respective contentions of the parties are quite straightforward. Plaintiff takes the position that the crucial May 12, 1930 transfer of motion picture rights from Hans Bartsch to defendant's predecessor in interest, Warner, did not include the right to exhibit "Wie Einst Im Mai" or "Maytime" on television. For this reason plaintiff contends that any and all television performances constitute infringements of her renewal copyright entitling her to relief.

Defendant M.G.M., on the other hand, takes the simple position that all rights to exhibit the film on television were relinquished by the May 12, 1930 transfer. It urges further that in any event Hans Bartsch made an absolute and unconditional transfer to it of any and all rights of whatsoever nature he received from persons owning an interest in "Wie Einst Im Mai" and retained nothing on which a claim of infringement can be based.

The first narrow issue posed by these contentions is whether the May 12, 1930 grant was broad enough to constitute a conveyance of television exhibition rights. More particularly, the question is whether the right to exhibit "Maytime" on television was embraced in a conveyance of "motion picture rights" authorizing Warner "to project, transmit and otherwise reproduce the said musical play or any adaptation or version thereof visually and audibly by the art of cinematography or any process analogous thereto . . . ."

III.

The parties recognize that the correct disposition of this issue requires a determination of the intent of the principals as manifested in the contract of May 12, 1930. As in Meyers v. Selznick Co., 373 F.2d 218, 222 (2d Cir. 1966), the words used by the parties in this crucial document are hardly so " 'plain and clear' as to exclude proof of surrounding circumstances and other extrinsic aids to interpretation." Accordingly the parties introduced evidence throwing light on the general practices of the motion picture industry in 1930. Unfortunately neither side was able to produce a witness who was directly involved in the negotiations or preparation of the particular grant with which we are directly concerned.

During 1930 the future possibilities of television were recognized by knowledgeable people in the entertainment and motion picture industries. There is no question that upon occasion rights to exhibit motion pictures on television were specifically bargained for and transferred during that year.[22] Plaintiff introduced in evidence several grants to Warner during this period containing a specific reference to the right to televise motion pictures. On the other hand, at about the same time Warner also obtained several broad grants of motion picture rights omitting any specific reference to television.

In the case at bar I do not deem the absence of any specific reference to television in the crucial 1930 transfer to Warner to be of any controlling significance. In the first place, of course, grants and assignments to Warner by others during the same period obviously are not indicative of the precise scope of Bartsch's grant to Warner, particularly in the absence of any evidence that Bartsch was aware of them.

Moreover, we are by no means left in the dark as to exactly what bundle of rights was actually embraced by the 1930 transfer. The pertinent language in the contract of May 12, 1930, is strongly suggestive of the conclusion that the transferor Bartsch relinquished "Maytime" television rights. The phrase "to project, transmit and otherwise reproduce the said musical play" appears to represent an attempt by the parties to exhaust all possibilities with respect to the exhibition of the film. It was generally understood in the industry during

---

[22] This was so although the showing of movies on television was not common practice until the 1950's; defendant M.G.M., for example, did not commence licensing its motion pictures for television until 1957 . . .

1930 that phrases such as the catch-all term "otherwise reproduce" were included in grants of film rights to assure an enlargement of the rights granted. And I have little difficulty on this record in reaching the conclusion that exhibition of the film on television is simply another way of projecting, transmitting and reproducing the play within the contemplation of the 1930 contract. This is true although, naturally enough, the parties who negotiated the grant were evidently not fully aware of the great commercial potential in motion picture entertainment through the medium of television.

In addition, defendant has established here that the exhibitions of the film on television qualify as reproductions of the play "by the art of cinematography or any process analogous thereto." The art of cinematography means generally the production of "a motion picture in any shape, form, size, color dimension" and thereafter making "use of that motion picture." The adjective "analogous" in this contract means "corresponding to something else" or "bearing some resemblance or proportion." Webster, New International Dictionary 94 (2d ed. 1954). The exhibition of a film through the television medium is certainly the utilization of a process analogous to or resembling the art of cinematography.

John Whittaker, defendant's well qualified expert witness, fully explained the respective techniques and mechanical operations of exhibiting a film in a theatre as compared with reproduction of a film image on a television screen in the home. His testimony was uncontradicted, since plaintiff did not produce an expert. The processes of theatre and home television exhibition are markedly similar. In a theatre the images in a motion picture film are produced by a projector casting rays of light against a screen. A shutter controls the various degrees of brightness which make up the picture seen by the audience. Similarly, the customary practice for exhibiting motion picture films over television requires the use of a standard projector, sound head and lenses like those which are used in the theatre.

A very small image is projected against a photosensitive electronic scanning system, rather than a standard screen, and the information by a process of transduction is converted into electrical energy, transmitted over the air in electrical impulses, and carried into the home where it is again converted by the viewer's set. The process of "unscrambling" or "descanning" the airwave transmission so as to cast the image on the television screen is quite similar to that which takes place on the theatre screen, except that on the set in the home an electronic shutter, rather than a mechanical shutter, is used to control the picture image. Finally, the audio or sound portions of the film are transmitted entirely by wires in the theatre, whereas, of course, in television the airwaves necessarily provide part of the medium of transmission between the wires at the beginning and the end of the process. The intervention of the airwaves results in only a split-second hiatus and does not prevent the receiver at home from communicating the sound just as rapidly as the transmission in a large theatre.

It is evident, therefore, that the process of exhibiting a motion picture over television provides a very close analogy to an exhibition in a theatre. This was true in 1930 from the point of view of the production and commercial end of the motion picture industry. And this is true today from the point of view of the technical and mechanical processes involved, as Whittaker's testimony firmly established. As plaintiff brought out on cross-examination, the only substantial difference between the theatre and home television exhibitions concerns the intervention of the airwaves in the transmission or communication process. While this factor prevents the two processes from being identical, it certainly does not destroy the close analogy between them.

Beyond this, the broad, sweeping phrase "by the art of cinematography or any process analogous thereto," like the expansive terms "project, transmit or otherwise reproduce," was evidently included in the contract as a means of enlarging the grant to Warner. In my view this protective language was sufficiently broad to assure that Warner obtained the television rights here in issue. This is a case like L.C. Page & Co. v. Fox Film Corp., 83 F.2d 196, 199 (2d cir. 1936), where "the genus embraced the later developed species." I therefore find that plaintiff's predecessor in interest, Hans Bartsch, relinquished all rights to exhibit "Maytime" on television by the express terms of the May 12, 1930 transfer to Warner.

There is yet a further reason why plaintiff cannot prevail in this action. As mentioned, on January 23, 1930, Bartsch obtained from several persons having an interest in "Wie Einst Im Mai" all motion picture rights "together with the sole and exclusive rights to use, adapt, translate, add to and change the said operetta or musical play and the title thereof in the making of motion picture photoplays, and to project, transmit and otherwise reproduce the said work or any adaptation or version thereof, visually and audibly by the art of cinematography or any process analogous thereto, and to copyright, vend, license and exhibit such motion picture photoplays throughout the world. . . ." On May 12 of the same year Bartsch turned around and for all practical purposes transferred to Warner any and all rights he had obtained on January 23. With minor variations not here material the May 12 transfer to Warner reiterated *in haec verba* the language delimiting the extent of the rights Bartsch had obtained on January 23. In short, Bartsch transferred to Warner nothing less nor more (i.e., everything) he had received from the prior owners.

"One method of ascertaining what has or has not been transferred is to see what has been retained by the grantor." Allied Chemical Corp. v. United States, 370 F.2d 697, 699 (2d Cir. 1967). Since Bartsch transferred to Warner, M.G.M.'s predecessor in interest, everything he obtained from *his* grantors, there was nothing for him to retain. He thus could not have retained the television rights. This is quite consistent with the testimony of Robert W. Perkins who, as counsel to Warner in 1930, approved the contract with which we are concerned upon the understanding that his employer had effectively obtained television rights, a conclusion which was based, among other things, on the identity between what was granted to Bartsch and what Bartsch granted to Warner.

Plaintiff points to a general reservation of rights in the 1930 transfer[37] as evidence of the fact that Bartsch did not specifically intend to relinquish unspecified rights, in particular the privilege to exhibit the film on television. Such a general reservation, however, was by no means unusual in assignments of motion picture rights of this type in 1930, and this particular provision is virtually useless in illuminating the specific intent of the parties as manifested by their contract. Warner obtained nothing more and nothing less than what was specifically relinquished. Bartsch retained nothing more and nothing less than what was specifically reserved. These observations scarcely illuminate the ultimate issue. I therefore find that Hans Bartsch unconditionally transferred to Warner any and all television rights he had secured from those owning interests in "Wie Einst Im Mai."

Since I have found for the defendant on this crucial question of the scope of the grant made in the assignment of May 12, 1930, it is unnecessary to consider the alternative claims that plaintiff is barred by laches and that the motion picture "Maytime," though based in whole or in part on the composition "Wie Einst Im Mai," nevertheless does not constitute an infringement within the meaning of the copyright law.

Judgement will be entered for defendant.

The foregoing opinion constitutes my findings of fact and conclusions of law pursuant to Rule 52, F.R.Civ.P.

It is so ordered.

---

[37] Paragraph 13 of Def. Ex. B. provides: "The rights which the Purchaser obtains from the Owner in 'WIE EINST IM MAI' and/or 'MAYTIME' are specifically limited to those granted herein. All other rights now in existence or which may hereafter come into existence shall always be reserved to the owner and for his sole benefit, but nothing herein contained shall in any way limit or restrict the rights which Purchaser has acquired or shall hereafter acquire from any other person, firm, or corporation in and to 'WIE EINST IM MAI' and/or 'MAYTIME'."

BARTSCH v.
METRO-GOLDWYN-MAYER, INC.
391 F.2d 150 (2d Cir. 1968)

Before LUMBARD, Chief Judge, and WATERMAN and FRIENDLY, Circuit Judges.

FRIENDLY, Circuit Judge:

This appeal from a judgement of the District Court for the Southern District of New York raises the question whether, on the facts here appearing, an assignee of motion picture rights to a musical play is entitled to authorize the telecasting of its copyrighted film. Although the issue seems considerably closer to us than it did to Judge Bryan, we affirm the judgment dismissing the complaint of the copyright owner.

In January 1930, the authors, composers, and publishers of and owners of certain other interests in a German musical play "Wie Einst in Mai," which had been produced in this country as "Maytime" with a changed libretto and score, assigned to Hans Bartsch

> The motion picture rights and all our right, title and interest in and in connection with such motion picture rights of the said operetta or musical play, throughout the world, together with the sole and exclusive rights to use, adapt, translate, add to and change the said operetta or musical play and the title thereof in the making of motion picture photoplays, and to project, transmit and otherwise reproduce the said work or any adaptation or version thereof, visually or audibly by the art of cinematography or any process analogous thereto, and to copyright, vend, license and exhibit such motion picture photoplays throughout the world; together with the further sole and exclusive rights by mechanical and/or electrical means to record, reproduce and transmit sound, including spoken words, dialogue, songs and music, and to change such dialogue, if extracted from said works, and to interpolate or use other dialogue, songs and music in or in connection with or as part of said motion picture photoplays, and the exhibition, reproduction and transmission thereof, and to make, use, license, import and vend any and all records or other devices required or desired for any such purposes.

In May of that year Bartsch assigned to Warner Bros. Pictures, Inc.

> the motion picture rights throughout the world, in and to a certain musical play entitled "WIE EINST IN MAI," libretto and lyrics by Rudolf Schanzer and Rudolph Bernauer, music by Walter Kollo and Willy Bredschneider, for the full period of all copyrights and any renewed and extended terms thereof, together with the sole and exclusive right to use, adapt, translate, add to, subtract from, interpolate in and change said

musical play, and the title thereof (subject so far as the right to use said title is concerned to Paragraph 7 hereof), in the making of motion picture photoplays and to project, transmit and otherwise reproduce the said musical play or any adaptation or version thereof visually or audibly by the art of cinematography or any process analogous thereto, and to copyright, vend, license and exhibit such motion picture photoplays throughout the world, together with the further sole and exclusive right by mechanical and/or electrical means to record, reproduce and transmit sound, including spoken words, dialogue, songs and music, and to change such dialogue, if extracted from said musical play, and at its own expense and responsibility to interpolate and use other dialogue, songs and music in or in connection with or as part of said motion picture photoplays, and the exhibition, reproduction and transmission thereof, and to make, use, license, import, vend and copyright any and all records or other devices made or required or desired for any such purposes.

By another clause Bartsch reserved the right to exercise for himself the rights generally granted to Warner Brothers insofar as these concerned German language motion pictures in certain countries and subject to specified restrictions:

but it is expressly understood and agreed that nothing herein contained shall in any way limit or restrict the absolute right of Purchaser to produce, release, distribute and/or exhibit the photoplay or photoplays produced hereunder based in whole or in part on "Wie Einst in Mai" and/or "Maytime," in all countries of the world, including the territory mentioned in this paragraph, at any time, and regardless of the right herein reserved to the Owner.

A further clause recited

The rights which the Purchaser obtains from the Owner in "Wie Einst in Mai" and/or "Maytime" are specifically limited to those granted herein. All other rights now in existence or which may hereafter come into existence shall always be reserved to the Owner and for his sole benefit, but nothing herein contained shall in any way limit or restrict the rights which Purchaser has acquired or shall hereafter acquire from any other person, firm or corporation in and to "Wie Einst in Mai" and/or "Maytime".

Warner Brothers transferred its rights to defendant Metro-Goldwyn-Mayer, Inc. early in 1935, which made, distributed and exhibited a highly successful motion picture "Maytime." The co-authors of the German libretto, one in 1935 and the other in 1938, transferred all their copyright interests and renewal rights to Bartsch, whose rights in turn have devolved to the plaintiff, his widow. The controversy stems from MGM's licensing its motion picture for television, beginning in 1958.

Although the district judge upheld MGM's contention that the 1930 assignment from Bartsch to Warner Brothers included the right to permit telecasting of the motion picture to be made from the musical play, he thought there was "a further reason why plaintiff cannot prevail in this action," namely, that Bartsch had granted all that he had. This does not do justice to plaintiff's argument. Her position is that in 1930 Bartsch not only did not but could not grant the right to televise the motion picture since, under the similar language of the assignment to him, it was not his to grant; her claim of infringement is based not on the 1930 assignment to Bartsch of the motion picture rights but on the authors' later assignments of the full copyright.

The district court, appearing to consider that defendant's rights turned on the authorization "to project, transmit and otherwise reproduce the said musical play or any adaptation or version thereof visually and audibly by the art of cinematography *or any process analogous thereto*," concluded that television came within the phrase we have italicized. We have grave doubt on that score. We freely grant that "analogous" is a broader word than "similar," and also that the first step in a telecast of a film, namely, the projection of the motion picture to an electronic pickup, is "analogous" to throwing the picture on a theatre screen. But to characterize the to us nigh miraculous processes whereby these images actuate airwaves so as to cause electronic changes in sets in millions of homes which are then "unscrambled" or "descanned" and thus produce pictures on television screens—along with the simultaneous electronic transmission of sound—as "analogous" to cinematography pushes the analogy beyond the breaking point. This is particularly so since the district court's construction would seem to lead to the conclusion that the assignment would entitle the assignee to "project, transmit and otherwise reproduce" the musical play by a live telecast—a right which pretty clearly was not granted and indeed has not been claimed.

As we read the instruments, defendant's rights do not turn on the language we have been discussing but rather on the broad grant, in the assignments to and from Bartsch, of "the motion picture rights throughout the world," which were spelled out to include the right "to copyright, vend, license and exhibit such motion picture photoplays throughout the world." The "to project, transmit and otherwise reproduce" language appears rather to have been directed at how the musical play was to be made into a photoplay. This may well have seemed a more vexing problem in 1930, due to uncertainties as to the best method for linking visual and audible reproduction, cf. Paramount Publix Corp. v. American TriErgon Corp., 294 U.S. 464, 55 S.Ct. 449. 79 L.Ed. 997 (1935), and whether a grant of motion picture rights to a play or novel included the right to sound reproduction, see L. C. Page & Co. v. Fox Film

Corp., 83 F.2d 196 (2 Cir. 1936), than today. Being unclear whether sound reproductions would require alterations in previous methods of converting a play into a photoplay, Warner Brothers sought and obtained a considerable degree of freedom in that regard. On this view the clause whose meaning has been so hotly debated is irrelevant to the point here at issue, and decision turns rather on whether a broad assignment of the right "to copyright, vend, license and exhibit such motion picture photoplays throughout the world" includes the right to "license" a broadcaster to "exhibit" the copyrighted motion picture by a telecast without a further grant by the copyright owner.

A threshold issue—which the pre-*Erie L. C. Page* decision was not required to take into account—is whether this question should be determined under state or federal law. The seventeenth paragraph of Bartsch's assignment says, somewhat unhelpfully, that "Each and every term of this agreement shall be construed in accordance with the laws of the United States of America *and* of the State of New York." [Emphasis supplied.] We hold that New York law governs. The development of a "federal common law" of contracts is justified only when required by a distinctive national policy and, as we found in T. B. Harms v. Eliscu, 339 F.2d 823, 828 (2 Cir. 1964), citing many cases, "the general interest that copyrights, like all other forms of property, should be enjoyed by their true owner is not enough to meet this . . . test." The fact that plaintiff is seeking a remedy granted by Congress to copyright owners removes any problem of federal jurisdiction but does not mean that federal principles must govern the disposition of every aspect of her claim.

Unfortunately, when we turn to state law, we find that it offers little assistance. Two other situations must be distinguished. This is not a case like Manners v. Morosco, 252 U.S. 317, 40 S.Ct.335, 64 L.Ed. 590 (1920), cited with approval, Underhill v. Schenck, 238 N.Y. 7, 143 N.E. 773, 33 A.L.R. 303 (1924), in which an all encompassing grant found in one provision must be limited by the context created by other terms of the agreement indicating that the use of the copyrighted material in only one medium was contemplated. The words of Bartsch's assignment, as we have shown, were well designed to give the assignee the broadest rights with respect to *its* copyrighted property, to wit, the photoplay. "Exhibit" means to "display" or to "show" by any method, and nothing in the rest of the grant sufficiently reveals a contrary intention.[1] Nor is this case like Kirke La Shelle Co. v. Paul Armstrong Co., 263 N.Y. 79, 188 N.E. 163 (1938), in which the new medium was completely unknown at the time when the contract was written. Rather, the trial court

---

[1] The plaintiff points to paragraph 13 of the agreement, reproduced in the text, as indicating an intention to exclude television rights. The provision limits the rights of the assignee to those "specifically . . . granted herein," and saves to Bartsch "all other rights now in existence or which may hereafter come into existence." We cannot read this as standing for more than the truism that whatever Bartsch had not granted, he had retained.

correctly found that, "During 1930 the future possibilities of television were recognized by knowledgeable people in the entertainment and motion picture industries," though surely not in the scope it has attained. While *Kirke La Shelle* teaches that New York will not charge a grantor with the duty of expressly saving television rights when he could not know of the invention's existence, we have found no case holding that an experienced businessman like Bartsch is not bound by the natural implications of the language he accepted when he had reason to know of the new medium's potential.[2]

Plaintiff, naturally enough, would not frame the issue in precisely this way. Instead, she argues that even in 1930 Warner Brothers often attempted to obtain an express grant of television rights and that its failure to succeed in Bartsch's case should persuade us that, despite the broad language, only established forms of exhibition were contemplated. She buttresses this argument by producing a number of 1930 assignments to Warner Brothers, some of which specifically granted the right to televise motion pictures and others of which granted full television rights, and by adducing testimony of the Warner Brothers lawyer who had approved the assignment from Bartsch that on many occasions Warner Brothers attempted to secure an express grant of such rights but did not always succeed.

However, this is not enough to show that the Bartsch assignments were a case of that sort. For all that appears Warner Brothers may have decided that, in dealing with Bartsch, it would be better tactics to rely on general words that were sufficiently broad rather than seek an express inclusion and perhaps end up with the opposite, or may have used a form regular in the industry without thinking very precisely about television, or—perhaps most likely—may simply have parroted the language in the grant from Bartsch's assignors to him on the theory it would thus be getting all he had, whatever that might be. Indeed, it is really the assignment to Bartsch rather than the one from him that must control. While plaintiff suggests that Warner Brothers may have furnished Bartsch the forms to be used with his assignors, this is sheer speculation. There is no showing that the form was unique to Warner Brothers; indeed the contrary appears.

With Bartsch dead, his grantors apparently so, and the Warner Brothers lawyer understandably having no recollection of the negotiation, any effort to reconstruct what the parties actually intended nearly forty years ago is

---

[2] In Ettore v. Philco Television Broadcasting Corp., 229 F.2d 481, cert. denied, 351 U.S. 926, 76 S.Ct. 783, 100 L.Ed. 1456 (1956), the Third Circuit, applying Pennsylvania law, held that a 1935 contract granting moving picture rights did not permit the grantee to televise the film. However, unlike Bartsch, the grantor, Ettore, was not an experienced businessman but a prize fighter, and the Court relied heavily on his lack of sophistication in determining whether it was fair to charge him with knowledge of the new medium. Id. at 491, n.14.

doomed to failure. In the end, decision must turn, as Professor Nimmer has suggested, The Law of Copyright § 125.3 (1964), on a choice between two basic approaches more than on an attempt to distill decisive meaning out of language that very likely had none. As between an approach that "a license of rights in a given medium (e.g., 'motion picture rights') includes only such uses as fall within the unambiguous core meaning of the term (e. g., exhibition of motion picture film in motion picture theaters) and exclude any uses which lie within the ambiguous penumbra (e. g., exhibition of motion picture film on television)" and another whereby "the licensee may properly pursue any uses which may reasonably be said to fall within the medium as described in the license," he prefers the latter. So do we. But see Warner, Radio and Television Rights § 52 (1953). If the words are broad enough to cover the new use, it seems fairer that the burden of framing and negotiating an exception should fall on the grantor; if Bartsch or his assignors had desired to limit "exhibition" of the motion picture to the conventional method where light is carried from a projector to a screen directly beheld by the viewer, they could have said so. A further reason favoring the broader view in a case like this is that it provides a single person who can make the copyrighted work available to the public over the penumbral medium, whereas the narrower one involves the risk that a deadlock between the grantor and the grantee might prevent the work's being shown over the new medium at all. Quite apart from the probable impracticality, the assignments are broad enough even on plaintiff's view to prevent the copyright owners from licensing anyone else to make a photoplay for telecasting. The risk that some May might find the nation's television screens bereft of the annual display of "Maytime," interlarded with the usual liberal diet of commercials, is not one a court can take lightly.

Affirmed.

MANNERS v. MOROSCO

258 F. 557 (2d Cir. 1919)
rev'd 252 U.S. 317 (1920)

Before WARD, HOUGH, and MANTON, Circuit Judges.

MANTON, Circuit Judge. The appellant is the author of "Peg O'My Heart." He is the husband of Laurette Taylor, the star of that very successful play as dramatized.

On January 19, 1912, the parties entered into a contract which in part provided and granted to the appellee "the sole and exclusive license and liberty to produce, perform and represent the said play in the United States of America and the Dominion of Canada." The third paragraph provided:

> "The party of the second part (appellee) agrees to produce the play not later than July 1, 1913, and to continue the said play for at least 75 performances during the season of 1913–1914 and for each theatrical season thereafter for a period of five years."

The fifth paragraph provides:

> "That the said party of the second part (appellee) further agrees that if during any one theatrical year such year to begin on the first day of October, said play has not been produced or presented for 75 performances, then all rights of the said party of the second part shall cease and determine and shall immediately revert to the said party of the first part."

After the contract was made, the play was produced and ran continuously and successfully for a period of 74 weeks up to May 30, 1914, in New York, with Laurette Taylor in the star part. On July 20, 1914, the parties entered into an agreement modifying in some respects the agreement of January 19, 1912. By the modification, arrangement was made for the production of the play without Laurette Taylor in the star part and for other productions in more than one company. It was further provided that the appellee be permitted to lease, stipulate, assign, transfer, or sell to any one, any of his rights under either contract. And it was specifically covenanted that the issue now presented between the parties as to the ownership of motion picture rights was to be determined by reference to the original contract. After the execution of this contract, a number of companies gave performances in various parts of the United States and Canada. Payment under the terms of the contract was duly made to the appellant.

When the theatrical season of 1917–1918 expired, the appellant, claiming that the appellee no longer had any interest in any of the producing rights, brought this action to restrain further production of the play by the appellee, both on the stage and in motion picture form. Two questions are presented by counsel on this appeal: First, the date, if any, of the termination of the contract; and, second, whether the appellee under the contract is entitled to the motion picture rights.

It is claimed by the appellant that only a license, revocable at his option, was contracted for with the appellee under the third paragraph of the first contract, and that the contract expired at the end of the theatrical season in May, 1918. But that is not what was contracted for. It was not an agreement for personal service or for a mere license, but was a bargain and sale of the sole and exclusive right to produce, perform, and represent the said play in the

United States and Canada. Property was thereby granted and conveyed. It may be intangible, but it has a value and is the subject of proprietorship. It is not a conveyance which is revocable at will or for a temporary period, but for the time provided for in the terms of the contract.

The third paragraph is a covenant setting forth the least that the appellee would do in performing the contract. In other words, it sets forth the appellee's assurance of his bona fide endeavor or attempt to make the play a success and thus secure to the appellant some substantial royalties. A mere reading of the paragraph will indicate that the parties fixed a minimum and not a maximum of endeavor on the part of the appellee to make for success. It is not an agreement of the most that the appellee agreed to do to make for success. In this connection, the fifth paragraph must be considered and read with the third paragraph. Plainly, if the appellee had failed to present 75 performances of the play "during any one theatrical year," then all rights of the appellee ceased and determined and the play reverted to the appellant. There is harmony between the first and third paragraphs and the intent of the parties that the appellee's rights should not be limited to any definite period is quite plain. The grant was perpetual if the obligations of the contract, particularly paragraphs 3 and 5, were complied with.

The modified contract made on July 20, 1914, reaffirmed the first contract and provided in the ninth paragraph that, at least four years after its date, the original contract was still in force, as a conveyance of all the production rights, and that neither party would produce the play in motion picture form without the consent of the other and until such time, when, after the expiration of four years, the question of motion picture rights should be determined pursuant to the terms of the original agreement.

This clearly negatives the claim of the appellant that under the third paragraph the contract expired after five years from January 19, 1912. An agreement for production rights binding the parties' heirs, executors, assignees, administrators, and successors, is an assignment and not a mere license.

Since the contract is not revocable by will by either party or otherwise limited as to its duration by its express terms or by the inherent nature of the contract itself with reference to its subject-matter, it is presumably intended to be permanent or perpetual in the obligation it imposes.

In determining the production rights conveyed, whether it included the right to produce in motion picture form or not, we must confine our study to the contract itself. The intention of the parties must be secured from the language employed in the instrument itself. Such intention means the accepted reasonable and judicial settled content of the words employed. If the parties have erred in the use of the words, this kind of action cannot grant relief. The words employed, "the sole and exclusive license and liberty to produce, perform and represent the said play," have received judicial construction. A motion picture performance is a stage representation of the play and violative of the rights of an owner of the exclusive right of production. Frohman v. Fitch, 164 App. Div. 231, 149 N. Y. Supp. 633.

Ordinarily, one may "produce or perform" a spoken play upon the stage, but "to represent" seems to be peculiarly appropriate to a motion picture representation of a play. Dramatic rights were held to include the motion picture rights in Frohman v. Fitch, supra, in the absence of other words narrowing the meaning of the contract. An author of dramatic composition is protected by section 4952 of the Revised Statutes of the United States as to not only the sole right of printing it, but also the sole right of "publishing, performing or representing it or causing it to be performed or represented by others." Nor need we be confined in our determination to a strict legal use of the words employed as heretofore judicially determined. It is apparent that the parties intended the results here pronounced. We think the parties intended a conveyance of the entire right to place the play before the American public in any form. It seems inconceivable that the parties intended to reserve to the appellant the right of production in motion picture form when they gave no such expression of reservation in the language of the contract, and particularly when the language employed indicated a comprehensive grant of all producing rights.

In paragraph 10 of of the first contract, the author reserved the right to print and publish the play, but his right was not to be exercised within six months after the production of such play in New York City unless by written consent of the manager. So, too, reservations were made as to leasing and subletting the play. By the tenth paragraph, the author reserved the right of publication in book form.

An expression in the contract of one or more things of a class implies the exclusion of all not expressed, although all would have been implied had none been expressed.

In view of what appears in this record of the cost and expense of successfully dramatizing this play and what appears to be a lucrative contract resulting to the appellant, this court should be reluctant to give a construction not warranted by the language nor intended by the parties, which would permit of competition by the appellant in the production of this play in motion pictures. Frohman v. Fitch, 164 App. Div. 231, 149 N. Y. Sup. 633.

Appellant, however, says that Klein v. Beach, 239 Fed. 108, 151 C. C. A. 282, supports his views. In that case, it was recited, "whereas the manager wishes to engage the services of the author to dramatize the said book for presentation on the stage," and the novelist granted to the author "the sole and exclusive right to dramatize the said book for presentation on the stage," and the parties agreed to grant to the manager "the sole and exclusive license and liberty to produce, perform and represent the said play or dramatic composition on the stage," the right to dramatize the novel for presentation on the stage was held not to carry the right to produce in motion pictures. This court, in considering Klein v. Beach, supra, said:

> "The turning point in this case, is the scope of the grant, whether by its terms it conferred upon Klein dramatic rights in the larger sense including presentation, not only by living actors, but also by motion pictures, or whether it was limited to the 'stage' proper."

This court approved Frohman v. Fitch, supra, and upon the authority of Kalem v. Harper, 222 U. S. 55, 32 Sup. Ct. 20, 56 L. ED. 92, Ann. Cas. 1913A, 1285, stated that the dramatic rights included motion picture rights, but such a conveyance of dramatic rights to have such meaning cannot be narrowed by other limitations. In Klein v. Beach, supra, stage rights only were granted, and this was made plain in the preamble and the provisions of the contract. This court there said in so holding: "In general it is quite clear that this was the prevailing purpose of the parties."

In the case at bar, no distinction is made between the producing rights which the appellant had and those which he conveyed, except where the parties themselves defined it, such as in paragraph 10, to wit, reserving the right to publish the play in book form under conditions there expressed.

We find no error in excluding the contract with Laurette Taylor. This was a contract for the services of Laurette Taylor to perform as a leading female character, not only in this play, but in other plays that might be suited to her talent and ability. It provided for a three-year period with an option of three more. It was no evidence indicating a limitation upon the contract between the parties to this litigation and was properly excluded.

The identity of the person who drew the agreement of January 19, 1912, was unimportant. The contract was bilateral. Responsibility for ambiguity in a contract should be borne by the party who caused it, but there is no ambiguity. It was not important to know the identity of the party who drew the contract.

Holding these views as we do, the decree must be affirmed.

WARD, Circuit Judge (dissenting in part). The grant in the contract under consideration is of an exclusive right "to produce, perform and represent" a play. There has been no judicial construction of any of these words so as to make them technical without reference to the terms of some particular contract. Harper Bros. v. Kalem Co., 169 Fed. 61, 94 C. C. A. 429 (Kalem Co. v. Harper Bros., 222 U. S. 55, 32 Sup. Ct. 20, 56 L. Ed. 92, Ann. Cas. 1913A,

1285), was not a case of contract but of infringement of copyright, the question being whether a moving picture show was a dramatization of an author's work. In Frohman v. Fitch, 164 App. Div. 231, 149 N. Y. Supp. 663, the exclusive right to "produce" a play was construed in the particular contract to cover moving picture rights, whereas in Klein v. Beach, 239 Fed. 108, 151 C. C. A. 282, we held the grant of an exclusive right to "produce, perform, and represent" a play "on the stage" did not cover moving picture rights. The other words "perform and represent" in that contract and in the contract now under consideration have appeared in our Copyright Act since 1870 (U. S. Rev. Stat. 4966), long before moving picture shows were dreamed of. Therefore the question is: When the parties used the words "produce, perform and represent" the play, what were they intending to cover by those words? It seems to me perfectly plain from the contract that they were intending to cover the spoken play only and, if so, the words they used, however large, must be confined to the thing they were contracting about.

The third article of the contract speaks of theatrical seasons, which exist for spoken and do not exist for movie plays.

The fourth article provides for royalties on the gross weekly receipts of the box office, which was held in Harper Bros. v. Klaw (D. C.) 232 Fed. 609, 612, to be inapplicable to "any method of photoplays in commercial use or known to witnesses or counsel." The trial judge refused to permit the plaintiff, over his objection and exception, to prove this fact.

The fifth article refers again to theatrical seasons.

The sixth article provides for the production of the play in first class theaters and on the road with Miss Taylor in the title role, which applies in my judgment to the spoken play only.

The eighth article provides that the rehearsals and productions shall be under the author's direction, which does not apply to movie shows.

The eleventh article provides that should the play fail in New York or on the road it should be released to stock theaters, which applies to the spoken play only.

On the other hand, I find not a word in the contract indicating an intention to transfer the movie rights though they were perfectly well known by both parties. Therefore though the words of the grant are large enough to cover them, I think the words are to be restricted to what the parties were contracting about, viz., the spoken play.

MANNERS v. MOROSCO
252 U.S. 317 (1920)

Mr. Justice HOLMES delivered the opinion of the Court.

This is a suit by the author of a play called *Peg O' My Heart* to restrain the defendant, Morosco, from representing the play in motion pictures, in violation of the plaintiff's copyright; and also, although this is a subsidiary question, from producing the play at all. The defendant justifies under an agreement of January 19, 1912, and a supplemental agreement of July 20, 1914, both set forth in the bill. The ground upon which the right to produce the play in any way was denied was that the agreement gave rights only for five years. This construction was rejected by the District Court and the Circuit Court of Appeals. Both Courts held also that the agreement conveyed the right to represent the play in moving pictures and on that ground dismissed the bill. 254 Fed. 737; 258 Fed. 557.

By the first agreement the plaintiff, party of the first part "does grant" to Morosco, the party of the second part, "the sole and exclusive license and liberty to produce, perform and represent the said play in the United States of America and the Dominion of Canada," subject to the terms and conditions of the contract. Morosco agrees "to produce the play not later than January first, 1913, and to continue the said play for at least seventy-five performances during the season of 1913–1914 and for each theatrical season thereafter for a period of five years." He agrees further to pay specified percentages on the gross weekly receipts as royalties, and that "if during any one theatrical year . . . said play has not been produced or presented for seventy-five performances, then all rights of the said party of the second part shall cease and determine and shall immediately revert to the said party of the first part." Morosco further agrees to present the play in first-class theatres with competent companies and with Miss Laurette Taylor (the stage name of the author's wife) in the title role; the play to have a production in New York and to be continued on the road for at least one season or longer if considered advisable by both parties. No alterations, eliminations or additions are to be made without the approval of the author and the rehearsals and production of the play are to be under his direction. The author to have the right to print and publish the play but not within six months after the production of the play in New York City without consent. Morosco is not to let or transfer his rights without the author's consent. "Should the play fail in New York City and on the road it shall be released for stock;" i. e., let to stock companies, with an equal division of royalties between plaintiff and defendant. By an addendum, after Miss Taylor should have finished her season her successor in the role of "Peg" for any subsequent tours shall be mutually agreeable to both parties.

The contract is declared binding upon the parties, "their heirs, executors, assigns, administrators and successors."

The second agreement, in order to adjust controversies and to modify the first, authorized Morosco "as long as this contract is in force" "to produce, perform and represent" the play with or in as many companies as he saw fit, without engaging Laurette Taylor and without consulting the plaintiff as to the cast, rehearsals or production of the play. Morosco also was authorized to let or sell any of his rights under the contracts, but he was not to be released from his personal liability to pay the royalties as specified in the contracts. The play might be released for stock whenever the net profits realized from all the companies producing the play should be less than $2,000, and then the royalties received from the stock theatres were to be divided equally. For four years from date neither party without consent of the other was to produce or give leave to produce the play by moving pictures and after that the rights of the parties were to be determined by and under the original agreement as if the supplemental agreement had not been made.

As to the duration of the defendant's rights we agree with the Courts below. We perceive no ground for converting the defendant's undertaking to continue the play for seventy-five performances during the season of 1913–1914, and for each season thereafter for five years, into a limit of the plaintiff's grant of rights. As was said in the District Court, it is a statement of the least the defendant was to do, not of the most that he was to have. The plaintiff was secured sufficiently by the forfeiture in case the play should not have been produced for seventy-five performances. The provisions in both contracts as to the release for stock are somewhat of an additional indication that it was expected that the arrangement was to last as long as the public liked the play well enough to make it pay, provided the defendant kept his half of the bargain performed.

On the question principally argued we are of opinion that the majority below was wrong. The thing granted was "the sole and exclusive license and liberty to produce, perform and represent" the play within the territorial limits stated, subject to the other terms of the contract. It may be assumed that those words might carry the right to represent the play in moving pictures if the other terms pointed that way, but to our mind they are inconsistent with any such intent. We need not discuss the abstract question whether, in view of the fact that such a mode of representation was familiar, it was to be expected that it should be mentioned if it was to be granted or should be excluded if it was to be denied. Every detail shows that a representation by spoken drama alone is provided for. The play is to be continued for seventy-five performances for the theatrical seasons named. This applies only to the regular stage. The royalties are adapted only to that mode of presentation. Harper Bros. v. Klaw (D. C.) 232 Fed. 609, 612. The play is to be presented in first-class theatres with a competent company and with Miss Laurette Taylor in the title role, which, of course, does not mean in moving pictures. The stipulations against alterations, eliminations or additions, and that the rehearsals and production of the play shall be under the direction of the author, denote the same thing, and clearly indicate that no other form of production is contemplated. The residuary clause, so to speak, by which the play is to drop to stock companies shows the lowest point to which the author was willing to let it go.

The Courts below based their reasoning upon the impossibility of supposing that the author reserved the right to destroy the value of the right granted, however that right may be characterized, by retaining power to set up the same play in motion pictures a few doors off with a much smaller admission fee. We agree with the premise but not with the conclusion. The implied assumption of the contract seems to us to be that the play was to be produced only as a spoken drama, with respect for the author's natural susceptibility concerning a strict adhesion to the text. We need not amplify the argument presented below against the reservation of the right in question. As was said by Judge Hough in a similar case:

> "There is implied a negative covenant on the part of the [grantor] . . . not to use the ungranted portion of the copyright estate to the detriment, if not the destruction, of the licensees' estate. Admittedly, if Harper Bros. (or Klaw and Erlanger, for the matter of that) permitted photo-plays of Ben Hur to infest the country, the market for the spoken play would be greatly impaired, if not destroyed." Harper Bros. v. Klaw (D. C.) 232 Fed. 609, 613.

The result is that the plaintiff is entitled to an injunction against the representation of the play in moving pictures, but upon the terms that the plaintiff also shall abstain from presenting or authorizing the presentation of the play in that form in Canada or the United States.

Decree reversed. Injunction to issue upon the condition that the plaintiff shall neither represent nor authorize the representation of the play Peg O' My Heart in moving pictures while the contract with the defendant remains in force.

Mr. Justice CLARKE dissenting.

The decision of this case involves the construction of the written contract of January 19, 1912, as modified by that of July 20, 1914, and, centering its attention upon the claim of the defendant to moving picture rights the court dismisses in a single paragraph provisions in these contracts which seem to me to so clearly limit the rights of the defendant to a term expiring possibly in May, 1918, but certainly not later than May, 1919, that I cannot concur in the conclusion arrived at by my Associates.

The court says:

> "As to the duration of the defendant's rights we agree with the Courts below. We see no ground for converting the defendant's undertaking to continue the play for seventy-five performances during the season of 1913–1914, and for each season thereafter for five years, into a limit of the plaintiff's grant of rights. As was said in the District Court, it is a statement of the least that defendant was to do, not of the most that he was to have."

This expression, that the third paragraph of the contract of January 19, 1912, "is a statement of the least that defendant was to do, not of the most that he was to have," is repeated in the opinion of each of the three courts as the sufficient reason for concluding, as the District Court said, that the contract gave to the defendant "all the rights mentioned for all time." It is not the first time that a catchy phrase has diverted attention from less picturesque realities.

My reasons for concluding that the rights of the defendant were limited, as the court says his obligations were limited, to a term expiring not later than the close of the theatrical season of 1918–1919, may be briefly stated.

The grant which it is concluded gave the defendant the exclusive license and liberty to "produce, perform and represent" the play involved "for all time" is in these words:

> "First. The party of the first part hereby grants . . . to the party of the second part, *subject to the terms, conditions and limitations hereinafter expressed*, the sole and exclusive license and liberty to produce, perform and represent the said play in the United States" and Canada.

In terms this is a "license," and in terms also it is subject to "conditions and limitations" to follow in the contract, which are found in the third and fifth paragraphs.

The third paragraph reads:

> "The party of the second part [defendant] agrees to produce the play not later than January 1st, 1913, and to continue said play for at least seventy-five performances during the season 1913–1914 and for each theatrical season thereafter for a period of five years."

The fifth paragraph provides that if the defendant shall fail to produce the play seventy-five times in any one theatrical year—

> "then all rights of the said party of the second part [the defendant] shall cease and determine and shall immediately revert to the said party of the first part."

This third paragraph expresses the agreement of the parties as to what the defendant was to do in consideration of the grant by the plaintiff in the first paragraph, and reading it and the fifth paragraph together, as one, we have the extreme extent and time limit of the defendant's obligation and the penalty forfeiture, is provided for the failure to perform at any time within that limit. The court says that the third paragraph expresses "the least (all) that the defendant was to do," so that his obligation under the contract ended with the five-year period, which obviously would be not later than the close of the theatrical season of 1918–1919. This being true, when did the reciprocal obligation of the plaintiff expire?

That the obligation of the plaintiff continued "for all time" is apparently derived wholly from the inference, as stated by the District Court, that the parties, if they had intended otherwise, "could readily have fixed a time limit in the first paragraph by the addition of words such as 'for ——— years from' or 'until' a stated date."

It is very true that the parties could have written their contract in a different form, and certainly with much more precision of statement, than that in which they did write it, but it is also true that in making it in their own way and terms they granted a general license in the first paragraph, but made it subject to the "terms, conditions and limitations" thereinafter to be expressed, and that they then went forward and expressed in the third paragraph the five-year limitation as we have seen it. The court holds that this five-year limitation applies to the defendant's obligation to perform but that it does not apply to the plaintiff's license to produce. I think it applies to both. Plainly the parties were undertaking to set down in their contract the mutual obligations which each intended to assume—those of the one in consideration of those of the other. The author granted the privilege of producing the play and the defendant agreed to produce it for at least 75 performances during each of five years. After that, the court concludes, the defendant was no longer bound by the contract to do anything which could advantage the plaintiff and therefore, clearly, the plaintiff should not continue thereafter under obligation to the defendant, unless the intention to be so bound is unmistakably expressed in his contract. The "natural and normal" inference is that when the obligation of one party to such a contract as we have here is ended it was the intention that the obligation of the other party should end also.

The inference that the license to produce continued after the obligation to produce expired, in my judgment, can be sustained only by neglecting the specific provision of the first paragraph, that the license granted is subject to the limitations which should follow, and which did follow in the third paragraph. It involves imposing, by judicial construction, heavy and unusual burdens upon the author of a successful dramatic composition in the interest of a commercial producer—a result which courts should not strain themselves to accomplish.

A penalty of forfeiture being provided for failure of the defendant to perform at any time, I cannot see any substantial reason for inserting the five-year limitation except to fix a limit for the expiration of all rights of both parties and this, it seems to me, was its only function.

The provision in the first contract that if the play should fail "in New York and on the road," and in the second that if the net profits for "one theatrical season" should be less than $2,000, the play should be "released for stock" and the royalties divided equally between the parties, would have ample scope for the application within the five-year period and therefore cannot properly be made the basis for the implied continuance of the license beyond that term.

For the reasons thus briefly stated, I think that the parties expressed with sufficient clearness their intention that their mutual relations should all terminate with the expiration of the five-year period, and therefore I dissent from the opinion of the court.

Mr. Justice PITNEY concurs in this opinion.

WARNER BROS. PICTURES, INC. v. COLUMBIA BROADCASTING SYSTEM, INC.
216 F.2d 945 (9th Cir. 1954)

Before STEPHENS and FEE, Circuit Judges, and CLARK, District Judge.

STEPHENS, Circuit Judge.

Dashiell Hammett composed a mystery-detective story entitled "The Maltese Falcon" which was published serially, and each installment was copyrighted by the publisher. Subsequently, Alfred A. Knopf, Inc., entered into a contract with the author to publish the work in book form, Knopf published the book and, in accord with the terms of the contract, copyrighted it.

In 1930, after publication in book form and after publication of all installments of the first serial thereof, Knopf and Hammett, designated as "Owners", for a consideration of $8,500.00, granted certain defined rights in and to The Maltese Falcon (called "writings" in the agreement) to Warner Bros., as "Purchaser".[1] Coincidentally, Knopf executed an instrument to Warner called

---

[1] The Hammett-Knopf-Warner contract, with certain formalities deleted as in the district court's memorandum decision of December 28, 1951, 102 F.Supp. 141, 143, is as follows:

   " . . . Warner as 'Purchaser' was granted the following rights inter alia 'in and to that certain story, hereinafter called "writings," entitled "Maltese Falcon" . . . : 1. (a) the exclusive . . . motion picture rights, including, common law and statutory copyright in the same . . . together with all benefits of the copyrights in such writings, the title and the

"Assignment of Copyright"[2] for a nominal consideration. The text of the
"assignment" shows on its face that it is not an assignment of the copyright

theme thereof, and of all remedies held thereunder, with respect to such motion picture
rights; (b) the exclusive right to make motion picture versions thereof . . . including the
exclusive right to show . . . photographs in motion, representing scenes or action taken
from or based upon said writings, or any adaptation thereof; (c) the exclusive right to
record and reproduce language, speech, songs, music, dancing, choreography and other
sounds in connection with . . . the production and exhibition of photoplays based upon
such writings . . . ; (d) the exclusive right for the purpose of such sound records and
photoplays, to adapt, use, dramatize, arrange, change, transpose, make musical versions of,
add to, interpolate in and subtract from said writings, the language, title and dialogue
thereof . . . ; (e) the exclusive right to record such writings, language and dialogue and
such adaptations, dramatizations, arrangements, change . . . and interpolations on sound
records and to reproduce the same from such sound records in synchronism with and/or
separately from such photoplays . . . ; (f) the right in the writings for production and use
upon the spoken stage . . . is reserved to the Owners, but all other now or hereafter
existing dramatic, exhibition or other presentation rights in the writings, and without
limiting the generality of the foregoing, including talking motion picture rights . . . as well
as the right to transmit and exploit scenes and pictures taken or adapted from or based
upon said writings, the language, title and dialogue thereof, by radio, television or
otherwise, together with the right to transmit and reproduce by radio, television or
otherwise, the writings, the language, title and dialogue thereof and the sound records
herein referred to in connection with the broadcasting of said motion picture versions . . .
are granted exclusively to the Purchaser . . . [and] 12. The Owners warrant and agree that
they will not cause or allow or sanction any publication or dramatization of said writings or
any arrangement, or revision or reissue thereof in any form in any parts of the world,
without first granting to the Purchaser, without further consideration, the silent and
talking motion picture rights and the mechanical and recording and reproducing rights
(and all the rights set forth in paragraph (1) hereof) and in and to any such arrangement,
revision or reissue above named.' "

[2] "Assignment of Copyright. Whereas, Dashiell Hammett is the author of a certain literary
composition entitled "Maltese Falcon", five installments of which have been published . . . and
have been copyrighted by Pro-Distributors Corporation; and

"Whereas, the Pro-Distributors Corporation has heretofore assigned to the Undersigned,
Alfred A. Knopf, Inc., the foregoing copyrights, and

"Whereas, the Undersigned published a novel, "Maltese Falcon" in book form, and registered the novel in United States Copyright Office . . . ,

"Now, Therefore, in consideration of the sum of One Dollar in hand paid and for other
valuable considerations now received, the Undersigned sells and assigns unto Warner Bros.
Pictures, Inc., its successors and assigns forever, the motion picture and talking motion picture
rights . . . in and to the said literary composition (hereinafter called 'writings') and all motion
picture rights in all copyrights thereof, as well as radio broadcasting and television rights, . . .
together with the sole and exclusive right to use, interpolate songs, music, sounds, words and
dialogue in, translate, adapt and change said writings and the title in the making of or in
conjunction with or separately and apart from motion picture photoplays, and to lease, vend
and exhibit the same throughout the world, and to copyright the same in its own name or
otherwise, including the right to record and reproduce sounds, language, dialogue and speech
taken, adapted and translated from the writings, in connection with and/or in synchronism with
and/or separately from the production and exhibition of photoplays based upon such writings,

but that it is a grant to Warner of specified rights to the use of the writings in The Maltese Falcon. Both the contract between Hammett-Knopf and Warner, and the "assignment" from Knopf, purport to grant to Warner certain defined and detailed exclusive rights to the use of The Maltese Falcon "writings" in moving pictures, radio, and television.

By the common law, the author of a writing possesses the sole and exclusive right to publish it, but upon and after the first publication the writing may be published by anyone including the author, since the writing has gone into the public domain. The copyright statute extends the author's sole and exclusive right in accordance with its terms and provisions. In other words, it reserves the writing from the public domain for the effective period of the copyright. What we have just said is what is meant by courts when they say: "When the copyright comes in, the common law right goes out."

No question as to the legality of the copyright on The Maltese Falcon or to its continuing effectiveness through all times in suit, or to its complete beneficial ownership by Hammett and Knopf together, is in issue. Therefore, at the effective moment of the grants by Hammett and Knopf to Warner, the latter became possessed of the sole and exclusive right to the writing which is within the copyright, less all limiting terms of the grants. The grants are limited to defined uses in motion picture, talking pictures, radio, and television.

It is claimed by Warner that it acquired the exclusive right to the use of the writing, The Maltese Falcon, including the individual characters and their names, together with the title, "The Maltese Falcon", in motion pictures, radio, and television. The use of the title is not in issue, since the grant to Warner specifically includes it.

It is the position of Hammett and the other defendants, all of whom claim some interest under him, that the rights acquired by Warner are those specifically mentioned in the conveying or granting instruments, and that the exclusive right to the use of the characters and/or their names were not

---

whether such records be on the film itself or on separate discs, or any other material or medium, by means of mechanical, electrical, photographic or other devices and improvements thereupon which are now or hereafter may be used in connection with the production and exhibition of motion pictures (hereinafter referred to as 'sound records') and to copyright in its own name or otherwise said sound records.

"The Undersigned agrees to obtain or cause to be obtained a renewal of such copyrights according to law in order to secure said rights in Warner Bros. Pictures, Inc., during any and all renewal terms, and the Undersigned hereby appoints Warner Bros. Pictures, Inc., its attorney-in-fact with an irrevocable power to do all acts and things for and in the name of the Undersigned to obtain such renewals.

"Dated: June 23, 1930."

mentioned as being granted; that the instruments, properly construed, do not convey any exclusive right to the use of characters with or without names, hence Hammett could use them in other stories. However, if, by reason of the silence in the instruments as to such claimed rights, the instruments should be held to be ambiguous on this point, the custom and practice demonstrate that such rights are not customarily parted with by authors, but that characters which are depicted in one detective story together with their names are customarily retained and used in the intricacies of subsequent but different tales.

Hammett did so use the characters with their names and did contract with others for such use. In 1946 he used The Maltese Falcon characters including Sam Spade, the detective and the leading character in the Falcon, by name, and granted to third parties the sole and exclusive right, except their use in the Falcon, to use that character by name (later orally enlarged to include other characters of the Falcon) in radio, television, and motion pictures. Under such claimed rights, radio broadcasts of "Adventures of Sam Spade", including "The Kandy Tooth" were broadcast in weekly half-hour episodes from 1946 to 1950.

Warner claims infringement of copyright and "unfair use and competition" by such re-use and, as well, for infringement of parts of the story and the whole of the writing inclusive of characters and their names. Hammett and the other defendants deny infringement or unfair use and competition on any count, and Hammett requests the court to declare his rights in the premises. Knopf is a nominal party asking and claiming nothing, and is made a plaintiff under the right granted Warner in the Hammett-Knopf-Warner contract.

The trial court denied relief to Warner, declared Hammett's rights, and assessed costs against Warner, who appeals.

The instruments under which Warner claims were prepared by Warner Bros. Corporation which is a large, experienced moving picture producer. It would seem proper, therefore, to construe the instruments under the assumption that the claimant knew what it wanted and that in defining the items in the instruments which it desired and intended to take, it included all of the items it was contracting to take. We are of the opinion that since the use of characters and character names are nowhere specifically mentioned in the agreements, but that other items, including the title, "The Maltese Falcon", and their use are specifically mentioned as being granted, that the character rights with the names cannot be held to be within the grants, and that under the doctrine of *ejusdem generis,* general language cannot be held to include them. As was said in Phillip v. Jerome H. Remick & Co., S.D., N.Y., Op. No. 9,999, 1936, "Such doubt as there is should be resolved in favor of the composer. The clearest language is necessary to divest the author of the fruits of his labor. Such language is lacking here."

The conclusion that these rights are not within the granting instruments is strongly buttressed by the fact that historically and presently detective fiction writers have and do carry the leading characters with their names and individualisms from one story into succeeding stories. This was the practice of Edgar Allen Poe, Sir Arthur Conan Doyle, and others; and in the last two decades of S.S. Van Dine, Earle Stanley Gardner, and others. The reader's interest thereby snowballs as new "capers" of the familiar characters are related in succeeding tales. If the intention of the contracting parties had been to avoid this practice which was a very valuable one to the author, it is hardly reasonable that it would be left to a general clause following specific grants. Another buttressing fact is that Hammett wrote and caused to be published in 1932, long after the Falcon agreements, three stories in which some of the leading characters of the Falcon were featured, and no objection was voiced by Warner. It is also of some note that the evidence shows that Columbia, long subsequent to the conveying instruments, dickered with Warner for the use of the Falcon on its "Suspense" radio program and, failing in its efforts, substituted "The Kandy Tooth" which uses the Falcon characters under license of Hammett. Warner made no claim against Columbia at or reasonably soon afterward. The conclusion we have come to, as to the intention of the parties, would seem to be in harmony with the fact that the purchase price paid by Warner was $8,500.00, which would seem inadequate compensation for the complete surrender of the characters made famous by the popular reception of the book, The Maltese Falcon; and that the intention of the parties, inclusive of the "Assignment," was not that Hammett should be deprived of using the Falcon characters in subsequently written stories, and that the contract, properly construed, does not deprive Hammett of their use.

Up to this point we have discussed the points at issue by construing the contract and by seeking the intention of the parties to it, and we have concluded that the parties never intended by their contract to buy and sell the future use of the personalities in the writing.

It will now be profitable to consider whether it was ever intended by the copyright statute that characters with their names should be under its protection.

The practice of writers to compose sequels to stories is old, and the copyright statute, though amended several times, has never specifically mentioned the point. It does not appear that it has ever been adjudicated, although it is mentioned in Nichols v. Universal Pictures Corp., 2 Cir., 1930, 45 F.2d 119. If Congress had intended that the sale of the right to publish a copyrighted story would foreclose the author's use of its characters in subsequent works for the life of the copyright, it would seem Congress would have made specific provision therefor. Authors work for the love of their art no more than other professional people work in other lines of work for the love of it. There is the financial motive as well. The characters of an author's imagination and the art of his descriptive talent, like a painter's or like a person with his penmanship, are always limited and always fall into limited patterns.[5] The restriction argued for is unreasonable, and would effect the very opposite of the statute's purpose which is to encourage the production of the arts.

It is our conception of the area covered by the copyright statute that when a study of the two writings is made and it is plain from the study that one of them is not in fact the creation of the putative author, but instead has been copied in substantial part exactly or in transparent re-phrasing to produce essentially the story of the other writing, it infringes.

It is conceivable that the character really constitutes the story being told, but if the character is only the chessman in the game of telling the story he is not within the area of the protection afforded by the copyright. The subject is given consideration in the Nichols case, supra, 45 F.2d at page 121 of the citation. At page 122 of 45 F.2d of the same case the court remarks that the line between infringement and non-infringement is indefinite and may seem arbitrary when drawn; nevertheless it must be drawn. Nichols v. Universal Pictures Corp., 2 Cir., 1930, 45 F.2d 119.

We conclude that even if the Owners assigned their complete rights in the copyright to the Falcon, such assignment did not prevent the author from using the characters used therein, in other stories. The characters were vehicles for the story told, and the vehicles did not go with the sale of the story.

We turn to the consideration of general infringement. It is agreed that a story entitled "The Kandy Tooth" is the closest to The Maltese Falcon, and from a practical standpoint if the Tooth does not infringe the Falcon, there has been no infringement.

We have set out in notes 8 and 9 at the end of this opinion, short summations of the two works. There is a sameness in the tricks of spinning out

---

[5] "He must be a poor creature that does not often repeat himself. Imagine the author of the excellent piece of advice, 'Know thyself', never alluding to that sentiment again during the course of a protracted existence! Why, the truths a man carries about with him are his tools; and do you think a carpenter is bound to use the same plane but once to smooth a knotty board with, or to hang up his hammer after it has driven its first nail? I shall never repeat a conversation, but an idea, often. I shall use the same types when I like, but not commonly the same stereotypes. A thought is often original, though you have uttered it a hundred times. It has come to you over a new route, by a new and express train of associations." The Autocrat of the Breakfast Table, by O. W. Holmes, M.D., p. 9, reprint of original edition.

the yarn so as to sustain the reader's suspense as to hinted mystery, and there is a similarity in the two stories in that there is a long complicated search for a lost article of fabulous value. The searches are filled with complications, fatalities, and moral delinquencies by characters in name, description, and action of some similarities. The script of the Tooth was not composed by Hammett and, except for a few expressions, is not written in the Hammett literary style.

We see no clear error in the trial court's holding that the similarities of the two stories do not go to the degree of constituting practically the same story. There is no textual copying; the mystery of the Tooth and the suspense to the reader would not be dulled through his having read the Falcon. In a phrase, they are different stories though of the same general nature.

Unfair Use and Competition

Warner claims the radio broadcasts, "The Adventures of Sam Spade" and the "Suspense" broadcast of "The Kandy Tooth," and others, wherein the characters of the Falcon were used by name and their peculiarities, constituted unfair use and competition. The trial court found against such contention and we think the conclusion does not constitute clear error.

It is patent that the characters of The Maltese Falcon could not fairly be used in such a manner as to cause the Falcon to be materially lessened in its commercial worth by degrading or cheapening them so that the public would not be interested in their capers. They could not be used in such a manner as to deceive the public or to "palm off" to the public the idea that they were really witnessing The Maltese Falcon when they viewed showings of the other stories. We think there was no reversible error in the court's conclusions on these points.

Although we have thought it necessary to arrive at some conclusions not entirely in accord with those of the district court, or to arrive at like conclusions through somewhat different reasoning, nevertheless we commend a reading of that court's opinion and notation of authorities cited. We are in complete accord with the order of the district court that the plaintiffs-appellants take nothing, and that defendants-appellees recover their costs.

The judgment in accordance with this opinion will settle all of the issues of the case, including all of Hammett's interest in the subject matter under Warner's claims. There is no justiciable controversy between Hammett and Knopf, the nominal plaintiff. It follows that no useful purpose could be served by considering Hammett's prayer for a declaration of his rights and his counterclaim for a declaratory judgment is therefore dismissed and the judgment running to him on it is reversed. Otherwise, the judgment is affirmed.[8, 9]

Reversed and affirmed in part.

(Text continued on page 424)

---

[8] The Maltese Falcon Story. The theme of the story of The Maltese Falcon is a complicated

search for a fabulously valuable bird figurine called The Maltese Falcon. The action of the story centers in San Francisco from elsewhere, with the leading actors, or characters gathering there intent upon the objective. An attractive, alluring woman of uncertain age and reputation, by name Brigid O'Shaughnessy, assuming a false name and great distress, in search of help, called upon private detective Sam Spade, a clever, laconic, rangy-looking man whose morals and practices are none too idyllic, and well if not too favorably known to the police. Brigid qualifies within the requisite of the proverbial monumental liar, but, though Spade is not deceived, she manages to withhold the truth from him. A dunderheaded policeman and his partner enter the tangled story. Effie Perine is Spade's secretary, one of those see-all, know-all, self effacing paragons of loyal efficiency. A mystical character of a man who apparently is cooperating with Brigid against three others of their search-party gets shot to death and Spade is under suspicion. The leader of the search-party is a fat man named Gutman, of infinite patience and possessed of untold money. He proposes to pay a large sum to Sam who represents that he can deliver the bird. An effeminate lackey of a man by the name of Cairo does Gutman's bidding. A young, boyish gunman is under Gutman's orders. The story runs on at accelerated tempo in mystery until the captain of a ship, just in from the Orient, appears at Spade's apartment with a package in hand and falls dead from the boy's bullets sent into him just before he entered Spade's place. All gather at Sam's for the delivery of the bird, supposed to be in the package, and for payment of the money. Sam gets the award and Gutman gets the bird, which is a worthless counterfeit of the genuine. Gutman maintains his sang-froid. Brigid and Sam have trespassed the conventions. Yet, as somehow it is revealed the lady herself was the author of the first fatality, she is delivered over by the benevolent Sam and is sent on her way to San Quentin prison. These characters are skillfully depicted in a running, attractive style and distinctly assume individualism as distinguished from mere other persons.

Warner claims ownership of all of this including the characterizations with the characters' names, and the story.

[9] The Kandy Tooth Story. The script opens with Sam Spade telephoning from jail to his faithful secretary, Effie Perine, early in the morning. Effie hurries to Sam who dictates his story. Dundy, the police officer, is present. Spade has received a telegram from the fat Caspar Gutman who had been marked "dead" from the end of The Maltese Falcon caper. The telegram is a warning about "an invidious pair of rogues", a dentist, and a charming woman named Hope Laverne, who have something to do with a "hidden tooth." Spade is bailed out by a mystery man who deposits $20,000.00 with the law. Gutman will shortly arrive in San Francisco. The dentist, so Spade dictated, had been ushered into his office by Effie and entreats him to get someone's "bridge." The dentist leaves. Spade contemplates "Hm-m-m . . . Beware the Hidden Tooth". In comes Hope Laverne, a character along the line of Brigid O'Shaughnessy, and she is, or claims to be, a sister of the dentist. Hope explains the brother's obsession about a dental bridge. She wants to find him. Spade goes to a hotel, gets information from a house detective, and finds the brother, badly beaten; the two walk on the street—the dentist collapses. Spade takes him into a newsreel theater. The show excites him—it's about white elephants and particularly Oriental in character. Spade and the dentist go back to Spade's room. There Laverne recites a story of a tooth having been extracted from the jaw of a sacred body long since the occupant of an Oriental tomb. The tooth was taken by international rogues and installed by the dentist in the bridgework of an innocent refugee. The rogues are now attempting to locate the refugee and regain the priceless tooth.

Hope calls Spade on the telephone for help, and he goes, but is attacked by a boy, brother of the gun-boy in The Maltese Falcon. They scuffle and Spade is felled by a gun butt. He comes to in the presence of the imperturbable Gutman and strange happenings ensue. Spade finally gets

"A.C. DEMANDS FOR TALENT EXCLUSIVES DUE FOR LEGAL TEST"
Variety (June 28, 1978), p. 1

Philadelphia, June 27.

Plan by Atlantic City's Resorts International Hotel Casino to put a 90-day 100-mile exclusivity lock on Don Rickles and other headliners under longterm pacts is getting knocks from Philly area bidders for big marquee names, the Latin Casino in Cherry Hill, N.J., and the Valley Forge (Pa.) Music Fair.

The A.C. site has already presented Steve Lawrence & Eydie Gorme, Bill Cosby, Rickles, Vic Damone and Ben Vereen, and has coming up Buddy Hackett, Victor Borge, Gene Kelly, Bob Newhart, Red Skelton and Alan King. Many have played the Latin Casino and/or Valley Forge.

Music Fairs exec Shelly Gross concedes that "area and time protection clauses" are standard (Valley Forge itself uses a rider in contracts nixing within 50 miles night club, arena, theatre and benefit performances, sans written permission, from date of signing to 30 days after engagement), but says "normal and reasonable" limitations have permitted Valley Forge and Latin to coexist.

"Many stars—Totie Fields, Liberace, Lou Rawls, the Spinners—have worked for both of us. We never object to Latin Casino bookings. If they have an act in the spring, we book it in the fall, and vice versa. We don't consider Atlantic City similarly competitive. We'd take an act a week after.

"Booking an act four weeks at a time with an unreasonable exclusion may violate restraint of trade laws. We put the various agencies on notice a year ago that if they illegally shut off our sources, we'd go to the courts.

"There's a mistaken idea that they pay more than we do, but we're more

---

the tooth in the ashes of the cremated body of the refugee, Herman Julius. $20,000.00 is paid upon delivery of the package containing the ashes. The tooth, by reason of a religious significance, is worth untold wealth to Gutman if he can produce it. A murder is committed; Hope and Sam had been more than friends. A Russian was mixed up in the plot. When Gutman saw that he had been duped through the delivery to him of the cremation residue, he took it as philosophically as when the bird in The Maltese Falcon turned out to be spurious. It develops that $20,000.00 had been put up for Sam's bail, and Sam puts up the same money as bail for Hope who gets into and out of jail. In some not very clear manner it all ends with no money gained by Spade, but Hope telephones her love after leaving jail, and Effie is not sure that the whole affair will net her a new ribbon for her typewriter.

than competitive on a per performance basis when you consider that we require only eight or nine shows, instead of 18 and sometimes more. We also think we offer the public a much better deal."

Although in their earliest years the Music Fairs presented only musical comedies and operettas, they added night club and concert style entertainers (Jack Benny, Wayne Newton, Robert Goulet, etc.) as much as 10 years ago. The Latin reversed that procedure by booking musicals, but abandoned the practice after a single summer.

Latin owners Dallas and Charles Gerson declined comment, but said they would issue a statement "at the proper time." However, the Latin's schedule for next season, usually firmed by this time of year, is still being put together.

Lee A. Daniels, "HARDY BOYS NAMED IN LITERARY SUIT"
The New York Times (June 10, 1980), p. A1

For nearly 80 years, Tom Swift, Nancy Drew, the Hardy Boys and the Bobbsey Twins have lived over at Grosset & Dunlap. But now the Stratemeyer Syndicate, the book-writing concern that turns out these and other children's adventure series, wants them to have a new home (at least in paperback) down the street at Simon & Schuster. However, a Federal judge will have to decide if the move is legal.

Stratemeyer, whose books have thrilled three generations of youngsters the world over, is being sued in Federal District Court in Manhattan by Grosset & Dunlap, its publisher since the early 1900's, for breach of contract.

In turn, the writing concern and the publisher it now wants to do business with, Simon & Schuster, are countersuing Grosset.

The major question in the complex nonjury trial before Judge Robert J. Ward is who will publish the new paperback editions of the syndicate's four immensely successful series for a new generation of youthful readers.

Grosset & Dunlap, which has published the hardcover editions for nearly 80 years, contends that a 1979 agreement between the Stratemeyer partnership and Simon & Schuster to publish the new stories in the series in paperback editions is a breach of Grosset's contract with the syndicate and infringes upon Grosset's copyright and trademark rights in the books and their characters.

Grosset is seeking punitive damages of $300 million, unspecified compensatory damages and a variety of declarations of its contractual rights and several injunctions against the Stratemeyer partnership and Simon & Schuster.

The Stratemeyer Syndicate and Simon & Schuster deny Grosset's claims and contend that Grosset had only a "limited license" to publish the syndicate's books in hardcover, not in paperback, and does not own any of the copyrights to the syndicate's work.

Spokesmen and lawyers for both sides have declined to comment on the issues or on the syndicate's operation while the case is being decided. Information about their positions was gained from papers filed with the court.

The association between Grosset and the syndicate started when Edward Stratemeyer, a dime-novel writer, created the Bobbsey Twins. Mr. Stratemeyer agreed to a contract with Grosset, formed his own syndicate, and hired ghost writers to turn out many of the volumes as the series grew popular.

The writers wrote under a contract of anonymity, signing away their rights for a flat fee. Pseudonyms were used. This is still the syndicate's method of operation as it continues to produce new volumes in the popular series.

Daughter Heads Syndicate

Mr. Stratemeyer's successor as head of the syndicate is his daughter, Harriet S. Adams, who is now 87 years old. She says she wrote at least 165 books in several of the series under various pseudonyms.

There have been 17 series, and they included the Rover Boys, The X Bar X Boys, the Blythe Girls and the Buck and Larry baseball stories.

From the beginning, however, the most successful of them were the four that now are at the center of the dispute in Federal Court.

A spokesman for Grosset declined to discuss sales volumes or revenues of the books. But Grosset has previously said that by the late 1960's the Bobbsey Twins had sold 50 million volumes, the Hardy Boys 26 million volumes, and Nancy Drew 30 million volumes. At that time, the annual sales figures for the three series totaled nearly 3 million volumes a year.

Statement of Payments

In papers it filed with the court, Grosset contends that for the years 1975 to 1979, it paid to the syndicate $2.5 million as its share of the revenue from book sales for the three series.

The relationship between Mr. Stratemeyer and Grosset was sealed by contract in 1910 and a second one in 1930, shortly before his death. Grosset contends the latter contract gave it "exclusive rights" to publish both hardback and paperback editions of most of the existing series of Stratemeyer books, and that new agreements made in 1934 and 1951 added new series to the contract and made provisions for the addition of still other series.

In addition, Grosset contends that a contract between it and the syndicate in 1954 gave it rights to a share of all revenues derived from subsidiary rights for foreign-language editions and another subsidiary rights.

Contract Disputes Cited

However, according to court papers filed by the syndicate and Simon & Schuster, a series of disputes between the syndicate and Grosset in the late 1970's over royalties, format and the terms of a new contract led lawyers for the syndicate to approach Simon & Schuster about publishing the concern's new books in paperback.

They agreed to a contract in February 1979. Simon & Schuster thus far has published in paperback four additions to the Hardy Boys series, two to the Nancy Drew series and a large-type edition, designed for beginning readers, to the Bobbsey Twins series. These volumes have not been published in hard cover.

Simon & Schuster contends that Grosset never had the rights to publish paperback editions of the Stratemeyer books, and that its earlier contract with the syndicate did not give it the automatic right to publish the syndicate's books forever.

NAMATH v. SPORTS ILLUSTRATED

80 Misc. 2d 531, 363 N.Y.S.2d 276 (Sup. Ct. N.Y. Co.)
aff'd 48 A.D.2d 487, 371 N.Y.S.2d 10 (1st Dept 1975)

HAROLD BAER, Justice:

This is a motion to dismiss the complaint which seeks substantial damages under Civil Rights Law, sections 50, 51. Plaintiff demands $250,000. in compensatory damages and $2,000,000. in punitive damages.

The defendant Time Incorporated publishes Sports Illustrated. In January, 1969, Sports Illustrated published photographs of the plaintiff. These photographs were admittedly newsworthy as plaintiff was the star quarterback of the "Jets" when they defeated the "Colts" in the Super Bowl. The gravamen of the plaintiff's complaint is that the magazine, in its advertising campaign during the latter half of 1972, used photographs in ten advertisements to promote subscriptions. He demands damages for violation of his right of privacy and the wrongful use of his photograph without his written consent (Civil Rights Law, §§ 50, 51).

It is apparent from a reading of the complaint that plaintiff seeks damages, not for violation of his right of privacy but because he was deprived of substantial income from a "property" right. He earns substantial income for endorsement of many products. The contention is that this defendant should not be permitted to use his name or photograph without his written consent and without remuneration to him. Plaintiff states that in 1972 his commercial endorsements brought him income "in excess of several hundred thousand dollars." "His grievance is not the invasion of his 'privacy'—privacy is the one thing he did not want, or need, in his occupation." (Concurring opinion, Desmond, J., in Gautier v. Pro-Football, Inc., 304 N.Y. 354, 361, 107 N.E.2d 485, 489.) In that case it was pointed out that "[c]laims based on use of a name or a picture 'for advertising purposes' . . . have received much more liberal treatment than those grounded on use 'for purposes of trade'." (Gautier v. Pro-Football, Inc., 278 App.Div. 431, 434, 106 N.Y.S.2d 553, 556.)

In connection with advertising, the Courts of this State have held that incidental use of a name or likeness is not in contravention of the statute (. . . Booth v. Curtis Publishing Co., 15 A.D.2d 343, 223 N.Y.S.2d 737, affd. 11 N.Y.2d 907, 228 N.Y.S.2d 468, 182 N.E.2d 812 . . .). It is the Booth case, supra, on which defendant mainly relies. In that case, *Holiday* Magazine had published a news article about a resort in the West Indies, accompanied by photographs of prominent guests. The plaintiff, Shirley Booth, the well-known actress, was photographed without objection, her picture appeared in the magazine and was republished six months later as part of an advertisement for *Holiday*. The Appellate Division held that there is no violation of the statute if the name and photograph are limited to establishing the news content and quality of the media:

> "Consequently, it suffices here that so long as the reproduction was used to illustrate the quality and content of the periodical in which it originally appeared, the statute was not violated, albeit the reproduction appeared in other media for purposes of advertising the periodical." (15 A.D.2d p. 350, 223 N.Y.S.2d p. 744.)

This was the extreme limit of "incidental use" and predicated upon the theory that the statute was not violated by a true and fair presentation in the news or from "incidental advertising" of the news medium in which she was properly and fairly presented.

There was a strong dissenting opinion by Justice Eager (p. 353, 223 N.Y.S.2d p. 747) based on the case of Flores v. Mosler Safe Co., 7 N.Y.2d 276, 196 N.Y.S.2d 975, 164 N.E.2d 853. However, as pointed out by Justice Breitel (now Chief Judge of the Court of Appeals), the Flores case involved the advertising for sale of defendant's products. It was a use for trade purposes and a classic example of collateral use. It was not a use incidental to the dissemination of news. The Booth decision, supra, emphasizes that the statute should be interpreted realistically, given effect to the purpose as well as the language of the statute (Booth v. Curtis, supra, 15 A.D.2d at p. 347, 223 N.Y.S.2d 907.).

This plaintiff raises the point that the defendant's advertisement was not an incidental use but became a collateral use with the passing of time, the makeup of the advertisements, the prominent use of plaintiff's name, the superimposed wording and the accompanying copy. He insists that these raise questions of fact that preclude summary judgment.

Photographs of Joe Namath appeared many times on the cover and in stories published by the defendant from July, 1965 through October, 1972. He admits that these were newsworthy and does not object to them. He does object to the use of his name and likeness in promotional material between September and December, 1972. In the defendant's promotional material, plaintiff's photograph was printed adjacent to a subscription application for *Sports Illustrated*. In most instances promotional material appeared alongside or below his picture. Magazines, popular with the male reader, included the words, "How to get Close to Joe Namath". In the publications read mostly by female subscribers, the inscription was, "The man you love loves Joe Namath". Plaintiff intimates that it may have been unobjectionable to him if they had substituted the word "football" where his name appeared. There is nothing degrading, derogatory or untruthful about the copy. The plaintiff does not doubt his popularity or newsworthiness or that the statement was fair comment. Admittedly, it was used to stimulate subscriptions but this is permissible and see Booth, supra, 15 A.D.2d p. 349, 223 N.Y.S.2d p. 743:

> "It stands to reason that a publication can best prove its worth and illustrate its content by submission of complete copies of or extraction from past editions. Nor would it suffice to show stability of quality merely to utilize for that purpose a current issue. Moreover, the widespread usage over the years of reproducing extracts from the covers and internal pages of out-of-issue periodicals of personal matter relating to all sorts of news figures, of public or private stature, is ample recognition that the usage has not violated the sensibilities of the community or the purport of the statute.

> . . .

> "To be sure, Holiday's subsequent republication of Miss Booth's picture was, in motivation, sheer advertising and solicitation. *This alone is not determinative of the question so long as the law accords an exempt status to incidental advertising of the news medium itself.*" (Emphasis supplied.)

The constitutionality of the New York statute has been under scrutiny. The realistic interpretation by the New York courts has avoided conflict with the First Amendment of the Constitution.

"The appellant argues that the statute should be declared unconstitutional on its face if construed by the New York courts to impose liability without proof of knowing or reckless falsity. Such a declaration would not be warranted even if it were entirely clear that this had previously been the view of the New York courts. The New York Court of Appeals, as the *Spahn* [Spahn v. Messner, Inc., 18 N.Y.2d 324, 274 N.Y.S.2d 877, 221 N.E.2d 543.] opinion demonstrates, has been assiduous in construing the statute to avoid invasion of the constitutional protections of speech and press." (Time, Inc. v. Hill, 385 U.S. 374, 397, 87 S.Ct. 534, 547, 17 L.Ed.2d 456.)

" . . . 'That books, newspapers and magazines are published and sold for profit does not prevent them from being a form of expression whose liberty is safeguarded by the First Amendment.' Joseph Burstyn, Inc. v. Wilson, 343 U.S. 495, 501–502, 72 S.Ct. 777, 780, 96 L.Ed. 1098". (Cited in Time, Inc. v. Hill, 385 U.S. p. 397, 87 S.Ct. p. 546.)

It is understandable that plaintiff desires payment for the use of his name and likeness in advertisements for the sale of publications in which he has appeared as newsworthy just as he is paid for collateral endorsement of commercial products. This he cannot accomplish under the existing law of our State and Nation. Athletic prowess is much admired and well paid in this country. It is commendable that freedom of speech and the press under the First Amendment transcends the right to privacy. This is so particularly when a petitioner seeks remuneration for what is basically a property right—not a right to privacy.

The motion to dismiss the complaint is granted.

NAMATH v. SPORTS ILLUSTRATED
48 A.D.2d 487, 371 N.Y.S.2d 10 (1st Dept 1975)

Before KUPFERMAN, J. P., and MURPHY, CAPOZZOLI, LANE and NUNEZ, JJ.

CAPOZZOLI, Justice:

Plaintiff sought substantial compensatory and punitive damages by reason of defendants' publication and use of plaintiff's photograph without his consent. That photograph, which was originally used by defendants, without objection from plaintiff, in conjunction with a news article published by them on the 1969 Super Bowl Game, was used in advertisements promoting subscriptions to their magazine, Sports Illustrated.

The use of plaintiff's photograph was merely incidental advertising of defendants' magazine in which plaintiff had earlier been properly and fairly depicted and, hence, it was not violative of the Civil Rights Law (*Booth v. Curtis Publishing Co.*, 15 A.D.2d 343, 223 N.Y.S.2d 737, aff'd, 11 N.Y.2d 907, 228 N.Y.S.2d 468, 182 N.E.2d 812).

Certainly, defendants' subsequent republication of plaintiff's picture was "in motivation, sheer advertising and solicitation. This alone is not determinative of the question so long as the law accords an exempt status to incidental advertising of the news medium itself". (*Booth v. Curtis Publishing Co.*, supra, p. 349, 223 N.Y.S.2d p. 744). Again, it was stated, at 15 A.D.2d p. 350, 223 N.Y.S.2d p. 744 of the cited case, as follows:

> "Consequently, it suffices here that so long as the reproduction was used to illustrate the quality and content of the periodical in which it originally appeared, the statute was not violated, albeit the reproduction appeared in other media for purposes of advertising the periodical."

Contrary to the dissent, we deem the cited case to be dispositive hereof. The language from the Namath advertisements relied upon in the dissent, does not indicate plaintiff's endorsement of the magazine Sports Illustrated. Had that been the situation, a completely different issue would have been presented. Rather, that language merely indicates, to the readers of those advertisements, the general nature of the contents of what is likely to be included in future issues of the magazine.

The order of the Supreme Court, New York County, entered on February 5th, 1975, granting defendants' motion for summary judgment dismissing the complaint herein, and the judgment entered thereon on February 10th, 1975, should be affirmed, with costs.

Order, Supreme Court, New York County, entered on February 5, 1975, and judgment entered thereon on February 10, 1975, affirmed. Respondents shall recover of appellant $60 costs and disbursements of this appeal.

All concur except KUPFERMAN, J. P., and MURPHY, J., who dissent in a dissenting opinion by KUPFERMAN, J. P.

KUPFERMAN, Justice (dissenting).

It is undisputed that one Joseph W. Namath is an outstanding sports figure, redoubtable on the football field. Among other things, as the star quarterback of the New York Jets, he led his team to victory on January 12, 1969 in the Super Bowl in Miami.

This feat and the story of the game and its star were heralded with illustrative photographs in the January 20, 1969 issue of Sports Illustrated, conceded to be an outstanding magazine published by Time Incorporated and devoted, as its name implies, to the activities for which it is famous. Of course, this was not the first nor the last time that Sports Illustrated featured Mr. Namath and properly so.

The legal problem involves the use of one of his action photos from the January 20, 1969 issue in subsequent advertisements in other magazines as promotional material for the sale of subscriptions to Sports Illustrated.

Plaintiff contends that the use was commercial in violation of his right of privacy under §§ 50 and 51 of the Civil Rights Law. See, in general, "The Muddled State of Law of Privacy" by J. Irwin Shapiro, N.Y.L.J., May 16 and May 19, 1975, p. 1, col. 3. Further, that because he was in the business of endorsing products and selling the use of his name and likeness, it interfered with his right to such sale, sometimes known as the right of publicity. *Haelan Laboratories v. Topps Chewing Gum*, 202 F.2d 866 (2nd Cir. 1953). Defendants contend there is an attempt to invade their constitutional rights under the First and Fourteenth Amendments by the maintenance of this action and that, in any event, the advertisements were meant to show "the nature, quality and content" of the magazine and not to trade on the plaintiff's name and likeness.

Initially, we are met with the determination in a similar case, *Booth v. Curtis Publishing Co.*, 15 A.D.2d 343, 223 N.Y.W.2d 737 (1st Dept.) *aff'd without op.*, 11 N.Y.2d 907, 228 N.Y.S.2d 468, 182 N.E.2d 812 (1962) relied on by Baer, J., in his opinion at Special Term dismissing the complaint.

The plaintiff was Shirley Booth, the well-known actress, photographed at a resort in the West Indies, up to her neck in the water and wearing an interesting chapeau, which photo appeared in Holiday Magazine along with photographs of other prominent guests. This photo was then used as a substantial part of an advertisement for Holiday.

Mr. Justice Breitel (now Chief Judge Breitel) wrote:

> "Consequently, it suffices here that so long as the reproduction was used to illustrate the quality and content of the periodical in which it originally appeared, the statute was not violated, albeit the reproduction appeared in other media for purposes of advertising the periodical." 15 A.D.2d at p. 350, 223 N.Y.S.2d at p. 744.

However, the situation is one of degree. A comparison of the Booth and Namath photographs and advertising copy shows that in the Booth case, her name is in exceedingly small print, and it is the type of photograph itself which attracted attention. In the Namath advertisement, we find, in addition to the outstanding photograph, in Cosmopolitan Magazine (for women) the heading "The Man You Love loves Joe Namath", and in Life, the heading "How to get Close to Joe Namath." There seems to be trading on the name of the personality involved in the defendants' advertisements.

This distinction between actual advertising use and use to inform, *cf. Bigelow v. Virginia*, 421 U.S. 809, 95 S.Ct. 2222, 44 L.Ed.2d 600 (1975) means that cases like *Time, Inc. v. Hill*, 385 U.S. 374, 87 S.Ct. 534, 17 L.Ed.2d 456 (1967) and *Cantrell v. Forest City Publishing Co.*, 419 U.S. 245, 95 S.Ct. 465 (1974) involving so-called "false light" portrayal are of only incidental interest. It is also a distinction accepted by Mr. Justice Breitel in that he recognized a right "to have one's personality, even if newsworthy, free from commercial exploitation at the hands of another . . . " *Booth v. Curtis Publishing Co., supra*, 15 A.D.2d at p. 351, 223 N.Y.S.2d at p. 745.

The complaint should not have been dismissed as a matter of law.

MURPHY, J., concurs.

CEPEDA v. SWIFT & COMPANY
291 F. Supp. 242 (E.D. Mo.1968)

MEMORANDUM OPINION AND ORDER

REGAN, District Judge.

All parties have filed motions for a summary judgment. As appears infra, we sustain defendants' motions and deny plaintiff's.

Orlando Cepeda is a professional baseball player in the celebrity category. He seeks actual and punitive damages for the allegedly "unauthorized use of his name, photograph, reputation and signature" for advertising purposes. The material facts bearing upon the issue of liability are not in dispute.

Wilson Sporting Goods Company is a manufacturer of baseballs and other sporting goods. Swift & Company is a wholesale meat processor. A division of Swift, St. Louis Independent Packing Company, markets bacon and franks under the brand name "Mayrose."

Admittedly, Cepeda entered into a contract with Wilson dated April 30, 1963, granting it "the exclusive right and license to manufacture, *advertise and sell baseballs*, baseball shoes, baseball gloves and baseball mitts *identified by his name, facsimile signature, initials, portrait*, or by any nickname popularly applied to him, and *to license others so to do.*" The contract required Wilson to pay Cepeda a royalty of 10 cents per dozen on Cepeda-identified baseballs sold by Wilson or its licensees, and different amounts on the other products covered by the contract, with a maximum of $1000 per year on total royalties payable to plaintiff. Although the payments to Cepeda have never reached the maximum in any one year, there is no question as to the fact that Wilson has made all payments due Cepeda under the contract and the renewals thereof.

A quantity of "official Orlando Cepeda baseballs" bearing Cepeda's facsimile signature were manufactured by Wilson and sold to Brown-Flatt Incentives which in turn resold the baseballs to Swift & Company (or to Swift's advertising agency acting on Swift's behalf). Wilson has conceded that at the time these baseballs were manufactured and sold it had knowledge not only that Brown-Flatt Incentives intended to sell the baseballs to or on behalf of Swift or its agents, but that the baseballs would be offered for sale to the general public through an advertising campaign conducted on behalf of Swift by its advertising agency (through which advertising campaign the general public would be advised that the baseballs in question could be purchased for the sum of $1.00 each together with a label or coupon from a product manufactured by Swift). Wilson agreed to provide appropriate copy and pictures of plaintiff for use by Swift. The advertising campaign was in fact conducted, and more than 12,000 baseballs were sold by Swift in the manner contemplated.

On the theory that one picture is worth a thousand words, we reproduce one of the advertisements of which plaintiff complains and which is fairly representative of all.

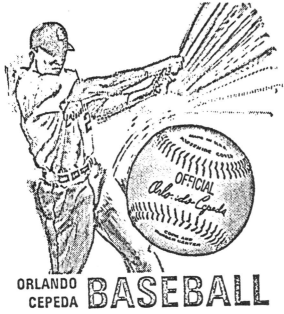

Official weight and size baseball with cork and rubber center, anchored and balanced winding. Hand stitched alum
tanned horsehide cover.

STOCK UP FOR THE SEASON! Just send in words
"SPECIAL OFFER" from package of MAYROSE FRANKS or
MAYROSE BACON with $1.00 check or money order (no
cash) for each ball.

Swift's television and radio advertisements, which have also been considered
on the motions for summary judgment, are not essentially different. The
following is a typical radio advertisement:

"The baseball season gets more exciting every day . . . just about as exciting as the offer you'll find on the specially marked packages of MAYROSE BACON and MAYROSE FRANKS! That's right . . . MAYROSE is offering an Orlando Cepeda autograph baseball for just $1.00 and the words 'SPECIAL OFFER' from a package of MAYROSE FRANKS or MAYROSE BACON! The Orlando Cepeda baseball is official size and weight, with cork and rubber center, anchored and balanced winding and hand-stitched, genuine horsehide cover. And remember . . . these wonderful Orlando Cepeda autograph baseballs are just $1.00 each with the words 'SPECIAL OFFER' from a package of MAYROSE FRANKS or MAYROSE BACON! These baseballs make great souvenirs for all of the baseball fans in the family, so get plenty for everyone. And, the whole family will enjoy sweet, tender MAYROSE BACON and juicy, flavorful MAYROSE FRANKS. Just look for the specially marked packages of MAYROSE BACON and MAYROSE FRANKS the next time you shop . . . enjoy the finest . . . MAYROSE . . . and get your Orlando Cepeda autograph baseballs."

Neither defendant questions the right of Cepeda to whatever commercial value there may be in the use of his name, portrait and reputation. See Munden v. Harris, 153 Mo.App. 652, 134 S.W. 1076, to the effect that no one may appropriate the commercial value in the use of another's name, picture or reputation without his consent. All parties start with the basic premise that this so-called "right of publicity" is a valuable property right which may not be violated with impunity, but which may be bargained away. See for example, Haelan Laboratories, Inc. v. Topps Chewing Gum, Inc., 2 Cir., 202 F.2d 866, 868.

The issue here is whether the use of plaintiff's name, picture and reputation admittedly made by Swift was authorized by Cepeda's contract with Wilson. Initially, Cepeda argues that under the contract Wilson had no right to license a meat processor (Swift) to advertise and sell the baseballs, on the theory that since Wilson is known to the public as a maker and seller of sporting goods and not as a premium house or promotion agent, the "reasonable interpretation" of the contract phrase "license others so to do" is that the only "others" Wilson could license to sell Cepeda baseballs are sporting goods retailers.

"In interpreting the contract we must be guided by the well-established rules that we cannot make contracts for the parties or insert provisions by judicial interpretation. We are to determine what the parties intended by what they said, and we cannot be concerned with what they might have said, or with what they perhaps should have said." Brackett v. Easton Boot and Shoe Company, Mo., 388 S.W.2d 842, 847. To interpret the contract as plaintiff urges would be to make a new contract for the parties, there being no language therein which restricts Wilson in its dealings to sporting goods retailers. The contract contains no restriction whatsoever against Wilson or its licensees using or selling Cepeda baseballs as "advertising premiums." We must give effect to the contract as written.

Plaintiff's basic contention is that the sole right he gave Wilson to use and license the use of his name and fame was "in connection with" baseballs and other designated baseball paraphernalia, and that defendants had no right to use his name "in connection with" meat products. However, the words "in connection with" are not contained in the contract.

Cepeda argues that Swift's major purpose was to increase its sales of hot dogs and bacon, and that the baseballs were "a mere vehicle to convey purchasers to defendant Swift's products", or, stated otherwise, that "plaintiff's reputation, goodwill, popularity and signature were being used as bait to lure his fans to defendant Swift's products."

The contract does not in any way restrict or limit either the method of merchandising the baseballs or the manner in which they may be advertised or sold. And the method actually used by Swift to sell the Cepeda-identified baseballs was reasonably calculated to assure that a substantial number of such baseballs would be sold. The more baseballs Swift purchased and sold, the more royalties Cepeda would receive, up to the contract maximum.

What Cepeda is really contending is that a merchant who sells or advertises Cepeda-identified baseballs must completely divorce such sales and advertisements from the sale or advertisement of all other products handled by him. Carried to its logical conclusion, Cepeda's argument would preclude even a sporting goods retailer from advertising Cepeda baseballs in conjunction with other sporting goods.

Granting that Swift's *purpose* in selling Cepeda baseballs was to promote its meat products, the fact is that Cepeda's name and portrait were used *only* to accurately describe and advertise the baseball bearing his name. And although a label from a Swift meat product was a part of the purchase price demanded of those who wished to purchase the baseball, it is nevertheless true that what Swift was actually selling were baseballs.

It is a matter of common knowledge that merchants advertise well-known products at cost or less for the purpose of "luring" customers into the advertisers' places of business where they might be expected to purchase not only the well-known products being used as "bait", but also other items as well. So, too, merchants frequently advertise a well-known product at an attractive price, subject to the customer making a purchase of a specific dollar amount of other merchandise, the purpose being, of course, to "lure" the customer into buying such other merchandise by means of the "bait".

We see no impropriety, under the contract, in Swift's similar utilization of

Orlando Cepeda baseballs for the purpose of increasing its dollar volume of sales of meat products. That Swift chose to insist upon proofs-of-purchase of one of its products as a condition of its sales of the baseballs at a reduced price did not exceed the scope of its license. This is true even though the more Cepeda baseballs Swift was able to sell in this manner, the more (or so it can be assumed) Swift's meat products would also be sold to enable the baseball customers to obtain the necessary labels to be used as part of the purchase price.

A careful examination of Swift's advertisements convinces us that the thrust thereof was to persuade the public to purchase Cepeda-identified baseballs and *thereby* increase Swift's sales of meat. Nothing in the advertisements would normally persuade a customer who had no interest in a Cepeda baseball to purchase any Swift meat product simply because the advertisements displayed plaintiff's name and portrait. In no sense of the word was the name or reputation of plaintiff used to promote or endorse the meat products as such.

In other words, it is clear that only those individuals who were desirous of purchasing Cepeda-identified baseballs would be induced by the advertisements to purchase Swift meat products, and they would do so solely because of the necessity of obtaining proofs-of-purchase to acquire what they really desired, namely, the Cepeda-identified baseballs.

Had Swift's advertisements merely offered the Cepeda-identified baseballs at an attractive price as a gesture of good will, without any requirement that a proof-of-purchase from a Swift product accompany the order, such use of the baseballs to improve Swift's public image and thereby *indirectly* increase its meat sales would differ only in degree from the use actually made.

In any event, there is no provision in the contract which precluded Swift from tieing-in sale of Cepeda-identified baseballs to Swift meat products, in the sense that a prospective purchaser of a baseball was required to pay, as a part of the purchase price, a portion of a label from a meat product.

Inasmuch as the contract clearly authorized the sale of Cepeda baseballs by any method whatsoever, we do not believe that Swift's use of such baseballs as "bait" creates liability where none would otherwise exist.

It follows from the foregoing that having granted Wilson the right to manufacture, advertise and sell Orlando Cepeda baseballs and to license others to do so, with no restriction as to the method of resale, plaintiff is precluded from now complaining that the use of his name, picture and fame to identify the baseballs and promote their sale was unauthorized, even though the sales thereof were "in connection with" the sale of meat products in the manner used by Swift.

The use of plaintiff's name disclosed by the undisputed facts was within the authorization of the contract. There being no genuine issue as to the material facts, we hold that plaintiff is not entitled to recover. Accordingly, the motions of defendants for summary judgment are hereby sustained and the motion of plaintiff for summary judgment is overruled. The Clerk is directed to enter judgment in favor of defendants and against plaintiff.

CEPEDA v.
SWIFT AND COMPANY
aff'd 415 F.2d 1205 (8th Cir. 1969)

Before VAN OOSTERHOUT, Chief Judge, and MEHAFFY and GIBSON, Circuit Judges.

MEHAFFY, Circuit Judge.

Orlando Cepeda, a citizen of Puerto Rico and a famous major league baseball player, brought this suit in state court against Swift and Company. Upon timely removal to federal court by Swift, Cepeda filed an amended complaint, joining as an additional defendant Wilson Sporting Goods Company. The action was grounded upon the asserted unauthorized use of plaintiff's name, likeness, photograph, signature and good will by Swift in an advertising campaign utilized by one of its divisions in the promotion of sales of meat products, namely Mayrose franks and bacon.

The complaint alleged that plaintiff has become a widely renowned athlete and, as a result, his right to associate his name through endorsement of products and in connection with promotions and sales of products is an asset of great value; that his right of privacy has been invaded and infringed by defendants in their unauthorized use of his name, photograph, etc.; that this unauthorized use has unjustly enriched defendant Swift; and that plaintiff is entitled to compensatory and punitive damages. In the second count of the complaint, plaintiff asserts that on April 30, 1963 he entered into an agreement with defendant Wilson through which Wilson acquired the right to use plaintiff's name, facsimile signature, initials, portrait, or any nickname popularly applied to him, in connection with the sale of baseballs, baseball shoes, baseball gloves and baseball mitts and to license others to do the same. The contract period was for two years with option to renew for an additional period of one, two or three years. On March 29, 1965, defendant Wilson notified plaintiff of its execution of its option to renew for a period of two years. Plaintiff further alleged that in 1967 Wilson, in disregard of plaintiff's rights, entered into an agreement with Swift by the terms of which Wilson sold baseballs to Swift and agreed that Swift could conduct an advertising campaign employing plaintiff's name and picture with the promotion and sale of Swift's meat products.

Swift did not advertise that Cepeda endorsed its meat products but merely offered Cepeda baseballs at a special price to those forwarding with their order a specified portion of the wrapper from certain products. The campaign was carried out and employed extensively by radio, television, newspapers, magazines and other advertising media in Missouri, Illinois and elsewhere. Plaintiff contends that the gist of Swift's advertising campaign was to associate plaintiff's name and good will inherent in it with defendant's products, asserting that Wilson at no time had his consent to use or assign his name in connection with the promotion and sale of meat products. Plaintiff also sought compensatory and punitive damages from defendant Wilson.

The record consists of numerous interrogatories, exhibits, affidavits and motions by each of the parties for summary judgment. The district court in a memorandum opinion and order reported at 291 F.Supp. 242 (E.D.Mo.1968) sustained the motions of defendants for summary judgment, overruled plaintiff's motion, and entered judgment if favor of defendants. We affirm the judgment of the district court.

The propriety of summary judgment by the court on issues involving interpretation of the contract is not challenged by either party. Such use of a summary judgment is desirable where, as here, the contract is unambiguous. Nor is it a matter of dispute that plaintiff has a valuable property right in his name, photograph and image and that he may sell these property rights. Therefore, the sole issue presented by this appeal is whether the contract between plaintiff and Wilson authorized the use of plaintiff's name and photograph in the manner in which they were used.

The pertinent part of the contract between plaintiff and Wilson reads as follows:

"1. Cepeda grants to Wilson the exclusive world right and license to manufacture, advertise and sell baseballs, baseball shoes, baseball gloves and baseball mitts identified by his name, facsimile signature, initials, portrait, or by any nickname popularly applied to him, and to license others so to do. During the term of this agreement Cepeda agrees not to grant any similar right or license to any other person, Cepeda shall sign all lawful documents which may be necessary to enable Wilson to secure federal, state or foreign registration of trade marks or trade names for products identified as herein provided."

The consideration for the contract was that Wilson should pay plaintiff a royalty of $1.00 per dozen on baseball catcher's or basemen's mitts, 60¢ per dozen on baseball gloves and 10¢ per dozen on baseballs sold by Wilson or its licensees, provided that the royalties should not be less than $50.00 per year nor more than $500.00 per year. When the contract was renewed, the maximum royalty was raised to $1,000 per year, but in no year have the royalties reached said maximum amounts. It is not in dispute that Wilson paid plaintiff all of the royalties for the Cepeda products manufactured and sold by it.

The thrust of plaintiff's argument is that the contract conveyed to Wilson the right to use his name only in connection with the sale of certain baseball products and that nowhere in the contract does plaintiff authorize his name to be used in connection with meat products or the promotion of meat products as was done here. We disagree. The contract plainly grants to Wilson the exclusive world right to manufacture, advertise and sell baseballs, baseball shoes, baseball gloves and baseball mitts identified by plaintiff's name, facsimile signature or picture, and the right to license others so to do. The contract nowhere contains any restriction on the manner in which baseballs could be advertised or sold. Plaintiff's argument is rooted in the concept that the intent of the parties was to restrict the advertising and sale of products. To accept plaintiff's interpretation of the contract would require a rewriting and the interpolation of words into the contract. This we cannot do when the language of the contract is so clear. The contract, being unambiguous as it is, needs no interpretation except to give the plain and simple words their plain and simple meaning. Contracts are not rendered ambiguous by the mere fact that the parties do not agree upon their proper construction. Our function is to enforce the contract as made.

It is perfectly clear to us that plaintiff contracted with Wilson and granted to it the exclusive world right and license to manufacture, advertise and sell baseballs. Wilson was also authorized to contract its rights to others and this is exactly what was done in this case. We further find that Swift did not exceed the authority granted to it by Wilson. The advertising material that Swift used was an offer to sell Orlando Cepeda baseballs for only $1.00 with the words "Special Offer" taken from a package of Mayrose franks or bacon. A number of the advertisements contained a picture of plaintiff in his baseball uniform either swinging a bat or catching a ball along with a picture of the baseball offered, a picture of the Mayrose products, and an explanation of the "Special Offer." However, as hereinbefore mentioned, a survey of all the advertisements reflects that Swift did not in any fashion attempt to indicate that plaintiff used or endorsed its meat products but simply offered for sale Cepeda baseballs for $1.00 when accompanied with a portion of the wrapper from one of its meat products.

We find that the interpretation of the contract by the district court is correct and that the defendants did not exceed their contractual authority.

The judgment of the district court is affirmed.

FACTORS ETC., INC. v.
PRO ARTS, INC.
597 F.2d 215 (2d Cir. 1978)

Before WATERMAN, INGRAHAM and MANSFIELD, Circuit Judges.

INGRAHAM, Circuit Judge:

Plaintiffs-Appellees, Factors Etc., Inc. (Factors) and Boxcar Enterprises, Inc. (Boxcar), sued Defendants-Appellants, Pro Arts, Inc. (Pro Arts) and Stop and Shop Companies, Inc. (Stop and Shop), for injunctive relief and damages based upon defendants' alleged misappropriation and unauthorized use of the name and likeness of Elvis Presley (Presley). The trial court granted the plaintiffs' preliminary injunction upon its findings that the exclusive right to market Presley memorabilia survived the death of Presley, and the Presley poster printed by defendants allegedly in derogation of this right was not privileged as the publication of a newsworthy event. This is an interlocutory appeal pursuant to 28 U.S.C. § 1292(a)(1).

Because the facts are not in dispute, we need not describe them in detail. During Presley's career as an entertainer, Colonel Tom Parker (Parker) served as his close friend, mentor and personal manager. This professional relationship between the two parties began on March 26, 1956, with the execution of the first contract between them. Parker immediately began the task of creating the "Elvis persona." In so doing, both he and Presley capitalized upon the marketing of merchandise bearing the Elvis name and likeness. Parker directed this effort until Presley's death, a task reflected by the numerous extensions of the contract between the two parties.

Boxcar Enterprises, a Tennessee corporation controlled by Presley and Parker,[2] was the vehicle through which the commercial Elvis Presley rights were marketed. Boxcar sublicensed other companies to do the actual manufacturing and distributing of each specific item, receiving royalties from the sales.[3]

On August 16, 1977, Elvis Presley died suddenly and unexpectedly. His father, Vernon Presley, was appointed executor of his estate. On August 18,

---

[2] Parker owned 56% of the shares; Presley and Tom Dishkin, President of Boxcar, each owned 22%.

[3] When Boxcar licensed a merchandising item, Presley received 20% of the royalties, Parker received 20%, and Dishkin received 10%. The remaining 50% went to Boxcar.

1977, two days after Presley's death, Boxcar granted Factors the exclusive license to exploit commercially the name and likeness of Elvis Presley. Factors paid Boxcar $100,000 on execution of the agreement against a guarantee of $150,000. Vernon Presley, as executor of the estate, signed the agreement licensing Factors, at the same time warranting that Boxcar was the sole and exclusive owner of the commercial Elvis Presley rights.[4] The agreement was also approved by Parker.

Immediately following Presley's death, Pro Arts decided that it too wanted a share in the market for Elvis Presley memorabilia. It purchased the copyright in the photograph of Presley from a staff photographer of the Atlanta (Georgia) Journal. On August 19, 1977, three days after his death, Pro Arts published a poster using the photograph and filed an application for registration of copyright. The poster is entitled "IN MEMORY" and below the photograph of Presley the poster bears the dates "1935–1977."

On the same day that the poster was published, Pro Arts began to market it. One of its first customers was co-defendant Stop and Shop Companies, which thereafter sold the poster through its Bradlees Stores Division in the Southern District of New York. On August 24, 1977, five days after its poster was placed on the market, Pro Arts notified Boxcar Enterprises that it was offering "a memorial 'Elvis' poster to meet the public demand." When Factors was informed of the letter, it replied to Pro Arts claiming the exclusive right to manufacture, sell and distribute all merchandise utilizing the name and likeness of Elvis Presley. Factors also warned Pro Arts that if it did not discontinue sale of the poster, it would be subject to a lawsuit for injunctive relief, damages and an accounting.

Instead of ceasing distribution of the poster, Pro Arts filed suit in the United States District Court for the Northern District of Ohio seeking a declaratory judgment of non-infringement of the rights claimed by Factors. When Factors discovered that it had been sued in Ohio, it responded by instituting this action against Pro Arts and Stop and Shop in United States District Court for the Southern District of New York. This later action was filed on September 26, 1977, just five days after Pro Arts' action.

Upon the filing of the complaint in this action, the district judge entered an "order to show cause" requiring Pro Arts to show cause why an injunction should not issue against it. Pro Arts responded with a motion to dismiss, stay or transfer the suit to the Northern District of Ohio. On October 13, 1977, the New York court filed an opinion and order of preliminary injunction against Pro Arts. The injunction restrained Pro Arts during the pendency of the

---

[4] Contemporaneous with this agreement, Vernon Presley wrote to Parker, asking him to "carry on according to the same terms and conditions as stated in the contractual agreement [between Presley and Parker] dated January 22, 1976" (See n. 1, *supra*).

action from manufacturing, selling or distributing (1) any more copies of the poster labeled "IN MEMORY . . . 1935–1977," (2) any other posters, reproductions or copies containing any likeness of Elvis Presley, and (3) utilizing for commercial profit in any manner or form the name or likeness of Elvis Presley. The order also denied Pro Arts' motion to dismiss, stay or transfer. Pro Arts has duly perfected this interlocutory appeal from the order.

. . . .

We now proceed to the determination of the principal issue in this case—whether or not the preliminary injunction was improvidently granted. In order to be granted a preliminary injunction under Rule 65(a), Fed.R.Civ.P., the movant must make " 'a clear showing of either (1) probable success on the merits *and* possible irreparable injury, *or* (2) sufficiently serious questions going to the merits to make them a fair ground for litigation *and* a balance of hardships tipping decidedly toward the party requesting the preliminary relief.' " *Triebwasser & Katz v. American Tel. & Tel. Co.*, 535 F.2d 1356, 1358 (2d Cir. 1976) (emphasis in original), *quoting Sonesta International Hotels Corp. v. Wellington Assoc.*, 483 F.2d 247, 250 (2d Cir. 1973). The trial court employed the first prong of the test, finding that Factors had demonstrated probable success on the merits and possible irreparable injury. Because Pro Arts does not challenge the trial court's finding of possible irreparable harm, we need only address the first of the two requirements, that of probable success on the merits.

In concluding that Factors would likely prevail on the merits at trial, the court found that Elvis Presley exercised his right of publicity during his lifetime by giving Parker the exclusive authority to exploit his image through Boxcar Enterprises. This exclusive authority survived Presley's death, after which it was validly assigned to Factors. For this reason Pro Arts was enjoined from manufacturing, distributing, selling or otherwise profiting from merchandise bearing the name or likeness of the late Elvis Presley.

It is beyond cavil that the grant or denial of preliminary injunctive relief " 'will not be disturbed [on appeal] unless there is an abuse of [the trial court's] discretion . . . or unless there is a clear mistake of law.' " *New York v. Nuclear Regulatory Commission*, 550 F.2d 745, 751 (2d Cir. 1977), *quoting Triebwasser & Katz v. American Tel. & Tel. Co.*, 535 F.2d at 1358. On appeal, Pro Arts alleges two errors of law on the part of the trial court. According to Pro Arts, the trial court erred first in concluding that the right of publicity could survive the death of the celebrity. Second, Pro Arts argues that even if the right did so survive, Pro Arts was privileged, as a matter of law, in printing and distributing its "memorial poster" of Presley, because the poster celebrated a newsworthy event.

The first issue, the duration of the so-called "right of publicity," is one of state law, more specifically the law of the State of New York. Because of the dearth of New York case law in this area, however, we have sought assistance from federal court decisions interpreting and applying New York law, as well as decisions from courts of other states.

As the district court noted, much confusion shrouds the so-called "right of publicity," largely because it has often been discussed under the rubric "right of privacy." As Dean Prosser has stated, the right of privacy embraces "four distinct kinds of invasion of four different interests of the plaintiff, which are tied together by the common name, but otherwise have almost nothing in common except that each represents an interference with the right of the plaintiff 'to be let alone.' " W. Prosser, Torts 804 (4th ed. 1971). Prosser has classified the four species of this tort as (1) intrusion upon the plaintiff's physical solitude or seclusion, *id.* at 807, (2) public disclosure of private facts, *id.* at 809, (3) false light in the public eye, *id.* at 812, and (4) appropriation of plaintiff's name or likeness for defendant's benefit, *id.* at 804.

The fourth type, appropriation of plaintiff's name or likeness for defendant's benefit, has in recent years acquired the label, "right of publicity." The distinguishing feature of this branch of the tort is that it involves the use of plaintiff's protected right for defendant's direct commercial advantage. The nature of the remedy also separates the right of publicity from the other three species of the tort. To protect his interest with respect to the first three, the injured party attempts to minimize the intrusion or publication of the damaging matter. In contrast, the right of publicity plaintiff does not necessarily object to the commercial exploitation—so long as the exploitation is at his behest and he is receiving the profits. This point was recently underscored by the Supreme Court in *Zacchini v. Scripps-Howard Broadcasting Co.*, 433 U.S. 562, 97 S.Ct. 2849, 53 L.Ed.2d 965 (1977). According to the Court, the interest protected:

> is closely analogous to the goals of patent and copyright law, focusing on the right of the individual to reap the reward of his endeavors and having little to do with protecting feeling or reputation.

Id. at 573, 97 S.Ct. at 2856.

> [The rationale is thus] "one of preventing unjust enrichment by the theft of good will. No social purpose is served by having the defendant get free some aspect of the plaintiff that would have market value and for which he would normally pay."

Id. at 576, 97 S.Ct. at 2857, quoting *Kalven*, Privacy in Tort Law—Were Warren and Brandeis Wrong? 31 Law & Contemp.Prob. 326, 331 (1966).

The State of New York provides a statutory right for the protection of a *living* person from commercial exploitation of his name and picture by others without his written consent. This statutory right, also called a "right of privacy," is predicated upon the classic right of privacy's theoretical basis which is to prevent injury to feelings. *Price v. Hal Roach Studios, Inc.*, 400 F.Supp. 836, 843 (S.D.N.Y.1975); *Lombardo v. Doyle, Dane & Bernbach*, 58 A.D.2d 620, 396 N.Y.S.2d 661 (1977). In *Haelan Laboratories, Inc. v. Topps Chewing Gum, Inc.*, 202 F.2d 866 (2d Cir.), *cert. denied*, 346 U.S. 816, 74 S.Ct. 26, 98 L.Ed. 343 (1953), we recognized that the right of publicity exists independent from the statutory right of privacy and that it can be validly transferred by its owner:

> We think that, in addition to and independent of that right of privacy (which in New York derives from statute), a man has a right in the publicity value of his photograph, i. e., the right to grant the exclusive privilege of publishing his picture, and that such a grant may validly be made "in gross," i. e., without an accompanying transfer of a business or of anything else. Whether it be labelled a "property" right is immaterial; for here, as often elsewhere, the tag "property" simply symbolizes the fact that courts enforce a claim which has pecuniary worth.

Id. at 868.

Since the landmark *Haelan Laboratories, Inc.* case, several decisions by courts applying New York law have labeled the right of publicity as a valid transferable property right, *see, e. g., Price v. Hal Roach Studios, Inc.*, 400 F.Supp. at 844; *Groucho Marx Productions, Inc. v. Playboy Enterprises, Inc.*, No. 77–1782 (S.D.N.Y. Dec. 30, 1977); *Lombardo v. Doyle, Dane & Bernbach*, 58 A.D.2d 620, 396 N.Y.S.2d 661 (1977), as well as recent decisions by courts applying the law of other states, *see, e. g., Cepeda v. Swift & Co.*, 415 F.2d 1205, 1206 (8th Cir. 1969); *Memphis Development Foundation v. Factors, Etc., Inc.*, 441 F.Supp. 1323, 1329 (W.D.Tenn.1977).

There can be no doubt that Elvis Presley assigned to Boxcar a valid property right, the exclusive authority to print, publish and distribute his name and likeness. In so doing, he carved out a separate intangible property right for himself, the right to a certain percentage of the royalties which would be realized by Boxcar upon exploitation of Presley's likeness and name. The identification of this exclusive right belonging to Boxcar as a transferable property right compels the conclusion that the right survives Presley's death. The death of Presley, who was merely the beneficiary of an income interest in Boxcar's exclusive right, should not in itself extinguish Boxcar's property right. Instead, the income interest, continually produced from Boxcar's exclusive right of commercial exploitation, should inure to Presley's estate at death like any other intangible property right. To hold that the right did not survive Presley's death, would be to grant competitors of Factors, such as Pro Arts, a windfall in the form of profits from the use of Presley's name and likeness. At the same time, the exclusive right purchased by Factors and the financial benefits accruing to the celebrity's heirs would be rendered virtually worthless.

Though no New York court has directly addressed this issue,[10] the only two cases on point agree with our conclusion that the right of publicity should survive the celebrity's death. *See Memphis Development Foundation v. Factors, Etc., Inc.*, 441 F.Supp. 1323 (W.D.Tenn.1977); *Price v. Hal Roach Studios, Inc.*, 400 F.Supp. 836 (S.D.N.Y.1975). Of these two cases the *Price* case is particularly persuasive since it is a decision of a United States District Court purportedly applying New York law. *Price* involved a dispute over the ownership of the commercial right to use the names and likenesses of Stanley Laurel and Oliver Hardy ("Laurel and Hardy") following the death of the renowned comedians. The exclusive right to exploit the comedy team commercially was assigned to co-plaintiff Larry Harmon Pictures Corporation by Stan Laurel during his lifetime, by Oliver Hardy's widow and sole heir under Hardy's will, Lucille Hardy Price, and by Laurel and Hardy's production company, Laurel and Hardy Feature Productions. Several years later, when the *Price* defendants sought to utilize the name and likenesses of Laurel and Hardy, the owners sued. The district court held that the deaths of the actors did not extinguish the right of publicity held by the grantee of the right. This conclusion was found to be inherent in the distinction between the right of publicity and the right of privacy:

> Since the theoretical basis for the classic right of privacy, and of the statutory right in New York, is to prevent injury to feelings, death is a logical conclusion to any such claim. In addition, based upon the same theoretical foundation, such a right of privacy is not assignable during life. When determining the scope of the right of publicity, however, one must take into account the purely commercial nature of the protected right. Courts and commentators have done just that in recognizing the right of publicity as assignable. There appears to be no logical reason to terminate this right upon death of the person protected.

400 F.Supp. at 844. In sum, we hold that Boxcar's exclusive right to exploit the Presley name and likeness, because exercised during Presley's life, survived his death.[11] The right was therefore validly transferred to Factors following Presley's death.

---

[10] We do note, however, dicta from a recent appellate division opinion, *Lombardo v. Doyle, Dane & Bernbach*, 58 A.D.2d 620, 396 N.Y.S.2d 661 (2d Dept. 1977), to the effect that "while a cause of action under the Civil Rights Law is not assignable during one's lifetime and terminates at death, the right to publicity, e. g., the property right to one's name, photograph and image is under no such inhibition."

[11] Because the right was exploited during Presley's life, we need not, and therefore do not, decide whether the right would survive the death of the celebrity if not exploited during the celebrity's life.

Pro Arts' final argument is that even if Factors possesses the exclusive right to distribute Presley memorabilia, this right does not prevent Pro Arts from publishing what it terms a "memorial poster" commemorating a newsworthy event. In support of this argument, Pro Arts cites *Paulsen v. Personality Posters, Inc.*, 59 Misc.2d 444, 299 N.Y.S.2d 501 (Sup.Ct.1968), a case arising out of the bogus presidential candidacy of the television comedian Pat Paulsen. Paulsen sued defendant for publishing and distributing a poster of Paulsen with the legend "FOR PRESIDENT." The court refused to enjoin sale of the poster because Paulsen's choice of the political arena for satire made him "newsworthy" in the First Amendment sense. We cannot accept Pro Arts contention that the legend "IN MEMORY . . . " placed its poster in the same category as one picturing a presidential candidate, albeit a mock candidate. We hold, therefore, that Pro Arts' poster of Presley was not privileged as celebrating a newsworthy event.

In conclusion we hold that the district court did not abuse its discretion in granting the injunction since Factors has demonstrated a strong likelihood of success on the merits at trial. Factors possesses the exclusive right to print and distribute Elvis Presley memorabilia, a right which was validly transferred to it from Boxcar following Presley's death. Pro Arts infringed this right by printing and distributing the Elvis Presley poster, a poster whose publication was not privileged as a newsworthy event.

We affirm the action of the district court and remand for further proceedings.

Supplemental Reading

Zacchini v. Scripps-Howard Broadcasting Co., 433 U.S. 562 (1977) (unauthorized broadcast of performer's entire act violated performer's right of publicity).

Memphis Development Foundation v. Factors Etc., Inc., 441 F. Supp. 1323 (W.D. Tenn. 1977), *rev'd*, 616 F.2d 956 (6th Cir. 1980).

Lugosi v. Universal Pictures, 25 Cal. 3d 813, 160 Cal. Rptr. 323, 603 P.2d 425 (1979) (the right of publicity of plaintiff, who never sought to exploit his name and likeness when alive terminated upon his death).

Meltzer v. Zoller, 520 F. Supp. 847 (D. N.J. 1981) (under Copyright Act of 1976, a work prepared by an independent contractor is not a work for hire unless it is included in one of the statutory categories, and the parties entered into an express written agreement designating the work as one for hire).

Brylawski, *Protection of Characters—Sam Spade Revisited*, 22 Bull. Copyright Soc'y 77 (1974).

Kerson, *Sequel Rights in the Law of Literary Property*, 12 Copyright Law Symp. 76 (ASCAP) (1963).

Felcher & Rubin, *Privacy, Publicity and the Portrayal of Real People by the Media*, 88 Yale L.J. 1577 (1979).

2 T. Selz and M. Simensky, *Entertainment Law*, 19–1 through 19–94 (1983).

Jazzy, *When Works Collide: Derivative Motion Pictures, Underlying Rights and the Public Interest*, 28 U.C.L.A. L. Rev. 715 (1981).

CHAPTER 6

REPRESENTATIONS,
WARRANTIES AND INDEMNITIES

Introduction

Representations, warranties and indemnities are common in enterprises other than the entertainment industry. This chapter explores the purposes of representations and warranties in general, and then analyzes those purposes in the context of the entertainment industry.

Representations and warranties in sample entertainment industry agreements will be examined with two questions in mind: what is the nature of the risk involved? and who should appropriately bear that risk? Insurance which is available in the entertainment industry to cover such risks, and the limitations and benefits of such insurance, are also considered.

Required Reading

Menzel v. List, 24 N.Y.2d 91, 298 N.Y.S.2d 979 (1969).

Kerby v. Hal Roach Studios, Inc., 53 Cal. App. 2d 207, 127 P.2d 577 (Cal. Dist. Ct. App. 1942).

Bright Tunes Music Corp. v. Harrisongs Music, Ltd., 420 F. Supp. 177 (S.D.N.Y. 1976).

Herbert Mitgang, "Publisher Rejects 'Offensive' Books," *The New York Times* (September 1, 1983), p. C17.

"ABC Paid Ali For Interview, But Denies He Was 'Employee'," *Variety* (March 5, 1980), pp. 51, 68.

Eric Page, "New Dispute Is Stirred by Doubleday-Davis Suit," *The New York Times* (February 26, 1980), p. C9.

Loew's Inc. v. Wolff, 101 F. Supp. 981 (S.D. Cal. 1951).

All contracts and union agreements referred to in the chapter "Concepts."

CONCEPTS

1. What is the purpose of representations and warranties? What does *Menzel v. List* (p. 453) suggest about the answer?

2. Consider Book Publishing Agreement, Parags. 36–42 (p. 864), and Acquisition of Rights Agreement, Parag. 6 (pp. 640–641). Are there any representations or warranties which seem unreasonable?

3. What does *Kerby v. Hal Roach Studios* (p. 458) indicate about the danger in representations regarding the right of privacy? What could the studio have done to avoid the problem?

4. What does *Bright Tunes Music Corp. v. Harrisongs Music, Ltd.* (p. 463) indicate about the danger in representations regarding copyright ownership?

5. What does *The New York Times* article of 9/1/83 (p. 467) suggest about a possible danger in representations regarding obscenity?

6. How does the purpose of representations and warranties relate to indemnity provisions?

   (A) Are Book Publishing Agreement, Parags. 87, 89 (pp. 876, 877) reasonable in scope?

   (B) If there are contractual representations and warranties, why does one need an indemnification paragraph? See Acquisition of Rights Agreement, Parag. 10 (p. 642). Do the *Variety* article, 3/5/80 (p. 469), and *The New York Times* article, 2/26/80 (p. 470), suggest an answer?

7. Does a purchase price place any limit on the amount of an indemnity so that a seller does not stand to lose more than could possibly be gained by a sale?

   (A) What does *Menzel v. List* (p. 453) suggest about the answer to this question?

   (B) What contractual provision could address this question?

8. If *Loew's v. Wolff* (p. 472) had been an option rather than an assignment, and the claim had arisen during the option period, what would Loew's choice have been?

   (A) What does the theory of "marketable title" suggest about a possible answer?

   (B) How could such an answer be incorporated by contract?

9. What is the impact of errors and omissions insurance policies?

   (A) Considering the types of problems addressed in questions 3 and 4 above, what types of risks are "E and O" policies designed to cover?

(B) What is their impact? See Writers Guild of America Basic Agreement (1970), (1977), (1981) Article 28 (pp. 522, 560, 593). What is the problem for an insurance company, and therefore for a producer, in Writers Guild of America Basic Agreement (1977), Article 28, Parag. 3, second full paragraph (p. 561)?

10. What difference does it make whether or not Muhammed Ali (p. 469) was an employee?

MENZEL v. LIST
24 N.Y.2d 91, 298 N.Y.S.2d 979 (1969)

BURKE, Judge.

In 1932 Mrs. Erna Menzel and her husband purchased a painting by Marc Chagall at an auction in Brussels, Belgium, for 3,800 Belgian francs (then equivalent to about $150). When the Germans invaded Belgium in 1940, the Menzels fled and left their possessions, including the Chagall painting, in their apartment. They returned six years later and found that the painting had been removed by the German authorities and that a receipt for the painting had been left. The location of the painting between the time of its removal by the Germans in 1941 and 1955 is unknown. In 1955 Klaus Perls and his wife, the proprietors of a New York art gallery, purchased the Chagall from a Parisian art gallery for $2,800. The Perls knew nothing of the painting's previous history and made no inquiry concerning it, being content to rely on the reputability of the Paris gallery as to authenticity and title. In October, 1955 the Perls sold the painting to Albert List for $4,000. However, in 1962, Mrs. Menzel noticed a reproduction of the Chagall in an art book accompanied by a statement that the painting was in Albert List's possession. She thereupon demanded the painting from him but he refused to surrender it to her.

Mrs. Menzel then instituted a replevin action against Mr. List and he, in turn, impleaded the Perls, alleging in his third-party complaint that they were liable to him for breach of an implied warranty of title. At the trial, expert testimony was introduced to establish the painting's fair market value at the time of trial. The only evidence of its value at the time it was purchased by List was the price which he paid to the Perls. The trial court charged the jury that, if it found for Mrs. Menzel against List, it was also to "assess the value of said painting at such an amount as you believe from the testimony represents its present value." The jury returned a verdict for Mrs. Menzel and she entered a judgment directing the return of the painting to her or, in the alternative, that List pay to her the value of the painting, which the jury found to be $22,500.

(List has, in fact, returned the painting to Mrs. Menzel.) In addition, the jury found for List as against the Perls, on his third-party complaint, in the amount of $22,500, the painting's present value plus the costs of the Menzel action incurred by List. 49 Misc.2d 300, 267 N.Y.S.2d 804.

The Perls appealed to the Appellate Division, First Department, from that judgment and the judgment was unanimously modified, on the law, by reducing the amount awarded to List to $4,000 (the purchase price he had paid for the painting), with interest from the date of the purchase. In a memorandum, the Appellate Division held that the third-party action was for breach of an implied warranty of *quiet* possession and, accordingly, held that the Statute of Limitations had not run on List's claim since his possession was not disturbed until the judgment for Mrs. Menzel. 28 A.D.2d 516, 279 N.Y.S.2d 608. In addition, the court held that the "applicable measure of damages was the price List paid for the painting at the time of purchase, together with interest", citing three New York cases.

List filed a notice of appeal as of right from the unanimous modification insofar as it reduced the amount of his judgment to $4,000, with interest from the date of purchase. The Perls filed a notice of cross appeal from so much of the Appellate Division's order as failed to dismiss the third-party complaint, denied costs and disbursements and fixed the date from which interest was to run on List's judgment. The Perls have now abandoned the cross appeal as to the failure to dismiss the third-party complaint and the denial of costs and disbursements, leaving only the issue as to the date from which interest should run.

List's appeal and the Perls' cross appeal present only questions of law for resolution, the facts having been found by the jury and affirmed by the Appellate Division (its modification was on the law as to the proper measure of damages and the running of interest). The issue on the main appeal is simply what is or should be the proper measure of damages for the breach of an implied warranty of title (or quiet possession) in the sale of personal property. The cases cited by the Appellate Division do not hold that the measure of damages is the purchase price plus interest. The *Staats* case . . . was an action for breach of a real property covenant in which there was dicta to the effect that the rule was the same for personal property. The dicta was compromised one year later by the same jurist (Chief Justice KENT who wrote the opinion in *Staats* in Blasdale v. Babcock, 1 Johns. 517 [1806], where it was held that the buyer was entitled to recover in damages the amount which he had been compelled to pay to the true owner, the actual value of the chattel. In Armstrong v. Percy, 5 Wend. 535, . . . the buyer recovered the purchase price but only because the chattel, a horse, was found to have depreciated in value below the price paid. In Case v. Hall & Van Elten, 24 Wend. 102, . . . there is contained a statement which is pure dicta to the effect that warranty damages are the purchase price (the action was in contract for goods sold and delivered). The parties have cited no New York case which squarely meets the issue and it is, therefore, concluded that, contrary to the counter assertions of the parties, neither "purchase plus interest" (Perls) nor "value at date of dispossession" (List) is presently the law of this State. In fact, there is a marked absence of case law on the issue. One legislative source has described this paucity of case law with the understatement that "[t]he implied warranty of title under the Uniform Sales Act [N.Y. Personal Property Law, Consol.Laws, c. 41, § 94] has seldom been invoked." (1955 Report of N.Y. Law Rev.Comm., Vol. 1, p. 387, n. 68, citing Pinney v. Geraghty, 209 App.Div. 630, 205 N.Y.S. 645, a case dealing with the effect of the vendor's ignoring a vouching-in notice.) Furthermore, the case law in other jurisdictions in this country provides no consistent approach, much less "rule", on this issue and it is difficult even to add up jurisdictions to pinpoint a "majority" and a "minority." One attempt to collect and organize the law in this country on this issue concludes that there are at least four distinct "rules" for measuring the damages flowing from the breach of a personal property warranty of title: purchase price plus interest; "value", without specification as to the time at which value is to be determined; value at the time of dispossession; and value at the time of the sale (Ann., Breach of Warranty of Title—Damages, 13 A.L.R.2d 1369). Interestingly enough, the annotator was able to find New York cases each of which used language which would apparently suggest that a different one of these four "rules" was the *the* rule. (Ann., *supra,* p. 1380) In the face of such unsettled and unconvincing "precedent", the issue is one which is open to resolution as a question which is actually one of first impression.

At the time of the sale to List and at the commencement of the *Menzel* replevin action, there was in effect the New York counterpart to section 13 of the Uniform Sales Act (N.Y. Personal Property Law, § 94 [PPL]) which provided that "In a contract to sell or a sale, unless contrary intention appears, there is

1. An implied warranty on the part of the seller that . . . he has a right to sell the goods . . .

2. An implied warranty that the buyer shall have and enjoy quiet possession of the goods as against any lawful claims existing at the time of the sale."

In addition, section 150 of the PPL provided for remedies for breach of warranty and subdivision 6 provided: "The measure of damages for breach of warranty is the loss directly and naturally resulting, in the ordinary course of events, from the breach of warranty". Subdivision 7 applies, by its terms, only to a breach of warranty of quality and is, therefore, not controlling on the question of damages for breach of warranty of title and quiet enjoyment. Thus, the Perls' reliance on this subdivision is misplaced. The Perls contend that the only loss directly and naturally resulting, in the ordinary course of events, from their breach was List's loss of the purchase price. List, however, contends that that loss is the present market value of the painting, the value which he would have been able to obtain if the Perls had conveyed good title. The Perls support their position by reference to the damages recoverable for breach of the warranty of quiet possession as to real property. However, this analogy has been severely criticized by a leading authority in these terms: "This rule [limiting damages to the purchase price plus interest] virtually confines the buyer to rescission and restitution, a remedy to which the injured buyer is undoubtedly entitled if he so elects, but it is a violation of general principles of contracts to deny him in an action on the contract such damages *as will put him in as good a position as he would have occupied had the contract been kept.*" (11 Williston, Contracts [3d ed.], § 1395A, p. 484 [emphasis added].) Clearly, List can only be put in the same position he would have occupied if the contract had been kept by the Perls if he recovers the value of the painting at the time when, by the judgment in the main action, he was required to surrender the painting to Mrs. Menzel or pay her the present value of the painting. Had the warranty been fulfilled, i.e., had title been as warranted by the Perls, List would still have possession of a painting currently worth $22,500 and he would have realized that price at an auction or private sale. If List recovers only the purchase price plus interest, the effect is to *put* him in the same position he would have occupied *if the sale had never been made.* Manifestly, an injured buyer is not compensated when he recovers only so much as placed him in *status quo ante* since such a recovery implicitly denies that he had suffered any damage. This rationale has been applied in Massachusetts in a case construing a statute identical in language to section 150 (subd. 6) of the PPL where the buyer was held entitled to the value "which [he] lost by not receiving a title to it as warranted. . . . His loss cannot be measured by the [price] that he paid for the machine. He is entitled to the benefit of his bargain" (Spillane v. Corey, 323 Mass. 673, 675, 84 N.E.2d 5 [1949]; see, also, Pillgrene v. James J. Paulman, Inc., 6 Terry 225, 226, 45 Del. 225–226, 71 A.2d 59 [1950] ["The purpose of compensatory damages is to place the buyer in as good condition as he would have occupied had the title been good."]). This measure of damages reflects what the buyer has actually lost and it awards to him only the loss which has directly and naturally resulted, in the ordinary course of events, from the seller's breach of warranty.

An objection raised by the Perls to this measure of damages is that it exposes the innocent seller to potentially ruinous liability where the article sold has substantially appreciated in value. However, this "potential ruin" is not beyond the control of the seller since he can take steps to ascertain the status of title so as to satisfy himself that he himself is getting good title. (Mr.

Perls testified that to question a reputable dealer as to his title would be an "insult." Perhaps, but the sensitivity of the art dealer cannot serve to deprive the injured buyer of compensation for a breach which could have been avoided had the insult been risked.) Should such an inquiry produce no reasonably reliable information as to the status of title, it is not requiring too much to expect that, as a reasonable businessman, the dealer would himself either refuse to buy or, having bought, inform his vendee of the uncertain status of title. Furthermore, under section 94 of the PPL, the seller could modify or exclude the warranties since they arise only "unless contrary intention appears". Had the Perls taken the trouble to inquire as to title, they could have sold to List subject to any existing lawful claims unknown to them at the time of sale. Accordingly, the "prospects of ruin" forecast as flowing from the rule are not quite as ominous as the argument would indicate. Accordingly, the order of the Appellate Division should be reversed as to the measure of damages and the judgment awarding List the value of the painting at the time of trial of the *Menzel* action should be reinstated.

On the cross appeal by the Perls, the issue is as to the time from which interest should run on the judgment in favor of List against the Perls. The Appellate Division indicated that interest should be recovered from the date of purchase in October, 1955, but it did so only in conjunction with its determination that the measure of damages should be the purchase price paid by List on that date. Manifestly, the present-value measure of damages has no necessary connection with the date of purchase and is, in fact, inconsistent with the running of interest from the date of purchase since List's possession was not disturbed until the judgment directing delivery of the painting to Mrs. Menzel, or, in the alternative, paying her the present value of the painting. Accordingly, List was not damaged until that time and there is no basis upon which to predicate the inclusion of interest from the date of purchase. Accordingly, on the cross appeal, the order of the Appellate Division, insofar as it directed that interest should run from the date of purchase, should be reversed and interest directed to be included from the date on which Mrs. Menzel's judgment was entered, May 10, 1966.

SCILEPPI, BERGAN, BREITEL and JASEN, JJ., concur.

FULD, C.J., and KEATING, J., taking no part.

Order reversed, with costs to third-party plaintiff-appellant-respondent, and case remitted to Supreme Court, New York County, for further proceedings in accordance with the opinion herein.

KERBY v. HAL ROACH STUDIOS, INC.

53 Cal. App. 2d 207, 127 P.2d 577 (Cal. Dist. Ct. App. 1942)

SHAW, Justice pro tem.

The plaintiff appeals from a judgment of nonsuit. No question is raised regarding the sufficiency of the complaint to present her case; hence we do not review its allegations.

The salient facts shown by the evidence are as follows: The plaintiff is an actress, concert singer, and monologist of many years' experience, both in the United States and Europe. For many years she has been and now is engaged in collecting American folk-lore, including legends, stories and songs, and in presenting them to the public on concert programs. Her character is conceded to be good. Defendant corporation is engaged in the business of producing motion pictures and defendant Seltzer is the head of its publicity department. In March, 1939, a motion picture which the corporation had produced was on exhibition in Los Angeles in the theater mentioned in the letter hereinafter set forth. For the purpose of advertising that picture the defendants caused a letter bearing plaintiff's name as apparent signer to be prepared, handwritten in a feminine hand and then reproduced mechanically on pink stationery, and also caused 1,000 copies of the letter so reproduced to be enclosed in pink envelopes, addressed in a feminine hand and sent by mail to 1,000 men householders selected by the mailing agency which addressed the envelopes. The date of mailing was March 8, 1939. All of this was done without plaintiff's knowledge or consent. The letter so sent reads as follows:

"Dearest:

"Don't breathe it to a soul, but I'm back in Los Angeles and more curious than ever to see you. Remember how I cut up about a year ago? Well, I'm raring to go again, and believe me I'm in the mood for fun.

"Let's renew our acquaintanceship and I promise you an evening you won't forget. Meet me in front of Warners Downtown Theatre at 7th and Hill on Thursday. Just look for a girl with a gleam in her eye, a smile on her lips and mischief on her mind!

"Fondly,

"Your ectoplasmic playmate,

"Marion Kerby."

At the time this letter was sent plaintiff was a resident of Los Angeles. At that time and during all of the year 1939 her name and address were listed in the Los Angeles City Directory and in the Los Angeles telephone directory, and she was the only person of that name so listed. The name at the end of this letter, in addition to being that of plaintiff, was also the name of the chief character in two works of fiction previously published and of the chief feminine character in the moving picture above mentioned.

The effects of the sending of this letter in the manner and to the persons above described are not depicted in the record except by excluded offer of proof and a showing that plaintiff had a large number of telephone calls and a personal visit in regard to it; but no evidence and little imagination and knowledge of human nature are necessary to enable anyone to understand what results should be expected. It could not but lead to misunderstandings between husbands and their wives who saw the letter and put the worst interpretation on it; it would arouse the expectation of lonesome males who were interested in the promised evening; and it must result in telephone calls and other communications from both irate wives and lonesome males and perhaps also from aggrieved but innocent husbands. It would also necessarily affect adversely the reputation of plaintiff with all who might read the letter and suppose her capable of writing and sending it. Apparently the defendants had no foresight in these matters, but they cannot for that reason escape the natural and probable consequences of their acts. The effect of all this on plaintiff does appear; she became terribly excited, nervous, unhappy; she had a feeling of disgrace and anguish; she was heartsick and didn't care what happened, whether she had the rest of a career or not; in the case of a lady caller plaintiff was afraid of being shot. Whereas she had fifteen paid engagements in the twelve months immediately preceding the publication, she had only two in seventeen months thereafter, but the evidence does not certainly show that this was due to the sending of the letter.

Does the law refuse all redress to one who has been thus grievously imposed upon and subjected to embarrassment, humiliation and scorn, merely to satisfy the desire of some business concern for publicity? We think not. Plaintiff rests her appeal here for redress upon her right of privacy and we think it may be so supported. The law regarding privacy is of somewhat recent development. In some states the right of privacy is not yet recognized as a justiciable right. But in California it has been accepted as a right the breach of which gives rise to a cause of action. (Melvin v. Reid, 931, 112 Cal.App. 285, 297 P.91, 92, where the law on this subject is quite fully discussed.) The case at bar differs in its facts from that just cited and from any other to which our attention has been called in which the right of privacy has been recognized and enforced, but that fact does not necessarily require us to hold that plaintiff has no right of action here. New sets of facts are continually arising to which accepted legal principles must be applied, and the novelty of the factual situation is not an unscalable barrier to such application of the law. As stated in Melvin v. Reid, supra, quoting from another case, "The right of privacy has been defined as the right to live one's life in seclusion, without being subjected to unwarranted and undesired publicity. In short, it is the right to be let alone." The court further said in Melvin v. Reid: "The right to pursue and obtain happiness is guaranteed to all by the fundamental law of our state. This right by its very nature includes the right to live free from the unwarranted attack of others upon one's liberty, property, and reputation. Any person living a life of rectitude has that right to happiness which includes a freedom from unnecessary attacks on his character, social standing, or reputation."

Here the plaintiff was, without her consent, plucked from her regular routine of life and thrust before the world, or at least 1,000 of its persons, as the author of a letter not written by her and of a nature to at least cast doubt on her moral character, and this was done in a manner to call down on her a train of highly undesirable consequences. This constituted as strong an invasion of the right of privacy as any of those described in the cases. As stated in Pavesich v. New England Life Ins. Co., 1905, 122 Ga. 190, 50 S.E. 68, 69 L.R.A. 101, 113, 106 Am.St.Rep.104, 126, 2 Ann.Cas. 561, the right of privacy includes protection against "mortifying notoriety," unless some legal justification for its infliction exists. The desire to advertise a business constitutes no such justification. A similar question was involved in Goodyear Tire & Rubber Co. v. Vandergriff, 1936, 52 Ga.App. 662, 184 S.E. 452, 454. There the respondent, Vandergriff, who was engaged in the trucking business and seems to have been a large user of tires, sued the Goodyear Tire & Rubber Company and several of its employees, and the defendants appealed from a judgment against them. One of the individual appellants telephoned to several tire dealers who were competitors of the Goodyear Company, falsely represented to them that the respondent, Vandergriff, was talking and thus obtained from these competitors the confidential prices they would have quoted to Vandergriff. Another of the appellants then telephoned to one of these competitors, objecting to the lowness of the prices so quoted, and falsely informed this competitor that Vandergriff had revealed the prices quoted to him by the competitor. The competitors sent representatives to call on Vandergriff because of the statement that he was in the market for tires, and he was also subjected to embarrassment, chagrin, contempt and ridicule because of this conduct of appellants. On these facts it was held that Vandergriff had a cause of action. While the decision was partly based on a statute forbidding false personation, the court held that there was an actionable invasion of Vandergriff's right of privacy, citing and following Pavesich v. New England Life Ins. Co., supra, and saying in this connection: " . . . placing the plaintiff in the position of having procured confidential prices on tires, and then betraying the confidence imposed in him by giving the quoted prices to competitors, had 'a tendency to bring the plaintiff into contempt or ridicule,' and 'entitles him to recover, without proof of special damage.' "

In Melvin v. Reid, 1931, supra, 112 Cal. App. 285, 297 P. 91, are listed certain qualifications and limitations of the right of privacy, but the present case does not come within any of them. The plaintiff's position as an actress and concert singer might have afforded justification for some sorts of publicity regarding her greater than that to which persons not so engaged must submit, but it in no wise justified the acts done by the defendants here.

Respondent contends that there is "nothing salacious, suggestive or immoral about the letter." Without going that far, a letter written and circulated as was this one might invade the right of privacy, but we cannot accede to this contention in all respects. To understand the full scope of the imputations made by the sending of the letter we must bear in mind all the circumstances of its sending. Plaintiff's name was signed at the end of it and this constituted an assertion that she had written it. It was handwritten in a feminine hand and on such stationery as women use in private correspondence, thus negativing any idea that it was a matter of business or anything but a personal communication to the addressee. It was sent to 1,000 male householders selected by the mailing agency. It may reasonably be inferred that many of these householders would be married and that few, if any, of them would have a personal acquaintance with plaintiff. The letter itself is of somewhat doubtful implications. While it does not directly assert or invite an improper relation between the writer and the person of the opposite sex to whom it is addressed, no great amount of imagination is necessary to read such a meaning into it, and it is easy to see how the wife of an addressee, if she saw the letter, might have done so. But apart from this, and giving the letter the most innocent meaning its words will reasonably bear, no modest woman of fine feelings and sensibilities would write such a letter as this to men whom she did not know. To suggest that a woman has written such a letter under such circumstances is to impute to her a laxness of character, a coarseness of moral fibre and a willingness to scrape acquaintance for no good purpose; and to spread such imputations abroad, as defendants have done, is as much an invasion of the right of privacy as was the publication of true but derogatory statements in Melvin v. Reid, 1931, supra, 112 Cal.App. 285, 297 P.91.

Defendants also contend that the letter "is plainly an advertisement and should have been so regarded by any reasonable person," advancing in support of this contention the claim that it was printed and that it fixed no time for the meeting proposed. The exact method by which the letter was reproduced does not appear, but the evidence does show that it was first typewritten, then handwritten by a woman clerk, and that the longhand letter was turned over to an engraving plant by which an engraved plate was made. It is a matter of judicial notice that by such methods prints can be made which, in the absence of close inspection, will pass for original handwriting, and we cannot assume that this letter was obviously a printed one. There is nothing in its words to refer to the motion picture or to warn any reader that it was merely an advertisement or other work of fiction. As to the rendezvous, the letter proposed that it be in the evening "on Thursday." The recipient would easily understand this to mean the next Thursday after receipt of the letter, and this would not be so vague as to make it obvious that frustration would meet any attempt to keep the appointment.

As already indicated, the letter was circulated by defendants for the purpose of advertising a moving picture, and as far as appears they had no intent to refer therein to plaintiff and did not know of her existence, although they might easily have discovered it. These facts, which are stressed by defendants, tend to show want of malice and might avert an award of punitive damages, but they constitute no defense to plaintiff's action. The letter did, in fact, refer to plaintiff in clear and definite fashion, and would reasonably have been so understood by anyone who knew of her existence. The wrong complained of is the invasion of plaintiff's right of privacy, and such an invasion is no less real or damaging because the invader supposed he was in other territory. The case bears considerable analogy, both as to the right invaded and the nature of the injury inflicted, to one of libel. It is well established that inadvertence or mistake affords no defense to a charge of libel, where the defamatory publication does, in fact, refer to the plaintiff . . . Corrigan v. Bobbs-Merrill Co., 1920, 228 N.Y. 58, 63, 126 N.E. 260, 262, 10 A.L.R. 662, 666. "The question is not so much who was aimed at as who was hit." Corrigan v. Bobbs-Merrill Co., supra.

The letter complained of here might very well have formed the basis of a charge of libel. It appears to come fully within the definition of libel in section 45 of the Civil Code. A libel need not be a statement directly referring to a person and stating something defamatory about him. It may as well be accomplished by falsely putting words into the mouth or attaching them to the pen of the person defamed and thus imputing to such person a willingness to use them, where the mere fact of having uttered or used the words would produce any of the results enumerated in section 45, supra.

We do not, however, rest our decision on the ground of libel, for several reasons. The appellant has not sought to uphold her action as one for libel, and the complaint, while possibly sufficient to charge a libel, is not so labeled and was obviously not drawn for that purpose. The record does not show whether or not plaintiff complied with the statute (Stats.1871–72 p. 533; Deering's Gen.Laws, 1937, Act 4317) requiring a bond for costs to be filed in an action for libel or slander, but the facts above recited imbue us with a strong suspicion that she did not; and if such be the case her action, if for libel, would be subject to dismissal on its return to the lower court, unless such bond were filed.

The judgment is reversed.

SCHAUER, P.J., and SHINN, J., concurred.

BRIGHT TUNES MUSIC CORP. v. HARRISONGS MUSIC, LTD.
420 F. Supp 177 (S.D.N.Y. 1976)

OPINION AND ORDER

OWEN, District Judge.

This is an action in which it is claimed that a successful song, My Sweet Lord, listing George Harrison as the composer, is plagiarized from an earlier successful song, He's So Fine, composed by Ronald Mack, recorded by a singing group called the "Chiffons," the copyright of which is owned by plaintiff, Bright Tunes Music Corp.

He's So Fine, recorded in 1962, is a catchy tune consisting essentially of four repetitions of a very short basic musical phrase, "sol-mi-re," (hereinafter motif A),[1] altered as necessary to fit the words, followed by four repetitions of another short basic musical phrase, "sol-la-do-la-do," (hereinafter motif B).[2] While neither motif is novel, the four repetitions of A, followed by four repetitions of B, is a highly unique pattern.[3] In addition, in the second use of the motif B series, there is a grace note inserted making the phrase go "sol-la-do-la-*re*-do."[4]

My Sweet Lord, recorded first in 1970, also uses the same motif A (modified to suit the words) four times, followed by motif B, repeated three times, not four. In place of He's So Fine's fourth repetition of motif B, My Sweet Lord has a transitional passage of musical attractiveness of the same approximate

---

1

2

---

[3] All the experts agreed on this.

4

length, with the identical grace note in the identical second repetition.[5] The harmonies of both songs are identical.[6]

George Harrison, a former member of the The Beatles, was aware of He's So Fine. In the United States, it was No. 1 on the billboard charts for five weeks; in England, Harrison's home country, it was No. 12 on the charts on June 1, 1963, a date upon which one of the Beatle songs was, in fact, in first position. For seven weeks in 1963, He's So Fine was one of the top hits in England.

According to Harrison, the circumstances of the composition of My Sweet Lord were as follows. Harrison and his group, which include an American black gospel singer named Billy Preston,[7] were in Copenhagen, Denmark, on a singing engagement. There was a press conference involving the group going on backstage. Harrison slipped away from the press conference and went to a room upstairs and began "vamping" some guitar chords, fitting on to the chords he was playing the words, "Hallelujah" and "Hare Krishna" in various ways.[8] During the course of this vamping, he was alternating between what musicians call a Minor II chord and a Major V chord.

At some point, germinating started and he went down to meet with others of the group, asking them to listen, which they did, and everyone began to join in, taking first "Hallelujah" and then "Hare Krishna" and putting them into four part harmony. Harrison obviously started using the "Hallelujah," etc., as repeated sounds, and from there developed the lyrics, to wit, "My Sweet Lord," "Dear, Dear Lord," etc. In any event, from this very free-flowing exchange of ideas, with Harrison playing his two chords and everybody singing "Hallelujah" and "Hare Krishna," there began to emerge the My Sweet Lord text idea, which Harrison sought to develop a little bit further during the following week as he was playing it on his guitar. Thus developed motif A and its words interspersed with "Hallelujah" and "Hare Krishna."

Approximately one week after the idea first began to germinate, the entire

---

[5] This grace note, as will be seen *infra*, has substantial significance in assessing the claims of the parties hereto.

[6] Expert witnesses for the defendants asserted crucial differences in the two songs. These claimed differences essentially stem, however, from the fact that different words and number of syllables were involved. This necessitated modest alterations in the repetitions or the places of beginning of a phrase, which, however, has nothing to do whatsoever with the essential musical kernel that is involved.

[7] Preston recorded the first Harrison copyrighted recording of My Sweet Lord, of which more *infra*, and from his musical background was necessarily equally aware of He's So Fine.

[8] These words ended up being a "responsive" interjection between the eventually copyrighted words of My Sweet Lord. In He's So Fine the Chiffons used the sound "dulang" in the same places to fill in and give rhythmic impetus to what would otherwise be somewhat dead spots in the music.

group flew back to London because they had earlier booked time to go to a recording studio with Billy Preston to make an album. In the studio, Preston was the principal musician. Harrison did not play in the session. He had given Preston his basic motif A with the idea that it be turned into a song, and was back and forth from the studio to the engineer's recording booth, supervising the recording "takes." Under circumstances that Harrison was utterly unable to recall, while everybody was working toward a finished song, in the recording studio, somehow or other the essential three notes of motif A reached polished form.

> "Q. [By the Court]: . . . you feel that those three notes . . . the motif A in the record, those three notes developed somewhere in that recording session?

> "Mr. Harrison: I'd say those three there were finalized as beginning there."

> . . . .

> "Q. [By the Court]: Is it possible that Billy Preston hit on those [notes comprising motif A]?

> "Mr. Harrison: Yes, but it's possible also that I hit on that, too, as far back as the dressing room, just scat singing."

Similarly, it appears that motif B emerged in some fashion at the recording session as did motif A. This is also true of the unique grace note in the second repetition of motif B.

> "Q. [By the Court]: All I am trying to get at, Mr. Harrison, is if you have a recollection when that [grace] note popped into existence as it ends up in the Billy Preston recording.

> . . . .

> "Mr. Harrison: . . . [Billy Preston] might have put that there on every take, but it just might have been on one take, or he might have varied it on different takes at different places."

The Bill Preston recording, listing George Harrison as the composer, was thereafter issued by Apple Records. The music was then reduced to paper by someone who prepared a "lead sheet" containing the melody, the words and the harmony for the United States copyright application.[9]

---

[9] It is of interest, but not of legal significance, in my opinion, that when Harrison later recorded the song himself, he chose to omit the little grace note, not only in his musical recording but in the printed sheet music that was issued following that particular recording. The genesis of the song remains the same, however modestly Harrison may have later altered it. Harrison, it should be noted, regards his song as that which he sings at the particular moment he is singing it and not something that is written on a piece of paper.

Seeking the wellsprings of musical composition—why a composer chooses the succession of notes and the harmonies he does—whether it be George Harrison or Richard Wagner—is a fascinating inquiry. It is apparent from the extensive colloquy between the Court and Harrison covering forty pages in the transcript that neither Harrison nor Preston were conscious of the fact that they were utilizing the He's So Fine theme.[10] However, they in fact were, for it is perfectly obvious to the listener that in musical terms, the two songs are virtually identical except for one phrase. There is motif A used four times, followed by motif B, four times in one case, and three times in the other, with the same grace note in the second repetition of motif B.[11]

What happened? I conclude that the composer,[12] in seeking musical materials to clothe his thoughts, was working with various possibilities. As he tried this possibility and that, there came to the surface of his mind a particular combination that pleased him as being one he felt would be appealing to a prospective listener; in other words, that this combination of sounds would work. Why? Because his subconscious knew it already had worked in a song his conscious mind did not remember. Having arrived at this pleasing combination of sounds, the recording was made, the lead sheet prepared for copy-

---

[10] Preston may well have been the "composer" of motif B and the telltale grace note appearing in the second use of the motif during the recording session, for Harrison testified:

> "The Court: To be as careful as I can now in summing this up, you can't really say that you or Billy Preston or somebody else didn't somewhere along the line suggest these; all you know is that when Billy Preston sang them that way at the recording session, you felt they were a successful way to sing this, and you kept it?
>
> "The Witness: Yes, I mean at that time we chose what is a good performance.
>
> "The Court: And you felt it was a worthy piece of music?
>
> "The Witness: Yes . . . ."

[11] Even Harrison's own expert witness, Harold Barlow, long in the field, acknowledged that although the two motifs were in the public domain, their use here was so unusual that he, in all his experience, had never come across this unique sequential use of these materials. He testified:

> "The Court: And I think you agree with me in this, that we are talking about a basic three-note structure that composers can vary in modest ways, but we are still talking about the same heart, the same essence?
>
> "The Witness: Yes.
>
> "The Court: So you say that you have not seen anywhere four A's followed by three B's or four?
>
> "The Witness: Or four A's followed by four B's."

The uniqueness is even greater when one considers the identical grace note in the identical place in each song.

[12] I treat Harrison as the composer, although it appears that Billy Preston may have been the composer as to part. (See fn. 10 *supra*). Even were Preston the composer as to part, this is immaterial.

right and the song became an enormous success. Did Harrison deliberately use the music of He's So Fine? I do not believe he did so deliberately. Nevertheless, it is clear that My Sweet Lord is the very same song as He's So Fine with different words, and Harrison had access to He's So Fine. This is, under the law, infringement of copyright, and is no less so even though subconsciously accomplished.

Given the foregoing, I find for the plaintiff on the issue of plagiarism, and set the action down for trial on November 8, 1976 on the issue of damages and other relief as to which the plaintiff may be entitled. The foregoing constitutes the Court's findings of fact and conclusions of law.

So Ordered.

Herbert Mitgang, "PUBLISHER REJECTS 'OFFENSIVE' BOOKS"

The New York Times (September 1, 1983), p. C17

Dodd, Mead & Company, the 144-year-old New York trade-book publisher, has cancelled two novels advertised in its fall 1983 catalogue and withdrawn a volume of verse that is already in print. Dodd, Mead was ordered to take these actions by its parent company, Thomas Nelson Inc. of Nashville, the world's largest Bible publisher, which considered some language in the books objectionable.

After being set in type, "Tip on a Dead Crab" by William Murray and "Skim" by Thomas Henege will not be published by Dodd, Mead, which was acquired a little more than a year ago by Thomas Nelson. In addition, about 5,000 copies of "The Devil's Book of Verse," edited by Richard Conniff, are not being shipped from Dodd, Mead's warehouse, on orders of Nelson.

Lewis W. Gillenson, president of Dodd, Mead, said that Nelson had insisted that certain "four-letter words, excessive scatology and language that took God's name in vain" had to be eliminated before the books could be published. Mr. Gillenson said that Sam Moore, president of Nelson, had asked him to "publish books that will not have offensive language in them."

The language considered not acceptable by Nelson included words or word combinations that used God, Christ or Jesus as expletives. Mr. Gillenson said that an executive of Nelson told him it was all right to print "damn" but not "goddamn." The four-letter word for copulation was forbidden, but the four-letter word for defecation was permitted.

The authors and their agents described the action as "censorship" and refused to make any changes in their books. Mr. Gillenson declined to call Dodd, Mead's refusal to publish "censorship"; he described his orders as a desire to save Nelson from embarrassment because its executives were "deeply involved in the Christian movement."

Dodd, Mead has informed John Cushman, agent for Mr. Henege, and Helen Brann, agent for Mr. Murray, that the two novelists could keep their advance money. In addition, Dodd, Mead will turn over the type and graphic designs of the unpublished books to the authors.

Mr. Murray, who writes "Letters From Italy" for The New Yorker and has written nine novels, said "Tip on a Dead Crab" is about people who live by gambling on horses.

"The 20 words they wanted changed in the new book were not in themselves of great artistic importance," he said. "But it's the ethics and morality of forcing changes that's wrong—no writer should put up with it. Of course, it's censorship."

Mr. Cushman said that his client, Mr. Henege—it is a pen name; his real name is Albert F. Gillotti, and he is a vice president of Banker's Trust in Europe—had been asked to remove the word "goddamn," which appears a number of times in his manuscript. Mr. Henege responded through his agent that he would not tolerate changes in "Skim," a thriller about international banking and political corruption.

Mr. Gillotti said: "When the accountants or salesmen who head conglomerates can tell an editor of a publishing subsidiary what he cannot accept for publication because the book might interfere with the stream of revenues from another part of his business—cigarettes, say, or food additives—then I fear for the future of independent thought in the United States."

"The Devil's Book of Verse," published Aug. 1, is a collection of poetry ranging from John Dryden to Cole Porter. Its editor, Mr. Conniff, a senior editor at Geo magazine, said there were objections to two poems. One by Ezra Pound, "Ancient Music," uses "goddamn" 10 times; the second, by an unknown author, contains four-letter words—to which Nelson did not object—but contains "goddamn."

Mr. Gillenson had asked Mr. Conniff to permit pages with the two offending poems to be removed from the book before it left the warehouse. Mr. Conniff said he refused to do so.

According to BP Report, a book-publishing newsletter, Nelson feared that its competitors in the religious-book field would call attention to Dodd, Mead's "offensive books" and damage the company's reputation with Christian booksellers.

Nelson acquired the faltering trade-book house in April 1982 for $4.5

million. Dodd, Mead's backlist is considered to be its most valuable editorial property. A fresh effort was being made to acquire modern works of fiction, but several New York literary agents yesterday expressed doubts that they would submit novels to Dodd, Mead in the future.

"ABC PAID ALI FOR INTERVIEW, BUT DENIES HE WAS 'EMPLOYEE' "

Variety (March 5, 1980), p. 51

Was Muhammad Ali an employee of ABC in March 1975 because the network paid him $5,000 in "expenses" for an interview with Howard Cosell and were his ad libs during that interview on March 29, 1975, prepared for him by the web?

ABC says no on both counts and has asked Ali to pay back $193,532 awarded the ex-champion by an arbitration panel called into the dispute by his union, the American Federation of TV & Radio Artists. The panel agreed with Ali that he was an employee and decided by a two-to-one vote that the ad libs were prepared.

ABC said no money was paid into pension funds for Ali because of the appearance and no other deductions were made. Ali, ABC said, was not on the show to entertain but as an expert. The high expense item was not divulged to the audience watching the "Wide World Of Sports" show on which the interview appeared and viewers might have been forgiven if they thought Ali was a "news source" and Cosell a "reporter."

Ali's Outburst

What brought ABC's payment to a news source to light was its anger that Ali sought $193,532 he had spent in defending a libel action brought against him by a man he accused of racism on the show and in press conferences before and after it. Ali was discussing his dissatisfaction with a man who had refereed his fights with Chuck Wepner and Joe Frazier. The referee, Tony Perez sued Ali for $1,000,000 and lost, but Ali picked up his own defense tab and later went to his union and they went to arbitration.

ABC said that under the AFTRA contractual code that determines ABC's relations with the union, the arbitration might have been binding, except that the panel made an "improper amendment and alteration of the code" by ignoring the evidence ABC presented that Ali was not an employee and its denial that the ad lib remarks had been prepared for Ali.

The suit noted that during the trial of the Perez charges, Ali had named

ABC in a "third-party complaint" and asked the trial judge to hold the network liable for any damages assessed against him if Perez won. The trial judge, ABC said, dismissed that action.

ABC is asking relief from the arbitration award and costs for its current action.

Eric Page, "NEW DISPUTE IS STIRRED BY DOUBLEDAY—DAVIS SUIT"

The New York Times (February 26, 1980), p. C9

A recent lawsuit by Doubleday & company against one of its own authors, Gwen Davis, has added fuel to the controversy surrounding last year's libel award against both Doubleday and Miss Davis.

The controversy, which is to be discussed further today at a seminar to be held by the Association of American publishers, has continued against a background of concern in the book and media worlds about the state of the First Amendment, of the nation's libel law and of the relationship between author and publisher.

The association's freedom to read committee is sponsoring the open seminar, "Can Fiction Be Libelous: How the Bindrim Decision Could Affect You," directed at publishers, authors, editors, lawyers and others concerned with creative writing. It is to be held at 2 P.M. in the eighth-floor auditorium of the Time-Life Building. Admission is $10. Among the book-world notables expected to take part are Kenneth D. McCormick, Miss Davis's editor at Doubleday, and Thomas C. Wallace, editor in chief of Holt, Rinehart & Winston.

Ruling by Supreme Court

The United States Supreme Court, without giving any reason, refused last December to review the $75,000 award won in a suit brought by Paul Bindrim, a California psychologist. He was the self-described real-life model for a fictional character—a bearded leader of nude encounter therapy sessions—in Miss Davis's 1971 novel, "Touching."

Then, on Feb. 15, Doubleday filed suit against Miss Davis for $138,000 in Federal Court in Manhattan. The sum includes the $75,000 award to Dr. Bindrim, which was set by a California appellate court last year; interest due him, and legal and other expenses incurred in the case by Doubleday, the publishing combine, which also owns a controlling interest in the Mets baseball team.

Doubleday contends that Miss Davis must pay the money because its contract with her stipulates that, in matters of libel as well as some others, she is to "indemnify and hold the publisher harmless from any claim, suit, or action, and any expense or damage in consequence thereof."

Similar clauses are standard in the publishing industry, and in recent years publishers have tended increasingly to invoke them; one effect of the suit, some lawyers in the field contend, is to underscore the hazard that the clauses represent to writers.

"I'm hurt and horrified; I can't believe this is happening," Miss Davis said recently, speaking from her California home. "It's as if the whole traditional relationship between author and publisher has been abandoned. I've discovered sadly that there's no justice—but I had hoped at least that there was mercy."

Mr. McCormick, Miss Davis's editor, could not be reached for comment yesterday, and a member of Doubleday's legal department declined to discuss the reasons for the action or its implications for publishers and writers.

Irwin Karp, counsel for the Authors Guild and Authors League, representing both book writers and playwrights, said, "It's unfortunate that the suit has been brought against Miss Davis; it's the sort of situation in which two parties who are natural allies in defending an important First Amendment principle should not be put in an adversary position at this point: in the libel suit Doubleday and she had both contended that the First Amendment protected her right to write the novel and Doubleday's right to publish it."

Decision Called 'Wrong-Headed'

Critics of the Supreme Court under Chief Justice Warren E. Burger have been contending that it has reduced the protections provided under the First Amendment. And though the Burger court has not dealt with questions of libel where fiction is involved, it is widely seen as having backtracked somewhat in the area of protections against libel in other contexts.

No comment about the Doubleday suit against Miss Davis, the author of 12 books, has been forthcoming from the Association of American Publishers, but the association's president, Townsend Hoopes, has called the libel award to Dr. Bindrim "one of the most destructive and wrong-headed decisions that any court has made in the area of First Amendment rights."

Reached at his Madison Avenue office, Mr. Wallace said yesterday that the libel award was "probably a very dangerous decision as far as the future of fiction in America is concerned; it makes it possible for people to claim they have been libeled in a work of fiction although the character portrayed in that work of fiction may be of a different color, race, physical makeup and even sex." The fictional character in "Touching" had a different name and was otherwise different from the real Dr. Bindrim.

LOEW'S INC. v. WOLFF
101 F. Supp. 981 (S.D. Cal. 1951)

JAMES M. CARTER, District Judge.

This case raises novel questions concerning literary property; and warranties, express and implied, in the sale thereof. The case arises under the diversity jurisdiction of this court.

On March 21, 1949, defendants, Victoria Wolf and Erich Wolff, sold to the plaintiff, Loew's Inc., a story in manuscript form entitled, "Case History." On that date, a regular form contract used by plaintiff was executed by the defendants. The present action is based upon alleged violations of certain provisions of this contract.

The facts, as disclosed at the trial which led up to the execution of this contract, are as follows:

Erich Wolff, a doctor, specializing in cardialgy, had met his former wife, Cathy, during chemistry lectures where she was a laboratory assistant at the institute at which he studied.

Following their marriage, she later became subject to spells of extreme melancholia and attempted suicide. He investigated shock treatment and radium treatment for ovarian glands. Following her second suicide attempt, she submitted to radium treatment which produced a marked change in her personality. A third suicide attempt followed and she died on May 22, 1942.

A year and a half later, Doctor Wolff read articles in medical journals describing a pre-frontal lobotomy operation for melancholia and the marked change it produced in a patient's personality. It will be noted that all of these matters, as testified to by Dr. Wolff, were factual matters and in the public domain.

Victoria Wolf, a short story writer and novelist met Erich Wolff in 1943. Late that year, he first discussed with her the operation on the brain, known as a pre-frontal lobotomy, as the basis of a story. She knew, and Erich Wolff told her, of the tragic experiences of Wolff and his former wife. Wolff told her of the lobotomy operation; its cure of melancholia, and its transformation of the character of the patient. Due to other commitments, Victoria Wolf was unable to write the story for Erich Wolff at that time.

After his discussion with Victoria Wolf, he then contacted Elsie Foulstone, also a writer, and discussed the possibility of her aiding him in preparing a draft of the story for motion picture purposes. He told her of the facts above and she wrote a synopsis of a story entitled, "Swear Not by the Moon," based on those facts, plus additional fictional matter. The end product did not please Erich Wolff and he relieved her of any further duties.

Nothing further was done about the story until some time in 1945, when Erich Wolff again contacted Victoria Wolf and prevailed upon her to work on the story. In that year Victoria Wolf wrote a synopsis of a story entitled, "Through Narrow Streets," which was based upon the doctor's former wife's experiences, the doctor's description of a lobotomy operation and her own research concerning it, and additional fictional matter.

Dissatisfied, she next wrote a revision entitled, "Brain Storm" and late in 1948 or early 1949, wrote a second revision entitled, "Case History," the story in suit. It was a combination of fact and fiction. As stated above, this story was sold to the plaintiff in March 1949 for $15,000.

The document executed by the parties was entitled "Assignment of All Rights." By its language, (Sec. 1) defendants Erich Wolff and Victoria Wolf transferred and sold to plaintiff all rights of every kind in and to the story and "the complete, unconditional and unencumbered title" thereto. Section 4 of the assignment provided that defendants represented and warranted that each was the "sole author and owner of said work, together with the title thereof,"[1] and "the sole owner of all rights of any and all kinds whatsoever in and to said work, throughout the world;" that each had "the sole and exclusive rights to dispose of each and every right herein granted;" that "neither said work nor any part thereof is in the public domain;"[2] that, "said work is original with me in all respects;" that "no incident therein contained and no part thereof is taken from or based upon any other literary or dramatic work or any photoplay, or in any way infringes upon the copyright or any other right of any individual, firm, person or corporation."

Section 5 provides for the appointment of the purchaser as lawful attorney, irrevocably, for the sole benefit of the purchaser to institute and prosecute any action to protect the rights granted herein.

By Section 6, the defendants guarantee and warrant that they will "indemnify, make good, and hold harmless the purchaser of, from and against any and all loss, damage, costs, charges, legal fees, recoveries, judgments, penalties, and expenses which may be obtained against, imposed upon or suffered by

---

[1] Sec. 8 provides that if two or more persons appear as signatories to the assignment, the agreement shall bind them jointly and severally. No point has been made that each states, "I am the sole author and owner of said work."

[2] This is an obviously fictitious provision and must have been so known by both parties. No story can exist without some matter, be it minute, from the public domain.

the purchaser by reason of any infringement or violation or alleged violation of any copyright or any other right of any person, firm or corporation, or by reason of or from any use which may be made of said work by the purchaser, or by reason of any term, covenant, representation, or warranty herein contained, or by reason of anything whatsoever which might prejudice the securing to the purchaser of the full benefit of the rights herein granted and/or purported to be granted."

Section 7 provides that the sellers "agree duly to execute, acknowledge and deliver, and/or to procure the due execution, acknowledgment and delivery to the purchaser of any and all further assignments and/or other instruments which in the sole judgment and discretion of the purchaser may be deemed necessary or expedient to carry out or effectuate the purposes or intent of this present instrument."

About three months after the execution of this instrument and the sale, Elsie Foulstone discovered that Erich Wolff had sold his story, and on July 1, 1949, plaintiff was notified that she claimed a portion of the proceeds of the sale because of the work she had done in 1944. On that same day plaintiff notified defendants' agent of the Foulstone claim. On July 30, 1949, plaintiff made a demand on defendants that they obtain a quitclaim and release from Foulstone within a reasonable time or they would be compelled to rescind their agreement of March 21st. On September 21, 1949, Elsie Foulstone filed action in the Superior Court of the State of California, County of Los Angeles, naming Erich Wolff, Victoria Wolf and Metro-Goldwyn-Mayer Pictures as defendants. The present plaintiff was not served and did not appear. Both of the present defendants were served and appeared in the Superior Court action.

On September 30, 1949, the plaintiff served defendant Erich Wolff with a notice of rescission. On October 1, 1949, defendant, Victoria Wolf, was served with a like notice. On February 28, 1950, the Superior Court rendered a judgment in favor of defendants finding that Elsie Foulstone had no valid claim or interest in or to the story, "Case History" which was sold to the plaintiff. The present action was filed on November 2, 1949, prior to the above mentioned judgment.

Plaintiff's complaint contains seven causes of action, some of which may be promptly disposed of, while others raise new and novel questions concerning expressed and implied warranties concerning the sale of literary property.

Plaintiff's complaint contains the following causes of action:

First cause of action, alleges breaches of certain express promises and warranties, to-wit,

1. That defendants did not own the complete, unconditional and unencumbered title to the story.

2. That defendants were not the sole owners or authors of said story.

3. That defendants did not have sole or exclusive rights to said story.

4. That defendants caused the assigned rights to be impaired.

5. That the story was not original with defendants.

6. That the use of said story by the plaintiff would violate the rights of another person.

7. That "Case History" was copied in large part from another work.

Plaintiff alleges the right to rescind, and that it rescinded, and claims the return of the purchase price.

Second cause of action is based upon the express warranties of the first cause and the additional theory that defendants agreed to sell plaintiff a "marketable and perfect" title to the story, "Case History," free from reasonable doubt.

Third cause of action alleges failure of consideration because of the breach by defendants of the warranties set forth in the first and second causes.

Fourth cause of action alleges defendants fraudulently induced plaintiff to enter into said contract and plaintiff was therefore entitled to and did rescind said contract.

Fifth cause of action alleges that plaintiff entered into said contract under a mistake of fact, relying on the express warranty of the first cause and the theory of "perfect and marketable" title in the second cause.

Sixth cause of action alleges that under provision 6 of the contract defendants agreed to indemnify and hold harmless the plaintiff in any action for all costs, losses, etc., incurred by plaintiff by reason of any infringement or violation or alleged violation of the right of another person. This cause of action is for damages for the decrease in value of the story and for all costs and attorneys' fees involved in this action.

Seventh cause of action alleges fraudulent representations, to-wit the express warranties above, and claims money damages.

At the conclusion of the trial, the court found:—

1. That "Case History" was a different story from "Swear Not By the Moon", and that the only points of similarity were factual matters from the public domain.

2. That Erich Wolff collaborated with Elsie Foulstone on the story, "Swear Not By the Moon."

3. That there had been proved no fraud or fraudulent representations on the part of the defendants, Erich Wolff and Victoria Wolf.

The court now finds:—

1. That defendants owned the complete, unconditional and unencumbered title to the story, "Case History".

2. That defendants were the sole owners and authors of said story.

3. That defendants had the sole and exclusive rights to said story.

4. That defendants did not cause the rights assigned to be impaired.

5. That the story was original with defendants.

6. That the use of the story by plaintiff would not violate any rights of Miss Foulstone.

7. That there was no fraudulent concealment of material facts.

These findings dispose of causes of action one, four and seven.

The second cause of action, in addition to setting forth express warranties which we have found were not breached rests on plaintiff's claim to a "marketable and perfect" title, free from reasonable doubt. This raises the question of the existence and validity of what will hereafter be referred to as "implied warranties."

The third and fifth causes of action raise the same question, since they incorporate the allegations of the second cause.[3]

The sixth cause of action will depend upon the interpretation given to provision 6 of the "Assignment."

I.

There Was No Warranty, Express or Implied,
of "Marketable and Perfect Title" to the Story.

A. There was no express warranty.

The plaintiff argues that an express warranty of "marketable and perfect" title, free from reasonable doubt, arose by the use of the words, "complete, unconditional and unencumbered title"; "sole author and owner of said work"; "sole owner of all rights of any and all kinds whatsoever in and to said

---

[3] Causes of action two, three and five, although entitled "rescission" are really claims for money after an alleged rescission by the act of the plaintiff. This court is not asked to rescind the contract between the parties. The plaintiff contends that prior to the judgment of the Superior Court, it has rescinded and that this judgment in no way affected that rescission. Even though this court found that defendants owned the complete, unconditional and unencumbered title to the story, it does not mean that this court found defendants had a "perfect and marketable title, free from reasonable doubt," at the time of the sale or at the time of the attempted rescission by the plaintiff. If such a warranty existed, either expressly or by implication, then the rescission by plaintiff might have been effective. Our question then is, "Did such a warranty exist?"

work, throughout the world"; and "I have the sole and exclusive right to dispose of each and every right herein granted." Nowhere in this most comprehensive instrument can be found the words "marketable, perfect or free from reasonable doubt." Thus, in order to find such an express warranty it must be found that the words actually used in the "Assignment of Rights" were or are synonymous with "marketable and perfect" title.

No case has been cited by counsel nor can any be found by this court which holds that the phrase "complete, unconditional and unencumbered title" is synonymous with "marketable and perfect" title. The common meaning of the word "complete" is "Filled up, with no part, item, or element lacking." It means that the "whole" title has been given and that no part or portion of it has been kept by the seller or sold to any other person. In two cases involving the sale of real estate, the words "complete title" were found to mean the instruments which constitute the evidence of title, and not to mean the estate or interest conveyed. Slidell v. Grandjean, 1883, 111 U.S. 412, 4 S.Ct. 475, 28 L.Ed. 321; Dingey v. Paxton, 60 Miss. 1038, at page 1054.

The warranty of "marketability of title" is a warranty found almost exclusively in connection with the sale of real property. Such words as "merchantable title," "clear title," "good title" and "perfect title" have been held in cases involving the sale of land to mean the same as "marketable title." None of these words can be found in the present instrument. As used in this assignment the word "complete" was not meant to be synonymous with the word "marketable or perfect." It was used to mean just what the word indicated, i. e. "whole title," that is, that no other person owned any interest in the property nor was any kept by the sellers. In this respect, the plaintiffs got what they bargained for. It seems evident that the remaining words used in the assignment are not synonymous with "marketable or perfect" title.

B. There was no implied warranty.

Plaintiff argues that the law implies the warranty of marketable title in the sale of literary property. In doing so, plaintiff wishes to have this court apply a well established doctrine used exclusively in the sale of real property to the sale of personal property. To support its contention, plaintiff cites the case of Hollywood Plays, Inc., v. Columbia Pictures Corp., 299 N.Y. 61, 85 N.E.2d 865, 10 A.L.R.2d 728. In this case, the plaintiff's sought damages for breach of a contract to purchase the motion picture, television, and radio rights to a play. The plaintiffs had purchased an interest in these rights from the trustee of one Woods, who had originally received 50 per cent of these rights by license from the proprietors of the copyright. In Woods' schedules in bankruptcy, he had listed his ownership as 25 per cent. There was no question but that Woods had owned 50 per cent up to two years before his adjudication in bankruptcy, and the plaintiffs contended that the insertion in his schedules of the lesser figure had been due to a mere error. No other explanation was forthcoming, and the plaintiffs relied on the fact that all of Woods' property had in fact, passed to his trustee, and had been included in the sale and assignment by the trustee to the plaintiffs. The New York court in reversing the lower courts, held that "the defendant was excused from performance because of a defect in plaintiffs' title." The court avoided the finding by the trial court that plaintiffs had actual title, and in our opinion erroneously declared the issue to be whether or not plaintiffs had an "unclouded title."

There are more than mere historical reasons for concluding that the doctrine of "marketable title" should be limited to cases involving the sale of real property. This doctrine has a basis in the traditional concepts of judicial fair play. Briefly, the doctrine developed because the courts at common law believed, and rightly so, that since the law required there be a recorded title in the sale of real estate, then that record title should be clear and free from reasonable doubt. A buyer, desiring to purchase the seller's land, would request that the seller deliver to him a "marketable" record of title to the property. If by searching the record, the title was free from reasonable doubt, it was proclaimed that the buyer had a "marketable" title and could not avoid the enforcement of the contract. If on the other hand, a defect appeared in the record title, then the common law courts felt that justice demanded that the seller either clear the record title or they would allow the buyer to avoid the contract. But the doctrine was not applied to the sale of personal property. At common law and with few exceptions the law as it exists today, there was no requirement that the sale of personal property be recorded. The doctrine of caveat emptor therefore prevailed. Without the application of this latter doctrine, it is highly doubtful that any sale of personal property would ever become final. There are no records to search. There is no way to ascertain that a cloud exists on the title. It is not a requirement that a record title be produced before a purchaser will buy the article in question. Thus, because of these difference between the sale of real and personal property, the courts neither then nor now could imply by law into a contract of sale of personal property the doctrine of "marketable" title. If they did so, then there would be no case in which the seller could rest in ease, for if any third person asserted a claim to the property the courts would be compelled to avoid the contract between the parties. To do this would be to place upon the seller an unsurmountable burden, and would leave the door open to allow a discontented purchaser to avoid any contract involving the sale of personal property.

For these reasons, in adopting the Uniform Sales Act the warranty of "marketable" title was conspicuously excluded. The implied warranties of title are found in Section 1733 of the Civil Code of California. There it is declared that the only implied warranties of title are, (1) that the seller has the *"right"* to sell; (2) "that the buyer shall have and enjoy *quiet possession* of the goods as against any lawful claims existing at the time of the sale", and (3) "that the goods shall be free at the time of the sale from any charge or encumbrance in favor of any third person . . . ". With these exceptions there are no other implied warranties of title in the sale of personal property and this court will not imply any others.

It is obvious that sales involving literary property are different in some respects from the sale of ordinary goods. The sale of literary property is more analogous to the sale of patents and patent rights. Both literary properties and patents are products of the mind, plus skill. Both utilize matters in the public domain. A review of patent cases confirms the position taken by this court.

In Consumers' Gas Co. v. American Electric Construction Co., 3 Cir., 1892, 50 F. 778, 780, the action was by an electric construction company against a gas company to recover the price of installing an electric plant. The gas company set up by affidavit of defense that a certain patentee had threatened it with a claim for damages for infringement of patent rights if it used the machinery installed by the plaintiff, and that by such use the defendant would also be liable to another patentee. The court held that these facts were no defense, declaring: "A purchaser of property, who has had the full use and enjoyment of the same, and is in the undisturbed possession thereof, in the absence of fraud, cannot withhold the purchase price because a third person claims to have a superior title thereto, or an adverse right therein, and threatens to bring suit to enforce the same, or because of an alleged liability on the part of the purchaser to a patentee for an infringement of letters patent, by reason of the use of the property." This case was followed in The Electron, 2 Cir., 1896, 74 F. 689.

It has also been held that the vendee of patent rights cannot maintain, as against an action for the price, the defense that he rescinded because he had been notified by a third party that the patent was an infringement and that he would be held liable therefor. In Tinsman v. Independent Harvester Co., 1917, 205 Ill.App. 239 it was held that the vendee must show the actual invalidity of the patent, or at least that he had been enjoined after reasonable defense.

The rule has been well put in the case of Computing Scales Co. v. Long, 66 S.C. 379, 44 S.E. 963, 964, 65 L.R.A. 294. There the court said: "If, however, the vendor at the time of the sale knew of a valid outstanding title or incumbrance, and failed to give notice to the vendee, the element of fraud is introduced, and the vendee may rescind without waiting for actual loss to come to him. . . . But mere dispute about the title, or the contingency of future loss, does not warrant a rescission, and, where the buyer returns the goods, and refuses to pay the purchase money, it is incumbent on him to show that there is a valid adverse claim, from which loss to him would inevitably occur. . . . The application of the rule may sometimes result in hardship, but to adopt any other would make it possible for a purchaser to escape from his contract upon any claim coming to his notice, however baseless or absurd it might be."

The above rules should be even more strictly applied in the sale of literary property and no court should be led into the pitfall of the real estate rule. In Golding v. R. K. O. Pictures, Inc., 1950, 35 Cal.2d 690, 710, 221 P.2d 95, Justice Schauer of the Supreme Court of California refers to the fact that there are approximately thirty-six basic plots in all writing. Consequently, assertions of similarity and of plagiarism are practically a concomitant of all story writing. To establish then, a rule permitting the purchaser of literary property to return the property and demand back the purchase price upon a mere assertion of similarity or plagiarism is to create a right without the support of reason or principle, the exercise of which would result in untold hardship. There can be no other conclusion but that the law will not imply a warranty of "marketable" title in the sale of literary property.

Since it is the opinion of this court that there was neither an express nor implied warranty of "marketability of title", the second cause of action is accordingly disposed of. Consequently, the third and fifth causes of action which are predicated upon there being a warranty of "marketable" title must likewise fail.

II.

Are Defendants Obligated to Reimburse Plaintiff for Any Expenses Incurred in This Suit Under Provision 6, of the "Assignment."

Plaintiff's sixth cause of action is predicated upon the theory that regardless of the outcome of the other causes of action, defendants have agreed, by virtue of provision 6 of the "Assignment of Rights" to "indemnify, make good and hold harmless the purchaser of, from and against any and all loss, damage, costs, charges, legal fees, recoveries, judgments, penalties and expenses which may be obtained against, imposed upon or suffered by the purchaser by reason of any infringement or violation or alleged violation of any copyright or any other right of any person, firm or corporation, or by reason of or from any use which may be made of said work by the purchaser, or by reason of the breach of any term, covenant, representation, or warranty herein contained, or by reason of anything whatsoever which might prejudice the securing to the purchaser of the full benefit of the rights herein granted and/or purported to be granted."

Plaintiff contends that by bringing this action they have incurred legal expenses and costs and that the story has become valueless because they have not used it according to their planned schedules, and that because of this loss and expense, defendants are liable under the above provision.

The answer to this contention lies in well established rules pertaining to the interpretation of contracts. The basic question is, "What was the intent of the parties"? Did defendants agree to reimburse plaintiff for any action brought by plaintiff against defendants, or any loss which plaintiff might inadvisably cause itself to suffer? We think not. The more logical interpretation would be that defendants agreed to reimburse plaintiff in the event the plaintiff were forced to defend an action brought by some third party. The plaintiff here was notified of the action filed in the California Superior Court. They refused to come in as party defendants. They expended no money in the defense of that action and incurred no loss thereby.

The expenses and any other loss which plaintiff might have incurred by bringing this action are self-imposed, and defendants are not liable therefor.

Supplemental Reading

Wrench v. Universal Pictures Co., 104 F. Supp. 374 (S.D.N.Y. 1952) (contract for sale of motion picture rights in stories may contain an implied warranty of marketability of title in the property even though no such warranty is formally expressed).

Official Comment to U.C.C. § 2–312(1)(a).

Part II

ENTERTAINMENT INDUSTRY AGREEMENTS

COLLECTIVE BARGAINING AGREEMENTS

DIRECTORS GUILD
OF AMERICA, INC.

———

BASIC AGREEMENT
OF 1973

Article 2

DISPUTES

Section 2–100 MATTERS SUBJECT TO ARBITRATION PROCEDURES

2–101

The following matters shall be subject to Arbitration Procedures as described in Section 2–400, except as otherwise provided in this Article:

(a) Alleged violations of the terms of the Basic Agreement.

(b) Disputes concerning interpretation of the terms of the Basic Agreement.

(c) Money claims for unpaid compensation.

Section 2–200 GENERAL

2–201 Courts

Nothing herein contained shall be construed to prevent, as between individual employer and employee, or the Guild, as the case may be, recourse to the courts at any time prior to the happening of any of the following events: (a) a final determination of the dispute by the Grievance Procedure or in any other manner, (b) mutual agreement to arbitrate, and (c) with respect to the employee if the Guild and the Employer have mutually agreed to arbitrate the same issue, question or matter.

2–202 Arbitration Requirement

Employer and the Guild will be bound to arbitrate any issue, question or matter arising between them under this Basic Agreement if arbitrable hereunder, except that neither the Employer nor the Guild shall be required to agree to such an arbitration in any case, (other than with respect to Directors creative rights as provided in Section 7–1500 [not included in this casebook]), where the Employer or the Guild feels that the issue, question or matter can best be determined by a court.

2–203 Rights

The pendency of any mutually agreed arbitration procedure shall not be deemed a waiver or limitation or suspension of any of the employee's or Employer's rights of suspension, termination or injunction except to the extent, if any, that such a waiver, limitation or suspension is required by and specifically agreed to in the agreement to arbitrate.

2–204 Additional Provisions Relating to Directors Creative Rights and Credits

With respect to additional arbitration provisions relating to the Directors Creative Rights, see Section 7–1500 [not included in this casebook], and with respect to credits, see Section 8–200 [casebook pp. 488–489].

Section 2–300 GRIEVANCE PROCEDURES

2–301 Matters Subject to Grievance Procedures

All matters of every sort concerning which dissatisfaction may arise between the Employer and the Guild or between the Employer and any person subject to this Agreement, shall be referred to the Grievance Procedures for full and friendly discussion, except matters pertaining to revisions or modifications of this Basic Agreement. Any matter with respect to which a party intends to request arbitration or institute court proceedings, except those involving suspension, termination or injunction, shall first be submitted to Grievance Procedures.

2–302 The Grievance Procedure

Within five (5) business days after written request by the Guild, an employee, or an Employer for a Grievance Procedure, an authorized representative of the Guild and an authorized representative of the Employer shall meet and in good faith attempt to settle and adjust the difference or dispute. If the matter shall not have been brought to a meeting as aforesaid within five (5) business days or shall not have been settled or adjusted to each party's mutual satisfaction within four (4) business days after said meeting, the Grievance Procedure may be deemed terminated and any party to the Grievance Procedure may proceed to request an arbitration pursuant to Paragraph 2–401 or may proceed in court.

Section 2–400 ARBITRATION

2–401 Procedures

If a dispute is not settled pursuant to the Grievance Procedure provided for in Paragraph 2–302 hereof, the Guild or the employee or the Employer, whichever is making the claim, may deliver to the other party or parties to the Grievance Procedure a written statement of the claim, which statement shall set forth the material facts and the alleged contract breach or violation involved and which statement shall request the other party's agreement to have the matter arbitrated. At the time of delivering the statement of claim, the claimant shall designate in writing the arbitrator selected by it. Within seven days thereafter, exclusive of Saturdays, Sundays, and holidays, the respondent shall by notice in writing indicate whether or not it agrees to proceed by arbitration, and, if agreeable to having the matter arbitrated, shall designate in writing the arbitrator selected by it. The two arbitrators so selected shall endeavor to agree upon a third arbitrator within a period of one week after the designation of the second arbitrator. If a third arbitrator is not agreed upon within such period, the third arbitrator shall be appointed by and pursuant to the rules of the American Arbitration Association upon the written request of either claimant or respondent. The rules of procedure in the arbitration shall be the applicable rules as then currently published and in effect of the American Arbitration Association, except to the extent that the same may be inconsistent with the provisions of this Article 2.

2–402 Decision and Award

In any arbitration pursuant to the provisions hereof the decision and award of the majority of the arbitrators shall be binding and conclusive upon all parties to said arbitration, including the individual employee involved, and any party thereto may have the award confirmed and made a judgment of a court of competent jurisdiction.

2–403 Costs and Expenses

The cost and expense of the arbitration shall be shared equally by the Guild or the individual member, if any, on the one hand, and the Employer on the other.

. . . .

Article 8

DIRECTORS' CREDITS FOR THEATRICAL MOTION PICTURES

. . . .

Section 8–200 ARBITRATION

8–201

Any dispute with respect to the credit provisions of Article 8 [for comparable provisions, in 1981 DGA Basic Agreement, see casebook pp. 502–503] shall be submitted to arbitration but not to grievance subject to the following provisions:

(a) The Guild shall act on behalf of itself and the Director or Directors.

(b) Within 24 hours after the Guild serves written notice upon the Employer of an alleged breach of such credit provisions an authorized representative of the Guild and an authorized representative of the Employer will meet in a good faith attempt to settle or resolve the dispute.

(c) In the event the parties shall fail to meet or shall otherwise fail to settle or resolve the dispute within 24 hours of the commencement of the meeting first held in accordance with Subparagraph (b) above, said dispute shall be submitted directly to arbitration, said arbitration to be commenced not later than five business days after the service of the written notice provided for in Subparagraph (b) above.

(d) The dispute shall be submitted to a single neutral arbitrator mutually selected from an authorized list of arbitrators to be approved by the parties hereto and made a part hereof.

In the event the parties are unable, within 48 hours after the service of the written notice provided for in Subparagraph (b) above, to agree upon a neutral arbitrator from the above list or otherwise, the arbitrator will automatically be the person next in sequence on the above list following the person last selected from said list to serve in such an arbitration and who is available and willing to serve and who is not disqualified because of personal interest or representation of a party having a personal interest in the dispute.

(e) Notwithstanding anything in this Basic Agreement to the contrary, the arbitrator shall have jurisdiction and power to award damages and/or to require the Employer to withdraw, cancel, change or re-do advertising materials already issued or prepared, or to require the company to change or re-do any film titles, or to order any other reasonable relief the arbitrator deems appropriate in the circumstances, whether relating to credit on the screen, in advertising or otherwise. Any award rendered by the arbitrator shall be binding on the parties hereto and upon the employee or employees involved and upon the loan-out company, if one is involved.

(f) Any court of competent jurisdiction may confirm, set aside, or modify any arbitration award hereunder in any proceeding brought for such purpose in accordance with applicable law.

(g) Any or all time limits set forth herein may be waived by the mutual consent of the parties.

(h) To the extent not inconsistent herewith, all other provisions of this Basic Agreement relating to arbitrations shall be applicable.

. . . .

DIRECTORS GUILD
OF AMERICA, INC.

BASIC AGREEMENT
OF 1981

Article 2

DISPUTES

Section 2–100 MATTERS SUBJECT TO GRIEVANCE AND ARBITRATION

2–101 Arbitrability

The following matters shall be subject to arbitration: All grievances, disputes or controversies over the interpretation or application of the BA and, in addition, all grievances, disputes or controversies over the interpretation or application of any Employee's personal services contract or deal memo with respect to (1) credit provisions, (2) cutting rights provisions, (3) preview rights provisions, (4) creative rights provisions (including, without limitation, all consultation and/or approval rights of any kind relating to any motion picture), (5) money claims for unpaid compensation seeking $300,000 or less, (6) cash per diem payments for Employees only; provided, however, that grievances, disputes or controversies over the interpretation or application of any personal service contract or deal memo shall not be arbitrable if they relate to (a) perquisites such as per diem (except as provided above), travel arrangements, secretarial services and the like, (b) compensation measured by net or gross proceeds, or (c) other provisions not referred to in (1) through (6) hereinabove.

The Arbitrator shall determine any dispute as to the arbitrability of any matter hereunder.

2–102 Limitation on Arbitrator's Power

The Arbitrator shall not have the power to vary, alter, modify or amend any of the terms of the BA or of any deal memo or personal service contract in making a decision or award.

2–103 Defenses, Setoffs and Counterclaims

(a) In any grievance or arbitration concerning a claim for unpaid compensation under an Employee's deal memo or personal service contract, the Employer may assert any and all defenses, counterclaims and setoffs, including any defenses based on a claim of suspension or termination.

(b) In any grievance or arbitration concerning a claim for unpaid minimum compensation under the BA only, the Employer may, but need not, assert any and all defenses including any defense based on a claim of suspension or termination and may, but need not assert any setoff or counterclaim not exceeding the amount claimed by the Guild. It is expressly agreed that any award by the Arbitrator concerning the matter at issue in such arbitration shall not be binding, res judicata or serve as collateral estoppel upon either the

Employer or Employee in any separate arbitration or court proceeding brought by the Employer or Employee, except that (i) the amount of any award and the amount of any setoff or counterclaim shall be credited against any liability of Employer to Employee or vice versa and (ii) Employer may not assert any claim, counterclaim or setoff against Employee in any subsequent arbitration or court proceeding if such matter was asserted in the arbitration, except to the extent the amount exceeds the amount claimed by the Guild in the arbitration.

Section 2–200 GRIEVANCE PROCEDURE

2–201 Time Limits

The Guild or an Employer may file a grievance over any matter subject to the disputes procedure of this Article 2; provided, however, that a joint filing by the Guild and the Employee shall be required if the grievance relates to arbitrable matters in the personal service contract or deal memo in excess of BA minimums, and provided further, however, that any grievance must be filed on or before the earlier of:

(a) Eighteen (18) months following the date on which the facts upon which the claim is based were discovered by the party bringing the grievance or arbitration proceeding; or

(b) Four (4) years following the date on which the event in dispute occurred.

2–202 Grievance Notice

The grievance shall be in writing, state the essential facts of the claim and refer to the contractual provisions alleged to have been breached.

2–203 Grievance Meeting

Within ten (10) working days after the filing of the grievance, an authorized representative of the Guild and an authorized representative of the Employer shall meet and attempt to settle the dispute or difference.

Section 2–300 ARBITRATION PROCEDURE

2–301 Parties

In any grievance or arbitration hereunder, only the Guild and the Employer shall be parties, except that in any grievance or arbitration involving claims for unpaid compensation under, or other arbitrable violations of, a personal service contract or deal memo, the Employee involved and the Employee's loan-out company, if any, shall also be parties.

2–302 Demand for Arbitration

If the dispute or difference is not settled at the meeting described in

Paragraph 2–203 above, or if the other party refuses or fails to meet, the party aggrieved (hereinafter "claimant") may deliver to the other party (hereinafter "respondent") a written demand for arbitration which shall set forth the basis of the dispute, the material facts, the position of the claimant, and the relief sought. Such demand must be served not later than sixty (60) days after the filing of the grievance. The arbitration shall proceed as described in the Arbitration Procedure set forth below.

2–203   Respondent's Statement of Its Position

The respondent shall promptly, within five (5) business days following receipt of the demand for arbitration, inform the claimant (the Guild in the case of a joint filing) of its representative and serve a written statement of its position.

2–304   Selection of the Arbitrator

(a) Within five (5) business days following the respondent's receipt of the demand for arbitration, the parties will attempt to mutually agree upon an Arbitrator. If the parties do not mutually agree upon an Arbitrator, the Arbitrator shall be selected from the following list of persons in rotation on an Employer by Employer basis.

LOS ANGELES	NEW YORK
Hermione Brown	James V. Altieri
Arnold Burk	Maurice C. Benewitz
Roger Davis	Milton Friedman
Dixon Dern	Walter Gelhorn
Martin Gang	Daniel House
Joseph Gentile	Mathew Kelly
Sam Kagel*	George Nicolau
Edward Mosk	Jesse Simons
Melville Nimmer	Janet Spencer
Sol Rosenthal	Arthur Stark
Arthur Rosett	
Murray Schwartz	
Charles Silverberg	
Myron D. Slobodien	
Payson Wolff	
Kenneth Ziffren	

Other Arbitrators may be added from time to time by mutual agreement between the Guild and the Employer.

---

*Not available for Expedited Arbitrations

(b) From July 1, 1981, to and including January 1, 1983, the Arbitrator shall be selected in rotation on an Employer by Employer basis starting from the top of the list down, and during the remainder of the term of this BA the Arbitrator shall be selected in rotation on the same basis starting from the bottom of the list up.

(c) If no person on the list is available to hear the dispute, an Arbitrator shall be mutually selected by the Guild and the Employer. If they fail to agree, the Federal Mediation and Conciliation Service shall select the Arbitrator.

(d) If more than one Employer is named as a respondent in any arbitration complaint, the Arbitrator selected shall be the one next in line from the list of the Employer most recently a party to any arbitration.

(e) Within five (5) business days following receipt by respondent(s) of the demand for arbitration the claimant(s) and the respondent(s) shall each have the right to exercise one (1) peremptory challenge of one of the two Arbitrators whose names are next in order on the list immediately following the name of the Arbitrator last selected.

(f) If the Arbitrator selected cannot serve, a substitute shall be selected in accordance with the procedure set forth in paragraphs (a), (b), (c) and (d), except the parties need not attempt to mutually agree on the substitute Arbitrator.

2–305 Situs of Arbitration

All arbitrations shall be in Los Angeles, absent agreement by the parties, except that they shall be in New York if the personal service agreement out of which the dispute arose was negotiated, entered into and production was based in New York and a majority of the witnesses required for the arbitration hearing reside regularly in and around the New York area. Any dispute as to where the arbitration should be held shall be determined by an Arbitrator in Los Angeles selected according to the method set forth herein. If the Arbitrator determines that Los Angeles is the proper situs for the arbitration, he or she shall hear the merits thereof, provided he or she is available.

2–306 Notification to Arbitrator

The claimant(s) shall notify the Arbitrator of his or her selection in writing with a copy to each respondent and at the same time furnish the Arbitrator with a copy of the BA, a copy of the demand for arbitration and the name, address and telephone number of the person who will represent the claimant(s) in the arbitration hearing.

2–307 Hearing

(a) Upon receipt of the demand for arbitration, the Arbitrator shall forthwith set the date for the arbitration hearing after contacting the parties' representatives for their available dates. If possible, the date for the hearing shall be within 15 to 30 days after the demand for the arbitration. The Arbitrator shall notify the parties of the time and place of the arbitration hearing.

(b) The arbitration hearing shall take place on the scheduled date. If either party fails to appear, the Arbitrator is specifically authorized and empowered to hear the matter on the evidence of the appearing party and enter an award based on such evidence.

(c) Each party shall bear the costs of presenting its own case. The fees of the Arbitrator and the hearing shall be allocated by the Arbitrator in his or her sound discretion.

(d) All hearings and deliberations conducted pursuant to the grievance and arbitration provisions of this Article 2 shall be closed to the public. Only authorized representatives of the Guild and Employer or witnesses called by the Arbitrator or by either party may attend.

(e) All written communication to and from the Arbitrator or writings filed in connection with the arbitration proceedings and all testimony and arguments at the arbitration shall be privileged.

2–308   Exchange of Information

The parties will cooperate in the exchange of information reasonably in advance of the hearing date regarding the expected utilization of documents and physical evidence. The introduction of documents or physical evidence shall not be precluded because they were not exchanged in advance of the hearing.

2–309   Award

The award of the Arbitrator shall be promptly furnished to the parties in writing and shall be final and binding on the Guild, the Employee and the Employer. An arbitration award interpreting any of the terms of this BA thereafter shall be binding upon the Guild and the Employer; provided, however, that in any subsequent arbitration between the Guild and the Employer involving an interpretation of the same term or terms of the BA, the Arbitrator may determine whether or not, as a result of the different combination of facts, the prior arbitration award is relevant or determinative of the issue in such subsequent arbitration.

Section 2–400   EXPEDITED ARBITRATION PROCEDURE

2–401

Notwithstanding any other provision of the BA, any personal service contract or any deal memo, the following Expedited Arbitration Procedure shall be followed if in the opinion of a party a grievance will become moot or damages will be increased by reason of delay if processed through the above Grievance and Arbitration Procedure.

(a) A Notice of Expedited Arbitration (so labeled by the claimant) shall be reduced to writing and given to the respondent and the first available Arbitrator listed in subparagraph 2–304 (a) who can hear the matter within two business days following the filing of the Notice of Expedited Arbitration. The Notice of Expedited Arbitration shall include the name, address and telephone number of the claimant's representative(s) and the name of the person who represents the respondent. A copy of the BA and any applicable available personal service contract and/or deal memo shall be given to the Expedited Arbitrator along with the Notice of Expedited Arbitration.

(b) Upon receipt of the Notice of Expedited Arbitration, the Arbitrator shall, by telephone or telegraph, notify the parties of the time and place of the Expedited Arbitration hearing.

(c) An Expedited Arbitration hearing shall not be continued, absent agreement of the parties, except upon proof of good cause by the party requesting such continuance. The unavailability of any witness shall not constitute good cause unless the witness' testimony is relevant to the issues in the arbitration and could not be received by means consistent with fundamental fairness which do not require the witness' presence at the hearing.

(d) Paragraphs 2–101, 2–102, 2–103, 2–201, 2–301, 2–304 (b) through (d), 2–305, 2–307 (b) through (e) and 2–309 of this Article 2 shall be applicable to this Expedited Arbitration Procedure, except that:

    (i)   the Expedited Arbitration hearing shall be commenced not later than on the second business day next following receipt of the Notice of Expedited Arbitration;

    (ii)   the Arbitrator's written award shall be issued with two (2) business days from the end of the Expedited Arbitration hearing; but failure to meet the deadline shall not oust the Arbitrator of jurisdiction; and

    (iii)   the award shall be served on the parties by messenger.

(e) Nothing contained in this Expedited Arbitration Procedure shall preclude the parties from discussing the settlement of the Expedited Arbitration, except that such discussion shall not delay the Expedited Arbitration Procedure.

(f) The failure of the claimant to serve the Notice of Expedited Arbitration within ten (10) business days following the date on which the facts upon which the claim is based were discovered by the party bringing the Expedited Arbitration shall constitute a waiver of the right to this Expedited Arbitration Procedure. If two or more claims are submitted to Expedited Arbitration and the Expedited Arbitration Procedure has been waived or is inapplicable to one or more claims, the same Arbitrator may determine the claims not subject to Expedited Arbitration, provided that such non-Expedited Arbitration claim or claims shall be determined in accordance with the regular Arbitration Proceedings, unless the parties agree otherwise.

(g) Any party to any arbitration hereunder may, if the circumstances hereinabove set forth exist, require that the arbitration be conducted as an expedited arbitration by serving appropriate notice to that effect.

(h) If the Expedited Arbitration involves multiple disputes or controversies the Expedited Arbitrator may, upon the request of a party, bifurcate or separate such disputes or controversies and render separate awards, each of which shall be deemed final.

Section 2–500 ARBITRAL REMEDIES

2–501 Authority of Arbitrator

The Arbitrator shall have the authority to grant or award one or more of money damages, orders to withdraw, cancel, change or re-do advertising material already issued or prepared, or to require Employer to change or re-do any film titles, or to order back pay or reinstatement, or to order any other reasonable relief the Arbitrator deems appropriate in the circumstances, whether relating to credit on the screen or in advertising or any other arbitrable matter, in the event the Arbitrator finds a breach of the BA or of those provisions of the personal service contract or the deal memo which are subject to arbitration pursuant to the provisions of Paragraph 2–101 hereof.

2–502 Consideration for Determining Remedies

In determining the appropriate remedy, the Arbitrator shall take into account such evidence as may be adduced by the claimant of similar prior violations by the respondent. The Arbitrator shall also take into account evidence of failure on the part of the claimant to notify the respondent promptly of the violation, and evidence of inadvertent breach.

2–503 Compliance with Arbitrator's Award

Should the Arbitrator issue an award which in whole or part is not self-executing, and a party fails to comply with such award, the party aggrieved thereby may, but need not, submit the matter to the Arbitrator who issued the award.

Section 2–600 COURT PROCEEDINGS

2–601 Arbitration Exclusive Remedy

Arbitration hereunder shall be the exclusive remedy in connection with claims for violation by the Employee, Guild or the Employer of the provisions of the BA and of the arbitrable provisions of any personal service contract or deal memo other than claims for compensation.

2–602 Claims for Compensation

(a) The Employee shall have the right, prior to commencement of an arbitration by any party entitled thereto, to commence action in any court of competent jurisdiction with respect to unpaid compensation in any amount, and in any event regarding the non-arbitrable portions of Employee's personal service contract. Upon the filing of such action, the further operation of the procedures and remedies described in this Article 2 shall cease to apply to such dispute. The Guild shall have the right, but not the obligation, to be party in any such action in court.

(b) The Guild shall have the right to take to grievance and arbitration any claim by the Guild of an Employer's breach of the BA, including a failure to pay minimum compensation, regardless of whether or not such claimed breach may also involve a breach by the Company of its contract with the Employee. Such proceeding shall not affect the right of the Employee to pursue remedies at law or in equity, except as limited by the provisions of the BA.

(c) If the Employee and the Guild make a claim for unpaid compensation in an arbitration proceeding, then to the extent of any unpaid non-contingent compensation in excess of $300,000, collection of such excess from the Employer shall be deemed waived. No Employee shall have the right to commence court proceedings to collect any unpaid compensation for which claim has been made in arbitration, including, but not limited to, compensation in excess of the jurisdictional amount of $300,000.

2–603 Petition to Confirm, Vacate or Modify Award

(a) Nothing in the BA shall preclude any court of competent jurisdiction from confirming, setting aside or modifying any award hereunder in accordance with applicable law.

(b) Service of a petition to confirm, set aside or modify an arbitration award hereunder may be served by certified or registered mail, return receipt requested.

Section 2–700 WITHDRAWAL OF SERVICES

2–701

Notwithstanding any provision of any personal service contract, deal memo or of the BA to the contrary, it shall not be a violation thereof for the Guild or any Employee (at the direction of the Guild) to withhold services from the Employer if the Employer fails or refuses to abide by the final award of any Arbitrator for any reason whatsoever.

. . . .

Article 4

DIRECTOR'S FREELANCE CONTRACTS

. . . .

4–110 Prohibition Against Credits and Offsets

Overscale cannot be used to credit or offset in any manner any payments required to be made to the Director. The only exception to the prohibition against crediting or offset of monies in excess of scale is the right of Employer to negotiate with the Director to credit or offset residuals against monies in excess of 200% of scale. However, the foregoing exception shall not be applicable to any residual or other additional compensation required to be paid under Article 20 of this BA.

No prepayment of residuals will be permitted unless set forth in the "deal memorandum" in the specific amounts which are to be prepaid. Residual compensation shall not otherwise be prepaid. Any prepayment of residual compensation shall be sent to the Director in care of the Guild and not combined with the other payments for his or her services.

The provisions of this Section shall be applicable only to "deal memoranda" and contracts of employment entered into after the date of execution of this BA.

. . . .

Article 6

SUSPENSION AND TERMINATION OF DIRECTORS

6–101

Except as expressly provided in this Article, the provisions of this BA with reference to the obligation of the Employer to furnish employment for the respective "guarantee" periods specified, or to provide for payment of salary in aggregate amounts herein specified, shall, of course, be subject to any and all rights of suspension and/or termination which the Employer may have by contract or otherwise in the event of any incapacity or default of the Director or, in the case of any interference, suspension or postponement of production by reason of strikes, acts of God, governmental action, regulations or decrees, casualties, or any other causes provided for in the so-called "force majeure" clause of such Director's contract of employment or the force majeure provisions of this BA. No suspension or termination of Director's services shall be permitted or effected by Employer under such force majeure clause or provisions unless the entire cast and the Director of Photography of the picture are likewise suspended or terminated, as the case may be. Subject to such rights of suspension and/or termination, the obligation of the Employer upon entering into a contract for the employment of a Freelance Director to furnish employment during any of the foregoing "guarantee" periods of employment shall be wholly satisfied by the payment of the agreed salary for the applicable minimum period. With respect to only theatrical motion pictures, or television films 61 minutes or more in length, the illness or incapacity for one week or less of a member of the cast or any other person in connection with the picture, shall not be considered "force majeure." With respect to television motion pictures: If the Director is employed on a film under 61 minutes in length, and he is suspended by reason of illness or incapacity of a member of the cast or any other person connected with the picture, then the Director may forthwith terminate the employment, but if such termination occurs the Employer may thereafter employ the same or another Director to fulfill the remaining portion of the guaranteed period of employment. The Employer further agrees that if despite such suspension the star of the picture or the Director of Photography is paid in whole or in part with respect to such picture, then the Director will be paid in the same pro rata amount as the star or the Director of Photography is paid. If there is a difference in the proportionate amount paid to the star and the Director of Photography then the higher proportionate amount shall be paid to the Director. The foregoing provision shall not apply to the continuation of payments to a term player or Director of Photography who is carried by the Employer under the provisions of a term contract.

. . . .

6–105 Payment To and Mitigation By Discharged Employees

If a Director is removed from a motion picture, the Employer shall forthwith deliver to the Guild for the Director all remaining unpaid non-deferred, non-contingent compensation as provided by the personal services agreement or deal memo.

If Employer disputes its obligation to pay said compensation to the Director, the amount in dispute shall be deposited with a mutually acceptable bank or other third party designated by an Arbitrator. Such escrow agent shall distribute the amount deposited, together with interest accumulated, if any, according to the provisions of any settlement agreement or, if the dispute is not settled, according to the award of an Arbitrator or judgment of a court of law.

If the Director is employed by third parties during the remaining period during which the Director was guaranteed employment in the motion picture, Employer shall be entitled to an offset of the compensation arising from such new employment for such remaining portion of the guaranteed period against the compensation remaining unpaid under the earlier agreement. Under the described circumstances, the Guild guarantees repayment from the Director to the extent herein provided. Employer agrees that the Director shall have no obligation to mitigate damages arising from his or her removal and that the only obligation of the Director in such event will be to repay or offset sums as herein set forth if the Director, in his or her sole discretion, actually accepts employment during the remaining guaranteed period of the motion picture.

. . . .

Article 8

DIRECTORS' CREDITS

. . . .

Section 8–200 CREDIT FOR DIRECTORS OF THEATRICAL MOTION PICTURES

8–201 Screen Credit

The Director shall be given credit on all positive prints in size of type not less than 50% of the size in which the title of the motion picture is displayed or of the largest size in which credit is accorded to any other person, whichever is greater, and no other credit shall appear on such card which shall be the last title card appearing prior to principal photography. If more than one Director is given such credit, in accordance with the provisions of Paragraph 8–101, then such 50% may be reduced to 30% for each. The Employer shall furnish to the Guild copies of the main and end titles as soon as the same are prepared in final form but before the prints are made for the purpose of checking compliance with the credit provisions of this BA. After such copies are furnished, there can be no changes relating to the term Director, Direction or any derivation thereof, without first giving the Guild notice of such proposed changes or elimination.

. . . .

8–203 Credits on Paid Advertising

The Employer shall accord credit for direction of a motion picture on all paid advertising issued or prepared by the Employer in the continental United States and prepared subsequent to final determination of directorial credit in the manner herein provided, it being understood that in such advertising prepared or issued prior to such final determination the Employer shall include such credit for direction as the Employer may in good faith believe to be proper, and if this varies from the credits as finally determined, then it will not be used subsequent to such determination, to the extent not theretofore distributed.

Copies of these credits as determined, with respect to motion pictures covered hereunder, shall be sent to all of the Employer's foreign sales and distribution offices, if any.

The foregoing obligations of Employer are subject to the following:

a. Size and Location of Credit

Except as stated otherwise in this Section 8–200, the location of the Director's credit shall be discretionary with the Employer, and the size of type of the Director's credit shall be no less than 15% of the size of type used for the title of the motion picture, but in no event less than the size and style of type for any credit accorded any persons other than actors.

. . . .

e. "Trade Paper" Advertising

The Director shall receive credit in size of type not less than 30% the size of type used for the title of the motion picture in any United States motion picture industry trade paper advertisement.

. . . .

g. Exceptions

(i) Subject to the provisions of (ii) below, none of the foregoing obligations under this Section 8–203 shall apply:

1) to group advertising, *i.e.*, where more than one motion picture is advertised;

2) to so-called "teaser" advertising, as that term is used in the motion picture industry;

3) to "trailer" advertising, as that term is used in the motion picture industry. Notwithstanding the foregoing, if credit is given for film or camera process (such as Panavision, Techni-

color or DeLuxe), or if the individual producer or writer is mentioned, then the Director's name shall be mentioned;

4) to other advertising on the screen, radio, or television, not to exceed (1) minute;

5) to special advertising relating only to the source material on which the motion picture is based, or to the author, or any member of the cast, or the individual producer, or any other personnel concerned in its production, or similar matters.

(ii) None of the exceptions under (i) above shall apply and the name of the Director shall also be mentioned if the name of any person other than two starring actors is mentioned, in any of the advertising listed above, with the exception only of congratulatory advertising or award advertising where no one is mentioned other than the person being congratulated or mentioned for the award.

. . . .

Article 11

ADDITIONAL COMPENSATION TO DIRECTORS FOR "FREE" TELEVISION FILMS

Section 11–100 ADDITIONAL COMPENSATION FOR RERUNS AND FOREIGN TELECASTS

. . . .

11–102 Foreign Telecasting Payments

(a) If the Employer desires to telecast any television motion picture in any part of the world outside the United States and Canada, the Employer shall pay additional compensation for such foreign telecasting of not less than 15% of the applicable "base amount" in effect on the date of commencement of principal photography, not later than 30 days after the Employer obtains knowledge of the first foreign telecast.

(b) When the Distributor's Foreign Gross, as defined herein, of any such television motion picture has exceeded $7,000 for a one-half hour picture, $13,000 for a one-hour picture, or $18,000 if such picture is one and one-half hours or more in length, the Director shall be entitled to the additional payment of not less than 10% of the applicable "base amount" in effect on the date of commencement of principal photography, not later than thirty (30) days after such Gross has been so exceeded.

(c) When the Distributor's Foreign Gross of any such television motion picture has exceeded $10,000 for a one-half hour picture, $18,000 for a one-hour picture, or $24,000 if such picture is one and one-half hours or more in length, the Director shall be entitled to the additional payment of not less than 10% of the applicable "base amount" in effect on the date of the commencement of principal photography, not later than thirty (30) days after such Gross has been so exceeded.

(d) The "base amounts" referred to and the applicable payments under subparagraphs (a), (b) and (c) above are as follows:

Effective Dates

Length of Program	7/1/81 Residual Base - % and Amount	7/1/82 Residual Base - % and Amount	7/1/83 Residual Base - % and Amount
7 minutes & under	748	838	930
	15% = 112	15% = 126	15% = 140
	10% = 75	10% = 84	10% = 93
	10% = 75	10% = 84	10% = 93
8–15 minutes	1,562	1,750	1,942
	15% = 234	15% = 263	15% = 291
	10% = 156	10% = 175	10% = 194
	10% = 156	10% = 175	10% = 194
16–30 minutes ·	3,872	4,336	4,813
	15% = 581	15% = 650	15% = 722
	10% = 387	10% = 434	10% = 481
	10% = 387	10% = 434	10% = 481
31–60 minutes	6,997	7,836	8,698
	15% = 1,050	15% = 1,176	15% = 1,305
	10% = 700	10% = 784	10% = 870
	10% = 700	10% = 784	10% = 870
61–90 minutes	10,121	11,336	12,583
	15% = 1,518	15% = 1,700	15% = 1,887
	10% = 1,012	10% = 1,134	10% = 1,258
	10% = 1,012	10% = 1,134	10% = 1,258

Length of Program	7/1/81 Residual Base - % and Amount	7/1/82 Residual Base - % and Amount	7/1/83 Residual Base - % and Amount
91–120 minutes*	13,246	14,836	16,468
	15% = 1,987	15% = 2,225	15% = 2,470
	10% = 1,325	10% = 1,484	10% = 1,647
	10% = 1,325	10% = 1,484	10% = 1,647

* Over 120 minutes, prorate payment based on 1 hour rate.

(e) After the Director has received a total of the amounts specified in subparagraphs (a), (b), and (c) above with respect to any picture, no further sums shall be payable for foreign telecasting of such picture.

(f) The term "foreign telecasting," as used herein, shall mean any telecast (whether simultaneous or delayed) outside the United States, its territories and possessions, and Canada other than a telecast on any of the following regularly affiliated stations of a United States television network as a part of the United States network television telecast: XEW–TV or XEQ–TV or XHTV or XHGC–TV, Mexico City; and ZBM, Pembroke, Bermuda, for CBS and NBC; and any network affiliate in Tijuana; and ZBF, Hamilton, Bermuda, for ABC.

(g) As used herein, the term "Distributor's Foreign Gross" shall mean, with respect to any television motion picture, the absolute gross income realized by the distributor of such picture for the foreign telecasting thereof and including, in the case of a "foreign territorial sale" by any such distributor, the income realized from such sale by such distributor but not the income realized by the "purchaser" or "licensee." The phrase "absolute gross income" shall not include:

(i) Sums realized or held by the way of deposits or security, until and unless earned, other than such sums as are non-returnable.

(ii) Sums required to be paid or withheld as taxes, in the nature of turnover taxes, sales taxes or similar taxes based on the actual receipts of the picture or on any monies to be remitted to or by the distributor, but there shall not be excluded from Distributor's Foreign Gross any net income, franchise tax or excess profit tax or similar tax payable by the distributor on its net income or for the privilege of doing business.

(iii) Frozen foreign currency until the distributor shall have either the right to use such foreign currency in or to transmit such foreign currency from the country or territory where it is frozen. In the event such currency may be utilized or transmitted as aforesaid, it shall be deemed to have been converted to United States dollars at the prevailing free market rate of exchange at the time such right to use or transmit accrues.

Distributor's Foreign Gross realized in foreign currency in any reporting period required hereunder shall be deemed to be converted to United States dollars at the prevailing free market rate of exchange at the close of such reporting period.

If any transaction involving any picture subject to a foreign telecast payment under this BA shall also include motion pictures, broadcast time, broadcast facilities or material (including commercial or advertising material) which are not subject to such payment, there shall be a reasonable allocation between the television motion pictures which are subject to foreign telecast payment and such other pictures, time, facilities or material, and only the sums properly allocable to pictures which are subject to a foreign telecast payment shall be included in the Distributor's Foreign Gross.

(h) The above formula for foreign telecasting is a minimum formula, and nothing herein shall preclude any Director from bargaining for better terms with respect to such foreign telecasting.

. . . .

Section 11–200 ADDITIONAL COMPENSATION FOR THEATRICAL EXHIBITION

11–201

Additional compensation shall immediately accrue and be payable to the Director of a television film when such film is used for theatrical exhibition as follows (excepting the "bridging" of television films for theatrical release, trailers, promos or Second Units, for which there will be no additional compensation):

If a television film is exhibited theatrically outside of the United States and Canada, then upon the release of such television film for theatrical exhibition the Director shall be paid an amount equal to One Hundred Percent (100%) of the applicable theatrical minimum. If such film is released theatrically in the United States or Canada the Director shall be paid One Hundred Fifty Percent (150%) of such applicable theatrical minimum; provided, however, that the maximum payment under the provisions of this Paragraph 11–201 for theatrical release of a television film shall be One Hundred Fifty Percent (150%) of applicable theatrical minimum.

The foregoing shall not apply to the incidental use of a television excerpt (as that term is generally used in the industry) in a theatrical exhibition. For use of such an excerpt in a theatrical motion picture the following payments will be made:

(i) Excerpt less than 30 seconds, $312.50;

(ii) Excerpt 30 seconds to 2 minutes, $625 per excerpt;

(iii) Excerpt over 2 minutes, $625 plus $250 for each additional minute or fraction thereof.

. . . .

Article 18

SUPPLEMENTAL MARKETS—THEATRICAL AND FREE TELEVISION MOTION PICTURES

18–101 Motion Pictures Covered

The provisions of this Article 18 relate and apply only to theatrical and free television motion pictures which are:

(a) produced by the Employer or within the provisions of Paragraph 18–116 [not included in this casebook], and

(b) the principal photography of which commenced on or after July 1, 1971, which motion pictures are, either during the term hereof or at any time thereafter, released in supplemental markets (as defined below); and

(c) produced by Employer with Directors, UPM's and First and Key Second Assistant Directors employed by Employer under the terms of this BA or in the employ of the actual Producer as described in Paragraph 18–116 (to which employment the provisions of the Paragraph apply).

18–102 Definitions

The term "Supplemental Markets", as used in this BA means only: The exhibition of motion pictures by means of cassettes (to the limited extent provided in subparagraph (a) of this Paragraph 18–102), pay-type CATV, or Pay Television, as those terms are hereafter defined in this Paragraph 18–102 and the exhibition of television motion pictures on any commercial carrier such as commercial airlines, trains, ships and buses (referred to herein as "in-flight").

(a) Cassettes: For the purposes of this Article 18, a cassette is any audio-visual device, including without limitation, cassette, cartridge, phonogram or other similar audio-visual device now known or hereafter devised, containing a motion picture (recorded on film, discs, tapes or other material) and designed for replay through a television receiver or comparable device. The sale or rental of cassettes for replay through a television receiver or comparable device in the home or in closed-circuit use such as in hotel rooms, constitutes "Supplemental Markets".

(b) Pay-Type CATV: Exhibition of motion pictures through a television receiver or comparable device by means of transmission by a

Community Antenna Television System (CATV) where, in addition to an obligatory general cable charge to the subscriber for the CATV service: (i) a charge is made for programs selected by the subscriber, or (ii) the subscriber has the option, by making payment, to receive special programming over one or more channels which are not available to the subscriber without such payment.

(c) Pay Television: Exhibition of motion pictures through a television receiver or comparable device by means of telecast, cable or closed circuit for which the viewing audience (whether by the individual viewer or by the hotel, motel, hospital or other accommodation where the viewer is) pays to receive the program by making a separate payment for such specific program. Exhibition in theatres or comparable places by means of telecast or cable is theatrical exhibition and shall not be considered Pay Television.

The term "Supplemental Markets" does not include the exhibition of a motion picture by cassette or otherwise over a television broadcast station in free television, or in theatrical exhibition (and for this purpose "theatrical exhibition" includes what has previously been considered to be the educational market), the exhibition of theatrical motion pictures on any commercial carrier (referred to herein as "in-flight") such as commercial airlines, trains, ships, and buses, and other uses which have been traditionally considered theatrical exhibition of theatrical motion pictures. Wherever reference is made in this Article 18 to pay-type CATV or pay television, such reference shall be deemed to include only those uses of motion pictures as to which a charge is actually made to the subscriber (which may be a hotel, motel or other accommodation) for the program viewed, or where the subscriber or viewer has the option, for a payment, to receive special programming over one or more special channels. [Where no program charge or special channel charge is made to the subscriber in addition to the obligatory general charge, the transmission of motion pictures by the CATV facility, including programming originated by the CATV facility, is free television exhibition for the purposes of this BA and such exhibition shall not be considered "Supplemental Markets" exhibition.]*

[With respect to theatrical motion pictures, the Employer has agreed to the inclusion of pay-type CATV and pay television in the "Supplemental Markets" because under the present pattern of distribution of theatrical motion pictures, pay-type CATV and pay television are supplemental to the primary market. The Employer reserves the right in future negotiations to contend that the pattern of release has changed so that pay-type CATV and/or pay television are no longer a "Supplemental Market" but constitute or are a part

---

*[Margin Note] Before Pay TV Committee.

of the primary market of distribution of theatrical motion pictures, and that therefore no additional payment pursuant to this Article should be made with respect to the release of theatrical motion pictures (including those covered by this BA) in said markets. The Guild reserves the right to contend in future negotiations that the method of employment and payment provided for in this BA is applicable and appropriate to employment directly for motion pictures intended primarily for release on pay-type CATV, pay television or cassettes, and that the provisions of this BA with respect to all kinds of "Supplemental Markets", whether they are or have become primary markets or not, shall be improved for the benefit of Employees hereunder for said markets. Nothing herein shall limit the scope of negotiations on said subjects.]**

18–103 Percentage of Accountable Receipts Payable

As to each motion picture referred to in Paragraph 18–101 above (herein sometimes called "Such Picture"), the Employer will pay additional compensation of one and 2/10 percent (1.2%) (hereinafter referred to as the "percentage payment") of the Employer's accountable receipts from the distribution of Such Picture in "Supplemental Markets". Such "percentage payment" is to be divided as follows: ½ of such amount to be paid to the Director; ⅓ of such amount to be paid to the Directors Guild of America-Producer Pension Plan (herein referred to as the "Pension Plan"); and a prorata share of 1/6 of such amount to be paid to the UPM, the First Assistant Director and the Key Second Assistant Director employed on such motion picture (such portion of such 1/6 prorata share to be based upon their respective minimum schedule wage rate hereunder). If more than one Director, UPM, or First Assistant Director renders service in connection with Such Picture, the allocations of their respective portion of the pro rata shares shall be determined by the Guild and the Employees shall be bound by such determination. Such percentage payment is to be computed as hereinafter provided and subject to the following provisions of this Article 18.

18–104 Definition of "Employer's Gross"

The term "Employer's gross", as used herein, means the worldwide total gross receipts derived by the distributor of Such Picture (who may be the Employer or a distributor licensed by the Employer) from licensing the right to exhibit Such Picture in Supplemental Markets; provided, however, that in the case of any Such Picture which is produced outside of the United States, if Such Picture is subject to this BA and if such production is under an arrangement (herein referred to as a "foreign production deal") pursuant to which a foreign producer or distributor provides or guarantees any of the financing for the production of Such Picture or furnishes any other consider-

---

**[Margin Note] DGA's position is that this paragraph should be deleted.

ation for such production and a foreign distributor acquires one or more foreign territories for the distribution of Such Picture in Supplemental Markets, then no monies from any such distribution in any such foreign territory shall be included in Employer's gross except to the extent such foreign producer or foreign distributor is obligated to account to Employer or to the distributor of Such Picture for such monies, and except for gross receipts received by such foreign distributor from such distribution in the United Kingdom.

If the distributor of Such Picture does not distribute Such Picture directly in Supplemental Markets, but employs a subdistributor to so distribute Such Picture, then the "Employer's gross" shall be the worldwide total gross receipts derived by such subdistributor from licensing the right to exhibit Such Picture in Supplemental Markets. In case of an outright sale of the Supplemental Markets distribution rights, for the entire world, or any territory or country, the income derived by the seller from such sale, but not the income realized by the purchaser or licensee of such rights, shall be the "Employer's gross". If any such outright sale shall include Supplemental Markets exhibition rights and other rights, then (but only for the purpose of the computation required hereunder) the Employer shall allocate to the Supplemental Markets exhibition rights a fair and reasonable portion of the sales price which shall, for the purpose hereof, be the "Employer's gross". In reaching this determination, Employer may consider the current market value of Supplemental Markets exhibition rights in comparable motion pictures.

If the Guild shall contend that the amount so allocated was not fair and reasonable, such claim may be determined by submission to arbitration as herein provided; and in the event the Arbitrator shall find that such allocation was not reasonable and fair, he or she shall determine the fair and reasonable amount to be allocated. If the outright sale includes Supplemental Markets distribution rights to more than one motion picture, Employer shall likewise allocate to each Such Picture a fair and reasonable portion of the sales price of the Supplemental Market rights; and if the Guild contends that such allocation is not fair and reasonable, the question may be determined by submission to arbitration as above provided. If the Arbitrator shall find that such allocation was not fair and reasonable, the Arbitrator shall determine the fair and reasonable amount to be so allocated to each Such Picture. Nothing with respect to the price received on the outright sale of only supplemental markets distribution rights in a single Such Picture shall be subject to arbitration except that, in the event of a dispute, there may be arbitrated the question of whether the price reported by the Employer to the Guild as having been received by the Employer on such outright sale is less than the amount actually received by the Employer on such outright sale.

It is recognized that the method of distributing cassettes may not be similar to the method of distributing theatrical motion pictures in television. However, for the purpose of determining the amounts payable for cassette distribution of motion pictures, it is the intent of the parties that the basis for determining Employer's gross from the cassette distribution shall be comparable to the basis used for determining the Employer's gross from the distribution of theatrical motion pictures in television. For example, gross receipts from cassettes sold at the retail level would not be Employer's gross hereunder. As a further example, if the Employer itself acts as a distributor and retailer, a reasonable allocation of the retail gross receipts shall be made as between the Employer as Distributor and the Employer as retailer, and only the former shall be deemed to be Employer's gross. The reasonableness of such allocation shall be subject to arbitration, and in such arbitration, generally prevailing trade practices in the cassette distribution industry with respect to dealings between non-related companies shall be relevant evidence.

The Employer's gross shall not include:

(a) Rebates, credits or repayments for cassettes returned (and in this connection the Employer shall have the right to set up a reasonable reserve for returns);

(b) Sums required to be paid or withheld as taxes, in the nature of turnover taxes, sales taxes or similar taxes based on the actual receipts of such motion picture or on any monies to be remitted to or by the Employer, but there shall not be excluded from Employer's gross any net income tax, franchise tax or excess profit tax or similar tax payable by the Employer or such Distributor on its net income or for the privilege of doing business.

18–105 Definition of "Accountable Receipts"

The term "accountable receipts", as used herein, means one hundred percent (100%) of the "Employer's gross".

Article 19

THEATRICAL MOTION PICTURES THE PRINCIPAL PHOTOGRAPHY OF WHICH COMMENCES AFTER JULY 1, 1981* AND RELEASED TO FREE TELEVISION

19-101 Motion Pictures Covered

As to all theatrical motion pictures the principal photography of which commenced prior to May 1, 1960, the Guild does not and will not make any claim for compensation for the exhibition of such motion pictures on television.

The provisions of this Article relate and apply only to theatrical motion pictures:

(a) produced by the Employer or within the provisions of Paragraph 19-111 [not included in this casebook];

(b) the principal photography of which commenced between July 1, 1981, and July 1, 1984, inclusive, which motion pictures are, either during the term hereof or at any time thereafter, released to free television; and

(c) produced by Employer with Directors employed by Employer under the terms of this BA or in the employ of the actual producer as described in Paragraph 19-111 (to which employment the provisions of this Article apply).

19-102 Percentage of Accountable Receipts Payable

As to each such motion picture, the Employer will pay (i) to the Directors Guild of America-Producer Pension Plan (herein referred to as the Pension Plan) an amount equal to one percent (1%) of the Employer's accountable receipts from the distribution of such motion picture on free television, computed as hereinafter provided, and (ii) one percent (1%) of such accountable receipts to be paid the Director of the motion picture on a pro rata allocation to each Director where there is more than one Director. In the latter case, in the event of any controversy as to the pro rata allocation of such 1%, the amount allocable to each Director shall be resolved by the Guild and each individual Director involved shall be bound thereby. The payment of the

---

*Note: With respect to theatrical motion pictures the principal photography of which commenced after April 30, 1960, and (i) prior to May 1, 1968, see the Directors Guild Basic Agreements of 1960 and 1964; (ii) between May 1, 1968 and May 1, 1973, see the Directors Guild Basic Agreement of 1968, as amended April 1, 1972; (iii) between May 1, 1973 and December 31, 1977, see the Directors Guild Basic Agreement of 1973; (iv) between January 1, 1978 and June 30, 1981, see the Directors Guild Basic Agreement of 1978.

1% to be paid to the Director or Directors shall be sent to the Guild for forwarding to such Director or Directors and compliance therewith shall constitute payment to the Director. Such 2% payment is hereinafter referred to as the "percentage payment". These payments are not subject to Health and Welfare or Pension contributions. The above is subject to the following conditions:

19–103 Definition of "Employer's Gross"

The term "Employer's Gross", as used herein, means the worldwide total gross receipts derived by the distributor of such motion picture (who may be the Employer or a distributor licensed by the Employer) from licensing the right to exhibit the motion picture on free television but shall not include:

(a) Sums realized or held by way of deposit as security, until and unless earned, other than such sums as non-returnable;

(b) Sums required to be paid or withheld as taxes, in the nature of turnover taxes, sales taxes or similar taxes based on the actual receipts of such motion picture or on any monies to be remitted to or by the Employer or such other distributor, but there shall not be excluded from Distributor's gross receipts any net income tax, franchise tax or excise profit tax or similar tax payable by the Employer or such Distributor on its net income or for the privilege of doing business.

(c) Frozen foreign currency until the Employer shall either have the right to freely use such foreign currency or Employer or Distributor has the right to transmit to the United States to Employer or Distributor such foreign currency from the country or territory where it is frozen. If such currency may be utilized or transmitted as aforesaid it shall be deemed to have been converted to United States dollars at the rate of exchange at which such currency was actually transmitted to the United States as aforesaid, or if not actually transmitted, then at the prevailing free market rate of exchange at the time such right to use or to transmit occurs.

Such gross income realized in foreign currency in any reporting period required hereunder shall be deemed to be converted to United States dollars at the prevailing market rate of exchange at the close of such reporting period, except that where such gross income has actually been transmitted to the United States, it shall be deemed converted to United States dollars at the rate of exchange at which such foreign currency was actually so transmitted.

Frozen foreign currency shall be deemed to be unblocked on the basis of "first-in, first-out" unless otherwise allocated by local foreign fiscal authorities. Allocation of such unblocked funds as between revenue which serves as the basis of determining payments hereunder and other revenue, shall be on a proportional basis, subject to different earmarking by local foreign fiscal authorities.

If the Distributor of the motion picture does not distribute the motion picture directly to free television, but employs a subdistributor to so distribute the motion picture, then the Employer's gross shall be the worldwide total gross receipts derived by such subdistributor from licensing the right to exhibit the motion picture on free television.

In case of an outright sale of the free television distribution rights, for the entire world, or any territory or country, the income derived by the seller from such sale, but not the income realized by the purchaser or licensee of such rights, shall be the Employer's gross. If any such outright sale shall include free television exhibition rights and other rights, then (but only for the purpose of the computation required hereunder), the Employer shall allocate to the free television exhibition rights a fair and reasonable portion of the sales price which shall, for the purpose hereof, be the Employer's gross. In reaching such determination Employer may consider the current market value of free television exhibition rights in comparable motion pictures.

If the Guild shall contend that the amount so allocated was not fair and reasonable, such claim may be submitted to arbitration as herein provided; and in the event the Arbitrator shall find that such allocation was not reasonable and fair, the Arbitrator shall determine the fair and reasonable amount to be so allocated.

If the outright sale includes free television distribution rights to more than one motion picture, Employer shall likewise allocate to each motion picture a fair and reasonable portion of the sales price of the free television rights; and if the Guild contends that such allocation is not fair and reasonable, the question may be determined by submission to arbitration as above provided. If the Arbitrator shall find that such allocation was not fair and reasonable, he or she shall determine the fair and reasonable amount to be so allocated to each motion picture. Nothing with respect to the price received on the outright sale of only free television distribution rights in a single motion picture shall be subject to arbitration except that in the event of a dispute, there may be arbitrated the question of whether the price reported by the Employer to the Guild as having been received by the Employer on such outright sale is less than the amount actually received by the Employer on such outright sale. Sums paid to any advertising agency in connection with any exhibition of a motion picture on free television shall not be included in Employer's gross.

19–104 Definition of "Accountable Receipts"

The term "accountable receipts," as used herein, means the balance of the Employer's gross after deducting an arbitrary forty percent (40%) of the Employer's gross for distribution fees and expenses; except that in the case of an outright sale of free television distribution rights, there shall be deducted only an arbitrary ten percent (10%) of the Employer's gross for sales commissions and expenses of sale.

. . . .

19–109   Crediting

If a participating Director's employment agreement with the Employer requires that the Director's compensation shall be based, in whole or in part, upon, or measured by a percentage of the gross receipts or revenues derived from the distribution of the motion picture, any payment due hereunder shall be credited pro rata against such percentage compensation. Where all or a part of a Director's compensation is a specified sum of money, including what is commonly known and referred to as a "deferment", such specified sum of money may not be credited against amounts payable by the Employer hereunder.

WRITERS GUILD

OF

AMERICA

1970

THEATRICAL AND

TELEVISION FILM

AGREEMENT

Article 12

MATTERS SUBJECT TO GRIEVANCE AND ARBITRATION (GENERAL)

A. GRIEVANCE AND ARBITRATION

Except as otherwise specifically provided in this paragraph or elsewhere in this Basic Agreement, the following matters shall be submitted to grievance and thereafter to arbitration as herein provided, and no other matters shall be submitted to grievance or arbitration:

. . . .

2. Any alleged breach of any of the terms or provisions of this Basic Agreement by the Guild or Company, except that violations of credit provisions as to photoplays shall be subject to the following conditions and limitations:

If the Grievance Committee decides or the arbitrator(s) decides that any such credit provision has been violated the Grievance Committee or arbitrator(s) shall have jurisdiction only to make a prospective decision or award and shall have no jurisdiction to award damages, penalties, or any monetary amount or to require the Company to withdraw, cancel, change or re-do advertising materials already issued or prepared, or to require the Company to change or re-do any film titles. Advertising shall be deemed, hereunder, to have been prepared when the Company has forwarded the finished copy therefor to the processor or publisher. The Company agrees, however, to revise advertising found improper which was prepared prior to the final decision of the Grievance Committee or the arbitrator(s), if such revision can physically and mechanically be made prior to the closing date of such processor or publisher and at reasonable expense, provided the processor or publisher has not yet commenced work on that part of the material which the change would affect. No award in any grievance or arbitration determining a question as to credits shall affect or be used or be admissible in any other action or proceeding of any nature whatsoever, but any court of competent jurisdiction may confirm, set aside or modify any grievance or arbitration award hereunder in any proceeding brought for such purpose in accordance with applicable law.

. . . .

Article 16

SEPARATION OF RIGHTS

A. THEATRICAL

. . . .

8. Writer's Right to Reacquire Literary Material. The provisions of this subsection 8. apply only to literary material (i) acquired by Company subject to the terms of this Basic Agreement, (ii) which is original, i.e., not based on any preexisting material, (iii) which has not been exploited in any medium, and (iv) which Company has decided it will not exploit in any medium in the future. As to such literary material if the writer who has written the same desires to purchase Company's right, title and interest therein, the Guild, on behalf of such writer may notify Company in writing of such desire. Within thirty (30) days following receipt of such written notice, Company shall notify the Guild of the terms and conditions, including the price at which it will sell its right, title and interest in such literary material; provided, however, that Company may instead notify the Guild that the literary material does not meet one or more of the conditions precedent specified in the first sentence of this subsection 8. The Company's decision that it has not decided not to exploit such literary material, and/or regarding the terms and conditions of the sale, shall not be subject to challenge by the Guild or by the writer on any grounds whatsoever whether in arbitration or otherwise even though Company does not in fact exploit or dispose of such material. The purchase price designated by Company shall not be in excess of the total direct costs previously incurred by Company in relation to such literary material and the possible exploitation thereof, including but not limited to the purchase price, if any, of the material, the payments for writing services in relation to the material, and all costs incurred by Company for the proposed production of a motion picture based on such material or for any other exploitation of such material. Within thirty (30) days following notice from the Company of the terms and conditions on which it will sell its right, title and interest in such literary material, including the purchase price, the Guild, on behalf of the writer may serve written notice of acceptance of such terms and conditions and immediately following service of such notice the parties shall proceed to close the transaction. Failure to effect such purchase in accordance with the procedure specified by the foregoing provisions shall result in the forfeiture of writer's right to purchase such material. At any time before receipt of notice of acceptance of the terms and conditions of sale, Company may dispose of such literary material or of any rights therein or with respect thereto or may itself elect to exploit such material, and in either such event the writer shall no longer have the right to acquire Company's right, title or interest in such material. Furthermore, if Company had previously granted some other person

or company the right or option to acquire such material or any rights therein, the writer of such literary material shall not have the right to purchase the same so long as such other right remains outstanding. In the event that more than one writer is involved in the writing of such literary material the Guild shall have the sole responsibility to determine which of such writers has the right to purchase as provided herein and all interested writers shall be bound by the decision of the Guild.

. . . .

Article 28

WARRANTY AND INDEMNIFICATION
(GENERAL)

1. Company and writer may in any individual contract of employment include provisions for warranties of originality and no violation of rights of third parties, indemnification against judgments, damages, costs and expenses including attorneys' fees in connection with suits relating to the literary material or the use of the literary material supplied by the writer or the use thereof by Company; provided, however, that the writer shall in no event

   a. be required by contract to waive his right to defend himself against a claim by Company for costs, damages or losses arising out of settlements not consented to by the writer; and Company reserves all of the rights it may otherwise have against the writer;

   b. be required to warrant or indemnify with respect to any claim that his literary material invaded the privacy of any person unless the writer knowingly used the name or personality of such person or should have known, in the exercise of reasonable prudence, that such person would or might claim that his personality was used in such material;

   c. be required to warrant or indemnify with respect to any material other than that furnished by the writer.

2. The Company shall indemnify such writer against any and all damages, costs and expenses, including attorneys' fees, and shall relieve the writer of all liability in connection with any claim or action respecting material supplied to the writer by the Company for incorporation into the writer's work.

3. The Company and the employee, upon the presentation of any such claim to either of them or the institution of any such action naming either or both of them as defendants, shall promptly notify the other of the presentation of any such claim or the institution of any such action giving such other party full

details thereof, but the pendency of any such claim or action shall not relieve the Company of its obligation to pay to the employee any monies due to the employee with respect to the literary material contributed by the employee.

WRITERS GUILD

OF

AMERICA

1973

THEATRICAL & TELEVISION

BASIC AGREEMENT

Article 12

MATTERS SUBJECT TO GRIEVANCE AND ARBITRATION
(GENERAL)

1. Article 12 A. 2. [casebook p. 518] is deleted and the following is substituted in its place and stead:

"2. Any alleged breach of any of the terms or provisions of this Basic Agreement by the Guild or the Company including, without limitation, violations of credit provisions. Provided, any dispute with respect to the credit provisions shall be submitted to arbitration but not to grievance subject to the following provisions.

"a. The Guild shall act on behalf of itself and the writer or writers and the loan-out company, if one is involved.

"b. Within 24 hours after the Guild serves written notice upon the Company of an alleged breach of the credit provision an authorized representative of the Guild and an authorized representative of the Company will meet in a good faith attempt to settle or resolve the dispute.

"c. In the event the parties shall fail to meet or shall otherwise fail to settle or resolve the dispute within 24 hours of the commencement of the meeting first held in accordance with Paragraph b. above, said dispute shall be submitted directly to arbitration, said arbitration to be commenced not later than 5 business days after the service of the written notice provided for in Paragraph b. above.

"d. The dispute shall be submitted to a single neutral arbitrator mutually selected from the authorized list of arbitrators approved by the parties hereto as follows:

Walter Bruington
Jack Dales
Roger Davis
Dixon Q. Dern
Sidney Justin
Leon Kaplan

In the event the parties are unable, within 48 hours after the service of the written notice provided for in Paragraph b. above, to agree upon a neutral arbitrator from the above list or otherwise, the arbitrator will automatically be the person next in sequence on the above list following the person last selected from said list to serve in such an arbitration and who is available and willing to serve and who is not disqualified because of personal interest or representation of a party having a personal interest in the dispute.

"e. Notwithstanding anything in this Basic Agreement to the contrary, the arbitrator shall have jurisdiction and power to award damages and/or to require the Company to withdraw, cancel, change or re-do advertising materials already issued or prepared, or to require the Company to change or re-do any film titles, or to order any other reasonable relief the arbitrator deems appropriate in the circumstances, whether relating to credit on the screen, in advertising or otherwise. Any award rendered by the arbitrator shall be binding on the parties hereto and upon the writer or writers involved and upon the loan-out company, if one is involved.

"f. Any court of competent jurisdiction may confirm, set aside, or modify any arbitration award hereunder in any proceeding brought for such purpose in accordance with applicable law.

"g. Any or all time limits set forth herein may be waived by the mutual consent of the parties.

"h. To the extent not inconsistent herewith, all other provisions of this Basic Agreement relating to arbitrations shall be applicable."

. . . .

Article 16

SEPARATION OF RIGHTS

1. The first sentence of paragraph A.8 [casebook p. 519] is revised to read as follows:

"8. Writers' Right to Reacquire Literary Material. The provisions of this subsection 8. apply only to literary material (i) acquired by Company subject to the terms of this Basic Agreement or the terms of the 1970 WGA agreement, (ii) which is original, i.e., not based on any pre-existing material, (iii) which has not been exploited in any medium, and (iv) which Company has decided it will not exploit in any medium in the future."

The fourth sentence of paragraph A.8 [casebook p. 519], sentence commencing "The Company's decision") is revised by adding the following at the end and as part of said sentence:

"; without limiting the generality of the foregoing, offering the literary material for sale, or negotiating for such sale, shall not be deemed to be an election not to exploit such literary material."

The fifth sentence of paragraph A.8 [casebook p. 519], sentence commencing "The purchase price . . . ") is revised to read:

"The purchase price designated by Company shall not be in excess of the total direct costs previously incurred by Company in relation only to such literary material, including payments for the acquisition of the literary material and for writing services connected therewith (including writing services in relation to treatments and screenplays based thereon), and fringe benefit costs in relation thereto, such as pension and health and welfare payments and social security payments, but exclusive of overhead and exclusive of costs of any other kind (e.g., costs relating to proposed production other than writing costs)."

WRITERS GUILD

OF

AMERICA

1977

THEATRICAL & TELEVISION

BASIC AGREEMENT

Article 1

DEFINITIONS

The following terms or words used herein shall have the following meaning:

. . . .

B. THEATRICAL

1. Writer and Professional Writer.

. . . .

b. A "professional writer" hereunder is a person who on or after March 2, 1977, sells or licenses to the Company the ownership of or rights to use literary material written by such writer, for use in the production of a motion picture, which literary material had not prior to such sale or license been published or exploited in any manner or by any medium whatever, and who at such time:

(1) has received employment for a total of 13 weeks as a motion picture and/or television writer, or radio writer for dramatic programs; or

(2) has received credit on the screen as a writer for a television or theatrical motion picture; or

(3) has received credit for three original stories or one teleplay for a program one-half hour or more in length in the field of live television; or

(4) has received credit for three radio scripts for dramatic radio programs one-half hour or more in length; or

(5) has received credit for one professionally produced play on the legitimate stage, or one published novel.

The Company may rely on the statement of the writer with respect to whether or not the material has theretofore been published or otherwise exploited.

It is understood that the employment of the writer need not be consecutive for the purpose of b. (1) above.

. . . .

C. TELEVISION

1. Writer and Professional Writer

. . . .

b. A "professional writer" means any person who has (a) received employment for a total of 13 weeks as a television, motion picture or radio writer, or (b) has received credit on the screen as a writer for a television or theatrical motion picture, or (c) has received credit for three (3) original stories or one (1) teleplay for a program one-half hour or more in length in the field of live television, or (d) has received credit for three (3) radio scripts for radio programs one-half hour or more in length, or (e) has received credit for one professionally produced play on the legitimate stage or one published novel.

Article 2

TERM AND EFFECTIVE DATE OF AGREEMENT

A. GENERAL

1. The term of this Basic Agreement shall commence on March 2, 1977 and shall continue to and including March 1, 1981.

2. With respect to all employment agreements with writers in effect on March 2, 1977 the terms of this Basic Agreement relating to minimum compensation and to rights in material shall apply only to services performed and literary material written under such employment contracts where the date of actual employment (i.e., the commitment date) was on or after March 2, 1977, except as specifically otherwise provided herein in Article 2, Section B or Section C [not included in this casebook].

3. With respect to literary material acquired from professional writers (as described herein) the terms of this Basic Agreement relating to minimum compensation and rights in material shall apply only to unpublished and unexploited literary material acquired from such professional writers on or after March 2, 1977.

. . . .

Article 11

GRIEVANCE AND ARBITRATION RULES AND PROCEDURES

. . . .

E. ARBITRATION OF DISPUTES CONCERNING CREDIT PROVISIONS

A dispute concerning the credit provisions of this Basic Agreement shall be submitted to an expedited arbitration proceeding governed by the following rules:

1. The Guild shall act on behalf of itself and the writer.

2. Within twenty-four (24) hours after the Guild serves written notice upon the Company concerning a dispute involving a credit provision, an authorized representative of the Guild and an authorized representative of the Company will meet in a good faith attempt to settle or resolve the dispute.

3. In the event the parties shall fail to meet or shall otherwise fail to settle or resolve the dispute within 24 hours after the 24 hours provided in subsection 2 above, the dispute shall be submitted to arbitration to be commenced not later than 5 business days after the service of the written notice provided for in subsection 2 above.

4. The dispute shall be submitted to a single arbitrator mutually selected from the authorized revolving list of arbitrators approved by the parties hereto as follows:

Roger Davis	Edward Mosk
Dixon Q. Dern	Ed Perlstein
Martin Gang	Gordon Stulberg
	Kenneth Ziffren

In the event the parties are unable, within 48 hours (not including weekends or holidays) after respondent's receipt of the written notice provided for in subsection 2 above, to agree upon an arbitrator from the above list or otherwise, the arbitrator will automatically be the person who is available and willing to serve, who is not disqualified because of personal interest in the dispute or representation of a party having a personal interest in the dispute, and who, at the expiration of said 48 hour period, is next in sequence on the above list following the person last selected from said list to serve in any arbitration under Article 11E. "Next in sequence" shall be determined on an industry-wide basis, not a company by company basis.

5. Notwithstanding anything in this Basic Agreement to the contrary, the arbitrator shall have jurisdiction and power to award damages, to order the Company to withdraw, cancel, change, or re-do advertising materials already issued or prepared, to require the Company to re-do any film titles, and to order any other reasonable relief the arbitrator deems appropriate in the circumstances whether relating to credit on the screen, advertising or otherwise. Any award rendered by the arbitrator shall be binding on the parties and upon the writer.

6. Any or all time limits set forth herein may be waived by the mutual consent of the parties.

7. To the extent not inconsistent herewith, all other provisions of the Basic Agreement relating to arbitrations shall be applicable.

Article 12

COURT PROCEEDINGS

A. Nothing in this Basic Agreement shall limit the rights of the Guild or any writer to assert any and all appropriate legal and equitable rights and remedies to which the Guild or such writer is entitled in courts of competent jurisdiction with regard to an alleged breach of Article 8 [not included in this casebook] and Schedule A [casebook pp. 578–586] of this Basic Agreement with respect to writing credit; subject, however, to the following conditions and limitations:

1. The Guild and the writer shall be bound by any court proceedings instituted by the Guild.

2. If the Guild or the writer commences any proceedings in court with respect to any such alleged breach prior to the submission of the dispute to arbitration hereunder, then neither the Guild nor the writer may submit such dispute to arbitration and no arbitrator shall have jurisdiction to consider the alleged breach of such credit provision.

3. If the Guild or the Company commences an arbitration proceeding hereunder with respect to any such alleged breach prior to the submission of the dispute to a court, then neither the Guild nor the writer shall thereafter commence any proceeding in court with respect to such alleged breach.

4. Any permissible court proceeding referred to in this Section A must be commenced by the Guild or the writer, if at all, within the applicable time limits specified in subsection 2. of Article 11.A [not included in this casebook].

. . . .

Article 15

TELEVISION EXHIBITION

A. THEATRICAL

. . . .

3. As to each such theatrical motion picture referred to in 2. above [not included in this casebook], (herein sometimes called "Such Picture"), the Company will pay to each participating Writer (as such term is hereinafter defined) as additional compensation, a pro-rata share of two per cent (2%) (hereinafter referred to as the "percentage payment") of the Company's accountable receipts from the distribution of Such Picture on free television, computed as hereinafter provided and subject to the following conditions:

a. The term "Producer's gross", as used herein, means the worldwide total gross receipts derived by the distributor of Such Picture (who may be the Company or a distributor licensed by the Company) from licensing the right to exhibit Such Picture on free television; provided, however, that in the case of any Such Picture which is produced outside of the United States, if Such

Picture is subject to this Basic Agreement and if such production is under an arrangement (herein referred to as a "foreign production deal") pursuant to which a foreign producer or distributor provides or guarantees any of the financing for the production of Such Picture or furnishes any other consideration for such production and a foreign distributor acquires one or more foreign territories for the distribution of Such Picture on free television, then no monies from any such distribution in any such foreign territory shall be included in Producer's gross except to the extent such foreign producer or foreign distributor is obligated to account to Company or to the distributor of Such Picture for such monies, and except for gross receipts received by such foreign distributor from such distribution in the United Kingdom.

If the distributor of Such Picture does not distribute Such Picture directly to free television, but employs a subdistributor to so distribute Such Picture, then the "Producer's gross" shall be the worldwide total gross receipts derived by such subdistributor from licensing the right to exhibit Such Picture on free television. In case of an outright sale of the free television distribution rights, for the entire world, or any territory or country, the income derived by the seller from such sale, but not the income realized by the purchaser or licensee of such rights, shall be the "Producer's gross". If any such outright sale shall include free television exhibition rights and other rights, then (but only for the purpose of the computation required hereunder) the Company shall allocate to the free television exhibition rights a fair and reasonable portion of the sales price which shall, for the purpose hereof, be the "Producer's gross". In reaching such determination Company may consider the current market value of free television exhibition rights in comparable motion pictures.

If the Guild shall contend that the amount so allocated was not fair and reasonable, such claim may be determined by submission to arbitration as herein provided; and in the event the Board of Arbitration shall find that such allocation was not reasonable and fair, it shall determine the fair and reasonable amount to be so allocated. If the outright sale includes free television distribution rights to more than one motion picture, Company shall likewise allocate to each Such Picture a fair and reasonable portion of the sales price of the free television rights; and if the Guild contends that such allocation is not fair and reasonable, the question may be determined by submission to arbitration as above provided. If the Board of Arbitration shall find that such allocation was not fair and reasonable, it shall determine the fair and reasonable amount to be so allocated to each Such Picture. Nothing with respect to the price received on the outright sale of only free television distribution rights in a single Such Picture shall be subject to arbitration except that in the event of a dispute, there may be arbitrated the question of whether the price reported by the Company to the Guild as having been received by the Company on such outright sale is less than the amount actually received by the Company on such outright sale. Sums paid to any advertising agency in connection with any exhibition of any Such Picture on free television shall not be included in Producer's gross.

Guild's right to elect. The parties further agree with reference to Article 15A3: If in the upcoming negotiations with SAG and DGA, the Company agrees to modify the basic substantive provisions regarding licensing of the theatrical motion pictures for exhibition on free television, Company will so notify the Guild and accord it the opportunity to elect that this subparagraph be modified in the same manner, as of the date on which the Guild so notifies the Company. Adjustments which statistically maintain the relative allocations of proceeds derived from post-1960 theatrical motion pictures licensed to television among SAG, DGA and WGA as established in 1960 (i.e., the ratio of 6, 2 and 2 of accountable receipts respectively) will not activate this provision, but an increase in the relative allocations to SAG, or DGA in such proceeds, will activate this provision, with any such increase to be accorded proportionately to WGA. Upon request the Guild shall be provided with the statistics upon which the adjustments have been made, and the Guild's right to activate this provision shall be arbitrable. The Guild shall give notice of its election within 60 days after receipt of the Company's Notice or after being provided with the statistics referred to, whichever is later. The election shall be limited to accepting the entire agreement reached with SAG or DGA on licensing theatrical motion pictures for exhibition on free television, and only such entire agreement, but with appropriate equivalent adjustment for writers for provisions peculiar to actors or directors as the case may be.

b. The term "accountable receipts", as used herein, means the balance of the Producer's gross after deducting an arbitrary forty per cent (40%) of the Producer's gross for distribution fees and expenses; except that in the case of an outright sale of free television distribution rights, there shall be deducted only an arbitrary ten per cent (10%) of the Producer's gross for sales commissions and expenses of sale.

c. Company's obligation shall accrue hereunder only after accountable receipts are received by Company but as to foreign receipts such obligation shall accrue only when such receipts can be freely converted to U.S. dollars and are remitted to the United States, and until such time no frozen foreign receipts shall be included in accountable receipts. Payment of amounts accruing hereunder shall be made quarterly on the basis of quarterly statements, as hereinafter provided. Upon request, and if permitted by the authorities of a foreign country, the Company will transfer to any Writer, in the currency of such foreign country, his share, if any, of frozen foreign receipts in such country, provided the writer will bear any costs involved; and such transfer shall be deemed to be payment to the writer of an equivalent number of U.S. dollars at the then current free rate for blocked funds of that category as determined by the Company. Concurrently with such transfer the writer will pay to the Company in U.S. dollars the total amount the Company is required to withhold from such payment under all applicable laws. If the Company utilizes frozen foreign currencies derived from exhibition of Such Picture on free television by conversion thereof to properties that may be freely exported and turned to account, the amount so utilized by the Company shall be deemed to have been converted to U.S. dollars at the then current free market rate for blocked funds of that category determined as above provided. Frozen foreign receipts from free television shall be deemed to be released on a first-in first-out basis, unless the authorities of the foreign country involved designate a specific period that would render such basis inapplicable. Such released funds shall be allocated between Such Picture and other motion pictures distributed by the distributor on free television in the same ratio that receipts, derived from the distribution of Such Picture on free television within the foreign country, bear to the total receipts derived from the distribution of Such Picture and all other motion pictures on free television within the foreign country, during the applicable period, unless the authorities of the foreign country involved require another method of allocation, in which case such other method shall be used. Foreign receipts shall be accounted for in U.S. dollars at the rate of exchange at which such receipts are actually converted and remitted, and should any discounts, taxes, duties or charges be imposed in connection with the receipt or remittance of foreign funds, only so much of such funds as remain thereafter shall be included in accountable receipts. Company shall not be responsible for loss or diminuation of foreign receipts as a result of any matter or thing not reasonably within the control of the Company. The Guild and the writers shall be bound by any arrangements made in good faith by the Company or for its account, with respect to the deposit or remittance of foreign revenue. Frozen foreign receipts shall not be considered trust funds and the Company may freely commingle the same with other funds of the Company. No sums received by way of deposits or security need be included in Producer's gross until earned, but when the Company is paid a non-returnable advance by a distributor, such advance shall be included in the Producer's gross.

d. If any license or outright sale of exhibition rights to Such Picture on free television includes as a part thereof any filmed commercial or advertising material, the Company shall be permitted to allocate a reasonable amount (in accordance with then current standard charges in the industry) to such commercial or advertising material, and the amount so allocated shall not be included in Producer's gross hereunder.

e. The term "Participating Writer", as used herein, means a writer who, while in the employ of the Company or in the employ of the actual Producing Company of Such Picture as described in paragraph h.(4) of this subsection 3 [casebook pp. 545–546]. (to which employment the provisions of this Basic Agreement apply), or a professional writer from whom the Company (or such actual producer) acquired literary material (to which acquisition the provisions of this Basic Agreement apply), participated in the writing of and received credit pursuant to the Theatrical Schedule A hereof for the writing of the story or screenplay upon which Such Picture was based. If such picture is a remake of a prior motion picture, and if any of the writers of the prior motion picture receive writing credit for the remake, such writers shall be deemed to be "participating writers" for the purposes of this article 15.A., but then only if their employment as writers for the prior motion picture, or if the purchase of literary material from them for the prior motion picture, was covered by and subject to a collective bargaining agreement with the Guild.

The "pro-rata share" payable to each Participating Writer shall be as follows:

(1) If the Participating Writer or Writers receive "written by" credit, 100% thereof shall be payable to the credited writer or writers receiving "written by" credit.

(2) If the Participating Writer or Writers receive either story or screenstory credit, or screenplay credit, but not both, 100% thereof shall be payable to the credited Participating Writer or Writers receiving story or screenstory, or screenplay credit, as the case may be; provided, however, that if the individual employment contract or purchase agreement with the other writer(s) (i.e., those who are not subject to this Basic Agreement) provides for payment to such writer or writerss of the additional compensation provided for in this Article 15.A., such writer or writers shall receive the share which would have been payable had such writer or writers been Participating Writers, as provided in clause (3) following.

(3) If the Participating Writer or Writers receive both "story by" or "screenstory by" and screenplay credit, 75% thereof shall be payable to the credited screenplay writer or writers, and 25% thereof to the credited story or screenstory writer or writers. In the event there is a minor credit, such as adaptation, the writer or writers receiving such minor credit shall be paid ten percent (10%) thereof which sum shall be deducted from the screenplay writer's share.

Any participating writers receiving the same screen credit referred to above shall share equally in such percentage amount specified.

If there are one or more participating Writers who receive screenplay credit and no credit is given for story or screenstory, then the pro-rata share which would have been payable to a participating Writer had he received such story or screenstory credit shall, subject to the provisions of the next following paragraph, be paid to the Participating Writers who receive such screenplay credit. The provisions of the immediately preceding sentence shall also apply with respect to the determination under the Producer-Writers Guild Theatrical Basic Agreements of 1960, 1963, 1970 and 1973 of "pro rata shares" payable to Participating Writers as therein defined.

If the Writer's services in Such Picture are performed for the Company on a loan-out basis, then for the purpose of this Article 15A the Company shall be deemed to be the employer, and the lender shall not have any responsibility hereunder with respect to Such Picture.

f. If the picture is licensed for network exhibition, payment with respect to the gross receipts from such license shall be made as follows:

(i) If under the terms of the license there is no possibility that the picture can or may be dropped out of the license, payment must be made within thirty (30) days after receipt of payment from the network with respect to such picture.

(ii) If there is a possibility that such picture can or may be dropped out of such license, then payment with respect to such picture shall be made within thirty (30) days after exhibition of such picture on television pursuant to such license, but not earlier than 30 days after receipt of payment from the network with respect to such picture.

Payment shall be accompanied with a written report of the license fee payable for such picture pursuant to the license and of the amount paid by the network for such picture.

With respect to exhibition of the picture on free television other than pursuant to a license for network exhibition, the following provisions of this subsection f. shall apply:

Within a reasonable time after the expiration of each calendar or fiscal quarter, but not exceeding sixty (60) days, Company will furnish or cause to be furnished to the Guild a written report showing the Producer's gross during the preceding quarter from the distribution of each Such Picture by Company on free television with respect to which Company is required to make payments hereunder (whether distributed by the Company or through another distributor).

Concurrently with the furnishing of each such report, the Company will make the payments shown to be due by such report. All payments shall be made by check payable to the order of the Writers entitled thereto, and shall be delivered to the Guild for forwarding to such Writers; and compliance herewith shall constitute payment to the Writers.

No such reports need be furnished with respect to any period during which there was no such Producer's gross. The Company shall make available for inspection by the Guild all distributor's statements and exhibitor's statements which are available to the Company insofar as they relate to such Producer's gross, and all the financial terms of contracts pertaining to such Producer's gross, and the Guild shall have the right, at reasonable times, to examine the books and records of the Company as to such Producer's gross pertaining to such distribution of any such picture, at whatever place or places such records are customarily kept by the Company. If the Guild requests that it be informed of the license fee paid under a license for the free television exhibition of the picture, or if the Guild requests that it be sent an extract of the financial terms of such a license, and if such information is not extensive in nature, the Company will forward such information or extract without making it necessary for the Guild to send a representative to the offices of the Company. In general, the Company will co-operate in furnishing such information to the Guild by mail or telephone, where doing so is not unreasonable or burdensome. If more than one picture is licensed in a single license agreement, the Company shall inform the Guild, at its request, of the identity of the pictures covered by the license, and shall make available to inspection by the Guild in the office where such license agreement is customarily kept a copy of the terms of such license showing the titles of the pictures licensed under such agreement and the license fee for each such picture. Company agrees to cooperate in responding to reasonable inquiries from the Guild as to whether any such picture is currently being distributed for telecasting on free television. An inadvertent failure to comply with the reporting provisions of this paragraph f. shall not constitute a default by the Company hereunder, provided such failure is cured promptly after notice thereof from the Guild is received by the Company.

Company shall make all social security, withholding, unemployment insurance, and disability insurance payment required by law with respect to the additional compensation provided for in this Article 15A.

If the Company shall fail to make any payment provided for in this Article 15A to be made to the Writer when and as the same becomes due and payable, it shall bear interest at the rate of ten per cent (10%) per annum on the unpaid balance thereof commencing to accrue ten (10) days after notice in writing to Company from the Guild of such delinquency.

The compensation payable under this Article 15A shall be excluded from the gross compensation upon which the Company contributions are to be made to the Pension Plan.

g. If a Participating Writer's employment agreement with the Company requires that the Writer's compensation shall be based, in whole or in part, upon, or measured by, a percentage of the gross receipts derived from the distribution of Such Picture, then such percentage compensation shall be credited against any amounts payable to the Writer hereunder, and likewise any payment due to the Writer hereunder shall be credited against such percentage compensation. Where all or a part of a Writer's compensation is a specified sum of money, commonly known and referred to as a "deferment", such deferment may not be credited against amounts payable by the Company to such Writer hereunder.

h. With respect to all Such Pictures, the following provisions shall be applicable:

(1) Television Distributor's Assumption Agreement:

Prior to the commencement of principal photography of each Such Picture, if the Company is not also the distributor on free television of Such Picture, Company shall obtain from the distributor having such free television distribution rights and deliver to Guild, a separate written agreement herein called "TELEVISION DISTRIBUTOR'S ASSUMPTION AGREEMENT", made expressly for the benefit of Guild as representative of the writers involved, by which such distributor agrees to assume and pay the amounts payable hereunder by reason of the exhibition of Such Picture on free television, when and as the same become due. Such agreement shall be substantially in the following form:

"TELEVISION DISTRIBUTOR'S ASSUMPTION AGREEMENT

In consideration of the execution of a DISTRIBUTION AGREE-MENT between _____ Company, and the undersigned Distributor, Distributor agrees that the motion picture presently entitled _____ is subject to the Writers Guild of America Theatrical and Television Basic Agreement of 1977 (hereinafter "Basic Agreement") and particularly to the provisions of Article 15A thereof, pertaining to additional compensation payable to writers when theatrical motion pictures are released to free television, and Distributor hereby agrees expressly for the benefit of the Writers Guild of America, West, Inc., herein called WGA, as representative of the writers whose services are included in such motion picture when telecast to make the additional compensation payment required thereby when such motion picture is exhibited on free television. Distributor for and on behalf of the Company shall make all social security, withholding, unemployment insurance and disability insurance payments required by law with respect to the additional compensation referred to in the preceding sentence.

It is expressly understood that the right of Distributor to license such motion picture for exhibition on free television, or to exhibit or cause or permit such motion picture to be exhibited on free television, shall be subject to and conditioned upon the prompt payment of such additional compensation, in accordance with Article 15A of the Basic Agreement. It is agreed that WGA, in addition to all other remedies, shall be entitled to injunctive relief against Distributor in the event such payments are not made.

Prompt payment:

(a) Network exhibition

If the picture is licensed for network exhibition, payment with respect to the gross receipts from such license shall be made as follows:

(i) If under the terms of the license there is no possibility that the picture can or may be dropped out of the license, payment must be made within thirty (30) days after receipt of payment from the network with respect to such picture.

(ii) If there is a possibility that such picture can or may be dropped out of such license, then payment with respect to such picture shall be made within thirty (30) days after exhibition of such picture on television pursuant to such license, but not earlier than 30 days after receipt of payment from the network with respect to such picture.

Payment shall be accompanied with a written report of the license fee payable for such picture pursuant to the license and of the amount paid by the network for such picture.

(b) Other free television exhibition

With respect to exhibition of the picture on free television other than pursuant to a license for network exhibition, the following provisions shall apply: Within a reasonable time after the expiration of each calendar or fiscal quarter, but not exceeding sixty (60) days, Distributor will furnish or cause to be furnished to WGA a written report showing the Producer's gross (as defined in Article 15A of the Basic Agreement) during the preceding quarter from the distribution of such picture by Distributor on free television with respect to which Distributor is required to make payments hereunder (whether distributed by the Distributor or through another distributor licensed by Distributor). Such report shall be accompanied by such payments as may be due.

Distributor shall also make available for inspection by WGA all Distributor's statements delivered to Company insofar as they relate to Producer's gross. WGA shall have the right at reasonable times and on reasonable notice to examine the books and records of Distributor as to Producer's gross. If Distributor shall fail to make such payments as and when due and payable, they shall bear interest at the rate of ten per cent (10%) per annum on the unpaid balance thereof commencing to accrue ten (10) days after notice in writing from WGA of such delinquency.

This DISTRIBUTOR'S ASSUMPTION AGREEMENT shall remain effective and binding upon Distributor as long as it remains the Distributor of such motion picture on free television, and thereafter in perpetuity only if it has provided or guaranteed any of the financing for the production of such motion picture, in accordance with and subject to the provisions of paragraph h.(3)(i) of Article 15A3. of the Basic Agreement.

Where there is more than one distributor the provisions of such paragraph h.(3)(iii) of Article 15A3., of the Basic Agreement shall apply to each distributor which neither provides nor guarantees any of the financing for the production of such motion picture.

The Distributor has, has not (strike whichever is inapplicable) provided or guaranteed financing for production of such motion picture.

DISTRIBUTOR

By————————————————

Date: ————————

Address: ————————"

An inadvertent failure on the part of any such distributor to comply with any of the reporting provisions of this paragraph h.(1) shall in no event constitute a default by the Company or such distributor or a breach of this Basic Agreement, provided that such failure is cured promptly after notice in writing thereof from the Guild.

In the event of the expiration or termination of any distribution agreement, the obligation of Company to obtain and deliver to the Guild such TELEVISION DISTRIBUTOR'S ASSUMPTION AGREEMENT shall apply as well to any subsequent distribution agreement entered into by Company and Company shall obtain and deliver an executed TELEVISION DISTRIBUTOR'S ASSUMPTION AGREEMENT within ten (10) days after the execution of each of such subsequent distribution agreement.

If, with respect of any Such Picture distributor is not liable in perpetuity to pay the television fees provided for hereunder, or if there is no distribution agreement made by Company with respect to any Such Picture granting television distribution rights to the distributor, then the Guild, prior to the commencement of principal photography of Such Picture, may require such further financial assurances from Company as it deems advisable to insure performance of Company's obligations to pay the television fees provided for herein, including without limitation the execution of security agreements, guarantees, or other protective agreements. If any member company of the Association of Motion Picture and Television Producers, Inc., becomes liable in perpetuity under a TELEVISION DISTRIBUTOR'S ASSUMPTION AGREEMENT to pay the television fees provided for hereunder with respect to Such Picture, the Guild will release and cause to be discharged of record all such security agreements, guarantees or other protective agreements entered into or obtained by or from Company, provided, however that Company's primary liability shall not be released thereby.

(2) Buyer's Assumption Agreement.

If the Company shall sell, transfer or assign its rights to exhibit on free television any Such Picture, it shall obtain from such buyer, transferee or assignee, a separate agreement made expressly for the benefit of the Guild as representative of the writers involved, requiring such buyer, transferee or assignee to comply with the provisions of this Basic Agreement with respect to additional compensation to writers by reason of the exhibition of Such Picture on free television, when and as the same become due. Such agreement shall be substantially in the following form:

"BUYER'S ASSUMPTION AGREEMENT

For a valuable consideration, the undersigned _____ (Insert name of Buyer, transferee or assignee) (hereinafter referred to as Buyer) hereby agrees with _____ (Insert name of Company) that all motion pictures covered by this agreement, a list of which is appended hereto, are subject to the Writers Guild of America Theatrical and Television Basic Agreement of 1977 (hereinafter "Basic Agreement") and particularly to the provisions of Article 15A thereof, pertaining to additional compensation payable to writers when theatrical motion pictures are released to free television and Buyer hereby agrees expressly for the benefit of the Writers Guild of America, West, Inc., hereinafter called WGA, as representative of the writers whose services are included in each such motion picture when telecast, to assume and be bound by Company's obligation thereunder to make the additional compensation payments required thereby when each such motion picture is exhibited on free television. Buyer for and on behalf of the Company shall make all social security, withholding, unemployment insurance, and disability insurance payments required by law with respect to the additional compensation referred to in the preceding sentence.

It is expressly understood that the right of the Buyer to license each such motion picture for exhibition on free television, or to exhibit or cause or permit such motion picture to be exhibited on free television, shall be subject to and conditioned upon the prompt payment of such additional compensation, in accordance with Article 15A of the Basic Agreement. It is agreed that WGA, in addition to all other remedies, shall be entitled to injunctive relief against Buyer in event such payments are not made.

Prompt payment:

(a) Network exhibition

If the picture is licensed for network exhibition, payment with respect to the gross receipts from such license shall be made as follows:

(i) If under the terms of the license there is no possibility that the picture can or may be dropped out of the license, payment must be made within thirty (30) days after receipt of payment from the network with respect to such picture.

(ii) If there is a possibility that such picture can or may be dropped out of such license, then payment with respect to such picture shall be made within thirty (30) days after exhibition of such picture on television pursuant to such license, but not earlier than 30 days after receipt of payment from the network with respect to such picture.

Payment shall be accompanied with a written report of the license fee payable for such picture pursuant to the license and of the amount paid by the network for such picture.

(b) Other free television exhibition

With respect to exhibition of the picture on free television other than pursuant to a license for network exhibition, the following provisions shall apply: Within a reasonable time after the expiration of each calendar or fiscal quarter, but not exceeding sixty (60) days, Buyer will furnish or cause to be furnished to WGA a written report showing the "Producer's gross" (as defined in Article 15A of the Basic Agreement) during the preceding quarter from the distribution of such Pictures by Buyer on free television with respect to which Buyer is required to make payments hereunder (whether distributed by Buyer or through another distributor licensed by Buyer). Such report shall be accompanied by such payments as may be due.

Buyer shall also make available for inspection by WGA all Distributor's statements delivered to Buyer insofar as they relate to Producer's gross. WGA shall have the right at reasonable times to examine the books and records of Buyer as to Producer's gross. If Buyer shall fail to make such payments as and when due and payable, they shall bear interest at the rate of ten per cent (10%) per annum on the unpaid balance thereof commencing to accrue ten (10) days after notice in writing from WGA of such delinquency.

Where there is more than one buyer the provisions of paragraph h. (3) (iii) of Article 15A 3. of the Basic Agreement shall apply to each Buyer.

BUYER

By_____

Date:_____

Address:_____ "

The Company agrees to deliver to the Guild an executed copy of the above referred to Buyer's Assumption Agreement within thirty (30) days after the sale, assignment or transfer of Such Picture, with the name and address of the purchaser or assignee.

Any inadvertent failure on the part of the buyer to comply with any of the reporting provisions of this subparagraph (2) shall in no event constitute a default by the Company or such Buyer or a breach of this agreement, provided that such failure is cured promptly after notice in writing thereof from the Guild.

Upon delivery of such Buyer's Assumption Agreement and on condition that the guild approves in writing the financial responsibility of the purchaser, assignee, or transferee, Company shall not be further liable for the keeping of any such records, or for the payment of such additional compensation for the exhibition of any such pictures on free television, it being agreed that the purchaser, assignee, or transferee, shall solely be liable therefor.

The Guild agrees that it will not unreasonably withhold its approval of the financial responsibility of any such purchaser, assignee or transferee, it being further agreed that if the Guild, within twenty-one (21) days of receipt of written notice of any such sale, assignment or transfer has not advised the Company that it disapproves the financial responsibility of such purchaser, assignee or transferee, the Guild will be deemed to have approved the financial responsibility thereof. In the event the Guild advises the Company within such twenty-one (21) day period that it disapproves the financial responsibility of any such purchaser, assignee or transferee and the Company disputes such disapproval, the Company shall have the right, at its election, to cause to be immediately submitted to arbitration, as herein provided, the issue of whether the Guild has unreasonably withheld the approval of the financial responsibility of such purchaser, assignee or transferee for payments due hereunder.

(3) Television Distributor's Liability:

With respect to any Such Picture, the following provisions shall be applicable to the distributor of Such Picture for telecasting on free television:

(i) Where the distributor has provided or guaranteed any of the financing for the production of Such Picture the obligations of the distributor under this Article 15A shall continue in perpetuity notwithstanding the expiration or termination of such distribution agreement, or any foreclosure of a chattel mortgage, security agreement, pledge, or lien on Such Picture. In the case of foreclosure, should such mortgagee, pledgee or security holder or a third party, who is neither the Company or distributor, acquire title to Such Picture and execute the Buyer's Assumption Agreement, and upon condition that the Guild, in its discretion, approves such purchaser's financial responsibility, then when the distributor ceases to be the distributor of Such Picture for telecasting on free television the distributor shall thereupon be released from any and all further obligations under this Article 15A with respect to Such Picture. Should any third party (other than in connection with any such foreclosure) acquire the rights of such distributor to the distribution of Such Picture on free television and execute a Television Distributor's Assumption Agreement pursuant to which it is liable in perpetuity to make the payments under this Article 15A then upon condition that the Guild in its discretion approves such third party's financial responsibility, such distributor shall thereupon be released from any and all further obligations under this Article 15A with respect to Such Picture. However such distributor shall not be liable for the payment of any television fees based on monies received by a foreign distributor under a "foreign production deal" as defined in subsection 3.a. of this Article 15A [casebook p. 531] with respect to which such foreign distributor or independent producer is not obligated to account to such distributor.

(ii) Where the distributor of Such Picture does not provide or guarantee any of the financing of Such Picture, the Television Distributor's Assumption Agreement shall be binding upon the distributor only as long as it is the distributor of Such Picture on free television.

(iii) Where there is more than one distributor or buyer of Such Picture on free television, the liability of any such distributor or buyer, which neither provides nor guarantees any of the financing for the production of Such Picture, for the payment of television fees under this Article 15A, shall be applicable only to such portion of Producer's gross as is derived by distributor or buyer as the case may be.

The distributor or buyer as used in this subparagraph (iii) refers to a distributor or buyer, as the case may be, under any distribution or sale agreement, as the case may be, with Company, as distinguished from an agreement between such distributor or buyer and its sub-distributor.

(4) Acquisition of Title by Company:

If Company was not the actual producer of Such Picture which was produced by a signatory Company but acquired title thereto by purchase, assignment, transfer, voluntary or involuntary, or by foreclosure of a chattel mortgage or security agreement or a pledgee's sale, Company shall nevertheless be obligated to make the payments herein provided when Such Picture is exhibited on free television, unless such payment required hereunder has already been paid.

(5) Financing-Distribution Agreement by Company:

The obligation of the signatory Company hereunder with respect to the payments provided for in this Article 15A shall also apply to any Such Pictures produced by an independent producer under a contract between the signatory Company and such independent producer for the production of such motion picture, and for the financing and distribution thereof by the signatory Company. However, such signatory Company shall not be liable for the payment of any television fees based on monies received by a foreign distributor under a foreign production deal as defined in paragraph a. of this subsection 3., with respect to which such foreign distributor or such independent producer is not obligated to account to such signatory Company. Nor shall such signatory Company be obligated to obtain any Television Distributor's Assumption Agreement from any foreign distributor referred to in paragraph a. of this subsection 3. except if such foreign distributor is obligated to account to such signatory Company pursuant to subparagraph (a) of this paragraph 3. with respect to monies as therein provided.

(6) Company Liability:

It is expressly understood and agreed that Company shall in all events remain bound hereunder to make the payments due by reason of the exhibition of each Such Picture on free television, irrespective of the assumption of such liability by any other person, firm or company as hereinabove provided, except as otherwise expressly provided in this Basic Agreement.

(7) Failure to Deliver Assumption Agreement:

The failure of Company to obtain and deliver an executed assumption agreement as provided in paragraph h. (1) and h. (2) and subparagraph (i) of this Article 15A3. shall be deemed a substantial breach of this Basic Agreement.

(8) Company's Dissolution:

If Company dissolves and is no longer in the business of producing motion pictures and if a distributor assumes all of the obligations of the Company under this Article 15A and the financial responsibility of the distributor is approved by the Guild in its discretion, the Company shall thereupon be released of any obligation with respect to any payments due hereunder; provided that if the distributor which assumes all of the obligations of the Company is a member company of the Association of Motion Picture & Television Producers, Inc. or if any such member company is permanently liable to pay the television fees provided for in this Article 15A with respect to the motion pictures for which the Company is liable to make such payment of television fees, then the financial responsibility of such distributor shall be conclusively deemed approved and such Company shall be released of any obligation with respect to any such payments.

(9) Networks and Television Stations:

No television network, station, sponsor or advertising agency shall be required to execute any Television Distributor's Assumption Agreement, or Buyer's Assumption Agreement, or a Literary Material Assumption Agreement, except, if it is the distributor of Such Picture on free television or the buyer of the Company's free television rights in Such Picture, as the case may be.

i. If the Company shall sell, transfer, assign or otherwise dispose of its rights in any story or screenplay (to which the provisions of this Article 15A3. apply, or may apply) prior to the production of a motion picture based thereon, to any person or company (hereinafter referred to as the "Buyer") other than a person or company with headquarters outside the United States, the Company shall obtain from the Buyer a separate agreement in substantially the following form:

"LITERARY MATERIAL ASSUMPTION AGREEMENT

_____ (hereinafter referred to as the "Buyer") agrees with _____ (Company) that the story, screenplay or story and screenplay covered by this Agreement is subject to the Writers Guild of America Theatrical and Television Basic Agreement of 1977 (herein the "Basic Agreement") and particularly to the provisions of Article 15A3. thereof pertaining to additional payments to Writers on release of a theatrical motion picture based thereon to free television (but excluding paragraph h. of said Article 15A3.) and the said Buyer hereby agrees, expressly for the benefit of the Writers Guild of America, West, Inc., (herein referred to as the Guild) as representatives of the Writers involved, to abide by and perform the provisions of said Basic Agreement and make the additional payments required thereunder, as aforesaid. For the purpose of applying such provisions of said Basic Agreement, the Writer or Writers of such material shall be treated in all respects as though the said material were written by such Writer or Writers while in the employ of the Buyer.

It is expressly understood and agreed that the rights of the Buyer to exhibit or license the exhibition of any motion picture based upon said material shall be subject to and conditioned upon the payment to the Writer or Writers involved of additional compensation, if any, required under subsection 3. (except paragraph h. thereof) of said Article 15A 3. of said Basic Agreement, and it is agreed that the Guild shall be entitled to injunctive relief and damages against Buyer in the event such payments are not made.

If the Buyer shall sell, transfer, assign or otherwise dispose of its rights in such material to any person or company with headquarters in the United States, it may obtain from the party acquiring such rights a separate agreement in the same form (including this sentence) as this agreement, and will notify the Guild thereof, together with the name and address of the transferee, and deliver to the Guild a copy of such assumption agreement; it being the intent hereof that the obligations herein set forth shall be continuing obligations on the part of such subsequent owners, of such material, so headquartered in the United States.

BUYER

By_____

Date:_____

Address:_____ "

The Company agrees to give notice to the Guild of such sale, transfer or assignment of the nature above mentioned, with the name and address of the Buyer, and to deliver to the Guild an executed copy of such assumption agreement. An inadvertent failure on the part of the Company to comply with any of the provisions of this paragraph i. shall in no event constitute a default by the Company hereunder or a breach of this Basic Agreement, provided that such failure is cured promptly after notice thereof from the Guild.

Upon delivery of such assumption agreement, Company, or any subsequent owner obtaining the execution of such an assumption agreement, shall not be further liable to the Guild or any Writer for the keeping of any such records or the payment of such additional compensation, or for compliance with credit obligations insofar as they relate to the broadcast of Such Picture on free television; and the Guild agrees to look exclusively to the party last executing such an assumption agreement for the keeping of such records, payment and compliance with credit obligations. If a company with headquarters outside the United States is a subsidiary of the Company, or the Company is the distributor of Such Picture for such a company, then for the purposes of this paragraph i. such company shall be deemed to be headquartered only in the United States.

j. Anything to the contrary herein notwithstanding, it is agreed that the provisions of this subsection 3. apply only if Such Picture is first exhibited on free television after Such Picture has had a bona fide theatrical release. For such purpose Such Picture may be regarded as having had a bona fide theatrical release even though such release has not fully completed, or shall not have been withdrawn from, its theatrical release, and even though Such Picture may have been released theatrically only domestically or theatrically only in foreign countries or territories. If Such Picture is exhibited on free television prior to the time that it has had a bona fide theatrical release, then the release of Such Picture to free television shall be governed by the provisions of the Basic Agreement then in effect between the parties hereto, but only with respect to the provisions thereof relating to additional compensation for television reruns on free television.

The provisions of this subsection 3. shall not apply to the televising of trailers or advertising a motion picture by shots, etc., substantially in the nature of a trailer, or to the use of stock shots, or to the televising of excerpts from theatrical motion pictures for news or review purposes. For any other use of excerpts from Such Picture in television programs, including television programs which consist substantially of excerpts from theatrical motion pictures, the Company shall pay the following aggregate one-time only sum to the writers determined by the Guild to be entitled to such compensation and prorated as determined by the Guild:

(a) 1 minute or less of excerpts—$125, or

(b) over 1 but not over 2 minutes of excerpts—$250, or

(c) over 2 minutes of excerpts—the amount referred to in (b) for the first two minutes and $100 for each minute or portion thereof in excess of 2 minutes.

No compensation shall be payable pursuant to this subparagraph j. to a writer of a motion picture from which an excerpt is derived if such writer writes material for and receives writing credit on the program into which such excerpt is inserted.

k. Notwithstanding the sooner termination of this agreement, the parties hereto agree that the terms and conditions of this subsection 3, shall apply and remain in full force and effect, and without change, to Such Pictures produced by the Company, the principal photography of which commenced between March 2, 1977 and March 1, 1981 both dates inclusive, regardless of when (either during or at any time after the expiration of the term of this Basic Agreement or of such period) Such Pictures are released to free television, and regardless of the terms or provisions of any Basic Agreement which is a modification, extension, or renewal of, or substitution for this Basic Agreement.

Article 15

TELEVISION EXHIBITION RE-RUNS
& FOREIGN TELECASTS OF TV FILMS

B. TELEVISION

. . . .

2. Foreign Telecasting Formula

a. In the event such television film is telecast in any part of the world outside the United States and Canada, the writers referred to in 1.b.(2) and (4) [not included in this casebook] above, shall be paid additional compensation for such foreign telecasting as follows:

(1) initial payment of not less than 15% of their applicable minimum compensation payable not later than 30 days after the Company obtains knowledge of the first foreign telecast, and in no event later than six months after the first foreign telecast.

(2) 10% of the applicable minimum when the Distributor's Foreign Gross exceeds $7,000.00 for half-hour pictures, $13,000.00 for one-hour pictures, or $18,000.00 for pictures in excess of one hour in length. Such payment to be made no later than thirty (30) days after such gross has been so exceeded, and

(3) a final payment of 10% of the applicable minimum compensation when the Distributor's Foreign Gross exceeds $10,000.00 for half-hour pictures, $18,000.00 for one-hour pictures, or $24,000.00 for pictures in excess of one hour in length. Such payments to be made no later than thirty (30) days after such gross has been so exceeded.

b. After the writer has received a total of 35% of his applicable minimum compensation with respect to any television film, no further sums shall be payable by reason of the Distributor's Foreign Gross received thereafter.

c. The term "foreign telecasting" as used herein, shall mean any telecast (whether simultaneous or delayed) outside the United States, its territories and possessions, and Canada, other than a telecast on any of the following regularly affiliated stations of a United States television network as a part of the United States network television telecast: XH-TV, Mexico City; ZBM, Pembroke, Bermuda, for CBS; XEW-TV or XEQ-TV or XH-TV or XHGC Mexico City, and ZBM, Pembroke, Bermuda for NBC; and XE-TV Tijuana; and ZFB, Hamilton, Bermuda, for ABC.

d. As used herein the term "Distributor's Foreign Gross" shall mean with respect to any television film, the absolute gross income realized by the distributor of such picture from the foreign telecasting thereof and including, in the case of a "foreign territorial sale" by any such distributor, the income realized from such sale by such distributor but not the income realized by the "purchaser" or "licensee." The phrase "absolute gross income" shall not include:

(1) Sums realized or held by the way of deposits or security, until and unless earned, other than such sums as are nonreturnable.

(2) Sums required to be paid or withheld as taxes, in the nature of turnover taxes, sales taxes or similar taxes based on the actual receipts of the television film or on any monies to be remitted to or by the distributor, but there shall not be excluded from distributor's foreign gross any net income, franchise tax or excess profit tax or similar tax payable by the distributor on its net income or for the privilege of doing business.

(3) Frozen foreign currency until the distributor shall have either the right to use such foreign currency in or to transmit such foreign currency from the country or territory where it is frozen. In the event such currency may be utilized or transmitted as aforesaid, it shall be deemed to have been converted to United States dollars at the prevailing free market rate of exchange at the time such right to use or transmit accrues.

Distributor's foreign gross realized in foreign currency in any reporting period required hereunder shall be deemed to be converted to United States dollars at the prevailing free market rate of exchange at the close of such reporting period.

e. If any transaction involving any television film subject to a foreign telecast payment under this Basic Agreement shall also include motion pictures, broadcast time, broadcast facilities or material (including commercial or advertising material) which are not subject to such payment, there shall be a reasonable allocation between the television films which are subject to a foreign telecast payment and such other pictures, time, facilities or material, and only the sums properly allocable to pictures which are subject to a foreign telecast payment shall be included in Distributor's Foreign Gross.

. . . .

3. Application of Excess

Company, at its option, may make any part or all of the additional payments for re-runs and foreign telecasts provided herein, at the time of employment of writer or at any time prior to the time the same is due (but only if the agreement between the Company and writer with respect thereto is set forth in writer's individual contract); provided that no part of writer's initial compensation which is at or less than twice the applicable minimum compensation herein set forth may be applied against such re-run and foreign telecast payments, or either.

. . . .

7. If a writer's individual employment contract contains a provision giving such writer a percentage or other participation in the receipts, revenues or profits of a television film, such payment may be credited against the minimum additional compensation for re-runs and foreign telecasts or either provided herein, but writer, in any event, shall be entitled to be paid not less than such minimum additional compensation for re-runs, and foreign telecasts, or either, as the case may be, and any payment on account thereof shall likewise be credited against such participation; provided that amounts received by writer as a percentage or other participation in the receipts, revenues or profits of the television film may not be credited against the minimum additional compensation for reruns or foreign telecasts until writer has received as compensation from all sources an amount equal to twice the applicable minimum compensation.

. . . .

13. Additional Compensation for Theatrical Exhibition

In the event a television film, based upon literary material to which this Basic Agreement applies, is exhibited theatrically, the writer or writers employed thereon who receive story and teleplay screen credit therefor shall be paid additional compensation as follows:

(i) If the television film is exhibited theatrically outside of the United States, an amount which in the aggregate shall not be less than the total minimum compensation applicable to such literary material as specified in Article 13B. 7.a., b., c. and e. of the Basic Agreement [not included in this casebook], or not less than the total minimum compensation applicable to such literary material as specified in Article 13A 1. [not included in this casebook] hereof, whichever is the greater;

(ii) If the television film is exhibited theatrically in the United States, or both in the United States and in a foreign country or territory, an amount which in the aggregate is not less than 150% of the total minimum compensation applicable to such literary material as specified in Article 13B. 7.a., b., c. and e. of the Basic Agreement, or not less than the total minimum compensation applicable to such literary material as specified in Article 13A 1. hereof, whichever is greater.

There is to be no duplication of the payments provided for in (i) and (ii) above; i.e., if the initial theatrical release of the television film takes place outside of the United States and payment is made pursuant to (i) above, then upon the subsequent theatrical release of the television film in the United States, the amount payable to the writer will be the difference between the amount provided for in (i) above and the amount provided for in (ii) above, and conversely, if the initial theatrical release of the television film takes place in the United States and payment is made pursuant to (ii) above; then no additional compensation will be payable if the television film is subsequently release theatrically outside of the United States. For the purposes of (i) and (ii) above, if two or more television films are combined for theatrical release, the applicable minimum provided for in Article 13A 1. shall be the minimum applicable to one theatrical motion picture of the cost of the combined television films. Such additional compensation shall be paid regardless of whether such film is exhibited alone or as a part of or in combination with other films; and if such film is combined with other television films, the additional compensation for such theatrical release shall be not less than the total minimum compensation applicable to the writing of all such television films or parts thereof which have been so combined. If more than one writer shares the story or teleplay credit, then all of the writers sharing each credit shall be considered a unit and shall participate equally and receive in the aggregate the theatrical exhibition payment applicable thereto except that in the case of a comedy-variety program the Guild shall determine the proportions in which such participating writers will share the theatrical exhibition payment, will notify the Company thereof and Company will make payments accordingly.

a. Such additional compensation for theatrical exhibition shall be payable whenever such television film (in whole or in substantial part) is placed in any theatrical exhibition.

b. All payments of such additional compensation for theatrical exhibition shall be made promptly by check payable to the order of the writer entitled thereto, and if not paid to the writer at the time of employment shall be delivered to Guild for forwarding to such writer, and compliance herewith shall constitute payment to the writer.

c. The Company at its option, may make the additional payment for theatrical exhibition at the time of the employment of the writer or at any time prior to the time the same is due (but only if the agreement between the Company and the writer with respect thereto is set forth in the writer's individual contract); provided that only such part of the compensation initially paid to the writer as shall exceed twice the applicable minimum compensation may be applied in prepayment of additional compensation for theatrical exhibition.

Any exhibition of a film, other than through the medium of free television or as covered by Article 51 (Supplemental Markets) [casebook pp. 559–578], shall constitute a theatrical exhibition and (subject to the provisions of subsection 16. of this Article 15B [not included in this casebook]) payment for such theatrical exhibition shall be as herein provided, except that this shall not apply to showings where no fee or admission charge is paid by the viewing audience.

If the Company licenses or grants to any third party the right to place in theatrical exhibition a television film produced after March 1, 1977 which exhibition is to be before a viewing audience which pays no fee or admission charge to view the same, Company will pay to the writer(s) entitled to story and/or teleplay credit an amount equal in the aggregate to 5% of the gross amounts received by Company derived therefrom; provided, however, the sums paid to the writer(s) hereunder shall in no event exceed the applicable amount otherwise payable to such writer(s) under the provisions of Paragraph 13 [not included in this casebook] had there been a fee or admission charge paid by the viewing audience. Where Company licenses or grants any such right to a subsidiary or other related entity, the gross amounts referred to in the preceding sentence shall be the amounts specifically paid to the Company subject to there having been good faith bargaining between the Company and such subsidiary or related entity. Company shall account to the writer(s) entitled to payments hereunder on no less than an annual basis; provided that no accounting need be made for any 12-month period following the 12-month period during which the Company received no gross amounts with respect thereto. There shall be no duplication of the payments provide for in this subparagraph, and the payments provided for in any other provision of Paragraph 13. That is, any payment made under this subparagraph shall be credited against any payment which may become due the writer(s) under all other provisions of Paragraph 13. Conversely, if a theatrical release payment is made to the writer(s) under the provisions of Paragraph 13 other than under this subparagraph then no further sum shall be payable under this subparagraph.

d. With respect to a television film or multi-part program whose aggregate length as initially broadcast on television is more than four (4) hours and which is exhibited theatrically in condensed form, for purposes of this paragraph 13 the total minimum compensation applicable to such literary material as specified in Article 13.B.7.a., b., c., and e. shall be specially determined as follows:

(1) If said film is exhibited theatrically outside of the United States, said minimum shall be based on the actual length of the film in its condensed, theatrical-release form but not less than four times the applicable sixty minute minimum;

(2) If said film is exhibited theatrically in the United States, or both in the United States and in a foreign country or territory, said minimum shall be based on the actual length of the film in its condensed, theatrical-release form, but no less than the sum of (a) four times the applicable 60-minute minimum plus (b) one-half of the difference between (i) the minimum applicable to the program in its initially broadcast length and (ii) four times the applicable 60-minute minimum.

The provisions set forth above in paragraph 13 relating to nonduplication of payments shall also apply to the foregoing special provisions.

e. If the Company shall sell, transfer, assign or otherwise dispose of its theatrical exhibition rights in any television film, it shall obtain from the buyer a separate agreement in substantially the form prescribed with respect to re-runs, requiring the buyer to comply with the provisions of this Basic Agreement with respect to additional compensation payable to the writer for theatrical exhibition of the film; and upon obtaining such agreement Company shall not be further liable to the Guild or writer for the payment of additional compensation for theatrical exhibition.

The excerpting of so-called "stock shots" by Company from television film for transposition to and use in otherwise separately produced theatrical film shall not be deemed to be an exercise of the theatrical exhibition rights by Company within the meaning of this paragraph.

If Company shall produce a film budgeted at $125,000.00 or more intended primarily for television release and it shall thereafter release such film theatrically in any country in the world, Company shall pay to writer any amount by which the established flat deal theatrical motion picture minimum for such film at the time of its production shall exceed the total of the minimum applicable compensation and minimum theatrical exhibition payments required to be made hereunder. The established flat deal theatrical motion picture minimum shall be the compensation set forth in Article 13A hereof.

. . . .

Article 16

SEPARATION OF RIGHTS

A. THEATRICAL

. . . .

8. **Writer's Right to Reacquire Literary Material.**

The provisions of this subsection 8. apply only to literary material (i) acquired by Company subject to the terms of this Basic Agreement or the terms of the 1970 or 1973 WGA agreement, (ii) which is original, i.e., not based on any pre-existing material, (iii) which has not been exploited in any medium, and (iv) which Company has decided it will not exploit in any medium in the future. As to such literary material if the writer who has written the same desires to purchase Company's right, title and interest therein, the Guild, on behalf of such writer may notify Company in writing of such desire. Within thirty (30) days following receipt of such written notice, Company shall notify the Guild of the terms and conditions, including the price at which it will sell its right, title and interest in such literary material; provided, however, that Company may instead notify the Guild that the literary material does not meet one or more of the conditions precedent specified in the first sentence of this subsection 8. The Company's decision that it has not decided not to exploit such literary material, and/or regarding the terms and conditions of the sale, shall not be subject to challenge by the Guild or by the writer on any grounds whatsoever whether in arbitration or otherwise even though Company does not in fact exploit or dispose of such material; without limiting the generality of the foregoing, offering the literary material for sale, or negotiating for such sale, shall not be deemed to be an election not to exploit such literary material.

The purchase price designated by Company shall not be in excess of the total direct costs previously incurred by Company in relation only to such literary material, including payments for the acquisition of the literary material and for writing services connected therewith (including writing services in relation to treatments and screenplays based thereon), and fringe benefit costs in relation thereto, such as pension and health and welfare payments and social security payments, but exclusive of overhead and exclusive of costs of any other kind (e.g., costs relating to proposed production other than writing costs).

Within thirty (30) days following notice from the Company of the terms and conditions on which it will sell its right, title and interest in such literary material, including the purchase price, the Guild, on behalf of the writer may serve written notice of acceptance of such terms and conditions and immediately following service of such notice the parties shall proceed to close the transaction. Failure to effect such purchase in accordance with the procedure specified by the foregoing provisions shall result in the forfeiture of writer's right to purchase such material. At any time before receipt of notice of acceptance of the terms and conditions of sale, Company may dispose of such literary material or of any rights therein or with respect thereto or may itself elect to exploit such material, and in either such event the writer shall no longer have the right to acquire Company's right, title or interest in such material.

In addition to the foregoing, but with respect only to literary material acquired by a Company on and after March 2, 1977, the writer may reacquire such literary material in accordance with the procedures set forth below, if production of a theatrical or television motion picture based on the literary material has not commenced upon expiration of the following applicable time period:

(a) If, during the five-year period after (i) the Company's purchase or license of the literary material (if written by a professional writer) or (ii) completion of the writer's services rendered in connection with the literary material, the Company has not had additional writing services rendered thereon or otherwise actively developed the literary material, and if, further, upon expiration of said five-year period, the Company is not engaged in negotiations for the sale or license of the literary material to a third party, then upon expiration of said five-year period; or

(b) If, upon expiration of the five-year period referred to in subparagraph (a) above, the Company is engaged in negotiations for the sale or license of the literary material to a third party but has not also had additional writing services rendered thereon or otherwise actively developed the literary material, and if said negotiations do not result in a sale or license thereof, then upon the conclusion of said negotiations; or

(c) If neither subparagraph (a) or (b) above applies, then upon expiration of the seven-year period after (i) the Company's purchase or license of the literary material (if written by a professional writer), or (ii) completion of the writer's services rendered in connection with the literary material.

If the writer does reacquire such literary material, such reacquisition is subject to all existing commitments, such a security interests, participations, options, turnaround rights, employment rights, etc.

At any time during the two-year period immediately following expiration of the applicable time period set forth above, the Guild may give the written notice provided in the second sentence of this Paragraph 8 (hereafter "Guild's notice"), and within 30 days thereafter Company shall give the written notice provided in the third sentence of this Paragraph 8 (hereafter "Company's notice"), stating the terms and conditions on which it will sell its right, title and interest in such literary material, including the purchase price. Upon the giving of Company's notice, the literary property shall be deemed literary material which the Company has decided it will not exploit in any medium in the future. The purchase price designated by Company shall not be in excess of the total direct costs previously incurred by Company in relation only to such literary material as set forth in the fifth sentence of Paragraph 8 above. Within 120 days of the giving of the Company's notice (during which period the Company shall not exploit, produce, sell or dispose of said material to any third person), the Guild, on behalf of the writer, may serve written notice of acceptance of such terms and conditions and immediately following service of such notice the parties shall proceed to close the transaction. Failure to effect such purchase in accordance with the procedure specified by the foregoing provisions by the end of such two-year period (i.e., the years commencing after the expiration of the applicable time period set forth above) shall result in the forfeiture of writer's right to purchase such material any time thereafter under any provision of this Paragraph 8. Within said two-year period the Guild on behalf of the writer may repeat the Guild's notice one or more times. All of the procedures and rights above described with respect to the first giving of the Guild's notice shall apply to the first such repeat notice. All of said procedures and rights shall also apply to the second and any subsequent repeat notices except that the Company shall not exploit, produce, sell or dispose of said material to any third person during any period between the giving of the Guild's second (or subsequent) repeat notice and the expiration of 120 days following the giving of the Company's respective notice.

Furthermore, if Company had previously granted some other person or company the right or option to acquire such material or any rights therein, the writer of such literary material shall not have the right to purchase the same so long as such other right remains outstanding. In the event that more than one writer is involved in the writing of such literary material the Guild shall have the sole responsibility to determine which of such writers has the right to purchase as provided herein and all interested writers shall be bound by the decision of the Guild.

. . . .

Article 28

WARRANTY AND INDEMNIFICATION
(GENERAL)

1. Company and writer may in any individual contract of employment include provisions for warranties of originality and no violation of rights of third parties, indemnification against judgments, damages, costs and expenses including attorneys' fees in connection with suit relating to the literary material or the use of the literary material supplied by the writer or the use thereof by Company; provided, however, that the writer shall in no event

a. be required by contract to waive his right to defend himself against a claim by Company for costs, damages or losses arising out of settlements not consented to by the writer; and Company reserves all of the rights it may otherwise have against the writer;

b. be required to warrant or indemnify with respect to any claim that his literary material defamed or invaded the privacy of any person unless the writer knowingly used the name or personality of such person or should have known, in the exercise of reasonable prudence, that such person would or might claim that his personality was used in such material;

c. be required to warrant or indemnify with respect to any material other than that furnished by the writer.

2. The Company shall indemnify such writer against any and all damages, costs and expenses, including attorneys' fees, and shall relieve the writer of all liability in connection with any claim or action respecting material supplied to the writer by the Company for incorporation into the writer's work or incorporated in the writer's work by employees or officers of the Company other than the writer.

3. The Company and the writer, upon the presentation of any such claim to either of them or the institution of any such action naming either or both of them as defendants, shall promptly notify the other of the presentation of any such claim or the institution of any such action giving such other party full details thereof, but the pendency of any such claim or action shall not relieve

the Company of its obligation to pay to the employee any monies due to the writer with respect to the literary material contributed by the employee.

The company shall name or cover the writer (including writers employed via loan out companies, if the insurer permits such coverage) as additional insured on its errors and ommissions policies respecting theatrical and television motion pictures.

. . . .

Article 51

SUPPLEMENTAL MARKETS

1. The provisions of this Article 51 relate and apply only to motion pictures as defined in Article 1.A.1. and 1.A.2 [not included in this casebook]:

a. produced by the Company or within the provisions of paragraph h. (4) of subsection 3., of this Article 51 [casebook p. 574], and

b. the principal photography of which commenced on or after March 2, 1977, which motion pictures are, either during the term hereof or at any time thereafter, released in supplemental markets (as defined below); and

c. based upon a story or screenplay (the word "screenplay" shall be deemed to include teleplay, for the purposes of this Article) written by a writer while in the employ of the Company or in the employ of the actual producing Company as described in paragraph h (4) of subsection 3. of this Article 51 (to which employment the provisions of this Basic Agreement apply as provided in Article 5 hereof [not included in this casebook]) or acquired by the Company (or such actual producing Company) from a professional writer (to which acquisition the provisions of this Basic Agreement apply as provided in Article 5 hereof), which writer or professional writer received or receives screen credit for authorship of such story or screenplay, as provided in the appropriate Theatrical or Television Schedule A, as the case may be.

2. DEFINITIONS.

The term "Supplemental Markets", as used in this Agreement means only: The exhibition of motion pictures by means of cassettes (to the limited extent provided in subparagraph a of this paragraph 2), pay-type CATV, or Pay Television, as those terms are hereafter defined in this paragraph 2 and the exhibition of television motion pictures on any commercial carrier such as commercial airlines, trains, ships, and buses (referred to herein as "in-flight").

a. Cassettes: For the purposes of this Agreement, a cassette is any audio-visual device, including without limitation, cassette, cartridge, phonogram or other similar audio-visual device now known or hereafter devised, containing a motion picture (recorded on film, disc, tapes or other material) and designed for replay through a television receiver or comparable device. The sale or rental of cassettes for replay through a television receiver or comparable device in the home or in closed-circuit use such as in hotel rooms, constitute the "Supplemental Market" for the purposes of this agreement.

b. Pay-Type CATV: Exhibition of motion pictures through a television receiver or comparable device by means of transmission by a Community Antenna Television System (CATV) where, in addition to an obligatory general cable charge to the subscriber for the CATV service: (i) a charge is made for programs selected by the subscriber, or (ii) the subscriber has the option, by making payment, to receive special programming over one or more channels which are not available to the subscriber without such payment.

c. Pay Television: Exhibition of motion pictures through a television receiver or comparable device by means of telecast, cable or closed circuit for which the viewing audience (whether by the individual viewer or by the hotel, motel, hospital or other accommodation where the viewer is) pays to receive the program by making a separate payment for such specific program. Exhibitions in theatres or comparable places by means of telecast or cable is theatrical exhibition and shall not be considered Pay Television.

The term "Supplemental Markets" does not include the exhibition of a motion picture by cassette or otherwise over a television broadcast station in free television, or in theatrical exhibition and for this purpose "theatrical exhibition" includes what has previously been considered to be the educational market, the exhibition of theatrical motion pictures on any commercial carrier (referred to herein as "In-flight"), such a commercial airlines, trains, ships and buses, and other uses which have been traditionally considered theatrical exhibition of theatrical motion pictures. Wherever reference is made in this Agreement to pay-type CATV or pay television, such reference shall be deemed to include only those uses of motion pictures as to which a charge is actually made to the subscriber (which may be a hotel, motel or other accommodation) for the program viewed, or where the subscriber or viewer has the option, for a payment, to receive special programming over one or more special channels. Where no program charge or special channel charge is made to the subscriber in addition to the obligatory general charge, the transmission of motion pictures by the CATV facility, including programming originated by the CATV facility, is free television exhibition for the purposes of this Agreement, and such exhibition shall not be considered "Supplemental Markets" exhibition.

With respect to theatrical motion pictures, the Company has agreed to the inclusion of pay-type CATV and pay television in the "Supplemental Markets" because under the present pattern of distribution of theatrical motion pictures, pay-type CATV and pay television are supplemental to the primary market. The Company reserves the right in future negotiations to contend that the pattern of release has changed so that pay-type CATV and/or pay television are no longer a "Supplemental Market" but constitute or are a part of the primary market of distribution of theatrical motion pictures, and that therefore no additional payment pursuant to this Article should be made with respect to the release of theatrical motion pictures (including those covered by this agreement) in said markets. The Guild reserves the right to contend in future negotiations that the method of employment and payment provided for in this Basic Agreement for writers of motion pictures are applicable and appropriate to employment and payment to writers of literary materials written directly for motion pictures intended primarily for release on pay-type CATV, pay television or cassettes, and that the provisions of this Agreement with respect to all kinds of "Supplemental Markets", whether they are or have become primary markets or not, shall be improved for the benefit of the writers of literary materials for said markets. Nothing herein shall limit the scope of negotiations on said subjects.

3. As to each such motion picture referred to in 1 above, (herein sometimes called "Such Picture"), the Company will pay to each participating Writer (as such term is hereinafter defined) as additional compensation, a pro-rata share of one and 2/10 percent (1.2%) (hereinafter referred to as the "percentage payment") of the company's accountable receipts from the distribution of Such Picture in "Supplemental Markets", computed as hereinafter provided and subject to the following conditions:

a. The term "Producer's gross", as used herein, means the worldwide total gross receipts derived by the distributor of Such Picture (who may be the Company or a distributor licensed by the Company) from licensing the right to exhibit Such Picture in Supplemental Market; provided, however, that in the case of any Such Picture which is produced outside of the United States, if Such Picture is subject to this Basic Agreement and if such production is under an arrangement (herein referred to as a "foreign production deal") pursuant to which a foreign producer or distributor provides or guarantees any of the financing for the production of Such Picture or furnishes any other consideration for such production and foreign distributor acquires one or more foreign territories for the distribution of Such Picture in Supplemental

Markets, then no monies from any such distribution in any such foreign territory shall be included in Producer's gross except to the extent such foreign producer or foreign distributor is obligated to account to Company or to the distributor of Such Picture for such monies, and except for gross receipts received by such foreign distributor from such distribution in the United Kingdom.

If the distributor of Such Picture does not distribute Such Picture directly in Supplemental Markets, but employs a subdistributor to so distribute Such Picture, then the "Producer's gross" shall be the worldwide total gross receipts derived by such subdistributor from licensing the right to exhibit Such Picture in Supplemental Markets. In case of an outright sale of the Supplemental Markets distribution rights, for the entire world, or any territory or country, the income derived by the seller from such sale, but not the income realized by the purchaser or licensee of such rights, shall be the "Producer's gross". If any such outright sale shall include Supplemental Markets exhibition rights and other rights, then (but only for the purpose of the computation required hereunder) the Company shall allocate to the Supplement Markets exhibition rights a fair and reasonable portion of the sales price which shall, for the purpose hereof, be the "Producer's gross". In reaching such determination Company may consider the current market value of Supplemental Markets exhibition rights in comparable motion pictures.

If the Guild shall contend that the amount so allocated was not fair and reasonable, such claim may be determined by submission to arbitration as herein provided; and in the event the Board of Arbitration shall find that such allocation was not reasonable and fair, it shall determine the fair and reasonable amount to be so allocated. If the outright sale includes Supplemental Markets distribution rights to more than one motion picture, Company shall likewise allocate to each Such Picture a fair and reasonable portion of the sales price of the Supplemental Markets rights; and if the Guild contends that such allocation is not fair and reasonable, the question may be determined by submission to arbitration as above provided. If the Board of Arbitration shall find that such allocation was not fair and reasonable, it shall determine the fair and reasonable amount to be so allocated to each Such Picture. Nothing with respect to the price received on the outright sale of only Supplemental Markets distribution rights in a single Such Picture shall be subject to arbitration except that in the event of a dispute, there may be arbitrated the question of whether the price reported by the Company to the Guild as having been received by the Company on such outright sale is less than the amount actually received by the Company on such outright sale.

It is recognized that the method of distributing cassettes may not be similar to the method of distributing theatrical motion pictures in television. However, for the purpose of determining the amounts payable for cassette distribution of motion pictures, it is the intent of the parties that the basis for determining Producer's gross from cassette distribution shall be comparable to the basis used for determining the Producer's gross from the distribution of theatrical motion pictures in television. For example, gross receipts from casettes sold at the retail level would not be Producer's gross hereunder. As a further example, if the Producer itself acts as a distributor and retailer, a reasonable allocation of the retail gross receipts shall be made as between the Producer as Distributor and the Producer as retailer, and only the former shall be deemed to be Producer's gross. The reasonableness of such allocation shall be subject to arbitration and, in such arbitration, generally prevailing trade practices in the cassette distribution industry with respect to dealings between non-related companies, shall be relevant evidence.

The Producer's gross shall not include:

(i) Rebates, credits or repayments for cassettes returned (and in this connection the Producer shall have the right to set up a reasonable reserve for returns);

(ii) Sums required to be paid or withheld as taxes, in the nature of turnover taxes, sales taxes or similar taxes based on the actual receipts of such motion picture or on any monies to be remitted to or by the Producer but there shall not be excluded from Producer's gross any net income tax, franchise tax or excess profit tax or similar tax payable by the Producer or such Distributor on its net income or for the privilege of doing business;

b. The term "accountable receipts" as used herein, means fifty percent (50%) of the "Producer's gross", except as follows:

(i) As to the Producer's gross from television motion pictures, the term "accountable receipts" as used herein means 100% of such gross.

(ii) As to any particular theatrical motion picture, if the Producer's gross from such motion picture exceeds $400,000, the "accountable receipts" of such motion pictures means 50% of the first $400,000 of such Producer's gross and 100% of such Producer's gross in excess of $400,000.

(iii) At the time, if any, that the producer's gross from Supplemental Markets of all motion pictures covered by collective bargaining agreements between the Guild and any motion picture producer or producers, heretofore, now or hereafter in existence, during any consecutive 12-month period equals $45,000,000, the term "accountable receipts" (as to any particular motion picture covered by this Agreement) shall mean 100% of the Producer's gross derived by such motion picture from Supplemental Markets after such date.

c. Company's obligation shall accrue hereunder only after Producer's gross is received by Company but as to foreign receipts such obligation shall accrue only when such receipts can be freely converted to U. S. dollars and are remitted to the United States, and until such time no frozen foreign receipts shall be included in Producer's gross. Payment of amounts accruing hereunder shall be made quarterly on the basis of quarterly statements, as hereinafter provided.

Upon request, and if permitted by the authorities of a foreign country, the Company will transfer to any writer, in the currency of such foreign country, his share, if any, of frozen foreign receipts in such country, provided the writer will bear any costs involved; and such transfer shall be deemed to be payment to the writer of an equivalent number of U. S. dollars at the then current free rate for blocked funds of that category as determined by the Company. Concurrently with such transfer the writer will pay to the Company in U. S. dollars the total amount the Company is required to withhold from such payment under all applicable laws. If the Company utilizes frozen foreign currencies derived from exhibition of Such Picture in Supplemental Markets by conversion thereof to properties that may be freely exported and turned to account, the amount so utilized by the Company shall be deemed to have been converted to U. S. dollars at the then current free market rate for blocked funds of that category determined as above provided. Frozen foreign receipts from Supplemental Markets shall be deemed to be released on a first-in first-out basis, unless the authorities of the foreign country involved designate a specific period that would render such basis inapplicable. Such released funds shall be allocated between Such Picture and other motion pictures distributed by the distributor in Supplemental Markets in the same ratio that receipts, derived from the distribution of Such Picture in Supplemental Markets within the foreign country, bear to the total receipts derived from the distribution of Such Picture and all other motion pictures in Supplemental Markets with the foreign country, during the applicable period, unless the authorities of the foreign country involved require another method of allocation, in which case such other method shall be used. Foreign receipts shall be accounted for in U. S. dollars at the rate of exchange at which such receipts are actually converted and remitted, and should any discounts, taxes, duties or charges be imposed in connection with the receipt or remittance of foreign funds, only so much of such funds as remain thereafter shall be included in accountable receipts. Company shall not be responsible for loss or diminution of foreign receipts as a result of any matter or thing not reasonably within the control of the Company. The Guild and the writers shall be bound by any arrangements made in good faith by the Company or for its account, with respect to the deposit or remittance of foreign revenue. Frozen foreign receipts shall not be considered trust funds and the Company may freely commingle the same with other funds of the Company. No sums received by way of deposits or security need be included in Producer's gross until earned, but when the Company is paid a non-returnable advance by a distributor, such advance shall be included in the Producer's gross.

d. If any license or outright sale of exhibition rights to such Picture in Supplemental Markets includes as a part thereof any filmed commercial or advertising material, the Company shall be permitted to allocate a reasonable amount (in accordance with then current standard charges in the industry) to such commercial or advertising material, and the amount so allocated shall not be included in Producer's gross hereunder.

e. The term "Participating Writer", as used herein, means a writer who, while in the employ of the Company or in the employ of the actual Producing Company of Such picture as described in paragraph h. (4) of this subsection 3. (to which employment the provisions of this Basic Agreement apply), or a professional writer from whom the Company (or such actual producer) acquired literary material (to which acquisition the provisions of this Basic Agreement apply), participated in the writing of and received credit pursuant to the Theatrical Schedule A hereof or the Television Schedule A hereof, as the case may be, for the writing of the story or screenplay, or story and teleplay, as the case may be, upon which Such Picture was based. If Such Picture is a remake of a prior motion picture, and if any of the writers of the prior motion picture receive writing credit for the remake, such writers shall be deemed to be "Participating Writers" for the purposes of this paragraph e, but only if their employment as writers for the prior motion picture, or if the purchase of literary material from them for the prior motion picture, was covered by and subject to a collective bargaining agreement with the Guild. The "pro-rata share" payable to each Participating Writer shall be as follows:

Seventy-five percent (75%) thereof shall be payable to the credited screenplay or teleplay writer or writers, twenty-five percent (25%) thereof shall be payable to the credited story or screenstory writer or writers. In the event there is a minor credit, such as adaptation, the writer or writers receiving such minor credit shall be paid ten percent (10%) thereof which sum shall be deducted from the screenplay writers' share. The Writer or writers receiving a "written by" credit shall be entitled to one hundred percent (100%) of the monies.

Any participating writers receiving the same screen credit referred to above shall share equally in such percentage amount specified.

If there are one or more participating Writers who receive screenplay or teleplay credit and no credit is given for story or screen-story, then the pro-rata share which would have been payable to a participating Writer had he received such story or screen-story credit shall, subject to the provisions of the next following paragraph, be paid to the Participating Writers who receive such screenplay or teleplay credit.

If the Writer's services in Such Picture are performed for the Company on a loan-out basis, then for the purposes of this Article the Company shall be deemed to be the employer, and the lender shall not have any responsibility hereunder with respect to Such Picture. With respect to any Such Picture, if there are one or more Participating Writers who receive credit as aforesaid and one or more Writers who perform services in connection with the writing of the story or teleplay or screenplay and receive screen credit in connection with Such Picture, but who are not subject to this Basic Agreement, then that portion of percentage payment of said one and two-tenths percent (1.2%) which would otherwise have been payable to such one or more Writers not subject to this Basic Agreement may be retained by Company, and the Company shall not be obligated to pay such portion to any such participating Writer receiving credit as aforesaid.

f. Within a reasonable time after the expiration of each calendar or fiscal quarter, but not exceeding sixty (60) days, Company will furnish or cause to be furnished to the Guild a written report showing the Producer's gross during the preceding quarter from the distribution of each Such Picture by Company in Supplemental Markets with respect to which Company is required to make payments hereunder (whether distributed by the Company or through another distributor).

Concurrently with the furnishing of each such report, the Company will make the payments shown to be due by such report. All payments shall be made by check payable to the order of the Writers entitled thereto, and shall be delivered to the Guild for forwarding to such Writers; and compliance herewith shall constitute payment to the Writers.

No such reports need be furnished with respect to any period during which there was no such Producer's gross. The Company shall make available for inspection by the Guild all distributor's statements and exhibitor's statements which are available to the Company insofar as they relate to such Producer's gross, and all the financial terms of contracts pertaining to such Producer's gross, and the Guild shall have the right, at reasonable times, to examine the books and records of the Company as to such Producer's gross pertaining to such distribution of any Such Picture, at whatever place or places such records are customarily kept by the Company. If the Guild requests that it be informed of the license fee paid under a license for the exhibition of Such Picture in Supplemental Markets, or if the Guild requests that it be sent an extract of the financial terms of such a license, and if such information is not extensive in nature, the Company will forward such information or extract without making it necessary for the Guild to send a representative to the offices of the Company. In general, the Company will cooperate in furnishing such information to the Guild by mail or telephone, where doing so is not unreasonable or burdensome. If more than one picture is licensed in a single license agreement, the Company shall inform the Guild, at its request, of the identity of the pictures covered by the license, and shall make available to inspection by the Guild in the office where such license agreement is customarily kept a copy of the terms of such license showing the titles of the pictures licensed under such agreement and the license fee for each such picture. Company agrees to cooperate in responding to reasonable inquiries from the Guild as to whether any such picture is currently being distributed for telecasting on pay television or in any other Supplemental Market as herein defined. An inadvertent failure to comply with the reporting provisions of this paragraph f. shall not constitute a default by the Company hereunder, provided such failure is cured promptly after notice thereof from the Guild is received by the Company.

Company shall make all social security, withholding, unemployment insurance, and disability insurance payments required by law with respect to the additional compensation provided for in this Article *51*.

If the Company shall fail to make any payment provided for in this Article *51* to be made to the Writer when and as the same becomes due and payable, it shall bear interest at the rate of one and one half percent (1½%) per month on the unpaid balance thereof commencing to accrue ten (10) days after notice in writing to Company from the Guild of such delinquency.

The compensation payable under this Article *51* shall be excluded from the gross compensation upon which the Company contributions are to be made to the Pension Plan.

g. If a Participating Writer's employment agreement with the Company requires that the Writer's compensation shall be based, in whole or in part, upon, or measured by, a percentage of the gross receipts derived from the distribution of Such Picture, then such percentage compensation shall be credited against any amounts payable to the Writer hereunder, and likewise any payment due to the Writer hereunder shall be credited against such percentage compensation. Where all or a part of a Writer's compensation is a specified sum of money, commonly known and referred to as a "deferment", such deferment may not be credited against amounts payable by the Company to such Writer hereunder.

h. With respect to all Such Pictures, the following provisions shall be applicable:

(1) Distributor's Assumption Agreement:

Prior to the commencement of principal photography of each Such Picture, if the company is not also the distributor in supplemental markets of Such Picture, Company shall obtain from the distributor having such Supplemental Markets distribution rights and deliver to Guild, a separate written agreement herein called "DISTRIBUTOR'S ASSUMPTION AGREEMENT", made expressly for the benefit of Guild as representive of the writers involved, by which such distributor agrees to assume and pay the amounts payable hereunder by reason of the exhibition of Such Picture in Supplemental Markets, when and as the same become due. Such agreement shall be substantially in the following form:

"DISTRIBUTOR'S
ASSUMPTION AGREEMENT

In consideration of the execution of a DISTRIBUTION AGREE-MENT between _____ Company, and the undersigned Distributor, Distributor agrees that the motion picture presently entitled _____, is subject to the Writers Guild of America Theatrical and Television Basic Agreement of 1977, as amended, (hereinafter "Basic Agreement") and particularly to the provisions of Article *51* thereof, pertaining to additional compensation payable to writers when motion pictures are released in supplemental markets and Distributor hereby agrees expressly for the benefit of the Writers Guild of America, West, Inc., herein called WGA, as representative of the writers whose services are included in such motion picture as released in supplemental markets to make the additional compensation payment required thereby when such motion picture is exhibited in supplemental markets. Distributor for and on behalf of the Company shall make all social security, withholding, unemployment insurance and disability insurance payments required by law with respect to the additional compensation referred to in the preceding sentence.

It is expressly understood that the right of Distributor to license such motion picture for exhibition in supplemental markets, or to exhibit or cause or permit shall motion picture to be exhibited in supplemental markets, shall be subject and conditioned upon the prompt payment of such additional compensation, in accordance with Article *51* of the Basic Agreement. It is agreed that WGA, in addition to all other remedies, shall be entitled to injunctive relief against Distributor in the event such payments are not made.

Within a reasonable time after the expiration of each calendar or fiscal quarter, but not exceeding sixty (60) days, Distributor will furnish or cause to be furnished to WGA a written report showing the

Producer's gross (as defined in Article *51* of the Basic Agreement) during the preceding quarter from the distribution of such picture by Distributor in supplemental markets with respect to which Distributor is required to make payments hereunder (whether distributed by the Distributor or through another distributor licensed by Distributor). Such report shall be accompanied by such payments as may be due.

Distributor shall also make available for inspection by WGA all Distributor's statements delivered to Company insofar as they relate to Producer's gross. WGA shall have the right at reasonable times and on reasonable notice to examine the books and records of Distributor as to Producer's gross. If Distributor shall fail to make such payments as and when due and payable, they shall bear interest at the rate of one and one-half per cent (1½%) per month on the unpaid balance thereof commencing to accrue ten (10) days after notice in writing from WGA of such delinquency.

This DISTRIBUTOR'S ASSUMPTION AGREEMENT shall remain effective and binding upon Distributor as long as it remains the Distributor of such motion picture in supplemental markets, and thereafter in perpetuity only if it has provided or guaranteed any of the financing for the production of such motion picture, in accordance with and subject to the provisions of paragraph h. (3)(i) of Article 51.3. of the Basic Agreement.

Where there is more than one distributor the provisions of such paragraph h.(3)(iii) of Article 51.3., of the Basic Agreement shall apply to each distributor which neither provides nor guarantees any of the financing for the production of such motion picture.

The Distributor has, has not (strike whichever is inapplicable) provided or guaranteed financing for production of such motion picture.

DISTRIBUTOR

By_____

Date: _____

Address: _____ "

An inadvertent failure on the part of any such distributor to comply with any of the reporting provisions of this paragraph h.(1) shall in no event constitute a default by the Company or such distributor or a breach of this Basic Agreement, provided that such failure is cured promptly after notice in writing thereof from the Guild.

In the event of the expiration or termination of any distribution agreement, the obligation of Company to obtain and deliver to the Guild such DISTRIBUTOR'S ASSUMPTION AGREEMENT shall apply as well to any subsequent distribution agreement entered into by Company and Company shall obtain and deliver an executed DIS-TRIBUTOR'S ASSUMPTION AGREEMENT within ten (10) days after the execution of each of such subsequent distribution agreement.

If, with respect to any Such Picture distributor is not liable in perpetuity to pay the supplemental markets fees provided for hereunder, or if there is no distribution agreement by Company with respect to any Such Picture granting supplemental markets distribution rights to the distributor, then the Guild, prior to the commencement of principal photography of Such Picture, may require such further financial assurances from Company as it deems advisable to insure performance of Company's obligations to pay the Supplemental Markets fees provided for herein, including without limitation the execution of security agreements, guarantees, or other protective agreements. If any member company of the Association of Motion Picture and Television Producers, Inc., becomes liable in perpetuity under a DISTRIBU-TOR'S ASSUMPTION AGREEMENT to pay the supplemental markets fees provided for hereunder with respect to Such Picture, the Guild will release and cause to be discharged of record all such security agreements, guarantees or other protective agreements entered into or obtained by or from Company, provided, however that Company's primary liability shall not be released thereby.

(2) Buyer's Assumption Agreement.

If the Company shall sell, transfer or assign its rights to exhibit in Supplemental Markets any Such Picture it shall obtain from such buyer, transferee or assignee, a separate agreement made expressly for the benefit of the Guild as representative of the writers involved, requiring such buyer, transferee or assignee to comply with the provisions of this Basic Agreement with respect to additional compensation to writers by reason of the exhibition of Such Picture in Supplemental Markets, when and as the same become due. Such agreement shall be substantially in the following form:

"BUYER'S ASSUMPTION AGREEMENT

For a valuable consideration, the undersigned _____ (Insert name of Buyer, transferee or assignee) (hereinafter referred to as Buyer) hereby agrees with _____ (Insert name of Company) that all motion pictures covered by this agreement, a list of which is appended hereto, are subject to the Writers Guild of America Theatrical and Television Basic Agreement of 1977, as amended, (hereinafter "Basic Agreement") and particularly to the provisions of Article 51 thereof, pertaining to additional compensation payable to writers when motion pictures are released to supplemental markets and Buyer hereby agrees expressly for the benefit of the Writers Guild of America, West, Inc., hereinafter called WGA, as representative of the writers whose services are included in each such motion picture when telecast, to assume and be bound by Company's obligation thereunder to make the additional compensation payments required thereby when each such motion picture is exhibited in supplemental markets. Buyer for and on behalf of the Company shall make all social security, withholding, unemployment insurance, and disability insurance payments required by law with respect to the additional compensation referred to in the preceding sentence.

It is expressly understood that the right of the Buyer to license each such motion picture for exhibition in supplemental markets, or to exhibit or cause or permit such motion picture to be exhibited in supplemental markets, shall be subject to and conditioned upon the prompt payment of such additional compensation, in accordance with Article 51 of the Basic Agreement. It is agreed that WGA, in addition to all other remedies, shall be entitled to injunctive relief against Buyer in event such payments are not made.

Within a reasonable time after the expiration of each calendar or fiscal quarter, but not exceeding sixty (60) days, Buyer will furnish or cause to be furnished to WGA a written report showing the "Producer's gross" (as defined in Article 51 of the Basic Agreement) during the preceding quarter from the distribution of such Pictures by Buyer in supplemental markets with respect to which Buyer is required to make payments hereunder (whether distributed by Buyer or through another distributor licensed by Buyer). Such report shall be accompanied by such payments as may be due.

Buyer shall also make available for inspection by WGA all Distributor's statements delivered to Buyer insofar as they relate to Producer's gross. WGA shall have the right at reasonable times to examine the books and records of Buyer as to Producer's gross. If Buyer shall fail to make such payments as and when due and payable, they shall bear interest at the rate of one and one-half per cent (1½%) per month on the unpaid balance thereof commencing to accrue ten (10) days after notice in writing from WGA of such delinquency.

Where there is more than one buyer the provisions of paragraph h.(3)(iii) of Article 51.3. of the Basic Agreement shall apply to each Buyer.

———————————————————————

       BUYER

       By——————————————————————

Date: _____

Address: _____ "

The Company agrees to deliver to the Guild an executed copy of the above referred to Buyer's Assumption Agreement within thirty (30) days after the sale, assignment or transfer of Such Picture, with the name and address of the purchaser or assignee.

Any inadvertent failure on the part of the buyer to comply with any of the reporting provisions of this subparagraph (2) shall in no event constitute a default by the Company or such Buyer or a breach of this Agreement, provided that such failure is cured promptly after notice in writing thereof from the Guild.

Upon delivery of such Buyer's Assumption Agreement and on condition that the Guild approves in writing the financial responsibility of the purchaser, assignee, or transferee, Company shall not be further liable for the keeping of any such records, or for the payment of such additional compensation for the exhibition of any Such Pictures in supplemental markets, it being agreed that the purchaser, assignee, or transferee, shall solely be liable therefor.

The Guild agrees that it will not unreasonably withhold its approval of the financial responsibility of any such purchaser, assignee or transferee, it being further agreed that if the Guild, within twenty-one (21) days of receipt of written notice of any such sale, assignment or transfer has not advised the Company that it disapproves the financial responsibility of such purchaser, assignee or transferee, the Guild will be deemed to have approved the financial responsibility thereof. In the event the Guild advises the Company within such twenty-one (21) day period that it disapproves the financial responsibility of any such purchaser, assignee or transferee and the Company disputes such disapproval, the Company shall have the right, at its election, to cause to be immediately submitted to arbitration, as herein provided, the issue of whether the Guild has unreasonably withheld the approval of the financial responsibility of such purchaser, assignee or transferee for payments due hereunder.

(3) Distributor's Liability:

With respect to any Such Picture, the following provisions shall be applicable to the distributor of Such Picture in Supplemental Markets:

(i) Where the distributor has provided or guaranteed any of the financing for the production of Such Picture the obligations of the distributor under this Article 51 shall continue in perpetuity notwithstanding the expiration or termination of such distribution agreement, or any foreclosure of a chattel mortgage, security agreement, pledge, or lien on Such Picture. In the case of foreclosure, should such mortgagee, pledgee or security holder or a third party, who is neither the Company or distributor, acquire title to Such Picture and execute the Buyer's Assumption Agreement, and upon condition that the Guild, in its discretion, approves such purchaser's financial responsibility, then when the distributor ceases to be the distributor of Such Picture in Supplemental Markets the distributor shall thereupon be released from any and all further obligations under this Article 51 with respect to Such Picture. Should any third party (other than in connection with any such foreclosure) acquire the rights of such distributor to the distribution of Such Picture in Supplemental Markets and execute a Distributor's Assumption Agreement pursuant to which it is liable in perpetuity to make the payments under this Article 51 then upon condition that the Guild in its discretion approves such third party's financial responsibility, such distributor shall thereupon be released from any and all further obligations under this Article 51 with respect to Such Picture. However, such distributor shall not be liable for the payment of any Supplemental Market fees based on monies received by a foreign distributor under a "foreign production deal" as defined in subsection 3.a. of this Article 51 with respect to which such foreign distributor or independent producer is not obligated to account to such distributor.

(ii) Where the distributor of Such Picture does not provide or guarantee any of the financing of Such Picture, the Distributor's Assumption Agreement shall be binding upon the distributor only as long as it is the distributor of Such Picture in Supplemental Markets.

(iii) Where there is more than one distributor or buyer of Such Picture in Supplemental Markets, the liability of any such distributor or buyer, which neither provides nor guarantees any of the financing for the production of Such Picture, for the payment of Supplemental Market fees under this Article 51, shall be applicable only to such portion of Producer's gross as is derived by distributor or buyer as the case may be.

The distributor or buyer as used in this subparagraph (iii) refers to a distributor or buyer, as the case may be, under any distribution or sale agreement, as the case may be, with Company, as distinguished from an agreement between such distributor or buyer and its sub-distributor.

(4) Acquisition of Title by Company:

If Company was not the actual producer of Such Picture which was produced by a signatory Company but acquired title thereto by purchase, assignment, transfer, voluntary or involuntary, or by foreclosure of a chattel mortgage or security agreement or a pledgee's sale, Company shall nevertheless be obligated to make the payments herein provided when Such Picture is exhibited in Supplemental Markets, unless such payment required hereunder has already been paid.

(5) Financing-Distribution Agreement by Company:

The obligation of the signatory Company hereunder with respect to the payments provided for in this Article 51 shall also apply to any Such Pictures produced by an independent producer under a contract between the signatory Company and such independent producer for the production of such motion picture, and for the financing and distribution thereof by the signatory Company. However, such signatory Company shall not be liable for the payment of any Supplemental Market fees based on monies received by a foreign distributor under a foreign production deal as defined in paragraph a. of this subsection 3. [casebook p. 562], with respect to which such foreign distributor or such independent producer is not obligated to account to such signatory Company. Nor shall such signatory Company be obligated to obtain any Distributor's Assumption Agreement from any foreign distributor referred to in paragraph a. of this subsection 3. except if such foreign distributor is obligated to account to such signatory Company pursuant to subparagraph (1) of this paragraph 3. with respect to monies as therein provided.

(6) Company Liability:

It is expressly understood and agreed that Company shall in all events remain bound hereunder to make the payments due by reason of the exhibition of each Such Picture in Supplemental Markets, irrespective of the assumption of such liability by any other person, firm or company as hereinabove provided, except as otherwise expressly provided in this Basic Agreement.

(7) Failure to Deliver Assumption Agreement:

The failure of Company to obtain and deliver an executed assumption agreement as provided in paragraph h.(1) and h.(2) and subparagraph (i) of this Article 51.3. shall be deemed a substantial breach of this Basic Agreement.

(8) Company's Dissolution:

If Company dissolves and is no longer in the business of producing motion pictures and if a distributor assumes all of the obligations of the Company under this Article 51 and the financial responsibility of the distributor is approved by the Guild in its discretion, the Company shall thereupon be released of any obligation with respect to any payments due hereunder; provided that if the distributor which assumes all of the obligations of the Company is a member company of the Association of Motion Picture & Television Producers, Inc. or if any such member company is permanently liable to pay the Supplemental Market fees provided for in this Article 51 with respect to the motion pictures for which the Company is liable to make such payment of Supplemental Market fees, then the financial responsibility of such distributor shall be conclusively deemed approved and such Company shall be released of any obligation with respect to any such payments.

(9) Networks and Television Stations:

No television network, station, sponsor or advertising agency shall be required to execute any Distributor's Assumption Agreement, or Buyer's Assumption Agreement, or a Literary Material Assumption Agreement, except if it is the distributor of Such Picture in Supplemental Markets or the buyer of the Company's Supplemental Markets rights in Such Picture, as the case may be.

i. If the Company shall sell, transfer, assign or otherwise dispose of its rights in any story, screenplay or teleplay (to which the provisions of this Article 51.3. apply, or may apply) prior to the production of a motion picture based thereon, to any person or company (hereinafter referred to as the "Buyer") other than a person or company with headquarters outside the United States, the Company shall obtain from the Buyer a separate agreement in substantially the following form:

"LITERARY MATERIAL ASSUMPTION AGREEMENT

_____ (hereinafter referred to as the 'Buyer') agrees with _____ (Company) that the story, screenplay, story and screenplay or story and teleplay covered by this Agreement is subject to the Writers Guild of America Theatrical and Television Basic Agreement of 1977 as amended, (herein the "Basic Agreement") and particularly to the provisions of Article 51.3. thereof pertaining to additional payments to Writers on release of a motion picture based thereon in the Supplemental Markets (but excluding paragraph h. of said Article 51.3.,) and the said Buyer hereby agrees, expressly for the benefit of the Writers Guild of America, West, Inc., (herein referred to as the Guild) as representatives of the Writers involved, to abide by and perform the provisions of said Basic Agreement and make the additional payments required thereunder, as aforesaid. For the purpose of applying such provisions of said Basic Agreement, the Writer or Writers of such material shall be treated in all respects as though the said material were written by such Writer or Writers while in the employ of the Buyer.

It is expressly understood and agreed that the rights of the Buyer to exhibit or license the exhibition of any motion picture based upon said material shall be subject to and conditioned upon the payment to the Writer or Writers involved of additional compensation, if any, required under subsection 3. (except paragraph h. thereof) of said Article 51.3. of said Basic Agreement, and it is agreed that the Guild shall be entitled to injunctive relief and damages against Buyer in the event such payments are not made.

If the Buyer shall sell, transfer, assign or otherwise dispose of its rights in such material to any person or company with headquarters in the United States, it may obtain from the party acquiring such rights a separate agreement in the same form (including this sentence) as this agreement, and will notify the Guild thereof, together with the name and address of the transferee, and deliver to the Guild a copy of such assumption agreement; it being the intent hereof that the obligations herein set forth shall be continuing obligations on the part of such subsequent owners of such material, so headquartered in the United States.

BUYER

By_____

Date: _____

Address: _____ "

The Company agrees to give notice to the Guild of such sale, transfer or assignment of the nature above mentioned, with the name and address of the Buyer, and to deliver to the Guild an executed copy of such assumption agreement. An inadvertent failure on the part of the Company to comply with any of the provisions of this paragraph i. shall in no event constitute a default by the Company hereunder or a breach of this Basic Agreement, provided that such failure is cured promptly after notice thereof from the guild.

Upon delivery of such assumption agreement, Company, or any subsequent owner obtaining the execution of such an assumption agreement, shall not be further liable to the Guild or any Writer for the keeping of any such records or the payment of such additional compensation, or for compliance with credit obligations insofar as they relate to the exhibition of Such Picture in Supplemental Markets; and the Guild agrees to look exclusively to the party last executing such an assumption agreement for the keeping of such records, payment and compliance with credit obligations. If a company with headquarters outside the United States is a subsidiary of the Company, or the Company is the distributor of Such Picture for such a company, then for the purposes of this paragraph i. such company shall be deemed to be headquartered only in the United States. The provisions of this subsection 3. shall not apply to the distribution or exhibition in relation to Supplemental Markets of trailers or advertising a motion picture by shots, etc., substantially in the nature of a trailer, or to the use of stock shots.

j. Notwithstanding the sooner termination of this agreement, the parties hereto agree that the terms and conditions of this subsection 3. shall apply and remain in full force and effect, and without change, to Such Pictures produced by the Company, the principal photography of which commenced between March 2, 1977 and March 1, 1981, both dates inclusive, regardless of when (either during or at any time after the expiration of the term of this Basic Agreement or of such period) Such Pictures are released in Supplemental Markets, and regardless of the terms or provisions of any Basic Agreement which is a modification, extension, or renewal of, or substitution for this Basic Agreement, subject however to the provisions of the third paragraph of subsection 2 of this Article 51.

4. If in the upcoming negotiations with SAG and DGA, the Company agrees to modify the basic substantive provisions regarding supplemental markets, Company will so advise the Guild and accord it the opportunity to elect that this Article be modified in the same manner, as of the date on which the Guild so notifies the Company. Adjustments which statistically maintain the relative allocations of proceeds derived from supplemental markets among SAG, DGA and WGA as established in existing collective bargaining agreements will not activate this provision, but an increase in the relative allocations to SAG or DGA in such proceeds will activate this provision, with any such increase to be accorded proportionately to WGA. Upon request the Guild shall be provided with the statistics upon which the adjustments have been made, and the Guild's right to activate this provision shall be arbitrable. The Guild shall give notice of its election within 60 days after receipt of the

Company's notice or after being provided with the statistics referred to, whichever is later. The election shall be limited to accepting the entire agreement reached with SAG or DGA on supplemental markets, and only such entire agreement, but with appropriate equivalent adjustment for writers for provisions peculiar to actors or directors as the case may be.

Theatrical Schedule A

THEATRICAL CREDITS

. . . .

9. A writer who has participated in the writing of the screenplay, or a writer who has been employed by the Company on the story, or who has sold or licensed literary material subject to this Basic Agreement, shall, for the purpose of this Basic Agreement, be considered a participant. As a participant, he shall be entitled to participate in the procedure for determination of screen credits, and in addition, in the case of a remake, any writer who has received credit either for story or screenplay in connection with the most recent production of such remake photoplay.

10. Prior to the final determination of screen credits, as provided herein, the work of participants not receiving screen credit may be publicized by the Company. After such a determination of screen credits only persons receiving screen credits or source material credit may be so publicized.

11. Before the writing credits for a motion picture are finally determined (and in the case of a motion picture produced in Company's studios in the Los Angeles area, no later than three (3) business days following completion of principal photography of such motion picture, except where circumstances make in impractical), the Company will send to each participant and to the Guild concurrently a written notice which will state the Company's choice of credit on a tentative basis, together with the names of all participants, their addresses last known to the Company and if a participant is then also a director or producer of the photoplay the notice will so indicate. Where the Company deems its record of participants incomplete, it may comply with the foregoing by giving notice to each writer whose name and address are furnished by the Guild within five (5) days after the Company's request for such information, in addition to giving notice to each participant shown on its own records.

The Company shall on such notice of tentative credits, for the information of the Guild and participants, state the form of any source material credit which Company intends to use in connection with the photoplay. Such credits shall not be subject to the provisions for protest and arbitration as hereinafter provided, but the Guild shall have the right to object to the form of such a credit.

At the Company's request, the Guild may, but shall not be obligated to, make a determination of screen credits and shall so notify the participants. When a Guild determination is so made, it shall be considered a final determination.

At the request of the Guild made to the Company on commencement of principal photography of such motion picture, the Company shall furnish the Guild with a list of all persons who, to the best of the Company's knowledge, are or were participants (see subsection 9. above) with respect to such motion picture. If thereafter any other writer is engaged by Company to render writing services in or in connection with such motion picture during the principal photography thereof, the Company will promptly notify the Guild of that fact. If the motion picture involved is a remake of an earlier motion picture produced by Company, the list of writers to be supplied by the Company pursuant to this paragraph shall include the name of any writer employed by the Company to render writing services with respect to the most recent prior production by Company of such earlier motion picture and who received screen credit for such writing services.

A casual or inadvertent failure by the Company to forward the notices, list, names or other information to the Guild or persons specified at the times or places designated pursuant to this subsection 11. shall not be deemed to be a breach of this Basic Agreement.

12. The notice specified in subsection 11. hereof, will be sent by telegraph to writers outside of Los Angeles area or by telegram, messenger or special delivery mail to writers in such area. In case of remakes the Company shall not be under any obligation to send any notice to any writer contributing to the screenplay or story of the original production unless such writer received screen credit in connection with such original production.

Notices may be sent by mail, telegram or personal delivery as above provided. If the notices are mailed, registered or certified mail shall be used, with return receipt requested; the failure of the addressee to sign or return the receipt shall not invalidate the notice.

13. The Company will keep the final determination of screen credits open until a time specified in the notice by the Company, but such time will not be earlier than six o'clock p.m. of the tenth business day following the next day after the dispatch of the notice above specified; provided, however, that if in the good faith judgment of the Company there is an emergency requiring earlier determination and the Company so states in its notice, such time may

be no earlier than six o'clock of the fifth business day following the next day after the dispatch of the notice above specified.

If within the time specified, a written request to read the script has not been delivered to the Company from any of the participants, or a written protest of the tentative credits has not been delivered to the Company from any participant or from the Guild, the tentative credits shall become final. Every protest, including that of the Guild, shall state the grounds or basis therefor in the notice thereof. The Guild agrees not to use its right of protest indiscriminately. In the event of an emergency and on Company's request, the Guild may reduce such "fifth business day" period. The Guild agrees to cooperate as fully as possible in considering such requests.

14. If a request to read the script is received by the Company from a participant within the time specified in subsection 13. hereof, or if a written protest of the tentative credits is received by the Company from a participant or the Guild within said period, the Company will withhold final determination of credits until a time to be specified by the Company which time will not be earlier than one hundred and twenty (120) hours, exclusive of Sundays and holidays, after the scripts are delivered to the Guild office in Los Angeles, or one hundred and twenty (120) hours after the Guild is notified that the scripts are available at the Company's studio, whichever is earlier. In the event of an emergency and on the Company's request, the Guild may grant a reduction of such one hundred and twenty (120) hour period. The Guild agrees to cooperate as fully as possible in considering such requests.

The tentative screen credits shall become final if no protest is timely made.

15. Upon receipt of a protest or request to read the script, the Company will deliver a copy of the script to the Guild office in Los Angeles for each participant who requests it, and the Company shall notify the participants and the Guild by telegraph informing them of the name of the protesting party and the new time set for final determination.

16. If a unanimous designation of credits as provided for in subsection 7. hereof [not included in this casebook] or a request for arbitration as hereinafter provided is not communicated to the Company within the time limit set for the final determination of credits, the Company may make the tentative credits final.

17. Any notice specified in the foregoing paragraphs shall, unless a specified form of service thereof is otherwise provided for herein, be sent by the Company by telegraphing, mailing or delivering the same to the last known address of the writer or may be delivered to the writer personally. If the notices are mailed, registered or certified mail shall be used with return receipt requested; the failure of the addressee to sign or return the receipt shall not invalidate the notice.

18. Unless a unanimous agreement has been reached in accordance with subsection 7. hereof, any participant or the Guild, may within the period provided for in subsection 14. hereof, file with the Company at its Studio and the Guild at its Los Angeles office a written request for arbitration of credits. In any case where automatic credit arbitration is required under this Schedule A the Guild will be deemed to have made a written request for arbitration of credits, at the time the Company submits the notice of tentative credits, and in such case Company will immediately make available to the Guild the material as provided for under this subsection.

The Guild through its arbitration committee shall make and advise the Company of its decision within the limitations of this Schedule A. Said decision shall be made and advised within twelve business days of the requests referred to in the immediately preceding paragraph; if in the good faith judgment of the Company there is an emergency requiring earlier decision and the Company so notifies the Guild, said decision shall be made and advised within ten business days of the requests referred to in the immediately preceding paragraph. In the event the decision of the arbitration committee is not rendered within said period, as the same may have been extended by the Company, the Company may make the tentative credits final, provided the terms and provisions of this subsection 18 have been fully complied with by the Company.

In the event of an emergency and upon the Company's request that the time for arbitration be shortened, the Guild agrees to cooperate as fully as possible. If the material is voluminous or complex, or if other circumstances beyond the control of the Guild necessitate a longer period in order to render a fair decision, and the Guild requests an extension of time for arbitration, the Company agrees to cooperate as fully as possible.

Prior to the rendition of the decision said committee may make such investigations and conduct such hearings as may seem advisable to it. Immediately upon receipt of said request for arbitration, the Company shall make available to Guild three (3) copies of the script, and three copies of all available material written by the participants and three copies of all available source material, provided, however that if three copies of any such material shall not be available, Company shall only be required to provide such copies as are available but in such case the time within which the committee may be required to render its decision as provided for herein shall be extended from ten days to twenty days. In addition, the Company shall cooperate with the arbitration committee to arrive at a just determination by furnishing all available information relative to the arbitration. Upon request of the arbitration committee, the Company shall provide the committee with a copy of the cutting continuity if it is available at the time of arbitration.

The decision of the Guild arbitration committee, and any Board of Review established by the Guild in connection therewith, with respect to writing credits, in-so-far as it is rendered within the limitations of this Schedule A, shall be final, and the Company will accept and follow the designation of screen credits contained in such decision and all writers shall be bound thereby.

19. The decision of the Guild arbitration committee may be published in such media as the Guild may determine. No writer or Company shall be entitled to collect damages or shall be entitled to injunctive relief as a result of any decision of the Committee with regard to credits. In signing any contract incorporating by reference or otherwise all or part of this Basic Agreement, any writer or Company specifically waives all rights or claims against the Guild and/or its arbiters or any of them under the laws of libel or slander or otherwise with regard to proceedings before the Guild arbitration committee and any full and fair publication of the findings and/or decisions of such Committee. The Guild and any writer signing any contract incorporating by reference or otherwise or referring to this Schedule A, and any writer consenting to the procedure set forth in this Schedule A, shall not have any rights or claims of any nature against any Company growing out of or concerning any action of the Guild or its arbiters or any of them, or any determination of credits in the manner provided in this Schedule A, and all such rights or claims are hereby specifically waived.

. . . .

22. In any publicity issued or released prior to the final determination of credits as herein provided, the Company may include such screenplay or screenplay and story credits as the Company may in good faith believe to be fair and truthful statement of authorship. After such final determination of credits, the Company shall not issue or release any publicity which shall state screenplay or screenplay and story authorship contrary to such determination. No casual or inadvertent breach of the foregoing shall be deemed to constitute a breach by the Company.

Writing credit, but not necessarily in the form specified in this Schedule A, shall be included in publicity releases issued by the Company relating to the picture when the producer and the director are mentioned, whether in the form of a production or presentation credit or otherwise, except where such release is restricted to information about such individual or individuals. The writing credit shall also be included in all other publicity and promotional matter, including screening invitations issued by the Company where the credit of the producer or director is included whether in the form of a production or presentation credit or otherwise. Prior to a final determination of credits the Company shall include those credits which it in good faith believes to be a fair and truthful statement of authorship.

Screenplay or screenplay and story credit in accordance with the final determination of such credit will be given on any paid advertising issued anywhere in the world, provided such advertising is prepared by the Company in the Continental United States and is controlled by the Company where such advertisement is used; it being understood that in such advertising prepared prior to final determination of screenplay and story credits, the Company shall include such screenplay or screenplay and story credit as the Company may in good faith believe to be a fair and truthful statement of authorship. After final determination of credits, the Company shall not prepare for issuance any advertising which shall state screenplay or screenplay and story authorship contrary to such final determination.

Where there is only a single writer on a project and if a paid advertisement is issued in which that writer would have received credit hereunder had there been a final determination of credit at that time, then such writer shall be given credit in such advertisement in accordance with the credit requirements of this Schedule A.

In forms of advertising covered hereunder the names of the individual writers accorded screenplay or screenplay and story credit for photoplay will appear in the same size and style of type as that in which the name of either the individual producer of the photoplay or, the director of the photoplay shall appear in such advertising, whichever is larger. Provided, however, that:

a. If three (3) or more writers share screenplay credit; then the Company shall not be required to use, for the advertising credit to which such three (3) or more writers are entitled, an area in excess of the minimum area that would be occupied by the names of the first two (2) of such writers, if only such first two (2) writers were entitled to share screenplay credit; it being understood that for such purpose the Company may diminish height of the type in which the names of the three (3) or more writers appear in addition to narrowing from side to side the names of such three (3) or more writers; it being further understood that for the purpose of determining which of the writers are the first two (2), the order in which such writers appear in the notification of the Guild's determination reached in its credit arbitration proceedings shall control; and

b. Where a writer entitled to screenplay credit is also entitled to credit as the director and/or producer of the photoplay, then the name of such writer need only be mentioned once in such advertising, provided, however, that he receives credit as a writer; provided further that the order of credit as between writer, producer and director shall be the same as the order with respect to which such credits are given on the screen; and

c. In giving such credit on twenty-four (24) sheets, the names of the individual writers shall in no event appear in type less than 3-½ inches in height, or if the screenplay or story credit is shared by more than two (2), in type less than 2-½ inches in height; and

d. In giving such credit in forms of advertising covered hereunder, other than on twenty-four (24) sheets the names of the individual writers shall in no event appear in type of a height less than 15% of the height of type used for the title of the photoplay, or if there are two (2) titles of the photoplay, the larger title of the photoplay. Company may seek a waiver of the double billing provision, in particular cases such as the "Beau Geste" ads and the Guild will not unreasonably withhold such waivers.

In all cases the location of the credit accorded to any writer under this subsection 22 shall be discretionary with the Company.

Where the title of the photoplay is in letters of varying sizes, the percentage above referred to shall be based on not less than the average size of all the letters in such title.

The foregoing obligation to accord advertising credit shall be limited to screenplay or screenplay and story or written by credit and shall not apply:

a) To so-called "teaser" advertising, except that if a 'Produced by" or "Directed by" credit is included, the writing credit shall also be included.

b) To advertisements less than four column inches in size, but if such advertising contains a "Produced by" or "Directed by" credit, the writing credit shall also be included.

c) To radio or the audio portion of television advertising.

d) Where credit is given neither to the individual producer nor director of the photoplay.

e) To special advertising relating only to the source material on which the picture is based, or author thereof, any member or members of the cast, the director, individual producer, or other personnel concerned in its production, or similar matters.

Advertising shall be deemed to have been prepared hereunder when the Company has forwarded the finished copy therefor to the processor or publisher. The Company agrees, however, to revise advertising prepared prior to the final determination of credits so as to show the screenplay or screenplay and story credit as finally determined, if such revision can physically and mechanically be made prior to the closing date of such processor or publisher and at reasonable expense, and provided the processor or publisher has not yet commenced work on that part of the material which the change would affect.

The Company shall require that all writing credits as they appear on the screen appear in any published version of the whole or substantial part of a picture script, and in any novel based on the screenplay, provided that with respect to any novel based on such screenplay the credit shall indicate that such novel is based on such screenplay. Such writing credit shall appear on the title page in the same size and style of type used for the writer of the novel. If the name of the writer of the novel appears on the cover the "screenplay" or "written by" credit shall also appear on the cover in the same size and style of type as the writer of the novel, provided, however, that the writing credit need not so appear if the writer of the screenplay is the writer of the novel. The contract with the publisher shall provide that this provision is for the express benefit of the writer and the Guild, and that the publisher will comply with such requirements. But the failure of a publisher to comply with any of such requirements shall not constitute a breach by the Company.

In connection with the radio or television broadcast of a half-hour or more in length, the whole or nearly the whole of the entertainment portion of which consists of the adaptation of a screenplay or substantial part thereof, the screenplay or screenplay and story credit as it appears on the screen shall be given either orally or visually.

Where the major writing contribution to a photoplay is in the form of narration, credit for such narration shall be given and worded in the following form: "narration written by." When a narration credit is given in lieu of a screenplay credit on any photoplay, then such narration credit shall be subject to all of the rights and limitations as are provided in this subsection 22. with respect to screenplay credit.

If hereafter the Company distributes or licenses the distribution of a souvenir program or theatrical program of a motion picture hereunder, or a phonograph record or phonograph album made from the sound track of a motion picture hereunder, and the individual producer or director of such picture is named in his capacity as such in such program or on the liner, cover or jacket of such album or records, then the writer shall also be named. The size of such credit as specified under this Schedule A shall be related to the size of the title as it is used in the listing of credit for such picture on such program, liner, cover or jacket. If Company includes the director or individual producer credits in any catalogue or sales brochure it issues to the public, the applicable writer's credit will also be included.

If in giving credits with relation to a product, the Company gives a "produced by" and also a "directed by" credit then Company shall require the writer's credits to be given in accordance with the provisions of this Schedule

A. The failure of a third party to comply with such requirement shall not constitute a breach by Company.

Where the Company supplies written handouts to reviewers and critics it will list writing credits, if they have theretofore been determined.

No casual or inadvertent breach of any of the foregoing shall be deemed to constitute a default, or a breach by the Company of this Basic Agreement.

WRITERS GUILD

OF

AMERICA

1981

THEATRICAL & TELEVISION

BASIC AGREEMENT

Article 11

GRIEVANCE AND ARBITRATION
RULES AND PROCEDURES

. . . .

E. ARBITRATION OF DISPUTES CONCERNING CREDIT PROVISIONS

Article 11.E.4. [casebook p. 530] shall be amended by substituting the following for the list of arbitrators:

List of Los Angeles arbitrators:

Ed Blau	Walter L.M. Lorimer
Arnold Burk	Ed Mosk
Roger Davis	Sol Rosenthal
Dixon Dern	Myron Slobodian
Martin Gang	Ken Ziffren

List of New York Arbitrators:

James Altieri	George Nicolau
Daniel Collins	Eva Robins
Milton Friedman	Arthur Stark
Walter Gellhorn	

Additional names will be added from time to time during the term of the contract by mutual agreement of the parties.

Article 11.E.4. [casebook p. 530] shall be amended by incorporating the following provision:

"The situs of the arbitration proceedings shall be Los Angeles, California unless the parties mutually agree to New York, New York or some other situs. If the parties agree to New York, New York, the arbitrator shall be selected from the New York list of arbitrators set forth in this Article 11.E."

Article 11 shall be amended by the addition of the following new section [casebook p. 530]:

"F. EQUAL STATUS OF PARTIES

It is understood that the Producers and the Guild are parties of equal status under this Agreement and in the administration of the arbitration processes throughout this Agreement. The equal status of the parties in the administration of the arbitration process shall be recognized in matters involving the determination of the availability of arbitrators, the selection of hearing dates, the retention of stenographic reporters, and insofar as applicable in all communications with the arbitrators."

. . . .

Article 16

SEPARATION OF RIGHTS

A. THEATRICAL

. . . .

Article 16.A.8. [casebook pp. 555–558] shall be amended to provide that:

8. Writer's Right to Re-Acquire Literary Material

The provisions of this subsection 8. apply only to literary material (i) which is original, i.e., not based on any pre-existing material, and (ii) which has not been exploited in any medium.

a) With respect to literary material acquired by Company subject to the terms of the 1970 or 1973 WGA agreement, if the writer who has written the same desires to purchase Company's right, title and interest therein, the Guild, on behalf of such writer may notify Company in writing of such desire. Within ninety (90) days following receipt of such written notice, Company shall notify the Guild of the terms and conditions, including the price at which it will sell its right, title and interest in such literary material; provided, however, that Company may instead notify the Guild that the literary material does not meet one or more of the conditions precedent specified in the first sentence of this subsection 8 or that the literary material is in active development at the time of the Company's notification to the Guild. If the Company proceeds in accordance with the foregoing proviso and the Guild disputes the factual basis upon which the Company relies for so proceeding, such dispute shall be subject to the grievance and arbitration provisions of this Agreement. However, the Company's decision regarding the terms and conditions of the sale shall not be subject to challenge by the Guild or by the writer on any grounds whatsoever whether in arbitration or otherwise.

The purchase price designated by Company shall not be in excess of the total direct costs previously incurred by Company in relation only to such literary material, including payments for the acquisition of the literary material and for writing services connected therewith (including writing services in relation to treatments and screenplays based thereon), and fringe benefit costs in relation thereto, such as pension and health fund payments and social security payments, but exclusive of overhead and exclusive of costs of any other kind (e.g., costs relating to proposed production other than writing costs).

Within thirty (30) days following notice from the Company of the terms and conditions on which it will sell its right, title and interest in such literary material, including the purchase price, the Guild, on behalf of the writer may serve written notice of acceptance of such terms and conditions and immediately following service of such notice the parties shall proceed to close the transaction. Failure to effect such purchase in accordance with the procedure specified by the foregoing provisions shall result in the forfeiture of writer's right to purchase such material. At any time before receipt of notice of acceptance of the terms and conditions of sale, Company may dispose of such literary material or of any rights therein or with respect thereto or may itself commence active development of such material, and in either such event the writer shall no longer have the right to acquire Company's right, title or interest in such material.

b) The provisions of 16.A.8. commencing with the fourth paragraph thereof [casebook pp. 556–557] shall apply to literary material acquired on and after March 2, 1977 but prior to March 2, 1981.

c) In addition to the foregoing, but with respect only to literary material acquired by Company on or after March 2, 1981, the writer may reacquire such literary material on the terms set forth below upon expiration of the five-year period following the later of (i) the Company's purchase or license of the covered literary material or (ii) completion of the writer's services rendered in connection with the literary material. The writer may reacquire such literary material pursuant to this paragraph only if it is not in active development at the time that the procedures for reacquiring the literary material are instituted.

Examples of active development for the purpose of this paragraph are:

(i) Employment of a writer to re-write the literary material;

(ii) Employment of a director, major actor or other key above-the-line element on a pay-or-play basis for a motion picture based upon the literary material;

(iii) A production designer, production manager or other supervisor is in active preparation for the production of the motion picture;

(iv) A unit production manager or other person is engaged to prepare a budget for the motion picture, or

(v) Production has commenced upon a theatrical or television motion picture based on the literary material.

The writer shall reacquire the literary material pursuant to the foregoing paragraphs upon payment to the company of all compensation actually paid by the Company to the writer for services in connection with the literary material, or for the purchase or license of the literary material in the case of a professional writer. The writer shall obligate the acquiring company to reimburse the Company for any other direct cost previously incurred by the Company in relation to such literary material (as described in the second subparagraph of this paragraph 8(a)) out of the first revenue after production costs have been recovered. The document by which the writer reacquires the literary material shall contain a provision setting forth the obligations referred to in the preceding sentence.

. . . .

Article 28

WARRANTY AND INDEMNIFICATION
(GENERAL)

Add the following to paragraph 1 [casebook p. 559]:

"d. be required to warrant or indemnify with respect to third party defamation, invasion of privacy or publicity claims, where the writer is requested by the Company to prepare literary materials which are based in whole or in part on any actual individual, whether living or dead, provided writer accurately provides all information reasonably requested by Company for the purpose of permitting the Company to evaluate the risks involved in the utilization of the material supplied by writer."

. . . .

Article 51

SUPPLEMENTAL MARKETS

Article 51.1.b. [casebook p. 559]: Change "1977" to "1981."

Article 51.2. [casebook p. 560]: The definitions of cassettes, pay-type CATV, and pay television shall conform to the definitions in Appendix B [not included in this casebook].

Article 51.2.c., second paragraph [casebook p. 560], shall be amended by inserting the following at the beginning of the last sentence:

"With respect to television films produced prior to March 2, 1981 except as provided in [New] Article 57, [not included in this casebook] . . . . "

Article 51.2.c. [casebook p. 560] shall be further amended by inserting a paragraph after the second paragraph reading:

"The release of theatrical films or television films for separate exhibition on domestic basic cable (i.e., other than as part of free television licensing) which films were produced on or after March 2, 1981 for free television or for theatrical release, shall be considered a release to a supplemental market and the writer shall be paid at 1.2% of the Company's accountable receipts."

Article 51.3.b. [casebook p. 564] shall be amended to read:

"The term accountable receipts as used herein means one hundred percent (100%) of the Producer's gross."

Delete (i), (ii) and (iii)—no longer applicable.

Theatrical Schedule A

THEATRICAL CREDITS

. . . .

Section 9 [casebook p. 578] shall be amended to read:

"A writer who has participated in the writing of a screenplay, or a writer who has been employed by the Company on the story, or who has sold or licensed literary material subject to this Basic Agreement, shall, for the purpose of this Basic Agreement, be considered a participant. As a participant, the writer shall be entitled to participate in the procedure for determination of screen credits. In addition, in the case of a remake, any writer who has received credit under this Agreement or a predecessor agreement to this Agreement, for story or screenplay or teleplay in connection with a prior version of the film previously produced for theatrical release, for free television exhibition or for pay television on the video cassette/video disc market shall also be considered a participant. The preceding sentence shall not apply if it conflicts with contractual commitments entered into prior to March 2, 1981."

Section 11 shall be amended by inserting the following after the first sentence [casebook pp. 578–579]:

"A copy of the final shooting script (or if such script is not available, the latest revised script available) will be sent with the notice of tentative credits to each of the participating writers."

Section 13, second paragraph [casebook p. 580]:

In the first sentence delete the words "a written request to read the script has not been delivered to the Company from any of the participants, or."

Section 14, [casebook p. 580] revise the first four lines to read:

"If a written protest of the tentative credits is received by the Company from a participant or the Guild within the time specified in subsection 13 hereof, the Company will withhold the final determination of credits until a time . . . "

Section 15, [casebook pp. 580–581] revise to read:

"Upon receipt of a protest, the Company shall notify the participants and the Guild by telegraph informing them of the name of the protesting party and the new time set for final determination."

Section 18, third paragraph, [casebook p. 581] shall be amended by adding the following sentence:

"The Company will not unreasonably deny the Guild's request for an extension of time. Agreement for extensions of time shall be in writing and shall specify the new date by which the Company will be advised of the arbitration decision."

Section 18, fourth paragraph, [casebook p. 582] shall be amended by inserting the following after the second sentence:

"If no final shooting script is available, Company will provide the Guild with a video cassette or print of the motion picture."

In Section 22 [casebook p. 582] provide that:

In any case in which there would be an obligation to accord an advertising credit to a writer if credit were given to the producer or the director, such obligation shall also exist if credit is given to the executive producer as an individual.

Add to paragraph 22(e) [casebook p. 585]:

"Writing credits shall be given as provided herein in advertising which features a quotation(s) from a review(s) of the motion picture if the name of an individual producer or director appears in any of the quotations; provided, however, if the name of individual producer or director in the quotation(s) shall be in the same size and style of type as the remainder of the quotation(s) then the writing credit need not conform in size or style of type to the name in the quotation but shall otherwise conform in size and style of type as provided in this paragraph 22."

PRODUCER

SCREEN ACTORS GUILD

CODIFIED

BASIC AGREEMENT

OF 1977

4. THEATRICAL MOTION PICTURES, THE PRINCIPAL PHOTOGRAPHY OF WHICH COMMENCED BETWEEN JANUARY 31, 1960 AND JANUARY 31, 1966 RELEASED TO FREE TELEVISION

A. With respect to theatrical motion pictures the principal photography of which commenced between January 31, 1960 and January 31, 1966 and released to free television, Producer agrees to pay to SAG a deferred compensation for rateable distribution to the actors appearing in such pictures, an amount equal to six percent (6%) of the world-wide total gross receipts from the distribution of such pictures on free television, after deducting a flat amount of forty percent (40%) of such total gross receipts for distribution fees and expenses. Where the Producer does not itself so distribute such picture but effects its distribution through another distributor, the percentage paid shall be based on such distributor's gross receipts from such distribution of such picture on free television, after deducting said flat amount of forty percent (40%) from such total gross receipts, payable only after they are received by the Producer, and after such forty percent (40%) deduction. Where Producer is paid advances by a distributor, the above percentage shall likewise be payable on the amount of such advances. Where Producer sells outright the right to exhibit on free television, SAG shall be paid promptly the above percentage on the gross amounts actually received by producer for such free television exhibition rights, after deducting a flat amount of ten percent (10%) of such gross amounts so received by Producer from such outright sale of free television exhibition rights, for sales commission and expenses of sale.

If any such outright sale shall include both free television exhibition rights and other rights with respect to one or more pictures, the Producer shall allocate to the free television exhibition rights covered by such sale, a fair and reasonable portion of the sale price (but only for the purpose of determining the percentage payment due hereunder) based on the sale of free television exhibition rights in comparable pictures. If SAG shall contend that the amount so allocated in any such outright sale for free television exhibition rights was not fair and reasonable as aforesaid, then such claim shall be submitted to arbitration as herein provided. In the event the arbitrators shall find that such allocation was not reasonable and fair as aforesaid, they shall determine the fair and reasonable amount to be so allocated. Where the sale is of the free television exhibition rights only in a group of pictures, Producer shall likewise make an allocation of a portion of the sales price to each picture. If SAG contends that such allocation is not fair and reasonable, the matter may be similarly submitted to arbitration, as above provided. In the event the arbitrators shall find that such allocation was not reasonable and fair, as aforesaid, they shall determine the fair and reasonable amount to be so allocated.

The provisions of the preceding paragraph shall not apply to any sale of free television exhibition rights only, in a single picture.

SAG shall not be entitled to any percentage payments provided above from any Producer with respect to any picture for which, under an agreement with SAG, any other party has theretofore made or theretofore become obligated to SAG to make any such percentage payment, except that as to pictures the principal photography of which commenced after August 1, 1965, the provisions of Section 6 hereof shall apply.

With respect to the monies payable under this Section 4 for the telecasting of a motion picture the principal photography of which commenced between February 1, 1960, and January 31, 1966, both dates inclusive, which is initially exhibited on television after August 1, 1965, the following definition of "rateable distribution" shall apply: _____.

With respect to actors whose compensation is based, in whole or in part, upon a percentage of Producer's gross receipts from such picture, the rateable distribution as to such actors shall be based upon and computed under provisions of subsection F of this Section. The monies so due shall be deducted from the total monies payable under this Section 4A with respect to such motion picture. The remaining monies shall be rateably apportioned among the cast entitled to participate, on a unit system, and each actor will receive that proportion of the monies to be distributed which his number of units bears to the total number of cast units.

Units will be assigned to actors entitled to participate as follows:

Actors employed by the day: Number of Days Worked or Guaranteed, Whichever is Longer	Units
One (1) day	1
Two (2) days	1½
Three (3) days	2
Four (4) days	2½

Five or more days shall be covered by the schedule below for all other actors.

All other actors: Number of Weeks Worked or Guaranteed, Whichever is Longer	Units
One (1) week*	3
Two (2) weeks*	4
Three (3) weeks or more	5

*In applying the foregoing schedule an actor who works or is guaranteed a fractional week in excess of one or two weeks shall be deemed to have worked a full additional week.

5. TELEVISION EXHIBITION OF THEATRICAL MOTION PICTURES, THE PRINCIPAL PHOTOGRAPHY OF WHICH COMMENCED AFTER JANUARY 31, 1966; SUPPLEMENTAL MARKETS EXHIBITION OF THEATRICAL MOTION PICTURES, THE PRINCIPAL PHOTOGRAPHY OF WHICH COMMENCED AFTER JUNE 30, 1971.

A. Schedule of Payments

With respect to each theatrical motion picture produced hereunder, the principal photography of which commenced after January 31, 1966, which is released by Producer for exhibition on free television anywhere in the world, Producer agrees to pay to each actor whose services are included in such motion picture when telecast compensation not less than the amounts set forth below.

With respect to each theatrical motion picture produced hereunder the principal photography of which commenced after June 30, 1971, which is released by Producer for exhibition in Supplemental Markets anywhere in the world, Producer agrees to pay to each actor whose services are included in such motion picture when so released compensation not less than the amounts set forth below; except, however, with respect to such motion pictures on which the principal photography commenced after July 1, 1971 but prior to June 30, 1974, the provisions of the 1971 Supplement to the Producer-Screen Actors Guild Basic Agreement of 1967 shall govern; except, further, that with respect to such motion pictures on which the principal photography commenced after July 1, 1974, but prior to July 1, 1977, the provisions of the Producer-Screen Actors Guild Memorandum Agreement of 1974 shall govern.

Where a theatrical motion picture, principal photography of which commenced after June 30, 1977 is released by Producer for exhibition both on free television and in Supplemental Markets anywhere in the world, the distributor's gross receipts from such combined exhibition shall be aggregated for the purpose of applying the formula set forth below.

The term "actor" means those persons covered by this Agreement and includes actors, professional singers, stunt players, airplane and helicopter pilots and puppeteers. Said compensation, herein called television and Supplemental Market fees, shall be computed on the following amounts (hereinafter referred to as base amounts) for the applicable length of engagement:

(1) Actors employed by the day:

Number of Days Worked or Guaranteed, Whichever is Longer	Base Amount
One (1) day	$100
Two (2) days	$150
Three (3) days	$200
Four (4) days	$250

Five or more days shall be covered by the schedule below for all other actors.

All other actors:

Number of Days Worked or Guaranteed, Whichever is Longer	Base Amount
One (1) week*	$300
Two (2) weeks*	$400
Three (3) weeks or more	$500

*In applying the foregoing schedule, an actor who works or is guaranteed a fractional week in excess of one week or two weeks shall be deemed to have worked a full additional week.

(2) Television and (if applicable) Supplemental Market fees shall be computed on the foregoing base amounts as follows:

(a) When such theatrical motion picture is initially exhibited either on free television or (if applicable) in Supplemental Markets anywhere in the world, the following percentages of the applicable base amounts shall be due: 30%.

In the following provisions of this subparagraph (a) the term "such gross receipts" means Distributor's gross receipts (as defined in subsection C below, and subject to the 50% limitation provided for in the first sentence of said subsection C with respect to gross receipts derived from Supplemental Markets) from the distribution of such motion picture on free television and (if applicable) in Supplemental Markets.

When such gross receipts of such motion picture amount to $125,000, the following additional percentage of the base amount shall be due: 10%.

When such gross receipts of such motion picture amount to $200,000, the following additional percentage of the base amount shall be due: 25%.

When such gross receipts of such motion picture amount to $300,000, the following additional percentage of the base amount shall be due: 22½%.

When such gross receipts of such motion picture amount to $400,000, the following additional percentage of the base amount shall be due: 22½%.

When such gross receipts of such motion picture amount to $500,000, the following additional percentage of the base amount shall be due: 20%.

After each additional full increment of $100,000 of such gross receipts of such motion picture in excess of $500,000, the following additional percentage of the base amount shall be due: 10%.

Notwithstanding the foregoing provisions of this subparagraph (a), as to such motion picture, principal photography of which commenced after January 31, 1966, but prior to July 1, 1971, if the first payment to an actor made after July 31, 1971 pursuant to this subparagraph (a) is a payment other than the payment due with respect to initial free television exhibition and other than payment due at the $125,000 level of gross receipts, such first payment made after July 31, 1971, shall be 2½ percentage points less than the applicable percentage specified in this subparagraph (a). For example, if the first such payment made to an actor after July 31, 1971, is the payment provided for at the $200,000 level of gross receipts, the payment shall be 22½% of the base amount; if the first such payment is the payment provided for at the $300,000 level of gross receipts, the payment shall be 20% of the base amount, and so forth. There shall only be one such reduction per actor for any particular motion picture.

(b) Prime Time Network Exhibition:

Not later than thirty (30) days after the first network exhibition on free television of any such motion picture in the United States, occurring in whole or in part during prime time, there shall be due and payable to actor (as a non-returnable advance against the payments due under the foregoing schedule) not less than 70% of the applicable base amount; provided that any amounts theretofore paid under this Section 5 shall be credited against such 70% payment.

Prime time shall mean 7:00 p.m. to 11:00 p.m.

As used herein, the term "network exhibition" shall mean the telecasting of such picture over the network facilities in the United States of NBC, CBS, or ABC, or any other network hereafter established, for the exhibition of entertainment product by any means, including CATV or satellite distribution; provided, however, that such newly-established network shall be deemed included as a "network" only if it exhibits substantially simultaneously (taking into account time changes and delays) in over-all markets substantially comparable to the markets in which the NBC, CBS, or ABC networks presently exhibit. A motion picture shall not be deemed telecast over a television network where it is telecast (i) on any single regional network presently established and (ii) where it is telecast on any single regional network which may hereafter be established and which does not include New York, Chicago or Los Angeles.

B. Definition of Supplemental Markets

The term "Supplemental Markets" as used in this Agreement means: the exhibition of theatrical motion pictures by means of cassettes (to the limited extent provided in paragraph (1) of this subsection B), pay-type CATV, or Pay Television, as those terms are hereafter defined in this subsection B.

(1) Cassettes: For the purposes of this Agreement, a cassette is any audio-visual device, including without limitation, cassette, cartridge, phonogram or other similar audio-visual device now known or hereafter devised, containing a theatrical motion picture (recorded on film, disc, tapes or other material) and designed for replay on a home-type television screen. The sale or rental of cassettes for replay on a home-type television screen in the home constitutes the "Supplemental Market" for the purposes of this Agreement, insofar as cassettes are concerned.

(2) Pay-Type CATV: Exhibition of theatrical motion pictures on home-type television screens by means of transmission by a community antenna television system (CATV) where, in addition to the obligatory general cable charge to the subscriber for the CATV service: (i) a further charge is made for programs selected by the subscriber, or (ii) the subscriber has the option, by making payment, in addition to the standard subscription charge, to receive special programming over one or more channels which are not available to the subscriber without such additional payment.

(3) Pay Television: Exhibition of theatrical motion pictures on a home-type television screen by means of telecast, cable or closed circuit in which the viewing audience pays to receive the program by making a separate payment for such specific program. Exhibitions in theatres or comparable places by means of telecast or cable is theatrical exhibition and shall not be considered Pay Television.

The term "Supplemental Markets" does not include the exhibition of a theatrical motion picture by cassette or otherwise over a television broadcast station or in theatrical exhibition, and for this purpose "theatrical exhibition" includes the educational market, the exhibition of theatrical motion pictures on any commercial carrier (referred to herein as "In-Flight"), such as commercial airlines, trains, ships and buses, and other uses which have been traditionally considered theatrical exhibition of theatrical motion pictures, other than the specific home use hereinabove defined as the "Supplemental Market" for cassettes.

Wherever reference is made in this Agreement to pay-type CATV or Pay Television, such reference shall be deemed to include only those uses of theatrical motion pictures as to which a charge is actually made to the subscriber for the program viewed, or where the subscriber has the option, by additional payment, to receive special programming over one or more special channels. Where no program charge or special channel charge is made to the subscriber in addition to the general charge, the transmission of theatrical motion pictures by the CATV or television facility, including programming originated by the CATV or television facility, is free television exhibition for the purposes of this Agreement, and such exhibition shall not be considered Supplemental Markets exhibition.

The Producers have agreed to the inclusion of pay-type CATV and Pay Television in the "Supplemental Markets" because, under the present pattern of distribution of theatrical motion pictures, pay-type CATV and Pay Television are supplemental to the primary theatrical market. The Producers reserve the right in future negotiations to contend that the pattern of release has changed so that pay-type CATV and/or Pay Television are no longer a Supplemental Market but constitute or are a part of the primary market of distribution of theatrical motion pictures, and that therefore no additional payment should be made with respect to the release of theatrical motion pictures (including those covered by this Agreement) in said markets. Nothing herein shall limit the scope of negotiations on said subject.

. . . .

D. Application to Pictures Initially Released Theatrically

The provisions of this Section 5 regarding additional compensation for free television exhibition apply only to a theatrical motion picture which is exhibited on free television after it has had a bona fide theatrical release. Such motion picture exhibited on free television that has not had a bona fide theatrical release shall be governed by the Screen Actors Guild Television Agreement in effect at the time of such exhibition but only with respect to the provisions relating to additional compensation for reruns and foreign telecasts, or as may otherwise be agreed upon between the Producer and the Guild. The provisions of this Section 5 shall not apply to the televising, or exhibition in Supplemental Markets, of trailers or advertising a motion picture by shots, etc., substantially in the nature of a trailer, subject to the limitations provided in Section 18 hereof.

20. PROHIBITION AGAINST CREDITING

No compensation paid to a player for his services in excess of the minimum may be credited against overtime, penalties or any other compensation otherwise due the player.

. . . .

25. SCREEN CREDITS

A. Producer agrees that a cast of characters on at least one card will be placed at the end of each theatrical feature motion picture, naming the actor and the role portrayed. All credits on this card shall be in the same size and style of type, with the arrangement, number and selection of players listed to be at the sole discretion of the Producer. All such credits shall be in a readily readable color, size and speed. The Guild will not unreasonably withhold waivers in connection with the foregoing. Any actor identified by name and role elsewhere in the picture need not be listed in the cast of characters at the end of the picture. This agreement regarding screen credits applies only to motion pictures on which principal photography commenced July 1, 1977, or thereafter.

B. Feature Motion Pictures

In all feature motion pictures with a cast of fifty or less, all players shall receive credit. In all other feature motion pictures not less than fifty shall be listed in the cast of characters required at the end of each feature motion picture in connection with theatrical exhibition, excluding players identified elsewhere in the picture. Stunt players need not be identified by role. The Guild, and only the Guild, may seek to arbitrate an alleged violation of this subsection B pursuant to the arbitration procedures set forth in this Section 25 C (3).

C. Billing

(1) Producer shall honor individually-negotiated billing for the screen as to placement, size and description as agreed upon in player's individual contract.

(2) In its distribution and licensing agreements with exhibitors, distributors, broadcasters, etc., Producer will include a provision prohibiting the licensee from eliminating or changing the billing as it appears on the positive prints of the motion picture.

(3) Disputes as to whether agreed-upon screen credit has been accorded shall be arbitrable. A panel of sole arbitrators for this purpose shall be agreed upon. The cost of such arbitrator shall be shared equally by the Guild and

Producer. The decision and award shall be in writing and shall be final and binding on the parties and players involved.

(4) The provisions hereof shall not apply to Schedule F players or when termination of a contract is involved as provided by Section 9 C(4)(b) of the Arbitration provisions.

(5) Liquidated Damages—as to Schedule A and B players, if a breach occurs and the facts are not in dispute or if breach is found by an arbitrator, damages in the following amounts shall be payable:

(a) In the case of a day player his daily rate but not in excess of the amount payable under (c) hereof.

(b) In the case of a three-day player in television, his three-day rate but not in excess of the amount payable under (c) of this subparagraph 5.

(c) In the case of a weekly free-lance player, his weekly rate (not exceeding the limits of Schedule B). Such liquidated damages shall be the exclusive remedy for such players.

(6) As to all other players subject to the provisions hereof, the arbitrator shall have the authority to award appropriate relief consisting of damages, correction of prints subject to (7) below, or both.

(7) Correction of Prints

(a) Theatrical Motion Pictures. Correction of prints may be awarded by the arbitrator in his discretion if Producer received notice of the claimed breach in sufficient time to make such correction before release. If correction is awarded, Producer shall be obligated to make such corrections as soon as is practical consistent with existing distribution commitments and in any event before any reissue. For this purpose television release of the film shall be considered a reissue.

(b) Television Motion Pictures. Correction of television prints with respect to the first broadcast or first rerun may be awarded by the arbitrator if Producer received notice of the alleged breach in sufficient time to make the necessary correction for the applicable run.

(8) Inadvertent oversight by Producer shall not be a defense to any claim of breach hereunder, but may be considered with respect to the issue of appropriate relief.

(9) All claims must be filed within one year after the first theatrical release of a theatrical film or within one year of the first television broadcast of a television film.

1977

SCREEN ACTORS

GUILD

TELEVISION

AGREEMENT

18. ADDITIONAL COMPENSATION
FOR RERUNS AND FOREIGN TELECASTS

. . . .

(c) Foreign Telecasting Formula

(1) If the Producer desires to acquire the right to telecast any television motion picture in any part of the world outside the United States and Canada, the employment contract of each player engaged therein shall contain a separate provision for additional compensation for such foreign telecasting which shall call for an initial payment of not less than 15% of his total applicable minimum salary payable not later than thirty days after Producer obtains knowledge of the first foreign telecast, and in no event later than six months after the first foreign telecast, and the payment of the sums referred to in (2) and (3) below.

(2) When the Distributor's Foreign Gross, as defined herein, of any such television motion picture has exceeded $7,000 for a one-half hour picture, $13,000 for a one-hour picture, or $18,000 if such picture is one and one-half hours or more in length, the player shall be entitled to the payment of not less than an additional 10% of his total applicable minimum salary payable not later than thirty (30) days after such gross has been so exceeded.

(3) When the Distributor's Foreign Gross of any such television motion picture has exceeded $10,000 for a one-half hour picture, $18,000 for a one-hour picture, or $24,000 if such picture is one and one-half hours or more in length, the player shall be entitled to the payment of not less than an additional 10% of his total applicable minimum salary payable not later than thirty (30) days after such gross has been so exceeded.

(4) After player has received a total of 35% of his total applicable minimum salary with respect to any picture, no further sums shall be payable for foreign telecasting of such picture.

(5) The provisions of this subsection (c) shall apply with respect to all television motion pictures produced on or after July 1, 1977. The provisions of prior Screen Actors Guild Television Agreements shall continue to apply as to all television motion pictures produced during the term of those respective Agreements.

(6) The term "foreign telecasting," as used herein, shall mean any telecast (whether simultaneous or delayed) outside the United States, its commonwealths, territories and possessions, and Canada other than a telecast on any of the following regularly affiliated stations of a United States television network as a part of the United States network television

telecast: ZBM, Pembroke, Bermuda, for CBS and NBC; and ZBF, Hamilton, Bermuda, for ABC; and XETV, Tijuana, Mexico for NBC.

(7) As used herein the term "Distributor's Foreign Gross" shall mean, with respect to any television motion picture, the absolute gross income realized by the distributor of such picture from the foreign telecasting thereof and including, in the case of a "foreign territorial sale" by any such distributor, the income realized from such sale by such distributor but not the income realized by the "purchaser" or "licensee". The phrase "absolute gross income" shall not include:

a) Sums realized or held by the way of deposits or security, until and unless earned, other than such sums as are nonreturnable.

b) Sums required to be paid or withheld as taxes, in the nature of turnover taxes, sales taxes or similar taxes based on the actual receipts of the picture or on any monies to be remitted to or by the distributor, but there shall not be excluded from distributor's foreign gross any net income, franchise tax or excess profit tax or similar tax payable by the distributor on its net income or for the privilege of doing business.

c) Frozen foreign currency until the distributor shall have either the right to use such foreign currency in or to transmit such foreign currency from the country or territory where it is frozen. In the event such currency may be utilized or transmitted as aforesaid, it shall be deemed to have been converted to United States dollars at the prevailing free market rate of exchange at the time such right to use or transmit accrues.

Distributor's Foreign Gross realized in foreign currency in any reporting period required hereunder shall be deemed to be converted to United States dollars at the prevailing free market rate of exchange at the close of such reporting period.

If any transaction involving any picture subject to a foreign telecast payment under this Agreement shall also include motion pictures, broadcast time, broadcast facilities or material (including commercial or advertising material) which are not subject to such payment, there shall be a reasonable allocation between the television motion pictures which are subject to a foreign telecast payment and such other pictures, time, facilities or material, and only the sums properly allocable to pictures which are subject to a foreign telecast payment shall be included in Distributor's Foreign Gross.

(8) The above formula for foreign telecasting is a minimum formula and nothing herein shall preclude any player from bargaining for better terms with respect to such foreign telecasting.

(d) Advance Payment for Residuals

Each contract between the Producer and the player shall contain a separate provision for such additional compensation for reruns or foreign telecasts. There shall be the following limitations on advance payment for television reruns or foreign telecasts:

(1) The Producer may not make any payment to a day player or term contract player for reruns or foreign telecasts at any time prior to the time of the use for which payment is made.

(2) Commencing with employment agreements entered into on or after July 1, 1977, covering all other players, the player may agree to an advance payment for reruns or foreign telecasts provided the same is separately stated and is paid in addition to such salary set forth in the player's contract and provided further that the salary at which advance payment for network prime time reruns is permitted and shall be the following:

Program Length	Per Week or Per Episode
one-half hour	$ 5,000.00
one hour	$ 7,500.00
over one hour	$10,000.00

(3) Other. For all other residual purposes (e.g., syndication, non-prime time network, theatrical and foreign), the salary at which advance payment is permitted shall be increased to $5,000 per week or per episode commencing with the 1978–79 season.

. . . .

(f) If a player's individual employment contract contains a provision giving such player a percentage or other participation in the receipts, revenues or profits of the television motion picture, such payment shall be credited against the minimum additional compensation for reruns and foreign telecasts provided herein, but the player, in any event, shall be entitled to be paid not less than such minimum additional compensation for rerun and foreign telecast, and any payment on account thereof shall likewise be credited against such participation. However, unless such rerun and foreign telecasting payments have been exceeded by profit participation payments, rerun payments shall be due and payable as provided in subsection (b) (3)b) of this Section 18, and foreign telecasting payments shall be due and payable as provided in subsection (c) of this Section 18, and any such payments shall likewise be credited against such participation. There shall be no duplication of crediting under this subsection (f), subsection (e) of Section 19, and subsection (e) of Section 20.

19. ADDITIONAL COMPENSATION
FOR THEATRICAL RIGHTS

(a) The rights granted to the Producer in a television motion picture shall be limited (except as provided in Section 20) to the right to exhibit such motion picture over free television anywhere. If the Producer desires to acquire the right to exhibit a television motion picture in theatrical exhibition anywhere in the world, such rights shall be the subject of individual bargaining between the Producer and the players appearing therein in accordance with the following provisions:

(b) For the purposes of this Section 19, the United States, its commonwealths, territories and possessions and Canada shall be deemed a single geographical area and all other countries as a separate geographical area.

(c) The employment contract of the player shall contain a separate provision for additional compensation for such theatrical rights, which shall be not less than the following:

(1) If theatrical exhibition takes place in either of the geographical areas specified in subparagraph (b) above, the additional compensation payable: a) with respect to a day player, the day player's total applicable minimum; and b) with respect to all other players, the free-lance player's total applicable minimum.

(2) If theatrical exhibition takes place in both of the geographical areas specified in subparagraph (b) above, 100% of the total applicable minimum shall be paid for each such area.

(3) In any event, the initial payment for theatrical exhibition in either of such geographical areas shall be 150% of the total applicable minimum; the extra 50% shall constitute a prepayment against the payment due for theatrical exhibition in the other area. Upon the later theatrical exhibition in such other area, the balance of such payment required under subparagraph (2) above, shall be paid to the player.

(4) Total applicable minimum is the total minimum salary for the type of contract under which the player was employed for the period of the player's employment in the television motion picture.

(5) The above formula is a minimum formula and nothing herein shall preclude a player from bargaining for better terms with respect to such theatrical rights.

(d) Limitation on advance payment of theatrical release compensation:

(1) The Producer may not make any payment to a day player or term contract player for theatrical exhibition at a time prior to the time of such theatrical exhibition.

(2) As to all other players, where the salary for the player's services provided in the player's contract is Five Thousand Dollars ($5,000) or more per week or per episode, the player may agree to an advance payment for theatrical exhibition, provided the same is separately stated and is paid in addition to such salary provided in the player's contract.

. . . .

(g) If a player's individual employment contract contains a provision giving such player a percentage or other participation in the receipts, revenues or profits of the television motion picture, such payment shall be credited against the minimum additional compensation for theatrical rights provided herein, but the player in any event shall be entitled to be paid not less than such minimum additional compensation and any payment on account thereof shall be credited against such participation. There shall be no duplication of crediting under this subsection (g), subsection (f) of Section 18, and subsection (e) of Section 20. Unless theatrical rights payments have been exceeded by profit participation payment, player shall be paid as provided in (e) above, and any such payments shall likewise be credited against such participation.

20. ADDITIONAL COMPENSATION— SUPPLEMENTAL MARKETS

(a) Definition

The term "Supplemental Markets", as used in this Agreement, means only: The exhibition of television motion pictures by means of cassettes (to the limited extent provided in subparagraph (1) of this paragraph (a), pay-type CATV, or Pay Television, as those terms are hereafter defined in this paragraph (a), and the exhibition of television motion pictures on any commercial carrier such as commercial airlines, trains, ships and buses (referred to herein as "In-Flight").

The rights granted to the Producer in a television motion picture shall include the right to exhibit such motion picture in the Supplemental Markets. This right shall exist not only with respect to television motion pictures produced during the term of this Agreement, but also with respect to all television motion pictures produced by the Producer between July 21, 1952 and June 30, 1977, subject to any restrictions provided in any player's individual employment contract.

(1) Cassettes: For the purpose of this Agreement, a cassette is any audio-visual device, including without limitation, cassette, cartridge, phonogram or other similar audio-visual device now known or hereafter devised, containing a television motion picture (recorded on film, disc, tapes or other material) and designed for replay on a home-type television screen. The sale or rental of cassettes for replay on a home-type television

screen in the home or in other closed-circuit use such as in hotel rooms, constitutes the "Supplemental Market" for the purposes of this Agreement. The foregoing definition does not include the exhibition of a television motion picture by cassette over a television broadcast station or in theatrical exhibition.

(2) Pay-Type CATV: Exhibition of television motion pictures on home-type television screens by means of transmission by a Community Antenna Television System (CATV) where, in addition to the obligatory general cable charge to the subscriber for the CATV service: (i) a further charge is made for programs selected by the subscriber, or (ii) the subscriber has the option, by making payment, in addition to the standard subscription charge, to receive special programming over one or more channels which are not available to the subscriber without such additional payment. Where no program charge or special channel charge is made to the subscriber, in addition to the general cable charge, the transmission of motion pictures by the CATV facility including programming originated by the CATV facility, is free television exhibition for the purposes of this Agreement, and such exhibition shall not be considered a "Supplemental Market".

(3) Pay Television: Exhibition of television motion pictures on a home-type television screen by means of telecast, cable or closed circuit in which the viewing audience pays to receive the program by making a separate payment for such specific program. Exhibitions in theatres or comparable places by means of telecast or cable is theatrical exhibition and shall not be considered Pay Television.

(b) Schedule of Payments

With respect to all television motion pictures produced under the terms of a collective bargaining agreement with the Guild between July 21, 1952, and June 30, 1977 and all television motion pictures produced during the term thereof, the Producer agrees to pay to each player whose services are included in such motion picture when distributed by or for the Producer for use in Supplemental Markets, compensation not less than the amounts provided herein. The term "player" means those persons covered by this Agreement, and with respect to those television motion pictures produced between July 21, 1952 and June 30, 1977, those players covered by a collective bargaining agreement with the Guild in effect at the time of production.

(1) Players employed for less than one week:

Number of Days Worked or Guaranteed, Whichever is Longer	Base Amount
One (1) day	$100
Two (2) days	$150
Three (3) days	$200
Four (4) days	$250

Five or more days shall be covered by the schedule below for all other players.

(2) All other players:

Number of Weeks Worked or Guaranteed, Whichever is Longer	Base Amount
One (1) week*	$300
Two (2) weeks*	$400
Three (3) weeks	$500

*In applying the foregoing schedule, a player who works or is guaranteed a fractional week in excess of one week or two weeks, shall be deemed to have worked a full additional week.

(3) *Supplemental Market Fees:*

Supplemental Market fees shall be computed on the foregoing base amounts, as follows:

a) When such television motion picture is initially released in any Supplemental Market, except "In-Flight", the player shall be paid 20% of the applicable base amount; and when the Distributor's gross receipts (as defined in subsection c) below) from the distribution of such television motion picture in such Supplemental Markets equals $62,500, the player shall be paid an additional 10% of the applicable base amount; provided, however, with respect to gross receipts from "In-Flight" distribution, 30% of the base amount shall be payable upon initial release of the picture for such market; and provided further, that the total payment or payments under this subparagraph a) shall not exceed thirty per cent (30%) of the applicable base amount.

b) When such gross receipts from the distribution of such television motion picture in Supplemental Markets amount to $125,000, the following additional percentage of the base amount shall be due: 10%.

c) When such gross receipts from the distribution of such television motion picture in Supplemental Markets amount to $200,000, the following additional percentage of the base amount shall be due: 25%.

d) When such gross receipts from the distribution of such television motion picture in Supplemental Markets amount to $300,000, the following additional percentage of the base amount shall be due: 22½%.

e) When such gross receipts from the distribution of such television motion picture in Supplemental Markets amount to $400,000, the following additional percentage of the base amount shall be due: 22½%.

f) When such gross receipts from the distribution of such television motion picture in Supplemental Markets amount to $500,000, the following additional percentage of the base amount shall be due: 20%.

g) After each additional full increment of $100,000 of such gross receipts in excess of $500,000, the following additional percentage of the base amount shall be due: 10%.

(c) Definition of Distributor's Gross Receipts

(1) In applying the formula set forth in this Section 20, for calculating Supplemental Market fees, Distributor's gross receipts shall be included in the formula at 100% of the actual amount of such gross receipts.

(2) As used herein, the term "Distributor's gross receipts" shall mean the absolute gross income received by all Distributors (as hereinafter defined) of such television motion picture from the Supplemental Market use thereof anywhere in the world, and including, in the case of a "foreign territorial sale" by any such Distributor, the income received from such sale by such Distributor but not the income received by the "purchaser" or the "licensee". "Distributor" as used in this Agreement, shall mean the Producer when it distributes such motion picture for Supplemental Market use through its own distribution facilities, and all other Distributors engaged by Producer to distribute such motion picture for Supplemental Market use.

It is recognized that the method of distributing cassettes may not be similar to the method of distributing theatrical motion pictures in television. However, for the purpose of determining the amounts payable to players for cassette distribution of television motion pictures, it is the intent of the parties that the basis for determining Distributor's gross receipts from cassette distribution shall be comparable to the basis used for determining the Distributor's gross receipts from the distribution of theatrical motion pictures in television. For example, gross receipts from cassettes sold at the retail level would not be Distributor's gross receipts hereunder. As a further example, if the Producer itself acts as distributor and retailer, a reasonable allocation of the retail gross receipts shall be made as between the Producer as Distributor and the Producer as retailer, and only the former shall be deemed to be Distributor's gross receipts. The reasonableness of such allocation shall be subject to arbitration and, in such arbitration, generally prevailing trade practices in the cassette distribution industry with respect to dealings between non-related companies, shall be relevant evidence.

(3) The Distributor's gross receipts shall not include:

a) Sums realized or held by way of deposit as security, until and unless earned, other than such sums as are non-returnable;

b) Rebates, credits or repayments for cassettes returned (and in this connection the Producer shall have the right to set up a reasonable reserve for returns);

c) Sums required to be paid or withheld as taxes, in the nature of turnover taxes, sales taxes or similar taxes based on the actual receipts of such motion picture or on any moneys to be remitted to or by the Producer or such other distributor; but there shall not be excluded from Distributor's gross receipts any net income tax, franchise tax or excess profit tax or similar tax payable by the Producer or such Distributor on its net income or for the privilege of doing business;

d) Frozen foreign currency until the Producer shall either have the right to freely use such foreign currency, or Producer or Distributor has the right to transmit to the United States to Producer or Distributor such foreign currency from the country or territory where it is frozen. If such currency may be utilized or transmitted as aforesaid it shall be deemed to have been converted to United States dollars at the rate of exchange at which such currency was actually transmitted to the United States as aforesaid, or, if not actually transmitted, then at the prevailing free market rate of exchange at the time such right to use or to transmit occurs. Frozen foreign currency shall be deemed to be unblocked on the basis of "first in, first out" unless otherwise allocated by local foreign fiscal authorities. Allocation of such unblocked funds as between revenue which serves as the basis of determining payments hereunder and other revenue, shall be on a proportional basis, subject to different earmarking by local foreign fiscal authorities.

(4) Allocation of Gross Receipts

If any agreement for distribution in the Supplemental Market includes more than one television motion picture, or includes both Supplemental

Market rights and other rights, the Producer shall make a reasonable allocation for the purpose of determining payments due hereunder. If the Guild contends that such allocation is not reasonable, then such claim shall be submitted to arbitration under Section 50 of this Agreement.

. . . .

(e) Effect of Player's Individual Contract

If a player's individual employment contract contains a provision giving such player a percentage or other participation in the receipts, revenues or profits of the television motion picture, such payment shall be credited against the minimum additional compensation for Supplemental Market use provided herein, but the player in any event shall be entitled to be paid not less than such minimum additional compensation, and any payment on account thereof shall be credited against such participation. There shall be no duplication of crediting under this subsection (e), subsection (f) of Section 18, and subsection (g) of Section 19. Unless Supplemental Market fees have been paid to a player in excess of his profit participation payment, the player shall be paid Supplemental Market fees as provided in this Section 20, and any such payments shall likewise be credited against such participation.

54. SCREEN CREDIT & BILLING

(a) (1) Producer agrees that a cast of characters on at least one card shall be placed at the end of each television motion picture naming the actor and the role portrayed. All credits on this card shall be in the same size and style of type with the arrangement, number and selection of players listed, to be at the sole discretion of Producer. All such credits shall be in a readily readable color, size and speed. The Guild will not unreasonably withhold waivers in connection with the foregoing. Any actor identified by name and role elsewhere in the picture, or any actor playing a major continuing role, and identified by name elsewhere in the picture, need not be listed in the cast of characters at the end of the picture. Such credits may be displayed over action or background; provided, however, that the cast of characters may not be superimposed over commercial background material except only for commercial background material presented on behalf of the single sponsor or alternate-week sponsor of a series.

(2) If the Guild contends that a particular credit is not in conformity with the credit requirements of this Section, the Guild shall give prompt notice to the Producer. If the parties cannot resolve the matter, the Guild may refer the matter to the Cooperative Committee at any time not later than fifteen (15) days after the program is televised. The Committee shall promptly meet and, if a majority of the Committee agrees that the credit requirements have been violated, the Producer, on notice from the Cooperative Committee, shall

correct or replace such credit with appropriate credits prior to any further use of the program involved. Any such dispute not so resolved by a majority of the Cooperative Committee within ten (10) days after the matter was considered by the Cooperative Committee may be submitted by the Guild to arbitration, as herein provided, to determine whether or not the credits given comply with the foregoing credit requirements, and if not, to require that the credits be corrected or replaced prior to the further use of the program involved.

(b) (1) Producer shall honor individually-negotiated billing for the screen as to placement, size and description as agreed upon in player's individual contract.

(2) In its distribution and licensing agreements with exhibitors, distributors, broadcasters, etc., Producer will include a provision prohibiting the licensee from eliminating or changing the billing as it appears on the positive prints of the motion picture.

(3) Disputes as to whether agreed-upon screen credit has been accorded shall be arbitrable. A panel of sole arbitrators for this purpose shall be agreed upon. The cost of such arbitrator shall be shared equally by the Guild and Producer. The decision and award shall be in writing and shall be final and binding on the parties and players involved.

(4) The provisions hereof shall not apply to Schedule F or when termination of a contract is involved as provided by Section 50(c)(4)b) of this Agreement.

(5) Liquidated Damages—As to Schedule A and B players, if a breach occurs and the facts are not in dispute or if breach is found by an arbitrator, damages in the following amounts shall be payable:

a) In the case of a day player his daily rate but not in excess of the amount payable under c) of this subparagraph (5).

b) In the case of a three-day player in television, his three-day rate but not in excess of the amount payable under c) of this subparagraph (5).

c) In the case of a weekly free-lance player, his weekly rate (not exceeding the limits of Schedule B).

Such liquidated damages shall be the exclusive remedy for such players.

(6) As to all other players subject to the provisions hereof, the arbitrator shall have the authority to award appropriate relief consisting of damages, correction of prints subject to subparagraph (7) below, or both.

(7) Correction of prints with respect to the first broadcast or first rerun may be awarded by the arbitrator if Producer received notice of the alleged breach in sufficient time to make the necessary correction for the applicable run.

(8) Inadvertent oversight by Producer shall not be a defense to any claim of

breach hereunder, but may be considered with respect to the issue of appropriate relief.

(9) All claims must be filed within one year after the first television broadcast of a television film.

SCREEN ACTORS GUILD

1980

TELEVISION AGREEMENT

1980

BASIC AGREEMENT

Part I

THEATRICAL AND TELEVISION

. . . .

5. Theatrical Motion Pictures Released to Free Television

Section 5 of the Basic Agreement [casebook pp. 598–603] is re-numbered as Section 5.1, and appropriate conforming amendments shall be made throughout the Basic Agreement.

A new section numbered 5.2 is added to the Basic Agreement as follows:

5.2 TELEVISION EXHIBITION OF THEATRICAL MOTION PICTURES, THE PRINCIPAL PHOTOGRAPHY OF WHICH COMMENCED AFTER OCTOBER 6, 1980.

A. With respect to theatrical motion pictures released to free television, the principal photography of which commenced after October 6, 1980, Producer agrees to pay to Screen Actors Guild a deferred compensation for rateable distribution to the actors appearing in said pictures, an amount equal to 3.6% of the worldwide total gross receipts from the distribution of such pictures on free television, which amount shall include pension and welfare contributions.

B. *Distribution Formula.* The amount received by Screen Actors Guild under the formula set forth in Paragraph A above shall be distributed as follows:

Units will be assigned to actors entitled to participate as follows:

(1) *Time Units*

With respect to each actor, units for time worked shall be computed as follows:

- Each day = 1/5 unit
- Each week = 1 unit
- No more than 5 time units may be credited to any player.

(2) *Salary Units*

With respect to each actor, units for total compensation received from the film shall be credited with units as follows:

(a) Day Player: Each multiple of daily scale equals 1/5 unit. A fraction of daily scale when more than 1/2 shall be credited as another 1/5 unit.

(b) All Other Players: Each multiple of weekly scale equals 1 unit.

A fraction of a multiple when more than 1/2 of weekly scale shall be credited as another weekly unit.

(c) No more than 10 salary units may be credited to any player.

(3) *Computation*

Each player shall be credited with the sum of time and salary units as computed above, and each player will receive that rateable proportion of the monies as the actors' number of units bears to the total number of units for the entire cast.

C. All of the provisions of Section 4G [not included in this casebook] and 5.1 of the Basic Agreement, except where inconsistent herewith, are incorporated herein.

6. *Theatrical Motion Pictures in Supplemental Market Use*

The provisions of new Section 5.2 of the Basic Agreement set forth in Paragraph 5 of this Part I of this Agreement are incorporated herein by reference and shall be applicable to the worldwide total gross receipts from the distribution of such theatrical motion pictures in supplemental markets.

Old Section 5 (renumbered as 5.1) is amended by adding the following at the end thereof:

" 'Distributor's Gross Receipts' shall mean one hundred percent (100%) of the Distributor's gross from Supplemental Markets after June 30, 1979."

7. *Additional Compensation for Reruns—Television Programs*

Section 18(b)(1)(b) of the Television Agreement [not included in this casebook] is amended as follows:

"(b) The ceilings (maximum rerun payments) for each television motion picture shall be as follows:

For Programs Produced
During the Period:

	10/6/80 through 12/31/81	1/1/82 through 6/30/83
½ hour program	$1550	$1600
1 hour program	$1900	$2200
1 ½ hour program	$2100	$2400
2 hour program	$2300	$2600
Over 2 hour program	$2800	$3000

8. *Advance Payment for Residuals—Television Programs*

Section 18(d)(2) [casebook p. 608] of the Television Agreement is amended to read as follows:

Commencing with employment agreements entered into on or after October 6, 1980, covering all other players, the player may agree to an advance payment for reruns or foreign telecasts provided the advance payment is separately listed and is paid in addition to the salary, which is separately and specifically set forth as salary (not including advances) in the player's contract and provided further that the salary, at which advance payments which are additional for network prime time reruns, is permitted shall be no less than the following:

Program Length	Salary Per Week or Per Episode
½ hour	$ 7,000
1 hour	$10,000
Over 1 hour	$12,500

Section 18(d)(3) [casebook p. 608] and 19(d)(2) [casebook p. 610] of the Television Agreement are amended by increasing the money breaks therein provided from $5,000 to $7,000.

9. *Additional Compensation—Supplemental Markets—Television Programs*

A new Section 20.1 is added to the Television Agreement as follows:

20.1 *Additional Compensation—Supplemental Markets; Television Programs Produced On or After October 6, 1980*

Payment for such use shall be the same percentage and computed in the same manner as payment for supplemental market exhibition of theatrical motion pictures as specified in Paragraph 6 of this Agreement.

. . . .

Part IV

GENERAL

. . . .

5. *Screen Credits—Television*

Producers agree to promptly cause a bulletin to be mailed to members of the Association of Motion Picture & Television Producers and the Alliance to remind such members of their obligations with respect to screen credits provided in Paragraph 54 of the Television Agreement [casebook pp. 615–616] and to periodically, at the Guild's request, thereafter so remind such members.

Part V

PAY TELEVISION, VIDEO DISCS/VIDEO CASSETTE MARKETS

. . . .

3. *Additional Compensation*

A. Pay Television—For covered programs released in the Pay Television Market anywhere in the world:

(1) For exhibition days on any system either in excess of ten or subsequent to one year from the date of the initial exhibition on such system, Producer shall pay 4.50% (plus Pension and Health and Welfare payments in accordance with the SAG Television Agreement) of the total world wide Distributor's gross as defined in Section 5C [not included in this casebook] of the Basic Agreement, except that in the case of covered programs the cast of which (exclusive of those members of the cast who would not be entitled to residuals if the program had been produced for free television) is four players or less, the total percentage shall be computed on the basis of 1% per player. The computation of the number of players in the cast, for purposes of determining the percentage payable, shall exclude off-camera announcers, provided however, that where the only performer(s) on a program is an off camera announcer(s), the percentage shall be ½ of 1% plus pension and welfare. However, off-camera announcers shall not be excluded for purposes of determining the rateable distribution provided in Part V, Paragraph 5 hereof [not included in this casebook].

(2) If any license, whether an initial or subsequent license, for a program on any system covers exhibition days in excess of ten, each such day shall be given equal monetary weight in determining the sums subject to the payment described in subparagraph (1) hereof. As an example, if the initial license encompasses seventeen exhibition days, 7/17th of the sums actually received from such license shall be subject to the appropriate payment under this Section 3. For further example, if a second or subsequent license is for ten days and covers the 9th thru 18th day, 8/10th of the sum actually received from such license shall be subject to the appropriate payment under this Section 3.

(3) Where a license covers exhibition days both within and outside the one year limitation set forth in Paragraph 2B above [not included in this casebook], all days shall be given equal monetary weight. For example, if a license is for fourteen days use in eighteen months, and five exhibition days occur after the one year period, each day of exhibition which actually occurs after the one year period shall be given equal monetary weight, and 5/14ths of the license fee shall be subject to the appropriate payment under this Part V, Section 3.

(4) The provisions of Section 18(d) [casebook p. 608] and Section 20(e) [casebook p. 615] of the SAG Television Agreement relating to the application of contingent compensation against the payments to any individual actor shall be applicable also to the payments required herein.

(5) (a) The provisions of Sections 5C and G [not included in this casebook] (renumbered as Sections 5.1C and G, respectively) and Section 4G [not included in this casebook] of the Basic Agreement relating to definition of distributor's gross receipts, effect of individual contracts, and reporting, and Paragraph 6 [not included in this casebook] of the Basic Agreement relating to responsibility for payments, are incorporated herein.

(b) Payment shall be made quarterly and each such payment shall be accompanied by the reports required under Section 5G of the Basic Agreement (new Section 5.1G).

B. *Video Disc/Video Cassette Market*

(1) For sales of a covered program in the video disc/video cassette market, the Producer shall pay 4.50% (plus Pension and Health and Welfare payments in accordance with the SAG Television Agreement) of the fee or other payment actually received by the Producer from net unit sales in excess of 100,000 units in the aggregate, except that in the case of covered programs the cast of which (exclusive of those members of the cast who would not be entitled to residuals if the program had been

produced for network television) is four players or less, the total percentage shall be computed on the basis of 1% per player. The computation of the number of players in the cast, for purposes of this paragraph only (but not for the purpose of determining rateable distribution provided in Paragraph 5 hereof), shall exclude off-camera announcer(s), provided however, that where the only performer(s) on a program is an off-camera announcer(s), the percentage shall be ½ of 1%, plus pension and welfare.

(2) The term "disc" as used in this paragraph shall refer to both video discs and video cassettes. The term "unit" shall refer to the disc or aggregate discs in each package released by the Producer for sale or rental. If a unit consists of more than one program, it shall be deemed a unit sale with respect to each such program. "Net Unit Sales" shall mean sales of units which are released by the Producer or its distributor for sale and are not returned, or are released by the Producer or its distributor for rental purposes.

(3) It is recognized that some companies hereunder may act both as producers and as distributors of disc units in covered sales. In such a case, the payments set forth above shall be based on either (i) the fee or other payment received by the subsidiary, division or other department of the company which serves as the production branch from the subsidiary, division or other department of the company which serves as the distribution branch, or (ii) where no separate subsidiary, division, or other department serves as the production branch, a reasonable allocation of the gross receipts of the company from covered sales attributable solely to fees or other payments which would be made to a production subsidiary, division or other department of the company if one existed, or would be made to an outside producer. The reasonableness of such allocation in (ii) above, or of the fee or other payment received by the production subsidiary, division or other department in (i) above, shall be determined in its license fee payments to outside producers for comparable disc units, or in the absence of such practice, by generally prevailing trade practice in the video disc industry.

(4) The provisions of Section 20(e) [casebook p. 615] of the SAG Television Agreement relating to application of contingent compensation against the payments to any individual actor shall be applicable also to the payments required herein.

Part VI

EXISTING TELEVISION PRODUCT TO BASIC CABLE

1. *Existing Television Product Released to Basic Cable*

The following shall be added as new Section 20.1 to the Television Agreement:

> "20.1 *Television Motion Pictures Produced Prior To October 6, 1980 and Exhibited on Basic Cable*
>
> (a) Producer shall pay to the Guild for rateable distribution to the players 4.50% of distributor's gross receipts plus pension and welfare with respect to any television entertainment programs produced prior to October 6, 1980 and released to basic cable. The foregoing provision, however, shall only apply to those television series programs that have run three (3) network seasons or less, which have not been placed in domestic syndication, nor exhibited on network non-prime time. The foregoing shall also be limited to television series programs and shall not apply to specials, movies of the week, multi-part novels for television, or any other single program.
>
> (b) Consent of the players must first be obtained by the Producer before the use provided in subparagraph (a) is permitted; however, in those instances where a player cannot be located, the Guild may act on behalf of such player.
>
> (c) Except as modified by this Section, all of the provisions of Section 20 of this Television Agreement shall apply to additional compensation payable with respect to the exhibition of television motion pictures in supplemental markets."

SUMMARY OF CHANGES
1983 SAG NEGOTIATIONS*
by
THE ALLIANCE OF MOTION PICTURE
& TELEVISION PRODUCERS

. . . .

14. *Supplemental Markets*:

(AFTRA, Exh. A *only*) Contribution under Exhibit D [not included in this

---

*[Draft only; not necessarily contract language—Ed.]

casebook] increased to 3.6% *including* pension and welfare for programs produced on or after July 1, 1983; for programs produced before November 16, 1973, can negotiate with performer to use product in "Supp. Mkt." as defined in Exh. D.

. . . .

16. *Money Breaks/Advance Payment for Residuals*:

New "Over 2-hour" program category of $17,000; status quo as to money breaks for other program lengths. (*Note*: "per episode" retained).

. . . .

36. *Product Made for Pay*:

Additional compensation increased from 4.5% to 6% of distributor's gross, *plus* pension and welfare.

New separate agreement for performers employed in pay-TV, videodiscs and cassettes, represented by joint SAG-AFTRA Committee, *provided* there is resolution of what the one agreement is and resolution of trust fund problem (pension and welfare).

. . . .

41. *Basic Cable*:

Original product for free TV which is released after 7/1/83 to Basic Cable generates 3.6% Supplemental Market payment, *including* pension and welfare.

SAMPLE INDIVIDUAL AGREEMENTS

ACQUISITION

OF RIGHTS

AGREEMENT

AGREEMENT

THIS AGREEMENT is made and entered into as of this day of _____, 19____, by and between _____ (the "Seller") and _____ _____ (the "Purchaser").

The Seller is the owner of the motion picture, television and allied rights in and to an original work entitled _____, written by _____ (Said work, with the theme, plot, characters, setting and story contained therein, shall hereinafter be referred to as the "Work".) The Purchaser desires to acquire the sole and exclusive motion picture, television and allied rights, as provided herein, in and to the Work.

Accordingly, the parties agree as follows:

1. *Grant of Rights.* The Seller hereby conveys, grants, and assigns to the Purchaser, forever and throughout the world, exclusively during the current and any renewed or extended term of copyright anywhere in the world and thereafter non-exclusively, the following rights in and relating to the Work, and any and all parts thereof including without limitation the characters contained therein whether as contained therein or otherwise:

1.1. All motion picture rights including, but not limited to, the rights to produce, project, exhibit, broadcast and transmit an unlimited number of motion pictures (including without limitation "remake" and "sequel" motion pictures, as said terms are commonly understood in the United States motion picture industry), theatrically, non-theatrically, on television, by means of cassettes and cartridges, and in all other media, now or hereafter known, and in all gauges and sizes. The term "motion picture," or words of similar import, as used in this Agreement, shall be deemed to mean and include any present or future kind of motion picture in any gauge, without or with sound recorded synchronously therewith, whether the same is produced on film or magnetic or video tape or wire or any other substance or by any other method or means now or hereafter used for the production, exhibition or transmission of any kind of motion picture, and whether the same is produced initially for theatrical, non-theatrical or television exhibition or transmission or otherwise. The first full length feature motion picture produced hereunder is sometimes hereinafter referred to as the "Motion Picture";

1.2. All television rights including, but not limited to, the rights to produce, project, exhibit, broadcast and transmit an unlimited number of television productions (including without limitation "series" and "specials," as such terms are commonly understood in the United States television industry), on television and in all other media now or hereafter known and in all gauges. The term "television production," or words of similar import, as used in this Agreement, shall be deemed to mean and include any present or future kind of television production, live or recorded, without or with sound recorded synchronously therewith, whether the same is produced on film or magnetic or video tape or wire or any other substance or by any other method or means now or hereafter used for the production, exhibition or transmission of any kind of television production, and whether the same is produced initially for television exhibition or transmission or otherwise;

1.3. So that the Purchaser shall be able to exploit fully the exclusive motion picture and television rights described in Paragraphs 1.1 and 1.2 above, the Seller agrees that such rights shall include without limitation the following exclusive rights:

1.3.1. To use, adapt, translate, subtract from, add to and change the Work and the title thereof, or any other title by which it (or any part thereof) has been or may at any time be known, in the making of motion pictures and television productions and/or as a part of or in conjunction with any such motion picture and television production;

1.3.2. To combine the Work in any manner with any other work or works in the making of motion pictures and television productions;

1.3.3. To use the Work and any part thereof, including without limitation the characters contained therein, and said titles and any similar titles, in conjunction with motion pictures and television productions based upon all or any part or parts of the Work and/or other literary, dramatic and/or dramatico-musical works, and/or in conjunction with musical compositions used for or in connection with such motion pictures and television productions, whether or not written for, or used in, or in connection with, or in any manner whatsoever apart from, any such motion pictures and television productions;

1.3.4. To project, transmit, exhibit, broadcast and otherwise reproduce the Work and any part or parts thereof pictorially and audibly by the art of cinematography or any process analogous thereto in any manner, including the right to project, transmit, reproduce and exhibit motion pictures and television productions and any part or parts thereof (including without limitation, by so-called "pay," "free," "free home," "closed circuit," "theatre," "toll," "CATV," or "subscription" television), and by the use of cartridges, cassettes, or other devices similar or dissimilar, and by so-called "EVR," "Cartrivision" or other similar systems and by any other process of transmission now known or hereafter to be devised;

1.3.5. To publish, use, copyright, vend, license, exhibit, perform and otherwise exploit, and license others to publish, use, copyright, vend, license, exhibit, perform and otherwise exploit, such motion pictures and television productions and the scripts of the same and any part thereof;

1.3.6. To record, reproduce and transmit sound, including spoken words, dialogue, music and songs, by any manner or means (including mechanical and electrical means and any other means now known or hereafter developed) whether extracted from or based upon the Work or otherwise, and to interpolate other spoken words, dialogue, music and songs, in or in connection with or as part of the production, reproduction, transmission, exhibition, performance or presentation of such motion pictures and television productions;

1.3.7. To make, copyright, publish, use, vend, license, perform and otherwise exploit, and license others to make, copyright, publish, use, vend, license, perform and otherwise exploit, in any manner, musical compositions, records, tapes and other sound-reproducing devices based in whole or in part on the Work or such motion pictures and television productions or such musical compositions, or any part or parts thereof, including the right to use the title of the Work and any similar titles in connection therewith;

1.3.8. To arrange for any and all merchandising and commercial tie-ups of any sort and nature arising out of or connected with the Work and/or the title thereof and/or the characters contained therein and/or said motion pictures and television productions; and

1.3.9. Generally to produce, reproduce, remake, reissue, transmit, exhibit and perform motion pictures and television productions of any and all kinds;

1.4. The right, but only for purposes of advertising and exploiting motion pictures and television productions, to make, publish and copyright, or cause to be made, published and copyrighted, in the name of the Purchaser or its nominees, in any and all languages, excerpts from the Work and synopses, scenarios and other versions of the Work and of any motion pictures or television productions made pursuant to this Agreement (each not exceeding 10,000 words in length), with or without illustrations of any type or kind whatsoever, on condition that then existing copyrights in the Work shall not thereby become invalidated. No use by the Purchaser of the name of the Seller shall be made in connection with any of the foregoing in such manner as would indicate that he is the author of any such synopses, scenarios or other versions. The Seller shall be appropriately indicated, however, to be the author of the Work;

1.5. The right, without additional compensation to the Seller, to broadcast and transmit by radio and television excerpts from and condensations of the Work and/or any motion pictures and television productions produced pursuant hereto in connection with advertising and publicity for any such motion picture or television productions; and

1.6. Solely for the purposes of advertising, publicizing and exploiting the rights granted to the Purchaser hereunder, the right to use, and to license, cause or permit others to use, the Seller's name, portrait, picture or likeness, and biographical data.

2. *Restrictions on Grant of Rights.*

2.1. The rights granted in Paragraph 1 above shall be deemed granted for a period (the "Grant Period") beginning on the date hereof and ending on the date _____ months thereafter, subject to extension as hereinafter provided.

2.2. The Purchaser shall have the right, but not the obligation, on or before the expiration of the _____ months period specified in Paragraph 2.1, to extend the Grant Period to a date which shall be _____ months from the date hereof by making the payment to the Seller specified in Paragraph 4.2 below and in the event that such payment is made, the Grant Period shall automatically be deemed extended until such date.

2.3. The Purchaser shall have the further right, but not the obligation, on or before _____ months from the date hereof, or, if the payment specified in Paragraph 4.2 below has been made, on or before _____ months from the date hereof, to extend the Grant Period in perpetuity by making the payment specified in Paragraph 4.3 below.

2.4. If the Grant Period has not been extended pursuant to Paragraph 2.2 above and/or pursuant to Paragraph 2.3 above, then this Agreement shall terminate, shall thereafter be deemed null and void, and all rights granted to the Purchaser hereunder shall revert to the Seller.

2.5. Notwithstanding anything contained herein to the contrary, if the Purchaser does not commence production of the Motion Picture within _____ years from the date hereof, then, upon the payment by the Seller to the Purchaser of a sum equal to the amount paid by the Purchaser to the Seller hereunder, this Agreement shall terminate, shall thereafter be deemed null and void, and all rights granted to the Purchaser hereunder shall revert to the Seller.

3. *Reserved Rights.* The Seller hereby specifically reserves the right to utilize and/or dispose of the following rights in the Work:

3.1. Stage productions with living actors performing in the immediate presence of an audience; *provided, however,* that the Seller shall not use and/or dispose of such stage production rights until ____ years from the date of this Agreement; *and provided further* that if the Motion Picture is produced and released or broadcast within such ____ year period, such ____ year period shall be extended automatically until five years from the date of the initial release or broadcast of the Motion Picture; and

3.2. Print publication rights in the Work other than the print publication rights granted in Paragraphs 1.3.5 and 1.4 above.

4. *Compensation.* In full consideration to the Seller for agreeing to and for performing all of the terms and conditions hereof, the Purchaser shall pay to the Seller, and the Seller shall accept, the following sums upon the following conditions:

4.1. Upon the complete execution of this Agreement, the sum of $____, receipt of which is hereby acknowledged;

4.2. On or before the date ____ months from the date hereof, if the Purchaser shall elect in its sole discretion to extend the Grant Period as provided in Paragraph 2.2 above, the sum of $____;

4.3. On or before the date ____ months from the date hereof, or, if the payment specified in Paragraph 4.2 has been made, on or before ____ months from the date hereof, if the Purchaser shall elect in its sole discretion to extend the Grant Period as provided in Paragraph 2.3 above:

4.3.1. The sum of $____, less the sums paid pursuant to Paragraphs 4.1 and 4.2 above, if the Purchaser at the time it makes such payment intends to release the Motion Picture initially on television; or

4.3.2. The sum of $____, less the sums paid pursuant to Paragraphs 4.1 and 4.2 above, if the Purchaser at the time it makes such payment intends to release the Motion Picture initially theatrically;

4.4. If the Purchaser makes the payment pursuant to Paragraph 4.3.1 above, and the Motion Picture is thereafter given a general theatrical release anywhere in the world, the Purchaser shall pay the Seller an additional sum of $____, within 30 days after the initial such general theatrical release.

5. *Contingent Compensation.* Provided the Seller fully and completely performs all the terms and conditions of this Agreement to be performed by him, if the following events occur, the Purchaser shall pay the Seller the following:

5.1. If the Motion Picture is produced and generally released, an amount equal to ____% of 100% of the "Net Profits" from the Motion

Picture. "Net Profits" shall be defined and payable pursuant to Exhibit A hereto, the terms of which are incorporated herein by reference;

5.2. If a feature-length sequel theatrical motion picture based in whole or in part on the Work is produced after the production of the Motion Picture, for each such sequel, an amount equal to $____, plus ____% of the net profits from such sequel motion picture (such net profits to be defined in a similar manner as that specified in Exhibit A hereto) and if a feature length remake theatrical motion picture based in whole or in part on the Work is produced after the production of the Motion Picture, for each such remake, an amount equal to $____, plus ____% of the net profits from each remake motion picture (such net profits to be defined in a similar manner as that specified in Exhibit A hereto);

5.3. If a television series based in whole or in part on the Work is produced:

5.3.1. With respect to each episode of such series (other than a daytime or "strip" television series) with a running time of one-half hour or less, the sum of $____; and with respect to any such episode with a running time in excess of one-half hour, but less than or equal to one hour, the sum of $____; and with respect to any such episode with a running time in excess of one hour, the sum of $____. Such sums shall be payable within 30 days after the initial broadcast of each such episode if such broadcast occurs on a national television network in the United States or within 4 months after the initial broadcast of each such episode if such broadcast occurs other than on a national television network in the United States;

5.3.2. If such series is a daytime or "strip" television series or show, the sum of $____ for each one-half hour of running time of each episode thereof. Such sums shall be payable within 30 days after the initial broadcast of each such episode if such broadcast occurs on a national television network in the United States or within 4 months after the initial broadcast of each such episode if such broadcast occurs other than on a national television network in the Unites States;

5.3.3. If any episode of any such series is rerun in the United States, a sum equal to 20% of the original flat fee payment pursuant to Paragraph 5.3.1 or 5.3.2 above for each of the first five reruns of each such episode, payable within 30 days after each such episode is rerun if such rerun occurs on a national television network in the United States or within 4 months after each rerun of each such episode if such rerun occurs other than on a national television network in the United States. Nothing shall be payable for any subsequent reruns;

5.4. If a television "special" or movie-of-the-week is produced and broadcast after the production of the Motion Picture, the sum $____ for each such program, payable within 30 days after the initial broadcast of each such program if such broadcast occurs on a national television network in the United States or within 4 months after the initial broadcast of each such program if such broadcast occurs other than on a national television network in the United States.

6. *Representations and Warranties.* The Seller hereby represents and warrants as follows:

6.1. All of the work was written by and is wholly original with the Seller; and the Work does not and will not, and any use of the Work contemplated hereunder will not, violate, conflict with, or infringe upon any rights whatsoever (including, without limitation, any copyright, common law or statutory, throughout the world; any right of publication, performance, or any other right in any work; and any right against libel, slander, invasion of privacy or similar right) of any person, firm or corporation;

6.2. The Work is fictitious and no real persons are depicted therein;

6.3. No claim has been made that the Work violates, conflicts with or infringes upon any rights whatsoever (including, without limitation, any copyright, common law or statutory, throughout the world; any right of publication, performance, or any other right in any work; and any right against libel, slander, invasion of privacy or similar right) of any person, firm or corporation;

6.4. There are no claims or litigation with respect to, concerning or purporting to affect adversely the Seller's right or title in or to the Work as herein represented and conveyed;

6.5. The Seller is the sole and exclusive owner throughout the world of the rights herein granted to the Purchaser and has the right to grant such rights exclusively to Purchaser. There is not now valid or outstanding, and the Seller will not hereafter grant, any right in connection with the Work which is or would be adverse to, or inconsistent with, or impair, the rights herein granted to the Purchaser, and he has not entered into any agreements with respect to the Work or disposed of any rights therein, except for a publishing agreement between the Seller and _____ (dated _____, 19___) and the rights granted in said publishing agreement are not in conflict with the rights granted to the Purchaser herein;

6.6. The Work was first published in the United States by _____ on _____ and copyright therein has been registered with the United States Copyright Office in the name of the Seller under the date of _____ and under Registration Number ____. The Work is protected by copyright in the United States and in those countries which are signatory or adhere to the Berne and Universal Copyright Conventions and is not in the public domain anywhere in the world where copyright protection is available;

6.7. With respect to the title _____, the Seller does not make any warranties except that he has not committed any act whereby the Purchaser's right to use such title for any purpose contemplated hereunder has been adversely affected.

7. *Versions of, Changes in and Sequels to the Work.*

7.1. The Seller warrants that neither he nor anyone authorized by him has heretofore published or authorized, and he agrees that he will not hereafter publish, or authorize the publication of, any version or sequel of the Work in any form unless such version or sequel is duly copyrighted in the United States and duly registered for copyright in the United States Copyright Office.

7.2. If any changes, revisions, additions, versions or sequels have heretofore been made or hereafter are made in or to the Work, including its title, for purposes of publication, translations or otherwise (including dramatic versions), originated by the Seller or by others under a license from the Seller, the Purchaser shall have the same rights in and to such changes, revisions, additions, versions and sequels as in the Work, it being understood and agreed that all such existing and future changes, revisions, additions, versions and sequels upon the creation thereof are and will constitute a part of the Work.

8. *Copyright Registration, Renewal, Extension and Grants of Rights.* Prior to the expiration of any copyright or copyrights in the Work or any part thereof (as the same may be extended), the Seller shall, to the extent legally permissible, renew or extend, or procure the renewal or extension of, such copyright or copyrights. The Seller hereby conveys, grants and assigns to the Purchaser all of the rights herein conveyed, granted and assigned for such renewal and extended terms as well as for the initial term. The Seller hereby irrevocably appoints the Purchaser or its designee(s) or assign(s) as his attorney-in-fact (acknowledging that such power is coupled with an interest) with the right, but not the obligation, to execute, deliver and record, on behalf of the Seller and in the name of the Seller, (a) any and all documents necessary or proper to secure the renewal or extension of any such copyright or copyrights and (b) all assignments and other documents necessary or proper to convey, grant, assign

and secure to the Purchaser all of the rights hereby conveyed, granted and assigned, for the term of such renewal or extensions as well as for the initial term. If the present copyright law of the United States or any other country where the Work is or may hereafter be protected shall be amended or changed or a new copyright law enacted, so that the term of copyright is extended, enlarged or created, the Purchaser shall be entitled to all of the rights hereby conveyed, granted and assigned to the Purchaser for such extended, or enlarged or created term.

9. *Additional Documents.* The Seller shall execute and deliver to the Purchaser, and obtain for and furnish to the Purchaser, any and all further documents necessary or proper to evidence or secure to the Purchaser the rights herein conveyed, granted and assigned, and to perfect the record thereof. Without limiting the generality of the foregoing, the Seller agrees to execute and deliver short-form assignments of any and all the rights, licenses, privileges and property herein conveyed, granted and assigned to the Purchaser, duly executed and acknowledged by the Seller, and the Seller hereby irrevocably appoints the Purchaser or its designee(s) or assign(s) as his attorney-in-fact (acknowledging that such power is coupled with an interest) with the right, but not the obligation, to execute such short-form assignments in his name; and further the Seller agrees to secure and deliver to the Purchaser a quitclaim or quitclaims of all rights, licenses, privileges and property herein granted to the Purchaser, duly executed and acknowledged by any persons, firms or corporations having any interest in the Work, if the Purchaser shall request the same.

10. *Indemnity.* The Seller shall indemnify and save harmless the Purchaser, its successors, licensees and assigns, and the officers, directors, employees, agents and representatives thereof, against any and all claims, demands, suits, losses, costs, expenses (including, without limitation, reasonable legal fees and expenses), damages or recoveries (including, without limitation, any amounts paid in settlement) suffered, made, incurred or assumed by the Purchaser, its successors, licensees, assigns or the officers, directors, employees, agents and representatives thereof, by reason of the breach or alleged breach of any warranty, undertaking, representation, agreement or certification made or entered into herein or hereunder by the Seller.

11. *Credits.*

11.1. With respect to any motion picture or television production produced hereunder, the Purchaser agrees to give the Seller credit on the screen on a card on which no other material shall appear except the credit afforded the screenwriter(s), in a size of type equal to the size of the screen credit given to the screenwriter, in substantially the following form:

11.1.1. If such motion picture or television production shall be entitled _____: "Based upon the _____ by _____".

11.1.2. If such motion picture or television production shall have a different title: "Based upon the ____ entitled '_____' by _____".

11.2. Subject to the paid advertising exceptions in agreements between the Purchaser and distributors of motion pictures based upon the Work, in all paid advertisements in which the screenwriter(s) of a motion picture based upon the Work receives credit, the Seller shall receive credit as specified in Paragraph 11.1.1 or 11.1.2 above, and such credit shall be at least in the same size and prominence as the credit accorded to such screenwriter.

11.3. No casual or inadvertent failure of the Purchaser to comply with the provisions of this Paragraph 11 and no breach by any other person, firm or corporation of any contract requiring observance of such credit requirements, shall be deemed a breach of this Agreement by the Purchaser.

12. *Purchaser's Control.* The Seller acknowledges the right of the Purchaser to make any changes in the Work in the preparation and exploitation of any motion pictures and television productions based upon the Work, and in this connection the Seller acknowledges and agrees that he will not have any right of approval or consultation with respect to any such changes or with respect to any element (casting, screenplay, directing, distribution, etc.) of any motion pictures or television productions produced hereunder. Without limiting the generality of the foregoing sentence, the Purchaser shall have all artistic control over and the right to cut, edit, add to, subtract from, arrange, rearrange and revise the Work in any manner. The Seller hereby waives any right of droit moral or any similar right with respect to the Work and agrees not to institute, support, maintain, or permit any action or lawsuit on the ground that any motion picture or television production produced hereunder, or any other exercise of any of the rights conveyed, granted and assigned by the Seller hereunder constitutes an infringement of any right of droit moral or any similar right, or is in any way a defamation or mutilation of the Work or any part thereof or of the reputation of the Seller, or contains unauthorized variations, alterations, modifications, changes or translations. The Seller shall not have any right to approve, or be consulted about, any arrangements made by the Purchaser (including without limitation all decisions relating to commencement, continuation, suspension and/or abandonment) with respect to the production, distribution, exhibition or other exploitation of any motion pictures or television productions produced hereunder.

13. *No Obligation to Produce; No Reversion.* Nothing herein or elsewhere contained shall obligate the Purchaser to produce any motion picture or

television production based upon the Work. Irrespective of whether or not the Purchaser shall make any motion picture or television production hereunder, it is expressly understood and agreed that, except as specifically provided in Paragraph 2 above, the rights granted in this Agreement to the Purchaser with respect to the characters and characterizations contained in the Work and all other rights granted herein shall belong exclusively, unconditionally and forever to the Purchaser, and under no circumstances whatsoever shall any of such rights revert to the Seller.

14. *Agency.* Seller hereby irrevocably designates _____ as his exclusive agent in connection with this Agreement. All payments or notices due Seller hereunder may be made to and in the name of and sent to such agent. Receipt by such agent shall be deemed receipt by Seller.

15. *Assignment.* The Purchaser may assign its rights hereunder to any person, firm or corporation, *provided, however,* that the Purchaser shall not be released from any of its obligations hereunder to the Seller unless the assignee assumes in writing all of such obligations.

16. *Governing Law.* This Agreement is made in the State of New York and shall in all respects be governed by and construed in accordance with the laws of that State applicable to contracts made and entirely performed therein.

17. *Notices.* Any payments, notices, documents, statements, or other writings (collectively referred to herein as "Notices") required or desired to be given hereunder shall be in writing and shall be sent to the parties hereto at the addresses given above, or to such other address as the Seller or the Purchaser may hereafter designate in writing in the manner provided above, and shall be sufficiently given by personal delivery thereof to the Purchaser or to the Seller, or by telegraphing or by mailing the same in a postpaid wrapper addressed to the other party as aforesaid, and the date of such delivery, telegraphing or mailing shall be the date of the giving of such Notices. Copies of all Notices to be given to Purchaser shall be sent to _____.

18. *Miscellaneous Provisions.*

18.1. The rights and remedies of the Seller in the event of a breach of this Agreement shall be limited to the right, if any, to recover damages in an action at law, and in no event shall the Seller be entitled by reason of any such breach to terminate this Agreement and the Seller shall not be entitled to and hereby waives the right in such event to equitable or injunctive relief or to enjoin, restrain, or interfere with the production, distribution, exhibition, or other exploitation of any motion picture or television production produced hereunder.

18.2. The failure of either party to this Agreement to object to or to take affirmative action with respect to any conduct of the other party which is in violation of this Agreement shall not be construed as the waiver of any rights or remedies in connection with such violation. No waiver by either party hereto of any breach by the other party of any term, covenant or condition of this Agreement shall be deemed a waiver of any other breach (whether prior to or subsequent) of the same or any other term, covenant or condition of this or any other agreement.

18.3. This Agreement constitutes the entire agreement between the parties with respect to the within subject matter and cannot be modified except by a written instrument signed by the party to be charged with the contents thereof.

18.4. Paragraph headings used herein are for convenience only, and shall not be deemed to be part of this Agreement.

IN WITNESS WHEREOF, the parties hereto have caused this instrument to be executed as of the day and year first above written.

_____

Seller:

_____

Purchaser:

By:_____

_____

ASSIGNMENT

KNOW ALL MEN BY THESE PRESENTS:

THIS INSTRUMENT is subject to all the terms and conditions of the Agreement dated _____, 197____, between _____ (referred to herein as "Purchaser"), and _____ _____ (referred to herein as "Seller"), and Exhibit A thereto, relating to the literary and/or dramatic work (the "Work") entitled "_____" written by Seller.

The undersigned Seller, for One Dollar in hand paid and for other valuable consideration now received, hereby sells and assigns unto Purchaser, and its successors and assigns forever, all MOTION PICTURE AND TELEVISION RIGHTS in and to the Work, and all parts thereof, and all MOTION PICTURE AND TELEVISION RIGHTS in all copyright thereof (and in any renewals or extensions thereof) including copyright registered in the United States Copyright Office in the name of Seller under date ____ ____, Entry No. _____; together with the sole and exclusive right to use, adapt, change, translate, add to, and take from the Work and the title in the making of motion picture and television productions of every kind or character and to lease, vend, exploit and exhibit (including exhibition on free and pay television) the same throughout the world and to copyright the same in Purchaser's name. Included in said MOTION PICTURE AND TELEVISION RIGHTS are: sound, musical and talking motion picture rights; cassettes, cartridge, and so-called "EVR," "Cartrivision" and other similar system rights, including transmission from recordings; rights in the characters contained in the Work; the right to record and reproduce sounds, music and speech, taken from the Work or other sources, accompanying motion pictures based on the Work or other sources and separately as commercial phonograph records; filmed and taped television rights; commercial tie-up rights; and the right to print and publish synopses, revised and/or abridged versions of the Work and any motion picture versions thereof which publicize or advertise such pictures.

The undersigned agrees, insofar as the undersigned now or later may have the power or authority so to do, to cause renewals or extensions of any copyright in the Work duly to be obtained, and the MOTION PICTURE AND TELEVISION RIGHTS herein granted are now assigned to Purchaser for the renewal or extended term of copyright and after such renewal or extension further or like documents of confirmation of assignment will be given to Purchaser if requested. The undersigned hereby appoints Purchaser as his irrevocable attorney-in-fact, with the right, but not the obligation, to execute and file all such documents and to do all acts necessary for the obtaining of such extensions or renewals and evidencing the continuation of the same rights in Purchaser for such renewed or extended terms as are now vested in Purchaser.

And the said Purchaser, and its successors and assigns, are hereby empowered to bring, prosecute, defend and appear in suits, actions and proceedings of any nature under or concerning said copyright or its renewals or extensions, or concerning any infringement thereof, and particularly infringement of or interference with any of the MOTION PICTURE AND TELEVISION RIGHTS now granted under said copyright or renewals or extensions, in the name of the copyright proprietor but at the sole cost and expense of said Purchaser which will indemnify the undersigned therein. Any recovery of costs from infringement or violation of any copyright or its renewals or extensions, so far as it arises from any violation of MOTION PICTURE AND TELEVISION RIGHTS hereby assigned, is now assigned to and shall be paid to said Purchaser and its successors and assigns.

Dated: . . . .

_____

Seller

STATE OF _____ } ss.:

COUNTY OF _____

On this ____ day of _____, 197____, before me came _____, to me known to be the individual described in and who executed the foregoing instrument, and duly acknowledged that he executed the same.

_____
Notary Public

_____

SCHEDULE I

ATTACHED TO AND HEREBY MADE A PART OF THE AGREEMENT BETWEEN
_____, A DIVISION OF _____ CORPORATION

_____
(Producer)

and_____
(Contractor)

DATED:_____

A. Definition of Gross Proceeds & Net Proceeds:

1. The term "gross proceeds" as used herein means all monies actually received by Producer from the broadcasting, distribution, exhibition and marketing (herein sometimes collectively called "distribution") of the programs (including the pilot, if any) produced during the term of the Agreement to which this Schedule is attached and from the lease, license, sale, disposition or other use (herein sometimes collectively a "use") of subsidiary rights and merchandising rights, both defined below, derived from such programs; except that the following shall not be included in gross proceeds:

   (i) any monies paid to Producer and thereafter refunded (and if any such monies have been included in computing any sums paid to Contractor, such payment shall be deemed an overpayment);

(ii) any monies in the nature of security or deposits, unless and until received by Producer and to be retained by it for its sole benefit absolutely and unconditionally;

(iii) any monies derived by Producer from the use of its facilities and personnel in connection with production, insertion and/or integration of television commercials.

If Producer sublicenses distribution of the programs to any subdistributor, gross proceeds shall relate to the monies actually received by such subdistributor to the extent that such subdistributor accounts therefor to Producer and makes payment thereof to Producer. If Producer engages any third party to act as its representative in licensing subsidiary rights and/or merchandising rights, gross proceeds shall relate to the monies actually received by such third party to the extent that such third party accounts therefor to Producer and makes payment thereof to Producer.

2. The term "net proceeds" as used herein means the amount remaining after the deduction from gross proceeds of

(i) all 'program production and distribution costs", and

(ii) all "costs and expenses relative to uses of subsidiary rights and merchandising rights"

all as defined and set forth below.

3. The following shall constitute "program production and distribution costs" which are chargeable against gross proceeds:

(a) *Production Costs*: Costs (other than costs which are covered by the Production Fee referred to in paragraph (b) below) incurred in connection with the production of each program, as follows:

(i) All payments, salaries and fees payable to any person, firm or corporation rendering services or supplying goods or materials for or in connection with any program, including, but not limited to publicity and casting charges; with respect to Producer's employees, the foregoing shall include, without limitation, severance, holiday and vacation pay, and Producer's then prevailing percentage of salaries paid to such personnel to cover any union welfare fund contributions, governmental contributions and/or other "fringe" benefit payments made for or on behalf of said personnel; if Producer incurs any retroactive salary or other increases (including, but not limited to fringe benefits) by reason of any collective bargaining agreement or by reason of the provisions of any government law, rule or regulation, such increases shall be treated as costs hereunder;

(ii) All monies payable to Contractor under this paragraph A3(a), exclusive of payments of net proceeds to Contractor under this Schedule;

(iii) Deferred monies, salaries or fees (including both those expressed in fixed amounts and those expressed in percentages) payable to any person, firm or corporation rendering services or supplying goods or materials for or in connection with any program;

(iv) The cost of all facilities, equipment and materials and other below-the-line elements used for each program whether or not furnished by Producer; in this connection it is agreed that, to the extent Producer furnishes such below-the-line elements (other than those furnished for the Production Fee, whether or not furnished on an as available basis), they shall be furnished, as available, at Producer's then prevailing rates (including, but not limited to, flat rate charges). If Producer is required to rent any equipment from third parties (including unavailable equipment which would have been furnished under the Production Fee if available, but excluding equipment required to be furnished under the Production Fee), the series shall be charged Producer's actual rental cost.

(v) Any additional or extraordinary costs (not actually reimbursed by insurance) incurred by reason of acts of God, force majeure, illness or other contingencies;

(vi) Bank charges relative to financing transactions (exclusive of penalties and/or interest charged because of late payment or non-payment); interest paid on interim and deficit financing but not to exceed the rate then prevailing among banks or other generally recognized lending institutions in the industry. If Producer itself furnishes such financing, Producer shall be entitled to charge, as an expense, interest on its unrecouped costs (including overhead), which interest shall be computed for each accounting period as of the last day of the period reported and calculated at one percent (1%) above the prime bank-lending rate in effect on the last day of such reported period. If interim or deficit financing shall have been secured by Producer for several program series (including the program series named in the body of the agreement to which this Schedule is attached), the interest chargeable as a cost hereunder shall be allocated accordingly;

(vii) Insurance premiums and other similar charges attributable to the programs;

(viii) Taxes, assessments or other similar liabilities imposed upon Producer by reason of production of the programs (excluding corporate income and franchise taxes levied on the income of Producer not directly related to the production of the programs hereunder);

(ix) All costs of trademark and copyright searches, services and registration and similar costs, and all costs in obtaining and maintaining Errors and Omissions insurance coverage attributable to the production of the programs (including, but not limited to, outside attorneys' fees and statutory fees);

(x) Any other costs, not referred to above, reasonably incurred in connection with production of the programs.

Costs referred to herein shall be computed in accordance with standard motion picture accounting principles. Contractor shall be given the benefit of volume and cash discounts actually received, but Producer shall be under no obligation to take advantage of any such discount.

(b) *Production Fee (Overhead)*:

(i) An amount (herein called either "the Production Fee" or "overhead") equal to twenty percent (20%) (except such percentage shall be thirty percent (30%) for 90-minute or longer television programs), increasable as provided below, of the total of (1) all production costs referred to in paragraph A3(a) above and (2) all costs and/or expenses incurred as a result of network repeat broadcasts made as part of the network first run broadcasts; except that for the purpose only of computing such Production Fee there shall be excluded any deferred cost referred to in paragraph A3(a)(iii) above until same is actually paid. The aforesaid twenty percent (20%) Production Fee shall increase by one percent (1%) in each succeeding production year. (E.g., the Production Fee shall be twenty-one percent (21%) with respect to programs produced for the second broadcast year of the series, twenty-two percent (22%) for programs produced for the third broadcast year of the series, etc.) The Facilities and Services Exhibit, attached hereto and hereby made a part hereof, details the services and facilities to be furnished by Producer for the Production Fee.

(ii) Anything to the contrary in paragraph (i) above or elsewhere in this Schedule I to the contrary notwithstanding, if Producer is no longer operating its present studios (the __ facilities at __ ____), the Production Fee will be adjusted to take into account the resultant added cost to Producer in renting, leasing or purchasing facilities and equipment required to be furnished by Producer for the Production Fee (as distinguished from those items to be furnished on an as available basis). In making such adjustment, however, Producer will credit against such added cost (in an amount not to exceed such added cost) the television facility fee which was most recently charged outside tenants by Producer for furnishing the particular facilities and equipment giving rise to such added cost. If such outside tenant television facility fee covers items in addition to such particular facilities and equipment, the credit (in an amount not to exceed such added cost) shall be the portion of such fee applicable to such particular facilities and equipment, which portion shall be determined by Producer's good faith allocation.

(c) *Distribution Costs*: All direct costs and expenses incurred in connection with the distribution of the programs, whether or not listed below, including, but not limited to:

(i) additional payments (including both those expressed in fixed amounts and in percentages, including, but not limited to, television rerun, theatrical reuse payments and/or any other payments required to be made to or on behalf of personnel used upon the programs by reason of any collective bargaining agreement and/or individual employment agreements), if any, required to be made with respect to any persons or firms who render services upon or furnish material for the programs, together with all taxes, fees, contributions and similar expenses attributable to such payments;

(ii) music synchronization license fees and performance fees, if any, paid in connection with the exercise of distribution rights hereunder;

(iii) all costs incurred in connection with the making of such duplicate tapes, prints and negatives of the programs as Producer may deem necessary, in its discretion, for the proper distribution of the programs, and in connection with the possession, storage and shipment of such prints and negatives, including laboratory and transportation charges, the cost of reels and containers, and insurance premiums on prints, negatives, reels and containers;

(iv) direct advertising, exploitation and publicity costs, including, but not limited to, the cost of newspaper, tradepaper, magazine, radio, television and direct mail advertising, the cost of campaign books and sales promotion books, the cost of press matter and synopses, and the cost of all advertising and promotion accessories customary in the trade; provided that, if any advertising or promotional materials relate to several program series, the costs thereof shall be fairly allocated as among all such program series;

(v) costs and expenses directly attributable to accommodating the programs for uses which may be made of them, including, but not limited to, any costs incurred in retitling the programs, removing commercial material, dubbing or subtitling programs for foreign distribution, or otherwise altering or editing the programs for any uses (whether for censorship purposes or otherwise); provided, if foreign language versions are made by a third party in exchange or partly in exchange for exhibition rights in a certain country or territory, Producer may allocate to gross revenues hereunder its estimated value of such syndication rights and, in addition, treat such allocated amount as a distribution expense hereunder;

(vi) direct cost of checking or audit, where, in Producer's discretion, an independent person or company is engaged by Producer to check or audit;

(vii) trade association fees;

(viii) all sums paid or accrued on account of sales, use, value of the programs, receipts, income, remittance and other taxes, however denominated, to any governmental authority including any cost (fairly apportioned to the programs hereunder) of contesting the same, and all sums paid or accrued on account of all duties, customs and imposts, costs of acquiring permits and other similar authority to secure the entry and exercise of the rights hereunder (excluding corporate income and franchise taxes levied on the income of the Producer);

(ix) all discounts, allowances and commissions incurred in connection with the distribution of the programs, including, but not limited to, any agency commissions, charged as a sales commission or otherwise in connection with the programs; provided that no agency sales commission shall be chargeable under this subclause (ix) in connection with first run broadcasts (including network repeat broadcasts made as a part of the first run broadcasts) of the programs hereunder;

(x) anything to the contrary notwithstanding, Contractor's profit participation will take effect only after Producer shall have fully recouped in cash all of its program production costs (including Production Fees) hereunder and, until such recoupment is effected, profit participation to others (including network, agencies, sponsors and individuals), if any, will be deducted as distribution expenses;

(xi) any other direct costs and expenses not referred to above directly attributable to the distribution of the programs.

(d) *Distribution Fees*: Distribution fees (herein expressly deemed a cost) to be retained by Producer with respect to the licensing of the programs in the following amounts:

(i) for network television broadcasting (i.e. broadcasting of the programs over a transcontinental network system of over sixty (60) stations within the fifty United States and the District of Columbia (herein the "United States Territory"), including delayed and/or supplemental broadcasting in connection therewith)—ten percent (10%)

of gross proceeds actually received during each "accounting period" (as defined below);

(ii) for syndicated television broadcasting (i.e. broadcasting of the programs on any basis other than network broadcasting) within the United States Territory:

(A) Ten percent (10%) of gross proceeds actually received during each accounting period pursuant to each separate licensing agreement which contemplates syndicated broadcasting of the programs over sixty (60) or more television stations within the United States Territory;

(B) Twenty-five percent (25%) of gross proceeds actually received during each accounting period pursuant to each separate licensing agreement which contemplates syndicated broadcasting of the programs over more than twenty-five (25) but less than sixty (60) television stations within the United States Territory;

(C) Forty percent (40%) of gross proceeds actually received during each accounting period pursuant to each separate licensing agreement which contemplates syndicated broadcasting of the programs over twenty-five (25) or fewer television stations within the United States Territory;

(D) The distribution fee for the licensing of programs in Puerto Rico shall be forty percent (40%) of gross proceeds actually received during each accounting period from Puerto Rico, except that the distribution fee shall be ten percent (10%) with respect to those programs, if any, which the U. S. network is licensed to broadcast in Puerto Rico as part of its network territory.

(iii) for television broadcasting within Canada:

(A) Twenty-five percent (25%) of gross proceeds actually received during each accounting period pursuant to each separate licensing agreement which contemplates broadcasting of the programs over the CBC (Canadian) English-speaking network;

(B) Forty percent (40%) of gross proceeds actually received during each accounting period pursuant to each separate licensing agreement which contemplates broadcasting of the programs in Canada, other than over the CBC (Canadian) English-speaking network,

except that the distribution fee shall be ten percent (10%) with respect to programs, if any, which the U. S. network is licensed to broadcast in Canada as part of its network territory;

(iv) for foreign television broadcasting (i.e. broadcasting on any basis in any area outside Canada and the United States Territory) - Fifty percent (50%) of the sums actually received by Producer during each accounting period pursuant to each licensing agreement which contemplates the broadcast of the programs in any such foreign area (herein sometimes referred to as "foreign territory");

(v) for theatrical distribution of programs, Producer's then applicable theatrical distribution fees;

(vi) for any exhibition of the programs over "theater" television facilities and/or "in-flight" and/or shipboard facilities, Producer's then applicable distribution fees;

(vii) for any "home movie exhibition" or any other exhibition not specified above—an amount equal to fifty percent (50%) of gross proceeds from each separate exhibition agreement covering such exhibition. The term "home movie exhibition" as used herein means exhibition of the programs to those present at the exhibition thereof in homes, schools, churches, clubs and the like.

The television distribution fees specified herein shall apply regardless of the type of telecast (whether free television, cable television, pay television, subscription television or other). The distribution fees specified herein shall constitute payment for any overhead costs incurred by Producer in distributing the programs. If Producer licenses distribution of the programs to a subdistributor, the distribution fees set forth hereinabove shall include such subdistributor's fees as well as Producer's. Anything to the contrary notwithstanding, if Producer grants distribution rights (as distinguished from subdistribution rights) to others, including the network, then, to the extent that the distribution fees charged by such others are greater than those set forth in this paragraph 3.(d), these paragraph 3.(d) distribution rates shall be increased accordingly. The aforesaid ten percent (10%) U.S. network distribution fee set forth in paragraph A.3.(d)(i) above shall include all payments made by Producer to an outside agency with respect to the initial network telecast of the programs (including network repeat telecasts which are part of the first run network broadcasts). All other agency commissions shall be charged as a cost in accordance with the provisions of paragraph A.3.(c)(ix) hereof.

It is specifically understood and agreed that the distribution fees indicated herein may be increased if the distribution fees charged by a majority of the major distributors (as such term is understood in the television and/or motion picture industry, as may be applicable), are increased. Such increase shall be the extent of such increase of the majority of such distributors.

(e) *"Barters"*: If programs are licensed partly or entirely on so-called "barter" basis (e.g. in exchange for commercial time), no gross proceeds will be deemed realized from the non-cash assets so received until such assets are converted into cash (the converted sums), with foreign funds to be treated as set forth in paragraph B.3. hereof. If Producer, its subsidiaries or affiliates exploit any such non-cash asset instead of converting it to cash, the fair market price of such asset shall be deemed gross proceeds. In any event, Producer shall be entitled to a distribution fee of forty percent (40%) of the U.S. converted sums or fifty percent (50%) of the foreign converted sums, as the case may be.

(f) *Claims or Proceedings*: Costs, including, but not limited to, reasonable attorney's and collection agency's fees and costs incurred in any claim or proceeding brought by or against Producer in connection with each program or the agreement to which this Schedule is attached, or any provision thereof or hereof; excluding, however, any costs of litigation incurred by Producer in an action brought by Contractor against Producer wherein Contractor is successful.

4. The following shall constitute "costs and expenses relative to uses of subsidiary rights and merchandising rights" which are chargeable against gross proceeds:

(i) any share of net proceeds paid to any performers or others for the use of their names, voices, likenesses, endorsements and/or biographical material in connection with any use of merchandising rights;

(ii) the amounts, if any, paid to writers and others for their services in rewriting, revising, changing the form of or otherwise developing the programs for the purpose of such use;

(iii) all royalties (including both those expressed in fixed amounts and in percentages) payable to any writers or other persons by reason of such exploitation; any payments which are accrued by reason of being deferred for payment at a later time other than any such deferred payments which are in the nature of a profit participation or payment of which is contingent upon subsequent receipt of gross proceeds;

(iv) all taxes (excluding corporate franchise and corporate income taxes not directly related to the exploitation of programs or rights hereunder) and governmental assessments no matter how characterized or described;

(v) all trademark costs, copyright costs and other costs incurred in connection with establishment and protection of the merchandising and subsidiary rights and costs of all insurance premiums (including, but not limited to, attorney's fees, statutory fees, and copyright and trademark searches and services) not otherwise reimbursed under paragraph 3.(a)(ix) hereof;

(vi) in the case of subsidiary rights (but not merchandising rights) any other direct costs and expenses incurred in connection with the exploitation of such subsidiary rights; no such other direct costs as herein referred to shall be chargeable with respect to exploitation of merchandising rights;

(vii) a handling fee (herein specifically deemed a cost) to be retained by Producer in an amount

(A) with respect to merchandising rights, equal to fifty percent (50%) of gross proceeds derived pursuant to each and every license relative to merchandising rights; provided that if Producer engages any third party to act as its representative in licensing of any merchandising rights, the handling fee referred to herein shall include such third party's handling fee or handling charges as well as Producer's. If Producer exploits a particular merchandising right itself (as distinguished from licensing a third party or parties), the gross proceeds derived from the exploitation of such merchandising right shall be the fair market price of such merchandising right. If a merchandising right is exploited through a subsidiary or affiliate, the gross proceeds shall be the negotiated license fee which shall be determined by the fair market price;

(B) with respect to subsidiary rights, equal to twenty-five percent (25%) of the gross proceeds derived pursuant to each and every license relative to subsidiary rights; provided that, if Producer engages any third party to act as its representative in licensing of any subsidiary right, the handling fee referred to herein shall include such third party's handling fee or handling charges as well as Producer's. If Producer exploits a particular subsidiary right itself (as distinguished from licensing a third party or parties), the gross proceeds derived from the exploitation of such subsidiary right shall be the fair market price of such subsidiary right. If a subsidiary right is exploited through a subsidiary or affiliate, the gross proceeds therefrom shall be the negotiated license fee which shall be determined by the fair market price.

5. (a) *Subsidiary Rights*: As used herein, "subsidiary rights" means, without limitation, any and all rights with respect to theatrical motion picture rights, radio broadcasting, legitimate stage performances, printed publications (including, but not limited to, hard-cover books, but excluding paperback books and comic books) and/or any other uses of a similar or dissimilar nature in any industry and/or field of endeavor whether or not now in existence or commercially feasible, but excluding any music publication, recording, performance or other music exploitation. The term "theatrical motion picture rights" as used herein, means the right to (and/or authorize others to) produce, exhibit (before paid admission audiences or otherwise), perform

(whether for profit or otherwise), sell, lease, license and otherwise dispose of, exploit and turn to account any one or more silent, sound, talking, dialogue and/or musical motion picture photoplays (based in whole or in part upon the programs or elements thereof) of any type now known or hereafter devised intended initially for theatrical exhibition as distinguished from television broadcasting. If Producer exploits a particular subsidiary right itself or through a subsidiary or affiliate (as distinguished from licensing a third party or parties), the gross proceeds derived from the exploitation of such subsidiary right shall be limited to the aforesaid fair market price or negotiated license fee of such subsidiary right, and Contractor shall have no obligations or liabilities with respect to the exploitation of such subsidiary right nor be otherwise entitled to any rights or benefits therefrom.

(b) *Merchandising Rights*: The term "merchandising rights" means, without limitation, any and all rights with respect to paperback books and comic books, cartoon and newspaper publication, toys, novelties, figures and figurines, trinkets, fabric, apparel, food, drinks and any other goods and services, whether of a similar or dissimilar nature, as well as commercial tie-in rights, premiums, giveaways, and the like, except that this term shall not include any merchandising rights with respect to subsidiary rights exploited by Producer or a subsidiary or affiliate or Producer. Merchandising rights also include any right to use the series title and/or the names, voices and/or likenesses of the leading series players in connection with phonograph records and sheet music, but do not otherwise include any music publication, recording, performance or other music exploitation rights.

(c) *Other Exclusions*: It is expressly agreed that subsidiary rights and merchandising rights shall in no event include (i) any use of stock footage (as that term is commonly used in the entertainment industry) from the programs; (ii) television broadcasting rights of any nature whatsoever and/or rights with respect to any distribution of the programs themselves by way of television broadcasting, theatrical exhibition and/or other means of exhibition, distribution or marketing whether now known or hereafter devised and/or (iii) any participation in any share of net proceeds derived from television programs other than the specific program or series covered by the agreement to which this Schedule is attached (including, but not limited to, so-called "spin-off" programs as that term is generally understood in the industry). If an episode of the series is produced with the intention of spinning-off another series or program(s), the cost and revenues attributable to such episode shall be handled in the same manner as provided herein, except that, for the purpose of computing Contractors's net profits hereunder (i) the production costs and fees attributable to such episode (the "spin-off") shall not exceed that of the highest cost (including overhead) episode produced during such production year, (ii) the initial telecast revenue of the spin-off episode shall be the per program fee (and repeat fee, if applicable) for such production year's programs (other than the pilot) and (iii) if the spin-off episode is subsequently distributed as part of another series, the amount, if any, by which the cost of the spin-off exceeds the revenue shall be credited.

B. Accounting:

1. Net proceeds hereunder shall be computed by Producer based upon the aggregate of gross proceeds derived from distribution of the programs and uses of subsidiary rights and merchandising rights during accounting periods (herein "accounting periods") as specified below. The first accounting period hereunder shall commence with the initial first-run network broadcast of any program to which this Schedule applies and shall continue through the end of Producer's third (3rd) fiscal quarter. Each twelve (12) month period thereafter shall constitute a separate accounting period. Producer shall render an accounting statement to Contractor within one hundred eighty days after the end of each accounting period during which any gross proceeds are received by Producer hereunder. Each said accounting statement shall set forth in reasonable detail: The gross proceeds received by Producer during the accounting period covered by such statement; the costs and expenses chargeable against such gross proceeds; and the computation of net proceeds, if any, which are available for distribution. Concurrently with the furnishing of any such statement, Producer shall pay Contractor its share of net proceeds, if any, payable to Contractor pursuant to said accounting statement. If, during any accounting period or periods, Producer incurs a net operating loss, such loss or losses shall be carried forward or carried back into one or more accounting periods in which net proceeds are realized and applied as a reduction of said net proceeds. Producer may, during the pendency of any claim brought or threatened against Producer by any third party with respect to any breach of any warranty or agreement made by Contractor under the agreement to which this Schedule is attached, withhold any sums payable to Contractor hereunder in an amount which, in Producer's reasonable business judgment, is sufficient to satisfy Contractor's liability to Producer in connection therewith. Producer may also, in each accounting statement, provide for reserves which, in Producer's reasonable business judgment, are sufficient to cover (i) any and all distribution, merchandising and subsidiary rights costs which Producer reasonably anticipates will be incurred or accrued within one (1) year from the end of the period covered by such accounting statement and/or (ii) the potential liability to Producer (in Producer's reasonable business judgment) from claims brought or threatened against Producer by any third party with respect to the programs.

2. Producer shall maintain books and records relative to gross proceeds and net proceeds derived from distribution of the programs and uses of subsidiary rights and merchandising rights. If Contractor so requests, Producer will

permit Contractor or any mutual agreeable independent certified public accountant to make an examination, at Contractor's expense, of such of its books and records as may be necessary to verify the accuracy of any statement submitted to Contractor by Producer hereunder, which examination with respect to each statement must take place, during reasonable business hours, at Producer's Hollywood office, only once during the six-month period subsequent to the delivery of such earnings statement. No examination may be made by or under the supervision of any past employee of Producer or its parent, associated or affiliated companies. Said examination may relate only to the sums contained on the last statement submitted to Contractor. No examination shall continue longer than thirty (30) days from and after the commencement thereof. A true copy of all reports made by Contractor's accountants, pursuant to the foregoing provision, shall be delivered to Producer at the same time such respective reports are delivered to Contractor by said accountants. Producer need not furnish Contractor with copies of any records inspected, but Contractor may copy said records or make extracts therefrom at its sole expense. Producer shall not be deemed in default hereunder in the event it is unable to include information in such statements for any country within the time limitation specified herein if such delay is occasioned because of wars, delays in transportation or other reasons beyond Producer's control. Each statement rendered hereunder shall be binding upon Contractor and not subject to objection for any reason unless such objection is made in writing stating the basis thereof and delivered to Producer within six (6) months from delivery of such earnings statement or, if an audit is commenced prior thereto, within thirty (30) days from the completion of such audit.

3. No sums shall be taken into consideration in computing gross proceeds hereunder until actually paid to or received by Producer in the Unites States in U.S. dollars. If any foreign receipts of the programs are frozen or unremittable and such receipts in foreign currency shall be transferred to Producer's account in any such foreign country, Producer will notify Contractor to such effect. Upon Contractor's written request and upon condition that the same shall be permitted by the authorities of such foreign country, Producer will transfer to Contractor, at Contractor's cost and expense, the same part of such foreign receipts as Contractor would be entitled to hereunder if the foreign receipts were transmitted to and paid in the United States in accordance with the terms hereof, such part of the aforesaid foreign receipts to be transferred by Producer to such bank as is designated by Contractor in the foreign country. Producer shall not be liable in any way for any losses caused by fluctuation in the rate of exchange or because of any failure to convert or remit any particular funds to the United States at any particular time or at a more favorable cost or rate of exchange than the cost or rate of exchange at which such conversion and remittance was accomplished, it being agreed that Con-

tractor shall be bound by whatever arrangements Producer may make for the conversion and remittance of foreign funds and by whatever cost or rate of exchange (official or unofficial) incurred or used for such conversion and remittance. Further, Producer makes no warranties or representations that any part of any such foreign currency may be converted into U.S. dollars or transferred to the account of Contractor in any foreign country.

4. If Producer, in its use of subsidiary rights hereunder, should combine or authorize others to combine elements contributed to the programs by Contractor with other elements derived from the programs and/or elements not derived from the programs, then only that portion of monies derived by or paid to Producer for such combined use which is paid for or reasonably allocated (by Producer) to the use of such program elements contributed by Contractor shall be included in gross proceeds hereunder.

If Producer, in its use of merchandising rights hereunder, should combine or authorize others to combine elements derived from the programs with other creative elements not derived from the programs, then only that portion of monies derived by or paid to Producer for such combined use which is paid for or reasonably allocated (by Producer) to the use of elements derived from the programs shall be included in gross proceeds hereunder.

C. Subordination:

Contractor agrees that Producer may, in connection with the financing (both interim and deficit) of the production of any programs to which this Schedule pertains, pledge, mortgage, assign and otherwise hypothecate said programs or the proceeds to be derived therefrom in whole or in part without Contractor's consent and Contractor agrees to and does hereby subordinate to any such production loans all sums which may become payable to Contractor by reason of Contractor's right to share in net proceeds hereunder, it being understood that by reason of such subordination such payments as may become due Contractor hereunder shall be postponed accordingly; provided, however, that

> (i) unless and until there shall be a foreclosure sale affecting such programs, Producer shall not be relieved of its obligations to make payments of the sums equal to any net proceeds becoming payable to Contractor hereunder, notwithstanding that the time of such payment may be postponed by reason of Contractor's agreement to subordinate as herein set forth; provided, however, that in the event of a foreclosure sale of such programs or the proceeds therefrom by reason of such hypothecation, Contractor shall be entitled to share in any equity remaining after such sale as if such equity were gross proceeds from such programs;

(ii) if Producer obtains a production loan for a number of programs, including both the programs covered by this Schedule and other programs, then Contractor does not agree, and shall not be required, to subordinate to such production loan any payments of net proceeds becoming due Contractor hereunder; provided, however, that if such production loan is severable (i.e. so that a default with respect to payment of sums borrowed for such other programs would not constitute a default with respect to the programs hereunder) then the provisions of this subclause (ii) shall not apply.

It is understood, of course, that any profits derived from production loans shall not be deemed gross proceeds hereunder. Contractor agrees from time to time and at any time to execute any consent or other instrument which any bank or lending institution may reasonably require to evidence Contractor's agreement to subordinate as hereinabove set forth.

D. Outright Sale:

If Producer elects to sell or otherwise make an outright entire disposition of (i) any program or program series, or the proceeds to be derived therefrom or (ii) the television distribution, theatrical distribution, merchandising or subsidiary rights, or the proceeds to the derived therefrom, in which Contractor is entitled to share in net proceeds (it being understood that Producer shall have right, in its sole discretion, so to do), Producer shall, in each instance, by giving Contractor written notice to such effect, elect to have such disposition made on either of the following bases:

(i) free and clear of any obligation to Contractor whatsoever on the part of purchaser or assignee, in which event, the purchase price or other consideration received by Producer from such disposition after deduction of costs and expenses, including, but not limited to, agents' commissions and reasonable attorney's fees directly attributable thereto, shall be included in computing gross proceeds hereunder and, in such event, neither Producer nor such purchaser or assignee shall be liable to make payments to Contractor based upon gross proceeds derived from the right or interest thus sold or disposed of, from and after the effective date of such disposition; or

(ii) subject to the obligation on the part of the purchaser or assignee to account for and to pay to Contractor, in the manner herein provided, any net proceeds becoming payable to Contractor hereunder from and after the effective date of such disposition, in which event, the purchase price or other consideration received by Producer from such purchaser or assignee shall not be included in computing gross proceeds hereunder and Contractor shall have no right whatsoever to participate in said purchase price or other consideration received by Producer and Producer shall be relieved of and discharged from and with respect to any and all obligations whatsoever which Producer would otherwise have under this Schedule (including, but not limited to, obligations to make accountings and/or payments to Contractor) from and after the effective date of such disposition with respect to the right or interest so sold or disposed of; provided that such purchaser or assignee shall have no right to treat the purchase price or other consideration paid or given by such purchaser or assignee (and any interest payments or other carrying or financing charges incurred in connection therewith) as a cost in determining any net proceeds thereafter becoming payable to Contractor.

Contractor shall have no right to dispute Producer's determination to proceed under (i) above with respect to any disposition. Further, if Producer gives Contractor notice of Producer's determination to proceed under (ii) above with respect to any disposition, such determination shall be binding upon Contractor unless Contractor notifies Producer in writing (which notice must be delivered to Producer within seven (7) business days after the date of Producer's notice) that Contractor has determined (acting in the exercise of sound business judgment) that the purchaser or assignee referred to in Purchaser's notice is financially irresponsible. If Contractor gives Producer such a notice, then Producer may elect to either proceed under (i) above with respect to such disposition or, notwithstanding Contractor's notice, to proceed under (ii); provided, however, that if Producer elects, notwithstanding Contractor's notice, to proceed under (ii) then, if such purchaser or assignee shall thereafter fail or refuse to make payments of any net proceeds becoming due Contractor in accordance with accountings rendered by such purchaser or assignee to Contractor (as the same may be adjusted if Contractor shall successfully contest the same in accordance with its rights hereunder), Producer shall, upon written notice of such default, be liable to make such payments; provided, further, that if, at any time subsequent to the effective date of such disposition, Contractor shall have received, as its share of net proceeds, amounts (whether paid by such purchaser or assignee or by Producer in the event of such purchaser's or assignee's default) equal to the share of net proceeds which Contractor would have received if Contractor had shared in the purchase price or other consideration for such disposition as specified in (i) above, then, thereafter, Producer shall have no further obligations or liability to make payments to Contractor under the foregoing provisions of this sentence.

E. Other Provisions:

1. Unless the agreement to which this Schedule is attached specifically provides to the contrary then, notwithstanding the net profit participation payable to Contractor hereunder, Contractor shall (i) have no right, title or interest of any kind or nature whatsoever in and to the programs or any

distribution, subsidiary, merchandising or other rights derived therefrom, and (ii) not be a partner or joint venturer with Producer.

2. Anything in this Agreement to the contrary notwithstanding, in preparing and filing corporate tax returns, Producer shall have the sole right to take the full amount of whatever credits, deductions or other benefits as may be available throughout the world with respect to, or relating to, taxes and fees paid in connection with the production, broadcasting, distribution, exhibition and marketing of the programs (including the pilot, if any) produced during the term of this Agreement, as well as in connection with the exploitation of the subsidiary and merchandising rights derived therefrom, and Contractor shall not have the right to share or participate in or to take any such credits, deductions or other benefits which Producer or its distributors or sub-distributors may take as aforesaid.

3. All gross proceeds derived from distribution of the programs and from uses of subsidiary rights and merchandising rights derived therefrom shall be received by Producer as its sole and absolute property and, as between Producer and Contractor, Producer's only obligation under this Schedule shall be to pay to Contractor sums equal to Contractor's share of net proceeds, if any, becoming payable hereunder. No fiduciary or separation of funds obligations of any sort are created by this Schedule or by the provisions of the agreement to which it is attached.

4. As between Contractor and Producer, Producer shall have complete authority to exploit its distribution, syndication and merchandising rights hereunder throughout the world in accordance with such method, policies and terms as it may determine in its uncontrolled discretion. Producer has not made any representations or warranties, express or implied, as to the amount of proceeds to be derived from the exploitation of the programs nor that there will be any sum payable to Contractor hereunder. Producer may exploit any or all of its rights hereunder either itself or through such distributor or subdistributors as it may determine in its uncontrolled discretion. Further, Producer may refrain from exploiting any or all of its rights in the programs anywhere or in any territory for any reason. Producer may license the programs for distribution in any media to any and all theatres or other agencies in which Producer may have an interest, directly or indirectly, upon such terms and fees as Producer may determine to be fair and proper under the circumstances.

5. Where distribution and/or merchandising and/or subsidiary rights in the programs are exploited by Producer hereunder together with other rights in the programs, or together with rights in other programs or properties, Producer's allocation, in good faith, of the revenues therefrom to gross proceeds

hereunder and of the expenses to distribution, merchandising and/or subsidiary rights expenses hereunder shall be final.

6. The titles of the paragraphs of this Schedule are for convenience only and are not intended to affect the interpretation of any paragraphs of this Schedule or of the Schedule itself.

_____,

A DIVISION OF_____

CORPORATION

By_____

FACILITIES AND SERVICES EXHIBIT

A. INCLUDED IN PRODUCTION FEE

In consideration for the payment of the "Production Fee" defined in the SCHEDULE I to which this Exhibit is attached, Producer shall furnish, without further charge except as noted, the following below-the-line services and facilities.

1. *STAGE SPACE*: Stage space, as reasonably required, during the regular production season of the series; such stage space shall be designated by Producer. Home base stages will be held by Producer during the regular production season, except that when layoffs or extended locations occur such stages will be made available to Producer for other production if needed; each home base stage will be struck clean, if requested by Producer, within a reasonable time after completion of the regular production season. Producer shall charge series (i.e., as direct cost) for all labor costs in connection with the following: set striking, folding and/or storage, cleaning any and all stages and sets after use by series; restoring, repairing and reconditioning sets, streets, sidewalks, catwalks and any other fixtures and facilities to their original condition if altered, damaged (except ordinary wear and tear) or destroyed during series use thereof; restoration and replacement of stairwells, pits, tanks or holes of any nature cut into Producer's stage floors.

2. *STANDING SETS*: Subject to Producer's reasonable discretion and with the exception of "home sets", all standing sets are available on a scheduled basis. Producer shall charge series for the costs of revamping and striking.

3. *OFFICE SPACE*: All office space reasonably necessary, such space to be designated by Producer and to include light, heat, water, janitorial services, and desks, chairs and office equipment as available from Producer studio inventory.

4. *EDITORIAL FACILITIES*: Necessary cutting rooms with normal equipment; necessary rooms for cutting of sound effects and music, as well as shipping and receiving; coding and splicing facilities.

5. *PROJECTION FACILITIES*: Projection rooms, equipped with standard 35mm equipment shall be furnished at reasonable times on each day, exclusive of Saturdays, Sundays and holidays. Producer shall charge series for projectionists' labor. Producer shall designate projection facilities to be furnished hereunder.

6. *DRESSING ROOMS*: Dressing room facilities for all stars; additional dressing rooms or portable dressing rooms for feature players, bit players, extras and the like, as available; dressing room space to be designated by Producer.

7. *DEPARTMENT HEADS*: Non-exclusive supervisorial and consulting services of the heads of the then existing following departments shall be furnished, as required: (a) Construction (including general superintendent (as distinguished from construction foreman), set estimating and mill supervision); (b) Camera; (c) Film Services; (d) Electrical; (e) Production Administration; (f) Property & Set Dressing; (g) Sound; (h) Transportation; (i) Wardrobe; (j) Grip; (k) Security; (l) Paint; (m) Mechanical; (n) Drapery; (o) Labor; (p) Communications; (q) Industrial Relations; (r) Operations Desk; (s) Accounting & Data Processing; (t) Production; (u) Art; (v) Storage Space; (w) Post Productions; (x) Music; (y) Special Effects.

8. *CAMERA*: One BNC or NC camera, or equivalent, complete with standards accessories (if three camera technique is used, then three cameras and crab dollies); additional lenses and accessories (including the Producer's viewscope) on an as available basis. Lenses and accessories not owned by Producer shall be rented, if available, and charged at actual cost.

9. *ELECTRICAL EQUIPMENT AND POWER*: All reasonable requirements of series for electrical equipment within its capacity with studio-owned equipment, including molevators, dimmers, generators and the like, as available. Series to be charged Producer's cost for globe burnouts, breakage and replacement. There is no charge for power at studio premises of Producer. Generators furnished, as available, for locations; charges for generators and generator operators are pro-rated among all series using Producer's facilities in accordance with Producer's standard policy.

10. *GRIP EQUIPMENT*: Standard complements of grip equipment including one crab dolly for each camera furnished (each dolly to be equipped with newly developed risers) as well as necessary diffusion, as available; studio-owned special grip equipment, as available; studio-owned backings, as available. Series shall be charged for gelatins at Producer's then prevailing rates.

11. *PROPERTY AND DRAPES*: Producer-owned properties and drapes as available. Series will be charged cost of refinishing and alterations, and for loss and damage, and for full cost of properties altered to the extent the same are not re-usable thereafter. Producer reserves the right to approve all refinishing and alterations. All materials and properties purchased, and drapes and properties manufactured, shall be and remain the property of Producer.

12. *WARDROBE*: Wardrobe owned by Producer, as available. Series will be charged for cleaning, alterations, loss and damage. All wardrobe purchased and manufactured shall be and remain the property of Producer.

13. *HOSPITAL*: Then available studio hospital and staff at _____ ("studio premises"), if any, shall be provided during normal production times; First Aid personnel and nurses on overtime or working on sets or on location shall be charged to series.

14. *PROCESS EQUIPMENT*: Use of studio-owned process equipment, as available, with any charge to activate such equipment to be charged to series.

15. *SPECIAL EFFECTS*: Studio-owned special effects equipment as available. Series shall be charged for any costs necessary for said items to be put in order or, if damaged to be restored.

16. *MAIL SERVICE*: Normal mail service on Producer's premises.

17. *TELEPHONE SERVICE*: No charge for toll free local calls or studio paging system. Series shall be charged for unit and long distance charges, telephone equipment rental, special connection charges and radio telephones.

18. *ACCOUNTING*: There will be no charge for Producer's internal accounting and data processing (for both above and below-the-line), nor for the furnishing of profit participation statements. Special payroll processes, preparation of tax returns or keeping books of account for joint ventures, etc., will not be provided.

19. *EXECUTIVE, BUSINESS, LEGAL, ETC., PERSONNEL*: Producer's executive, business, administrative, legal and contract administration personnel in connection with the negotiation, handling and administration of production contracts, sales contracts and the like. The foregoing shall not include executive producers, producers, associate producers and others normally charged directly to a series, who shall continue to be so charged.

B.

In addition to the direct costs set forth in paragraph A.3.(a) of SCHEDULE I, the following items shall be charged as direct costs to the series (and not included in the Production Fee).

1. *TRANSPORTATION*: Producer shall furnish available studio-owned transportation equipment to series at standard industry rates.

2. *STOCK FOOTAGE, SOUND EFFECTS LIBRARY, ETC.*: Producer shall furnish available stock footage, the use of transparency background material, the use of studio-owned sound effects library, and leader stock at its then prevailing rates, subject to a ten foot minimum charge for furnished stock footage or transparency background material.

3. *OFFICE SUPPLIES*: Stationery and office supplies, multilith or other reproduction processes shall be charged to the series at Producer's cost.

4. *LOCATION LABOR*: Location auditor, series' cost estimators, department heads and others whose services are used on location will be charged to the series.

5. *MAINTENANCE*: Producer shall charge the series for all costs (labor and materials) of repairing or replacing (in case of destruction or loss) any equipment furnished by Producer hereunder.

SCREENPLAY

LOANOUT AGREEMENT

LOAN-OUT AGREEMENT

July 1, 19____

c/o _____

_____

_____

Attn:

Re: _____

Gentlemen:

The undersigned _____ Corporation wishes to engage from you the screenwriting services of _____ (the "Writer"), including, without limitation, the preparation of a long treatment (the "Treatment"), in connection with a screenplay (the "Screenplay") based upon the literary work (the "Work") entitled "_____" by _____ for a full length feature theatrical motion picture (the "Motion Picture") tentatively entitled "_____", and you wish to supply such services for the undersigned.

Therefore, you and the undersigned hereby agree as follows:

1. *Services.*

    1.1. As of the date of this agreement, you shall cause the Writer to begin writing the Treatment of the Screenplay. You shall cause the Writer to deliver to the undersigned the Treatment (minimum of 75 to 100 pages) on or before August 1, 19__.

    1.2. You shall cause the Writer to be available to the undersigned whenever and wherever the undersigned may direct during the 30 day period following the delivery of the Treatment to discuss changes in and revisions of the Treatment.

    1.3. On or before the end of the period described in Paragraph 1.2 above, you shall cause the Writer, upon notification from the undersigned, to begin writing a first draft (the "First Draft") of the Screenplay. You shall cause the Writer to deliver to the undersigned the First Draft, incorporating revisions, changes and/or suggestions given him by the undersigned, on or before the date 14 weeks from the date of such notice.

    1.4. You shall cause the Writer to be available to the undersigned whenever and wherever the undersigned may direct during the 40 day period following the delivery of the First Draft to discuss changes in and revisions of the First Draft.

1.5. The undersigned shall have the right, but not the obligation, on or before the end of the period described in Paragraph 1.4 above (as such period may be extended pursuant to Paragraph 1.9 below), to require you to cause the Writer to write a second draft (the "Second Draft") of the Screenplay. If the undersigned elects to exercise its right pursuant to this paragraph 1.5, it shall so notify you, and you shall cause the Writer to deliver to the undersigned the Second Draft, incorporating revisions, changes and/or suggestions given him by the undersigned, on or before the date 4 weeks from the date of such notice.

1.6. You shall cause the Writer to be available to the undersigned whenever and wherever the undersigned may direct during the 30 day period following the delivery of the Second Draft to discuss changes in and revisions of the Second Draft.

1.7. The undersigned shall have the right, but not the obligation, on or before the end of the period described in Paragraph 1.6 above (as such period may be extended pursuant to Paragraph 1.9 below), to require you to cause the Writer to write a third draft (the "Third Draft") of the Screenplay. If the undersigned elects to exercise its right pursuant to this Paragraph 1.7, it shall so notify you, and you shall cause the Writer to deliver to the undersigned the Third Draft, incorporating revisions, changes and/or suggestions given him by the undersigned, on or before the date 4 weeks from the date of such notice.

1.8. You shall cause the Writer to be available to the undersigned whenever and wherever the undersigned may direct during the 30 day period following the delivery of the Third Draft to discuss changes in and revisions of the Third Draft.

1.9. The undersigned shall have the right, but not the obligation, on or before the end of each of the periods described in Paragraphs 1.4, 1.6 and 1.8 above, to require you to cause the Writer to perform polishing and rewriting services in connection with the Screenplay (the product of such services each time the undersigned requires such polishing and rewriting services is referred to herein as the "First Rewrite", the "Second Rewrite", etc.). If the undersigned elects to exercise its right pursuant to this Paragraph 1.9, it shall notify you in writing, and you shall cause the Writer to deliver to the undersigned the product of such polishing and rewriting services incorporating revisions, changes, and/or suggestions given him by the undersigned, on or before the date 2 weeks from the date of such notice.

1.10. At any time during which the Writer is required to perform writing services pursuant to Paragraphs 1.1, 1.3, 1.5, 1.7 and 1.9 above, he shall perform services exclusively for you in supplying the Writer's services to the undersigned and shall not perform services of any kind whatsoever for any person, firm or corporation other than you and the undersigned, or for or on his own behalf, without the express written consent of the undersigned. His services hereunder during the periods described in Paragraphs 1.2, 1.4, 1.6 and 1.8 shall be non-exclusive to the undersigned, but such services shall be made available to the undersigned consistent with the terms and conditions set forth in said Paragraphs 1.2, 1.4, 1.6 and 1.8.

1.11. Notwithstanding anything to the contrary in Paragraphs 1.3 through 1.9 above, to the extent the undersigned has not required the Writer's writing services in connection with the Screenplay as specified in such Paragraphs, the undersigned shall have the right, but not the obligation, to require the Writer to perform such services at any time, subject to his then existing contractual professional writing commitments. If the undersigned elects to exercise its right pursuant to this Paragraph 1.11, it shall so notify you in writing and you shall cause the Writer to perform such services, subject to such commitments existing on the date of such notice. If the Writer is unable to perform such services due to such conflicting commitments, you shall so notify the undersigned promptly after receiving the undersigned's notice requiring such services, and your notice shall set forth the earliest date thereafter that the Writer will be available to perform and complete such services.

1.12. You hereby acknowledge and agree that time is of the essence in the performance of the Writer's services hereunder.

2. *Grant of Rights.* You hereby grant to the undersigned throughout the world the following rights exclusively for the current and any renewed or extended term of copyright anywhere in the world and thereafter non-exclusively (provided that the rights granted pursuant to Paragraph 2.4 below shall be granted exclusively to the undersigned forever):

2.1. All rights of any kind and nature, whether now or hereafter known, in and to the product of the Writer's services hereunder;

2.2. Without limiting the generality of Paragraph 2.1 above, the rights granted hereunder include, but are not limited to: (a) copyright (for the original term and any renewals and/or extensions thereof); (b) motion picture, television, performing, recording, phonographic recording, television spin-off series, novelization, and merchandising and other ancillary rights; (c) the right without any limitation whatsoever to negotiate, distribute, transmit, publicize, exhibit and exploit the product of the Writer's services hereunder (whether as part of the Screenplay or the Motion Picture or otherwise) anywhere in the world by any means, method or media now or hereafter known (including without limitation the rights to release the Motion Picture theatrically anywhere in the world, to telecast the Motion Picture for an unlimited number of runs in the United States and Canada, to telecast the Motion Picture anywhere else in the world, to distribute and exhibit the Motion Picture on means of transportation, and to license or assign any of the foregoing rights); (d) the right to use all or any of the product of the Writer's services hereunder (whether as part of the Screenplay or the Motion Picture or otherwise) in connection with all mechanical, performing or other rights now or hereafter known which might or could be used in the production, recording, transmission, exhibition, exploitation and publicity of any production in any medium now or hereafter known; (e) the right in the exercise of any of said rights to adapt, change, arrange, translate, add to or interpolate in or take from the product of the Writer's services hereunder; and (f) the right to traffic and deal in any other manner in all of the product of the Writer's services hereunder;

2.3. You acknowledge and agree that since for copyright purposes the Writer is performing his services hereunder as an employee-for-hire of the undersigned and the product of such services shall be deemed a work-for-hire for the undersigned, the undersigned shall have the right to obtain copyright (and to renew copyright) in the name of the undersigned or the undersigned's designee on all of the product of the Writer's services hereunder, and you hereby acknowledge that the undersigned shall have the right to secure copyright (and to renew copyright) as aforesaid to said material and to do all things in connection therewith which you or the Writer might otherwise yourselves do or perform; and

2.4. The right to use, license, cause or permit others to use the Writer's name, sobriquet, picture, likeness and biography in connection with the Screenplay and/or the Motion Picture and/or the exercise of any of the other rights of the undersigned hereunder and advertising and publicity in connection therewith (whether or not the Screenplay and/or the Motion Picture shall consist substantially of the product of his services hereunder). You acknowledge and agree that the undersigned shall have the sole and exclusive right to issue publicity concerning the Writer with respect to the Screenplay, the Motion Picture and/or any other product of his services hereunder, provided that an incidental reference to the Writer's services hereunder and/or to the Motion Picture shall not be a breach hereof.

3. *Representations and Warranties.*

3.1. You hereby represent and warrant:

3.1.1. You have an exclusive employment agreement with the Writer which will be in full force and effect throughout the period the Writer's services are required hereunder; you have the right to enter into this agreement and to supply the Writer's services as contemplated hereunder; you have the right to grant all rights herein granted by you; and no provision for rights granted, for the Writer's employment or services hereunder, or for the use of his name, sobriquet, picture, likeness or biography as herein contemplated does now or will hereunder violate, conflict with or infringe upon any rights whatsoever of any person, firm, or corporation;

3.1.2. The Writer will be the sole author of the material delivered and/or suggested by him hereunder; all of such material is or will be wholly original with him and not copied in whole or in part from any work other than the Work, and such material will not violate, conflict with or infringe upon any rights whatsoever (including, without limitation, any copyright, literary, dramatic, photoplay, or common law rights; rights of privacy; or rights against libel or slander) of any person, firm or corporation.

3.2. Your representations and warranties herein shall apply only to material which the Writer contributes to the Screenplay and/or the Motion Picture, and shall not apply to material supplied by the undersigned (including, without limitation, the Work) or to any extraneous material inserted in the Screenplay and/or the Motion Picture by the undersigned, its associates, successors, designees, licensees or others.

4. *Indemnities.*

4.1. You agree to indemnify and save harmless the undersigned, its successors, licensees and assigns, and the officers, directors, employees, representatives and agents thereof, against any and all claims, demands, suits, losses, costs, expenses (including, without limitation, reasonable legal fees and expenses), damages or recoveries (including, without limitation, any amounts paid in settlement) suffered, made, incurred or assumed by the undersigned, its successors, licensees, assigns, or the officers, directors, employees, representatives and agents thereof, by reason of the breach or alleged breach of any warranty, undertaking, representation or agreement made or entered into herein or hereunder by you.

4.2. The undersigned agrees to indemnify you and the Writer and to save each of you harmless against any and all claims, demands, suits, losses, costs, expenses (including, without limitation, reasonable legal fees and expenses), damages or recoveries (including, without limitation, any amounts paid in settlement) suffered, made, incurred or assumed by you or the Writer by reason of any changes in the Screenplay by the undersigned, its successors, licensees or assigns, or any material used in or in connection with the Motion Picture other than material supplied by the Writer.

5. *Compensation.* Provided you and the Writer fully and completely perform all the terms and conditions of this agreement, and in full consideration to you for entering into this agreement and for performing all the terms and conditions thereof, the undersigned shall pay to you and you shall accept the following:

5.1. The sum of $____,000, payable upon delivery of the Treatment, receipt of which is hereby acknowledged;

5.2. The sum of $____,000, payable $____,000 when the Writer begins writing the First Draft, $____,000 7 weeks thereafter and $____,000 upon delivery of the First Draft pursuant to Paragraph 1.3 above.

6. *Contingent Compensation.* Provided you and the Writer fully and completely perform all the terms and conditions of this agreement, if the following events occur, the undersigned shall pay to you and you shall accept the following:

6.1. If the undersigned notifies you that it is exercising its right pursuant to Paragraph 1.5 or 1.11 above to require you to write the Second Draft, the sum of $____,000, payable $____000 when the Writer begins writing the Second Draft and $____000 upon delivery of the Second Draft pursuant to Paragraph 1.5 or 1.11 above as the case may be;

6.2. If the undersigned notifies you that it is exercising its right pursuant to Paragraph 1.7 or 1.11 above to require you to write the Third Draft, the sum of $____,000 payable $____,000 when the Writer begins writing the Third Draft and $____000 upon delivery of the Third Draft pursuant to Paragraph 1.7 or 1.11 above as the case may be;

6.3. If the Motion Picture is produced and if the undersigned has not made any of the payments pursuant to Paragraphs 6.1 and 6.2 above and if the Writer receives sole "Screenplay By" credit pursuant to Paragraph 8 below, then an additional sum of $____,000 upon such final credit determination;

6.4. If the Motion Picture is produced, released and if there are net profits ("Net Profits") as defined in paragraph D(a)(2)(THIRDLY) of a document annexed thereto and made a part hereof as Exhibit A then:

6.4.1. If the Writer receives sole "Screenplay By" credit pursuant to Paragraph 8 below:

6.4.1.1. A contingent deferment in the amount of $____,000, defined and payable *pari passu* with other contingent deferments from the gross receipts from the Motion Picture (as defined in Exhibit A) pursuant to paragraph D(a)(2)(THIRDLY) of Exhibit A;

6.4.1.2. An amount equal to ____% of 100% of the Net Profits from the Motion Picture.

6.4.2. Notwithstanding anything to the contrary in Paragraph 6.4.1 above, if the Writer shares "Screenplay By" credit with a third party or parties, you shall receive, in lieu of the amounts set forth in Paragraph 6.4.1, one-half of such amounts as set forth therein;

6.5. It is expressly understood that if the Writer receives no "Screenplay By" credit pursuant to Paragraph 8 below, you shall not receive any further payments pursuant to Paragraphs 6.3 and/or 6.4 above;

6.6. If any payments are required pursuant to the Writers Guild of America 1973 Theatrical and Television Basic Agreement (the "Basic Agreement") in connection with the exploitation of any rights in, ancillary to or derived from the Motion Picture, then any such payments shall, to the maximum extent permitted by the Basic Agreement, be credited against the payments, if any, thereafter becoming due pursuant to Paragraph 6.4.1.2 above (as such payments may be reduced pursuant to Paragraph 6.4.2 above), and any payments pursuant to Paragraph 6.4.1.2 above (as so reduced) shall be credited against any payments thereafter becoming due pursuant to the Basic Agreement.

7. *Statements.* You shall receive statements and have audit rights pursuant to the terms of Exhibit A annexed hereto. Statements shall be accompanied by the payment of the sums, if any, payable to you pursuant to Paragraph 6.4 above, as reflected by such statements.

8. *Credit.* Provided you and the Writer fully and completely perform all the terms and conditions of this agreement, if the Motion Picture is produced and released, the Writer shall receive screen credit for his services hereunder in accordance with the terms of the Basic Agreement. Any paid advertising credit required by the Basic Agreement shall be subject to the undersigned's standard paid advertising exclusions and artwork title exceptions. No casual or inadvertent failure of the undersigned to comply with this Paragraph 8, and no failure of any other person(s), firm(s) or corporation(s) to meet their contractual obligations to comply with this Paragraph 8, shall constitute a breach of this agreement by the undersigned.

9. *Control of Production.* As among you, the Writer and the undersigned, the undersigned shall have complete control (including without limitation all decisions relating to commencement, continuation, suspension, and/or abandonment) of the financing, production, distribution and exploitation of the Motion Picture. Without limiting the generality of the foregoing sentence, the undersigned shall have all artistic control over and the right to cut, edit, add to, subtract from, arrange, rearrange and revise the Screenplay and any other product of the Writer's services hereunder, whether in connection with the Motion Picture or otherwise, in any manner.

10. *Suspension; Termination.*

10.1. The undersigned shall have the right to suspend this agreement (including without limitation the writing and reading and consultation periods pursuant to Paragraph 1 above), and to refrain from paying any consideration hereunder during the period of any of the following contingencies:

10.1.1. Mental, physical or other disability incapacitating the Writer from performing the terms hereof or complying with each and all of his obligations to be performed hereunder;

10.1.2. If, prior to the completion of the Writer's services hereunder, the undersigned has been interfered with in any manner whatsoever thereby preventing the undersigned from using the product of the Writer's services hereunder or from preparing or producing the Motion Picture, including by reason of any legislative, executive or judicial act (whether or not valid), boycott, labor controversy (including but not limited to a threat of lockout, boycott or strike), armed conflict (whether or not there has been an official declaration of war or official statement as to the existence of a state of war), invasion, occupation, interventions of military authorities, delay of a common carrier, inability without fault to obtain sufficient material, labor, transportation, power or other sufficient material, labor, transportation, power or other essential commodity required in the conduct of the business of the undersigned or the person, firm or corporation financing the Motion Picture, or by reason of the death, illness, incapacity or disability of the director or any principal member of the cast of the Motion Picture, or by reason of any cause, thing or occurrence of a similar or dissimilar kind not within the undersigned's control, or if for any reason a substantial group of distributors or exhibitors handling motion pictures in the United States shall cease distribution or exhibition for one week or more; or

10.1.3. In the event of the Writer's failure, refusal or neglect to perform any of his required services hereunder to the full limit of his ability as, when and whenever instructed and directed by the undersigned, and in the manner herein provided, or otherwise to perform in full the terms of this agreement.

10.2. The undersigned shall have the right, but not the obligation, to terminate the Writer's services hereunder and any financial obligations thereafter accruing to you hereunder at any time during the continuance of any contingency referred to in Paragraph 10.1.1 above if, prior to the completion of the Writer's services hereunder, any contingency or contingencies referred to in Paragraph 10.1.1 continue for a consecutive period of seven days or for an aggregate period of fourteen days; or at any time during the occurrence of any contingency referred to in Paragraph 10.1.2 above if any contingency or contingencies referred to in said Paragraph 10.1.2 continue for a consecutive or aggregate period of 8 weeks or more; or at any time during the continuance of, and for up to 30 days following the end of, any contingency referred to in Paragraph 10.1.3 above. In the event that the undersigned has suspended the payment of consideration by reason of occurrence of any contingency referred to in Paragraph 10.1.2 above, you shall also have the right to terminate the Writer's services hereunder at any time during the occurence of such contingency in the event that the suspension for such contingency continues for a period or aggregate of periods of 8 weeks or more, provided that you notify the undersigned in writing after the expiration of said period or aggregate of periods of your desire to terminate, and provided further that the Writer is then ready, willing and able to resume the performance of his services hereunder; but if the undersigned should lift and terminate the suspension of compensation to you hereunder (subject to further suspension for other proper cause) commencing as of one week following receipt by the undersigned of said notice, the Writer's services and your and his other obligations hereunder shall not be terminated but shall continue in full force and effect.

10.3. The exercise by the undersigned of its termination rights pursuant to Paragraph 10.2 above based on a failure or refusal by the Writer pursuant to Paragraph 10.1.3 above shall not preclude the undersigned from recovering by appropriate action the damages, if any, resulting from such failure or refusal.

11. *Assignment.* The undersigned shall have the right to assign this agreement or its rights and obligations hereunder to any person, firm or corporation, provided that such assignment shall not release the undersigned from its obligations hereunder unless the assignee assumes in writing the obligations of the undersigned. You shall not have the right to assign this agreement, *provided, however,* that any sums payable to you hereunder shall be assignable

to any person, firm or corporation, provided, however, that, in the event you assign said sums, the undersigned shall only be obligated to make payments under this agreement to one person, firm or corporation, as the case may be.

12. *No Obligation to Produce or Release the Motion Picture.* The undersigned shall not be obligated actually to utilize the Writer's services hereunder, or to include the product of his services hereunder in the Motion Picture or to produce or release the Motion Picture, or to continue distribution or release of the Motion Picture once released; *provided, however,* that the undersigned shall, subject to its rights of termination pursuant to Paragraph 10.2 above, pay you all compensation payable pursuant to Paragraph 5 above.

13. *Morals Clause.* If at any time the Writer's conduct, either while he is rendering services or in his private life, is without due regard to social conventions or public morals or decency, the undersigned may delete or refrain from giving any credit otherwise required pursuant to Paragraph 8 above in connection with the Writer's services theretofore or thereafter rendered hereunder.

14. *Agency.* You hereby irrevocably designate _____ as your exclusive agent in connection with this agreement. All payments due you hereunder shall be made to and in the name of such agent. Receipt of such payments by such agent shall be deemed receipt by you.

15. *Notices.* Any notices, documents, statements or other writings (collectively referred to herein as "Notices") required or desired to be given hereunder will be in writing and shall be sent to you at your address set forth above, and to the undersigned, at _____, Attn: Legal Department-Motion Pictures, or to such other address as you or the undersigned may hereafter designate in writing in the manner provided above, and shall be sufficiently given by personal delivery thereof to the addressee, or by mailing or by telegraphing the same in a post-paid wrapper addressed to the addressee as aforesaid, and the date of such delivery, telegraphing or mailing shall be the date of the giving of such Notices. Copies of all Notices to be given to the undersigned shall be sent to _____.

16. *Miscellaneous.*

16.1. This agreement is made in New York and all negotiations in connection with this agreement shall be deemed to have occurred in New York. This agreement shall be construed in accordance with the laws of the State of New York applicable to contracts entirely made and performed therein.

16.2. You and the undersigned intend to enter into a formal Writer's Loanout Agreement on the terms and conditions standard in the current motion picture industry in the United States, but not inconsistent with and subject to the terms and conditions contained herein. Until such time, if any, as more formal agreements are drawn and executed, however, this letter agreement shall serve as a complete, binding and enforceable contract with respect to the subject matter contained herein.

16.3. You acknowledge and agree that the Writer's services hereunder are unique, that the undersigned's damages at law are inadequate if the Writer should breach this agreement, and that the undersigned shall be entitled to injunctive relief to prevent any such breach.

16.4. Your rights and remedies in the event of any breach of this agreement by the undersigned shall be limited to your rights, if any, to recover money damages in an action at law, and in no event shall you be entitled by reason of any such breach to terminate this agreement and you shall not be entitled and hereby waive the right in such event to equitable or injunctive relief or to enjoin, restrain or interfere with the distribution or exhibition of the Motion Picture or the exercise of any of the other rights of the undersigned hereunder.

16.5. Your grant of rights hereunder is irrevocable, and all rights granted hereunder shall remain vested in the undersigned, its successors and assigns, whether this agreement expires or is terminated, or whether the Writer's services hereunder are terminated for any cause or reason whatsoever.

16.6 The failure by you or by the undersigned to object to or to take affirmative action with respect to any conduct of the other which is in violation of this agreement shall not be construed as the waiver of any rights or remedies in connection with such violation. No waiver by either you or the undersigned of any breach by the other of any term, covenant or condition of this agreement shall be deemed a waiver of any other breach (whether prior to or subsequent) of the same or any other term, covenant or condition of this or any other agreement.

16.7. If any provision of this agreement is declared invalid or unenforceable, such provision shall be deemed modified to the extent necessary and possible to render it valid and enforceable. In any event, the unenforceability or invalidity of any provision shall not affect any other provision of this agreement, and this agreement shall continue in full force and effect, and be construed and enforced, as if such provision had not been included, or had been modified as above provided, as the case may be.

16.8. Paragraph headings used herein are for convenience only, and shall not be deemed a part of this agreement.

If the foregoing sets forth our agreement, please so indicate by signing in the space provided below.

Very truly yours,

_____CORPORATION

By_____

Authorized Agent

Accepted and Agreed to:

_____

By_____

Authorized Officer

_____

ARTISTS INDUCEMENT LETTER

(Date)

(Address)

Re: (Title)

Gentlemen:

Reference is made to the agreement(s) of even date herewith (herein called the "Lending Agreement") between (_____) (herein called "Lender") and you covering the lending of the services of the undersigned by Lender to you.

As an inducement to you to enter into the Lending Agreement and as a material part of the consideration moving to you for so doing, the undersigned hereby represents, warrants and agrees as follows:

1. That the undersigned has heretofore entered into an agreement (herein called the "Employment Agreement") with Lender covering the rendition of the undersigned's services for Lender and that Lender has the right and authority to enter into the Lending Agreement and to furnish to you the rights and services of the undersigned upon the terms and conditions therein specified;

2. That the undersigned is familiar with each and all of the terms, covenants and conditions of the Lending Agreement and hereby consents to the execution thereof; that the undersigned shall perform and comply with all of the terms, covenants and conditions of the Lending Agreement on the part of the undersigned to be performed and complied with, even if the Employment Agreement should hereafter be terminated or suspended; that the undersigned shall tender to you all of the services provided for under the Lending Agreement and hereby confirms that there have been granted to Lender all of the

rights granted by Lender to you under the Lending Agreement; that the undersigned is performing his services pursuant to the Lending Agreement as your employee-for-hire for copyright purposes; that all notices (as defined in the Lending Agreement) served upon the Lender in accordance with the Lending Agreement shall be deemed notices to the undersigned of the contents thereof;

3. That the undersigned has read and is familiar with all of the representations and warranties made by Lender in the Lending Agreement, and hereby makes such representations and warranties as though the undersigned were a party to the Lending Agreement, and hereby agrees jointly and severally with Lender to indemnify and hold you harmless from and against any and all loss, damage, costs, legal fees and expenses, claims, recoveries, judgments and expenses which may be suffered by you by reason of any violation or claim of violation by the undersigned of any of the representations, warranties, covenants or other agreements by the undersigned contained herein;

4. That the undersigned hereby waives any right of droit moral or any similar right with respect to the (_____) (as defined in the Lending Agreement) for which services are being rendered and with respect to any other product of his services hereunder and under the Lending Agreement and agrees not to institute, support, maintain, or permit any action or lawsuit on the ground that any motion picture or television production produced hereunder, or any other exercise of any of the rights conveyed, granted and assigned by the undersigned hereunder and by Lender under the Lending Agreement constitutes an infringement of any right of droit moral or any similar right, or is in any way a defamation or mutilation of any of the product of the services of the undersigned hereunder or under the Lending Agreement or of the reputation of the undersigned, or contains unauthorized variations, alterations, modifications, changes or translations;

5. That the undersigned is under no obligation or disability by law or otherwise which would prevent or restrict the undersigned from performing and complying with all of the terms, covenants and conditions of the Lending Agreement on the part of the undersigned to be performed or complied with;

6. That the undersigned will look solely to Lender or its associated or subsidiary companies and not to you for all compensation and other remuneration in connection with any and all services and rights which the undersigned may render and grant to you hereunder and under the Lending Agreement and in connection with any use which you may make of the product of the services of the undersigned hereunder and under the Lending Agreement.

7. That you shall be entitled to equitable relief against the undersigned by injunction or otherwise to restrain, enjoin and/or prevent the violation or breach by the undersigned of any obligation of the undersigned to be per-

formed as provided in the Lending Agreement and/or the violation or breach by the undersigned of any obligations or agreements under this present instrument;

8. That if Lender should be dissolved or should otherwise cease to exist or for any reason whatsoever should fail, be unable, neglect or refuse to perform and observe each and all of the conditions of the Lending Agreement requiring performance or compliance on its part, the undersigned shall, at your election, be deemed substituted as a direct party to said Lending Agreement in the place and stead of Lender and further that in the event of a breach or threatened breach of said Lending Agreement by Lender or by the undersigned you shall be entitled to legal and equitable relief by way of injunction or otherwise against Lender or against the undersigned or against both of us in your discretion in any event without the necessity of first resorting to or exhausting any rights or remedies which you may have against Lender; all of the foregoing to be to the same extent and with the same force and effect as if the undersigned were a direct party to said Lending Agreement in the first instance and as if in such Lending Agreement the undersigned had personally agreed to render the services therein provided to be rendered by the undersigned and to perform and observe each and all of the terms and conditions of the said Lending Agreement requiring performance or compliance on the part of Lender or the undersigned or both of us;

9. That the undersigned will indemnify and hold you harmless from and against any and all taxes which you may have to pay and any and all liabilities (including judgments, penalties, interest, damages, costs and expenses including reasonable legal fees and expenses) which may be obtained against, imposed upon, or suffered by you or which you may incur by reason of your failure to deduct and withhold from the compensation payable under the Lending Agreement any amounts required or permitted to be deducted and withheld from the compensation of an employee under the provisions of the Federal Income Tax Act, the Federal Social Security Act, any state and/or city income tax and/or unemployment insurance acts and/or any amendment thereof and/or any other statutes heretofore or hereafter anywhere enacted requiring the withholding of any amount from the compensation of any employee.

Very truly yours,

_____

(Name)

NETWORK
TELEVISION AGREEMENT

AGREEMENT

c/o _____

_____

_____

Re:_____ (Working title)

Gentlemen:

This will confirm the agreement between _____ as Packager, and Network with respect to the development and prospective production of a two-hour pilot program and a series of one-hour programs based on the above-named property.

1. *DEVELOPMENT*

Network has ordered and Packager has agreed to deliver to Network a two-hour pilot teleplay based on the above-named property, which will be written by _____. As full compensation for the teleplay, Network will reimburse Packager for its direct, out-of-pocket costs up to $____, plus direct out-of-pocket employer fringe expenses thereon. In addition, Network will reimburse Packager up to $____ subject to substantiation, for the reasonable and necessary travel and living expenses incurred by _____ and _____ in connection with a research trip to _____. Packager will deliver the first draft teleplay on or before _____, 19__, and the final teleplay, including all rewrites and revisions as required by Network, but not exceeding the number permitted by the applicable WGA agreement, on or before a date to be mutually agreed upon as soon thereafter as possible.

2. *PILOT:*

(a) Network will have the exclusive and irrevocable option, exercisable within sixty (60) days after delivery of the final teleplay, to order a two-hour color film pilot program based on the final teleplay. If ordered, Packager will produce said pilot in ____ and deliver same to Network by furnishing elements in accordance with the attached Schedule of Color Film Delivery Requirements within fourteen (14) weeks from Network's exercise of its pilot option.

(b) If Network orders the pilot, Network will pay Packager, as full compensation for the pilot and the rights granted hereunder to Network, the sum of $____ flat, including all development costs, with protection for the first two leads over $____, subject to pre-approval by Network. Payment will be made pursuant to the following schedule: $____ upon the exercise by Network of its pilot option and the balance divided into thirds and payable, one-third on commencement of principal photography, one-third less all of Network's development costs, on completion of principal photography and the balance upon delivery of the pilot in accordance with the attached SCHEDULE OF COLOR FILM DELIVERY REQUIREMENTS.

(c) If Network orders the pilot, Network will have the exclusive right to make an initial and one repeat telecast of the pilot in the broadcast territory at any time during the two year period following delivery of the pilot, in any time period or format (alone, with other pilots, as part of the series or in conjunction with any other material) without restriction.

(d) If Network does not exercise its pilot option, the rights in the property and teleplay granted to Network by Packager will automatically revert to Packager, but if Packager at any time makes any use or disposition of the teleplay or any part thereof, Network shall be entitled to recoup its development costs, less rewrite costs, if any, from the first monies derived by Packager for any such use or disposition of the teleplay.

3. *REQUIREMENTS.*

(a) With respect to the pilot and if Network exercises its series option, all series programs hereunder, Network will have prior approval of all key creative elements, including but not limited to title, format, openings and closings, executive and line producers, directors, headwriters (if any), writers, story editors, outlines, scripts, (to the extent they vary from approved outlines), principal cast, including guest stars, theme or featured music, etc. Submissions and approvals shall be made with a view to facilitating timely delivery of the programs, and not exercised in a manner intended to frustrate the deal. The format of the series may not be changed from that approved for the pilot unless such change is specifically approved by Network. _____ is hereby approved as Executive Producer of the pilot and series programs.

(b) Network will have full creative consultation rights regarding all other elements of the pilot and all series programs and Packager will give due consideration to Network's advice.

(c) Network may conduct audience tests of the pilot during series option period on a non-broadcast basis (including direct projection, CATV and cable television), provided no charge is made to view the pilot. Such use for audience testing purposes will not be deemed a broadcast or run. Packager will not screen or authorize the screening of the pilot to anyone outside of Packager's organization during the series option period unless Network has consented in writing.

(d) The producer(s) and executive producer (if any) of the pilot, and those pilot performers who are cast in continuing roles (as well as any other pilot personnel who are mutually agreed to be essential to the series) shall, subject to Network's continuing approval, be furnished by Packager for each series program for at least the first five years of the series term for which Network exercises its options and Packager will endeavor to obtain talent for all series years.

(e) Packager will advise Network at the time a continuing performer's name is submitted to Network for approval if Packager has been unable to obtain the right to employ the performer for the series term (including all option years) and Network may disapprove employment of such performer. A continuing performer under this agreement is one who is employed for the series for not less than the equivalent of 6/13ths (to the nearest whole number) of the new programs of the applicable broadcast year.

(f) Packager will obtain a hold upon the services of the producer and continuing cast (and of any other personnel essential to the proposed series, as may be determined in each case) for a start of the series in accordance with Network's series start options.

(g) During Network's series option period and if Network exercises its series option, continuing until the end of the series term, pilot performers in continuing roles will not appear in continuing roles on any other television series and will not portray on television any character portrayed by them in the pilot or series.

(h) If Packager fails for any reason to make timely delivery of the pilot or, if Network orders the series, of any series program, Network's options and other deadlines for series start, increasing series orders, etc., shall be extended in good faith to compensate for the delay, with due consideration for customary network practices and policies, including the possibility of carrying over the project for all or part of the next succeeding broadcast year. The foregoing shall be in addition to any other remedies Network may have.

4. *SERIES OPTIONS:*

(a) If Network exercises its option with respect to the pilot, Network will have the exclusive and irrevocable option to order the first broadcast year of the series of one-hour programs based on the pilot, exercisable as follows:

(i) For a Fall 19__ series start, by written notice to Packager on or before May 1, 1978;

(ii) For a mid-season 19__/__ start, by written notice to Packager on or before November 15, 19__.

(b) If Network exercises its option for the first broadcast year of the series, Network shall have six (6) successive additional annual options to extend the term for an additional broadcast year, each such option being exercisable on or before May 1 preceding the applicable broadcast year. If Network does not exercise any one of its options for an additional broadcast year of the series, or if it fails to increase its initial order for a Fall start of the series to a total of at least 22 new programs, then it shall lose its right to order such series for any subsequent broadcast year.

(c) If Network exercises all of its annual options for the series and if Packager desires to continue broadcast of new programs of such series after the last optional broadcast year, Network shall have the right of first negotiation with respect thereto for a period of thirty (30) days commencing on January 15 of the last broadcast year of the term, followed by a right of first refusal for one year after the expiration of the last such broadcast year.

(d) Notwithstanding any other provision, if Packager fails for any reason to make timely delivery of programs for the start of any applicable broadcast season, Network may, without penalty for doing so and in addition to any other remedy, elect to reduce its minimum order at the rate of one new program for each week of late delivery.

5. *SERIES ORDER PATTERN:*

(a) If Network exercises its option for a series start in the Fall of 19__, its initial order will be 13 new one-hour programs (which, at Network's election, may consist of either 13 new programs or 12 new programs plus the pilot). Network shall have the right to order 9 additional new programs by giving Packager notice to such effect on or before a date to be negotiated in good faith.

(b) If Network exercises its option for a series start in mid-season 19__/__, its initial order will be 13 new one-hour programs (which, at Network's election, may consist of either 13 new programs or 12 new programs plus the pilot). Network shall have the right to order up to four additional new programs by giving Packager notice to such effect on or before a date to be negotiated in good faith.

(c) If Network exercises its option for a series start in mid-season and its series option for the 19__-__ broadcast season, Network's initial order for the latter will be 17 new one-hour programs with the right to order 5 additional new programs, exercisable by giving Packager notice to such effect on or before November 14, 19__. Network shall have the further right to order up to 4 additional new programs by giving Packager notice to such effect on or before a date to be negotiated in good faith.

(d) In each subsequent broadcast year for which Network exercises its series option, Network's initial order will be 22 new one-hour programs. Network will have the right to order up to 4 additional new programs by giving Packager notice to such effect on or before a date to be negotiated in good faith.

(e) During the first and each subsequent broadcast year of the series, Network may telecast repeats of the programs as needed.

(f) If Network orders more than the minimum number of new programs for a broadcast year, Network may accomplish the initial broadcast of one or more of the extra programs in any subsequent broadcast year of the series but Network may not reduce the minimum order applicable to the later year.

6. *SERIES PAYMENTS:*

(a) For each new series program ordered by Network and furnished by Packager, including the right to make the initial and one repeat telecast of each program, Network will pay Packager the following applicable amounts:

Broadcast Year	Payment For Two Runs
1st year	$____ flat
2nd year	$____
3rd year	$____
4th year	$____
5th year	$____
6th year	$____
7th year	$____

(b) In addition to the foregoing applicable amounts, if in the first broadcast year of the series the compensation for the first two leads exceeds $____ in the aggregate per new series program, Network will reimburse Packager for the amount of such excess over $____ provided Network has pre-approved such arrangements. Network will continue to reimburse Packager in the same amount as determined in the first broadcast year for each subsequent broadcast year during which such payments are made to the first two leads.

(c) If Network does not telecast the second run of any program, Network will be entitled to the benefit of Packager's savings of out-of-pocket talent residuals and other expenses which Packager would otherwise have incurred if the second run had been telecast by Network.

(d) The foregoing applicable amounts for each new series program are predicated on the series being produced in _____.

(e) Network and Packager will negotiate in good faith an annual pre-production advance applicable to Network's series order.

7. *PAYMENT SCHEDULE:*

Payment for each new series program will be advanced and payable, subject to receipt of Packager's invoices, as follows:

⅓ will be advanced within ten (10) days after commencement of principal photography.

⅓, less a pro-rata share of the pre-production advance, if any, made by Network, will be advanced within ten (10) days after completion of principal photography,

The balance shall be paid within ten (10) days following delivery as specified in the attached SCHEDULE OF COLOR FILM DELIVERY REQUIRE-MENTS.

8. *COST PROTECTION:*

Except for programs for the first broadcast year of the series, Network will protect Packager against certain union governmental and industry-wide production cost increases in accordance with the provisions of paragraph S of the attached ADDITIONAL TERMS AND CONDITIONS. The Cost Protection Date shall be February 1, 19__

9. *PERFORMANCE GUARANTEE:*

With respect to the production of the pilot and, if applicable, the series programs, Network shall have the continuing right to require Packager to furnish Network with a guarantee of Packager's financial ability to perform and complete its obligations pursuant to this agreement. The guarantee will be in a form satisfactory to Network to assure that Network will receive delivery of the completed programs in compliance with this agreement and to protect monies advanced by Network towards production of the programs in the event of Packager's failure to perform for any reason. In each case, the guarantee will be furnished to Network promptly upon Network's request therefor.

10. The foregoing together with the attached ADDITIONAL TERMS AND CONDITIONS shall constitute a binding agreement between the parties. All controversies or questions arising under or with respect to this agreement shall be determined in accordance with the New York laws applicable to contracts made and to be performed wholly in New York.

11. *RESERVED RIGHTS:*

Packager reserves all rights in and to the programs, series and property for its use and disposition, subject to the rights granted to Network and subject to the restrictions on Packager's exercise thereof imposed by this agreement, but Packager shall not exercise any reserved rights in a manner which may interfere with, limit or restrict in any way the full enjoyment of rights granted to Network and Packager shall not exercise distribution, subsidiary or other reserved rights in the broadcast territory during the term of this agreement, except that Packager may exercise merchandising, music and publishing rights. Packager's exercise of merchandising rights will be subject to Network's reasonable approval from the standpoint of significant impairment of sponsorship sales; Packager will not grant any merchandising rights without Network's prior approval while there is available for sale a principal sponsorship of the series and Packager will not knowingly grant any merchandising rights for any products competitive to those products authorized for advertising of any one-minute sponsor of the series.

12. The foregoing together with the attached ADDITIONAL TERMS AND CONDITIONS shall constitute a binding agreement between the parties. All controversies or questions arising under or with respect to this agreement shall be determined in accordance with the New York laws applicable to contracts made and to be performed wholly in New York.

Your signature together with ours below will constitute this our agreement.

ACCEPTED AND AGREED:

By_____

NETWORK

By_____

Date

ADDITIONAL TERMS AND CONDITIONS

A. As used herein, the first broadcast year of the series will commence with the first broadcast thereof on the Network and will continue until the commencement of the next broadcast season in the Fall. (The word "Fall" as used in this agreement will include September and October.) The second and each succeeding broadcast year will commence in the Fall, and continue until the following Fall. Each broadcast year will have approximately 52 weeks more or less, depending on the scheduling by Network of commencement of the new broadcast season and except for any first broadcast year starting in the Winter/Spring ("Mid-season"). (The word "Mid-season" as used in this agreement will include Winter and Spring.) Network will have the right to extend each broadcast year by one week for each broadcast omitted due to preemptions or withholdings, but only up to a maximum of 3 weeks for programs omitted because of Network's preemptions or withholdings. All broadcast years of the series constitute the "series term."

B. During the series term Network will have the exclusive right to broadcast the series on a network basis or otherwise in the broadcast territory on free television (including the right to license community antenna and similar systems and the usual supplemental and delayed broadcasts within sixty (60) days after the network transmission) on any sustaining or sponsored basis, on behalf of any product or services, on any day, at any hour and with first runs and reruns in any mix, all as Network may from time to time determine. The broadcast territory will consist of the U.S., its territories and possessions excluding Puerto Rico.

"Network basis" as used herein means a broadcast, transmission or exhibition by means of simultaneously interconnected television devices, methods and improvements, now or hereafter known, without limitation (except by means of direct sale to community antenna or pay television systems which will not be authorized by Network or Packager during the term of the agreement); the television devices, methods and improvements referred to herein include but are not limited to, so called "booster" and "translator" stations and relay systems, as well as antenna systems which receive and retransmit or redistribute (with or without amplification) television signals by wire or cable connection or otherwise to television receiving sets.

C. Network will have the right to make one initial broadcast and unlimited repeat broadcasts of each program, to intersperse new and repeat program broadcasts and to make repeat broadcasts as needed up to a maximum of fifty-two (52) new and repeat broadcasts in each broadcast year of the series. Network will have the right to select repeats from any year's programs. Programs of the series will not be broadcast more frequently than once-per-week, except in connection with schedule changes and to permit transition between broadcast years. If a program is broadcast more than twice, the parties will negotiate in good faith the amount to be paid by Network for the third and subsequent runs.

D.1. Packager may license programs of the series in Canada (subject to Paragraph D 3 below) but Packager will not pre-release any program earlier than four (4) days prior to its scheduled initial United States broadcast.

D.2. A "principal sponsor" for the purposes of this agreement is one who buys the equivalent of at least one-sixth of the commercial time accompanying the series over at least 13 weeks of the broadcast year.

D.3. Packager will not license programs of the series for broadcast during the series term by any station anywhere whose Grade A or Grade B Contour (or both), determined in accordance with the Rules and Regulations of the Federal Communications Commission, covers any part of Detroit, Michigan, or San Diego, California.

E.1. Packager will comply with, and all programs (pilot and series) to be produced will be subject to Network's prior absolute approval with respect to their compliance with, Network's standard and practices, rules, regulations, and legal responsibilities and with the established broadcasting, business and advertising policies of Network generally applicable to program suppliers of which Packager is informed, including without limitation the Network and NAB codes and the rules and regulations of Network's Departments of Broadcast Standards and Compliance and Practices. The programs will also conform to the established advertising and business policies of any principal sponsor, provided Network has notified Packager of such sponsor and its advertising and business policies prior to the production of the programs involved. All submissions and approvals will be made with a view to meeting the delivery dates of the programs hereunder. Packager will furnish Network with written reports providing such information as Network reasonably requests in order that Network or any station may comply with the rules and regulations of the Federal Communications Commission respecting the contents of the programs. Timing, commercial format, number and length of commercials, and commercial integration will be as designated by Network.

E.2. Packager will sign the Packager's Disclosure Letter furnished him by the Compliance and Practices Department as a condition precedent to its receiving payment pursuant to this agreement. Furthermore, Packager will insert the following language in all contracts between the Packager and any talent who appear in the broadcast performance of the Program and who are hired by the Packager:

> "Artist understands that it is a Federal offense, unless disclosed to his or her employer or to the network prior to broadcast, to:
>
> 1. Give or agree to give to any member of the production staff, anyone associated in any manner with the programs or any representative of the network any portion of his or her compensation or anything else of value for arranging his or her appearance on the program.
>
> 2. Accept or agree to accept anything of value, other than his or her regular compensation for services on the program to promote any product, service or venture on the air, or use any prepared material containing such a promotion where player knows the writer received consideration for it."

In addition, Packager will insert the following language in all contracts between the Packager and talent who do not appear in the broadcast performance of the program:

> "I affirm that neither I nor anyone acting for me gave or agreed to give to the producer, anyone associated in any manner with the program or any representative of Network, any portion of my compensation for services to the program or anything else of value, for arranging my being engaged in connection with the program. In addition, I affirm that neither I nor anyone acting for me received or agreed to receive anything of value from any person for arranging his or her appearance on the program. I understand Network policy prohibits payments for arranging personal appearances and that failure to disclose to Network any such arrangement constitutes a Federal crime.

"I am aware it is a Federal offense, unless disclosed to Network prior to broadcast, for me to accept or agree to accept anything of value other than my regular compensation for services to the program for promoting any product, service or venture on the air. I am also aware that it is a Federal offense to use any prepared material containing such a promotion where I know the writer received consideration for it and fail to disclose this to Network prior to broadcast.

"I shall notify the Network Compliance and Practices Department immediately if any person attempts to induce me to do anything in violation of the foregoing or which is in any way dishonest."

E.3. Packager recognizes Network's policy of equal employment opportunity and that Network applies such policy to all aspects of its operations and further that Packager asserts that in all aspects of its production activity there will likewise be no discrimination because of race, creed, religion, sex or national origin.

F.1. Subject to the terms of this agreement, Packager will furnish everyone and everything necessary for the development, production and delivery of programs hereunder and to Network's right to broadcast the programs and will comply with the requirements of all applicable union agreements. Packager will become a party to the then-current WGA Theatrical and Television Basic Agreement prior to Packager's commencement of performance under this agreement.

F.2. The series will be substantially equivalent in technical, entertainment, and production quality to the pilot upon which it is based, consistent with the reduction of the shooting schedule for each program necessarily involved in the production of a full series as compared to the longer shooting schedule contemplated for the presentation or pilot and will conform to, include and satisfy any particular terms of the format or description of the series (such as use of guest stars in episodes, shooting schedule, location schedule, special effects and the like) given by Packager to Network. All programs will be in color.

F.3. Packager will make delivery of each program in the series as specified in Schedule of Color Film Delivery Requirements annexed hereto not later than fourteen (14) days prior to its scheduled broadcast date.

F.4. Unless otherwise specified in the agreement, Packager will commence delivery of new programs hereunder no later than fourteen weeks following Network's order of the series. Packager will endeavor to make earlier delivery if possible. However, Packager will not be required to commence delivery of such new programs more than four weeks prior to the date of the first scheduled broadcast of the applicable series; it is understood that, at Network's request, Packager will use all reasonable efforts to deliver one or two such programs earlier than four weeks prior to such initial broadcast date.

F.5. Timely delivery requires that Network will have delivery of at least four new programs prior to scheduled commencement of each broadcast season and delivery of each remaining new program at least two weeks prior to its scheduled telecast.

G. Except as otherwise stated in this agreement, the property, the series and every program thereof (including the pilot) will be exclusive to Network in the broadcast territory for all broadcast and non-broadcast uses during the period from the date of this agreement to the expiration of Network's option for the series, and if Network exercises its option for the series, thereafter until the end of the series term. Except as expressly permitted by this agreement, Packager shall not make or permit any use of such property, series, program or elements thereof in the broadcast territory during such period without Network's prior written approval.

H.1. Events of force majeure, Act of God, preemptions or default will be defined and handled as follows:

(a) Any event beyond Packager's control preventing timely delivery of programs and broadcasting rights thereto will be called "Packager's unexpected event". These include Act of God, force majeure, war, etc., death or incapacity of or morals clause violation by a star or labor difficulties preventing production. Any event beyond Network's control and any of the following which prevent broadcasting of programs hereunder will be called "Network's unexpected event": Governmental act preventing customary network broadcasting, Act of God, event of force majeure, labor difficulties impairing broadcasting or threats thereof, war, and Network's appropriation of the time period for a program of public importance or Network's appropriation of the time period for an event such as a parade, game, holiday, political or exceptional program.

(b) Where Packager's unexpected event prevents delivery, Network may broadcast a rerun or omit broadcasting. In addition, Network may (i) reduce the programs ordered or (ii) require delivery after the event abates and either substitute it for a scheduled rerun or extend the series term to accommodate it or use it as a program of the minimum of any succeeding production year. Further, if delivery of 2 consecutive programs or 4 in the aggregate is so prevented in the broadcast year, Network may cancel production of the then-remaining programs of that year.

Notwithstanding the provisions of the preceding paragraph if any star of the series dies or becomes disabled so that said star is unable to perform in the series, Network will also have the right to terminate the series by written notice to Packager exercisable within 30 days of such death or disability. In the event of such termination, Network shall be entitled to refund of all monies paid by it with respect to any programs of the applicable series broadcast year which have not been telecast; Network's sole obligation will be to pay in full only for programs containing said star's performance which it elects to telecast after the star's death or disability and which are completed and delivered in accordance with the series delivery schedule.

(c) If an Network's unexpected event prevents Network from broadcasting, Network may exercise one or more of these rights: (i) Reduce the programs ordered or any guaranteed reruns for that season, (ii) require continued production and delivery and substitute the new programs for scheduled reruns or extend the series term to accommodate affected programs or use the affected programs against the minimum of any subsequent broadcast year, or (iii) cancel production and delivery of the balance of programs for that broadcast year. Network will reimburse all of Packager's accountable out-of-pocket direct costs incurred by reason of Network's unexpected event (not previously reimbursed and not exceeding the balance by Network for the affected programs). Packager will endeavor to reduce or eliminate such costs.

H.2. If appropriation of the time period under (a) of H. 1 affects only a portion of the network, Network may subsequently broadcast the program on such affected portion (in addition to regular broadcast on the unaffected portion) without liability to Packager beyond reimbursement to Packager of any rerun payments thereby necessarily incurred.

H.3. Packager or Network may terminate for the other's breach of any material representation, warranty, term or condition of the agreement, unless the breach is cured within 10 days of notice from the other. If Packager breaches, Network may, in lieu of terminating, exercise the rights that Network would have as though the breach were due to Packager's unexpected event, or suspended its obligations to accept and pay for the programs during the period Packager remains in default and Network may extend the term hereof for a period equal to all or any part of the period of the breach. Network may terminate the term at any time during the period of default and suspension. Rights hereunder are cumulative and in addition to those at law and in equity.

I. During each broadcast year, series stars and other major continuing performers will be exclusive in television and radio to the series, except for performances rendered prior to the first broadcast year (and performances rendered prior to the series option period) and except further that such performers may perform in guest appearances to the extent stated below. Each such performer may make not more than three (3) guest appearances on television or radio programs during each thirteen (13) weeks provided that (i) such person is not then in default of obligations with respect to programs hereunder; (ii) such services will not interfere with the services of such person in programs hereunder; (iii) such person will not portray any character portrayed by such person in any program hereunder; (iv) such person will not appear in the premiere of any program on other than the Network and will not appear in any other program opposite the time of a Network premiere of a series; (v) such person will not appear on any program the time of broadcast of which is within one hour before or one-half hour after the regularly scheduled broadcast time period of the applicable program hereunder; and (vi) such person will not appear on any program presented on behalf of any product or service conflicting with the categories of products or services (limited to three categories) advertised or authorized to be advertised on the series by a principal sponsor. Network will furnish Packager with a list of such products or services with respect to which Network has granted sponsors such protection, at Packager's request. Notwithstanding anything to the contrary, the provisions of this paragraph shall be subject to applicable AFTRA or SAG limitations on exclusivity for the appropriate performances fees.

J. During each production year of the series, the star and other continuing performers will perform in leads-in and leads-out without additional compensation and Packager will use its best efforts to have such performers perform in commercials for use only on the programs at scale or double scale compensation. Packager will advise Network at the time Packager submits the name of such performer to Network for its approval if Packager is unable to obtain the agreement of such performer to do commercials at scale, and Network shall have the right to disapprove such performer on such basis. If however, Network approves such person, Network shall pay or cause the sponsor to pay the commercial fee requested by such person for commercials actually done. Such performers will not enter into commercial tie-ups during the term without Network's prior reasonable approval.

K. If the series is on film, Network will, at the end of each broadcasting year, but subject to the rights of Network and each principal sponsor, respectively, to retain one 16mm print for reference and file purposes only and subject to damage or loss occurring while under Network's control, return to Packager all prints delivered pursuant to items I (b) 1 and I (b) 2 of the Film Delivery Schedule, and Packager may purchase from Network at fair value any 16mm d. b. prints which Network has paid for and Network may still have on hand. Network will destroy any of such prints which Packager does not purchase from Network and upon Packager's request, furnish Packager with an affidavit of any such destruction or with respect to any lost prints.

L. Packager will clear at the source all necessary recording and performing rights to enable Network to broadcast the programs as provided herein, except that performing rights need not be cleared by Packager (i) where the same are controlled by ASCAP or BMI and Network then has a blanket license from such in effect at the time of broadcast of the programs or (ii) where the music is in the public domain. Network will be responsible for clearing the performing rights of which are controlled by ASCAP or BMI if Network then has a license therewith at the time of such broadcast. Packager will submit to Network a list of music specifying the composer, publisher and type of use not less than ten (10) days before use. If Network clears any rights to music at Packager's request, Packager will pay Network its then standard fee for such service.

M. Packager hereby grants to Network the right to use and license others to use the title of the series and titles of programs, the names of Packager, executive producer, if any, producer, director, performers and important creative personnel and other production personnel, and the sobriquet, biography, picture, likeness and voice of each for informative purposes or in connection with the advertising and publicizing of the programs hereunder (either alone or in conjunction of advertising and publicizing of Network's services and the products or services of any licensee or sponsor of the programs hereunder, but not as an endorsement of any such product or service) or in connection with the exploitation by Network of the rights herein granted to it. Network may open mail addressed to program or production personnel and reply to non-personal mail; personal mail will be forwarded to the addressee. Excerpts from programs (including performances therein) may be used as promos and trailers as Network elects, subject to Network's reimbursing Packager for applicable union-mandated fees, if any, for such use.

Stars and continuing performers will be available at reasonable times for normal publicity activities, including photography sessions at Network's gallery and press interviews; they will also participate in the annual Network press trip to Los Angeles.

N. Except where Network's indemnity of Packager is applicable, Packager will indemnify and hold harmless Network, the stations over which the programs are broadcast, each sponsor of the programs and its advertising agency, and their officers, directors, agents, and employees, from and against liability, actions, claims, demands, loss or damage (including reasonable attorneys' fees) based on, caused by or arising of (i) the use of the programs and the property and any material and performances contained therein in accordance with this agreement or (ii) the breach of any warranty or provision of this agreement by Packager. The aforesaid indemnity extends to liability, claims, actions, demands, loss and damage based upon the alleged or actual submission to Network of a basic idea, format or property similar to that of the series or any program hereunder by anyone else, even if before network's negotiations with Packager for this series. Except for public domain material, Packager warrants the originality of the basic idea, format and property and Packager's conception and development thereof. Network's review and approval of the series and the idea, format and material furnished by Packager hereunder will not constitute a waiver of Packager's indemnity with regard thereto.

Network will indemnify and hold harmless Packager, its officers, directors, agents and employees to the same extent with respect to material furnished by Network or any sponsor of the series or acts done by Network or by Packager at Network's direction.

Packager will, in addition and to the extent that such insurance is available to producers generally, maintain in full force and effect during the full term a television producer's liability (error and omissions) policy issued by a reputable company approved by Network, insuring Packager's obligations hereunder for $____/$____ for each program. Packager will furnish Network with a certificate of insurance for the policy prior to commencement of production of any program hereunder; a copy of all notices thereunder concerning the property, program or series will be sent to Network promptly.

Packager will also obtain and maintain in effect at its expense standard form cast and film or tape "negative" insurance, naming Network as loss payee as Network's interest may appear (from monies paid or advanced by Network for the program). Packager will deliver certificates of such insurance to Network before commencing production. In addition, Packager will carry adequate comprehensive general liability and damage insurance, workmen's compensation and other employers' insurance required by law.

Termination of this agreement will not affect the continuing obligations of an indemnitor. The indemnitor may and, upon written request of the indemnitee, will assume the defense of any claim, demand or action (for which indemnity is provided) against such indemnitee and will, upon request of the indemnitee, allow the indemnitee to cooperate in the defense thereof. The indemnitee will give the indemnitor prompt notice of any claim, demand or action arising under the provisions of any indemnity. If the indemnitee settles any claim, demand or action for which indemnity is provided without the prior written consent of the indemnitor, the indemnitor shall be released from all and any liability under said indemnity in that instance. The provisions of this paragraph are applicable in any case where an indemnity is provided under this agreement.

O. Network will have no obligation to broadcast the pilot or series or any one or more of the programs hereunder and Network may elect only to pay for it or them as provided in this agreement. If Network exercises this pay or play right, Packager will, at Network's request discontinue production forthwith, incur no further expense on the programs and endeavor to minimize those expenses already incurred; Network's payment will be reduced by the amount of any savings Packager is able to effect.

P. Packager represents and warrants:

(i) Packager has the right to enter into this agreement and grant the rights herein granted;

(ii) Packager has not done and will not do any act or enter into any agreement which would violate any of the rights granted to Network hereunder or interfere with the performance of Packager's obligations;

(iii) Network will not be liable for any fees or commissions to any agent or representative of Packager or any person whose services are furnished by Packager or to any other party and Packager will hold Network harmless with respect thereto;

(iv) On delivery of each program the program will be free and clear of any encumbrance including any lien or tax which is not subordinate and subject to all rights granted to Network herein; and

(v) All music recording and synchronizing rights required for Network's broadcast are controlled by ASCAP or BMI or are in the public domain, or are controlled by Packager; and

(vi) The exercise by Network in accordance with the terms of this agreement of the rights granted to it herein will not violate or infringe any rights of any person, firm or corporation.

Q. Network may assign this agreement or any part hereof to any entity controlling, controlled by or under common control with Network, or acquiring a substantial portion of Network's business who will assume Network's obligations, but such assignment will not relieve Network of its liability. Packager will not assign, pledge, mortgage, hypothecate, or otherwise encumber in any manner any program or property hereunder, except subject to Network's rights.

R. If at any time the conduct of any person whose services or the product of whose services Packager furnishes hereunder, either while rendering services hereunder or in such person's private life, is without due regard to the best interests of Network and any principal sponsor of the program, or to social conventions or public morals or decency, or if such person commits any act or becomes involved in any situation or occurrence which shocks, insults or offends the community or reflects unfavorably upon such person or Network or any principal sponsor of the series, or if publicity is given to any such conduct, commission or involvement on the part of such person, which occurred previously, Network may require Packager to furnish a replacement for such person who will be subject to Network' approval. If such conduct, commission or involvement is that of Packager or a person whose services are of the essence to this agreement, Network will have the right to terminate this agreement. Network may delete any credit given to such person (or Packager, if its conduct is involved) in connection with any services theretofore or thereafter rendered, regardless of whether the services are terminated.

S.1 Except for programs ordered in the first year of the series, and subject to Paragraph S.2. and S.3. below, Network will reimburse Packager with respect only to the following listed items for net increases in Packager's actual new and repeat program costs which become effective on or after the "Cost Protection Date" elsewhere in this agreement specified:

(a) New or increased minimum union wage scale payments pursuant to industry-wide collective bargaining agreements with the labor organization having jurisdiction which require Packager to increase the compensation of any person whose services are furnished by Packager to bring such person's compensation up to applicable minimum scale;

(b) New or increased minimum pension and welfare fund payments or contributions based upon the compensation payable to persons whose services are furnished by Packager hereunder pursuant to industry-wide collective bargaining agreements with the labor organization having jurisdiction;

(c) New or increased costs by reason of any new or increased federal, state or municipal old age, unemployment or disability insurance taxes, or employer tax payments based upon the compensation payable to persons whose services are furnished by Packager hereunder;

(d) Increases resulting from an industry-wide increase in sound recording royalties, raw stock and laboratory charges.

S.2. Reimbursement pursuant to Paragraph S.1. above is limited to said governmental or union scale increases which are not to commence until after the Cost Protection Date; but there shall be no such reimbursement for the first year of any such union-mandated increase which takes effect in steps over the term of a labor agreement if the term of the applicable labor agreement expires prior to the Cost Protection Date (even though the new labor agreement is not agreed to until after the Cost Protection Date and regardless of whether or not the union scale increase is retroactive).

S.3. (i) Reimbursement pursuant to Paragraph S.1. above is limited to net increases, considering all of the listed items together. Conversely, if there is a net decrease in Packager's expenses after said Cost Protection Date, considering all of the listed items together, the applicable license fee payable by Network to Packager hereunder will be reduced by the amount of such net decrease.

(ii) Network will not reimburse Packager for agency commissions on reimbursements under Paragraph S.1. above.

T. If during the term any element(s) forming a part of the series (or any element submitted for inclusion in the series which is not rejected by Network) becomes the basis for a new series, Network will have an exclusive hold on such spin-off series throughout the series term. Network will also have the right of first negotiation (as herein defined) with respect to any such spin-off for a period of thirty (30) days commencing at any time after the end of the last broadcast year of series telecast and if Network and Packager do not reach agreement on the terms for such spin-off series, Network will have a first refusal (as herein defined) for one year after the end of such first negotiation.

U. As used in this agreement, "first negotiation" will mean that Packager will first negotiate exclusively with Network during a period of 20 business days (unless a longer period is otherwise expressly provided in this agreement) before negotiating with anyone else. The right of "first refusal" will mean that Network will have the first opportunity to enter into an agreement with Packager on terms at least as favorable to Network as those offered to Packager by another person which Packager is willing to accept or those offered by Packager to such person which such person is willing to accept. Network will have 10 days from the receipt of written advice of the details of any such offer within which to exercise such right of first refusal by notifying Packager in writing that Network will require Packager to enter into a contract with Network on substantially the same terms. If Network fails to exercise the right within the 10-day period, Packager may enter into the commitment with such other person. If Packager fails to enter into such commitment, the terms hereof will apply to any next and each subsequent offer received by or made by Packager.

V. If packager fails, or by way of anticipatory breach will fail, to perform and deliver as required by this agreement, Network may take over production for the period of the failure and Packager will be liable for costs incurred by Network. Packager will require persons on and connected with the series to perform for Network during the take-over period or Network may so require in Packager's name. Any dispute between the parties arising under this paragraph will be promptly and finally determined by arbitration pursuant to AAA rules.

Schedule of
COLOR FILM DELIVERY REQUIREMENTS

I. Each new film will be deemed delivered when:

(a) the following items are deposited in a laboratory approved by Network:

1. 35mm original color negative, titled, edited and assembled and conformed to final edited work print, meeting contract requirements.

2. 35mm sound track negative from original three stripe magnetic master synchronized with assembled picture negative;

3. one 16mm color reversal intermediate negative, fully color and density corrected, made by direct reduction from 35mm original negative, or one 16mm color duplicate negative, fully color and density corrected, made by reduction from a 35mm color interpositive; and

4. one 35/32mm sound track negative transferred from original three stripe magnetic master and synchronized with assembled 16mm picture negative; and

(b) the following items are delivered to Network in Los Angeles or New Jersey, as Network designates:

1. two 35mm composite prints, fully color and density corrected, meeting Network's technical standards for network television transmission, on cores and in containers;

2. three 16mm composite prints, fully color and density corrected, meeting Network's technical standards for network television transmission, on reels and in containers;

3. one 35mm fully color corrected interpositive, one 35mm work print and one 35mm magnetic track, as required by Network to enable Network to prepare promotional trailers;

4. two copies of corrected final shooting script;

5. five copies of detailed music cue sheets;

6. copy of Packager's instructions to the laboratory and acknowledgment by laboratory of delivery of Items (a) 1–4;

7. selection of both black and white negatives with proofs, and color transparencies, in 35mm, 2¼" × 2¼" or 4" × 5" size. These will be of different scenes and cast photographed during production, suitable for publicity, gallery and news purposes, when requested by Network; but not more than an average of three days (one day for regular series) still coverage per new film will be requested.

8. Packager will adhere to format supplied by Network and will deliver elements as designated (i.e., trailer; montage/teaser; bumpers, etc.) at Packager's expense.

II. Additional 16mm color prints requested by Network will be made by contact from the 16mm reversal color intermediate or the 16mm color internegative. Such 16mm prints made at Network's request will be paid by Network at the lowest available rate.

III. If Network requires black-and-white production, the film delivery requirements will be the appropriate elements in accordance with Network's standard specifications for black-and-white films.

* IV. Unless otherwise specified in the agreement, Packager will commence delivery of new films no later than fourteen (14) weeks following Network's order of the series. Packager will endeavor to make earlier delivery if possible. However, Packager shall not be required to commence delivery of such new films more than four (4) weeks prior to the date of the first scheduled telecast of the applicable series; it being understood that, at Network's request, Packager will use Packager's best efforts to deliver one or two such films earlier than four (4) weeks prior to such initial telecast date.

V. Network and 25% sponsors shall have the right to retain one (1) 16mm print of the film program each for reference and file purposes only.

---

*Applicable only to series.

MINIMUM

BASIC PRODUCTION CONTRACT

MINIMUM BASIC PRODUCTION CONTRACT*

(The terms contained in this Contract and the accompanying Schedule are the Minimum Terms to which the Author is entitled. While the Author may obtain terms more favorable, no provision of the Contract or Schedule may be waived by the Author in consideration of a greater interest or more favorable terms under any other provision thereof.)

THIS CONTRACT, made and entered into as of the _____ day of _____, 19____, by and between _____, whose address is _____, hereinafter collectively referred to as the "Producer"** , and _____ whose address is _____ hereinafter collectively referred to as the "Author".

WITNESSETH:

WHEREAS, the Author, a member of the Dramatists Guild of the Authors League of America, Inc. (hereinafter called the "Guild"),† has been preparing the book, music and/or lyrics‡ of a certain play or other literary property, now entitled _____ (hereinafter referred to as the "Play"); and

WHEREAS, the Producer is in the business of producing plays and desires to produce the Play in the United States and Canada and to acquire the Author's services in connection therewith;

Now, THEREFORE, in consideration of the premises and the mutual promises and covenants herein contained, and other good and valuable consideration, it is agreed:

FIRST: The Author hereby:

(a) Warrants that he is the Author of the book, music and/or lyrics* of said Play and has the right to enter into this agreement;

(b) Agrees that on compliance with this Contract, the Producer shall have the exclusive right to produce the Play on the speaking stage in the United States and Canada and acquire the Author's services in connection therewith;

(c) Agrees that he will perform such services as may be reasonably necessary in making revisions;

---

*Copyright © 1955, 1961, by The Authors League of America, Inc.

**Where the Producer is a partnership the agreement shall be with the partnership and each individual general partner.

†Strike out what is not appropriate.

‡The phrase "The Dramatists Guild, Inc." is substituted for, and in place of, the phrase "The Dramatists Guild of the Authors League of America, Inc." wherever the latter appears in this contract with the same effect as if such phrase had been physically changed to read "The Dramatists Guild, Inc."

*Strike out what is not appropriate.

(d) Agrees that he will assist in the selection of the cast and consult with, assist and advise the Producer, director, dance director, conductor and scenic and costume designers in the problems arising out of the production;

(e) Agrees that he will attend rehearsals of the Play as well as out-of-town performances prior to the New York opening of the play, provided, however, that he may be excused from such attendance on showing reasonable cause.

SECOND: Although nothing herein shall be deemed to obligate the Producer to produce the Play, nevertheless, unless the Producer produces and presents the Play on the speaking stage under his own management in a regular evening bill (other than a try-out performance) in a first class theatre in a first class manner, with a first class cast and a first class director, on or before the _____ day of _____, 196___ or one year from the date hereof (whichever date occurs first), his right to produce the Play and to the services of the Author shall then automatically and without notice terminate.

THIRD: In consideration of the foregoing and of the Author's services in writing the Play and the Author's agreement to perform services in connection with its production as hereinabove provided, the Producer agrees to pay:

(a) Until the production of the Play, and so long as he desires to maintain his right to produce, a fixed monthly compensation (no part of which shall in any event be returnable to the Producer) of $____ or $200 (whichever amount shall be greater), each to the Bookwriter, Composer and Lyricist*, commencing with the signing of this Contract, and monthly thereafter, until the production of the Play or the termination of this Contract under SECOND above, whichever event shall occur first; provided however, that if subdivision (b) is not selected, or that, if selected, it does not become operative, then (i) if the Producer pays $____ or $500 (whichever amount be greater) on the signing of this Contract, such payment shall be in lieu of payments for the first three months and (ii) the monthly payment for the next three months shall be $____ or $100 (whichever amount be greater) and (iii) the monthly payment for the next six months shall be $____ or $200 (whichever amount be greater).

Where the Contract provides that the musical has not been completed, or is in the process of being written, at the time this Contract is being signed, the payments specified in this subdivision shall commence only when a "completed musical work" is submitted to the Producer. The production date in paragraph SECOND shall be one year from the date such "completed musical work" is submitted. Solely for the purpose of determining when such payments shall commence and when the said period shall begin to run, a "completed" musical shall be deemed to mean a book of at least 80 pages, single-spaced, plus a score consisting of music and lyrics for at least 12 songs.

---

*Strike out what is not appropriate.

*(Check and
initial al-
ternative
desired)*

The following subdivision (b)
☐ *shall*
☐ *shall not*
*be included in this Contract as
part of the parties' agreement.*

(But subdivision (b) shall not apply if the parties select alternative (d)(i) below.)

(b) (1) Provided that the Producer has made, or shall make, comparable arrangements with the director, choreographer, actors, and with respect to the fees of the Producer himself, and subject to the conditions hereinafter set forth, and the Author agrees to accept, compensation for not more than 30 consecutive weeks of performances (including all out-of-town performances prior to the New York opening, New York preview performances, New York performances, and road performances after the New York run) commencing with the first performance of the Play out-of-town, and if there are no out-of-town performances, then commencing with the first New York performance as follows:

    (i)   One-half of the compensation provided for each said week in subparagraphs (c), (d) (ii), or (e) below, as the case may be, or 4% of the gross weekly box office receipts for each of such weeks, whichever is greater, provided that

    (ii)   when compensation has been paid for an aggregate of thirty weeks under (i) above, full compensation shall thereafter be paid to the Author, pursuant to provisions of (e) below.

(2) If the "Production Expenses" (as hereinafter defined in Paragraph TWELFTH) shall have been recouped prior to the end of the thirtieth week in which reduced compensation may be paid under Clause (1) above, said Clause (1) shall become inoperative at the end of the week in which such recoupment shall take place, and full compensation shall thereafter be paid to the Author pursuant to the provisions of subdivisions (c), (d) (ii) and (e) below, as the case may be. It is understood that "Production Expenses" as defined in Paragraph TWELFTH, do not include the principal amount of any bond or any security or collateral deposited therefor, but for the purposes of this Paragraph THIRD (b), "Production Expenses" shall include management fees and office charges, subject to the limitations of THIRD (b) (5) (iv) paid during the period commencing two weeks prior to the opening of rehearsals and terminating with the official New York opening.

(3) In determining whether "Production Expenses" have been recouped, there shall be taken into account as income to the Producer, applicable to the recoupment of such expenses, all income to the Producer derived directly or

indirectly from the production of the Play, including not only income from the first-class performances and other activities controlled by the Producer (such as the sale of souvenir programs, payments from music publishers and the like) but also, and without limiting the generality of the foregoing: (i) the share of net receipts paid to the Producer pursuant to Paragraph SEVENTH hereof, during any week in which compensation is paid under (1) above, and (ii) the share of net receipts to which the Producer shall thereafter become entitled (pursuant to Paragraph SEVENTH) with respect to any disposition of rights specified therein, made during or prior to any such week, although such share of net receipts is not actually paid, or does not become payable to the Producer, until after the termination of such week.

(4) If "comparable arrangements" are not made with each and every one of the following:

Director, choreographer, actors and Producer (including any general partner, "persons in control" of a corporate Producer as herein defined, or person(s) otherwise participating in the production with, or in association with, the Producer),

with respect to the period in which compensation shall be paid to the Author under Clause (1) above, then this entire subdivision (b) shall become inoperative and full compensation shall be paid to the Author pursuant to subdivision (c), (d) (ii) or (e) below, as the case may be.

(5) "Comparable arrangements" (as used in this subdivision (b)) shall mean arrangements contained in written contracts executed prior to the first rehearsal by the Producer:

(i) *With the director*—Whereby the director shall receive as compensation, during the period in which Clause (1) is in effect, one-half of the percentage of weekly box office receipts which he is to receive during the New York run, but such compensation during said period shall not be required to be reduced below 1% of the gross weekly box office receipts.

(ii) *With the choreographer*—Whereby the choreographer shall receive as compensation, during the period in which Clause (1) is in effect, one-half of the percentage of weekly box office receipts which he shall receive during the New York run, but such compensation during said period shall not be required to be reduced below one-half of 1% of the gross weekly box office receipts.

(iii) *With actors*—Whereby the actor shall receive as compensation, during the period in which Clause (1) above is in effect, one-half of the guaranteed salary and/or one-half of the percentage of weekly box office receipts (or other compensation measured thereby) which he shall receive during the New York run, but such compensation during said period shall not be required to be reduced below $2,000 per week; further provided that no such arrangement need be made with any actor who is to receive less than $2,000 during the New York run and is not to receive any percentage of the box office receipts (or compensation measured thereby).

(iv) *With respect to Producers' Fees*—That during the period in which Clause (1) above is in effect, any management fee and/or percentage of gross weekly box office receipts payable to the Producer (or any general partner, "persons in control" of a corporate Producer as herein defined, or person(s) otherwise participating in the production with or in association with, the Producer) shall be one-half the amount of the management fee or percentage of box office receipts, payable during the New York run, except that in no event shall such management fee and/or percentage of gross weekly box office receipts during the period in which Clause (1) is in effect exceed one-half of one percent of the gross weekly box office receipts. In addition, during the period in which Clause (1) is in effect, the Producer shall not pay or make any charge for office expenses in excess of $350 per week.

Provided further that in no event shall the compensation of any of the persons named in (i), (ii), (iii) and (iv) above, during the period in which Clause (1) is in effect, be required to be reduced below such percentage or amount which bears the same proportion to the compensation which such person shall receive during the remainder of the New York run, as the compensation to be paid to the Author under THIRD (b) (1) (i) bears to the compensation paid to him under THIRD (c), (d) (ii) and (e).

(6) Nothing herein contained shall be deemed to require the Producer to make the foregoing arrangements or any other arrangements with the director, choreographer, actors, or with respect to Producer's fees in connection with the production, and the Author shall have no right to compel the Producer to make such "comparable arrangements"; it being understood that the foregoing provisions are set forth as a condition upon the happening of which this subdivision (b) shall become operative and if "comparable arrangements" referred to in Clause (5) above are not made, the only consequence shall be that this subdivision (b) shall be deemed inoperative and full compensation shall be paid to the Author pursuant to subparagraphs (c), (d) and/or (e) below, as the case may be.

(7) It is understood that the Author has elected this subdivision (b) on the Producer's representation and agreement that the "comparable arrangements" with the other persons referred to above will be arrived at, and carried out, by the Producer in good faith, and will be bona fide arrangements in order to

permit the recoupment of "Production Expenses" as promptly as possible; it being understood that if "comparable arrangements" are made, or carried out, in such manner, that any of said other persons shall, in fact, receive more during said period than they would have by a good faith compliance herewith, then the Author would suffer damages to the extent of the one-half of the full compensation he will have foregone during said period by reason of his acceptance of this subdivision (b).

(8) The Producer agrees to furnish to the Author and to the Guild within ten days after the execution thereof and no later than two weeks before the commencement of rehearsals, copies of all contracts (and amendments thereto) with the director, choreographer and actors (referred to in (5) above) respecting arrangements for their compensation, and any contracts concerning production or management fees (referred to in (5) above); he shall also furnish to them at the same time a schedule listing all members of the cast and the director and the amount and terms of compensation to be paid to each during the New York run; the Producer shall also submit to the Guild prior to the New York opening, a statement or budget of the "Production Expenses" of the Play and shall submit promptly to the Author and to the Guild weekly statements of operating expenses for each week during the run of the Play; the Producer shall also submit to the Guild copies of all financial statements or reports issued by the Producer to stockholders, limited partners, joint venturers or other backers, including a copy of the final financial statement with respect to the production.

Upon written request of the Author or the Guild the Producer agrees that either of them may examine, or cause to be examined by independent public accountants, the books of the Producer during and/or after the run of the Play insofar as they relate to the production of the Play, provided that not more than one such examination shall be made in any six-month period and that no examination may be made more than eighteen months after the close of the last performance of the first-class run; it being understood that the purpose of such examination shall be to determine whether the foregoing provisions of this subdivision (b) have been performed.

(c) For each week of out-of-town performances prior to the New York opening and for preview performances in New York prior to the official opening, 6% or ____% (whichever is greater) of the gross weekly box office receipts. Such payments shall not exceed $1,500 in any one of the first four weeks of such out-of-town performances prior to the New York opening, provided that if any of said weeks is not a full calendar week then the maximum for such shorter week shall be prorated, except that said $1,500 limitation shall not apply in the event subdivision (b) hereof is elected and operative.

(d) For the first three consecutive weeks beginning with the official New York opening, the amounts fixed in that one of the following alternatives which has been checked in the box in the margin and initialed by the parties:

(N.B. If this alternative (d) (i) is selected, subdivision (b) of this Paragraph THIRD *shall be deemed deleted from this Contract.)*

☐ (i) The sum of $6000 to be paid to the order of the Guild, in escrow for the benefit of the Author, at least one week prior to the first rehearsal. The Producer shall send to the Author and the Guild at least ten days prior thereto written notice of the date of the first rehearsal. The Guild shall pay said sum to the Author immediately after the New York opening.

If the Producer has not paid the $6000 as herein provided, compensation at the rates specified in the first sentence of subdivision (c) hereof except that the Author shall have the option to terminate the contract by written notice sent to the Producer and the Guild within three days after the default.

The Guild shall repay said $6000 to the Producer whenever the Producer has notified the Guild in writing that he has abandoned any intention to produce the play in New York, and in such event the Producer shall have no right later to produce the play in New York unless the Producer shall have given 64 out-of-town performances within a period of 80 days. If the play is then produced in New York the Author shall be entitled to compensation at the rates specified in the first sentence of subdivision (c) hereof.

☐ (ii) 6% or ____% (whichever is greater) of the gross weekly box office receipts.

(e) For each week of New York performances commencing with the fourth successive consecutive full calendar week after the New York opening, 6% or ____% (whichever is greater) of the gross weekly box office receipts.

(f) For each week of road performances, after the New York run, the compensation at the rates specified in the first sentence of subdivision (c) hereof, provided that, if such payment would result in there being no operating profits (as hereinafter defined) for a particular week, then the Author shall receive only such compensation for that week as shall not result in an operating loss, except that in no week shall the Author receive less than $500.

(g) The payments required to be made pursuant to subdivision (a) may be deducted from the percentage compensation payable pursuant to any of the foregoing subdivisions, but can in no event be deducted from the fixed payment provided for in subdivision (d) (i).

FOURTH: (a) If the Producer has produced the Play for one of the periods specified in Section 2 of the annexed Schedule and has otherwise complied with this Contract, he shall have the exclusive right to produce the Play on the speaking stage in the United Kingdom of Great Britain and in Ireland (hereinafter called "British Isles") for a consecutive run as theatrically understood, in a regular evening bill, upon all the terms and conditions which apply to a New York production, at any time up to and including six months after the close of the first class production in New York, upon sending the Author, in care of the Guild, written notice within one month after said closing performance accompanied by a payment of $500, of his intention so to produce the play, except that such payment need not be made if the Producer has produced the play in the United States for at least 208 performances and all other provisions of the contract have been complied with.

(b) The Producer shall pay to the Guild for the account of the Author 6% or ____% (whichever is greater) of the gross weekly box office receipts.

(c) The payments made in accordance with subdivision (a) hereof may be deducted from the compensation to be paid under subdivision (b).

(d) Provided the Producer has complied with the provisions of subdivision (a) hereof, he may produce the Play in association with or under lease to a British producer subject to the Author's written consent. In such case the Producer's obligation to make the payments herein provided shall remain unimpaired. Such contract between the Producer and the British producer shall require the Play to be produced in the manner and on the terms provided in subdivisions (a) and (b) hereof.

(e) If the Producer has not produced the Play in the British Isles within the period hereinabove provided, then the Author shall thereafter have the sole right to produce or authorize the the production of the Play, provided, however, that if the Producer has otherwise complied with this Contract the Author shall pay the Producer 25% of the net proceeds received by him as the result of any contract for the production of such Play made within five years after the New York opening, including any proceeds from subsidiary rights.

FIFTH: (a) The portion of any gross receipts or net profits due to the Author shall belong to the Author and shall be held in trust by the Producer as the Author's property until payment. The trust nature of such fund shall not be questioned, whether the monies are physically segregated or not. In the event of breach of trust hereunder, the Author may, at his option, pursue his remedies at law or in equity in lieu of the arbitration procedure established by this Contract.

(b) Within 7 days after the end of each calendar week the Producer agrees to forward to the Guild for the Author's account the amount due as compensation for such week and also, within such time, to furnish to the Guild daily box office statements for each Author, of each performance of the Play during such week, signed by the Treasurer or Treasurers of the theatre in which performances are given, and countersigned by the Producer or his duly authorized representative. Box office statements and payments due for plays presented more than 500 miles from New York City may be so furnished and paid within 14 days after the end of each week; for plays presented in the British Isles, within 21 days. In cases where the Author's compensation depends on operating profits or losses, weekly operating statements shall be sent to the Guild for each Author with his check.

(c) All checks shall be sent to the Guild. Checks for payments due under Paragraphs THIRD (a) and (d)(i) and FOURTH (a) shall be drawn to the order of the Guild. All other checks shall be drawn to the order of the Author or, where he indicates in writing to the Producer and the Guild that he is represented by an agent, to the agent, provided the agent is a member in good standing of the Society of Authors' Representatives, Inc.

SIXTH: (a) The Producer, recognizing that the Play is the artistic creation of the Author and that as such the Author is entitled to protect the type and nature of the production of his creation, hereby agrees:

(i) Under his own management to rehearse, present and continue to present the Play, including road companies thereof, with a cast, director, conductor and dance director mutually agreeable to him and to the Author, and to announce the name of the Author as sole Author of the book, music and/or lyrics* of the Play upon all programs and in all advertising matter in which the name of the Producer appears. After the opening of the Play any change in the cast or any replacement of a director, conductor or dance director shall likewise be subject to the mutual consent of the parties. The Author may designate another person to act on his behalf with respect to such approvals and appointments. If the Author is not available for consultation in the United States, the provisions of this subdivision shall not apply unless he shall have designated another person to act on his behalf who is available for consultation in the United States.

(ii) To rehearse, produce, present and continue to present the Play, including road companies, thereof, with only such additions, omissions or alterations as may be specifically authorized by the Author. The Author shall make no additions, omissions or alterations in the manuscript of the Play as contracted for production without the consent of the Producer. Any change of any kind whatsoever in the manuscript, stage business or performance of a play made by anyone shall be deemed to be a part of the

---

*Strike out what is not appropriate.

Play and shall belong to the Author of the book, music or lyrics, as the case may be. The Author shall not be obligated to make payment to any person suggesting or making any such changes unless he has entered into a bona fide written collaboration agreement to do so. The Author shall without any obligation to the Producer be entitled to use any parts of the play omitted.

(b) Where the approval or consent of the Author is required, Composers, Lyricists and Book Writers, respectively, shall vote as separate units, with one vote to each unit.

(c) In any case where, after the play has run in New York for at least three weeks, the Producer, because of some emergency, requests the approval of the Author to make changes or replacements as provided in subdivision (a)(i), and the Producer is unable to obtain any Composer's, Lyricist's or Book Writer's response to such request 72 hours after having sent him and the Guild telegrams requesting the same, then such Composer's, Lyricist's or Book Writer's right to vote shall be forfeit and the votes of the others shall control.

(d) The Producer may complain to the Guild that the Author is unreasonable in refusing to make changes or additions. In such event the Guild shall appoint a representative or representatives and, if they so advise, shall lend its best efforts to prevail upon the Author to make the suggested changes, it being understood, however, that the Guild shall have no power to compel the Author to agree to such changes.

SEVENTH: Although the Producer is acquiring the Author's services solely in connection with the production of the Play, the Author recognizes that by a successful production the Producer makes a contribution to the value of uses of the Play in other media. Therefore, although the relationship between the parties is limited to play production as herein provided, and the Author alone owns and controls the Play with respect to all other uses, nevertheless, if the Producer has produced the Play as provided in Section 2 of the annexed Schedule, the Author agrees:

(a) That he will not authorize or permit any outright sale of the right to use said Play for any of the purposes described in subdivisions (c), (d) and (e) hereof and during the period therein specified without the Producer's prior consent. In no event shall there be any outright sale of any such rights prior to the first class production of the Play, except that an outright sale of motion picture rights prior to such first class production may be permitted if made subject to the provisions of Section 61 of the annexed Schedule.

(b) That he will use his best efforts to exploit the Play for any of the purposes described in subdivisions (c), (d) and (e) hereof.

(c) That the Producer shall receive the percentage of net receipts (regardless of when paid) specified hereinbelow if during any of the periods there set forth any of the following rights are disposed of: motion picture; or with respect to the continental United States and Canada any of the following: radio; television; second class touring performances; foreign language performances; condensed and tabloid versions; so-called concert tour versions; commercial uses; grand opera; and, if Paragraph THIRD (b) is not selected or, if selected, does not become operative, stock performances and amateur performances:

> If before the expiration of 10 years after the last performance hereunder of the last first class run of the Play: 40%

> If within the next succeeding 2 years: 35%

> If within the next succeeding 2 years: 30%

> If within the next succeeding 2 years: 25%

> If within the next succeeding 2 years: 20%

(d) That, if Paragraph THIRD (b) is selected and becomes operative, subdivision (c) above shall not apply to stock and amateur performances and the Producer shall receive the percentage of net receipts (regardless of when paid) specified hereinbelow if, during the period there set forth, any of the following rights are disposed of with respect to the continental United States and Canada: stock performances; amateur performances; Off-Broadway performances:

> If before the expiration of 5 years after the last performance hereunder of the last first class run of the Play: 40%

(e) That if the Producer has produced the Play in the British Isles in accordance with the provisions of Paragraph FOURTH hereof and Section 14 of the annexed Schedule and has otherwise complied with all the terms and conditions of this Contract, then he will have the same financial interest in the right to use said Play for any of the purposes specified in subdivisions (c) and (d) hereof (other than motion picture rights) when they are exploited in the British Isles as therein provided with respect to the United States.

*EIGHTH: The Author shall have the exclusive right without limitation to negotiate and contract for all performances or for any of the other purposes specified in subdivisions (c) and (d) of Paragraph SEVENTH, outside the Continental United States, Canada or the British Isles, and, provided Producer is entitled to share in subsidiary rights pursuant to Paragraph SEVENTH, shall pay to the Producer ____ of the net proceeds he receives from such contracts so executed within 7 years after the New York opening.

NINTH: All compensation from whatever source derived: (except for the

---

*[Margin Note] See Paragraph TENTH.

advance provided in Paragraph TENTH (f)) shall be shared as follows:

Name	Share
_____	_____
_____	_____
_____	_____
_____	_____

TENTH: Additional Clauses: To the extent that any provision of the additional clauses contained in this Paragraph TENTH conflicts with any printed portion of this Contract, the provision of these additional clauses shall prevail:

(a) *Definitions*:

1. "Bookwriter/Lyricist" shall mean _____

2. "Composer" shall mean _____

3. "Author" shall mean the Bookwriter/Lyricist and Composer collectively.

4. "Owner" shall mean _____

5. "Work" shall mean _____

6. "Play" shall mean the book, music and lyrics of the dramatico-musical play written by the Bookwriter/Lyricist and the Composer based upon the Work.

7. "Gross weekly box office receipts", as used in Section 9 of the schedule of Additional Production Terms and elsewhere in this Contract, shall, subject to approval of The Dramatists Guild, mean all receipts from all sources whatsoever derived from the sale of tickets to the Play after the deduction of only the following:

With respect to the United States and Canada:

(i) Federal, state and/or city admissions taxes and any other similar taxes now or hereafter imposed on admissions;

(ii) Fees or commissions paid in connection with theatre parties or benefits, subscription group sales, American Express or similar credit card plans, automated ticket distribution or remote box offices (but not ticket brokers);

(iii) Those sums approximately equivalent to the former 5% New York City Amusement Tax, the net proceeds of which are actually paid over to the pension and welfare funds of the various theatrical unions; and

With respect to the United Kingdom, library discounts, entertainment taxes, and value added taxes; provided, that if The Dramatists Guild and the League of New York Theatres shall agree on a definition of gross weekly box office receipts different from that contained herein, then such definition, to the extent that it shall be expressly inconsistent with the definition contained herein, shall prevail with respect to all gross weekly box office receipts thereafter received.

(b) *Representations and Warranties*:

1. The Bookwriter/Lyricist hereby represents, warrants and agrees that:

(i) He is the sole author of the book of the Play (the "Book") and the lyrics of the Play (the "Lyrics") and the Book and Lyrics are original with him and have not been copied in whole or in part from any other work except insofar as they are based on, or taken from, material in the public domain or in the Work; the Book and Lyrics do not violate, conflict with or infringe upon any rights whatsoever of any person, firm or corporation;

(ii) He has the right to enter into this Contract and to dispose of the rights granted by him herein and while the Producer has rights hereunder, the Bookwriter/Lyricist will not grant or authorize rights inconsistent with the rights granted to Producer hereunder;

(iii) The Book and Lyrics are not in the public domain, and he will take all steps necessary to secure copyright protection for the Book and Lyrics in the United States and in countries signatory or adherent to the Universal Copyright Convention, and he will register his claim to copyright in the Book and Lyrics in the United States Copyright Office;

(iv) There has not been, and he does not know of, any claim or legal proceeding alleging that the Book and/or Lyrics, or any use thereof, violates, conflicts with or infringes upon the rights of any person, firm or corporation;

(v) No representation or warranty is made hereunder with respect to the title of the Play, except that the Bookwriter/Lyricist represents and warrants that the right to use such title has not been affected by any act or omission on his part and that, to the best of his knowledge and belief, no claim has been made to the effect that he does not have the right to use or grant the use of the title and that to the best of his knowledge and belief said title may be legally used by the Producer herein.

2. The Composer hereby represents, warrants and agrees that:

(i) He is the sole author of the music of the Play (the "Music"); the Music is original with him and has not been copied in whole or in part from any other work except insofar as it is based on musical material in the public domain; the Music does not violate, conflict with or infringe upon any rights whatsoever of any person, firm or corporation;

(ii) He has the right to enter into this Contract and to dispose of the rights granted by him herein and while the Producer has rights hereunder, the Composer will not grant or authorize rights inconsistent with the rights granted to Producer hereunder;

(iii) The Music is not in the public domain, and he will take all steps necessary to secure copyright protection for the Music in the United States and in countries signatory or adherent to the Universal Copyright Convention, and he will register his claim to copyright in the Music in the United States Copyright Office;

(iv) There has not been, and he does not know of, any claim or legal proceeding alleging that the Music and/or the titles of any portions thereof, or any use thereof, violates, conflicts with or infringes upon the rights of any person, firm or corporation;

(v) No representation or warranty is made hereunder with respect to the title of the Play, except that the Composer represents and warrants that the right to use such title has not been affected by any act or omission on his part and that, to the best of his knowledge and belief, no claim has been made to the effect that he does not have the right to use or grant the use of the title of the Play or the titles of any portion of the Music, and that to the best of his knowledge and belief said titles may be legally used by the Producer for the purpose of exercising the rights granted to the Producer herein.

3. _____ hereby represents, warrants and agrees that:

(i) He is the sole author of the Work; the Work is original with him and has not been copied in whole or in part from any other work except insofar as it is based on material in the public domain; the Work does not violate, conflict with or infringe upon any rights whatsoever of any person, firm or corporation;

(ii) The Owner has the right to enter into this Contract and to dispose of the rights granted by them herein and while the Producer has rights hereunder, the Owner will not grant or authorize rights inconsistent with the rights granted to Producer hereunder;

(iii) The Owner has taken all steps necessary to secure copyright protection for the Work in the United States and in countries signatory or adherent to the Universal Copyright Convention, and the Owner's claim to copyright in the Work has been registered in the United States Copyright Office;

(iv) There has not been, and he does not know of, any claim or legal proceeding alleging that the Work, or any use thereof, violates, conflicts with or infringes upon the rights of any person, firm or corporation.

(c) *Indemnification:*

1. The Bookwriter/Lyricist will indemnify and hold harmless the Producer and/or the Composer and their successors and assigns against any expenses (including reasonable attorneys' fees), damages or losses (including any amounts paid in settlement, but only if the Bookwriter/Lyricist consents thereto in writing) suffered or incurred by the Producer and /or Composer by reason of the breach of any of the Bookwriter/Lyricist's representations or warranties contained herein as sustained finally by a court of competent jurisdiction; provided, however, that nothing contained herein shall be deemed to alter the rights and obligations of the parties under Section 41 of the Schedule of Additional Production Terms.

2. The Composer will indemnify and hold harmless the Producer and/or the Bookwriter/Lyricist and their successors and assigns against any expenses (including reasonable attorneys' fees), damages or losses (including any amounts paid in settlement, but only if the Composer consents thereto in writing), suffered or incurred by the Producer and/or Bookwriter/Lyricist by reason of the breach of any of the Composer's representations or warranties contained herein as sustained finally by a court of competent jurisdiction; provided, however, that nothing contained herein shall be deemed to alter the rights and obligations of the parties under Section 41 of the Schedule of Additional Production Terms.

3. _____ will indemnify and hold harmless the Producer and/or the Composer and their successors and assigns against any expenses (including reasonable attorneys' fees), damages or losses (including any amounts paid in settlement, but only if _____ consents thereto in writing), suffered or incurred by the Producer and/or Composer by reason of the breach of any of _____s representations or warranties contained herein as sustained finally by a court of competent jurisdiction; provided, however, that nothing contained herein shall be deemed to alter the rights and obligation of the parties under Section 41 of the Schedule of Additional Production Terms.

4. The Producer agrees that he will indemnify and hold harmless the Author and/or Owner and their respective successors and assigns against any claims, demands, suits, losses, costs, expenses (including reasonable attorneys' fees), damages and recoveries suffered or incurred by the Author and/or Owner by reason of the use in the Play of any material (including, but without limitation, all literary and musical material) not contributed or written by the Author or _____

(d) *Grant of Rights:*

1. The Author and Owner grant exclusively to the Producer the right to produce and present all professional live stage performances of the Play throughout the United States and Canada, provided, however, that the only performances which shall be presented outside of New York prior to the official opening in New York shall be performances presented either during the so-called "tryout tour" (as that term is understood in the theatrical industry) or at regional theatres, but in any event presented by the company which the Producer intends to perform the initial run in New York (the "New York Company").

2. If the Producer presents the New York Company in a first-class production in New York for at least the number of performances described in Section 2 of the Schedule of Additional Production Terms attached hereto and incorporated by reference herein (it being understood that regional theatre performances shall not be included in computing such number of performances), or if the Producer presents the New York Company in an Off-Broadway production in New York for at least 64 performances, then the Producer shall continue to have professional live stage performance rights (including without limitation Off-Broadway performance rights) as defined in Article II of such Schedule.

3. The Producer shall have the right to authorize one or more radio and/or television presentations of excerpts from the Play (each such presentation not to exceed ten (10) minutes and such presentation not to be serialized) for the sole purpose of exploiting and publicizing the productions of the Play; provided, however, that the Producer receives no compensation or profit (other than reimbursement for out-of-pocket expenses) for authorizing such radio or television presentations.

(e) *Production Date*

All rights granted to the Producer hereunder shall terminate and revert to the Author and Owner, as their interests may appear, automatically, unless the Play has been presented for its initial performance on or before the date (the "Initial Presentation Date") six months from the date this Agreement has been fully executed, and countersigned by The Dramatists Guild, Inc., provided that the Producer shall have the right, but not the obligation, to extend the Initial Presentation Date to the date (the "Extended Presentation Date") twelve months from the date this Agreement has been fully executed, and countersigned by The Dramatists Guild, Inc., if, on or before the Initial Presentation Date, the following have occurred:

1. The Producer has a letter from a theatre in New York City, indicating that space is available for presentation of the Play;

2. The Producer has prepared a budget for production of the Play of not less than $__,000, which budget is part of the information to be made available by the Producer to prospective investors in the Producer's production of the Play;

3. The Producer has in final form, cleared by any governmental regulatory agencies whose clearance may be required, offering documents which Producer intends to make available to prospective investors in the Producer's production of the Play;

4. The Producer has a firm commitment from _____ (or another director approved by the Author) to perform services as the director of the Play; and

5. The Producer has firm commitments from one or more co-producers who have been approved by the Author.

(f) *Advance:*

The Producer shall pay to the Author in lieu of the sums provided in Paragraph THIRD (a) and subject to Paragraph THIRD (g) hereof and any other provisions of this Contract applicable to advances, as non-returnable advances against royalties, the following amounts, in each instance to be divided and paid 50% to the Bookwriter/Lyricist and 50% to the Composer:

1. Upon execution of this Contract, an aggregate amount equal to $__,000;

2. If the Producer elects to extend the Initial Presentation Date through the Extended Presentation Date pursuant to Paragraph TENTH (e) above, on or before the Initial Presentation Date, an additional aggregate amount equal to $__,000.

(g) *Compensation:*

1. The Producer shall pay to the Author and Owner as percentage compensation under Paragraph THIRD (c), (d) and (e) an aggregate of __% of the gross weekly box office receipts commencing with the first paid public performance of the Play hereunder. All such compensation shall be divided and paid as follows:

(i)   3/7ths to the Bookwriter/Lyricist;

(ii)   3/7ths to the Composer;

(iii)   1/7th to the Owner.

2. At any time that the Play is presented in a theatre in New York having fewer than 300 seats or at a theatre outside New York having a schedule of ticket prices scaled so that the gross weekly box office receipts based on eight performances at capacity would not exceed $__,000, the percentage compensation payable to each of the Bookwriter/Lyricist, Composer and Owner shall be

reduced proportionately to an aggregate of __% of the gross weekly box office receipts.

(h) *Subsidiary Rights and Division of Proceeds Therefrom:*

The Producer shall be entitled to the following maximum participation in the net receipts derived by the Author and Owner from the exploitation of rights in the Play as set forth in Paragraphs SEVENTH and EIGHTH hereof, notwithstanding anything to the contrary therein:

1. If the Producer shall have presented the Play in one or more first-class theatres of 500 seats or more for the number of performances described in Section 2 of the annexed Schedule (it being understood that regional theatre performances shall not be included in computing such number of performances), then the Producer's percentage participation shall be 40%; or

2. If the Producer shall have presented the Play in New York in a theatre with fewer than 500 seats for the number of performances indicated below, then the Producer's percentage participation shall be as specified below:

Number of Performances Following Official New York Opening	Producer's Percentage Participation
____	0%
____	10%
____	20%
____	30%
__ and more	40%

3. The Proceeds (other than the advances described in Paragraph TENTH (f) hereof) payable to the Author and Owner hereunder from the sale, lease, license or other disposition of any rights in and to the Play, including, but without limitation, the rights referred to in Paragraphs SEVENTH, EIGHTH, and TENTH (h) and (1) hereof, shall be divided among the Bookwriter/ Lyricist, Composer and Owner in the same proportion as the compensation payable to them as described in Paragraph TENTH (g)(1) hereof. Prior to the aforesaid division, however, the percentage participation, if any, payable to the Producer under Paragraphs SEVENTH, EIGHTH, TENTH (h), and TENTH (1) hereof shall first be deducted and paid to the Producer.

4. The Producer shall not be entitled to receive any percentage or share of any monies or proceeds derived by the Bookwriter/Lyricist and/or the Composer or any other person authorized by either of them from the publication, mechanical reproduction, synchronization and small performing rights in the separate Music and Lyrics or from any rights in and to such separate Music and Lyrics as are customarily granted to music publishers or from any use of

whatsoever kind or nature of the separate Music and Lyrics for motion pictures, radio and television purposes or otherwise, all of which the Bookwriter/Lyricist and/or the Composer shall be entitled to receive for their respective accounts, provided, however, that nothing in this Paragraph TENTH (h) shall impair or modify the provisions of Paragraph TENTH (1) hereof. Any reference contained in this Contract to separate numbers, separate Music and Lyrics, separate musical compositions or separate synchronization of Music and Lyrics shall be deemed to refer to the non-dramatic use of the Music and Lyrics apart from any other portion of the Play (such as, but not limited to, the book, staging, sets and costumes).

5. If there is a merger of all elements of the Play pursuant to Paragraph TENTH (j) below, then, except as part of a disposition of rights in the Play, the Bookwriter/Lyricist and Composer each hereby agree that they and their music publisher or anyone claiming through them will not consent to the license of the synchronization rights of the separate musical compositions of the Play for motion picture or television production; provided, however, if by the end of the fifth year following the close of the New York Company there has been no disposition of the motion picture or television rights in the Play, then the Bookwriter/Lyricist and Composer (and their music publisher) shall be free at any time during the next five years to license synchronization rights in the separate musical compositions of the Play so long as not more than one such composition is used in any one motion picture or television presentation and such composition does not contain the title of the Play or the name of characters of, or incidents from, the Play; and provided, further, that if by the end of the tenth year following the close of the New York Company there has been no disposition of motion picture or television rights in the Play, then the Bookwriter/Lyricist and Composer (and their music publisher) shall be free at any time thereafter to license synchronization rights in the separate musical compositions of the Play for motion picture and television purposes without restriction.

6. Insofar as the Producer may do so, the Producer does hereby agree to grant to the publisher who shall publish the Music and Lyrics the right to use the art work of the Play on sheet music, folios and advertising at a reasonable charge therefor. Said publisher may also have the right to use production photographs of the Play provided that it obtains at its expense the necessary clearance from those persons whose photographs, names or likenesses are depicted or used therein.

(i) *Restriction on the Use of the Work:*

1. The Owner shall not authorize any stage performance of the Work in the United States or Canada during the period in which the Producer is entitled to present the Play hereunder, subject, however, to any and all rights in the Play

heretofore granted by the Owner to Dramatists Play Service ("DPS"). Notwithstanding said grant to DPS, the Owner shall, if given appropriate notice by the Producer, use their best efforts to assist in arranging with DPS to protect the Play from competition by withholding the Work from stock or amateur performances within a reasonable radius of cities in which the Producer plans to present the Play.

2. Provided there has been any disposition of motion picture or television rights in the Play on or before the date five years from the close of the New York Company (it being understood that if there is no such disposition by such date, the following restrictions shall not apply), during the period in which the Producer is entitled to his percentage participation pursuant to Paragraphs SEVENTH, EIGHTH and TENTH (h) hereof, the Owner agrees:

(i) Not to authorize any motion picture or television use of the Work (except for the customary rights granted by authors to producers of live stage performances for publicity and advertising purposes); and

(ii) Not to authorize the presentation of any other musical version of the Work.

Following the termination of Producer's percentage participation, there shall be no restrictions whatsoever on the Owner's right in their sole and absolute discretion, to authorize any presentation of, or creation of any new versions of, the Work in any and all media, and neither the Producer nor the Composer shall have any right of participation whatsoever in any amounts derived from such disposition by the Owner.

(j) *Control of the Play and Disposition of Rights Therein:*

1. In the event that this Contract shall terminate for any reason prior to the first paid public performance of the Play, the Author and Owner hereby agree that the rights in the Book, Lyrics and Music and the Work shall be as follows:

(i) All rights in and to the Book and Lyrics shall be retained by the Bookwriter/Lyricist for his own use, free from any claim by the Producer or the Composer;

(ii) All rights in and to the Music shall be retained by the Composer for his own use, free from any claim by the Producer or the Bookwriter/Lyricist;

(iii) All rights in and to the Work shall remain the sole property of the Owner for their own use, free from any claim by the Producer or the Composer.

2. The Bookwriter/Lyricist and the Composer agree that there shall be a

complete merger (subject to Paragraph TENTH (j) (3)) of the Book, Music and Lyrics, and they shall be deemed a single work, upon the first paid public performance of the Play. Upon such merger, all rights in the Play shall be jointly controlled by the Bookwriter/Lyricist and the Composer, who hereby agree to act in good faith, in cooperation with each other, and to exercise their best efforts in order to exploit the Play for all of the purposes described in this Contract. If the Producer is entitled to any of his percentage participation pursuant to Paragraphs SEVENTH, EIGHTH, TENTH (h), and/or TENTH (1) hereof, and if the Bookwriter/Lyricist and the Composer disagree about any such exploitation, such disagreement shall be submitted for resolution to The Dramatists Guild or to another arbitrator mutually agreeable to the Bookwriter/Lyricist and the Composer.

3. Notwithstanding Paragraph TENTH (j)(2) above, the Owner shall have the right, in their sole and absolute discretion, to combine any material from the Book with the Work in any manner whatsoever and to dispose of said Work with such added material in any manner they shall determine subject only to the restrictions agreed to by the Owner with respect to the Work as set forth in Paragraph TENTH (i) above. Neither the Producer nor the Composer shall be entitled to participate in any proceeds derived by the Owner from the disposition of the Work with such added material.

4. If the Book shall be published separate and apart from the Lyrics and the Music or if the Book shall be published with the Lyrics but not the Music, the proceeds therefrom shall inure solely to the Bookwriter/Lyricist.

5. All rights in and to any of the Music and Lyrics which are deleted from the Play prior to the official opening in New York or deleted from the Play during the first ten performances following said opening, shall revert to the Composer and Bookwriter/Lyricist, respectively, for their use, free from any claim by the Producer or the other.

(k) *Approvals*:

1. Except as expressly provided otherwise in this Paragraph TENTH (k), all rights or approval given to the Author under the provisions of this Contract shall be exercised jointly by the Bookwriter/Lyricist and the Composer.

2. The Author shall have the right to approve the musical director and the orchestrator engaged for the original New York production of the Play.

3. The Composer shall have sole approval of the contents of the Music; and the Bookwriter/Lyricist shall have sole approval of the contents of the Book and Lyrics.

4. The Author shall have the right to approve all bookings for any pre-New York tour and any theatre in New York in which the Producer intends to

present the Play. The Author hereby approves the_____

5. With respect to all approvals which the Author has under this Contract, if the Author fails to send the Producer written notice disapproving any item or element submitted in writing for the Author's approval, within three business days after such item or element has been so submitted to the Author, the Author will be deemed to have approved such item or element. If the Bookwriter/Lyricist and the Composer disagree about any item or element submitted for their approval, the Producer shall have the right, but not the obligation, to resolve such disagreement by indicating in writing his agreement with the position of the Bookwriter/Lyricist or the Composer, as the case may be, which position shall prevail.

(l) *Cast-Album Uses*:

If the Play is presented in New York, the Producer, in cooperation with the music publisher, shall have the right to arrange for the disposition of the right to make a recorded "cast-album" of the Play (including, but not limited to, dialogue from the Play for introductory or bridging purposes) in which the cast of the Play is used; provided, however, that any such disposition shall be made subject to the approval of the Author. The Producer shall share in revenue derived from the "cast-album" only to the extent of his percentage participation pursuant to Paragraph TENTH (h) above. The Bookwriter/ Lyricist, the Composer, and the Producer shall each be entitled to receive a copy of all statements regarding royalties payable in respect of the "cast-album" which shall be sent by the recording company issuing such album, and the Producer's contract with such recording company shall so provide. It is expressly understood and agreed that the aforesaid arrangements and division of proceeds shall not be deemed to refer to or include any arrangements for or division of proceeds from the mechanical rights in the Music and Lyrics. The Producer shall have no interest or share in such mechanical rights proceeds.

(m) *Ownership of Copyright*:

Copyright in the Book shall be in the name of the Bookwriter/Lyricist, and copyright in the Music and Lyrics shall be in the names of the Composer and the Bookwriter/Lyricist or their designees.

(n) *Billing*:

1. The Author shall be accorded billing whenever and wherever the title of the Play appears, including but not limited to all theatre programs, houseboards, billboards, displays, posters, circulars, announcements and advertisements (other than ABC and teaser ads) under the control of the Producer, in substantially the following form:

(Title of the Play)

Book and Lyrics by _____

Music by _____

2. The billing for the Bookwriter/Lyricist and the Composer shall be in equal size and prominence and shall appear on a separate line (or lines) not shared with any other element of the production, shall follow immediately the title of the Play, and the names of the Author in such billing shall be in type of a size and prominence at least 75% of that of the size and prominence of the title of the Play or the names of the stars, whichever is larger.

3. Billing for _____ as Author of the Work shall be discretionary with the Producer.

4. No person, other than stars, shall receive billing credit which shall precede the aforesaid credits and no person other than the stars shall be accorded billing more prominent than that accorded to the Author.

5. Wherever the Author is entitled to receive credit hereunder (aside from theatre programs and houseboards), and all credits in connection with the Play therein are accorded in a so-called "billing box", the size of the Author's credits therein shall be determined by the size of the title of the Play in said billing box.

6. The provisions for size, prominence, order, and requirements of credits shall not be applicable with respect to the use in advertising or other publicity in any medium of quotations from published reports or critics' reviews.

7. In his contracts with third parties who have control over anything relating to billing, the Producer shall require compliance with the credit provisions hereof. No casual or inadvertent failure to comply with the provisions of this Paragraph TENTH (n), and no breach by any third party of an agreement between the Producer and such third party, shall constitute a breach of this Contract by the Producer if the Producer takes reasonable steps to remedy such failure promptly after receiving written notice thereof.

8. The Bookwriter/Lyricist and the Composer each hereby consent to the use of their respective names, likenesses and biographical resumes in connection with the exercise by the Producer of his rights hereunder and advertising and publicity relating thereto, including without limitation as part of or in connection with the "cast-album" described in Paragraph TENTH (1) above, and its manufacture, distribution, advertising, and/or sale.

(o) *Transportation and Living Expenses*:

1. (i) When the Bookwriter/Lyricist and/or the Composer accompanies the Play on its pre-Broadway tour and/or (ii) when the Bookwriter/Lyricist and/or Composer takes a trip at any time at the Producer's request in connection

with the Play and/or (iii) when the Bookwriter/Lyricist and/or Composer is not a resident of New York and comes to New York for the rehearsal of the Play, or comes to New York at any other time at the Producer's request, the Producer shall furnish each of the Bookwriter/Lyricist and/or Composer, as the case may be, first-class transportation on each such tour, trip or travel, including return to the residence of the Bookwriter/Lyricist and/or Composer if the Bookwriter/Lyricist and/or Composer is not a resident of New York and shall pay each of the Bookwriter/Lyricist and/or Composer, as the case may be, Sixty Dollars ($__.00) a day (including travel days) toward the living expenses of the Bookwriter/Lyricist and/or Composer throughout each such tour, trip or stay in New York. The Bookwriter/Lyricist and Composer shall also be entitled to attend the opening of all companies of the Producer, if any, following the New York run of the Play and the Producer shall pay each of the Bookwriter/Lyricist and Composer the same per diem living allowance and furnish to each the same transportation expenses for each such opening as provided above.

2. During any out-of-New York tryout of the Play, the Producer, at his sole expense, shall furnish a piano for the Composer's use.

(p) *House Seats*:

1. For each regular evening and matinee performance of the Play in New York City (that is, except for benefit and theatre performances), the Bookwriter/Lyricist and the Composer shall each be entitled to purchase three adjoining pairs of house seats all in the first ten rows of the center section of the orchestra. For benefit and theatre party performances in New York City, the Bookwriter/Lyricist and the Composer shall each be entitled to purchase one pair of house seats in the first ten rows of the center section of the orchestra. The Bookwriter/Lyricist and the Composer shall also be entitled to purchase five additional pairs of house seats in the center section of the orchestra, for the official opening performance of the Play in New York. All tickets shall be purchased at regular box office prices. Such tickets shall be set aside and made available for purchase by such person or his designee until 6:00 p.m. of the day preceding the scheduled commencement of each evening performance of the Play, and until 12:00 noon of the day preceding the scheduled commencement of each matinee performance of the Play.

2. The Bookwriter/Lyricist and the Composer each acknowledges and agrees that the theatre tickets made available hereunder cannot, except in accordance with the regulations promulgated by the Office of the Attorney General of the State of New York, be resold at a premium, and that complete and accurate records will be maintained by each of them, which may be inspected at reasonable times by a duly designated representative of the

Producer and/or the Attorney General of the State of New York, with respect to the disposition of all tickets made available hereunder.

(q) *Title Changes*:

No changes in the title of the Play shall be made except with the approval of the Author. The title of the Play shall be the property of the Author.

(r) *Agency (Bookwriter/Lyricist and Owner)*:

The Bookwriter/Lyricist and the Owner hereby employ and designate _____, exclusive agent with respect to their interest in the Play (whether or not the Play is produced hereunder) and any and all rights and uses therein of any nature whatsoever, including but not limited to all production rights and all rights specified in Paragraphs SEVENTH, TENTH (h) and (1) of this Contract. The Bookwriter/Lyricist and Owner hereby authorize and direct the Producer (and any person, firm or corporation acquiring any rights in the Play) to pay all monies due to them hereunder (hereinafter referred to as "said monies") to and in the name of the said Agent, and to accept the receipt of the said Agent as full evidence and satisfaction of said payments. In return for services rendered and to be rendered, the Bookwriter/Lyricist and Owner agree to pay to and hereby authorize the said Agent to receive and retain ten percent (10%) of all said monies, including but not limited to their share of subsidiary and motion picture rights, whether or not the Producer participates therein, except that with respect to the proceeds from amateur performances, such percentages so received and retained shall be twenty percent (20%). All payments to the said Agent hereunder shall be computed and based upon the gross sums payable to the Bookwriter/Lyricist and Owner before the computation and deduction of the Producer's share, if any, of the remaining net proceeds. With respect to the proceeds from the sale of motion picture rights, it is expressly understood that there shall be deducted from the aforesaid ten percent (10%) the Bookwriter/Lyricist's and Owner's pro rata share of the three and one-half percent (3-½%) (or such lesser percent as may be) payable to the Negotiator's Fund.

Anything hereinabove to the contrary notwithstanding, whenever this Contract requires payment to be made to The Dramatists Guild or to the Negotiator on behalf of the Bookwriter/Lyricist and/or Owner, payment shall be so made.

The Producer further agrees that if at any time the Bookwriter/Lyricist and Owner shall not be obligated to pay commissions to _____ with respect to any disposition of rights in the Play, the Bookwriter/Lyricist and Owner may designate another agent in lieu of _____ and such agent shall be entitled to receive commissions with respect to the Bookwriter/Lyricist's and Owner's

share of any such proceeds in the same manner as is provided above for
_____.

(s) *Agency (Composer)*:

The Composer hereby employs and designates _____, as his sole and exclusive agent with respect to his interest in the Play (whether or not the Play is produced hereunder) and any and all rights and uses therein of any nature whatsoever, including but not limited to all production rights and all rights specified in Paragraphs SEVENTH, TENTH (h) and (1) of the Contract. The Composer does hereby authorize and direct the Producer (and any person, firm or corporation acquiring any rights in the Play) to pay all monies due or to become due to him hereunder (hereinafter referred to as "said monies") to and in the name of the said Agent as full evidence and satisfaction of said payments. In return for services rendered and to be rendered, the Composer agrees to pay to and does hereby authorize the said Agent to receive and retain ____% of all said monies, including but not limited to his share of subsidiary and motion picture rights, whether or not the Producer participates therein, except that with respect to the proceeds from amateur performances, such percentage so received and retained shall be twenty percent (20%). All payments to the said Agent hereunder shall be computed and based upon the gross sums payable to the Composer before the computation and deduction of the Producer's share, if any, of the remaining net proceeds. With respect to the proceeds from the sale of motion picture rights, it is expressly understood that there shall be deducted from the aforesaid ____% the Composer's pro rata share of three and one-half percent (3-½%) (or such lesser amount as may be) payable to the Negotiator's Fund.

Anything hereinabove to the contrary notwithstanding, whenever this Contract requires payment to be made to The Dramatists Guild or to the Negotiator on behalf of the Composer, payment shall be so made.

Any claim, controversy or difference between the Composer and his Agent or the Producer and the aforesaid Agent, arising out of or relating to this Contract or in connection with the Play shall be settled by arbitration in New York, New York in accordance with the rules then obtaining of the American Arbitration Association, and judgment upon the award rendered may be entered in any court of the forum having jurisdiction thereof.

(t) *Orchestration*:

The amount which the Producer may deduct from the compensation of the Author pursuant to Section 8(e) of the Schedule of Additional Production Terms is hereby fixed at $__ per week.

(u) *No Obligation to Producer*:

Nothing herein contained shall be deemed to obligate the Producer to produce and present the Play.

(v) *Headings*:

Headings contained in this Contract are included for convenience only and are not to be deemed a part of this Contract.

(w) *Stage Manager's Script*:

Prior to the final close of the Play under this Contract, or prior to one (1) month after the New York opening, whichever is earlier, the Producer shall deliver to each of the agents of the Bookwriter/Lyricist and Composer as the Bookwriter/Lyricist's and Composer's property, respectively, a neat and legible script of the Play as produced on the New York opening containing lighting, costume and property plots and scene diagrams, as well as all other details and information customarily contained in a "stage manager's script".

(x) *Union Rules*:

Pursuant to the rules and regulations of the United Scenic Artists, Scenic Designing Artists and Theatrical Costume Designer's Contracts, the Bookwriter/Lyricist and the Composer each undertakes and agrees that he will not sell, lease, license or authorize the use of any of the original designs of scenery and costumes created by the designers under the standard union agreements for productions of the Play hereunder, without both the designers' consent and the Producer's consent.

(y) *Licenses; Assignments*:

1. The Producer shall have the right to co-present any production hereunder and/or to license any of its rights hereunder to any other person, firm or corporation.

2. The Producer shall have the right to assign this Contract to any partnership in which the Producer and/or any partnership or corporation owned or controlled by the Producer, is a general partner, or to any corporation owned or controlled by the Producer and/or any partnership or corporation owned or controlled by the Producer, or to any joint venture in which the Producer and/or any partnership or corporation owned by the Producer is one of the joint venturers.

3. Paragraphs 1 and 2 of this Paragraph TENTH (y) are both subject to Section 49 of the Schedule of Additional Production Terms.

(z) *Notices:*_____

_____

(aa) *Governing Law*:

This Contract shall be deemed made in the State of New York, and shall be governed by, and construed in accordance with, the laws of such State applicable to contracts made and entirely performed therein.

(bb) *Entire Agreement*:

This Contract sets forth the entire agreement of the Producer, the Bookwriter/Lyricist, the Owner, and the Composer with respect to the Play and may not be altered, modified or changed except in writing signed by the party to be charged with the contents thereof.

(cc) *Out-of-Town Run*:

Prior to the official New York opening of the Play, if any, the Producer shall present the New York Company in not fewer than 24 performances in the aggregate outside of New York City.

ELEVENTH: Any claim, dispute or controversy arising between the Producer and the Author under, or in connection with, or out of the Contract or the breach thereof, shall be submitted to arbitration as specified in Article XIII of the annexed Schedule unless the Author selects other remedies as permitted by Paragraph FIFTH (a) hereof. The Guild shall receive notice of such arbitration and shall have the right to be a party to the same.

TWELFTH: The following words and phrases when used in this Contract or the annexed Schedule shall mean and include as follows:

Author: Each Dramatist, Collaborator or Adaptor of the Play and each Composer, Lyricist, Novelist or Author of any other literary or musical material used in the Play but not including a person whose service is only that of a literal translator.

Commercial Uses: Toys, games, figures, dolls, novelties or any physical property representing a character in the Play or using the name of a character or the title of the Play or otherwise connected with the Play or its title, provided the Author has consented to such use.

Contract: This contract and the Schedule of Additional Production Terms annexed thereto.

End of first class run: Whenever the Producer has lost his right to reopen the play or has in writing declared that he will not reopen it.

New York: The theatrical district of the Borough of Manhattan of the City of New York.

Off-Broadway Performances: Performances in theatres located in the City of New York which are classified pursuant to the terms of the minimum basic contract of Actors Equity as "Off-Broadway."

Continental United States: shall be deemed to include the States of Hawaii and Alaska, geographical inconsistencies notwithstanding.

Production Expenses: Fees of designers and directors; cost of sets, curtains, drapes and costumes; cost or payments on account of properties, furnishings and electrical equipment; premiums for bonds and insurance; unrecouped advances to authors; rehearsal charges, transportation charges, reasonable legal and auditing expenses, advance publicity and other expenses actually incurred in connection with the production and presentation preliminary to the opening of the Play in New York, including any out-of-town losses, but there shall not be included any compensation to the Producer or to any person rendering the services of a producer other than a charge for office expenses not to exceed $250 per week commencing two weeks before the opening of rehearsals and continuing until the New York opening. No items charged as production expense shall be charged against operating profits, or vice versa.

Weekly Operating Profits: The difference between the Producer's share of the box office receipts (after meeting any theatre minimum guaranty) and the total weekly expenses determined as follows: $500 for Author's minimum compensation, salaries of the cast, business manager, press agent, orchestra, and miscellaneous stage help, compensation payable to the directors, transportation charges, office charge not to exceed $450, advertising, rentals, miscellaneous supplies, and all other reasonable expenses of whatever kind actually incurred in connection with the weekly operation of the Play as distinguished from production costs, but not including any compensation to the Producer or a person rendering the services of a producer, nor any monies paid by way of percentage of the receipts or otherwise for the making of any loan or the posting of any bond.

THIRTEENTH: This Contract shall be binding upon and inure to the benefit of the respective parties hereto and their respective successors in interest (except as herein otherwise limited), but shall be effective only when countersigned by the Guild. No change or modification of this Contract shall be effective unless reduced to writing, signed by the parties hereto, and countersigned by the Guild. If the Producing Managers Contract is assigned by the Guild pursuant to paragraph XXI thereof, (i) this Contract shall be deemed to have been amended as of the date of such assignment so that the name of the assignee shall be substituted in place of the words "Guild", "Dramatists Guild" or "The Dramatists Guild of the Authors League of America, Inc." wherever such words shall appear; (ii) the name of the Council or governing body of said assignee shall be deemed to have been substituted in place of the name of the Council of the Guild wherever it shall appear; and (iii) such assignee and its governing body shall succeed to and assume all rights, privileges, duties and obligations of the Dramatists Guild of the Authors League of America, Inc. and its Council under this Contract.

FOURTEENTH: Should any part, term or provision of this agreement be decided by the courts to be in conflict with any law of the state where made or of the United States, the validity of the remaining portions or provisions shall not be affected thereby.

FIFTEENTH: In making proof of the execution of this Contract or of any of the terms thereof, for any purpose, the use of a copy of this Contract filed with the Dramatists Guild shall be sufficient provided (a) that the copy produced from the files of the Guild need not have attached to it the particular printed copy of the Schedule of Production Terms annexed thereto at the time of deposit with the Guild but may be produced with any identical printed copy of said Schedule, and (b) that at any time after two years from the date of execution hereof there may be produced from the files of the Guild, in lieu of the copy of this Contract originally deposited therein, a microfilm of said copy.

IN WITNESS WHEREOF, the parties hereto have hereunto set their hands and seals the day and year first above written.

_____

Author of the Book

_____

Lyricist

_____

Composer

_____

Producer*

In consideration of the execution of this Contract by the Author, the

_____

*Where this contract is signed by a corporate Producer, the officer signing should state his office and the corporate seal should be affixed. Where the officer signing for the corporation is other than the President, a certified copy of a resolution should be furnished showing the authority of said person so to sign.

Where this contract is signed by a partnership, all the general partners must sign and the partnership name should also be stated.

(If Producer is a corporation, the following must be signed by the person or persons in control thereof, i.e., the person or persons (a) owning or controlling a majority of its stock or a majority of its voting stock; or (b) using their name as part of the corporate title; or (c) rendering services in connection with the play as Producer or (d) whose name is included in publicity, advertising or programs as Producer or co-Producer of the play.)

undersigned (if more than one, then the undersigned jointly and severally) hereby agrees to be jointly liable with the Producer for the full performance of each and every covenant and provision of this Contract on the Producer's part to be performed, including but not limited to the payment of all monies due the Author hereunder.

COUNTERSIGNED:

THE DRAMATISTS GUILD OF THE AUTHORS LEAGUE OF AMERICA, INC.

By: _____

Schedule of
ADDITIONAL PRODUCTION TERMS*
Article I

THIS SCHEDULE

SECTION 1.

This schedule of additional Production Terms shall be deemed part of the foregoing Production Contract.

Article II

THE PRODUCTION OF THE PLAY

SECTION 2. *How Rights Acquired.*

The Producer shall have the exclusive right to make a first class production of the Play in the United States and Canada under his own management provided the Play is produced within the period and in the manner specified in Paragraph SECOND of the Production Contract and such contract is otherwise complied with in all respects and the Play has been so presented for one of the following periods: (1) for 21 consecutive performances in New York; (2) for 64 consecutive performances, whether outside of or in New York, provided that breaks may be made in performances outside of New York because of the necessities of travel so long as the 64 performances shall have been given within 80 days of the first performance; or (3) one performance in New York if the Producer has made the payment provided for in subdivision (d) (i) of Paragraph THIRD of the Production Contract. Such exclusive production rights shall continue only so long as the Producer shall continuously produce

*Copyright 1955, 1961, by the Authors League of America, Inc.

the Play as herein provided and otherwise fully comply with the Contract, subject to the reopening rights as specified in Section 5 hereof.

If Paragraph THIRD (b) is selected and becomes operative, each preview performance given in New York within ten days of the official New York opening (even though not consecutive), shall be considered a "consecutive performance in New York" for the purpose of determining whether the play has been presented for the period "21 consecutive performances in New York," provided that the Author is paid the specified compensation for such preview performance, and that the gross of each is at least 65% of the capacity of the theatre (computed at the box office prices announced for the New York run), and that there shall not actually have been 21 or more consecutive performances in New York after the official New York opening.

SECTION 3. *Association with Others.*

The Producer shall not use the name of any person, firm or corporation as participating in the production of the Play unless such person, firm or corporation is a party to the Producing Manager's Contract with the Guild and the Author has consented in writing.

SECTION 4. *Closing.*

The Producer shall in each instance immediately upon determining to close a run of a Play, give written notice thereof to the Author.

SECTION 5. *Reopenings.*

(a) Provided the producer has acquired exclusive first class production rights by compliance with one of the alternatives set forth in Section 2 of this Schedule, he may within 4½ months after the close of the initial first class run of the Play, notify the Author in writing of his intention to reopen the first class production of the Play in the United States and/or Canada. In such case he may so reopen the Play provided that simultaneously with sending the notice of intention he pays $100 to the Author, plus $100 each month thereafter until the first performance of the renewed run takes place.

(b) The Producer may so present the Play not later than 6 months after the date of mailing said notice, provided that if such 6-month period shall expire between May 1st and September 14th the Producer may reopen the Play not later than September 15th next following.

(c) If the Producer shall have produced the Play for a renewed run as permitted by this Section, and shall thereafter have presented the Play for at least 21 consecutive first class performances in New York, or 64 first class performances outside of New York, or partly inside and outside New York within a period of 80 days, then the Producer shall continue to be entitled to further reopening rights, in each instance under the procedure defined in this Section.

(d) If the Play is first produced outside of New York within the period and in the manner specified in the Production Contract, for at least 3 consecutive performances, and the Producer closes the Play within 1 month after said third performance, he may reopen the Play provided he does so not later than 3 months after the closing and gives the Author written notice of his intention so to do within 30 days after the closing. No further payment, as required by Paragraph THIRD (a) of the Production Contract, need be made by the Producer for the first month after closing, but the Producer shall pay $200 per month for the next two successive months. All the provisions of this Section shall apply to this reopening.

SECTION 6. *Author's Decisions.*

In all cases where the approval or consent of the Author is required, an unresolved disagreement among several Authors of the Play shall be controlled by a majority of the Authors, unless a different method of decision is provided for in the Production Contract. In the event of a tie vote the President of the Guild shall, upon the request of the Producer or Authors, or any of them, appoint a single arbitrator to pass upon such unresolved disagreements.

SECTION 7. *Revue Sketches.*

(a) Any sketch or number of a revue and any songs or musical numbers in any musical play which shall not have been used on opening night in New York or within 3 weeks thereafter, or having been so used shall be omitted from the play for 3 successive consecutive weeks, may be withdrawn by the Author and used by him for any purpose, free of any claim by the Producer, subject only to such participating interest in additional uses as the Producer may theretofore have acquired.

(b) If a sketch, song or other contribution of one or more Authors is omitted from a condensed or tabloid version of a play, then the Author or Authors whose work is so omitted shall nevertheless share in the proceeds from such version, provided their said respective contributions shall have been included in at least one-half of the then prior presentations of the New York run of the Play. In such cases, each Author shall share in the proceeds of the condensed or tabloid version in the same proportion that his original Play compensation bears to the total compensation due under the Production Contract.

SECTION 8. *Musical Scores.*

(a) The Producer shall in the first instance furnish all necessary orchestral scores, conductor's scores, orchestra parts and vocal parts at his own expense.

(b) The orchestral score, conductor's score, orchestra parts and vocal parts shall belong jointly to the Lyricist and Composer of the play immediately upon delivery thereof to the Producer. Such scores and parts may be used by the Lyricist and Composer at any time after the close of the first class run of the play, whether or not the deductions or payments referred to in (e) or (f) of this Section have been completed.

(c) The Composer and Lyricist alone shall have the right to contract for the publication of the music and lyrics of a musical production or any part thereof, without prejudice to the right of the Producer to arrange for separate payment to him by the Publisher. The Composer and Lyricist alone may permit reproduction of the music and lyrics or any part thereof by discs or any other means or devices.

(d) The Producer shall, at the request of the Composer and Lyricist, or the Guild, make available to the Guild as soon as feasible after the opening, the said orchestral score for the purpose of making a copy thereof. Upon the close of the run of each company the Producer shall deliver to the Composer and Lyricist the complete orchestral score, conductor's score, orchestra parts, vocal parts and prompt book; provided, however, that the Producer may make and retain a copy of such score, parts and prompt book but not for use or sale.

(e) The Producer may deduct from the compensation of the Composer and Lyricist (but not from payments required by Paragraph THIRD (a), (d)(i), or (f) of the Production Contract) such amount as may be fixed in the Production Contract, but not more than $100 in each week, until a sum equal to 50% of the Producer's actual expenditure for the orchestral score, conductor's score, orchestra parts and vocal parts shall have been recovered by him. The Producer shall pay to the Guild the monies so deducted until there shall have been presented to the Guild evidence of his actual expenditures for such scores and parts, whereupon the Guild shall pay him the monies held by it to the extent of 50% of such actual expenditures. The deduction so made, unless otherwise agreed upon, shall be borne by the Composer and Lyricist according to their respective percentages of compensation.

(f) The Composer and Lyricist may at their option pay outright to the Producer at any time a sum equal to 50% of his expenditures for such scores and parts or such remaining balance thereof as may then be unpaid.

Article III

COMPENSATION, DEDUCTIONS AND EXPENSES

SECTION 9. *Basis of Computation.*

Where percentage weekly compensation is based upon gross weekly box office receipts, the percentage shall be computed upon receipts from all sources whatsoever, including any and all sums over and above regular box office prices of tickets received by the Producer, or by anyone in his employ, from speculators, ticket agencies, ticket brokers or other persons, and any other additional sums whatsoever received from the production of the play. Should the play be performed by more than one company, percentage compensation accruing from each company shall be computed and paid separately.

SECTION 10. *Adaptor's Compensation.*

Where an English language adaptation is made from a foreign language play or from other literary property, the Adaptor shall receive at least ⅓ of the minimum compensation payable to the Author.

SECTION 11. *Repertoire.*

If the play is produced in repertoire, percentage compensation shall be computed in groups of 8 performances, such 8 performances to constitute a week for the purpose of this Contract, except that the time for payment or mailing shall be as agreed upon in the Production Contract, but in no event later than 4 days after the end of every calendar month in which the play is performed, regardless of the number of performances.

SECTION 12. *Deductions.*

No deductions shall be made from compensation due by the Producer to the Author on account of a debt due by the Author to the Producer unless an agreement in writing providing therefor shall have been made between the Author and Producer and filed with the Guild; except, however, that such deduction may be made if it is less than $100, and a memorandum signed or initialed by the Author acknowledging his indebtedness, and receipted by the Producer or his representative, shall accompany the statement for the week in which the deduction is made.

SECTION 13. *Expenses.*

The Producer shall pay such reasonable hotel and traveling expenses as the Author may incur in making trips outside New York City (or to New York City if a non-resident) to attend rehearsals and out-of-town performances prior to the opening and the New York opening, and at any other time when the presence of the Author is required by the Producer.

Article IV

FOREIGN PRODUCTIONS OF THE PLAY

SECTION 14. *Production in the British Isles.*

The Producer shall have the exclusive right to make a first class production of the Play in the British Isles provided the Play is produced within the period and in the manner specified in Paragraph FOURTH of the Production Contract, and the Play, if first produced in London, runs there for 21 consecutive performances or is presented for a total of 64 performances within 80 days after the first performance, partly in London and partly outside of London, or, if it is first produced outside of London, runs for at least 64 performances outside of London within 80 days after the first performance. Such production right shall continue only so long as the Producer shall continuously produce the Play as herein provided and otherwise fully comply with the Contract, subject to reopening rights specified in Section 15 of this Schedule.

SECTION 15. *British Reopenings.*

(a) Provided the Producer has acquired exclusive first class production rights by compliance with one of the alternatives set forth in Section 14 of this Schedule, he may, within 3 months after the close of the initial first class British run of the Play, notify the Author in writing of his intention to reopen the first class production of the Play in the British Isles. In such case he may reopen the Play provided that simultaneously with sending the notice of intention he pays $100 to the Author, plus $100 each month thereafter until the first performance of the renewed run takes place. In such event the Play shall be so produced within 3 months after the mailing of said notice but if such 3-month period shall expire between August 1st and October 14th, the Producer may reopen the Play not later than October 15th next following.

(b) If the Producer shall have reopened the Play under subdivision (a) hereof and shall thereupon have produced the Play for 21 consecutive first class performances in London, or 64 such performances outside of London, within a period of 80 days, he shall continue to be entitled to further first class productions until the first class run in the British Isles shall cease, in each instance under the procedure set forth in subdivision (a) hereof.

SECTION 16. *Foreign Uses.*

If the Author disposes of any foreign uses, he shall reserve in his contract for his own use, all motion picture and television rights in such foreign territory (including the British Isles) and such contract shall provide that the exercise of such reserved rights by any other person in the foreign territory shall not be deemed competitive with any rights so disposed of.

Article V

THE NEGOTIATOR

SECTION 17. *The Negotiator.*

The person heretofore acting as Negotiator under the Minimum Basic Agreement of 1946 shall continue to act as Negotiator.

SECTION 18. *Replacement of Negotiator.*

The present Negotiator shall serve until removed by a ⅔ vote of the Council of the Guild or by a ⅔ vote of the Producers who have signed the Producing Manager's contact taken on 10 days' prior written notice. The vote of the Producers shall be cast by the Producers present in person or by proxy at a meeting duly called for that purpose and attended by no less than 25 signatory Producers.

SECTION 19. *Temporary Negotiator.*

If the Negotiator dies, resigns, is removed or is for any reason unable to perform his duties, the Council of the Guild may forthwith appoint, by a ⅔ vote, a temporary Negotiator with all the rights and duties of Negotiator (except that his compensation shall be fixed by the Guild) to act during the incapacity of the Negotiator or until his successor is appointed.

SECTION 20. *Alternate Negotiator.*

The Guild Council may appoint an alternate Negotiator who shall have the right to sign checks in conjunction with the Guild. The Council shall have the right to change the alternate from time to time. The alternate's signature shall be used in lieu of the Negotiator's only when the Negotiator is not available owing to illness or temporary absence.

SECTION 21. *Selection of New Negotiator.*

Any new Negotiator shall be selected by the joint vote of the Council of the Guild by a ⅔ vote and a ⅔ vote of the Producers signatory to the Producing Manager's Contract, to be cast at a meeting of the Producers specially called for that purpose and attended by no less than 25 signatory Producers.

SECTION 22. *Disqualification of Negotiator.*

If it appears that the Negotiator, by reason of his relations with any Producer who has received motion picture financing directly or indirectly, or his representation of any Author or Producer of the particular play involved, or for any other reason whatsoever, might, in the disposal of motion picture rights in connection with any play, act in a dual capacity or occupy a position possibly conflicting with complete representation of the Author, the General Advisory Committee may, at its option, or upon the request of the Author or Producer involved, replace the Negotiator by a substitute Negotiator to act in connection with the disposal of the motion picture rights of the particular play involved.

SECTION 23. *Duties of Negotiator.*

The Negotiator shall act as representative of the Author in connection with the disposal of world motion picture rights in a play or part thereof and shall have the right generally to offer the same to motion picture producers, and to carry on negotiations therefor subject to such written instructions as may be issued to him by the General Advisory Committee. He shall have the right to consummate such sale or lease after consultation with the Producer and subject to the Author's approval, and to receive and distribute the monies resulting therefrom as provided herein. In consulting with the Producer, the Negotiator shall report the details of offers received by him for such rights and the terms and conditions of any proposed contract for the sale or lease thereof. All contracts shall be countersigned by the Guild.

If such rights are disposed of prior to the production of the Play, the motion picture contract must be signed before the beginning of rehearsals. In such a case the contract shall be on the basis of a minimum guaranteed payment or an advance, plus or on account of percentage payments based on the picture receipts or the box office receipts of the Play, or both, and shall be subject to the approval of the Guild and the Producer.

SECTION 24. *Disposition of Proceeds.*

All monies received from the disposal of motion picture rights shall be forthwith deposited by the Negotiator in the Chemical Bank New York Trust Company (or such other depositary entitled to receive city or state funds as may be designated by the Guild) in a special account to the credit of "The Dramatists Guild, Negotiator's Account"; and withdrawals therefrom shall be made by check signed by the Negotiator or by the alternate Negotiator, or by the Temporary Negotiator and countersigned by a person designated by the Guild. There shall first be deducted from such monies $3\frac{1}{2}\%$ thereof; and the balance shall thereupon be paid to the party or parties entitled thereto. The Negotiator shall make and deliver a check for the aforesaid $3\frac{1}{2}\%$ to the order of The Dramatists Guild of The Authors League of America, Inc., and the Guild shall deposit the same in a separate account.

SECTION 25. *The $3\frac{1}{2}\%$ Fund.*

At the end of each calendar year a statement shall be prepared showing what part of the $3\frac{1}{2}\%$ fund remains on hand, after the payment of the

Negotiator's compensation and expenses and any expenses of the Guild attributable to the fund. The balance shall be apportioned to each play for the motion picture rights for which monies were received during that year, and shall be paid to the person or persons against whom it was charged as hereinafter provided in Section 37.

SECTION 26. *Compensation of Negotiator.*

The Negotiator's compensation shall be determined by the Guild, but shall in no event exceed $20,000 a year. In addition the Guild may pay him no more than $15,000 a year for his expenses. If the $3\frac{1}{2}\%$ of the monies derived from the disposition of motion picture rights exceeds $25,000 the Guild may pay him an additional amount as compensation up to 1% of the gross picture proceeds of any pre-production lease of motion picture rights out of any surplus held by the Guild in its special account attributable to the Play for which such picture rights have been sold. But the payments to the Negotiator for compensation and expenses shall in no case exceed said $3\frac{1}{2}\%$.

Article VI

MOTION PICTURE AND OTHER USES

SECTION 27. *Cooperation by Author.*

The Author agrees to cooperate with the Negotiator and shall promptly transmit to the Negotiator all offers for the motion picture rights received directly by him, and shall disclose to the Negotiator any arrangements actual or contemplated, between the Author and any motion picture producer with whom negotiations may be pending for the disposal of the motion picture rights. Moreover, the Author agrees that unless the Producer shall consent thereto, he will not insist on any commitment or agreement with a Motion Picture Producer for his personal services as author, actor, director, or in any other capacity, as a condition of disposition of the motion picture rights to such Producer.

SECTION 28. *Rights of Producer.*

If the Producer deems himself aggrieved by any disposition of motion picture rights, his sole recourse shall be against the Author and then only for fraud or wilful misconduct; the Author's refusal to grant the right to make a motion picture sequel or sequels of the Play or of the picture made therefrom shall not be a basis for the Producer deeming himself aggrieved; and in no event shall the Producer have any recourse, in law or in equity, against any purchaser or lessee of such rights, or against anyone claiming thereunder, or against the Negotiator, the Guild, or other Producers who voted for the selection of the Negotiator.

SECTION 29. *Conflicts.*

The motion picture release date shall not interfere with either the New York or the road run of the Play. Such release date shall be fixed by the Author, and the Producer shall be advised thereof by telegraph or mail. If the Producer files no objection with the Negotiator within 3 days after such notification is sent or given (Saturdays, Sundays and legal holidays excepted), the release date will be deemed to be satisfactory to him. If within the period specified he states in writing his reasons for objecting, the Negotiator shall give due consideration to his objections and shall then fix a release date which shall be binding and conclusive on the parties.

SECTION 30. *Revues.*

A separate song or sketch from a revue may be disposed of for motion picture purposes only at the expiration of 18 months after the close of the first class run, except that if the Producer shall, within 5 days after notice to him thereof, object thereto, then the approval of the General Advisory Committee described in Section 35 hereof shall first be obtained. Unless otherwise agreed among the Authors, the Authors' share of the proceeds shall be participated in only by the Authors of the song or sketch so disposed of.

SECTION 31. *Restrictions on Author.*

Unless the Producer consents in writing, the Author shall not permit the release of the additional rights hereinbelow referred to until the following times:

(a) Stock presentations, Amateur presentations, Musical Comedy, Operetta and Grand Opera based upon the Play, Foreign Language performances in the United States, Radio, Television, Second Class Touring Rights, Condensed and Tabloid versions, Concert Tour versions, and Off-Broadway performances: at any time after the end of the first class run, provided, nevertheless, that selected songs from a musical production may be released for radio at any time.

(b) Commercial Uses: At any time after the initial performance of the Play.

(c) Publication of Music: Simultaneously with or at any time after the initial first class performance of the Play.

(d) Mechanical Reproduction of Music: At any time after the initial first class performance of the Play.

SECTION 32. *Producers' Participation in Sequels.*

If the motion picture producer, in the original contract for motion picture rights, is granted the right to make one or more motion picture sequels upon additional compensation, then, if and when such additional compensation is paid, unless a lower percentage is specified in the Production Contract, the Producer shall receive ½ of the respective percentages provided in Paragraph SEVENTH of the Production Contract.

SECTION 33. *Rights in Case of New Producer.*

(a) In any instance in which the Producer of the first run of the play shall be entitled to share in the motion picture proceeds and no motion picture rights shall have been sold, the Author must in each instance, before granting to any other Producer the right to revive the first class run or himself revive it, offer to the Producer who first produced the play the right so to revive the run upon the same terms, provisions and conditions as he shall be willing to accept from another producer or, if so to be revived by the Author, then upon the same compensation terms as originally provided. Such offer must be submitted in writing to the Producer by registered mail, and if the said Producer shall not in writing accept the said offer within 10 days after the mailing of such notice, then he will be deemed to have rejected the offer so to revive the Play, and the Author shall then be free to produce it himself or to grant such rights to another producer within 90 days thereafter on terms at least as favorable to the Author as those offered to the Producer and rejected by him.

(b) If the motion picture rights have not been disposed of within 5 years after the close of the first class run and, the Producer not having exercised the option granted in subdivision (a) hereof, the Author or a new Producer produces a revival of the play or a new version thereof after the expiration of said 5 years, then the percentages to which the original Producer shall be entitled as provided in Paragraph SEVENTH (c) of the Contract shall be cut in half. If such revival or new version runs for any of the periods specified in Section 2 of this Schedule, the Producer who shall have produced such revival or new version shall receive one-half of the percentages above specified, but in such case the periods of participation shall run from the termination of the first class run of the revival or new version.

(c) In the event of such revival or production of a new version, and in the event that such new Producer or the Author shall not have produced the Play in accordance with Section 2 hereof, so that no right to participate in the proceeds of a motion picture lease or sale of other uses shall have accrued to such new Producer, then the full participation of the Producer who shall first have produced the play shall remain unimpaired.

SECTION 34. *Defaults by Producer.*

(a) If the Producer is in default to a member of the Guild in the payment of compensation or other monies accruing from the production of any play, the

Guild may file with the Negotiator a memorandum to that effect, and the Negotiator shall thereupon withhold from the Producer's share the amount stated in such memorandum and shall forthwith notify the Producer in writing thereof. Unless the Producer demands arbitration thereon, within 10 days after the mailing of such notice, the Negotiator shall make payment of the amount shown to be due in such memorandum.

(b) If the Producer shall have furnished a bond, and the Guild shall have drawn on such bond because of the Producer's defaulted obligations on any play, and the Producer shall have failed to replenish the bond after notice and demand according to its terms, the Guild may file with the Negotiator a memorandum to that effect, stating the amount so to be replenished, and the Negotiator shall thereupon withhold from the Producer's share the amount stated in such memorandum, and shall forthwith notify the Producer in writing thereof. If the Producer within 10 days advises the Negotiator in writing that he disputes the claim of the Guild in whole or in part, the Negotiator shall continue to withhold the disputed amount pending determination by arbitration; otherwise he may pay over such amount to the Guild, to apply on such bond.

SECTION 35. *General Advisory Committee.*

The General Advisory Committee established pursuant to the Producing Manager's Contract shall, in addition to any powers specifically granted to it in this Schedule, have the following powers:

(a) For the purpose of effectuating and facilitating the provisions of this contract relating to the negotiation, lease or sale of motion picture rights, instructions in writing shall be issued from time to time to the Negotiator by the Committee. The instructions contained in Appendix A hereto annexed shall remain in force until changed by the General Advisory Committee. When new instructions are issued they shall take the place of the old.

(b) The Committee shall issue directives to establish principles to prevail with respect to outright disposition of uses of the Play and shall define the extent of second class touring rights.

(c) Such instructions and directives may embody, but are not limited to, minimum conditions but they shall not conflict with, nor operate or be construed as, a contradiction or limitation of either the spirit or the letter of this Contract.

(d) Two members and two alternates to the General Advisory Committee shall be appointed to a Special Subcommittee whose function shall be to review and study the relations between agents and parties to the Production Contracts, and the problems which have arisen and may arise in connection with such relations; and further, to make recommendations for the improvement of such relations and the solution of such problems, which recommendations may include recommendations for the immediate amendment of the existing Producing Manager's contracts with the Guild.

The Producer Members and the Guild Members of the General Advisory Committee shall, respectively, designate one of their members and one alternate to serve on the Committee. The General Advisory Committee shall prescribe rules for the calling of meetings, quorums and other matters of Subcommittee procedure.

Article VII

RESERVATION OF RIGHTS

SECTION 36. *Reservation of Rights.*

The Author shall retain sole and complete title, both legal and equitable, in and to the Play and all rights and uses of every kind except as otherwise specifically herein provided. The Author reserves all rights and uses now in existence or which may hereafter come into existence, except as specifically herein provided. Any rights reserved shall not be deemed competitive with any of the Producer's rights and may be exercised by the Author at any time except as otherwise specifically provided. All contracts for the publication of the music and lyrics of any play shall provide that the copyright be in the names of the Composer and Lyricist.

Article VIII

AGENTS

SECTION 37. *Employment and Commission.*

(a) The Author may employ an Agent for the disposal of uses of the play referred to in this contact. The commission of such Agent shall not exceed 10% of the amount of such sale or lease except for amateur performances, for which the commission shall not exceed 20%, and except as hereinafter provided in relation to motion picture uses. Such commissions shall be deducted from the proceeds of any sale or lease in which the Producer shares before payment is made to the Producer.

(B) If the Producer has not consented to the Agent also representing him with respect to motion picture uses, the Agent's commission with respect to such use or uses shall not exceed 10% of the proceeds of such sale or lease to which the Author is entitled, and shall be deducted only from the Author's share; if the Producer shall consent to the Agent also representing him, then the Agent's commission shall not exceed 10% of the proceeds of such sale or lease and shall be deducted from the proceeds in which the Producer shares before payment is made to the Producer.

In the event of a sale or lease for motion picture use, the 3½% paid into the Negotiator's fund shall be deducted:

(i) From the Agent's commission, if such commission is deducted from the proceeds of the disposition of motion picture rights before payment to the Producer, or

(ii) From the Agent's commission and the Producer's share of the proceeds of the disposition (in accordance respectively with the Author's and the Producer's interests in the entire proceeds), if the Agent's commission is deducted only from the proceeds to which the Author is entitled, provided that nothing herein shall be construed to permit the deduction of more then 3½% of the Producer's share of such proceeds if he has not consented to the Agent's also representing him, or

(iii) From the Author's share and the Producer's share of the Proceeds of the disposition in accordance with their respective interests, if the Author had no agent.

SECTION 38. *Restrictions in Appointments.*

In no event shall the Author appoint the Producer, or any corporation in which the Producer has an interest, or any employee of the Producer, or the attorney for the Producer, or a member of a firm of attorneys representing a Producer, as his Agent or as his representative. No Author's Agent or officer, directing head or employee of an Agent shall, with respect to the same play, act in the dual capacity of Agent and Producer (the word "Producer" as herein used shall include any person having executive direction or a majority stock interest in the Producer, if a corporation or who is one of the general partners of any partnership, general or limited) in making a Production Contract; and if he does so act, he shall be deemed to have abandoned his agency insofar as the Play in question is concerned, and shall not be entitled to collect or receive any monies or commissions in connection with such Production Contract.

SECTION 39. *Payments.*

All monies derived from the disposal of the rights referred to in Article VI shall be paid to the Author's agent, but only if the agent is the Dramatists' Play Service, Inc., or is a member in good standing of the Society of Author's Representatives, Inc. Otherwise such monies shall be paid to the Guild which shall pay such monies directly to the Author, Agent and Producer as their respective interests shall appear.

SECTION 40. *Restrictions.*

Neither the Author nor the Producer shall make any claim for commissions in connection with any disposition of the Play for any purpose. Nor shall the Producer be reimbursed for any expenses or disbursements claimed by him unless the Author, prior to the expenditure thereof, shall have agreed upon the repayment of such disbursements in writing and such agreement shall have been countersigned by the Guild.

Article IX

CLAIMS FOR INFRINGEMENT

SECTION 41. *Claims by Third Parties.*

In the event that libel or any infringement of or interference with the rights of any third party is claimed because of the production of the Play, then the Producer and Author shall jointly conduct the defense of any action arising therefrom and shall share equally the expenses thereof, unless the infringement, libel or other interference shall be found to have been caused by either the Author or Producer singly, in which event no part of the expenses shall be paid by the other, and either shall be entitled to all legal remedies he may have against the other. Whenever an Author writes a Play at the request of a Producer, from an idea or from material supplied him by said Producer, and an action is brought on the grounds of plagiarism, then the Producer shall defend the action at his own expense and pay any and all damages that may be found as the result of the plagiarism and pay any judgment rendered against the Author on account thereof. In no event shall the Author be responsible for any material in the Play not written by him. Upon any suit being brought against the Author or Producer alone, such person shall promptly inform the other of that fact.

Article X

SPECIAL CONCESSIONS AND GUILD APPROVAL

SECTION 42. *Reduction of Compensation.*

(a) If the Producer has presented the play for any of the periods specified in Section 2 hereof, has paid in full all compensation due for such periods, and has otherwise complied with this Contract, there may, with the written consent of the Author and the Guild, be a reduction of future compensation payable under Paragraph THIRD (c) after 8 weeks of out-of-town performances and under Paragraph THIRD (e)—except that, in the case of dramatic productions, this shall not be applicable during the period in which Production Expenses are being recouped under subdivision (e)(i). One reduction, of not more than two weeks' duration, may be made without the consent of the Guild, provided that an agreement, in writing, for such reduction be signed by both of the parties and filed with the Guild within one week after the reduction is agreed upon; if not so signed and filed, it shall be null and void.

(b) If Paragraph THIRD (b) is selected and becomes operative, there shall, during the period in which reduced compensation is paid pursuant to Clause (1) thereof, be no reductions of compensation, under any circumstances under the provisions of Section 42 (a) or otherwise.

SECTION 43. *Other Concessions.*

When special circumstances arise as the result of which the Author or Producer desires specific concessions in this Contract other than financial ones, they or either of them may so advise the other and the General Advisory Committee, in care of the Guild, in writing. The Committee may in its discretion allow such concessions as it deems appropriate and the particular provisions of the Contract in the particular case will be modified accordingly.

SECTION 44. *Conditions.*

The Guild or the General Advisory Committee, as the case may be, may prescribe conditions for the granting of concessions but they agree that no discrimination shall be exercised in any particular case, it being the intention that special or specific concessions made to one Producer or Author shall be made to others similarly situated if warranted by the circumstances. The Guild, or the Committee, as the case may be, may nevertheless from time to time adopt a new or different policy respecting a request for concessions without regard to prior decisions, provided that no such change in policy shall be made by the Guild acting alone without the consent of the General Advisory Committee. In prescribing such conditions on making concessions, the Guild, or the Committee, as the case may be, shall not be bound by concessions granted prior to June 1, 1961, if Paragraph THIRD (b) is elected and becomes operative.

SECTION 45. *The Guild's Approval.*

In any case where the approval of the Guild is required, such approval shall not be unreasonably withheld; but in no event shall the Guild be liable in any matter involving exercise of discretion.

Article XI

TERMINATION

SECTION 46. *Upon Notice by Author.*

If the Producer at any time fails to make any payment when due (time being of the essence of this Contract); or fails to comply with or fulfill any of the other terms of this Contract or of the Production Contract, the Author may, at his option, call upon the Producer, by notice sent by registered mail or by telegraph, to correct such failure or breach within 3 days after the mailing or telegraphing of such notice. If the Producer fails to correct such breach within the aforesaid 3 days, all his rights under the Contract shall cease and terminate forthwith, upon the expiration of the 3 days, and all rights in the play shall thereupon revert to the Author. Sundays and legal holidays shall not be included in computing such 3-day period. In the event that the Producer shall have his office or place of business more than 100 miles from the place from which the notice is sent, then such notice shall be sent by telegraph. There shall be no termination or reversion of rights under this Section except after such notice.

SECTION 47. *Automatically and Without Notice.*

All rights granted to the Producer under the Contract shall terminate automatically and without notice if and when the Producer fails to produce the play within the time and in the manner provided in Paragraph SECOND of the Production Contract; or fails to complete the number of performances referred to in Section 2 of this Schedule; or fails to make any payment due under Paragraph THIRD (a) within 10 days after it becomes due; or becomes bankrupt, or commits, undergoes or permits any of the other acts set forth in Article XII hereof.

SECTION 48. *Effect of Termination.*

Whenever for any reason the Contract has terminated hereunder, all rights of the Producer shall cease and terminate. In such case the Producer shall forthwith return to the Author all manuscripts, scores, "parts" and other literary or musical material in his possession or under his control, except that he may retain one copy of the manuscript, but not for use or sale.

Article XII

ASSIGNMENT AND BANKRUPTCY

SECTION 49. *Assignability of Rights.*

Neither the Contract nor the rights granted thereby to the Producer shall be assigned or sublet by the Producer, by operation of law or otherwise, without his first having obtained the consent in writing of the Author and of the Guild; except that an assignment may be made to a corporation, which is a signatory to the Producing Manager's Contract and in which the Producer has the controlling interest or of which he is the directing head or to a partnership, all the general partners of which have signed such Producing Manager's Contract, provided that any assignee shall assume all of the obligations of this Contract and that the Producer shall remain personally liable for the fulfillment thereof in the same manner as though no such assignment had been made. A copy of any assignment shall be filed with the Guild.

SECTION 50. *Bankruptcy, etc.*

If the Producer files a petition in bankruptcy or is adjudicated a bankrupt, or makes an assignment for the benefit of his creditors, or takes advantage of any state or federal insolvency act, or liquidates his business in any manner whatsoever, or if a receiver is appointed for his property and business and remains undischarged for a period of 20 days, or if the Producer (being a corporation) becomes a party, without the written consent of the Guild first obtained, to any merger, consolidation or reorganization, or if the corporate existence of the Producer is terminated by voluntary or involuntary dissolution, the Producer's rights under the Contract shall cease and terminate as provided in Article XI hereof.

Article XIII

ARBITRATION

SECTION 51. *Obligation to Arbitrate.*

Any claim, dispute, or controversy arising between the Producer and the Author under, or in connection with, or out of, the Contract, or the breach thereof, shall be submitted to arbitration. Failure by a Producer to pay any amount claimed to be due by an Author or by the Guild is evidence of a dispute entitling the claimant to an arbitration. Judgment upon the award rendered may be entered in the highest Court of the forum, State or Federal, having jurisdiction.

All arbitrations shall be conducted in the City of New York before the Theatrical Production Arbitration Board herein created and in accordance with the procedures herein set forth except where the Author and Producer agree to hold the arbitration outside New York. In such event, the arbitrators shall be selected from the panel of the American Arbitration Association and the arbitration shall be held in accordance with the rules of said Association.

SECTION 52. *The Theatrical Production Arbitration Board.*

The Board shall consist of 24 permanent members. 8 shall be chosen by the Guild Council (to be known as the Author's Slate); 8 by a majority of signatory Producers (to be known as the Producer's Slate), said selections to be made within 30 days after 25 Producers have become signatories to the Producing Manager's Contract. Within 20 days thereafter, a majority of the 16 persons so chosen shall appoint any 8 additional persons as public members (to be known as the Public Slate), provided such persons have never been a member of the Guild or produced a play. All such persons shall serve for the duration of the term of this Contract and any extensions thereof.

SECTION 53. *Replacements.*

In the event of the death, resignation, illness, incapacity or unavailability of any member, a temporary or permanent successor shall be appointed: by the Council of the Guild, if the vacancy is in the Author's Slate; by a meeting of the signatory Producers, if it is in the Producer's Slate; by a majority of the members of the Author's and Producer's Slates, jointly, if it is in the Public Slate.

SECTION 54. *Rules.*

The Board, by a majority vote of all members, shall have full power to establish such rules and procedures as it may deem necessary not inconsistent herewith. In the absence of such rules, the procedure under this Article shall be in accordance with the commercial arbitration rules then obtaining of the American Arbitration Association, except as hereinbelow otherwise provided.

SECTION 55. *The Complaint.*

The party aggrieved, whether Author, Producer or Guild (hereinafter referred to as the "Complainant") shall file with the American Arbitration Association five copies of a written complaint setting forth the claim, dispute, difficulty, misunderstanding, charge or controversy to be arbitrated and the relief which the complainant requests. A copy of the complaint shall be mailed by the American Arbitration Association to the party complained against (hereinafter referred to as the "Respondent") and another to the Guild.

SECTION 56. *The Answer.*

The Respondent shall, within 8 days of the mailing to him of the complaint, file five copies of a written answer with the American Arbitration Association and the American Arbitration Association shall mail one copy to the Complainant and another to the Guild. Where the copy of the complaint is mailed to a Respondent at an address more than 500 miles from New York, he shall have 3 additional days to file his answer. If no written answer is filed within such period, the Respondent nevertheless will be deemed to have entered a general denial of the allegations of the complaint.

SECTION 57. *Participation by the Guild.*

The Guild may file a complaint and demand arbitration, with or without the Author's consent; and the Author, in such event, shall be a party to the arbitration, and shall not discontinue the arbitration without the consent of the Guild.

SECTION 58. *Selection of Arbitrators.*

(a) The Author, or the Guild, if it has initiated the arbitration, shall appoint one arbitrator from the Author's Slate and the Producer shall appoint one arbitrator from the Producer's Slate. These two arbitrators shall be appointed within 10 days from the date of the mailing of the complaint to the Respondent.

(b) If either the Author or the Producer fails to appoint an arbitrator within 10 days after the mailing of the complaint as aforesaid, then such appointment shall be made promptly from the Author's Slate by the Guild and from the Producer's Slate by the American Arbitration Association.

(c) Immediately after the appointment of the aforesaid 2 arbitrators, the third arbitrator shall be appointed within 5 days by the 2 arbitrators to be chosen from among the persons on the Public Slate. The American Arbitration Association shall appoint from members of its panels any arbitrator or arbitrators required where for any reason appointment has not been made from the slates herein provided for.

SECTION 59. *Power of Arbitrators.*

The arbitrators are empowered to award damages against any party to the controversy in such sums as they shall deem fair and reasonable under the circumstances, to require specific performance of a contract, to grant any other remedy or relief, injunctive or otherwise, which they deem just and equitable. The arbitrators are also empowered to render a partial award before making a final award and grant such relief, injunctive or otherwise, in such partial award as they deem just and equitable. The arbitrators shall determine and indicate in their written award by whom and in what proportion the cost of arbitration shall be borne.

SECTION 60. *Special Arbitration.*

If the Author or Producer demand an immediate arbitration upon a complaint by either alleging violation, in the case of Dramatic Productions of Paragraphs FIRST (e), or SIXTH (a) or (b), or in the case of Dramatico-Musical Productions of Paragraphs FIRST (e) or SIXTH (a), of the Production Contract, and five copies of the complaint are filed with the Guild at any time after 10 days before the date for which rehearsals have been scheduled, the arbitration procedure outlined in this Article shall be accelerated as follows:

(a) The arbitration hearing shall be held within 3 days after the filing of the complaint.

(b) The complaint shall be delivered or telegraphed to the Respondent by the American Arbitration Association. The Respondent must file five copies of his answer with the American Arbitration Association within 24 hours thereafter.

(c) The name of the arbitrator appointed by the Complainant shall be set forth in the complaint and the name of the arbitrator appointed by the Respondent shall be set forth in the answer. If either person so named shall be unavailable a substitute shall be forthwith named by the Author or Producer, as the case may be. The third arbitrator shall be appointed by the persons so selected within 24 hours after the receipt of the answer by the American Arbitration Association. The American Arbitration Association shall appoint from members of its panels any arbitrator or arbitrators required where for any reason appointment has not been made from the Slates herein provided for.

Article XIV

MISCELLANEOUS

SECTION 61. *Prior Disposition of Motion Picture Rights.*

Should an Author sell or lease the motion picture rights in a play or other literary property prior to the making of a contract for its production upon the speaking stage in the United States (except as provided in Section 23), then no contract shall be made for the production of said play upon the speaking stage in the United States until 1 year after such sale or lease of the motion picture rights.

SECTION 62. *Compromise.*

Should the Guild claim that the Producing Manager's Contract has been violated because of a breach of this Contract, it shall be no defense in any proceeding instituted by the Guild that a compromise has been made between the Producer and the Author, unless the Guild has been a party thereto.

SECTION 63. *Disciplining of Author.*

If, as the result of an arbitration wherein the Producer is complainant, an award is rendered against the Author, the Guild may discipline the Author in such manner as in its discretion it shall deem advisable.

SECTION 64. *Debt by Author.*

If the Author is indebted to the Guild or to a Producer, the Guild may file with the Negotiator a memorandum to that effect, and the Negotiator shall thereupon withhold from the Author's share the amount of such indebtedness and shall pay the same over to the Guild.

Article XV

AMENDMENTS AND NOTICES

SECTION 65. *Procedure for Amendments.*

The provisions of this Schedule relating to the Motion Picture Negotiator, the General Advisory Committee and the Theatrical Industry Arbitration Board may be amended at any time in any respects, including but not limited to the manner of the appointment of said Negotiator, Committee or Board, or members thereof or successors thereto, or their powers. Any amendment to become effective shall be approved by the Guild in the manner required by its Constitution and by a ⅔ vote of Producers signatory to valid and subsisting Producing Manager's Contracts in person or by proxy at a meeting specially called for said purpose on 10 days' notice, provided that at least 25 Producers shall have attended. Such amendment so adopted shall be binding upon the Guild and its members and upon all the Producers signatory to the Producing Manager's Contract, but shall be effective only as to transactions or controversies arising subsequent to the date of such approval.

SECTION 66. *Notices.*

Upon signing the Contract the Producer shall supply the Guild in writing with his address. Notices provided to be given him hereunder shall be sent to the address so furnished and a notice so mailed sent by registered mail shall be deemed due notice to the Producer. All notices provided in the Contract to be given to the Author shall be sent to him at the address stated in the Production Contract, by registered mail, with a copy to the Guild.

Appendix A
to
SCHEDULE OF THE ADDITIONAL PRODUCTION TERMS
Instructions to the Negotiator

Procedure to Be Followed in the Sale or Lease of Plays for Motion Picture Production

It is recognized that with regard to procedure to be followed in the disposition of the screen rights to plays, theatrical productions are divided into two groups, those completely or substantially financed by motion picture producers and those not so financed (herein referred to as "financed independently of the motion picture industry"). The distinction takes on significance where the disposition of motion picture rights is concerned. The significance lies in the fact that the producer who has motion picture backing (by reason of financial, employment or other contractual relations) occupies a dual position. He is both buyer and seller. As a result of this dual role, it is impossible for him, however strict and unexceptionable his conduct, to escape criticism. This duality does not exist, however, for the producer whose production is financed independently of the motion picture industry. You should bear this distinction in mind in carrying out your duties. It is suggested that you request every producer to make a voluntary disclosure to you of any relationship that he may have which conflicts with the basic relationship of being jointly interested with the author in the proceeds of motion picture monies.

I Plays Produced by Producers Independently of Motion Picture Backing

You will offer the producer full opportunity to satisfy you that he is certain of his own knowledge that neither all nor any substantial part of his financial backing is directly or indirectly derived from any motion picture producer. You will not, in this connection, be required to exact any onerous legal proof of the producer, but will rely on your own best judgment, remembering, however, that the burden of proof is on the producer. In the event of the producer's electing to take advantage of this opportunity and of his satisfying you that no substantial part of the financing of the play in question was derived from the motion picture industry, it is recognized that his interest in securing the highest price, or the best conditions of sale, or both, is identical with that of the author and that it is to the author's advantage to have the constant benefit of the producer's advice and experience throughout the negotiations of the screen rights to the play.

In the event of the producer's refusal or failure to satisfy you as above, you will decide all questions of his participation in negotiations according to your own best judgment. As provided in Article VI, Section 28 of the Schedule of

Additional Production Terms, you are not to be in any way liable for the exercise of discretion.

The producer having complied with the requirements of Article II, Section 2, of the Schedule of Additional Production Terms, you shall, upon request of either the author (or his agent) or the producer, call a conference between the author (or his agent), the producer and yourself to the end of fixing a price at which the play may be offered for sale to the motion pictures; and shall thereafter offer the play for such sale at the price established.

If at any time during the negotiations for the sale or lease of a play it is, in your opinion or in the opinion of either the author (or his agent) or the producer, advisable either to reduce or to raise the price at which the play is to be held for picture sale, you will again call for a conference for the establishment of a new price. At no time shall the holding price of any play be changed in either direction without affording the author and producer full opportunity to confer. Any offer received by you must be forthwith communicated to the author, or his agent, and the producer.

It is desirable that the sales price shall be mutually satisfactory to both author and producer. In the event the author decides to accept a definite offer which is unsatisfactory to the producer then, except in the event of the contingency provided for in the second succeeding paragraph, the following procedure shall be followed: You shall forthwith advise the producer by telegram of the price, method of payment and release date. This offer may be accepted by you unless the producer shall, within 24 hours (exclusive of Saturdays, Sundays and holidays) of the giving of the notice, advise you by telegram that the offer is rejected, giving his reasons therefor. If the producer rejects the offer he shall have a period not to exceed 5 days from the date of the notification from the producer above referred to in which to submit to you a definite offer (a) from a party of financial standing capable of making the payments set forth in the offer at the respective times therein provided for, (b) for a price in excess of that acceptable to the author and (c) on other terms at least as favorable to the author as those contained in the offer which the author is willing to accept. If within the prescribed period of time the producer brings in such offer, same shall be accepted. If within the prescribed period of time the producer fails to bring in such offer then the offer acceptable to the author shall be accepted. In the event the author and producer do not agree as to whether or not the offer brought in by the producer is (a) from a party of financial standing capable of making the payments set forth in the offer at the respective times therein provided for, (b) for a price in excess of that acceptable to the author and (c) on terms at least as favorable to the author as those contained in the offer which the author is willing to accept, then it is agreed as follows:

You shall have the right in your sole discretion (i) to determine said issue or (ii) to request the American Arbitration Association to appoint two persons who, together with you will constitute the arbitrators to determine said issue. If you by reason of your relationship with either author or producer or for any other reason whatsoever, occupy a position as a result of which you may not be able unbiasedly to determine said issue, then if requested by either author or producer or on your own volition you shall request the American Arbitration Association to appoint three persons who, without you, will constitute the arbitrators to determine said issue, which determination shall hereafter also be referred to as a determination under (ii) hereof. The determination by you under the contingency provided for in (i) or the determination of the majority of the three persons referred to in (ii) shall be binding and conclusive upon the author and the producer. In the event alternative (ii) is adopted, the arbitration shall take place on two days' notice, Sundays and holidays excluded, and the cost of said arbitration shall be borne by the author and producer in equal proportion. Except as hereinbefore provided for, the rules and regulations of the American Arbitration Association shall apply to any determination made under alternative (ii) but any determination made under (i) shall be made by you without any formal hearing. You shall have the right to make the decision under alternative (i) before provided for except in such situations where in your uncontrolled determination the question involved is a close one.

The exception referred to in the second preceding paragraph is as follows: In the event the producer is associated with or employed by a motion picture producer or has been financed wholly or in substantial part by a motion picture producer or an officer thereof, then you shall not be obligated to offer the producer any period in which to bring in a definite offer in excess of that acceptable to the author, but except as aforesaid, the provisions of the foregoing paragraph shall apply.

If at any time during the negotiations for the sale or even after the consummation of the sale you or the author find any reasonable grounds for doubting the veracity of the producer's statement of his financial backing, you or the author shall forthwith report said doubts to the Council of the Guild and either the author or the Guild may then demand an arbitration under the terms of the Minimum Basic Production Contract or the Producing Manager's Contract (as the case may be), to establish the fact of misrepresentation, if any.

II   Plays Financed by Motion Picture Producers in Whole or in Part

The phrase "motion picture backer" as hereinafter employed is construed as describing any motion picture producer or affiliate or officer or employee thereof, contributing, in whole or in part, to the financing of the production of the play to be sold. The phrase "motion picture backed producer" as hereinafter employed is construed as describing any producer whose production is financed in whole or in substantial part, through employment or other contractual relations, by a motion picture backer.

Such productions fall into three classifications, as follows:

(1) That in which the producer has in writing disclosed to the author, upon signing the original production contract, the fact that he is, or desires to be, motion picture financed;

(2) That in which the producer does not make such disclosure upon signing the production contract, but makes it before the date of the play's first rehearsal;

(3) That in which the producer has made no such disclosure at any time but is not, at the time of negotiations for the play's sale to motion pictures, able to satisfy the Negotiator of his complete independence of motion picture financing.

The object of such classification is to protect the interests of all three parties and to avoid the complications which result from motion picture financing of which the author is not aware.

III Procedure in Case Production Falls Under Above Classification (1)

It is desirable from all points of view that the producer whose production is to be financed by motion picture capital should in writing disclose to the author either the fact of such financing, or his desire or intention, to obtain such financing, prior to the signing of the original theatrical production contract. When such disclosure is made and the author signs the production contract, it shall be assumed that the author is satisfied with such financing and you will accord the motion picture backers the protection provided in the following procedure.

The producer having complied with the terms and conditions as listed in Article II of the Schedule of Additional Production Terms, you shall decide when, in your judgment, acting as the author's representative, a holding price at which the screen rights to the play are to be offered for sale or lease should be fixed and after full consultation with both producer and author you will arrange with the author to fix that price.

If the fixing of this price gives you any reason to suspect collusion between the motion picture producer and the author which might operate against the spirit and content of the Minimum Basic Production Contract, or the interest of the producer, or the author's best financial interest, you will forthwith report your suspicions to the Council of the Guild as a violation of the Minimum Basic Production Contract.

The price being fixed to your satisfaction, however, you will

(a) Immediately offer the rights at this price to the motion picture backer, with the stipulation that he shall have forty-eight (48) hours in which to accept or reject the price named.

(b) If at the end of said forty-eight (48) hours the motion picture backer, does not accept the play at the price named, then the play may be offered in the open market with the rejected price as a minimum, and no further opportunity will be given to, or bids received from the motion picture producer to meet or better any other bids from any other motion picture corporation in excess of the price rejected by him.

(c) If the play is not sold in the open market at the price named, or better, you and the author may by agreement reduce the holding price. If you do so, however, the procedure hereinbefore outlined may be repeated, and successively thereafter if found to be necessary.

If at any time following a rejection by the motion picture company, the author and Negotiator elect to demand of the motion picture company an offer as evidence of its interest in the property and the motion picture company does not submit any such offer within one week on the Negotiator's request to do so, then the play shall be considered free and clear of any obligation to the motion picture company which financed it and shall be offered in the open market and no further opportunity will be given to, or bids received from the motion picture backer to meet or better any other bids from any other motion picture producer in excess of the price rejected by him.

If the motion picture company does so manifest its interest by making an offer, this offer must be submitted as a fixed sum, or a fixed sum plus a percentage of receipts, together with a summary of the terms of the proposed contract which shall be acceptable to the Negotiator. The author shall by the terms of such offer have one week in which to accept or reject it. If the author rejects it, however, he may still use it as a minimum holding price at which to offer the property on the open market but no bid will be received from the motion picture backer in excess of such holding price. If, however, no offers are received in excess of this holding price, the author may, if he wishes, offer the play in the open market at a sum at or below the price set by the motion picture backer and rejected by the author. In this instance, however, the motion picture backer will be free to file offers with you in competition with any other motion picture company and no bid from such backer shall be received in such competition in excess of such minimum holding price. But if the author receives a bid from any other motion picture company at the same price as that offered by the backer, the backer's bid (if kept open) shall receive preference, provided that the other terms of the contract offered by the backer are as favorable as those offered by the other motion picture company.

In all cases of such motion picture financed productions, you will at all times keep the author fully informed of all facts relating to sale or lease, including (but not by way of limitation) offers received, steps in negotiation, execution of the contract and consummation of the sale, but you will not reveal any such facts to anyone other than the author, and the Guild; and you will particularly caution the author against disclosing any such information to the motion picture backed manager.

IV Procedure Under Classification (2)

When the producer has made no written disclosure of motion picture financing upon signing the production contract, but has made it between that date and the date of the first rehearsal of the play, then the author shall have the right to choose between instructing the Negotiator either to follow the above procedure or instructing him to proceed as in the ensuing paragraph.

V Procedure Under Classification (3)

Where the producer has not at any time in writing disclosed to the author the fact of any motion picture financing, or cannot, at the time of the negotiations for the play's sale or lease to pictures, satisfy the Negotiator of his independence of motion picture financing, or has received motion picture backing at some time after the date of the first rehearsal and prior to the offering for sale or lease, whether such backing is disclosed or not, then the Negotiator shall use his utmost efforts to secure a competitive open market for the picture rights to the play without any of the advantages to the motion picture backer as set forth in the above machinery. In such cases the author, of course, will be doubly cautioned against disclosing any offers to the producer.

MOTION PICTURE PRE-SALE/

LIVE THEATRICAL

FINANCING AGREEMENT

MEMORANDUM OF AGREEMENT made this 1st day of August 19____ by and among Financier/Distributor ("F/D"), Bookwriter, Composer, Lyricist, Producer A, and Producer B relating to the musical play tentatively entitled "_____" ("the Play"). Bookwriter, Composer and Lyricist are herein referred to as "the Authors" and Producer A and Producer B are herein referred to as "the Producers".

The Authors have written the book, music and lyrics of a musical play entitled "_____" ("the Play") and have granted to the Producers the right to produce and present the Play in the British Isles and, if such production shall take place, in the United States and Canada. The arrangements between the Authors and the Producers are set forth in Exhibit A annexed hereto.

The Producers intend to commence rehearsals of the production of the Play in the British Isles on August 21, 19____, but in no event later than October 15, 19____, and have contracted for the booking of the Play at the _____ Theatre in the West End of London.

The British production of the Play is to be directed by _____, who will also share in the proceeds derived from the exploitation of the subsidiary rights in the Play.

1. *Financing of the British Production.* The Producers represent and warrant that the estimated production requirements of the production of the Play in the British Isles are $____,000 plus an involuntary overcall of 20%. The Producers represent and warrant that they have obtained binding and valid commitments for subscriptions in the total amount of $____,000 (plus the involuntary overcall of 20%). F/D agrees to subscribe (or cause to be subscribed) the remaining amount of $____,000 (plus the involuntary overcall of 20%); and F/D hereby agrees to make payment (or cause payment to be made) of such subscription to the Producers upon the execution of this Agreement. F/D further agrees to make payment of the involuntary overcall (or cause to be made) promptly following demand by the Producers. F/D agrees to execute the investing agreement annexed hereto as Exhibit B and, subject to and as modified by this Agreement, the rights of F/D with respect to its investment in the British production shall be governed by the provisions of Exhibit B, but the Producers agree that they shall have the same fiduciary responsibilities to F/D, with respect to the investment made by F/D, as the Producers would have under the standard form of investing agreement for a Broadway Play. (F/D hereby acknowledges and agrees that the Producers have advanced certain moneys for the pre-production costs of the Play, and the Producers shall be entitled to be reimbursed for such advances out of the production funds supplied by F/D and the other investors in the British production. F/D further acknowledges and agrees that the Producers are to receive ____% of the gross box office receipts of the British production of the

Play to be divided ____% to each of the Producers and ____% to _____ Associates Limited, in consideration for certain production services to be supplied by that company. _____ Associates Limited is also to receive a fee of £____ per week, commencing eight weeks prior to the commencement of rehearsal and continuing until three weeks after the close of the British production.)

2. *British Show Album.* F/D shall have the exclusive right to record the show album of the British production of the Play and to distribute said show album worldwide. In consideration therefor F/D agrees to pay to the publisher of the music and lyrics of the Play a mechanical royalty to be negotiated between F/D and said publisher, and in addition agrees to pay a royalty of ____% of 90% (with the customary exceptions) of the retail selling price of said album to the Authors, to be accounted for by the Authors as provided in paragraph VI of Exhibit A annexed hereto. Any artists' royalties measured by the selling price of the album shall be deducted from said royalty, and the recording costs shall be charged against said royalty.

3. *Publication of the Music and Lyrics.* F/D acknowledges that Composer and Lyricist (the authors of the music and lyrics of the Play) have a binding agreement with Music Publishing Co., Inc. for the publication of the music and lyrics. F/D, Composer, Lyricist and Music Pub. have heretofore negotiated an arrangement for the participation by F/D in the proceeds from said publication rights pursuant to a separate memorandum from F/D to Composer, Lyricist, and Music Pub.

4. *U.S. and Canadian Production.* As provided in paragraph 8(a) of Exhibit X annexed hereto, the Producers have the right to produce and present the Play in New York at any time within one year following the last performance of the Play in the West End of London (subject to the conditions set forth in Exhibit X). If the Producers shall elect to exercise such right, then they shall so notify F/D and F/D shall have the right, at its option, to invest all or any part of the production financing of such production on terms which shall be in accordance with the usual provisions for investment in musical productions in the United States and Canada. (In this connection, the Producers agree that the British production of the Play shall be entitled to receive ____% of the gross box office receipts of the Play in the United States and Canada and ____% of the net profits of the Play in the United States and Canada.)

5. *U.S. Show Album.* If the Producers shall elect to produce the Play in the United States (and regardless of any investment by F/D pursuant to paragraph 4 above) then the Producers shall in the first instance negotiate in good faith with F/D for an arrangement whereby F/D shall have the right to record and distribute the show album of the production of the Play in the United States. In such negotiations, the Producers shall have the right to

request an investment by F/D in the production of the Play in the United States. If such negotiations shall not result in a binding contract, then F/D shall, nevertheless, have a right of first refusal on the show album rights of the American production on the terms offered to any other person and acceptable to such person.

6. *Grant of Motion Picture Rights.* The Authors hereby grant, assign and transfer to F/D all motion picture and allied television rights in and to the Play. The Producers hereby confirm and ratify such grant. On a date which shall be one year from the close of the production of the Play in the West End of London, or 90 days following the opening of such Play in New York, whichever first occur, F/D shall notify the Authors and the Producers if it intends to produce a motion picture based upon the Play ("the Picture"). If it shall elect to do so, then F/D shall pay, upon the date of such notification, the sum of $____,000. If it shall elect not to produce the Picture, then all motion picture and allied television rights hereby granted, assigned and transferred to F/D shall terminate and revert to the Authors.

If F/D shall elect to produce the Picture pursuant to the foregoing, then, in order to retain the motion picture and allied television rights, F/D shall thereafter pay to the Authors the sum of $____,000 on each anniversary date following the first payment of $____,000 until the commencement of principal photography of the Picture (and failure to make any such annual payment shall result in the termination and reversion of the motion picture and allied television rights); *provided, however,* that if principal photography of the Picture shall not have been commenced by F/D within five years from the opening of the Play in the West End of London, then the motion picture and allied television rights hereby granted, assigned and transferred to F/D shall terminate and revert to the Authors.

7. *Release Date of the Picture.* If F/D shall produce the Picture, then the Picture shall not be released until

(a) five years from the opening of the Play in the West End of London; or

(b) three and one-half years from the opening of the Play in the United States or Canada;

whichever date shall first occur *provided, however,* as follows: if all first-class companies of the Play shall have permanently closed in the British Isles and the United States and Canada, then the permissible release date shall be deemed the date of such permanent closing; and, if the production of the Play in the United States or Canada shall not commence within one year following the close of the Play in the West End of London, then F/D shall have the right to release the Picture upon such date; and if during the production of the Play in the United States and Canada there shall be, with respect to the original company of the Play, any 20 weeks of performances out of any 30 consecutive weeks during which the Play shall run at less than 60% of the capacity of the theatre or theatres in which such company is running, then the three and one-half year period referred to in subparagraph (b) above shall be deemed to be two and one-half years.

8. *Compensation for Motion Picture Rights.* If F/D shall produce the Picture, then F/D shall pay to the Authors (to be divided as set forth in Exhibit A and subject to the conditions provided in Exhibit A) ____% of the distributors' net profits of the Picture throughout the world and ____% of the distributors' net profits from all remakes and sequel motion pictures less any payments made by F/D pursuant to paragraph 6 above. Such payments shall be made quarterly for the first two years following the release of the Picture and of each such remake and sequel, semi-annually for the third year, and annually thereafter. The definition of distributors' gross receipts shall be the normal definition included in production-distribution agreements negotiated by F/D. The Authors of the Play and their representatives shall have the normal right of access to the books and records of F/D relating to distributors' gross receipts for auditing purposes.

9. *Engagement of Producer A and Producer B as Producers of the Picture.* If F/D shall produce the first Picture hereunder, then it shall engage Producer A and Producer B (or any companies ("their Companies") supplying their respective services) as the producers of the Picture. The compensation payable to Producer A and Producer B (or their Companies) (to be divided equally between them or their Companies) shall be $____,000 (payable one-quarter six weeks prior to commencement of principal photography of the Picture, one-quarter upon the commencement of the principal photography of the Picture, one-quarter upon the conclusion of the principal photography of the Picture, and one-quarter upon the delivery of the Picture), plus $____,000 payable out of the first net profits, if any, of the Picture *pari passu* with any other deferments, plus an amount equal to ____% of the net profits, if any, of the Picture; *provided, however,* that there shall be first charged against the ____% share of net profits payable to Producer A and Producer B (or their Companies) all compensation payable to the Authors pursuant to paragraph 8 above and any other share of gross receipts or net profits payable to any other persons providing materials, services or rights to the production of the Picture, it being understood that all shares of gross receipts paid prior to reaching net profits are deemed part of negative cost and are recoupable as part of negative cost without bearing interest, and that such shares of gross receipts recouped as negative cost shall not subsequently be charged against net profits payable to A and B; but, *provided further however,* that the share of net profits payable to A and B (or their Companies) shall in no event be reduced to an amount

which shall be less than _____% of 100% of the net profits of the Picture. The term "net profits" shall have the meaning set forth in the Exhibit A.

A and B agree to make themselves available upon reasonable notice by F/D to perform such production services and in the event that either of them shall be unavailable to perform such services then F/D shall not be obligated to engage such person, but the compensation of the other producer shall not be reduced thereby.

10. *Engagement of Composer and Lyricist to Write Additional Music and Lyrics for the Picture.* If F/D shall elect to produce the Picture as above provided, then F/D shall have the right, but not the obligation, to request C and L to write additional songs to be used in the Picture provided that all additional songs shall first be offered to C and L for composition. F/D agrees to pay to C and L the sum of $_____,000 as the composition fee for each such song so commissioned. The publication rights of such music and lyrics shall be granted to Music Pub. subject to the agreement referred to in paragraph 3 above. If C and L shall elect not to compose and deliver said songs or shall fail to deliver such songs, then F/D shall be free to commission songs from another composer or composers and to interpolate said songs in the Picture on condition that publication rights to all additional songs composed by another composer shall belong to F/D as set forth in the separate memorandum specified in Paragraph 3 above. If C and L shall deliver such songs, as requested by F/D, then no music or lyrics shall be interpolated in the Picture other than the music and lyrics written by C and L, the music contained in the play, or public domain music, or incidental music identified with the period of the play. If F/D wishes to employ a composer to write bridge, gap and/or tag music for the Picture, F/D shall give Composer the first opportunity to write such music and shall have the right to employ another composer to write such music only if F/D and C are unable to agree after good faith negotiations upon the terms upon which C will write such music, provided that F/D shall not offer to such other composer terms more favorable than the last terms offered to C to write such music.

11. *Play Director as Director of the Picture.* F/D acknowledges the provisions of paragraph 23(a) of Exhibit X, and F/D agrees to negotiate in good faith with _____ for his services as director of the Picture, but if after such good faith negotiations F/D and _____ are unable to agree upon the terms upon which _____ will perform his services as director of the Picture, F/D shall be free to employ any other person as director of the Picture.

12. *Formal Agreement.* This Memorandum of Agreement sets forth only the main provisions of the arrangements among the parties hereto and, accordingly, it is agreed that a formal agreement incorporating these and other normal reasonable terms shall be prepared and executed by the parties hereto. If the

parties cannot agree on the provisions of such formal agreement, then this Memorandum of Agreement shall be binding on the parties hereto and any ambiguity or omission shall be resolved by arbitration in New York, New York pursuant to the rules of the American Arbitration Association with a sole arbitrator who shall be experienced in the theatrical and motion picture business. The arbitrator in such proceeding shall have the right and authority to resolve any ambiguity or impose any terms which have been inadvertently omitted in this Memorandum of Agreement by reference to the normal and usual terms of the theatrical and motion picture business, and such determination shall be final and binding upon the parties.

Financier/Distributor

By_____

_____
Composer

_____
Lyricist

_____
Bookwriter

_____
(for himself and _____ Productions, Inc.)
Producer A

_____
(for himself and _____ Films Ltd. and _____ Films Productions Limited)
Producer B

EXHIBIT "A"

This Exhibit is attached to and made part of the agreement dated _____, between _____ _____ and F/D, relating to Picture now entitled _____.

TABLE OF CONTENTS

I. *APPLICATION OF GROSS RECEIPTS*

Gross Receipts shall be applied to the following categories on a continuing basis and in the herein listed order of priority:

A. *Fees*

F/D distribution fees per Paragraph III.

B. *Expenses*

F/D distribution costs per Paragraph IV.

C. *Other Participations*

Amounts F/D may be contractually obligated to pay (whether as a deferment [other than those specified in E below], a gross receipts participation, or otherwise, but excluding any sums payable by way of net profit participations which come out of the Participant's share of net profits as may be provided in this agreement) to any person including Participant, and excluding any share of net profits payable to Participant or F/D hereunder, for rights or services in connection with Picture, based or dependent on all or any part of percentage of the gross receipts (whether or not such gross receipts are defined or computed in the same manner as set forth herein) and which are not included in the computation of negative cost, are called participations. In computing share of Participant hereunder, a participation shall be deductible hereunder (notwithstanding the order of priority in this Paragraph I) if, when and to the extent that F/D obligation to pay it accrues, whether or not such payment has then become due or been made and regardless of whether F/D has recovered its negative cost.

D. *Negative Cost*

Negative cost of Picture per Paragraph V., provided that amount deemed interest herein shall be recoupable before negative cost.

E. *Deferments*

All amounts payable pursuant to a contract approved in writing by F/D to any person entitled to same out of first net profits or immediately prior to there being such net profits, provided such amounts shall not be a percentage of net profits, unless there is a different order of payment specified under this agreement.

F. *Net Profits*

Net profits are the gross receipts, if any, remaining after deduction of items specified in Paragraph A through E inclusive.

II. *GROSS RECEIPTS*

A. *Sources*

For accounting purposes, Gross Receipts means all receipts received by F/D on behalf of the Picture as:

(1) F/D Film Rental

(2) Film rental from Subdistributors.

(3) Receipts from Flat Sale(s).

(4) Receipts (less all costs) from copyright infringers or similar causes of action.

(5) Receipts from theatre box office operated by F/D (such as in four-wall or road show exhibitions) to extent receipts from all such engagements taken as a whole exceed costs incurred for all such engagements. If such costs exceed such receipts, the excess cost shall be deductible as a distribution cost.

(6) Subsidies or prizes provided that if use of such amounts is a condition to receipt thereof, such amount is not included until actually used.

(7) Music royalties computed in accordance with Schedule A attached hereto.

(8) Royalties from audio visual cassettes, discs and similar devices, computed in accordance with Schedule B attached hereto.

(9) Receipts from merchandising (including sale or license of souvenir programs and booklets), and receipts (less all costs) from exercise of book publication rights.

If the costs relating to II.A (4), (5) and (9) above, and applicable distribution fees, if any, exceed receipts from II.A (4), (5) or (9) above, such costs shall be deductible as a distribution cost.

B. *Gross Receipts Exclusions*

The following are excluded from Gross Receipts:

(1) Box office receipts of any theatre or other exhibitor (except as specified in Paragraph II.A(5) hereof); and receipts of: broadcasters and other transmitters including, but not limited to, radio and television (TV), i.e. both "free" and "pay"; book or music publishers; wholesale or retail distributors, licensors or sellers of audio visual cassettes, video discs or any similar devices hereafter devised; record or tape producers, distributors or stores; and merchandisers or any other similar user; whether or not any or all of such foregoing entities are owned, operated or controlled by F/D.

(2) Amounts collected as taxes or for payment of taxes such as admission, sales, use or value added taxes.

(3) Film rental contributed to charitable organizations.

(4) Receipts from remakes, sequels, TV series or other derivative uses of Picture other than as specified in Paragraph II.A hereof.

(5) Salvage value or receipts derived from print stocks, stock footage, stills, props, sets, wardrobe, or other items included in negative cost. Notwithstanding the foregoing, any sums received from the sale of stock footage or the sale of cars purchased specifically in connection with the Picture and sold after completion of photography shall be included in the Gross Receipts of the Picture without a distribution fee.

III. *DISTRIBUTION FEES*

F/D shall retain for its own account as its distribution fee for the Picture the following percentages of Gross Receipts:

A. *Theatrical Gross Receipts*
30% U.S. and Canada
35% U.K.
40% Foreign
15% Flat Sales

B. *Non-Theatrical Gross Receipts*
50% Worldwide

C. *Free TV*
25% U.S. Network (a network is defined as ABC, CBS or NBC.)
35% U.S. Syndication and Canada
40% Foreign

D. *Merchandising*
50% inclusive of subdistributors fees, plus out of pocket costs (including royalties to third parties).

E. *Book Publication Rights*
15% plus royalties to third parties.

F. *All Other Receipts*
The theatrical fee for the Territory shall be applicable except no such fee shall be applied against infringement recoveries, subsidies or music royalties included in Gross Receipts.

G. *Fee Computation*
Gross Receipts for purpose of computing F/D distribution fee excludes all items specified in Paragraph II.A (4), (6) and (7) hereof.

IV. *DISTRIBUTION COSTS*

F/D shall deduct and retain the costs of distribution for its own account from Gross Receipts, which costs shall be the aggregate of following costs, expenses, and charges (costs) paid or incurred by F/D or a subdistributor thereof for:

A. *Ad and Publicity Costs*

Advertising, promoting, exploiting and publicizing (collectively "ad" or "advertising"), including cost of ad space, time, physical material used for production of or broadcasting ads and commercials, shipping, integrating and monitoring of ads and commercials, preparation and distribution of ad and promotional material, salaries, fees, and travel and business expenses of F/D advertising and marketing executives in connection with the Picture, personalities connected to Picture, and publicists, press representatives and field exploitation persons appropriately allocated to the Picture, and regardless if incurred by or paid to F/D employees or other persons, previews, screenings, premieres, entertainment of press and personalities, research and tests of ad concepts and effectiveness, press books and kits, trailers, stills and other accessories and publicity releases, advertising allowances to theatres or other exhibitors regardless of how effected, other advertising and publicity costs whether directed to the consumer or the exhibitor, institutional costs, and an amount equal to 10% of all such costs under this Paragraph A.

There shall be included in such 10% overhead the salaries of any executive officer or employee of F/D, except that salaries of regular employees of F/D rendering services in connection with field exploitation and salaries and fees of special publicists and advertising personnel shall not be included.

Any rebates, refunds, discounts or other sums paid back to F/D in connection with such advertising costs shall be credited back to advertising expenses.

B. *Conversion*

Costs, discounts and expenses incurred in obtaining remittances of receipts to the U.S., including costs of contesting imposition of restricted funds.

C. *Checking*

Checking theatre attendance and receipts, and investigating unauthorized usage of Picture, whether payable to or incurred by F/D employees or other persons.

D. *Claims*

Claims and litigation (such as infringement, unfair competition, anti-trust, privacy and defamation) arising out of distribution of Picture, including attorney and auditor fees.

E. *Collections*

Costs incurred in connection with collection of Gross Receipts including attorney and auditor fees and costs, and liability incurred by F/D in connection therewith.

F. *Copyright and Royalties*

Copyright, trademark and patent costs in connection with Picture and protection thereof. Royalties payable to manufacturers of sound recording and reproduction equipment, to extent not included in negative cost.

G. *Other Versions*

To make, deliver, and use foreign, video cassettes, video discs, or any other media versions of Picture, or titles thereof, or to make changes required by censorship and rating considerations, to the extent not included in negative cost.

H. *Residuals*

Residuals are costs incurred and payments required under applicable collective bargaining agreements by reason of or as a condition to use or exhibition of Picture in television or any other media. To extent such payments are made to or on behalf of Participant and Participant is thereafter entitled to net profits, such payments shall be deemed a credit against such net profits to extent not prohibited by the applicable collective bargaining agreement. Any payments made to Participant hereunder prior to payment of residuals are deemed a credit against such residuals to extent not prohibited by applicable collective bargaining agreement. In neither event may credit, when applicable, be deducted a second time against Participant.

I. *Insurance*

Insurance coverage for any risk of loss with respect to the Picture.

J. *Trade Dues*

Allocable portion of dues, assessments, including legal fees and costs and contributions to MPAA or similarly constituted or substitute organizations throughout the world (including legal fees to counsel respecting anti-trust matters and matters formerly handled by AMPTP prior to F/D's withdrawal therefrom).

K. *Licenses*

All licenses, duties, fees or any other amounts required to permit use of Picture.

L. *Prints*

Prints and video cassettes or video discs of Picture including lab, labor, service and materials, titles, discs, dubbing, subtitling, gauge reductions, inspection, repair, shipping, storage, delivery and insurance thereon.

M. *Taxes*

Taxes and governmental fees of any nature and however characterized including costs of contesting, interest and penalties thereon (other than F/D or subdistributor corporate income taxes), imposed directly or indirectly on the Picture or any part thereof or on the Gross Receipts or the license, distribution or exhibition of Picture, or collection, conversion, or remittance of monies connected therewith.

N. *Transportation*

Transportation, shipping, reels and containers and related charges.

O. *General*

All other costs customarily incurred by F/D in connection with the distribution and exploitation of motion pictures or customarily treated as cost of distribution, and which are not included in cost of production of the Picture.

V. *NEGATIVE COST ITEMS*

A. *Cost of Production*

(1) The Cost of Production (or negative cost) is the aggregate of all costs, charges, claims and expenses paid or incurred in connection with the development, production and delivery of the Picture and its trailer, including payments required to be made at a later date following production of Picture, determined in the customary manner F/D accounts for production costs at time Picture is produced. F/D Studio facilities shall be used to the extent they reasonably meet production requirements, and all charges in connection therewith shall be included in cost of production in accordance with the then-current F/D facilities charge schedule. Insurance recoveries related to items in negative cost shall be credited to cost of production.

(2) Participations in Gross Receipts shall be deemed included in cost of production regardless of whether obligation is fixed or dependent upon Gross Receipts provided that participations in Gross Receipts shall be included in cost of production only to extent F/D obligation to pay said participation accrues before any net profits pursuant hereto have been derived.

(3) There shall be no double deductions; i.e., any item in cost of production cannot again be charged as a distribution cost and vice versa.

B. *Overhead*

Overhead of 15% of the aggregate of amounts determined pursuant to A(1) & (2). F/D overhead charge shall accrue and be included in the cost of production concurrently with the incurring of the respective items of direct cost of the Picture.

C. *Interest*

(1) Interest on aggregate of amounts determined pursuant to Paragraphs V.A. and B. shall be deemed to be at an annual rate equal to 125% of U.S. prime rate of Chemical Bank of New York, as the same may vary from time to time, such interest commencing from respective dates on which amounts chargeable to cost of production are incurred or paid and continuing until the mid-point of an accounting period with respect to which said amounts are recouped as herein provided.

(2) If any principal photography of the Picture shall occur outside of the U.S., then in lieu of the rate specified above, the rate of interest with respect to funds expended in any country outside the U.S. shall be at an annual rate equal to 125% of the prime rate, or equivalent thereof, charged by the principal bank in the applicable country, as the same may vary from time to time.

D. *Overbudget*

An additional amount by which the cost of production exceeds the approved Picture budget by the lower of __,000 or 10% of the budget shall be deemed included in cost of production, but such excess overbudget amount shall not itself bear interest. Excess costs incurred due to force majeure, written direction from F/D, and retroactive increases to scale personnel under collective bargaining agreements are excluded from overbudget computation.

VI. *ACCOUNTING*

A. *General*

F/D shall render statements to Participant showing in summary form the appropriate calculations relating to treatment of Gross Receipts. Such statements may be on billing or collection basis as F/D may elect from time to time. Whenever Gross Receipts are derived or costs incurred in connection with transactions involving the Picture and other motion pictures, F/D shall allocate same based on its reasonable opinion and with respect to trailers and shorts utilized with the Picture outside of the U.S. and Canada, 3% of such receipts for trailers and 5% thereof for shorts shall be conclusively deemed reasonable with respect thereto.

B. *Books*

F/D shall keep books of account at its NY office with respect to the distribution of the Picture. Said books, to the extent they have not become incontestable or have not been previously examined, may be examined at Participant's expense once in each 12-month period (the first of which commences upon issuance of first statement hereunder) by a national firm of reputable CPA's, the selection of which is subject to F/D approval, not to be unreasonably withheld. No such examination may continue beyond a period of 30 days after commencement thereof. A copy of the report of such examination shall be delivered to F/D at such time it is made available to Participant.

C. *Withholdings*

All amounts payable to Participant under this Agreement shall be subject to all laws and regulations now or hereafter in existence requiring the reporting, deduction or withholding of payments for income or other taxes payable by or assessable against Participant. F/D shall have the right to make such deductions and withholdings, and the payment or reporting thereof to the governmental agency concerned in accordance with F/D's good-faith determination of such laws and regulations shall constitute payment hereunder to Participant, and F/D shall not be liable to Participant for the making of such reports, deductions and/or withholdings or the payment thereof to the governmental agency concerned. In any such event, Participant shall make and prosecute any and all claims which it may have (and which it desires to make and prosecute) with respect to the same directly with the governmental agency having jurisdiction thereof.

D. *Statements*

F/D shall give Participant quarterly statements relating to the distribution of the Picture for the first two years after date established by F/D and reflected in its records in its usual fashion as the date of first general release of Picture in the U.S. Such statements shall be for the applicable accounting period and be given within 60 days thereafter and accompanied with payment of amount, if any, shown due Participant. After expiration of such period, statement shall be given semi-annually for next two years and then annually (if any compensation is payable to Participant) hereunder or if none due, then on Participant's written request, provided such request is not effective unless made at least 1 year after the last such request or statement. Such semi-annual and annual statements shall be given within 120 days after the applicable accounting period and accompanied with payment of amount, if any, shown due Participant.

If the Picture is generally re-issued in U.S. theatrically, then F/D shall resume quarterly statements for one year from the date of such re-issue and if the Picture is exhibited, i.e. broadcast on prime time network television in the U.S., F/D shall account for such network television broadcast by issuing a quarterly statement within 60 days after the applicable quarterly accounting period accompanied by payment, if any, shown due Participant.

E. *Incontestability*

Statements shall be subject to correction or amendment at any time. F/D shall keep the books of account referred to in Paragraph B above for at least 24 months after the last transaction reflected in a statement for the first time. Each statement shall be deemed conclusively correct and binding on Participant as to the transactions reflected therein for the first time on the expiration of a period of 24 months after the date sent. The inclusion of any item from a prior statement on a subsequent statement shall not render such prior-appearing item contestable or recommence the running of the applicable 24-month period with respect thereto. If Participant serves written notice on F/D within the applicable 24-month period, objecting in specific detail to particular items and stating the nature of the objection, then insofar as such specified items are concerned, statements shall not be deemed conclusively correct and binding.

F. *Address*

All statements shall be deemed sent when mailed to Participant at then current address for notices hereunder.

G. *Reserves*

F/D shall have right to establish appropriate reserves and adjust same from time to time for any distribution costs, uncollected accounts or other items which F/D reasonably anticipates will be deductible from Gross Receipts hereunder. F/D agrees to liquidate any reserves hereunder within a reasonable period of time.

H. *Tax Credits*

F/D and/or its subsidiaries and subdistributors, and/or _____ shall have sole right to take the full amount of whatever credits (including without limitation investment tax credits), deductions or other benefits that may be available to them throughout the world, with respect to taxes and excises payable with respect to the Picture or any activity related thereto, without any accounting, credit or payment obligation to Participant.

I. *Creditor-Debtor*

There is a Creditor-Debtor relationship between F/D and Participant with respect to payment of amounts due Participant hereunder and nothing contained herein shall be construed to create an agency, trust or fiduciary obligation with respect to such amounts or to prevent F/D from commingling any such amounts with any other funds or give Participant a lien on the Picture and Participant waives any right to claim to the contrary. F/D obligation to pay Participant hereunder shall not bear interest nor entitle Participant to gains which may accrue to such funds prior to payment to Participant.

VII. *MISCELLANEOUS*

A. *No Representation*

F/D has no obligation to distribute Picture and if it does so, Participant acknowledges that F/D has not made any representations with respect to the amount of Gross Receipts, deferments, or net profits, if any, which will or may be derived from distribution of the Picture.

F/D, however, agrees to use its best efforts to distribute the Picture in all territories throughout the world as soon as reasonably practicable consistent with sound business policies and practices and subject to F/D's policies regarding release of motion pictures and subject to the requirements of censorship boards or other constituted authorities or bodies and contingencies beyond F/D's control which may restrict, prohibit or postpone release or distribution of the Picture.

B. *Control of Distribution and Marketing*

(1) As between F/D and Participant, F/D shall have exclusive and perpetual control of the distribution, marketing, advertising, publicizing, exploitation, sale, or other disposition of the Picture and may distribute, or withhold or withdraw the Picture from distribution at its sole discretion with respect to one or more countries or media. F/D may distribute the Picture with other pictures whether or not F/D has any ownership interest or participation in such other pictures.

(2) F/D owns all rights to the Picture and the copyrights thereof and its Gross Receipts and net profits including the right to hypothecate them and Participant shall have no right, title, or interest therein except nothing specified in this Paragraph B(2) shall release F/D from making payments to Participant to extent required hereunder.

(3) F/D can make percentage or flat sales and grant others rights to distribute the Picture on terms determined by F/D, and may make and cancel contracts, adjust and settle disputes, and give allowances and rebates to distributors, licensees, exhibitors or other persons whether or not any such entity is owned, operated, or controlled by F/D.

(4) F/D shall have complete discretion in determining extent, if any, to which it will audit or check payments to F/D or press claims for amounts which, if collected, would become Gross Receipts.

C. *Sale of All Rights*

(1) If F/D sells all its right, title and interest in Picture (other than through merger or consolidation), Participant may elect that:

(a) The net sum received by F/D shall constitute Gross Receipts hereunder but further income of purchaser would not be included in Gross Receipts, or,

(b) the sum received by F/D shall not be included in Gross Receipts and all receipts and expenses (other than purchase price paid F/D) of the purchaser relating to the Picture shall be treated for purposes of accounting to Participant, as though they were receipts and expenses of F/D, provided that upon assumption by purchaser of such obligation, the sale shall be deemed a novation and F/D shall thereafter have no obligation of any kind to Participant, provided, however, that F/D is not relieved for a period of two years after the sale hereunder unless such sale is made to a major U.S. distributor or the sale is made after three years from the U.S. initial release of the Picture.

(2) Such election shall be made within 7 days after F/D notifies Participant in writing that it proposes to make such sale and identifies the purchaser and purchase price. Participant shall be deemed to have elected alternative (a) above, unless F/D receives written notice of Participant's election of alternative (b) above within 7 days after issuance of F/D notice. If a price change subsequently occurs and it is substantial and adversely affects the elected alternative, the above procedure is to be repeated.

D. *Assignment by Participant*

Participant may assign Participant's right to receive percentage compensation hereunder, at any time after the release of the Picture. However, F/D shall only be obligated to honor one such assignment, and then only if it is an assignment of all (as distinguished from part) of Participant's right to receive such percentage compensation thereafter. Nothing herein contained shall be deemed to preclude Participant from making a partial assignment or to preclude the first assignee (of all of Participant's said right) from making a subsequent complete or partial assignment; however, F/D shall not be obligated to pay in accordance with any such partial or subsequent assignment unless a single person is designated as a disbursing agent, to whom F/D may make all such payments thereafter, regardless of any further assignment(s). F/D's obligation to pay in accordance with any such assignment, or designation of a disbursing agent, shall be further conditioned on F/D's receipt of written notice thereof, in form satisfactory to F/D. F/D's payment in accordance with any such assignment or designation shall be deemed to be the equivalent of payment to Participant hereunder. Participant's rights to examine F/D's books of account shall not be assignable without F/D's prior written consent. F/D shall have first refusal with respect to any proposed assignment of Participant's right to receive percentage compensation hereunder and Participant shall notify F/D of terms of any such proposed assignment and F/D shall have 7 days within which to elect to accept such terms. Participant shall make no change in said terms adverse to his own interest without giving F/D the opportunity to accept such other terms. The preceding two sentences shall not apply to family gifts or transfers by operation of law.

E. *Third Party Beneficiary*

Nothing herein contained shall be deemed to create a third party beneficiary agreement.

F. *Headings*

Headings are for convenience only and are of no effect in construing contents of this Agreement.

VIII. *DEFINITIONS*

A. *Applicable Distribution Fees*

The following applies for purposes of determining distribution fees under Paragraph III. A, B, C and E hereof:

(1) *Theatrical*
Theatrical is exhibition in theatres, airlines, other transportation media, armed forces, V.A., Red Cross and similar institutional use, pay, cable and subscription television, audio visual cassettes and similar devices, for transmission of audio and visual image whether now known or hereafter devised.

(2) *Non-Theatrical*
Non-theatrical exhibition means exhibition in 16mm, 35mm gauge or lower in or by schools, hospitals, college campuses, prisons, individuals, oil companies, public libraries, railroads, private institutions, social clubs, churches, and similar usages excluding theatrical exhibitions.

(3) *Free TV*

(4) *Flat Sale*
"Flat Sale" is a license by F/D to any person for exhibition in theatres of the Picture for a period in excess of one year for a territory or area in consideration of the payment of a specified amount not fixed by a percentage of receipts of such person and without any obligation of such person to account for or report to F/D the amount of any proceeds or expenses of such distribution or licensing.

B. *Conversion*

The conversion of foreign currency into U.S. dollars shall be made at average weighted rate of exchange utilized by F/D for all pictures for which remittances have been received by F/D in the U.S. during the applicable accounting period.

C. *Film Rental*

Film Rental is amounts received by F/D for license or privilege to exhibit Picture in any and all media and manner including theatrical, free TV, non-theatrical exhibitions, cable or pay TV, cassette or other audio-visual device and any other manner or means or media, whether now known or hereafter devised, but excluding amounts received from flat sales, advance payments or security deposits (unless earned by exhibition or broadcast or forfeited), and refunds, rebates, or adjustments granted other persons by F/D.

D. *Gross Receipts*

Amounts are not deemed Gross Receipts or received unless paid in U.S. dollars in the U.S. or payable in a foreign currency which is not restricted and could be remitted in U.S. dollars to the U.S., if F/D, in the exercise of reasonable discretion could do so, it being agreed that if restricted funds are used by F/D in the foreign territory involved, such sums shall be credited to the Gross Receipts of the Picture. Gross Receipts from armed forces exhibitions shall be subject to the applicable distribution fees in Paragraph III.A hereof with respect to the territories where such exhibitions shall occur. Gross Receipts from airlines and other transportation media exhibitions shall be subject to the applicable distribution fees in Paragraph III.A hereof with respect to the territories where the agreements relating to such exhibitions are entered into.

E. *Here*

Here as prefix in words such as hereof and hereunder refers to this Exhibit "A".

F. *Includes*

Includes (and equivalents included or including) and such as, are illustrative and not limitative.

G. *Or*

Or is not only disjunctive but also conjunctive.

H. *Participant*

Person who has entered into this agreement with F/D.

I. *Person*

Any corporation, partnership, or other business entity or natural person.

J. *F/D*

F/D means _____ Corporation, a Delaware corporation, its divisions and owned or controlled subsidiaries engaged in the business of distributing motion pictures for exhibition in theatres and for broadcasting over television stations but shall not include: any person distributing the Picture for purposes other than exhibition in theatres or by television stations; exhibitors or others who may actually exhibit the Picture to the public; radio or television broadcasters; cable operators; wholesale distributors or retailers of video discs, video cassettes or similar devices; book or music publishers; phonograph record producers or distributors; merchandisers, etc. whether or not any of the foregoing are subsidiaries or affiliates of F/D.

K. *Restricted Funds*

(1) Amounts which would otherwise be included in Gross Receipts but which are not because they are payable in foreign currency and not received pursuant hereto are restricted. Such restricted amounts shall not be deemed Gross Receipts hereunder nor accounted for hereunder unless and until they have been received by F/D in U.S. dollars in the U.S. or unless used by F/D in the foreign territory involved.

(2) As and when percentage compensation becomes payable to Participant under this agreement, Participant may notify F/D in writing that Participant elects to require settlement of Participant's share of restricted funds remaining in any foreign country in the currency of such country. Such notice shall also include a designation of a bank or other representative in such country to whom payment may be made for Participant's account. Such payment shall be made to such representative as and when Participant has obtained any required permission. Such payment shall be made at Participant's expense and shall, to the extent thereof, be deemed the equivalent of the inclusion in Gross Receipts of the restricted funds of which such payment represents Participant's share, and shall satisfy F/D's obligations to Participant with respect to such restricted funds and Participant's share thereof.

(3) On Participant's written request, F/D shall report to Participant the amount of restricted funds (if any) which under this Paragraph have not yet been included in Gross Receipts as of the closing date of the most recent statement which has then been furnished to Participant under Paragraph VI.D hereof.

L. *Subdistributor*

A Subdistributor is a person licensed by F/D for the purpose of distributing the Picture for exhibition in theatres and for broadcasting over television stations in a specific area other than U.S. and Canada Territory, with an obligation to report Gross Receipts and expenses to F/D regardless of whether based on percentage or fixed basis. Subject to provisions relating to restricted currency of Paragraph K, all such receipts and expenses shall be treated as though receipts and expenses of F/D and the licensing or other arrangement between F/D and each such subdistributor shall be of no relevance hereunder. Cinema International Corporation shall be deemed a Subdistributor.

M. *Territory*

This is:

(1) U.S. is the United States, together with any other countries which are licensed by or through the distributing organization(s) servicing the U.S. for F/D.

(2) Canada is Canada and any other countries licensed by or through F/D's Canadian distribution organization.

(3) The United Kingdom (U.K.) is United Kingdom of Great Britain and Northern Ireland, Republic of Ireland, Channel Islands, Isle of Man, Gibraltar, Malta, and ships and aircraft flying British flag, and British camps wherever situated.

(4) Foreign is all countries (other than U.S., U.K. and Canada) and any other areas in the universe.

(5) All foregoing references to countries include their territories and possessions, and political subdivisions.

N. *This Agreement*

This is the agreement to which this exhibit is attached, this exhibit, and any other attached amendments, exhibits and schedules.

Schedule A
ROYALTIES REFERRED TO IN II . A . (7) OF THIS AGREEMENT

1. (a) If Participant is not entitled to receive any composers' or lyricists' royalties or otherwise share in music publishing royalties, then, insofar as F/D shall have exclusive, worldwide perpetual publication, performing, recording (including, without limitation, "original soundtrack album"), synchronization and all other rights in all unpublished musical compositions written for or used in or in connection with the Picture, F/D may license any or all of such rights to a music publishing company of its choosing, including an F/D subsidiary or affiliate company, provided that such license agreement shall require payment by said publishing company of the following royalties, which shall be included in Gross Receipts of the Picture without the application of distribution fees:

(i) Piano or orchestration copies sold in U.S. and Canada—two cents (2¢) per copy;

(ii) Net receipts of publisher from performing fees, excluding U.S. and Canada—sixteen and two-thirds percent (16⅔%); and

(iii) Net receipts of publisher worldwide from all sources other than the types listed in (i) and (ii)—sixteen and two-thirds percent (16⅔%).

(b) If Participant is not entitled to receive any artists' and/or producer royalties in respect of phonograph records derived from the soundtrack of the Picture, then insofar as F/D shall have all rights, worldwide, to the use and exploitation of the soundtrack of the Picture for phonograph records, tapes, transcriptions or any other form or medium of any nature whatsoever, F/D agrees that if F/D grants record rights to any record company, F/D shall endeavor to obtain the best available royalties in good-faith negotiation with such record company and, in any event, shall obtain not less than the following royalties, or, if such record company is a F/D subsidiary or affiliate company, then the following royalties shall likewise govern:

A royalty of 5% of 90% of the suggested retail price or 10% of 90% of the wholesale price (whichever is customarily paid at the time involved) of records manufactured, sold, paid for and not subject to return, such royalty to be computed in accordance with such record company's usual practice in computing such royalties, including, without limitation, reductions and deductions normally taken in accordance with the regular accounting practices of such record company. To the extent that royalties may be payable to any artists in connection with such record, such royalties shall reduce the royalty payable hereunder. The royalty payable hereunder with respect to foreign distribution of records, budget-line albums, reel-to-reel tapes, tape cartridges and sales by record clubs shall be at reduced rates in accordance with such record company's then-current practice. No royalties shall be due hereunder for promotional copies of records or for records sold below the cost of manufacture. Costs incurred by such record company in connection with the production of such record or records shall be charged to the royalty payable hereunder in the same proportion that the royalty payable hereunder bears to the total royalties payable.

Any record royalties payable hereunder shall be included in Gross Receipts of the Picture, without the application of distribution fees.

Notwithstanding anything to the contrary in this Paragraph 1, if F/D shall have the rights therein set forth in any country or territory of the world and derives monies from the exercise of said rights in such country or territory, the royalties applicable thereto, computed in accordance with the provisions of this Paragraph 1, shall be included in Gross Receipts of the Picture.

Schedule B
ROYALTIES REFERRED TO IN II . A . (8) OF THIS AGREEMENT

All royalties received by F/D from the sale or license of audio visual cassettes, video discs or any similar device shall be included in the Gross Receipts of the Picture under this Agreement.

To the extent F/D grants to its subsidiary or affiliated company, e.g., _____ the right to sell or license audio visual cassettes, video discs or any similar device, then there shall be included in the Gross Receipts of the Picture under this Agreement a royalty in an amount equal to 20% of the sums actually received by _____ by virtue of the aforesaid grant of video-cassette-disc rights.

RECORD

AGREEMENT

AGREEMENT dated _____ ____, 198__, by and between _____ ("Company") and _____ ("Artist").

1. *Term.*

Company hereby engages Artist's exclusive services as a recording artist for recording phonograph records embodying Artist's performances for an initial period commencing as of the date hereof and expiring six (6) months after the delivery of the First Album (as the term "First Album" is hereinafter defined), but in no event shall the initial period expire later than ten (10) years after the date hereof. Artist hereby grants to Company _____ (__) separate, consecutive and irrevocable options, each to renew this agreement for a period commencing consecutively upon the expiration of the preceding period and expiring six (6) months after Artist's delivery to Company of the last album (as the term "album" is hereinafter defined) to be delivered during each such option period in satisfaction of the Recording Commitment (as the term "Recording Commitment" is hereinafter defined) therefor, but in no event shall any of such option periods expire later than ten (10) years after the date hereof; provided, however, that the fourth option period, if applicable, shall expire upon the delivery of the _____ Album (as the term "_____ Album" is hereinafter defined). Each such option period shall be upon all of the terms and conditions of this agreement, except as otherwise specifically set forth herein. Each option shall be exercised, if at all, by Company giving Artist written notice at any time prior to the expiration of the then-current period. Artist accepts such engagement and agrees to perform this agreement to the best of Artist's ability.

2. *Recording Commitment.*

(a) During the initial period and each option period of the term hereof, Artist agrees to record and deliver to Company a sufficient number of Masters (as the term "Master" is hereinafter defined) as shall constitute the number of albums set forth below (the "Recording Commitment"):

Contract Period	Number of Albums
Initial Period	_____
First Option Period	_____
Second Option Period	_____
Third Option Period	_____
Fourth Option Period	_____

(b) The album to be delivered in satisfaction of the Recording Commitment for the initial period is hereinafter referred to as the "First Album", and the successive albums to be delivered in satisfaction of the Recording Commitment after the delivery of the First Album are hereinafter referred to as the Second Album, the Third Album, the Fourth Album, the Fifth Album, the

Sixth Album, the Seventh Album and the Eighth Album. No multiple albums (as the term "multiple album" is hereinafter defined) shall be recorded, delivered or released hereunder in satisfaction of the Recording Commitment hereof without Company's and Artist's prior written consent, which may be withheld in either party's sole discretion; provided, that if Company consents to the delivery of any multiple album hereunder, then such multiple album shall, subject to paragraph 5 below, be deemed a single album for all purposes hereunder.

(c) The First Album shall be delivered to Company within four (4) months after the date hereof. Each album, if any, to be delivered in satisfaction of the Recording Commitment hereof after the First Album shall be delivered no sooner than eight (8) months and no later than twelve (12) months after delivery of the immediately preceding album delivered in satisfaction of the Recording Commitment.

(d) Subject to paragraph 14 hereof, time is of the essence in Artist's delivery of Masters in satisfaction of the Recording Commitment and failure to make timely delivery of any Masters shall constitute an "event of default" under paragraph 11 hereof. Company's exercise of an option or failure to suspend its obligations hereunder shall not constitute a waiver of any of Company's rights to undelivered Masters unless Company waives such rights in writing. In the event that Artist is delinquent in the delivery of any Masters hereunder, the next delivered Masters shall be deemed to satisfy the most delinquent requirements first, and Artist may not commence recording of the Masters constituting any particular album to be delivered in satisfaction of the Recording Commitment until Artist has delivered to Company all the Masters constituting each prior album of the Recording Commitment unless Company shall otherwise agree in writing.

3. *Royalties and Advances.*

(a) Artist shall be entitled to a royalty on net sales of records embodying Masters, computed and paid pursuant to the provisions of Exhibit A attached hereto. Such royalty shall include Artist's royalties and all royalties payable to other artists, producers and other persons rendering services in connection with the recording of the Masters which become or may become due by reason of Company's exploitation of the Masters; provided, however, that Company shall make and be solely responsible for payments to the AFM Music Performance Trust Fund and Special Payments Fund, as well as to any similar funds whose contributions are based upon the sale of records.

(b) Provided that Artist is not then in material breach of this agreement, Company shall pay to Artist the following amounts as recoupable advances against royalties payable in accordance with paragraph 3(a) hereof and Exhibit A hereto:

(i) _____ Dollars ($____) in respect of the First Album, payable as follows: _____ Dollars ($____) within seven (7) days after full execution hereof and the balance, subject to paragraph 4(c) below, thirty (30) days after the delivery of the First Album.

(ii) Company agrees to pay Artist a "Sales Advance" in connection with each album (other than the First Album) to be delivered in satisfaction of the Recording Commitment hereof, computed as follows: the Sales Advance shall equal _____ percent (____%) of the royalties accrued to Artist's royalty account (after allowance for reasonable reserves) with respect to net sales through normal retail channels in the United States of the "Previous Album" (as the term "Previous Album" is hereinafter defined) as of the "Qualifying Date" (as the term "Qualifying Date" is hereinafter defined), but not less than the minimum amount nor more than the maximum amount set forth below with respect to each such album:

Album	Minimum Advance	Maximum Advance
Second Album	$ _____	$ _____
Third Album	$ _____	$ _____
Fourth Album	$ _____	$ _____
Fifth Album	$ _____	$ _____
Sixth Album	$ _____	$ _____
Seventh Album	$ _____	$ _____
Eighth Album	$ _____	$ _____

The "Previous Album" shall be the album of the Recording Commitment delivered by Artist to Company immediately prior to the delivery of the album for which the "Sales Advance" is being made, and the "Qualifying Date" shall be the date nine (9) months after the release in the United States of the "Previous Album". No Sales Advance shall be due in connection with any "Greatest Hits" or "Best of"-type album which Company may release and any such "Greatest Hits" album, "Best of"-type album or any other re-packaged album shall not be considered a Previous Album for the purposes of any Sales Advance. The Sales Advance with respect to each album of the Recording Commitment shall be payable in accordance with paragraph 3(c) hereof.

(c) Not later than Artist's written notice to Company that Artist has commenced recording a particular album in a recording studio, Artist shall give Company written notice whether Artist will record such album under Company's recording license (in which event, Company shall advance recording costs therefor in accordance with the provisions contained below) or if Artist will record such album under Artist's or a third party's recording license (in which event, Company shall not pay or be responsible for any such recording costs, and Artist shall pay same and indemnify and hold Company harmless therefrom); if Artist fails to make such election, then Artist shall be deemed to have elected to have Company pay such recording costs. The Sales Advance for each album to be delivered by Artist in satisfaction of the Recording Commitment for each option period hereof, if applicable, shall be paid as follows:

(i) In the event that the Qualifying Date for the Previous Album occurs prior to the commencement of recording the applicable album, Company shall pay to Artist, within fourteen (14) days after Artist gives Company written notice that Artist has commenced recording such album in a recording studio, an amount equal to one-half (½) of the amount, if any, by which the Sales Advance for such album as set forth in paragraph 3(b)(ii) above exceeds the sum of one hundred fifteen percent (115%) of the aggregate recording costs (excluding any advances paid to the individual producer) for the Previous Album and the advance to be paid to the producer of the applicable album. Subject to paragraph 4(c) below, the balance of the Sales Advance shall be paid to Artist within (14) days following delivery by Artist to Company of such album; provided, that Company shall have the right to withhold a portion thereof for up to thirty (30) days after delivery in an amount reasonably related to the estimated amount of recording costs for which Company has not been invoiced as of the date when Company makes such payment.

(ii) In the event that the Qualifying Date for the Previous Album shall not have occurred prior to the commencement of recording of the applicable album hereunder but occurs prior to delivery of such album, Company shall pay to Artist within fourteen (14) days after Artist gives Company written notice that Artist has commenced recording such album in a recording studio, an amount equal to one-half (½) of the amount, if any, by which the Minimum Advance for such album as set forth in paragraph 3(b)(ii) above exceeds the sum of one hundred fifteen percent (115%) of the aggregate recording costs (excluding any advance paid to the producer) for the Previous Album and the advance to be paid to the producer of the applicable album. Subject to paragraph 4(c) below, Company shall pay to Artist, within fourteen (14) days following delivery by Artist to Company of such album, an amount equal to the amount by which the Sales Advance for such album exceeds the amount paid by Company to Artist upon commencement of recording of such album; provided, that Company shall have the right to withhold a portion thereof for up to thirty (30) days after delivery in an amount reasonably related to the estimated amount of recording costs for which Company has not been invoiced as of the date when Company makes such payment.

(iii) In the event that the Qualifying Date for the Previous Album shall not have occurred prior to the commencement of recording of the applicable album hereunder and shall not have occurred prior to the delivery thereof, Company shall pay to Artist, within fourteen (14) days after Artist gives Company written notice that Artist has commenced recording such album in a recording studio, an amount equal to one-half (½) of the amount, if any, by which the Minimum Advance for such album as set forth in paragraph 3(b)(ii) above exceeds the sum of one hundred fifteen percent (115%) of the aggregate recording costs (excluding any advance paid to the producer) for the Previous Album and the advance to be paid to the producer of the applicable album. Subject to paragraph 4(c) below, Company shall pay to Artist, within fourteen (14) days following delivery by Artist to Company of such album, an amount equal to the amount by which the Minimum Advance for such album exceeds the amount paid by Company to Artist upon commencement of recording of such album; provided, that Company shall have the right to withhold a portion thereof for up to thirty (30) days after delivery in an amount reasonably related to the estimated amount of recording costs for which Company has not been invoiced as of the date when Company makes such payment. Thereafter, within fourteen (14) days after the Qualifying Date for the Previous Album, Company shall pay to Artist the amount, if any, by which the Sales Advance for such album exceeds the amounts theretofore paid by Company to Artist or on Artist's behalf with respect to such album.

(iv) Notwithstanding anything to the contrary contained herein, Company shall not have the obligation to pay any amounts due in connection with the commencement of recording a particular album hereunder earlier than five (5) months following the delivery by Artist to Company of the Previous Album.

(d) Artist hereby grants Company the option, exercisable at any time after the date hereof by written notice to Artist, to guarantee for the exclusive recording services of Artist, payment to Artist of no less than Six Thousand Dollars ($6,000) during each consecutive twelve (12) month period during the term hereof with the first such period commencing as of the date on which Company exercises such option and expiring one (1) year after such date. Accordingly, in such event, if the aggregate of royalties, advances and recording session fees paid to Artist by Company hereunder during any such twelve (12) month period has not equalled or exceeded Six Thousand Dollars ($6,000), Artist shall give Company written notice thereof. Within thirty (30) days after Company's receipt of such notice, Company shall pay to Artist an amount equal to such deficit. Any such payments made to Artist pursuant to this paragraph 3(d) shall be an advance against any and all royalties or other monies (other than mechanical copyright royalties) payable to Artist by Company pursuant to this agreement. If California law is hereafter changed to provide for a different minimum compensation requirement than Six Thousand Dollars ($6,000) per annum as a requisite for injunctive relief, then each of the foregoing references to "Six Thousand Dollars ($6,000)" shall each automatically be deemed amended to such new figure as of the effective date of such change.

4. *Recording Procedure.*

(a) Artist shall schedule and conduct recording sessions only after first obtaining Company's written approval of the individual producer, the places of recording, the selections to be recorded and the Authorized Budget (as the term "Authorized Budget" is hereinafter defined). Artist shall request such approvals at least thirty (30) days prior to the proposed first date of recording. If Company disapproves any of the foregoing, Artist shall promptly submit alternative proposals, but in all instances allowing Company a reasonable period of review prior to the proposed first date of recording.

(b) Artist shall engage artists, producers, musicians, recording studios or other personnel or facilities for the recording sessions hereunder, but only after having submitted a written estimate of all recording costs (as the term "recording costs" is hereinafter defined) to be incurred in connection therewith and having obtained a written authorization therefor signed by one of Company's officers. Such estimate shall provide for payment to Artist of minimum union scale only for Artist's services and shall not contain a charge for arrangements or orchestrations supplied by Artist. The aforesaid written authorization to conduct such session or sessions shall indicate the maximum amount which Artist may expend for the session or sessions authorized (the "Authorized Budget"). The granting of authorizations and the approval of Authorized Budgets shall be entirely within Company's discretion; provided, that Company agrees to approve an Authorized Budget for any particular album which does not exceed ninety percent (90%) of the advance for such album pursuant to paragraph 3(b) hereof (as same may be reduced pursuant to the provisions of this agreement) and is otherwise in conformity with the requirements hereof. Company shall have the right to have a representative attend all recording sessions conducted pursuant to this agreement. Without limiting Company's other rights or remedies in such event, if it reasonably appears to Company that the recording costs for any Masters will exceed the Authorized Budget therefor, Company shall have the right to require Artist to discontinue recording unless Artist can establish to Company's reasonable satisfaction that Artist can and will pay or reimburse Company for any recording costs in excess of the Authorized Budget.

(c) Company agrees to advance recording costs for the production of each particular album of the Recording Commitment in an amount not in excess of the Authorized Budget therefor. Artist will deliver copies of substantiating invoices, receipts, Form B's, any required AFTRA forms (if applicable), vouchers and similar satisfactory documentary evidence of such costs, and if Artist fails to do so, Company's obligation to pay further recording costs will be suspended until delivery thereof. Artist agrees to deliver, or cause the individual producer of the Masters to deliver, Form B's, W-4's and any required AFTRA forms (if applicable) to Company within seventy-two (72) hours after each session hereunder so that Company may timely make all required union payments, and Artist agrees to deliver all other invoices, receipts, vouchers and documents within one (1) week after Artist's receipt thereof. If Company incurs late-payment penalties by reason of Artist's failure to make timely delivery of any such materials, Artist will reimburse Company for same upon demand and, without limiting its other rights and remedies, Company may deduct an amount equal to all such penalties from monies otherwise payable to Artist under this agreement. Company shall be responsible for late-payment penalties caused solely by Company's acts or omissions. In the event that Company, in its sole discretion, shall pay any recording costs for any Masters hereunder in excess of the Authorized Budget in respect thereof, Artist shall repay any such excess upon demand and, without limiting its other rights and remedies, Company may deduct same from any advances, royalties, mechanical copyright royalties payable with respect to Controlled Compositions (as the term "Controlled Composition" is hereinafter defined) and/or other monies payable to Artist pursuant to this agreement.

(d) For each Master, Artist shall deliver to Company a two-track stereo tape, all multi-track master tapes (including, but not limited to, any twenty-four (24) track master tapes) and, upon Company's request, a monaural tape. The two-track stereo tapes for the Masters constituting each album to be delivered hereunder shall be assembled on one (1) [or, if necessary, on two (2)] master tape reels. Artist shall not own or control, directly or indirectly, any additional copies of the Masters; provided, however, Artist shall have the right to retain safety copies of the Masters. All original session tapes and any derivatives or reproductions thereof shall also be delivered to Company or maintained at a recording studio or other location designated or approved by Company, in Company's name and subject to Company's control.

(e) All recording costs shall be recouped from all royalties otherwise payable hereunder and shall also be deemed a prepayment of the delivery portion of the advance for the album for which such recording costs were paid.

5. *Mechanical Copyright Royalties.*

(a) Company shall be responsible for payment of mechanical copyright royalties for the United States directly to the copyright proprietors of the selections embodied in the Masters. Artist shall assist Company in obtaining from the copyright proprietors mechanical licenses issued to Company for the United States for all selections embodied in Masters delivered hereunder which are not Controlled Compositions (as the term "Controlled Composition" is hereinafter defined); provided, however, that Artist shall cause the copyright proprietors to issue to Company mechanical licenses for the United States for all selections embodied in Masters delivered hereunder which are not subject to the compulsory license provisions of the United States Copyright Act; provided, that Company's personnel shall handle the actual paperwork required in connection therewith. A selection which is not a Controlled Composition is hereinafter referred to as a "Non-Controlled Composition". Such mechanical licenses as Artist is required to cause to be issued to Company shall be at rates and upon terms no less favorable to Company than those contained in the then-current standard mechanical license issued by The Harry Fox Agency, Inc. Such licenses shall name Company as licensee, and copies thereof shall be delivered to Company concurrently with the delivery to Company of the Masters to which they relate. Notwithstanding anything to the contrary contained in Exhibit A hereto, statements as to mechanical copyright royalties hereunder, together with payment of accrued mechanical copyright royalties otherwise payable in respect of such quarterly period, less reserves, shall be sent no later than forty-five (45) days following the close of each calendar quarter.

(b) As used in this agreement, the term "Controlled Composition" means a selection embodied in a Master recorded or released hereunder, which selection is (i) written or composed, in whole or in part, by Artist, or (ii) owned or controlled, in whole or in part, directly or indirectly, by Artist, or by any person owned or controlled by Artist, or in which Artist has a direct or indirect income interest. Notwithstanding the foregoing, with respect to any Controlled Composition which is co-written by Artist with another individual or individuals ("Third Party Writers"), if the Third Party Portion thereof (as the term "Third Party Portion" is hereinafter defined) is not subject to the provisions of the immediately preceding subpart (ii) of this paragraph 5(b), then the Third Party Portion only of such Composition shall not be deemed a Controlled Composition hereunder under for purposes of this paragraph 5. As used herein, the "Third Party Portion" of a selection subject to the foregoing sentence shall be that percentage of the rights in the applicable selection which is not owned by a person described in subpart (ii) of this paragraph 5(b), but in no event shall the Third Party Portion be greater than a fraction of such selection, the numerator of which is the number of Third Party Writers of such selection and the denominator of which is the total number of writers and composers of such selection. All Controlled Compositions are hereby licensed to Company for the United States at a rate per selection equal to seventy-five percent (75%) of the Controlled Composition Applicable Statutory Rate (as the term "Controlled Composition Applicable Statutory Rate" is hereinafter defined) and such mechanical copyright royalty shall be payable with respect to net sales of records hereunder, except that no mechanical copyright royalties shall be payable with respect to any records as to which no royalties are payable pursuant to Exhibit A hereto or with respect to any Controlled Composition which is one (1) minute or less in duration; provided, however, that Company shall pay mechanical copyright royalties with respect to fifty percent (50%) of Album Free Goods (including, without limitation, Special Album Free Goods), as the term "Album Free Goods" is defined in Exhibit A hereto. As used herein, the "Controlled Composition Applicable Statutory Rate" with respect to a particular selection shall mean the minimum statutory mechanical copyright rate in effect as of the date of delivery of the first Master embodying such selection; provided, that the Controlled Composition Applicable Statutory Rate with respect to the selections embodied on a particular "Greatest Hits" or "Best of"-type album shall be the minimum statutory rate in effect on the date of initial United States release of such "Greatest Hits" or "Best of"-type album but only with respect to sales of such "Greatest Hits" or "Best of"-type album.

(c) (i) Notwithstanding the provisions of paragraphs 5(a) and 5(b) above, with respect to net sales of records in the United States, the maximum aggregate copyright royalty rate payable by Company in respect of any album hereunder (the "Maximum Aggregate Album Rate") containing one (1) disc record or the tape equivalent thereof, regardless of the number of selections embodied therein or the playing time thereof, shall be ten (10) times the minimum statutory mechanical copyright royalty rate in effect as of the date of manufacture of each respective copy of such album (the "Non-Controlled Composition Applicable Statutory Rate"), the maximum aggregate copyright royalty rate payable by Company in respect of any single record hereunder embodying two (2) or fewer selections, regardless of the playing time thereof, shall be two (2) times the Non-Controlled Composition Applicable Statutory Rate (the "Double Maximum Aggregate Single Rate"), and the maximum aggregate copyright royalty rate payable by Company in respect of any single record hereunder embodying three (3) selections, regardless of the playing time thereof, shall be three (3) times the Non-Controlled Composition Applicable Statutory Rate (the "Triple Maximum Aggregate Single Rate"). With respect to multiple albums, the maximum aggregate copyright royalty rate payable by Company with respect thereto, regardless of the number of selections embodied therein or the playing time thereof, shall be the Maximum Aggregate Multiple Album Rate. As used herein, the "Maximum Aggregate Multiple Album Rate" for a particular multiple album shall be the Maximum Aggregate Album Rate which would be applicable to a single disc album delivered on the date such multiple album was manufactured multiplied by a fraction, the numerator of which is the suggested retail list price of such multiple album in disc form and the denominator of which is Company's then prevailing suggested retail list price for single disc albums (the "Multiple Album Factor"). Accordingly, with respect to records sold in the United States, in the event that the actual aggregate mechanical copyright royalty rate which Company is required to pay in respect of any album, multiple album or single record hereunder shall exceed the applicable Maximum Aggregate Album Rate, Maximum Aggregate Multiple Album Rate, Double Maximum Aggregate Single Rate or Triple Maximum Aggregate Single Rate, as applicable, to the extent Company is unable to recover all of such excess from the mechanical copyright royalties payable with respect to Controlled Compositions, if any, embodied thereon, Company shall have the right to deduct an amount equal to the additional payments to be made by Company as a result thereof from any royalties, mechanical royalties payable with respect to Controlled Compositions embodied on other records hereunder, or other sums payable under this agreement.

(ii) Notwithstanding the foregoing, in the event that there shall be more than ten (10) Masters embodied on a single disc album delivered by Artist hereunder, which album embodies both Controlled Compositions and Non-Controlled Compositions, then the Maximum Aggregate Album Rate for such album shall be the actual aggregate rate at which such mechanical copyright royalties would have been payable with respect to such album had such album embodied only ten (10) Masters and such ten (10) Masters consisted first of the Masters on such album which embody Non-Controlled Compositions and, if there are fewer than ten (10) such Masters on such album, sufficient additional Masters on such album which embody Controlled Compositions. By way of example, if an album embodied twelve (12) Masters of which seven (7) embodied Controlled Compositions and five (5) embodied Non-Controlled Compositions, and the Controlled Composition Applicable Statutory Rate and the Non-Controlled Composition Applicable Statutory Rate for such album were both four cents ($.04), then the Maximum Aggregate Album Rate for such album would be thirty-five cents ($.35) (i.e. five (5) Non-Controlled Compositions at four cents ($.04) each and five (5) Controlled Composition at three cents ($.03) each).

(d) Notwithstanding anything to the contrary contained herein, the maximum aggregate mechanical copyright royalty payable by Company for all Controlled Compositions embodied on any album hereunder containing one (1) disc record or the tape equivalent thereof, regardless of the number of Controlled Compositions embodied thereon or the playing time thereof, shall be seventy-five percent (75%) of ten (10) times the Controlled Composition Applicable Statutory Rate for such album ("Maximum Aggregate Controlled

Composition Album Rate"), the maximum aggregate mechanical copyright royalty payable by Company for all Controlled Compositions embodied on any single record hereunder embodying two (2) or fewer Controlled Compositions, regardless of the playing time thereof, shall be seventy-five percent (75%) of two (2) times the Controlled Composition Applicable Statutory Rate for such single record (the "Double Maximum Aggregate Controlled Composition Single Rate"), and the maximum aggregate mechanical copyright royalty payable by Company for all Controlled Compositions embodied on any single record hereunder embodying three (3) Controlled Compositions, regardless of the playing time thereof, shall be seventy-five percent (75%) of three (3) times the Controlled Composition Applicable Statutory Rate for such single record (the "Triple Maximum Aggregate Controlled Composition Single Rate"). With respect to multiple albums, the maximum aggregate mechanical copyright royalty by Company for all Controlled Compositions embodied thereon, regardless of the number of Controlled Compositions embodied thereon or the playing time thereof, shall be the Maximum Aggregate Controlled Composition Multiple Album Rate. As used herein, the "Maximum Aggregate Controlled Composition Multiple Rate" shall be the Maximum Aggregate Controlled Composition Album Rate which would be applicable to a single disc album delivered on the date such multiple album was delivered hereunder multiplied by the Multiple Album Factor.

(e) Notwithstanding anything to the contrary contained herein, in the event that the aggregate of the mechanical copyright royalties payable with respect to all Controlled Compositions and Non-Controlled Compositions embodied on any particular single disc album shall be less than the mechanical copyright royalties which would have been payable if such album had been constituted of ten (10) Controlled Compositions, then Company shall pay to Artist or Artist's designee the amount of such deficit as additional Controlled Composition mechanical copyright royalties hereunder. The provisions of the first sentence of this paragraph 5(e) shall not be applicable with respect to any Mini-LP (as the term "Mini-LP" is hereinafter defined).

(f) No mechanical copyright royalties shall be payable in respect of Controlled Compositions which are arrangements of selections in the public domain. Notwithstanding the foregoing, in the event any such arrangement is credited by ASCAP or BMI, then such arrangement shall be licensed to Company at a mechanical copyright royalty rate equal to the Controlled Composition Applicable Statutory Rate with respect to the original composition multiplied by the percentage utilized by the applicable performing rights society or organization (ASCAP or BMI) in determining the credits to be given to the publisher of such arrangement for public performances thereof; provided, that unless and until Artist furnishes to Company a copy of the letter from the performing rights society or organization setting forth the percentage of the otherwise applicable credit which the publisher will receive for such public performances, Company shall not be obligated to pay any copyright royalty with respect to any such arrangement.

(g) Any assignment made of the ownership or copyrights in, or the rights to license or administer the use of, any Controlled Composition shall be subject to the terms and provisions hereof.

6. Grant of Rights.

(a) Artist acknowledges and agrees that Company is and shall be the owner throughout the universe (the "Territory") of all right, title and interest in and to all Masters and all other recordings embodying the results and proceeds of Artist's recording services, whether or not delivered hereunder, which are made or delivered during the term hereof, and all records and reproductions made therefrom during and from their creation, including, without limitation, the worldwide copyrights therein and thereto (but excluding the copyrights of the musical compositions embodied therein) and the exclusive right to copyright same as "sound recordings" in the name of Company, to renew and extend such copyrights (it being agreed that for this purpose Artist is deemed Company's employee for hire), and to exercise throughout the Territory all rights of the copyright proprietor thereunder. To the extent, if any, that Artist may be deemed an "author" of such "sound recordings", Artist further grants to Company a power of attorney, irrevocable and coupled with an interest, for Artist and in Artist's name, to apply for and obtain, and on obtaining same, to assign to Company, all such copyrights and renewals and extensions thereof, which power of attorney may only be exercised if Artist fails to execute and deliver to Company any document which Company may reasonably submit to Artist for execution. Artist further agrees to execute and deliver to Company, and to cause each other person rendering services in connection with the Masters to execute and deliver to Company, written assignments to Company (in a form satisfactory to Company) of all sound recording copyright rights (including renewal and extension rights) such person may have. Without limiting the foregoing, but subject to the terms and conditions contained in this agreement, Company shall have the exclusive and perpetual right throughout the Territory to control Masters and all other recordings hereunder, and may sell, lease, license, and otherwise exploit such Masters or other recordings hereunder or refrain therefrom, throughout the Territory upon such terms and conditions, in such records, and in such forms and versions, as it may in its sole discretion determine. Artist acknowledges that records embodying Masters may be released under any trademark, trade name or label designated by Company; provided, that the initial release in the United States of each album delivered hereunder shall be on Company's then-current top-line "pop" label.

(b) Company shall have the right to use and publish, and to permit others to use and publish, the name (including any professional name by which the person involved is or may become known) and likeness of and biographical material concerning Artist (including the individual members of Artist) and the name (including any professional name by which the person involved is or may become known) of the individual producer(s) and all others rendering services in connection with Masters, for advertising and purposes of trade in connection with the promotion and sale of records made hereunder, or Company may refrain from the foregoing. Except in connection with records which may have been recorded for third parties prior to the commencement of the term hereof and which third parties own and have the right to exploit as of the date hereof without the consent of Artist, this right shall be exclusive to Company in the Territory during the term of this agreement and non-exclusive thereafter. During the term hereof, Company may bill, advertise, and describe Artist for the Territory as, and Artist agrees to utilize Artist's reasonable efforts in other aspects of Artist's career to be billed, advertised and described as an "Exclusive 'Company' Artist", or by a similar designation. Artist will deliver to Company any photographs of and biographical material concerning Artist, label data and any other material which Artist may own or control which Company reasonably may require to exploit and promote records embodying Masters hereunder. Company agrees that, notwithstanding anything to the contrary contained herein, any and all likenesses and photographs of and biographical material concerning Artist shall be subject to Artist's approval; provided, that such approval shall be deemed given with respect to any material submitted by Artist and provided further that such approval shall be deemed given with respect to any such material which Artist does not disapprove in writing within five (5) business days after Artist has been notified that such material is available for review at Company's offices. Company shall have the right to utilize such approved or submitted photographs, likenesses and biographical material; provided, however, that if Artist objects to any previously approved or submitted photographs, likenesses or biographical material and shall provide Company with replacements therefor, then after such replacements have been provided Company shall not utilize those photographs, likenesses and biographical material to which Artist has objected. Unless such failure is persistent, Company's inadvertent failure to comply with the foregoing requirements with respect to photographs, likenesses and biographical material shall not be deemed a breach hereof; provided, that after Company's receipt of written notice of any such failure, it shall use reasonable efforts to prospectively comply with the foregoing provisions with respect to such photographs, likenesses and biographical material.

(c) Company has not made, and does not hereby make, any representation or warranty with respect to the quantity (if any) of sales of records embodying

Masters. Artist recognizes and acknowledges that the sale of phonograph records is speculative and agrees that the judgment of Company and its subsidiary and affiliated companies in regard to any matter affecting the sale, distribution and exploitation of said records shall be binding and conclusive upon Artist. Artist warrants and agrees that Artist will not make any claim, nor shall any liability be imposed upon Company based upon any claim, that more sales could have been made or better business could have been done than was actually made or done by Company or any of its licensees.

7. *Release Commitment.*

(a) Provided Artist is not then in material breach hereunder, Company shall release each album of the Recording Commitment in the United States not later than the latter of (i) ninety (90) days after delivery of such album (including the delivery of all required materials and information in connection therewith and the granting of all necessary consents and approvals in connection therewith), and (ii) nine (9) months after release by Company of the immediately preceding album delivered by Artist to Company in satisfaction of the Recording Commitment hereof; provided, that in the event that the last day on which Company would be obligated pursuant to the foregoing to release any album hereunder falls between October 1 and December 31 of any year, then Company shall not be obligated to release such album in the United States prior to the third week of January of the next succeeding year; provided, however, if the gross sales (without regard to reserves for this purpose only) in the United States through normal retail channels of the immediately preceding album is more than two hundred fifty thousand (250,000) units as of the date on which a particular album is delivered hereunder, the foregoing suspension shall only apply if Company is obligated to release such album pursuant to the provisions hereof between November 1 and December 31 of any year. Upon Company's failure to release any album as aforesaid, Artist's sole remedy shall be the right for thirty (30) days after the expiration of such ninety (90) day or nine (9) month period (as such period may be suspended and extended as set forth herein) to notify Company in writing of such failure. If Company fails to release any album in the United States within sixty (60) days after such notice, Artist shall have the right (as Artist's sole remedy) for thirty (30) days after the expiration of such sixty (60) day period to terminate the term hereof by written notice to Company. Artist's failure to notify Company within any of the time periods set forth herein shall be a waiver of Artist's right to terminate the term hereof as aforesaid.

(b) In the event that Artist shall have the right to terminate the term of this agreement as a result of Company's failure to release an album hereunder and shall properly exercise such right in accordance with subparagraph 7(a) above then, at Artist's election, to be exercised by written notice to Company no later than one hundred twenty (120) days after such termination, Artist shall have the right to purchase such unreleased album from Company; provided, however, that in the event Company shall have commenced the manufacture of copies of such album prior to Company's receipt of Artist's such notice with the intention of releasing such album (and Company, in fact, thereafter releases such album within ninety (90) days after receipt of such notice), then such notice shall be of no force and effect and Company shall have no obligation to sell such album to Artist. The purchase price for any such unreleased album shall be all sums paid by Company pursuant to paragraphs 3 and 4 with respect to such unreleased album (hereinafter referred to as the "Purchase Price") and the Purchase Price shall be paid to Company concurrently with the transfer of all rights in the album to Artist. Further, concurrently with the transfer of such rights, Artist shall execute Company's standard form master purchase agreement.

8. *Exclusivity; Re-recording Restrictions.*

(a) During the term of this agreement:

(i) Artist shall not enter into any agreement or make any commitment which would interfere with Artist's performance of any of the terms and provisions hereof.

(ii) Artist shall not perform for the purpose of making phonograph records for distribution or sale in the Territory by or for any person other than Company.

(iii) Except with respect to master recordings recorded by Artist prior to the date hereof which are owned by third parties as of the date hereof and which any such third party has the right to commercially exploit without Artist's permission as of the date hereof, Artist shall not directly or indirectly authorize the use of Artist's name (including Artist's current professional name or any professional name hereafter used by Artist with Company's prior written consent), photograph, likeness or other identification, voice or other sound effects, or performance, for or in of connection with the production, sale, advertising or exploitation of phonograph records in the Territory by or for any person other than Company.

(iv) Notwithstanding anything to the contrary contained herein, Artist shall not, without Company's prior written consent, promote, advertise, endorse or otherwise utilize Artist's name (whether legal or professional, and whether presently or hereafter used by Artist) and/or likeness and/or logo (whether presently or hereafter used by Artist) in connection with the sale, distribution, advertising or other exploitation of any blank tapes, including, without limitation, reel-to-reel tapes, cartridges or cassettes, whether for financial remuneration, promotional consideration or otherwise.

(v) In the event Artist makes any sound recordings for motion pictures, television, radio or any medium, or if Artist performs as a member of the cast in making sound recordings for a live theatrical presentation, Artist agrees that Artist will do so only pursuant to a written contract prohibiting the use of such recordings, directly or indirectly, for phonograph record purposes.

(vi) Prior to the applicable Restriction Date (as the term "Restriction Date" is hereinafter defined), Artist shall not utilize or authorize any third party to utilize in any medium any audio-visual reproduction of Artist's audio performance of a particular selection if such selection is embodied on any Master delivered by Artist to Company hereunder during the term hereof.

(b) Artist agrees that Artist shall not perform in any manner any selection (or portion thereof) recorded hereunder, whether or not released by Company, for the purposes of making records for distribution or sale in the Territory by or for any person other than Company, at any time prior to the later of the following dates (such later date, with respect to any such selection, is hereinafter sometimes referred to as the "Restriction Date"): (i) five (5) years after the date of delivery to Company of the last Master embodying such selection, and (ii) two (2) years after the expiration or termination of the term of this agreement or any subsequent agreement between Company and any person relating to Artist's recording services. Notwithstanding the foregoing, the Restriction Date with respect to any musical composition embodied on a Master which has not been commercially released during the term hereof or within one (1) year thereafter shall be the date one (1) year after the expiration of the term hereof; provided, however, that in the event that any such composition was also embodied on one or more other Masters which was commercially released during the term hereof or within one (1) year thereafter, then the Restriction Date shall be as set forth in the first sentence of this paragraph 8(b) with respect to such composition.

(c) Artist shall not at any time manufacture, distribute or sell, or directly or indirectly authorize the manufacture, distribution or sale in the Territory by any person other than Company of phonograph records embodying (i) any performance rendered in any manner by Artist during the term of this agreement, or (ii) any performance rendered in any manner by Artist after the expiration or termination of the term of this agreement of a selection recorded hereunder, whether or not released by Company, if such performance is rendered prior to the Restriction Date applicable thereto. Furthermore, Artist shall not record or directly or indirectly authorize to be recorded for any purpose any such performance without in each case taking all reasonable measures necessary to prevent the manufacture, distribution or sale in the Territory at any time by any person other than Company of phonograph records embodying such performance. Specifically, but without limiting the generality of the foregoing, if, after the expiration or termination of the term of this agreement, Artist performs for any purpose any selection recorded hereunder prior to the Restriction Date applicable thereto, Artist will do so only pursuant to a written contract containing an express provision that neither such performance nor any recording thereof will be used directly or indirectly for the purpose of making phonograph records for distribution or sale in the Territory. Upon Company's request, Artist shall promptly deliver to Company a true and correct copy of the pertinent provisions of each such contract.

(d) Company may take such action as it deems necessary, in Artist's name (with Artist's consent, which shall not be unreasonably withheld) and/or in its own name, to enforce or protect its rights under this agreement, including, without limitation, taking action against any person who uses the performances, name, photograph, likeness, other identification, voice and/or sound effects of Artist in violation of Company's rights under this agreement. Artist shall reasonably cooperate with Company in any controversy or litigation which may arise with a third party relating to Company's rights under this agreement.

9. *Warranties and Representations.*

Artist represents, warrants and agrees that:

(a) Artist is free to enter into and perform this agreement, and is not under any restriction or obligation which will impair Artist's full performance of Artist's obligations hereunder or impair Company's full enjoyment of Company's rights hereunder. Without limitation of the foregoing, Artist specifically warrants and represents that no selection recorded or to be recorded by Artist hereunder is or will be subject to any re-recording restriction under any previous recording contract to which Artist may have been a party, and that neither Artist nor any other person rendering services in connection with Masters is or will be a party to any contract which would in any way impair the rights granted to Company hereunder.

(b) Each Master shall be free of all liens and encumbrances, and there will be no claims, demands or actions pending or threatened with respect thereto other than any such liens, encumbrances, claims, demands or actions arising from Company's acts or omissions.

(c) Neither any name(s) utilized by Artist, the Masters, any of the selections embodied therein, any other matters or materials supplied by Artist hereunder, nor any exploitation or use of any of the foregoing, shall violate or infringe upon any civil, personal or proprietary rights of any person, including, without limitation, trademarks, trade names, copyrights and rights of privacy and publicity.

(d) Artist shall not, at any time prior to the date occurring nine (9) months after the termination or expiration of the term hereof, sell, license or otherwise exploit in any manner whatsoever, or authorize any third party to sell, license or otherwise exploit, any recordings embodying the performances of Artist which are now or are hereafter owned or controlled by Artist, and any selections embodied in such recordings are and shall be subject to paragraph 8(b) above.

(e) The selections embodied in Masters shall be available for mechanical licensing to Company in accordance with paragraph 5 above.

(f) Artist is, and shall remain, a member in good standing of any appropriate union(s) with which Company may at any time have an agreement lawfully requiring such union membership.

(g) All Masters shall be produced under and in conformity with all union agreements to which the Masters may at any time be or become subject. All musicians and other persons rendering services in the production of Masters will be paid the sums required to be paid to them under appropriate union agreements, and the contributions to appropriate union pension or similar trust funds required thereby will be made. The foregoing representations and warranties are respectively included for the benefit of AFM, AFTRA, all other appropriate unions, their respective members whose performances are embodied in the Masters, and Company, and may be enforced by such unions, their respective designees or by Company. Company shall make and be solely responsible for payments to the AFM Music Performance Trust Fund and Special Payments Fund, as well as to any similar funds whose contributions are based upon the sale of records.

(h) Company's acceptance and/or utilization of Masters or other matters or materials hereunder shall not constitute a waiver of any of Artist's representations or warranties in respect thereof.

(i) Artist agrees to use Artist's best good faith efforts to record and produce commercially acceptable Masters hereunder.

10. *Indemnification.*

(a) Artist agrees to indemnify and hold Company harmless from and against any liability, damage, cost or expense (including costs and reasonable attorneys' fees) occasioned by or arising out of any claim, demand or action which is inconsistent with any agreement, representation, grant or warranty made or assumed by Artist hereunder, which claim, demand or action is reduced to final non-appealable adverse judgment or settled with Artist's written consent, which consent shall not be unreasonably withheld. Company agrees to give

Artist notice of any claim, demand or action to which the foregoing indemnity applies, and Artist may participate in the defense of same at Artist's expense, through counsel of Artist's choice; provided, that the final control and disposition of same (by settlement, compromise or otherwise) shall remain with Company. Artist agrees to pay Company on demand any amounts for which it may be responsible under the foregoing indemnity and, without limiting any of its other rights or remedies, upon the making or filing of any claim, demand or action subject hereto, Company shall be entitled to withhold sums payable under this agreement, in an amount reasonably related to the potential liability, plus costs and reasonable attorneys' fees; provided, that Company shall not so withhold any monies if Artist posts a bond which has been reasonably approved in all aspects (form, amount, duration, surety, etc.) by Company. Further, at such time, if ever, as such withheld monies become payable to Artist, Company shall pay Artist interest on such withheld and payable funds at the rate prevailing at Security Pacific National Bank in Los Angeles, California, for regular passbook savings accounts from time to time during the period in which such monies are so withheld. With respect to any claim or demand, monies may not be withheld hereunder for more than one (1) year after Company has received written notice of such claim or demand unless legal action with respect to such claim or demand is filed and served within such one (1) year period. Artist will, at Company's request, cooperate fully with Company in any controversy which may arise with third parties or litigation which may be brought by third parties concerning this agreement or any of Company's rights hereunder. If Artist fails to consent to a proposed settlement, Company shall nonetheless have the right to enter into such proposed settlement but, in such event, Artist shall not be liable for the amount of the settlement, but shall be liable for expenses (including costs and reasonable attorneys' fees) which Company incurred up to and including the date as of which the claim is settled. Alternatively, if Artist fails to consent to a proposed settlement and Company elects not to enter into such settlement agreement in accordance with the immediately preceding sentence, Artist shall, at Company's written request, thereafter directly bear all costs of defense and shall promptly reimburse Company for all expenses incurred by Company (including costs and reasonable attorneys' fees) up to and including the date as of which Artist failed to consent to such proposed settlement and, if Artist fails to promptly undertake such future costs and reimburse Company for such accumulated expenses, Company may settle such claim in its sole discretion and Artist's indemnification shall apply to such settlement. Notwithstanding the foregoing, if any claim or demand as to which Artist has undertaken the costs of defense results in a final, unappealable judgment which is not adverse to Company or Artist, then Artist shall give Company written notice thereof and Company shall promptly reimburse Artist for one-half (½) of the amounts for which Artist had theretofore reimbursed Company in respect of such claim or demand pursuant to this paragraph 10(a).

(b) Company agrees to indemnify and hold Artist harmless against any liability, damage, cost or expense (including costs and reasonable attorneys' fees) occasioned by or arising out of any claim, demand or action inconsistent with any agreement, representation or warranty made or assumed by Company hereunder which is reduced to final non-appealable judgment or settled with Company's written consent, which consent shall not be unreasonably withheld. In all relevant respects, and provisions of paragraph 10(a) hereof shall be applicable to the scope of such indemnification.

11. *Force Majeure; Defaults and Remedies.*

(a) If Company's performance hereunder is delayed or becomes impossible or commercially impracticable by reason of any force majeure event, including, without limitation, any act of God, fire, earthquake, strike, civil commotion, acts of government or any order, regulation, ruling or action of any labor union or association of artists affecting Company and/or the phonograph record industry, Company, upon notice to Artist, may suspend its obligations hereunder for the duration of such delay, impossibility or impracticability, as the case may be. In the event any force majeure suspension exceeds six (6) consecutive months, Artist may terminate the term of this agreement upon ten (10) days written notice to Company; provided, that any such termination by Artist shall be effective only if the force majeure event does not affect a substantial portion of the United States recording industry, in no way involves Artist's acts or omissions, and Company fails to terminate the suspension within ten (10) days after its receipt of Artist's notice. Company shall not withhold payment of royalties during any such suspension unless the force majeure event materially impairs Company's ability to calculate and/or pay royalties.

(b) Each of the following shall constitute an event of default hereunder:

(i) Artist's voice and/or playing ability becomes impaired as determined by a physician reasonably designated by Company and Artist (provided that Artist shall not thwart Company's rights under this paragraph 11(b) by failing to designate a physician) or Artist ceases to seriously pursue Artist's career as an entertainer or Artist attempts to assign this agreement or Artist fails, refuses or neglects to fulfill any of Artist's material obligations hereunder.

(ii) In the event Artist commences a voluntary case under any applicable bankruptcy, insolvency or other similar law now or hereafter in effect or consents to the entering of an order for relief in any involuntary case under such law or consents to the appointment of or taking possession by a receiver, liquidator, assignee, trustee or sequestrator (or similar appointee) of Artist or any substantial part of Artist's property or Artist makes any assignment for the benefit of creditors or takes any act (whether corporate or otherwise) in furtherance of any of the foregoing.

(iii) If a court having jurisdiction over the affairs or property of Artist enters a decree or order for relief in respect of Artist or any of Artist's property in an involuntary case under any applicable bankruptcy, insolvency or other similar law now or hereafter in effect or appoints a receiver, liquidator, assignee, custodian, trustee or sequestrator (or similar appointee) of Artist or for any substantial part of Artist's property or orders the winding up or liquidation of Artist's affairs and such decree or order remains unstayed and in effect for a period of fifteen (15) consecutive days.

(c) On the occurrence of any event of default, Company, in addition to its other rights or remedies, may, by notice to Artist, elect to (i) suspend its obligations to Artist hereunder for the duration of such event (except that Company shall not suspend its obligation to pay royalties earned hereunder if Artist's failure to perform Artist's obligations is caused by reasons beyond the reasonable control of Artist), and/or (ii) terminate the term of this agreement by written notice to Artist given at any time (whether or not during a period of suspension based on such event or based upon any other event), and thereby be relieved of all liability other than any obligations hereunder to pay royalties in respect of Masters delivered prior to termination.

(d) Artist acknowledges that Artist's performance hereunder, and the rights granted Company herein, are of a special, unique, extraordinary and intellectual character which gives them peculiar value, the loss of which cannot be reasonably or adequately compensated in damages in an action at law, that a breach by Artist of this agreement will cause Company irreparable injury and that, subject to paragraph 14 hereof, Company is not obligated to accept the performance of Artist hereunder from or to render performances due to Artist hereunder for any party or person other than Artist, including, without limitation, any successor in interest to Artist. Company shall be entitled to seek injunctive and/or other equitable relief to prevent a breach of this agreement by Artist, which relief shall be in addition to any other rights or remedies which Company may have, whether for damages or otherwise.

12. *Promotional Activities of Artist.*

Artist will, from time to time, at Company's request, whenever same will not unreasonably interfere with other professional activities of Artist, appear at photographic sessions in connection with the creation of artwork, poster and cover art to be used for the advertising, marketing and promotion of records hereunder; appear for interviews with representatives of the press and Company's publicity personnel; and advise and consult with Company regarding Artist's performances hereunder. Artist will also, if requested by Company, and subject to Artist's reasonable availability, make personal appearances on radio and television and elsewhere and record taped interviews, spot announcements, trailers and electrical transcriptions, all for the purpose of advertising, exploiting and/or promoting records hereunder. Artist shall not be entitled to any compensation for such services, except as may be required by applicable union agreements; provided, however, that Company shall reimburse Artist for the reasonable travel and living expenses incurred by Artist in connection with the rendition by Artist of services rendered at Company's direction pursuant to this paragraph 12 pursuant to a budget approved by Company in advance. Notwithstanding the foregoing provisions of this paragraph 12, Artist's failure to comply with the requirements of this paragraph 12 in any instance shall not constitute a breach of this agreement unless Artist consistently refuses or fails to comply with such requirements and/or unless Artist refuses or fails to perform a reasonable amount of such requirements with respect to any album of the Recording Commitment.

13. *Life Insurance.*

Company shall have the right at any time during the term hereof to obtain insurance on the life of Artist at Company's sole cost and expense, with Company being the sole beneficiary thereof. Artist agrees to fully cooperate with Company, at Company's sole cost and expense, in connection with the obtaining of such a policy, including, without limitation, Artist's submission to a physical examination and the completion of any and all documents necessary or desirable in respect thereof. Neither Artist nor Artist's estate shall have any right to claim the benefit of any such policy obtained by Company. The uninsurability of Artist shall not be deemed a breach of this agreement by Artist.

14. *Miscellaneous.*

Company may assign this agreement to (a) any parent, subsidiary, sister corporation or other affiliate of Company, (b) a person acquiring all or substantially all of the phonograph record assets of Company, or (c) an entity into which Company may merge; provided, however, that in the event of any such assignment, Company shall remain secondarily liable hereunder and, accordingly, Artist shall first be obligated to exhaust Artist's remedies against the applicable assignee before proceeding against Company hereunder. The foregoing shall not prohibit or in any way restrict Company from assigning or licensing any of its rights hereunder in the ordinary course of business. This agreement is personal to Artist and may only be assigned by Artist to a corporation or other entity which is wholly owned and controlled by Artist, such restriction to be binding on each successive assignee. This agreement is entire, and all negotiations and understandings are merged herein. No approvals or consents by either party hereunder shall be unreasonably withheld unless otherwise specifically provided herein. This agreement cannot be modified except by an instrument in writing, executed by both Company and Artist. A waiver of a breach by either party in any one instance shall not constitute a waiver of any subsequent breach, whether or not similar. Nothing herein contained shall constitute a partnership between or joint venture by the parties hereto, or constitute either party the agent or employee of the other. This agreement is not intended for the benefit of any third party, except as is otherwise provided in paragraph 9(g). Company shall not be deemed in default or breach of this agreement unless it is given written notice thereof and same is not cured within fifteen (15) days after such notice. Artist shall not be deemed to be in default or breach of this agreement unless Artist is given written notice thereof and same is not cured within fifteen (15) days after such notice; provided that the foregoing shall not be applicable to any breach which cannot be cured (e.g. breach of a re-recording restriction or a provision of paragraph 11(b)(ii) above), and further provided that nothing contained herein shall prevent Company from seeking immediate injunctive relief. Nothing in this agreement shall be construed so as to require the commission of any act contrary to law, and wherever there is any conflict between any provision of this agreement and any present or future statute, law, ordinance or regulation, the latter shall prevail, but in such event the provision of this agreement affected shall be curtailed and limited only to the extent necessary to bring it within legal requirements. The headings of the paragraphs hereof are for convenience only and shall not be deemed to limit or in any way affect the scope, meaning or intent of this agreement or any portion hereof. This agreement shall be governed by the laws of the State of _____ applicable to contracts made and to be wholly performed in the State of _____. Any claim, dispute or disagreement with respect to this agreement shall be submitted to the courts of the State of _____ or the federal courts within the State of _____, which courts shall have exclusive jurisdiction thereof. Any process in any action or proceeding commenced in such courts may, among other methods, be served upon Artist by delivering or mailing the same, via registered or certified mail, return receipt requested, addressed to Artist at the address set forth in paragraph 16 hereof or such other address as Artist may designate pursuant to paragraph 16 hereof. Any such delivery of mail service shall be deemed to have the same force and effect as personal service within the State of _____.

15. *Definitions.*

(a) "Person" means a person, firm or corporation; (b) "Master" means a fully mixed, edited, equalized and leadered fifteen (15) i.p.s. one-quarter inch or thirty (30) i.p.s. one-half inch tape recording, theretofore unreleased, which (i) has been accepted by Company as technically and commercially satisfactory for the production and sale of records, (ii) in Company's reasonable good faith opinion does not constitute a libel, slander or other invasion of third-party rights, and does not violate Company's standards of decency or constitute an obscenity, (iii) embodies a performance featuring only Artist, of a selection not previously recorded by Artist, (iv) has been completely recorded by Artist during the term hereof in a first-class recording studio, (v) has a playing time of not less than two (2) minutes, and (vi) unless Artist is solely an instrumentalist, does not embody solely an instrumental performance; (c) "delivery", or words of like connotation, shall mean, with respect to each particular Master, the delivery to Company of all necessary approvals, permissions, label copy information, licenses and consents required to enable Company to release records embodying such Master, the physical tender of such Master to Company's offices in _____, and Company's acceptance of such Master as complying with this paragraph 15(c); (d) "selection" or "composition" means a single musical composition, including a medley, and all components thereof (musical or otherwise); (e) "phonograph record" or "record" means all forms of reproductions now or hereafter known, manufactured or distributed primarily for home use, school use, juke-box use or use in means of transportation, including records of sound alone and audio-visual records; provided, however, that, subject to paragraph 18 below, and to Company's right to license the right to embody a particular Master in audio-visual devices intended primarily for home use (e.g. videodiscs, videocassettes) in connection with Company's issuance of a license for the inclusion of such Master in a feature film or other audio-visual program, neither Company nor Artist shall exploit any audiovisual devices intended primarily for home use embodying the musical performances of Artist without the prior written consent of the other party hereto; (f) a "Video Song" means a film, videotape or other device utilized for the reproduction of a combination of Artist's audio performance of one (1) musical selection and a visual rendition of Artist's performance (or other visual accompaniment); (g) "recording costs" shall refer to all direct costs incurred in the production of Masters, through the final lacquer master (but, if the final lacquer master is cut at any studio owned by Company _____ then such mastering costs shall not be recoupable hereunder), including, without limitation, all sums paid to the individual producer(s), musicians, vocalists, conductors, arrangers, orchestrators, copyists and engineers; transportation costs, hotel, living expenses, immigration clearances and per diems incurred in connection with the attendance of artists (including Artist), the individual producer(s), musicians and other essential personnel at recording sessions and the preparation therefor; payments to a union or guild trustee or fund based on services at recording sessions (and not based on sales of records hereunder); payments for studio or rehearsal hall rental; payments for tape, editing, mastering, mixing and other similar functions; reference dubs; equalizing time; and all other costs and expenses incurred hereunder, which are now or hereafter generally recognized as recording and mastering costs in the phonograph record industry; (h) "album" shall mean a set of no less than eight (8) and no more than twelve (12) Masters having an aggregate playing time of thirty-two (32) to forty (40) minutes and a "multiple album" shall mean a package containing two (2) or more albums which are sold as a unit; (i) "Mini-LP" shall mean a set of no less than four (4) and no more than seven (7) Masters having an aggregate playing time of not less than fifteen (15) minutes which bears a suggested retail list price ("SRLP") in the applicable country of the Territory which is (i) with respect to the United States and Canada, at least two dollars ($2.00) less than the SRLP of the majority of Company's or Company's licensee's, as applicable, then-current newly-released albums in the applicable country, and (ii) with respect to any particular country in the Territory but outside of the United States and Canada, eighty percent (80%) or less of the SRLP of the majority of the then-current newly-released albums of Company's licensee in such country; (j) "single" or "single record" shall mean a set of three (3) or fewer Masters; (k) "mid-price record" shall mean a record which is released under any label designation, _____ and bears a SRLP in the applicable country of the Territory of at least sixty-five percent (65%) but not more than eighty percent (80%) of the SRLP of the majority of Company's or Company's licensee's, as applicable, then-current newly-released records; (1) "budget record" shall mean a record which is released under any label designation, _____ and bears a SRLP in the applicable country of the Territory of less than sixty-five percent (65%) of the SRLP of a majority of Company's or Company's licensee's, as applicable, then-current newly-released records; (m) "sampler record" shall mean a record embodying Masters together with other recordings which is intended for sale at a price which is less than fifty percent (50%) of the price of then-current newly-released albums; (n) "net sales" shall mean the cumulative number of records sold by Company or Company's branches or affiliates to independent third parties, for which Company has been paid, less records returned for credit at any time for any reason, including at Company's request, and less all credits, cancellations, exchanges or other adjustments; (o) "net royalties" or "net receipts" shall mean (i) gross advances paid by Company's licensees which are specifically paid in respect of Masters hereunder, and (ii) gross royalties earned by Company [in excess of the gross advances described in the preceding clause (i)] in respect of uses of the Masters by Company's licensees of records embodying Masters, for which Company has been paid or has otherwise received a credit to Company's account, less Company's following expenses in respect of same: costs of collection, shipping, taxes, payments to any unions or guilds (or their trust funds), and mechanical copyright royalties; (p) "term" refers to the initial period and any option period for which Company has exercised an option under paragraph 1 hereof; (q) "period of the term" means the initial period, or an option period for which Company has exercised an option under paragraph 1 hereof.

16. *Notices.*

All notices required hereunder or which either party desires to serve upon the other shall be in writing and shall be deemed given when addressed as set forth below and when delivered personally, with a receipt signed by a principal or officer of the deliveree; when deposited, postage prepaid, in the United States mails (certified or registered mail, return receipt requested, in all cases other than royalty statements); when deposited, toll prepaid, in any telegraph office in the United States; or when transmitted via telex. Addresses for notices shall be as follows:

TO ARTISTS:

_____

_____

TO COMPANY:

_____

_____

or such other address as either party may designate by notice given as aforesaid; provided, however, that notice of a change of address shall be effective only after receipt thereof.

17. *"Greatest Hits" Albums.*

(a) Notwithstanding anything to the contrary contained herein, during the term hereof, upon Company's request, Artist shall record and deliver to Company no more than two (2) Masters featuring the performances of Artist (each of such Masters is hereinafter referred to as a "New Greatest Hits Master") to be included in each "Greatest Hits" or "Best of" album (both such types of albums being herein referred to as a "Greatest Hits Album") released by Company in the United States during the term hereof. Each New Greatest Hits Master shall (i) embody the performance of Artist of a musical composition not theretofore recorded by Artist, (ii) subject to Artist's prior professional commitments, be delivered to Company no later than sixty (60) days after Company's request therefor, and (iii) be in addition to (and, accordingly, shall not be deemed delivered in partial satisfaction of) Artist's Recording Commitment set forth in paragraph 2 hereof. Company shall pay for the costs of recording each such New Greatest Hits Master up to the amount of an "Authorized Budget" therefor to be approved in writing by Company.

(b) (i) Artist shall have the right to approve the selections to be embodied in any Greatest Hits Album released in the United States during the term hereof and the sequencing thereof, which approval shall not be unreasonably with-held; provided, however, that the "A" side of any single record that has appeared in the Top 75 of the *Billboard* "Pop" Chart (or the equivalent charts in *Cashbox*) shall be deemed approved by Artist. Artist shall be deemed to have approved any selection not disapproved in writing by Artist within five (5) business days after Artist's receipt of Company's request for such approval.

(ii) Company shall consult with Artist with respect to the selections to be embodied in any Greatest Hits Album released in the United States after the term hereof and the sequencing thereof; provided, however, that Company's inadvertent failure to so consult with Artist shall not constitute a breach of this agreement.

(c) Provided that Artist is not then in default of any of Artist's material obligations hereunder, with respect to each Greatest Hits Album, if any, released by Company in the United States which embodies all New Greatest Hits Masters requested therefor by Company, if any, as permitted herein, Company shall pay to Artist, as an advance against royalties hereunder, the amount, if any, by which _____ Dollars ($____) exceeds the unrecouped balance in Artist's royalty account hereunder as of the date of release of such Greatest Hits Album in the United States.

(d) Notwithstanding anything to the contrary contained herein, in the event that Artist fails to record and deliver any New Greatest Hits Master requested by Company pursuant to paragraph 17(a) above in the time period provided therein, Company shall have the right to release the applicable Greatest Hits Album, as provided herein, prior to Artist's delivery to Company of such New Greatest Hits Master and, in such event, Company shall have no obligation to pay Artist any advance whatsoever in respect of such Greatest Hits Album.

(e) With respect to each Greatest Hits Album, if any, to be released by Company in the United States after the term hereof, Company shall consult with Artist and with Artist's new record company, if any, in good faith, to coordinate the release of such Greatest Hits Album in the United States with the release of other albums featuring solely the performances of Artist with the intention that Company shall not release such Greatest Hits Album in the United States within four (4) months following the release of any such other album; provided, however, that if Company delays the release of any such Greatest Hits Album until four (4) months after the release of any such other album embodying solely the performances of Artist, then Company shall have the right to release such Greatest Hits Album at any time after the expiration of such four (4) month period.

18. *Video Songs*

If Company and Artist mutually decide to provide one (1) or more Video

Songs during the term hereof (which neither Company nor Artist is under any obligation whatsoever to do), the following shall be applicable:

(a) The selection(s) to be embodied in each Video Song (the "Compositions") shall be designated by Company.

(b) Each Video Song shall be shot on a date or dates and at a location or locations to be mutually designated by Company and Artist.

(c) The producer and director of each Video Song, and the concept or script for each Video Song, shall each be approved by both Company and Artist. Company shall engage the producer, director and other production personnel for each Video Song, and shall be responsible for and shall pay the production costs of each Video Song in an amount not in excess of a budget to be established in advance by Company and Artist (the "Production Budget"). Artist shall be responsible for and shall pay the production costs for each Video Song which are in excess of the Production Budget therefor if such excess is incurred as a result of Artist's acts or omissions. If such excess production costs are incurred solely as a result of causes other than Artist's acts or omissions, Artist shall not be obligated to pay such excess costs but Company shall have the right to recoup such excess costs from Gross Video Receipts (as the term "Gross Video Receipts" is hereinafter defined). In the event that Company pays any production cost for which Artist is responsible pursuant to the foregoing (which Company is in no way obligated to do), Artist shall promptly reimburse Company for such excess upon demand and, without limiting Company's other rights and remedies, Company may deduct an amount equal to such excess from any monies otherwise payable to Artist hereunder. One-half (½) of the production costs for which Company is responsible pursuant to this paragraph shall be recoupable from royalties (other than mechanical copyright royalties) payable to Artist under this agreement or any other agreement between Company and Artist (or any person furnishing Artist's recording services) with respect to Artist's recording services, and the other one-half (½) thereof shall be non-recoupable from record royalties (but all production costs of Video Songs which are paid or incurred by Company, to the extent that same are not recouped from record royalties, shall be recoupable from Gross Video Receipts as set forth in paragraph 1(q) of Exhibit A hereto).

(d) Company shall be the sole owner of all rights in and to each Video Song (including the Territory copyrights therein and thereto) for the Territory.

(e) Artist shall fully cooperate with the producer, director and all other production personnel in the production of each Video Song and, to the extent required, shall render Artist's services as a visual performer in connection with each Video Song.

(f) Artist shall issue (or shall cause the music publishing companies having the right to do so to issue) (i) worldwide, perpetual synchronization licenses to Company for the use of all Controlled Compositions in Video Songs, and (ii) perpetual licenses to Company for public performance in the United States (to the extent that ASCAP and BMI are unable to issue same) of all Controlled Compositions in Video Songs, each such license to be issued at no cost and to be effective as of the commencement of production of the applicable Video Song (and Artist's execution of this agreement shall constitute the issuance of such licenses by any music publishing company which is owned or controlled by Artist or by any person owned or controlled by Artist). In the event that Artist shall fail to cause any such music publishing company to issue any such license to Company, and if Company shall thereupon pay any fee to such music publishing company in order to obtain any such license, then Company shall have the right to deduct the amount of such license fee from any and all monies otherwise payable to Artist hereunder.

(g) Company shall have the right to use and allow others to use each Video Song for advertising and promotional purposes with no payment to Artist. As used herein, "advertising and promotional purposes" shall mean all uses for which Company receives no monetary consideration from licensees in excess of a reasonable amount as reimbursement for the actual costs incurred by Company for tape stock, duplication of the Video Song and shipping.

(h) Company shall also have the right to use and allow others to use the Video Songs for commercial purposes. As used herein, "commercial purposes" shall mean any use for which Company receives monetary consideration in excess of a reasonable amount as reimbursement for the actual costs incurred by Company for tape stock, duplication of the Video Song and shipping.

(i) Company shall have the right to use and publish, and to permit others to use and publish, Artist's name and likeness and biographical material concerning Artist, in each Video Song and for advertising and purposes of trade in connection with the Video Songs; provided, that such materials (other than the Video Songs themselves) shall be subject to Artist's approval as set forth in paragraph 6 (b) above.

(j) In the event that, at any time from and after the date when Company and Artist schedule the commencement of production of a particular Video Song but prior to the completion of Artist's services with respect to such Video Song, Artist is prevented from commencing or continuing such services as set forth herein by reason of injury or sickness, Artist shall (i) immediately notify Company of such circumstances, (ii) immediately procure the attention of a duly-qualified physician, (iii) obtain and provide to Company such physician's certificate detailing fully the nature of such incapacity and the circumstances in which such incapacity arises, (iv) submit to such examinations with respect to such incapacity as shall be required by Company or Company's insurance carrier, and (v) cooperate with Company and Company's insurance carrier with respect to any insurance claim in connection with such incapacity; provided, however, that Company shall not require Artist to fulfill any obligations under this paragraph 18(j) in excess of those required by Company's insurance carrier. Notwithstanding the provisions of paragraph 18(c) above, if and to the extent that Company recovers from Company's insurance carrier any production costs for a particular Video in excess of the Production Budget therefor, for which excess costs Artist is responsible pursuant to paragraph 18(c) above and which have been previously charged against Artist's account hereunder or for which Artist has theretofore reimbursed Company, Company shall, upon such recovery, re-credit Artist's account or reimburse Artist, as applicable, in the amount of such recovery.

19. *Release of Product After Term.*

Notwithstanding anything to the contrary contained herein, in the event that Company shall exercise all of the options provided for in paragraph 1 above, then Artist shall not authorize any person or company (other than Company) to release any recording embodying Artist's performances until nine (9) months following the delivery by Artist to Company of the last album required to be delivered in satisfaction of the Recording Commitment hereof.

20. *Marketing Restrictions.*

Notwithstanding anything to the contrary contained herein:

(a) Except with respect to so-called "intransit" uses, no more than two (2) Masters shall be coupled on any particular record embodying master recordings featuring artists other than Artist for release in the United States and Canada during the term hereof without Artist's written consent.

(b) Company shall not distribute copies of any album hereunder on a budget-line label in the United States prior to the date which is eighteen (18) months after the initial release in the United States of such album unless Company shall pay Artist royalties with respect to any such copies distributed prior to the expiration of such eighteen (18) month period at the rate set forth in paragraph 1(a) of Exhibit A hereto without reduction in such rate pursuant to paragraph 1(k)(iv) of Exhibit A hereto.

(c) Company shall not distribute copies of any album hereunder as mid-price records in the United States prior to the date which is nine (9) months after the initial United States release of such album unless Company shall pay Artist royalties with respect to any such copies distributed prior to the expiration of such nine (9) month period at the rate set forth in paragraph 1(a) of Exhibit A hereto without reduction in such rate pursuant to paragraph 1(k)(v) of Exhibit A hereto.

(d) Company shall not sell records hereunder as premiums in connection with other products or services without Artist's written consent, which may be withheld for any reason.

(e) Company shall not sell copies of any album hereunder as "cut-outs" (i.e. records which have been deleted from Company's catalogue) or as overstock in the United States until twelve (12) months after the initial release of such album in the United States.

(f) Company shall not, during the term hereof, authorize the use of any Master hereunder for any non-phonograph record use (including, without limitation, in the soundtrack of a motion picture or television program or in a commercial advertising a product other than records hereunder) without the written consent of Artist, which consent may be withheld for any reason.

(g) No "live" recordings of Artist's performances may be made or utilized by Company without Artist's written consent, which may be withheld for any reason.

21. *Merchandising.*

It is expressly understood and agreed that no so-called "merchandising rights" are granted to Company hereunder and, accordingly, without limiting the generality of the foregoing, Company shall not have the right to use or license others to use Artist's name and/or likeness in connection with anything other than the promotion and exploitation of Masters and Video Songs hereunder, in accordance with all the terms and provisions hereof, it being understood that Company shall have no right to and shall not derive any profit from such promotional activities.

22. *Editing and Remixing.*

Company shall not edit, cut, remix or in any way alter Masters delivered hereunder except as to (a) non-disc configurations, and then solely for timing purposes, and (b) single records throughout the Territory. In respect of United States single records, if a representative of Artist specifically designated in writing for this purpose is available in Burbank, California, such representative shall have the right to edit, remix or cut Masters for single records (if necessary), and if such individual fails to do so within ten (10) days after receipt of Company's request, Company may edit, remix or cut such Masters as it deems appropriate (subject to such individual's approval, which approval shall be deemed given if written objection is not given to Company within five (5) days after receipt of the item, stating the basis of the objection). If such individual edits, remixes or cuts for a single record and Company does not approve such editing, remixing or cutting, Company may re-edit, remix or re-cut same (subject to such individual's approval, which approval shall be deemed given if written objection is not given to Company within five (5) days after receipt of the item, stating the basis of the objection) or re-submit same to Artist's representative for re-editing, remixing or re-cutting in accordance with the above ten (10) day procedure. The individual producer of the Master involved is hereby designated for purposes of this paragraph 22, until further notice to Company, as the person authorized on Artist's behalf to edit, remix or cut Masters for single records in accordance with the procedure set forth herein.

23. *Sideman Performances.*

Notwithstanding anything to the contrary contained herein, Artist shall have the right, during the term hereof, to perform as a background sideman, background vocalist or background instrumentalist for the purpose of making phonograph record master recordings which are recorded by featured artist(s) other than Artist and are released by record companies other than Company on the following terms and conditions:

(a) Artist's such performance shall be only in a background capacity and under no circumstances shall Artist perform as a featured artist, including, without limitation, in a duet performance;

(b) No such performance shall interrupt, delay or interfere with Artist's rendition of services hereunder or with any professional engagement to which Artist is committed which is intended to aid in the promotion of the phonograph records embodying Masters hereunder;

(c) No such performance shall be rendered in connection with the recording of any musical composition embodied on a Master theretofore or thereafter delivered by Artist hereunder.

(d) No such performance shall be rendered on any recording of which Artist is an individual producer.

(e) Artist's name and likeness, and biographical material concerning Artist, shall not be utilized in any manner in connection with the manufacture, sale or other exploitation of any such phonograph records embodying Artist's performances or in connection with the advertising thereof, except that Artist's name may be printed on the liner notes of any album embodying Artist's such performances in type no larger or more prominent than that used for any other background musician, background vocalist or background instrumentalist whose performances are embodied therein and, in such event, Company shall receive a courtesy credit in the customary manner.

24. *Acknowledgement.*

Artist acknowledges that the foregoing agreement for Artist's services covered by the AFTRA Phonograph Code may include provisions which relate to the following: Music Publishing, Audio-Visual Production, Merchandising and Mechanical Royalties.

By_____

_____

_____

—————

Exhibit A

ROYALTY PROVISIONS

The following provisions constitute an integral part of the agreement between _____ ("Company") and _____ ("Artist") dated _____ ____, 198____ (the "Agreement").

1. Company agrees to pay to Artist a royalty based on one hundred percent (100%) of the net sales of phonograph records embodying Masters, computed on the suggested retail list price ("SRLP") of such records (except as otherwise provided), as follows:

(a) (i) With respect to net sales (in tape and disc configuration) through normal retail channels in the United States (such net sales being hereinafter referred to as "U.S. Net Sales") of the First Album and the Second Album, _____ percent (____%) with respect to the first _____ ( ) U.S. Net Sales of each of said albums, _____ percent (____%) with respect to U.S. Net Sales of each of said albums in excess of _____ ( ) but not in excess of _____ ( ), ____ percent (__%) with respect to U.S. Net Sales of each of said albums in excess of _____ ( ) but not in excess of _____ ( ), ____ percent (__%) with respect to U.S. Net Sales of each of said albums in excess of _____ ( ) but not in excess of _____ ( ) and ____ percent (__%) with respect to U.S. Net Sales of each of said albums in excess of _____ ( ), computed separately on an album-by-album basis.

(ii) With respect to U.S. Net Sales of the Third Album and the Fourth Album, ____ percent (__%) with respect to the first _____ ( ) U.S. Net Sales of each of said albums, ____ percent (__%) with respect to U.S. Net Sales of each of said albums in excess of _____ ( ) but not in excess of _____ ( ), ____ percent (__%) with respect to U.S. Net Sales of each of said albums in excess of _____ ( ) but not in excess of _____ ( ), ____ percent (__%) with respect to U.S. Net Sales of each of said albums in excess of _____ (   ) but not in excess of _____ (   ) and ____ percent (__%) with respect to U.S. Net Sales of each said albums in excess of _____ (   ), computed separately on an album-by-album basis.

(iii) With respect to U.S. Net Sales of the Fifth Album and the Sixth Album, ____ percent (__%) with respect to the first _____ (   ) U.S. Net Sales of each of said albums, ____ percent (__%) with respect to U.S. Net Sales of each of said albums in excess of _____ (   ) but not in excess of _____ (   ), ____ percent (__%) with respect to U.S. Net Sales of each of said albums in excess of _____ (   ) but not in excess of _____ (   ), ____ percent (__%) with respect to U.S. Net Sales of each of said albums in excess of _____ (   ) but not in excess of _____ (   ) and ____ percent (__%) with respect to U.S. Net Sales of each of said albums in excess of _____ (   ), computed separately on an album-by-album basis.

(iv) With respect to U.S. Net Sales of the Seventh Album and the Eighth Album, ____ percent (__%) with respect to the first _____ (   ) U.S. Net Sales of each of said albums, ____ percent (__%) with respect to U.S. Net Sales of each of said albums in excess of _____ (   ) but not in excess of _____ (   ), ____ percent (__%) with respect to U.S. Net Sales of each of said albums in excess of _____ (   ) but not in excess of _____ (   ), ____ percent (__%) with respect to U.S. Net Sales of each of said albums in excess of _____ (   ) but not in excess of _____ (   ) and ____ percent (__%) with respect to U.S. Net Sales of each of said albums in excess of _____ (   ), computed separately on an album-by-album basis.

(v) The only net sales to be considered for purposes of escalating the royalty rates pursuant to paragraphs 1(a)(i), 1(a)(ii), 1(a)(iii), and 1(a)(iv) above shall be those U.S. Net Sales for which a royalty is payable under this paragraph 1(a). Without limiting the foregoing, net sales subject to paragraphs 1(b) through (p) of this Exhibit A shall not be considered. None of the foregoing escalations shall result in an increase in any royalty rates contained herein other than for United States net sales under this paragraph 1(a), even though other royalties may be based on the royalty rates set forth in this paragraph 1(a). No re-packaged or other records not consisting solely of theretofore unreleased Masters shall be considered for purposes of the foregoing escalations.

(vi) As used herein, the "Base U.S. Album Royalty Rate" for a particular album recorded and delivered in satisfaction of the Recording Commitment of the Agreement (and each Master embodied therein) shall mean a royalty rate equal to the royalty rate for the first U.S. Net Sale of such album as set forth in this paragraph 1(a).

(b) The United States royalty rate for each Master contained on a "Best of" or "Greatest Hits" album shall be the highest rate attained by such Master (in accordance with paragraph 1(a) above) at the time the "Best of" or "Greatest Hits" album is initially released, and such rates shall not thereafter escalate for any reason whatsoever. The royalty rate applicable to each New Greatest Hits Master in each country of the Territory shall be the rate in effect in such country for the album released during the contract period in which such "Greatest Hits" or "Best of" album is released in such country.

(c) With respect to net sales of single records through normal retail channels in the United States, ____ percent (__%) with respect to singles derived from the First through Fourth Albums and ____ percent (__%) with respect to singles derived from the Fifth through Eighth Albums. As used herein, the "Base U.S. Single Royalty Rate" for each Master hereunder shall mean the royalty rates set forth in this paragraph 1(c) with respect to such Master as embodied on single records in the United States.

(d) (i) With respect to net sales of each album of the Recording Commitment (in disc and tape configuration) through normal retail channels in Canada and with respect to each Master initially embodied thereon as embodied on other albums (including records sold for export to licensees in Canada), the royalty rate shall be ____ percent (__%) of the Base U.S. Album Royalty Rate for the applicable album of the Recording Commitment.

(ii) With respect to net sales of single records through normal retail channels in Canada (including records sold for export to licensees in Canada), the royalty rate shall be ____ percent (__%) of the Base U.S. Single Royalty Rate.

(e) (i) With respect to net sales of each album of the Recording Commitment (in disc and tape configuration) through normal retail channels in the United Kingdom, West Germany and Australia and with respect to each Master initially embodied thereon as embodied on other albums (including records sold for export to licensees in said countries), the royalty rate shall be ____ percent (__%) of the Base U.S. Album Royalty Rate for the applicable album of the Recording Commitment.

(ii) With respect to net sales of single records through normal retail channels in the United Kingdom, West Germany and Australia (including records sold for export to licensees in said countries), the royalty rate shall be ____ percent (__%) of the Base U.S. Single Royalty Rate.

(f) (i) With respect to net sales of each album of the Recording Commitment (in disc and tape configuration) through normal retail channels in France and Japan and with respect to each Master initially embodied thereon as embodied on other albums (including records sold for export to licensees in said countries), the royalty rate shall be ____ percent (__%) of the Base U.S. Album Royalty Rate for the applicable album of the Recording Commitment.

(ii) With respect to net sales of single records through normal retail channels in France and Japan (including records sold for export to licensees in said countries), the royalty rate shall be ____ percent (__%) of the Base U.S. Single Royalty Rate.

(g) (i) With respect to net sales of each album of the Recording Commitment (in disc and tape configuration) through normal retail channels in the Territory but outside of the United States, Canada, the United Kingdom, Australia, West Germany, France and Japan and with respect to each Master initially embodied thereon as embodied on other albums (including records sold for export to licensees in any of such other countries), the royalty rate shall be ____ percent (__%) of the Base U.S. Album Royalty Rate for the applicable album.

(ii) With respect to net sales of single records through normal retail channels in the Territory but outside of the United States, Canada, the United Kingdom, Australia, West Germany, France and Japan (including records sold for export to licensees in any of such other countries), the royalty rate shall be ____ percent (__%) of the Base U.S. Single Royalty Rate.

(h) Notwithstanding anything to the contrary contained herein, the royalty rate payable for records sold in the form of pre-recorded tapes or any other form (other than disc) shall be the otherwise applicable royalty rate; provided, that if Company's price to its subdistributors of any record sold in pre-recorded tape form (or any form other than disc) shall be eighty percent (80%) or less of Company's price to its subdistributors for the corresponding record in disc form, then the royalty rate at which royalties are computed with respect to such pre-recorded tapes (or other form other than disc) shall be eighty percent (80%) of the otherwise applicable rate based upon the actual SLRP of such pre-recorded tapes (or other form other than disc).

(i) Notwithstanding anything to the contrary contained herein, with respect to records sold via direct mail or through a mail order operation (including, without limitation, record club plans) by licensees of Company, Artists's royalty shall be one-half (½) of the net royalty paid Company by its licensees in connection with such sales.

(j) (i) Notwithstanding anything to the contrary contained herein, with respect to sales of records in any configuration (including, without limitation, tapes, discs or CD LPs) by non-affiliated licensees of Company (at present, only so-called "audiophile" recordings), Artist's royalty shall be one-half (½) of the net royalty paid Company by such licensees in connection with such sales.

(ii) The royalty rate in respect of net sales of copies of any album hereunder in so-called "compact disc" configuration (such net sales being herein referred to as "CD Sales") shall be as follows: (A) with respect to CD Sales of any album which is delivered and/or initially released hereunder on or before the date which is three (3) years after the date hereof (each such album being herein referred to as a "CD LP"), the royalty rate with respect to CD Sales thereof in each country of the Territory which take place within three (3) years after the initial release thereof [such three (3) year period with respect to each CD LP being herein referred to as the "Initial CD Release Period" applicable thereto] shall be the royalty rate applicable to the first net sale of such album through normal retail channels in the applicable country pursuant to this Exhibit A but shall be based on the SRLP of such album in vinyl disc configuration (the vinyl disc album corresponding to a particular CD LP being referred to as the "Vinyl LP") in the applicable country or, if a particular CD LP does not have a Vinyl LP in a particular country, then the royalty rate therefor in such country shall be based on the SRLP of the majority of Company's or Company's licensee's (as applicable) full-priced newly-released albums in vinyl disc configuration in such country, and (B) with respect to CD Sales of each CD LP which take place after the Initial CD Release Period applicable thereto, and with respect to CD Sales of albums hereunder which are not CD LPs, the royalty rate shall be negotiated in good faith by Company and Artist and shall be consistent with the then-current practice in the United States recording industry applicable to adjustments of royalty rates applicable to albums sold in "compact disc" configuration; provided, that Company shall have the absolute right to exploit CD LPs in "compact disc" configuration after the Initial CD Release Period and to exploit all other albums in "compact disc" configuration even prior to the conclusion of such good-faith negotiations. Except as provided to the contrary in this paragraph 1(j)(ii), the royalty payable hereunder in respect of CD Sales shall be pro-rated, reduced, computed and paid in accordance with the provisions of this Agreement.

(k) Notwithstanding anything to the contrary contained herein:

(i) With respect to the following types of records, the royalty rate shall be one-half (½) of the otherwise applicable royalty rate, based on the SRLP of the record involved, unless otherwise indicated: (A) records sold as premiums in connection with other products or services and the SRLP for premiums shall be deemed the net amount received by Company from an actual sale of such record; and (B) records sold to governmental agencies or institutions (including, without limitation, their agencies and departments, but excluding Armed Forces Post Exchanges and similar retail-type facilities).

(ii) With respect to records sold via television and/or radio advertisements through mail order, telephone order or special retail outlets (such as "K-Tel"-type packages), by licensees of Company, the royalty shall be one-half (½) of the net receipts received by Company from its licensees. Notwithstanding the foregoing, in the event that Company shall sell records directly (and not through licensees) via television and/or radio advertisements or through mail or phone order in the United States, then such sales for purposes of paragraph 1(a) of this Exhibit A shall be deemed sales through normal retail channels for all purposes (including, without limitation, for purposes of escalating royalties pursuant to paragraph 1(a) of this Exhibit A and for purposes of getting the benefit of escalated royalties) and, accordingly, Artist shall be paid royalties with respect thereto in accordance with paragraph 1(a) hereof but only with respect to eighty-five percent (85%) of such net sales.

(iii) With respect to records sold through Armed Forces Post Exchanges, ship's stores and other military facilities ("PX Records"), the royalty rate shall be the otherwise applicable royalty rate, based on the SRLP of the record involved in the Armed Forces Post Exchanges, ship's stores and other military facilities, as applicable; provided, that with respect to PX Records sold in the Territory but outside of the United States, the royalty rate shall be three-fourths (¾) of the otherwise applicable royalty rate, based on the SRLP of the record involved in the Armed Forces Post Exchanges, ship's stores and other military facilities, as applicable.

(iv) With respect to budget records, the royalty rate shall be one-half (½) of the otherwise applicable royalty rate.

(v) With respect to mid-price records, the royalty rate shall be three-fourths (¾) of the otherwise applicable royalty rate.

(vi) With respect to Mini-LPs, the royalty rate shall be three-fourths (¾) of the otherwise applicable royalty rate with respect to records in album configuration.

(vii) In the event that Company shall sell or license third parties to sell "records" via telephone, satellite, cable or other direct transmission to the consumer over wire or through the air, such sales shall be deemed sales of such "records" through normal retail channels for all purposes (including, without limitation, for purposes of escalating royalties pursuant to paragraph 1(a) of this Exhibit A and for purposes of getting the benefit of escalated royalties) and, accordingly, Artist shall be paid royalties with respect thereto at the rates and in the manner set forth in paragraph 1(a), 1(b), 1(c), 1(d), 1(e), 1(f) or 1(g), as applicable, of this Exhibit A, but with respect to any such sales in the United States royalties shall only be paid with respect to eighty-five percent (85%) of such sales. For purposes of calculating royalties payable in connection with such sales, the SRLP of such "records" shall be deemed to be the then-current SRLP of tape copies of such records, and the same packaging deduction shall be made for such sales in accordance with paragraph 1(n)(ii) of this Exhibit A as is applicable to tape copies of such records.

(l) As to Masters embodying performances of Artist together with the performances of another royalty artist or artists (provided, that any such joint recordings shall require the approval of Artist and Company, which approval may be withheld by either party for any reason), the royalty otherwise payable hereunder, and the recording costs otherwise chargeable against Artist in respect of such Masters, shall be prorated on the basis of the number of royalty artists (including Artist) whose performances are embodied on such Masters, and for purposes of such proration any artist performing as a group shall be deemed one (1) artist. In the event Company couples Masters with recordings which are not Masters, the amounts otherwise payable to Artist hereunder shall be multiplied by a fraction, the numerator of which is the number of Masters which are embodied in the record involved and the denominator of which is the aggregate number of recordings (including Masters) embodied in such record.

(m) No royalties shall be payable in respect of (i) records furnished on a no-charge basis or sold for less than fifty percent (50%) of Company's (or its licensees') posted wholesale list price to disc jockeys, publishers, employees of Company (or its licensees), motion picture companies, radio and television stations and other customary recipients of free, discounted or promotional records; (ii) records sold by Company (or its licensees) at close-out or cut-out prices or for scrap (and, as used herein, "scrap" shall mean a sale to a third party for purposes of utilizing the raw material of which the records are made), or at less than Company's (or its licensees') inventory cost; (iii) records (or fractions thereof) given away or shipped on a so-called "no-charge" or "freebie" basis or sold for fifty percent (50%) or less of Company's (or its licensees') posted wholesale list price to distributors, subdistributors, dealers and others whether or not such records are intended for sale to third parties; (iv) sampler records; and (v) if Company, or its licensees sell records at a discount from Company's, or its licensees', as applicable, posted wholesale list price (but for more than fifty percent (50%) of such price), the number of records (or fractions thereof) determined by applying such discount to the total number of records shipped. For convenience, those records sold at a discount in lieu of or in addition to records furnished on a so-called "no-charge" basis (definitionally determined herein as the percentage amount of such discount multiplied by the number of records sold at such discount) and records furnished on such a so-called "no-charge" basis are collectively sometimes referred to herein as "Free Goods". References in this agreement to "records for which no royalties are payable hereunder", or words of similar connotation, shall include, without limitation, all Free Goods. Free Goods embodying albums or Mini-LPs hereunder are sometimes referred to herein as "Album Free Goods", and Free Goods embodying single records hereunder are sometimes referred to herein as "Single Free Goods". Company and Artist acknowledge and agree that, with respect to each album and Mini-LP hereunder, fifteen percent (15%) of the aggregate units of each album and Mini-LP sold by Company hereunder or shipped by Company hereunder shall be Album Free Goods. Company and Artist acknowledge and agree that, with respect to each single record hereunder, twenty-three percent (23%) of the aggregate units of such single record sold by Company or shipped by Company hereunder shall be shipped by Company hereunder as Single Free Goods. In addition to the foregoing Album Free Goods, Company shall have the right to ship Special Album Free Goods (as the term "Special Album Free Goods" is hereinafter defined) but not in excess of ten percent (10%) of all records embodying each album and Mini-LP sold by Company or shipped by Company hereunder. In addition to the foregoing Single Free Goods, Company shall have the right to ship Special Single Free Goods (as the term "Special Single Free Goods" is hereinafter defined) but not in excess of ten percent (10%) of the aggregate units of each single record sold by Company or shipped by Company hereunder. In the event that Company shall ship Free Goods and/ or Special Free Goods (as the term "Special Free Goods" is hereinafter defined) in excess of the limits set forth above, Company shall not be deemed in breach hereof, and Company's only obligation to Artist in such event shall be to pay Artist royalties as provided herein in respect of such excess Free Goods or Special Free Goods, as applicable. From time to time, Company may conduct special programs with respect to the marketing and merchandising of recordings of various artists which may include Artist hereunder, or special "impact" programs concerning the marketing and merchandising of recordings hereunder, and all of said special programs may involve the distribution of additional Free Goods; all such additional Free Goods shipped pursuant to any such special program are herein referred to as "Special Free Goods", all additional Album Free Goods shipped pursuant to any such special program are herein referred to as "Special Album Free Goods", and all additional Single Free Goods shipped pursuant to any such special program are herein referred to as "Special Single Free Goods".

(n) Notwithstanding anything to the contrary contained herein, the following shall be excluded from the base against which the applicable royalty percentage rate is to be applied:

(i) All sales, use, excise, transactional, V.A.T. and other similar taxes included in the retail or other applicable price of records; and

(ii) In the case of records sold in or with jackets, cartridges, cassettes, boxes, reels or other devices or containers, an amount equal to ten percent (10%) of the SRLP for single-pocket albums, Mini-LPs, 7-inch single records in special sleeves, and 12-inch single records, fifteen percent (15%) thereof for multi-fold albums or albums with cardboard sleeves or special inserts or attachments, twenty percent (20%) thereof for tapes, and twenty-five percent (25%) thereof for CD LPs.

(o) Company may license Masters for phonograph record use or for any other type of use on a flat fee, royalty rate or cent rate basis, in which event, in lieu of any other payment due hereunder, Company shall credit Artist's royalty account with fifty percent (50%) of the net royalties actually received by Company.

(p) One-half (½) of Company's net receipts, if any, which are specifically referable (in reports to Company) for United States public performances of Masters less any portion thereof which is payable by Company to producers with respect to such public performances; provided, that if Artist receives payment in respect thereof from a third party, Company shall pay Artist such amount as shall provide Artist with a total (including the share received by Artist from third parties) equal to one-half (½) of the aggregate amount paid to Company, Artist and any individual producers.

(q) (i) Notwithstanding anything to the contrary contained herein, as to the use of Video Songs for commercial purposes Artist shall be paid a royalty equal to one-half (½) of Company's Net Video Receipts, as the term "Net Video Receipts" is hereinafter defined.

(ii) As used herein, "Gross Video Receipts" shall mean one hundred percent (100%) of monies actually received by Company (or credited to Company's account) in the United States from the exploitation of Video Songs throughout the Territory; provided, that monies actually received by Company or credited to Company's account shall be subject to adjustment for returns, refunds, credits, settlements, allowances, rebates and discounts.

(iii) As used herein, "Net Video Receipts" shall mean Gross Video Receipts less:

(A) All production costs and distribution costs (as the terms "production costs" and "distribution costs" are hereinafter defined) paid or incurred by Company in connection with Video Songs;

(B) Any and all payments required to be made to third parties, including, without limitation, to unions or guilds or to the publishers of Non-Controlled Compositions (but expressly excluding any "Royalty Participant", as the term "Royalty Participant" is hereinafter defined) in connection with the production and/or exploitation of Video Songs; and

(C) All sales, gross receipts, foreign withholding, excise, use, value added, personal property or similar taxes paid or incurred by Company with respect to the production or exploitation of Video Songs.

(iv) Artist shall be solely responsible for and shall pay any and all monies payable to the producer(s) of the master recording(s) embodied in Video Songs (the "Video Masters") and to any other third parties (except the publishers of Non-Controlled Compositions which are embodied in the applicable Video Song(s) and any unions or guilds) who are entitled to a royalty or any other payment in respect of Company's exploitation of Video Masters (each such third party being hereinafter referred to as a "Royalty Participant") if the applicable Royalty Participant is entitled to any monies in connection with the applicable Video Song. Notwithstanding the foregoing, in the event Company shall pay or be required to pay any such monies directly to any Royalty Participant, then Artist's royalties hereunder shall be reduced by an amount equal to all such payments.

(v) As used herein, (A) "distribution costs" of Video Songs shall mean all costs paid or incurred by Company in connection with the distribution of Video Songs other than Company's general overhead expenses, and (B) "production costs" of Video Songs means all direct costs incurred in the production of Video Songs through the final 1-inch master tape or film, including, without limitation, all sums paid to or for production companies (including, without limitation, payments to or for producers, directors, writers and associate producers); payments to or for technical crews (including, without limitation, payments to or for cameramen, videomen, maintenance engineers, audio crew members and equipment); payments to or for lighting crews (including, without limitation, payments for or to lighting directors, gaffers, electricians, best boys, grips and equipment); payments to or for set construction crews and material; payments for or to production crews (including, without limitation, payments for or to production managers and assistants, secretaries, floor managers, art directors, prop masters, make-up and wardrobe personnel and materials, go-fers and script girls); location and police permits and fees (including hall and studio rental); cartage; equipment rental; transportation costs, hotel expenses, living expenses and per diems incurred in connection with location scouting and the attendance of artists and all production personnel at pre-production, production and post-production sessions for Video Songs and the preparation therefor; insurance premiums paid in connection with the production of Video Songs; taxes and contingencies (including fees or mark-ups payable to any production company or any other person in connection with Video Songs); payments for tape, film or other stock; payments for on-line and off-line editing, mixing, Quantel or other special effects, color correction, audio track transfer or dubbing, title cards and similar functions; creation of one (1) ¾-inch videocassette with SMPTE code from the

1-inch master videotape; payments to all extras, sidemen and other persons appearing in Video Songs in respect of the production and use thereof; payments to any union or guild or union or guild trustee or fund in respect of Video Songs; and all other costs and expenses incurred with respect to Video Songs which are now or hereafter generally recognized as production costs of audio-visual programs.

(vi) In the event Company couples Video Songs with video songs which are not Video Songs hereunder, the amounts otherwise payable to Artist hereunder with respect to such coupled Video Songs shall be multiplied by a fraction, the numerator of which is the number of Video Songs involved and the denominator of which is the aggregate number of video songs (including Video Songs) involved, and each selection embodied on each Video Song and video song involved shall count as one (1) Video Song or video song for such purposes. If one (1) or more Video Songs are produced together with one (1) or more video songs which are not Video Songs so that some or all of the production costs are jointly attributable to all of such Video Songs and other video songs, then only a fraction of such joint production costs shall be chargeable against Artist in respect of such Video Song(s), the numerator of which is the number of Video Songs involved in such joint production and the denominator of which is the aggregate number of video songs (including Video Songs) involved in such joint production; any production costs incurred in such a joint production which are reasonably attributable solely to the Video Songs or the other video songs involved shall be attributed solely to the applicable Video Songs or video songs and shall not be apportioned as joint production costs as aforesaid.

(vii) In the event that Company shall manufacture and distribute in the United States videocassettes and/or videodiscs embodying one or more Video Songs, then Company shall pay to Artist a royalty, subject to the proration provisions of subparagraph 1(q)(vi) above, equal to ____ percent (__%) of Company's wholesale price to subdistributors of such videodiscs or videocassettes, as applicable. Such royalty shall be inclusive of all royalties that may be payable to all third parties (other than unions or guilds), including, without limitation, producers of the Masters embodied on each Video Song, producers and directors of the visual portion of such Video Song, and publishers of both Controlled Compositions and Non-Controlled Compositions. In the event that Company shall make any such payments to third parties with respect to any such videocassettes or videodiscs, Company shall have the right to deduct such payments from royalties otherwise payable to Artist with respect to each videodisc or videocassette.

(r) (i) For purposes of sales outside the United States, the SRLP shall be the SRLP from time to time of such records in the country of manufacture or the country of sale, as Company is paid. If there are no SRLPs of records in any particular country, then for the purposes of computing royalties hereunder the prices of records in such country generally regarded as the equivalent thereof shall be deemed the SRLPs of such records. Royalties on foreign sales shall be computed in the national currency of the country involved, and shall be deemed earned only when monies from sales on which such royalties are based are received by Company in the United States (or credited against an advance theretofore so received) at the dollar equivalent of the rate of exchange at which Company is paid, net of Artist's proportionate share of any and all applicable foreign taxes. In the event Company does not receive payments in United States dollars in the United States as a result of governmental restrictions and elects to accept payment in a foreign currency, Company may deposit Artist's royalties in such foreign currency to Artist's account (and at Artist's expense) in a depository selected by Artist. Deposit as aforesaid of payments representing royalties applicable hereto shall satisfy Company's obligations hereunder for the sales to which such royalty payments are applicable.

(ii) Notwithstanding anything to the contrary contained herein with respect to records sold in any country of the Territory in which governmental or other authorities place limits on the royalty rates permissible for remittances to the United States in respect of records sold therein, the royalty rate payable to Artist hereunder in respect of sales of records in each such territory shall equal the lesser of (A) the otherwise-applicable royalty rate payable in respect of records sold therein, and (B) the effective royalty rate permitted by such governmental or other authority for remittances to the United States, *less* (C) the sum of (1) a royalty equivalent to two percent (2%) of the retail list price (or other applicable base against which the applicable royalty percentage rate is applied pursuant to the terms hereof), and (2) such monies as Company or its licensees shall be required to pay to all applicable union funds in respect of said sales.

(s) Company may at any time elect to utilize a different method of computing royalties from that specified above so long as such method or methods are applicable to substantially all persons similarly engaged by Company, and provided that no such method reduces the net monies due Artist. In the event that Company shall no longer designate a SRLP for records hereunder in the United States, then for the purpose of computing royalties hereunder (i) with respect to sales of single disc albums through normal retail channels in the United States, the SRLP of such albums shall be deemed to be a dollar amount computed by multiplying Company's price to subdistributors (before consideration of any discount resulting from the distribution of Album Free Goods) for such albums by a fraction, the numerator of which is $8.98 and the denominator of which is $5.92 (which is Company's current price to subdistributors before consideration of any discount resulting from the distribution of

Album Free Goods for albums with an $8.98 SRLP), and (ii) with respect to the sale of single records through normal retail channels in the United States, the SRLP of such single records shall be deemed to be a dollar amount computed by multiplying Company's price to subdistributors for such single records (before consideration of any discount resulting from the distribution of Single Free Goods) by a fraction, the numerator of which is $1.99 and the denominator of which is $1.265 (which is Company's current price to subdistributors before consideration of any discount resulting from the distribution of Single Free Goods for single records with a $1.99 SRLP).

2. No royalties shall be payable to Artist unless and until Company is in a "recouped position" (i.e. Company has recouped from royalties otherwise payable hereunder, in accordance with the Agreement, all recoupable recording costs, advances, expenses, and other charges incurred or borne by Company under the Agreement which are recoupable in accordance with the terms and conditions thereof). If, at Artist's request, Company makes payment to Artist or a third party designee of Artist of amounts not provided for in the Agreement (which Company is in no way obligated to do), such payments shall also be recoupable as aforesaid unless Company agrees otherwise in writing. Prior to final determination thereof, Company may withhold a reasonable reserve against returns, etc., such reserve to be established by Company in its sound discretion, based on, among other factors, Artist's sales experience. Company shall not retain a reserve in excess of _____ percent (__%) of royalties otherwise payable for any particular accounting period. Company shall then include the amount so withheld as a part of the gross royalties payable with respect to the next accounting period hereunder, which such gross royalties shall be subject to the withholding of reserves in accordance with the immediately preceding sentence hereof, and so forth. Company agrees that, in the United States, records which are returned shall be charged to Artist's account in the same royalty-bearing to non-royalty bearing ratio as such records were originally credited to Artist's account.

3. (a) Within sixty (60) days after June 30 and December 31 of each year during which applicable phonograph records are sold, Company shall render a statement of accrued royalties earned under the Agreement during the preceding calendar half-year, less all amounts chargeable thereagainst (including, to the extent lawful or as permitted hereunder, all or any portion of any indebtedness then owing by Artist to Company) under the Agreement. Notwithstanding the foregoing, Company shall not have the right to recoup from royalties payable hereunder with respect to a given semi-annual accounting period advances or other recoupable payments paid to Artist or to third parties on Artist's behalf by Company hereunder after the close of such semi-annual accounting period unless Artist has requested that a payment scheduled to be made prior to the close of such semi-annual accounting period be

delayed until after the close of such semi-annual accounting period. Simultaneously with the rendering of its statement, Company shall pay Artist the net amount, if any, shown to be due thereon, less any deductions or withholdings required by law or any union or guild rules or regulations. Artist shall be deemed to have consented to each statement, and such statement shall become final and binding upon Artist, two (2) years after the rendition thereof unless Artist renders specific written objection thereto within such period; and if Company gives Artist written notice that it denies the validity of the objection, unless suit is instituted within one (1) year of the date Company gives such notice.

(b) Artist may designate a certified public accountant who may audit the books and records of Company concerning the distribution and sale of records embodying Masters. Said examination shall be at Artist's sole cost and expense, conducted during normal business hours and upon reasonable notice, and may not be conducted more than once annually. The books and records for a particular accounting period may only be audited as aforesaid during the two (2) years following rendition of the statement for such period. Further, such examination shall be conditioned upon the accountant's agreement to Company that he will not voluntarily disclose any findings to any person other than Artist, or Artist's attorney or other advisers and that he is not being compensated on a contingent fee basis.

MERCHANDISING AGREEMENT

LICENSING AGREEMENT
—with—

_____

AGREEMENT dated _____, 19____, between _____, a New York corporation having an office at _____ (hereinafter referred to as Licensor and _____ (hereinafter referred to as "Licensee") whose address is_____

_____

WITNESSETH:

WHEREAS, Licensor has rights to the name, likeness, character, symbol, design and visual representations listed on Schedule A hereof (which name, likeness, character, symbol, design and visual representations and/or each of the individual components thereof shall hereinafter be referred to as the "Property"), and

WHEREAS, Licensee desires to utilize the Property upon and in connection with the manufacture, sale and distribution of the articles described on Schedule A hereof;

NOW, THEREFORE, in consideration of the premises and the mutual covenants of the parties hereinafter set forth, it is agreed as follows:

1. Licensor hereby grants to Licensee, and Licensee hereby accepts the right, license and privilege of utilizing the Property, upon the terms and conditions hereinafter set forth, solely and only upon and in connection with the manufacture, sale and distribution of the articles listed on Schedule A hereof. Schedule A and all its terms and conditions are hereby incorporated in and made a part of this Agreement. Nothing in this Agreement shall be construed to prevent Licensor from granting any other licenses for the use of the Property or from utilizing the Property in any manner whatsoever, except that Licensor agrees that except as provided herein it will grant no other licenses in the territory effective during the term of this Agreement for the use of the Property in connection with the sale of the articles described on Schedule A hereof, provided however that if the articles licensed hereunder are limited as to suggested retail selling price, size or other characteristic, Licensor shall have the right to license to others the use of the Property for similar articles so long as such other licenses shall exclude the right to merchandise articles within the limitations expressly granted to the licensee hereunder.

2. The term of this Agreement shall be for the period set forth on Schedule A hereof, unless sooner terminated in accordance with the provisions hereof.

3. The license granted hereunder shall be for the territory set forth on Schedule A hereof. Licensee agrees that it will not make, or authorize any use,

direct or indirect, of the Property in any other area, and that it will not knowingly sell articles covered by this Agreement to persons who intend or are likely to resell them in any other area.

4. Licensee agrees to pay to Licensor as royalty a sum equal to the per cent set forth on Schedule A hereof of all net sales by Licensee or any of its affiliated, associated or subsidiary companies of the articles covered by this Agreement. The term "net sales" shall mean gross sales price on actual shipments by Licensee less quantity and trade discounts and returns for defective or damaged merchandise, but no deduction shall be made for cash or other discounts or uncollectible accounts. No costs incurred in the manufacture, sale, distribution or exploitation of the articles shall be deducted from any royalty payable by Licensee. Said royalty shall also be paid by Licensee to Licensor on all articles distributed by Licensee or any of its affiliated, associated or subsidiary companies even if not billed, such as free introductory offers, samples, etc., such royalty to be based upon the usual billing price for such articles if sold to the distributee.

5. Licensee agrees to pay to Licensor the minimum advance royalty set forth on Schedule A hereof as a non-returnable advance guarantee against royalties to be paid to Licensor during the term of this Agreement, to be paid on execution of this Agreement. No part of such minimum advance royalty shall in any event be repayable to Licensee, except as set forth in paragraphs 15 and 17 hereof.

6. Licensee agrees that the articles covered by this Agreement shall be of a high standard and of such style, appearance and quality as to be adequate and suited to their exploitation to the best advantage and to the protection and enhancement of the Property and the good will pertaining thereto, that such articles will be manufactured, sold and distributed in accordance with all applicable Federal, State and local laws, and that the policy of sale, distribution and exploitation by Licensee shall be of a high standard and to the best advantage and that the same shall in no manner reflect adversely upon the Property. The quality and style of such articles as well as of any carton, container or packing or wrapping material shall be subject to the written approval of Licensor. To this end Licensee shall, before selling or distributing any of the articles, furnish to Licensor free of cost, for its written approval, a reasonable number of samples of each article, its cartons, containers and packing and wrapping material. Such approval shall not be unreasonably withheld. In the event Licensor fails to approve in writing any of the samples of the articles furnished to Licensor within 21 days from the date of submission thereof, the articles shall be deemed to be disapproved. After samples have been approved pursuant to this paragraph, Licensee shall not depart therefrom in any respect without the prior written consent of Licensor. From time to time after Licensee has commenced selling the articles and upon

Licensor's written request, Licensee shall furnish without cost to Licensor not more than twenty-four additional random samples of each article being manufactured and sold by Licensee hereunder, together with any cartons, containers and packing and wrapping material used in connection therewith.

7. Within 30 days after the initial shipment of the articles covered by this Agreement, and promptly on the 15th day of each calendar month thereafter, Licensee shall furnish to Licensor complete and accurate statements certified to be accurate by Licensee showing the number, description and gross sales price, itemized deductions from gross sales price and net sales price of the articles covered by this Agreement distributed and/or sold by Licensee during the preceding calendar month, together with any returns made during the preceding calendar month. Such statements shall be furnished to Licensor whether or not any of the articles have been sold during the preceding calendar month. Royalties in excess of the aforementioned minimum advance royalty shall be due on the 15th day of the month following the calendar month in which earned and payment in U.S. currency shall accompany the statements furnished as required above. The receipt or acceptance by Licensor of any of the statements furnished pursuant to this Agreement or of any royalties paid hereunder (or the cashing of any royalty checks paid hereunder) shall not preclude Licensor from questioning the correctness thereof at any time, and in the event that any inconsistencies or mistakes are discovered in such statements or payments, they shall immediately be rectified and the appropriate payment made by Licensee.

8. Licensee agrees to keep accurate books of account and records at its principal place of business covering all transactions relating to the license hereby granted, and Licensor and its duly authorized representatives shall have the right at all reasonable hours of the day to an examination of said books of account and records and of all other documents and material in the possession or under the control of Licensee with respect to the subject matter and terms of this Agreement and shall have free and full access thereto for said purposes and for the purpose of making extracts therefrom. Upon demand of Licensor Licensee shall at its own expense furnish to Licensor a detailed statement by an independent certified public accountant showing the number, description, gross sales price, itemized deductions from gross sales price, and net sales price of the articles covered by this Agreement distributed and/or sold by Licensee to the date of Licensor's demand. All books of account and records shall be kept available for at least two years after the termination of this license.

9. (a) Licensee recognizes the great value of the good will associated with the Property, and acknowledges that the Property and all rights therein and good will pertaining thereto belong exclusively to Licensor, and that the Property has a secondary meaning in the mind of the public. Licensee agrees

that it will not during the term of this Agreement or thereafter attack the title or any rights of Licensor in and to the Property or attack the validity of this license. Licensor hereby indemnifies Licensee and undertakes to hold it harmless against breach by Licensor of any warranty or representation made by Licensor hereunder arising solely out of the use by Licensee of the Property as authorized in this Agreement, provided that prompt notice is given to Licensor of any such claim or suit and provided, further, that Licensor shall have the option to undertake and conduct the defense of any suit so brought.

(b) Licensee agrees to assist Licensor to the extent necessary in the procurement of any protection or to protect any of Licensor's rights to the Property, and Licensor if it so desires may commence or prosecute any claims or suits in its own name or in the name of Licensee or join Licensee as a party thereto. Licensee shall notify Licensor in writing of any infringements or imitations by others of the Property on articles similar to those covered by this Agreement which may come to Licensee's attention, and Licensor shall have the sole right to determine whether or not any action shall be taken on account of any such infringements or imitations. Licensee shall not institute any suit or take any action on account of any such infringements or imitations without first obtaining the written consent of Licensor to do so. All costs and expenses, including legal fees, incurred in connection with any such suits which are so instituted by Licensee with the consent of Licensor shall be borne solely by Licensee.

10. (a) Except for the rights licensed hereunder by Licensor to Licensee, Licensee hereby indemnifies and shall hold harmless Licensor and the performers and other personnel in or associated with any motion picture and/or television series produced and distributed by or for Licensor or its licensees relating to or based in whole or in part on the Property, and the person or firm whose property is being licensed hereunder, and parent, subsidiary and affiliated companies, and co-producers and co-venturers of Licensor and, where applicable, sponsors of any such television series and their respective advertising agencies, and officers, directors, agents and employees of each of the foregoing and all persons connected with and/or employed by them and each of them, from and against the costs and expenses of any and all claims, demands, causes of action and judgements arising out of the unauthorized use of any patent, process, method or device or out of infringement of any copyright, trade name, patent or label or invasion of the right of privacy, publicity, or other property right, or failure to perform, or defect in or use of the licensed articles, or infringement or breach of any other personal or property right, of any person, firm or corporation, by Licensee, its officers, employees, agents or anyone directly or indirectly, acting by, through, on behalf of, pursuant to contractual or any other relationship with Licensee in connection with the preparation, manufacture, distribution, advertising, pro-

motion and/or sale of the licensed articles and/or any material relating thereto and/or naming or referring to any such performers, personnel, marks and/or elements. With respect to the foregoing indemnity, Licensee shall defend and hold harmless all of the aforesaid parties and each of them, at no cost or expense to them whatsoever, including but not limited to attorney's fees and court costs. Licensor shall have the right to defend any such action or proceeding with attorneys of its own selection.

(b) Licensee shall obtain and maintain at its cost and expense standard Product Liability Insurance from a qualified insurance company licensed to do business in the State of New York naming Licensor and each and all of the parties indemnified in sub-paragraph (a) of this paragraph as additional named insureds, which policy shall provide protection against any and all claims, demands and causes of action arising out of any defects or failure to perform, alleged or otherwise, in the licensed articles or any material used in connection therewith or any use thereof; the amount and coverage shall be a minimum of $500,000/$1,000,000 for bodily injury and $100,000 for property damage. The policy shall provide for ten days notice to Licensor by registered mail from the insurer return receipt requested in the event of any modification, cancellation or termination. Licensee agrees to furnish to Licensor a certified copy of the policy providing such coverage within thirty days after the date of this Agreement and in no event shall Licensee manufacture, distribute or sell the licensed articles prior to receipt by Licensor of such evidence of insurance.

(c) Licensee further agrees to obtain and maintain at its cost and expense throughout the term of this Agreement Advertiser's Liability Insurance, the form of which must be acceptable to Licensor, from a qualified insurance company licensed to do busines in the State of New York naming Licensor and each and all of the parties indemnified in sub-paragraph (a) of this paragraph as additional named insureds; the amount and coverage shall be a minimum of $500,000/$1,000,000. The policy shall provide for ten days notice to Licensor by registered mail from the insurer return receipt requested in the event of any modification, cancellation or termination. Licensee agrees to furnish to Licensor a certified copy of the policy providing such coverage within thirty days after the date of this Agreement and in no event shall Licensee manufacture, distribute or sell the licensed articles prior to receipt by Licensor of such evidence of insurance.

11. Licensee agrees that it will cause to appear on or within each article sold by it under this license and on or within all advertising, promotional or display material relating to the Property such copyright notice as may be designated by Licensor, and where such article or advertising, promotional or display material bears a trade-mark or service mark, appropriate statutory notice of registration or application for registration thereof approved by Licensor shall be used. In the event that any article is marketed in a carton, container and/or

packing or wrapping material, each and every tag, label, imprint or other device containing any such notice and all advertising, promotional or display material bearing the Property shall be submitted by Licensee for Licensor for written approval prior to use by Licensee. Such approval shall not be unreasonably withheld. Items not approved in writing by Licensor within 21 days shall be deemed disapproved. Licensee agrees to cooperate fully and in good faith with Licensor for the purpose of securing and preserving Licensor's rights in and to the Property. In the event there has been no previous registration of the Property and/or articles and/or any material relating thereto, Licensee shall at its expense at Licensor's request register such as a copyright, trademark and/or service mark in the appropriate class in such name as Licensor may designate. It is agreed that nothing contained in this Agreement shall be construed as an assignment or grant to the Licensee of any right, title or interests in or to the Property, it being understood that all rights relating thereto are reserved by Licensor except for the license hereunder to Licensee of the right to use and utilize the Property only as specifically and expressly provided in this Agreement. Licensee hereby agrees that at the termination or expiration of this Agreement Licensee will be deemed to have assigned, transferred and conveyed to Licensor any trade rights, equities, good will, titles or other rights in and to the Property which may have been obtained by Licensee in pursuance of any endeavors covered hereby, and that Licensee will execute any instruments requested by Licensor to accomplish or confirm the foregoing. Any such assignment, transfer or conveyance shall be without other consideration than the mutual covenants and considerations of this Agreement. Licensee hereby agrees that its every use of such Property shall inure to the benefit of Licensor and that Licensee shall not at any time acquire any rights in such Property by virtue of any use it may make of such Property.

12. (a) Licensee agrees that during the term of this license it will at the sole cost and expense of Licensee diligently and continuously manufacture, distribute and sell the articles covered by this Agreement and that it will use its best efforts to make and maintain adequate arrangements for the distribution of the articles throughout the territory. Licensor shall have the right to terminate this license if Licensee shall, for any reason, fail to carry on efficiently and in good faith the manufacture, distribution, sale and exploitation of the articles listed on Schedule A hereof in accordance with the terms and intent of this Agreement if such failure or refusal continues for a period of 15 days after Licensor shall have served notice upon Licensee, such termination to be effective on expiration of said 15 day period unless in the interim Licensee has remedied any such default and gives notice thereof to Licensor.

(b) Licensee agrees that it will sell and distribute the articles covered by this Agreement outright at a competitive price and not more than the price generally and customarily charged the trade by Licensee and not on an approval, consignment or sale or return basis, and only to jobbers, wholesalers and distributors for sale and distribution to retail stores and merchants and through mail order outlets, and to retail stores and merchants for sale and distribution direct to the public. Licensee shall not knowingly without prior written consent of Licensor sell or distribute such articles to jobbers, wholesalers, distributors, sponsors of a radio or television program, retail stores or merchants whose sales or distribution are or will be made for publicity or promotional tie-in purposes, combination sales, premiums, giveaways or similar methods of merchandising or whose business methods are questionable. In the event any sale is made at a special price to any of Licensee's subsidiaries or to any other person, firm or corporation related in any manner to Licensee or its officers, directors or major stockholders, there shall be a royalty paid on such sale based upon the price generally charged the trade by Licensee. Licensee agrees to sell to Licensor if requested to do so by Licensor such quantities of the articles at as low a rate and on as good terms as Licensee sells similar quantities of the articles to the general trade, and Licensor agrees to respect Licensee's resale prices (if any) upon resale by Licensor except for resales to Licensor's employees. If a sponsor or advertiser of any television series relating to the Property or any part or parts thereof, desires quantities of the licensed articles as an aid or device to advertise or promote its products or services and if Licensee is unable to agree with such sponsor or advertiser on the terms thereof, then Licensor shall have the right to license another person, firm or corporation to manufacture the licensed articles for such advertiser or sponsor only and solely as such an aid or device.

(c) It is agreed that if Licensor should convey an offer to Licensee to purchase the articles listed on Schedule A hereof in connection with a premium, giveaway or other promotional arrangement, Licensee shall have 10 days within which to accept or reject such an offer. In the event that Licensee fails to accept such offer within the specified 10 days, Licensor shall have the right to enter into the proposed premium, giveaway or promotional arrangement using the services of another manufacturer, provided, however, that in such event Licensee shall have a 3 day period within which to meet the terms offered by such manufacturer for the production of such article.

13. In all cases where Licensee desires artwork involving articles which are the subject of this license to be executed, the cost of such artwork and the time for the production thereof shall be borne by Licensee. All artwork and designs involving the Property, or any reproduction thereof, shall, notwithstanding their invention or use by Licensee, be and remain the property of Licensor and Licensor shall be entitled to use the same and to license the use of the same by others, subject to this license. The form and content of all advertising and promotional material shall be subject to the written approval of Licensor.

Such approval shall not be reasonably withheld. Failure of Licensor to approve in writing within 21 days constitutes disapproval thereof.

14. If Licensee shall not have commenced in good faith to manufacture and distribute in substantial quantities the licensed articles within the period set forth on Schedule A hereof, Licensor in addition to all other remedies available to it hereunder may terminate this license with respect to any article or class or category thereof which has not been manufactured and distributed during such period, by giving written notice of termination to Licensee. Such notice shall be effective 30 days after notice is mailed to Licensee, unless Licensee in the interim shall have begun the manufacture and distribution of such article. If Licensee files a petition in bankruptcy or is adjudicated a bankrupt or if a petition in bankruptcy is filed against Licensee which is not dismissed within 30 days or if it becomes insolvent, or makes an assignment for the benefit of its creditors or an arrangement pursuant to any bankruptcy law, or if Licensee discontinues its business or if a receiver is appointed for it or its business, who is not discharged within 30 days, the license hereby granted shall automatically terminate forthwith without any notice whatsoever being necessary. If Licensee shall violate any of its other obligations under this Agreement, Licensor shall have the right to terminate the license hereby granted upon 15 days notice in writing, and such notice of termination shall become effective unless Licensee shall remedy the violation within said 15 day period and reasonably satisfy Licensor that such violation has been remedied. In the event this license is terminated under this paragraph, Licensee, its receivers, representatives, trustees, agents, administrators, successors and/or permitted assigns shall have no right to sell, exploit or in any way deal with or in any articles covered by this Agreement, or any carton, container, packing or wrapping material, advertising, promotional or display material pertaining thereto, except with and under the special consent and instructions of Licensor in writing which they shall be obliged to follow. Termination of the license under the provisions of this paragraph shall be without prejudice to any rights which Licensor may otherwise have against Licensee. Upon the termination of this license, notwithstanding anything to the contrary herein, all royalties on sales theretofore made shall become immediately due and payable and no minimum advance royalties shall be repayable.

15. In the event that any of the articles listed on Schedule A hereof conflicts with a similar product of a manufacturer, seller or distributor who may hereinafter be a participating sponsor, as hereinafter defined, of a program on which the Property in any form appears or is used, or with any product of a subsidiary or affiliate of such a participating sponsor, then Licensor shall have the right to terminate this Agreement as to such article or articles by written notice to Licensee effective not less than 30 days after the date such notice is given. As used herein, a "participating sponsor" shall be deemed to mean any

person, firm or corporation sponsoring not less than 50% of at least a 14-minute radio or television program segment for a fixed non-cancellable period of at least 13 weeks, or not less than 25% of at least a 14-minute radio or television program segment for a fixed non-cancellable period of at least 26 weeks. In the event of such termination, Licensee shall have 60 days after the effective date of such termination to dispose of all such articles on hand or in process of manufacture prior to such notice, in accordance with the provisions of this Agreement. However, in the event such termination is effective as to all the articles subject to this Agreement and the advance guarantee for the then current year has not been fully recouped from actual royalties by the end of said 60-day disposal period, Licensor shall refund to Licensee the difference between the advance guarantee which has been paid for such contract year and the actual royalties which have been earned by Licensor during said year. The refund provision contained in the preceding sentence pertains only to termination occurring pursuant to this paragraph and shall not affect the applicability of any other paragraph to such termination except as expressly contradicted herein. Licensee acknowledges and agrees that nothing contained in this Agreement shall preclude the Property from being sponsored on any television or radio program by any type of a manufacturer, seller or distributor nor shall any such sponsorship be deemed to be in derogation of any rights being granted Licensee under this Agreement.

16. Sixty (60) days before the expiration of this license and, in the event of its termination, 10 days after receipt of notice of termination or the happening of the event which terminates this Agreement where no notice is required, a statement showing the number and description of articles covered by this Agreement on hand or in process shall be furnished by Licensee to Licensor, and Licensor shall have the right to take a physical inventory to ascertain or verify such inventory and statement, and refusal by Licensee to submit to such physical inventory by Licensor or its duly authorized representatives shall forfeit Licensee's right to dispose of such inventory, Licensor retaining all other legal and equitable rights it may have in the circumstances. After termination of the license under the provisions of the preceding paragraph hereof, and except as otherwise provided in this Agreement, Licensee may dispose of articles covered by this Agreement which are on hand or in process at the time notice of termination is received for a period of 60 days after notice of termination, provided advances and royalties with respect to that period are paid and statements are furnished for that period. Licensee may dispose of articles covered by this Agreement which are on hand at the time this Agreement expires by its terms for a period of 60 days after such expiration date provided advances and royalties with respect to that period are paid and statements are furnished for that period. During such 60 day period, Licensor may itself use or license the use of the Property in any manner at any time

anywhere in the world. Notwithstanding anything to the contrary herein, Licensee shall not manufacture, sell or dispose of any articles covered by this license after its termination based on the failure of Licensee to affix notice of copyright, trademark or service mark registration to the articles, cartons, containers or packing or wrapping material, or advertising, promotional or display material, or because of the departure by Licensee from the quality and style thereof approved by Licensor or because of any other material breach of this Agreement by Licensee. Except as aforesaid, after the expiration or termination of this license, all rights granted to Licensee hereunder shall forthwith revert to Licensor, which shall be free to license others to use the Property in connection with the manufacture, sale and distribution of the articles covered hereby and Licensee will refrain from further use of the Property or any further reference to it direct or indirect or anything deemed by Licensor to be similar to the Property in connection with the manufacture, sale or distribution of Licensee's products. Licensee acknowledges that its failure (except as otherwise provided herein) to cease the manufacture, sale or distribution of the articles covered by this Agreement or any class or category thereof at the termination or expiration of this Agreement will result in immediate and irremediable damage to Licensor and to the rights of any subsequent Licensor licensee. Licensee acknowledges and admits that there is no adequate remedy at law for failure to cease manufacture, sale or distribution, and Licensee agrees that in the event of such failure Licensor shall be entitled to equitable relief by way of temporary and permanent injunctions and such other further relief as any court with jurisdiction may deem just and proper.

17. Licensor makes no warranty or representation as to the amount of gross sales or net sales or profits Licensee will derive hereunder. Licensor makes no warranty or representation concerning the quality of the motion picture referred to on Schedule A hereof or that production of said motion picture will be completed or that said motion picture will be released. If said motion picture is not completed and release thereof commenced in the United States within three years after the date of this Agreement, by reason of fire, earthquake, labor dispute, lock-out, strike, act of God or public enemy, any municipal ordinance, state or federal law, governmental order or regulation, or any other cause beyond Licensor's control, including but not limited to the death, illness or incapacity of the director or of any principal member of the cast of said motion picture, this Agreement shall terminate at the expiration of said three year period and Licensor's only liability shall be to return to Licensee the unrecouped portion if any of the minimum advance guarantee theretofore paid by Licensee to Licensor provided Licensee demands said refund within thirty days after the expiration of said three year period in

which event Licensor shall make said refund within thirty days after receiving said demand.

18. The license hereby granted is and shall be personal to the Licensee, and shall not be assignable by any act of the Licensee or by operation of law. Licensee shall have no right to grant any sub-licenses. Any attempt by Licensee to grant sub-licenses or to assign, or part with possession or control of this license or any of its rights hereunder shall constitute a material breach of this Agreement. Licensor shall have the right to assign this Agreement, in which event Licensor shall be relieved of any and all obligations hereunder, provided such assignee shall assume this Agreement and all rights and obligations thereunder in writing.

19. All notices or other communications required or desired to be sent to either party hereto shall be in writing and shall be sent by Registered or Certified Mail, return receipt requested, or sent by telegram, or by personal delivery to an officer, at the address first above stated for such party. Either party may change the address to which notices and other communications are to be sent by notice in writing to the other party.

20. This Agreement does not constitute either party the agent of the other, or create a partnership or joint venture between the parties, and Licensee shall have no power to obligate or bind Licensor in any manner whatsoever.

21. This Agreement, whenever called upon to be construed, shall be governed by the laws of the State of New York.

22. No waiver or modification of any of the terms of this Agreement shall be valid unless by an express agreement in writing subscribed by the parties hereto. No waiver by either party of a breach or a default hereunder shall be deemed a waiver by such party of a subsequent breach or default of like or similar nature. There are no representations, warranties, covenants, undertakings or promises other than those contained in this Agreement and Schedule A hereof, which represent the entire understanding of the parties.

IN WITNESS WHEREOF, the parties hereto have duly executed this Agreement as of the day and year first above written.

LICENSEE

By_____

By_____

LICENSOR*

_____

*This Agreement is not binding upon Licensor unless signed by an officer thereof.

BOOK PUBLISHING

AGREEMENT

PUBLISHING AGREEMENT

————,

(hereinafter called the "Publisher")
and

————,

(hereinafter called the "Author")
agree:

FIRST: The Author

A. shall deliver to the Publisher two copies of the literary work now entitled _____ (hereinafter called the "Literary Work") in Final Form on or before _____, 19____.

B. makes the warranties and representations set forth in Part Two (36-45) of the Basic Agreement, except as otherwise specifically stated in *THIRD* (C) of this Publishing Agreement;

C. grants and assigns to the Publisher:

(i)   the trade edition rights;

(ii) all other primary rights; and

(iii) the shares, provided in *THIRD* (A) of this Publishing Agreement, of the proceeds received on disposition of the secondary rights; and

D. agrees not to offer any other full-length work for publication prior to delivery of the Literary Work in Final Form and that the Publisher shall have the first opportunity to consider the Author's next (*i.e.*, written after the Literary Work) full-length work for publication on mutually satisfactory terms. If, within 60 days following submission of the final manuscript of such work to the Publisher, or within 60 days after the publication of the Literary Work, whichever shall be later, Publisher and Author are unable in good faith to agree upon terms for publication, the Author shall be free thereafter to submit the manuscript of such next work to other publishers, provided, however, that the Publisher shall retain the first option of publishing the work on terms no less favorable to the Author than those offered by any other publisher.

SECOND: The Publisher

A. shall publish same in book form on acceptance by it of the Literary Work on or before _____ 19____. For purposes of computing the royalty on the first hardcover publication, the list price shall be at least ____, even though Publisher's actual list price is lower.

B. shall copyright the Literary Work in the United States in the name of the Author;

C. shall pay the Author

    (i)   royalties at the following rates, for sales of the trade edition (less returns):_____;

    (ii)   50% of the net proceeds received on disposition of the other primary rights, except as otherwise provided herein;

    (iii) in accordance with the special provisions in Part Five of the Basic Agreement, for sales by mail order, at special discount, as unbound sheets for export from reduced printings, to book clubs, or as excess stock, or for any mass market paperback reprint, quality paperback or textbook editions of the Literary Work published by the Publisher itself under one of its own imprints or for publication of part of the Literary Work by the Publisher in another work.

THIRD: The Publisher and the Author

A. agree to share the net proceeds received on disposition of the following secondary rights as follows and that Publisher is authorized exclusively on behalf of the Author to dispose of such secondary rights as are preceded by an asterisk:

Dramatic Rights	__% to Author	__% to Publisher
Motion Picture Rights	__% to Author	__% to Publisher
Allied Motion Picture Rights	__% to Author	__% to Publisher
Educational Picture Rights	__% to Author	__% to Publisher
Radio Rights	__% to Author	__% to Publisher
Television Rights	__% to Author	__% to Publisher
First Periodical Rights	__% to Author	__% to Publisher
Commercial Rights	__% to Author	__% to Publisher
Foreign Language Rights	__% to Author	__% to Publisher
British Commonwealth Rights	__% to Author	__% to Publisher

B. agree to be bound by all of the terms and conditions of the Basic Agreement which follows and which is made an integral part of this Publishing Agreement; and

C. agree to the following special provisions, which shall prevail over any conflicting provisions in the Basic Agreement:_____

_____

_____(L.S.)
Author

By_____
Authorized Signature

Soc. Sec. #:_____

Citizenship:_____

Dated _____ 19____

BASIC AGREEMENT

TABLE OF CONTENTS

Part One
DEFINITION OF TERMS

As used in this Basic Agreement and in the Publishing Agreement:

Primary Rights.

1. "Primary Rights" shall mean all of the rights defined in Part One (2) through (13) inclusive. The territory within which such rights are exercisable is set forth in Part Three (46). "Secondary Rights" as and to the extent expressly defined in Part One (15) through (23) inclusive are excepted from implied comprehension within the definitions of Primary Rights.

Trade Edition Rights, Trade Editions.

2. "Trade Edition Rights" shall mean the exclusive right to publish, or authorize others to publish, trade editions of the Literary Work referred to in the Publishing Agreement. "Trade Editions" shall mean the first edition of the Literary Work in book form, and all other editions in book form except those referred to in the next paragraphs.

Book Club Rights.

3. "Book Club Rights" shall mean the exclusive right to authorize book clubs to print and sell the Literary Work in book form.

Mass Market Paperback Reprint Rights.

4. "Mass Market Paperback Reprint Rights" shall mean the exclusive right, after the publication of the first trade edition, to publish, or to authorize others (not including book clubs) to publish, other editions of the Literary Work in formats designed primarily for mass market distribution through such channels as chain store outlets and news and magazine wholesalers.

Quality Paperback Edition Rights.

5. "Quality Paperback Edition Rights" shall mean the exclusive right, after the publication of the first trade edition, to publish, or authorize others to publish, other editions of the Literary Work at less than the catalog retail price of the most recent trade edition, but at more than the catalog retail price of any mass market paperback reprint edition which has been authorized.

Textbook Rights.

6. "Textbook Rights" shall mean the exclusive right to publish, or to authorize others to publish, the Literary Work in textbook form, for distribution to or use in educational or other similar institutions.

Book Selection Rights.

7. "Book Selection Rights" shall mean the exclusive right, after publication of the first trade edition, to include, or to authorize others to include, in anthologies and other works in book form, including, without limitation, in dramatic form, selections from, parts of, and/or photographs, charts, maps, drawings, index, illustrations and other illustrative or decorative material from the Literary Work, to the extent that the Publisher deems appropriate, provided that no such selection to be included in any one book shall exceed approximately 10,000 words from or 10% of the length of a work of prose (whichever is shorter), one short story from a collection of stories, three complete poems from a collection of poems, or one act from a play.

Abridgment or Condensation Rights.

8. "Abridgment or Condensation Rights" shall mean the exclusive right, after the publication of the first trade edition, to publish, or to authorize others to publish, either as part of a book (as distinguished from a periodical), or as a separate book publication, an abbreviated version of the Literary Work, not exceeding two-thirds of the original version in length, all of which must be (i) in the original text, if it is an abridgment, or (ii) approved in writing by the Author, if it is a condensation.

Periodical Selection Rights.

9. "Periodical Selection Rights" shall mean the exclusive right, subject to any limitations required under any prior disposition of first periodical rights, to authorize others to publish in magazines or newspapers selections from, parts of, and/or photographs, charts, maps, drawings, index, illustrations and other illustrative or decorative material from the Literary Work, for the purpose of aiding or exploiting the sale of the Literary Work, provided that no such selection to be included in any one magazine or newspaper shall exceed approximately 2,000 words from a work of prose, one short story from a collection of stories, two complete poems from a collection of poems or one scene from a play.

Second Periodical Rights.

10. "Second Periodical Rights" shall mean the exclusive right, after the publication of the first trade edition, to publish, or to authorize others to publish, the Literary Work in magazines or newspapers—either in full as a serial, or in an abbreviated version (abridged or condensed) which shall exceed approximately 30,000 words or one-half of the length of the Literary Work (whichever is less), or as a selection which shall exceed approximately 2,000 words from a work of prose, one short story from a collection of stories, two complete poems from a collection of poems, or one scene from a play.

Transcription Rights.

11. "Transcription Rights" shall mean the exclusive right to use the Literary Work, or any portion thereof, as a basis for phonographic, tape, wire, magnetic, electronic, light wave amplification, photographic, microfilm, microfiche, electronic audio-video, or audio-visual recordings, slides, filmstrips, transparencies, programming for any method of information storage, reproduction or retrieval, and for any other forms or means of copying or recording (now known or hereafter devised) the text of the Literary Work, including recordings made for the blind.

Digest Rights.

12. "Digest Rights" shall mean the exclusive right, either simultaneously or after the publication of the first trade edition, to publish, or to authorize others to publish, in any magazine—whether devoted exclusively to abbreviated versions, or consisting primarily of other material—an abbreviated version (abridged or condensed) of the Literary Work, which version shall be complete in one issue and shall not exceed approximately 30,000 words or one-half of the length of the Literary Work, whichever is less.

Other Publishing Rights.

13. "Other Publishing Rights" shall mean all publishing rights not specifically enumerated herein, whether now in existence or hereafter coming into existence.

Secondary Rights.

14. "Secondary Rights" shall mean all the rights defined in Part One (15) through (23) inclusive. The territory within which such rights are exercisable is set forth in Part Three (47).

Dramatic Rights.

15. "Dramatic Rights" shall mean the exclusive right to use, or to authorize others to use, the Literary Work, title, plot, episodes, events, scenes and characters depicted therein, in whole or in part, for (i) writing a dramatic version thereof, or a drama in any way based thereon and (ii) producing or performing either of the above on the stage.

Motion Picture Rights.

16. "Motion Picture Rights" shall mean the exclusive right to use, or to authorize others to use, the Literary Work, title, plot, episodes, events, scenes and characters depicted therein, in whole or in part, for the purpose of making motion pictures primarily for exhibition in regular commercial channels, and the right to grant the allied motion picture rights.

Allied Motion Picture Rights.

17. "Allied Motion Picture Rights" shall mean (i) the exclusive right to condense, or to authorize others to condense, the Literary Work, or the commercial motion picture treatment thereof, into not more than 7,500 words, for the purpose of promoting motion pictures based on the Literary Work, and (ii) such limited radio or television rights as are customarily granted for the purpose of using those mediums to promote motion pictures based on the Literary Work.

Educational Picture Rights.

18. "Educational Picture Rights" shall mean the exclusive right to use, or to authorize others to use, the Literary Work, in whole or in part, in making motion pictures primarily for exhibition for educational purposes.

Radio Rights.

19. "Radio Rights" shall mean the exclusive right to use, or to authorize others to use, the Literary Work, title, plot, episodes, events, scenes and characters depicted therein, in whole or in part, for AM, FM or other broadcasting.

Television Rights.

20. "Television Rights" shall mean the exclusive right to use, or to authorize others to use, the Literary Work, title, plot, episodes, events, scenes and characters depicted therein, in whole or in part, for broadcast performances on television other than closed circuit television for private viewing by limited audiences.

First Periodical Rights.

21. "First Periodical Rights" shall mean the exclusive right, before the publication of the first trade edition, to publish, or to authorize others to publish, the Literary Work in magazines or newspapers—either in full as a serial, or in an abbreviated version (abridged or condensed) which shall exceed approximately 30,000 words or one-half of the length of the Literary Work (whichever is less), or as a selection which shall exceed approximately 2,000 words from a work of prose, one short story from a collection of stories, two complete poems from a collection of poems, or one scene from a play.

Commercial Rights.

22. "Commercial Rights" shall mean the exclusive right to use, or to authorize others to use, in whole or in part, the Literary Work, the title of the Literary Work, and the names and characterizations of characters created in

the Literary Work, as a basis for (i) trademarks or trade names for other products, or (ii) toys or games.

Foreign Language Rights.

23. "Foreign Language Rights" shall mean the exclusive several rights to authorize others to translate the Literary Work in whole or in part, and to adapt same for translation into one or more foreign languages, and to publish and sell, or to authorize others to publish and sell, such translations in any part of the world.

British Commonwealth Rights.

23(a). "British Commonwealth Rights" shall mean the exclusive several rights to publish and sell and to authorize others to publish and sell the Literary Work in the English language in the British Commonwealth and the traditional British market as constituted at the date of this agreement exclusive of Canada, Australia and Israel.

Author's Unshared Secondary Rights.

24. "Author's Unshared Secondary Rights" shall mean all secondary rights as to which, under Part *THIRD* (A) of the Publishing Agreement, the Author is to retain all the proceeds from disposition.

Shared Secondary Rights.

25. "Shared Secondary Rights" shall mean all secondary rights as to which, under Part *THIRD* (A) of the Publishing Agreement, the Author and the Publisher are to share the proceeds from disposition.

Sale or Disposition of Rights.

26. A "Sale," "Disposition" or "Grant" of rights shall include an assignment, transfer, bargain or license of the rights referred to or of any interest or option relating to such rights.

Proceeds on Disposition of Primary Rights.

27. "Proceeds on Disposition of the Primary Rights" shall mean the gross amount received on the sale or disposition of such primary rights, less any costs and expenses incurred by the Publisher in connection with or by reason of such sale or disposition.

Proceeds on Disposition of Secondary Rights.

28. "Proceeds on Disposition of the Secondary Rights" shall mean the gross amount received from the sale or disposition of such secondary rights, less any commissions which may be paid for services rendered in connection with such

disposition, either to the Author's agent designated in the Publishing Agreement or to any agent authorized by the Publisher to dispose of such secondary rights. Moreover, if either (i) any other persons shall have rendered services which contributed to the value of any of the secondary rights and shall have become entitled to receive a share of the proceeds of disposition thereof (e.g., a dramatizer, a theatrical producer or a translator of the Literary Work), or (ii) upon a sale of the motion picture rights a portion of the proceeds shall be payable to the Dramatists Guild of the Authors League of America, Inc., then the amounts paid to such other persons shall also be deducted from the gross amount received from the sale or disposition of such secondary rights in order to determine the amount to be shared between the Author and the Publisher.

Final Form.

29. "Final Form" shall mean a complete, legible, typewritten manuscript of the Literary Work (including photographs, charts, maps, drawings or index, if any of these are required), acceptable to the Publisher in content and form and ready for the printer.

Agreed Publication Date.

30. "Agreed Publication Date" shall mean the date on which the Publisher has agreed in the Publishing Agreement to publish the Literary Work.

Actual Publication Date.

31. "Actual Publication Date" shall mean the date on which the Publisher first offers the first trade edition of the Literary Work for sale to the public.

Base Royalty Rate.

32. "Base Royalty Rate" shall mean the royalty rates provided in **Part** *SECOND* (C)(i) of the Publishing Agreement.

Mail Order Sales.

33. "Mail Order Sales" shall mean copies of the Literary Work sold directly to the consumer through (i) the medium of mail order coupon advertising, or (ii) direct-by-mail circularization.

Special Discount Sales.

34. "Special Discount Sales" shall mean any sales at a discount of 50% or more from the catalog retail price. Sales to book clubs shall not be included under special discount sales.

Agreement.

35. "Agreement" (or "this agreement") shall mean the Publishing Agreement and this Basic Agreement.

Part Two
AUTHOR'S WARRANTIES

Except as otherwise specifically stated in Part *THIRD* (C) of the Publishing Agreement, the Author warrants and represents that:

Sole Author and Proprietor.

36. He is the sole Author and proprietor of the Literary Work.

Authority to Grant.

37. He has full power and authority to make this agreement and to grant the rights granted hereunder, and he has not previously assigned, transferred or otherwise encumbered the same; and that he has no prior agreement, commitment, or other arrangement, oral or written, to write or participate in writing any other book-length work and will enter into no such agreement, commitment, or other arrangement until after delivery of the manuscript of the Literary Work in Final Form.

Not Previously Published.

38. The Literary Work has not been previously published.

Not in Public Domain.

39. The Literary Work is not in the public domain.

No Infringement.

40. The Literary Work does not infringe any statutory or common law copyright.

Not Libelous.

41. The Literary Work does not invade the right of privacy of any third person, or contain any matter libelous or otherwise in contravention of the rights of any third person; and, if the Literary Work is not a work of fiction, all statements in the Literary Work asserted as facts are true or are based upon reasonable research for accuracy.

Not Unlawful.

42. The Literary Work contains no matter which is obscene or matter the

publication or sale whereof otherwise violates any federal or state statute or regulation thereunder, nor is it in any other manner unlawful.

Permissions.

42(a). The Author agrees that should he incorporate in the Literary Work any writings, drawings, photographs or other material either previously published or not, either of his own or another artist or writer, he shall prior to delivery of the Literary Work in Final Form obtain and, whenever requested by Publisher, shall deliver to the Publisher proper and complete written permission and authorization from the owner of the common law or statutory copyright or other right to use the same in the Literary Work or for the purpose of promoting or advertising the Literary Work throughout the world.

Investigation by Publisher.

43. The Publisher shall be under no obligation to make an independent investigation to determine whether the foregoing warranties and representations are true and correct; and any independent investigation by or for the Publisher, or its failure to investigate, shall not constitute a defense to the Author in any action based upon a breach of any of the foregoing warranties.

Effect of Warranties and Representations.

44. The warranties and representations of Author hereunder are true on the date of the execution of this agreement and shall be true on the date of the actual publication of the Literary Work, and at all intervening times. The Publisher may rely conclusively on the truth of the warranties and representations herein in dealings with any third party in connection with exercise or disposition of any rights in the Literary Work.

Warranties to Survive Termination.

45. Each of the foregoing warranties and representations shall survive the termination of this agreement.

Part Three
EXTENT OF GRANT

Territorial Extent of Primary Rights.

46. Under the grant of primary rights, the Publisher and its grantees shall have the exclusive right of publication throughout the world in the English language under its own name and under various trade names and imprints.

Territorial Extent of Secondary Rights.

47. The secondary rights are world-wide rights, and all provisions as to the

disposition of such secondary rights and the sharing of the proceeds thereof shall apply equally in all countries of the world—provided, however, that to the extent that the Author is unable to grant world-wide dramatic rights, because of the requirements in the Minimum Basic Agreement of the Dramatists Guild of the Authors League of America, Inc., the territorial extent of dramatic rights shall be as broad as the Author is able to grant thereunder. If the Publisher shares in the proceeds derived from the disposition of Second Periodical, radio or television rights, he shall not participate in any portion derived from sales outside the territory given under the grant of primary rights.

Duration of Grant.

48. All rights granted under this agreement are, except where expressly subject to earlier termination, to continue in effect during (i) the full term of the copyright of the Literary Work in the United States in effect under the laws of the United States at the time, (ii) any renewals of that copyright, and (iii) any extensions either of such original copyright or of a renewal thereof.

Author's Rights.

49. All rights not expressly granted by the Author to the Publisher are reserved by the Author. The Author shall not exercise or dispose of any rights reserved to him in such a way as substantially to destroy, detract from, impair or frustrate the value of any rights granted herein to the Publisher, nor shall he publish or permit to be published during the term of this agreement any book or other writing based substantially on subject matter, material, characters or incidents in the Literary Work without the written consent of the Publisher. The Author warrants and represents that he has not granted and will not grant to any person (except to the Publisher), permission, authority, right or license for publication or distribution of the Literary Work in the open English language market, in a mass-market or quality paperback edition, sooner than the latter of one year following the publication of any British hard-cover trade edition or three months following the publication of the first United States mass market paperback reprint edition. The Author warrants that the Literary Work will be his next book (whether under the Author's own name or otherwise), that he will not undertake to write any other work for publication in book form before delivery to the Publisher of the complete manuscript of the Literary Work in Final Form, and agrees that in no event will he publish or authorize publication of any other book-length work of which he is an author or co-author until six months after publication of the Literary Work. The Author further agrees not to submit any full-length work or proposals therefor in any form to the Publisher or to any third party until he has

delivered to the Publisher the complete manuscript of the Literary Work in Final Form.

Disposition or Exercise by Publisher of Primary Rights.

50. The Publisher shall have the exclusive right, but shall not be obligated, to dispose of or exercise any or all of the primary rights in and to the Literary Work. During the Author's lifetime, however, such right shall be subject to the Author's consent in case of disposition of mass market paperback reprint rights, such consent not to be unreasonably withheld. The Publisher shall notify the Author promptly after each disposition of primary rights, and, at the Author's request, the Publisher shall furnish the Author with copies of any contracts made with respect to disposition of any primary rights.

Disposition of Author's Unshared Secondary Rights.

51. The Author shall have the exclusive right to dispose of the Author's unshared secondary rights, and shall notify the Publisher promptly after each such disposition.

Disposition of Shared Secondary Rights.

52. If the Author has designated an agent in the Publishing Agreement, that agent shall have the exclusive right to dispose of all of the shared secondary rights as to which he has authority from the Author. The terms and conditions of any such disposition of rights by the agent shall be subject to the Publisher's written approval. The name and address of such agent, together with a representation by the Author as to any special limitations on the agent's authority, shall be set forth in the Publishing Agreement.

Disposition by Publisher of Shared Secondary Rights.

53. If the Author has not designated an agent in the Publishing Agreement, the Publisher shall have the exclusive right, but shall not be obligated, as agent for the Author to dispose of all of the shared secondary rights; or if the Author has designated an agent with limited authority, the Publisher shall have the exclusive right, but shall not be obligated, as agent of the Author to dispose of the shared secondary rights as to which the agent does not have authority from the Author. The Publisher may appoint an agent to dispose of any rights of which the Publisher is thus authorized to dispose. Where Publisher is specifically authorized to dispose of rights such authorization shall be deemed an agency coupled with an interest.

Approval of Disposition or Exercise Not to Be Unreasonably Withheld.

54. Neither the Publisher nor the Author shall unreasonably withhold consent where such consent is requested in connection with disposition or

exercise of rights under this agreement. The Author and the Publisher shall each have the right to receive copies of any contracts thus made with respect to the said rights.

Author's Consent.

55. When the Author's written consent or approval is required or requested under this agreement, if the Author has died, or if the Author does not answer the Publisher's request for such consent or approval within a reasonable time, or if after reasonable diligence the Publisher has not succeeded in informing the Author that such consent or approval is desired, the Author shall be deemed to have given his consent.

Author's Name and Likeness.

56. The Publisher may use the name and likeness of the Author on the cover and jacket, and generally in connection with the advertising and promotion of the Literary Work.

Author to Execute Documents.

57. The Author shall, when requested by the Publisher, execute all documents which may be necessary or appropriate to enable the Publisher to exercise or deal with any of the rights granted hereunder.

Licenses Without Fee.

57(a). The Publisher is authorized to license publication of the Literary Work in Braille, or photographing, microfilming or large type editions of the Work for sale to the physically handicapped, or extracts of the Work containing not more than approximately five hundred (500) words, or ten thousand (10,000) words in connection with motion picture licenses, without compensation therefor. In the event compensation is received, it shall be shared as provided in Part *SECOND* (C) (ii) of the Publishing Agreement.

Part Four
COPYRIGHT

Copyright in the United States.

58. The Author authorizes the Publisher to take all appropriate measures to copyright the Literary Work in the United States in the name of the Author. Any agreement made by the Author or his agent or by the Publisher to dispose of the first periodical rights to the Literary Work must require either (i) that the copyright for the first periodical publication shall be taken out in the Author's name, or (ii) if such copyright is to be taken out in the name of another, that such copyright holder shall assign the copyright to the Author,

and in the latter case the Author agrees to deliver such assignment of copyright to the Publisher before the agreed publication date.

Notice.

59. The Publisher shall print the appropriate notice required to comply with the applicable copyright laws of the United States and the provisions of the Universal Copyright Convention in each copy of the Literary Work published by it.

Renewal.

60. The Author agrees that, during his lifetime and provided that this agreement has not been previously terminated, he shall be obligated to make good and seasonable application for the renewal or for any extension of any copyright in the Literary Work, and to execute all instruments which the Publisher may require in order to confirm the Publisher's rights in the Literary Work during the period of the renewal or of any extension of the copyright. The Author shall direct his executor by Will to fulfill the terms of this agreement and to make timely application for renewal of copyright.

Protection of Copyright in Disposition of Other Rights.

61. Any agreement made by the Author or by the Publisher to dispose of any rights in and to the Literary Work must require the licensee or grantee of the Author or of the Publisher respectively to take all necessary and appropriate steps to protect the then existing copyright in and to the Literary Work.

Foreign Copyright.

62. The Publisher may take such steps as it deems appropriate to copyright the Literary Work in any other countries, but the Publisher shall be under no obligation to procure copyright in any such countries, and shall not be liable to the Author for any acts or omissions by it in connection therewith. The Author may copyright the Literary Work in any foreign country if the Publisher fails to take steps to obtain such a copyright within 30 days after receiving a written request from the Author to do so.

Part Five
ROYALTIES AND OTHER PAYMENTS

Computation of Royalties Generally.

63. Royalties shall be computed on the basis of the number of copies actually sold by the Publisher, less returns. No royalties shall be computed on copies given away for review or promotion, nor on copies given to the Author.

On Mail Orders and Special Discounts.

64. On mail order sales and special discount sales the royalty shall be 5% of the net amount actually received from such sales.

On Sheet and Export.

65. On unbound sheet sales and sales for export of the trade editions of the Literary Work, royalties shall be calculated on the net amount actually received from such sales.

On Sales from Reduced Printings.

66. On sales made out of any new printings or bindings of 2,500 copies or less, made more than one year after publication date, royalties shall be computed at one-half the base royalty rates provided hereunder.

Royalty Statements and Payments.

67. The Publisher shall render royalty statements and make accounting and royalty and other payments to the Author (i) in February for the preceding period April 1 to September 30, and (ii) in August for the preceding period October 1 to March 31.

Details to Be Shown.

68. Royalty statements shall state the number of copies sold during the period covered. If the Author so requests, the Publisher shall, within 30 days after rendering the royalty statement, advise the Author in available detail of the number of copies printed, bound, sold, and given away during the period covered by the royalty statement, as well as the approximate number of salable copies on hand at the end of said period.

Book Club Sales.

69. On all sales to book clubs, the amount allocated as royalty or other compensation to the Publisher shall be divided equally between the Author and the Publisher.

Certain Primary Rights Exercised by Publisher.

70. On the exercise of quality paperback reprint edition or textbook edition rights by publication under one of its own imprints royalties (but no further advance) shall be paid to the Author at the following rates based on the catalog retail price: (i) 6% on the first 10,000 copies sold within the United States, exclusive of sales specified in subparagraph (iii) below, and (ii) 7½% on all copies sold within the United States thereafter, exclusive of the sales specified in subparagraph (iii) below, and (iii) 3% on mail order sales, copies sold outside the United States, in bulk to book clubs, or other special

discounts. On the exercise of mass market paperback reprint rights, book club rights, book selection rights, abridgment or condensation rights, or any other primary rights, by publication under one of its own imprints, the Author shall receive one-half of the fair market value of such rights at the time of exercise.

Excess Stock Sales.

71. When the Publisher believes that copies of the Literary Work are not readily salable at regular prices within a reasonable time, the Publisher may (but not earlier than 12 months from the actual publication date) dispose of such copies as surplus at the best price obtainable. Upon such disposition, the Author shall receive in lieu of all other royalties hereunder the excess over the Publisher's manufacturing costs up to 10% of the net proceeds of such disposition.

Payment of Advances.

72. The payment of advances to the Author, including such payment following delivery of the manuscript, shall not be deemed to be evidence either that the manuscript of the Literary Work is in content or form acceptable to the Publisher, or that the Author has complied with his warranties or other agreements hereunder.

Repayment of Advances.

73. Any advance royalties or other sums paid to or on behalf of the Author under this agreement or otherwise, and any other payments due from the Author to the Publisher, may be applied in reduction of any payments due to the Author under this agreement.

Security Interest.

74. To secure the advances made to Author, and payment of any other sums which may be or become due to Publisher hereunder, Author hereby grants to Publisher (i) a security interest under the Uniform Commercial Code in the manuscript to be delivered by him to Publisher hereunder, said security interest to attach to the manuscript as and when it is written, and to any and all outlines, drafts, notes, and written background material relating thereto; and (ii) the right to immediate possession, at any time upon demand, of the said manuscript, outlines, drafts, notes, permissions, consents, and background material. Author agrees to execute and deliver to Publisher, in form requested by Publisher, a financing statement and such other documents which Publisher may require to perfect its security interest in the said manuscript, outlines, drafts, notes and background material.

Reserve for Returns.

75. Any amounts payable to the Author hereunder shall be subject to such reserve for returns of copies of the Literary Work as the Publisher shall establish in its reasonable discretion.

Author's Right to Examine Books of Account.

76. The Author may, upon written request, examine the books of account of the Publisher in so far as they relate to the Literary Work, for the period of two years immediately preceding such examination.

Author's Agent.

77. If the Author has an agent, as indicated by the inclusion of an agent's name and address in the Publishing Agreement, until receipt by the Publisher of written notice by the Author canceling the agent's authority hereunder, all payments accruing to the Author under this agreement shall be made to such Author's agent, and the receipt by the Author's agent shall constitute a full and valid discharge of the Publisher's obligations for such payments under this agreement. Author's agent is fully authorized to do and perform all acts on behalf of the Author in all matters arising out of or under this agreement, and the Publisher may conclusively rely upon such authority until actual receipt by Publisher of written notice, signed by the Author, canceling or limiting such authority. No such revocation or limitation shall affect the validity of any act of the agent prior to receipt of such notice by the Publisher to the extent that the Publisher has relied thereon.

Part Six
DELIVERY OF MANUSCRIPT AND CORRECTION OF PROOFS

Failure of Author to Deliver Work in Final Form.

78(a). Timely delivery of the Literary Work in Final Form is essential to the Publisher and is of the essence of this agreement. If the Author fails to deliver the Literary Work in Final Form within the time specified, the Publisher shall have an option to give the Author a notice in writing terminating this agreement, and in such event the Publisher may then recover and the Author agrees to repay on demand all amounts advanced to the Author.

(b). Additionally, the Publisher shall not be obligated to accept or publish the Literary Work if, in its sole editorial judgment, such work is not satisfactory to it. Provided, however, that if the Author shall, within the time specified, have delivered the Literary Work in what he represents to be its completed form, the Literary Work shall be deemed to be acceptable in content and form to the Publisher unless, within 90 days after receipt thereof by the Publisher, the Publisher shall give to the Author a notice in writing stating that in its editorial judgment the work is not acceptable to it, in which case this agreement shall thereupon terminate and the Publisher may then recover and the Author agrees to repay on demand all amounts advanced to the Author. If Publisher so elects, in lieu of such notice, it may give written notice to the Author stating the particular respects in which the submitted manuscript is unacceptable, including, without limitation, reservations or questions of the Publisher concerning matters within any of the warranties, representations and agreements contained in Paragraphs 36-42. Any written request by or on behalf of the Publisher for changes in or for substantiation or confirmation of any statement in the Literary Work shall be deemed, without any need expressly to say so, to constitute notice that the manuscript is then unacceptable to the Publisher without responses satisfactory to the Publisher, and that it has not been accepted. If such request be made of the Author or his agent, unless the Publisher shall otherwise agree in writing, failure of the Author, within 60 days after the date of such request, to respond to the satisfaction of the Publisher in respect to all subject matter of such request shall have the same significance and effect as failure to deliver a manuscript in Final Form within 60 days after a notice as provided in the first sentence of this Paragraph 78. Correspondingly, a 90-day period within which the Publisher may reject a Literary Work in the exercise of its editorial judgment or for non-compliance to its satisfaction with a request for changes, substantiation or confirmation, shall run from the last date on which the Author purports to have submitted responses in compliance with the Publisher's request for changes, substantiation or compliance. A request for changes or substantiation or confirmation as aforesaid shall not preclude other similar requests prior to the elapse of such 90-day period, or within a new like period after the receipt by Publisher of Author's tendered compliance with Publisher's request.

Delay for Author's Illness.

79. If, however, because of illness or any other factor beyond his control, the Author is unable so to deliver the Literary Work, the date for such delivery shall be extended for a reasonable time. If after the elapse of such reasonable time the Author continues to fail or is unable to deliver the Literary Work or to satisfy the Publisher's request(s) for changes or substantiation, the Publisher may give written notice of termination, effective at the expiration of 60 days or such longer period as the Publisher may specify in such notice, and if the Author shall fail to deliver the manuscript in Final Form within such 60 days or specified longer period, as the case may be, this agreement will be terminated at the expiration of said period, and the Publisher may recover all amounts advanced to the Author. If the Author dies prior to acceptance by the Publisher whether or not following delivery of the manuscript in Final Form, the Publisher, in its sole discretion, may terminate this agreement upon giving

a written notice of termination to the Author's personal representatives within 90 days of receipt by Publisher of notice of his death, in which case the Publisher may then recover from such personal representatives all amounts previously advanced hereunder.

Failure to Deliver Photos, Charts, etc.

80. If the Author fails to deliver photographs, charts, maps, drawings, or the index, in cases where any of these are required for the Literary Work, the Publisher shall have the right (but not the obligation) to cause the same to be prepared and to charge the cost of such preparation to the Author.

Correction of Proofs.

81. The Publisher shall supply the Author with one set each of galley and, at its option, page proofs, and the Author shall return each set of proofs with his corrections to the Publisher within 21 days of receipt thereof. The Publisher shall also proofread the proofs. If, because of his own fault, the Author shall fail to return the corrected proofs within the 21-day period herein specified, the Publisher may publish the Literary Work without the Author's approval of the proofs—provided, however, that if, because of illness or any other factor beyond his control, the Author informs the Publisher that he is unable so to return the corrected proofs, his time for correcting such proofs shall be extended for another 21-day period, and after that period the Publisher may publish the Literary Work without the Author's approval of the proofs.

Cost of Author's Alterations.

82. If, in the correction of galley and page proofs, the Author requests changes from the text of his manuscript, the Author agrees to pay to the Publisher the cost of such changes, over 15% of the original cost of composition, provided that, at the Author's request, the Publisher shall submit an itemized statement of such charges, and shall make available corrected proofs for the Author's inspection at the Publisher's office.

No Obligation to Publish.

83(a). Notwithstanding anything contained herein to the contrary, in no event shall the Publisher be obligated to publish the Literary Work if, in its sole and absolute judgment, the Literary Work contains libelous or obscene material, or its publication would violate the right of privacy, common law or statutory copyrights, or any other rights of any person. In such event, Publisher shall be entitled on demand to the return of all monies advanced to the Author hereunder, and to terminate this agreement. Notwithstanding any request by Publisher for change or substantiation, nothing in this agreement shall be deemed to impose upon the Publisher any duty of independent investigation or relieve the Author of any of the obligations assumed by him hereunder.

(b). The Publisher shall not be obligated to publish the Literary Work if, whether before or after acceptance thereof, supervening events or circumstances since the date of this agreement have, in the sole judgment of the Publisher, materially adversely changed the economic expectations of the Publisher in respect to the Literary Work at the time of the making of this agreement, and in such event all of the Publisher's rights in and to the Literary Work shall terminate and revert to the Author on the giving by the Publisher to the Author of notice of its decision, or, if the Publisher fails to do so, by the Author pursuant to Paragraph 84, and in any such event, the Author shall be entitled to retain all payments to the Author theretofore made under this agreement.

Part Seven
DELAYS IN PUBLICATION

Delays Due to Publisher's Fault.

84. The Publisher, in its sole and absolute discretion, shall have the right to re-schedule publication of the Literary Work beyond the agreed publication date for a reasonable time and also in the event of late delivery by the Author of the manuscript in Final Form. Thereafter, if publication of the Literary Work is delayed in the absence of excusable circumstances the Author's sole and exclusive remedy shall be to give the Publisher a notice in writing, stating that if the Publisher fails to publish the Literary Work within 180 days after the date of such notice, then all of the Publisher's rights in and to the Literary Work shall terminate at the end of such 180-day period; and if, in such event, the Publisher shall fail to publish the Literary Work within such 180-day period, all of the Publisher's rights in and to the Literary Work shall terminate and revert to the Author, and the Author shall be entitled, as liquidated damages and in lieu of all damages and remedies, legal or equitable, to retain all payments theretofore made to Author under this agreement.

Delays Not Due to Publisher's Fault.

85. If publication is delayed beyond the agreed publication date because of acts or conditions beyond the control of the Publisher or its suppliers or contractors, including (by way of illustration and not by way of limitation) war, shortages of material, strikes, riots, civil commotions, fire or flood, the agreed publication date shall be extended to a date six months following removal of the cause of the delay.

Part Eight
DISPUTES

Disputes Between Parties.

86. In the event of any dispute under this agreement arising between or among the parties, any party may request any other party to agree to submit such dispute to arbitration in the City of New York in accordance with the then rules of the American Arbitration Association. Absent an agreement to arbitrate, exclusive jurisdiction for the determination of any such dispute solely between or among parties to this agreement is hereby vested in the Supreme Court, New York County, or, at the election of either party if the jurisdictional prerequisites at the time exist, in the United States District Court for the Southern District of New York, and each party hereto agrees to submit to the jurisdiction of either such court in the City and State of New York for the determination of any such dispute, and hereby consents (in addition to service of process by any other means provided at the time by law) to service of process on him or it, as the case may be, by registered mail, first class postage prepaid, return receipt requested, addressed to the defendant named in such process at the address to which notices may be given pursuant to Paragraph 106 of this agreement, and that notice by mail so given shall be deemed to confer jurisdiction upon such court.

Part Nine
INDEMNIFICATION AND DEFENSE
OF LITIGATION

Indemnification by Author.

87. The Author shall indemnify and hold the Publisher harmless against any loss, liability, damage, cost or expense arising out of or for the purpose of avoiding any suit, proceeding, claim or demand or the settlement thereof, which may be brought or made against the Publisher by reason of the publication, sale, or distribution of, or disposition of rights in respect to, the Literary Work, based on the contents of the Literary Work, except in connection with matters inserted in the Literary Work by or at the direction of the Publisher or involving solely controversies arising out of or based on commercial transactions between the Publisher and the customer.

Notice of Suits Brought.

88. Prompt notice of any such non-excepted suit, proceeding, claim or demand brought or made against the Publisher or Author shall be given to the Author or Publisher respectively.

Cost of Defending Suits.

89. If any such non-excepted suit, claim or demand is brought or made, the Publisher may elect (i) to undertake the defense thereof, or (ii) to notify the Author to undertake the defense. If the Publisher does so notify the Author, the Author shall undertake such defense; and in such cases the Publisher may, at its option, join in the defense. In all the foregoing events the cost and expense of any defense shall be borne by the Author, unless (a) such suit, claim or demand arises solely out of an act or omission of the Publisher, in which case the cost and expense shall be borne by the Publisher, or (b) the Author has, pursuant to notification from the Publisher, undertaken the defense and the Publisher at its option elects to join with the Author in the defense, in which case the total cost and expense (including reasonable counsel fees) shall be shared equally by the Publisher and Author.

Publisher May Withhold Payments.

90. Whenever any such non-excepted suit, claim or demand is instituted, the Publisher may withhold, payments due to the Author under this, or any other, agreement between the Author and the Publisher, subject, however, to the Author's right to draw on such sums to defray his expenses in connection with such suit, claim or demand. If a final adverse judgment is rendered in such a suit and is not discharged by the Author, the Publisher may apply the payments so withheld to the satisfaction and discharge of such judgment.

Part Ten
INFRINGEMENT BY OTHERS

Suits, by Publisher or Author.

91. If during the existence of this agreement the copyright, or any other right in respect to the Literary Work, is infringed or violated, the Publisher may, at its own cost and expense, take such legal action, in the Author's name if necessary, as may be required to restrain such infringement and to seek damages therefor. The Publisher shall not be liable to the Author for the Publisher's failure to take such legal steps. If the Publisher does not bring such an action, the Author may do so in his own name and at his own cost and expense. Money damages recovered for an infringement shall be applied first toward the repayment of the expense of bringing and maintaining the action, and thereafter the balance shall be divided equally between the Author and Publisher.

Part Eleven
WITHDRAWAL FROM PUBLICATION

If Discontinued or Out of Print.

92. If, at any time after the expiration of two years from the actual publication date, either of the following events occurs:

(i) the Publisher notifies the Author in writing that the Publisher intends to discontinue publication of both the trade and textbook editions of the Literary Work; or

(ii) the Publisher allows all editions of the Literary Work to go out of print and does not place any edition on sale within six months after the Author has made a request therefor in writing, and if there is no English language or foreign language reprint edition authorized by Publisher available or contracted for,

the Author may by a notice in writing (a) revoke the Publisher's right to publish any further copies of the trade editions of the Literary Work; (b) revoke the grant to the Publisher of such of the other primary rights as the Publisher has not already exercised or disposed of; (c) revoke any power given to the Publisher to dispose of such secondary rights as have not already been disposed of; and (d) revoke any grant of rights made to the Publisher in the Publishing Agreement to share in the proceeds on disposition of such secondary rights as have not already been disposed of. In such event the Author shall have the right to purchase any available plates or film of the Literary Work at cost, and/or any remaining copies or sheets of the Literary Work at the Publisher's manufacturing cost. If the Author does not purchase such plates, copies or sheets, the Publisher may melt the plates, and may sell the copies or sheets at any price and retain the proceeds of such sale.

Part Twelve
BREACH BY PUBLISHER

Termination for Substantial Breach.

93. Except as otherwise specifically provided in this agreement, if the Publisher shall commit a substantial breach of this agreement and shall fail to remedy the breach within 60 days after receiving a written notice by registered mail from the Author requesting the Publisher to remedy such breach, the Author may by a notice in writing (i) revoke the Publisher's right to publish the trade editions of the Literary Work, if it has not already been published at such time; (ii) require the Publisher to cease further publication of the trade editions of the Literary Work, if it has already been published at such time, but in such event the Publisher shall be permitted to sell all copies of those

editions of the Literary Work which have already been printed or are in the process of being printed; (iii) revoke the grant to the Publisher of such of the other primary rights as the Publisher has not already exercised or disposed of; (iv) revoke any power given to the Publisher to dispose of such secondary rights as have not already been disposed of; (v) revoke any grant of rights made to the Publisher in the Publishing Agreement to share in the proceeds on disposition of such secondary rights as have not already been disposed of. In such event the Author shall have the right to purchase any available plates or film of the Literary Work at cost, and/or remaining copies or sheets of the Literary Work already printed at the Publisher's manufacturing cost. If the Author does not purchase such plates, copies or sheets, the Publisher may melt the plates, and may sell the copies or sheets at any price and retain the proceeds of such sale. Any right of the Author pursuant to Paragraph 76 shall survive such termination.

Part Thirteen
BANKRUPTCY OR INSOLVENCY OF PUBLISHER

Bankruptcy, Receivership, Assignment for Creditors.

94. If the Publisher is finally adjudicated a bankrupt, or if a receiver is appointed, or if an assignment is made for the benefit of creditors, the Author may by a notice in writing (i) revoke the Publisher's right to publish the trade editions of the Literary Work, if it has not already been published at such time; (ii) require the Publisher to cease further publication of the trade editions of the Literary Work, if it has already been published at such times, but in such event, if the Author consents in writing, the Publisher shall be permitted to sell all copies of those editions of the Literary Work as have already been printed or are in the process of being printed (provided that if the Author has died, or if the Author does not answer the Publisher's request for such consent within a reasonable time, or if after reasonable diligence the Publisher has not succeeded in informing the Author that such consent is desired, the Author shall be deemed to have given his consent); (iii) revoke the grant to the Publisher of such of the other primary rights as the Publisher has not already exercised or disposed of; (iv) revoke any power given to the Publisher to dispose of such secondary rights as have not already been disposed of; and (v) revoke any grant of rights made to the Publisher in the Publishing Agreement to share in the proceeds on disposition of such secondary rights as have not already been disposed of. For the purposes of this PART THIRTEEN, "the Publisher" shall include successors in interest of the Publisher, including a trustee in bankruptcy, a receiver, or an assignee for the benefit of creditors. In such event the Author shall have the right to purchase all copies or sheets of the Literary Work in the possession of the Publisher and the plates therefor, at the then fair market value as determined by arbitration under the rules of the

American Arbitration Association. If the Author does not purchase such plates, copies or sheets, the Publisher may melt the plates, and sell the copies or sheets at any price and retain the proceeds of such sale.

Part Fourteen
MISCELLANEOUS PROVISIONS

Publisher Shall Determine Style, etc.

95. The format, style of printing and binding, and all other matters relating to the manufacture, sale, distribution and promotion of the Literary Work shall be determined at the sole discretion of the Publisher. The Publisher may not make any changes in the manuscript of the Literary Work without the consent of the Author, except that the Publisher may make changes (i) in the capitalization and punctuation of the Literary Work, to make it conform to the Publisher's accepted style, or (ii) in the spelling and punctuation of a British edition of the Literary Work, to make it conform to American usage.

Title Changes.

96. The title of the Literary Work as set forth in the Publishing Agreement may be changed by mutual agreement of the Author and the Publisher.

Single Author to Represent.

97. When there is more than one author, any one (and an alternate) may be designated in the Publishing Agreement to act on behalf of all the authors jointly, and the Publisher may rely on the acts of the Author or his alternate so designated as representative of and binding upon all the Authors; and in the absence of such designation, the Publisher may deal with any one of the Authors as the agent and representative of all; and may rely on the acts of such Author-representative as binding on all the Authors. When there is more than one author, unless the Publishing Agreement specifies otherwise or until receipt by the Publisher of contrary instructions, the Publisher may assume that all Authors share equally in proceeds payable hereunder and may either issue separate checks in equal amounts payable to each Author severally or single checks payable jointly to all Authors.

Price Changes.

98. The Publisher may change the catalog retail price of the trade editions provided its royalties on trade editions sales are calculated on a retail price not less than the minimum price fixed in the Publishing Agreement.

Free Copies for Author; Purchases by Author.

99. The Publisher shall present the Author with ten free copies of the first

trade edition, and one free copy of any other edition published by the Publisher, upon publication. The Author shall have the right to purchase additional copies of the trade editions for his own use, and not for resale, at a 40% discount from the catalog retail price.

Publisher to Execute Documents.

100. If any of the rights granted to the Publisher revert to the Author, the Publisher shall execute all documents which may be necessary or appropriate to revest all such rights in the Author.

Acceptance of Agreement.

101. The agreement shall be binding on the Publisher only when it is accepted by an authorized officer of the Publisher.

Laws Applicable to Agreement.

102. The agreement shall be construed in accordance with the laws of the State of New York.

Agreement Binding on Successors in Interest.

103. The agreement shall be binding upon and inure to the benefit of the executors, administrators and assigns of the Author, and upon and to the successors and assigns of the Publisher.

Modification of Agreement.

104. The agreement may not be modified, altered or changed except by an instrument in writing signed by the Author and the Publisher.

Waivers Are Not Cumulative.

105. No waiver of any term or condition of this agreement, or of any breach of this agreement or of any part thereof, shall be deemed a waiver of any other term or condition of the agreement or of any later breach of the agreement or of any part thereof, nor shall publication or continued publication or payment by the Publisher following notice or claim of facts which, if true, would constitute a breach of warranty, representation or agreement of the Author, constitute or imply any waiver by the Publisher of any defenses, rights or remedies of the Publisher.

Notices.

106. All notices to be given hereunder by either party shall be in writing and shall be sent by registered mail to the other party at the respective addresses as they are given in the Publishing Agreement, unless said addresses are changed by either party by a notice in writing to the other party.

Singular Shall Include Plural.

107. Wherever required by the context, the singular shall include the plural, and the plural the singular, and the masculine shall include the feminine and the neuter. The "Author" shall include the "Authors" if there are more than one.

Captions, Table of Contents, etc.

108. Captions or marginal notes, and the table of contents of this agreement are for convenience only, and are not to be deemed part of the agreement.

Part III

APPLICATION OF ENTERTAINMENT INDUSTRY CONCEPTS

WRITING ASSIGNMENTS

FIRST WRITING ASSIGNMENT: DRAFTING COUNTERPROPOSAL TO WAMEX'S FIRST OFFER

You are representing Dan Sing Starr ("Starr"), a leading proponent of physical fitness for children.

Ms. Starr has been approached by Warner-Amex Satellite Entertainment Corporation ("Wamex") about developing cable programming involving her specialty.

Following is a summary of Ms. Starr's background, which, in turn, is followed by Wamex's first offer.

As a writing assignment, please prepare a written memorandum setting forth the basic business points for Starr's counterproposal to the first offer from Wamex. Your counterproposal should be fair and reasonable from *both* the viewpoints of Starr and Wamex so that it is likely to be accepted by Wamex (Starr does not like to pay legal fees for lengthy negotiations).

BACKGROUND

Ms. Starr and her husband (with whom she is now fighting in an acrimonious divorce proceeding) have co-authored three books, published in paperback two, four and six years ago, the most recent of which was a non-fiction bestseller (8 weeks on the *Times* "Best Seller" list, rising to number 3), describing exercise programs, and advocating physical fitness, for children.

In addition, she has had two records which have been released, one three years ago which sold 200,000 copies and one late last year which so far has sold 350,000 copies, each along with a separate booklet (also co-authored with her husband), setting forth an exercise program for children, the first from ages four through eight, and the second from ages eight through twelve. She is considering doing a subsequent recording for ages twelve through sixteen, but nothing definite has yet been set.

In addition, for the last five years, Ms. Starr has been writing a weekly column on health and children for newspaper syndication.

At present, she is also busy running classes for children in New York City. During her classes, she generally has a woman present who sings folk songs as back-ground for class activities.

Her annual income from her various activities is presently in the low six figures.

┌─────────────────────────────┐
│   FIRST OFFER BY WAMEX   │
└─────────────────────────────┘

1. The term of this agreement will be the three year period commencing on the earlier of the January 1 or July 1 following the signature of this agreement. During the term, Ms. Starr will be exclusive to Wamex for cable television (including pay cable) and video disk and cassette projects.

2. Within six months of the start of the term Ms. Starr will prepare and submit to Wamex two proposals, one for an exercise series for children, and the other a dance series for children.

3. If Wamex elects to produce either or both series, Ms. Starr will write, produce, and direct each episode, for which she will receive $15,000 per episode for a series of half hour episodes, or $25,000 per episode for a series of 60 minute episodes.

4. It is understood that a series commitment by Wamex is conditional upon Wamex being able to arrange for partial production financing through the presale by Wamex of video disk and cassette rights to the series.

5. Wamex will own the copyright to the series, each episode therein, and all rights derived therefrom in all media throughout the world.

6. If a series is produced, Starr will receive an amount equal to 5% of the net profits derived by Wamex from the licensing of video disk and video cassette rights to the series.

7. If a series is ordered by Wamex, Starr will deliver episodes on the production schedule, and within the budget, set by Wamex.

8. If the series is ordered and produced, Starr will receive credit reflecting her contributions. Wamex has the right to use Starr's name, image, and likeness in promotion and publicity for a series, and to reflect Starr's exclusive relationship with Wamex during the three year period referred to in paragraph 1 above.

9. If Starr is required to perform services in connection with the series, or promotion in connection therewith, beyond 100 miles from New York City or her then location (whichever is closer to the place services hereunder are to be performed), she will be provided with one first class roundtrip transportation ticket and reimbursed for reasonable living expenses up to $100 per day.

10. Starr represents and warrants that all material in the series will be

original with her; that no person, firm, or corporation will have or make any claims in connection with such material; and that nothing contained in the series will be harmful to any viewer.

SECOND WRITING ASSIGNMENT: HYPOTHETICALS

Following are seven sets of hypothetical contract situations, and three sets of hypothetical litigation situations, which will give you an opportunity to apply in practice the principles which we have been discussing during the first part of the course.

CONTRACT HYPOTHETICALS

In each contract situation, there is a first offer from each side in the negotiation. You, representing one side in the deal, will be expected to prepare a reasonable compromise position on each deal point, for presentation to the class. Another student, representing the other side of the deal, will also have prepared a reasonable compromise position on each deal point, which may agree with your compromise offer, or be an alternative compromise. Other members of the class will also be expected to offer alternative compromise suggestions if they have any.

You will be expected to justify the compromise you have suggested, as to why you feel it is reasonable. Anyone presenting an alternative should likewise be prepared to discuss the reasoning behind the compromise suggestion: what was at stake in each side's opening offer, and how does the compromise meet these considerations?

As part of the assignment, each set of negotiators should agree between themselves *before* class on the germane business background of their respective clients, and the business assumptions upon which they both are operating. For example, these factors might include the costs of creating or producing or distributing the creative product involved; the amount paid or received for the last deal; or the success of recent projects, both artistically and commercially. These factors should be prepared in writing and distributed to the class on the day of the negotiations. The description can be as long or as short as each set of negotiators deems necessary. For an example of a short set of assumptions, see "Background" for the Writing Assignment.

Following the class discussion, the students representing the two sides of the deal should agree between themselves on the final compromise positions for each deal point (including all deal points covered in the first offer, and any other deal points either side feels are material) and reflect these final compromises in a written summary. Each side will then prepare a proposed contract incorporating these mutually agreed compromises, using the relevant sample contract precedent which is part of these materials. The contract will be due *4 weeks* from the date of the class presentation.

LITIGATION HYPOTHETICALS

In the litigation situations, there are background facts set forth, and the type of motion which has been made.

You, representing the plaintiff or the defendant, will be expected to present an oral argument to the class on the issues which you intend to present in support of, or in opposition to, the pending motion. Each set of litigators should agree between themselves before class on the relevant issues they intend arguing. These issues should be prepared in writing and distributed to the class on the day of the argument. Other members of the class will be expected to comment on the issues as presented, offering additional arguments in support of, or in opposition to, these issues.

Each side will then be expected to write a memorandum of law in support of his or her client's position, which will be due *four weeks* from the date of the class presentation.

Representatives of both sides in the litigation hypotheticals may agree, before the class in which they present the issues on their side, on any additional background facts which they deem relevant, with these stipulated facts to be handed to the class on the day of their presentation.

Hypothetical Situations

Contract Hypotheticals:

Industry Branch	Parties
Live theatrical	● authors/producer
	● authors & producer/movie studio
Television	● rights owner/producer
	● producer/network
Book publishing	● author/publisher
Music	● recording artist/recording company
	● recording artist/merchandising company

Litigation Hypotheticals:

Industry Branch	Parties
Film	• writer-director/film studio
Music	• recording artist & record company/split off record artist & his record company
Book publishing and live theatricals	• heirs of famous star/theatre producer & writer

Contract Hypothetical
LIVE THEATRICAL BRANCH

Agreement A
Minimum Basic Production Contract

Minimum Basic Production Contract ("MBPC") between Connie Truller ("CT") and Ema Warbler ("EW") ("Authors") and Holly Geld ("HG"), producer, relating to "Women's Rites" ("Play").

```
┌─────────────────────────────────────────────┐
│   HG's FIRST OFFER TO CT AND EW              │
└─────────────────────────────────────────────┘
```

1. Authors will complete book/music/lyrics in form satisfactory to HG within 12 months.

2. Advances:

   (a) To Authors: $5,000 payable $1,000 now, $2,000 on delivery of satisfactory book/music/lyrics, and $2,000 on first day of rehearsals.

   (b) To CT as director's advance: $5,000 payable, $1,000 on delivery of satisfactory book/music/lyrics, $2,000 on start of casting and $2,000 in equal weekly installments during rehearsals.

3. Royalties based on gross weekly box office receipts:

   (a) Authors: 2% to CT, 4% to EW

   (b) Director: 2%

   (c) Automatic waiver in loss weeks

4. Production date: 18 months after Authors deliver satisfactory book/music/lyrics, subject to extension for a further 18 months on payment of additional $2,500 advance, either 18 or 36 months' date subject to extension for up to 6 months on month-to-month basis at $200 per month to accommodate availability of star or theatre.

5. Cast album rights: HG to participate in income as one of the subsidiary rights, plus, if HG arranges cast album deal, gets 10% commission off-the-top.

6. Authors cannot dispose of motion picture rights without getting purchaser to agree to negotiate with HG to produce motion picture.

7. Billing:

   (a) Stage: Authors on same line, 50% of title; CT as director, 50% of title

(b) Film: "Originally produced on Broadway by HG," separate card, main titles, HG's name 100% size of title

8. Expenses: $75 per day and economy class transportation if and when Authors required to travel more than 250 miles from New York.

9. Orchestration fees: $100 per week from Authors' royalties.

CT's AND EW's
FIRST OFFER TO HG

1. Authors will deliver first draft book/music/lyrics with 12 months, subject to CT's other work opportunities.

2. Authors will make reasonable changes requested by HG if requests agreed to by them.

3. Advances to Authors:

   (a) $7,500 payable $3,750 on signing and $3,750 on delivery of first draft book/music/lyrics.

   (b) At HG's option, $2,500 in one year to extend rights another year if no production by then, provided filed SEC papers by end of one year.

   (c) $300 per month for month-to-month extensions at the end of the second year (up to 6 months) to accommodate availability of a signed star and theatre booked for set opening date.

4. Director's fee: fee, not an advance; $10,000, payable $5,000 now, $2,500 on delivery of book/music/lyrics, $2,500 on start of rehearsals, but not later than 1 year from delivery of book/music/lyrics.

5. Royalties: Authors: 9% (3% for each of book/music/lyrics);
   Director: 3%

6. Production date: 1 year after delivery of first draft book/music/lyrics, with 1 year extension if SEC documents filed and $2,500 paid, with up to further 6 month extension to accommodate availability of signed star and theatre.

7. Subsidiary rights:

   (a) HG participates in income only if Play runs for 21 performances from official New York opening.

   (b) Cast album: Authors control disposition, but money part of subsidiary rights income if HG entitled to share.

   (c) No music publishing income as part of subsidiary rights sharing.

8. Billing:

(a) Authors: line below title, 100% size of title.

(b) Director: last credit, 100% size of title.

9. Expenses:

(a) $125 per day plus hotel plus first-class transportation.

(b) Piano available to EW, in tune, during rehearsals and out-of-town tryouts.

(c) Authors have right to be present during all rehearsals and out-of-town tryouts.

10. Orchestration fees: $75 per week, until 50% of cost paid.

Agreement B
Theatrical Investment Agreement/Pre-Sale Motion Picture Rights

Theatrical Investment Agreement/Pre-Sale Motion Picture Rights among Connie Truller ("CT"), Ema Warbler ("EW") ("Authors"), Holly Geld ("HG") (stage producer), and UniPar Motion Pictures, Inc. ("UP") relating to "Women's Rites" ("Play").

> ## UP's FIRST OFFER TO AUTHORS AND HG

1. If it approves of book/music/lyrics for the Play, UP will invest actual production budget, up to $3 million, as a limited partner in a partnership of which HG is the sole general partner.

2. UP has approval over two most major cast members for Play.

3. If budget over $3 million, obligation to invest contingent on HG having in a bank the amount needed to meet the actual production budget which must include $100,000 for out-of-town losses plus a 10% reserve.

4. Authors, and CT as director, and HG must agree to waive royalties in loss weeks.

5. UP gets 60% of net profits from theatrical production.

6. UP gets presentation credit above the title in second position after HG, 100% of size of title.

7. UP gets music publishing rights.

8. UP has option to invest in UK production or any other companies producing Play under HG control.

9. UP has cast album rights:

(a) Pay music publisher $0.20 per LP.

(b) Pay HG and Authors record royalty of 10% of retail in U.S., reducible by artists' royalties.

10. UP, at its election, has motion picture and television rights in the Play: if UP wants to exercise these rights, pay $25,000 within 1 year after close of last first-class company, and additional $225,000 on commencement of principal photography, and 10% of net profits. Payments go to limited partnership producing Play to recoup production costs of Play and/or be part of net profits.

11. If UP produces motion picture, it has soundtrack album rights for $0.20 per album into gross receipts of Picture and 20% of music publishing net profits into gross receipts of Picture.

12. UP has free synchronization licenses if it produces any motion picture or television productions using music from the Play.

13. Credits on first motion picture produced by UP: single card reflecting original Broadway production produced by HG, directed by CT, book/music/lyrics by CT/EW.

14. All decisions relating to production and distribution of motion picture by UP in its sole discretion.

FIRST OFFER BY CT, EW AND HG TO UP

---

1. UP committing to put up entire production budget for the Play.

2. Authors will consult with UP about casting the Play, but Authors' decision final.

3. UP gets 50% of net profits from the Play.

4. In playbills, UP gets "produced in association with" credit, ⅔ of HG's credit.

5. UP gets to administer music publishing rights for administration fee of 10% in the U.S. and not more than 20% combined U.S. and foreign, with normal royalties to EW as composer/lyricist, and with music publisher's net split ⅓ to UP, ⅓ to HG and ⅓ to EW.

6. UP can have cast album rights of cast album released within three

months after New York opening at 2.5¢ per song and royalty of 15% of retail in U.S., reducible by artists' royalties but not below 10% of retail royalty.

7. Motion picture rights:

(a) Must exercise option within twelve months after New York opening or six months after close New York company, whichever occurs first.

(b) With exercise, pay $500,000, plus $500,000 on commencement of principal photography but not later than one year after first $500,000 payment.

(c) 10% of gross receipts after breakeven, rising to 15% of gross receipts after breakeven plus $5,000,000.

(d) Payments go 75% to Authors and 25% to HG, not into gross receipts of limited partnership producing Play.

(e) First motion picture must have general theatrical release in U.S. before any other rights used.

(f) No theatrical motion picture release until close of last first-class live theatrical company.

(g) Motion Picture Credits:

- Authors: separate card "Based on" following screenplay writers' card
- CT: separate card "originally directed on Broadway by"
- HG: separate card as original Broadway producer
- All names 100% of title

(h) Must hire:

(I)   EW to write any new songs, not fewer than 3, at $10,000 each, with same music publishing deal as for Play.

(II)   Must use at least 8 songs from Play.

(III)   CT to write screenplay at $250,000, plus 5% of net profits.

(IV)   CT to direct at $250,000, plus 10% of net profits.

(V)   HG to produce at $250,000, plus 10% of net profits.

8. Remake and sequel rights: 50% of money for first motion picture.

9. Television rights:

(a) Specials: $5,000 per ½ hour running time,

(b) TV Series: $1,500 per ½ hour running time each episode; $2,000 per 1 hour; $2,500 per 90 minutes; plus 10% escalations per year of new episodes, compounded.

(c) 100% of initial payment over each of first 5 reruns at 20% each.

10. No print publication rights or merchandising rights granted to UP; reserved to Authors.

Contract Hypothetical
TELEVISION BRANCH

Agreement A
Rights Acquisition Agreement

Rights Acquisition Agreement between Phillerton Syndicate, Inc. ("PSI"), syndicator of a newspaper cartoon strip written by D.R.T. Riter but in which PSI owns the copyright, and Animart, Inc. ("AI"), a producer of animated films, which wants to do a television program based on the strip.

FIRST OFFER TO PSI's AI

---

1. AI will acquire only the right to produce one 60-to-90 minute TV Special for broadcast on United Television Network ("UTN") based on political satire cartoon strip entitled "Under Cover Agent" ("Strip").

2. Copyright in Special will be in PSI's name.

3. PSI wants $100,000 for rights from first monies received by AI from UTN.

4. Beyond two UTN runs, all profits will be divided 50/50 between PSI and AI (of PSI's share, 50% goes to D.R.T. Riter, cartoonist of Strip).

5. PSI reserves all rights in Strip other than right to make one Special for UTN; PSI may exercise TV rights in Strip after 3 years from date of first telecast of UTN Special.

6. "Presentation" credit for PSI on screen and in all ads.

7. Special must be broadcast within one year, or rights revert to PSI.

8. AI and/or UTN will spend not less than $50,000 for advertising and promotion for first telecast of Special.

ANIMART's FIRST OFFER TO PSI AI'S

---

1. AI to obtain exclusive television rights in the Strip.

2. For the first television program, AI will pay PSI 5% of the budget, as AI gets monies from TV distributor.

3. Copyright will be in AI's name.

4. AI has right to produce next theatrical picture based on Strip, and any

further TV program (special or series) as long as each further TV program is produced within 2 years of broadcast of most recent TV program.

5. AI gets all rights in media, including screenplay publication rights and merchandising rights.

6. AI pays PSI 40% of the net profits from the first television program.

7. Screen credit for PSI, "Based on cartoon strip created by D.R.T. Riter, distributed by PSI", size and placement in AI's discretion.

Agreement B
Television Network Agreement

Television Network Agreement between United Television Network ("UTN") and Animart, Inc. ("AI") for step deal development of possible animated television Special to be produced by AI, based on syndicated newspaper cartoon strip written by D.R.T. Riter ("DRT").

> ### UTN's FIRST OFFER TO AI

1. 90-minute script within 9 weeks, with UTN option, if it elects to go forward, to cut back to 60-minute program or expand to 120 minutes.

2. UTN to exercise its option on script length within 60 days after delivery of the script.

3. UTN option to order program within 60 days after receiving final script.

4. If UTN passes on program, AI may not sell to another network until 1 broadcast season passes, and then only if UTN gets reimbursed for its development expenses.

5. License fee for 2 runs: $500,000 for 60 minutes.

6. If UTN orders Special, AI must deliver within 1 year, with UTN to have 2 runs within the following 2 broadcast seasons.

7. UTN has options for 3 further runs at $100,000, $75,000, and $50,000 respectively, each option to be exercised by May 1 of last broadcast season's rights.

8. If UTN exercises all 3 options on further runs, then UTN has right of first negotiation-last refusal on any other TV uses.

9. If UTN orders Special, it has a right of first negotiation-last refusal on any other TV shows based on Strip.

10. UTN has exclusivity on the program and all elements therein and all characters therein in U.S. during term of UTN's rights.

11. UTN has all key creative approvals.

12. If UTN orders the Special, AI must supply a completion guarantee from a financially responsible person or company.

AI's FIRST OFFER TO UTN

1. AI will deliver a 90-minute script within 9 weeks, followed by a 30-day reading and option period in which UTN can decide on 60–, 90– or 120–minute program.

2. UTN to advance script costs (including WGA Pension & Welfare payments and any other fringes) against license fee.

3. If UTN passes on the program after the first draft script then UTN has no further rights.

4. If UTN goes forward past first draft, second draft will be delivered within 4 weeks unless UTN asks for a longer script (120 minutes), when second draft will be delivered within 6 weeks; followed by a 30-day reading and option period, and 2 weeks for rewrite, if any, plus another 30-day option period.

5. If at the end of any option period, UTN does not proceed with the next step, then UTN will be deemed to have passed, and Paragraph 3 above applies.

6. If UTN orders Special, delivery within one year subject to extension for events beyond AI's control.

7. UTN has 2 runs in 2 seasons, staring with the season of delivery.

8. License fee is $800,000 if Special is 60 minutes; $1,200,000 if 90 minutes; or $1,600,000 if 120 minutes; payable ⅓ with program order, ⅓ on completion of principal photography, and ⅓ on delivery, with script advance from last payment.

9. Options for 3 further runs, one per season, at $150,000 for third run, $175,000 for fourth run and $200,000 for fifth run, each option to be exercised within 30 days after last broadcast.

10. No further rights or options, except right of first negotiation for any other TV programs produced by AI based on Script.

11. Commercial TV exclusivity only, during term of UTN's license.

12. UTN will have right to approve any screenplay writer other than DRT, and the director.

13. AI will supply a net worth statement, but will not be obligated to supply a completion guarantee if net worth statement exceeds $500,000.

Contract Hypothetical
BOOK PUBLISHING BRANCH

Book Publishing Agreement

Book Publishing Agreement between Dr. Hart Bern ("HB"), noted heart surgeon, and Vanity Press Incorporated ("VPI"), publisher.

```
┌─────────────────────────────┐
│  HB's FIRST OFFER TO VPI    │
└─────────────────────────────┘
```

1. HB will prepare cookbook for people with hypertension.

2. HB will deliver manuscript within 18 months, subject to extension if HB required to consult on too many cases to deliver on time.

3. Manuscript may include recipes previously published by HB in newsletters, magazine articles, etc.

4. VPI must publish within 6 months after delivery of manuscript, or rights revert to HB.

5. VIP will pay HB $25,000 advance, against royalty of 10% retail cover price on first 5,000 copies, 12½% next 5,000 copies and 15% over 10,000 copies in hardcover.

6. Softcover: 50%/50% on first $100,000 received by VPI, 60%/40% on receipts over $100,000.

7. Copyright in HB's name.

8. VPI will not publish any other special diet cookbooks within 6 months before or within two years after HB's book is published.

9. VPI must spend not less than $25,000 for advertising and promotion.

```
┌─────────────────────────────┐
│  VPI's FIRST OFFER TO HB    │
└─────────────────────────────┘
```

1. VPI acquires worldwide right to publish cookbook on hypertension in all languages, and all other rights in all media.

2. HB will deliver acceptable manuscript within 12 months.

3. VPI will pay HB $2,500 advance on delivery of satisfactory manuscript, against 50% of VPI's net receipts from all sources (excluding 25,000 copies to be given to Healthy Foods Limited ("HFL"), a manufacturer of health food

products, in exchange for HFL giving $100,000 to VPI to help cover book production costs).

4. Where HFL distributes items in recipes, HB will, in his recipes, mention HFL trademark with ingredients, not just generic ingredient.

5. VPI will have 12 months from delivery of satisfactory manuscript within which to publish, or HB can buy back rights for publisher's investment to date (including advance), and subject to obligation to HFL (25,000 hardcover copies).

6. HB represents:

   (a) Recipes are all tested and will not create health problems for people with hypertension.

   (b) Recipes are all original with Dr. Bern and not copied from anyone else.

   (c) At least 50% will not have been published previously in newsletters or elsewhere.

7. HB will update the book as required by VPI and/or by new medical advances or information; any loss on out-of-date editions will be part of the 50/50 net computation.

8. VPI will own the copyright.

9. HB to supply an index, or pay for the cost of indexing recipes.

Contract Hypothetical
MUSIC BRANCH

Agreement A
Recording Agreement

Recording Agreement between R.B. Trory ("RB"), new recording artist, and Spun Gold Records ("SG"), the home of the stars.

FIRST OFFER BY SG TO RB
---

1. Two-year term, plus SG has four one-year options to extend.

2. RB to record and deliver minimum of 24 3½-minute sides per year, satisfactory to SG.

3. SG will pay all recording costs, including AFM minimum session fees to RB, as advance against RB royalties; producer's and other artists' royalties deductible from royalty to RB.

4. Cost of art work for jackets is also an advance against RB royalties.

5. Royalties: 7% retail or 14% wholesale, at SG election, for U.S. record sales; ½ for tape; ½ of each respectively outside U.S.—first 2 years; rising to 7½% (subject to all reductions) for first option year extension; 8% second option year; 9% third option year; 10% fourth option year.

6. SG has exclusive merchandising rights to RB during term, with right to sell inventory for 2 years after end of term.

7. SG owns P (copyrights in RB's performances), and may continue to use RB's performances after end of term.

8. Sides recorded in excess of minimum may, at SG's option, be applied against future year's minimum to be recorded.

9. SG to designate songs to be recorded by RB, arrangements, accompaniment, producer.

10. RB must sign music publishing agreement with Hitter Miss Music Publishing Corporation, sister company of SG.

FIRST OFFER BY RB TO SG
---

1. One-year term, plus SG may have two one-year options to extend.

2. RB to deliver a minimum of twelve 3½-minute masters per year.

3. RB to select music, accompaniment; producer to be mutually approved.

4. No studio or recording costs charged against royalties.

5. Artwork for record covers to be submitted to RB for approval.

6. Royalties:

First Year:	10% retail or 20% wholesale for U.S. sales; ½ for foreign sales.
Second year:	12% retail or 24% wholesale for U.S. sales; ½ for foreign sales.
Third year:	14% retail or 28% wholesale for U.S. sales; ½ for foreign sales.

7. Advance: $10,000 on signing; to exercise option for the second year, $40,000; to exercise option for the third year, $75,000.

8. No merchandising rights.

9. RB to own P (copyright in RB's performances).

10. Any reserves on SG accountings must be self-liquidating within one year.

11. SG obligated to release 1 album or 2 singles per year.

12. SG must take and pay for a full page advertisement within 30 days after signing in *Cashbox* or *Billboard* and in weekly *Variety* and also upon release of each record.

13. SG to make a $50,000 advertising contribution to each live tour.

14. RB can terminate agreement if SG breaches agreement and fails to cure within seven days after notice.

Agreement B
Merchandising License Agreement

Merchandising License Agreement between R. B. Trory ("RB") and Hartcell Distributors ("HD").

FIRST OFFER BY HD TO RB

---

1. HD has exclusive worldwide merchandising rights to RB's name, voice, image, likeness, and signature.

2. Five year term.

3. Right to sublicense.

4. HD pays royalty of 5% of gross amounts received by HD, net of returns.

5. Semi-annual accountings within 60 days after end of each semi-annual period.

6. One year to dispose of inventory on hand at end of term.

7. HD owns copyright in any artwork or packaging created or designed during term.

8. No representation by HD regarding the amount of sales HD might generate.

FIRST OFFER BY RB TO HD

1. HD getting a U.S. license to manufacture and sell t-shirts, posters, and decals.

2. One year license, renewable for up to total of five years in one-year extensions provided RB has received annual royalties of not less than $100,000 for year 1, $200,000 for year 2, $300,000 for year 3, and $400,000 for year 4.

3. $25,000 cash advance on signing.

4. No sublicensing.

5. Royalty of 5% retail price on t-shirts, 10% of retail on posters and decals.

6. Monthly accountings within 30 days after end of each month.

7. Sixty days before end of term, HD to supply RB with an inventory list— HD has the right to dispose of inventory for up to 60 days after end of term, subject to continued timely accountings.

8. Quality control: RB has a right of approval over artwork, packaging, product; RB has right of approval over prototypes, plus random samples from each production run.

9. HD will handle no other rock singers during term.

10. HD will not challenge RB's ownership and control over name, image and likeness.

11. HD will sue at HD's expense any unauthorized competitors.

12. HD will spend not less than $100,000 advertising each year.

13. RB owns copyright in any artwork or packaging containing his name, image or likeness.

Litigation Hypothetical
FILM INDUSTRY

Jean Pierre Truffle is a world famous director whose films are distributed internationally. Early last year, Truffle entered into an agreement with Warner Communications in Paris to make a film at Warner's studio outside Paris for initial release in France and subsequent distribution in Europe and the rest of the world.

Truffle had written a widely-read short story which he agreed to license to Warner as the basis for the film. Warner agreed to give him a "based upon" credit for the short story in addition to giving him directorial credit.

As part of the negotiations, Truffle agreed to accept union scale compensation for his directorial services in exchange for final cut of the film. On Truffle's last deal, he received $1,000,000 as a director, plus the right to three cuts and previews, but not final cut.

Truffle completed the film at Warner's Paris studio. Fifty prints of the film were made in preparation for the planned distribution of the film in France, and shortly thereafter, in the United States. Twenty-five prints were kept in Paris and twenty-five were sent to New York in preparation for distribution.

Unbeknownst to Truffle, Warner executives who had screened the film did not think it would be commercially successful without substantial re-editing and restructuring of the story line, including a happy ending instead of Truffle's downbeat conclusion. To remedy the situation, and without telling Truffle, one-half hour of film footage was deleted and new footage added to each of the fifty prints made of the film.

Prior to release of Truffle's re-edited film in Paris, Truffle learned that his film would be released in a substantially different form than the form he originally edited. Truffle sued in Paris to enjoin the film's release. Among other claims, he alleged that Warner had violated his "right of integrity," recognized under French law as part of his "moral rights." A French court granted his request for an injunction.

Shortly thereafter, and despite the French court's decision, Warner commenced preparations to release its re-edited version of Truffle's film in New York, containing the contractually agreed upon "based upon" and "directed by" credits.

Truffle's American lawyers now seek preliminarily to restrain release of the film in New York. Warner moves to dismiss Truffle's claim.

Litigation Hypothetical
MUSIC INDUSTRY

"ICE" is the name of a rock group which has recorded four record albums for CBS Records. The albums have ranged from moderately successful to triple platinum. The group had been unknown prior to its contract with CBS. The group consists of three members: Ed Ray, the vocalist, Dave May and Claude Fay. All of the group's records have been produced by John Steinway, a staff CBS record producer well known for discovering new talent and turning them into stars.

Last year, the group's CBS record contract expired. Although May and Fay wanted to continue with CBS records, Ray wanted to sign with Warner Records, believing that CBS had significantly underpaid the royalties due to the group under its CBS contract.

When the members of the group were unable to decide which company to go with, May and Fay signed with CBS and Ray signed with Warner.

May and Fay, with a new vocalist, are planning to release their new rock album under the name "ICE" next month.

During the past week, May and Fay discovered that Ray has formed a new country and western band under the name "ICE", and that Warner is planning to release the group's first album nationally at the end of this month.

May and Fay, with CBS, immediately bring suit, commenced by a motion for a preliminary injunction against Ray and Warner to restrain their use of the name "ICE."

In their responsive motion papers, Ray and Warner claim that plaintiffs have no right to prevent their use of the name "ICE". Ray and Warner also bring their own counter-motion against plaintiffs, seeking from the court a declaratory judgment adjudging their right to continue use of the name "ICE," or in the alternative, that under the court's powers of equity, it fashion an appropriate remedy recognizing the interests of all parties.

Litigation Hypothetical

BOOK PUBLISHING AND LIVE THEATRICAL INDUSTRIES

Jane Crawford, a famous German movie star who moved to Hollywood in the 1930's, died last year. During her lifetime she was an actress of international reknown, who appeared not only in films, but also on the stage and in television.

During her lifetime, Ms. Crawford rejected numerous endorsement opportunities. She did, however, near the end of her life, enter into an agreement with the author Kirk Truman for him to write her authorized biography, on condition that it not be published until after her death. She agreed that, provided this condition were met, the book could be publicized using her name and indicating that the biography was authorized.

For entering into the agreement, Ms. Crawford received $50,000, plus an additional $50,000 to be paid to her estate on publication. Both sums were advances against royalties to be paid her estate. Thereafter, she spent numerous hours with Truman, giving him the details of the life.

After Ms. Crawford's death and publication of her biography, a Broadway play was produced entitled "An Evening With Jane Crawford." The play starred an actress who was made up to resemble Ms. Crawford, and who spoke in a heavy Germanic accent. The play consisted of the actress relating a number of incidents from Ms. Crawford's life that first appeared in Ms. Crawford's biography.

Learning about the play, Ms. Crawford's estate and Mr. Truman move for a preliminary injunction to stop the play. The producers move for summary judgment dismissing plaintiffs' claim.

TABLE OF CASES

Principal cases are set in italic type. Cases cited or discussed
are set in Roman type. References are to pages.

INDEX

[References are to text pages in Part One.]

A

[References are to text pages in Part One.]

C

I

[References are to text pages in Part One.]

M

MUTILATION OF ARTIST'S WORKS
(See also ARTISTIC CONTROL)
Editing film for television specifications 172–174; 190–192

N

NAMES
Contract for use of 266–270
Credits (See CREDITS)
Exclusive right to (See GRANT OF RIGHTS)
Format and style suggesting implied approval 242–253
Service marks, names applicable as 295–296
Tradenames (See TRADEMARKS AND TRADENAMES)

O

OBSCENE MATERIAL
Publication withdrawn by publisher 467–469

P

"PALMING OFF"
Imitations of established stars, advertisements utilizing 193–201
Name of star substituted in credits 292–300
Test for 196–197

PAY OR PLAY ARRANGEMENTS (See COMPENSATION)

PEN NAMES (See TRADEMARKS AND TRADENAMES)

PHOTOPLAYS (See MOTION PICTURE INDUSTRY)

PLAGIARISM
Melodies, unconscious infringement of copyright through use of same
    melody 463–466

POOLING AGREEMENTS
Exhibitors establishing
    Anti-competition factors 32–35

PRICE FIXING
ASCAP/BMI
    Blanket licensing of music for network use constituting 84–140
Block booking 37–39, 71
Clearances and runs 29–32
Dramatists' Guild basic agreement viewed as 78–83, 368